WILD MAMMALS
IN CAPTIVITY

WILD MAMMALS IN CAPTIVITY

Principles and Techniques

EDITORS

Devra G. Kleiman

Mary E. Allen

Katerina V. Thompson

Susan Lumpkin

MANAGING EDITOR

Holly Harris

THE UNIVERSITY OF CHICAGO PRESS

CHICAGO AND LONDON

The University of Chicago Press, Chicago 60637
The University of Chicago Press, Ltd., London
© 1996 by The University of Chicago
All rights reserved. Published 1996
Paperback edition 1997
Printed in the United States of America
10 09 08 07 06   6 7

ISBN 0-226-44003-6   (paperback)

Library of Congress Cataloging-in-Publication Data

Wild mammals in captivity : principles and techniques / editors, Devra
    G. Kleiman ... [et al.].

        p.   cm.
    Includes bibliographical references and index.
    1. Captive mammals.   2. Captive mammals—Housing—Design and
construction.   I. Kleiman, Devra G.
    SF408.W55   1996
    636.088'9—dc20   95-21376
                                                        CIP

Gerald M. Durrell died in January 1995 while this volume was in press. We dedicate this book to him, a pioneer in the zoo and conservation community. Gerald Durrell's ideas and actions set the stage for the recent revolution in the mission of zoos (which we hope this volume embodies), while his writings transformed the lives of many individuals, leading them to seek careers in wildlife conservation and biology. It is difficult to overestimate the impact that Gerald Durrell has had within the zoo community; we have all been touched profoundly by his passion and love for nature. The following quotation is from Gerald Durrell (1990); we think it epitomizes his deep conviction that we humans can preserve and restore this Earth after centuries of destruction.

"The World is as delicate and complicated as a spider's web. If you touch one thread you send shudders running through all the other threads. We are not just touching the web, we are tearing holes in it. Now think of the web as a safety net. The thin strands of survival. Help us tend it, repair it, hold it together."

—Before Another Song Ends

CONTENTS

APPENDIXES

ACKNOWLEDGMENTS

For a volume that took over ten years to reach fruition, it is obvious that there will be numerous organizations and individuals to thank.

From 1986, the following institutions provided grant support in excess of $10,000 each:

Geraldine Dodge Foundation
Prospect Hill Foundation
Smithsonian Institution Smithson Society
Friends of the National Zoo
Robert and Helen Kleberg Foundation

We would have been unable to begin or complete the editing of this volume without the generous support of the above institutions; we are profoundly grateful.

Additionally, we had numerous smaller contributions from zoos and other institutions ($5,000 or less). We thank the Wildlife Conservation Society (then the New York Zoological Society), Digital Equipment Corporation, Chicago Zoological Park (Brookfield), American Zoo and Aquarium Association, Wildlife Preservation Trust International, Zoological Society of Philadelphia, New England Aquarium, Denver Zoological Gardens, Lincoln Park Zoological Gardens, Kansas City Zoological Gardens, Columbus Zoological Gardens, San Antonio Zoological Gardens and Aquarium, San Francisco Zoological Gardens, Audubon Park and Zoological Garden, St. Louis Zoological Park, Cincinnati Zoo and Botanical Garden, Los Angeles Zoo, and Calgary Zoo, Botanical Garden, and Prehistoric Park.

We thank the following individuals who reviewed chapters and provided helpful suggestions to authors: Mary Allen, Jeanne Altmann, Cheri Asa, Anne Baker, Rob Baldwin, Jon Ballou, Ben Beck, Marc Bekoff, Joel Berger, Judith Block, Gordon Burghardt, Mitchell Bush, Ann Byers, John Byers, Kathy Carlstead, Scott Citino, William Conway, Sue Crissey, Carolyn Crockett, George Day, Scott Derrickson, Jim Doherty, Betsy Dresser, Barbara Durrant, Nathan Flesness, Ed Gould, Ted Grand, Holly Harris, Ric Hider, Robert Hoage, Robert Hoffmann, Jo Gayle Howard, Michael Hutchins, David Jessup, William Karesh, Devra Kleiman, Fred Koontz, Karl Kranz, Bob Lacy, William Lasley, John Lucas, Susan Lumpkin, Terry Maple, Hal Markowitz, Jill Mellen, Charlie Menzel, Dennis Meritt, Richard Montali, Stephen O'Brien, Glenn Olsen, Janis Ott-Joslin, Michael Power, Kathy Ralls, Sam Ridgeway, Miles Roberts, Michael Robinson, Carlos Ruiz-Miranda, Dietrich Schaaf, Christian Schmidt, John Seidensticker, David Stepherdson, Lisa Stevens, Jay Sweeney, Katerina Thompson, Ron Tilson, Duane Ullrey, Bruce Watkins, Wendy Westrom, and Bill Xanten.

Several authors provided contributions that ultimately could not be included in the volume for a variety of reasons; we thank them for their time and effort: Russell Greenberg, Gail Foreman, Bill Karesh, Lee Werle, Jan Anderson, Derek Crabbe, Ron Tilson, Allen Biunczik, and Michael Don Carlos.

Finally, we thank J'Amy Allen, Brian Stafford, Melissa Popper, Mary Hagedorn, and Camilla Carroll for their editorial, indexing, proofing, and other assistance and Zoo Atlanta for providing us with some of Holly Harris's time. This volume would never have been published without the support of Susan E. Abrams, University of Chicago Press, who was there when the original plan was "hatched." Norma Roche did a superb job of copy-editing, and Jean McConville helped enormously with standardization of nomenclature as well as copy-editing. The tolerance of the National Zoological Park is gratefully acknowledged; NZP provided incalculable support for this project, including staff administrative time and the use of facilities and office supplies and equipment.

We expect that we have forgotten some important contributions to the production of this volume; we thank all who have contributed whether recognized here or not.

FOREWORD

About thirty years ago, while Lee Crandall was working on the classic *Management of Wild Mammals in Captivity*, I (G. D.) was in the process of setting up my own zoo.

I had made a number of animal collecting expeditions to West Africa and South America in the late 1940s and 1950s and discovered that, while with relative ease I could keep and sometimes breed delicate creatures in rough wooden traveling crates, the animals died within months of being handed over to a large "modern" zoo. I took a long, close look at the average zoo and became severely disillusioned. It seemed most zoos were characterized by a lack of interest in the science of zoology, lack of consideration for animal welfare, and most of all, lack of concern for the perilous state of some of these animals in the wild. I could see the enormous potential value of zoos to wildlife conservation, but few of the zoos of the day could see it for themselves. I decided I would try to set up my own zoo with properly run breeding colonies of endangered species. Foiled by petty bureaucracy in England, I went to Jersey, a self-governing island in the English Channel, which was busy developing a tourist industry and which greeted my somewhat unusual idea with enthusiasm. I wanted to create a zoo that not only displayed animals and educated people, but also addressed the ever-increasing problem of preserving the world's wildlife.

The Jersey Zoological Park opened in 1959, and Crandall's milestone volume was published five years later. In his Introduction, Crandall (1964, vii) mentioned zoos' "new prominence in the field of propagation of threatened species." This is what the Jersey Zoo was all about, and to further the work, I had just established the Jersey Wildlife Preservation Trust (JWPT), which now became the "owner" and "director" of the collection and its activities. The JWPT has a worldwide membership and sibling trusts in the United States and Canada, all dedicated to saving endangered animal species by breeding them in captivity and reestablishing them in the wild.

Crandall (1964, viii) had made another perceptive comment: "The zoological garden is a moving, fluid entity, changing . . . constantly in concept and execution." Zoos first appeared in Egypt and China several thousand years ago; in China they were rightly known as "Gardens of Intel-

ligence." Since then there have been zoological collections throughout the ages as people learned the pleasures of observing wild animals as well as hunting them. But only relatively recently was the connection made between zoos and conservation.

Devra Kleiman points out here that while Crandall believed in the *potential* for zoos to contribute to wildlife conservation, twenty years later there was a revolution going on in the zoo world—zoos were making an *actual* contribution to conservation, and in a major way. That was when the notion of this book was first being discussed by Kleiman and her colleagues, about ten years ago. Today we would go further and say that the breeding of wild animals in captivity is an *indispensable* part of the conservation effort and that the zoos of the world are and will be *vital* forces in the struggle to save biodiversity on this planet. It cannot be said too strongly that without the aid of good zoos, many species of animals will soon disappear forever.

The current volume was born of the need to update Crandall's work, as he foresaw, but in "concept and execution," it is quite different. It is a book for zoo people entering the twenty-first century because it synthesizes the theoretical and practical knowledge of wild mammals in captivity acquired so rapidly and abundantly in the last three decades and directs us toward ideas and activities whose true values are only just being realized, like metapopulation management, manipulation of reproduction and genetics, and the research capacity of zoos.

There is danger on the horizon, however. Anti-zoo elements in Britain and other European countries have wormed their way into the public consciousness. For the moment, there seems to be less of a threat in North America and Australia, and zoos in developing countries, like India, are now experiencing massive popular appeal. But in Britain and Europe the zoo community itself has contributed to the state of affairs by responding defensively to the criticisms or, worse, by not responding at all. There is no reason for this apathy, for good zoos have good stories to tell and should be trumpeting their achievements in breeding endangered species and educating their visitors in conservation and environmental matters.

It is sadly true that there are bad zoos in the world, some

very, very bad. Motivated by greed, the owners cruelly exploit animals to titillate the public. They, the owners, should be put out of business. Other zoos are careless of animal welfare and operate only because of desultory visits by an ill-informed, entertainment-seeking public and perhaps some lip service to the conservation role of zoos. There is no place for these menageries in the world today.

And yet other zoos, with the best-intentioned directors and staffs, remain substandard with respect to animal welfare and conservation. Why haven't they the resources required to bring them up to scratch? Part of the answer lies in the fact that too many members of their governing bodies are appallingly ignorant of the work the zoos are doing. One such person took us on a tour of a zoo (it shall remain nameless) of which he was a prominent board member. "What a beautiful Barbary sheep," we said. "Hey, that's not a barbarian sheep," he replied, "it's called a Hoofed Mammal." Furthermore, too many zoo boards are still in the Dark Ages when it comes to understanding the role of a modern zoo. They believe a zoo's main function is to entertain people rather than save animals, which explains why giant pandas can still be peddled around the world's zoos like piebald prostitutes.

Animals of endangered species are as valuable as—more valuable indeed than—Ming vases or van Goghs. You cannot put a price on them. That is why it is heartening to see the good zoos and the animals' countries of origin now exchanging or lending rare creatures to one another instead of treating them as merchandise.

We now know that this book will be seized upon with glee by all zoo directors and mammal curators, just as Crandall's was, and that their staffs will fight over who gets to borrow it first. But one of our greatest hopes is that it finds its way into the libraries of the businessmen, politicians, and others who sit on the boards and councils of their local zoos, not so much for its facts and figures, but for its clear message of what zoos are and should be doing in global conservation.

Wild Mammals in Captivity has had a lengthy gestation period, and Kleiman and her colleagues are to be warmly congratulated on the birth of this important book. No doubt its longevity will rival Crandall's, and any offspring it has will guide us well into the future.

Gerald and Lee Durrell
Jersey Wildlife Preservation Trust

PREFACE

DEVRA G. KLEIMAN

The impetus for the development of this volume was the realization that Crandall's *Management of Wild Mammals in Captivity* (1964) was nearly twenty years old. The insight came during a dinner with University of Chicago editor Susan E. Abrams (Chicago had published the first Crandall), John Eisenberg, and me, perhaps in 1981. The idea of doing a Crandall sequel emerged at that time, although none of us knew who could do it or how it could be done. It seemed as though there had been such an explosion of information that (1) a single person could never write the entire book, and (2) one volume would never suffice. It is interesting that in his Foreword to Crandall's book, Fairfield Osborn, then President of the New York Zoological Society, indicated that there was only one ideal author who could have written the original book—and that person was Crandall.

Thoughts of developing an updated Crandall sloshed around in our collective unconsciousnesses for a while, and we talked with several colleagues that we thought might be interested in shouldering such a burden. Finally, my postdoctoral student, Susan Lumpkin, expressed considerable interest in pursuing the project. Susan, now Director of Communications for the Friends of the National Zoo (FONZ), became the book's first editor and with me developed a proposal that was used to gain support from funding agencies. Susan and I developed the concepts for the organization and structure of the volume(s), proposed the appointment of an international editorial advisory board, on which I would be the chief editorial advisor, and began to seek authors to write the chapters.

We decided to develop a multivolume work, with the first volume including major reviews of subjects important for managing wild mammals in captivity and subsequent volumes organized taxonomically, as in the original Crandall book. We doubted that we could do a taxonomic summary of what was known about wild mammals in captivity in a single volume.

In thinking about the structure of the first volume, we realized that there had been some major advances in management since Crandall's time that did not necessarily result from changes in diet or housing, but grew out of our new conceptual approaches to managing animals. The zoo community had taken a quantum leap in management with the development of species survival plans for endangered species, demographic and genetic management were commonly being used, and artificial methods of promoting and controlling reproduction were becoming more and more the norm.

Nonetheless, in reviewing Crandall's original volume, it became clear that he was far ahead of his contemporaries conceptually. In 1964, in his Introduction, Crandall stated, "The zoological garden of today has progressed far beyond the scope and status of the mere menagerie," a still often-quoted concept. Crandall had also recognized the potential for zoos to contribute to conservation, suggesting in his Introduction that zoos had recently come into prominence through their propagation of threatened species. By 1984, twenty years later, when this volume was first taking shape, further progress had been supplanted by an actual revolution in the declared missions of zoos; it was now clear that zoos could be major actors in the development of the science of conservation biology and in the actual practice of species and environmental preservation. I doubt that Crandall could have visualized how powerful zoos would become in setting priorities for the conservation movement in the last two decades of the twentieth century. Zoos finally realized that they had the money, the motivation, the organization, and the constituencies to make a major contribution to saving the world's endangered species and their habitats. Credit for propelling zoos onto center stage in the environmental movement probably should go to three individuals, George Rabb, Ulysses S. Seal, and William Conway, who had the vision, the authority, and the perseverance to drag U.S. zoos, "kicking and screaming," into the twenty-first century.

Crandall's 1964 volume covered a lot of ground. He provided information on systematics and natural history as they affected the management of a species in captivity. He then discussed specifics of captive management, including exhibit areas and housing, restraint, diets, and methods for breeding a species. Where the information was available, he provided life history data such as estrous cycles, gestation periods, and longevities. It is interesting to see so much discussion of captive longevities in Crandall as we now seek methods to reduce the longevities of genetically overrepresented animals.

Crandall also discussed at length the history of species or taxa in captivity, a subject that would probably be much less relevant today. In 1964, however, there were some species for which zoos had had experiences of only a handful of specimens. For example, only four platypuses had been held in U.S. zoos by 1964. Crandall's emphasis on the more charismatic mammals would be echoed by a comparable book today; happily, we have a lot more information on some taxa (for example, bats and elephant shrews) for which Crandall had almost no data. But there was still an emphasis on popular groups of large animals: Crandall devotes a total of 267 pages to the "hoofed stock" (perissodactyls, artiodactyls, and elephants) compared with 145 pages for the carnivores, 115 pages for the primates, and a *total* of 125 pages for the seven orders that include the rodents, insectivores, chiropterans, marsupials, edentates, and pholidotes.

The uneven distribution of focus, sometimes due to popularity, sometimes to lack of knowledge at the time, is still a bit surprising. All bats were covered in five pages, as were all callitrichid primates, today among the most popular of exhibits in zoos. The elephant shrews as a family were allotted one page, the Lemuridae two pages. Yet, several single species were discussed in incredible depth, especially considering the fact that the U.S. had minimal experience of them. Giant pandas, of which there had been a total of nine in the United States through 1964, were given six pages, and platypuses were allotted ten pages.

There have been major advances made since 1964 in the management of mammals in captivity, and the growth in the available literature attests to this. Additionally, numerous taxonomic accounts of mammalian groups have been published that provide a considerable update in management techniques relative to Crandall's time. Finally, communication about advances in management techniques has speeded up enormously, through international and national zoo organizations, regular conferences (Jersey Wildlife Preservation Trust in 1992 organized the Sixth World Conference on Breeding Endangered Species in Captivity, having organized the first one in 1972), zoo journals that publish new information rapidly, bibliographic retrieval services, and studbooks, Taxon Advisory Groups (TAGs), and Species Survival Plans (SSPs), as well as the ever-present facsimile machines (Fax) and computers with electronic mail.

Indeed, the easy availability of information about the management of individual taxa was a major reason that we decided not to do a direct update of Crandall, but chose to concentrate more on the changes in the conceptual approaches to keeping mammals in captivity. We wanted to present overviews of topics that would provide a framework within which a reader could add and assimilate both general and specific information. We wanted to develop less of a cookbook with specific recipes, and more of a primer that explained the basic principles of cooking. Thus, we have overviews of socialization techniques; training; marking and identification techniques; principles of exhibitry; the biopark concept; methods of dealing with surplus; contraception; parental care; behavioral development; artificial techniques of reproduction; genetic research and its applications; and development and use of simple data collection procedures.

This volume consists of forty-eight chapters and five appendices. It grew exponentially as Susan and I spoke with colleagues about new topics that needed to be covered and as our authors found that they could not restrict themselves to our page limits. Time passed as we waited, patiently at first, and then less so, for completed manuscripts. Some authors changed jobs or were unable to complete their chapters, and new authors had to be recruited. More challenges arose when Susan accepted her current position with FONZ in 1987, and reluctantly concluded that she could not oversee completion of the volume while working full-time. We looked for editorial and organizational assistance, but with insufficient money, could not get the full-time help required. In 1988, Holly Harris, our current coordinating editor, joined the project; and in 1990, Mary Allen came on as a scientific co-editor. Katerina Thompson joined the editorial group in 1993 and helped us add some important new chapters, revise others, and polish the entire volume. However, time constraints and limited funding again created further challenges to overcome. Finally, as we prepared to send the volume to the publisher, we asked authors to update their chapters in order to provide the most current information possible.

Now, at long last, more than ten years after its conception, *Wild Mammals in Captivity* is born. I feel compelled to comment that the magnitude of the task of coordinating and producing a publication that involves seventy-eight authors and seven such diverse aspects of zoological management required tremendous patience and cooperation from all those involved. Crandall spent seven years producing his book, but I realize that he did not have seventy-eight authors eagerly awaiting publication of their major reviews. I feel confident that the wait was worth it—both for our authors and our audience.

The taxonomic authority followed in this book is *Mammal Species of the World* (2d ed.; Washington, D.C.: Smithsonian Institution Press, 1993), edited by D.E. Wilson and D.M. Reader.

PART ONE

Basic Husbandry

INTRODUCTION
Mary E. Allen

Zoos, unlike museums, have the unique challenge of maintaining living collections. They are charged with the humane treatment and daily maintenance of the animals in their care. The level of sophistication in the husbandry of zoo animals has progressed substantially since Crandall's original volume. Improvements in animal care have resulted from an increased awareness of both the physical and the psychological needs of captive animals and the realization that recruitment from the wild is no longer an option. Part 1 assembles practical and basic information about zoo animal management that can be directly applied to the daily management of mammal collections.

This volume, *Wild Mammals in Captivity: Principles and Techniques,* appropriately begins with a chapter on ethics and animal welfare, currently a top priority in zoo animal management. In chapter 1 Mench and Kreger present a historical overview of the changing relationship between animals and humans and how this relationship colors the attitudes of zoo visitors toward animals and the zoos that house them. Visitors are likely to have more favorable impressions of "natural" exhibits, which, if appropriately designed, can do much to educate and inform them. The challenge to zoos, however, is the construction of environments that not only appeal to visitors but also fulfill the real needs of the animals living in them.

Zoo animal medicine has made remarkable advances in just twenty years. Major zoos now employ at least two full-time veterinarians, and these professionals have dramatically improved the health of collections. The basic foundation for a successful captive animal program is preventive medicine. Hinshaw, Amand, and Tinkelman review the essentials of such a program in chapter 2, which include screening methods for disease, vaccinations, and quarantine requirements. They emphasize the importance of health records, nutrition, dentistry, sanitation, and pest control. Chapter 3 by Bush presents current knowledge of safe and humane methods of capture, handling, and anesthesia for zoo mammals. Accepted methods of animal restraint and anesthesia are based on methods used for domestic species. Undomesticated zoo mammals, however, present unique challenges; the zoo veterinarian, as a specialist, must refine and modify handling and anesthesia methods so that they are safe for both zoo mammals and animal handlers.

Nurseries that include public viewing areas attract visitor interest. However, the hand-rearing of zoo mammals is currently discouraged. Read and Meier present the philosophy of hand rearing in chapter 4 and summarize the essential components of the care of neonatal mammals, including husbandry, medical care, and record keeping. To be prepared for the eventuality of hand rearing, zoos should have established neonatal care protocols in place before they are presented with an orphaned neonate.

Record keeping in zoos has become essential to the effective management of zoo mammals. Medical management, breeding records, inter-zoo loan agreements, and necropsy records require accurate and consistent animal identification. Rice and Kalk present a variety of identification techniques in chapter 5, ranging from simple natural marks and tattoos to more innovative options, such as electromagnetic microchips. They also discuss the suitability of the different techniques and their application to different mammal species.

For mammals in captivity we remove many of the choices that face animals in nature: we provide food, shelter, and medical care, establish breeding pairs, and make decisions about group composition. Zoo staff must frequently move individual animals to optimize genetic diversity. This increases the importance of understanding and properly organizing the socialization processes that accompany moves or introductions. The two chapters on socialization techniques and appropriate methods of introduction emphasize the relevance of the prior social experiences of the animals, their spatial and temporal requirements, group composition, and habitat characteristics, as well as staff expertise. In both chapters the authors place emphasis on the physical and psychological well-being of zoo mammals. Watts and Meder review the unique challenges of primate socialization and introduction in chapter 6, emphasizing the importance of slow, stepwise introductions to minimize injuries and promote compatibility. In chapter 7 Kranz applies many of these same principles to a discussion of the introduction and socialization of other mammals. The dramatic increase in animal shipments makes particularly useful to zoo managers the practical information on crate training provided by Kranz. Careful planning and design can eliminate injuries and deaths of animals in shipment.

Animals in zoos are neither "wild" nor truly domesticated. With few exceptions, including elephants and marine mammals, zoo mammals were, until recently, rarely trained to be tractable. There is now increasing recognition of the benefits of training and learned behaviors for many other zoo mammals. Blood sampling, hoof trimming, semen collection, and other procedures that usually require anesthesia can be safely performed with appropriate conditioning and training. In chapter 8 Mellen and Ellis provide an overview of the concepts of learning, reinforcement, and motivation, followed by descriptions of the many techniques and applications of training that enable zoo staff to manipulate animals safely. They also discuss the psychological benefits to the animals and the educational benefits to the visiting public of animal demonstrations.

Finally, in chapter 9, Flanagan and Tsipis cover the practical aspects of zoo security, in the context of the safety and security of both the visiting public and the animals. Every zoo emergency requires the expertise of either security or veterinary personnel, and some situations call for both. The authors, from their perspectives of veterinarian and security officer, offer constructive guidelines and protocols that emphasize the responsibilities and training of zoo staff, the importance of sound exhibit design, and the roles of both security staff and emergency response teams.

1

Ethical and Welfare Issues Associated with Keeping Wild Mammals in Captivity

JOY A. MENCH AND MICHAEL D. KREGER

There was an exhibition at the Zoological Park in the Bronx yesterday which had
for many of the visitors something more than a provocation to laughter. There were laughs in it enough, too,
but there was something about it that made the serious minded grave. Even those who laughed the most
turned away with an expression on their faces such as one sees after a play with a sad ending
or a book in which the hero or heroine is poorly rewarded.
"Something about it that I don't like," was the way one man put it.
NEW YORK TIMES, 9 SEPTEMBER 1906

"Something about it that I don't like." Those words were uttered in response to the remarkable sight of a Congo pygmy, Ota Benga, being exhibited in a cage at the Monkey House along with an orangutan that he had been given as a companion. Ota had previously been on display at the St. Louis World's Fair, along with thousands of other native people collected from around the world by early-twentieth-century explorers. This human exhibition was designed to be the anthropological counterpart of Carl Hagenbeck's enormous animal circus, also on display at the fair, and in addition was to serve an avowedly scientific purpose: to collect measurements that would enable scientists to determine the characteristics that distinguished "primitive" from "civilized" man. Hundreds of thousands of visitors flocked to see Ota Benga at the zoo until protests by the Baptist clergy (combined with Ota's unruly behavior) forced Bronx Zoo director William T. Hornaday to release him to the care of the Howard Colored Orphan Asylum (Bradford and Blume 1992).

"Something about it that I don't like." Thankfully, the exhibition of human curiosities is now a rare occurrence. However, modern zoo visitors may find themselves experiencing similar uncomfortable and contradictory feelings when they stand outside of an animal exhibit, particularly if the animal appears to them to be "bored" or "unhappy." Such feelings are symbolic of an important change in our

ideas about the relationship between humans and animals, and indicate a progressive enlargement of our moral concerns beyond traditional boundaries such as nation, race, or species.

Historically, animals have been viewed in Western culture primarily in the context of their usefulness to human beings. Human needs for food, draft power, entertainment, enlightenment, or companionship have therefore been the paramount considerations in the treatment of animals, and this has been reflected not only in custom but in law. Domesticated animals were viewed as property, which could be purchased, used, and disposed of at the owner's discretion as long as the legal rights of other persons were not infringed in the process. Even wild animals did not escape notions of utility (Thomas 1983). This is not to suggest that cruel treatment of animals was considered acceptable.[1] However, kindness to animals was advocated not because it was a duty owed directly to animals themselves, but because it improved human character.

Although concern about the treatment of animals grew steadily (Thomas 1983), it was not until the nineteenth cen-

[1] It may have been common, however, at least according to our current notions of cruelty. For graphic descriptions of human (mis)treatment of animals historically, see Carson (1972), Ryder (1989), and Turner (1992).

tury that attitudes toward animals began to change significantly. This change led ultimately to the growth of the organized animal protection movement, as well as to the adoption of legislation that regulated the treatment of animals with the explicit intention of diminishing the pain or suffering experienced by the animals.

A number of factors propelled this change (Turner 1980; Sperling 1988). Innovations in technology and manufacturing resulted in the growth of cities and a reduction in the labor force required for food production. A large urban middle class emerged that had little daily contact with food or pest animals, but that was affluent enough to keep animals primarily for companionship. There seems little doubt that the growth of pet keeping has both paralleled and fostered more empathetic views of animals (Serpell 1986).

A second factor was the growth of animal experimentation. By the nineteenth century vivisection was common in medical and veterinary schools in Europe, and physiologists like François Magendie conducted public demonstrations in which animals were subjected to procedures such as invasive surgery and slow suffocation. Since effective anesthetics (for either humans or animals) were not available until the 1850s, most of these experiments were carried out on fully conscious animals, provoking widespread revulsion and a heightened sensitivity to the issue of animal pain. The ensuing passionate arguments concerning the utility and morality of animal experimentation are still with us today.

But perhaps the most critical factor was the emergence of a new and explicitly scientific perspective on the natural world. The development of this perspective can be traced to the elaboration during the eighteenth century of a classification scheme based on the structural characteristics of animals and plants (Thomas 1983). This increased attention to structural relationships among organisms laid the foundation for Darwin's theory of evolution, which shattered long-held assumptions about human uniqueness. It is the growing appreciation of the continuity and commonalities between animals and humans resulting from the study of evolutionary biology that has fostered much of the current debate about the treatment of animals in our society.

ETHICS AND ANIMALS

Humans have long pondered the basis for their superiority over animals (Thomas 1983). Characteristics that have been suggested as distinguishing humans from animals have ranged from the fanciful to the serious: dancing, laughter, cooking, manners, religion, a convoluted gut (in order that sublime contemplation can occur during the leisurely digestion of food), hair that grays, ears that wiggle, cerebral laterality, an immortal soul, politics, an upright posture, a protruding nose, the use of tools, reason, and language. These distinctions have often been used to justify the unique legal and moral status of human beings.

Recently, however, philosophers have begun to ask whether traits like these are truly significant in the sense that they entitle humans to different ethical consideration. Why is it morally acceptable to use animals for scientific experiments or to keep them in zoos for educational purposes when it is not acceptable to use humans in this way? If it is because humans have speech or reason, then how should we view humans who do not have these attributes, for example, infants or individuals who are brain-damaged? Clearly, the answers to these questions will also have an effect on how society deals with difficult problems in human ethics such as abortion and euthanasia.

Two philosophers have been particularly prominent in this debate about the treatment of animals: Peter Singer, the author of *Animal Liberation* (1990), and Tom Regan, the author of *The Case for Animal Rights* (1983). Regan and Singer have been called the "midwives" of the animal rights movement in the United States (Jasper and Nelkin 1992), since they gave the movement a coherent agenda and an ethical foundation. They (and others) have posed a fundamentally new question about animals: In addition to their value to humans, do animals have a value in and of themselves, and do they therefore possess interests that entitle them to be treated as objects of moral concern? If so, what duties do we owe them?

Singer argues that the ability to experience suffering and pleasure *(sentience),* which is shared by humans and many animals, is the necessary and sufficient condition for having morally relevant interests: "It would be nonsense to state that it was not in the interests of a stone to be kicked along the road by a schoolboy. A stone does not have interests because it cannot suffer. Nothing that we could do to it could possibly make any difference to its welfare . . . [but] a mouse, for example, does have an interest in not being kicked along the road, because it will suffer if it is."

Singer contends that all sentient creatures are entitled to have their interests in avoiding suffering and experiencing pleasure weighed equally with those of other sentient beings in situations in which a conflict of interest might occur, such as when animals are raised for meat production. According to Singer, denying such equal consideration on the basis of species alone constitutes *speciesism,* which is analogous to racism or sexism in that it uses arbitrary and morally irrelevant characteristics to define the boundaries of moral concern.

Tom Regan, on the other hand, views sentience as only one of the attributes that entitle animals to moral consideration. According to Regan, animals (particularly mammals) also have perceptions, memories, emotions, desires, beliefs, self-consciousness, intentions, and a sense of the future. As such, they are what Regan terms *"subjects of a life,"* who have a right not to be harmed by having their interests (whether those interests consist of choosing a mate, discovering a new type of food, or living a long life) disturbed by others.

It is worth emphasizing that neither Regan nor Singer is advocating equal treatment for animals, as is sometimes mistakenly claimed. Both are well aware that there would be little point in giving pandas the right to vote or dogs the right to a public education, since such rights are irrelevant to the animals and could not be exercised. Neither do they believe that the like interests of humans and animals are necessarily of equal weight. This is illustrated by Regan in one of his dog-in-a-lifeboat scenarios, in which four normal, *manity in the Victorian mind.* Baltimore: Johns Hopkins University Press.

United States Department of Agriculture (USDA). 1992. *Animal Welfare Enforcement Fiscal Year 1992.* Animal and Plant Health Inspection Service, Hyattsville, Maryland.

Varner, G. E., and Monroe, M. C. 1991. Ethical perspectives on captive breeding: Is it for the birds? *Endangered Species Update* 8 (1): 27–29.

Walker, S. 1983. *Animal thought.* London: Routledge & Kegan Paul.

Wemmer, C., and Derrickson, S. 1987. Reintroduction: The zoo-biologists dream. Prospects and problems of reintroducing captive bred wildlife. *AAZPA Annual Conference Proceedings,* 48–65. Wheeling, W.Va.: American Association of Zoological Parks and Aquariums.

White, A. 1984. *Rights.* Oxford: Oxford University Press.

White, J., and Barry, S. 1984. *Science education for families in informal learning settings: An evaluation of the Herp Lab project.* Washington, D.C.: National Zoological Park.

Wolf, R. L., and Tymitz, B. L. 1981. Studying visitor perceptions of zoo environments: A naturalistic view. *Int. Zoo Yrbk.* 21: 49–53.

Yerke, R., and Burns, A. 1991. Measuring the impact of animal shows on visitor attitudes. *AAZPA Annual Conference Proceedings,* 532–39. Wheeling, W.Va.: American Association of Zoological Parks and Aquariums.

Zeehandelaar, F. H., and Sarnoff, P. 1971. *Zeebongo: The wacky wild animal business,* 176. New Jersey: Prentice-Hall.

2

Preventive Medicine

KEITH C. HINSHAW, WILBUR B. AMAND, AND CARL L. TINKELMAN

THE IMPORTANCE OF PREVENTIVE MEDICINE

The purpose of this chapter is to review the essential elements of a preventive medicine program for captive wild mammals. These elements include stock selection, quarantine, routine health monitoring and maintenance, nutrition, enclosure design, pest control, sanitation, and an employee health program. The overall goals of a preventive medicine program are to prevent disease from entering the animal collection, to assure that the animals are properly maintained, and to avoid dissemination of disease to other institutions, or to free-ranging populations if collection animals are to be part of a reintroduction program (Norton 1993).

Preventive medicine must be the foundation of the animal health program at any animal facility. Once a wild animal becomes ill, it can be very difficult to perform diagnostic tests or to treat it successfully. Signs of illness in a captive wild animal may not become obvious until the animal is in extremely poor health. As an example, a 17-year-old leopard, *Panthera pardus*, at our facility showed no symptoms of the tumor (a bronchogenic carcinoma) that occupied 75% of his lung tissue until it partially occluded his esophagus.

Diagnosis and treatment of captive wild animals usually require physical or chemical restraint (including general anesthesia)—procedures that are stressful to healthy animals and may exacerbate an illness or even result in the death of an ill animal. Some bacterial and parasite problems, once established in an exhibit or group of animals, are almost impossible to eradicate and may result in one or more of the following: (1) increased mortality in the animal collection, (2) poor reproductive performance, (3) poor display animals for the visiting public, (4) increased restrictions on shipping animals out of the collection, and (5) health risks to zoo personnel.

STOCK SELECTION AND ANIMAL HISTORY

Preventive medicine should start before animals arrive at the facility. Proper selection of animal stock prevents many potential problems. Inquiries should be made regarding an animal's health history as well as the health problems of its parents, siblings, offspring, and cagemates. Questions should be asked regarding (1) the animal's parasite history, (2) chronic health problems that require periodic medical intervention, (3) unsightly skin lesions or intermittent lameness, (4) behavioral disorders such as regurgitation or self-mutilation, and (5) any evidence of exposure to infectious disease. Animals intended for propagation should be free from reproductive disorders and heritable defects such as poor body conformation, malformed teeth, or hoof abnormalities. An exception might be considered if the overall genetic contribution that the animal can make to the captive population outweighs the potential perpetuation of the defect. Consideration should also be given to whether a female animal has given birth previously and what has become of her offspring (e.g., did it survive, did the mother raise it, did it become a physically and behaviorally normal adult?). Useful information on a male would include whether the animal has had access to reproductively active females, has exhibited normal breeding behavior, any offspring sired and their status, and whether semen has been collected and evaluated.

It is always valuable to talk to the person who actually cares for the animal as well as the consulting veterinarian. They should be able to supply information on the animal's housing and dietary history, response to medications and immobilizing agents, and behavior patterns. At this time, obtain a copy of any medical records for review prior to the animal's shipment. State and federal regulations often require specific tests prior to shipment, such as serological screening for brucellosis or equine infectious anemia. Results of these tests, as well as results of tests for other potential health problems, should be reported before the animal leaves for your facility.

Another important issue is the vaccination status of the animal. The efficacy of a vaccine depends on the animal's immune competence. The most beneficial response to the vaccine develops in a healthy animal under minimal stress. Transport to a new facility and the subsequent adjustment sign and dimensions of these components will vary according to the species exhibited and the physical attributes of the exhibit itself. Direct contact between the public and animals, as well as public feeding of animals, should never be allowed unless supervised by employees or trained volunteers (see Coe, chap. 16, and Seidensticker and Doherty, chap. 18, this volume).

Barriers enclosing animals should be visible to them and recognizable as barriers. For example, woven mesh fencing is adequate to contain a number of antelope species. However, when startled, some nervous animals, such as lechwe, *Kobus leche,* or gazelles, *Gazella* spp., may kill themselves by running into an otherwise familiar barrier in order to avoid a noxious stimulus. A number of great apes have drowned in relatively shallow water barriers due to their unfamiliarity with the barriers and the absence of underwater support structures into which they could climb.

The zoo perimeter should be fenced to prevent unwanted entry by humans and other animals. The fence should have a minimum height of 2.5 m and be constructed of material that will discourage climbing by people and wild animals. The bottom should be buried at least 0.25 m deep, or firmly attached to a slab or curb, to prevent burrowing through by packs of feral dogs and other wildlife. Nearby vegetation should be trimmed and maintained so that large limbs do not overhang the fence, allowing intrusion or damage to the fence structure during severe weather conditions. Regular inspections of the perimeter fence for damage and intruders should be performed by the security staff during their scheduled rounds. The security of fencing, walls, and moats can be greatly enhanced by the addition of lighting to permit night security personnel to watch for nocturnal predators and intruders.

Special attention should be given to the construction and maintenance of gates. The gate should tightly abut the fence and, when locked, should not warp, leaving an inviting gap at the top or bottom.

Locks are used throughout zoos. The number of keys and locks can quickly get out of hand, resulting in a very heavy and cumbersome key ring. The number of keys can be easily controlled through the use of a master key system. Each area can use a unique key while a master key can be reserved for management and/or security personnel.

A comprehensive design will work to eliminate potential areas of escape or routes into the exhibit by intruders. Nevertheless, animals spend 24 hours per day seeking ways to get out of their exhibits, and occasionally humans and other animals seek ways to get in.

STANDARD OPERATING PROCEDURES

Employees must be provided with training in the safest way to perform their duties. Written operational procedures as well as individual training should be given to each new employee. All employees should review safety and operational procedures on a regular basis. Procedures may need to be updated or revised to accommodate new animals or facility conditions. All changes should be recorded in writing and made available to all concerned staff. Written procedures

should specify the manner in which each employee shall perform his or her assigned duties. Specific details should be given on the manner of feeding, shifting, and cleaning animal cages, the use of disinfectants and medications, and tool and safety equipment use.

Regularly scheduled lectures should present various safety topics appropriate for the whole staff; examples include proper lifting, personal protection, zoonoses, hygiene, and chemical safety. Complete information on all chemicals used in the zoo must be easily available to the staff. This information should include the composition, toxicity, and reactivity of the chemical, safety measures or protective equipment needed, and procedures to follow in the event of accidental exposure.

Safety problems should be reported in writing by employees as soon as a problem is noticed. If possible, the employee should correct the problem on the spot. When this is not possible, the employee should be encouraged to suggest corrective measures. In the case of serious or recurring safety problems, a thorough investigation into the problem should be conducted and a resolution devised.

SECURITY STAFF

The most effective security is provided by the physical presence of zoo personnel. Keepers, public assistance/information personnel, and law enforcement officers should be in evidence throughout the zoo to prevent incidents and to observe animal behavior. It is vitally important to have adequate personnel on staff to care for the animals and to police the public. Numerous studies have shown that vandalism is discouraged if the potential vandals feel that they are under surveillance.

The number of security personnel and their positions within the zoo's organizational structure will vary among institutions. All institutions should realize the importance of delegating responsibility for security to a specific individual or department. There are two types of security officers: those with police powers and those without. Security officers with police powers are bound by laws that vary depending upon the political subdivision and/or state involved. The use of these officers will not be dealt with here. Zoos that typically use security personnel without police powers must develop security procedures within their own institutions. However, certain basic principles are applicable in any institution.

The security department's basic policy should be protection through prevention. In a small institution, this may be accomplished by animal keepers performing certain security functions; larger institutions may hire a private security company. Officers hired from a private security company are less likely to be knowledgeable about the zoo and its programs. They may be best used in areas where money is handled, such as at the admissions gate or in public concession areas. For zoos operating their own security force, it is recommended that the specific duties assigned to the security officers provide adequate stimulation during the entire shift. Security personnel should be able to administer minor first aid, complete accident/injury reports, and provide in-

SECTION A

Location: _____ PIC: _____ OPR Div.: _____

Incident: ☐ occurred   ☐ was reported   ☐ was discovered
on ___/___/___ at   ☐ am   ☐ pm

Brief description of incident: _____
_____

Reported by other than person completing form:

Name: _____

Who is ☐ employee # _____ or non-employee at: _____

_____

Address   City   State   Zip   Phone

SECTION B

☐ CLASS I
   ☐ Accident ☐ Non-auto ☐ Auto
     ☐ Personal ☐ Non-personal
   ☐ Fire
   ☐ Lost Child
   ☐ School Truancy
   ☐ Participant/visitor illness
   ☐ Inappropriate conduct
     ☐ Adult ☐ Youth
   ☐ Violation of Park
     Rules and Regulation
     Cite # _____
   ☐ Other _____

☐ CLASS II
   ☐ Theft: ☐ Non-auto ☐ Auto
   ☐ Burglary
   ☐ Assault
   ☐ Vandalism/Criminal mischief
   ☐ Disorderly conduct
   ☐ Offense against family or child
     ☐ Witnessed   ☐ Reported
   ☐ Sexual Misconduct
   ☐ Criminal Trespass
   ☐ Other _____

ACTIONS TAKEN	ASSISTANCE REQUESTED
☐ Counsel/Advise employee ☐ Counsel/Advise visitor/participant ☐ Apply First Aid/CPR ☐ Requested assistance ☐ Other _____	☐ None ☐ Fire ☐ Police ☐ Medical-EMT ☐ Parent, relative, guardian ☐ Child Protective Services ☐ Truancy officer ☐ Supervisor

_____   _____
Name of employee completing form   Emp. #

Fig. 9.1. A sample incident report.

formation for visitors, in addition to performing general security duties such as routine patrolling and making building checks.

Security personnel can likewise play an important public relations role. Often they provide a visitor's first contact with the zoo staff, and sometimes the only one that a member of the public will have during his or her zoo visit. The officer's conduct will influence the public's perception of the zoo's concern for its visitors, its efficiency, and the overall competency of its staff. As a consequence, security personnel should be carefully screened before they are hired to ensure that only applicants who are able to project the proper image and perform the required duties are selected. Training is critical to ensure that the officers know the zoo's goals and objectives. Training will identify the officers' duties and the procedures to be followed in their performance. Continuing in-service training will also help keep the officers informed and motivated.

Security staff must be easily identifiable by visitors. Emergency phones, first-aid stations, and security offices should be visible. Security officers, like all zoo staff, should wear uniforms. Photo identification cards should be worn visibly by all employees. Good grooming and a properly worn uniform will project competence and professionalism.

Both security staff and other zoo employees should continually be alert for hazardous conditions within the zoo, such as misuse of equipment or chemicals, broken windows, water or gas leaks, broken guardrails, and downed or dangerous tree limbs. A written report should be submitted to the appropriate supervisor and department to identify repair needs.

Each security officer should be familiar with the law enforcement agency with jurisdiction over the zoo. It is the responsibility of the zoo security personnel to learn what support the local agency can offer, to determine the procedures followed by the local police department, to make the acquaintance of those officers responsible for providing police protection to the zoo, and to ensure that the police officers are fully informed of the zoo's emergency procedures. It is important to maintain a good relationship with outside agencies that may be helpful in an emergency situation.

Security programs must function to protect the zoo and

SECTION C

PERSON #1

☐ Employee Injured: ☐ Yes
☐ Non-employee ☐ No

| Race | Name-Last, | First, | MI. |

| Sex | Address | Street-Apt. No. | |

| Age | City | State | Zip |

PERSON #2

☐ Employee Injured: ☐ Yes
☐ Non-employee ☐ No

| Race | Name-Last, | First, | MI. |

| Sex | Address | Street-Apt. No. | |

| Age | City | State | Zip |

PERSON #3

☐ Employee Injured: ☐ Yes
☐ Non-employee ☐ No

| Race | Name-Last, | First, | MI. |

| Sex | Address | Street-Apt. No. | |

| Age | City | State | Zip |

SECTION D

☐ Public property ☐ Private property
  ☐ non-vehicle ☐ non-vehicle
  ☐ vehicle ☐ vehicle

☐ Loss of materials/supplies
☐ Loss/repair of equipment
☐ Loss/repair of vehicle
☐ Loss/repair of building/structure
☐ Loss/replacement of land improvements
☐ Loss of financial assets
☐ Other (specify) _____

VALUE OF LOSS/REPAIR:
☐ Less than & $500 ☐ $2,500-$5,000
☐ $500-$1,000 ☐ $5,000-$10,000
☐ $1,000-$2,500 ☐ over $10,000

SECTION E

IDENTIFY KEY PERSON ASSISTING:
  ☐ None

Name: _____
  Last First MI

Emp.# _____ Badge # _____ or

Address Street Apt. No.

City State Zip Phone
Brief description of outcome: _____

SECTION F

DOCUMENTS ACCOMPANYING REPORTS
☐ Police report or Case File # _____
☐ Supervisors Report of Vehicle Accident
☐ 1st report of employee injury
☐ Participant injury/Medical Assistance report
☐ Supplemental Incident Report

☐ Work order
☐ Witness statement(s)
☐ Report of Inventory Loss
☐ Other

_____ _____
Signature Date

FIG. 9.1 (cont.)

its visitors from the small number of visitors who refuse to cooperate in obeying rules and safeguarding the property of the zoo and all its visitors, thus making everyone feel safe. The public should be monitored, and unruly groups should be identified and pointed out to the security staff. Security officers must extend fair and equal treatment to all. They must maintain a position of neutrality and act with firmness. Diplomacy and courtesy are the keys to any situation involving people.

A sound management practice is that of reporting in writing all incidents and injuries requiring the attention of zoo personnel. Visitors typically experience such nuisances as insect bites and minor scrapes. Occasionally, however, a more serious injury occurs that may involve the hospitalization of a visitor and, eventually, a claim against the zoo. Clear, informative, and accurate reports will be essential in determining the zoo's liability and resolution of the claim. Employee injuries may be much more diverse and require clear, concise, and accurate reporting. A person familiar with the particular work environment (usually the employee's supervisor) should help complete the report, detailing the circumstances of the incident. Figure 9.1 is a sample report form.

DEALING WITH EMERGENCIES

In spite of good planning and clearly understood and practiced procedures, emergencies will occur in every zoo. Although the possible scenarios are limitless, they may include animal escapes, feral dogs mauling zoo specimens, zoo visitors entering enclosures with dangerous animals, fires, severe weather, even chemical spills or explosions. Because of the range of possibilities, the plan for response must be adaptable and suited to the personnel, facilities, and equipment available. In all cases the following priorities apply:

1. Ensure public safety.
2. Ensure the safety of the zoo and affiliated personnel.
3. Ensure the safety of the animal collection.
4. Prevent or minimize damage to facilities and equipment.

All zoo personnel should be aware of their individual responsibilities in the event of any kind of emergency at any time of the day or night. The number of people involved in managing an emergency will vary with the size and scope of the collection, as well as with the nature of the specific emergency. In a large zoo, employee responsibilities may need to be designated in advance to ensure an efficient response.

Animal-Related Emergencies

Emergency Response Teams. Four separate needs must be addressed in an animal emergency: (1) capture or containment of the animal(s) involved, (2) crowd control and the treatment of human injuries, (3) communication, and, if necessary to prevent human injury, (4) destruction of the animal(s). Each of these needs should be addressed by a different "team" of personnel. Prior delegation of authority and responsibility prevents confusion and facilitates an efficient response.

During an emergency, leadership should be delegated to the most senior staff member present. All responding teams should be working toward the same goals: preventing or minimizing injury to people and animals, and preventing damage to facilities. The decisions made during each emergency will be influenced by the skills and abilities of the staff present at the scene. The best outcome will occur when there is cohesiveness of staff, good training, and strong leadership.

Capture or Containment of the Animal. If an animal escapes from its enclosure, rapid containment or immobilization will prevent injury to visitors and staff as well as to the animal itself. The people most capable of dealing with an escaped animal are the keepers who routinely care for it and the veterinary staff. Together these people constitute the first "team" that should respond in every escaped animal emergency. They are also the ones most familiar with the animal's normal behavior and with the facility or area in which it is housed. The animal section personnel must have access to capture equipment such as nets, crates, ropes, elephant hooks, and snare poles. They should also have keys and a working knowledge of the facility. With luck, they will be able to confine the animal by utilizing secondary containment structures or by shifting it into an empty cage or pen.

The veterinary staff can respond with equipment to effect chemical restraint should it be necessary (see Bush, chap. 3, this volume). A capture gun, blow darts, or even a pole syringe can be used to restrain specimens that cannot be safely contained in any other manner. In order to prevent confusion, a list of all potentially dangerous species within the collection should be made, together with the preferred drug and dose to be used on each. During an emergency there will be no time to refer to the literature or to the animal's medical record for the anesthetic regimen of choice.

The use of chemical restraint and remote delivery equipment should be limited to the veterinary staff. These people use the equipment regularly and are familiar with the effects of the various restraint drugs. In most cases, the minimum time to effect sedation is 5 minutes. Depending on the species, conditions, and restraint agent(s) used, it may take 15 minutes or more to achieve immobilization, particularly in an excited animal. Animals under the influence of chemical agents but which are not yet fully immobilized can be even more dangerous to humans due to the inhibition of their normal fear response. Unnecessary staff as well as curious members of the public should be kept away from the scene.

Public Safety. Until the situation is under control, it is important to keep the scene of the emergency free of unnecessary people. This can be especially difficult during hours of public visitation. A team of employees should be assigned to respond to all emergency calls to provide crowd control and support. These people should come from areas of the zoo unlikely to be involved in dangerous animal emergencies, such as the administration, education, children's zoo, or bird department staffs. This team should clear the area of both visitors and employees not engaged in the capture attempt and rope off the area.

All zoo gates should be closed to prevent additional access by the public and to hinder further escape of the animal. A zoo representative should remain at each gate to allow the entry of emergency vehicles and, when needed, to accompany them to the site. Access for emergency vehicles can be difficult in most zoos. Hills, sharp corners, overhanging branches, narrow walkways, and new construction may impede emergency vehicles. Staff familiar with the layout of the zoo can guide them on the quickest route to the scene. In some circumstances, zoo vehicles will be needed to transport people into and out of an area.

First aid may need to be administered both to zoo employees and to members of the public. Personnel ordinarily assigned to crowd control should be trained in first aid so that they can provide emergency first aid while waiting for an ambulance. With this training, they can also give first aid for the minor injuries, bee stings, and so forth that occur regularly in a zoo. Certified first aid training is available in every major United States city through the American Red Cross. Zoo personnel trained in first aid are invaluable during emergencies and for day-to-day zoo-related medical problems.

Emergency Communication. Good communication is critical in the management of an emergency. From the first call for help to the dissemination of information after the event, information must be concise and accurate. Until the problem is resolved, emergency communications take priority over all other communications. Small zoos may rely on word of mouth to spread the news of a problem needing immediate attention. Whistles can be carried by all keeper staff and utilized to summon assistance when necessary. The telephone can be used to summon emergency support from outside the zoo. Larger zoos may have telephone systems and two-way radios that are used routinely to communicate within the zoo. Public address systems can be used to mobilize staff as well as to encourage the public to seek safety away from the emergency site and/or direct them to safety within a building. In addition to safeguarding their well-being, removing onlookers from the area provides improved access for emergency vehicles. All gates to the zoo should be closed to additional visitors until the emergency situation is under control. A zoo employee should be stationed at each gate to explain the emergency and to suggest that the situation will be under control shortly.

Each zoo should develop an exact schedule of who is to be notified by whom in the event of an animal escape. We suggest that each employee be instructed to call a central switchboard operator and state his or her name, the location, and the nature of the emergency. If the employee is alone, visual contact with the animal should be maintained and a messenger (even a member of the public) should be sent to get help. The switchboard operator should then notify a predetermined schedule of animal maintenance supervisors. Notification can be accomplished by telephoning or using radios to contact the appropriate individuals, by announcing a coded phrase over a public address system, by activating all or certain designated pagers, or by setting off a siren. Minimally, the list of people to be contacted would include the personnel of the animal section involved, the veterinary staff, the shooting team, and the personnel responsible for crowd control.

A list of emergency telephone numbers should be available to employees at all times. Most critically, the person acting as switchboard operator should have ready access to phone numbers that may need to be called during an emergency. Appropriate zoo personnel, local hospitals, public utilities, police, fire, ambulance, and maintenance/repair services should be listed. Additionally, personal pager numbers should be provided in the event that zoo personnel are otherwise unavailable. Key staff may be required to carry radios or pagers at all times in order to respond rapidly to an emergency. During "off" hours when no switchboard operator is present, security guards, as well as any personnel observing an emergency situation, should be able to contact appropriate emergency response team members.

The success of the entire procedure is dependent upon the reaction of the person in the position of switchboard operator/dispatcher. Training is the key that will guarantee an effective response to any emergency situation. Zoo personnel should develop procedures appropriate for their zoo in advance, when time and thought can be given to formulating precise and clear procedures to prevent panic and confusion. These procedures should be readily available in writing to whomever is operating the switchboard at any given time.

Public Information. During and after an emergency, employees may be asked about the situation by members of the public or the news media. It is essential that zoo employees completely understand the responsibility they bear to themselves, to any animal involved in an emergency, to fellow employees, zoo visitors, and the public at large, to the zoo, and to its governing institution in this situation. In order to protect the essential interests and well-being of all parties concerned, employees must refrain from giving personal interpretations of the incident. Individual employees will not have all the facts, nor be able to assess fully the circumstances surrounding an emergency. Releasing partial information, the names of individuals involved, or speculating as to the cause of the emergency will do a terrible disservice to all involved.

An emergency at the local zoo will immediately draw media attention. The media, as well as the general public, have a right to know the facts surrounding any incident. Although the zoo director will ultimately assume the role of spokesperson, the director may be busy managing the problem when the press first arrive. In this event, one person should be designated as a spokesperson to answer all inquiries. The spokesperson should be careful not to release the names of any victims or minors until relatives have been notified. It is extremely important that blame or responsibility for an incident not be discussed until an investigation has occurred.

Shooting Team. Whenever a dangerous animal threatens human life, it should be destroyed immediately. A "shooting team" should respond to all emergencies involving potentially dangerous animals. These people will have no responsibility to capture or restrain the animal, nor should they have to deal with crowd control. Their entire attention should be devoted to the situation at hand, and they should be able to respond immediately should circumstances dictate.

People authorized to use firearms must be responsible, familiar with the behavior of potentially dangerous animals, and familiar with firearms and safety practices. They should undergo regular training at a firing range with the weapons to be used in the event of an animal escape. Access to firearms should be limited to members of the shooting team and should be approved in advance by the institution. Shotguns loaded with large buckshot or slugs and rifles using ammunition appropriate to the size of the potentially dangerous animals in the collection should be available. Shooting team members should destroy an animal only when instructed to do so by the most senior animal section representative on site or when human life is immediately threatened.

Some zoos have "kill lists" identifying animals that are to be destroyed whenever they breach secondary containment. Although this may simplify the decision-making process, it may result in needless animal destruction. Even the most dangerous of species may try to hide or retreat when in unfamiliar surroundings. It is very possible that the animal can be safely immobilized and returned to its enclosure.

Other Emergencies

There are many threatening conditions that may require a rapid and organized response to minimize injury to people and animals or damage to facilities. Severe weather such as hurricanes, tornadoes, flooding, or earthquakes not only can severely damage the zoo, but also will do serious damage to the local community. Resources and equipment to clean up after catastrophic weather conditions will be directed to the community as a whole, and the zoo will be a low priority unless it presents a threat to the community. Portable generators, chain saws, gasoline, fresh water, and an adequate supply of foodstuffs should be maintained by the zoo at all times. Staff may be needed around the clock to deal with problems occurring during severe weather. Normal access to the zoo may be limited or cut off due to flooding, downed trees, or damaged roadways.

Fire in an animal facility requires quick thinking and discretionary judgement on the part of the employee discovering the problem. The fire department should be called immediately and directed to the zoo entrance nearest the fire that allows the passage of its vehicles. The switchboard operator should also notify appropriate zoo personnel to assist at the scene. The public should be evacuated from the area. If the fire is within an animal facility, attempts should be made to remove animals threatened by the fire. If possible, employees should attempt to extinguish the fire with a fire extinguisher. Circuit breakers to the affected area should be turned off.

Bomb threats should be immediately referred to the law enforcement agency having jurisdiction. Generally, in a bomb threat emergency, zoo staff should follow the same evacuation procedures as for a fire, except that all radio communications in the area should cease immediately. Visitors overhearing conversation concerning a bomb threat could panic, creating yet another problem.

Emergency Procedures Manual

Written emergency procedures are critical. Training cannot begin, nor can there be assurance of uniformity, if a reference text or manual is not available to each employee. A copy of the zoo's emergency procedures should be given to each new employee hired. It should be clear to the employee that he or she is responsible for understanding the material. Emergency procedures should be discussed regularly during employee training sessions. Various scenarios should be given as examples, and the employees should discuss their response in each hypothetical situation. Practices or "drills" involving a variety of situations and conditions should be conducted periodically. After each drill (or actual emergency) all responding individuals should gather within 24 to 48 hours to critique the response. Any improvements resulting from this critique should be promptly incorporated into the written procedure manual.

The key to the management of any zoo emergency is common sense. Common sense and the ability to translate training programs and established procedures into effective action appropriate to the situation make security programs effective.

REFERENCES

Brand, M., ed. 1984. *Security for libraries: People, buildings, collections.* Chicago: American Library Association.

Emergency procedures manual, Houston Zoological Gardens. 1988. Houston, Tex.: Houston Zoological Gardens.

Madison, A. 1970. *Vandalism: The not-so-senseless crime.* New York: Seabury Press.

Rosberg, R. R., ed. 1980. *Security risk management.* Boston: Dorison House Publishers.

Sausman, K. 1982. *Zoological park and aquarium fundamentals.* Wheeling, W.Va.: American Association of Zoological Parks and Aquariums.

Strobl, W. M. 1973. *Security: Theft protection, security development, fire protection, emergency and disaster planning, and guard organization.* New York: Industrial Press.

PART TWO

Nutrition

INTRODUCTION
Mary E. Allen

Scientific management of zoo animal populations requires attention to many facets of biology, including social interactions, behavioral requirements, microhabitat characteristics, population genetics, reproductive viability, and preventive medical programs. There can be little doubt, however, that nutrition is one of the most critical components of animal management, and yet one that has received insufficient attention in the zoological community. Zoo mammals must be fed daily. We have not only an opportunity, but an obligation, to assure that their diets promote health and longevity. As of 1994, only six zoos in North America had employed trained nutritionists, and a handful of others had engaged nutritional consultants. Given the variety of species maintained in zoos and the lack of nutritional research on most zoo animals, this must be considered a rather small beginning.

This part provides an introduction to the fundamental principles of nutrition. While the chapters emphasize practical aspects of feeding zoo mammals, the authors reinforce the importance and contribution of basic research in nutritional sciences. In chapter 10, Oftedal and Allen discuss how the constraints of captivity dictate what and how we feed zoo animals. Many zoo professionals hold the view that we must provide "natural" diets whenever possible; that fresh foods, such as produce and prey, are superior to manufactured foods. However, Oftedal and Allen point out that few zoo mammals demonstrate "nutritional wisdom" with respect to food choice. Specific nutrients are required, not necessarily specific foods, although the physical form of foods, dietary diversity, and food presentation methods may be important in promoting normal feeding behavior. This chapter reviews the step-by-step process of dietary evaluation and includes discussions of dry matter content, feed label information, the use of supplements, computer programs, nutrient interrelationships, and the establishment of nutrient standards.

Most animal care staff working in zoos do not have training in nutrition. Chapter 11 on essential nutrients by Allen and Oftedal provides basic information about the nutrients, indications of deficiencies and toxicities, and quantitative requirements. While nutrient requirements have not been quantitatively defined for most zoo mammals, extrapolation from the known requirements of domestic animals can be useful. The chapter also explains the basis for the expression of requirements. The major constituents of foods are defined, as are the methods used to determine them analytically.

The remaining three chapters in this section apply basic nutritional principles to the feeding of herbivores, carnivores, and omnivores. Oftedal, Baer, and Allen point out in chapter 12 that most herbivores in zoos are fed diets that are very similar to those fed to domestic herbivores. Fortunately, zoo herbivores adapt readily to pelleted diets and hays, since relying on fresh browse and produce as major sources of essential nutrients is both expensive and ineffective. The authors discuss the different approaches that apply to the feeding of "bulk and roughage feeders" versus "concentrate selectors." Practical discussions of pellet formulation, the use and quality assessment of hay, and the use of browse and produce are included.

Zoos have progressed considerably since the days when carnivores were fed slabs of meat, with dire consequences to their health. Manufactured feeds, such as dry kibbled dog foods and frozen meat-based diets, are widely used for canids and felids. In chapter 13, Allen, Oftedal, and Baer make a distinction between the "obligate" or strict carnivore and the facultative carnivore. With respect to the domestic cat, the peculiarities of strict carnivore requirements are fairly well defined. However, there are specialist carnivores such as pinnipeds and anteaters about which we know little. As with the cat, unique requirements may exist for these species that would set them apart from other, facultative carnivores. Nutritional research is needed on these little-studied species.

There is a common belief among non-nutritionists that if foods consumed by wild mammals could be chemically defined through sampling and analysis, we would know with some certainty how and what to feed in captivity. Chapter 14 by Oftedal and Allen on the feeding and nutrition of omnivorous mammals explains that while knowledge of food choice and composition in the wild is helpful, it does not provide sufficient quantitative information to aid in dietary formulation for captive omnivores. Our tendency to feed fruits and vegetables to captive primates stems from our knowledge that fruits, leaves, and other plant parts are consumed by many primates in the wild, yet cultivated produce bears little resemblance nutritionally to the plants consumed by wild primates. The use of produce, browse, and insects in diets for omnivores is discussed in the context of heightened interest in increasing dietary diversity and promoting more normal behaviors.

Nutritional studies in zoos are usually initiated in response to specific health problems, and gradually, some of these problems are being solved. However, basic research on nutritional physiology and digestive strategies is also essential for improving the management of zoo mammals, and some of this research may need to be accomplished in the wild under natural conditions.

10

Nutrition and Dietary Evaluation in Zoos

OLAV T. OFTEDAL AND MARY E. ALLEN

NUTRITION AS A SCIENTIFIC FIELD

As a science, the study of nutrition has advanced rapidly in the past hundred years. In the nineteenth century the nutritional importance of such major food constituents as protein, fat, carbohydrate, and fiber was recognized, and there was much interest in some of the major minerals. But it was not until the twentieth century that the essentiality of vitamins, amino acids, fatty acids, and many trace minerals was demonstrated. The total number of nutrients (vitamins, minerals, amino acids, fatty acids) that are required by mammals is now known to be about 45–47, depending on species. The estimated nutrient requirements of most species of domestic and laboratory animals and of humans have been published by the National Research Council of the U.S. National Academy of Sciences (table 10.1).

Advances in nutritional research have led to a wide array of practical improvements in animal management and feed manufacture. Important relationships have been demonstrated between nutrient intakes and rates of growth, reproductive performance, digestive function, and disease processes. Technological advances in feed manufacture have resulted in improved stability of nutrients during the processing, storage, and use of animal feeds. The characteristics of feeds and feed by-products are better understood, and, as a consequence, the production of higher-quality diets at lower cost is now possible.

In the fields of human medicine, laboratory animal research, and animal agriculture, the importance of nutrition is well recognized. Unfortunately, much misinformation and unfounded speculation about nutrition is disseminated through the popular press, thanks largely to the contributions of self-proclaimed "experts" who lack professional training in nutritional sciences (see Jarvis 1983). However, a large number of training programs in nutrition are now available. In North America about a hundred colleges and universities currently offer graduate training in the nutritional sciences (American Institute of Nutrition 1989).

Despite the rapid advances being made in the nutrition of domestic and laboratory animals, zoo animal nutrition remains a new and a relatively unexplored field. Although H. L. Ratcliffe pioneered the concept of complete, formulated diets at the Philadelphia Zoo in the 1930s (e.g., Ratcliffe 1940, 1947, 1966), most curators and keepers have had implicit faith that diets that approximate the kinds of foods eaten in the wild will be adequate for the majority of zoo animals. Thus monkeys have been fed fruits and vegetables, carnivores slabs of meat, and insectivores trays of mealworms *without regard to nutritional composition*. Some zoo animals managed to survive for many years on these diets, so the diets became commonplace and accepted.

Captive animals may adapt to substandard diets for prolonged periods as long as additional nutrient demands such as those associated with growth, reproduction, or disease do not arise. Aside from early reports of severe metabolic bone disease in large carnivores and monkeys (e.g., Bland Sutton 1888), there was little recognition until the late 1960s and 1970s that nutrient deficiencies might be widespread in zoo animals, or that the reproductive performance of zoo animals might be curtailed by inappropriate diets (e.g., Crawford 1968). In two volumes of the International Zoo Yearbook, volumes 6 (1966) and 16 (1976), much attention was given to the nutrition of zoo animals. J. D. Wallach argued that nutritional problems were ubiquitous in zoos (Wallach 1970, 1971), but unfortunately he included many speculative diagnoses and unwarranted conclusions in his argument. C. T. Robbins's books on wildlife nutrition (1983, 1992) represented a major contribution to the field of nondomestic animal nutrition. In North America, the first zoos to hire professionally trained nutritionists were the Metro Toronto Zoo in 1975, the National Zoological Park in 1978, and the Chicago Zoological Society in 1980.

Given that capture in the wild is no longer an appropriate method of stocking most types of zoo animals, and that zoos must therefore design breeding programs that will sustain captive animal populations, the goal of zoo feeding programs must be to provide nutritional support for all stages of life, including gestation, lactation, and early postnatal

TABLE 10.1.   National Research Council Publications on the
Nutrient Requirements of Domestic and Laboratory Animals

Title	Edition	Year
Nutrient Requirements of Beef Cattle	6th	1984
Nutrient Requirements of Cats	2d	1986
Nutrient Requirements of Fish	2d	1993
Nutrient Requirements of Dairy Cattle	6th	1989
Nutrient Requirements of Dogs	2d	1985
Nutrient Requirements of Goats	1st	1981
Nutrient Requirements of Horses	5th	1989
Nutrient Requirements of Laboratory Animals	4th	1995
Nutrient Requirements of Mink and Foxes	2d	1982
Nutrient Requirements of Nonhuman Primates	1st	1978
Nutrient Requirements of Poultry	9th	1994
Nutrient Requirements of Rabbits	2d	1977
Nutrient Requirements of Sheep	6th	1985
Nutrient Requirements of Swine	9th	1988

Note: This list includes the most recent revisions as of 1995.

growth. It can no longer be assumed that traditional zoo diets are adequate, even when little evidence of frank nutritional deficiency is observed. Marginal nutrient intakes are apt to be manifest first as increased susceptibility to disease, reduced fertility, lower neonatal viability, suboptimal milk production, and retarded rates of growth. In the absence of careful dietary evaluation, it is unlikely that the nutritional component of these problems will be recognized.

DIETARY CHOICE IN THE WILD AND IN CAPTIVITY

Mammals exhibit a wide range of morphological, physiological, and behavioral adaptations geared to the acquisition and utilization of a diverse array of foods. In the wild, both the temporal and the spatial distribution of food resources are typically complex, so that food acquisition may require a large proportion of an animal's daily time budget. In most habitats seasonal variation in food quantity and quality is pronounced, whether driven by changes in temperature, in precipitation, or (in marine habitats) in oceanic currents. Thus mammals may often confront periods of food scarcity. If these periods occur in a regular seasonal pattern, nutritionally costly processes (e.g., intensive lactation and the early postweaning period) may be confined to the periods of nutrient abundance.

Captivity removes much of the complexity and seasonality of food resources. Human beings tend to feed during discrete meals and, almost without thought, have imposed a similar feeding pattern on virtually all species kept in zoos. Animals are fed discrete meals at specific and predictable times, year in and year out. Diets are prepared according to some agreed-upon formula, and vary only as much as individual feeders may differ in their common practices. The amounts fed are geared to produce animals that are in good condition at all times. Seasonality in weight tends to occur only in animals such as temperate-zone deer, seals, and bears that retain seasonal patterns of food intake driven by day length or reproductive cycles.

Thus little similarity remains in the patterns of food availability faced by captive animals and animals in the wild.

Captive mammals are also typically fed on items of importance in human agriculture: commercially available fruits and vegetables, commercially caught fish, meat and dairy products, dog and cat foods, grass and legume hays, and livestock feeds (with or without minor modifications). Such products are only superficially similar to foods available in the wild.

Captive animals are therefore faced with feeding choices very different from those of animals in the wild, and there is no a priori reason to suppose that the choices made in captivity bear any resemblance to choices made in the wild, or that those choices optimize nutrient intakes. On the contrary, nutritionists in zoos have seen countless cases in which the choices made by zoo animals result in nutritionally imbalanced diets. Unfortunately, little scientific evidence exists in support of the notion that zoo animals possess "nutritional wisdom" that enables them to self-select the most appropriate nutrient levels. Unless and until zoos are able to replicate the exact seasonal, temporal, spatial, and nutritional complexity of diets encountered in the wild, animals will be faced with choices that they have not evolved to make. Zoo personnel have no option but to exercise the power of making dietary decisions for the animals in their care. This is the fundamental challenge facing the zoo nutritionist: making the right choices.

THE PROCESS OF DIETARY EVALUATION

Even though food is a central component of animal care and represents a large part of zoo budgets, decisions about diets are often made by diverse staff members. Keepers, curators, veterinarians, and directors may propose, institute, or modify diets for animals. The lack of central responsibility for animal diets usually results in little attention to nutritional concerns unless a major health problem occurs. Even when nutrient deficiencies are diagnosed, detailed dietary evaluation is rarely undertaken. Nutrient supplements may be added without any clear understanding of actual nutrient intakes, either before or after the initiation of supplementation. An important role of the zoo nutritionist is to emphasize the importance of dietary evaluation as a means of improving animal management.

Dietary evaluation is a complicated and time-consuming task, involving measurement of food intake, estimation of nutrient contents, evaluation of label and analytical data, decisions on appropriate nutrient standards, and interpretation of discrepancies between actual and target nutrient levels. Fortunately, a number of computer programs have been devised for evaluating animal diets, including ones developed by zoo nutritionists that contain many typical zoo food items in the data base. While such programs greatly facilitate dietary evaluation, they do not obviate the need for an educated interpretation of the computer output.

Given the vital importance of the evaluation process to an understanding of the nutritional status of a zoo animal, it is appropriate to describe the steps involved in some detail. Any dietary evaluation should consider the following components:

• The diet as presented: form, diversity of ingredients, method of presentation, and use of supplements

• The diet as consumed: the relative amounts of different components consumed by individual animals
• Nutrient composition data: the nutrient levels in the individual foods that are consumed
• Dietary analysis: nutrient levels for the entire diet, as calculated by computer programs
• Appropriate nutrient standards: how nutrient requirements are established, and their limitations
• Dietary revision: implementation of proposed changes

The following discussion of these components is presented in general terms; comments on the diets of specific types of mammals are included in the following chapters on the nutrition and feeding of herbivores (chap. 12), carnivores (chap. 13), and omnivores (chap. 14).

The Diet as Presented

The physical forms of dietary components vary greatly among zoo animal diets: diets may be composed of fresh, canned, frozen, dried, liquid, gel-based, pelleted, and/or extruded products. The physical forms of foods can greatly influence palatability, storage characteristics, spoilage and nutrient stability, digestive function, and feeding behaviors. For example, high-moisture foods are typically prone to bacterial or fungal growth unless treated with antimicrobial agents. By contrast, some manufactured foods (such as pelleted feeds) produced by grinding, mixing, compacting, and drying are quite stable for many months at room temperature if kept dry. Animals with reduced dentition or poor oral health may have difficulty with hard or fibrous foods. Digestive anatomy and physiology may also dictate whether a food form is appropriate. Animals with fermentation chambers, whether in the foregut or hindgut, may require relatively fibrous foods (e.g., hay or browse) to ensure normal microbial fermentation.

While dietary diversity may not be essential from a nutritional perspective, it may play a central role in the stimulation of feeding behavior, especially among primates and other mammals that in the wild spend many hours per day in feeding activities. The effort to minimize costly and nutritionally imbalanced items in an animal diet should be counterbalanced by an attempt to provide diverse feeding opportunities. Even grazing mammals may develop behavioral vices if hay, browse, or other feedstuffs that require prolonged chewing are not regularly available.

The manner of food preparation and presentation can have important nutritional and health implications. Meat, fish, and dairy-based diets can spoil rapidly if warmed before feeding (e.g., premature thawing of frozen foods) or after placement in the exhibit (e.g., due to high ambient temperatures in summer). Prolonged storage of foods prior to use may lead to oxidative changes that reduce levels of vitamins and affect palatability. Poorly designed feeders may lead to needless waste or exclusion of low-ranking animals from choice foods or feeding sites. For example, poorly designed hayracks may allow the high-quality leaves of alfalfa hay to fall on wet or soiled ground, from which they are not eaten, even though alfalfa leaves are preferred by many herbivores.

When evaluating a diet, special attention should be paid to the use of vitamin or mineral supplements. Compositional data for commercial supplements are usually provided on the label or on information sheets supplied with the product. Commercially available supplements vary greatly in composition and are not interchangeable. The supplementation levels recommended by manufacturers may not be appropriate when these products are included in zoo animal diets. Moreover, products marketed specifically for zoo animals frequently contain highly imbalanced nutrient levels. In our experience, the use of inappropriate supplements in excessive amounts is a common cause of excessive or imbalanced vitamin and mineral levels in zoo animal diets. In most cases it is preferable to balance a diet using nutritionally complete feeds rather than relying on accurate disbursement and good mixing of small amounts of supplements.

The Diet as Consumed

When animals are housed in groups, it is common practice to feed amounts somewhat in excess of consumption to ensure that all individuals have access to food. The net effect of this practice is that animals may pick and choose among foods and may ingest a diet that is quite different from the diet that was offered. Intake of individual food items can be measured by weighing the amount of each item offered and the amount remaining uneaten after a meal is finished. With individuals fed alone, this is a relatively easy task, so long as the animal does not throw food from the cage (e.g., some primates), no food is thrown into the cage by zoo visitors, there is no natural vegetation in the enclosure that the animal may be eating (e.g., some ungulates), and vermin such as sparrows, squirrels, or mice do not also partake of the provided meal. Animals housed and fed in groups present more of a problem since it is often impossible to determine who eats what. In such cases observations at feeding times by keepers or volunteers can provide valuable information about food preferences or dominance hierarchies within a group. Sometimes an animal can be separated from its group for a few days for measurement of food intake, but the stress of separation and the change in enclosure size or structure may influence its activity, behavior, and pattern of food consumption.

The measurement of food consumption requires an appreciation of the confounding factors mentioned above, as well as changes in food moisture content. The error caused by moisture loss or gain is easily overlooked. Moist foods will lose water when left at room temperature, especially when exposed to sun or wind or during winter when air is dry. Moisture losses are accelerated when fruits, vegetables, and other foods are chopped or diced. Some dry feeds will pick up moisture, both from humid air and from water on cage floors. Weight changes in feed pans between feeding and pan removal represent the combined effects of moisture changes and food disappearance. One way to correct for moisture losses or gains is to prepare a duplicate feed pan that is kept under the same environmental conditions as the actual feed pan, except that animals do not have access to it. Such "control" pans are valuable as indicators of the magnitude of moisture change, but are not precise. True moisture losses or gains will depend upon the length of time that individual items are exposed to air, which in turn depends on if and when they are eaten.

Given the problem of moisture change, the most accurate method of measuring intake is to determine the dry matter content of the foods offered as well as that of refusals. Food samples and uneaten foods can be dried to constant weight in a drying oven and intake of each food type calculated on a dry matter basis. Because some kinds of foods are highly variable in moisture content, one must ensure that the samples collected are in fact representative of the items offered. The importance of dry matter determination depends on the type of diet and the conditions under which it is fed.

Data on the Nutrient Composition of Foods

The nutrient composition of a diet is typically estimated from data on the nutrient compositions of the individual food items constituting the diet, and is only as accurate as the data on which the estimate is based. Unfortunately, zoo animal diets often contain feedstuffs that are not routinely used in the nutrition of either domestic animals or humans. Zoo nutritionists attempt to obtain analytical data on these foods, but there is as yet no comprehensive publication of such data on zoo feeds.

Data on nutrients in foods can be found in a number of useful publications. The Agricultural Research Service of the United States Department of Agriculture (USDA) produced a publication on human food composition entitled *Composition of Foods* (Agriculture Handbook no. 8) (Watt and Merrill 1963). The data in this handbook are periodically updated and expanded, and are published in revised sections on specific groups of foods (e.g., dairy and egg products, baby foods, fats and oils.) These can be obtained from the U.S. Government Printing Office, Washington, D.C. 20402. *McCance and Widdowson's The Composition of Foods* (Holland et al. 1992) and *Bowes and Church's Food Values of Portions Commonly Used* (Pennington 1989) provide additional information in a somewhat different form. While extremely useful for human foods such as fruits, vegetables, meats, dairy products, and eggs, these publications do not include animal feeds. Animal nutritionists often formulate pelleted or extruded feeds using ground products and by-products such as ground corn, alfalfa meal, soybean meal, and meat and bone meal. Additional animal feedstuffs include whole grains, hays, pasture grasses, browse plants, and mineral supplements. An *Atlas of United States and Canadian Feeds* was published by the National Research Council (NRC) in 1976; updated and more complete information may be found in the various subcommittee reports of the NRC Committee on Animal Nutrition (see table 10.1). NRC publications may be obtained from the National Academy Press, 2101 Constitution Avenue N.W., Washington, D.C. 20418. The annual reference issue of the weekly publication *Feedstuffs* also contains tables of nutrient composition, including useful tables of mineral supplements. Information on the nutritional composition of Asian, African, and South American foods and animals feeds is also available (Leung and Flores 1961; Leung et al. 1965; Leung, Busson, and Jardin 1968; Gohl 1975).

Some types of zoo foods, such as whole prey, various browse plants, and specialty zoo feeds, are not listed in standard human or animal food tables. In some cases, information on the chemical composition of unusual food items can be found in scientific papers and theses (e.g., Southgate 1973; Gaulin and Craker 1979; Milton and Dintsis 1981; Ullrey, Robinson, and Whetter 1981; Hume 1982; Oftedal and Boness 1983; Sauer 1983; Altmann, Post, and Klein 1985; McCullough and Ullrey 1985; Allen 1989; Allen and Oftedal 1989; Bernard and Ullrey 1989; Ullrey and Bernard 1989; Warnell 1988). Additional sources of nutrient composition information may be found in the chapters on herbivores (chap. 12), carnivores (chap. 13), and omnivores (chap. 14) in this volume. Information on commercial feeds can sometimes be obtained directly from manufacturers. Some companies provide data on the nutrient composition of their products in addition to what is required on the feed label by law. Detailed data provided by manufacturers, however, can represent calculated levels of nutrients, nutrients that are added to the base ingredients, such as those from vitamin and mineral premixes, or actual analytical data determined by laboratory testing. It is necessary to contact company representatives to clarify this point.

Label information can be of some value if nothing else is available. Labels typically provide guaranteed minimum levels of certain nutrients (e.g., crude protein, crude fat) and maximum levels of others (e.g., crude fiber, ash). Label guarantees are governed by the American Association of Feed Control Officials. In many cases the actual values will be close to the guaranteed levels, but this is not always the case. Information on ingredient composition is also provided on feed labels. State and federal laws govern the listing of ingredients on feed tags and labels, but the applicability of those laws depends on the type of feed (livestock vs. pet vs. other), the state of origin (especially if locally made), and whether the feed is shipped in interstate commerce. The ingredients that appear on the product label or in promotional material should be listed in descending order of predominance by weight.

Regulations also permit manufacturers to list feed ingredients under "collective terms." Collective terms such as "plant protein products" and "animal protein products" may be used in place of more specific terms such as soybean meal, corn gluten meal, meat and bone meal, or fish meal. Collective terms are governed by federal regulations and can be used only for livestock and poultry feeds. The use of collective terms is not permitted for laboratory or zoo animal foods or for pet foods. This classification based on ingredient origin permits manufacturers to use ingredients that are readily available or inexpensive at the time of manufacture, thereby reducing production costs. The Code of Federal Regulations contains additional information on laws governing feed labels.

The most reliable source of information on foods used in a zoo is analysis by a reputable laboratory. Laboratory analysis is important as a check on the declared composition of feeds and as a means of assessing the quality of highly variable foods such as hay, browse, and fish. Unfortunately, the costs of analysis are quite high for some nutrients, and it is not uncommon to pay $150 or more per sample for a routine battery of nutrient assays. Vitamin assays are often difficult, subject to analytic error, and expensive. Unusual foods may present sampling and analytic problems with which a commercial laboratory is unfamiliar. The most accurate analyses are undoubtedly those conducted in research laboratories using standard analytic procedures. Nutritionists at local universities or government laboratories may be willing to conduct a limited number of analyses as a public service.

Samples selected for analysis must be representative. Sampling may be particularly problematic in foods that are not homogeneous, such as fish and other prey, hay, and browse. For example, when sampling cases of frozen fish, it is necessary to take fish from boxes selected randomly. In addition, fish should be taken from both the middle and the ends of the boxes. A band saw is usually required unless entire cases of fish are thawed to permit removal of individual fish. A truckload of hay may include some bales that are weedy, others that are rain-damaged, and others in which much of the leafy material has been lost during handling; thus samples must be collected from many bales (see Oftedal, Baer, and Allen, chap. 12, this volume). Particular problems may arise in sampling for the analysis of trace minerals and labile nutrients, such as many vitamins (Harris and Karmas 1975; Wolf 1987; Machlin 1991).

The appropriate preservation methods for samples sent for analysis vary depending on the sample. For example, fresh browse should first be frozen, then shipped overnight in insulated containers with dry ice. Frozen foods should also be shipped overnight on dry ice. Dry feeds and forages can be shipped via regular mail.

The selection of a laboratory should be made carefully since there can be great variation among commercial laboratories with respect to methods used, reliability, and cost. Experienced food chemists or nutritionists can be consulted regarding the reputation of a particular laboratory and the suitability of its methods if the user is unfamiliar with them. A check on the precision of a laboratory can be accomplished by sending two matched samples of a feed for the same analyses. The sensitivity of the methods used by a particular laboratory can be checked by sending two matched samples, one of which has had a nutrient added in a known quantity.

Some foods used in zoo animal diets can contain toxins that may be harmful to animals (see Oftedal, Baer, and Allen, chap. 12, this volume). Reviews of food safety and of toxins in foods and animal feeds can be found in Graham (1980), Broquist (1985), Cheeke and Shull (1985), Mehansho, Butler, and Carlson (1987), and Fowler (1989). Laboratories that specialize in analysis of toxins should be used when toxins are suspected.

Dietary Analysis by Computer

The nutrient composition of a diet can be calculated by hand from the amounts of individual foods used and their nutrient levels, but this method is very time-consuming even if a calculator is used. Given that hundreds of individual calculations may be involved in a single dietary evaluation, nutritionists rely heavily on computer programs and data bases that have been developed for this purpose. Although a number of computer programs are commercially available and can be adapted for evaluations of zoo animal diets, many are limited by a restricted data base (e.g., only human foods or only ingredients for domestic animal feeds) or by

the types of dietary manipulations that can be performed. The most useful programs allow calculation of dietary composition on both fresh weight and dry weight bases and identify calculations involving missing data (unknown values) for specific nutrients.

The accuracy of the data base is crucial to any computer analysis of animal diets. The paucity of information on some key nutrients is a particular problem. For example, the selenium content is not known for many feeds used in zoo animal diets. A computer-generated dietary analysis may indicate that a diet is low in selenium, but the low figure may simply reflect an absence of selenium values in the data base. The well-intended supplementation of such a diet with selenium might result in toxic levels. Data entered by users should also be scrutinized for errors, such as entry of nutrient data in the wrong units (e.g., as milligrams rather than micrograms, or amount per pound rather than per kilogram) or with a decimal place shift (e.g., 0.01% instead of 0.1%).

The rapid calculation of nutrient levels made possible by computer programs is particularly valuable when a quick dietary diagnosis is needed, as with an ailing animal. However, computer analyses also require correct interpretation. A professionally trained nutritionist relies on knowledge about digestive processes, nutrient metabolism, interactions among nutrients, nutrient stability, factors that affect nutrient requirements (e.g., species, age, growth rate, reproductive status, clinical conditions), and nutrient toxicities to apply the results of these analyses. At least one program ("The Animal Nutritionist," N-Squared Computing, Silverton, Oregon) allows comparison of nutritional values with estimated nutrient requirements as published by the various NRC subcommittees (see table 10.1). This ability is useful given the diverse array of zoo animals that may be of interest. For example, the diet for a fennec fox, *Vulpes (= Fennecus) zerda,* can be compared with the nutrient requirements of the domestic dog. While the exact requirements of many species are not known, such comparisons with related species can point out major dietary deficiencies. It is important to understand, however, how requirement levels are estimated, and the inherent limitations in these estimates that may make cross-species comparisons inappropriate.

The Development and Use of Nutrient Standards

In the United States, the Committee on Animal Nutrition of the National Research Council periodically releases reports on the nutrient requirements of laboratory and domestic animals (see table 10.1). Each report represents the judgment of a subcommittee of experts and is based on a review of available scientific literature. These reports are revised and updated periodically as new data become available. Similar reports are prepared in some other countries, such as the publications of the Agricultural Research Council in Great Britain (e.g., Agricultural Research Council 1980).

Nutrient requirements for domestic animals are determined through feeding experiments in which specific responses (such as growth and composition of tissues, biochemical indices, and reproductive performance) are monitored. Given the normal variation in the nutrient composition of natural feed ingredients and the chemical and metabolic interactions that may occur among nutrients and other chemical compounds, nutritionists often opt to use rigorously defined diets in their attempts to define nutrient requirements. Whereas a "practical diet" is composed of natural feed ingredients, a "purified diet" contains a limited number of relatively well defined constituents, and a "chemically defined diet" contains nutrients in pure chemical form (e.g., starch or sucrose, individual amino acids, individual vitamins and minerals). Nutrient requirements of animals are often determined using purified and chemically defined diets in which factors that adversely affect nutrient availability are avoided or minimized. As such, these minimal nutrient requirements are best-case scenarios; the same nutrient levels in practical diets may fail to meet requirements due to reduced nutrient availability. In utilizing nutrient requirement estimates, a nutritionist must be aware of the conditions under which the requirements were estimated and determine whether any corrections or allowances need to be made in evaluating practical diets.

Interrelationships among specific nutrients can profoundly affect the utilization of nutrients by animals. For example, calcium metabolism is regulated by vitamin D, vitamin E requirements are increased with increasing dietary polyunsaturated fatty acids, vitamin K requirements may be increased in the presence of excess vitamin E, and copper, molybdenum, and sulfur interactions are well established. A review of this topic can be found in Wise (1980).

Interactions between nutrients and nonnutritive food components, sometimes called secondary plant compounds, may also affect the availability of nutrients. One of the best-known examples is the effect of oxalic acid on calcium availability. Leafy green plants such as spinach and rhubarb greens, tropical grasses, legumes, shrubs, and trees contain calcium oxalates in varying amounts. Mineral deficiency signs, urolithiasis, and poisoning have been described in animals consuming high concentrations of oxalates (Barry and Blaney 1987), although there are species differences in the ability to detoxify oxalates. Phytic acid is another plant compound that can adversely affect mineral absorption by animals (Graf 1986). Phytic acid (phytate) serves as a phosphorous storage compound for plants and is present in high concentrations in grains and seeds. As much as 90% of seed phosphorus may exist as phytate-phosphorus. In this form, the phosphorus is not readily available to animals. In addition, phytates can complex with other minerals such as iron, calcium, and magnesium, and as a consequence, the availability of those minerals may also be reduced. Other secondary plant compounds found in foods, such as tannins and alkaloids, are discussed by Oftedal, Baer, and Allen, (chap. 12, this volume). Knowledge of interrelationships among nutrients and nonnutritive food components is essential in the evaluation of zoo animal diets.

The requirements published by the NRC are updated periodically as additional information is generated through controlled studies. The estimates for some species (e.g., dairy cattle, pigs) are based on a large number of studies and are thus relatively tightly defined. Other species (e.g., horses, goats, rabbits) have received less research attention because of their lesser economic importance and hence more restricted research funding. Research conducted by nutritionists employed by feed manufacturers is rarely published,

as it is considered proprietary information. Thus, although much research has been conducted on diets for dogs, the published literature is surprisingly meager. Differences in the estimated nutrient requirements of different species reflect, in part, differences in the amount of published information available for different species.

Many breeds of domestic and laboratory animals have undergone intensive genetic selection in an effort to improve growth rates, productivity, and reproductive output. Rapid weight gain, marbling of muscle tissues with fat, high and sustained milk yields, and large litter size may not be relevant criteria for the dietary management of zoo animals, although they may be crucial to the farmer rearing cattle and swine. The nutrient requirements for rapid growth of beef cattle in feed lots may be quite different from those for young wildebeest roaming in a mixed-species African plains exhibit. Longevity is usually not an objective in domestic animal operations, although it often is in zoos.

Estimates of domestic animal nutrient requirements can serve as useful guidelines for evaluating zoo animal diets, but a number of factors exist that make direct application difficult. Growth, fattening, lactation, pregnancy, illness, and old age may influence nutrient requirements, and need to be taken into account. Requirements for certain nutrients may also be elevated under conditions of stress. When nutrient standards derived from studies of domestic animals are applied to exotic animals, a margin of safety should be included, at least for some nutrients. For example, the amounts of vitamin E required by domestic animals may not be sufficient for some species of zoo animals, especially those that are prone to myopathy (Brady and Ullrey 1976; Hume 1982; Ullrey et al. 1983). A cautious approach is warranted until sound research can demonstrate whether perceived differences between exotic and domestic animals are real or not.

Nutrient losses due to chemical instability during manufacture, transport, or storage of feeds should be considered in establishing target nutrient levels. For example, some vitamins are labile when exposed to heat, light, oxygen, or a combination thereof (Bender 1978; National Research Council 1973). Stability may also be influenced by mineral content (due to a catalytic effect), moisture content, and feed pH. Nutrient levels in diets should include an allowance for losses, and vulnerable feeds should not be stored for long periods of time before being used.

Dietary Revision

A number of basic principles apply when dietary changes are implemented. Dietary changes should be made in stepwise fashion, with the rate of change depending on both the magnitude of change and the type of animal being fed. A small change (e.g., deletion of a minor component) can be made stepwise over the course of several days, but a wholesale change should be made more gradually over a period of a week or more. Gradual change is especially important for herbivorous animals since the fermentation compartments of the digestive tract are especially sensitive to changes in constituents that support fermentation (see Oftedal, Baer, and Allen, chap. 12, this volume). Some individual animals are reluctant to accept dietary changes and are apt to go off feed if confronted with rapid change. If possible, dietary changes should be made in the absence of other potential disturbances. Construction in the vicinity of the enclosure, periods of high visitor density, introductions of new individuals into a group, and other potential causes of stress should be taken into account when dietary changes are contemplated or attempted.

The person responsible for the purchase of animal food should be consulted well in advance of any dietary change since a gradual change may require that a stockpile of the old feed be kept on hand. When new animals are obtained via purchase or loan, information concerning their usual diet should be obtained from their previous caretakers. When possible, a supply of the products previously fed should be shipped with the animals to permit a gradual changeover to the intended diet.

New food items can sometimes be disguised by mixing them with familiar dietary ingredients or with other particularly attractive foods. For example, a new herbivore pellet may not be accepted by all individuals. If mixing with the old pellet is ineffective, "sweet-feed" (a grain mix for horses that contains molasses) may be used for a few weeks to induce consumption of the new pellet. Alternatively, chopped fruits or vegetables may be mixed with the new pellet to improve acceptance.

Good record keeping and attention to feeding behavior are especially important when dietary changes are implemented. The role of keepers is paramount when diets are changed because keepers are usually most familiar with the typical behavior, preferences, and physical condition of individual animals. Input from keepers is extremely useful in planning dietary changes, and their attitude may ultimately determine the success or failure of implementation. The reasons for any proposed dietary change should be made clear well in advance of the change. If possible, keepers should strive to tabulate information on feed acceptance and intake on a daily basis so that the success of the dietary change can be more accurately evaluated.

Dietary change may sometimes come about inadvertently, through ingredient substitutions made by feed manufacturers. If the ingredient composition of a feed is not fixed via purchasing specifications, the manufacturer may change ingredient composition from one lot of feed to the next in response to changing ingredient costs. These changes may cause palatability problems and feed refusal, which could have serious consequences during periods of high energy or nutrient demand, as during rapid growth, lactation, or illness. The use of fixed-composition ("fixed formula") feeds can reduce lot-to-lot or manufacturer-to-manufacturer variation and is hence advisable when feasible (see Oftedal, Baer, and Allen, chap. 12, this volume).

CONCLUSION

As so many factors must be considered in dietary evaluation, decisions concerning animal diets should be made carefully and with input from a variety of zoo staff, including a nutritionist. Zoo animal nutrition is a new and exciting field of scientific endeavor, and much more research is needed, even with regard to very basic questions. Unfortunately, only a handful of the persons who work in zoos have training in nutrition. We hope that the nutrition chapters in this volume will help to increase awareness of the importance of nutrition to zoos and stimulate students to consider a career in this rapidly developing area.

REFERENCES

Agricultural Research Council. 1980. *The nutrient requirements of ruminant livestock.* Slough, England: Commonwealth Agricultural Bureaux.

Allen, M. E. 1989. Nutritional aspects of insectivory. Ph.D. thesis, Michigan State University, East Lansing.

Allen, M. E., and Oftedal, O. T. 1989. Dietary manipulation of the calcium concentration of feed crickets. *J. Zoo Wildl. Med.* 20:26–33.

Altmann, S. A., Post, D. G., and Klein, D. F. 1985. Nutrients and toxins of plants in Amboseli, Kenya. *Afr. J. Ecol.* 25:279–93.

American Institute of Nutrition. 1989. The directory of graduate programs in nutritional sciences. *J. Nutr.* 119:D1–D92.

Barry, T. N., and Blaney, B. J. 1987. Secondary compounds of forages. In *The nutrition of herbivores,* ed. J. B. Hacker and J. H. Ternouth, 91–119. Marrickville, N.S.W., Australia: Academic Press.

Bender, A. E. 1978. *Food processing and nutrition.* New York: Academic Press.

Bernard, J. B., and Ullrey, D. E. 1989. Evaluation of dietary husbandry of marine mammals at two major zoological parks. *J. Zoo Wildl. Med.* 20:45–52.

Bland Sutton, J. 1888. Rickets in monkeys, lions, bears, and birds. *J. Comp. Med. Surg.* 10:1–29.

Brady, P. S., and Ullrey, D. E. 1976. White muscle disease in wild mammals. *Proceedings of the Annual Meeting of the American Association of Zoo Veterinarians,* St. Louis, Mo., 269–84. Philadelphia: American Association of Zoo Veterinarians.

Broquist, Harry P. 1985. The indolizidine alkaloids, slaframine and swainsonine: Contaminants in animal forages. In *Annual review of nutrition,* vol. 5, ed. R. E. Olson, E. Buetler, and H. P. Broquist, 391–409. Palo Alto, Calif.: Annual Reviews.

Cheeke, P. R., and Shull, L. R. 1985. Natural toxicants in feeds and poisonous plants. Westport, Conn.: AVI Publishing.

Crawford, M. A. 1968. *Comparative nutrition of wild animals.* Symposia of the Zoological Society of London, no. 21. New York: Academic Press.

Fowler, M. E. 1989. *Medicine and surgery of South American camelids.* Ames: Iowa State University Press.

Gaulin, S. J., and Craker, L. E. 1979. Protein in vegetative and reproductive tissues of several neotropical species. *J. Agric. Food Chem.* 27:791–95.

Gohl, Bo. 1975. *Tropical feeds: Feeds information summaries and nutritive values.* FAO Agricultural Studies, no. 96. Rome: Food and Agriculture Organization of the United Nations.

Graf, E. 1986. Phytic acid, chemistry and applications. Minneapolis, Minn.: Pilatus Press.

Graham, H. D. 1980. *Safety of foods.* 2d ed. Westport, Conn.: AVI Publishing.

Harris, R. S., and Karmas, E. 1975. *Nutritional evaluation of food processing.* 2d ed. Westport, Conn.: AVI Publishing.

Holland, B., Welch, A. A., Unwin, D. H., Buss, D. H., Paul, A. A., and Southgate, D. A. T. 1992. *McCance and Widdowson's The composition of foods.* 5th ed. Letchworth, Herts., U.K.: Royal Society of Chemistry.

Hume, I. D. 1982. *Digestive physiology and nutrition of marsupials.* New York: Cambridge University Press.

Jarvis, W. T. 1983. Food faddism, cultism, and quackery. In

Annual review of nutrition, vol. 3, ed. W. J. Darby, H. P. Broquist, and R. E. Olson, 391–409. Palo Alto, Calif.: Annual Reviews.

Leung, W. W., Busson, F., and Jardin, C. 1968. *USHEW/FAO food composition table for use in Africa.* Bethesda, Md.: National Center for Chronic Disease Control, U.S. Department of Health, Education, and Welfare.

Leung, W. W., Butrum, R. R., Chang, F. H., Rao, M. N., and Polacchi, W. 1965. *USHEW/FAO food composition table for use in East Asia.* Bethesda, Md.: National Institute of Arthritis, Metabolism, and Diseases, U.S. Department of Health, Education, and Welfare.

Leung, W. W., and Flores, M. 1961. *INCAP-ICNND food composition table for use in Latin America.* Bethesda, Md.: National Institutes of Health.

Machlin, L. J. 1991. *Handbook of vitamins.* 2d ed. New York: Marcel Dekker.

McCullough, D. R., and Ullrey, D. E. 1985. *Chemical composition and gross energy of deer forage plants on the George Reserve, Michigan.* Research Report no. 465, February 1985. East Lansing: Michigan State University Agricultural Experiment Station.

Mehansho, H., Butler, L. R., and Carlson, D. M. 1987. Dietary tannins and salivary proline-rich proteins: Interactions, induction, and defense mechanisms. In *Annual review of nutrition,* vol. 7, ed. R. E. Olson and H. P. Broquist, 423–40. Palo Alto, Calif.: Annual Reviews.

Milton, K., and Dintsis, F. R. 1981. Nitrogen-to-protein conversion factors for tropical plant samples. *Biotropica* 13:177–81.

National Research Council. 1973. *Effect of processing on the nutritional value of feeds.* Washington, D.C.: National Academy of Sciences.

———. 1976. *Atlas of United States and Canadian feeds.* Washington, D.C.: National Academy of Sciences.

Oftedal, O. T., and Boness, D. J. 1983. Fish quality: The net result. *Proceedings of the Annual Meeting of the American Association of Zoo Veterinarians,* 47–51. Philadelphia: American Association of Zoo Veterinarians.

Pennington, J. A. T. 1989. *Bowes and Church's food values of portions commonly used.* 15th ed. New York: Harper and Row.

Ratcliffe, H. L. 1940. Diets for a zoological garden: Some results during a test period of five years. *Zoologica* 25:463–72.

———. 1947. Scientific diets for the zoo. *Fauna* 9:26–28.

———. 1966. Diets for zoological gardens: Aid to conservation and disease control. *Int. Zoo Yrbk.* 6:4–23.

Robbins, C. T. 1983. *Wildlife feeding and nutrition.* New York: Academic Press.

———. 1992. *Wildlife feeding and nutrition.* 2d ed. New York: Academic Press.

Sauer, J. J. C. 1983. A comparison between *Acacia* and *Combretum* leaves utilized by giraffe. *S. Afr. J. Anim. Sci.* 13:43–44.

Southgate, D. A. T. 1973. Fibre and the other unavailable carbohydrates and their effects on the energy value of the diet. *Proc. Nutr. Soc.* 32:131–36.

Ullrey, D. E., and Bernard, J. B. 1989. Meat diets for performing exotic cats. *J. Zoo Wildl. Med.* 20:20–25.

Ullrey, D. E., Robinson, P. T., and Whetter, P. A. 1981. Composition of preferred and rejected *Eucalyptus* browse offered to captive koalas, *Phascolarctos cinereus* (Marsupialia). *Aust. J. Zool.* 29:839–46.

Ullrey, D. E., Schmitt, S. M., Cooley, T. M., Ku, P. K., and Whetter, P. A. 1983. Vitamin E and selenium, an update for captive wild animals. *Proceedings of the Annual Meeting of the American Association of Zoo Veterinarians,* Louisville, Ky., 37–39. Philadelphia: American Association of Zoo Veterinarians.

Wallach, J. D. 1970. Nutritional diseases of exotic animals. *J. Am. Vet. Med. Assoc.* 157:583–99.

———. 1971. Nutritional problems in zoos. *Proceedings, Cornell Nutrition Conference for Feed Manufacturers,* 10–19.

Warnell, K. J. 1988. Feed intake, digestibility, digesta passage, and fecal microbial ecology of the red panda *(Ailurus fulgens).* M.S. thesis, Michigan State University, East Lansing.

Watt, B. K., and Merrill, A. L. 1963. *Composition of foods.* (Agriculture Handbook no. 8). Washington, D.C.: U.S. Department of Agriculture.

Wise, A. 1980. Nutrient interrelationships. *Nutr. Abs. Rev.,* ser. A, 50 (5): 319–32.

Wolf, W. R. 1987. Quality assurance for trace element analysis. In *Trace elements in human and animal nutrition,* 5th ed., ed. W. Mertz, 57–78. New York: Academic Press.

11

Essential Nutrients in Mammalian Diets

MARY E. ALLEN AND OLAV T. OFTEDAL

Nutritional evaluation of a diet requires assessment of a multitude of nutrients. Appropriate nutrient levels are important both to ensure appropriate digestive function and to fulfill specific metabolic needs. Nutritional research has established that a wide variety of nutrients are required by animals, and that the specific levels required may vary considerably from species to species (tables 11.1 and 11.2). In this chapter we present some basic information on the nutrients thought to be required by zoo mammals, with some comments on nutrient analysis and deficiencies. Interrelationships of nutrients are discussed in chapter 10. A more detailed review of the nutrients may be found in animal nutrition texts such as Church and Pond (1988) and Maynard et al. (1979).

EXPRESSION OF NUTRIENT REQUIREMENTS

An animal's daily requirement for nutrients is influenced by its body size, physiological state, activity level, age, health status, and other factors. For practical reasons, animal nutritionists usually express the amount of a nutrient in a diet as a percentage or as a concentration. The nutrient requirements of animals are also commonly expressed in this way. However, this method of expressing nutrient requirements does not account for the fact that a high-energy diet will generally be consumed in lesser quantities than will a low-energy diet. Thus, expression of nutrient requirements based on the energy density of a diet is actually more precise, since, under normal circumstances, animals will adjust food intake to meet their caloric requirements (see Oftedal and Allen, chap. 14, this volume).

We can rarely achieve precision when feeding zoo animals because of this uncertainty about level of intake. While animals under normal circumstances usually will not consume energy in excess of their requirements, obesity in pets and zoo animals is not uncommon. Zoo animals in a group situation tend to be fed in excess of their requirements to ensure that the youngest or most subordinate animals will obtain sufficient food, but some animals (particularly domi-

nant animals) may consume energy in excess of their needs and become obese.

In contrast, low levels of food intake may occur in animals that experience pronounced seasonality in food intake in the wild. Even in captivity, the effects of photoperiod, temperature, and other factors may induce periods of chronic energy deficit and weight loss attributable to depressed intake.

THE MAJOR CONSTITUENTS OF FOODS

Food is composed both of major constituents, such as fats, proteins, and carbohydrates, and of specific essential nutrients, such as amino acids, fatty acids, minerals, and vitamins. Labels on manufactured feeds usually include some information on the concentrations of the major constituents, often expressed as minimum or maximum values. These listings are typically based on the "proximate analysis" system, which includes analyses for moisture, crude fiber, crude protein, crude fat, and ash (Maynard et al. 1979). The difference between the sum of these constituents and 100% is calculated and termed "nitrogen-free extract" or "carbohydrate." The proximate analysis system provides a reasonable estimate of most of the major constituents as long as fiber levels are low and there is not much nonprotein nitrogen. For foods high in fiber, other systems of fiber analysis are more appropriate (Van Soest 1994), and "carbohydrate" cannot be measured accurately by difference. We first present a discussion of some of the characteristics of the major food constituents, followed by a discussion of the essential minerals and vitamins.

Water

The moisture in foods is important as a supplemental water source for many animals. In species that do not drink water, water requirements must be met by water in food, either directly or via oxidation of organic constituents to produce metabolic water. The water requirements of mammals depend on a variety of factors, but are especially influenced

TABLE 11.1.   Estimated Nutrient Requirements for Growth of Some Omnivores and Carnivores

Nutrient	Mouse[a]	Rat[b]	Pig[c]	Dog[d]	Cat[e]
Protein (%)	20.0	16.7	20	15	24
Arginine (%)	0.33	0.48	0.44	0.50	1.0
Histidine (%)	0.22	0.31	0.28	0.18	0.3
Isoleucine (%)	0.44	0.69	0.59	0.36	0.5
Leucine (%)	0.78	1.19	0.78	0.58	1.2
Lysine (%)	0.44	1.02	1.06	0.51	0.8
Methionine + cystine (%)	0.56	1.09	0.53	0.39	0.75
Phenylalanine + tyrosine (%)	0.44	1.13	0.86	0.72	0.85
Threonine (%)	0.44	0.69	0.62	0.47	0.7
Tryptophan (%)	0.11	0.22	0.16	0.15	0.15
Valine (%)	0.56	0.82	0.62	0.39	0.6
Fat (%)					
Linoleic acid (%)	0.76	0.67	0.11	1.0	0.5
Arachidonic acid (%)	ND	ND	ND	ND	0.02
Minerals					
Calcium (%)	0.56	0.56	0.78	0.59	0.8
Phosphorus (%)	0.33	0.33	0.67	0.44	0.6
Potassium (%)	0.22	0.40	0.29	0.44	0.4
Sodium (%)	0.06	0.06	0.11	0.06	0.05
Chloride (%)	0.06	0.06	0.09	0.09	0.19
Magnesium (%)	0.06	0.06	0.044	0.04	0.04
Iron (ppm)	39	39	89	32	80
Copper (ppm)	6.7	5.6	5.6	2.9	5.0
Manganese (ppm)	11	11	3.3	5.1	5
Zinc (ppm)	11	11	89	36	50
Iodine (ppm)	0.17	0.17	0.16	0.59	0.35
Selenium (ppm)	0.17	0.17	0.28	0.11	0.1
Vitamins					
Vitamin A (IU/kg)	2,670	2,560	1,940	3,710	3,300
Vitamin D (IU/kg)	1,100	1,100	220	404	500
Vitamin E (IU/kg)	36	30	12	22	30
Vitamin K (ppm)	1.1	1.1	0.56	ND	0.1
Thiamin (ppm)	5.6	4.4	1.1	1.0	5
Riboflavin (ppm)	7.8	3.3	3.3	2.5	4
Pantothenic acid (ppm)	18	11	10	9.9	5
Niacin (ppm)	17	17	14	11	40
Pyridoxine (ppm)	8.9	6.7	1.7	1.1	4
Folic acid (ppm)	0.56	1.1	0.33	0.2	0.8
Biotin (ppm)	0.22	0.22	0.06	ND	0.07
Vitamin B_{12} (ppb)	11	56	17	26	20
Choline (ppm)	2,220	833	440	1,250	2,400

Note: Requirements per kg diet (dry matter basis).

Abbreviations: ND, requirement not demonstrated.

[a] For young, growing mouse (National Research Council 1995).

[b] For young, growing rat (National Research Council 1995).

[c] For 10–20 kg growing pig (National Research Council 1988).

[d] For 3 kg growing beagle puppy (National Research Council 1985).

[e] For 10–20-week-old-kitten consuming a diet with 5.0 kcal ME/g diet dry matter (National Research Council 1986).

by thermoregulatory needs. Since evaporation of water requires a substantial amount of heat energy, many mammals use evaporative cooling as a method of heat loss (Schmidt-Nielsen and Schmidt-Nielsen 1952; Schmidt-Nielsen 1979). Because the amount of water evaporated may be great, such animals require access to large amounts of water when heat-stressed. Other factors that influence water requirements include the need to excrete electrolytes and renal wastes, the

ability of the kidneys to produce concentrated urine, and the need for water for milk production.

The water content of foods has important implications for food storage since high-moisture foods are subject to microbial and fungal proliferation in the absence of suitable deterrents. Hay that is insufficiently dry will tend to become moldy, for example. Water content is particularly high in some types of produce (up to 90-95% of many commercial

TABLE 11.2. Estimated Nutrient Requirements for Growth of Some Domestic Herbivores

Nutrient	Horse[a]	Sheep[b]	Cattle[c]
Protein (%)	14.5	14.7	16
Lysine (%)	0.60	ND	ND
Fat			
Linoleic acid (%)	0.5	ND	ND
Minerals			
Calcium (%)	0.68	0.51	0.52
Phosphorus (%)	0.38	0.24	0.31
Potassium (%)	0.30	0.65	0.65
Sodium (%)	0.10	0.13	0.10
Chloride (%)	UNK	UNK	0.20
Magnesium (%)	0.08	0.15	0.16
Sulfur (%)	0.15	0.2	0.16
Iron (ppm)	50	40	50
Copper (ppm)	10	9	10
Manganese (ppm)	40	30	40
Zinc (ppm)	40	27	40
Iodine (ppm)	0.1	0.45	0.25
Selenium (ppm)	0.1	0.15	0.30
Cobalt (ppm)	0.1	0.15	0.10
Vitamins			
Vitamin A (IU/kg)	2,000	1,085	2,200
Vitamin D (IU/kg)	800	427	300
Vitamin E (IU/kg)	80	15	25
Thiamine (ppm)	3	NR	ND
Riboflavin (ppm)	2	NR	NR

Note: Requirements per kg diet (dry matter basis).

Abbreviations: UNK, quantitative requirement unknown; ND, requirement not demonstrated; NR, not required.

[a] For 4-month-old and/or growing foal (National Research Council 1989a).

[b] For 4-month-old lamb (National Research Council 1985); median value used when range of values given.

[c] For 3–6-month-old calf (National Research Council 1989b).

fruits and vegetables), increasing food bulk and diluting the levels of other nutrients. In most cases animals are able to adjust their intake of foods to compensate for different water contents so long as sufficient quantities are available. One common mistake is to substitute one food in an animal diet for another with a different moisture content without adjusting the amount fed. In relation to nutrient content, high-moisture foods are usually expensive, and are thus financially wasteful.

Nutritionists commonly express nutrient levels in feeds on a dry matter (moisture-free) basis to avoid the confounding effect of water in nutritional calculations. It is a mistake to compare the nutrient levels of various feeds without taking into account differences in water content. Nutrient requirements are also typically expressed either on a dry matter basis or in relation to a dry-type (ca. 10% moisture) food. As the convention adopted may vary in different publications, it is essential that this be determined before tables of nutrient requirements are used.

The importance of dry matter in dietary evaluation can be illustrated by an example. Suppose that chemical analysis indicates that monkey biscuits contain 18 g protein and 9 g water per 100 g, while the same amount of a canned marmoset diet contains 8.6 g protein and 60 g water. At first

glance, one might conclude that the monkey biscuits are higher in protein content. While this is technically true, the difference between the two feeds is attributable to the diluting effect of water in the higher-moisture product. An animal can compensate for this difference by eating more of the high-moisture diet and thereby obtaining an equivalent amount of energy or nutrients. The diluting effect of water can be removed by calculating nutrient levels on a dry matter (moisture-free) basis. On a dry matter basis, the concentration of protein is very similar in the two products, 22 g per 100 g monkey biscuits and 21.5 g per 100 g canned diet.

Crude Fiber

Crude fiber is an antiquated measure of the fiber level in a food, but it is still widely used by manufacturers since it has a legal definition. Crude fiber is the residue remaining after a food has been subjected to sequential acid and alkaline digestion. This procedure was devised in the nineteenth century as a crude approximation of the human digestive process, and was meant to isolate the indigestible materials in foods. More recently another fiber analysis system has come into widespread use, especially in analysis of high-fiber foods for herbivores (Van Soest 1994). In this "detergent fiber" system, food is boiled with a neutral detergent to remove cell contents, leaving only the cell wall. The residue is termed "Neutral Detergent Fiber" (NDF), and consists primarily of cellulose, hemicellulose, and lignin. A second analytic procedure involves treatment with an acidic detergent solution, which removes primarily cell contents and hemicellulose. The resulting "Acid Detergent Fiber" (ADF) is thus mostly cellulose and lignin, and the difference between NDF and ADF is a measure of hemicellulose content. Hemicellulose and cellulose can be digested by microbial fermentation in herbivorous mammals (see Oftedal, Baer, and Allen, chap. 12, this volume), but lignin is virtually indigestible. Lignin is usually measured by treatment of ADF with sulfuric acid, which removes the cellulose; cellulose content can then be estimated as ADF minus lignin.

While the details of these fiber analyses and their interpretation in different kinds of foods are beyond the scope of this chapter (see Van Soest 1994; Southgate 1973), it is important to recognize that fiber plays an important role in digestive processes and as a source of energy. Cellulose is the most abundant organic material on this planet, and herbivorous mammals that are able to utilize cellulose as a primary energy source can exploit foods that are largely indigestible to other mammals. Although monogastric species with relatively simple digestive tracts do not rely on fiber as a primary source of energy, digestion of fiber by humans and other primates can be substantial (Van Soest 1978; Milton and Demment 1988). As mammals do not secrete the enzymes necessary for digesting cellulose (cellulases), they must rely on symbiotic microorganisms in the gut (bacteria, protozoa, and fungi) that can ferment cellulose and other carbohydrates, producing volatile fatty acids (VFAs). The volatile fatty acids are then absorbed and used as an energy substrate by the host mammal. In herbivores that rely on microbial fermentation, appropriate levels of fiber (and some other nutrients such as nitrogen) must be supplied to the microbes or severe gastric disorders may arise (see Oftedal, Baer, and Allen, chap. 12, this volume).

Crude Protein

Crude protein is an approximation of the amount of protein in a food based on an analysis of total organic nitrogen (TN) by the Kjeldahl method. The assumptions are made that all organic nitrogen in the food is contained in protein, and that the nitrogen content of protein is 16% (hence the conversion, percentage protein = $100 \times TN/16$ or $TN \times 6.25$). For some foods, other conversion factors are used. For example, for grains, the factor used in calculating protein from nitrogen is about 5.8, and for seeds and nuts, the factor ranges from 5.2 to 5.7 (Watt and Merrill 1963). Milton and Dintzis (1981) report that more appropriate factors for converting nitrogen to protein in tropical leaves are between 4.0 and 5.0. "Crude protein" tends to overestimate true protein content because some of the organic nitrogen in foods is in nonprotein form (e.g., nucleic acids, creatinine, uric acid, urea, free amino acids). The protein content of foods is of great practical importance since many foods used in zoo animal diets do not contain adequate levels of protein to support optimal growth or reproduction.

Proteins are composed primarily of amino acids. Much of a mammal's "protein" requirement is actually a requirement for certain essential amino acids, although dietary proteins also supply other, nonessential amino acids that are used as a source of organic nitrogen for synthesis of tissue proteins. The essential amino acids are those that cannot be synthesized in the mammalian body, or that cannot be synthesized at a sufficient rate to support maximal growth. Of the ten major essential amino acids (arginine, histidine, isoleucine, leucine, lysine, methionine, phenylalanine, threonine, tryptophan, and valine), methionine may be partially replaced by cystine, and phenylalanine by tyrosine. Certain other amino acids may be required in some species for maximal growth (e.g., proline), and domestic cats (and probably other felids) require the free amino acid taurine in the diet. Lysine and tryptophan, as well as the sulfur-containing amino acids methionine and cystine, are quite low in the proteins of some plant products, a fact that must be considered in formulating pelleted feeds. Ruminants and other herbivores with foregut fermentation obtain essential amino acids from microbial proteins and hence may not require a dietary source per se (see Oftedal, Baer, and Allen, chap. 12, this volume).

Crude Fat

Crude fat is a measure of the amount of lipid material (primarily triglycerides) in foods. The exact value obtained in a lipid analysis depends on the extraction method used, since different extraction procedures extract somewhat different combinations of polar and nonpolar lipids. The fat content of a food is useful in predicting its energy content. Fat contains about 9 kcal/g of metabolizable energy, as compared with about 4 kcal/g for proteins and carbohydrates; high-fat foods are therefore high in energy content. Some lipids, however, such as some waxes and aromatic oils found in plants, may not be readily digested or metabolized and thus provide little metabolizable energy. Overestimates of energy content can result if these substances are recovered in the fat extraction. Mammals do not have a dietary requirement for fat per se, although they do require certain essential fatty acids. Linoleic acid meets the essential fatty acid requirements of most animals that have been studied, although the domestic cat (and perhaps other specialized carnivores) requires arachidonic acid as well. Fat sources are used in feed manufacture to improve palatability (especially for carnivores), to increase the energy content of feeds, and to facilitate the manufacturing process (since the fat serves to lubricate the feed as it passes through the manufacturing equipment).

Ash

Ash content is determined by incinerating a food sample at a high temperature (e.g., 600°C) in a muffle furnace. The incineration process destroys all organic material, leaving only mineral matter. Ash is thus a crude check on the level of minerals in a feed, but is not very informative without additional mineral analyses.

Carbohydrate

In the proximate analysis system, carbohydrate content is calculated by difference from the other analytic results: carbohydrate (also termed "nitrogen-free extract") = 100% − (percentage moisture + percentage crude fiber + percentage crude protein + percentage crude fat + percentage ash). Since the value obtained is influenced by errors in all the other measurements, it is not very accurate, and is rarely used in animal nutrition. It is commonly reported in some of the older human food tables, however, and may give a reasonable approximation of actual carbohydrate content in foods low in fiber content. The carbohydrates in foods include simple sugars (monosaccharides), complex sugars (disaccharides and oligosaccharides), and polymeric compounds such as starch, hemicellulose, and cellulose. Hemicellulose and cellulose are usually considered part of the fiber complex as they are resistant to digestion in the absence of fermentation.

Gross Energy

The digestion and metabolism of the fat, protein, carbohydrate, and fiber constituents of foods release energy. The total amount of chemical energy in food that theoretically could be used by an animal is termed "gross energy." Gross energy can be measured directly by combustion of food with oxygen in a bomb calorimeter. The calorimeter measures the amount of heat produced in calories. A calorie is the amount of heat required to raise the temperature of 1 gram of water by 1 degree Celsius (by convention, from 14.5° to 15.5°C), and a thousand calories is termed a Calorie (with a capital C) or, to avoid confusion, a kilocalorie (kcal). In much of the world, energy in food is expressed according to the *Système International d'Unités*, or SI, as kilojoules (kJ). One kcal equals 4.184 kJ.

Animals are unable to extract all of the gross energy in foods. The most obvious energy loss is through the feces. "Digestible energy" is the amount of energy in ingested food minus the amount lost in feces. Since the digestibility of a food is largely a function of the composition of the food, digestible energy values are assigned to individual foodstuffs in food composition tables designed for animal feeding. However, digestibility is also a function of the animal being fed, so digestible energy values determined for cattle, sheep, pigs, or horses may not be accurate for zoo animals.

Energy is also lost in urine. For example, if a mammal ingests protein and catabolizes the amino acids to release energy, the nitrogen produced has to be excreted in the urine. In mammals this nitrogen is mostly incorporated into urea, which in itself contains energy. About 15% of the energy in catabolized protein is lost as urinary urea (Kleiber 1975). "Metabolizable energy" (ME) is defined as the energy in ingested food minus the energy excreted as feces, urine, and methane. Methane energy losses are of practical importance only for herbivores with substantial fermentation (see Oftedal, Baer, and Allen, chap. 12, this volume). Thus, for most mammals, metabolizable energy is the energy in food minus the energy in feces and urine.

In human nutrition, it is common to calculate the metabolizable energy content of foods (in human food tables, sometimes referred to as "food energy" or "available energy") using conversion factors that account for typical energy losses associated with the digestion and metabolism of proteins, fats, and carbohydrates. The factors most commonly used are 4.0, 9.0, and 4.0 kcal per gram of protein, fat, and carbohydrate respectively. These factors give fairly reasonable energy estimates when applied to low-fiber foods that are fed to captive omnivorous and carnivorous species. However, such factors are of little practical value for foods that are high in fiber and of low digestibility. Moreover, they do not take into account energy gained and lost via microbial fermentation of fiber and other food constituents in herbivores.

A large number of additional terms are used to describe the energetics of animals, but are not of much practical significance in the feeding of zoo mammals. Both Brody (1945) and Kleiber (1975) provide detailed descriptions of animal energetics.

MINERALS OF NUTRITIONAL IMPORTANCE IN ZOO DIETS

All life forms, whether animal, plant, or microbial, require minerals for synthesis of structural materials, as constituents of fluids and tissues, and as components of enzymatic machinery (Underwood 1981). In ecosystems, the degree of abundance or depletion of different mineral nutrients can have profound effects on plant and animal communities. It should be no surprise, therefore, that dietary levels of minerals can be very important to zoo animals.

At present, twenty-two mineral elements are believed to be essential for the higher forms of animal life (Underwood 1981). Of these, seven are major or "macro-minerals" (calcium, phosphorus, sodium, chlorine, potassium, magnesium, and sulfur) and the rest are "trace minerals" that are found in animal tissues in only trace amounts. Concentrations of macro-minerals are usually given as percentages,

while trace minerals of practical importance are expressed as parts per million (ppm) or mg/kg, on either a fresh or dry weight basis. The trace minerals of the most practical significance for zoo mammals are iron, copper, zinc, manganese, selenium, cobalt, and iodine. A number of other "new trace minerals" (e.g., chromium, silicon, vanadium, nickel, arsenic, lead) are thought to be essential for mammals in minute amounts (Mertz 1986, 1987), but these are not likely to be deficient in zoo animal diets and will not be discussed further.

The most widely employed method for mineral analysis is atomic absorption spectroscopy, although other chemical and instrumental procedures are often used (J. C. Smith 1987). In the past fifteen years the methodology for analyzing trace minerals has progressed rapidly, leading to changes in the accepted normal concentrations in tissues and foods (Mertz 1986). While mineral composition data can be of great value in evaluating zoo diets, sampling must be done carefully to avoid inadvertent environmental contamination, especially in the case of trace minerals (Wolf 1987). Contrary to popular belief, analysis of the mineral content of hair is rarely instructive with respect to establishing mineral status because of airborne and other sources of contamination. Hair analysis is also retrospective, since mineral incorporation occurs in the hair follicle. Blood, liver, or other tissue analyses are usually more revealing.

In the past sixty years great advances have been made in research on mineral metabolism and requirements. Space permits only a brief discussion of the minerals that may be important in diets for captive wild mammals. For more detailed discussions of the distribution, absorption, metabolism, requirements, and toxicities of minerals, see Underwood (1977, 1981), Mertz (1986, 1987), National Research Council (1980), and the Nutrient Requirements series of the National Research Council.

Calcium and Phosphorus
Calcium and phosphorus are required in relatively large amounts and in appropriate ratios during both growth (for bone development) and lactation (for milk production). Over 98% of all calcium in the body is in the skeleton, part of which represents a labile reserve. Calcium phosphate in bone provides structural support for the vertebrate body. In soft tissues calcium plays critical roles in muscle contraction, nerve function, blood clotting, and the activation of many enzymes (Maynard et al. 1979; Church and Pond 1988). Prolonged deficiency can lead to severe metabolic disorders as bodily stores are depleted and homeostatic mechanisms fail. Phosphorus is also found in high concentrations in the skeleton in association with calcium. Phosphorus is ubiquitous in the body and is a critical component of countless metabolic reactions. Parathyroid hormone, calcitonin, and vitamin D metabolites regulate calcium and phosphorus homeostasis.

Calcium requirements are usually about 0.5–0.8% of dietary dry matter for growth and lactation, as compared with phosphorus requirements of 0.3–0.7% (see table 11.1). Because imbalances of the ratio of calcium to phosphorus lead to poor absorption of and exacerbate deficiencies of both minerals, preferred dietary levels are typically expressed as a desired range of 1:1–2:1 in the calcium:phosphorus ratio. Unfortunately, many kinds of foods are low in calcium and have calcium:phosphorus ratios of less than 1. Excessive use of unsupplemented fruits, seeds, or grains, muscle meats, and insects can have particularly severe consequences for zoo animals. Demineralization of bone, tetany, and eventual death may occur as animals deplete skeletal stores. Appropriate amounts of calcium and phosphorus are especially critical during early growth and peak lactation (see table 11.1).

Excessive dietary calcium may lead to a reduction in the absorption of phosphorus, magnesium, and zinc. If dietary zinc levels are low or marginal, excessive calcium may induce clinical zinc deficiency. Grains and plant protein sources contain more phosphorus than calcium, but much of the phosphorus may be unavailable if it is present in phytate molecules. Low levels of phosphorus in soil may result in low phosphorus content in both pasture plants and hays. Phosphorus deficiency may well be the most critical mineral deficiency in grazing livestock (Allaway 1975).

Magnesium

Magnesium is found in high concentrations in skeletal tissues. This element functions to activate enzymes that are involved in muscle contractions and nerve conduction, as well as in the synthesis of proteins, carbohydrates, fats, and nucleic acids. Signs of deficiency include vasodilation, hyperirritability, convulsions, and calcification of soft tissues. While magnesium deficiency is usually not a problem in zoo animals, deficiency can occur in ruminants grazing lush spring pastures that are low in available magnesium. In practical feeding situations, magnesium toxicity is not usually seen.

Sodium

Appropriate dietary levels of sodium are essential to the maintenance of electrolyte balance and osmotic pressure. Sodium is a major extracellular cation. In domestic animals deficiencies are most likely to occur when animals are lactating, growing, or working intensively. Perspiration may represent a significant sodium loss in animals that sweat. Sodium-deficient animals may show a craving (pica) for salt. Sodium toxicity can occur if animals are not given access to fresh water. Extremely arid conditions (drought) or frozen water supplies may contribute to the development of sodium toxicity. Estimated sodium requirements for domestic mammals typically range from 0.05% to 0.13% of dietary dry matter (see tables 11.1 and 11.2), although working horses may need 0.3% (National Research Council 1989b).

Chloride

Chloride, the ionic form of chlorine, is an important extracellular anion that, in conjunction with bicarbonate, potassium, and sodium, plays an integral role in controlling acid-base balance. Chlorine is involved in digestion via gastric secretion of hydrochloric acid, and it catalyzes certain enzymes. Deficiencies and toxicities are rare. Estimated requirements are about 0.04–0.2% of dietary dry matter.

Potassium

Potassium is a major intracellular cation with an important role in the maintenance of acid-base balance and osmotic pressure. Deficiencies are uncommon since potassium is ubiquitous in living plant and animal tissues. Potassium deficiency can occur, however, in herbivores ingesting diets that are low in forage and high in concentrates, since grains are poor sources of potassium. Estimated requirements range from 0.1% to 0.8% of dietary dry matter.

Sulfur

Sulfur is a component of some amino acids and B vitamins. Sulfur-containing amino acids provide important structural cross-linkages in proteins, including connective tissue and hair proteins. Nonruminant mammals do not appear to have a sulfur requirement per se, since inorganic sulfur cannot be substituted for most preformed sulfur-containing compounds in the diet. In contrast, ruminants can use inorganic as well as organic sulfur because microbes in the ruminoreticulum use inorganic sulfur to synthesize sulfur-containing amino acids and B vitamins. Microbial synthesis of sulfur-containing amino acids requires that sufficient nitrogen also be available. The dietary ratio of nitrogen to sulfur is especially important for animals that synthesize large amounts of high-sulfur proteins, such as wool-producing animals like llamas, alpacas, and sheep. An appropriate nitrogen:sulfur ratio for these animals is 10:1. For other ruminants, appropriate ratios are 12:1–15:1.

Iron

Although iron is the most abundant elemental constituent of our planet (the molten core is predominantly iron), mammals require only trace amounts (Underwood 1977; Mertz 1987). Much of the iron in the body is found in hemoglobin. The remainder exists in myoglobin, in enzymes, and in transport and storage forms. The body normally regulates iron balance by controlling iron absorption, since it lacks effective means of excreting excess iron. The overall iron content of a diet may be less informative than the type of iron, since some forms of iron are poorly absorbed. Among natural sources, heme iron is readily absorbed. Among dietary supplements, iron in the form of ferrous sulfate is better absorbed than is iron in the ferrous carbonate form, although reagent-grade ferrous carbonate is a better source of available iron than is ferrous carbonate derived from ores. Ferric oxide, which is not absorbed by the gut, may be added to some animal feeds as a coloring agent. Some dietary compounds, such as phytates and oxalates, may lead to the formation of inert ferric precipitates.

Although iron deficiency is rare in healthy animals receiving solid foods, dietary iron may be important for animals that have become anemic as a consequence of blood loss. Many mammalian milks, including cow's milk, contain low concentrations of iron. Use of cow's milk in hand-rearing programs may lead to iron deficiency if iron supplements or access to soil are not provided. Abnormal accumulations of iron pigments in the livers of rock hyraxes (*Procavia capensis*) and lemurs (Lemuridae) have been reported, but the specific etiology is unclear (Rehg et al. 1980; Gonzales et al.

1984). Estimated iron requirements range from about 40 to 100 ppm in dietary dry matter.

Copper

Copper is important in connective tissue and in melanin synthesis. Copper-containing enzymes play a role in the mobilization of iron from body stores; hepatic iron accumulation is one consequence of copper deficiency. Deficiencies of copper are rare but may occur in ruminants fed forages produced on molybdenum-rich soils. In cases of suspected copper deficiency, the dietary concentrations of molybdenum, sulfate, and copper must be carefully assessed, as the interactions among these nutrients are complex. Excesses of dietary zinc can induce copper deficiency in some species. Zinc-coated cages have been implicated in a report of apparent copper deficiency in young rhesus macaques, *Macaca mulatta,* that were observed licking their cages (Obeck 1978). Among domestic species, some breeds of sheep appear particularly susceptible to excess dietary copper. There is also evidence that wombats, *Vombatus ursinus,* are intolerant of excess dietary copper (Barboza 1989). For domestic ruminants, the dietary requirement for copper ranges from 1 to 10 ppm, depending on molybdenum and sulfate levels in the diet. Nonruminants require about 5–10 ppm in dietary dry matter.

Iodine

Seventy to eighty percent of the body's iodine is found in the thyroid gland. The one known function of iodine is as a component of thyroxine and triiodothyronine, the thyroid hormones that regulate tissue metabolism. Deficiencies of iodine result in an enlargement of the thyroid gland (goiter) and consequently affect metabolism. Growth is sometimes severely retarded. In regions where soil iodine is found in low concentrations, and if diets are not sufficiently supplemented, iodine deficiency may be endemic. Goitrogens, such as thioglycosides, that are found in certain plants (e.g., *Brassica* spp.) may induce iodine deficiency. Goiter may also occur with iodine toxicity. Iodine is found in high concentrations in marine products. Dietary supplements containing kelp may deliver dangerously high dietary levels of iodine if used without care. Estimated iodine requirements range from about 0.05 to 1.0 ppm in dietary dry matter.

Cobalt

Vitamin B_{12} contains 4% cobalt. Although mammalian tissues are unable to synthesize vitamin B_{12}, microbes in the digestive tracts of herbivores can synthesize this vitamin if sufficient dietary cobalt is present. A specific cobalt need, other than for vitamin B_{12} synthesis, has not been established. In North America, soils low in cobalt in New England, the South Atlantic coastal plain, and parts of the Midwest produce legumes and grasses with cobalt levels insufficient to meet the requirements of domestic ruminants (Allaway 1975). The relatively high cobalt requirement of ruminants (about 0.1 ppm) is due in part to the inefficiency of the production of vitamin B_{12} from cobalt in the rumen and in part to the inefficiency of absorption of the vitamin in the small intestine (R. M. Smith 1987).

Zinc

Zinc is widely distributed in the body and is found in especially high concentrations in the retina and prostate. Zinc is a cofactor in many metabolic pathways and is involved in such vital functions as protein synthesis, glucose tolerance, immune competency, wound healing, and DNA and RNA synthesis. Both male and female rats require higher dietary levels of zinc for reproduction than for growth, but this does not appear to be true of all species (Hambidge, Casey, and Krebs 1986). Signs of zinc deficiency include growth retardation, anorexia, changes in skin and hair, and impaired reproductive function in both males and females, although males are more severely affected in some species. The zinc content of both plant and animal materials varies greatly. Plants that are high in zinc may also be high in phytate, so that the availability of the zinc is low (Hambidge, Casey, and Krebs 1986). Zinc deficiency is therefore more likely when diets do not contain animal sources. Deficiencies of zinc may occur with dietary excesses of calcium, cadmium, or copper. While zinc is relatively nontoxic, excess dietary zinc may interfere with the absorption and utilization of iron and copper. Estimated zinc requirements range from about 40 to 90 ppm in dietary dry matter.

Manganese

Manganese is involved in the development of the organic matrix of bone, in gluconeogenesis, and in fat mobilization. It is concentrated in the skeleton, but high concentrations are also present in the liver, kidneys, and pancreas. Mammals appear to require higher dietary levels of manganese for reproduction (especially fetal development) than for growth. Ataxia and loss of equilibrium in the newborn are among the first signs of manganese deficiency in rats, with neonatal deaths and loss of reproductive function in more severe deficiencies (Hurley and Keen 1987). Other manifestations include impaired growth, skeletal abnormalities, and defects in lipid and carbohydrate metabolism. Manganese is widespread in foods, but some grains (such as corn) contain low levels. In a practical feeding situation, manganese deficiency is not likely to occur except in poultry, which appear to have higher dietary requirements than do the mammals that have been studied. Estimated manganese requirements of domestic and laboratory mammals are quite variable, ranging from less than 10 to about 40 ppm in dietary dry matter.

Selenium

A primary known function of selenium in mammals is as a component of the enzyme glutathione peroxidase (Burk 1978). This enzyme protects cells from oxidative destruction by detoxifying peroxides. Signs of selenium deficiency include skeletal muscle degeneration, necrosis (white muscle disease), and calcification. The liver may also undergo pathological changes. Pasture plants and hays grown on low-selenium soils in the United States (e.g., the Northeast, the South Atlantic seaboard, the Pacific Northwest, and the Great Lakes region), Canada, and elsewhere must be supplemented with an appropriate selenium source (e.g., sodium selenite or sodium selenate) if selenium deficiency is to be avoided. Some range plants accumulate selenium, resulting in extremely high or toxic levels (Brown and Shrift 1982); however, this problem is not of practical concern in zoo animal diets. High concentrations are also found in marine fish and shellfish (Bernard and Ullrey 1989). Animal tissue levels of selenium are thought to reflect amounts of dietary selenium consumed (National Research Council 1983). Some cetacean and pinniped milks contain high (0.7–1.5 ppm, dry matter basis) selenium levels (Ullrey et al. 1984; Oftedal and Boness 1983). Selenium toxicity can occur when animals ingest levels as low as 10 times the requirement; therefore, the amounts of supplemental selenium added to diets must be carefully controlled. Vitamin E may offer some protection against low dietary selenium levels in some animals. Estimated selenium requirements range from about 0.05 to 0.3 ppm in dietary dry matter.

Other Trace Minerals

Deficiencies of other trace minerals (including such noted toxic materials as arsenic and lead) can be induced experimentally in very clean environments but rarely if ever occur under natural conditions. Toxicity may be a practical problem, however. For example, animals may consume lead-based paint out of boredom. In 42 primate deaths at the National Zoo over an 18-year period, the pathological findings were consistent with lead poisoning. The primates apparently ingested lead from cage bars (Zook and Parasch 1980). Raw rock phosphate contains extremely high levels of fluoride. The use of this form of phosphate as a phosphorus supplement in manufactured feed has resulted in fluoride toxicosis in domestic species.

VITAMINS IN ZOO DIETS

Vitamins are essential to maintain health and to support growth and reproduction in mammals. Vitamins are usually divided into two categories, fat-soluble and water-soluble, based on the observed solubility of these compounds in nonpolar and polar solvents respectively. The fat-soluble vitamins (vitamins A, D, E, and K) are entirely organic and contain only carbon, oxygen, and hydrogen. Water-soluble vitamins (thiamin, riboflavin, niacin, B_6, pantothenic acid, biotin, folic acid, B_{12}, and vitamin C) may also contain inorganic constituents and nitrogen. Symbiotic bacteria in the rumen, cecum, and colon of herbivores synthesize vitamin K and the water-soluble vitamins (except vitamin C). Therefore, animals with well-developed fermentation systems may be able to satisfy some or all of their requirements for these nutrients through bacterial contributions. With a few exceptions, the water-soluble vitamins are tolerated in high concentrations by animals. The B vitamins are generally not stored in the body (exceptions are vitamin B_{12} and riboflavin), and excesses are usually excreted by the kidney. By contrast, some of the fat-soluble vitamins are highly toxic if consumed in excess.

Remarkable advances have been made in the past thirty years in the characterization of the structure, chemistry, and physiological roles of the vitamins (Lawson 1978; Machlin 1980, 1991). However, quantitative analysis of vitamins in feeds is still relatively difficult and expensive, precluding routine analysis of zoo diets. The fat-soluble vitamins are now usually analyzed by high-pressure liquid chromatography (HPLC). A variety of methods are used to analyze B vitamins, including microbiological assays, biological assays, and spectrophotometric and enzymatic techniques. Interpretation of analytic data on vitamin content requires familiarity with the shortcomings of the available laboratory techniques. Requirements for vitamins A, D, and E are usually expressed in International Units (IU) per kg diet. Requirements for the other vitamins are usually expressed in μg or mg/kg diet. In their natural forms many vitamins are quite labile in the presence of oxygen, heat, or light, so losses during food manufacture may be substantial (Harris and Karmas 1975). When vitamins are added to foods, they are often chemically or physically stabilized (esterified, coated with a gelatin or starch matrix, antioxidants added) to extend shelf life.

Vitamin A

Vitamin A, or retinol, is found in a preformed state only in animal tissues and products. However, chemical precursors of retinol—provitamin A compounds—such as carotenes and carotenoids are synthesized by plants. The provitamin A compounds vary greatly in biopotency due to differences in their structure and stereochemical properties. For example, in the rat, the relative biopotencies are: retinol, 100; beta-carotene, 50; cryptoxanthin, 29; alpha-carotene, 25; gamma-carotene, 14; and xanthophyll, 0 (Ullrey 1972). There are species differences in the transport and storage of carotenoids (Sebrell and Harris 1967; Ullrey 1972; McDowell 1989). Cattle, horses, and humans may absorb significant amounts of carotenes and deposit them in lipid stores, producing yellow coloration of the fat. Pigs, dogs, sheep, goats, American bison, white-tailed deer, and rats first convert the carotenes to retinol, then transport and deposit this compound. Thus, these species have white fat. The cat is not able to use carotenes effectively and must consume retinol to satisfy its requirements. It is probable that wild felids, and perhaps some other obligate carnivores, share this unique characteristic.

Vitamin A plays a major metabolic role at the cellular level and in vision. It is also responsible for maintaining epithelial cell integrity and bone development. Depending on the species, deficiencies result in excessive lacrimation or xerophthalmia, corneal ulceration, exophthalmos, and/or blindness (McDowell 1989). Epithelial cells fail to differentiate normally, and the resulting replacement of ciliated cells with squamous cells in the trachea is usually associated with decreased resistance to infection.

Most estimated requirements for vitamin A range from 1,000 to 6,000 IU/kg diet; requirements may vary somewhat across species and are typically higher for reproduction than for growth (cf. National Research Council Nutrient Requirements series). Formulated diets usually contain high vitamin A levels to compensate for losses of vitamin A during manufacture and storage.

The carotenes and carotenoids are responsible for imparting color to some foods. Yellow and green plants are usually good sources of provitamin A compounds, although sunlight will destroy much of the vitamin A activity in sun-cured forages. When ingested by herbivorous animals, provitamin A compounds are converted to vitamin A in the intestine and liver. Carnivorous animals may derive much of their needed vitamin A by consuming the stores in the livers of their prey. Reports of extremely high vitamin A concentrations in the livers of polar bears, *Ursus maritimus,* and some seals no doubt reflect the concentration of this nutrient higher in the food chain (Rodahl 1949b).

Supplemental vitamin A should be used judiciously since this vitamin is highly toxic if consumed in excess. Vitamin A toxicity is relatively easily produced due to the small difference between requirements and toxic levels. In mammals, the safe upper limit for vitamin A may be no more than 10–30 times the requirement level (National Research Council 1987). Anorexia, weight loss, vomiting, headache, alopecia, skin exfoliation, hemorrhage, and skeletal malformation may be indicative of vitamin A toxicity, although the signs differ somewhat depending on whether overdosing with vitamin A has been acute or chronic.

Given the reported high liver concentrations in some pinnipeds and polar bears (Rodahl and Moore 1943), it is possible that some animals may have a high tolerance for vitamin A. However, Rodahl (1949a) suggests that polar bears may develop hypervitaminosis A when consuming entire seals (including livers). It has been reported that therapeutic levels of vitamin A (200,000 IU/kg diet) reversed persistent dermatitis in captive polar bears (Foster 1981); in most animals this dosage would produce toxicity.

Vitamin D

Vitamin D is intimately involved in the homeostatic control of calcium and phosphorus levels in the circulation and in the absorption of dietary calcium. Vitamin D occurs in two principal structural forms, vitamin D_2 (ergocalciferol) and vitamin D_3 (cholecalciferol), each of which undergoes biochemical modification (hydroxylation) after ingestion. Vitamin D_2 originates with the irradiation of ergosterol in plant tissues. Appreciable amounts of vitamin D_2 are found only after irradiation of injured (cut) plants or in the dead, lower leaves of plants; in living tissues ergosterol is apparently protected from the effects of irradiation (McDowell 1989). The vitamin D_2 content of hay increases considerably during field drying in direct sun, whereas there is little vitamin D_2 in artificially dried hay. The other form, vitamin D_3, originates in the skin of animals by ultraviolet irradiation of 7-dehydro-cholesterol. Vitamin D_3 passes directly from the epithelium to the circulation, and may also be absorbed from the digestive tract after ingestion of skin secretions during grooming. Vitamin D_3 is also ingested by predators consuming vertebrate prey.

Both of these compounds are hydroxylated in the C-25 and C-1 positions in the liver and kidney respectively. The resulting metabolically active compounds, 1,25 dihydroxy-ergocalciferol and 1,25 dihydroxy-cholecalciferol, exert a number of effects, including the synthesis of a calcium-binding protein in the gut mucosa. If there is insufficient synthesis of this protein, calcium absorption and transport are impaired.

Vitamin D deficiency is manifested by abnormally formed bones in animals. Rickets is the term traditionally used when the bones of young, growing, vitamin D–deficient animals become soft and pliable. Osteomalacia is the term used for the softening of bone in adult animals receiving insufficient exposure to sunlight or inadequate amounts of dietary vitamin D. Since vitamin D is not stored in appreciable amounts in most vertebrates, signs of deficiency may occur in only a few weeks or months, although onset of signs may be delayed due to slow vitamin D turnover in the body. Calcium homeostasis is rigidly regulated by the body. A decrease in plasma levels of calcium and magnesium with resultant tetany occurs when animals are severely deficient in vitamin D. Nutritional secondary hyperparathyroidism may also be seen as the parathyroid gland attempts to compensate for the insufficient plasma levels of calcium by increasing its output of parathyroid hormone, which stimulates the production of 1,25 dihydroxy-vitamin D.

Intakes of vitamin D of 10 to 100 times the requirement may result in demineralization of bone and precipitation of mineral in soft tissue (National Research Council 1987). Renal insufficiency may ultimately result due to calcification of the kidney. Some plants *(Solanum malacoxylon, Cestrum diurnum,* and *Trisetum flavescens)* are known to contain 1,25-dihydroxyvitamin D-glycoside. This compound, once absorbed, mimics the action of 1,25-dihydroxyvitamin D, bypassing the renal feedback control normally responsible for preventing vitamin D toxicity. Hypercalcemia, osteopetrosis, lameness, and dystrophic calcinosis of blood vessels, tendons, and ligaments may result.

Requirements for vitamin D range from about 200 to 1,000 IU/kg diet, assuming there is no or little exposure to sunlight. When assessing dietary levels of vitamin D, knowledge of dietary calcium and phosphorus concentrations is also necessary, since vitamin D influences the utilization of these minerals. Species differences exist in the biological activity of the two forms of the vitamin. Vitamin D_2 is apparently utilized less effectively than vitamin D_3 by some New World primates (National Research Council 1978). Vitamin D binding proteins in the echidna, *Tachyglossus aculeatus,* and some other species also bind vitamin D_3 preferentially. In light of these apparent taxonomic differences, it is wise to use vitamin D_3 if supplemental dietary vitamin D is necessary.

Vitamin E

Alpha-tocopherol is the most active natural form of vitamin E. There are a variety of isomers and esters of alpha-tocopherol that differ in biopotency (see Machlin 1980). Plants, especially their seed oils, contain the greatest concentrations of alpha-tocopherol, while animal tissues contain relatively little. Many factors influence the vitamin E content of foods, including fatty acid composition, presence of antioxidants, food processing methods, storage conditions, and season of harvest. It is therefore difficult to interpret laboratory data unless sufficient sample information is available.

Vitamin E functions in the body as an antioxidant. In this role, the vitamin E compounds undergo destruction as they protect cell membranes from oxidative changes due to the presence of free radicals. In the absence of sufficient vitamin E, unsaturated fatty acids in cell membranes will be damaged, resulting in vitamin E deficiency signs: skeletal and cardiac muscle myopathies, fat degeneration, red blood cell hemolysis, anemia, and encephalomalacia in some species (McDowell 1989). Some of these signs resemble those of selenium deficiency. There is evidence that selenium and the sulfur-containing amino acids may spare vitamin E to some extent. Vitamin E is considered a relatively safe vitamin with respect to oversupplementation. However, it has been reported that chicks fed 2,200 IU/kg diet (as all-*rac*-alpha-tocopheryl acetate) exhibited reduction in growth, a reduced hematocrit, and increased blood clotting times.

Estimated vitamin E requirements range from about 15 to 100 IU/kg diet. Additional vitamin E may be necessary in animals whose health is compromised due to parasite burdens or infection and in animals that receive a high-fat diet, especially if the fat is rich in polyunsaturated fatty acids. Stressed or heavily worked animals may also have higher requirements. An ester form of vitamin E such as RRR- or all-*rac*-alpha-tocopheryl acetate is usually preferred for supplementation because of its relatively high biological activity and stability. The efficacy of a water-soluble ester (D-alpha-tocopheryl polyethylene glycol succinate, or TPGS) for use with zoo animals is also under investigation.

Vitamin K

Vitamin K occurs naturally in two forms: vitamin K_1, synthesized by plants, and vitamin K_2, synthesized by microorganisms. Vitamin K_3 is a synthetic form and is called menadione. Vitamin K is required to maintain the action of blood-clotting proteins because it is involved in the addition of calcium binding sites to their precursor proteins. A deficiency of vitamin K is unlikely in healthy animals fed natural or manufactured rations, since the vitamin is ubiquitous in foods and is also synthesized by gut microbes. Dietary supplements may be necessary when animals are fed intestinally active antibiotics or sulfa drugs, or if coprophagy is prevented in animals that normally absorb nutrients from ingested feces. Ingestion of moldy sweet clover hay may induce vitamin K deficiency because of the presence of coumarin derivatives that are vitamin K antagonists. Menadione should be added to the diet at the level of 2–5 mg/kg diet when the presence of vitamin K antagonists is suspected or when intestinally active drugs are used. The naturally occurring forms of vitamin K are generally considered nontoxic. Anemia and porphyrinuria may occur when menadione is fed in excess.

The B Vitamins

The B vitamin complex includes thiamin, riboflavin, pantothenic acid, niacin, vitamin B_6, biotin, and vitamin B_{12}. Most of the B vitamins are widely distributed in plant tissues (thiamin, riboflavin, pantothenic acid, niacin, vitamin B_6, folic acid) or animal and microbial tissues (riboflavin, pantothenic acid, vitamin B_6, biotin, folic acid, vitamin B_{12}). Many of the B vitamins function as coenzymes that are important at the cellular and subcellular levels in decarboxylation, oxidation-reduction, transamination, deamination, phosphorylation, and isomerization reactions. Many of the deficiency signs are similar within and among species because of the wide range of functions of these vitamins. De-

ficiency signs often include central nervous system signs (incoordination, convulsions, peripheral nerve dysfunction). Listlessness, impaired growth, anemias, rough pelage, diarrhea, and anorexia may also occur.

There are some classic signs of B vitamin deficiency that are nutrient- or species-specific (McDowell 1989). For example, "black tongue" in dogs parallels signs (dermatitis and oral lesions) seen in humans with pellagra, and results from a deficiency in niacin. In pigs, a "goose-stepping" gait characterizes a pantothenic acid deficiency. A biotin deficiency results in scaly dermatitis; this was first discovered when raw egg whites were fed to rats. A protein in the egg white, avidin, was later discovered to be responsible for binding the biotin, rendering it unavailable. If sufficient raw or spray-dried egg whites are consumed, a biotin deficiency will be induced. Cooking the egg white denatures avidin. Although egg yolks contain substantial amounts of biotin, the use of raw or spray-dried egg whites should be avoided in diets for zoo animals.

Although all vertebrates require B vitamins at the tissue level, herbivores may obtain substantial amounts from microbial synthesis in the digestive tract. Supplemental B vitamins are rarely added to diets for domestic ruminants. Bacterial synthesis in the foregut usually supplies ample amounts of most of these nutrients, although in certain circumstances thiamin and niacin synthesis may be inadequate (National Research Council 1989a). It is not known whether production of the B vitamins by rumen microbes is sufficient in zoo animals, especially in small ruminants with relatively fast rates of digesta passage and low fiber intakes. Furthermore, diets fed to zoo ruminants may also be used for monogastric herbivores. Although cecal and colonic microbes may produce sufficient amounts of B vitamins in these animals, the efficiency of absorption of these nutrients in the hindgut is not well understood. Therefore, diets for zoo carnivores, omnivores, and herbivores should contain added B vitamins. Estimated requirements for B vitamins for some domestic mammals are listed in table 11.1.

From a practical standpoint, the B vitamin that has received the most attention in zoo animal management is thiamin. Thiamin, or vitamin B_1, plays a critical role in carbohydrate and energy metabolism as well as in fatty acid, DNA, and RNA synthesis. Deficiencies of thiamin are rare except in animals such as pinnipeds that consume raw fish containing thiaminases (Fujita 1954). In addition, certain plants (e.g., bracken fern and sweet potato leaves) contain antithiamin compounds that, when consumed, may lead to thiamin deficiency, although for zoo animals this is rarely a concern. Animals that are thiamin-deficient may vomit, refuse to eat, and have labored breathing. Rapid heartbeat, cardiac failure, and death will occur if thiamin supplementation is not provided. As with most B vitamins, thiamin may be supplemented at 1,000 or more times the requirement level without toxic effects (National Research Council 1987). Estimated requirements range from about 0.5 to 5.0 mg/kg diet dry matter.

Vitamin C

Some mammals are unable to synthesize ascorbic acid (vitamin C) because they lack L-gulonolactone oxidase, the enzyme that catalyzes the final step in the biosynthetic pathway. Although this enzyme is present in most mammals that have been studied, it is missing in anthropoid primates, bats, and guinea pigs (Chatterjee 1973; Birney, Jenness, and Ayaz 1976; Birney, Jenness, and Hume 1980; Jenness, Birney, and Ayaz 1980; Milton and Jenness 1987). In monotremes, ascorbic acid biosynthesis occurs in the kidney, just as it does in many fishes, amphibians, and reptiles (Birney, Jenness, and Hume 1979). In some marsupials biosynthesis occurs in both the liver and the kidney, but in placental mammals ascorbic acid is synthesized only in the liver (Birney, Jenness, and Hume 1980; Jenness, Birney, and Ayaz 1980; Hume 1982). In the absence of data indicating that a given mammalian species can synthesize ascorbic acid, it is prudent to provide a dietary source. Some animals with low levels of synthetic activity may require an additional dietary source of vitamin C to avert deficiency (Jenness, Birney, and Ayaz 1978; Hanssen et al. 1979).

Vitamin C plays an important role in many biochemical oxidation-reduction reactions, as well as in the synthesis of collagen, the structural protein in cartilage. The essentiality of vitamin C for humans was borne out by the widespread prevalence of scurvy among sailors and polar explorers who had no access to fresh foods containing vitamin C (Carpenter 1986). Deficiency signs include listlessness, soreness of joints, bones, and muscles, weakening of collagenous structures, abnormal bone growth, anorexia, and increased susceptibility to infectious disease (McDowell 1989). Bruising, swollen and bleeding gums, and petechial hemorrhages are also classic signs of vitamin C deficiency in susceptible species.

Vitamin C deficiency in zoo animals is most apt to arise due to omission of vitamin C from the diet (e.g., in milk formulas for bats) or due to the instability of vitamin C in manufactured feeds. Since canned primate food does not contain vitamin C, and since the vitamin C in extruded monkey biscuits deteriorates rapidly, fruits, vegetables, and browse provide an essential source of vitamin C in primate diets. Leafy materials of the cabbage family (kale, cabbage, brussels sprouts, mustard greens), citrus fruits, rose hips, and some types of browse are especially good sources of vitamin C (Sebrell and Harris 1967; Dash and Jenness 1985; Milton and Jenness 1987; McDowell 1989). Vitamin C is generally considered one of the least toxic nutrients. Given the relative instability of vitamin C, high levels may need to be added to manufactured foods to assure that adequate levels reach the animals being fed. However, stabilized forms of vitamin C have recently been developed that may prolong shelf life. Recommended dietary levels for vitamin C range from about 100 to 200 mg/kg diet dry matter (National Research Council 1978, 1995).

Myoinositol and Choline
Myoinositol and choline are two other nutrients that are usually included in discussions of the water-soluble vitamins. Among other functions, myoinositol and choline are involved in fat metabolism and transmission of nerve impulses (Holub 1986; Zeisel 1981). Requirements for inositol are not well established. Although supplemental choline may not be necessary in many mammalian diets, it may be

included as a safety measure at levels from 200 to 2,000 mg/kg diet dry matter.

REFERENCES

Allaway, W. H. 1975. *The effects of soils and fertilizers on human and animal nutrition.* Agriculture Information Bulletin no. 378. Washington, D.C.: U.S. Department of Agriculture.

Barboza, P. S. 1989. The nutritional physiology of the Vombatidae. Ph.D. thesis, The University of New England, Armidale, N.S.W.

Bernard, J. B., and Ullrey, D. E. 1989. Evaluation of dietary husbandry of marine mammals at two major zoological parks. *J. Zoo Wildl. Med.* 20:45–52.

Birney, E. C., Jenness, R., and Ayaz, K. M. 1976. Inability of bats to synthesize L-ascorbic acid. *Nature* 260:626–28.

Birney, E. C., Jenness, R., and Hume, I. D. 1979. Ascorbic acid biosynthesis in the mammalian kidney. *Experientia* 35:1425–26.

———. 1980. Evolution of an enzyme system: Ascorbic acid biosynthesis in monotremes and marsupials. *Evolution* 34: 230–39.

Brody, S. 1945. *Bioenergetics and growth.* New York: Reinhold Publishing Company. (Reprinted 1974.)

Brown, T. A., and Shrift, A. 1982. Selenium: Toxicity and tolerance in higher plants. *Biol. Rev.* 57:59–84.

Burk, R. F. 1978. Selenium in nutrition. *World Rev. Nutr. Diet.* 30:88–106.

Carpenter, K. J. 1986. The history of scurvy and vitamin C. Cambridge: Cambridge University Press.

Chatterjee, I. B. 1973. Evolution and biosynthesis of ascorbic acid. *Science* 182:1271–72.

Church, D. C., and Pond, W. G. 1988. *Basic animal nutrition and feeding.* New York: John Wiley and Sons.

Dash, J. A., and Jenness, R. 1985. Ascorbate content of foliage of eucalypts and conifers utilized by some Australian and North American mammals. *Experientia* 41:952–55.

Foster, J. W. 1981. Dermatitis in polar bears: A nutritional approach to therapy. *Proceedings of the Annual Meeting of the American Association of Zoo Veterinarians,* 58–60. Philadelphia: American Association of Zoo Veterinarians.

Fujita, A. 1954. Thiaminase. In *Advances in enzymology,* ed. F. F. Nord, 389–421. New York: Interscience Publishers.

Gonzales, J., Benirschke, K., Saltman, P., Roberts, J., and Robinson, P. T. 1984. Hemosiderosis in lemurs. *Z. Biol.* 3:255–65.

Hambidge, K. M., Casey, C. E., and Krebs, N. F. 1986. Zinc. In *Trace elements in human and animal nutrition,* 5th ed., vol. 2, ed. W. Mertz, 1–137. New York: Academic Press.

Hanssen, I., Grav, H. J., Steen, J. B., and Lysnes, H. 1979. Vitamin C deficiency in growing willow ptarmigan *(Lagopus lagopus lagopus). J. Nutr.* 109:2260–76.

Harris, R. S., and Karmas, E. 1975. Nutritional evaluation of food processing. 2d ed. Westport, Conn.: AVI Publishing.

Holub, B. J. 1986. Metabolism and function of myo-inositol and inositol phospholipids. *Annu. Rev. Nutr.* 6:563–97.

Hume, I. D. 1982. *Digestive physiology and nutrition of marsupials.* New York: Cambridge University Press.

Hurley, L. S., and Keen, C. L. 1987. Manganese. In *Trace elements in human and animal nutrition,* 5th ed., vol. 1, ed. W. Mertz, 185–223. New York: Academic Press.

Jenness, R., Birney, E. C., and Ayaz, K. L. 1978. Ascorbic acid and l-gulonolactone oxidase in lagomorphs. *Comp. Biochem. Physiol.* [B] 61:395–99.

———. 1980. Variation of L-gulonolactone oxidase activity in placental mammals. *Comp. Biochem. Physiol.* [B] 67:195–204.

Kleiber, M. 1975. *The fire of life: An introduction to animal energetics.* Rev. ed. Huntington, N.Y.: Robert E. Krieger.

Lawson, D. E. M. 1978. *Vitamin D*. London: Academic Press.

Machlin, L. J. 1980. *Vitamin E: A comprehensive treatise*. New York: Marcel Dekker.

———. 1991. *Handbook of vitamins*. 2d ed. New York: Marcel Dekker.

Maynard, L. A., Loosli, J. K., Hintz, H. F., and Warner, R. G. 1979. *Animal nutrition*. 7th ed. New York: McGraw-Hill.

McDowell, L. R. 1989. *Vitamins in animal nutrition*. San Diego: Academic Press.

Mertz, W. 1986. *Trace elements in human and animal nutrition*. 5th ed., vol. 2. New York: Academic Press.

———. 1987. *Trace elements in human and animal nutrition*. 5th ed., vol. 1. New York: Academic Press.

Milton, K., and Demment, M. W. 1988. Digestion and passage kinetics of chimpanzees fed high and low fiber diets and comparison with human data. *J. Nutr.* 118:1082–88.

Milton, K., and Dintzis, F. R. 1981. Nitrogen-to-protein conversion factors for tropical plant samples. *Biotropica* 13:177–81.

Milton, K., and Jenness, R. 1987. Ascorbic acid content of Neotropical plant parts available to wild monkeys and bats. *Experientia* 43:339–42.

National Research Council. 1978. *Nutrient requirements of nonhuman primates*. Washington, D.C.: National Academy of Sciences.

———. 1980. *Mineral tolerance of domestic animals*. Washington, D.C.: National Academy of Sciences.

———. 1983. *Selenium in nutrition*. Rev. ed. Washington, D.C.: National Academy of Sciences.

———. 1987. *Vitamin tolerance of animals*. Washington, D.C.: National Academy of Sciences.

———. 1989a. *Nutrient requirements of dairy cattle*. 6th rev. ed. Washington, D.C.: National Academy Press.

———. 1989b. *Nutrient requirements of horses*. 5th rev. ed. Washington, D.C.: National Academy Press.

———. 1995. *Nutrient requirements of laboratory animals*. 4th rev. ed. Washington, D.C.: National Academy of Sciences.

Obeck, D. K. 1978. Galvanized caging as a potential factor in the development of the "fading infant" or "white monkey" syndrome. *Lab. Anim. Sci.* 28:698–704.

Oftedal, O. T., and Boness, D. J. 1983. Considerations in the use of fish as food. In *Proceedings of the Third Annual Dr. Scholl Conference on the Nutrition of Captive Wild Animals*, ed. T. P. Meehan and M. E. Allen, 149–61. Chicago: Lincoln Park Zoological Society.

Rehg, J. E., Burek, J. D., Strandberg, J. D., and Montali, R. J. 1980. Hemochromotosis in the rock hyrax. In *Comparative pathology of zoo animals*, ed. R. J. Montali and G. Migaki, 113–20. Washington, D.C.: Smithsonian Institution Press.

Rodahl, K. 1949a. *The toxic effect of polar bear liver*. Norsk Polar Institutt Skrifter no. 92.

———. 1949b. Toxicity of polar bear liver. *Nature* 164:530.

Rodahl, K., and Moore, T. 1943. The vitamin A content and toxicity of bear and seal liver. *Biochem. J.* 37:166–68.

Schmidt-Nielsen, K. 1979. *Animal physiology*. 2d ed. Cambridge: Cambridge University Press.

Schmidt-Nielsen, K., and Schmidt-Nielsen, B. 1952. Water metabolism of desert mammals. *Physiol. Rev.* 32:135–66.

Sebrell, W. H., and Harris, R. S. 1967. *The vitamins*. New York: Academic Press.

Smith, J. C. 1987. Methods of trace element research. In *Trace elements in human and animal nutrition*, 5th ed., vol. 1, ed. W. Mertz, 21–56. New York: Academic Press.

Smith, R. M. 1987. Cobalt. In *Trace elements in human and animal nutrition*, 5th ed., vol. 1, ed. W. Mertz, 143–76. New York: Academic Press.

Southgate, D. A. T. 1973. Fibre and the other unavailable carbohydrates and their effects on the energy value of the diet. *Proc. Nutr. Soc.* 32:131–36.

Ullrey, D. E. 1972. Biological availability of fat-soluble vitamins: Vitamin A and carotene. *J. Anim. Sci.* 35:648–57.

Ullrey, D. E., Schwartz, C. C., Whetter, P. A., Rajeshwar Rao, T., Euber, J. R., Chenn, S. G., and Brunner, J. R. 1984. Blue-green color and composition of Stejneger's beaked whale *(Mesoplodon stejnegeri)* milk. *Comp. Biochem. Physiol.* [B] 79:349–52.

Underwood, E. J. 1977. *Trace elements in human and animal nutrition*. 4th ed. New York: Academic Press.

———. 1981. *The mineral nutrition of livestock*. Slough, England: Commonwealth Agricultural Bureaux.

Van Soest, P. J. 1978. Dietary fibers: Their definition and nutritional properties. *Am. J. Clin. Nutr.* 31:S12–S20.

———. 1994. *Nutritional ecology of the ruminant*. 2d ed. Ithaca, N.Y.: Comstock Publishing Associates, Cornell University Press.

Watt, B. K., and Merrill, A. L. 1963. *Composition of foods*. (Agriculture Handbook no. 8). Washington, D.C.: U.S. Department of Agriculture.

Wolf, W. R. 1987. Quality assurance for trace element analysis. In *Trace elements in human and animal nutrition*, 5th ed., vol. 1, ed. W. Mertz, 57–78. New York: Academic Press.

Zeisel, S. H. 1981. Dietary choline: Biochemistry, physiology, and pharmacology. *Annu. Rev. Nutr.* 1:95–121.

Zook, B. C., and Parasch, L. H. 1980. Lead poisoning in zoo primates: Environmental sources and neuropathological findings. In *The comparative pathology of zoo animals*, ed. R. J. Montali and G. Migaki, 143–52. Washington, D.C.: Smithsonian Institution Press.

12

The Feeding and Nutrition of Herbivores

OLAV T. OFTEDAL, DAVID J. BAER, AND MARY E. ALLEN

THE IMPORTANCE OF PLANT FIBER FERMENTATION

Unlike omnivores and carnivores, which usually consume rather digestible, low-fiber foods, many mammalian herbivores consume plant material with a moderate to high fiber content. Because mammals lack the endogenous enzymes necessary for digestion of the fiber components, they must rely on anaerobic fermentation of the fiber by symbiotic gastrointestinal (GI) microorganisms. One or more segments of the digestive tracts of mammalian herbivores are usually modified to form fermentation chambers that can support a large and active population of bacteria, protozoa, and fungi (Hungate 1966; Stevens 1988). These microbial species metabolize nutrients in ingested feeds and in salivary and GI secretions while producing wastes (such as volatile fatty acids [VFAs]) that are then metabolized by the host animal. The "microbial ecology" of this fermentation system can be described in terms such as the influx of necessary substrates and nutrients, stability of species composition, changes in environmental factors (e.g., pH, dissolved gases), and rates of removal of microbial wastes (the end products of fermentation, VFAs) (Prins 1977; Savage 1977). As the health of the host animal is highly dependent on the stability and productivity of this microbial system, the feeding of herbivores is often constrained by the needs of the microbial inhabitants. Rapid changes in diet that lead to disruptions in microbial fermentation systems can lead to severe medical disorders such as bloat, rumenitis, acidosis, and diarrhea (Stevens 1988).

This chapter is not intended to be a comprehensive treatise on the physiology and nutrition of herbivores. Several recent publications review various aspects of herbivore digestive processes, morphology, and physiology (Van Soest 1994; Church 1984; McDowell 1985; Milligan, Grovum,

At the time of writing, David Baer was with the Department of Zoological Research, National Zoological Park, Smithsonian Institution, Washington, D.C.

and Dobson 1986; Hacker and Ternouth 1987; Stevens 1988; Dobson and Dobson 1988; Robbins 1993; Gordon and Illius 1994).

THE DIVERSE DIGESTIVE SYSTEMS OF HERBIVORES

Two types of mammalian herbivores are often distinguished by the location of the major fermentation region in the digestive tract. Foregut fermenters have evolved fermentation systems that precede the acid- and enzyme-producing regions of the stomach and the small intestine. In ruminants, for example, the first three "gastric" chambers (rumen, reticulum, and omasum) promote fermentation by retaining food materials in a microbial "bath" that is buffered by saliva. These chambers are located anterior to the acid-secreting chamber (abomasum). Large food particles are recycled to the mouth for further grinding during rumination, thereby reducing particle size and increasing the exposure of fiber and other nutrients to microbial enzymes (Akin 1986). Thus, food materials that pass through the omasum into the glandular stomach (abomasum) have already been highly modified by microbial activity. Moreover, microbial cells themselves pass into the abomasum for digestion and are an important nutrient source for the ruminant. Other examples of foregut fermenters include camelids, hippopotamuses, kangaroos and wallabies, colobine monkeys, and sloths. Although the extent of compartmentation of the foregut varies among different mammalian groups, and although many foregut fermenters do not ruminate, the fermentation process is very similar to that described for ruminants.

In foregut fermenters, food is first digested by microbes and only afterward by the herbivore. Therefore, the art of feeding these animals is, in part, the art of feeding microbes. One must consider what kinds of materials are most satisfactory for maintaining the stability and productivity of the fermentation system. Some highly soluble and rapidly fermentable foodstuffs (e.g., sugars in fruits) can lead

TABLE 12.1.   Comparison of Gastrointestinal Anatomy and Function of Concentrate Selectors (Browsers) and Bulk and Roughage Feeders (Grazers)

	Concentrate selectors	Bulk and roughage feeders
Foregut weight, filled (as % of body weight)	10–12	13–15
Normal extent of rumenreticulum fill (%)	50–60	Almost 100
Stratification of digesta in rumen	No	Yes
Relative size of reticulum (compared with rumen, etc.)	Spacious	Not very spacious
Dorsal attachment of rumen dorsal sac	No	Yes
Caudal extension of rumen into pelvic inlet	No	Yes
Expansion of ventral sac of rumen into right side	No	Yes
Rumen pillars	Relatively weak	Powerful
Rumen-reticular opening	Remarkably wide	Narrower
Overall rumen appearance	S-shaped	Compartmentalized chambers
Zones of unpapillated mucosal surface	Not significant	Extensive
Rumination pattern	Intermittent, irregular, short duration	Long periods

Source: Data of Hofmann 1973.

to a highly disruptive, explosive fermentation, whereas low-quality, highly lignified hay may not support adequate fermentation.

The other major type of mammalian herbivore is the hindgut fermenter. In some hindgut fermenters, such as rabbits, koalas, and some rodents, the cecum is enlarged to serve as a fermentation chamber. In other hindgut fermenters, such as equids, rhinoceroses, elephants, and wombats, fermentation occurs primarily in a voluminous colon (Hume and Warner 1980; Stevens 1988). In hindgut fermenters, food is digested in the stomach and small intestine by host secretions before it enters the fermentation system. Thus, the fermentation process in the hindgut depends on the influx of materials that escape gastric and enzymatic digestion. Because the prefermentation digestive processes regulate the composition of fermentation substrates, the fermentation systems of hindgut fermenters are somewhat less prone to adverse consequences from rapid diet change. Nonetheless, a sudden influx of rapidly fermentable food residues (such as may occur if starch escapes upper tract digestion) may lead to microbial disruption and onset of diarrhea.

In attempting to understand the functional differences among the digestive systems of various herbivores, nutritionists and comparative physiologists are especially interested in the fates and passage rates of different-sized food particles through the GI tract. Even among ruminants, for example, differences in the relative size and anatomical characteristics of the foregut may influence the length of time that food particles remain exposed to microbial fermentation. Hofmann (1973, 1988) proposed that differences in gastrointestinal structure among ruminants are correlated with dietary specialization (as summarized in table 12.1). He argued that some browsing species (such as dik-diks, *Madoqua* spp., duikers, *Cephalophus* spp., and bongos, *Tragelaphus euryceros*) are "concentrate selectors," while those that graze on grasses (such as wildebeest, *Connochaetes* spp., sable antelope, *Hippotragus niger,* and oryx, *Oryx* spp.) are "bulk and roughage feeders." Hofmann further postulated that concentrate selectors tend to have small fermentation regions and anatomical features that facilitate rapid passage of large food particles. They

tend to avoid plant material that is very high in fiber, instead choosing more rapidly fermentable foods such as young leaves, flowers, and fruits. In contrast, bulk and roughage feeders have voluminous fermentation regions and anatomical features that facilitate the retention of large particles for more extensive fermentation. They tend to ingest predominantly high-fiber food (such as coarse, mature grasses). Although the functional significance of these differences has recently been questioned, especially with regard to fiber digestion and rates of digesta passage (Gordon and Illius 1994; Robbins, Spalinger, and Van Hoven, in press), the feeding strategies of browsers, grazers, and intermediate feeders are clearly different. While extremes in feeding strategy certainly exist, many ruminants undoubtedly fall somewhere in between and may combine certain features of both: for example, the giraffe, *Giraffa camelopardalis* (Baer, Oftedal, and Fahey 1985).

Among hindgut fermenters there can also be substantial differences in diet selection in response to variation in digestive function. Some large species, such as equids and elephants, are able to retain substantial amounts of fibrous material in the colonic fermentation system and have adopted a strategy of consuming large amounts of relatively indigestible, high-fiber foods (Foose 1982; Owen-Smith 1988). By contrast, small species with predominantly cecal fermentation are apt to select vegetation of higher digestibility.

NUTRITIONAL REQUIREMENTS OF HERBIVORES

Like other mammals, herbivores require a wide array of nutrients. The nutritional requirements of herbivores, however, are influenced by their symbiotic microbes in a number of ways. The fermentation process leads to the production of volatile fatty acids that are absorbed and utilized as an energy source by the host animal. In foregut fermenters, the microbes may use both protein constituents and nonprotein nitrogen to synthesize amino acids and proteins that are then available for utilization by the host. Thus, foregut fermenters are less sensitive than other animals to the amino acid composition of ingested foods. In domestic ruminant diets, urea or other nonprotein nitrogen sources (biuret, am-

TABLE 12.2.   Recommended Nutrient Content of Rations
for Père David's Deer

Nutrient	Concentration in diet[a]
Protein	16%
Calcium	0.60%
Phosphorus	0.40%
Magnesium	0.20%
Sodium chloride	0.50%
Potassium	0.80%
Vitamin A	6,000 IU/kg
Vitamin D	500 IU/kg
Vitamin E	130 IU/kg
Iron	50 ppm
Copper	10 ppm
Zinc	50 ppm
Manganese	40 ppm
Iodine	0.7 ppm
Cobalt	0.1 ppm
Selenium	0.2 ppm

Source: Adapted from Oftedal 1983.

Note: For manufactured feeds containing approximately 10% moisture.

[a]IU, International Units; ppm, parts per million.

monium salts) are often used as substitutes for protein, thereby reducing feed costs. Microbes also synthesize vitamins that may substitute for dietary vitamins. Mature ruminants, for example, are thought to have little or no dietary requirement for B vitamins or vitamin K, since these vitamins are produced in substantial amounts by ruminal microbes and can be absorbed in the small intestine. Hindgut fermenters may not be able to absorb all of the vitamins produced posterior to the small intestine. Mammals that practice coprophagy reingest the amino acids and vitamins synthesized in the hindgut and may reduce their dietary requirements in this way (Hornicke and Bjornhag 1980). Recommended nutrient levels for a foregut fermenter, Père David's deer, *Elaphurus davidianus,* are given in table 12.2.

ESTABLISHING A DIETARY MODEL FOR HERBIVORES

In the wild, herbivores ingest foods that vary widely in nutritional composition. Although vegetation is ubiquitous in many habitats, there are pronounced differences in composition among plant parts (leaves, twigs, flowers, flower buds, and fruits), and these differences may be exacerbated by both phenological changes (e.g., maturation of leaves) and seasonal effects. Differences also exist among plant types (e.g., grasses vs. legumes) and among plant species. Habitat characteristics, including soil type and composition, may influence the nutrient content of vegetation. Chemical constituents of some plants serve as feeding deterrents and may be highly noxious or even toxic. Although there have been numerous studies of the feeding behavior of herbivores such as white-tailed deer, *Odocoileus virginianus,* and moose, *Alces alces,* it is difficult to interpret the individual feeding choices made or to relate these to nutritional properties of the plants (Robbins 1993). Thus, data on the feeding behavior of wild herbivores are of value only in a general fashion.

It may be helpful to determine the extent to which a given species consumes high-fiber foods (e.g., mature grasses, mature leaves) and its degree of reliance on grazing versus browsing. However, studies completed in the wild rarely provide sufficient detail on nutrient intakes to allow formulation of a captive diet that would match the diet of the free-ranging animal.

In practice, zoo herbivores are best fed in a manner akin to that associated with domestic species. The extensive information available on the feeding of cattle, sheep, and goats provides a solid foundation for the feeding of ruminants, and information on horses can be employed in the development of feeding standards for large hindgut fermenters such as zebras, rhinos, and elephants. Domestic rabbits provide a model of a small, cecotrophic hindgut fermenter. While there are no good domestic models for herbivorous primates (e.g., colobus, *Colobus* spp., langurs, *Presbytis* spp., and howler monkeys, *Alouatta* spp.), herbivorous marsupials (e.g., kangaroos, wallabies, *Macropus* spp., and wombats, *Vombatus* spp.), or herbivorous carnivores (e.g., giant pandas, *Ailuropoda melanoleuca,* and red pandas, *Ailurus fulgens*), application of principles learned in the feeding of domestic species may help in making estimates about appropriate diets for these animals. Fortunately, nutritional research is under way on representatives of these dietary groups (e.g., Dierenfeld et al. 1982; Hume 1982; Watkins, Ullrey, and Whetter 1985; Warnell 1988; Barboza 1989; Fulton et al. 1991; Barboza and Hume 1991), and revisions and improvements to traditional zoo diets can be expected.

Diets for ungulates and many other herbivores are typically composed of some combination of hay, pelleted feed, browse, hydroponic grass, and produce. We will discuss each of these products in turn.

Hay Use and Assessment

Hays are forages that are harvested and dried for storage. Because hays often provide a major portion of dry matter intake for zoo herbivores, they are important nutrient sources. Hays are especially valuable as a source of fiber to support microbial fermentation and as a means of providing behavioral occupation. In the wild, herbivores often spend many hours each day in feeding activities. In captivity, animals that are fed relatively concentrated diets that can be consumed in minutes rather than hours may develop behavioral vices, especially chewing on exhibit or stall materials and excessive licking or grooming activities. Because consumption of hay requires prolonged periods of chewing, its use may help to prevent development of these vices.

Proper drying and curing of freshly cut forage is a critical step in producing high-quality hay (Barnes 1973; Reid 1973; Van Soest 1994; Church and Pond 1988). Once cut, hay must be dried prior to baling. If hay is too wet when it is baled, bacteria and mold can begin to grow. These microorganisms can reduce feed intake and may produce toxins that can adversely affect animal health. Hay that becomes wet from rain or dew may also have reduced nutritional value. If hay is baled when it is too dry, however, leaves may fracture and fall off the stems, reducing nutritional value. When overdried hay is offered to herbivores, feed intake

TABLE 12.3. Composition of Sun-Cured Legume and Grass Hays at Various Stages of Maturity

Hay	Crude protein	Fiber Fractions			Ca	P	Ca:P
		NDF	ADF	Lignin			
Legumes							
Alfalfa							
Early vegetative	23.0	38	28	5	1.80	0.35	5.1
Early bloom	18.0	42	31	8	1.41	0.22	6.4
Full bloom	15.0	50	37	10	1.25	0.22	5.7
Vetch, *Vicia* spp.							
Early vegetative	21.1	39	27	7	—	—	—
Late vegetative	19.6	43	30	8	—	—	—
Full bloom	16.0	—	—	—	1.02	0.28	3.6
Grasses							
Sudan							
Early vegetative	15.6	53	29	3	0.77	0.36	2.1
Early bloom	10.0	61	34	4	0.35	0.31	1.1
Full bloom	10.1	63	38	4	0.40	0.30	1.3
Timothy							
Early vegetative	17.8	48	25	3	0.52	0.39	1.3
Early bloom	10.7	61	34	6	0.51	0.29	1.8
Full bloom	7.7	69	42	8	0.36	0.24	1.5

Source: Fonnesbeck et al. 1984.
Note: Given as percentage of dry matter, with the exception of Ca:P ratio. NDF, neutral detergent fiber; ADF, acid detergent fiber; Ca, calcium; P_1 phosphorus.

also may be adversely affected. The time required for drying hay appropriately depends to a large extent on the local weather conditions and the method of drying. Most commonly, hay is left in the field to be dried by the sun; this method is known as sun curing. The minimum dry matter content of hay should be 85%. Beyond a maximum dry matter content of 93%, hay may be subject to excessive leaf fracture.

Some other nutritional changes occur during the curing process. Sun curing in the field generally increases the vitamin D_2 content of hay. This increase is a result of phytochemical conversion of vitamin D_2 precursors to a more biologically active vitamin D_2 compound (Morrison 1956). However, there is a concomitant loss in the vitamin A activity of the hay resulting from the oxidative destruction of carotenes, the precursors of vitamin A. During excessive drying, the losses of carotenes can be substantial (Morrison 1956). Once cured to the proper dry matter content, hay that is stored under dry conditions will remain relatively stable with respect to its nutritional value (Church 1984).

The two most commonly used types of hays are grass hays and legume hays (Heath, Metcalfe, and Barnes 1973). Taxonomically, grass hays derive from plants in the family Poaceae (Gramineae), whereas legume hays derive from plants in the family Fabaceae (Leguminosae). Examples of grass hays include Sudan, timothy, coastal Bermuda, fescues, bluegrass, prairie, ryegrass, canary, and Johnson. The most commonly used legume hay is alfalfa (called lucerne in Europe and Australasia). Other legume hays include clovers, lespedeza, lupines, and vetches. Hay producers often grow mixtures of legume and grass hays.

Legume hays and grass hays have several important nutritional similarities and differences (table 12.3). In general, legume hays are higher in crude protein, calcium, magnesium, and sulfur than grass hays. Grass hays are generally higher in manganese and zinc (Church and Pond 1988). Differences in fiber levels between legumes and grasses are also important and can influence voluntary feed intake. Legumes are generally higher in lignin and lower in NDF and hemicellulose than grasses (Van Soest 1994). In ruminants, voluntary feed intake is negatively correlated with NDF content (Mertens 1973). Because legumes are frequently lower in NDF than grasses, voluntary intake of legumes can be higher than that of grasses (Mertens 1973; Van Soest 1994). Some of these nutritional differences are dependent on local soil conditions, amount and type of fertilizer used, and growing conditions.

The mineral and crude protein content of hays can be affected by soil fertilization (Woodhouse and Griffith 1973; Allaway 1975; Van Soest 1994; Church and Pond 1988). Adjustments of soil pH and fertilization are often necessary to produce high-quality hays, especially grass hays. The more common nutrients in fertilizers include nitrogen, phosphorus, potassium, calcium, and magnesium. Sulfur fertilization may be used on some crops. Nitrogen fertilization can increase the crude protein content of the hay and is especially important when growing grass hays. Fertilization with nitrogen and phosphorus may also improve the palatability of certain hays (Rhykerd and Noller 1973). The type and amount of fertilizers that should be used depend on local soil and growing conditions. Thus soil testing and the advice of local agricultural extension agents can be important components of a sound hay-producing operation.

Regional variations among hays, especially in mineral content, should also be considered in developing a feeding program (Allaway 1975; Underwood 1981). The mineral content of hay is often related to soil mineral levels. Soil concentrations of nutritionally important minerals such as cobalt, molybdenum, iodine, and selenium vary greatly across geographic areas. For example, the soils in parts of Florida and California contain naturally occurring high levels of molybdenum, whereas in other parts of the country high molybdenum levels may be a consequence of industrial contamination. Forages grown in these areas may contain high levels of molybdenum, which may chemically combine with copper and sulfur. As a consequence of these mineral interactions, animals consuming this forage may develop an induced copper deficiency (Underwood 1981). An observed copper deficiency in animals at the San Diego Wild Animal Park was attributed to excessive molybdenum in pasture plants (D. E. Ullrey, pers. comm.). Selenium deficiency is another soil-related problem of regional importance. Hays grown in much of the Pacific Northwest, Florida, New England, the Mid-Atlantic states, and the Midwest often contain less than 0.1 ppm (dry matter basis) selenium. When such hays are used in zoo feeding programs, they should be supplemented with pelleted feeds enriched with selenium (e.g., 0.4 ppm).

An important factor influencing the nutritional value of both legume and grass hays is degree of maturity at cutting (Morrison 1956; Van Soest 1994) and, hence, stage at cutting is an important criterion in establishing hay grades (Rohweder 1980). As the plants mature, there is usually a decrease in the relative amount of leaf and an increase in the amount of stem. With the onset of flowering, nutrients are also diverted from the vegetative portion (leaf) to the reproductive portion (flower buds). These changes may result in decreased concentrations of crude protein and soluble carbohydrates in the vegetative portion and an increase in lignin content (see table 12.3). Levels of certain minerals such as calcium, potassium, and phosphorus may also decline. The net result is a decrease in palatability, digestibility, and nutritional value of hay as its maturity at cutting advances (Van Soest 1994).

Hay that is fed to zoo animals should be of high quality. Hay vendors often view zoos as an unsophisticated market that will accept low-quality hay and may attempt to deliver substandard material. Each shipment of hay should be inspected prior to acceptance, and if the hay is not acceptable it should be rejected. A lack of firmness in this regard encourages unscrupulous or careless behavior by vendors.

Quality can be evaluated initially by sight and smell upon the hay's arrival at the zoo (Morrison 1956; Rohweder 1980). The hay should contain minimal amounts of weeds, and it should not appear excessively bleached. Bleaching may indicate improper field drying. Hays, especially alfalfa hay, should appear leafy, and the leaves should not readily fall off the stems when a bale is opened. The amount of leaf may indicate the stage of growth at the time of cutting, but excessive leaf fall may also indicate that the hay is too dry. A number of flowers on legume hay and well-developed heads on grass hay may indicate late cutting (Rohweder 1987). Stems should feel pliable; stems that feel brittle or snap when they are bent may indicate that the hay is too dry or that the hay was too mature at the time of cutting. Excessive dustiness indicates mold. If the hay smells musty, or if it creates a choking sensation when smelled closely, mold growth may be a problem. These methods for evaluating hay are subjective, but they provide some indications as to how the hay was cured and handled and may help identify certain kinds of problems.

Nutrient testing permits further evaluation of hay quality, so long as the sampling is done in systematic fashion. At least fifteen individual bales should be sampled in cross-section with an appropriate forage sampler, such as a hay core sampler attached to an electric drill. Nutritional analyses on each hay delivery should include dry matter, crude protein, fiber fractions (NDF, ADF, and lignin), calcium, and phosphorus. Data should also be obtained on the trace mineral levels (including copper and selenium) of hay samples, but such data need not be obtained for each delivery once baseline levels are established for a specific hay-producing region. Objective information on the nutrient content of hay is important to ensure that only high-quality hay is used.

The choice of type of hay to use will depend on local availability and price. If high hay quality is not certain, use of legume hay is usually safer than use of grass hay, so long as the legume hay is free of mold, weeds, and insect infestations. Grass hays often require fertilization and close management for high nutritive value. A low-quality, overmature legume hay will provide more crude protein than an improperly managed grass hay. Another practical problem relates to the relatively high ratio of calcium to phosphorus in legume hays. In some parts of the United States, the calcium: phosphorus ratio in legume hays can approach 10. If the hay represents a large proportion of the diet, this imbalance may cause metabolic problems in the animals consuming it (Underwood 1981). There are at least two solutions to this problem. First, a nutritionally complete pellet can be formulated to help balance calcium and phosphorus in the diet. The proportion of pellet and hay can be manipulated to suit the type of herbivore that is being fed. Second, a mixture of legume and grass hays can be offered to the animals. The narrower calcium:phosphorus ratio of the grass hay helps to compensate for the imbalance of the legume hay.

Formulation of Pelleted Feeds

The use of pelleted feeds in feeding zoo herbivores has become widespread. In a survey of Père David's deer diets, it was found that ten of thirteen institutions were using pelleted diets and two were using a grain-molasses mix (Oftedal 1983). A pelleted feed is manufactured by mixing a predetermined set of ground ingredients, using a pellet mill to force this mixture through a die containing holes of specified size, and drying the resultant product to firmness. Pelleting is somewhat of an art in that appropriate ingredients and operating conditions are required to produce a pellet that will not crumble during packaging, transport, and feeding. Pelleted feeds are usually formulated using ingredients that are available locally at a reasonable price, and may include such materials as ground corn, wheat, or other grains, alfalfa meal, soybean meal, soybean or corn oil, fiber sources (e.g., soybean hulls, wheat bran, ground corncobs), calcium supplements, trace mineral premix, and vitamin premix.

Pelleted feeds are often formulated to be either "complete feeds" (with an ADF level of 15% or more), which do not require much supplementation with hay, or "concentrates" (with an ADF level of 9% or less), which must be fed in limited amounts and with substantial amounts of hay to maintain normal fermentation. Complete feeds are especially appropriate for feeding groups of animals, since social interactions may lead to some animals eating most of the pellets and other animals getting the bulk of the hay. An herbivore that overeats a concentrate runs the risk of rumenitis or other gastrointestinal disorders.

Pelleted feeds have a number of advantages that have increased their popularity. Their composition can be altered to suit particular needs (e.g., high protein or high selenium levels) by adjusting the ingredient mixtures. They are easily transported, stored, and used. There is minimal concern about nutrient stability if reasonable stock rotation and relatively cool and dry storage conditions are maintained. Pellet size can be varied; larger pellets (1/2 inch or greater) usually result in less waste and are less likely to be consumed by wild birds. If fed in sufficient amounts, pelleted feeds can reduce the need for tight control over nutrient levels in other diet components, such as hay. The most practical solution to the problem of unpredictable hay quality may be to set rather generous nutrient standards for the pelleted feed component. While this does not alleviate the need to avoid moldy or weedy hay, it does make monitoring of protein or fiber levels in hay less critical. Given the difficulty of consistently acquiring high-quality hay, an increase in the quality and amount of pellets used may be one of the simplest but most important nutritional contributions made to herbivores in zoos.

A wide range of pelleted diets are commercially available. While zoo herbivores may be fed rations designed for domestic species (such as horses, cattle, and sheep), this is usually not advisable for several reasons. Ungulates in zoos are most often maintained in mixed age and sex groups, in which each age and sex may have somewhat different nutrient requirements. By contrast, domestic animals are usually fed according to age and sex class, so that commercial feeds are designed for a specific purpose (e.g., early growth, fattening, maintenance, breeding, heavy lactation). Thus, a dairy cow feed may be inappropriate for a weanling fawn, and a horse maintenance feed may be unsuitable for a lactating gazelle. Captive wild herbivores may also have higher requirements for some nutrients, such as vitamin E and trace minerals, than domestic species. Finally, it is common in formulating pelleted feeds for exotic species to provide a margin of safety in nutrient levels to cover possible (but unknown) interspecies differences in nutrient requirements. The usual practice in feeding domestic animals, especially those reared for production purposes, is to use the cheapest feed ingredients that can still achieve the desired production level, so that the product can be priced competitively. This practice may reduce nutrient levels in feeds to minima that are appropriate for the target domestic species, but that may be below levels required by exotic zoo species.

The ideal pelleted feed will vary from location to location and from one feeding context to the next. Pellet formulation and manufacture should take into account a number of factors, including the proportion of the diet that will consist of pellets, the composition of hay or other feeds to be used in conjunction with the pellets, the types of herbivores to be fed (e.g., foregut vs. hindgut fermenters), the age, sex, and species groups to be fed, and the need for specific levels of particular nutrients (e.g., vitamin E, selenium, copper, calcium). Palatability characteristics of specific ingredients, desired pellet size and hardness, local availability of ingredients, and ingredient costs also should be considered.

One way of purchasing pelleted feeds is to have the zoo nutritionist specify the exact ingredient composition of the product to be manufactured (Oftedal and Allen 1987). Such products are often called fixed-formula or open-formula feeds, since the exact amounts and ingredients are openly declared. One advantage of fixed-formula feeds is that various manufacturers or vendors can bid competitively, and whoever gets the bid should in theory supply the same product. This practice may reduce the variability in feed characteristics as vendors change from year to year, and provides a more solid base of information against which to judge changes in animal performance. Of course, some unscrupulous or careless manufacturers may attempt to switch formulations to keep costs down as the availability and price of ingredients change, and inclusion of substandard ingredients may result in reduction of quality. Manufacturers usually prefer to sell variable- or closed-formula products, that is, products for which ingredient or nutrient specifications are set in a general way only, such that the precise formulation is known only to the manufacturer. Such specifications permit changes in product composition from batch to batch. Manufacturers are typically reluctant to release detailed compositional data on these products for fear that competitors may copy their formulas and steal market share. One of the great frustrations for the zoo nutritionist is the inability to get detailed information about products being used in the zoo. Often the only recourse is to send feed samples to a commercial laboratory for nutrient analyses, but these are apt to be costly and may be of questionable reliability unless care is taken in the selection of a reputable laboratory.

Formulating and evaluating a pelleted feed is obviously a task beyond the expertise of curatorial and veterinary staff, and requires input from both zoo nutritionists and feed manufacturers. Although relatively few zoos have staff nutritionists, assistance can often be obtained from consultants, university faculty, and scientists employed by feed manufacturers. While a pelleted diet developed for one animal collection may be usable at another zoo, careful consideration is in order before this choice is made.

Considerations in Use of Browse

Browse is commonly used as supplemental forage at many zoos, although the supply is usually limited by the cost and the effort involved in obtaining it. Browse consists of leaves, twigs, shoots, flowers, and fruits, usually harvested on zoo grounds or in the local area. Browse is usually offered immediately after cutting, although it may be preserved for a limited time by spraying with water or for a longer time by shock-freezing. Most commonly, browse is offered to hoofstock and primates. Other herbivores, such as koalas, *Phascolarctos cinereus*, and pandas may also be offered browse. Browse can stimulate naturalistic feeding behaviors and thus has a high occupational value (Gould and Bres 1986). Some types of browse are relatively nutritious and can provide substantial amounts of some nutrients, including plant fiber. Unfortunately, little is known about the nutrient values of most plant species used for browse. Browse availability varies seasonally and geographically, and harvesting practices are more apt to reflect availability than nutritional considerations. This is an area in which considerable nutritional research is needed.

One significant problem with the use of browse is that secondary plant compounds may be present at dangerously high levels in some species (Kingsbury 1964). Secondary plant compounds are chemicals produced by plants that are not used for primary plant metabolism (Rosenthal and Janzen 1979). They function as feeding deterrents and have evolved to protect plants from the many phytophagous and herbivorous animals that can quickly defoliate them. The thousands of different secondary compounds can be separated, based on chemical structure, into different classes. Some of these compounds can be more harmful to animals than others. For instance, some secondary compounds may be bitter or cause mild digestive disorders, while others may be toxic and lead rapidly to death.

Mention of some of the more common types of secondary compounds may illustrate the complexity of the problem. The most common refractory substance is *lignin*. Lignin reduces the activity of microbial enzymes and the accessibility of microbes to the fiber matrix, thus reducing fiber digestibility (Jung and Fahey 1983). *Tannins* are found at high levels in a number of tropical and temperate species, including the leaves and seeds (acorns) of oaks. Tannins bind with ingested proteins and reduce protein digestibility. It has recently been discovered that some herbivores secrete prolinerich polypeptides in saliva that help to reduce the adverse effects of tannins (Robbins et al. 1987; Mehansho, Butler, and Carlson 1987). The *alkaloids* are a large and diverse group of compounds, including some that are highly toxic (e.g., solanine in deadly nightshade) and others that are relatively nontoxic (e.g., caffeine). According to one estimate, 15–20% of all vascular plants contain alkaloids (Robinson 1979). *Cyanogenic glycosides* release cyanide when metabolized by plant enzymes after plant tissues are crushed or damaged. Acute poisoning often occurs when cyanogenic glycoside–rich plants such as wild cherry, chokecherry, sorghum, or acacias are ingested by livestock (Kingsbury 1964). Some bamboos may also contain substantial levels. *Saponins* are widely distributed among plants, and are found at especially high levels in leguminous plants. Saponins may irritate mucous membranes and depress food intake. *Glucosinolates* are especially abundant in plants of the mustard or cabbage family (Brassicaceae or Cruciferae) and are known to produce goiter in humans and animals. Feeding large amounts of kale can produce goiter in cattle and sheep (Van Etten and Tookey 1979).

Given the array of potential toxins, and given uncertainties about the factors that influence variations in their concentrations within and among different plants, browse use should be approached with some caution. Since potential toxicity is dose-related, a prudent approach is to feed modest quantities of any species of browse and to introduce each species into a diet gradually. While the literature on toxic plants is useful in assessing risks, almost all data are for domestic animals and humans. Toxicity problems are usually most prevalent in livestock when food supplies are limited and feeding choices are restricted (Kingsbury 1964). While zoo herbivores are usually provided with substantial amounts of non-browse items, boredom may play a role in inducing consumption of items that would not normally be eaten. The possibility of toxic secondary compounds in bamboo and eucalyptus warrants further investigation since these plants constitute such a large fraction of the diets of such species as giant and red pandas, bamboo lemurs, and koalas. While species-specific detoxification mechanisms may exist in these specialized herbivores, these animals also may exercise greater selectivity in feeding in the wild than is possible in the captive setting.

Hydroponic Crops as an Alternative Feed

Another type of forage that some zoos have used in the past, and that some zoos are currently using, is hydroponically grown grasses or sprouts (Oyarzun 1980). These crops are produced by sprouting seeds, such as soybeans, sunflower seeds, barley, or oats, in trays of water located in an environmentally controlled chamber. Temperature, lighting, watering systems, and in some cases fertilization are automatically controlled. The crop of sprouts typically develops within 7 days.

Historically, it was thought that hydroponic crops contained factors that improved animal growth, performance, and reproduction. These factors became known as "grass factors" or "grass juice factors." Subsequently, scientific research has led to the identification of some of these factors. One growth promoter was found to be copper sulfate, which was being added as a preservative (Scott, Nesheim, and Young 1976). Plant estrogens may also serve as growth promoters since these compounds can be biologically active as estrogens in animals that consume the plants. While some plant estrogens may promote animal growth, others may be responsible for acute and chronic infertility in some livestock (Moule, Braden, and Lamond 1963; Kingsbury 1964; Barry and Blaney 1987).

There are several important nutritional and economic factors to consider with regard to the use of hydroponically grown crops. Water is the major component of hydroponically grown crops, representing approximately 90% of their fresh weight (table 12.4). On a dry matter basis, some hydroponically grown crops are high in crude protein and are a good source of carotenes. However, hydroponically grown crops are consistently low in calcium and contain an inverse ratio of calcium to phosphorus (table 12.4) (Oyarzun 1980). Given their high moisture content, an animal would need to eat large amounts of hydroponically grown crops for them to have any substantial effect on its total nutrient intake. The high level of nitrates that has been reported in some types of hydroponic sprouts (Fasset 1973) may also pose a potential health problem. Hydroponic units can be expensive to purchase, maintain, and operate (Oyarzun 1980). The cost of the seeds is relatively

TABLE 12.4.   Composition of Hydroponic Crops and Leafy Greens (% of Dry Matter)

Item	Dry matter	Crude protein	Calcium	Phosphorus
Hydroponic crops				
Barley	9.4	18.2	0.18	0.58
Sunflower	10.8	26.8	0.22	0.80
Soybean	11.9	46.2	0.25	0.69
Leafy greens				
Lettuce	4.1	26.8	0.46	0.49
Kale	15.4	21.2	0.87	0.36

low, but the unit may require extensive operator time. Other leafy greens may be more nutritionally complete, easier to handle, better able to fulfill behavioral requisites, and less expensive.

Should Produce Be Used for Herbivores?

In zoos, herbivores are commonly fed a combination of fresh fruits and vegetables. The reasons for this are sometimes obscure, but probably include the belief that since many herbivores consume food materials in the wild that are botanically "fruits" or that are "green and leafy," captive animals should be fed something comparable. However, virtually all produce sold for human consumption is relatively low in plant fiber, and is thus quite different in composition from the materials usually eaten by herbivores in the wild (Oftedal and Allen, chap. 14, this volume). Commercial fruits are also high in sugars, which may lead to explosive fermentation in foregut fermenters. At least in ruminants and horses, ingestion of substantial amounts of fruits and some vegetables (including cabbage and kale) can lead to bloat and intestinal torsions. Use of fruits and other readily fermentable materials is thus risky and should be rigidly controlled. We believe that commercially available fruits are inappropriate for most herbivore diets and that vegetables should be used only in moderate amounts. Because produce items are expensive on a dry matter basis, reduction in their use may also result in significant savings in feed costs. Although produce use may have some positive behavioral effects, other foods (such as hay and browse) may be more appropriate for this purpose.

SPECIFIC RECOMMENDATIONS FOR THE FEEDING OF HERBIVORES

1. The basic diet for most ungulates and other strict herbivores should consist of pellets and hay. The pellets should be formulated to complement the amount and composition of hay used. Free water should be provided at all times when dry diets are fed.
2. Hay quality should be carefully evaluated with each shipment. The quality of hay becomes more critical as its proportion of the total diet increases. Moldy or weed-infested hay should never be fed.
3. Pellets should be formulated by a nutritionist familiar with the peculiarities of zoo animals. Nutrient levels should reflect the needs of the sex, age, or species group with the highest estimated requirements.
4. Special attention should be paid to levels of protein, fiber, vitamin E, calcium, phosphorus, copper, and selenium,

since both the target levels and the actual content in pellets and hay are apt to differ from one situation to the next. Deficiencies should not be addressed through the use of top-dressed supplements, as these can rarely be delivered with any accuracy.

5. When browse and/or produce are provided for behavioral occupation, the amounts and types used should be carefully limited in view of the potential for digestive effects and/or toxicity.
6. Some herbivores, such as colobus monkeys, pandas, and koalas, require special diets, as discussed elsewhere (cf. Watkins, Ullrey, and Whetter 1985; Barboza and Hume 1991; Fulton et al. 1991; Allen, Oftedal, and Baer, chap. 13, this volume). The development of relatively high fiber formulated products (such as extruded biscuits) may permit substantial improvements over traditional zoo diets (Fulton et al. 1991).

REFERENCES

Akin, D. E. 1986. Chemical and biological structure in plants related to microbial degradation of forage cell walls. In *Control of digestion and metabolism in ruminants: Proceedings of the Sixth International Symposium on Ruminant Physiology*, ed. L. P. Milligan, W. L. Grovum, and A. Dobson, 139–57. Englewood Cliffs, N.J.: Prentice-Hall.

Allaway, W. H. 1975. *The effects of soils and fertilizers on human and animal nutrition.* Agriculture Information Bulletin no. 378. Washington, D.C.: U.S. Department of Agriculture.

Baer, D. J., Oftedal, O. T., and Fahey, G. C. 1985. Feed selection and digestibility by captive giraffe. *Zoo Biol.* 4:57–64.

Barboza, P. S. 1989. The nutritional physiology of the Vombatidae. Ph.D. thesis, The University of New England, Armidale, N.S.W.

Barboza, P. S., and Hume, I. D. 1991. Designing diets for herbivorous marsupials. In *Proceedings of the Eighth Dr. Scholl Conference on the Nutrition of Captive Wild Animals*, ed. T. P. Meehan, S. D. Thompson, and M. E. Allen, 1–12. Chicago: Lincoln Park Zoological Society.

Barnes, K. K. 1973. Mechanization of forage harvesting and storage. In *Forages: The science of grassland agriculture*, ed. M. E. Heath, D. S. Metcalfe, and R. F. Barnes, 522–31. Ames: Iowa State University Press.

Barry, T. N., and Blaney, B. J. 1987. Secondary compounds of forages. In *The nutrition of herbivores*, ed. J. B. Hacker and J. H. Ternouth, 91–119. Orlando, Fla.: Academic Press.

Church, D. C., ed. 1984. *Livestock feeds and feeding.* 2d ed. Corvallis, Oreg.: O & B Books.

Church, D. C., and Pond, W. G. 1988. *Basic animal nutrition and feeding.* New York: John Wiley and Sons.

Dierenfeld, E. S., Hintz, H. F., Robertson, J. B., Van Soest, P. J., and Oftedal, O. T. 1982. Utilization of bamboo by the giant panda. *J. Nutr.* 112:636–41.

Dobson, A., and Dobson, M. J. 1988. Aspects of digestive physiology in ruminants. Ithaca, N.Y.: Cornell University Press.

Fasset, D. W. 1973. Nitrates and nitrites. In *Toxicants occurring naturally in foods*, 2d ed, ed. National Research Council, 7–25. Washington, D.C.: National Academy of Sciences.

Fonnesbeck, P. V., Lloyd, H., Obray, R., and Romesburg, S. 1984. IFI tables of feed composition. Logan: International Feedstuffs Institute, Utah State University.

Foose, T. J. 1982. Trophic strategies of ruminant vs. nonruminant ungulates. Ph.D. thesis, University of Chicago, Chicago, Ill.

Fulton, K. J., Roberts, M., Allen, M. E., Baer, D. J., Oftedal, O., and Crissey, S. 1991. The red panda SSP diet evaluation project. In *Proceedings of the Eighth Dr. Scholl Conference on the Nutrition of Captive Wild Animals*, ed. T. P. Meehan, S. D. Thompson, and M. E. Allen, 149–63. Chicago: Lincoln Park Zoological Society.

Gordon, I. I., and Illius, A. W. 1994. The functional significance of the browser-grazer dichotomy in African ruminants. *Oecologia* 98:167–75.

Gould, E., and Bres, M. 1986. Regurgitation and reingestion in captive gorillas: Description and intervention. *Zoo Biol.* 5: 241–50.

Hacker, J. B., and Ternouth, J. H., eds. 1987. *The nutrition of herbivores*. New York: Academic Press.

Heath, M. E., Metcalfe, D. S., and Barnes, R. F., eds. 1973. *Forages: The science of grassland agriculture*. 3d ed. Ames: Iowa State University Press.

Hofmann, R. 1973. The ruminant stomach: Stomach structure and feeding habits of East African game ruminants. Nairobi, Kenya: East African Literature Bureau.

———. 1988. Morphophysiological evolutionary adaptations of the ruminant digestive system. In *Aspects of digestive physiology in ruminants*, ed. A. Dobson and M. J. Dobson, 1–20. Ithaca, N.Y.: Cornell University Press.

Hornicke, H., and Bjornhag, G. 1980. Coprophagy and related strategies for digesta utilization. In *Digestive physiology and metabolism in ruminants*, ed. Y. Ruckebusch and P. Thivend, 707–30. Westport, Conn.: AVI Publishing.

Hume, I. D. 1982. *Digestive physiology and nutrition of marsupials*. New York: Cambridge University Press.

Hume, I. D., and Warner, A. C. I. 1980. Evolution of microbial digestion in mammals. In *Digestive physiology and metabolism in ruminants*, ed. Y. Ruckebusch and P. Thivend, 665–84. Westport, Conn.: AVI Publishing.

Hungate, R. E. 1966. *The rumen and its microbes*. New York: Academic Press.

Jung, H. C., and Fahey, G. C. 1983. Nutritional implications of phenolic monomers and lignin: A review. *J. Anim. Sci.* 57: 206–19.

Kingsbury, J. M. 1964. *Poisonous plants of the United States and Canada*. Englewood Cliffs, N.J.: Prentice-Hall.

McDowell, L. R., ed. 1985. Nutrition of grazing ruminants in warm climates. Orlando, Fla.: Academic Press.

Mehansho, H., Butler, L. G., and Carlson, D. M. 1987. Dietary tannins and salivary proline-rich proteins: Interactions, induction and defense mechanisms. *Annu. Rev. Nutr.* 7:423–40.

Mertens, D. R. 1973. Application of theoretical mathematical models to cell wall digestion and forage intake in ruminants. Ph.D.thesis, Cornell University, Ithaca, N.Y.

Milligan, L. P., Grovum, W. L., and Dobson, A., eds. 1986. *Control of digestion and metabolism in ruminants: Proceedings of the Sixth International Symposium on Ruminant Physiology*. Englewood Cliffs, N.J.: Prentice-Hall.

Morrison, F. B. 1956. Feeds and feeding. 22nd ed. Clinton, Iowa: Morrison Publishing.

Moule, G. R., Braden, A. W. H., and Lamond, D. R. 1963. The significance of estrogens in pasture plants in relation to animal production. *Anim. Breeding Abstr.* 31:139–57.

Oftedal, O. T. 1983. Nutrition: Feeding and handrearing. In *The biology and management of an extinct species, Père David's deer*, ed. B. B. Beck and C. Wemmer, 53–77. Park Ridge, N.J.: Noyes.

Oftedal, O. T., and Allen, M. E. 1987. Specifications for feeds used in zoo animal diets. In *Proceedings of the Sixth and Seventh Dr. Scholl Conferences on the Nutrition of Captive Wild Animals*, ed. T. P. Meehan and M. E. Allen, 13–27. Chicago: Lincoln Park Zoological Society.

Owen-Smith, R. N. 1988. *Megaherbivores: The influence of very large body size on ecology*. New York: Cambridge University Press.

Oyarzun, S. E. 1980. Hydroponic crops: A valuable alternative for feeding zoo animals? In *Proceedings of the First Annual Dr. Scholl Nutrition Conference: A Conference on the Nutrition of Captive Wild Animals*, ed. E. R. Maschgan, M. E. Allen, and L. E. Fisher, 91–114. Chicago: Lincoln Park Zoological Society.

Prins, R. A. 1977. Biochemical activities of gut microorganisms. In *Microbial ecology of the gut*, ed. R. T. J. Clarke and T. Bauchop, 73–183. New York: Academic Press.

Reid, J. T. 1973. Quality hay. In *Forages: The science of grassland agriculture*, ed. M. E. Heath, D. S. Metcalfe, and R. F. Barnes, 532–48. Ames: Iowa State University Press.

Rhykerd, C. L., and Noller, C. H. 1973. The role of nitrogen in forage production. In *Forages: The science of grassland agriculture*, ed. M. E. Heath, D. S. Metcalfe, and R. F. Barnes, 416–24. Ames: Iowa State University Press.

Robbins, C. T. 1993. *Wildlife feeding and nutrition*. 2d ed. New York: Academic Press.

Robbins, C. T., Mole, S., Hagerman, A. E., and Hanley, T. A. 1987. Role of tannins in defending plants against ruminants: Reduction in dry matter digestion. *Ecology* 68 (6): 1606–1615.

Robbins, C. T., Spalinger, D. E., and Van Hoven, W. In press. Adaptation of ruminants to browse and grass diets: Are anatomical-based browser-grazer interpretations valid? *Oecologia*.

Robinson, T. 1979. The evolutionary ecology of alkaloids. In *Herbivores: Their interactions with secondary plant metabolites*, ed. G. A. Rosenthal and D. H. Janzen, 413–48. New York: Academic Press.

Rohweder, D. A. 1980. Forage quality as related to animal needs and forage evaluation. In *Proceedings of the First Annual Dr. Scholl Nutrition Conference: A Conference on the Nutrition of Captive Wild Animals*, ed. E. R. Maschgan, M. E. Allen, and L. E. Fisher, 283–300. Chicago: Lincoln Park Zoological Society.

———. 1987. Quality evaluation and testing of hay. In *Proceedings of the Sixth and Seventh Annual Dr. Scholl Conferences on the Nutrition of Captive Wild Animals*, ed. T. P. Meehan and M. E. Allen, 48–62. Chicago: Lincoln Park Zoological Society.

Rosenthal, G. A., and Janzen, D. H., eds. 1979. *Herbivores: Their interaction with secondary plant metabolites*. New York: Academic Press.

Savage, D. C. 1977. Interactions between the host and its microbes.In *Microbial ecology of the gut*, ed. R. T. J. Clarke and T. Bauchop, 277–310. New York: Academic Press.

Scott, M. L., Nesheim, M. C., and Young, R. J. 1976. Nutrition of the chicken. Ithaca, N.Y.: M. L. Scott and Associates.

Stevens, C. E. 1988. Comparative physiology of the vertebrate digestive system. New York: Cambridge University Press.

Underwood, E. J. 1981. The mineral nutrition of livestock. Slough, England: Commonwealth Agricultural Bureaux.

Van Etten, C. H., and Tookey, H. L. 1979. Chemistry and biological effects of glucosinolates. In *Herbivores: Their interactions with secondary plant metabolites,* ed. G. A. Rosenthal and D. H. Janzen, 471–500. New York: Academic Press.

Van Soest, P. J. 1994. *Nutritional ecology of the ruminant.* 2d ed. Ithaca, N.Y.: Comstock Publishing Associates, Cornell University Press.

Warnell, K. J. 1988. Feed intake, digestibility, digesta passage, and fecal microbial ecology of the red panda *(Ailurus fulgens).* M.S. thesis, Michigan State University, East Lansing.

Watkins, B. E., Ullrey, D. E., and Whetter, P. A. 1985. Digestibility of a high-fiber biscuit-based diet by black and white colobus *(Colobus guereza). Am. J. Primatol.* 9:137–44.

Woodhouse, W. W., and Griffith, W. K. 1973. Soil fertility and fertilization of forages. In *Forages: The science of grassland agriculture,* ed. M. E. Heath, D. S. Metcalfe, and R. F. Barnes, 403–15. Ames: Iowa State University Press.

13

The Feeding and Nutrition of Carnivores

MARY E. ALLEN, OLAV T. OFTEDAL, AND DAVID J. BAER

CHARACTERISTICS OF MAMMALIAN CARNIVORES

In its broadest usage, the term "carnivore" refers to any species that obtains most or all of its nutrients from animal sources, either by predation or by scavenging. Other terms are sometimes employed for carnivores that are specialized to feed on specific types of prey: "piscivores" feed on fish, while "insectivores" feed on insects and other invertebrates.

Carnivores may consume a variety of prey species. Within the order Carnivora, Van Valkenburgh (1989) distinguished four groups based on the amount of vertebrate meat in the diet relative to other constituents: (1) the meat group (more than 70% vertebrate meat); (2) the meat/bone group (more than 70% vertebrate meat plus large bones); (3) the meat/nonvertebrate group (50–70% vertebrate meat plus fruit and/or insects); and (4) the nonvertebrate/meat group (fruit and/or insects and less than 50% vertebrate meat). For purposes of dietary management, "strict carnivores" that eat only animal prey may be distinguished from "facultative carnivores" that eat predominantly animal prey but also consume significant amounts of nonanimal foods. Strict carnivores are found in many mammalian orders, including Carnivora, Cetacea, Chiroptera, Edentata, Insectivora, Marsupialia, and Pinnipedia. In theory, a distinction may be made between "facultative carnivores" and "omnivores" depending on whether animal prey is the predominant food or only one of many food types eaten. In practice, however, this distinction is not very important, as the diets provided in zoos for facultative carnivores and omnivores may be quite similar.

The dentition of carnivores reflects the types of prey captured and consumed (Vaughan 1978; Van Valkenburgh 1989). Members of the Carnivora that feed on vertebrate prey typically have well-developed incisors and shearing

At the time of writing, David Baer was with the Department of Zoological Research, National Zoological Park, Smithsonian Institution, Washington, D.C.

carnassial teeth that facilitate effective grasping and tearing of flesh. Most pinnipeds have simple pointed teeth suitable for grasping and holding fish and aquatic invertebrates, but not for shearing flesh. However, the cusped cheek teeth of the crabeater seal, *Lobodon carcinophagus*, which feeds mainly on krill, reportedly help to filter the small crustaceans from the water. The many cusped tooth surfaces of shrews and other small insectivores help them to grasp the rigid exoskeletons of insect prey. Insectivores that feed on social insects (such as giant anteaters, *Myrmecophaga tridactyla*, echidnas, *Tachyglossus aculeatus*, numbats, *Myrmecobius fasciatus*, and aardvarks, *Orycteropus afer*) typically have reduced dentition but are equipped with a long serpentine tongue that is used to collect ants and termites from tunnels and cavities.

In contrast to this diversification of dentition, the digestive systems of carnivores are universally simple (Clemens 1980; Stevens 1988). There is no compartmentation of the stomach or large intestine, and the cecum, if present, is small. In most species the small and large intestines are rather short, providing a limited surface area for absorption of the products of digestion. These features are consistent with the observation that carnivore diets are usually highly digestible and do not require prolonged retention or microbial fermentation. The pinnipeds appear to differ from terrestrial carnivores in that the small intestines of many species are extremely long, typically 10 to 20 times body length (Bryden 1972; King 1983). The physiological significance of this feature is not known.

METABOLIC ADAPTATIONS OF CARNIVORES

The difference between facultative and strict carnivores may be illustrated by comparing the domestic dog (Canidae: *Canis familiaris*) and the domestic cat (Felidae: *Felis catus*). Many canids have rather broad feeding habits, including a variety of fruits and other plant parts in their diets. By contrast, the felids show no tendency to omnivory; they are all essentially predators (Ewer 1973). Nutritional studies indicate that the domestic dog and the domestic cat differ markedly in nutrient requirements and in nutrient metabolism (Graham-Jones 1965; Morris and Rogers 1983; National Research Council 1985, 1986). The most obvious differences occur in nitrogen and amino acid metabolism. The growing cat appears to require higher levels of most essential amino acids as well as more nitrogen from nonessential amino acids to compensate for high obligatory nitrogen losses (Rogers and Morris 1982; National Research Council 1986). When dietary nitrogen intake is low, the cat has only a limited ability to regulate transaminases and urea cycle enzymes, so that nitrogen losses remain elevated (Morris and Rogers 1983); by contrast, the dog is able to conserve nitrogen when dietary levels are low. The cat is also especially sensitive to arginine deficiency, which produces rapid elevation of blood ammonia levels and consequent ammonia toxicity. These metabolic peculiarities of the cat appear to be adaptations to a diet that is consistently high in protein. By contrast, most canid species appear to subsist on fruit and other low-protein foods from time to time, and cannot afford to be dependent on a high dietary intake of protein.

The relatively high level of methionine (and cystine) required by cats is thought to reflect in part a need for precursors for the synthesis of the sulfur-containing amino acid taurine. Yet the cat differs from most animals in requiring a dietary source of taurine as well, even when dietary levels of methionine and cystine are adequate. Cats have a reduced ability to synthesize taurine, even though they excrete high levels of taurine in bile (as conjugated bile salts) (National Research Council 1986). Taurine deficiency leads to central retinal degeneration and has also been associated with acute cardiomyopathy (Pion et al. 1987). It was discovered recently that a commercial canned cat food induced taurine deficiency in leopard cats, *Felis bengalensis*, even though assayed taurine levels in the diet were above the levels thought adequate for domestic cats (Howard et al. 1987).

In the wild, felids rarely encounter much carbohydrate in animal prey. Thus it is not surprising that the domestic cat lacks a hepatic glycolytic enzyme, glucokinase, that is present in the dog and in omnivores such as the laboratory mouse and rat (Morris and Rogers 1983). Although the cat can digest and utilize soluble carbohydrate by other pathways, this species derives most of its blood glucose from specific amino acids via gluconeogenic pathways (Morris and Rogers 1983).

The cat also requires preformed vitamin A in its diet since it cannot convert the plant provitamin A compounds (carotenoids such as beta-carotene) to retinol. Its vitamin A requirements may be satisfied by consumption of whole prey, including viscera. A dietary source of niacin is also essential for the cat. In other species of mammals that have been studied, metabolic conversion of the amino acid tryptophan to niacin can at least partially satisfy the niacin requirement, but in the cat this conversion does not occur (National Research Council 1986). This is of little consequence in the wild since whole prey are rich sources of niacin.

Another unusual characteristic of the cat is that its essential fatty acid requirements cannot be met solely by linoleic and/or linolenic acids, as in most mammals studied. Cats also require a long-chain fatty acid, arachidonic acid, that is available only from animal sources (National Research Council 1986). This requirement appears to stem from low activity of the hepatic desaturase enzymes required to convert linoleic to arachidonic acid. By contrast, there is no evidence that dogs or other more omnivorous species require arachidonic acid (National Research Council 1985).

These unique features of the cat may be viewed as derived traits associated with an extreme degree of carnivory. Canids appear to retain a broader array of metabolic pathways for the processing of nutrients, indicating a greater degree of dietary flexibility. Facultative carnivores need the diversity of metabolic pathways that is characteristic of species that feed on a broad array of foods.

The observed metabolic peculiarities of the cat suggest that other strict carnivores may also possess particular metabolic adaptations, but virtually nothing is known about those species. It is probably safe to assume that other felids are similar to the domestic cat, but what about fish and marine invertebrate feeders such as seals, Phocidae, sea lions, Otariidae, walrus, *Odobenus rosmarus*, and sea otters, *Enhydra lutris*? Do the restricted diets of obligate piscivores or insectivores imply metabolic adaptations? Until detailed nutritional studies are conducted on these specialized carnivores, we can only speculate about their nutrient requirements and hope that attempts to mimic natural diets are reasonably close.

THE NUTRIENT COMPOSITION OF WHOLE PREY

The composition of specific tissues of animals may differ substantially from that of the whole body. Much of the data base for human foods refers only to the parts of the animal consumed by humans; for example, muscle meat, fish fillets, crabmeat. The animal by-products that are typically included in feeds for domestic animals have been processed, and flesh or oil destined for human consumption has often been removed. Hence published data on whole prey, either vertebrate or invertebrate, are hard to find.

Terrestrial vertebrates are the predominant prey of many mammalian carnivores. The vertebrate carcass is generally similar in nutrient composition across species, at least with respect to major nutrients (table 13.1). Protein concentrations are typically quite high. Calcium and phosphorus are usually present in adequate amounts and in a satisfactory ratio. The water and fat content of prey, however, may vary according to such factors as developmental state, reproductive condition, and seasonal changes. Prey with substantial stored fat are especially high in energy content. At the extreme, polar bears, *Ursus maritimus*, feeding on seal blubber ingest large amounts of fat and relatively little protein (Nelson 1983).

Marine mammals feed on a variety of fish as well as marine invertebrates such as squid and krill. Whole fish (including heads, viscera, and scales) are in some respects similar in composition to terrestrial vertebrates (table 13.2). Fish typically contain substantial amounts of protein. The fat content of fish varies greatly depending on the species of

TABLE 13.1.   Nutrient Composition (Dry Matter Basis) of Selected Vertebrates

Species	Mass(g)	% dry matter	% crude protein	% fat	% ash	% Ca	% P	Source[a]
Rat								
Adult	280.0	34.0	59.7	23.6	15.7	4.0	1.8	1
Pup	5.9	14.0	77.1	7.1	15.7	—	—	2
Mouse								
Adult	27.6	31.5	58.3	23.9	11.0	3.4	1.8	1
Pup	1.6	16.7	74.9	12.6	12.6	—	—	2
Pup	3.9	26.7	50.3	35.5	8.0	4.0	1.6	1
Pup	5.9	25.8	59.2	23.6	9.8	2.3	1.9	1
Chick	34.3	33.0	67.9	16.8	8.2	1.7	0.9	1

[a] 1, M. E. Allen, D. J. Baer, and D. E. Ullrey, unpub.; 2, Widdowson 1950

TABLE 13.2.   Nutrient Composition (Dry Matter Basis) of Selected Whole Fish

Species	% dry matter	% crude protein	% fat	% ash	% Ca	% P	Source[a]
Atlantic herring	26.8	53.7	26.1	—	—	—	1
	33.5	40.6	36.4	—	—	—	1
	27.7	45.4	34.0	8.1	1.7	1.3	2
Atlantic mackerel	27.2	64.3	11.0	—	—	—	1
	40.5	31.4	51.1	—	—	—	1
Spanish mackerel	33.8	33.5	41.5	5.2	1.2	1.1	2
Butterfish	24.1	59.8	22.0	—	—	—	1
	36.4	32.1	48.6	—	—	—	1
Capelin	16.8	63.6	10.7	12.2	2.2	2.0	2
	20.8	56.0	19.0	9.6	1.2	1.3	2
Great Lakes smelt	18.7	57.2	4.8	—	—	—	1
	23.5	57.0	7.7	—	—	—	1
Columbia River smelt	22.7	43.9	42.9	5.8	1.1	1.1	2
	22.4	51.5	37.6	7.3	1.9	1.3	3
Squid (*Loligo* spp.)	18.8	65.4	11.4	6.4	0.1	1.2	2
	21	76	10	—	—	—	4

[a] 1, Oftedal and Boness 1983; 2, Bernard and Ullrey 1989, with phosphorus values corrected per D. E. Ullrey (pers. comm.); 3, M. E. Allen, D. J. Baer, and D. E. Ullrey, unpub.; 4, Geraci 1986.

TABLE 13.3.   Nutrient Composition (Dry Matter Basis) of Selected Invertebrates

Species	% dry matter	% crude protein	% fat	% ash	% Ca	% P	Source[a]
American cockroach	33.3	63.5	—	5.6	0.57	0.74	1
Fruit fly	29.6	70.1	12.6	4.5	0.10	1.05	1
House cricket	29.9	66.1	17.3	6.1	0.18	0.86	1
Mealworm larva	36.1	48.4	41.7	4.6	0.07	0.60	1
Wax moth larva	43.9	30.8	61.5	1.8	0.03	0.39	1
Termite *(Grigiotermes)*	33.7	18.7	1.5	59.9	—	—	2
Common earthworm	17.4	64.9	7.2	10.3	1.18	0.90	1
Tubifex worm	—	46.1	15.1	6.9	0.19	0.73	1

[a] 1, Allen 1989; 2, Redford and Dorea 1984.

fish and season of catch (table 13.2; Oftedal and Boness 1983; Bernard and Ullrey 1989). Some trace minerals, such as selenium, are present in fairly high concentrations in whole fish. Some species of fish are also high in the fat-soluble vitamins A and D (Allen and Baer 1989). Vitamin E probably also occurs in ample amounts in fresh fish; however, since it is a natural antioxidant and since fish oils oxidize readily, much of the vitamin E originally present may be destroyed prior to feeding, even after just a few weeks of frozen storage. In many types of fish substantial postmortem losses of thiamin may also occur.

Few detailed reports have been published on the body composition of invertebrates, and only some of these deal

with prey species important to wild or captive exotic animals (Allen 1989). Recent data suggest that insects and other terrestrial invertebrates are typically high in protein, very variable in fat, and low in calcium (table 13.3). Some of the variations may be due to the life stage of the invertebrate; for example, larval forms of some species tend to contain large amounts of fat. Although marine invertebrates such as mollusks and crustaceans may contain calcified structures, most terrestrial invertebrates utilize chitinous materials for structural support (e.g., the insect cuticle or exoskeleton) and rigidity (e.g., cutting mouthparts) (Richards 1951; Chapman 1982). The low calcium content seen in chemical analyses of insects is related to their lack of cal-

TABLE 13.4.   Nutrient Composition (Dry Matter Basis) of Selected Meat-Based Commercial Diets and Muscle Meats

Food	Form	% dry matter	% crude protein	% fat	% ash	% Ca	% P	Source[a]
Commercial Products								
Feline[b]	Frozen	41.6	37.2	39.6	9.1	2.7	1.2	1
Feline[c]	Frozen	40.6	37.6	38.4	8.7	2.2	0.4	1
Feline[d]	Canned	36.7	39.3	42.3	6.1	1.2	0.8	1
Canine[e]	Frozen	31.9	49.4	24.7	11.3	2.0	1.7	1
Meateater[f]	Frozen	28.5	51.3	31.7	7.3	1.6	1.3	1
Polar bear[g]	Frozen	32.5	46.8	38.3	6.5	1.5	1.2	1
Dog food[h]	Dry	92.5	27.0	9.4	6.8	1.6	0.7	1
Meats								
Horsemeat[i]	Frozen	28.2	71.0	20.9	3.8	0.07	0.5	1,2
Beef[j]	Raw	28.7	76.2	21.9	3.6	0.02	0.7	3
Pork[k]	Raw	27.1	75.6	20.0	3.9	0.02	0.8	3
Chicken[l]	Raw	24.5	87.3	12.6	3.9	0.05	0.7	3

[a] 1, M. E. Allen, D. J. Baer, and D. E. Ullrey, unpub.; 2, Ullrey and Bernard 1989; 3, Bodwell and Anderson 1986.
[b] Nebraska Brand Feline Diet
[c] Spectrum Feline Diet (Beef)
[d] ZuPreem Canned Feline Diet
[e] Nebraska Brand Canine Diet
[f] Western Plateau Meateater Diet
[g] Western Plateau Polar Bear Diet
[h] Purina Hi-Pro Dog Chow
[i] Nebraska Brand Horse Meat
[j] Beef round
[k] Pork ham
[l] Chicken flesh, dark and light combined

cified structures; in the adult mammal, 98% of body calcium is found in the bony skeleton. In areas with calcium-rich soils, invertebrates such as earthworms and grubs that ingest soil may contain substantial amounts of calcium in their digestive tracts and therefore may be a better source of minerals for an insectivorous predator than insects such as crickets or beetles (Bilby and Widdowson 1971; Allen 1989). It is not clear how bats and other insectivorous species that feed on flying insects obtain sufficient calcium, especially during lactation and other periods of high calcium demand.

USE OF MEAT AND MEAT-BASED DIETS

In the wild, carnivores typically eat all or most of the prey they capture and kill, including bones, fat, viscera, and other parts. Muscle meats are quite different in composition from whole prey (table 13.4). Although they are typically good sources of amino acids, some minerals (e.g., sodium, potassium, iron, selenium, and zinc), and some B vitamins (e.g., niacin, B_6, and B_{12}), they are very low in calcium (calcium: phosphorus ratios are about 1:15 to 1:30), manganese, and fat-soluble vitamins (vitamin D, vitamin E, and in most cases, vitamin A) (Bodwell and Anderson 1986; National Research Council 1986; Ullrey and Bernard 1989).

Use of muscle meats as the sole diet of carnivores such as wolves, *Canis lupus*, and tigers, *Panthera tigris*, was once widespread in zoos, and remains common among pets, with a predictable result: severe and often fatal nutritional bone disease (Slusher, Bistner, and Kircher 1965; Scott 1968; Gorham, Peckham, and Alexander 1970; Dietrich and Van Felt 1972; Fowler 1986). In both exotic and domestic ani-

mals, pathological bone conditions resulting from dietary imbalances of calcium, phosphorus, and vitamin D are manifested most frequently in growing or lactating animals. Although awareness of the problems associated with such diets is now common among zoo staff, slab meat is still often used with problem eaters.

The feeding of unsupplemented muscle meats also may lead to vitamin A deficiency in some circumstances. Exotic felines are believed to be similar to domestic cats in being unable to covert beta-carotene to vitamin A. Alopecia, anorexia, follicular hyperkeratosis, and general unthriftiness have been observed in cats fed insufficient vitamin A (Scott 1968; National Research Council 1986). Neurological signs are reportedly associated with vitamin A deficiency in lions, *Panthera leo* (O'Sullivan, Mayo, and Hartley 1977).

In the United States, commercially prepared, complete carnivore rations are now widely used for felids and other carnivores in zoos. These diets typically are prepared using horsemeat or beef and cereal grains balanced with mineral and vitamin premixes and are available as frozen or canned products. They are quite similar in proximate analysis to whole vertebrate prey (table 13.4). Most are formulated to comply with recommended nutrient levels for either domestic cats or dogs, although supplemental vitamins or minerals may be included at higher concentrations. Given the potential toxicity of vitamin A, the high vitamin A levels ($\geq$30,000 IU vitamin A/kg diet dry matter) in some of these products may be a matter of concern (see below).

Nutritional and metabolic bone disease has largely disappeared in zoo carnivores with the use of commercial meat-based diets. However, oral disease associated with the exclusive feeding of soft diets has become a significant problem (Fagan 1980). When consumed for prolonged periods, rations that require no chewing or tearing may contribute to excessive dental plaque and calculus formation. This in turn may lead to gingivitis, loose teeth, abscesses in the oral cavity, and ultimately, bacteremia. It has been suggested that recurrent sepsis resulting from dental infections may contribute to or cause compromised renal function, liver abscesses, or endocarditis (Robinson 1986).

The optimal method of adding abrading qualities to captive diets in order to reduce plaque formation is not known. Wolves fed a dry extruded dog food had approximately half the plaque of wolves fed a soft diet (Vosburgh et al. 1982). Haberstroh et al. (1984) evaluated the effects of using beef femur bones with some muscle still attached as supplements to the soft diet of Amur tigers, *Panthera tigris altaica*. The tooth surface areas covered by plaque and calculus were significantly reduced relative to those of a control group when bones were fed twice weekly, but not when bones were fed only once per week. Use of bones with attached meat is a common method of providing occupation to large cats in zoos.

In some zoos, rats, chickens, rabbits, or other vertebrate prey are offered on a regular or periodic basis instead of or in addition to the commercial preparations. While presumably better for oral health, these items are costly and may inadvertently introduce parasites or infectious diseases. Excessive use of live or whole prey may also produce a "spoiled" carnivore that refuses to eat other foods, even when a dietary shift is desired for medical reasons (e.g., to reduce protein intakes in an animal with kidney disease). Although they are extremely expensive (e.g., $300 or more per kg dry matter), neonatal or suckled mouse or rat pups are sometimes used as food for small carnivorous or omnivorous mammals. When live pups are purchased without mothers from suppliers, they are usually subjected to prolonged starvation before being used, a practice that is not only cruel but may deplete their nutrient levels. Suppliers will sometimes agree to provide mothers with the litters.

Whenever meat-based diets are used, proper storage, handling, and preparation methods are imperative. Meat-based products and dead rodents are very susceptible to bacterial growth and subsequent spoilage. Frozen products should be thawed under refrigeration, not at room temperature, so that temperature at the surface (where bacterial growth is apt to be greatest) remains low. Feeding times should be set so as to minimize exposure of food to high ambient temperatures. Coordination of feeding times with commissary delivery of thawed meat-based products and prompt removal of uneaten food may reduce spoilage. Personnel who prepare the food should be instructed in proper and hygienic food-handling methods.

Some mammals may be particularly susceptible to bacterial contaminants in raw meat or meat-based products. Nichols (1989) described a number of fatal cases involving small mammals (bandicoots, *Isoodon macrourus*, tree shrews, *Tupaia* spp., elephant shrews, *Elephantulus rufescens*) that were fed raw horsemeat-based diets. *Streptococcus zooepidemicus* was cultured both from the animals (at necropsy) and from the horsemeat-based diet that was fed. This organism is common in horses but may not produce clinical or pathological signs in affected horses that would lead to carcass rejection by inspectors. The small mammals that died of septicemia in this study were behaviorally stressed, very old, or very young. Such conditions may increase susceptibility to food-borne bacteria, as may the fact that small mammals do not normally encounter horsemeat and horsemeat-borne bacteria in the wild. If horsemeat-based products are included in small mammal diets, it may be advisable to use only canned products or to cook products containing raw horsemeat.

Captive canids are often fed the same meat-based products as captive felids. This practice is neither necessary nor appropriate in most cases. Canids and other facultative carnivores do not require the high levels of fat and protein these diets usually contain (see table 13.4). Obesity and renal stress may result from prolonged feeding of high-fat and high-protein diets, at least in older animals or animals with compromised kidney function (Lewis and Morris 1984). Dry dog foods should be used to a greater extent in carnivore diets to provide more appropriate nutrient levels, reduce disease risks, improve oral health, and reduce costs. However, dry foods are often less readily accepted than canned or meat-based diets, as many dog and cat owners have learned. Given the benefits of nutritionally balanced dry foods, it is worth the effort to induce their acceptance. Initial acceptance may be improved by mixing them with meat-based foods or by soaking them with various meat exudates or fluids. Introduction of the dry dog food at an early age and omission of more palatable food items may also improve acceptance.

Most bear species are quite omnivorous in the wild and can presumably be fed diets similar to those fed to canids. There is some evidence that large amounts of dry dog food may predispose some bears to loose stools, at least if grass or other fiber sources are not available (Boness et al. 1985).

USE OF FISH AND MARINE INVERTEBRATES

The species of fish used in zoo feeding programs vary locally and seasonally according to availability, but often include various species of herring, mackerel, butterfish, whitefish, smelt, and whitebait; commonly used marine invertebrates include clams, krill, shrimp, and squid (Oftedal and Boness 1983; Geraci 1986; Bernard and Ullrey 1989; Allen and Baer Associates, unpub.).

Fish quality is a major concern in the feeding of obligate piscivores, since it can be adversely affected by many factors surrounding the handling, freezing, and frozen storage of fish (Symes 1966). Time from catch to freezing, rate of freezing, freezer temperature, duration of frozen storage, and type of packing all may influence nutrient losses, bacterial proliferation, and generation of potentially toxic compounds. Routine evaluation of the quality of fish received from vendors is an essential component of fish purchasing.

Fish should be stored at about $-20°F$ or lower, and stock should be rotated so that most species of fish are stored no longer than 4 to 6 months (Geraci 1981, 1986). The method of thawing of frozen fish also can be important.

Thawing fish under running water or in standing water may cause water-soluble nutrients to be lost. Thawing at room temperature may result in excessive desiccation and promote bacterial growth. Ideally, fish should be thawed under refrigeration and used immediately (Geraci 1986).

A variety of fish species should be fed in order to compensate for nutrient variability and seasonal variation in fish composition, especially in migratory fish species. Some fish, such as mackerel, are believed to be responsible for producing scromboid poisoning in animals that eat them.

Because of the preponderance of polyunsaturated fatty acids in fish lipids, they tend to undergo oxidative rancidity rapidly. Vitamin E helps to retard this oxidative deterioration, but at the cost of destruction of the vitamin (Machlin 1980). Supplemental vitamin E can be used to compensate for potential oxidative losses. Gel capsules containing vitamin E can be placed in the mouths or gills of feed fish. Dosages of 50 to 100 IU vitamin E/kg fish appear to be reasonable (Geraci 1981, 1986; Oftedal and Boness 1983). Omission of vitamin E supplementation has been linked to vitamin E deficiency in pinnipeds (Oftedal and Boness 1983).

Some species of fish contain enzymes that destroy thiamin, one of the B vitamins. Thiaminases have been reported in clams, carp, herring, smelt, mackerel, and other species (Neilands 1947; Fujita 1954; National Research Council 1982). Thiamin deficiencies have been seen in marine mammals that were fed unsupplemented fish (Geraci 1972; Rigdon and Drager 1955; White 1970). When fish are fed, thiamin supplements should be included at a level of 25–30 mg/kg fish (Geraci 1986).

CHARACTERISTICS OF INSECT DIETS

The insects and invertebrates most commonly used in mammal diets include crickets, grasshoppers, mealworm larvae, wax moth larvae, and earthworms. In captivity, some insectivorous mammals, such as tarsiers, *Tarsius* spp., and insectivorous bats, may be loath to accept substitute foods and are therefore fed live insects (Allen and Oftedal 1989; Rasweiler 1977; Wilson 1988). However, most species, including shrews, Soricidae, tenrecs, Tenrecidae, and hedgehogs, Erinaceidae, can be maintained and bred on diets consisting of nutritionally balanced frozen or canned meat-based products. Usually such animals are offered insects as supplements only. Colonies of Asian musk shrews, *Suncus murinus,* have been successfully maintained for many generations on diets of pelleted mink food and extruded cat food in a ratio of approximately 80:20 (Dryden and Ross 1971; G. L. Dryden, pers. comm.).

Given the severely unbalanced calcium:phosphorus ratios of feed insects (see table 13.3), supplemental calcium should be provided when insects represent a significant part of the daily ration (e.g., 50% or more of diet dry matter). Poorly mineralized bone and rickets may result from prolonged consumption of low-calcium, high-phosphorus insects, especially in young, growing animals (Allen 1989). Crickets can be effectively supplemented by feeding them a diet containing at least 8% calcium (Allen and Oftedal 1989). This diet apparently accumulates in the guts of crickets that eat it, yielding crickets that contain 1.4% calcium and 0.83% phosphorus.

When high-fat insects (e.g., some larval forms) are fed, they should be used sparingly to avoid very high fat intakes and consequent dilution of other nutrients. Wax moth larvae may contain more than 50% fat on a dry matter basis. Some geophagous insects (earthworms, some termites, some grubs) contain very high levels of mineral constituents, as indicated by their ash content (Redford and Dorea 1984; Allen 1989). The potential positive or negative effects of very high mineral intakes on insectivorous mammals undoubtedly depend on the individual minerals ingested. There are relatively few data on the vitamin content of insects, so the importance of vitamin supplementation is not known.

SPECIAL DIETARY PROBLEMS

Choosing the appropriate diet for a carnivore will depend on a number of factors, including the extent to which the species is an obligate carnivore, the type and composition of prey consumed in the wild, and the individual animal's food preferences, intake patterns, and condition (see Oftedal and Allen, chap. 10, this volume). Nutrient standards are usually based on those developed for dogs and cats (see table 11.1, chap. 11), although the extent to which these are appropriate for specialized fish-eating and insect-eating mammals is not known.

Large carnivores in the wild frequently are faced with "feast or famine"; that is, large kills are interspersed with several days of fasting. Many zoos routinely fast their large cats 1 day per week. Although there is little scientific evidence to support this as a universal practice, occasional fasting is probably beneficial for animals that receive little exercise and are prone to obesity.

The cystinuria commonly seen in maned wolves, *Chrysocyon brachyurus*, may be linked to diet. Excessive urinary cystine levels were found in thirty-four out of forty-two captive and wild maned wolves in South America (Bovee et al. 1981). Four of the wolves had cystine stones, and three died due to the obstructions. When renal clearance studies were performed on five of the wolves, abnormalities (dibasic aminoaciduria) were found in all the animals. Although relatively omnivorous in the wild, maned wolves in zoos are typically fed meat-based diets better suited for felids. There is some evidence that reduction of protein content in the diet, combined with an increase in vegetable matter, may reduce the recurrence of cystine stones in afflicted domestic dogs, perhaps via alkalinization of the urine (Lewis and Morris 1984). Although available data are not conclusive, it seems advisable to reduce cystine intake via reduction of dietary protein content, thereby reducing cystine excretion rates. A number of zoos have reduced protein and fat intakes of maned wolves by substituting dry dog food for meat-based products.

Other types of uroliths (e.g., calcium oxalates or urates, or magnesium ammonium phosphates) may present persistent problems among some zoo carnivores, especially mink, *Mustela vison*, small-clawed otters, *Amblonyx cinereus*, and foxes, *Vulpes vulpes* (Calle 1988; Calle and Robinson 1985; Karesh 1983; Keymer, Lewis, and Don 1981; Long 1985).

The etiology of the diverse urolithiasis syndromes in zoo carnivores is poorly understood and has been little studied, but dietary correlates are often suspected. In a study of domestic ferrets, *Mustela putorius*, Edfors, Ullrey, and Aulerich (1989) reported that the incidence of urinary calculi could be controlled by diet.

Another controversial issue involves the use of very high doses of vitamin A for polar bears. The very high level of vitamin A found in polar bear liver (about 20 million IU/kg) has been implicated in the poisoning of both polar explorers and their dogs (Rodahl and Moore 1943; Rodahl 1949b). Apparently vitamin A is concentrated in certain polar food chains, leading to particularly high levels in some species of seals and the polar bears that feed on them. Rodahl (1949a) estimated that a polar bear consuming a single bearded seal, *Erignathus barbatus*, liver would ingest 30 to 100 million IU of vitamin A, and suggested that this amount might produce toxic signs in the bears if consumed regularly. However, livers of other species of seals may contain much less vitamin A (Ball et al. 1992). Foster (1981) used massive doses of vitamin A (200,000 IU vitamin A/kg diet) therapeutically in captive polar bears in an attempt to treat a persistent dermatitis that was unresponsive to other measures. It seems likely that such massive doses could have adverse long-term effects. Hypervitaminosis A has been reported in captive mink fed whale liver (Friend and Crampton 1961). Signs included impaired reproduction, hemorrhage, weight loss, and bone fractures. Alopecia and peeling skin are also fairly specific signs of vitamin A toxicity in mammals and humans (Rodahl 1949a).

Some obligate carnivores may have a higher requirement for vitamin A than domestic animals (Heywood 1967), but further experimental studies are required. However, the high levels of vitamin A included in some commercial carnivore diets may be a matter of concern, especially when these diets are fed to facultative carnivores and other mammals. It is not known whether the hepatic fibrosis (veno-occlusive disease) prevalent in captive cheetahs, *Acinonyx jubatus*, and snow leopards, *Uncia uncia*, is related to diet, but hypervitaminosis A has been suggested as one of several possible dietary associations (Gosselin et al. 1989; Munson and Worley 1991).

Although the giant panda, *Ailuropoda melanoleuca*, and the red panda, *Ailurus fulgens*, are taxonomically in the order Carnivora, both species are specialized bamboo feeders (Schaller et al. 1985; Johnson, Schaller, and Hu 1988). Their morphological adaptations to a bamboo diet include widely flared zygomatic arches, robust cheek teeth with broad crushing surfaces, and modifications to wrist bones to enhance forepaw dexterity (Davis 1964; Roberts and Gittleman 1984). The gastrointestinal tract gives little indication of herbivory, however. The stomach is simple, the intestines are short and without sacculation, and there is no cecum (Flower 1870; Raven 1937; Davis 1964). The lack of any apparent site for retention and fermentation of plant fiber in the digestive tract is consistent with digestion trials that indicate poor fiber utilization (Dierenfeld et al. 1982; Mainka, Zhao, and Li 1989; Warnell 1988). This is a puzzling digestive strategy because bamboo leaves are very high in fiber fractions such as cellulose, hemicellulose, and lignin. It is not clear what level of fiber is most appropriate for panda diets in captivity. Many, but not all, zoos utilize bamboo as a fiber source while also feeding a wet "gruel" as well as fruits, vegetables, and other foods as sources of additional nutrients (Oftedal and Dierenfeld 1982; Warnell, Crissey, and Oftedal 1989). The difficulty and cost of obtaining fresh bamboo year round and the recognition that soft gruels predispose carnivores to dental problems have stimulated a search for alternative diets for pandas. In cooperation with the Red Panda SSP, a wide range of U.S. zoos are currently using a "high-fiber" biscuit as a replacement for gruel and as a partial substitute for the fiber contained in bamboo.

SUMMARY AND RECOMMENDATIONS

Commercial canned, frozen, or dry diets formulated for domestic dogs and cats can provide a basis for the diets of many carnivorous and insectivorous zoo mammals. Prey items such as rats, mice, chicks, fish, or invertebrates may also be fed on a regular basis. Since whole prey are extremely expensive compared with prepared diets, in most cases such items need not represent more than 30% of the diet dry matter.

Effective diets should also provide some stimulation to teeth and gums to prevent gingivitis and oral abscesses. The use of large bones with meat attached is recommended for zoo felids and canids. Rodent prey or small rib bones may be offered once or twice per week to small carnivorous mammals.

Insects tend to be low in calcium content, and hence a plan of supplementation with calcium is essential. More research is needed both on the nutrient composition of insects and other invertebrates and on the metabolic peculiarities of insectivorous mammals.

When fish represent a significant part of the ration, thiamin and vitamin E supplements should be given in carefully controlled amounts based on documented daily food consumption. Fish should be periodically analyzed to determine when differences in composition, especially in fat content, might dictate changes in the amounts of fish offered. Rigorous standards should be applied in judging acceptability of fish for the feeding of piscivorous mammals.

It is essential that all personnel involved in handling, preparing, and distributing meat and fish be instructed in appropriate and sanitary methods of food handling. Such foods should be dated upon arrival and used in a timely fashion.

REFERENCES

Allen, M. E. 1989. Nutritional aspects of insectivory. Ph.D. thesis, Michigan State University, East Lansing.

Allen, M. E., and Baer, D. J. 1989. Fat soluble vitamin concentrations in fish commonly fed to zoo animals. Proceedings of the Annual Meeting of the American Association of Zoo Veterinarians, Greensboro, N.C., 104. Philadelphia: American Association of Zoo Veterinarians.

Allen, M. E., and Oftedal, O. T. 1989. Dietary manipulation of the calcium concentration of feed crickets. *J. Zoo Wildl. Med.* 20: 26–33.

Ball, M. D., Nizzi, C. P., Furr, H. C., Olson, J. A., and Oftedal, O. T. 1992. Fatty acyl esters of retinol (vitamin A) in the liver of the harp seal *(Phoca groenlandica)*, hooded seal *(Cystophora cristata)*, and California sea lion *(Zalophus californianus)*. *Biochem. Cell Biol.* 70:809–13.

Bernard, J. B., and Ullrey, D. E. 1989. Evaluation of dietary husbandry of marine mammals at two major zoological parks. *J. Zoo Wildl. Med.* 20:45–52.

Bilby, L. W., and Widdowson, E. M. 1971. Chemical composition of growth in nestling blackbirds and thrushes. *Br. J. Nutr.* 25:127–34.

Bodwell, C. E., and Anderson, B. A. 1986. Nutritional composition and value of meat and meat products. In *Muscle as food*, ed. P. J. Bechtel, 321–69. New York: Academic Press.

Boness, D. J., Allen, M. E., Oftedal, O. T., and Holden, M. M. 1985. The effects of dry dog food on the stool condition of spectacled bears, *Tremarctos ornatus*. Abstracts of the Annual Meeting of the American Association of Zoo Veterinarians, Scottsdale, Ariz., 83a.

Bovee, K. C., Bush, M., Dietz, J., Jezyk, P., and Segal, S. 1981. Cystinuria in the maned wolf of South America. *Science* 212:919–20.

Bryden, M. M. 1972. Growth and development of marine mammals. In *Functional anatomy of marine mammals*, ed. R. J. Harrison, 1–79. New York: Academic Press.

Calle, P. P. 1988. Asian small-clawed otter *(Aonyx cinerea)* urolithiasis prevalence in North America. *Z. Biol.* 7:233–42.

Calle, P. P., and Robinson, P. T. 1985. Glucosuria associated with renal calculi in Asian small-clawed otters. *J. Am. Vet. Med. Assoc.* 173:1159–62.

Chapman, R. F. 1982. *The insects: Structure and function.* 3d ed. Cambridge, Mass.: Harvard University Press.

Clemens, E. T. 1980. The digestive tract: Insectivore, prosimian, and advanced primate. In *Comparative physiology: Primitive mammals*, ed. K. Schmidt-Nielson, L. Bolis, and C. R. Taylor, 90–99. Cambridge: Cambridge University Press.

Davis, D. 1964. *The giant panda: A morphological study of evolutionary mechanisms.* Fieldiana (Zoology Memoirs) no. 3. Chicago: Natural History Museum.

Dierenfeld, E., Hintz, H. F., Robertson, J. R., Van Soest, P. J., and Oftedal, O. T. 1982. Utilization of bamboo by the giant panda. *J. Nutr.* 112:636–41.

Dietrich, R. A., and Van Felt, R. W. 1972. Juvenile osteomalacia in a coyote. *J. Wildl. Dis.* 8:146–48.

Dryden, G. L., and Ross, J. M. 1971. Enhanced growth and development of captive musk shrews, *Suncus murinus*, on an improved diet. *Growth* 35:311–25.

Edfors, C. H., Ullrey, D. E., and Aulerich, R. J. 1989. Prevention of urolithiasis in the ferret *(Mustela putorius furo)* with phosphoric acid. *J. Zoo Wildl. Med.* 20:12–19.

Ewer, R. F. 1973. *The carnivores.* Ithaca, N.Y.: Cornell University Press.

Fagan, D. A. 1980. Diet consistency and periodontal disease in exotic carnivores. In *Proceedings of the First Annual Dr. Scholl Nutrition Conference*, ed. E. R. Maschgan, M. E. Allen, and L. E. Fisher, 241–48. Chicago: Lincoln Park Zoological Society.

Flower, W. H. 1870. On the anatomy of *Ailurus fulgens. Proc. Zool. Soc. Lond.* 1870:752–69.

Foster, J. W. 1981. Dermatitis in polar bears: A nutritional approach to therapy. *Proceedings of the Annual Meeting of the American Association of Zoo Veterinarians*, 58–60. Philadelphia: American Association of Zoo Veterinarians.

Fowler, M. E. 1986. Metabolic bone disease. In *Zoo and wildlife medicine*, 2d ed., ed. M. E. Fowler, 69–90. Philadelphia: W. B. Saunders.

Friend, D. W., and Crampton, E. W. 1961. The adverse effect of raw whale liver on the breeding performance of female mink. *J. Nutr.* 73:317–20.

Fujita, A. 1954. Thiaminase. In *Advances in enzymology*, ed. F. F. Nord, 389–421. New York: Interscience Publishers.

Geraci, J. R. 1972. Experimental thiamine deficiency in captive harp seals *(Phoca groenlandica)* induced by eating herring *(Clupea harengus)* and smelts *(Osmerus mordax)*. *Can. J. Zool.* 50:179–95.

———. 1981. Dietary disorders in marine mammals: Synthesis and new findings. *J. Am. Vet. Med. Assoc.* 179:1183–91.

———. 1986. Marine mammals: Nutrition and nutritional disorders. In *Zoo and wild animal medicine*, 2d ed., ed. M. E. Fowler, 760–64. Philadelphia: W. B. Saunders.

Gorham, J. R., Peckham, J. C., and Alexander, J. 1970. Rickets and osteodystrophia fibrosa in foxes fed a high horsemeat ration. *J. Am. Vet. Med. Assoc.* 156:1331–33.

Gosselin, S. J., Setchell, K. D. R., Harrington, G. W., Welch, M. B. B., Pyylypiw, H., Kozeniauskas, R., Dollard, D., Tarr, M. J., and Dresser, B. L. 1989. Nutritional considerations in the pathogenesis of hepatic veno-occlusive disease in captive cheetahs. *Zoo Biol.* 8:339–47.

Graham-Jones, O. 1965. *Canine and feline nutritional requirements.* London: Pergamon Press.

Haberstroh, L. I., Ullrey, D. E., Sikarski, J. G., Richter, N. A., Colmery, B. H., and Myers, T. D. 1984. Diet and oral health in captive Amur tigers *(Panthera tigris altaica)*. *J. Zoo Anim. Med.* 15:142–46.

Heywood, R. 1967. Vitamin A in the liver and kidney of some Felidae. *Br. Vet. J.* 123:390–96.

Howard, J., Rogers, Q. R., Koch, S. A., Goodrowe, K. L., Montali, R. J., and Bush, M. 1987. Diet-induced taurine deficiency retinopathy in leopard cats *(Felis bengalensis)*. Proceedings of the Annual Meeting of the American Association of Zoo Veterinarians, 496–98. Philadelphia: American Association of Zoo Veterinarians.

Johnson, K. G., Schaller, G. B., and Hu, J. 1988. Comparative behavior of red and giant pandas in the Wolong reserve, China. *J. Mammal.* 69:552–64.

Karesh, W. B. 1983. Urolithiasis in Asian small-clawed otters. Proceedings of the Annual Meeting of the American Association of Zoo Veterinarians, Tampa, Fla., 42–44. Philadelphia: American Association of Zoo Veterinarians.

Keymer, I. R., Lewis, G., and Don, P. L. 1981. Urolithiasis in otters and other species. *Verhandlungsbericht des XXIII International Symposium über die Erkrankungen der Zootiere*, 391–401.

King, J. E. 1983. *Seals of the World.* 2d ed. Oxford: Oxford University Press.

Lewis, L. D., and Morris, M. L. 1984. *Small animal clinical nutrition.* Topeka, Kans.: Mark Morris Associates.

Long, G. G. 1985. Urolithiasis in ranch foxes. *J. Am. Vet. Med. Assoc.* 179:863–65.

Machlin, L. J. 1980. *Vitamin E: A comprehensive treatise.* New York: Marcel Dekker.

Mainka, S. A., Zhao, G., and Li, M. 1989. Utilization of bamboo, sugar cane, and gruel diet by two juvenile giant pandas *(Ailuropoda melanoleuca)*. *J. Zoo Wildl. Med.* 20:39–44.

Morris, J. G., and Rogers, Q. R. 1983. Nutritionally related metabolic adaptations of carnivores and ruminants. In *Plant, animal, and microbial adaptations to terrestrial environments*, ed. N. S. Margaris, M. Arianoutsou-Faraggitaki, and R. J. Reiter, 165–80. New York: Plenum Publishing.

Munson, L., and Worley, M. B. 1991. Veno-occlusive disease in snow leopards *(Panthera uncia)* from zoological parks. *Vet. Pathol.* 28:37–45.

National Research Council. 1982. *Nutrient requirements of mink and foxes.* 2d rev. ed. Washington, D.C.: National Academy Press.

———. 1985. *Nutrient requirements of dogs.* Rev. ed. Washington, D.C.: National Academy Press.

———. 1986. *Nutrient requirements of cats.* Rev. ed. Washington, D.C.: National Academy Press.

Neilands, J. B. 1947. Thiaminase in aquatic animals of Nova Scotia. *J. Fish. Res. Board Can.* 7:94–99.

Nelson, R. A. 1983. Feeding strategies and metabolic adjustments of the polar bears. In *Proceedings of the Third Annual Dr. Scholl Conference on the Nutrition of Captive Wild Animals,* ed. T. P. Meehan and M. E. Allen, 93–96. Chicago: Lincoln Park Zoological Society.

Nichols, D. K. 1989. Food-borne bacterial disease caused by uncooked horsemeat products. In *Proceedings of the Sixth and Seventh Annual Dr. Scholl Conference on the Nutrition of Captive Wild Animals,* ed. T. P. Meehan and M. E. Allen, 5–10. Chicago: Lincoln Park Zoological Society.

Oftedal, O. T., and Boness, D. J. 1983. Considerations in the use of fish as food. In *Proceedings of the Third Annual Dr. Scholl Conference on the Nutrition of Captive Wild Animals,* ed. T. P. Meehan and M. E. Allen, 149–61. Chicago: Lincoln Park Zoological Society.

Oftedal, O. T., and Dierenfeld, E. S. 1982. The giant panda: An herbivorous carnivore. In *Proceedings of the Second Annual Dr. Scholl Conference on the Nutrition of Captive Wild Animals,* ed. T. P. Meehan, B. A. Thomas, and K. Bell, 159–64. Chicago: Lincoln Park Zoological Society.

O'Sullivan, B. M., Mayo, F. D., and Hartley, W. J. 1977. Neurologic lesions in young captive lions associated with vitamin A deficiency. *Aust. Vet. J.* 53:187–89.

Pion, P. D., Kittleson, M. D., Rogers, Q. R., and Morris, J. G. 1987. Myocardial failure in cats associated with low plasma taurine: A reversible cardiomyopathy. *Science* 237:764–68.

Rasweiler, J. J. 1977. Bats as laboratory animals. In *Biology of bats,* ed. W. A. Wimsatt, 519–617. New York: Academic Press.

Raven, H. C. 1937. Notes on the anatomy and viscera of the giant panda. *Am. Mus. Novit.* 877:1–23.

Redford, K. H., and Dorea, J. G. 1984. The nutritional value of invertebrates with emphasis on ants and termites as food for mammals. *J. Zool.* (Lond.) 203:385–95.

Richards, A. G. 1951. *The integument of arthropods.* Minneapolis: University of Minnesota Press.

Rigdon, R. H., and Drager, G. A. 1955. Thiamine deficiency in sea lions fed only frozen fish. *J. Am. Vet. Med. Assoc.* 127:453–55.

Roberts, M. S., and Gittleman, J. G. 1984. *Ailurus fulgens. Mammal. Species* 222:1–8.

Robinson, P. T. 1986. Dentistry in zoo animals. In *Zoo and wild animal medicine,* ed. M. E. Fowler, 533–47. Philadelphia: W. B. Saunders.

Rodahl, K. 1949a. The toxic effect of polar bear liver. *Norsk Polar Institutt Skrifter,* no. 92.

Rodahl, K. 1949b. Toxicity of polar bear liver. *Nature* 164:530.

Rodahl, K., and Moore, T. 1943. The vitamin A content and toxicity of bear and seal liver. *Biochem. J.* 37:166–68.

Rogers, Q. R., and Morris, J. G. 1982. Do cats really need more protein? *J. Small Anim. Pract.* 23:521–32.

Schaller, G. B., Hu, J., Pan, W., and Zhu, J. 1985. *The giant pandas of Wolong.* Chicago: University of Chicago Press.

Scott, P. P. 1968. The special features of nutrition of cats, with observations on wild Felidae nutrition in the London Zoo. *Symp. Zool. Soc. Lond.* 21:21–36.

Slusher, R., Bistner, S. I., and Kircher, C. 1965. Nutritional secondary hyperparathyroidism in a tiger. *J. Am. Vet. Med. Assoc.* 147:1109–15.

Stevens, C. E. 1988. *Comparative physiology of the vertebrate digestive system.* New York: Cambridge University Press.

Symes, J. D. 1966. *Fish and fish inspection.* London: Lewis and Co.

Ullrey, D. E., and Bernard, J. B. 1989. Meat diets for performing exotic cats. *J. Zoo Wildl. Med.* 20:20–25.

Van Valkenburgh, B. 1989. Carnivore dental adaptations and diet: A study of trophic diversity within guilds. In *Carnivore behaviour, ecology, and evolution,* ed. J. L. Gittleman, 410–36. Ithaca, N.Y.: Cornell University Press.

Vaughan, T. A. 1978. *Mammalogy.* Philadelphia: W. B. Saunders.

Vosburgh, K. M., Barbiers, R. B., Sikarski, J. G., and Ullrey, D. E. 1982. A soft versus hard diet and oral health in captive timber wolves *(Canis lupus). J. Zoo Anim. Med.* 13:104–7.

Warnell, K. J. 1988. Feed intake, digestibility, digesta passage, and fecal microbial ecology of the red panda *(Ailurus fulgens).* M.S. thesis, Michigan State University, East Lansing.

Warnell, K. J., Crissey, S. D., and Oftedal, O. T. 1989. Utilization of bamboo and other fiber sources in red panda diets. In *Red panda biology,* ed. A. R. Glatston, 51–56. The Hague, Netherlands: SPB Academic Publishing.

White, J. R. 1970. Thiamine deficiency in an Atlantic bottle-nosed dolphin *(Tursiops truncatus)* on a diet of raw fish. *J. Am. Vet. Med. Assoc.* 157:559–62.

Widdowson, E. M. 1950. Chemical composition of newly born mammals. *Nature* 166:626–28.

Wilson, D. E. 1988. Maintaining bats for captive studies. In *Ecological and behavioral methods for the study of bats,* ed. T. H. Kunz, 247–64. Washington, D.C.: Smithsonian Institution Press.

14

The Feeding and Nutrition of Omnivores with Emphasis on Primates

OLAV T. OFTEDAL AND MARY E. ALLEN

In common usage, the term "omnivore" implies both dietary breadth and consumption of a relatively digestible diet of plant and animal origin. This simplification disguises the diversity of dietary strategies among animals that might be classed as omnivores and the degree to which they specialize on particular kinds of foods. For example, rodents that feed predominantly on seeds, bats that rely on nectar, primates that consume a high proportion of plant exudates, and viverrids that eat mostly fruit may be viewed as specialized granivores, nectarivores, gummivores, and frugivores respectively. Because the chemical, physical, and nutritional characteristics of seeds, nectar, gum, and fruit are very different, each of these taxa may have quite different anatomical, digestive, and metabolic adaptations that facilitate feeding on their preferred foods. To lump them all together as omnivores may overlook important variation among them. Unfortunately, the comparative nutrition of such dietary specialists is relatively unexplored. In this chapter we will primarily discuss aspects of the feeding and nutrition of generalist omnivores. In a few cases information on specific nutrient requirements for particular taxa will be discussed.

Although zoo collections include omnivorous species from a variety of mammalian orders (including marsupials, rodents, bats, and omnivorous species in the Carnivora), the most numerous omnivores in zoos are primates. In a review of field studies of the natural diets of 131 primate species, Harding (1981) concluded that fruit was consumed by 90% of the species, soft plant foods (immature leaves, buds, shoots, flowers) by 79%, mature leaves by 69%, invertebrates by 65%, seeds by 41%, and other animal foods (including eggs) by 37%. Species in each of the major primate groups consumed insects on at least an occasional basis. Primates typically feed on a broad array of plant and animal foods, and variation among primate diets is probably best described in terms of the relative proportions of different plant and animal foods rather than as specialization on particular foods (Hladik 1981). The complexity of primate diets has provoked great interest in the factors influencing feeding habits and foraging behavior in the wild (e.g., Clutton-Brock 1977; Harding and Teleki 1981; Kamil and Sargent 1981; Milton 1980, 1981; Rodman and Cant 1984; Janson 1988; Oftedal 1991).

Of course, some primates are highly folivorous (such as colobines and indriids). Although these species are more aptly considered herbivores, aspects of their feeding and nutrition will be mentioned here to avoid misunderstandings concerning the appropriateness of feeding diets developed for omnivorous primates to their nonomnivorous relatives.

THE USE OF INFORMATION ON DIETS IN THE WILD

The observation that omnivores (especially primates) consume a broad and complex diet in nature has led to two common ideas: (1) that it is preferable to offer an animal a broad array of food items in captivity, and (2) that animals possess "nutritional wisdom" that enables them to select a nutritionally balanced diet from among this broad array of foods. Unfortunately, there is little scientific evidence to support either notion, and in fact there are many examples from diverse taxa of unintended nutritional problems that have arisen with "cafeteria-style" feeding programs (see Oftedal and Allen, chap. 10, Allen and Oftedal, chap. 11, this volume).

Field studies of the foraging behavior of animals can provide insight into the kinds of food eaten, but it is usually difficult, if not impossible, to measure quantitatively the proportions of different foods in the natural diet. Food consumption of wild animals is usually expressed as the time spent feeding on particular foods, although actual ingestion rates may differ greatly from one food to another (Hladik 1977; Milton 1984; Oftedal 1991). Both the kinds and amounts of foods consumed by free-living animals vary according to availability. Large dietary differences can be expected among animals in different habitats and in different seasons. It is rarely possible to define the "normal" levels of fiber, protein, calcium, or other nutrients in the diets of primates or other omnivores with broad and complex diets. It is therefore necessary to rely on nutrient requirement estimates obtained by research on laboratory and domestic omnivores such as mice, rats, guinea pigs, pigs, and laboratory primates. Data on human nutrient needs may also be helpful, especially with respect to great ape diets.

DIGESTIVE AND METABOLIC ADAPTATIONS OF OMNIVORES

The digestive tracts of generalist omnivores must be able to deal with a variety of foods, including materials of both plant and animal origin. Thus one would not expect to find in these animals either the extreme simplicity of the guts of terrestrial carnivores or the complex compartmentation of the guts of herbivores. Most omnivorous mammals have a simple stomach, a small intestine of moderate length, and modest development of the colon and/or cecum that permits some degree of retention of digesta with associated fiber fermentation (Chivers and Hladik 1980; Hume 1982; Milton and McBee 1983; Martin et al. 1985; Stevens 1988). The sacculation of the colon in many primates (including humans) may further assist in retaining fermentable fiber fractions. Of course, some primates (such as colobines) have a capacious and compartmentalized stomach (analogous to that of a ruminant: Bauchop and Martucci 1968), while others (such as indriids) have a greatly enlarged cecum and colon, but these folivorous species are more aptly considered herbivores (see Oftedal, Baer, and Allen, chap. 12, this volume).

Although many rodents feed on nuts, seeds, and other relatively digestible foods, there are many others that depart from the omnivorous pattern, and these species should be fed accordingly (Landry 1970). The great diversity in the structure of the digestive tracts of these species indicates specialization for a wide variety of diets. Outpocketings and special glandular areas in the stomach are characteristic of some insectivorous species (such as grasshopper and burrowing mice, *Onychomys* and *Oxymycterus*), while other species such as the hamsters (e.g., *Cricetus, Cricetulus, Mesocricetus, Phodopus*) have compartmentalized stomachs (Vorontsov 1979). Herbivorous rodents such as porcupines (e.g., *Hystrix*), voles and lemmings (e.g., *Clethrionomys, Microtus, Lemmus*), muskrats *(Ondatra)*, beavers *(Castor)*, and capybaras *(Hydrochoeris)* have highly enlarged ceca and/or colons, as would be expected in species relying on fiber fermentation for a substantial proportion of their energy requirements (Vorontsov 1979, Stevens 1988).

Fermentation may also be of importance for species that feed extensively on gums, such as pygmy marmosets, *Callithrix (= Cebuella) pygmaea*, sugar gliders, *Petaurus breviceps*, and some galagos and cheirogaleid lemurs (Nash 1986; Power 1991). Gums are complex carbohydrates that apparently require microbial fermentation to be digested. The well-developed ceca and long colons of sugar gliders and Leadbeater's possum, *Gymnobelideus leadbeateri*, are thought to reflect the need for fermentation of ingested gums (Hume 1982). The relatively long retention times of digesta observed in pygmy marmosets may similarly relate to gum fermentation (Power 1991).

The dietary breadth of most omnivores implies that these animals must be able to adapt to a wide array of metabolic substrates. For example, seasonal or site variation in the availability of ripe fruits, flowers, insects, and other animal prey may result in considerable shifts in the intake of carbohydrate, fat, protein, and fiber. Omnivores cannot afford to be without sugar-digesting enzymes (unlike ruminants, which lack sucrase) or to have a limited ability to conserve nitrogen via regulation of metabolic pathways (unlike felids: see Allen, Oftedal, and Baer, chap. 13, this volume).

One metabolic adaptation that is commonly thought to be associated with fruit eating is the loss of the ability to synthesize vitamin C (ascorbic acid). Since fruits and other moist plant materials such as leaves and flowers typically contain substantial amounts of vitamin C (Milton and Jenness 1987), species that feed on these foods may not require the enzymatic machinery (specifically, L-gulonolactone oxidase) to produce this vitamin. In agreement with this theory, anthropoid primates have a demonstrated dietary requirement for vitamin C. However, a survey of the mammalian species that do and do not have the ability to synthesize vitamin C suggests that the loss of synthetic ability is not tightly linked to frugivory (table 14.1). For example, all bats that have been studied are unable to synthesize appreciable amounts of vitamin C, even though the studied species include insectivorous (e.g., *Eumops, Myotis, Pteronotus*), fish-eating *(Noctilio)*, blood-feeding *(Desmodus)*, and nectar-feeding (e.g., *Glossophaga*) bats as well as predominantly frugivorous species (e.g., *Artibeus, Sturnira*, and *Pteropus*) (Birney, Jenness, and Ayaz 1976). It is hard to argue that the guinea pig, *Cavia porcellus*, which requires a dietary source of vitamin C, has a diet that is distinctively different from those of the thirty-nine other species of rodents that can synthesize this vitamin (table 14.1; Jenness, Birney, and Ayaz 1980). Perhaps the only conclusion that can be drawn is that species that seasonally consume diets that are low in vitamin C (such as seeds and dried grasses) must rely on endogenous vitamin C synthesis. The provision of supplemental vitamin C, therefore, is an important component of the nutritional management of captive omnivores, and especially of bats and primates.

NUTRITIONAL REQUIREMENTS OF OMNIVORES

Although controlled studies have been conducted on only a limited number of rodents, primates, and the domestic pig, it is highly likely that most omnivorous mammals require a dietary source of the full suite of nutrients (including amino acids, fatty acids, vitamins, and minerals) described in chapter 11 of this volume. One possible exception involves species that practice coprophagy (reingestion of feces), including lagomorphs, some rodents, and sportive lemurs (*Lepilemur*: Hladik 1978). Microbial fermentation in the gut results in the production of essential amino acids (as microbial protein) and some vitamins, but in most mammals this fermentation occurs in a region of the hindgut (cecum or colon) from which absorption of most nutrients is limited or negligible. However, if the microbial end products are reingested via coprophagy, microbial protein, amino acids, and synthesized vitamins can be digested and/or absorbed

TABLE 14.1.   Vitamin C Synthetic Ability in Mammals

Order	Able to synthesize vitamin C	Unable to synthesize vitamin C
Monotremata	Tachyglossidae (1 species)	
	Ornithorhynchidae (1 species)	
Marsupialia	Burramyidae (1 species)	
	Didelphidae (1 species)	
	Dasyuridae (3 species)	
	Macropodidae (6 species)	
	Peramelidae (2 species)	
	Petauridae (2 species)	
	Phalangeridae (1 species)	
	Vombatidae (1 species)	
Insectivora	Soricidae (2 species)	
Chiroptera		Molossidae (4 species)
		Mormoopidae (4 species)
		Natalidae (1 species)
		Noctilionidae (1 species)
		Phyllostomatidae (15 species)
		Pteropodidae (1 species)
		Vespertilionidae (13 species)
Primates	Lorisidae (1 species)	Callitrichidae (2 species)
		Cebidae (2 species)
		Cercopithecidae (4 species)
		Hominidae (1 species)
Scandentia	Tupaiidae (1 species)	
Lagomorpha	Leporidae (5 species)	
Rodentia	Chinchillidae (1 species)	Caviidae (1 species)
	Dasyproctidae (1 species)	
	Geomyidae (1 species)	
	Heteromyidae (2 species)	
	Muridae (26 species)	
	Octodontidae (1 species)	
	Sciuridae (6 species)	
	Zapodidae (1 species)	
Carnivora	Canidae (1 species)	
	Felidae (1 species)	
	Mustelidae (2 species)	
	Procyonidae (1 species)	
	Ursidae (1 species)	
Artiodactyla	Bovidae (3 species)	
	Cervidae (1 species)	
	Suidae (1 species)	

Sources: Yess and Hegsted 1967; Chatterjee et al. 1975; Birney, Jenness, and Ayaz 1976; Jenness, Birney, and Ayaz 1978, 1980; Birney, Jenness, and Hume 1980; Flurer and Zucker 1989.

in the small intestine. Thus coprophagous species are apt to be less sensitive to dietary deficiencies of essential amino acids, some B vitamins, and vitamin K. The extent to which nutrients of fecal origin can replace dietary nutrients probably depends on a variety of as yet unidentified factors. In the rat, the dietary requirement for vitamin K depends on factors that influence the intestinal (microbial) synthesis of this vitamin and the extent of coprophagy (National Research Council 1995).

Nutrient requirements are affected by such factors as rate of growth, reproductive output, and metabolic needs. For example, on a dry diet (10% moisture) containing highly digestible protein of balanced amino acid composition, the protein requirements of rats are about 5.0% of the diet for maintenance and 15% for growth; laboratory mice have been reported to require about 18% protein for growth and

18% for reproduction under these conditions (National Research Council 1995).

In primates, the relationship of protein requirements to growth and adult maintenance stages is somewhat different. Within a primate species, protein requirements decrease with age if the requirements are expressed as the amount of protein required per kg body weight (table 14.2). However, the amount of energy required per kg body weight also decreases with age, so the amount of food eaten (relative to body weight) will decrease with age. The percentage of protein required in the diet will therefore depend on the relationship between the protein and energy contents of the diet. One way of examining this relationship is to express protein requirements as a percentage of metabolizable energy (ME) in the diet (table 14.2). During early growth, the protein requirement is a large percentage of ME, but this

TABLE 14.2. Estimates of the Amounts of High-Quality Protein Required by Various Primate Species at Different Stages of Life

Species	Age class	Body weight (kg)	Estimated protein requirements Intake (g/kg BW)	Estimated protein requirements % of ME in diet	Source[a]
Callithrix jacchus	Adult	0.41	4.6	7.4	1
Saimiri sciureus	2–3 wk. infant	0.15	18	15	2
	2–3 mo. infant	0.3	7.3	7.1	
	9 mo. juvenile	0.5	4.3	5.8	
Cebus albifrons	5–6 wk. infant	0.4	5.2	7.0	3,4
	3 mo. infant	0.6	4.2	6.4	
	7 mo. infant	1.0	3.3	5.2	
	Adult	2.8	1.8	7.5	
Macaca mulatta	1–7 mo. infant	1.1	3.4	5.5	5
Homo sapiens	1–6 mo. infant	6	2.2	8.0	6
	6–12 mo. infant	9	1.6	6.6	
	1–3 yr. child	13	1.2	4.9	
	7–10 yr. child	28	1.0	5.6	
	Young woman	58	0.8	8.4	
	Pregnant woman	58	1.0	9.6	
	Lactating woman (1st 6 mo.)	58	1.1	9.6	

Source: Adapted from Oftedal 1991.

Note: All studies were conducted with milk proteins (e.g., casein, lactalbumin) except human estimates, which are based on mixed diets. BW, body weight; ME, metabolizable energy.

[a] 1, Flurer, Krommer, and Zucker 1988; 2, Ausman et al. 1979; 3, Samonds and Hegsted 1973; 4, Ausman and Hegsted 1980; 5, Kerr et al. 1970; 6, National Research Council 1989.

percentage declines with increasing age and body weight. However, in at least some primate species, protein requirements (as a percentage of ME) subsequently increase. For example, the human protein requirement, expressed as a percentage of ME, is higher in an adult woman (8.4%) than in a child (4.9%) (table 14.2). The explanation is that although the estimated protein requirement of a woman (0.8 g/kg/day) is lower than that of a child (1.0–1.2 g/kg/day), the difference in energy requirements is even more substantial (38 kcal/kg/day for a woman vs. 90–100 kcal/kg/day for a young child) (National Research Council 1989). A similar pattern has been observed in captive cebus monkeys, *Cebus* spp.: relative to body weight, the adult protein requirement (1.8 g/kg) is lower than that of the juvenile (3.3 g/kg), but as a percentage of ME, the adult requirement is higher (7.5% of ME from protein vs. 5.2% of ME from protein). This counterintuitive finding of a lower protein requirement (as a percentage of ME) in the growing animal is attributable to the slow growth rates of most primates (especially humans). Species with rapid growth rates do require higher protein concentrations in the diet during growth than for adult maintenance.

Although it is most accurate to express dietary requirements in relation to metabolizable energy concentration, this method is useful only if an extensive data base of ME values in foods is available. ME values are not known for many zoo animal foods. It is not certain how well ME values measured or estimated for human foods or livestock feeds (see discussion in Blaxter 1989) apply to particular species of zoo animals. An alternative method of expressing nutrient requirements relative to metabolic body size (e.g., g protein per kg$^{0.75}$ per day) makes an adjustment for the metabolic effects of body size that is appropriate for some, but

not all, nutrients (Mitchell 1962). Moreover, this method requires that daily food intake be determined for each animal, which is usually not feasible in a zoo. In dealing with zoo animal diets it is more practical to express nutrient requirements as a percentage of dietary dry matter than as a percentage of metabolizable energy. The estimated nutrient requirements of omnivorous laboratory animals (e.g., rat, mouse, pig) have been listed in this manner in chapter 11 of this volume.

Since human nutrient requirements may be similar to those of apes and other anthropoid primates such as rhesus macaques or cebus monkeys, it is interesting to compare the recommended nutrient levels for humans with the requirements that have been estimated for nonhuman primates (table 14.3). This comparison involves the conversion of both sets of estimates to a dry matter basis. The human recommendations cannot be considered true minimal requirements since they include allowances for the bioavailability of nutrients in typical diets and have been increased to encompass expected variability among individuals. Even with these adjustments, however, the human recommendations for most nutrients are lower than the estimated requirements of nonhuman primates. This fact most likely reflects our lack of knowledge of the nutrient requirements of those species rather than a difference between human and nonhuman primates.

Because most of the nonhuman primate requirements are not well defined, animal managers and nutritionists must rely on "practical levels" that are thought to be sufficient based on experience with primate colonies in research facilities. These practical levels are apt to be considerably higher than minimal requirements as they usually include allowances for ingredient variation and other margins of

TABLE 14.3. Comparison of Nutrient Levels Recommended for Humans and for Nonhuman Primates

	Humans					Nonhuman primates (all stages)
	Infant (0.5–1 yr.)	Young child (1–3 yr.)	Young woman (19–24 yr.)	Pregnant woman	Lactating woman (1st 6 mo.)	
Energy intake (kcal/day)	850	1,300	2,200	2,500	2,700	—
Dry matter intake (g/day)	179	325	550	625	675	—
Protein (%)	7.8	4.9	8.4	9.6	9.6	16.3
Calcium (%)	0.34	0.25	0.22	0.19	0.18	0.54
Phosphorus (%)	0.28	0.25	0.22	0.19	0.18	0.43
Magnesium (%)	0.034	0.025	0.051	0.051	0.053	0.16
Iron (ppm)	56	31	27	48	22	196
Zinc (ppm)	28	31	22	24	28	11
Iodine (ppm)	0.28	0.22	0.27	0.28	0.30	2.2
Selenium (ppm)	0.08	0.06	0.10	0.10	0.11	—
Vitamin A (IU/kg)	6,985	4,103	4,848	4,267	6,420	10,900
Vitamin D (IU/kg)	2,235	1,231	727	640	593	2,170
Vitamin E (IU/kg)	22	18	15	16	18	54
Vitamin K (ppb)	56	46	109	104	96	—
Vitamin C (ppm)	196	123	109	112	141	109
Thiamin (ppm)	2.2	2.2	2.0	2.4	2.4	—
Riboflavin (ppm)	2.8	2.5	2.4	2.6	2.7	5.4
Niacin (ppm)	33.5	27.7	27.3	27.2	29.6	54
Vitamin B_6 (ppm)	3.4	3.1	2.9	3.5	3.1	2.7
Folic acid (ppb)	196	154	327	640	415	217
Vitamin B_{12} (ppb)	2.8	2.2	3.6	3.5	3.9	—

Note: Calculated from National Research Council 1978, 1989, expressed on a dry matter basis, based on a dry matter content of 92% in manufactured primate diets and a caloric content in both human and primate diets of 4 kcal/g dry matter (4.75 kcal/g for infant). Comparable bioavailability of nutrients in mixed human diets and primate diets is also assumed.

safety. Of course, in feeding zoo animals, the primary goal is to ensure that nutrient levels are somewhat in excess of requirements, rather than to feed the lowest possible levels of nutrients. It is important to remember, however, that some nutrients are toxic if fed in excess (see Allen and Oftedal, chap. 11, this volume). Although it is generally preferable to set the estimated requirement levels too high rather than too low, the concentrations of minerals and vitamins A, D, and E in the diet should be monitored to ensure that toxicities do not develop. Careful monitoring is especially important for diets that contain vitamin and mineral supplements.

Diets for omnivores, and especially primates, often contain considerable quantities of commercial fruits that are of low protein content, raising concern about the potential for protein deficiency. It is unlikely that protein deficiency is a common occurrence in primates, as the protein requirements of primates are rather low (Oftedal 1991), especially in comparison with those of other species such as domestic pigs and cats (see Allen and Oftedal, chap. 11, this volume). Once the period of milk dependency is past, growing and nonreproductive primates appear to require a minimum of 7–10% protein (dry matter basis) if fed a plant-based manufactured diet containing proteins of balanced amino acid composition and 85% digestibility (Oftedal 1991). Although information on the requirements of reproductive primates is very limited, pregnant and lactating primates appear to require about 12.5% dietary protein, although it is possible that species that produce milks of high protein content may have higher protein requirements during lactation

(Oftedal 1991). The National Research Council (1978b) recommendation of 16% protein (dry matter basis) for primates at all stages of life appears reasonable and safe; the suggestion that New World monkeys may require up to 25% protein is not supported by available data (Flurer and Zucker 1985; Oftedal 1991).

Vitamin D is considered a dietary essential for animals, including primates and other omnivores (see Allen and Oftedal, chap. 11, this volume). Vitamin D is of special concern in the diets of New World primates, which do not appear to utilize vitamin D_2 as effectively as they do vitamin D_3 (Lehner et al. 1966; Hunt, Garcia, and Hegsted 1967; Hay and Watson 1977). Exposure to sunlight or to artificial light with an appropriate spectrum (285–315 nm) can satisfy requirements for vitamin D by permitting cutaneous photobiogenic conversion of vitamin D precursors to vitamin D. Primates housed indoors without artificial light of the appropriate spectrum must derive all of their vitamin D_3 from dietary sources. Infants relying solely on milk (Ullrey 1986) and adults that are offered inadequate sources of dietary vitamin D_3 may be at risk of deficiency.

USE OF MANUFACTURED FEEDS

In formulating manufactured feeds it is usually safest to err on the high side for a given nutrient, adding a margin of safety to cover losses during manufacture and storage, any interspecific differences in requirements, and the possible dilution of the diet by offered supplemental foods. Analytic data for commercial primate feeds illustrate that some nu-

TABLE 14.4. Comparison of the Nutrient Composition of Commercial Primate Diets with Estimated Nutrient Requirements of Nonhuman Primates

	NRC requirements[a]	Target nutrient levels[b]	Commercial primate diets		
			Mean	Range	n
Dry matter (%)					
Dry diets			91.7	89.2–93.6	5
Canned diets			41.7	41.1–42.3	2
Fat (%)		4.0	5.5	2.7– 9.8	7
Protein (%)	16.3	15–20	21.2	16.0–26.1	7
Neutral detergent fiber (%)		10–20	20.9	14.0–25.7	6
Acid detergent fiber (%)		5–15	8.0	4.9–14.0	6
Acid lignin (%)			1.7	0.8– 2.4	6
Ash (%)			6.8	5.6– 8.3	7
Gross energy (kcal/g)			4.63	4.43–4.89	5
Metabolizable energy (kcal/g)[c]			3.91	3.49–4.24	7
Calcium (%)	0.54	0.9	1.29	0.98–1.84	7
Phosphorus (%)	0.43	0.6	0.66	0.40–0.92	7
Magnesium (%)	0.16	0.15	0.18	0.10–0.29	7
Sodium (%)		0.2	0.40	0.19–0.71	7
Potassium (%)		0.8	1.05	0.83–1.44	7
Iron (ppm)	196	150	492	111–1140	7
Copper (ppm)		10	17.6	14.0–22.6	7
Zinc (ppm)	11	60	196	106–505	7
Manganese (ppm)		30	89	31–176	7
Selenium (ppm)		0.2	0.36	0.07–0.59	7

Source: Adapted from Oftedal 1991.

Note: All values except dry matter percentage expressed on a dry matter basis.

Protein = total nitrogen × 6.25. Analytical data on commercial primate diets provided by Allen and Baer Associates, Olney, Md. 20832.

[a] Requirements as estimated by the U.S. National Research Council (1978).

[b] Suggested minimum nutrient levels based on practical zoo primate diets that include produce and a commercial product.

[c] Metabolizable energy (ME) values for the products calculated assuming ME values of 4 kcal/g for protein and carbohydrate nitrogen-free extract and 9 kcal/g for fat.

trients are included at higher levels than the NRC estimated requirements (table 14.4). These feeds vary considerably in composition, in part because some feeds have been targeted to specific taxa and also because the ingredients and mineral premixes used by various manufacturers are different. In general, feeds formulated for some New World primates (i.e., cebids, callitrichids, and *Callimico*) are high in protein (>20% on a dry matter basis), while diets for folivorous primates (e.g., *Colobus*, langurs, howler monkeys) are high in fiber fractions. Although there may not be much scientific justification for feeding high protein levels to New World monkeys, when these feeds are included in mixed diets containing low-protein foods such as fruits, the additional protein may help counteract the diluting effect of the low-protein foods. Suggested "target" nutrient levels for primate diets (that include both produce and commercial products) based on practical experience are also included in table 14.4.

Manufactured feeds are typically formulated to provide all essential nutrients and thus can form the nutritional foundation of a mixed diet. Guinea pigs, and possibly some other caviomorph rodents, as well as primates may need diets supplemented with vitamin C, either directly or via inclusion of vitamin C–rich foods (such as kale, cabbage, or citrus). This need is due to the normal loss of vitamin C, a highly labile nutrient, during the manufacture and storage of feeds. Manufacturers of commercial primate feeds are

aware of these expected losses and thus add additional amounts of this vitamin to compensate. However, an outbreak of scurvy in rhesus macaques and squirrel monkeys recently occurred that was traced to a mechanical failure in spraying the appropriate amount of vitamin C on the outside of commercial monkey biscuits during manufacture (Ratterree et. al. 1990). In practical zoo animal diets, reliance on a biscuit as the primary source of vitamin C is rare. Primates are usually offered fruits and vegetables, many of which are excellent sources of vitamin C.

Most practical feeds for primates are either canned or extruded, although baked biscuits have also been used successfully. Other omnivores are usually fed extruded (e.g., dry dog and cat foods), canned, or pelleted (such as rat, mouse, guinea pig, and rabbit feeds) products. Raw meat and frozen meat products are not recommended given the susceptibility of some species to *Streptococcus* and other meat-borne pathogens (see Allen, Oftedal, and Baer, chap. 13, this volume).

Highly folivorous primates (*Alouatta* spp., *Presbytis* spp., *Pygathrix* spp., *Colobus* spp.) that are adapted to consume diets high in fiber can benefit from the use of commercial biscuits specifically formulated to contain high levels of dietary fiber. Commercial primate biscuits vary markedly in fiber fractions (see table 14.4), and biscuits containing 5–7.5% acid detergent fiber (ADF) would be considered inappropriately low in fiber for use in the diets of highly folivorous species. When combined with leafy greens and suitable browse, a commercial product containing at least 12% ADF helps to contribute the fiber that is essential for proper gastrointestinal tract function in folivorous primates. These animals also benefit from frequent feedings, at least twice per day, which tend to encourage a continuous fermentation of plant fiber. As with all herbivores, major changes to the diets of folivorous primates must always proceed slowly, taking place over the course of 10 to 14 days (see Oftedal, Baer, and Allen, chap. 12, this volume).

USE OF PRODUCE AND BROWSE

Because of the common perception that omnivores feed on a broad array of foods, zoo diets for these species often include a variety of produce items, such as leafy greens (e.g., kale, cabbage, lettuce, spinach, celery), fruits (e.g., apples, bananas, grapes, oranges), seeds and grains (e.g., sunflower seeds, corn, oats, wheat, peanuts), and root crops (e.g., carrots, potatoes, sweet potatoes), as well as some miscellaneous items (e.g., hydroponic grass, leaves and branches from trees, mealworms, crickets, mouse pups). The specific mix of produce and miscellaneous items fed to a particular species generally reflects ideas about food selection in the wild, demonstrated food preferences in captivity, observed effects on fecal consistency, established feeding practices, and local market availability. Historically, nutritional considerations have not been the primary criteria by which the particular items in a given diet are selected.

There are undoubtedly valid reasons for introducing diversity into animal diets, including behavioral stimulation, reduction of boredom-associated stereotypic behaviors, improvement in exhibit quality, and reduced dependence on one or a few feeds as the sole source of nutrients. For example, the feeding of a variety of browse plants (maple, beech, willow, bamboo, kudzu, and mulberry) to captive gorillas reduced aberrant behavior (regurgitation and reingestion of gastric contents), increased the time devoted to feeding, and undoubtedly increased the fiber content of the diet (Gould and Bres 1986). It is important, however, that the offering of diversity does not undermine the nutritional balance of the ingested diet. For example, golden lion tamarins, *Leontopithecus rosalia*, appear to prefer such items as bananas, grapes, and raisins to a nutritionally complete canned product, and if offered sufficient quantities of the "treats," will fail to consume much of the complete feed, resulting in potential nutritional imbalances (Power 1992).

One way to avoid this problem is to restrict the amount of produce offered so that it provides no more than 30% of the ingested dry matter in the daily diet. This is still a considerable amount if one considers that most produce items contain only 10–20% dry matter, as compared with about 40% dry matter in canned feeds and 90% dry matter in dry feeds (see table 14.4). Thus, if a primate consumes a diet containing by weight 72% produce and 28% dry feed, about 30% of the dry matter comes from the produce. The equivalent values for a diet based on a canned product are about 53% produce and 47% canned feed.

While the figures above represent useful guidelines, the distinction must be made between the offered diet and the consumed diet. Primates and other omnivores usually will not consume all food items in the proportion in which they are offered. Therefore, assessments of the nutritional adequacy of a diet should be based on what is actually eaten, rather than only on what is offered. In order to assure adequate intake of complete feeds (canned or biscuit), these items can be offered early in the day when animals are likely to be most hungry. Multiple feedings throughout the day, with most produce offered late in the day, may also help to assure adequate intake of nutrients.

A common misconception is that fruits and vegetables produced for human consumption are similar to the plant materials consumed by primates and other omnivores in the wild. A comparison of some foods commonly fed to primates with the average composition of food types as eaten in the wild (by the red howler, *Alouatta seniculus*) demonstrates that market produce is higher in water and lower in fiber fractions (table 14.5). Commercial fruits typically contain low concentrations of both protein (2–6% of dry matter) and calcium (0.03–0.3% of dry matter), but this is not true of fruits in the wild. The common notion that fruits are low in fiber fractions results from our familiarity with commercial fruits; field studies demonstrate that the fruits eaten by primates in the wild may be as high in fiber fractions as are the leaves they eat (Calvert 1985; Oftedal 1991; Barton et al. 1993).

Commercial fruits are also high in sugars and other soluble carbohydrates that ferment rapidly. To avoid the risk of explosive fermentation, gastritis, and bloat, highly folivorous primates such as colobus monkeys, langurs, and proboscis monkeys that have an elaborate foregut fermentation system should probably not be fed fruits (see Oftedal, Baer, and Allen, chap. 12, this volume).

Given that money spent on produce is primarily payment for the harvest, transport, and marketing of water (75–92% of the weight of most produce), and given that most primates would benefit more from foods of structural complexity and high fiber content, some zoos are developing programs to harvest and feed browse such as bamboo and tree branches. While such programs may be beneficial, neither the nutritional benefits nor the potential toxicological risks have been adequately assessed (see Oftedal, Baer, and Allen, chap. 12, this volume). In the wild, folivorous primates exhibit considerable selectivity in feeding, but in captivity they may not be able to make appropriate choices due to lack of prior experience, the limited amounts offered, or the unfamiliar sensory, physical, or chemical properties of the browse species offered. For example, langurs fed a diet including *Acacia* leaves developed digestive disturbances, and some animals died after the gastrointestinal tract became impacted with ropes of indigestible *Acacia* fiber (Ensley et al. 1982).

USE OF INSECTS AND "TREAT" FOODS

It is common practice to use small, palatable food items to promote normal foraging behavior and to provide diet diversity. Captive callitrichids are usually offered crickets, mealworm larvae, or other insects as part of the daily diet. These and other omnivorous species may also capture insect

TABLE 14.5.   Comparison of Some Foods Eaten by Primates in Zoos and in the Wild

Food type	Dry matter	Protein	Fiber fractions[a]			Ca	P
			NDF	ADF	AL		
Market produce used in primate diets[b]							
Apples	12.8	2.3	17.4	12.6	3.8	0.04	0.06
Green beans	10.7	17.9	28.0	25.1	2.2	0.57	0.44
Cabbage	8.9	14.7	20.6	21.9	1.7	0.64	0.38
Carrots	12.2	7.7	15.2	16.5	1.5	0.31	0.31
Kale	12.3	32.5	19.3	24.7	4.6	1.43	0.58
Foods eaten in the wild by red howler monkeys[c]							
Flowers	25.1	14.4	50.6	35.8	17.1	0.49	0.30
Fruits	23.7	7.0	53.8	35.2	16.6	0.64	0.16
Mature leaves	36.5	16.6	57.2	40.5	20.4	1.36	0.14
Young leaves	32.2	21.2	54.4	36.4	21.1	0.29	0.28

Note: Values are expressed on a dry matter basis.

[a] NDF, neutral detergent fiber; ADF, acid detergent fiber; AL, acid lignin.

[b] All data except calcium and phosphorus from unpublished study on fiber digestion of *Colobus guereza* (see Oftedal, Jakubasz, and Whetter 1982); calcium and phosphorus values from Watt and Merrill 1963.

[c] Unpublished data of M. S. Edwards, S. D. Crissey, O. T. Oftedal, and R. Rudran, as cited in Oftedal 1991.

pests such as cockroaches that invade cages seeking food scraps, but the nutritional consequences of such behavior are hard to quantify.

Insects are good sources of protein and fat but provide little calcium (Allen 1989). When primates are offered insects as only a small part of an otherwise well balanced diet, calcium deficiency is of little concern. For example, 130 grams of diet (as-fed basis, consisting of canned marmoset diet and produce) consumed by a 500-gram tamarin could safely contain 3–5 grams of insects without significantly reducing the overall calcium content of the diet. In diets for other insectivorous primates, such as tarsiers, *Tarsius,* insects may represent the entire diet. Crickets and mealworm larvae, when fed as the sole diet, should be supplemented with a source of calcium so that the ratio of calcium to phosphorus is at least 1:1. This can be accomplished by dusting the insects with powdered calcium carbonate or by feeding a diet to the insects that contains at least 8% calcium. When crickets are fed diets containing 8% calcium for at least 48 hours, their gastrointestinal tracts become filled with calcium (Allen and Oftedal 1989). The dusting method is widely used in zoos and appears effective with crickets if the insects are eaten promptly. Otherwise, the crickets will begin to groom themselves, effectively removing the calcium.

Other "treats" commonly fed to captive primates are seeds and nuts. While these items are highly palatable, largely due to their high fat content, their use in diets for omnivores should be closely monitored. When seeds and nuts represent a large part of the consumed diet of psittacines, inadequate intakes of lysine, calcium, available phosphorus, sodium, manganese, zinc, iron, iodine, selenium, vitamins A, D, E, and K, riboflavin, pantothenic acid, available niacin, vitamin B$_{12}$, and choline may result (Ullrey, Allen, and Baer 1991). These same nutritional imbalances can be seen when primates are fed excessive amounts of seeds and nuts (M. Allen, pers. obs.). More appropriate "treats" for omnivorous mammals include low-sugar, high-fiber breakfast cereals, unbuttered, unsalted popcorn, and

herbivore pellets. These items are particularly useful in encouraging foraging when broadly scattered in enclosures. In this way, time spent searching and eating is extended, and the "treats" have a beneficial, rather than a deleterious, effect on the nutritional composition of the total diet.

CONCLUSIONS

The fact that omnivorous species of primates and other mammals may select items from a broad array of plant and animal foods in the wild should not be taken to mean that they must be offered a similar array of foods in captivity. Given the differences in composition between market produce and plants eaten in the wild, and the fact that we have little understanding of the factors affecting food choice in the wild, it is difficult if not impossible to replicate the natural diet. A more practical approach is to provide a diet that will meet estimated nutrient requirements while also providing sufficient fiber for normal digestive function and sufficient diversity to provide behavioral stimulation. Of course, each diet may need to be somewhat species-specific, reflecting tendencies to dietary specialization or predominance of particular kinds of food in the natural diet.

REFERENCES

Allen, M. E. 1989. Nutritional aspects of insectivory. Ph.D. thesis, Michigan State University, East Lansing.

Allen, M. E., and Oftedal, O. T. 1989. Dietary manipulation of the calcium content of feed crickets. *J. Zoo Wildl. Med.* 20 (1): 26–33.

Ausman, L. M., Gallina, D. L., Samonds, K. W., and Hegsted, D. M. 1979. Assessment of the efficiency of protein utilization in young squirrel and macaque monkeys. *Am. J. Clin. Nutr.* 32: 1813–23.

Ausman, L. M., and Hegsted, D. M. 1980. Protein requirements of adult cebus monkeys *(Cebus albifrons). Am. J. Clin. Nutr.* 33: 2551–58.

Barton, R. A., Whiten, A., Byrne, R. W., and English, M. 1993.

Chemical composition of baboon food plants: Implications for the interpretation of intra- and interspecific differences in diet. *Folia Primatol.* 61:1–20.

Bauchop, T., and Martucci, R. W. 1968. Ruminant-like digestion of the langur monkey. *Science* 161:698–700.

Birney, E. C., Jenness, R., and Ayaz, K. M. 1976. Inability of bats to synthesize L-ascorbic acid. *Nature* 260:626–28.

Birney, E. C., Jenness, R., and Hume, I. D. 1980. Evolution of an enzyme system: Ascorbic acid biosynthesis in monotremes and marsupials. *Evolution* 34:230–39.

Blaxter, K. L. 1989. *Energy metabolism in animals and man.* Cambridge: Cambridge University Press.

Calvert, J. J. 1985. Food selection by western gorillas *(G. g. gorilla)* in relation to food chemistry. *Oecologia* 65:236–46.

Chatterjee, I. B., Majumder, A. K., Nandi, B. K., and Subramanian, N. 1975. Synthesis and some major functions of vitamin C in animals. *Ann. N.Y. Acad. Sci.* 258:24–47.

Chivers, D. J., and Hladik, C. M. 1980. Morphology of the gastrointestinal tract in primates: Comparisons with other mammals in relation to diet. *J. Morphol.* 166:337–86.

Clutton-Brock, T. H. 1977. *Primate ecology: Studies of feeding and ranging behaviour in lemurs, monkeys, and apes.* New York: Academic Press.

Ensley, P. K., Rost, T. L., Anderson, M., Benirschke, K., Brockman, D., and Ullrey, D. 1982. Intestinal obstruction and perforation caused by undigested *Acacia* sp. leaves in langur monkeys. *J. Am. Vet. Med. Assoc.* 181:1351–54.

Flurer, C. I., Krommer, G., and Zucker, H. 1988. Endogenous N-excretion and minimal protein requirement for maintenance of the common marmoset *(Callithrix jacchus). Lab. Anim. Sci.* 38:183–86.

Flurer, C. I., and Zucker, H. 1985. Long-term experiments with low dietary protein levels in Callithricidae. *Primates* 26:479–90.

———. 1989. Ascorbic acid in a New World monkey family: Species difference and influence of stressors on ascorbic acid metabolism. *Z. Ernaehrungswiss.* 28:49–55.

Gould, E., and Bres, M. 1986. Regurgitation and reingestion in captive gorillas: Description and intervention. *Zoo Biol.* 5: 241–50.

Harding, R. S. O. 1981. An order of omnivores: Nonhuman primates in the wild. In *Omnivorous primates: Gathering and hunting in human evolution,* ed. R. S. O. Harding and G. Teleki, 191–214. New York: Columbia University Press.

Harding, R. S. O., and Teleki, G. 1981. *Omnivorous primates: Gathering and hunting in human evolution.* New York: Columbia University Press.

Hay, A. W. M., and Watson, G. 1977. Vitamin D$_2$ in vertebrate evolution. *Comp. Biochem. Physiol.* [B] 56:375–80.

Hladik, C. M. 1977. A comparative study of the feeding strategies of two sympatric species of leaf monkeys: *Presbytis senex* and *Presbytis entellus.* In *Primate ecology: Studies of feeding and ranging behaviour in lemurs, monkeys, and apes,* ed. T. H. Clutton-Brock, 323–53. New York: Academic Press.

———. 1978. Adaptive strategies of primates in relation to leafeating. In *The ecology of arboreal folivores,* ed. G. G. Montgomery, 373–95. Washington, D.C.: Smithsonian Institution Press.

———. 1981. Diet and evolution of feeding strategies among forest primates. In *Omnivorous primates: Gathering and hunting in human evolution,* ed. R. S. O. Harding and G. Teleki, 215–54. New York: Columbia University Press.

Hume, I. D. 1982. *Digestive physiology and nutrition of marsupials.* New York: Cambridge University Press.

Hunt, R. D., Garcia, F. G., and Hegsted, D. M. 1967. Vitamin D$_2$ and D$_3$ in New World primates: Production and regression of osteodystrophia fibrosa. *Lab. Anim. Care* 17:222–34.

Janson, C. H. 1988. Intra-specific food competition and primate social structure: A synthesis. *Behaviour* 105:1–17.

Jenness, R., Birney, E. C., and Ayaz, K. L. 1978. Ascorbic acid and l-gulonolactone oxidase in lagomorphs. *Comp. Biochem. Physiol.* [B] 61:395–99.

———. 1980. Variation of L-gulonolactone oxidase activity in placental mammals. *Comp. Biochem. Physiol.* [B] 67: 195–204.

Kamil, A. C., and Sargent, T. D. 1981. *Foraging behavior: Ecological, ethological, and psychological approaches.* New York: Garland Press.

Kerr, G. R., Allen, J. R., Scheffler, G., and Waisman, H. A. 1970. Malnutrition studies in the rhesus monkey. I. Effect on physical growth. *Am. J. Clin. Nutr.* 23:739–48.

Landry, S. O. 1970. The rodentia as omnivores. *Q. Rev. Biol.* 45: 351–72.

Lehner, N. D. M., Bullock, B. C., Clarkson, T. B., and Lofland, H. B. 1966. Biological activity of vitamins D$_2$ and D$_3$ fed to squirrel monkeys. *Fed. Proc.* 25:533.

Martin, R. D., Chivers, D. J., MacLarnon, A. M., and Hladik, C. M. 1985. Gastrointestinal allometry in primates and other mammals. In *Size and scaling in primate biology,* ed. W. L. Jungers, 61–89. New York: Plenum Press.

Milton, K. 1980. *The foraging strategy of howler monkeys.* New York: Columbia University Press.

———. 1981. Food choice and digestive strategies of two sympatric primate species. *Am. Nat.* 117:496–505.

———. 1984. The role of food-processing factors in primate food choice. In *Adaptations for foraging in nonhuman primates,* ed. P. S. Rodman and J. G. H. Cant, 249–79. New York: Columbia University Press.

Milton, K., and Jenness, R. 1987. Ascorbic acid content of Neotropical plant parts available to wild monkeys and bats. *Experientia* 43:339–42.

Milton, K., and McBee, R. H. 1983. Rates of fermentative digestion in the howler monkey, *Alouatta palliata* (Primates, Cebidae). *Comp. Biochem. Physiol.* [A] 74:29–31.

Mitchell, H. H. 1962. *Comparative nutrition of man and domestic animals.* New York: Academic Press.

Nash, L. T. 1986. Dietary, behavioral, and morphological aspects of gummivory in primates. *Yrbk. Phys. Anthropol.* 29:113–37.

National Research Council. 1978. *Nutrient requirements of nonhuman primates.* Washington, D.C.: National Academy of Sciences.

———. 1989. *Recommended dietary allowances.* 10th ed. Washington, D.C.: National Academy Press.

———. 1995. *Nutrient requirements of laboratory animals.* 4th rev. ed. Washington, D.C.: National Academy of Sciences.

Oftedal, O. T. 1991. The nutritional consequences of foraging in primates: The relationship of nutrient intakes to nutrient requirements. *Phil. Trans. R. Soc. Lond. B* 334:161–70.

Oftedal, O. T., Jakubasz, M., and Whetter, P. 1982. Food intake and diet digestibility by captive black and white colobus *(Colobus guereza)* at the National Zoological Park. *Proceedings of the Annual Meeting of the American Association of Zoo Veterinarians,* New Orleans, La., 33. Philadelphia: American Association of Zoo Veterinarians.

Power, M. L. 1991. Digestive function, energy intake, and the response to dietary gum in captive callitrichids. Ph.D. thesis, University of California at Berkeley.

———. 1992. Nutritional consequences of diet self-selection by captive golden lion tamarins. *AAZPA Regional Conference Proceedings,* 147–51. Wheeling, W. Va.: American Association of Zoological Parks and Aquariums.

Ratterree, M. S., Didier, P. J., Blanchard, J. L., Clarke, M. R., and

Schaeffer, D. 1990. Vitamin C deficiency in captive nonhuman primates fed commercial primate diet. *Lab. Anim. Sci.* 40: 165–68.

Rodman, P. S., and Cant, J. G. H., eds. 1984. *Adaptations for foraging in nonhuman primates.* New York: Columbia University Press.

Samonds, K. W., and Hegsted, D. M. 1973. Protein requirements of young cebus monkeys *(Cebus albifrons* and *apella). Am. J. Clin. Nutr.* 26:30–40.

Stevens, C. E. 1988. Comparative physiology of the vertebrate digestive system. New York: Cambridge University Press.

Ullrey, D. E. 1986. Nutrition of primates in captivity. In *Primates: The road to self-sustaining populations,* ed. K. Benirschke, 823–35. New York: Springer-Verlag.

Ullrey, D. E., Allen, M. E., and Baer, D. J. 1991. Formulated diets versus seed mixtures for Psittacines. *J. Nutr.* 121:S193–S205.

Vorontsov, N. N. 1979. *Evolution of the alimentary system in myomorph rodents.* (Translated from Russian). New Delhi, India: Indian National Scientific Documentation Centre.

Watt, B. K., and Merrill, A. L. 1963. *Composition of foods.* Agriculture Handbook no. 8. Washington, D.C.: U.S. Department of Agriculture.

Yess, N. J., and Hegsted, D. M. 1967. Biosynthesis of ascorbic acid in the acouchi and agouti. *J. Nutr.* 92:331–33.

PART THREE

Exhibitry

INTRODUCTION
Katerina V. Thompson

Zoo exhibitry has transcended the "stamp collection" menageries of the past. Through creative exhibit design, zoos now strive to educate visitors about biology, ecology, and the grave threats to our planet's biodiversity. This part summarizes modern approaches to exhibit design, both philosophical and practical, and provides a glimpse of the future of zoo exhibitry.

Conservation goals have evolved from preservation of individual species to preservation of entire ecosystems. Zoos have assumed an important role in educating the public about the critical loss of biodiversity that is occurring. By exhibiting animals in their natural contexts, zoos can reinforce the message of the interdependency of animals and their ecosystems. As Robinson argues in chapter 15, exhibiting animals in inappropriate social and ecological contexts presents a greatly distorted view of the natural world. To counter these false impressions, zoos must evolve into Bio-Parks, with exhibits that integrate elements of zoology, botany, and human culture.

Coe emphasizes in chapter 16 that all exhibits are educational, in the sense that zoo visitors, whether actively or passively, come away with distinct impressions. The task for zoo exhibit designers is to identify the message they wish to convey and find an effective means of transmitting that message to zoo visitors. Coe further outlines a process for designing new exhibits that draws from the collective expertise of the entire zoo staff.

Although the use of plants in and around zoo exhibits has greatly increased in recent years, the result, all too often, is a haphazard mixture of plant and animal life that lacks a coherent ecological message. In chapter 17, Jackson presents philosophical arguments for the use of plants, both living and dead, to increase the effectiveness of zoo exhibits.

Seidensticker and Doherty stress in chapter 18 that exhibits can achieve their educational objectives only by taking into account both the natural history and biological needs of the animals and the expectations of zoo visitors. They further provide guidelines for identifying and correcting ineffective exhibits.

Zoos must have means of containing animals, for the safety of the animals as well as that of zoo visitors. In the past, animals were displayed behind barriers that evoked comparisons to human prisons. Hancocks has been instrumental in promoting and implementing unobtrusive barriers for zoo exhibits. In chapter 19 he urges the use of barriers that blur the boundaries between the animals and zoo visitors in order to bring visitors (figuratively) into the animal's world.

In a style reminiscent of Crandall's original volume, Thomas and Maruska in chapter 20 contribute an account derived from their considerable experience in the zoo world. They review the potential advantages of mixed-species exhibits, enumerate steps for creating them, and provide examples of species combinations that have been successful at various zoos.

Modern technological advances have allowed the development of exhibits that are functional as well as attractive. The chapters by Maple and Perkins, Rosenthal and Xanten, and Boness provide highly practical advice on the technical aspects of exhibit design. In chapter 21 Maple and Perkins describe ways of furnishing exhibits that can meet the physical needs of the animals and encourage the expression of natural behaviors. Rosenthal and Xanten provide a "nuts-and-bolts" guide to exhibit design in chapter 22, with consideration for both the animals within and the staff that must maintain the exhibit and care for the animals. In the final chapter, chapter 23, Boness gives detailed guidelines for designing and maintaining aquatic exhibits.

The chapters in this section not only provide information that can be used to improve the educational impact of exhibitry but also provide the basis for enhancement of the environment of zoo animals to maintain behavioral diversity.

15

The BioPark Concept and the Exhibition of Mammals

MICHAEL H. ROBINSON

The concept of the BioPark as a derivative of the zoological park was foreshadowed by Boyden (1969), who suggested the creation of a holistic Biological Center. His idea was innovative and progressive, but was apparently ignored. More recently, zoos have made enormous strides toward naturalistic exhibits and biologically valid populations (social groupings) of animals. Despite this spectacular progress, zoos are still a distorted mirror of the natural world. The distortion stems from the heart of zoo programs, which tend to ignore the complementary half of life on earth: the plant kingdom. Zoos often distort the reflection of the animal world simply by placing so much emphasis on vertebrate animals. It is grossly unnatural to separate the biology of animals from the biology of plants. In reality, animals and plants are inextricably interdependent and intertwined.

The human tendency to separate things is part of our capacity to classify and bring order to our world. It is a basis of much of our intellectual success, but it often stands in the way of our understanding the connectivities of life. Over the centuries, history, logistics, and practicalities have separated plants into botanical gardens and animals into zoos and aquariums, just as these forces have traditionally divided academic biology into botany and zoology. In both cases the urge to compartmentalize has reinforced the other separating factors. In the field of what I call bioexhibitry (Robinson 1988), we have lodged all the glorious public presentation-content of anatomy, morphology, physiology, and paleontology in museums while keeping the living collections in "gardens." It is highly significant that we use the noun "garden," qualified by the appropriate adjective, to signify both those places where living plants are exhibited and those where living animals are exhibited.

In the BioPark these archaic separations do not exist. Holism, the condition of the living world, is restored as a powerful educational device. This change means much more than the creation of "habitat" exhibits. What it really means is the creation of exhibits that explain, elucidate, and ex-

emplify the interconnectedness of life. It means putting humans and our biology in the context of the rest of life. The ultimate progression in biological education is from the knowledge of ourselves to the mystery of other organisms. But the first step toward the BioPark is simply integrating plants into the exhibit. Most zoos present plants as a decorative backdrop to their animals as if they were inert objects irrelevant to animal ecology. If we are truly to educate people for a twenty-first century in which biological factors will dominate much of our decision making, we will have to show them how dynamic global ecology really is. How can we do this, and how can we use mammal exhibits, in particular, for this purpose?

To our relatively naive mammalian eyes, mammals are conspicuously dominant among animals. The multitudinous invertebrate species need as much emphasis as the mammals in the BioPark. This may seem an almost heretical viewpoint in a book devoted to mammals in captivity. But in terms of species, insects outnumber mammals by a minimum of a hundred to one. And this comparison emphasizes insects alone; the function of ecosystems depends heavily on even smaller animals and prokaryotes. Mammals have evolved complex specializations in a host of dependencies, interdependencies, and interactions with invertebrates, plants, protozoa, bacteria, viruses, and so on. The BioPark continues to capitalize on the fascination of mammals; however, it also focuses on their complex evolutionary relationships with a host of other organisms.

It is time to end the isolationism of simply exhibiting mammals against a naturalistic backdrop. The following suggestions for BioPark exhibits of mammals are meant to stimulate further ideas, not to be exhaustive or comprehensive. They are original only in the sense that they have resulted from personal brainstorming in connection with this chapter. These ideas must have occurred to others, and they may already be enshrined in exhibits at zoos around the world; if so, I missed them.

MAMMAL-PLANT AND PLANT-MAMMAL INTERACTIONS

Some of the most complex specializations in the plant world are adaptations for seed dispersal. Plants have not only invented aerodynamics to disperse their seeds, but have also used animals as dispersal agents through a wide range of adaptations that signifies a long evolutionary interaction. They have evolved attractants, including color and odor, to ensure that animals notice and carry off fruits, and even fruiting strategies that stimulate food hoarding. All of these strategies ensure the propagation of plants by parasitizing animal behavior. Plants have pandered to the dietary addictions of many mammals by loading fruits with sugars and fats. One example of such an interaction involves Asian one-horned rhinos, *Rhinoceros unicornis*. These animals in the wild consume so much plant material that they defecate up to 25 kg of dung daily. This dung is often deposited at particular sites to form accretionary dung piles or middens. Since rhinos eat fruits as well as grasses and leaves, the seeds of some trees pass through the rhino's intestinal tract and out with the dung. Transport through the gastrointestinal tract assists germination in some species. The middens then become seedbeds. In Nepal, stands of trewia trees mark the sites of rhino middens (Dinerstein and Wemmer 1988). At certain times of the year, rhino dung contains up to 25 trewia seeds per kg. While it would clearly be bad housekeeping to allow rhino dung to accumulate in exhibits, simulated dung piles (fiberglass) could illustrate the volume of plants that rhinos consume and subsequently disperse. Seedbeds of *Trewia nudifolia* could illustrate the process of seed dispersal. The tree itself could be grown in a warm and well-lit large mammal house.

Scatter hoarding is a mammalian response to extreme seasonal climates in the temperate regions and to plant fruiting strategies in the Tropics. By simple manipulation of feeding schedules it can be illustrated with any collection of agoutis, *Dasyprocta* spp., or acouchis, *Myoprocta* spp. In Southeast Asia the bearded pig, *Sus barbatus,* responds to spatial and temporal variations in fruit abundance by wide-scale migration rather than by hoarding. Although it is unlikely that bearded pigs could be common zoo exhibits, the phenomenon could be highlighted in graphics connected to rodent scatter hoarding. Opportunities for many questions arise: Did primitive humans store food? What about animals other than rodents? When animals bury food, do they find all the caches? How can you test this? Since the methodology of experimental ecology and biology should be one of the things that we explain to BioPark visitors, these are good questions to answer.

Tinbergen's (1972) famous study of scatter hoarding by red foxes is a marvelous piece of comprehensible field biology that suggests some further demonstrations in mammal exhibits. In these elegantly simple nondestructive experiments, hen's eggs were buried above the tideline on a sandy shore close to a gull colony. During the breeding season this colony was constantly raided by red foxes, *Vulpes vulpes,* which scatter-hoarded eggs and chicks. The buried hen's eggs tested whether the foxes could locate the eggs even if they had not buried them. If the answer was positive, then a good inference would be that foxes can recover hoarded food during times of shortage. Out of 100 buried eggs and 100 filled-in dummy (eggless) caches, foxes found and ate 8 eggs, and hedgehogs, *Erinaceus* spp., found and ate 12 eggs. Footprints in the sand enabled each cache discovery process to be reconstructed. When the experiment was carried out, the fox population around the colony had been reduced to one fox who was a rabbit "specialist." Thus, egg predation should have been at a low ebb. In these circumstances, the discovery rate is convincing. Coatis, *Nasua nasua,* raccoons, *Procyon* spp., opossums, *Didelphis* spp., and otters, *Lutra annectens,* are all capable of locating hidden hen's eggs at some depth (Rand and Robinson 1969).

There is an interesting link between plants' germination strategies and human use of plant propagules for food in everything from primitive diets to haute cuisine. Some fruits and seeds are loaded with high-energy materials like starches, sugars, and fats. This strategy allows rapid germination and early growth, enabling seedlings to outcompete competitors in the struggle for light. (Many of our major sources of cooking oil spring to mind: olives, coconuts, palmnuts, sunflower seeds, and so on.) In a primitive hunter-gatherer diet these substances could not be present in the excessive quantities that cause obesity and cardiac and circulatory problems in modern "civilized" diets. Our addictions to sweet things and high-cholesterol foods probably had an adaptive function in our "wild" state; however, they are now maladaptive.

An exhibit on human dietary problems can lead nicely into the problem that cellulose digestion poses for most herbivores. Everybody these days has heard of cellulose and knows the "healthy" foods that contain fiber. The cell walls of all plants consist of cellulose, a carbohydrate made up of glucose molecules. Cellulose is more abundant in plants than starch and is the most abundant organic material on earth. Despite this, no vertebrate produces enzymes capable of digesting cellulose. Mammals depend exclusively on the bacterial flora of their intestines to deal with cellulose. Since bacteria are widely perceived as harmful, this is a good story to tell. Herbivores have evolved a wide range of mechanisms and behaviors to facilitate bacterial digestive action. These should be a focus of attention in the exhibition of mammals. The teeth of herbivores are often highly adapted in structure and growth patterns to allow for the extensive grinding of plant materials required to expose cell contents otherwise encapsulated in cellulose. Jaw articulations have evolved to allow for lateral and rotatory movements in the milling action of the molars and premolars. Elephants' teeth illustrate dramatically and beautifully the evolution of massive grinding surfaces. Open-rooted continuous growth allows for the replacement of wearing surfaces, cusps of stronger material enhance the grinding, and so on.

Further cellulose-based mammalian adaptations include complex intestinal devices like the highly specialized stomachs of ruminants and the comparatively great length of the gut in all herbivores. Ruminants' adaptations allow the animals to graze rapidly when exposed to danger and chew later in comparative safety. This process can be seen in well-designed and managed hoofstock exhibits. The process of coprophagy in rabbits also fits nicely into an explication of cellulose digestion. The capacity of the giant panda, *Ailuropoda melanoleuca,* to cope with cellulose and lignin exemplifies its relatively recent "conversion" from a much more omnivorous diet. It has to process food in bulk because its digestive efficiency is so low.

Somewhere in an exhibit on the "cellulose problem" is the place for dealing with the digestion of wood and chitin. Both these substances are found in the diets of mammals but, as in the case of cellulose, are not digestible by autochthonous enzymes. Chitin, which makes up a substantial part of the exoskeletons of insects, figures heavily in the diets of insectivorous bats, anteaters, pangolins, *Manis* spp., aardvarks, *Orycteropus afer,* and less specialized insectivores. No vertebrate enzyme can degrade it down to its constituent sugars. Bat feces are rich in unprocessed chitin. Recently a bacterial enzyme capable of digesting chitin was found in bat guano (M. Tuttle, pers. comm.). Guano deposits not only have great economic value to humankind as sources of fertilizer but also have an extraordinarily rich bacterial flora. Since they contain masses of undigested chitin, it is not surprising that bacteria there have evolved chitinase. Perhaps someday we can make alcohol from processing wastes at shrimp canneries by way of bacterial fermentation, using bat guano–derived species. All this suggests that a bat guano exhibit would be appropriate in a bat exhibit.

Wood forms a considerable part of the diets of animals such as beavers, *Castor* spp., particularly in winter when leaves and soft plant parts are not available. As in the case of cellulose, it is subject to bacterial fermentation in the large intestine, particularly the cecum. Termites, pests to us because of their destruction of wood, are important decomposers in many ecosystems. Termites cannot themselves digest wood; they rely on protozoans within the intestine to make the nutrients available "secondhand." The great success of these insects hinges on their intestinal flagellates.

Another intimate interaction between plants and animals is that involved in pollination. Terrestrial plants either use animals to carry their pollen from one flower to another or scatter immense quantities of pollen into the wind. Mammals, particularly bats, are important pollinators of nocturnal flowers. The characteristics of bat-pollinated flowers can easily be illustrated by graphics or, better still, models associated with bat exhibits. Attracting bats requires massive flowers, predominantly white, pendent, with heavy odor, and with massive nectar production. All these features relate to the physiological characteristics and sensory specializations of the pollinator.

Finally, plants' responses to mammalian leaf-eaters should be considered. The defensive adaptations of plants have evolved over millions of years and may be at least as complex, specialized, and diverse as the defenses of animals against their predators. They range from the chemical to the mechanical. Thorns, spines, and urticating hairs are simple and obvious defenses against browsers; they are familiar to anyone who has picked blackberries. The silica content of grasses is a less obvious line of defense. Complex secondary compounds are even further from our own everyday experience; however, the link between current interests in hallucinogens and plant antimammal defenses is perhaps exploitable for biological education. Thorns and spines can be part

of a giraffe exhibit even if secondary compounds cannot. The link between plant defenses and the evolution of mammalian teeth, tongues, and palatal structures could be the basis for a fascinating display.

COMPARATIVE ANATOMY AND PHYSIOLOGY

Functional anatomy is also an exciting field. My favorite examples of mammalian structures that can be easily highlighted include the tail of the pygmy hippo, *Hexaprotodon (=Choeropsis) liberiensis,* and the elephant's nose. Pygmy hippos have arborescent hairs on their short and stubby tails (Kranz 1982). The function of this unusual adaptation becomes immediately apparent in our hippo enclosures. The animals spread dung in Jackson Pollock patterns on the walls; the arborescent hairs help in this marking behavior since they increase the dispersing power of the rotating tail during defecation. Again, we could use simulations of hippo dung-scatter on vertical surfaces to illustrate this marking behavior (Nile hippos, *Hippopotamus amphibius,* also mark but do not have the specialized hairs).

A stuffed elephant in a museum conveys little information about the sensitive perfection of the trunk, and an elephant skeleton, even less. But watching elephants at the zoo provides direct insights into this extraordinary derivative of the mammalian nose. The device can be seen in action, grasping small objects with precision, heaving large logs, and throwing dirt on the elephant's back; it makes drinking from a standing position possible and facilitates a social sniff-test of companions or strangers. All that is needed to complete the lesson is comparison with the tapir's, *Tapirus* spp., incipient trunk and a suitable model to illustrate the mechanisms involved. The electronic control technology now applied to children's toys could surely build a joystick-controlled, life-size elephant's trunk. An exhibit illustrating the comparative anatomy of the nose could range from proboscis monkeys, *Nasalis* spp., elephant shrews, aardvarks, mandrills, *Mandrillus sphinx,* echidnas, koalas, *Phascolarctos cinereus,* coatis, and star-nosed moles, *Condylura cristata,* to dolphins. Such an exhibit would establish a feeling for comparative rhinology. It could be argued that we do not really need living animals to do any of this, that a film or videotape would serve as well, but these media severely diminish both the spectacle and the magnificence.

Of course there are many other themes that could be illustrated in the elephant house alone. Despite years as a professional biologist, I am enchanted by skeletal structures. The way limbs work is an exciting theme for an exhibit, which could include the mechanics of ponderous legs and a comparison of elephants' legs with those of *Apatosaurus* or with those of extinct giant birds. Internally, the relative and absolute sizes of the elephant's vital organs could be compared with those of our own. If an elephant had a brain as proportionally large as our own, its head would have to be much, much bigger. This could be demonstrated most memorably by putting models next to the living animal.

The subject of flight suggests another impressive range of possibilities. Here comparisons among mammals, birds, and aircraft are clearly very instructive. Gliding flight has evolved in several families of mammals; true flight, only in bats. Variations in the aspect ratios of bats' wings parallel those that humans have designed to solve exactly the same functional problems. It would be relevant to put a model of an F16 next to an enclosure of fast-flying bats and a 747 next to the flying foxes.

Perhaps even more relevant to visitors' interests is some comparative physiology. Water conservation in mammals is just one example of a piece of physiology that can lead easily from the known to the unknown. Our omnipresent experiences as humans include urination, defecation, and perspiration. They govern our behavior in many ways and influence our architecture, both public and private. Perspiration has given rise to an enormous industry and massive advertising campaigns that no one escapes. The problems of desert animals in conserving water strongly affect each of these processes. Water conservation has become an important aspect of human planetary management. A comparison between our economies and those of camels, *Camelus* spp., and jerboas and gerbils, could be a significant one. Comparative volumes of urine outputs, comparative fecal viscosities, and sweat volume comparisons all touch a chord in our own awareness of bodily functions. One might even imagine a display of fecal volumes, balanced for body weight comparisons, inspiring some interest!

Even more directly relevant to a large number of zoo visitors is the physiology of pregnancy, parturition, lactation, and the rearing of young. Mothers and offspring figure prominently in our audience. What we share exclusively with our fellow mammals can be epitomized in our curiosity about our style of reproduction. Questions like, How long does it take? How is the baby born? Where are the breasts? How long to weaning? Do animals need toilet training? and even, How do you know the panda is pregnant? all spring to our audiences' minds. These natural (no pun intended) focuses of interest are seldom exploited. We can educate this way, and we should. Fortunately prudery is gone forever and we can be explicit about life's major processes—perhaps not yet about animal sex organs and copulations, but certainly about family life and care.

Milk and lactation can illustrate just one aspect of a BioPark approach to these subjects. The milk composition of animals varies considerably and reflects the evolutionary pressures of different ecologies and lifestyles (Oftedal and Tedman 1987; Oftedal and Jenness 1988). The difference between cow's milk and human milk should be well known, but isn't. By comparison, the difference between those relatively dilute milks and the supergrowth qualities of hooded seal, *Cystophora cristata*, milk is startling. Imagine being able to wean a baby that is larger than a human child at weaning after only a few days (Bowen, Oftedal, and Boness 1985)! Pumping "high-octane" milk in large volumes is an adaptation that makes sense, and its existence is an interesting fact that is more than a trivial pursuit. Models in the form of old-fashioned milk bottles comparing mammal milks for cream, water, carbohydrate, and protein content could be a dazzling display. So could a "Find the Nipple" game, with visitors marking their quiz cards as they walked through the mammal exhibits. We could also explain that we do urinalysis for zoo mammals in a fundamentally similar way to human pregnancy testing. The prospects here are endless.

Certainly we should also raise the theme of juvenile dependence. The extended period of dependence in humans is, arguably, one of the foundations of our species' ascendancy. This is a fact seldom adumbrated outside the exclusive circle of evolutionary biologists and zoologists. "Life with Mother" graphs, standardized to life span years as a common unit, would be a striking feature in a mammal exhibit. So would details of the proportion of life devoted to reproductive readiness.

ADAPTIVE COLORATION

One of the striking characteristics of most mammals is that they are covered with hair, fur, or wool that is colored in various patterns. Coloration can range from straight background-matching camouflage to very complex patterns. There are clearly a number of exciting questions to be raised about the adaptive functions of coloration. For instance, what about the odd assortment of black-and-white mammals? Giant pandas, colobus monkeys, *Colobus* spp., skunks, Malayan tapirs, *Tapirus indicus*, zebras, *Equus* spp., and ruffed lemurs, *Varecia variegata*, are strikingly black-and-white. Is there a general explanation? The differences between the sexes in coloration and between adult and juvenile stages all provide a basis for teaching biology.

PRIMATE EXHIBITS AND ANTHROPOLOGY

Because the boundary between biology and anthropology is blurred, and the overlap between these fields is probably even greater than that between experimental psychology and ethology, the BioPark could readily deal with humans' place in nature (to paraphrase Sir Arthur Sherrington). In most zoos there is a Great Ape House, which is the ideal setting for a Hall of Humankind. The exhibit could illustrate with direct comparisons our affinities with the great apes, including a display on anatomy and molecular genetics. We could use models to map out the stages of human ancestry since we diverged from the great apes. One of the most effective devices I have seen to illustrate some striking differences between humans and gorillas, *Gorilla gorilla*, is a sport jacket tailored to fit an adult male gorilla. When a zoo visitor tries it on, the differences in chest expansion and arm length become immediately and laughably obvious. An exhibit devoted to human evolution could emphasize language, tool use, and self-identification as well as showing some examples of these aspects of ape behavior, including attempts to teach apes sign language.

ETHOLOGY AND MAMMAL EXHIBITS

The subject of animal behavior studies and their place in biology can be dealt with by any existing zoo without its being transformed into a BioPark. But this is rarely done to any extent beyond dealing with the communicative aspects of behavior. This usually means signs showing the facial and body expressions of wolves, *Canis lupus*, and the displays of prairie dogs, *Cynomys* spp. These are often well done, informative, and even exciting, but it all usually stops there. Asking questions about the perceptual world of animals could be crucially important in shaping our attitudes toward animals, but this is seldom attempted. It is clear that many zoo visitors are anthropomorphic in their attitudes toward animals, which can cloud their judgment on issues of animal welfare. Perhaps much worse are the visitors with what Steve Kellert (1980) has labeled a "dominionistic" attitude. Unfortunately, we reinforce these attitudes by presenting visitors with a human-dominated picture of the world.

Increasingly throughout the zoo world, we design and build exhibits to be naturalistic. But "naturalistic" means natural-looking through our eyes, at our scale and viewpoint, within the limitations of our perceptions. This is unfortunate, since we now know enough of the sensory and perceptual worlds of many animals to present a cat's, wolf's, or deer's-eye view of the world. The Hollywood trick of presenting the familiar world as if we were shrunk to the size of a cat or mouse needs to be applied to zoo exhibits, along with a different color balance or a black-and-white viewpoint. Objects that are close or far away could be blurred according to what we know of distance vision in the animal involved. A further step would be to give emphasis to the objects that the species in question finds particularly relevant in its "umwelt." All this would help to place a species in its own world and not in a confused version of our world.

This kind of knowledge is probably the only solid foundation for developing logically humane attitudes toward animals. It is particularly important with respect to our attitudes toward mammals, since consciously, and often in a totally unsophisticated way, we identify more with them than with birds, reptiles, amphibians, or fishes. In my experience, letters complaining about zoo conditions are overwhelmingly concentrated on mammals, rarely about birds, and seldom about any other vertebrates. I have never known anyone to complain that a snake enclosure is too small and that the animals are bored or stressed. It is mammal-based anthropomorphisms that abound.

One aspect of the perceptual world of most mammals that we rarely appreciate is their world of odors. Nearly all our relatives, near and far, are basically macrosmatic. Our sense of smell, by contrast, is relatively poor and has probably deteriorated in the course of our civilizing process. Since many mammals have both conspicuous scent glands and equally conspicuous scent-marking behavior, mammal exhibits should be a perfect place to highlight odor communication (birds, reptiles, and amphibians, by contrast, show little such behavior). At the simplest level this odor exhibitry could range from emphasizing urine marking "flags" in cat exhibits to providing suitable small posts for musk deer, *Moschus* spp., to mark with their infraorbital glands. We normally assiduously scrub off the salt crystals that accumulate where the big cats scent-mark with urine; on the contrary, we should signpost them.

Many natural history museums have exhibitions in this respect; several have odor exhibits where one can test one's nose on the "perfumes" of beavers (castorin), musk-producing mammals, civets (civetone), and skunks. To this list we could add polecats, otters, maned wolves, *Chrysocyon brachyurus,* and many others. Even our close relatives, the gorillas, have a powerful body odor. Every time I watch visitors entering our elephant house I am struck by their tendency to react negatively to the smell, despite our high standards of hygiene. The smell is wholly natural and should not be offensive; the reaction is probably culturally conditioned. We have reduced our own natural odors with cosmetic compounds, and people who have never been in a cattle shed, stable, or barnyard have lived in an unnaturally odor-depleted world. Of course, when we are dealing with the functions of scents in mammals, we should spread our intellectual net to discuss tracker and drug-sniffing dogs, truffle-hunting pigs, and the functions of floral odors.

We certainly need to encourage visitors to be concerned about all life on earth. Primitive attitudes, not necessarily culturally acquired but perhaps atavistic, condemn some animals to be regarded as ugly, mean, or otherwise repellent. This is true not just of snakes, spiders, scorpions, and many "bugs," but also of some mammals. Our unscientific classifications of repellent creatures, including predators and scavengers, need great revision if we are to become real custodians of life on earth. We need to make heroes of weasels as well as pandas, of bats as well as bears. Developing humane attitudes toward plants will be even more difficult, as even the most extreme proponents of "animal liberation" propose that we should continue to kill and eat plants.

MAMMALS AND HUMANS

Throughout our history as a species humans have reacted to animals as sources of high-quality protein, clothing and materials for building shelters, and teeth and bone for tools. We have spent at least 99% of our existence as hunter-gatherers, and even after the Neolithic revolution and the beginnings of civilization, a substantial proportion of us remained hunter-gatherers. (It is said that 2,000 years ago about half of all humans were still hunter-gatherers.) This long period during which we were, ecologically speaking, merely upright and virtually naked omnivorous mammals, dependent on the natural carrying capacity of the environment, has left its mark on our culture. Much of the art and ceremony of hunter-gatherers relates to "the other mammals in their lives." Prehistoric art concentrates on mammals. Other vertebrates crop up in the art of desert and desert-fringe dwellers, but in general, mammals predominate. This art should be represented next to the living animals in mammal collections as a reminder of our ancient dependencies. It includes not only rock art, petroglyphs, and carvings, but also dance masks and metal objects. In fact, the tradition continues all the way through to relatively recent Oriental watercolors.

Even more striking is the dependence of the process of civilization on the two great Neolithic biological "discoveries": domestication and cultivation. Both involved genetic engineering by selection; domestication clearly involved behavioral manipulation as well (Price 1984; Clutton-Brock 1981, 1989). The list of domesticates and cultivars constitutes a tiny fraction of the species that were available at the human/natural world interface. For domestication as "walking larders," mammals were predominant. As hunting companions, guards, and rodenticides, mammals again were predominant. Information about domestication belongs in every BioPark. (Cultivation deserves an even more prominent place!) The domestic breeds of dogs are an admirably explicit example of selection's effects. How we used and continue to use the dog's predatory behavior makes a great story; I would like to see a sheepdog exhibit in every BioPark. Animals that were not chosen for domestication provide an interesting lesson in the characters of preadaptation. Cheetahs, *Acinonyx jubatus*, which are marvelous exhibits, were candidates for domestication, as Egyptian art shows us again and again. Can we explain why they never made the grade, and the broader lesson of that failure?

The prospect of integrating the BioPark with art collections from galleries and museums and with materials from anthropological exhibits is greatest at this point in our culture where humans and mammals meet. Somewhere in this story belongs the story of the history of zoos. In the zoo profession we talk and write papers about the history of zoos, but seldom exhibit our own evolution. The progress made since the first edition of Crandall (1964) deserves an exhibit to illustrate our increasing awareness of the needs of "wild mammals in captivity." We should preserve, somewhere in the future BioPark, a white-tiled "public urinal style" cage as an awful example of what once was. My own view is that it should be presented in the context of what was the low-income standard of human habitation during that period of zoo design. Slums and Victorian zoos were contemporaries. There is some powerful human social history to be taught alongside the history of bioexhibits.

* * *

Most of the examples detailed in the sections above are not original, and they are certainly not innovative, but this approach to exhibiting mammals in zoos as a basis for a whole range of holistic biological lessons has never been consistently applied. If zoos are to become the basis of information transfer, we will have to be consistently biological.

REFERENCES

Bowen, W. D., Oftedal, O. T., and Boness, D. J. 1985. Birth to weaning in four days: Remarkable growth in the hooded seal, *Cystophora cristata. Can. J. Zool.* 63:2841–46.

Boyden, S. 1969. The concept of a biological centre. *Int. Zoo Yrbk.* 9:199–201.

Clutton-Brock, J. 1981. *Domesticated animals from early times.* London: British Museum (NH) and Heinemann.

———. 1989. *The walking larder: Patterns of domestication, pastoralism, and predation.* London: Unwin Hyman.

Crandall, L. S. 1964. *The management of wild mammals in captivity.* Chicago and London: University of Chicago Press.

Dinerstein, E., and Wemmer, C. M. 1988. Fruits rhinoceros eat: Dispersal of *Trewia nudifolia* (Euphorbiaceae) in lowland Nepal. *Ecology* 69:1768–74.

Kellert, S. 1980. *Public attitudes toward critical wildlife and natural habitat issues.* 0234-101-00-623-4. Washington, D.C.: U.S. Government Printing Office.

Kranz, K. 1982. A note on the tail hairs from a pigmy hippopotamus *(Choeropsis liberiensis). Zoo Biol.* 1:237–41.

Oftedal, O. T., and Jenness, R. 1988. Interspecific variation in milk composition among horses, zebras, and asses (Perissodactyla: Equidae). *J. Dairy Res.* 55:57–66.

Oftedal, O. T., and Tedman, R. A. 1987. The behavior, physiology, and anatomy of lactation in the Pinnipedia. 1:175–245.

Price, E. O. 1984. Behavioral aspects of animal domestication. *Q. Rev. Biol.* 59:1–32.

Rand, A. S., and Robinson, M. H. 1969. Predation of iguana nests. *Herpetologia* 25:172–74.

Robinson, M. H. 1988. Bioscience education through bioparks. *BioScience* 38 (9): 630–34.

Tinbergen, N. 1972. *The animal in its world.* London: George Allen and Unwin.

16

What's the Message? Education through Exhibit Design

JON CHARLES COE

*Despite excellent intentions, even the best zoos may be creating animal stereotypes that are
not only incorrect, but that actually work against the interests of wildlife preservation. . . .
The sight of caged animals does not engender respect for animals.*

(SOMMER 1972)

*Unfortunately, the incarceration and exhibition of animals in zoos can perversely increase the sense of human
separation and alienation from wild animals, encouraging feelings of superiority and unalterable difference.
Somehow these barriers need to be diminished and a sensitive focus on the ways in which our
species destiny is inextricably linked with the welfare of nonhuman animals could help.
In addition, it would be advisable to accelerate the trend toward naturalistic exhibitry.*

(KELLERT 1986)

Why consider exhibit design in a volume about captive mammals? More than anything else, exhibits are a zoo's (or aquarium's) natural voice, the best means to communicate to the public our message about the animals that are so important to us. But we have often presented the wrong message.

We have a large audience and, collectively, a large voice. The American Association of Zoological Parks and Aquariums (AAZPA) estimated that 104 million people visited member institutions in 1991 (AAZPA 1992). These visitors represent 104 million educational opportunities. Assuming that each visitor spends 2 hours at a facility, and that communication at some level (conscious or subconscious) is possible every minute, then we could have over 12 billion communication opportunities in only a year! And these are direct, real-life experiences not reduced to television. The potential for zoos to teach people about wildlife and, more importantly, to create a vivid personal experience of wildlife is unparalleled.

Exhibit construction and renovation also represents a major investment of capital and time. *USA Today* estimated that in 1993 North American zoos and aquariums would spend $1.2 billion on capital improvements, a threefold increase over the previous decade (Jones 1993). This sum is considerably higher than the AAZPA calculation. Whatever the actual figure, however, the portion of that investment going into mammal displays is very significant.

Since the subject of this volume is wild mammals, I will focus on exhibitry techniques for this group and will generalize about most other groups. Also, I will concentrate on exhibit design as experienced by viewers; animal concerns and requirements are discussed elsewhere in this volume. For sources of specific information on the design and evaluation of educational materials (especially materials oriented to cognitive learning) and for exhibit design information beyond the scope of this chapter, see the reference list at the conclusion of the chapter.

This chapter will address exhibit design in a holistic manner with emphasis on those features believed to enhance affective learning and appreciation. Unfortunately, this area is not well understood and is under-studied. Yet these factors may be at the heart of the sentiments above expressed by Sommer and Kellert. While quantitative evaluations lag far behind applications, exhibits that attempt to immerse visitors in the exhibit setting are being built and opened at an accelerating rate across the United States. They are gaining enormous public acceptance as well as peer awards. It is my goal to discuss the basic premises behind these and other

FIG. 16.1.   Visitors observing gorillas at Zoo Atlanta. This exhibit was modeled to simulate an encounter with gorillas in the wild. (Photo by Jon Coe 1993.)

exhibit approaches so that zoo professionals can make informed choices based on their professional and institutional needs rather than blindly copying changing styles. I will also discuss an integrative design process to help realize the best options available.

PRESENTATION AND PERCEPTION

Can context affect perception? Imagine seeing a leopard pacing in a smelly, rusty cage in a room with peeling paint. In contrast, imagine observing the same leopard lying peacefully high in a thorn tree overlooking the Serengeti plain. Our feelings at the latter site would undoubtedly be excitement, awe, and wonder. We might pay a great deal of money for such an experience, although I doubt if we would pay much to participate in the former scenario.

Let us first define some useful terms:

Context: Exhibit viewers' perceptual surroundings. This includes everything that exhibit viewers perceive while experiencing an exhibit.

Content: The intended communication. Basically, this is what interpretive signs say. It is the information that the zoo or aquarium wants visitors to perceive, understand, and remember.

Message: The actual communication received and remembered by zoo visitors. This consists of the (cognitive) information, concepts, or ideas that the visitor gleans from the actual interpretive information, filtered through the (affective) context of the setting and the distractions, prejudices, or attitudes of the visitors themselves.

The message that counts most is the one visitors remember. If we, as designers, were first to select the message we wanted remembered, what sort of exhibit would we wrap around this message to convey it as memorably as possible?

Let's look at some examples of how context, content, and message interact. In older facilities, the implicit message of the barred cages may be that the incarcerated animals are dangerous felons. If there is an odor, the public might think the animals are unclean and uncouth. These assumptions would mislead them about the true character of the species exhibited. Even attractive remedial graphics would probably be overwhelmed by the contrary message signaled by an appalling exhibit context.

Now let's imagine a visitor walking along the pathway of a typical modern, "naturalistic" or "barless" zoological exhibit. The shrubs are neatly sheared. The public is watching bears against a setting of artificial rockwork, separated from them by a large, obvious moat. The whole setting (context) seems very safe, familiar, and predictable.

Now imagine a very different exhibit context. Visitors walk along narrow pathways through a rugged, wild-looking landscape of overhanging trees and dense herbaceous growth, immersed in a simulation of the animals' natural habitat. They look across invisible barriers to see a family of gorillas feeding in the shade of a large tree (fig. 16.1). The animals totally dominate the encounter. We have observed visitors in this context speaking in hushed voices. One rarely hears the rude, disrespectful comments commonly heard in front of older-style great ape exhibits (Hutchins, Hancocks, and Crockett 1984).

ZOO EXHIBIT STYLES

Precedents

Most early captive animal exhibits, whether public menageries and circuses or royal collections, were displays of human power over nature (Fisher 1967). Linnaeus's *Systema Naturae* reinforced this stereotype by isolating specimens from their natural context. This human-dominated or homocentric approach is in fact still the dominant form of animal exhibition today. Yet how can we convince the public of

FIG. 16.2.   The design innovations of the Hagenbeck family are many, but perhaps their vast multispecies panoramas such as this one at the Stellingen Zoo are best remembered. (Photo courtesy of Paul Joslin.)

the importance of wild habitat conservation when the primary message they receive from us is that "wild animals live at the zoo?"

In 1907, Carl Hagenbeck (1909) revolutionized the ways in which zoos presented wild animals. Hagenbeck's innovations in moat design are discussed by Hancocks (chap. 19, this volume). His dramatic panoramas, often showing predator/prey juxtapositions, are widely celebrated. These exhibits were also complex designs with overlapping sight lines that allowed visitors to move among the dramatic landscapes in coordinated visual sequences (fig. 16.2). These innovations are fundamental to modern "immersion" exhibit design. Hagenbeck rejected the intellectual order of Linnaean collections. His appeal was visual, subjective, and enormously successful. His style, however, was based more on the romantic landscaping style of the time than on a desire to illustrate the animals' natural habitats, although he had traveled the world on collecting trips.

The Hagenbeck family's work was so widely copied that, unfortunately, many of their substantive innovations became trivialized or lost. The Hagenbeck family were responsible for the precedents of many concepts being rediscovered by zoos today, including integrated master planning, ethnocultural displays, marketing and visitor service innovations, and advances in animal management and training (Coe 1995b).

Modernist Styles

The influence of the modernist movement on zoos began in the 1930s and is still important (Hancocks 1971). Modernist architects viewed buildings as "machines for living." Technological advances in industrialized nations led to the view that technology and science could provide for all human (and animal) needs. The resulting hard-edged exhibits, while extending longevity, also presented the animals as subordinate to an insensitive, machine-like type of care,

however untrue this may actually have been (Coe 1986). Architecture continued to define the context within which animals were seen. When modern art and architecture were combined, animals were sometimes presented as living inside a modern sculpture (fig. 16.3).

Modernism (sometimes thought of today as "functionalism") is still a widely used approach to animal exhibitry and is almost universally the style of choice in nonpublic areas of zoos and aquariums. The Lester Fisher Great Ape House at Lincoln Park Zoo is an excellent example of this approach used properly. Exhibit features function as artificial analogues to natural counterparts even though they make no attempt to look natural. Apparently, the exhibits are well liked by the public and well used by the great apes. What a shame that no one has studied the effect this exhibit has on public attitudes compared with the other great ape and landscape immersion exhibits that are discussed later.

High-Technology Exhibits

High-technology features are found in many new zoos and aquariums. Large graphic images, neon lights, and interactive gadgets share the contextual realm with the animals exhibited at the St. Louis Zoo's Living World. Such elements become attractions in their own right as well as contributing collectively to an overall high-tech and thus homocentric ambience. This atmosphere can be exciting and familiar to a generation that receives most of its information and entertainment from television. However, rapid technological advances make obsolescence a problem.

When used on a small scale, high-tech appliances such as binocular microscopes and plastic models of digestive systems can be useful interpretive aids. Also, many features of landscape immersion exhibits depend on advanced technology. Realistic artificial rocks and trees made of gunite, fiberglass, and epoxy, subtle sound systems, and huge curved aquarium windows are examples of such technology. There-

FIG. 16.3.   This polar bear exhibit of the modernist style resembles a modern sculpture more than a wild animal habitat. (Photo by Jon Coe 1993.)

fore, the definition of the high-tech style is based on the ultimate appearance of the exhibit rather than the level of technology used to create it.

Hybrid Styles

Every zoo more than a generation old is probably a hybrid of many different styles. Some facilities were conceived as hybrids embodying features of museums, aquariums, and zoological parks.

While designers may argue eloquently about which exhibit design styles are best, most zoo professionals must also be concerned about the integration of older and newer styles. Many zoos have fine historic buildings that have been renovated with much more modern habitat exhibits inside. In other situations, historic buildings that are no longer suitable for animals have been converted to facilities to serve the public. Also, naturalistic exhibits can contain interpretive shelters that feature high-tech presentations. Success comes from integration of style and function over time.

Landscape Immersion and the New Naturalism

The concept of displaying wild animals in simulations of their natural habitats would seem so obvious as not to require a name, much less an explanation. Yet, until fifteen years ago (with exceptions such as the Arizona Sonora Desert Museum), the closest zoos came to natural habitat presentations was to display wildlife in simulations of human gardens with lawns, hedges, and flower beds. A countermovement away from homocentric styles in zoo exhibit design emerged in the 1970s (Jones, Coe, and Paulson 1976; Coe 1982, 1983, 1985, 1986). In this approach, the landscape dominates the architecture, and the animals appear to dominate the public. What allowed for this dramatic change? First, advances in parasite control made it possible to keep more species on natural substrates. Second, the popularity of field scientists such as George Schaller, Dian

Fossey, and Jane Goodall resulted in a flood of images of and information about wildlife in dramatic native habitats. Third, some visionary zoo directors endorsed the goal of highly naturalistic exhibits, although they did not have the technical skills to achieve it. Finally, a new generation of exhibit designers who were both landscape architects and conservationists redefined the common "exhibit with gorillas" to mean "natural landscape with gorillas." Instead of studying other zoos' gorilla exhibits, they set out to understand and re-create the landscape in which gorillas are naturally found (Jones, Coe, and Paulson 1976). This biocentric perspective places the visitor in the gorillas' habitat, not the other way around—a substantial philosophical leap from the older homocentric models that had dominated animal displays for 4,000 years. This increasing interest in highly realistic exhibits also supported a virtual revolution in exhibit fabrication technology.

In landscape (or habitat) immersion exhibits, the zoo becomes a series of "mini-safaris." The visitor "leaves" the familiar grounds of an urban park called a "zoological garden" and becomes "immersed" in the simulated habitat of the animals, separated from them by invisible barriers. Every effort is made to remove or obscure contradictory elements such as buildings, service vehicles, large crowds of people, or anything that would detract from the image or experience of actually being in the wilderness.

The landscape immersion approach depends heavily upon plantings and has given substantial impetus to the new profession of "zoo horticulture" (Coe 1983). With proper design and horticultural maintenance, exhibits improve over time as plantings grow, rather than deteriorating with age as buildings do. Since landscape immersion exhibits appear to be works of nature, they may be as resistant to stylistic obsolescence as wildlife displays.

What is the difference between immersion exhibits and the "naturalistic" exhibits that date back to Hagenbeck's time? Exhibits that feature artificial rockwork and general-ized plantings are often termed "naturalistic" in contrast to architectural enclosures of bars and bare walls. "Natural habitat" exhibits attempt to realistically re-create specific animal habitats. However, as in museum dioramas, the viewer is often outside this setting and in a totally different context, such as a museum hall or park. "Immersion" ex-hibits not only attempt to re-create the specific look and feel of the animals' habitats, but to place the viewer in the habi-tats as well. As these highly realistic exhibits become more common, the more generic term "naturalistic" is often ap-plied to them as well.

GUIDELINES FOR THE CREATION OF LANDSCAPE IMMERSION EXHIBITS

I have attempted to develop an approach to the design of plant and animal exhibits that uses aspects of human be-havior to predispose visitors to respect animals and habi-tats. While these concepts are more fully developed else-where (Coe 1985), they result in the following practical steps (Jones 1982):

1. Invent an exhibit scenario that fully describes the exhibit context, just as a cinematic or theatrical scenario sets the scene for a performance. The scenario should establish the place being re-created in terms of geography, geology, bioregion, and habitat. There may also be a cultural context, such as a research station, national park shelter, safari camp, or even a shipwreck on the Skeleton Coast.
2. Immerse the visitors in the scenario, whether it is in-tended to simulate a natural landscape or a cultural setting.
3. Conceal all features that distract from the exhibit sce-nario, such as barriers and service buildings. Essential ob-jects such as viewing windows, railings, and interpretive features must be designed to fit believably within the scenario.
4. Design the exhibit in such ways that the animals appear to dominate the scene. Always present the animals re-spectfully if you expect visitors to treat them respectfully. Try to avoid creating situations in which the public looks down on the animals. If possible, place the animals higher than the visitors.
5. Control views so that visitors can never see the entire ani-mal area. Clever use of views and sight lines can make the animals' areas look limitless by "borrowing" appropriate distant landscapes as exhibit backdrops.
6. Integrate many types of habitat-appropriate species of animals and plants, creating as complete as possible an experience of the replicated habitat.

While these specific concepts were first put into practice at the Woodland Park Zoo, similar approaches were devel-oped (without supporting theoretical discussions) at the Arizona Sonora Desert Museum, Chicago's Brookfield Zoo, and the North Carolina Zoological Park. In fact, the Afri-can plains panorama at the then Bronx Zoo beautifully em-bodied most of these concepts as early as 1941 (Bridges 1966). More recently, "immersion" exhibits such as Jungle World, Himalayan Highlands, and Ethiopian Highlands at the Bronx Zoo/Wildlife Conservation Park, Ford African Rainforest and other exhibits at Zoo Atlanta, Amazonia at the National Zoological Park, Tiger River and other new exhibits at the San Diego Zoo, Brookfield Zoo's Habitat Af-rica, and Busch Gardens' Myombe Reserve, to name only a few recent examples, have followed this approach. Each institution has reinterpreted the concept with its own team of talented designers and staff to suit its own site and pro-gram requirements. The immersion approach has long since grown beyond the domain of any one group of designers or institutions. Even aquariums are minimizing the perceptual barriers between aquatic and terrestrial worlds with im-mense viewing windows and transparent tubes that allow visitors to walk through aquatic habitats. The Sea Cliffs ex-hibit at the Aquarium Wildlife Conservation Center is a fine example of this approach with marine mammals.

Popular as they have become, these super-naturalistic exhibits are not without faults. Controversy continues be-tween the supporters of "naturalistic" and of more "func-tional" approaches to design (Forthman-Quick 1984). De-tractors claim that animals in naturalistic exhibits are too difficult to see or too far away from viewers, and that con-venient artificial behavioral enrichment devices cannot be used because they do not look "natural" enough. Closer in-spection shows, however, that these problems usually result from specific design faults rather than failings inherent in the approach, and that much more "naturalistic" enrich-ment devices can usually be found. It must also be under-stood that there can be better or worse design solutions in any style.

Others decry the high cost of immersion exhibits, claim-ing that "too much money is spent on window dressing." Immersion exhibits are not necessarily more expensive per unit area than other types of well-made exhibits; however, they do tend to be larger than traditional exhibits. Indeed, the costs of all types of exhibits vary greatly and have risen rapidly in the last two decades.

Research Supporting Immersion Exhibits
While there is a growing body of literature on museum and graphic exhibit evaluation, there has been surprisingly little published work on the evaluation of animal exhibits in zoos and aquariums from an educational perspective. In addi-tion, many studies use very indirect or overly simplified methods, usually with predictably ambiguous results. How-ever, some recent work seems to support the growing move-ment toward highly realistic and immersion exhibits.

A study by Finlay, James, and Maple (1988) using both laboratory and field techniques confirmed the earlier labo-ratory findings of Rhoads and Goldsworthy (1979; cited in Finlay, James, and Maple 1988) that "an animal's environ-ment has a significant effect upon the characteristics which are attributed to the animal." Finlay concludes:

> Designers must lessen the perceptual clues that remind people that they are in a zoo. The findings of this study sup-ports Coe's (1985) argument that to be maximally effective the perceptual context created must be totally free of contra-dictory clues, such as obviously man-made barriers. This notion is at the heart of the concept of "landscape immer-sion." (Jones, Coe, and Paulson 1976)

In a parallel unpublished preference study conducted by Birney in 1989, visitors clearly ranked photos of naturalistic zoo exhibits as preferable to those of modernist exhibits (B. Birney, pers. comm.).

While these studies evaluated some of the premises of the landscape immersion approach, others have focused on the overall educational effectiveness of three exhibits considered state-of-the-art by present standards. Balan, Clinesmith, and Lang (1988) prepared a thorough evaluation of the Tiger River exhibit at the San Diego Zoo that considered both the exhibit graphics and the overall immersion exhibit itself. Of the 100 individuals or groups surveyed, "25% learned of the need to conserve the resources, plants, animals and beauty of rainforests," and 66% suggested a type of action when asked what could be done to conserve rainforests. Overall, 100% of respondents rated the effects and atmosphere good or very good, and 65% correctly identified that the exhibit was about rainforests. One hundred percent said they would revisit Tiger River. The authors concluded that Tiger River met both the cognitive and affective objectives established when the exhibit was being designed.

The San Diego Zoo also installed an innovative interactive environmental sound system in its new gorilla exhibit that was shown to improve the immersion experience of visitors who were not even consciously aware of its presence (Ogden and Lindburg 1991).

Perhaps the most extensive analysis of a highly realistic immersion exhibit was carried out by Bronwyn and Ford (1991). The survey results were obtained from questionnaires completed by 1,614 students visiting old or new gorilla exhibits at the Melbourne Zoo. Although attitudes and interests varied with age, the results suggest that the immersion exhibit helped students to appreciate ecological processes, enabling them to generalize about the animal as part of a community and appreciate the need for habitat preservation. The naturalistic enclosure also "positively affected the students' perceived value of the study of wild gorillas" and "their personal commitment to conservation" compared with the older, barren exhibit. Also, "students who saw the gorillas in the naturalistic enclosure were more positive in their attitudes to the zoo" (Bronwyn and Ford 1991).

While these results support the educational value of immersion exhibits, there is clearly a fertile field for additional work on both the theoretical basis for and practical value of these multidimensional exhibits.

Suggested Design Process

Design projects often fail to meet expectations because of a lack of understanding of and support for the design approach taken. Why? Because a broad consensus was not established to support it. Often there is little integration of exhibits. In addition, there is little integration of the roles of the people involved: animal managers, public service staff, educators, grounds and facilities staff, and designers. The design process itself may be the key to integrating these roles (Shettel-Neuber 1985).

Let's consider a design process that integrates all elements with a stake in the project. This process begins with a series of workshops. Workshop technology has advanced greatly, and experienced facilitators know how to bring people together and develop a consensus. The workshop process moves through the steps in the design and development process in a way that everyone can understand. It allows the full participation of all interested parties and maintains a record of all issues considered. The process encourages group and individual accountability and responsibility. It develops a shared sense of authorship and encourages a support constituency for the concepts that are selected. This process can accommodate large or small groups and can be done in-house. If the project is complex, it is best to bring in a professional facilitator who really understands how to make the system work.

Whether a design process applies to the planning of an entirely new zoo or aquarium or only to the detailed design and fabrication of some small interpretive unit, the process is basically the same. The first step is for the group to define the goals and objectives they wish to achieve. They should begin with institution-wide goals, establishing and clarifying the most important things that the facility has to say to its public—its "message." Where does the institution hope to be in ten or twenty years? What major national and international trends will affect its success? What are the goals and objectives of its subareas, including the proposed exhibit or facility? How does the project fit in with other institutions in the area? How do nearby exhibits integrate with the proposed project? What exactly *is* the proposed exhibit or project? The definition of the problem is 80% of the solution. The project definition, sometimes called the "scope," the construction budget, and the project schedule must be carefully integrated and should all be established at the same time.

Next, the primary theme or scenario for the exhibit is selected. There can also be several secondary and tertiary themes, which may parallel the primary theme or weave tangentially into it to add enrichment, complexity, and interest or to make points not clearly stated in the primary theme.

The selection of the exhibit style follows. Which approach best tells our story? Which most clearly establishes a context for the message we want the public to take with them and remember years from now? The design style selected could be familiar or totally original to the project. However, do not seek originality for its own sake, nor let conservatism keep you from going in an unfamiliar direction. Remember, the ultimate goal is to communicate a message.

As the design evolves, the group should ask, How does the public approach the exhibit? What transitional elements exist? How does the design of public viewing areas support the public's understanding of the message and the theme? What about the other areas within the exhibit context, the foreground, background, and transitional areas? Do they also support the message, or do distracting elements undermine the concept that we are trying to transmit? Does the exhibit experience have a clear beginning and a dramatic ending, and does it make that story relevant to the public?

Just as the design process must integrate all the different people who have responsibility within a project, so must the design integrate all of the elements within the project with the message that you wish to give. All areas must be integrated both aesthetically and functionally, including public areas, animal exhibit areas, off-exhibit and service areas, and support structures such as buildings and utilities. How will time and use affect the exhibit? Will the message be strengthened? How will operations, maintenance, and future programs affect it? It is my experience that the effectiveness of many new exhibits is limited because they are maintained in old ways. Design philosophy and management philosophy must support each other (Coe 1993).

Interpretation

Once an exhibit concept has been developed, how are the messages implicit in the design made explicit? There is a wide range of choices. At the most direct level there is the guide interpreter. Wolf and Tymitz (1979) have found that this kind of interaction establishes the strongest and most lasting impressions on the public. There are also self-guided tours, in which visitors are provided with guidebooks, audiocassettes, or other keys that explain what they are seeing as they go. There must be enough information provided to interpret the exhibit, yet graphic panels must not be so large or so conspicuous that they detract from the exhibits themselves. Birney (1982) found that animal exhibits with both graphic interpretation and narration by a guide were more effective in visitor education than animal exhibits with or without graphics alone. Sometimes additional kinds of support, such as sound (Ogden and Lindburg 1991) and video, are provided. These can be very effective because they give the public something active to experience if the animals happen to be inactive. Monitors and similar appliances must be designed and located in such a way that they neither contrast adversely with the exhibit nor encourage visitors to congest circulation lanes or block the views of other people. Medium- or high-tech interactive devices have great teaching potential, but designers must be sure that the activity generated around these facilities does not distract from the exhibit message and that staff can provide the technical maintenance required.

Evaluation

How is the finished exhibit to be evaluated? Cognitive and affective objectives must be clearly established early in the design process. The finished project should be measured against these objectives after opening and over time. How successfully does the exhibit meet the needs of animals and staff? How effectively does it communicate to the public? Informal evaluation is relatively simple, but the findings may be fragmentary and misleading. More scientific methods of evaluation should also be used, and such evaluations should be conducted by qualified, impartial researchers using techniques of greater or lesser sophistication depending on the information that is desired.

Screven (1988, 1990) argues persuasively that informational and interpretive graphics should be mocked up and tested in place (formative evaluation) before expensive, permanent graphics are produced and installed. Others suggest that multiple sets of graphics featuring various themes should be alternated to maintain the interest of repeat visitors.

Certainly the price of new exhibits and the rate at which they are being constructed justifies the expenditure of modest sums for far more research into the effectiveness of existing exhibits and how and why some exhibits fail.

Modification and Improvement

As those who have worked at zoos and aquariums know, a design project does not end on opening day; it only begins. Modification and improvement after opening should be expected and planned for in advance. We must evaluate and modify in order to learn how to plan better exhibits. We must also experiment with the design process used in order to bring about better results in the future.

CONCLUSIONS

Educational considerations in the design of facilities are paramount if we are to carry out our intentions effectively. We must clearly identify our messages and objectives and establish a supportive context in which the public will receive those messages through the exhibits they experience. We must break through the insensitivity of many urban visitors in ways they enjoy and find memorable and that encourage them to return. We must use our voice to empower and to activate. We must develop a methodology that will enable the appropriate staff to be involved in the design, implementation, and evaluation of our projects. We must support a comprehensive view, one that integrates all of these goals with the myriad other events that are going on around the zoo and which are important to its success. This comprehensive view must look beyond temporary considerations of style toward zoo exhibits that are more aesthetically, educationally, and operationally successful.

REFERENCES

AAZPA. 1992. *Zoos and aquariums in the Americas.* 50. Wheeling, W.Va.: American Association of Zoological Parks and Aquariums.

Balan, P., Clinesmith, S., and Lang, G. 1988. San Diego Zoo Tiger River evaluation report. Prepared for San Diego Zoo Education Department, San Diego, Calif.

Birney, B. A. 1982. Dosage versus distribution: The support of docents on zoo visitor's acquisition of knowledge. *AAZPA Annual Conference Proceedings,* 275–91. Wheeling, W.Va.: American Association of Zoological Parks and Aquariums.

Bitgood, S. 1987. Selected bibliography on exhibit design and evaluation in zoos. *Visitor Behavior* 2 (1): 8. Psychology Institute, Jacksonville State University, Ala.

Bitgood, S. 1990. The role of simulated immersion in exhibition. Technical Report no. 90–20. Center for Social Design, P. O. Box 111, Jacksonville, Ala. 36265.

Bitgood, S., and Patterson, D. 1987. Principles of exhibit design. *Visitor Behavior* 2 (1): 4–6. Psychology Institute, Jacksonville State University, Ala.

Bitgood, S., Patterson, D., and Benefield, A. 1986. "Understanding your visitors: Ten factors that influence visitor behavior. *AAZPA Annual Conference Proceedings* 726–43. Wheeling, W.Va.: American Association of Zoological Parks and Aquariums.

Bridges, W. 1966. *Gathering of animals: An unconventional history of the New York Zoological Society.* New York: Harper & Row.

Bronwyn, B., and Ford, J. C. 1991. Environmental enrichment in zoos: Melbourne Zoo's naturalistic approach. *Thylacinus* 16 (1): 12–17.

Coe, Jon C. 1982. "Bringing it all together: Integration of context, content, and message in zoo exhibit design. *AAZPA Annual Conference Proceedings*, 268–74. Wheeling, W.Va.: American Association of Zoological Parks and Aquariums.

———. 1983. A greensward for gorillas. *AAZPA Annual Conference Proceedings*, 117–21. Wheeling, W.Va.: American Association of Zoological Parks and Aquariums.

———. 1985. Design and perception: Making the zoo experience real. *Zoo Biol.* 4:197–208.

———. 1986. Towards a coevolution of zoos, aquariums and natural history museums. *AAZPA Annual Conference Proceedings*, 366–76. Wheeling, W.Va.: American Association of Zoological Parks and Aquariums.

———. 1995a. Environmental enrichment and facility design: Making it work. In *First Conference on Environmental Enrichment*, ed. D. Shepherdson, J. Mellen, and M. Hutchins. Washington, D.C.: Smithsonian Institution Press. In press.

———. 1995b. The evolution of zoo animal exhibits. In *The ark evolving: Zoos and aquariums in transition*, ed. C. Wemmer. Front Royal, Va.: Conservation and Research Center (Smithsonian Institution). In press.

Finlay, T., James, L., and Maple, T. 1988. Zoo environments influence people's perceptions of animals. *Environ. Behav.* 20 (4): 508–25.

Fisher, J. 1967. *Zoos of the world: The story of animals in captivity.* New York: Natural History Press.

Forthman-Quick, D. L. 1984. An integrative approach to environmental engineering in zoos. *Zoo Biol.* 3:65–78.

Hagenbeck, C. 1909. *Beasts and men: Being Carl Hagenbeck's experience for half a century among wild animals.* Translated by H. S. R. Elliot. New York: Longman Green.

Hancocks, D. 1971. *Animals and architecture.* London: Hugh Evelyn.

Hutchins, M., Hancocks, D., and Crockett, C. 1984. Natural solutions to the behavioral problems of captive animals. *Der Zoologische Garten* 54:28–42.

Jones, D. 1993. Wild kingdom competition grows fierce. *USA Today*, sect. B., 10 August.

Jones, G. 1982. Design principles for presentation of animals and nature. *AAZPA Annual Conference Proceedings*, 184–92. Wheeling, W.Va.: American Association of Zoological Parks and Aquariums.

Jones, G. R., Coe, J. C., and Paulson, D. R. 1976. *Woodland Park Zoo: Long range plan, development guidelines and exhibit scenarios.* Jones & Jones for Seattle Department of Parks and Recreation.

Kellert, S. 1986. The educational potential of the zoo and its visitor. Paper presented at Conference on Informal Learning in Zoos, Philadelphia Zoo, 26 September 1986.

Klein, L. 1986. *Exhibits: Planning and design.* New York: Madison Square Press.

Ogden, J. J., and Lindburg, D. G. 1991. "Do you hear what I hear?" The effect of auditory enrichment on zoo animals and visitors. *AAZPA Annual Conference Proceedings*, 428–35. Wheeling, W.Va.: American Association of Zoological Parks and Aquariums.

Ogden, J. J., Lindburg, D. G., and Maple, T. L. 1993. The effects of ecologically relevant sounds on zoo visitors. *Curator* 36: 147–56.

Screven, C. G. 1988. Teaching science to voluntary visitors and the role of evaluation. In *Science learning in the informal setting*, ed. P. Heltne and L. Marquardt, 230–39. Chicago: The Chicago Academy of Sciences.

———. 1990. Uses of evaluation before, during, and after exhibit designs. *ILVS Rev.* 1 (2): 33–66.

Serrell, B. 1983. Making exhibit labels, a step by step guide. Nashville, Tenn.: American Association for State and Local History.

Shettel-Neuber, J. 1985. The Whittier Southeast Asian exhibits: A post occupancy evaluation and comparison with older exhibits. Technical Report no. 86–80, Center for Social Design, Jacksonville, Ala.

Sommer, R. 1972. What do we learn at the zoo? *Mus. Hist.* 81 (7): 36.

Wolf, R., and Tymitz, B. 1979. "Do giraffes ever sit?" A study of visitor perceptions at the National Zoological Park. Prepared for the Smithsonian Institution, Washington, D.C.

17

Horticultural Philosophies in Zoo Exhibit Design

Donald W. Jackson

NATURALISTIC DESIGN CONCEPTS

A zoo horticulturist tends to see elephants, giraffes, and most other zoo animals in a slightly different light than does the typical zoo visitor. The trunks of elephants and long necks of giraffes, which make these animals such efficient browsers out on the hot, harsh plains of the Serengeti, also work surprisingly well at deftly plucking succulent leaves from the tree branches within their exhibits.

We wouldn't think of parking our cars beneath the dripline of a favorite shade tree at home. Ruts would soon develop, and the soil would quickly become so compacted as to hinder seriously the tree's growth and vitality. A full-grown rhino weighs a good bit more than most cars, and the tendency of these animals to rub against the tree's bark or browse the leaves simply adds to the compacting problem. Unlike rhinos, however, our cars do not also depend on the same trees to protect them from the hot summer sun or to give them a bit of privacy.

These scenarios represent real-life problems for the zoo horticulturist. Naturalistic exhibits obviously must be designed to successfully address plant-animal interactions while at the same time satisfying the often broad-ranging educational needs of the visiting public. We have a further responsibility, however, that is commonly neglected in even the most well-thought out exhibits in this country and abroad. Without question, few would disagree with the concept of simulating each animal's natural habitat as closely as possible. Unfortunately, zoo exhibits that could arguably be classed as "state of the art" in many other ways fail to truly develop this philosophy to its fullest potential.

The rigid design concepts associated with commercial or residential landscape architecture usually fail to immerse the zoo visitor in the most naturalistic setting possible. As a result, such designs seldom realize a cohesive and integrated exhibit space that fully meets the needs of the animal collection while at the same time paying adequate attention to the humanistic requirements of zoo patrons of all ages. While the large majority of our exhibits certainly are successful, incorporating landscape design as an integral part of exhibit planning can improve them.

Simulating a West African Rainforest

The thematic conceptualization and plant selection process for a West African lowland gorilla, *Gorilla gorilla gorilla*, exhibit can be used to illustrate this concept (Jackson 1990a). The leaves of plants indigenous to West Africa tend to have four main morphological characteristics in common: a relatively large leaf surface, a smooth and often waxy cuticle or upper surface, a depressed or "gutterlike" midrib, and an extended or "drip" tip. Although there are exceptions, by far the large majority are broad-leaved evergreens, as contrasted with plants found in more temperate climates. Depending on the cold-hardiness requirements zone in which the zoological institution is located, a wide range of plant species can be recommended to lend a feeling of authenticity to such an exhibit. Some excellent choices might include smooth sumac, *Rhus glabra*, staghorn sumac, *R. typhina*, American elder, *Sambucus canadensis*, princess tree, *Paulownia tomentosa*, or the tree of heaven, *Ailanthus altissima* (Bailey 1976). Depending on the latitude of the exhibit, many magnolias could also be used: a small sampling includes the southern magnolia, *Magnolia grandiflora*, cucumbertree magnolia, *M. acuminata*, bigleaf magnolia, *M. macrophylla* (whose leaves can measure a full 12–32 inches in length), and umbrella magnolia, *M. tripetala* (Jackson 1990b).

The Quest for Unique Plant Simulators

Although all of these plants are excellent simulators, they are rarely utilized to their fullest extent. To give further examples, the Chinese toon, *Cedrela sinensis*, and the Ural false spirea, *Sorbaria sorbifolia*, are infrequently encountered in North American zoos. This is especially unfortunate as the latter readily colonizes due to a rhizominous root system, grows extremely fast, and produces large, fleecy flower panicles up to a full 10 inches in diameter during most zoos' peak attendance periods from late June into July. It is also virtually insect and disease free, transplants readily, and is cold-hardy well up into Canada (Dirr 1983). Although neither species is easily available within the nursery trade (the usual source for most zoos), it is possible to obtain them. Botanical gardens can also be considered as a potential, although somewhat limited, resource, as can planting bare-root material. Although neither of these resources should form the nucleus for obtaining an exhibit's plant material, they should be considered viable options for truly spectacular species.

A number of truly spectacular herbaceous perennials are underutilized when zoos attempt to simulate the world's habitats. Although a species such as gunnera, *Gunnera manicata,* has fairly specific cultural requirements (it is not terribly cold-hardy throughout much of the continental United States), it will often mature to 6 feet or more in height, and boasts gigantic reniform to peltate (more or less rounded) leaves that can easily measure 2.5–3 feet in diameter (Wyman 1986).

The Use of Tropical Plants in Temperate Exhibitry

For exhibits that simulate the West African tropics, bananas, *Musa* × *paradisiaca,* are an excellent choice (Meggers, Ayensu, and Duckworth 1973). Banana rootstocks can be purchased from Florida suppliers for a nominal cost and grown easily when sufficiently fertilized. Another simulator of rainforested regions, the papaya, *Carica papaya,* (Graf 1976) is nearly as impressive and can be readily propagated from the seeds of fruit purchased at the corner grocery. In the southern United States, both bananas and papayas planted in spring will easily reach a full 15 feet in height (with a trunk diameter of at least 8 inches for bananas and 3–4 inches for papayas) by the time colder temperatures return each autumn. Even in more northern regions, both species should exceed 8 feet in height by the time late-season frosts arrive (Jackson 1990a).

Although gunnera, bananas, and papaya could all be treated as annuals, the ideal is to have glasshouse or polyhouse facilities available for the overwintering of the first two species and the propagation of the latter. Although such space usually must be rented or purchased, its overall impact is priceless, since it allows a much broader and infinitely more impressive range of plants to be used. The total cost of any major tropical exhibit inevitably ranges well into the millions of dollars; therefore, the financial investment to utilize a glasshouse or polyhouse is arguably low considering its long-term value to the exhibit. A wide range of other truly tropical plants can likewise be overwintered and planted along public walkways during the frost-free months to create a "rainforest experience" for the visiting public (Ehrlinger 1983). Much of the labor used in the spring planting of tropical plants, as well as moving them back into polyhouses for the winter, can be provided by volunteers.

Accurately Portraying Developing Nation Forestry and Agricultural Practices in Naturalistic Exhibits

The emphasis in tropical exhibits and landscaping is usually on how the forest should appear (e.g., on simulating rainforests). Planners of tropical exhibits should also consider the integration of exhibit components that will demonstrate the adverse effects of slash-and-burn agriculture. Although small areas of the zoo landscape are frequently charred and appropriately labeled to identify them as simulating this forestry practice, any attempt at recreating the associated agricultural practices of developing African nations is all too seldom accomplished at a level reflecting its importance. Vegetables, such as corn, are frequently planted in long, neat rows (a practice common in much more highly developed nations), and the overall selection of species is not nearly as representative as it could be.

The local farmers' markets in major United States metropolitan areas often contain a wealth of tropical vegetables that can increase both the aesthetic and educational value of such an exhibit. Farmers' markets can also act as "nursery sources" for seasonal landscape plantings. Numerous tropical fruits can be planted throughout a naturalistic African landscape and can be found growing, weeks later, up in the branches of a neighboring tree as tropical vines or lianas. They can be extremely inexpensive and effective landscape components during the warmer months of the year, but are killed by frosts later in the year.

Simulation of the African gingers, *Aframomum gigantieum* and *A. subsericeum,* is easily achieved by purchasing ginger tubers at the local farmers' market and planting them in selected landscape areas. Plantings of ginger are an easy, inexpensive, and visually effective way to simulate these naturally important food sources of the lowland gorilla.

UNDERSTANDING THE ECOLOGICAL "BIG PICTURE"

Whether we are walking in the hot, steamy forests of Cameroon, West Africa, or the Blue Ridge Mountains of North Carolina, many of the most obvious floristic features remain the same (Campbell 1926). The landscaping of a naturalistic exhibit does not begin and end with the simple selection of plants to represent a specific region of the world. There must be a thoughtful landscape design plan. The placement of trees, shrubs, herbaceous species, and cultivars within exhibits is as important as the actual plant list. We often choose nursery materials that will function as good simulators, but fall short by having their locations within the exhibit look far too artificial and planned. Typically we see static "arrangements" of plants along pedestrian walkways, when both the species diversity and placement should be infinitely more random. Likewise, instead of using more natural ground cover materials such as leaves (saved from the previous autumn), hardwood or cypress "bagged" mulch is all too frequently used.

If one were to survey the botanical interrelationships within the northern deciduous forest biome in West Virginia, Virginia, Ohio, or Michigan (Alexander 1971), maple, *Acer* sp., ash, *Fraxinus* spp., beech, *Fagus grandifolia,* and oak, *Quercus* spp., would all be present (Blake 1942). The percentage of each tree species would vary from woodlot to woodlot and would be dependent on a broad range of factors (Clapham 1973). Such factors would range widely from disturbances such as fire or logging to the type of soil represented throughout the area (Brady 1974) and whether or not it had a hardpan or a fragipan (Foth and Turk 1972) incorporated within its overall profile. Even when one takes into consideration the rhizominous root systems of colonizing species such as the American elder or elderberry, Mother Nature seldom permits trees and shrubs to mature and prosper in anything close to resembling a pure stand. There is almost always an invading specimen or two that has grown up and become part of the woodlot's overall botanical "mix."

Incorporating the Principles of Forest Silvics into Exhibit Design

It is unfortunate that these basic principles of forest silvics are not more widely understood and simulated within the landscape designs of our naturalistic exhibits (Burglund 1975; Campbell 1926). These ecological principles apply within the forests of the People's Republic of China (Zhang Jingwei 1982) just as they do throughout the woodlots of the northeastern United States (Walter 1986). An orderly grouping of a dozen equally spaced viburnums surrounding a larger, "specimen" magnolia or birch makes no more sense in the landscaping of a red panda, *Ailurus fulgens,* exhibit than it does in a red fox, *Vulpes vulpes,* or American black bear, *Ursus americanus,* exhibit, despite the fact that plant species of each genus are native to both countries (Takhtajan 1989).

Regardless of a region's botanical composition, not all trees grow straight and true, and for that matter, not all are even alive! The forest floor is covered with leaves, branches, and logs in various states of decomposition or decay. Although these characteristics should obviously become second nature to our exhibits as well, they frequently give way to the more conventional methodology inherent in residential or commercial landscape plantings. All too often, we participate in the grand opening of a multimillion-dollar exhibit only to see each tree planted either at right angles to the ground or, at best, canted or angled a mere few degrees off center. Seldom do we experience the pleasure of seeing a sizable tree "planted" with its uppermost branches nearly touching the ground, with its root system largely exposed as if it had been blown over in a gale but nonetheless remained alive despite a few broken branches. Such a design statement would leave an undeniable impression on zoo visitors.

The felling of a sizable tree in any forest would cause at least a minor gap in the canopy above and permit a few more rays of precious sunlight to filter down onto the floor below. As a result of this disturbance, it would be reasonable to expect a few saplings and shrubs to start growing up through the branches of the fallen giant, each one fighting for dominance before the canopy slowly but surely begins to close, allowing only shade-tolerant species to survive. Although examples of plant "succession" such as this are relatively easy to simulate within the landscaping of zoo exhibitry, they are usually neglected. Aside from the realism that they would infuse into a naturalistic red panda (Ehrlinger 1985) or Canadian lynx, *Felis lynx,* enclosure, we could also capitalize on them as an educational opportunity.

Designing with "Dead" Trees

Another improvement we could easily make in our attempts at horticultural realism would be not to simply hire a tree service to cut down each and every large tree that dies within the confines of our exhibits. A better alternative is to carefully excavate around the base of the dead tree with a backhoe and simply winch it over with the cable of a good-sized tow truck attached to its upper branches. The size of the tree as well as its placement within the exhibit will dictate whether or not this can be safely accomplished. Leaving a large tree uprooted and lying on its side along a public walkway is much more impressive to the visiting public than having it sawed into sections and hauled away.

This concept, in fact, can easily be taken a step further to "planting" a few dead trees throughout an exhibit. As curator of horticulture at another zoological institution, I hoisted a dead 22-inch-in-diameter southern magnolia high over existing landscaping and set it into a pre-dug hole to the side of a viewing area before opening the new multimillion-dollar exhibit. The base of the tree was then set in concrete and the hole refilled. Such a skeletal snag makes a wonderful foundation for vines.In fact, if such a specimen is located in an area that is somewhat distant from the public's view, pole beans can be planted at its base after the threat of frost has passed in the spring and encouraged to climb freely up the trunk and into its network of branches. The bean pods blend in with the vegetable's leaves from a distance and somewhat resemble a tropical liana or a patch of southern kudzu, *Pueraria lobata.* This strategy works whether one is striving to simulate a lowland gorilla habitat in Cameroon or an Okefenokee Swamp habitat in southern Georgia (Jackson 1990b).

Vines, Vines, and More Vines

Pole beans actually have a dual use, as they can be replanted each year to provide an annual cover on fences and the like, or used as a quick-growing screen until other, more permanent vines have had time to establish themselves. I have utilized pole beans within the confines of a guenon exhibit with excellent success. The beans had a number of weeks to become established before the animals were introduced into their new surroundings. They provided the small primates with nutritious forage on which to browse, and also provided environmental enrichment opportunities that lessened their destruction of other trees and shrubs within their exhibit.

Although pole beans and other seasonal vegetables can be very effective in simulating the tropical lianas of Cameroon, Sumatra, or even Brazil, it is equally important to include cold-hardy or "permanent" vine species as well. Although vines are by no means overused as a landscape component in exhibits that feature animals from temperate regions, they tend to be underutilized even in the display of rainforest animals. Wild grapes are common in prime second-growth ruffed grouse, *Bonasa umbellus,* or white-tailed deer, *Odocoileus virginianus,* habitats (Nowak 1991) in Pennsylvania and upstate New York. Similarly, vegetative climbers of all shapes and descriptions could be included in landscape designs for the habitats of animals native to tropical regions. A large array of vine species are available within the horticultural trade that would be excellent simulators for the habitats of any number of rainforest-dwelling animals, from the western lowland gorilla and okapi, *Okapia johnstoni*, to the siamang, *Hylobates syndactylus* (Nowak 1991). Just a small sampling of the most noteworthy species includes trumpet vine, *Campsis radicans* and *C.* × *tagliabuana*, climbing hydrangea, *Hydrangea anomala petiolaris*, Virginia creeper, *Parthenocissus quinquefolia* (Heriteau and Cathey 1990), silver lace vine, *Polygonum aubertii*, and the various clematis cultivars, *Clematis* × *jackmanii* (Dirr 1983).

PLANT-ANIMAL INTERACTIONS

Interactions between animals and their exhibit plantings are poorly understood, yet such information is critical for maximizing the educational and aesthetic impact of exhibits and protecting the health and well-being of the animals. An example of wise selection of horticultural species and cultivars for use in and around animal exhibits involves the ornamental shrub oleander, *Nerium oleander*. Oleander possesses narrow, 3–5-inch-long, glossy, dark green evergreen leaves, and is one of the most common landscape plants used in "Deep South" gardens, but its intolerance to cold winter conditions effectively precludes its use in northern regions. It is tolerant of drought as well as the windswept and salt-spray conditions so prevalent along oceanfront property (Dirr 1983). It is also able to tolerate growing in polluted areas, has an impressively fast, almost weedlike growth rate, and is resistant to the ravages of a wide range of insect and disease pests. Although this plant has so many positive attributes, they make little practical difference, as all parts of the plant are significantly poisonous, including even the smoke from its burning and the water in which its cut flowers have been placed. This plant is among the most common causes of poisonous plant ingestions reported by poison control centers in states where it is common as a landscape ornamental (Lampe and McCann 1985). I would not consider planting this species anywhere within a zoological park, to say nothing of in or around an animal exhibit, for fear that a leafy branch might find its way into the exhibit of a leaf-eating animal.

Two additional areas of plant-animal interaction are in need of further study. First, behavioral enrichment is a topic of considerable recent interest among animal managers, and exhibit plantings have great potential for providing enriched environments for captive animals. Animal managers and zoo horticulturists should work cooperatively to plan naturalistic exhibits that promote the expression of normal behaviors.

Second, there is much disagreement among animal managers concerning philosophies of mutual coexistence between plants and animals within exhibits. Opinions range from the dedicated and determined plant "protectionist" stance to the far opposite end of the spectrum. Frequently, funds designated for the protection of valuable mature trees within exhibits are cut from the construction budget. Exhibit construction itself results in considerable damage to trees (e.g., from heavy earthmoving equipment passing under the tree's dripline and compacting the soil). The design and construction of an efficient, cost-effective, and aesthetically pleasing structure that will, for example, protect a mature oak tree from the ravages of a full-grown male elephant is not a trivial task.

Many commercially available resources for lessening the negative impacts of plant-animal interactions in zoos have yet to be exploited to their fullest potential. The recent technological advances that allow well-drained and wear-resistant turf for professional sports can be adapted for use in a Serengeti plains exhibit, for example. Lessening damage to turf is clearly a common concern, whether that damage is wrought by football spikes or antelope hooves. Likewise, the recent knowledge gained by the horse industry in intensively managed pastures in states such as Kentucky may be useful in the design of zoo grassland exhibits. Such modern technological advances that have broad application to zoo horticulture include new turfgrass cultivars (and their corresponding nutritional consequences), drainage systems, and fertilization regimes.

INTRODUCTION PLANTINGS

Introduction plantings could also be called "transition" or even "mood" plantings, as they break the ice, so to speak, and usher visitors toward an upcoming naturalistic exhibit as they proceed on their "safari" through the zoo. Introduction plantings are not usually part of the zoo's primary landscaping as are the plants placed along public walkways. An introduction planting could easily be located at a zoo café or restaurant just outside the boundary of the park's colobus monkey, *Colobus guereza*, western lowland gorilla, or orangutan, *Pongo pygmaeus*, exhibit (Nowak 1991). Characteristically, petunias, geraniums, or some other showy summer flowering annual would be planted in the adjoining landscape beds in an attempt to provide the area with seasonal color. However, this type of display planting does nothing to set the stage and start transforming the visitor's mindset for the exhibit to come.

A more effective strategy would be to use tropical-looking flowers such as cannas, *Canna* × *generalis*, or cultivars of rose mallow hibiscus, *Hibiscus* × *moscheutos* (with their gigantic dinner plate–sized blooms). These introduction plantings would help the visitor "adjust" to the "tropics" before entering the actual exhibit. Additions of bananas, palms, large-foliaged hostas, and even bear's breech, *Acanthus mollis latifolius* (Brickell 1981), would help to add different sizes and textures to the plantings, yet still be very much in keeping with the theme of a nearby tropical exhibit. Permanent plantings must also be considered within the overall framework of introduction plantings, as it is of no inspiration at all for visitors to be greeted with bald cypress trees, *Taxodium distichum*, outside of an Australian outback enclosure or Colorado blue spruce adjacent to a Florida Everglades or South Carolina coastal marsh exhibit.

CONCLUSION

From the exclusion of poisonous plants to eliminating species like the persimmon, *Diospyros virginiana*, along walkways due to the prolific production of its large, messy fruit, a great deal of planning and forethought should go into the landscape design of any new, state-of-the-art zoo exhibit. The design of landscaping to complement a zoo's naturalistic exhibits must above all be based on a firm commitment to assure always that the most innovative and exciting horticultural methods possible are employed toward attaining the desired goal of truly naturalistic exhibitry.

REFERENCES

Alexander, M. 1971. *Principles of field biology.* Syracuse: State University of New York-College of Environmental Science and Forestry.

L. H. Bailey Hortorium Staff, Cornell University. 1976. *Hortus third: A concise dictionary of plants cultivated in the United States and Canada.* New York: Macmillan.

Blake, S. F. 1942. *Floras of the world.* U.S. Department of Agriculture Publication no. 401. Washington, D.C.: U.S. Government Printing Office.

Brady, N. 1974. *The nature and properties of soils.* New York: Macmillan.

Brickell, C., ed. 1981. *The American Horticultural Society encyclopedia of garden plants.* New York: Macmillan.

Burglund, J. 1975. *Silvics.* Syracuse: State University of New York-College of Environmental Science and Forestry.

Campbell, D. 1926. *An outline of plant geography.* New York: Macmillan.

Clapham, W. B. 1973. *Natural ecosystems.* New York: Macmillan.

Dirr, M. 1983. *Manual of woody landscape plants.* Champaign, Ill.: Stipes Publishing Company.

Ehrlinger, D. 1983. Animal exhibit landscaping: Use of hardy and nonhardy plants in animal habitat representation. Paper presented at the Association of Zoological Horticulture/American Association of Arboretums and Botanical Gardens Conference, San Diego, Calif.

————. 1985. Horticultural considerations in the planting of a red panda exhibit—Cincinnati Zoo. Paper presented at the Association of Zoological Horticulture/American Association of Zoological Parks and Aquariums Conference, Cincinnati, Ohio.

Foth, H. D., and Turk, L. M. 1972. *Fundamentals of soil science.* New York: John Wiley and Sons.

Graf, A. B. 1976. *Exotica (Series Four): International pictorial cyclopedia of exotic plants from tropical and near-tropic regions.* East Rutherford, N.J.: Roehrs Company.

Heriteau, J., and Cathey, H. M. 1990. *The National Arboretum book of outstanding garden plants.* New York: Simon and Schuster.

Jackson, D. 1989. The Ford African Rainforest: A horticultural experience. Paper presented at the American Association of Zoological Parks and Aquariums Southeast Regional Conference, Atlanta, Ga.

————. 1990a. Landscaping for realism. *Arnoldia* (Harvard University) 50 (1): 13–21.

————. 1990b. Landscaping in hostile environments. *Int. Zoo Yrbk.* 29:10–15.

Lampe, K. F., and McCann, M. A. 1985. *American Medical Association handbook of poisonous and injurious plants.* Chicago: University of Chicago Press.

Meggers, B., Ayensu, E. S., and Duckworth, W. D., eds. 1973. *Tropical forest ecosystems in Africa and South America: A comparative review.* Washington, D.C.: Smithsonian Institution Press.

Nowak, R. 1991. *Walker's mammals of the world.* 5th ed. 2 vols. Baltimore: Johns Hopkins University Press.

Takhtajan, A. 1989. *Floristic regions of the world.* Trans. T. J. Crovello. Berkeley: University of California Press.

Walter, H. 1986. *Vegetation of the earth and ecological systems of the geo-biosphere.* Berlin: Springer-Verlag.

Wyman, D. 1986. *Wyman's gardening encyclopedia.* New York: Macmillan.

Zhang Jingwei (Chang King-wai), ed. 1982. *The alpine plants of China.* Beijing: Science Press; New York: Gordon and Breach Science Publishers.

18

Integrating Animal Behavior and Exhibit Design

John Seidensticker and James G. Doherty

VISITORS AND WINDS OF CHANGE IN MAMMAL EXHIBITION

Animal exhibits are the heart and soul of the zoo. As in a museum, a zoo's primary educational tool is the exhibit. The essential difference is that in the zoo, the "objects" exhibited are living, breathing, feeding, defecating, and sometimes reproducing. The maintenance of a zoo's exhibition programs is complicated by the requirements of these living "objects." While zoos have continued to seek improvements in the care of animals maintained in exhibits, more recently animal management has been driven by the animal welfare expectations of an increasingly demanding public (Holden 1988). It is not surprising, then, that zoo research programs are being driven by the requirements of the animals, especially mammals, kept in confinement on public view. In a large measure, the future of zoos as credible educational institutions for the general public will depend on the strength of this research and the successful implementation of the animal management plans that result.

The presence of visitors vastly complicates animal exhibition as compared with the management of mammals maintained in other confined environments. Visitor presence can influence the behavior of animals living in exhibit spaces (Glatston et al. 1984; Jordan and Burghardt 1986; Chamove, Hosey, and Schaetzel 1988; Thompson 1989; Baldwin 1992; Carlstead 1991). Visitors come to zoos and view animal exhibits with varied expectations; these expectations have been shaped by changes in our values and perceptions of animals and conservation since the decades following World War II.

Visitors coming to zoos today live in an increasingly urbanized society, with little direct contact with agriculture and farm animals and with shrinking opportunities to live in and experience wilderness (Conway 1969). In many urban settings and for many visitors, zoo animals are as close as they can get to the real thing. The utility of animals is not a predominant interest for these visitors. Rather, animals living in zoos can evoke strong feelings in visitors about animals they have loved and lost, including pets and backyard acquaintances; about animals they have heard about or glimpsed occasionally but do not understand (bats, for example); about familiar animals they have been able to recognize since childhood but really know little about (lions, tigers, bears, elephants); and about other wonderful animals from far-off, exotic lands. We cannot ignore the fact that, for some zoo visitors, zoo animals evoke images of themselves, friends and acquaintances, and their own life experiences (e.g., Fulghum 1989, 159–161). Their perceptions of animals come primarily from television, where most programs present animals inaccurately and often anthropomorphically. Also, most animals on television are "free" and not "imprisoned" in zoos.

Kellert's (1976) surveys of perceptions of animals in American society revealed that zoo enthusiasts were very moralistic in their attitudes toward the treatment of animals. "Zoo enthusiasts, for example, strongly objected to rodeos, killing animals for fur, and utilitarian exploitation of animals. This group also revealed strong humanistic attitudes and, somewhat surprisingly, were not particularly naturalistic or ecologistic in their attitudes toward animals . . ." (544). A humanistic attitude is distinguished by a strong personal affection for individual animals. The most striking feature of the moralistic attitude is its great concern for the welfare of animals based on ethical principles opposing exploitation and the infliction of any harm. Fifty-five percent of the United States population is estimated to be strongly oriented toward these moralistic and humanistic attitudes (Kellert 1989).

Increasing urbanization in the United States, coupled with an increase in leisure time following World War II, has propelled a rising interest in the quality of life. Interest in conventional conservation, that is, concern for the efficient and wise use of resources, has turned into a concern for and interest in the environment. Environmental quality has become an integral part of our search for better health and a higher standard of living (Hays 1987). These concerns are mirrored in the evolution of some zoo exhibits and exhibition strategies. Zoo visitors, supporters, and critics now demand better environments, better health, and higher standards of living for the animals maintained in exhibits and in confinement generally.

The new exhibition programs, with roots in the environmental movement, foster biological and conservation literacy. The concepts of natural cycles, biological diversity, carrying capacity, ecosystems, stressed ecosystems, global change, and endangered species have become central in animal exhibition themes and fuel many zoo programs.

WHAT STORIES DO EXHIBITS TELL?

Animal exhibits communicate messages or "stories" to zoo visitors, as is masterfully discussed by Coe (1985; see also Coe, chap. 16, this volume). Curators and designers can plan the message and measure the efficacy of the presentation. Or they can muddle through. Indeed, muddling through in developing exhibits has many virtues, as we describe below, as long as there is a conscious choice of a message and the objective of the exhibit's story line is formulated in advance. Unfortunately, failure to recognize what is being communicated by animals in exhibits has been an oft-repeated folly.

Zoos may have fine mammal collections and significant research and conservation programs, but if the visitor experience consists of exhibits that appear empty, or exhibited animals that appear to visitors to be uncomfortable or stressed in some way, the take-home message is just that: "We didn't see anything." "Something is wrong with that animal." "The zoo doesn't care about the animals." If this is the case, the zoo has obviously lost its opportunity to promote positive changes in knowledge, attitudes, awareness, and actions toward wildlife. Associated interpretative materials will not and cannot retrieve this lost opportunity.

The Victorian zoological garden sought to present "the animal" as a simple display of a beautiful, interesting, or unusual object to the visitor. In this respect, zoos differed little from museums. There has been, however, a revolution in zoo animal exhibition with a de-emphasis on animals as objects and an increased emphasis on *animals engaged in natural behaviors,* living in natural or naturalistic environments (table 18.1) and seeming to be at home in the exhibit space (Hediger 1970; Hutchins, Hancocks, and Crockett 1984; Forthman-Quick 1984; Greene 1987). Zoo exhibits are windows to real animals doing real things, although at a somewhat reduced scale. Exhibits that appear to place the wild animal and the zoo visitor together in the same habitat—landscape immersion—are attempts to break down the visitors' sense of security by reminding them that wild animals are really wild (Greene 1987). Robinson (1988) has taken the point further, by stressing the "inextricable links between plants and animals" (630), so that the visitor comes away with a recognition of the interdependence of biological systems.

Animals and their behavior are the subject of this chapter and our focus in animal exhibition. For us, the message of animals in zoos today is the experience of ecology and behavior they provide for visitors (see Lueders 1989). Animals in zoos can help visitors gain perspective on the world and their place in it. We should be trying to get the visitor to

TABLE 18.1. Polakowski's Definitions for "Natural" Zoo Exhibit Habitats

Exhibit Type	Definition
Realistic Natural Habitat	Reproduces the real habitat in general appearance, land formation, plant life, and animal activity.
Modified Natural Habitat	Uses the elements of the real habitat but substitutes plants and trees, uses existing or modified land forms, and integrates the habitat into the existing surroundings.
Naturalistic Habitat	Makes little or no attempt to duplicate elements of the real habitat. Involves a stylistic use of natural materials. Often the main purpose is to decorate the space.

Source: Polakowski 1987, 90.

look hard at animals. As Ann Zwinger (1989) has stressed, once you really look at an animal and see it, ask questions about it, get an answer, and learn something about it, it becomes yours. "And once it becomes yours, you'll never destroy it . . ." (Zwinger 1989, 72).

Conway's (1968) "How to Exhibit a Bullfrog" is a metaphor of what the exhibition of animals might be and what we should be trying to accomplish with the exhibition of animals.

THE ANATOMY OF ANIMAL EXHIBITION

One of us (J.S.) recently served as an advisor for a well-known zoological park in the design of a new exhibit complex for jaguars, *Panthera onca.* The designers were working to obtain for the visitor a visual image of a jaguar lying on a log in the sun at the edge of a tropical river backwater. Think of the beautiful Coheleach (1982, 63) painting or that classic photograph of a jaguar in Perry (1970, 123). The space allotted for this was less than 300 square feet, and the designers were insistent that this was adequate; the design for the complex had also proceeded too far to allocate more space.

From studies conducted with carnivores living in exhibit spaces at the National Zoological Park (Carlstead, Seidensticker, and Baldwin 1991; Baldwin 1992; Carlstead, Brown, and Seidensticker 1993), we predicted that this exhibit, because of its small size, would produce excessive stereotypic behaviors in the jaguar maintained in that space. Visitors, rather than being thrilled, inspired, and learning something about jaguars, would take home a negative message: a big cat in a beautiful but too small cage alone, and obviously not comfortable.

The point is that exhibited animals are not objects, and they are not static. However, zoo professionals have available only a very small data base with which to make judgments concerning the welfare of animals in confined environments. This frequently puts curators in a difficult position in discussions with designers and architects of new exhibits, and creates conflict. The animal person "knows" there may be a problem, but has little in the way of empirical evidence to support those concerns.

Analyzing successful, as well as unsuccessful, mammal exhibits is an essential undertaking in building more successful exhibits. Even with the growing literature on zoo exhibit design, there is little information on exhibits that have been perceived as less than successful, or as actual failures. This complicates the analysis of those elements that have contributed to the creation of successful exhibits and those that have not worked (Petroski 1985). Indeed, there is also no well-established "industry standard" or objective criteria by which to judge an exhibit a success, a failure, or in need of help.

Animal Management Models

In our experience, there are four animal exhibition/management/research models under which zoos now operate (S. Lumpkin and J. Seidensticker, unpub.), with considerable tension among their proponents. In practice, none is purely applied.

The *zoo exhibit animal management model* is one inherited from the past and can be summarized by the phrase "Zoos are for people." For a very long time, animal management and exhibit design meant little more than holding a wild beast in an enclosure, usually a small cage or pit, and feeding it whatever it could live on that was cheap and available. Painting backdrops on cage walls, using glass rather than wire or bars, or adding cage decorations enhanced visitor perceptions, but did not change the basic model. This model is exemplified by the jaguar in the example above. The animal, not its behavior, is considered the focus.

The *ethological animal management model* can be summarized as "Zoos are for wild animal species that move and do things." Ethology is the study of whole patterns of animal behavior in natural environments, stressing evolutionary adaptations. The essential premise of this model is that zoo animals should be managed so that their lives differ as little from those of their wild conspecifics as possible. In other words, zoo managers should try to duplicate or simulate the species' spatial, social, and environmental requirements and challenges. This model's most influential early spokesperson was Hediger (1950, 1955, 1970). The ethological model does not demand that the animal's environment in confinement *look* naturalistic or that animals be allowed to manage their own affairs, only that the effects be like those in nature. For example, the replacement of the males in a lion, *Panthera leo*, pride can be a bloody affair in the wild (Schaller 1972). Introductions can be managed in a zoo setting that are not traumatic and that still result in stable social groups. The idea that the animal's environment should look naturalistic is a later innovation (Hutchins, Hancocks, and Crockett 1984).

The ethological management model is a problem-solving approach. Thus, if a species does not breed in confinement, this model assumes that changes in the captive social or physical environment to make it more like that in the wild would promote breeding. When it became apparent that inbreeding in the zoo setting was causing serious harm, breeding management plans were developed to mimic natural mating systems more closely.

The ethological model is best elucidated by comparing it with the medical model described next: the ethological model might prescribe quiet isolation for a nervous pregnant female with a history of maternal neglect that is about to give birth, since parturient females in the wild seek solitude, while the medical model might prescribe tranquilizers and prepare a plan for removing and hand-rearing the young.

The *medical animal management model* predates the ethological model and is responsible for many advances in zoo animal care and husbandry, including standards for sanitation, nutrition, and preventive medical care. The medical model stresses the reduction of environment complexity to make the captive environment cleaner and safer and to give managers greater control over the health of the animal. The medical animal management model emphasizes direct human technological intervention rather than approximating the wild condition: it fixes the animal so it can adjust to the conditions of confinement rather than fixing the conditions of confinement.

The use of techniques for "assisted" reproduction is a manifestation of the medical management model. Up to now, these techniques have generally been used when the application of ethological management, at its current state of knowledge, has not worked or has not been tried to improve captive propagation of a particular species.

The *humane animal management model* assumes that zoos are welfare states that take care of individual animals from cradle to grave. This management model is equally unconcerned with the zoo visitor and with animal populations or species as a whole. Rather, individual animals are managed like house pets, and somewhat anthropocentric assumptions are made about what animals need in order to be "happy" in confinement. This model demands intensive health care for animals, but generally is opposed to any invasive research that might cause temporary stress or pain, even in the interest of advancing medical care for the species.

This model is sympathetic to many aspects of ethological management but not to any ethologically related practices that might be perceived as potentially injurious or stressful to individual animals. This stance can lead to protectiveness of individuals that interferes with the animals' displaying behaviors required for normal social interactions or reproduction. The humane animal management model also dictates that animals can choose whether they want to be on exhibit or off, a choice that confounds exhibition strategies.

The Zoo and the Animal Exhibition System

Successful and improved exhibition of mammals, in our view, can be developed through a multifactorial perspective. This is by no means a novel idea. We present a diagram of the "animal exhibition system" in the wider zoo system in figure 18.1.

As important and central as successful animal exhibition is in zoos, it is, of course, only a part of a zoo's overall operations. There are four interdependent components that together constitute what we term "the animal exhibition system": (1) the zoo visitor looking at the exhibit; (2) the animals the zoo visitor sees in that exhibit and what those animals are doing; (3) the exhibit space, including the aesthetics of that space and how the space controls the presentation of the animals; and (4) the husbandry system that is responsible for the care of the animals. What the visitor sees

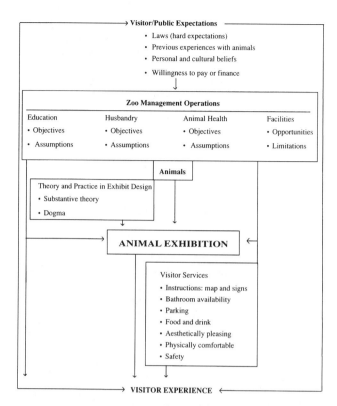

Fig. 18.1. The animal exhibition system in the context of the wider zoo. What the visitor sees in an exhibit is only part of the visitor experience. The curator's responsibility and the zoo's obligation is to enable the visitor to see animals engaged in natural behaviors.

in an exhibit is only part of the visitor experience; the zoo visitor's experience may be largely influenced by variables that are outside and beyond the control of the animal exhibition system (figure 18.1).

When someone makes a decision to visit the zoo, that person is usually already highly motivated. Once at the zoo, the visitor's expectations are strongly influenced by a hierarchy of needs: physiological needs, safety needs, social needs, and needs for self-esteem, self-actualization, and creativity. Unpleasant encounters with excessive trash, dirty bathrooms, poor directional signs, and failure to see animals that were expected can lead to great disappointment, or what can be termed "cognitive dissonance": a situation in which a person experiences something that was neither expected nor desired (Massie 1979). Curators have a very important stake in encouraging excellence in those programs that strongly influence the visitor experience.

Zoo designers can use cognitive dissonance in a positive way by devising means to "grab" zoo visitors, raise the hair on the backs of their necks, and give them a real jolt with exhibits based on landscape-immersion techniques (Coe 1985; Greene 1987).

Research and Animal Exhibition

How should research on the exhibition of mammals proceed to find the right mix of elements from the four management models so as to optimize conditions for both visitors and animals? One can begin with questions deriving from

the four components of the animal exhibition system: the visitors, the animals and activities that the zoo visitor sees in the exhibit, the exhibit space, and the care of the animals on exhibit by animal keepers.

Questions about zoo visitors:
• What and how do animal exhibits communicate to the zoo visitor?
• What do zoo visitors do and want to do at the zoo?
Questions about the animals and the exhibit space:
• What is a suitable exhibit space to feature the animal's behavior?
• What are the sources of stress to animals living in exhibits, and how does this stress affect them behaviorally and physiologically?
Questions about care and the animal keepers:
• What changes in animal management procedures can be implemented to promote excellence in animal exhibition?

These questions emphasize action on two levels: (1) increased research to understand the animal exhibition system, and (2) increased use of opportunities to implement improvements in the animal exhibition system. It is no surprise to zoo researchers that so often their findings are only slowly or never implemented, as this gap between research findings and practice exists in the management of most natural resources.

Difficulty in applying new substantive findings comes from the lack of a linkage between those who make the discoveries and those who care for the animals daily or who design exhibits. This linkage can be forged by developing husbandry protocols that are jointly authored by researcher and animal management and keeper staff, protocols that seek to meet articulated and agreed-upon objectives. Performance plans for researchers, managers, and keeper staff can contain statements to this effect. In our view, the essential linkage lies in establishing exhibition objectives.

Setting Exhibition Objectives

"It was Fauna's conviction, born out of long experience, that most people, one, did not know what they wanted; two, did not know how to go about getting it; and three, didn't know when they had it . . ." (Steinbeck 1954, 116). So it is with opportunities and constraints in establishing and meeting objectives for animal exhibits.

Should animal exhibition objectives be framed largely as an exercise in consumer (visitor) satisfaction, as visitor education, or in terms of the activity of the animals themselves? While obviously related, these questions address different dimensions of the zoo management system.

Consumer or visitor satisfaction objectives have their origins in economics. We can think of the yield of an exhibit, or a cluster of exhibits (or even the entire zoo experience) in terms of social benefits and aesthetic value, which can be measured in dollars. Most zoo visitors, as do most opera audiences, partake of an aesthetic experience and are willing to pay for it. Persons who dislike crowds, for example, or who are not satisfied with exhibit styles, or with the animals they see or do not see, simply would not be willing to pay again for that experience. Other visitors, however, might not care about crowding and might return again and again.

The aesthetic experience the former visitors have might not be less, but might differ qualitatively.

Managers establishing objectives usually seek to balance the total number of visitors in attendance, or rate of visitor attendance per day or per hour, or to maintain a sustained flow of visitation throughout the day or through the seasons. Value from a group of exhibits might be better maximized by providing opportunities to satisfy visitors of both low and high tolerance to visitor crowding. The consumer or economic perspective can also be used when seeking financial support from an expanded constituency, for example, by comparing zoos with professional sporting events or other forms of outdoor recreation and informal education.

Objectives concerning the effect of an exhibit on knowledge acquisition, attitude change, and subsequent visitor behavior originate from an expansion of zoos' concerns from entertainment to education and conservation. A good recent example of setting objectives and follow-up monitoring involves the African Rock Kopje exhibit at the San Diego Zoo. As Derwin and Piper (1988) explain, "The broad goal of the exhibit was to communicate the concept and beauty of the interdependent ecosystem and to increase the knowledge and appreciation of wildlife in people of all ages" (438).

An exhibit complex may have both cognitive (intellectual) and affective objectives (Shettel 1989). Among the cognitive objectives for the African Rock Kopje exhibit were that visitors be able to describe the kopje as an ecosystem, identify the secret life that makes the kopje a viable environment, and describe the physical or behavioral adaptations to the kopje of the hyrax, *Procavia capensis,* klipspringer, *Oreotragus oreotragus,* and pancake tortoise, *Malacochersus tornieri,* and explain these adaptations' survival value. "Affective objectives included requirements that visitors speak of and behave toward plants and animals with respect, express appreciation for nature and wildlife, and support conservation efforts when given the opportunity..." (Derwin and Piper 1988, 439).

Monitoring of visitors leaving the kopje exhibit revealed that they were unable to answer the cognitive questions if they had not read the interpretive signs. Interactive elements significantly helped cognitive recall. Younger visitors were more likely to use interpretive elements than to read panels; older visitors were more likely to read panels (Derwin and Piper 1988).

A major problem in defining objectives for informal learning in zoos is how little we know about what actually happens in zoos in terms of knowledge acquisition, or how that is influenced by levels of exhibit naturalism, conservation information, and interactive learning opportunities (S. Kellert, pers. comm., 1987). We cannot yet measure progress or the effect of zoo programs on informal learning. However, this is presently a major area of research in zoos (and other informal learning centers): we seek to understand learning styles in different people, how these change with age, and how to utilize this understanding in the presentation of animals and ancillary materials. We suspect that there are many lessons for us in the world of advertising. Morgan and Gramann (1989) provide a useful introduction to this topic.

The third dimension in establishing objectives in the exhibition of animals is the animals. What they are doing and how they are presented to the visitor are often influenced by the tensions generated among the four animal management models described above. To move beyond these tensions, we need to establish the following propositions and work from them: (1) what zoo visitors learn and how they feel about their visit to the zoo are strongly related to the animals they see and what these animals are doing, and (2) zoos have a vital concern and obligation to seek ways to improve zoo visitors' animal-viewing experience.

Such propositions may seem trivial, self-evident. They are not. Rather, they establish a base for evaluating and for proposing improvements in exhibits. Objectives for exhibits and exhibit operations can be formulated in terms of animals and what those animals are doing. Curators can ask, for example: Can visitors always see the animals maintained on exhibit? What are those animals doing? Are they behaving in the ways we want and expect them to in exhibit spaces? If not, what is wrong, and how can we fix it? Or, if an exhibit works, why does it work, and what does it take to keep it working? These are operational questions, and from these objectives, routines, improvements, and innovations can be established.

The pitfall in animal exhibition is that exhibition and ancillary activities such as interpretive programs are too often viewed *as an activity and not as a result.* The "consumer" is the visitor, not the animals, or the exhibit, or the interpretive programs themselves. The challenge is to define aggressively the results desired, and then monitor to see that they are achieved.

"DADDY, WHERE ARE THE ELEPHANTS?"

There are probably no more than a dozen of the approximately 4,000 mammal species that are recognized by the vast majority of people no matter where they live or what languages they speak. Most people, if ever exposed to them, remember to name elephants, lions, tigers, bears, giant pandas, and "monkeys." Indeed, the first exposition of a large exotic animal in North America was a lion in 1720; the first dromedary camel, *Camelus dromedarius,* was exhibited in 1721, the first orangutan, *Pongo pygmaeus,* in 1789, and the first Indian elephant, *Elephas maximus,* in 1796 (Vail 1934). These animals are nearly always included in zoo exhibition programs. Why are some animals favorites of zoo visitors and others ignored?

Public Preference and Perception
Kellert (1989), in a national (United States) survey, found the most-liked animals to be the dog, horse, swan, robin, butterfly, trout, salmon, eagle, elephant, turtle, cat, ladybug, and raccoon; the least-liked included the cockroach, mosquito, rat, wasp, rattlesnake, bat, vulture, shark, lizard, crow, coyote, and wolf. Note that the most preferred species were the dog and horse; the most preferred wild mammal was the elephant. Morris and Morris (1966, 200), based on a mail survey solicited over British television, found the top ten animal favorites among children to be the chimpanzee,

monkey, horse, bushbaby, panda, bear, elephant, lion, dog, and giraffe.

Important factors in these human preferences have been investigated by Morris and Morris (1966), Kellert (1989), and Kaplan and Kaplan (1989), among others (see Hoage 1989). Kellert (1989, 22) found the following factors to be important in public preferences for different species: "size (usually, the larger the animal, the more preferred); aesthetics (considered 'attractive'); intelligence (thought not only to have the capacity for reason but also for feelings and emotion); danger to humans; likelihood of inflicting property damage; phylogenetic relatedness to humans; cultural and historical relationship to humans; relationship to human society (pet, domestic farm animals, game, pest, native wildlife, exotic wildlife); texture (body appearance and structure; generally, the more unfamiliar to humans, the less preferred); mode of locomotion (generally, the more unfamiliar to humans, the less preferred); economic value of the species to humans." Morris and Morris (1966) examined the appeal that giant pandas have for zoo visitors and identified the following elements: flat face; large eyes; little or no tail; sits up vertically; can manipulate small objects; killer turned nonkiller; apparently harmless and friendly toward human beings; sexless; playful; appears clumsy; appears to be very soft; outline is rounded; is black-and-white; is a giant; has an easy name; has a historical precursor (teddy bear); is rare; comes from a remote and mysterious habitat; has a strange history of discovery; and is immensely valuable.

"Perhaps the greatest challenge confronting a wildlife educator is to encourage people to see animals 'as animals'—that is, without prejudice or preconceived notions or anthropomorphic projections . . ." (Hoage 1989, xiii). In our view, this is the major educational goal for zoos.

Active Animals and Visitor Viewing Opportunities

Like the management of all natural resource systems, the management of the animal exhibition system operates within biological, socioeconomic, and technological constraints. The manager's constant challenge is to understand these constraints and, within them, identify opportunities for change and improvement. For example, a common exhibition strategy in North America is to feature local, medium-sized mammals such as raccoons, *Procyon lotor*, or Virginia opossums, *Didelphis virginiana*. These animals are readily available and are usually inexpensive to obtain and maintain. We know that visitors value that with which they are familiar. The technology of producing exhibit spaces for these animals usually is not complicated. However, most medium-sized North American mammals are nocturnal and/or crepuscular in their activity and, when not active, retire to the protection of burrows. That is a biological constraint, and no amount of ancillary interpretative material will fix it. Nor can one design an exhibit to rectify this fact of life.

It is not surprising that large or active or "social" animals engage zoo visitors' attention longer than small or inactive animals. Bitgood, Patterson, and Benefield (1986) have defined eight factors that influence visitor behavior at zoo exhibits in terms of "attracting power"—the percentage of passersby who stop to view an exhibit—and "holding power"—the length of time that visitors stop and look at the exhibit. Holding power is correlated with animal motion, animal size, visitor participation, the presence of an animal infant, and ease of viewability. Attracting power is directly related to visitors' perceptions of the species' characteristics—perceived dangerousness and attractiveness are examples—and inversely related to the number of visually competing stimuli. Attracting and holding power both depend on visitor fatigue, satiation, and placement of exits.

An understanding of visitor perception and behavior at zoos is beginning to be included in exhibit design. Beautiful exhibits without animals are not what zoos are about. In our view, a reasonable objective is that visitors have a 90–95% chance of seeing an animal in an exhibit space engaged in natural behaviors. To accomplish this there must be a correct match between the animal's characteristics, the animal's needs, the exhibit space, and animal management procedures.

WONDERFUL ANIMALS DOING INTERESTING THINGS

Grant Jones (1982) has set out the principles for getting it right for the visitor, particularly as this can be accomplished through landscape immersion techniques (appendix 18.1). The curator's responsibility is selecting and getting it right for the animal. There are six variables (modified from Burghardt 1975) that are directly linked to wonderful animals doing interesting things in animal exhibits: (1) the animal keepers and their presentation to and interaction with the exhibit animals, (2) animal management procedures, (3) the actual physical characteristics of the exhibit space, (4) the environment (temperature, sun/shade, wind, etc.) in the exhibit space, (5) visitor numbers and their presentation to the animals, and (6) the animal species selected for exhibition and the characteristics of those species.

Matching Exhibit Spaces and Animal Needs

Hediger (1970, 524) characterized facilities for keeping animals in zoos as either "kennels" or "territories." By kennels he meant "a jail-like narrow cage in which an animal, most frequently a single one, is kept by force and viewed in this situation as a living specimen. 'Territory' on the other hand means the natural division of space, with species-specific habitat organization for the use of an animal or of a social unit of animals." A reading of Hediger (1950) is a necessary start for anyone trying to move the exhibition of animals beyond a kennel mode into a territorial mode. Since Hediger proposed the use of the word "territory" in this way, the term has taken on a more restricted meaning as "an area occupied more or less exclusively by an animal or group of animals by means of repulsion through overt defense or advertisement" (Wilson 1975, 597). Hediger's point is that the old-style cages, or kennels—even if they had glass or wire fronts for public viewing and painted backdrops—were very little different from museum displays, "a kind of solid box in which the animal was housed as a living specimen until its death and it became ready for the museum. The

TABLE 18.2. Eisenberg's Feeding and Substrate Matrix for Mammals

	Fossorial	Semifossorial	Aquatic	Semiaquatic	Volant	Terrestrial	Scansorial	Arboreal
Piscivore and squid-eater	−	+	+	+	+	−	−	−
Carnivore	+	+	+	+	+	+	+	+
Nectarivore	−	−	−	−	+	−	+	+
Gummivore	−	−	−	−	−	−	+	+
Crustacivore and clam-eater	−	−	+	+	−	−	−	−
Myrmecophage	+	+	−	−	−	+	+	+
Aerial insectivore	−	−	−	−	+	−	−	−
Foliage-gleaning insectivore	−	−	−	−	+	−	−	−
Insectivore/omnivore	+	+	−	+	−	+	+	+
Frugivore/omnivore	+	+	−	+	+	+	+	+
Frugivore/grainivore	+	+	−	+	−	+	+	+
Frugivore/herbivore	+	+	−	+	−	+	+	+
Herbivore/browser	+	+	−	+	−	+	+	+
Herbivore/grazer	+	+	+	+	−	+	+	−
Planktivore	−	−	+	−	−	−	−	−
Sanguivore	−	−	−	−	+	−	−	−

Source: Eisenberg 1981, 248.

Note: +, species adapted for this substrate and dietary specialization exist in the class Mammalia; −, no mammals are adapted for this substrate and dietary specialization. (See Eisenberg 1981 for definitions of terms utilized here.)

death chambers of the menageries were, in a way, the anterooms or waiting rooms of the museums. . . . There really was not much difference in the manner of presentation: the living animal in its narrow cage was provided with food, the stuffed one with preservative" (Hediger 1970, 521).

Moving the exhibition of zoo mammals beyond the "anteroom" mode has become more viable and exciting with our expanding experience of animals living in the wild through field studies. Significant exhibit improvements cannot be achieved without reference to natural history studies of the species in the wild (Maple 1981; Hutchins, Hancocks, and Crockett 1984). We must give consideration to the following variables as outlined in *The Mammalian Radiations* (Eisenberg 1981): (1) body size of adults, (2) relative brain weight, (3) basic metabolic rate, (4) geographic range, (5) diet type, (6) prey size, (7) diversity of foods eaten, (8) food-finding strategy, (9) activity patterns, (10) substrate utilization, (11) vegetation or habitat type(s) utilized, (12) mating system, (13) rearing system, (14) foraging system, (15) refuging system, and (16) antipredator system. The usefulness of behavioral studies in the maintenance of wild mammals in confinement and in developing captive breeding programs cannot be overemphasized (Eisenberg and Kleiman 1977).

Eisenberg's concepts of the "macroniche" and the "behavioral system" are central to the process of selecting mammal species to exhibit and establishing environmentally appropriate exhibit spaces. In seeking modal strategies among mammals, Eisenberg (1981, 247) devised a means of classifying living mammals into categories according to their utilization of certain environmental substrates and dietary preferences. His resulting matrix includes 8 categories of adaptations for substrate utilization and 16 categories of modal tendencies in dietary specialization. Of 128 possible modal strategies that result from this matrix, Eisenberg concluded that mammals utilize 64, or half, of them (table 18.2). Activity cycles and fluctuations in body temperature that derive from energy conservation needs and antipredatory strategies are affected by these modal strategies.

In captivity, daily feeding schedules can synchronize many rhythmic behaviors in mammals and can also result in circadian rhythms similar to those of light-dark cycles (cited in Zielinski 1986). Food-entrained rhythms have been demonstrated for herbivorous and omnivorous species. Some carnivores hunt for foods that have daily rhythms of availability. While learning to anticipate food delivery time in the zoo, they remain nocturnally active and spend most of the day resting and sleeping (Zielinski 1986; Baldwin 1992).

The restricted daily feedings experienced by many zoo mammals can result in activity cycles consisting of active periods that anticipate food delivery followed by subsequent long rest periods. The adaptive significance or theory of entrainment matters little when one is attempting to improve a mammal exhibit. Food delivery schedules that improve visitor viewing opportunities are preferable. (We discuss other aspects of foraging behavior below.) For some species, changing nocturnal cycles to diurnal ones can never be achieved, and it may be best to reconsider the species selected for exhibition in the first place. Or in some cases, especially when there is a conservation commitment to a species, an exhibit strategy can be chosen that will balance an exhibit with high holding power (diurnally active, social animals) with one in which the mammals predictably will be less active.

Understanding these major niche dimensions—substrate, diet, and activity cycle—is the first step in moving mammal exhibition beyond the kennel. This knowledge can be used to select species for exhibition that will not spend their days in burrows or otherwise out of view. A review of the mammals will demonstrate that this is not an easy task for many groups.

Eisenberg (1981, 441) emphasizes that an animal's social life may be divided into behavioral phases, which should be identified and targeted in the exhibition of mammals. He also suggests that it is useful to treat the social organizations of the two sexes differently. It is usually not possible to optimize an exhibit space for all behavioral phases for both sexes except for mammals that live in stable mixed-sex social groups.

The exhibition of coatis, *Nasua narica*, can be used as an example. There is nothing natural or constructive in the exhibition of a pair of coatis. Males are mainly solitary and can pose a danger to young coatis. Females live in small bands consisting of females and offspring, joined only during the breeding season by males (see Russell 1981, 1983a, 1983b). Targeting of the behavioral system of the coati would focus on the foraging system, refuging system, and antipredator strategy of a female band or bands. (At the National Zoological Park we have been able to maintain two bands together in one exhibit space equipped with two dens.) The exhibit would not include mating or rearing unless the male was held in a separate area and seasonally introduced to the group.

A surprising number of "solitary" carnivores are maintained in zoo exhibits as male-female or same-sex pairs. For some species, this is simply wrong behaviorally: adults are never found together except briefly for mating. In others, siblings remain together for extended periods of time after dispersal, or resident adults might utilize the same refuging or foraging areas if they are restricted by limited or highly clumped resources. We must ask, What social group is being presented in the exhibit space? Is that grouping correct for the species? At what phase in its life cycle? How long does this social grouping endure? Have the visitors been so informed?

The refuging phase in the life of a mammal is extremely important as it relates to mammalian exhibits because many mammals spend a considerable time sleeping, hibernating or estivating, or overwintering. Eisenberg points out that refuging may be strongly phasic. For example, the rearing requirements for young may be unlike the conditions necessary for adult survival, and male and female refuging areas may be radically different. Even in species with a more or less permanent social life, a single refuging area may be spatially subdivided by the age and sex classes (Eisenberg 1981, 419).

Unfortunately, the natural history literature on refuging is nonexistent for most species or lacking in the details that might be useful. We have benefited by asking field-workers to describe the characteristics of the lay-up places where they find their radio-tagged animals and encouraging them to include this information in their published accounts. A reasonable objective and a real challenge in animal exhibition is that the animal be comfortable staying in the exhibit on public view.

There is a very small body of literature available on just what mammals do in their exhibit spaces (e.g., Byers 1977; Mahler 1984; Forthman-Quick and Pappas 1986; Blasetti et al. 1988; Baldwin 1992). The improvement of existing exhibits requires an attempt to understand how animals adapt to the confines in which they live. In other words, we must seek to analyze behavior patterns as phenotypic adaptations to local conditions: the conditions of the exhibit space. The first step is to document what animals do in their exhibits and where and when they do it. Second, we must seek to understand how proximate conditions influence their behavior in their exhibits. And third, we must under-stand how the characteristics (morphological and physiological) of the species themselves are manifested in the behavior the visitor sees. We can then begin to understand why some exhibits work and other do not and, with this understanding, what animals' needs are and what we can do to fix exhibits that do not work.

Using these ideas for exhibit design and improvement is not as difficult as it may seem. A useful starting point is to fold the sixteen factors listed above into five primary design considerations:

1. Select species that are "exhibitable" in the facility available. An asocial, nocturnal, burrow-using mammal, for example, is not exhibitable in an outdoor enclosure open for daytime viewing.
2. Ensure that the macroniche of the species is considered in the exhibit design and that the exhibit is environmentally appropriate for the species.
3. Establish and explicitly state which behavioral system or systems are to be featured while the animal is in the exhibit space. Optimize the opportunity for animals to engage in nonaggressive social interactions during public viewing hours.
4. Provide appropriate species-specific resting or refuging sites for the mammals in the exhibit space.
5. Manipulate food type, amount, and distribution and timing of deliveries to optimize vigilance, food-seeking behavior, and with some species, feeding behavior (see below).

Animal Management Procedures and Environmental Enrichment

The kennel approach to zoo mammal management required only ensuring that the animals were fed and cleaned; animal keepers usually had their experience in custodial or farm work. This approach to husbandry did not recognize the effects that confinement had on the animals or the considerable effects that animal keepers have on the lives of the animals in their care. We present three recent examples of how modifications in animal management routines have significantly improved the behavior of confined mammals and likely visitor experience.

Mellen (1991) found a positive correlation between reproductive success in small nondomestic cats, *Felis* spp., and husbandry style. The more time keepers spent interacting with cats they cared for, the more likely the cats were to reproduce successfully. This result of increased "socialization" characterized by daily human-animal interactions beyond routine cleaning, feeding, and weighing—so that cats learned to feel "comfortable" with the inevitable presence of their keepers—was counterintuitive and contrary to what has been a noninteraction policy of actively minimizing contact between keepers and animals in many zoos. Mellen recommended that keepers not make pets out of the cats under their care, but encourage positive, "friendly" behavior from the cats; these interactions can be developed through cage mesh.

A second focus in improving management and housing for confined mammals has been "environmental enrichment": the provisioning of confined mammals with more things to do in their environment. In what has become a classic study, Chamove and colleagues (1982) added deep woodchip litter to otherwise unexciting primate cages: "The presence of woodchips as a direct-contact litter decreased inactivity and fighting, and increased time spent on the ground. Placing food in the deep litter led to further behavioral improvements. The use of frozen foods improved food distribution and reduced fighting in most situations, especially when the food was buried in the litter. With time, the litter became increasingly inhibitory to bacteria . . ." (Chamove et al. 1982, 308).

At the National Zoological Park, "Smokey Bear" *(Ursus americanus)* engaged in a high incidence of stereotypic pacing behavior. Hiding food in the exhibit as an alternative to his once- or twice-a-day standard feeding regimen was a very successful means of reducing the stereotypic pacing and inducing him to spend time searching for and finding food (Carlstead, Seidensticker, and Baldwin 1991). The total additional keeper time needed for this change in husbandry procedure was 20 minutes each day. In contrast, an automatic feeder in the bear's exhibit was ineffective in reducing stereotypic pacing.

Experimental evidence from sloth bears, *Melursus ursinus,* brown bears, *Ursus arctos,* and American black bears suggests that environmental stimuli that elicit manipulative behaviors are essential for guiding feeding-motivated behaviors into functional foraging sequences. Food that is hidden in manipulable objects, or that requires some complex activity to acquire (e.g., fishing or scanning an area while walking), requires the animal to constantly modify its behavior based on the stimuli it encounters, and thus to develop contingencies between behavior and its consequences (Carlstead, Seidensticker, and Baldwin 1991; Shepherdson et al. 1993). (Contingencies = "learning or more broadly, any process whereby the favorable results of some pattern of behavior produces changes in the animal that cause this behavior to be repeated or to increase in frequency" [Griffin 1984, 21]). Attempts to stimulate normal bear behavior by outfitting enclosures with feeding devices that dispense snacks at unpredictable intervals demonstrate an understanding of the high motivation of bears to feed, but they fail to allow bears to develop behavioral contingencies. The dispensed food is merely retrieved from highly predictable locations and requires no complex behaviors to obtain (Carlstead, Seidensticker, and Baldwin 1991).

A captive environment usually presents conditions to which all species must adapt, such as the presence of humans, imposed feeding regimes and a lack of foraging opportunities, veterinary medical procedures, space limitations, forced social groupings, and unchanging surroundings. Compared with the wild, confinement offers few opportunities for an animal to learn to cope with aversive conditions. Enrichment provides animals with behavioral options for responding to the environment. Data indicate that rearing in a socially or physically enriched environment, as well as experience with complex environments as an adult, promotes normal species-specific behavior, increases activity and exploration, reduces emotionality, and facilitates coping ability (research reviewed in Carlstead and Seidensticker 1989).

The behavioral benefits of enriching the environment of zoo animals by providing enclosure furnishings, toys, feeding devices, and scatter feeding have been extolled and are resulting in a general trend toward "occupational therapy" for confined mammals (Holden 1988). In our own experience, for example, the conflicting results of scatter feeding and a feeding device for bears have shown there is no one panacea. Each species or functional husbandry group (a group of species that are essentially treated the same from a husbandry point of view) should be examined to determine what is best for that group or species.

CONCLUSION

In seeking integrated principles for exhibiting mammals, we have examined those factors that affect what mammals do or do not do in exhibit spaces. Throughout this chapter we have sought to identify the dimensions that influence the mammal-zoo visitor interaction.

Exhibits fail when the life history characteristics of the mammals exhibited have not been carefully evaluated in relation to the objective of the exhibit, and when animal requirements have not been fully identified and included in the design of the exhibit space. Unfortunately, there are a multitude of examples of these shortcomings in most zoos. We have described an approach for identifying and fixing exhibits that are not working.

Improvements in animal management and in the exhibit space should be based on the characteristics and needs of the animal and the zoo's obligation to the visitor. Ask these simple questions: Can the visitor see the animals, and are they engaged in natural behavior?

APPENDIX 18.1 JONES'S PRINCIPLES FOR THE PRESENTATION OF ANIMALS AND NATURE IN ZOOS

1. Have animals at or above eye-level of viewers.
2. Don't surround animals with viewers; provide a number of smaller overlooks without overlapping lines of sight; avoid single overlooks; place overlooks on secondary pathways.
3. Allow the animal to remove itself from situations it finds stressful; allow the animal to choose between hot and cool, high and low, dry and wet, and off/on exhibit.
4. Don't display social animals in solitary confinement; display social animals in social groups.
5. Don't display deformed or disfigured animals.
6. Don't display animals using human artifacts; provide abundant occupational alternatives using features that are found in the animal's natural habitat that are suitable for the animals' physical and mental capabilities.
7. Don't exhibit the animal in a setting totally unrelated to its origins or adaptations; recreate or replicate a landscape typical of the animal's natural habitat(s) without distortion, or exaggeration, faithful in all possible details.
8. Make it impossible for the viewer to determine what contains the animal.
9. Immerse the viewer in the replicated landscape even before seeing the animal; make overlooks and adjacent circulation areas appear to be extensions of the animal's habitat; don't build perceptual barriers by placing the humans in a familiar man-made setting and the animals in a naturalistic setting.

10. Don't display animals from different habitats together in a natural habitat setting; combine compatible animals from the same habitat and use this opportunity to demonstrate and interpret inter-relationships between these species. An exception to this is when it is useful to point out adaptive characteristics the two species share.

11. Relate adjacent exhibits into habitat complexes and thus, form transitional or ecotonal areas between exhibits of adjacent habitat zones.

12. Don't design the buildings first and animal exhibits and holding areas second; plan all these elements concurrently as interrelated parts.

    Source: Jones 1982, 189-90.

REFERENCES

Baldwin, R. 1992. Behavior of carnivores in outdoor exhibits at the National Zoological Park. M.S. thesis, George Mason University, Fairfax, Va.

Bitgood, S., Patterson, D., and A. Benefield. 1986. Understanding your visitors: Ten factors that influence visitor behavior. *AAZPA Annual Conference Proceedings,* 726–43. Wheeling, W.Va.: American Association of Zoological Parks and Aquariums.

Blasetti, A., Boitani, L., Riviello, M. C., and Visalberghi, E. 1988. Activity budgets and use of enclosure space by wild boars *(Sus scrofa)* in captivity. *Zoo Biol.* 7:69–79.

Burghardt, G. M. 1975. Behavioral research on common animals in small zoos. In *Research in zoos and aquariums,* 103–33. Washington D.C.: National Academy of Science.

Byers, J. A. 1977. Terrain preferences in the play behavior of Siberian ibex kids *(Capra ibex sibirica). Z. Tierpsychol* 45: 199–209.

Carlstead, K. 1991. Fennec fox *(Vulpes zerda):* Environmental conditions influencing stereotypic behavior. *Int. Zoo Yrbk.* 30: 202–7.

Carlstead, K., Brown, J. L., and Seidensticker, J. 1993. Behavioral and adrenocortical responses to environmental changes in leopard cats *(Felis bengalensis). Zoo Biol.* 12:321–31.

Carlstead, K., and Seidensticker, J. 1989. Behavioral and physiological response to confined environments in domestic and nondomestic felids. Report, National Zoological Park, Smithsonian Institution, Washington, D.C.

Carlstead, K., Seidensticker, J., and Baldwin, R. 1991. Environmental enrichment for zoo bears. *Zoo Biol.* 10:3–16.

Chamove, A. S., Anderson, J. R., Morgan-Jones, S. C., and Jones, S. P. 1982. Deep woodchip litter: Hygiene, feeding, and behavioral enhancement in eight primate species. *Int. J. Stud. Anim. Prob.* 3:308–18.

Chamove, A. S., Hosey, G. R., and Schaetzel, P. 1988. Visitors excite primates in zoos. *Zoo Biol.* 7:359–69.

Coe, J. C. 1985. Design and perception: Making the zoo experience real. *Zoo Biol.* 4:197–208.

Coheleach, G. 1982. *The big cats.* New York: Harry N. Abrams.

Conway, W. G. 1968. How to exhibit a bullfrog: A bed-time story for zoo men. *Curator* 11:310–18.

———. 1969. Zoos: Their changing roles. *Science* 163:48–52.

Derwin, C. L., and Piper, J. B. 1988. The African Rock Kopje Exhibit evaluation and interpretive elements. *Environ. Behav.* 20: 435–51.

Eisenberg, J. F. 1981. *The mammalian radiations.* Chicago: University of Chicago Press.

Eisenberg, J. F., and Kleiman, D. G. 1977. The usefulness of behavioral studies in developing captive breeding programmes for mammals. *Int. Zoo Yrbk.* 17:81–89.

Forthman-Quick, D. L. 1984. An integrative approach to environmental engineering in zoos. *Zoo Biol.* 3:65–77.

Forthman-Quick, D. L., and Pappas, T. C. 1986. Enclosure utilization, activity budgets, and social behavior of captive chamois *(Rupicapra rupicapra)* during the rut. *Zoo Biol.* 5:281–92.

Fulghum, R. 1989. *All I really need to know I learned in kindergarten.* New York: Villard Books.

Glatston, A. R., Geilvoet-Soeteman, E., Hora-Pecek, E., and Hooff, J. A. R. A. M. van. 1984. The influence of the zoo environment on social behavior of groups of cotton-topped tamarins, *Saguinus oedipus oedipus. Zoo Biol.* 3:241–53.

Greene, M. 1987. No rms, jungle vu. *The Atlantic Monthly* 260 (6):62–78.

Griffin, D. A. 1984. *Animal thinking.* Cambridge, Mass.: Harvard University Press.

Hays, S. P. 1987. Beauty, health, and permanence: Environmental politics in the United States, 1955–1985. Cambridge: Cambridge University Press.

Hediger, H. 1950. *Wild animals in captivity.* New York: Dover Publications.

———. 1955. *Psychology of animals in zoos and circuses.* New York: Dover Publications.

———. 1970. The development of the presentation and the viewing of animals in zoological gardens. In *Development and evolution of behavior,* ed. L. P. Aronson, E. Tobach, D. S. Lehrman, and J. S. Rosenblatt, 519–28. San Francisco: W. H. Freeman.

Hoage, R. J., ed. 1989. *Perceptions of animals in American culture.* Washington, D.C.: Smithsonian Institution Press.

Holden, C. 1988. Animal rights: Uncle Sam wants happy chimps. *The Washington Post,* 16 October, C-3.

Hutchins, M., Hancocks, D., and Crockett, C. 1984. Naturalistic solutions to behavioral problems of captive animals. *Der Zoologische Garten* 54:28–42.

Jones, G. R. 1982. Design principles for presentation of animals and nature. *AAZPA Annual Conference Proceedings,* 184–92. Wheeling, W.Va.: American Association of Zoological Parks and Aquariums.

Jordan, R. H., and Burghardt, G. M. 1986. Employing an ethogram to detect reactivity of black bears *(Ursus americanus)* to the presence of humans. *Ethology* 73:89–115.

Kaplan, R., and Kaplan, S. 1989. *The experience of nature.* Cambridge: Cambridge University Press.

Kellert, S. R. 1976. Perception of animals in American society. In *North American Wildlife Conference* 41:533–46. Washington, D.C.: Wildlife Management Institute.

———. 1989. Perceptions of animals in America. In *Perceptions of animals in American culture,* ed. R. J. Hoage, 5–24. Washington, D.C.: Smithsonian Institution Press.

Lueders, E., ed. 1989. *Writing natural history: Dialogues with authors.* Salt Lake City: University of Utah Press.

Mahler, A. E. 1984. Activity budgets and use of exhibit space by South American tapir *(Tapirus terrestris)* in a zoological park setting. *Zoo Biol.* 3:35–46.

Maple, T. L. 1981. Evaluating captive environments. *Proceedings of the Annual Meeting of the American Association of Zoo Veterinarians,* 4–6. Philadelphia: American Association of Zoo Veterinarians.

Massie, J. L. 1979. *The essentials of management.* 3d ed. Englewood Cliffs, N.J.: Prentice-Hall.

Mellen, J. D. 1991. Factors influencing reproductive success in small captive exotic felids *(Felis* spp.): A multiple regression analysis. *Zoo Biol.* 10:95–110.

Morgan, J. M., and Gramann, J. H. 1989. Predicting effectiveness of wildlife education programs: A study of students' attitudes and knowledge towards snakes. *Wildl. Soc. Bull.* 17:501–9.

Morris, R., and D. Morris. 1966. *Men and pandas.* New York: McGraw-Hill.

Perry, R. 1970. *The world of the jaguar.* New York: Taplinger.

Petroski, H. 1985. *To engineer is human: The role of failure in successful design.* New York: St. Martin's Press.

Polakowski, K. J. 1987. *Zoo design: The reality of wild illusions.* Ann Arbor: University of Michigan, School of Natural Resources.

Robinson, M. H. 1988. Bioscience education through bioparks. *BioScience* 38:630–34.

Russell, J. K. 1981. Exclusion of adult male coatis from social groups: Protection from predation. *J. Mammal.* 62:206–8.

———. 1983a. Altruism in coati bands: Nepotism or reciprocity. In *Social behavior of female vertebrates,* ed. S. K. Wasser, 263–98. New York: Academic Press.

———. 1983b. Timing of reproductive effort in coatis in relation to fluctuation in food resource availability. In *The ecology of a tropical forest: Seasonal rhythms and long-term changes,* E. G. Leigh Jr., A. S. Rand, and D. M. Windsor, eds., 413–31. Washington, D.C.: Smithsonian Institution Press.

Schaller, G. B. 1972. *The Serengeti lion.* Chicago: University of Chicago Press.

Shepherdson, D. J., Carlstead, K., Mellen, J. D., and Seidensticker, J. 1993. The influence of food presentation on the behavior of small cats in confined environments. *Zoo Biol.* 12:203–16.

Shettel, H. 1989. Front-end evaluation: Another useful tool? *AAZPA Annual Conference Proceedings,* 434–39. Wheeling, W.Va.: American Association of Zoological Parks and Aquariums.

Steinbeck, J. 1954. *Sweet Thursday.* New York: Bantam Books.

Thompson, V. D. 1989. Behavioral response of 12 ungulate species in captivity to the presence of humans. *Zoo Biol.* 8:275–97.

Vail, R. W. G. 1934. *Random notes on the history of the early American circus.* Worcester, Mass.: American Antiquarian Society.

Wilson, E. O. 1975. *Sociobiology: The new synthesis.* Cambridge, Mass.: Belknap Press of Harvard University Press.

Zielinski, W. J. 1986. Circadian rhythms of small carnivores and the effect of restricted feeding on daily activity. *Physiol. Behav.* 38:613–20.

Zwinger, A. 1989. Field notes and the literary process. In *Writing natural history: Dialogues with authors,* ed. E. Leuders, 67–90. Salt Lake City: University of Utah Press.

19

The Design and Use of Moats and Barriers

David Hancocks

In the 1870s and 1880s the German architectural firm Ende and Bockmann created for the Zoological Gardens of Imperial Berlin the most impressive and elaborate zoo architecture that has ever existed (Hancocks 1971). Perhaps their most splendid work was the Elephant House, a huge edifice that, like much of Germany's best and worst, fell to the firepower of World War II.

Many zoo designers throughout nineteenth-century Europe sought exotic flavoring by producing copies of Islamic mosques and Chinese pagodas. The Berlin Elephant House was designed to simulate a Hindu temple (fig. 19.1). (We should not be surprised that foreign places of worship were treated in this sacrilegious manner; it was not uncommon for people from other lands and cultures to be put on display in zoos in the last century [see Mench and Kreger, chap. 1, this volume].) Richly ornamented and decorated with lavish murals, the building was solidly constructed of expensive materials. The interior was equally grand, designed to awe and impress. Somber and magnificent as a cathedral, and for very similar reasons, the Elephant House expressed pride of ownership, not of relics but of living beasts taken from Asian rainforests and African savannas.

It is worth examining this architectural phenomenon more closely. It takes a little time to look beyond the symbolism and the elaborate ornamentation to notice the space provided for the animal. The elephant itself is no longer awesome, as it was in the wild forests; it cannot compete with the magnificence of the architecture. Moreover, it barely has room to do anything other than turn around. This very elaborate Elephant House, like many zoo buildings, had only two simple goals: symbolically, it had to impress the visitors, and functionally, it had to contain the animals.

Zoo exhibits all tend to be equally efficient in their functional role of containing wild beasts. This efficiency, for the greater part of zoo history, has been achieved by heavy-handed means. Zoo animals typically have been restrained in gloomy cages made of stout iron bars, or kept in pits that are damp and dark (figs. 19.2, 19.3). Perhaps this was excusable a hundred years ago and more. Zookeepers were equally in the dark, with virtually no information about diets, diseases, behaviors, sociality, breeding, play, or anything of the animals' natural histories. Generally, in the wild, animals were being studied only through the sights of rifles.

So little was known about the animals that it was not possible to design for their needs. With no other information to guide them, some zoo architects, like Ende and Bockmann, designed buildings that reflected the legendary history or culture of the animals' countries of origin, creating an exotic atmosphere, suitably foreign and mysterious. Another school of thought based itself on recognition of the academic and scientific value of the collection. It considered classical styles to be more appropriate. The Monkey House at the Jardin des Plantes, built in the 1820s, is a clear example. (The French in particular seemed to have welcomed this approach. The Menagerie at Versailles, which set the pattern for so many others, clearly reflected the French academics' desire to master and exclude nature, using geometric patterns and radial symmetry to emphasize and demonstrate the superior finesse of humankind.)

Despite the astonishing amount of time, money, and energy that went into zoo construction throughout the nineteenth century, little real progress was made. Dozens of new zoos were built, but they tended only to copy each other. They varied only in scale and detail, not in concept or philosophy.

Early in the twentieth century, Carl Hagenbeck, in association with the Swiss architect Ursus Eggenschwiler, devised spectacular changes. In 1907 he opened the world's first barless zoo, at Hamburg, Germany, employing such design techniques as hidden moats, borrowed landscapes, naturalistic bands of vegetation, and artificial concrete mountains to create illusions of vast panoramas in which animals were kept separately but seen one against the other (Hagenbeck 1909).

FIG. 19.1.   The Berlin Elephant House, which simulated a Hindu temple, focused on the elaborate ornamentation rather than on providing space for the animal. (Illustration from the Zoological Society of London; reprinted from Hancocks 1971.)

FIG. 19.2.   Behind these unsubtle iron restraints at the Paignton Zoo is another unpleasant reminder of captivity: a grid of metal spikes set in the concrete floor. This technique is as unappealing as it is unsafe. (Photo by David Hancocks.)

Hagenbeck borrowed the idea of the "ha-ha" (the word obviously has onomatopoeic derivation, and should probably be spelled ah-ha!), a sunken ditch often employed in the landscaping of English country mansions to keep domestic stock out of the formal garden area, but extended the concept on a monumental scale. To discover what dimensions were needed for the ha-has, or moats, Hagenbeck made many experiments, testing and measuring the jumping and leaping powers of various animals by hanging favorite food items at different heights on long poles.

Whether for reasons of expense, lack of know-how, or timidity, Hagenbeck's ideas were not widely copied. London Zoo, with its Mappin Terraces, made an early but clumsy attempt. Over the years, several other zoos tried to adopt his principles, but amateurishly and without conviction. Vincennes Zoo, Paris, in 1934 made a more effective effort to build on his revolutionary ideas, but this was a rare exception. Indeed, Hagenbeck's sense of spectacle has rarely been equaled.

The idea of using moats as hidden devices to contain animals did not gain wide popularity until the 1950s, when outdoor grottoes became the vogue (fig. 19.4). Probably hundreds of them were built during the major phase of zoo building that followed World War II, especially in North America, where there was a new affluence, and in Germany, where the zoos had been destroyed by bombing. These grottoes, like the equally ubiquitous pits of the nineteenth-century zoos, were used principally for large mammals, es-

FIG. 19.3.   At their simplest, and worst, when used only to confine, barriers get between the viewers and the message that wild animals deserve care and respect. This particular example of insensitivity and degradation is from the Paignton Zoo. (Photo by David Hancocks.)

FIG. 19.4.   All the barriers at these bear exhibits in the Chaffee Zoo, Fresno, are so visually dominant and so conspicuously placed that they overpower any aesthetic appreciation for the animals on display. (Photo by David Hancocks.)

pecially bears, or, when built in the round (with an island in the middle), for monkeys. Sometimes made of bricks or concrete, but most often of rocks, either real or artificial, these exhibits were heralded as naturalistic and humane. Yet invariably these fanciful versions of caves and hills, devoid of anything alive except the pacing animal, were featureless and bland places.

Typically, the moats were set up like giant drains. The rockwork was oppressive and pervasive, built as clumsy replicas of arbitrarily invented geological formations. The grottoes' lack of subtlety was worsened by their monotonous repetition in zoos all over the world. The animals were kept contained in the open air, but nothing else was achieved.

Unfortunately, the mania for these grottoes coincided with the Disinfectant Period of zoo architecture. Heini Hediger (1950, 1955) pleaded long and eloquently for a naturalistic approach in the zoo, from diets to exhibits. But his was a lone voice crying in the wilderness. The Philadelphia and Frankfurt zoos represented the antithesis of Hediger's thinking, with their scientific biscuits and their tiled rooms for the habitation of apes, hygienically separated from people by the modern miracle of toughened glass. All too often, the end result resembles a cross between a bus station and a public restroom (fig. 19.5). Nonetheless, this type of housing became essential for any zoo wishing to adopt a modern, scientific pose. Marlin Perkins enthusiastically broadcast a special edition of "Wild Kingdom" from

FIG. 19.5.   Public areas and animal display areas at the National Zoo are separated by a keeper area, rigidly defined by columns and bars painted bright yellow and an untidy tangle of hoses. (Photo by David Hancocks.)

FIG. 19.6.   Rows of reptile cages at Chester Zoo. This banal approach is unfortunately typical. It creates fatigue and boredom, and destroys any interest in exploration or discovery. (Photo by David Hancocks.)

Seattle when Woodland Park Zoo opened the first Feline House to use glass for containing lions, tigers, and other big cats (Hancocks 1979). Immediately behind the glass was another technological wonder: a stainless steel mesh, activated electronically, that dropped automatically if the glass was broken. All this impressed Dr. Perkins mightily, but it did little for the cats, in their tiled rooms, with nothing to do and nowhere to get out of view.

Glass panels brought more than sterile enclosures; they also prevented any possibility of hearing or smelling the animals, provided an excellent membrane for tapping to disturb the animals, added the frustration of reflections, and imposed a very effective psychological barrier between the animals and the visitors (fig. 19.6).

At the same time that glass panels and tiled walls were in full fashion, the media were launching an increasingly vociferous campaign against keeping zoo animals in cages. Desmond Morris (1968) wrote bitterly (and accurately) about the "naked cage," arguing for more complex environments that matched animals' behavioral and psychological needs. For the most part, however, journalists concentrated their anger on the idea of keeping animals behind bars. With their connotations of jails and dungeons, iron bars are an ugly and visible public face.

Thus, for several reasons, *barriers* have been one of the few zoo problems toward which architects have been expected to apply creativity and inventiveness. Rather than concentrating on the quality of the enclosed space, or the development of zoo design philosophies, the architectural profession has been expected to limit itself to more technical matters, and especially to devising efficient means of containment. This emphasis on technical aspects of enclosure has resulted in much literature on dimensions, construction, and types of moats and barriers, particularly in publications such as *Der Zoologische Garten* and *International Zoo Yearbook,* and especially by German and Swiss architects.

Because methods of enclosure have had so much attention, the spaces contained *within* the barriers have been largely ignored. Close, even myopic, attention has been given to the possibility of physical escape. However, rarely is anything done to help the animals escape from the public eye if they want to, or escape from threats by other animals, or escape from the monotony of an unyielding and inappropriate environment. Note the difference between figure 19.7a, a traditional barrier design focusing on containment alone, and figure 19.7b, a design that takes into account the total exhibit.

Interestingly, this emphasis on barriers extends to zoo

FIG. 19.7. (*Top*) Sometimes designers go to great lengths, as in this example at the now defunct Stone Zoo, Massachusetts, to make the limits of enclosure as visible as possible. (*Bottom*) Disguised and camouflaged barriers in both the foreground and background of the lion exhibit at Seattle's Woodland Park Zoo, designed by Jones and Jones, help give the illusion of unconfined animals in a natural environment. (Photos by David Hancocks.)

FIG. 19.8.   A very successfully obscured moat barrier at Melbourne Zoo, attractively planted, minimizes the sense of separation between visitor and animal spaces. (Photo by David Hancocks.)

organizations, in which a self-imposed class structure typically separates keepers from managers, dividing not only work duties in the organization but also people's minds and conversations and the sharing of problems, hopes, frustrations, and ideas. It is significant, for example, to compare the enthusiasm applied to animal enrichment programs by zookeepers with that applied to acquisition loans of pandas by zoo directors.

Another problem of separation is the zoo-typical arrangement of exhibits by taxonomy. Natural history institutions have always tended to subdivide, rather than to create holistic views of, the natural world. Instead of integration, we invariably find the botanical gardens on one side of town and the zoological gardens on the other, and a natural history museum somewhere between the two. Within zoos, all the birds are characteristically put in one building, all the reptiles in another, and so on. The mammals are further separated into categories, so that people go to one place to see all the cats, to another to see all the bears, and to yet another to see all the pachyderms, or monkeys, or deer. It all goes against the grain of nature.

Barriers in the zoo, whether symbolic, physical, organizational, or intellectual, need to be used in such a way that they classify and distinguish, rather than merely dissect and separate. Their use should always be questioned, never taken for granted.

In a few cases physical barriers can be eliminated. For example, walk-through exhibit paddocks, with public pathways delineated by rails only about 12 inches (30 cm) high, are common in Australian zoos (figure 19.8). In the late 1980s one such two-acre (0.8 hectare) paddock, in the Healesville Sanctuary, Victoria, contained fifteen to twenty eastern grey kangaroos, *Macropus giganteus,* approximately the same number of red kangaroos, *Macropus rufus,* and several Cape Barren geese, *Cereopsis novaehol-*

landiae. In Northern Hemisphere zoos these animals would be securely separated from the public by a fence of more substantial proportions. It is not that people are different in their zoo-going behaviors in Australia than in America, just that designers and administrators tend to stick with the tried and true.

In an ideal situation we would have no barriers at all, so that people could experience wildlife as if on a walking safari in Zambia (fig. 19.9). Understandably there is a strong wish among many zoo designers for a completely invisible barrier: an electronic force-field or some other device. Antwerp Zoo experimented, quite successfully (Hancocks 1971), with very bright lights shining into interior exhibition spaces: the small birds in the enclosure would not fly into the darkness of the public area. This method, however, has other drawbacks (breeding may be affected, for example), is not suitable for many animals, and is certainly not dependable for either dangerous or rare species.

For safety's sake—that of visitors, staff, and animals—physical barriers that cannot be crossed must be used. Useful data are always available from other zoos and in the technical literature about dimensions of fences and moats that have proven successful. But it must be remembered when making such comparisons that circumstances differ from place to place, and that there can be wide discrepancies between the abilities of individual animals.

At Woodland Park Zoo, for example, a moat at the rear of a large, open gorilla, *Gorilla gorilla,* exhibit was constructed to maximum dimensions taken from other zoos with well-established records for effectively containing adult gorillas (fig. 19.10). A short time after moving into this enclosure, one of the male gorillas escaped via this moat. The important difference between the Woodland Park exhibit and those from which the moat dimensions had been taken

FIG. 19.9. In the African savanna exhibit at Woodland Park Zoo, the simple device of raising the horizon above eye level means that barriers and service buildings in the background are kept out of view. (Exhibit design and photo by Jones and Jones.)

FIG. 19.10. A tangle of vegetation and fallen trees obscures the public moat fronting Woodland Park Zoo's gorilla exhibit, and a hidden moat at the rear ensures a view of "borrowed" vegetation, designed to replicate a slash-and-burn forest clearing. (Exhibit design by Jones and Jones, photo by David Hancocks.)

was the presence of shrubs and trees of various sizes. The male gorilla, having surveyed the situation, pulled a hawthorn tree (*Crataegus* sp.; about 4-inch [10 cm] caliper) out of the ground, dropped it into the moat, then used it as a ladder to climb out the other side. That moat is now protected on the inside edge with a low-voltage electric wire, which the gorilla, after inspecting and touching it only once, now ignores.

Electric cables, or hot wires, have been used not only to contain animals but also to exclude them, notably to protect vegetation inside exhibit areas. In the right circumstances,

the right thinness of wire, particularly when used with camouflage-painted insulators, can be virtually invisible from a short viewing distance.

But there are problems with hot wires. Vegetation has to be kept clear of them, otherwise the system shorts out. Some animals have learned how to short-circuit the wires by using sticks or, as with elephants, by lifting them with their tusks. Other animals seem able to withstand surprisingly high voltages. An orangutan, *Pongo pygmaeus*, at Woodland Park Zoo used to sit with his hand on an electrified windowpane, watching with interest as the electric shocks rhythmically jolted his arm muscles. Chimpanzees, *Pan troglodytes*, in particular, seem to have hands as tough as boot leather. An electrified fence of six high-voltage cables proved no deterrent at the Chimpanzee Consortium at the Holloman Air Force Base, New Mexico (Wilson and Wilson 1969). The animals seemed oblivious to the electric shocks, climbing and swinging upon the fence without any apparent discomfort.

In the absence of electronic or magnetic force fields, some zoo people talk with fondness of "one-way glass." Such a product does not exist. Recently, glass with anti-reflecting coating has become available, but all glass reflects light, and thus images, to some degree or other. To overcome this, the light level on the viewing side must be much lower than that on the exhibit side, and if possible the glass must be angled so that it reflects only a dark, blank surface toward the viewer.

As noted earlier, glass brings many other problems, and is certainly not an invisible barrier. Indeed, when not used properly, glass can be as great a visual barrier as solid metal. A glass-paneled fence at the Toronto Zoo, for example, enclosing a lion, *Panthera leo*, draws immediate attention to itself not only through the repetitive row of metal columns supporting the supposedly invisible glass panes, but also by reflecting sunlight.

Piano-wire screens have also been used to try to create almost invisible barriers. Thin wire is strung very tightly between an upper and a lower horizontal support; the effect is rather like looking through a harp. When the eye focuses on distant objects the wires blur almost entirely from view. The technique can be most effective, but its use is limited to small animals that cannot pry the strands apart, for although the wire is very strong in linear tension, it cannot resist side pressure and is thus easily parted.

The price paid for such a light, fine barrier can be seen in the heavy top and bottom beams needed to withstand such tension. This problem is exacerbated when the beams are insensitively placed so that they are very noticeable; their bulk negates the benefit of such a visually delicate viewing screen. The small cat exhibits at the Arizona-Sonora Desert Museum in Tucson, Arizona are good, and early, examples of how piano-wire screens can be used effectively. Recent experiments at the Desert Museum have employed a catenary cable, as with a suspension bridge, rather than large horizontal beams, to hold the piano wire. This method dispenses with the need for a bulky supporting structure.

A virtually invisible fence system has been devised by Ken Stockton, Curator of Design and Planning at the Desert Museum, using multistrand wire ropes of extremely small diameter that are *tied* together to make a mesh of surprising strength. Mesh fences in the past either required welding, and thus a larger-diameter wire, or the application of clamps at each junction, which are highly visible as well as unreliable. Hand-woven wire netting, often employed in circuses and occasionally in zoos, also requires a larger-diameter wire, and has very high costs in labor. The tied mesh fence, especially when coated with a matte black finish, is to all intents and purposes invisible, particularly when seen against vegetation. There are plans to use this material at the Desert Museum for animals as strong and heavy as javelina, *Pecari (= Tayassu) tajacu.*

Location and context are also essential factors in determining the success (and invisibility) of any wire screens or fences. The landscape treatment, for example, should be identical on each side of the barrier. In the Bird House at the St. Louis Zoo, renovated in the late 1970s, piano-wire screens were used extensively and, as a novelty, placed in curved lines rather than the traditional straight patterns (fig. 19.11). The high expense of creating these transparent barriers was defeated, however, by the placement of deco-

FIG. 19.11. The Bird House at St. Louis Zoo used piano-wire screens extensively, but then drew attention to these minimalist barriers with different landscape treatments on each side. (Photo by David Hancocks.)

rative plants in black soil up to the very edge of the piano-wire screen on the public side, while on the other side the exhibition spaces were treated quite differently, usually with white or red sand floor coverings. No method could have more clearly drawn attention to a barrier that should have been inconspicuous.

Landscaping, if treated as an afterthought, is likely to exaggerate or highlight the presence of barriers. English zoos, especially, seem to delight in placing incongruous rows of flowers in front of exhibits, nicely emphasizing the differences between a pretty, domesticated human world on one side of the barrier and the usually sterile emptiness of the zoo animals' world on the other (fig. 19.12a). It is more difficult, but more satisfactory, to use landscape architecture to integrate the two sides. This technique promotes a sense of *immersion* in the landscape, resulting in much more effective exhibits and a much better informed public (Hancocks 1968; Jones, Coe, and Paulson 1976; see also Coe, chap. 16, this volume) (compare figure 19.12b with figure 19.12a). Placing people and animals in replicas of wilderness habitats is the best philosophy in moving toward nonimpedimentary barriers.

Barriers, it must be remembered, do more than keep the animals in: they must also keep people out. Someone with intimate knowledge of camels employed an effective minimalist barrier at the Toronto Zoo. It is merely a shallow retaining wall, constructed so that the camel area is about 18 inches (45 cm) higher than the public area (fig. 19.13). The camels will not, of course, step down from that height. But teenage *Homo sapiens* think nothing of stepping up and beyond such a minor obstacle, gaining easy and rapid access to the paddock and a situation of potential danger.

Clumsy approaches to barrier design in zoos are much more common than simplicity or elegance. Mesh panels are

FIG. 19.12.   *(a)* The English are particularly adept at this sort of thing: the enclosing grid of a barren cage for chimpanzees, at Longleat, is complemented and ridiculed by a neat little row of pretty flowers. *(b)* Moat edges need not be geometrical hard edges. This example of skillful treatment of a water moat edge, designed by Ted McToldridge, is at Santa Barbara Zoo. (Photos by David Hancocks.)

FIG. 19.13.   A minimal and unobtrusive barrier is sufficient to contain camels at the Toronto Zoo, but offers no impediment to humans who may choose to trespass into the enclosure. (Photo by David Hancocks.)

fixed on top of metal bars, or double layers of chain-link are fabricated, so that it is impossible to see through. This approach is ridiculous, but not at all uncommon. Moats, all too often, are big square-cut ditches, straight-lined, their concrete faces in open view. The lines of moats are also sometimes emphasized by adding bricks or rocks (fig. 19.14). Paignton Zoo, England, set grids of iron spikes in the concrete floor of its pachyderm exhibit, to keep the animals from getting close to walls or moats. They are painful to behold, both aesthetically and by association (see fig. 19.2). If moats are to be invisible to viewers, they must be designed with care and attention to detail. A design trick common in German zoos is to gently ramp the ground away from the public path, up to the edge of the moat, perhaps some 20 feet (6 meters) away. The angle of elevation obscures the moat from view. The disadvantage is that the barrier, and thus the exhibit, is placed even farther away from the public. Moats are greedy with land in any case.

The natural desire of people is to get as close as possible to the animals. Indeed, one of the few advantages of old-fashioned bars and chain-link fences is that they do allow closeness. Sometimes they also provide the only climbing

device within the animal's environment. Closeness, however, as anyone who has traveled on a crowded subway train can attest, is an ambivalent benefit. The animals in the zoo may not appreciate it at all.

Moats and barriers must separate people and animals for several reasons other than just preventing physical escape or entry: reasons such as health (people sneezing on animals, animals defecating on people), flight distance, safety (from thrown objects, for example), and diet control (people giving food to animals). It is admittedly difficult to achieve these objectives without creating a barrier that is noticeable or intrusive. But a few rules may help.

Avoid the straight lines of convenience.
Vary the angles of fences to avoid monotony; follow contour lines rather than bisecting them; and for safety as well as visual considerations, do not create acute or 90-degree angles within the enclosure.

Out of sight, out of mind.
Use every available technique to hide the barriers; use terrain to put them out of sight lines, obscure them with vegetation.

Diversify and confuse.
Use several different techniques so that one function is not repetitively obvious; disguise barriers as natural features: moats as river edges (fig. 19.15), walls as rock cliffs (fig. 19.16); introduce plantings or other screenings occasionally; hide distant fences by painting them flat black (*not* green) or camouflage colors and patterns.

Blur the barriers.
Ensure that transitional landscaping on each side of the barrier is complementary (ideally, identical); destroy the visual lines of demarcation (fig. 19.17); in nocturnal houses use artificial shadow patterns to extend beyond the plane of glass and into the public area.

Integration, not separation.
Look for opportunities to make visual connections across the barriers; use hidden moats at the back of exhibits so that the borrowed landscape extends the view; use barriers to protect areas of vegetation inside enclosures that are the same as those in the public area; incorporate landscape features such as termite mounds, rocks, logs, and so on, on *both* sides of the barrier.

Select the viewpoints.
Locate barriers at the best views, and obscure side barriers and other viewing areas from public view; never, never allow views across to other viewers.

With each of these design techniques it is essential to recognize the fact that one is copying from nature. Ugly, inappropriate, dissatisfying, ineffective exhibits are invariably the results of ignoring the axiom that *Nature is the Norm* (Hancocks 1980).

It is ridiculous to invent geological formations, producing artificial rock walls in colors, textures, and shapes that do not exist in nature. Planting flowers in rows or circles is equally false, unnecessary, and draws attention where it is neither wanted nor needed. Planting plans should aim to re-

FIG. 19.14. Attention is sometimes brought to the lines of demarcation by the addition of unsavory objects. In these instances at *(a)* London Zoo and *(b)* Calgary Zoo, jagged rocks have been set along the edges of the moats. (Photos by David Hancocks.)

flect accurately all aspects of natural landscapes, in detail and in character (see Jackson, chap. 17, this volume). One cannot improve on nature. The message that zoos must impart, in every way, is that we all must learn to respect and design with nature.

Thanks to such pioneers as George Schaller, Jane Goodall, and Dian Fossey, we have good information about many typical zoo animals in nature: about their lifestyles, behaviors, social biology, and ecology. One can now attempt to replicate their natural conditions. This undertaking can be difficult for architects and designers who need to stamp their design personalities on their work—unless they can recognize that replicating nature is, in fact, a far greater challenge, more difficult than inventing new ideas, more worthwhile than relying on divine inspiration.

We all know how different, and how much more satisfying, it is to watch an animal in the wild than an animal in the zoo. Thus, zoo designers need to look to nature to find the

FIG. 19.15.   Water moats typically have clearly defined geometric edges. It is much more satisfying to simulate nature, as in this primate exhibit at Woodland Park Zoo. (Exhibit design by Jones and Jones, photo by David Hancocks.)

FIG. 19.16.   This primate exhibit at Woodland Park Zoo, designed by Jones and Jones, carefully mimics the superficial untidiness of nature, and is intended to simulate an area of fallen trees and exposed earth banks created by flash flood torrents. This provides a legitimate reason for the presence of dead trees (as climbing apparatus) and earth banks (as enclosing barriers). (Photo by David Hancocks.)

answers, not to other zoos. We must find specific examples to duplicate, and use intelligence and design skills to create scenes and details that are as compelling as nature by virtue of their authenticity.

Zoo designers must literally cross the boundaries so that they can find out what the animals need and want; they must redefine the boundaries so that zoo exhibits can explain and integrate; they must blur the boundaries, deliberately, so that people and animals share the same naturalistic environment. Finally, zoo designers must recognize that barriers are not mere lines between two worlds, separating us and them. When the barrier problem is perceived as part of a total ecological design philosophy, the barriers shift from being control mechanisms that restrain animals in one place for our viewing expediency to become integral components of one total, holistic, and naturalistic zoo environment.

REFERENCES

Hagenbeck, C. 1909. *Beasts and man.* London: Longman.
Hancocks, D. 1968. *Zoological gardens.* Thesis, Bachelor of Architecture, University of Bath.

FIG. 19.17.   Between the viewer and this coyote is a virtually invisible fence; a hand-tied, anodized stainless steel cable forming a 2-inch (5-cm) square mesh, using overhand knots. This prototype at the Arizona-Sonora Desert Museum employs 27-lb. (12-kg) cable wire 0.012 inches (0.3 mm) in diameter.

———. 1971. *Animals and architecture*. New York: Praeger.

———. 1979. *75 years: A history of Woodland Park Zoological Gardens*. Seattle: Woodland Park Zoological Gardens.

———. 1980. Bringing nature into the zoo: Inexpensive solutions for zoo environments. *Int. J. Stud. Anim. Prob.* 3:170–77.

Hediger, H. 1950. *Wild animals in captivity: An outline of the biology of zoological gardens*. London: Butterworth.

———. 1955. *Studies of the psychology and behavior of animals in zoos and circuses*. London: Butterworth.

Jones, G., Coe, J. C., and Paulson, D. R. 1976. *Woodland Park Zoo: Long range plan, development guidelines and exhibit scenarios*. Seattle: Department of Parks and Recreation.

Morris, D. 1968. Must we have zoos? Yes, but . . . *Life*, 9 December, 78–86.

Wilson, W. L., and Wilson, C. D. 1969. *Colony management and proposed alterations in the light of existing conditions at the Chimpanzee Consortium*. New Mexico: Holloman Air Force Base.

20

Mixed-Species Exhibits with Mammals

WARREN D. THOMAS AND EDWARD J. MARUSKA

The idea of mixing different species in the same enclosure is nearly as old as the idea of holding exotic animals in captivity. It simply makes good sense, and is a practical use of facilities, to have one enclosure serve as the holding quarters for more than one species. During the evolution of zoos, certain mixed-species approaches to animal display became standard. Large flight cages contained many different bird species, reptile gardens often combined different crocodilians, and the typical "snake pit" showed a number of species together.

The idea of combining mammal species has taken a little longer to develop and has had its share of problems and complications (fig. 20.1). The question that one must ask is whether there are sufficient positive returns or advantages to showing species jointly to compensate for the risk inherent in placing them together in the same enclosure. Looking at the positive side, the advantages are quite striking:

1. The same physical facility can be utilized for multiple species, thereby reducing the necessity for and expense of separate enclosures for each individual species.
2. Combining species in the same enclosure presents a more interesting and educational display to the public. Mixed-species exhibits provide an opportunity for direct comparison of the sizes and adaptations of different species, and often the movements and dynamics of the different species together create a much more appealing, exciting exhibit.
3. The combination of multiple species within a single enclosure can provide a stimulus to the animals through their contact with each other. The level of activity increases, and as long as the activity is not antagonistic, this can have a positive effect on the physical and mental health of the animals.

The negative side of combining species is that one always runs the risk of interspecific agonism or even violent

encounters. Aggression can be overt, manifested in displacement, competition for position and space within the enclosure, and competition for food, or it can be subtle, evidenced simply as intimidation by social dominance or as stress. These negative factors must be carefully weighed, considered, and controlled in order to combine multiple species successfully.

Three general principles can be used as guides in developing mixed-species exhibits:

1. The difficulty of combining species is inversely proportional to the size of the exhibit: the larger the exhibit, the fewer the problems. Therefore, if the space is large enough, a combination of more than one large species is usually successful; for example, giraffes, *Giraffa camelopardalis*, can be combined with antelope; bison, *Bison bison*, with pronghorns, *Antilocapra americana*; rhinos with antelopes. This has been done frequently in drive-through game and wild animal parks during the last three decades.
2. Most zoos feel that, for educational purposes, only animals from the same geographic region should be exhibited together.
3. The smaller the enclosure, the more critical the selection of the animals placed within it to ensure natural behavior. Within this concept some specific guidelines can be suggested.

GUIDELINES FOR SPECIES SELECTION

1. The animals to be combined should not occupy exactly the same ecological niche in situ because they will compete. Arboreal species can often be placed with terrestrial forms, or aquatic species with terrestrial or arboreal forms, because in each case they would live in different sections of the exhibit. In some cases animals have been combined that have two different lifestyles, one diurnal and the other nocturnal, which also results in a noncompetitive situation.

At the time of writing, Warren D. Thomas was with the Los Angeles Zoo, Los Angeles, California.

ever, exceptions may be made when another theme is present (e.g., nocturnal exhibits).

FACTORS IN THE SUCCESS OF MIXED-SPECIES EXHIBITS

There are several things that can be done within the exhibit itself to improve the chances of success. Anything the animals might compete over should be provided in abundance. For example, if the species are arboreal, the zoo manager should ensure that there are more branches and perching areas available than are needed; too few will result in competition. It also pays to have visual barriers so animals can occasionally get out of visual contact with other animals sharing the enclosure. (Visual barriers are important not only for mixed-species exhibits but also for single-species exhibits that tend to have aggressive inhabitants). Heavily planted or rock-decorated enclosures provide many areas for hiding or seclusion, which in turn decreases aggressive contacts. Of course, the plants and rocks should be placed in such a way that the animals are still on view to the public. Any method that can be devised to exclude one species from a portion of the exhibit will allow the other species the use of that portion undisturbed. Small-tipped branches could be exploited by a very tiny animal, but would exclude a heavier one. The use of upright barriers spaced so that a smaller animal can get between them but a larger animal cannot is also a good method of separating areas. Another technique that has been utilized but not fully exploited is the use of light intensities—one portion of the display can be more brilliantly lit than the rest of the exhibit, creating differentially desirable zones for each species.

Feeding times are crucial. If possible, the species should be separated for feeding. If they cannot be fed separately and eat essentially the same food, it is necessary to have enough feeding stations dispersed throughout the enclosure to ensure that each animal obtains a fair share and that competition is kept to a minimum. At the Cincinnati Zoo, consideration of widely diverse food habits has allowed successful exhibition of a troop of colobus monkeys, *Colobus polykomos*, with a pair of aardwolves, *Proteles cristatus*, for the past several years in a 6 m long by 6 m wide by 5 m high exhibit. Upon introduction, the male colobus made some threatening overtures that lasted several minutes. There was no response from the aardwolves, and after the initial threatening behavior from the male colobus, both species totally ignored each other.

Animal managers must be constantly sensitive to behavioral changes that occur with reproductive cycles. While these changes do represent a problem, it is one that can be controlled. For example, a group of markhor, *Capra falconeri*, were compatibly housed with Celebes crested macaques, *Macaca nigra*, until the markhor young were born. The level of harassment of the markhor females and young escalated to the point that it became necessary to separate the species, or there would have been severe losses among the markhor young. A similar situation occurred in a relatively small enclosure that combined suni antelope, *Neotragus moschatus*, with spot-nosed guenons, *Cercopithecus ascanius schmidti*, with the same result (fig. 20.3).

FIG. 20.1.   A small group of male gerenuk has been introduced into the giraffe exhibit at the Los Angeles Zoo. The combination so far has proved workable.

2. When combining animals that occupy similar niches or have similar lifestyles, competition can be averted by choosing animals of markedly different size: for example, bongos, *Tragelaphus eurycerus isaaci*, and yellow-backed duikers, *Cephalophus sylvicultor*; or gaur, *Bos gaurus*, and axis deer, *Axis axis*. The larger animals tend to accept the presence of the smaller ones once they become accustomed to them, and do not dominate them. It should be noted that some smaller species may harass larger ones due to an aggressive or territorial nature, so size alone is not the sole determining factor.

3. Belligerent species should be avoided unless there is an immense amount of space. Certain species are inherently antagonistic to other species, and it is extremely difficult to work them into a multiple-species display unless it is very large. Examples are the hartebeest genera, *Damaliscus* and *Alcelaphus*; male springbok, *Antidorcus marsupialis*; and male zebra, *Equus* spp. (fig. 20.2).

4. As a general rule, primates are difficult to work in with other animals because in captivity they are usually aggressively territorial. Further, because primates are so inquisitive, they tend to "worry" or harass other species.

5. One cannot mix closely related species without running the risk of hybridization.

6. Mammal species from the same zoogeographic area are generally used together for their educational value; how-

FIG. 20.2.   Zebras and giraffes sharing an exhibit at the Los Angeles Zoo. The stallion frequently had to be removed because of his aggression toward the giraffes.

INTRODUCTIONS: SETTING UP A NEW MIXED-SPECIES EXHIBIT

The initial phases of setting up a mixed-species exhibit are crucial. Many species will live together compatibly once they become accustomed to each other; however, getting the animals sufficiently accustomed to each other's presence that neither species threatens or provokes antagonistic behavior is often a formidable task.

There are no short cuts during this early establishment phase. It takes time, patience, and thorough knowledge of both species' behavior and of each animal involved. There can be wide variation in individual responses. For example, it is easy to state that all male zebras, or all male springbok, are very aggressive and difficult to work into mixed-species displays. Yet there are exceptions. The converse is also true: eland, *Taurotragus* spp., for example, are generally very easy-going and docile, but some individuals are totally intolerant of other species close by. Knowledge of each individual animal's temperament reduces the chance of problems when species are combined.

The introduction must be carried out in a slow, carefully orchestrated fashion. The ideal situation is to have a brand new area to which neither of the species has been exposed, thereby avoiding the problem of established territorial identification. Additionally, the animals will show as much wariness toward the new area as toward the new species to which they are being introduced, which will dissipate their attention.

If, however, this is not the case, and one desires to introduce a new species into an enclosure that already has an-

FIG. 20.3.   Schmidt's spot-nosed guenons and suni antelope have been maintained together at the Los Angeles Zoo. The antelope did demonstrate some signs of stress.

other species in residence, the original residents must be removed from the exhibit before the new residents are added. The new group must be given sufficient time to become totally adjusted to and comfortable with the area in the absence of the original residents. The length of time needed before reintroduction of the original residents is dependent on the species involved, and can best be determined by careful observation. The new animals must be calm, well adjusted, and have established a normal, undisturbed behavioral pattern. At this point you can start the slow, careful introduction of the original inhabitants.

Sometimes you can use the strengths and weaknesses of each species in order to have them combine well. For example, it is possible to combine a small animal with an aggressive personality with a larger animal with a nonaggressive personality; for example, the ring-tailed coati, *Nasua nasua*, and the spectacled bear, *Tremarctos ornatus*; or a variety of species with the gelada baboon, *Theropithecus gelada* (e.g., at the Henry Doorly Zoo in Omaha, the Bronx Zoo/Wildlife Conservation Park, the Los Angeles Zoo, and the Gladys Porter Zoo in Brownsville, Texas). The gelada is a much more passive animal than almost any of the other baboons.

Sometimes it is only necessary to allow the animals to become visually (and probably olfactorily and auditorily) acquainted with each other through a wire barrier. At other times more elaborate manipulations must be made. It is axiomatic that the younger the animals are, the greater the chance of success. Like humans, older animals become resistant to change (although, since all animals are individuals, exceptions occur.)

In very large enclosures, gaur have been very successfully combined with a number of other species, but this is much more difficult in smaller enclosures. We were, however, successful at the Los Angeles Zoo in introducing juvenile gaur (a male and two females) to blackbuck, *Antilope cervicapra* (a male and three females) in an enclosure 55 m long by 23 m wide. The gaur were in residence in the display first. The two species were placed in visual contact for several days before being released together, with observers monitoring their actions. After about 40 minutes of chasing, all individuals settled down to peaceful coexistence. A short time later, one male and three female axis deer were introduced into the same enclosure, creating barely a ripple (Crotty 1981).

A more complicated introduction was accomplished between a pair of white rhinoceroses, *Ceratotherium simum simum*, and one male and two female Damara zebras, *Equus burchellii antiquorum*. Their enclosure was 34 m long by 15 m wide, relatively small in comparison to the bulk of the animals. There were certain facts we knew ahead of time. White rhinos in general (and these individuals in particular) tend to be quite placid and tolerant animals once they are familiar with their surroundings; however, the addition of another species could have sent them into a panic. The zebras were the more challenging species as they tend to be easily agitated; this was particularly evident in the three individuals being introduced. Zebras may work themselves into a veritable frenzy once this state is triggered, and they are often injured in the process. To avoid this, it was necessary to bring both species to a point at which they totally accepted and avoided each other. The yard already had a large pool and a group of boulders to act as a visual barrier. Further, part of the yard was separated from the rest with telephone poles set wide enough apart for the zebras, but not the rhinos, to pass through. The zebras were released into the display and given approximately 3 weeks to become familiar with the area and to settle down. During this time the rhinos were locked in their barn, out of sight and out of contact with the zebras.

After 3 weeks the rhinos were reintroduced into the exhibit. Between the rhino barn and the yard was a holding area separated from the yard by upright metal posts set close enough that the rhinos could not pass through. The first step in reintroducing the rhinos was to turn them loose in this intermediate area. Here both species had visual, olfactory, and auditory contact and could come close to each other. After about a week of this contact, the animals were virtually ignoring each other. In the next phase, we locked one of the rhinos in the barn and turned the other one out into the holding area, leaving the gate of the holding area open so that the rhino had access to the yard where the zebras were. As the rhino was psychologically attached to his locked-in mate, he stayed close by the barn, but became totally accustomed to the gate being left open, as did the zebras. This step lasted 2 days. Then we reversed the procedure, putting the other rhino out under the same conditions. This rhino also refused to leave the holding area, and became accustomed to the gate being left open and seeing the zebras walk by without a barrier in between. Next we put both rhinos into the holding area with the gate open. At that point the two rhinos slowly walked out into the yard, showing absolutely no apprehension, as they had become thoroughly familiar with having the gate open and seeing the zebras. The zebras simply moved out of the rhinos' way, going in and out behind the telephone-pole barrier and the boulders. None of the zebras' actions were so quick or violent as to upset the rhinos, and quite soon even the zebras' nervousness diminished. This became a compatible group that could be combined, separated, and recombined without problems. The entire introduction procedure took approximately 2 months, but to have rushed through any of the steps along the way would have invited disaster.

PRIMATES IN MIXED-SPECIES EXHIBITS

Primates pose special problems for mixed-species exhibits. Even in the absence of overt aggression between the primates and other species in the exhibit, there may be evidence that one of the species is under stress; often it is in the best interests of the animals' welfare to separate the species. Stress can often be manifested in subtle ways, such as animals declining in condition for no obvious reason, a lowered food intake, a psychological manifestation such as self-mutilation (see Carlstead, chap. 31, this volume), or a pathological manifestation such as gastric ulcers.

An example of this was chronicled at the Los Angeles Zoo, with a combination of silver langurs, *Trachypithecus* (=*Presbytis*) *cristatus*, and giant squirrels, *Ratufa bicolor*, in an exhibit 18 m long by 12 m wide by 5 m high. The animals appeared to get along quite well together. However, based on a detailed behavioral study done by the Los Angeles Zoo Research Division and the physical condition of the squirrels (e.g., rough hair coat and some anorexia), it became obvious that the squirrels were under a low, but detrimental, level of stress, even though the langurs rarely were close enough even to touch them.

TABLE 20.1.   Small Mixed-Species Exhibits

Species	Have been combined with these species in various zoos	Remarks
Chevrotain (Greater mouse deer), *Tragulus napu*	Bali mynah, *Leucopsar rothschildi*	
Golden lion tamarin, *Leontopithecus rosalia*	Giant toad, *Bufo marinus* Iguanas, *Iguana* sp. Screech owls, *Otus* spp. Basilisks, *Basilisous* spp. Red-capped cardinal, *Paroaria gularis* Two-toed sloth, *Choleopus didactylus* Hairy armadillo, *Chaetophractus* spp. Acouchi, *Myoprocta acouchy (=pratti)* Degus, *Octodon degus* Pygmy marmoset, *Callithrix (=Cebuella) pygmaea*	Iguanas ate plants Male hairy armadillo occasionally caught and ate acouchis and birds
Diana monkey, *Cercopithecus diana*	Rock hyrax, *Procavia capensis*	
Titi monkey, *Callicebus* spp.	Acouchi, *Myoprocta acouchy (=pratti)* Degus, *Octodon degus* Rock cavy, *Kerodon rupestris* Pygmy marmoset, *Callithrix (=Cebuella) pygmaea* Black-tailed marmoset, *Callithrix argentata*	Rock cavy aggressive to titis Marmosets intimidated titis
Owl monkey, *Aotus trivirgatus*	Three-banded armadillo, *Tolypeutes matacus*	
Goeldi's monkey, *Callimico goeldii*	Rock cavy, *Kerodon rupestris* Degus, *Octodon degus* Nutria, *Myocastor coypus*	
Black-and-white lemur, *Varecia variegata*	Ring-tailed lemur, *Lemur catta*	
Bushbaby, *Galago* spp.	Tree shrew, *Tupaia* spp. Brush-tailed porcupine, *Hystrix cristata* Zorilla, *Ictonyx striatus*	Predation by tree shrews on bushbaby young and vice versa. Predation by zorillas on bushbabies. Zorillas removed.
Nubian ibex, *Capra nubiana*	Patas monkey, *Erythrocebus patas*	
Golden-headed lion tamarin, *Leontopithecus chrysomelas*	Three-banded armadillo, *Tolypeutes* spp. Acouchi, *Myoprocta acouchy (=pratti)*	

There are, however, successful mixed-primate exhibits. Such combinations not only make interesting displays but may also help solve behavioral problems within established exhibits. For example, the Los Angeles Zoo had a successful breeding group of gelada baboons, but when the breeding male died there was no other male readily available in North America to replace him. The one remaining male in the group, which at that point contained six adult females with accompanying young, was about 5 years old. This young male simply had not matured sufficiently to establish dominance in the troop. The entire family fell into chaos, with constant fighting and antagonistic behavior among the females and also among the young. To restore order and, we hoped, trigger the 5-year-old male to mature quickly, we created a diversion by moving in two female chimpanzees, *Pan troglodytes*. After a transition period of introduction, the effect on the baboons was dramatic. All internal strife and fighting came to an abrupt halt as the baboons became more concerned about what the chimps were doing. Fur-

ther, within a week, the "outside intruders" seemed to trigger the young male baboon to assume dominance within the troop, and social order was quickly reestablished. Of course, it certainly helped his transition to dominance that the females appeared more concerned about the presence of the chimps than anything else at that moment. The combined display made an interesting exhibit, and the compatible relationship between the chimps and baboons was maintained for many years. Eventually, there was concern over the fact that there had been no reproduction in the gelada group since the combination was established, and it was thought that underlying stress might be suppressing breeding activity. After a thorough reproductive evaluation of the male gelada, it was determined that he was indeed infertile, but there was insufficient evidence that the causative agent was the presence of the chimpanzees. For other, unrelated reasons, this exhibit was eventually disbanded.

Animal body size often has little to do with whether a

TABLE 20.1.   *Continued*

Species	Have been combined with these species in various zoos	Remarks
Greater mouse lemur, *Microcebus coquereli*	Fat-tailed lemur, *Cheirogaleus medius*	
Large tree shrew, *Tupaia tana*	House shrew, *Suncus murinus* Lesser tree shrew, *Tupaia minor*	
Potto, *Perodicticus potto*	Senegal galago, *Galago senegalensis*	
Hammer-headed bat, *Hypsignathus mon-strosus*	Big fruit bat, *Artibeus jamaicensis* Nectar-eating bat, *Carollia perspicillata* Sugar glider, *Petaurus breviceps*	
Slender loris, *Loris tardigradus nordicus*	Chevrotain, *Tragulus napu*	
Prehensile-tailed porcupine, *Coendou pre-hensilis*	Degus, *Octodon degus*	Occasional problems with quills in degus
Sumatran orangutan, *Pongo pygmaeus abelii*	White-handed gibbon, *Hylobates lar*	
Prevost's squirrel, *Callosciurus prevostii*	Leopard tortoise, *Geochelone pardalis* Bali mynah, *Leucopsar rothschildi* Glossy starling, *Aplonis panayensis* Echidna, *Tachyglossus aculeatus* Plantain squirrel, *Callosciurus notatus* Giant squirrel, *Ratufa* spp. Mouse deer, *Tragulus* spp. Sugar glider, *Petaurus breviceps* Small-clawed otter, *Amblonyx cinereus*	Competition for nest sites with other squirrels and curtailed reproduction. Squirrels developed stress ulcers with otters
Japanese macaque, *Macaca f. fuscata*	Blue sheep, *Pseudois nayaur szechuanensis* California sea lion, *Zalophus californianus*	
Black-tailed marmoset, *Callithrix argentata*	Golden-headed lion tamarin, *Leontopithecus chrysomelas* Titi monkey, *Callicebus* spp. Goeldi's monkey, *Callimico goeldii* Acouchi, *Myoprocta pratti* Degus, *Octodon degus* Rock cavy, *Kerodon rupestris*	All-male group Black-tails intimidated titis All-male group
Gorillas, *Gorilla gorilla*	Colobus monkey, *Colobus* spp.	
Olive baboons, *Papio papio*	Meerkat, *Suricata suricatta*	
Barbary apes, *Macaca sylvanus*	Small-clawed otters, *Amblonyx cinereus*	

Note: Exhibits with two species in 500 m² or less

combination of species does or does not work. The Gladys Porter Zoo inadvertently had a pair of stump-tailed macaques, *Macaca arctoides,* get onto an island exhibit of orangutans, *Pongo pygmaeus,* which included some formidable, fully adult males. At first the animals appeared compatible, but a short time later the stump-tailed macaques had to be removed from the island because they were seriously intimidating the orangs. The male stump-tailed macaque would sit in the hallway of the indoor enclosure and refuse to let any of the orangs come in, even though the male orang outweighed him by nearly 300 pounds. A similar situation was reported in an exhibit that combined titi monkeys, *Callicebus* sp., with marmosets at the National Zoo (W. A. Xanten, pers. comm.).

With the present emphasis on large tropical zoo exhibits, greater experimentation with mixed-primate exhibits needs to occur. The Cincinnati Zoo has successfully exhibited four Sumatran orangutans, *P. pygmaeus abelii,* and two white-handed gibbons, *Hylobates lar.* Since their introduction

into a large, tree-studded exhibit, 53 m by 23 m, there has been a continuing playful interaction between the male gibbon and several orangs. In other exhibits, the inclusion of carefully placed, lightly electrified barriers prevents escapes and also ensures a security zone. The Cincinnati Zoo is currently testing the introduction of a troop of six patas monkeys, *Erythrocebus patas,* into a bonobo, *Pan paniscus,* exhibit measuring 52.3 m long by 29.2 m wide. The exhibit is hilly and also has many fallen trees that provide additional visual barriers. The patas monkeys have generally remained on the nonexhibit side of the dry moat, which is protected from the bonobos' entrance by strategically placed hot lines that allow only the smaller patas monkeys to enter. With time, the patas monkeys are becoming better adjusted to the exhibit, and occasionally they may be seen walking among a group of four resting bonobos with no interaction. The exhibit also houses six rock hyraxes, *Procavia* sp. In an inside display, 7 m long by 4 m wide by 5 m high, with prominent rocky areas and large artificial trees, a pair of diana

TABLE 20.2.   Large Mixed-Species Exhibits

Species	Combined with two or more species	Remarks
Koala, *Phascolarctos cinereus*	Echidna, *Tachyglossus aculeatus* Sugar glider, *Petaurus breviceps* Potoroo, *Potorous tridactylus*	Reproduction all spp.
Dik-dik, *Madoqua kirkii*	African golden weaver, *Ploceus subaureus* Black-winged red bishop, *Euplectes hordeaceus* Golden-breasted starling, *Cosmopssarus regius* Speckled pigeon, *Columba guinea*	
California sea lion, *Zalophus californianus*	Northern elephant seal, *Mirounga angustirostris* (female) Capybara, *Hydrochaerus hydrochaeris* Celebes macaque, *Macaca nigra* Gelada, *Theropithecus gelada*	All spp. kept in breeding groups except elephant seals. Pool with two islands; geladas on one and macaques on the other.
Bettong, *Bettongia penicillata*	Goffin cockatoo, *Cacatua goffini* Aru Island sulphur-crested cockatoo, *Cacatua g. eleonora*	
Bongo, *Tragelaphus euryceros*	Yellow-backed duiker, *Cephalophus sylvicultor* Bat-eared fox, *Otocyon megalotis*	All spp. were kept together in large groups
North American bison, *Bison bison*	North American wapiti, *Cervus canadensis* Pronghorn, *Antilocapra americana* Longhorn cattle, *Bos taurus*	
Giraffe, *Giraffa camelopardalis*	Zebra, *Equus burchellii* Common eland, *Taurotragus oryx*	Male zebras often must be separated; very common grouping seen in many zoos
Giraffe, *Giraffa camelopardalis*	Combined singly with the following: Lesser kudu, *Tragelaphus imperbis* Greater kudu, *Tragelaphus strepsiceros* Gerenuk, *Litocranius walleri* Grant's gazelle, *Gazella granti* Thomson's gazelle, *Gazella thomsonii* Ostrich, *Struthio camelus* Sitatunga, *Tragelaphus spekeii* Nyala, *Tragelaphus angasii*	Bushbuck family and many of the gazelles are quite tolerant
Aardwolf, *Proteles cristatus*	Black-and-white colobus, *Colobus guereza* Hyrax, *Procavia capensis*	

monkeys, *Cercopithecus diana*, share their space with three tree hyraxes, *Dendrohyrax* sp.

WHY USE MIXED-SPECIES EXHIBITS?

A few additional comments are in order. Mixing animals just for the sake of mixing them has limited justification. Where possible, they should be combined with some thought to their natural, overlapping ranges in the wild; there will also be times when other factors should be considered when arriving at a given combination. The factors to be considered should be determined by the animal manager.

One argument often voiced against mixed-species exhibits is the prospect of cross-contamination with parasites and diseases. We find this threat of little consequence if the proper safeguards have been observed beforehand. Introducing animals of a new species that have undergone proper veterinary screening and health precautions offers no more problems, by and large, than introducing a new animal of the same species.

Perhaps the most commonly voiced criticism is that the inherent risk of antagonistic interactions is so great that it is

difficult to justify the mixed-species display technique. We reject this premise because we believe that if it is properly approached, if all guidelines are strictly adhered to, and if one proceeds slowly and cautiously, the end result of the mixed-species technique far outweighs the risk and effort required to bring it to fruition.

Mixed-species displays have been a common feature of zoological gardens for quite some time, and are likely to remain so for practical, educational, and aesthetic reasons. In table 20.1 we list several known workable combinations of two different species in the same enclosure. Table 20.2 lists several examples of mixed-species displays in which more than two species have been involved. If the selection of species is handled judiciously, and there is a continuous monitoring of the dynamics of the exhibit, the mixed-species display will be a success, and will be more appealing and meaningful to the viewer than a single-species display.

REFERENCES

Crotty, Michael J. 1981. Mixed exhibit species at the Los Angeles Zoo. *Int. Zoo Yrbk.* 21:203–6.

TABLE 20.2.   *Continued*

Species	Combined with two or more species	Remarks
Aardvark, *Orycteropus afer*	Mongoose lemur, *Lemur mongoz* Egyptian fruit bat, *Rousettus aegyptiacus* Giant fruit bat, *Pteropus giganteus*	
Barbary macaque, *Macaca sylvanus*	Aoudad, *Ammotragus lervia* Small-clawed otter, *Amblonyx cinereus*	
Gaur, *Bos gaurus*	Axis deer, *Axis axis* Blackbuck, *Antilope cervicapra*	Best to do when animals are young, especially gaur. Must be done in careful stages.
Springhaas, *Pedetes capensis*	Potto, *Perodicticus potto* Senegal galago, *Galago senegalensis*	
Gelada, *Theropithecus gelada*	Combined singly with the following: Aoudad, *Ammotragus lervia* Nubian ibex, *Capra nubiana* Rock hyrax, *Procavia* spp.	
Mixed deer	Mule deer, *Odocoileus hemionus* White-tailed deer, *Odocoileus virginianus* Fallow deer, *Dama dama* Sika deer, *Cervus nippon* Barasingha deer, *Cervus duvauceli*	Combined of breeding groups, of each sp. Area 3 acres. Very little aggression and no hybridization as long as there was adult male for each species.
Bonobo, *Pan paniscus*	Patas monkey, *Erythrocebus patas* Rock hyrax, *Procavia capensis*	
Olive baboon, *Papio papio*	Meerkat, *Suricata suricatta*	
Gorilla, *Gorilla gorilla gorilla*	Colobus monkey, *Colobus* spp.	
Nilgai, *Boselaphus tragocamelus*	Combined singly with the following: Axis deer, *Axis axis* Blackbuck, *Antilope cervicapra*	
Red kangaroo, *Macropus rufus*	Dama wallaby, *Macropus eugenii* Emu, *Dromaius novaehollandiae* Cassowary, *Casuarius* spp.	Many combinations of macropods have been successful where there is significant size difference. Ratites work in well.

Note: Exhibits with two or more species in 1,500 m² or more.

Hediger, H. 1950. *Wild animals in captivity,* 111–12. London: Butterworth Publications.

———. 1955. *Psychology and behavior of captive animals in zoos and circuses,* 81–87. New York: Criteria Books.

Public zoo records:

Brownsville, Texas, 1983
Cincinnati, Ohio, 1987
Hanover, Germany, no date
Milwaukee, Wisconsin, 1973
New York/Bronx Zoo, New York, 1980
Omaha, Nebraska, 1986
Pretoria, South Africa, 1969
San Diego, California, 1983
Singapore, 1986
Zurich, Switzerland, 1979

21

Enclosure Furnishings and Structural Environmental Enrichment

Terry L. Maple and Lorraine A. Perkins

"In every good zoo the animal does not feel itself in any way a prisoner, but—as in the wild—it feels more like the tenant or owner of that unit of space to which the animal instinctively lays claim."

(Hediger 1969)

Zoo biologists have accepted the responsibility of collaborating with architects and engineers to design exhibits that enhance the lifestyles of captive animals. Indeed, the public's growing interest in animal welfare demands that zoos carefully consider programs and techniques that will contribute to the "psychological well-being" of the entire collection (e.g., Erwin and Deni 1979; Segal 1989). The zoo profession has responded to this challenge with considerable enthusiasm.

During the past decade, zoos have become increasingly naturalistic, providing opportunities to exhibit and manage mammals in appropriate social groupings (Coe 1985; Coe, chap. 16, this volume; Hancocks 1980; Hancocks, chap. 19, this volume; Hutchins, Hancocks, and Crockett 1984; Maple and Hoff 1982; Ogden, Lindburg, and Maple 1993). It is within such naturalistic surroundings that species-typical behavior patterns flourish. In complex environments where stressors (i.e., environmental stimuli that challenge the organism) occur at optimal frequencies and magnitudes, captive mammals emit natural behaviors, successfully breed, rear their offspring, and reach their normal life span. Psychopathology (e.g., stereotypic pacing, self-mutilation, bizarre deprivation acts, coprophagia) (see Carlstead, chap. 31, this volume) is rarely observed in effective simulations of the natural habitat (Clarke, Juno, and Maple 1982; Erwin and Deni 1979; Maple 1979; Maple and Finlay 1986). The wide-ranging scope of such naturalistic habitats has been clearly described by Ewer (1973):

> The area . . . must contain all the necessities of life. A sufficiency of food, water and shelter are the most obvious requirements but provision must also be made for the estab-

lishing of normal social relationships. . . . It is therefore necessary to take account not only of food requirements but also of social organization and breeding behaviour when considering living space and its utilisation. (254)

There are a multitude of environmental variables that contribute individually and collectively to the well-being of captive mammals. Some of these variables may be classified as elements of the physical environment (Maple 1979). One such class of variables, "enclosure furnishings," is an important source of environmental enrichment. This chapter is primarily concerned with the many ways that such furnishings (including nest boxes, loose browse, manipulable objects, and toys) can be utilized to improve the quality of life in captivity. In addition, we briefly review feeding practices in zoos as an opportunity for environmental enrichment.

A captive mammal may live in an environment that consists of a single public room and adjoining night quarters, or it may be provided with spacious outdoor exercise yards. We recognize that "total available living area" is only one of many characteristics of space. Environmental psychologists, studying human subjects, evaluate the effectiveness of a room in terms of its color, ambient environment (noise, temperature, illumination, odor), size, and shape. These variables are not unimportant to animals, but we know much more about their effects on people (Heimstra and McFarling 1974). A strong statement about the shape of zoo environments was issued by Hediger (1969):

> The most inadequate home of all . . . is the corner of a cubical space in which three planes are joined together. . . . The cube is a false starting point for zoo architecture. (196)

212

FIG. 21.1.   Apes build comfortable nests in the wild, which can be simulated with movable materials and flexible cage furnishings in captivity. (Photo by J. Fowler.)

Completely flat surfaces at right angles (e.g., "the cube") are as rare as straight lines in the wild. Hediger regarded the cubic form a "monstrous humanization," committed because it is the cheapest, simplest, and most familiar mode of construction. One salient disadvantage of cubic environments is the ease with which animals can be "cornered" by adversaries, thus contributing to morbidity and mortality.

While human beings evaluate the effects of furnishings in terms of "efficiency, comfort, beauty and value" (Heimstra and McFarling 1974), we propose that it is "comfort, appropriateness, and inherent utility" that make furnishings such an important aspect of the animal's environment (fig. 21.1). If they provide comfort by virtue of the animal's preference, fit the animal's needs and abilities, and promote activity and interaction, furnishings will contribute to the well-being of captive mammals.

In the pages that follow we have elected to emphasize the published research literature rather than the practitioners' unpublished lore. While the latter is an important source of ideas (and should not be ignored), management and design decisions should be based on reliable data generated by systematic observations. One limitation to this approach is that many captive mammals have not yet been the subject of scientific research. As a result, reports of nonhuman primate taxa will be more frequently cited herein than studies of any other mammalian group.

A NATURALIST'S PERSPECTIVE

Many wild mammals spend much of their time feeding and foraging. By contrast, captive mammals receive food infrequently, often in single daily servings, and are largely inactive as a result. Jane Goodall (1968) discovered that the chimpanzees, *Pan troglodytes*, of the Gombe Stream spent 6 to 8 hours each day feeding, traveling from 1 to 10 miles each day in search of food. According to Rodman (1979), Bornean orangutans, *Pongo pygmaeus pygmaeus*, engaged in feeding activity for 45.9% of each day, and traveled for

11.1% of each day. The pattern for the mountain gorilla, *Gorilla gorilla beringei*, is similar (Harcourt and Stewart 1984; Maple and Finlay 1987). By reference to field data, it is possible to alter the way in which captive animals are fed and thereby increase their activity levels to approach wild norms. Individual feeding bouts can be prolonged by the provision of food that is difficult to process (e.g., artichokes, pineapples, coconuts). More frequent feedings and distribution of food throughout an enclosure effectively provide diversion and relieve boredom (Bloomsmith 1989). Feeding innovations are best accomplished in physical settings that are large, complex, and natural. Some innovations are also possible in restricted settings.

By studying the activity budgets of wild animals and comparing their schedules with those of their captive counterparts, it is possible to determine whether the captive setting is conducive to the expression of species-typical behavior (cf. Forthman-Quick and Pappas 1986). In fact, appropriate (i.e., "natural") behaviors are most likely to occur in naturalistic surroundings. Unfortunately, many captive mammals are deprived of the benefits of a naturalistic habitat. As Harcourt (1987) recently suggested:

> The fault lies partly with zoo management, which sometimes appears to disregard knowledge gained from studies of species in the wild, and partly with the fieldworker, who disregards both the special problems of captivity and the necessity of making his knowledge available to the zoo manager. (248–49)

It should be acknowledged that some mammals are relatively inactive by nature. For example, African lions, *Panthera leo*, are known to spend 20 hours a day conserving energy (Estes 1993; Schaller 1972). Howler monkeys, *Alouatta* spp., and walrus, *Odobenus rosmarus*, spend 70% and 67% of each day at rest respectively (Sims 1993). For animals such as these, enrichment strategies may be employed to ensure that their activity does not fall below its expected duration, or to elicit activity when it can do the most good (e.g., to educate the public).

FIG. 21.2.   Ropes or artificial lianas provide opportunities for species-appropriate locomotion and movement through vertical space. (Photo by T. Maple.)

The naturalist's perspective (always based on accurate field data) provides a context within which zoo designers and programmers can solve problems. For example, in essentially "hard" environments, furnishings are provided to *soften* the enclosure. "Hard architecture" was characterized by Sommer (1974) as lacking in permeability and unchangeable, inducing distortions in behavior and psychological withdrawal (Maple and Archibald 1993).

CRITERIA FOR ENRICHMENT

Virtually any mammalian taxon can benefit from the presence of appropriate enclosure furnishings. The provision of usable surfaces, objects, toys, and manipulable and movable materials gives the animals sources of novelty, variability, complexity, and stimulus change. The amount of usable space can be increased by the judicious placement of enclosure furnishings that enable individuals to move vertically and horizontally throughout the entire enclosure (figure 21.2). Without access to the vertical dimension, many animals are limited to a terrestrial lifestyle within space defined by area but not by volume (Maple 1979, 1980; Maple and Stine 1982). Even predominantly horizontal animals can benefit from vertical space. For a variety of mammalian taxa, enclosure furnishings provide greater opportunities for locomotor activity and exercise.

Which mammalian taxa benefit most from enrichment? There is some evidence that more "intelligent" animals express a greater need for stimulation and therefore do not suffer boredom gladly. Big-brained taxa such as monkeys and apes, carnivores, elephants, and marine mammals should reap relatively greater benefits from enclosure enrichment.

Likewise, the hypothetical constructs "exploration" and "curiosity" can be applied here. For example, Glickman and Sroges (1966) discovered that nonhuman primates and carnivores were more likely to investigate novel objects than were other zoo animals. Furthermore, Parker (1969) found

that among the nonhuman primates, the apes exhibited the highest levels of curiosity and exploration.

If we choose to ignore the hierarchical data from comparative psychology, applying instead an ecological approach, omnivores and opportunists are more exploratory by nature; herbivores are far less inclined to explore. (In part, this is because the preferred foods of omnivores/opportunists are less abundant and, hence, more difficult to find.) By almost any standard of measurement, it is possible to differentiate animals in terms of their proclivities and needs. Male mammals are generally more exploratory than females (unless they are monogamous), while young mammals are always more manipulative and playful than adults (cf. Mitchell 1982).

It should be emphasized, however, that enrichment strategies can be tailored to benefit all captive animals, regardless of the magnitude of their curious, exploratory, or manipulative propensities. Fortunately, enclosure enrichment strategies for many mammal species have been well documented.

Among the smaller mammals, the highly intelligent and intensely curious mongooses, *Herpestinae,* are likely to be especially prone to boredom (synonyms: dullness, doldrums, weariness; Random House Dictionary of the English Language 1987). As Rasa (1975) observed, "Unfortunately, many zoo cages are devoid of anything that could interest a normal mongoose and, as a result, the inmates squat apathetically in a nestbox or pace up and down, oblivious to all around them, a classic case of motor stereotypism" (66).

The Oxford American Dictionary (1980) defines "enrichment" as "the improvement of quality by adding things." The extent of environmental enrichment is limited only by our imaginations and the inherent qualities of the enrichment device. Enrichment is by nature a dynamic process, but some sources of stimulation have proved hazardous to health. Water, for example, if provided in shallow, moving pools, is highly desirable. By contrast, many great apes have drowned in deep water moats (Brown, Dunlap, and Maple 1982).

Cement culverts and other visual barriers ("buffers") have been used in primate breeding colonies to provide cover and escape from adversaries, but the same effect can be obtained with grassy hills or berms. Where the topography is favorable, berms function as attractive natural "furnishings" that facilitate social relations among group-living mammals. Similarly, artificial rockwork can be shaped to provide specialized enclosure furnishings that promote activity, interaction, and security. For example, rock promontories may be used as lookouts by mammalian taxa as diverse as prairie dogs, *Cynomys* spp. (Egoscue 1975), patas monkeys, *Erythrocebus patas* (Bloomstrand and Maple 1987), and meerkats, *Suricata suricatta* (Wemmer and Fleming 1975).

MANIPULABLE OBJECTS AND MATERIALS

A comprehensive study of objects and their influence on primate behavior was conducted by Wilson (1982), who observed gorillas and orangutans residing in forty-one zoos in seven European countries. She searched for a relationship between the animals' activity levels and the variables of enclosure size, usable surface area, frequency of feeding, number of companions, and the presence of objects. For both pongid taxa, the factors most closely associated with activity were the number of companions and the presence of objects. The presence of objects proved to be more important than the actual size of the enclosure, and movable objects were more effective than immovable ones. As Wilson concluded, "Space is not enough; there must be something in the space" (208). In a recent study of twenty-nine orangutans in nine American zoos, Perkins (1992) essentially confirmed Wilson's findings.

Natural branches and vinelike ropes have been used by Snowdon and Savage (1989) to improve cages for marmosets and tamarins. These naturalistic furnishings were arranged so as to provide variation in textures, diameters, and degrees of firmness; when grasped, their give was not uniform. Nest boxes and containers for food and water were also placed high to contribute further to the arboreal orientation of space. The configuration of ropes and branches was changed quarterly.

Both social and solitary play can be induced by movable objects within an enclosure. For example, Rasa (1975) discovered that golf and Ping-Pong balls induced play in mongooses. Apparently, the balls resemble eggs, which the animals normally break and eat. They also played with dangling strings, small cardboard boxes, and pieces of newspaper or cloth. At Zoo Zurich in Switzerland (C. Schmidt, pers. comm.), ropes and sacks are routinely hung from the tops of wire cages for many species. Perhaps the ultimate hanging toy is the huge tractor tire that was suspended from the ceiling of the elephant house in Zurich. This massive object was provided for a bull elephant that had to be routinely isolated from human beings and elephants alike. Of course, these must be regarded as functional, albeit unnatural, solutions. At the Basel (Switzerland) Zoo, zoo biologist Jorg Hess has distributed great quantities of rolled newsprint throughout the enclosures of great apes. Such enclosures

FIG. 21.3.   Boomer balls, new at left and used at right. (Photo courtesy of M. A. Bloomsmith.)

take on a messy appearance, but the apes don't seem to mind!

Working at Zoo Atlanta, our collaborators have recently experimented with the introduction of hard rubber balls (known as "boomer balls") into the enclosures of a variety of mammals (fig. 21.3). These objects have been particularly effective in Atlanta with bears, large cats, and potbellied pigs, *Sus scrofa*. Since boomer balls often stimulate playful activity, it is appropriate to refer to them as "toys." Other observers have discovered that boomer balls are especially effective in water, where they bounce in response to an animal's movements.

While Gilbert and Wrenshall (1989) reported success with a "wolf"-sized nylaball introduced to groups of cynomolgus macaques, *Macaca fascicularis*, Line (1987) reported almost no interaction with nylaballs by individually housed rhesus macaques, *M. mulatta*. It may be safely concluded that the balls are more effective when the environment is conducive to sustained movement.

Working at the Topeka (Kansas) Zoo, Tripp (1985) examined the complexity of an environment for orangutans by comparing three exhibit conditions: (1) no manipulables or edibles, (2) manipulables present, and (3) manipulables and edibles present. The greatest activity was associated with the third condition. Both manipulation and locomotion were stimulated by the experimental enrichment procedure. These experimental data provide support for the earlier comments of comparative psychologist Robert M. Yerkes (1925), who wrote:

> If the captive cannot be given opportunity to work for its living, it should at least have abundant chance to exercise its reactive ingenuity and love of playing with things. . . . The greatest possibility of improvement in our provisions for captive primates lies in the invention and installation of apparatus which can be used for play or work. (229)

Other behavioral pioneers have advocated occupational opportunities for enriching the lives of captive mammals, including Garner (1896), Morris (1961), and Kortlandt (1960). These esteemed observers clearly recognized that such complex creatures need stimulating surroundings to be

Fig. 21.4.   Polar bear grasping fishsicle. (Zoo Atlanta photo.)

mentally and physically healthy. In nature, food acquisition is a challenging, time-consuming task. Too often we overlook feeding as a potential source of enrichment. A successful simulation of the natural habitat requires some attention to feeding and foraging behaviors. For example, prey catching has been simulated for polar bears, *Ursus maritimus*, by the use of "fishsicles" (fig. 21.4). A fish is frozen in a water-filled bucket, then thrown into the enclosure pool, stimulating pursuit and manipulation of the ice-encased fish by a determined bear (Law and Boyle 1986). Pieces of fruit and vegetables can also be encased in ice to lengthen processing time.

Live food (e.g., fish) influences the behavior of small felids in captivity (Shepherdson et al. 1993). For example, fishing cats, *Prionailurus viverrinus*, at the Metro Washington Park Zoo in Portland, Oregon, slept less and were more active, emitted previously unrecorded hunting behaviors, and utilized more of their enclosure when presented with live fish. The authors concluded, "An environment in which an animal can find food as a consequence of its natural exploration and foraging behavior is an essential key to approximating natural habitats and to improving animal welfare" (215).

The provision of simple browse (cf. Maple 1980; Akers and Schildkraut 1985) can contribute to reductions in the expression of coprophagia and regurgitation/reingestion (R & R) behavior. In a study by Gould and Bres (1986), the provision of browse increased feeding time from 11% to 27% of the day. However, browse alone does not completely suppress behaviors such as R & R, which may have a long developmental history and resist complete extinction. Chamove and his associates (1982) discovered that the addition of deep woodchip litter reduced aggression and increased the activity of monkeys living in laboratory cages. Experience at Zoo Atlanta and other zoos indicates that straw seeded with raisins and other tidbits provides similar benefits. Browse can also be suspended from cage tops or

from tree limbs. Animals with horns or antlers will use this browse for sparring, cleaning, and scratching as well as tearing off pieces for consumption.

Smith, Lindburg, and Vehrencamp (1989) observed captive lion-tailed macaques, *Macaca silenus*, to record their response to two methods of food presentation: (1) bite-sized portions and (2) whole foods. With the presentation of whole foods (e.g., broccoli, papaya, bananas, grapes, carrots, yams, apples, oranges), mean dietary diversity, feeding time, and total food consumption increased. As the authors concluded, whole foods "more closely mimic [conditions] in nature and . . . are therefore more likely to contribute to psychological well-being" (64).

The great apes prefer straw and leafy cuttings as nesting materials. While the large-bodied apes rest and sleep upon nests, smaller mammals may deeply immerse themselves within the loose material. For example, Rosenthal (1975) reported that water opossums, *Chironectes minimus*, housed at the Lincoln Park Zoo in Chicago utilized deep straw at once as a "nest and safe retreat."

Absorbent substrates are necessary for many small mammals, but there is no universally acceptable material. For example, Dryden (1975) determined that excelsior (wood-wool), cotton, and paper strips were unsatisfactory substrates for the Asian musk shrew, *Suncus murinus*. The subtleties of mammalian husbandry are evident from Dryden's explanation: "The animals become entangled in excelsior and cotton and are frightened by the rustling noise produced when moving through dry paper" (14). Throughout Europe, woodwool has been used as a nesting material for the great apes (fig. 21.5). It has the advantage of being easily raked up, since it tends to stay together in a tangled mass (unlike straw). However, while experienced animals do not typically consume woodwool, it has been known to cause serious constipation when ingested by inexperienced animals (C. Schmidt, pers. comm.).

Hutchins, Hancocks, and Crockett (1984) described the

FIG. 21.5.   At Apenheul in the Netherlands, gorillas are provided with large quantities of woodwool for nesting. (Photo by T. Maple.)

use of sand and red gravel as a substrate for the floor of a caracal, *Caracal,* enclosure at Woodland Park Zoo in Seattle. In addition, the enclosure was furnished with volcanic rocks, dead tree branches, and dried sagebrush. When given the opportunity to spend time in the enriched enclosure or in an adjacent sterile alternative, the animals elected to spend 80% of their time in the naturalistic habitat. The use of a sand substrate in the old feline house at Zoo Atlanta significantly contributed to healthier feet (R. McManamon, pers. comm.). It is well known that softer substrates are better for captive elephants, whose lives are frequently shortened by chronic foot disease.

Bloomstrand et al. (1986) evaluated a food-puzzle enrichment device invented by Dr. Ken Riddle and concluded that it was a cost-effective way to occupy time. It is a simple puzzle box for captive apes requiring the animal to push a peanut through a kind of finger maze in order to obtain the reward. In the presence of this device, chimpanzees spent less time engaged in coprophagia and other undesirable behaviors. However, some aggression was induced by competition over access to the device, prompting the authors to suggest that chimpanzees in groups would need several workstations. Another food puzzle was developed for Zoo Zurich by Kurt Rothfelder, who called it a "holzrugel" or "wooden, round thing" (fig. 21.6). The device, cut from a tree branch, is loaded with raisin paste. The apes obtain the mixture by "fishing" in the hole with a stem.

In the mid- to late 1970s a series of reports described devices that allowed zoo animals to "work" for food rewards (Markowitz 1975, 1978, 1979). Markowitz and his collaborators' approach established conditions in which captive animals can exert some degree of "control" over their environment. Markowitz's deployment of interactive devices such as "tic-tac-toe" games and "flying meatballs" is legendary. For example, Foster-Turley and Markowitz (1982) designed an interactive display for Asian small-clawed river otters, *Amblonyx cinereus.* Live crickets were offered as the

FIG. 21.6.   A holzrugel is probed with a small stick to obtain a food reward. (Zoo Atlanta photo.)

food reward. Placement of the apparatus led to an increase in activity within the enclosure. Furthermore, the otters continued to hunt crickets even when other food was readily available.

The technical apparatus designed by Markowitz for use in zoo environments has received some criticism (Hutchins, Hancocks, and Crockett 1984) on the grounds that the devices are artificial and unnatural. However, as Forthman-Quick (1984) concluded, the technical approach of Markowitz and the naturalistic approach favored by many zoo designers are not mutually exclusive. As Markowitz himself has demonstrated (1982), automatic feeders and prey-catching devices can be hidden within a landscape and/or effectively naturalized. The evidence indicates that activity and natural hunting responses can be induced and regulated by established contingencies of reinforcement. The state of this art is very natural indeed, and it ought to be carefully

FIG. 21.7.   Captive chimpanzees in Bastrop, Texas, probe "honey pot" with tree branches. (Photo by T. Maple.)

FIG. 21.8.   A drumming device was constructed by staff for the use of chimpanzees at Zoo Zurich. (Photo by T. Maple.)

considered as one way to achieve an environmental enrichment effect.

The suggestion that interactive enrichment devices send the wrong message to zoo visitors, that is, that animals "*depend* upon their caretakers who then *exploit* them for entertainment," no longer rings true. The technology pioneered by Markowitz is a promising management tool when applied appropriately. However, in highly naturalistic environments, toys and equipment may detract from the carefully crafted illusion of realism. In very hard environments, such as laboratory settings, aesthetics are far less important. In the modern zoo, technology should be always be creatively unobtrusive.

In our opinion, "passive naturalism" does not improve upon the interactive technology of Markowitz. The next generation of enrichment devices will surely blend computer-based technology and landscape immersion techniques. Animals can benefit from opportunities to manipulate their environments in all of the varied ways that our creativity permits (fig. 21.7).

Some of the best examples of naturalistic occupational devices are the artificial termite mounds that can be observed now in many zoos throughout the world. Nash (1982) described such a device in operation at Edinburgh's Scottish National Zoological Park, where it was equally appreciated by the chimpanzees and the public. The chimpanzees' regular use of the termite mound enabled local behavioral scientists to study chimpanzee tool use. Termite mounds have also been used by dwarf mongooses, *Helogale parvula*, which break eggs by propelling them through their back legs against the hard surface of the mound. The availability of a termite mound can stimulate natural behaviors in a variety of creatures (Bloomstrand et al. 1986; Besch 1981; Poulson 1974). Apes will also use a termite mound as a resonating drum. Large oil barrels and other artificial devices have also served as a stimulus to drumming (fig. 21.8).

Of course, a captive animal will eventually habituate to the presence of any enrichment device that is unchanging. As van Hooff (1967) observed: "Only those devices serve to occupy them most fully that (1) have an inherent amount of complexity or variability, (2) permit them to perform some natural activity [e.g., nesting or climbing; fig. 21.9] or (3) which render a nondevaluating reward" (35).

SCRATCH POSTS, NEST BOXES, AND SLEEPING PLATFORMS

Many small animals find security and comfort in locations where they can sleep individually or collectively, depending on their natural inclinations. The astute zoo biologist will

FIG. 21.9. An unnatural, but functional, climbing structure in use at the Bastrop chimpanzee facility in Texas. (Photo by T. Maple.)

provide sufficient sleeping places to accommodate changes in social relationships brought forth by sexual maturity or other factors, biological or otherwise. With regard to small felids, Leyhausen (1961) noted that few zoos have adequately housed these animals. He advised that indoor enclosures should contain a variety of tree trunks with intact branches, pieces of rock, and broad boards for elevated resting. Small cats, according to Leyhausen, also require cover and a variety of different pathways through the exhibit. Meyer-Holzapfel (1968b) successfully bred the shy European wildcat, *Felis silvestris,* by providing sleeping boxes immediately upon the animals' arrival. However, Leyhausen also noted that too much "furniture" could interfere with necessary cleaning. This point has been emphasized by Thomas (1986), who urged a "balance" between aesthetics, an animal's needs, and maintenance.

Animals that engage in scent marking will use their enclosure furnishings as signposts. In this manner, furnishings induce natural behavior patterns. The expression of such behaviors can be both amusing and fascinating in a zoo setting (Rasa 1975). For many taxa (for example, marmosets and tamarins), excessive cleanliness masks olfactory cues and inhibits breeding.

Both bears and cats benefit from scratch posts, which can be bolted to enclosure walls or, if large enough, placed on the floor of the enclosure. Sections of dead hardwoods work very well for this purpose. Scratch posts are also desirable for elephants, which use them to stimulate their sensitive skin (fig. 21.10). In addition to scratch posts, other naturalizing elements that are important to both elephants and rhinos are pools of clean water, mud wallows, and sandboxes. (Markowitz [1982] once enriched an elephant habitat by installing a car wash system so that the animals could get wet simply by pulling a chain!)

As browsers, both elephants and black rhinos, *Diceros bicornis,* eventually tear deadfall apart. Where there are no available manipulable materials, these animals will rub their tusks and horns against the hard surfaces of walls and doors, a behavior pattern that can lead to injury or loss. Rhinos, bison, and many other horned ungulates characteristically spar with deadfall, which must be regarded as a source of arousal. For animals that are naturally curious and manipulative, whole trees can be uprooted and provided as "megabrowse." Eisenberg (1975) discovered that providing rotten or hollow logs helped to prevent stereotypic locomotion by captive *Solenodon paradoxus.* However, since solenodons are inclined to poke their long snouts and slender appendages into crevices, logs and branches must be devoid of sharp projections or cracks. Maki and Bloomsmith (1989) found that uprooted oak trees were used by captive chimpanzees for up to 5 months. The animals sit and move about in the deadfall, consume the bark, leaves, and root ball, and manipulate all parts of the tree.

For many large animals, private denning areas are required if offspring are to be reared normally. In wild polar bears, for example, the mother is normally solitary, and the den protects her helpless offspring from cannibalism by adult males. In the zoo environment, maternity dens are conducive to normal parenting. When animals must be separated to follow management protocols, enlightened cage design can reduce the stress of isolation. Barnett, Hemsworth, and Winfield (1987) recently determined that the chronic physiological stress syndrome experienced by tethered pregnant pigs could be ameliorated by modifications in stall design. Wemmer (1974) noted at least three advantages of the polar bear dens designed for the Brookfield Zoo: (1) the animals used them readily and thus did not have to be confined during parturition; (2) the dens simulated the natural conditions of darkness and body-fitting contour; (3) the small den size acted to conserve body heat.

Variations in the placement or number of nest boxes have not been the subject of systematic inquiry. However, volume

FIG. 21.10. Elephants using vertical dead tree as rubbing post at Zoo Zurich. (Photo by T. Maple.)

15 (1975) of the *International Zoo Yearbook* contains a section devoted to small mammals, edited by J. F. Eisenberg and D. G. Kleiman, with many descriptions of enclosure furnishings and enrichment materials. For large mammals, details regarding enclosure design are widely scattered and largely unavailable. The best sources for ideas on enclosure design are still the works of Hediger (1950, 1969), the recent symposia distributed by the Paignton Zoological and Botanical Gardens (e.g., Michelmore 1976), and the 32 volumes of the *International Zoo Yearbook*. (see also Kenyon and Robinson, appendix 2, this volume).

As a rule, group-living mammals require multiple nest boxes. For example, at Zoo Zurich (C. Schmidt, pers. comm.), multiple nest boxes have been required for the red panda, *Ailurus fulgens*, river otters, *Lutra* spp., and other small carnivores. (Spotted hyenas, *Crocuta crocuta*, require multiple dens for the same reasons). The species-typical flight distance and normal spatial requirements will determine the appropriate location for an individual's nest box. Angled nest boxes, such as those with an L shape, are more natural and provide a greater sense of privacy and security (cf. Eisenberg 1975). For small mammals, the dimensions of a nest box can be important; greater security is provided if the nest box is snug. Nest boxes appear to be especially important for carnivorous and omnivorous mammals (Meyer-Holzapfel 1968a). Wooden nest boxes last a few years, while hard plastic materials are longer-lasting and easier to clean.

The sleeping platforms provided in zoos rarely conform to the animal's body contour, and we have seen few examples of "comfortable" furniture in mammalian night quarters. We believe that an animal's comfort is important, and for this reason, we do not advocate the use of metal sleeping platforms. Wooden platforms are more comfortable, but they are difficult to clean. Some of the new plastic polymers and resins are promising substitutes. Polypropylene has been successfully utilized for sleeping platforms at the Yerkes Primate Research Center of Emory University (Swenson, pers. comm.). At Woodland Park Zoo, a chain-link bed was designed for use in the zoo's innovative gorilla facility. The flexible chain was vinyl-coated, attached to a metal frame, and bolted to the walls. Filled with straw, these beds are truly flexible and comfortable, resembling sloping nests in the wild. The gorillas apparently agree. Suspended cargo nets, woven from natural fibers, may also be provided as a kind of hammock for nonhuman primates.

CONCLUDING REMARKS

Enclosure furnishings must be provided if captive mammals are expected to behave naturally and normally. Furnishings can be an important component of a complex captive environment. When zoo animals are housed in hard, inappropriate enclosures, it is very difficult to send a meaningful conservation message. If zoo visitors cannot see the connection between zoo animals and their habitat, we have failed to generate conservation awareness.

Zoo biologists should be actively in touch with the findings of field biologists. In fact, one way to ensure better exhibit programming (largely the responsibility of curators) is for zoo management to encourage field visits by zoo personnel. The more that we know about an animal's habits in nature, the better our chances of designing appropriate and effective zoo environments. When a zoo exhibit has been finished and opened, it is still useful to check and recheck its environment against the standards of the wild. The reliability and validity of this approach requires objective data. Post-occupancy evaluations should be encouraged (cf. Ogden 1989).

There are still many zoo animals for which we have very few field data to apply. More details will be required for enlightened design. Moreover, our captive environments must be increasingly flexible so that enclosure enrichment devices can be evaluated and adjusted. This too is the job of zoo biology. We are simply not studying our zoo animals enough.

The most effective furnishings produce behavior patterns that are typical of wild animals. Brachiating primates, such as gibbons and orangutans, will emit such behaviors when the environment provides opportunities for their expression. In many zoos, orangutans and gibbons cannot possibly brachiate. The animals are therefore prevented from expressing a natural behavior pattern, and the public is deprived of seeing one of their most unique behavioral attributes.

Landscape realism is an important educational tool in zoos, and is good for the animals too. However, to keep activity levels high, we should not ignore the promise of interactive technology. It is very likely that future zoo exhibitry will benefit from naturalistic landscapes blended with computer technology. This may be a particularly important combination in night houses, where zoo animals typically spend two-thirds of their lives. For very active animals, such as elephants, providing opportunities to engage in nocturnal problem-solving may be the most cost-effective way to contend with enforced idleness. Elephants, rhinos, and hippos should be provided with opportunities for activity at night, but only a few zoos have elected to do it.

In our opinion, good zoo environments are the product of multiple disciplines. Unfortunately, many zoos lack diversity among their professional staff. Teams comprising psychologists, zoologists, architects, engineers, horticulturists, and educators are better prepared for innovation. Such diversity in programming and design should be encouraged in the development of every zoo. Innovative enclosure furnishings will be developed in the same way.

Zoo professionals should also pay attention to recent advances in biomedical settings. Markowitz, for example, has shifted his attention to laboratory primates (e.g., Markowitz and Line 1989), but his work is likely to continue to be of value to zoo animals and zoo biologists alike.

Modern zoo design is increasingly naturalistic, depending as it must on the findings of field biology and environmental psychology. As we learn more about the many ways in which the physical environment influences animal behavior, the art and science of zoo biology will continue to advance.

REFERENCES

Akers, J. S., and Schildkraut, D. S. 1985. Regurgitation/reingestion and coprophagy in captive gorillas. *Zoo Biol.* 4:99–100.

Barnett, J. L., Hemsworth, P. H., and Winfield, C. G. 1987. The effects of design of individual stalls on the social behavior and physiological responses related to the welfare of pregnant pigs. *Appl. Anim. Behav. Sci.* 18:133–42.

Besch, D. A. 1981. Chimp island residents tap tool-using talents. *Animal Kingdom,* June–July, 30–33.

Bloomsmith, M. A. 1989. Feeding enrichment for captive great apes. In *Housing, care, and psychological well-being of captive and laboratory primates,* ed. E. F. Segal, 336–56. Park Ridge, N.J.: Noyes.

Bloomstrand, M. A., and Maple, T. L. 1987. Management of Af-rican monkeys in captivity. In *Comparative behavior of African monkeys,* ed. E. L. Zucker. New York: Alan R. Liss.

Bloomstrand, M. A., Riddle, K., Alford, P., and Maple, T. L. 1986. Objective evaluation of a behavioral enrichment device for captive chimpanzees (*Pan troglodytes*). *Zoo Biol.* 5:293–300.

Brown, S. G., Dunlap, W. P., and Maple, T. L. 1982. Notes on water contact by a captive male lowland gorilla. *Zoo Biol.* 1:243–50.

Chamove, A. L., Anderson, J. R., Morgan-Jones, S. C., and Jones, S. P. 1982. Deep woodchip litter: Hygiene, feeding, and behavioral enhancement in eight primate species. *Int. J. Stud. Anim. Prob.* 3:308–19.

Clarke, A. S., Juno, C. J., and Maple, T. L. 1982. Behavioral effects of a change in the physical environment: A pilot study of captive chimpanzees. *Zoo Biol.* 1:371–80.

Coe, J. C. 1985. Design and perception: Making the zoo experience real. *Zoo Biol.* 4:197–208.

Dryden, G. L. 1975. Establishment and maintenance of shrew colonies? *Int. Zoo Yrbk.* 15:12–18.

Egoscue, H. J. 1975. The care, management and display of prairie dogs in captivity. *Int. Zoo Yrbk.* 15:45–48.

Eisenberg, J. F. 1975. Tenrecs and solenodons in captivity. *Int. Zoo Yrbk.* 15:6–12.

Erwin, J., and Deni, R. 1979. Strangers in a strange land: Abnormal behaviors or abnormal environments? In *Captivity and behavior,* ed. J. Erwin, T. L. Maple, and G. Mitchell, 1–28. New York: Van Nostrand Reinhold.

Estes, R. D. 1993. *The safari companion.* Post Mills, Vt.: Chelsea Green.

Ewer, R. F. 1973. *The carnivores.* New York: Cornell University Press.

Forthman-Quick, D. L. 1984. An integrative approach to environmental engineering in zoos. *Zoo Biol.* 3:65–78.

Forthman-Quick, D., and Pappas, T. C. 1986. Enclosure utilization, activity budgets, and social behavior of captive chamois (*Rupicapra rupicapra*) during the rut. *Zoo Biol.* 5:281–92.

Foster-Turley, P., and Markowitz, H. 1982. A captive behavioral enrichment study with Asian small-clawed river otters (*Aonyx cinerea*). *Zoo Biol.* 1:29–44.

Garner, R. L. 1896. *Gorillas and chimpanzees.* London: Osgood McIlvaine.

Gilbert, S. G., and Wrenshall, E. 1989. Environmental enrichment for monkeys used in behavioral toxicology studies. In *Housing, care, and psychological well-being of captive and laboratory primates,* ed. E. F. Segal, 244–54. Park Ridge, N.J.: Noyes.

Glickman, S. E., and Sroges, R. W. 1966. Curiosity in zoo animals. *Behaviour* 26:151–88.

Goodall, J. 1968. The behavior of free-living chimpanzees in the Gombe Stream Reserve. *Anim. Behav. Monogr.* 1:161–311.

Gould, E., and Bres, M. 1986. Regurgitation and reingestion in captive gorillas: Description and intervention. *Zoo Biol.* 5:241–50.

Hancocks, D. 1980. Bringing nature into the zoo: Inexpensive solutions for zoo environments. *Int. J. Stud. Anim. Prob.* 1:170–77.

Harcourt, A. H. 1987. Behavior of wild gorillas and their management in captivity. *Int. Zoo Yrbk.* 26:248–55.

Harcourt, A. H., and Stewart, K. J. 1984. Gorillas' time feeding, aspects of methodology, body size, competition, and diet. *Afr. J. Ecol.* 22:207–15.

Hediger, H. 1950. *Wild animals in captivity.* London: Butterworths.

———. 1969. *Man and animal in the zoo.* London: Routledge and Kegan Paul.

Heimstra, N. W., and McFarling, L. H. 1974. *Environmental psychology.* Monterey, Calif.: Brooks/Cole.

Hooff, J. A. R. A. M. van. 1967. *The care and management of captive chimpanzees with special emphasis on the ecological aspects.* Aeromedical Research Laboratory Technical Report no. 67.

Hutchins, M., Hancocks, D., and Crockett, C. 1984. Naturalistic solutions to the behavioral problems of captive animals. *Der Zoologische Garten* 54:28–42.

Kortlandt, A. 1960. Can lessons from the wild improve the lot of captive chimpanzees? *Int. Zoo Yrbk.* 2:76–80.

Law, G., and Boyle, H. 1986. Notes on polar bear management at Glasgow Zoo. *Ratel* 13 (6): 174–76.

Leyhausen, P. 1961. Smaller cats in the zoo. *Int. Zoo Yrbk.* 3: 11–21.

Line, S. W. 1987. Environmental enrichment for laboratory primates. *J. Am. Vet. Med. Assoc.* 190:854–59.

Maki, S., and Bloomsmith, M. A. 1989. Uprooted trees facilitate the psychological well-being of captive chimpanzees. *Zoo Biol.* 8:79–88.

Maple, T. L. 1979. Great apes in captivity: The good, the bad, and the ugly. In *Captivity and behavior,* ed. J. Erwin, T. L. Maple, and G. Mitchell, 239–72. New York: Van Nostrand Reinhold.

———. 1980. *Orangutan behavior.* New York: Van Nostrand Reinhold.

Maple, T. L., and Archibald, E. A. 1993. ZooMan: Inside the zoo revolution. Atlanta: Longstreet.

Maple, T. L., and Finlay, T. W. 1986. Evaluating the environments of captive nonhuman primates. In *Primates: The road to self-sustaining populations,* ed. K. Benirschke, 479–88. New York: Springer-Verlag.

———. 1987. Post-occupancy evaluation in the zoo. *Appl. Anim. Behav. Sci.* 18:5–18.

Maple, T. L., and Hoff, M. P. 1982. *Gorilla behavior.* New York: Van Nostrand Reinhold.

Maple, T. L., and Stine, W. W. 1982. Environmental variables and great ape husbandry. *Am. J. Primatol,* suppl. 1, 67–76.

Markowitz, H. 1975. New methods for increasing activity in zoo animals: Some results and proposals for the future. In *Centennial symposium on science and research,* 151–62. Topeka, Kans.: Hill's Division, Riviana Foods.

———. 1978. Engineering environments for behavioral opportunities in the zoo. *Behav. Analyst* 1:34–47.

———. 1979. Environmental enrichment and behavioral engineering for captive primates. In *Captivity and behavior,* ed. J. Erwin, T. L. Maple, and G. Mitchell, 217–38. New York: Van Nostrand Reinhold.

———. 1982. *Behavioral enrichment in the zoo.* New York: Van Nostrand Reinhold.

Markowitz, H., and Line, S. 1989. Primate research models and environmental enrichment. In *Housing, care, and psychological well-being of captive and laboratory primates,* ed. E. F. Segal. Park Ridge, N.J.: Noyes.

Meyer-Holzapfel, M. 1968a. Abnormal behavior in zoo animals. In *Abnormal behavior of animals,* ed. M. W. Fox, 476–503. Philadelphia: W. B. Saunders.

———. 1968b. Breeding the European wild cat at Berne Zoo. *Int. Zoo Yrbk.* 8:31–38.

Michelmore, A. P. G., ed. 1976. *Zoo design 1.* Paignton, Devon, England: Paignton Zoological and Botanical Gardens, Ltd.

Mitchell, G. 1982. *Behavioral sex differences in nonhuman primates.* New York: Van Nostrand Reinhold.

Morris, D. 1961. A new approach to the problem of exhibiting small mammals in zoos. *Int. Zoo Yrbk.* 3:1–9.

Nash, V. J. 1982. Tool use by captive chimpanzees at an artificial termite mound. *Zoo Biol.* 1:211–22.

Ogden, J. J. 1989. A post-occupancy evaluation: Naturalistic habitats for captive lowland gorillas. Masters' thesis, Georgia Institute of Technology.

Ogden, J. J., Lindburg, D. G., and Maple, T. L. 1993. Preference for structural environmental features in captive lowland gorillas. *Zoo Biol.* 4:381–96.

Parker, C. E. 1969. Behavioral diversity in ten species of nonhuman primates. *J. Comp. Physiol. Psychol.* 87:930–37.

Perkins, L. A. 1992. Variables that influence the activity of captive orangutans. *Zoo Biol.* 11:117–86.

Poulson, H. 1974. Keeping chimpanzees occupied in captivity. *Int. Zoo News* 21:19–20.

Rasa, O. A. E. 1975. Mongoose sociology and behaviour as related to zoo exhibition. *Int. Zoo Yrbk.* 15:65–73.

Rodman, P. 1979. Individual activity patterns and the solitary nature of orangutans. In *The great apes,* ed. D. A. Hamburg and E. R. McCown, 235–55. Menlo Park, Calif.: Benjamin Cummings.

Rosenthal, M. A. 1975. Observations on the water opossum or yapok in captivity. *Int. Zoo Yrbk.* 15:4–6.

Schaller, G. B. 1972. *The Serengeti lion.* Chicago: University of Chicago Press.

Segal, E. F., ed. 1989. *Housing, care, and psychological well-being of captive and laboratory primates.* Park Ridge, N.J.: Noyes.

Shepherdson, D. J., Carlstead, K., Mellen, J., and Seidensticker, J. 1993. The influence of food presentation on the behavior of small cats in confined environments. *Zoo Biol.* 12:203–16.

Sims, G. 1993. Life in the slow lane. *Nat. Wildl.*

Smith, A., Lindburg, D. G., and Vehrencamp, S. 1989. Effect of food preparation on feeding behavior of lion-tailed macaques. *Zoo Biol.* 8:57–65.

Snowdon, C. T., and Savage, A. S. 1989. Psychological well-being of captive primates: General considerations and examples from callitrichids. In *Housing, care, and psychological well-being of captive and laboratory primates,* ed. E. F. Segal, 75–88. Park Ridge, N.J.: Noyes.

Sommer, R. 1974. *Tight spaces.* Englewood Cliffs, N.J.: Prentice-Hall.

Thomas, W. D. 1986. Housing and furniture. In *Primates: The road to self-sustaining populations,* ed. K. Benirschke, 463–64. New York: Springer-Verlag.

Tripp, J. K. 1985. Increasing activity in captive orangutans: Provision of manipulable and edible materials. *Zoo Biol.* 4:225–34.

Wemmer, C. 1974. Design for polar bear maternity dens. *Int. Zoo Yrbk.* 14:222–23.

Wemmer, C., and Fleming, M. J. 1975. Management of meercats in captivity. *Int. Zoo Yrbk.* 15:73–77.

Wilson, S. F. 1982. Environmental influences on the activity of captive apes. *Zoo Biol.* 1:201–9.

Yerkes, R. M. 1925. *Almost human.* New York: Century.

22

Structural and Keeper Considerations in Exhibit Design

MARK A. ROSENTHAL AND WILLIAM A. XANTEN

In this chapter we will discuss some general considerations that zoo planners should address when designing exhibits so that they will be easy and safe to maintain. Not only should the animal's biological and psychological needs be taken into account, but the people who daily manage and maintain the exhibit should also be considered. The animal keepers as well as the maintenance personnel are responsible for the upkeep of the exhibit; therefore, the more thought and consideration given to the construction of the area, the easier it will be for them to maintain and to manage responsibly. The need for preplanning cannot be overstated, since it is in this phase that the basic issues of exhibit design are addressed. Once concrete has been poured and set, for example, it is impossible to repitch the floors for better drainage without expensive change orders.

STRUCTURAL CONSIDERATIONS FOR THE VIEWING EXHIBIT

Walls

Wall composition and form will vary depending on the animal species and how they are to be exhibited. Square territories do not exist in nature, but in most exhibits the walls meet at perpendicular angles—the perfect place to catch dirt and debris. Rounding the corners of walls is an expensive option, but rounded corners accumulate less dirt and are easier to clean. A rounded joint at the junctions of walls and floors can eliminate a crevice where pests can hide or fecal matter can gather.

Walls may be made of precast concrete, which can be treated in many ways, each of which has advantages and drawbacks. When applying paint to walls, care should be taken to ensure that the preliminary application is done correctly or peeling may rapidly occur. Nothing detracts more from an exhibit's visual appeal than peeling paint. All paint for animal exhibits should be nontoxic, since many animals bite, lick, or peel off paint and ingest it. At one zoo, the mandrills, *Mandrillus sphinx*, ate old paint off the bars,

leading to lead poisoning in some of the troop members. In elephant and rhinoceros areas, no paint should be applied because the animals rub against the walls; a concrete stain is preferable.

Tile, available in many colors, can also be used as a wall covering and is easy to clean and maintain. However, the appearance of tile may be too antiseptic. Brick may be relatively inexpensive as a wall covering, depending on the type chosen, but it often requires tuck-pointing or sealing as the years go by. Brick is also hard to clean and has a rough surface. Fiberglass is a material that can be colored and is easily cleaned. Also, fiberglass, like tile, brick, and reinforced concrete, provides little space where insect pests can find shelter.

Wood walls offer the advantage of being easily replaced when damaged, and there are a wide variety of woods available, depending on the size of the construction budget. However, wood walls do offer abundant places for pests to shelter. In a giraffe, *Giraffa camelopardalis*, exhibit, wood was used as a façade on top of the concrete walls. The giraffes did not damage the wood, but mice and cockroaches used it for shelter. When using wood, it is also important to consider the type of animal in the exhibit. Elephants and rhinoceroses can damage wood planking by gouging it with their tusks or trying to remove planks using their horns. Wood can be cleaned, but after a long period of daily cleaning and spray from animal urine, certain woods may absorb water and rot more quickly.

Walls should be covered with sealants to waterproof the surfaces. This treatment makes general cleaning much easier. At one zoo, a concrete block wall was not sealed properly, and over the years, the constant use of water on the surface resulted in a leaching of the limestone in the mortar joints, leaving an efflorescence that could not be cleaned.

Murals are often used as a backdrop on walls. Because they can be expensive to replace or touch up when damaged, they need to be sealed for protection against washing and animal urine. Many species mark their living areas with urine. The long-term damaging effects of urine on the wall surface include discoloration and staining, especially on wood walls.

Wall coverings of artificial rockwork also must be sealed, and depressions should be created to permit adequate drainage to floor drains when the wall is washed and cleaned. Rockwork should incorporate pathways to allow keepers to climb the rock safely to clean the upper portions of the exhibit.

Fencing

In many outdoor mammal exhibits, fencing is used to enclose and thus define territories. A number of fencing types are available, such as chain-link, hog wire, welded mesh, metal horizontal bars, and wood palisades. The type of animal to be exhibited and budget considerations typically influence the type of fencing chosen.

Long-term maintenance of fencing is also a prime consideration in deciding the type of material to be used. Strength and tension are best when the fence runs in a straight line. Wire fencing that is too loose may result in animal injury. In ungulate enclosures, fencing should be attached to the paddock side of the posts to create an unbroken interior surface; this prevents an animal from running along the fence line and injuring itself on protruding posts. The designer needs to consider the animal's strength in the final choice of materials. Hediger (1964, 53) states, "Overexcitement weakens all barriers." Fencing for ungulates should be 6 to 8 feet high. Depending upon geographic location and the presence of indigenous predators, the designer may need to incorporate barriers to ward off digging and climbing predators.

The location and size of transfer gates along a fence perimeter should be considered carefully. The gates must allow the animal manager to gain access to them safely for opening and closing. Too small an opening in the transfer gate may result in herd animals bunching up as they attempt to move from one paddock to another. However, the larger the gate, the more difficult it may be to operate manually. Gates can be of the swing or slide variety and should be large enough to drive a vehicle through.

Floors

One of the most important factors in exhibit design is the slope of the floor and its drainage. During cleaning, excess water should drain rapidly. It is both frustrating and time-consuming to have large puddles of water or cleaner accumulate on a floor because of improper drainage. Poorly drained floors may need to be squeegeed down to get rid of excess water that has gathered in low spots and to prevent algae buildup. The slope to the drain should be ¼ inch to the foot as a minimum, and should not exceed ½ inch. To test whether an exhibit has an adequate slope to the drain, a bucket of water should be poured onto the floor from anywhere in the exhibit; if it does not flow easily toward the drain, the slope is poor.

Floors of most exhibits should have a nonskid texture, since good footing can prevent potentially dangerous falls. This can be accomplished in a variety of ways. A broom finish, lightly or heavily applied to a freshly poured cement floor, provides a degree of firm footing. When paint is used for floors, only specialized paints that withstand daily wear by the animals or animal keepers should be used.

Paddocks

Drainage should be a major consideration in paddock construction. A poorly drained yard results in unsightly pools of standing water; this condition not only is detrimental to general animal health but also requires animal keepers to spend more time in paddock maintenance. Both the top and subsurface substrates should be material that will promote good drainage. When the top substrate does not allow adequate drainage, water starts to erode the soil and form small gullies. If this condition develops, the yard should be graded and sloped to facilitate water runoff to a drainage area.

Ceilings

Skylights are excellent for exhibits that have plants or for animals that depend on photoperiods for specific activities, such as reproduction. Skylights should be of a type that does not block the ultraviolet rays. Wire mesh or barred ceilings are good sites from which to hang a variety of ropes, vines, or logs in an exhibit. If the ceiling is to be solid concrete, preplanning of light fixtures and hooks for hanging items is required. Suspended ceilings need to be high enough to prevent animals in the exhibit from reaching them; otherwise, zoo staff may be constantly looking for escaped animals above the suspended ceiling.

Keeper Access Doors

Keeper access doors to animal exhibits should be large enough for any keeper to gain entry without having to crawl or stoop. The doors should also be large enough to allow the entry of exhibit materials such as soil, rocks, plants, and dead trees, as well as equipment needed for daily maintenance (e.g., high-pressure washers or ladders). All doors should have a viewing window to allow keepers to look into the exhibit before entering, thus preventing animal escapes.

Off-Exhibit Holding Areas

Holding areas are essential for proper animal management, but many exhibits lack adequate off-exhibit holding areas. The two basic types of holding areas are those that are directly connected to an exhibit and those that are separated from the exhibit area.

Holding areas that are adjacent to the exhibit can be utilized for day-to-day transfer of animals during cleaning. In addition, animals can be separated for feeding and for sleeping, and when introductions are performed, introduction screens or doors can be placed between the exhibit and holding areas. Actual introductions thus can be done out of public view in the holding areas. Holding areas are also useful for isolating animals to obtain individually identified samples of urine or feces. For outdoor exhibits, holding areas in the rear may provide greater security at night. In addition, separate nighttime holding areas for ungulates allow paddocks to recover from the damage caused by grazing, browsing, and trampling of the substrate. Holding facilities that are separate from the exhibit are indispensable for holding surplus animals, or for situations that require separation of an animal from the exhibit. They are particularly important for females that are due to give birth, for introducing individuals that may initially fight, or for animals under medical treatment.

The adage that "nature abhors a vacuum" applies especially to animal holding areas. Certainly, any design for new or remodeled exhibits should include maximum holding facilities and, if at all possible, allow room for additional expansion at some later date. Design of a holding facility should follow the basic rules for any animal containment area: the plans should include proper drainage, lighting, water, climate control and/or ventilation (if indoors), shade (if outdoors), and pools (for aquatic animals). In addition, sufficient capability for shifting animals within the holding area needs to be provided. Holding areas need to be located in areas accessible to staff and have facilities for vehicles and equipment to load and unload animals and exhibit furnishings.

Movement of Animals from Exhibit to Holding Areas

The ability to transfer animals easily from one exhibit to another or between holding areas is of paramount importance in proper animal management. Such moves must be accomplished with a minimum of stress to the animals, as well as being safe and relatively easy for the keepers. The proper design of shifting facilities must first take into account the species' natural behavior. Doors should preferably be located at the junctions of walls, since most mammal species run to a corner or can be forced into a corner. Door operating mechanisms should be located at the opposite end of the exhibit from the door, as mammals tend to move away from keepers and not toward them.

Arboreal mammals, such as primates, should have shift doors located at heights that promote natural behaviors. Elevated doors must still allow keepers to reach them, and should have a wide shelf just below the bottom of the doorsill to support crates for catching animals. These shelves also provide a resting site for the animals and a secure anchor for limbs and vines.

Runs should be designed to allow keepers access to at least one side, and should have either sliding or guillotine doors where the holding or exhibit cage entrances are located. This design allows an animal to be directed from the run into the holding cage and prevents it from doubling back on the keeper. Shifting animals through cages should be avoided since the keeper may lose control over the animal once it is in a larger area. Squeeze cages can be built into runs so that the animals are habituated to them. Squeeze cages can also be built as a connection between two rows of holding cages.

Clear identification of shift doors is extremely important. Color coding and numbering of the doors and operating mechanisms makes shifting easier and safer for both the animal and the keeper. Door size is an important consideration. Doors that are too small may cause injuries to the sides and back of an animal moving through them; doors that are too large may not be usable for crates because additional materials will be needed to block the entrance and prevent animals from escaping around the sides of the crate. Low overhangs above doors can prevent the effective use of crates with guillotine doors.

Most carnivores and primates should be provided with either guillotine or sliding doors. Manually operated doors are the least expensive to build and to maintain, but are not recommended for great apes, who often grab the door as it is being closed and throw it back open. Without strong track stops, the door may be thrown off the track, possibly injuring the keeper. Some primates can actually push guillotine doors up unless the doors are extremely heavy and have a slot at the bottom to prevent fingers from slipping under the door. Care must be taken with large cats and primates with long tails that guillotine doors do not fall on them. Sliding doors eliminate the problem of injury, but are harder to operate. Guide tracks often become clogged, making operation even more difficult. Consideration needs to be given to horizontal space when designing sliding door placement and operation.

Guillotine doors can be operated by a cable with a handle that lifts the door when pulled and lowers it when slowly released. Doors operated in this manner must be light enough for the keeper to operate or have counterbalances provided. Another method of operation uses a cable attached to a ratchet that can be turned with a crank. This method can be dangerous if the door is very heavy and drops too fast for the keeper to maintain a hold on the crank handle. Animals and keepers can be seriously injured by this type of door.

Hydraulic, pneumatic, and electrically operated doors have recently become widely used in great ape and pachyderm facilities. Hydraulic and pneumatic doors are generally of the sliding type and have the advantage of being stoppable at any point during movement by releasing the operating switch. They can also be fitted with automatic pressure stops, which prevent animals from being crushed should they get trapped in the doorway.

Electrically operated doors are used to a lesser degree because, like manually operated doors, they can be forced open during operation if a chain drive is used. Worm screw drives can eliminate this problem, but they are very expensive to design and build. In all cases, manual overrides should be provided in case of mechanical failure.

Manually operated sliding doors are preferred for ungulate stalls and for small mammal enclosures. They are easily operated, inexpensive, and offer great flexibility; the size of the door opening can be controlled to aid in crating and reducing drafts, and the door can be closed quickly if needed.

Sliding and guillotine doors increase the total usable area of a stall or exhibit. This is particularly important in small mammal exhibits, where space is usually at a premium. A swinging door should never be used where animals are moved into or out of an exhibit or holding area. Swinging doors for keeper access should open into the enclosure to allow keepers a barrier between themselves and the animal; also, should the animal hit the door, it will be forced backward into a closed position. Swinging doors opening into the enclosure can also be designed to swing closed if they are accidentally left open by a forgetful keeper, thus preventing an escape. If available space prevents positioning a door to open inward, other options (such as a sliding door) may be used.

Dutch doors, swinging doors that are divided in the

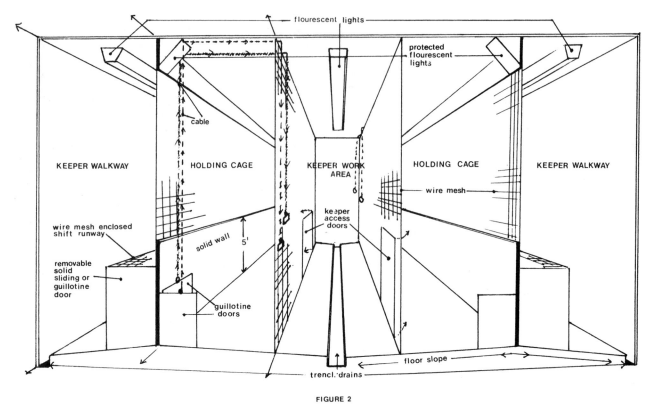

FIGURE 2

Fɪɢ. 22.1.   Generalized plan for animal/keeper holding, shift, and work areas (median horizontal section).

middle, are also used in ungulate barns and in small mammal exhibits. They allow the keeper to open the upper half and view the enclosure with little risk while preventing terrestrial small mammals from escaping. Again, it is preferable that these doors open inward.

Another door design recently used has been the garage door, although it is not widely used. This design is not recommended due to its complexity (at least two hinged sections) and the possibility of binding if it is hit by large mammals.

Door thickness and strength depend on the strength and size of the species. Heavy solid metal or barred doors are generally used for large carnivores, pachyderms, and great apes. Lightweight alloys may be used if they meet structural strength requirements. Thick lexan has been used successfully with great apes and can also be used with large carnivores. Reinforced concrete doors have been incorporated into pachyderm facilities with excellent success. Wooden doors are generally adequate for most ungulates. Hollow-core doors offer a lightweight alternative and can be quite strong if properly designed. However, they tend to rust from the inside out unless properly rustproofed; they also harbor rodents and cockroaches unless totally sealed.

Keeper Service Areas

Planners often forget the service areas when designing an exhibit. From a keeper/manager standpoint, this oversight can cause major problems with morale and overall opera-

tional efficiency. Service areas should be roomy, well lighted, well ventilated, and have proper drainage. Once these four criteria have been met, other needs are much simpler to provide.

Corridors and entry doors must be sufficiently wide for access by crates, food deliveries, and exhibit materials. Service areas should have access by ramps rather than stairs; steep steps and ladders should be avoided. Floors should have the proper pitch to allow good drainage, and non-skid materials or brushed concrete should be used to eliminate slipping. Trench drains are preferable since they drain quickly and are easy to maintain (fig. 22.1).

Adequate storage areas for food, tools, and exhibit materials are crucial for proper care of the exhibits. Freezer space provides for long-term bulk storage of foods, which saves time, prevents spoilage, and requires fewer food deliveries.

Racks are necessary for holding a variety of tools in accessible, secure areas. Hose racks should be located in convenient areas near the hose bibs and in sufficient numbers to allow the use of a short length of hose (less than 25 feet). Automatic hose racks are a convenience and, if located on the ceiling or high on the walls, save space along corridor walls. Automatic hose racks may break down, however, rendering them useless. Thus, stationary hose racks, which require hand coiling of the hose, may be preferable even though they occupy more space and are more time-consuming.

The introduction and removal of animals and materials to and from exhibit areas needs consideration during design. Work areas must provide sufficient space between the rear of the exhibit and the rear wall of the service area. The advantages of designing wide and high doors into the exhibits can be negated by corridors that are too narrow or too low to allow access with exhibit materials or crates. Designers often overlook the need for overhead room, for example, for crates' guillotine doors. The installation of rings or hooks for attachment of chains or ropes to secure crates against a door frame is also useful, especially for large, powerful mammals such as cats, bears, great apes, large ungulates, and pachyderms.

Designers also need to consider the possibility of animal escapes. What happens when an animal gets loose? Is there a safety vestibule? Dangerous animal sections should always have a safety gate before the entrance. A slide bolt in addition to other locking devices can add a secondary measure of safety to the gate.

Ideally, the keeper should have an unobstructed view of the entire area. An animal keeper was saved in one instance when he noticed footprints on the floor of the bear service area just before he opened the safety gate leading into the service corridor. He determined that the bears had escaped from the den and was able to summon help. Blind angles should be avoided if possible; mirrors can be used to see around corners. For small mammals, netting or wire mesh should cover any ceilings where there are overhead lights, ducts, or pipes in order to confine the escapees to a level that allows easy recapture. In areas housing large cats, bears, or primates, hiding areas (especially above or beneath cages) should be eliminated; good lighting is essential.

Service areas should make a keeper's daily work easier; discussions with keepers prior to design and construction usually elicit excellent ideas and lead to trouble-free facilities.

Utilities

Plumbing. Designing a good drainage system is important at the outset; future alterations can be costly. Attention should be given to selecting the proper size and number of drains and the location of each in and out of the exhibit. Drains placed on the outside of the exhibit are accessible to both keepers and maintenance personnel while the animal remains on display. The floor must pitch correctly to each drain, or it will render the drain totally ineffective.

Trench drains must be wide enough to accept a shovel or pitchfork in order to clean out waste. Catch baskets and strainers can be handy since they allow the waste to collect in one spot and prevent it from entering and blocking main pipes. In one great ape exhibit, an open drain is located inside the enclosure and is large enough to accept produce such as apples and oranges. The keeper can hose the entire area with the animals still on display and later retrieve the uneaten food and waste from the large, cone-shaped strainer.

If drains are located inside exhibits, the covers must be secured so that the animals cannot remove them. In one case, a polar bear, *Ursus maritimus,* removed a metal drain cover and broke a pane of glass in its underwater viewing area. Apes also can use their hands and strength to remove covers that are not securely attached.

When constructing pools, place the overflow drain at the end opposite to the pool fill fixture. As water is added to the pool and drained by the overflow, it will cause maximum water movement and help skim debris from the water surface.

The location of hose bibs, or connections, depends on the type of animal exhibited. Dangerous animals should have connections located outside their exhibit. Usually, if a hose bib is located in a central area, the hose can better serve a large number of exhibits. There should be enough hose bibs to avoid a keeper having to manage 100 feet of hose on a daily basis. With nondangerous animals, hose bibs can be located within the exhibit.

Hot water is useful for cleaning exhibits, but budget may play a role in the size of the water heater installed. Mixing valves are needed when temperate water is used, for example, when bathing elephants.

Self-filling water bowls are excellent for hoofstock. One type allows the animal to fill the bowl by pressing a lever with its snout. Since some antelopes and gazelles may have trouble with this type, another that may be preferable is regulated by a float device that automatically fills the bowl when the water level drops. However, primates and carnivores are capable of destroying self-filling water bowls with their teeth, hands, or paws. For them, "lick-it" watering devices are more effective: the animal licks the device or presses a small lever that releases water for as long as the lever is depressed. When the action is stopped, the water ceases to flow. In order to reduce the possibility of a carnivore defecating into its water container, the container should be located above floor level. The precise height will depend on the size of the animal.

Adequate water pressure is important since it gives keepers the volume of water they need when using hoses or filling pools. Cutoff valves should be easy to reach, and in a safe place away from direct contact with the animals. Main clean-out spots for pipes should be located so that maintenance crews can get to them easily. Zoo managers must provide adequate access to the key plumbing area to permit regular maintenance; pest control personnel may also need to have access to plumbing areas to lay traps or spray.

Electrical Systems. When designing the electrical systems of an exhibit, the future needs of the section should be considered. Adding power for unplanned additional electrical loads can be costly. Keepers, veterinarians, and maintenance people all need to use electrical power. A sufficient number of receptacles should be provided so that devices such as power sprayers or medical equipment can be plugged in near where they are needed.

The standard receptacle in the United States is 120 volts, grounded. This 15-ampere or 20-ampere receptacle has a slot for a matching grounding prong on the plug. For heavier-duty items such as water heaters or air conditioners, a 240-volt, 20-ampere grounded receptacle with heavier wire should be considered. The demand on an electrical system depends on the number of loads of current in operation and the level of energy consumption. Grounding guards against fire and shock, and helps to ensure that a faulty circuit is not dangerous. When placing receptacles outside, it is best to waterproof them with a special cover plate and gasketed doors that seal the receptacle sections when not in use.

There are other types of special receptacles for greater safety, for example, those in which a plug can be inserted only by rotating a solid cover that protects the slots, or on which the cover snaps back into place when the plug is withdrawn. Locking receptacles have a device that grips the prongs of a plug to prevent it from being pulled out accidentally; this is especially useful with equipment that is moved frequently while in use.

Incandescent bulbs emit light when the fixture is turned on and the filament inside the bulb becomes hot and luminous. Fluorescent lights work on a principle different from that of incandescent bulbs. The cost of installation of fluorescents may be greater, but the lighting is more uniform. Fluorescents produce less heat, eliminating heat buildup in smaller exhibits. Fluorescents also use energy more efficiently, which saves money. Fluorescent tubes designed for special uses, such as growing plants indoors, are available. In certain exhibits, the use of heat lamps or sunlamps may be necessary; this may necessitate incorporating special fixtures into the initial design of the exhibit.

A number of different types of switches are available. Dimmers are full-range switches that have variable settings, from a faint glow to full brightness, providing a convenient way to adjust the lighting level. They also save electricity and, when set at lower ranges, make bulbs last longer. A dimmer switch must be matched to the type of lighting it controls. Incandescent dimmers do not work on fluorescent lights, but special dimmers can be purchased to use with fluorescents.

A timer switch, which turns lights on and off at preset times, is controlled by a built-in electric clock and can be operated manually. Timer switches are ideal in nocturnal sections for controlling photoperiods.

An outdoor switch should come with a weatherproof cover that makes it impervious to water and the elements. When access to light switches must be limited for safety or security, locking switches can be used; these are turned on and off by inserting a special key. Light-handle switches, with small bulbs that glow when the handle is turned off, make switches easy to see in darkened areas.

The locations of receptacles, switches, and fixtures should make them easy for keepers and maintenance personnel to use and service. In one instance, safety switches were located on the inside of a gate, making it necessary for the keeper to open the safety gate before turning on lights—a potentially dangerous situation. Service panels and electric meters also need to be in locations that do not require an acrobat to reach them. In one zoo, fluorescent lights were placed above a series of small-mammal exhibits, but only one small door was placed in the ceiling to give access to them. The limited space on top of the exhibits forced the electrician to crawl on his belly to service the lights. Receptacles need to be high enough above the ground so that they are not sprayed when floors are washed down. Fixtures should not be placed where animals can reach them. In one orangutan, *Pongo pygmaeus*, exhibit, wire mesh prevented the adults from reaching the exhibit sunlamps, but the youngsters were easily able to extend their arms out far enough to damage the fixtures. Luckily, the animals did not injure themselves. Fixtures located within animal enclosures must have a strong enough protective cover to take all types of abuse. Certain types of heavy-duty plastic, which are also used in prison construction, can be used.

Ventilation. Adequate ventilation is needed for animals and zoo staff. The size and number of animals in an enclosure will determine the required rate of air exchange. Proper ventilation assures adequate drying of exhibit and work areas, which, along with good drainage, limits the buildup of algae and prevents mildew. If possible, ventilation should be controlled separately for each exhibit. All controls should be out of the reach of animals but easily accessible to staff and maintenance crews.

Waste Disposal

Disposing of daily accumulations of waste products from a variety of mammals probably poses one of the most difficult logistic problems facing the modern zoo. There are basically two types of animal waste: soluble materials that can be flushed into the sewer system, and nonsoluble materials that must be disposed of by other methods.

Disposal through the sewer system normally involves washing down exhibits, flushing fecal and food materials into a drain. Strainer baskets, placed in the drains to catch large particles that do not break up in the water, prevent sewer stoppages. The baskets can then be emptied into garbage containers (fig. 22.2).

There are a number of manual disposal methods for waste, involving carts, wheelbarrows, tubs, buckets, and manure pits. Manual disposal systems are simple and relatively inexpensive; the drawbacks are, of course, that they take much time and energy.

Over the past few years, a number of innovative mechanical methods for waste removal have been tried, with varying degrees of success. One of the most recent has been the use of conveyors that carry waste material (including browse and straw) from inside a building to an outside pit or dumpster. These conveyors can be belts, buckets, or a baffle-type design; all have the potential to break down, and all require maintenance to keep them operating efficiently.

One of the most difficult disposal issues is that of waste from Permanent Post Entry Quarantine (PPEQ) animals. Manure produced by PPEQ animals must be sterilized prior to leaving zoo grounds. This can be done by composting or chemical sterilization. Incinerating the manure is another approach; however, many municipalities have limitations on burning. Most zoos have areas on the grounds for composting or have approved sites elsewhere for storing manure. Zoos should contact the United States Department of Agriculture to obtain information regarding regulations for the disposal of certain types of manure before major planning occurs.

A large, centrally located collection pit can be used for disposing of large amounts of fecal matter from ungulates and pachyderms. Small amounts of waste can be collected by wheelbarrows, dump scooters, or front-end loaders. Waste can then be removed on a weekly basis to a composting site (either on or off zoo grounds) using a VAC-haul truck.

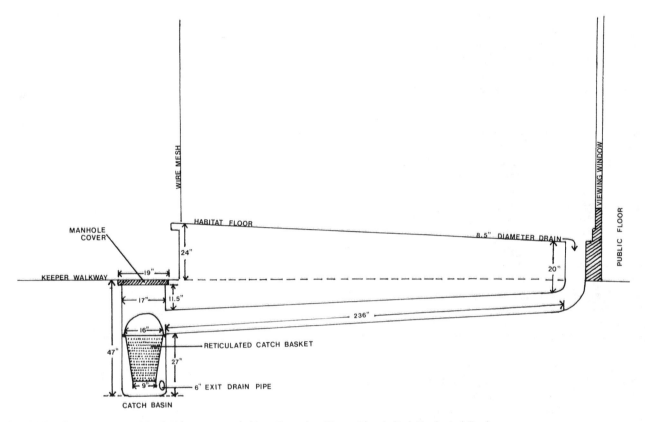

FIG. 22.2. Drainage system, North Side orangutan habitat, Great Ape House, Lincoln Park Zoological Gardens.

Manure can also be placed in a sealed vat, where bacterial action produces methane gas. If large amounts of gas are produced, the gas can then be used to augment other fuels for heating. Unfortunately, this technique has met with poor response due to the initial costs of the equipment and the limited use of methane gas in the United States.

Another innovative (and successful) approach to waste disposal used by some zoos is to sell the composted animal waste to the public for fertilizer. This strategy not only disposes of quantities of manure but also generates revenue from a normally unwanted and expensive disposal item. Obviously, certain manure cannot be sold without being treated.

PEST CONTROL

Pest control in animal exhibits is an ongoing problem. Pests such as mice, *Mus musculus,* rats, *Rattus norvegicus,* or cockroaches, *Blattella germanica,* need the following conditions to proliferate: (1) shelter, (2) accessible food, and (3) a temperate water source. These items are all easily found in many zoo exhibits and near service areas. Controlling pests is possible if problem areas are identified and a regular integrated pest control program is initiated.

Keepers usually will not visit and inspect areas that have difficult access. Therefore, all utilities, such as electrical vaults and plumbing mains, must be accessible for treatment. Hollow artificial rocks, logs, and trees in exhibits need access ports for spraying insecticide or inserting rodent bait stations.

Small-mammal exhibits should be sealed as tightly as possible to prevent rodents from entering. In one small-mammal exhibit, a pair of rock elephant shrews, *Elephantulus rupestris,* shared their area with a population of mice. When food was placed in the exhibit, the mice were the first to feed, consuming not only the shrew diet but also the potted plants. After the exhibit was sealed with a finer mesh on the ceiling, the plants thrived and the keepers were able to reduce the amount of food given by half.

It is important to seal utility pipes and electrical conduits that open in the floor, walls, or ceiling. Rodents use these artificial pathways to travel from section to section. Entry doors to exhibits and service areas should be flush to the ground to prevent rodents from entering. A mouse can enter through a mesh size that is as small as 8 mm. Whenever possible, cracks, crevices, and shelters where roaches can hide should be sealed or eliminated. Proper design should be coupled with an active management program, in which exhibit and service areas are regularly treated. Pest control is a never-ending battle.

SAFETY

Safety is an important part of exhibit design for animal keepers who work with dangerous animals. Alarms are important in areas where keepers work with animals such as bears, elephants, large cats, and large ungulates. The alarm buttons should be placed in areas that keepers can get to in an emergency situation. Alarms should not only sound in the entire section, but should also be heard outside the immediate area and in a central administrative area. The object of the alarms is to immediately alert as many people as possible that an emergency situation exists. If more than one area has alarms, then the central emergency control should be able to pinpoint exactly where the alarm has been activated, using different alarm sounds for different sections; for example, bear exhibits can use a siren while the elephant house uses a horn. Phones with outside lines are important safety features to permit calling within the zoo or summoning fire and police assistance.

With large animals such as elephants, rhinoceroses, or large ungulates, escape routes out of the exhibit can save human lives. Some zoos use small doors for keepers that the larger animal cannot pass through, allowing keepers an escape route in addition to the entry door of the exhibit. Bars that are spaced properly can contain a rhinoceros but allow room for a keeper to escape.

Blind spots are very dangerous. An animal may be out of the keeper's sight, giving a false impression that it is safe to enter an area. Some polar bear exhibits have convex mirrors located in the corners of the dens that allow the keeper to see every space in the area. The proper placement of viewing ports also can assure optimum viewing.

With dangerous animals, all doors to the exhibit should have double locking devices. Key-retaining locks ensure that the keeper does not place the lock on a shelf and forget to replace it. When designing new exhibits, it is preferable to use a master key for the section so that, in an emergency, one master key will allow staff to gain access to all areas.

ACKNOWLEDGMENTS

Special thanks to Eric Meyers for preparation of artwork and Lois Wagner for typing the manuscript.

REFERENCES

Collins, L. 1982. Propagation and conservation centers. In *Zoological parks and aquariums fundamentals*, ed. K. Sausmen, 141–68. Wheeling, W.Va.: American Association of Zoological Parks and Aquariums.

Curtis, L. 1982. Design features of mammal exhibits. In *Zoological parks and aquarium fundamentals*, ed. K. Sausmen, 59–76. Wheeling, W.Va.: American Association of Zoological Parks and Aquariums.

Doherty, J. 1977–78. The world of darkness in the Bronx Zoo. *AAZPA Regional Workshop Proceedings*, 256–59. Buffalo, N.Y.: American Association of Zoological Parks and Aquariums.

———. 1983. Animal management in the Carter Giraffe Building in the Bronx Zoo. *AAZPA Annual Conference Proceedings*, 317–24. Wheeling, W.Va.: American Association of Zoological Parks and Aquariums.

Goss, L., and Kuenzer, D. 1978. Primate and cat building. *AAZPA Annual Conference Proceedings*, 97–101. Wheeling, W.Va.: American Association of Zoological Parks and Aquariums.

Hediger, H. 1964. The problem of confined space. In *Wild animals in captivity*, 43–60. New York: Dover Publications.

———. 1969. Building for animals. In *Man and animal in the zoo: Zoo biology*, 183–216. New York: Seymour Lawrence/Delacorte Press.

Manton, V. 1975. Design of paddocks for herd animals. *Proceedings of the First International Symposium of Zoo Design and Construction*, 152–54. Paignton, England: Paignton Zoological and Botanical Gardens.

McIntyre, M. 1982. Carter Giraffe Building to open to general public at New York Zoological Park. *Animal Keeper's Forum* 9:105.

National Extension College. 1980. Housing and zoo design. In *Animal management*, 53–64. Cambridge, Mass.: National Extension College.

Rudolph, T. 1984. For all you do . . . This one's for you. *Animal Keeper's Forum* 11:339.

———. 1986. Animal exhibits design. *Animal Keeper's Forum* 5:160–61.

Simmons, L. 1977–78. New building for the management of great cats. *AAZPA Regional Workshop Proceedings*, 256–259. Indianapolis, Ind.: American Association of Zoological Parks and Aquariums.

23

Water Quality Management in Aquatic Mammal Exhibits

Serious concern for water quality in zoo exhibits is a recent phenomenon, as the use of pools, streams, and water moats in zoo exhibits is clearly on the increase. One can see this by simply perusing recent issues of zoo newsletters, annual reports, or magazines. Up until 10–15 years ago the major form of water treatment was to empty and refill the pool. The condition of the water at the time of emptying may have been the equivalent of anything from a Wisconsin lake in August, when algae blooms make it look like pea soup, to the influent to a wastewater treatment plant. No monitoring, other than visual and olfactory, was ever done to assess the quality of the water.

Such a laissez-faire attitude about the environment of captive animals might be justifiable for an outdoor terrestrial exhibit, where the air in which the animal lives is continuously exchanged with nonexhibit air, and excrement settles to the ground where it can be removed easily. However, it is not acceptable in an aquatic exhibit, where the water is isolated from a larger body of water, and urine and feces either dissolve or form fine particles that remain suspended in the water.

Whenever isolated indoor terrestrial exhibits have been designed, the standard practice has been to include a continuously operating treatment system for air exchange. Likewise, a continuously operating treatment system for water exchange is standard in the exhibition of fishes and invertebrates in aquariums. Zoos, however, have been much slower to include such systems in aquatic mammal exhibits or terrestrial mammal exhibits containing pools or moats. During the past decade many zoos have made improvements voluntarily; others were forced to do so by U.S. federal regulations.

In this chapter, I discuss the definition of good water quality, describe methods of treatment, borrowing heavily from drinking water and wastewater treatment practices as well as water treatment practices in aquariums, and discuss various methods of water treatment with respect to aquatic mammal husbandry.

WHAT IS GOOD WATER QUALITY?

What is good water quality? To answer this question, one must first identify one's objectives. In the past, the highest priority of a zoo was usually simply to have a species on display; animal health and exhibit quality were secondary. Today, that philosophy has changed in most zoos, and we may assume that the two main reasons for maintaining good water quality in exhibits are to promote animal health and to maintain an appropriate sensory environment for both the animal and the visitor. In exhibits with moats or decorative ponds that are not used frequently by animals, the presence of pathogens is less likely, so greater emphasis may be placed on appearance.

Animal Health

Pathogens. Maintaining good animal health entails keeping the environment free of pathogens and in balance with the chemical and physical conditions of the species' natural habitat. Requirements vary from species to species. The organisms that are pathogenic to captive animals may or may not be the same as those that cause disease in the wild. It is a well-known, though poorly documented, fact that the array of microorganisms associated with an animal changes when it is brought into captivity; some organisms that are not typically pathogenic may become so. A good example of this is the fungus *Fusarium solani*, which is quite prevalent in water containing organic material but is not usually associated with skin disease. Captive gray seals, *Halichoerus grypus*, that were stressed by unusually warm water developed skin lesions, with *Fusarium* appearing to be the primary agent (Montali et al. 1981). Some of the known pathogens of both captive and wild aquatic mammals are listed in table 23.1.

Considering the diversity of microorganisms and their unpredictable pathogenicity, it is difficult to establish criteria for water quality in terms of specific organisms. As a byproduct of the special status given to marine mammals by

TABLE 23.1.   Some Organisms Known to Be Pathogenic
to Aquatic Mammals

Bacteria

Acinetobacter parapertussis	*Leptospira pomona*
Aeromonas hydrophila	*Micrococcus* sp.
Alkalescens dispar	*Neisseria meningitidis*
Citrobacter sp.	*Pasturella mutacida*
Clostridium perfrigens	*Pasturella hemolyticum*
Clostridium botulinum	*Pseudomonas aeruginosa*
Corynebacterium pyrogenes	*Salmonella enteritidis*
Erysipelothrix rhusiopathiae	*Serratia* sp.
Escherichia coli	*Staphylococcus aureus*
Klebsiella pneumoniae	*Vibrio alginolyticus*

Fungi

Actinobacillus sp.	*Fusarium solani*
Aspergillus sp.	*Histoplasma* sp.
Blastomyces sp.	*Mucor* sp.
Candida albicans	*Nocadia* sp.
Coccidiomyces sp.	

Viruses

San Miguel sea lion virus	Gray whale enterovirus
Pox virus	Sei whale adenovirus
Phocine distemper virus (a morbillivirus)	

Sources: Wilson, Dykes, and Tsai 1972; Cusick and Bullock 1973;
Sweeney 1974; Sweeney and Gilmartin 1974; Fowler 1978; Wagner
and Mann 1978; Diamond, Ewing, and Cadwell 1979; Smith and
Skilling 1979; Tangredi and Medway 1980; Stroud and Roelke 1980;
Dunn, Buck, and Spotte 1982; Harwood 1989.

the U.S. Marine Mammal Protection Act of 1972 (Public
Law 92-522) and the Marine Mammal Protection Act
Amendments of 1988 (Public Law 100-711), the U.S. Department of Agriculture (USDA) developed regulations for
keeping marine mammals in captivity (*Federal Register* 44
[122]: 36868–36883; 49 [126]: 26674–26686). These regulations deal with the issue of pathogens in broad terms,
drawing upon standards from public health laws pertaining
to drinking water and swimming pools. The standards are
based upon tests of coliform bacteria as indicators of the
probability that pathogens are present in quantities sufficient to cause disease (Cheremisinoff, Cheremisinoff, and
Tratner 1981). Thus, facilities holding marine mammals
must be tested weekly for coliform bacteria. The maximum
acceptable level is 1,000 colonies per 100 ml of water. There
are questions about the validity of coliform tests as indicators of the presence of pathogens (Slanetz, Bartley, and Metcalf 1965), but these tests provide a guideline until we have
better methods. Zoos should adopt similar testing for other
aquatic or semiaquatic mammal exhibits and any exhibit
pools or moats into which animals might excrete waste.

As with many improvements to animal husbandry, testing water for coliforms can be costly. These tests should be
performed by someone with laboratory experience in microbiology to ensure the use of proper techniques. Commercial
laboratories generally charge between $15 and $30 to analyze each water sample. Sometimes local water treatment
plants will do the tests at no charge because of the large
number of tests they perform daily anyway. If an institution
has a sufficient number of aquatic exhibits, there may be justification for a laboratory on site. The currently accepted

testing methods may be found in *Standard Methods for Examination of Water and Wastewater Treatment* (1979).

Chemical and Physical Parameters. Criteria for chemical and physical parameters of water are not specified in
the USDA marine mammal regulations, mainly because we
know very little about chemical compounds that are potentially harmful to aquatic mammals. However, the content of
the water supplying most aquatic exhibits in zoos is indirectly under control, since it is also used by people and is
regulated with respect to human exposure. Research on the
effects of certain heavy metals and pesticides is being done
on aquatic mammals in the wild (e.g., Helle, Olsson, and
Jensen 1976; Reinjders 1979; Helle et al. 1983; see also the
special issue of *Ambio*, 1992 21 [8]: 494-608).

Some compounds, such as ammonia, nitrate, and nitrite,
that are found in natural water supplies are regulated in
drinking and swimming water because they are measures of
pollution or may be toxic in high enough concentrations (Lee
1970; Culp and Culp 1974). The U.S. Environmental Protection Agency's recommended maximum levels of ammonia,
nitrate, and nitrite are 0.05 mg/liter of water, 10 mg/l, and
1 mg/l respectively (*Federal Register* 40:59566–59588).
These substances are present in any water containing animal excreta, organic debris from the environment, or un-
consumed food items. There are no data on how these
compounds affect captive aquatic mammals, and in most
zoos they are not even monitored. Over a 9-day period during which several different filter media were tested, levels
of nitrate and ammonia in the sea lion, *Zalophus californianus*, exhibit at the National Zoo in Washington, D.C.,
exceeded the EPA criteria for human drinking and swimming water by an order of magnitude (Boness, unpub.).

Chemicals added to water may also be toxic in high
enough concentrations. For example, copper toxicity has
been reported in marine mammals (McDevitt 1986), yet
copper is often used as an algicide. Adding chlorine to public water supplies has been an accepted treatment practice
for many years. It is now being questioned because of potentially harmful by-products that may be produced by chemical reactions between the chlorine and organic material in
the water (Sontheimer 1980; Jolley, Brungs, and Cumming
1980; Maugh 1981). As will be discussed later, chlorine
treatment has been adopted by many institutions housing
aquatic mammals, and many zoos use water that has already been heavily treated with chlorine. The USDA regulations that now require monitoring of coliform bacteria in
marine mammal pools also require monitoring of chlorine
levels, which few zoos did in the past. The regulations do
not set limits, however, because there is no conclusive information on the effects of chlorine on the animals' health.
Most swimming pools do not exceed total chlorine levels of
1.0 part per million (ppm) during operating hours because
higher levels cause skin and eye irritation. However, this
level may be excessive for zoo exhibits because aquatic animals spend most of their time in the water.

Another issue concerning the chemical composition of
exhibit pools is the use of freshwater for animals, including
pinnipeds, cetaceans, the sea otter, *Enhydra lutris*, and the
polar bear, *Ursus maritimus*, that naturally inhabit salt or
brackish water. Many zoos house these animals in fresh-

water because it is less expensive to build and operate a freshwater pool than a saltwater one. This long-standing practice continues because little effort has been made to examine the health problems related to it. Evidence from eye opacities suggests that further investigation is warranted. Pinnipeds that developed eye opacities in freshwater either lost the opacities or had them markedly reduced when exposed to saltwater for varying lengths of time (Ulmer 1962; Hubbard 1968; Ronald and Ray, cited in Hubbard 1968). Additionally, according to a questionnaire to which twenty-five zoos replied, 67% (100 of 149) of the seals kept in freshwater were reported to have had eye opacities, whereas only 22% (27 of 124) housed in saltwater did (Boness, unpub.). Five out of six zoos that had freshwater exhibit pools but gave their animals saltwater baths said that the baths reduced or alleviated the opacities in individual animals. Due to the uncertainty of the ill effects of keeping marine mammals in a freshwater environment, perhaps a conservative approach should be taken: house marine mammals in a marine environment.

The problem of eye opacities in captive pinnipeds is undoubtedly complex and involves more than a single factor. In addition to housing pinnipeds in a marine environment, a plausible argument has been made for painting pools a dark color to reduce the intensity of sunlight reflection (Bellhorn, Dolensek, and Flynn 1977). At present, there are no data to evaluate this hypothesis.

Temperature is the most likely physical property of water to affect an animal's health. Although we know the normal temperature ranges for most aquatic animals in their natural environment, for most we do not know the limits of their tolerance. The manatee, *Trichechus manatus*, is one species for which we know at least the lower temperature limit: about 16°C (Jenkins 1978). It is common for animals to be housed at warmer water temperatures than in their natural environment because of the high cost of cooling water. When the limits are pushed too far in this direction, health problems may result, as previously mentioned with the relationship between a *Fusarium* infection and water temperature in gray seals (Montali et al. 1981). It is common knowledge that high water temperatures correlate with aberrant losses of hair in polar bears. Unusually high air or water temperatures might trigger molting at a time when it would not normally occur (see Watts 1992).

Visual Quality

Animal health concerns should clearly take precedence over the aesthetic quality of an exhibit; however, the two goals should be complementary. Aesthetically, good water quality means being able to see the animal in the water. Visual clarity is directly related to the amount of particulate matter suspended in the water. Turbidity is a quantitative measure of the relative amount of material in suspension. Two standard units of measurement commonly used are nephelometric turbidity units (NTU) and Jackson turbidity units (JTU). The degree to which suspended material needs to be removed for good viewing depends on the angle of viewing and the angle and intensity of ambient light. Observing from above the pool does not require as low a level of turbidity as does viewing horizontally through an underwater

port. Good visibility at the bottom of a pool 6 m deep at the National Zoo was obtained when turbidity readings were between 3 and 4 NTU. For comparable viewing from an underwater window, turbidity needed to be no more than about 2 NTU.

Criteria for acceptable visual clarity in exhibit pools cannot and generally should not be legislated. Each institution must make its own judgment. Certainly zoo visitors will make their opinions known if the clarity is not adequate.

METHODS OF WATER TREATMENT

Water systems in aquatic mammal exhibits are usually one of three types (fig. 23.1): (1) a complete flow-thru system, in which water is continuously pumped into and out of the primary holding pool at a rate high enough to preclude the need for water treatment, (2) a partial flow-thru system, in which a percentage of the water is continuously turned over but the remainder of the water is recirculated and treated (e.g., Spotte 1980; Nightingale 1981), or (3) a closed-loop system, in which the primary pool is filled with water that is recirculated through a treatment process for a given amount of time before being discarded. The type of system designed depends on the quality and cost of the water source. The ideal system is a complete flow-thru, but it is usually cost-effective to operate such a facility only along a coast that is free of local pollution. More often, even zoos and oceaniums along a coast use a partial flow-thru system. Inland facilities almost always use a closed-loop design because the source of water is normally the public drinking water supply, which is expensive and sometimes limited. The following information pertains to partial flow-thru and closed-

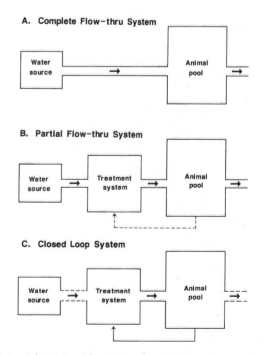

Fig. 23.1.   Schematics of three types of water systems for aquatic animal pools. Solid lines and arrows indicate continuous water flow; dotted lines and arrows represent periodic or optional flow. (From Boness 1985.)

loop systems, which are the most commonly used in zoos and aquariums.

As indicated in the previous section, the two main reasons for water treatment in aquatic exhibits are to remove pathogens and chemicals that may be harmful to animals and to remove particulate matter. The technology used by zoos to accomplish this evolved from drinking water and wastewater treatment. It must be kept in mind that there are two fundamental differences between water systems in zoos and their predecessors: animals spend all or a large proportion of their time in the treated water, and animal exhibits are usually closed-loop or partial flow-thru systems, whereas water treatment plants are complete flow-thru systems. In this latter aspect, aquatic exhibits are more like swimming pools, but swimming pools have predictable times when people will not be in them, and the amount of excreta added to them is generally minimal. One therefore cannot simply apply swimming pool treatment design to aquatic mammal exhibits.

Removal of Suspended Solids

Turbidity results from the presence of solids that remain suspended in the water column. Mechanical filtration, the primary method used to reduce turbidity, traps the suspended solids in a filter medium while allowing the water to pass through it. When the filter medium contains enough solid particles to impede water flow, the particles are backwashed into the waste disposal system.

Small particles are the most difficult to remove. Most suspended solids have negative ionic charges, which tend to make the smaller particles more stable than the larger ones (Cheremisinoff and Young 1975). Filtration of these small suspended solids can occur only when the individual particles join to form aggregates, or flocs. This process occurs naturally and can be enhanced by moderate agitation of the water (Spotte 1979), but only if the ionic charges are not so great as to produce repulsion (Cheremisinoff and Young 1975). In order for strongly charged particles to form aggregates, chemicals must be added either to neutralize the charge (a process known as coagulation) or to bridge the gap produced by the repelling forces (a process known as flocculation). Figure 23.2 gives the sizes of some suspended solids commonly found in pools and indicates whether they can be removed directly by mechanical filtration or require prefiltration flocculation or coagulation.

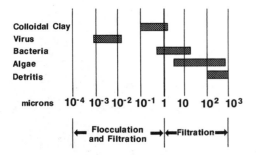

FIG. 23.2.   Sizes of various substances that might be found in suspension in aquatic mammal pools and the kind of treatment required to remove them. (Adapted from Cheremisinoff and Young 1975.)

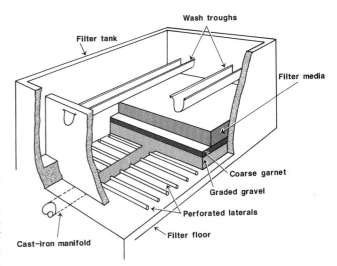

FIG. 23.3.   An illustration of a gravity filter. (Adapted from Culp and Culp 1974.)

Filter Types. Filter types may be classified in several ways. I will distinguish between gravity or low-rate filters (fig. 23.3) and pressure or high-rate filters (fig. 23.4). The major distinctions between them are outlined in table 23.2. Water treatment plants were initially slow to use pressure filters because the surface of the filter media cannot be seen and because they are susceptible to media upset from rapid pressure changes (Culp and Culp 1974). These problems were reduced by the development of monitoring instruments that are installed on the influent and effluent lines of pressure filters to allow monitoring of turbidity and changes in pressure across the filter. As a result, pressure filters are now commonly used in water and wastewater treatment plants and public swimming pools.

Determining which type of filter to use in an aquatic mammal exhibit depends on the size of the exhibit pool, the space available for the treatment system, and the funds available to operate and maintain the system. Pressure filters can filter at a rate 3 to 5 times greater than gravity filters per unit area of filter (table 23.2). Therefore, if the amount of water to be filtered is large relative to the space available and operating costs are not of concern, a pressure filtration system is the logical choice. However, pressure filters are substantially more expensive to operate and maintain because high-capacity pumps are required to circulate the water through the filter.

Most zoos designing aquatic exhibits today use pressure filters (e.g., Spotte 1980; Nightingale 1981; Monroe 1986), but judging from conversations with curators at several zoos, a word of caution about operating pressure filtration systems is appropriate: The systems are complex and delicate enough to require trained staff to operate them. Asking inexperienced staff to learn to operate a pressure filter by trial and error will result only in poor quality water and possibly expensive repairs.

Filter Media. The medium used most often in mechanical filtration is silica sand (0.3 to 1.0 mm in diameter), but anthracite (0.6 to 0.8 mm) and calcium carbonate (0.4 to 0.7 mm) are also used (Culp and Culp 1974; Cheremisinoff

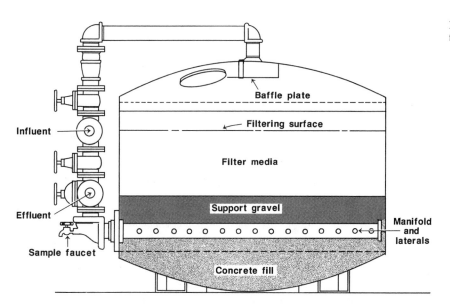

Fig. 23.4.   An illustration of a pressure filter. (Adapted from Baylis 1956.)

Table 23.2.   Some Characteristics of Gravity and Pressure Filters

| | Filter type | |
Characteristic	Gravity	Pressure
Construction	Open-topped: concrete or steel	Closed cylinder: steel or plastic
Filtration rate	2–4 gpm/ft^2	3–15 gpm/ft^2
Means of monitoring operation	Process can be observed directly from open top	Requires instruments on influent and effluent lines
Stability of media	Fairly stable because media are not exposed to sudden pressure changes	Vulnerable to major disturbance due to sudden pressure changes
Relative cost of operation	Low, because gravity is used to circulate water to the filter	High, because high-capacity pumps must circulate water to the filter.

and Young 1975). The size of the filter medium is important because the medium must prevent passage of suspended material, hold the particles loosely so that they can be easily backwashed out of the filter, and be able to hold a considerable volume of suspended matter without its clogging the filter. Anthracite and sand are equally effective for turbidity reduction. However, anthracite, which is less dense than sand and has different requirements for backwashing velocity, retains filtration efficiency at higher filtration rates and requires less frequent backwashing than does sand. Calcium carbonate medium, in principle, reacts with carbon dioxide in low-pH water to form calcium bicarbonate, which reduces the acidity of the water and prevents corrosion (Cheremisinoff and Young 1975). However, there is evidence from aquariums that a layer of microbes and organic slime will form around calcium carbonate particles, rendering them ineffective chemically. Calcium carbonate is soft and disintegrates easily and therefore must be replenished periodically, making it a relatively expensive medium to use. Moreover, as most filtration systems for aquatic exhibits consist of noncorrodible plastic or fiberglass piping and epoxy-coated stainless steel filters, corrosion due to low pH should not be a problem.

Greater filtration efficiency can be obtained by using dual- or mixed-media filters (Culp and Culp 1974; Spotte 1979). In a dual-media filter, a coarser grain is placed on top of a finer grain (usually anthracite on sand). In a mixed-media filter, there are at least three sizes of particles, which are layered from largest at the top to smallest at the bottom. After the first backwash of a newly laid filter, the distribution of particles should be as illustrated in figure 23.5: rather than their being completely layered, there should be an intermixing of the different-sized media. The net effect of this mixing is that the suspended solids penetrate into the bed, but still get trapped by the predominantly small medium at the bottom of the filter. This increases the functional surface area of the filter and allows longer filter runs before backwashing is necessary. In a single-medium filter only the upper several centimeters of medium collect the suspended solids.

Diatomaceous Earth Filters. Diatomaceous earth (DE) filters are used in aquariums (Spotte 1979) and to a limited extent for water treatment (Culp and Culp 1974). A few zoos have used them for aquatic mammal exhibits, but not without problems (Friedman et al. 1984; L. Cahill, pers. comm.). DE filters consist of a filter element that is precoated with a layer of DE and then continuously fed with a slurry of DE. These filters can remove smaller particles than either gravity or pressure sand or anthracite filters, but successful filtration with DE is highly dependent on proper precoating and slurry feed (see Spotte 1979 for a good discussion of this). If the particulate load is too heavy, replacement of the DE must be so frequent that the system becomes expensive and cumbersome to operate. Furthermore, disposal

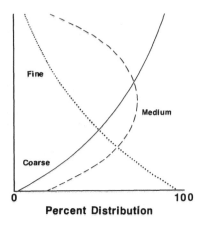

Percent Distribution

Fig. 23.5. Proper distribution of media in a mixed-media filter. The y axis represents the vertical dimension of the filter. (Adapted from Culp and Culp 1974.)

of the used DE powder may be a problem. Because heavy particulate loads are likely to be found in most aquatic mammal pools, DE filters are better thought of as a means of secondary filtration, following sand. However, if the goal is to reduce turbidity beyond what can be accomplished by sand filtration, a less expensive alternative to DE is the use of flocculants preceding sand filtration.

Flocculation. Flocculation is the process whereby a substance that will form long-chain compounds, or polymers, is added to water to bridge the distance between the ionic charges of small suspended particles, causing them to aggregate. The aggregations are then large enough to be removed by mechanical filtration. The most widely used inorganic flocculants are calcium, aluminum, and iron salts (Cheremisinoff and Young 1975). Aluminum sulfate (alum) is the flocculant most widely used at zoos and water treatment plants.

An appropriate method of mixing the flocculant and a proper water environment are as important as the flocculant itself (Culp and Culp 1974; Cheremisinoff and Young 1975). Thus, a mixing chamber is recommended. The specifications for this chamber and the water environment in it depend on the choice of flocculant and other aspects of the treatment system. Among the variables that are important to consider are: the amount of mixing time, the degree of agitation of the water, water temperature, and pH.

Removal of Dissolved Solids

Mechanical filtration reduces turbidity and removes solid organic matter that serves as nutrients for bacteria and algae, but it does little to remove dissolved compounds that contribute to the pollution of the water. This is particularly a problem in a closed-loop system, in which organic material that goes into solution in the water is added at a rate faster than it can be removed (Spotte and Adams 1979). Spotte and Adams measured total organic carbon (TOC) in two marine mammal systems, one with pressure sand filtration and the other with DE filtration, and found that TOC continued to increase at a high daily rate despite the mechanical filtration. In principle, the dissolved organics can be removed by physical adsorption, oxidation reactions, or ion exchange. However, the efficiency of these procedures in

large systems remains questionable, and the cost is likely to be high (Adams and Spotte 1980, 1982). Nevertheless, I shall briefly describe these treatment methods, as they may prove to be useful in small aquatic mammal exhibits or reptile and amphibian exhibits. They are used successfully in aquariums (Spotte 1979).

Physical Adsorption. Physical adsorption of dissolved solids is most often accomplished using activated carbon filtration. Adsorption occurs as the activated carbon attracts compounds to its surface and they accumulate there. This method is heavily used in water treatment because the carbon preferentially attracts organic compounds over others (Culp and Culp 1974). Activated carbon comes in powder (PAC) or granular (GAC) form (Tchobanoglous 1972). Even though PAC has a greater surface area and therefore more adsorption capacity per unit volume than GAC, GAC is a better medium because it wets rapidly, does not float, and is hard and dense so that it does not deteriorate appreciably in water (Culp and Culp 1974).

The rate of adsorption of organic compounds by GAC is dependent upon contact time (Culp and Culp 1974; Spotte 1979) and the amount of pore surface area (Morris and Weber 1964). A biological slime, formed by bacteria that naturally build up in the GAC filter, eventually coats the carbon grains and reduces transport of compounds to the carbon surface (McCreary and Snoeyink 1977). However, the buildup of heterotrophic bacteria in water treatment plants is encouraged in Europe because there is actually a net increase in the removal of ammonia with this biological activity (Sontheimer 1980).

The major problem with using GAC is cost. Once the pore sites on the carbon grains are full, the GAC is no longer effective and must be replaced (Adams and Spotte 1980). The frequency of replacement is dependent on the concentration of dissolved organic matter in the water. In a closed-loop system housing aquatic mammals, the amount of dissolved organic matter is high because the animals eat, defecate, and urinate in the water (Spotte and Adams 1979). Another problem arises because many zoos use chlorine as a disinfectant and/or oxidant, and activated carbon adsorbs chlorine (Kovach 1971). When they are used in tandem, the GAC counteracts the intended function of the chlorine, and the adsorption of chlorine increases the rate at which the GAC becomes spent. This problem would not occur if ozone were used as a disinfectant and oxidant in conjunction with GAC treatment in marine mammal systems (Adams and Spotte 1980). It remains to be determined whether such a combination of treatments would be more cost-effective than ozonation alone.

Oxidation. Dissolved organics may be removed from water by chemical alteration through oxidation. Chlorine and ozone are the two most commonly used oxidants in water treatment. The main oxidizing role of chlorine in water treatment is the removal of ammonia (Sontheimer 1980). Adams and Spotte (1980) demonstrated a reduction in organic carbon in closed-loop marine mammal systems by superchlorination. This procedure requires removing the animals from an exhibit and boosting chlorine levels extremely high (10 to 25 ppm). Even under such extreme chlorine treatment, however, the reduction in organic material

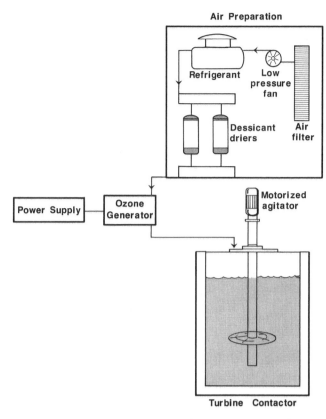

Air Preparation

Refrigerant

Low pressure fan

Dessicant driers

Air filter

Power Supply

Ozone Generator

Motorized agitator

Turbine   Contactor

FIG. 23.6.   The essential components of an ozonation system for disinfection of water. (Adapted from Cheremisinoff, Cheremisinoff, and Tratner 1981.)

was less than that with either ozonation or activated carbon filtration. In view of this result and concern over the potential carcinogenic effects of by-products of the oxidation process between chlorine and organic compounds (Jolley, Brungs, and Cumming 1980; Maugh 1981), the use of chlorine for removal of dissolved organics is not recommended.

Ozone's (O_3) high instability in water makes it a stronger oxidant than chlorine because it reacts with oxidizable compounds almost immediately upon contact (Cheremisinoff, Cheremisinoff, and Tratner 1981). The technology for ozonation has improved to the point that an ozone generator for commercial water treatment will fit on a tabletop. An ozonation system consists of four parts: an ozone generator, an air or gas preparation device, an electrical power supply, and a contact chamber (fig. 23.6). Ozone is produced by passing cool, dry air ($-40°C$ dew point) over an electrical field (usually 60 Hz with variable voltage). About 1% of the oxygen in the air is converted to ozone, which is then carried to a contact chamber and mixed with the water (Cheremisinoff and Young 1975; Cheremisinoff, Cheremisinoff, and Tratner 1981). Using pure oxygen instead of ambient air increases the efficiency of the ozone generator: 3–4% of the pure oxygen will be converted to ozone. The relatively new method of producing an ozonelike oxidant, photozone, may prove even more efficient (about 10% of pure oxygen is converted) (Lohr and Gratzek 1981).

Ozonation is more expensive than chlorination. There are no published cost analyses of ozone treatment of aquatic

mammal exhibits, but the costs for treating drinking water and wastewater have been determined. At dosages of 1.5–3.0 mg ozone per liter water (mg/l), the cost of ozonation is between \$1.75 and \$3.95 per 1,000 gallons of water (Miller et al. 1978). A comparison of the costs of ozonation versus chlorination of wastewater at the same plant showed that chlorination was between 30% and 60% cheaper, depending on the type of chlorine used (Yao 1972).

In a test of the effect of ozonation on dissolved organics in a marine mammal pool, dosages of about 4.0 mg/l did not significantly reduce the level of total organic carbon (Adams and Spotte 1980). However, when used in conjunction with activated carbon filtration, the ozone doubled the efficiency of the removal of TOC by the carbon.

Ion Exchange. Dissolved pollutants can be removed by ion exchange between an electrochemically charged substrate and the pollutant (Spotte 1979). To accomplish this, water must pass through a contact chamber containing an ionic resin. Spotte (figs. 3–16 in Spotte 1979) illustrates the use of a pressure filter as an ion exchange chamber.

The size of the exchange particles, competition from nonpollutant ions in the water, and the type of exchange material, among other factors, affect the ion exchange process. Smaller grains of exchange material are more effective than larger ones, probably because they provide more surface area (Spotte 1979). Treatment of dissolved organics is inhibited in saltwater because chloride ions in the water compete with the organic material for the exchange ions. For example, the effectiveness of ammonium ion removal at a fish hatchery was reduced by an order of magnitude when distilled water was changed to water with a salinity of 5% (Johnson and Sieburth 1974). Ion exchangers must be appropriate for the specific pollutant being removed. The ammonium ion is removed by a basic cationic exchanger, whereas nitrate, phosphate, and sulfate ions are removed by a basic anionic exchanger (Spotte 1979).

Spotte (1979) believes that ion exchange treatment should be used more often than it is in aquariums because when used properly it can remove 90% of the ammonium, nitrate, and phosphate ions. Its benefit for aquatic mammal facilities is less certain. In a laboratory test of water from a marine mammal pool at Mystic Marinelife Aquarium, two synthetic ionic resins reduced total organic carbon by only 10% after 77 to 96 hours of contact. It is not clear how much of the organic carbon was in the form of dissolved matter, but the amount of suspended matter was deliberately reduced prior to the test.

Removal of Pathogens

Water is usually disinfected by one of three methods: chlorination, ozonation, or ultraviolet radiation. Chlorine has been the predominant disinfectant used for drinking water, wastewater, and water in aquatic mammal facilities because of its residual effect on microorganisms and its relatively low cost (Culp and Culp 1974; Cheremisinoff, Cheremisinoff, and Tratner 1981). In this section I will briefly discuss each treatment method and its pros and cons in relation to aquatic mammal exhibits.

Chlorination. Chlorine is available in three forms: as a gas, and as either solid (calcium) or liquid (sodium) hypochlorite. Chlorine gas is much less expensive to use than the hypochlorites, but because it is considerably more dangerous, it is not often used. Gaseous chlorine can be lethal to humans at dosages as low as 430 ppm (Cheremisinoff, Cheremisinoff, and Tratner 1981).

In water, both gaseous and liquid chlorine react to form HOCl (hypochlorous acid) and H^+ plus OCl^- (hypochlorite ion). HOCl and OCl^- are known as free chlorines. The relative amount of HOCl to OCl^- is dependent on the pH of the water, and the chlorine itself alters pH; gaseous chlorine lowers pH and hypochlorites raise pH when added to water. Above pH 7.5, OCl^- predominates; below, HOCl predominates (Culp and Culp 1974). Chlorine is a very active oxidizing agent, and it readily reacts with ammonia and other nitrogenous materials to form chloramines, or combined chlorines.

Free chlorines are much more effective disinfectants than combined chlorines (Kabler et al. 1963; Chambers 1971). Among the two forms of free chlorine, HOCl is a better disinfectant than OCl^- because HOCl can penetrate the cell walls of organisms and OCl^- cannot (Culp 1978). Both types of chlorines have drawbacks. Combined chlorines are more toxic than free chlorines (see section 7 in Jolley, Brungs, and Cumming 1980), but free chlorines used in the presence of humic and fulvic acid or some algae can produce carcinogenic trihalomethanes (Oliver 1980; Briley et al. 1980). And even though chlorine is a good bactericide, many protozoans, yeasts, cysts, and viruses are resistant to it (Hammer 1975).

Breakpoint chlorination is generally believed to be the most effective technique of chlorine disinfection (fig. 23.7). When chlorine is first added to a system, it reacts with ammonia and nitrogenous waste to form combined chlorines. With time and increased chlorination, the ammonia levels decline, so that the addition of more chlorine results in the formation of a free chlorine residual. The point at which the combined chlorine residual is at a low is called the breakpoint. Breakpoint curves are unique to each water system because they are dependent on the initial concentrations of nitrogenous material and other oxidizable substances in the water.

Breakpoint chlorination is possible in an aquatic mammal facility, but, because ammonia is added continuously via the animals' waste products and because the animals are in the water all the time, careful monitoring of chlorine levels is required to stay beyond the breakpoint once it is achieved. The relatively high chlorine residuals that might be required to stay at breakpoint should not be a problem because free chlorine appears not to be toxic, but if breakpoint is lost and these high residuals become mainly combined chlorine, one has a serious problem. Depending on the concentration of nitrogenous material added to the pool on a daily basis (a direct function of the number of animals in the pool), whether or not there are precursors of trihalomethanes present, and the bacterial load of the system, it may be more feasible in an aquatic mammal exhibit just to use a low level of combined chlorines to keep bacteria levels down.

Chlorine should always be administered to the pool through a high-quality injection system. Manually adding

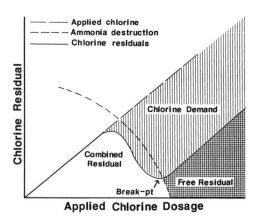

FIG. 23.7.   Theoretical breakpoint chlorination curve. (Adapted from Cheremisinoff, Cheremisinoff, and Tratner 1981.)

any type of chlorine is unsafe and does not properly distribute the chemical in the pool. Injection of a weak acid (e.g., muriatic acid) or base (soda ash), depending on the type of chlorine, should accompany chlorine injection to maintain a relatively constant pH. Injection systems should never be left unattended for long periods of time, and, ideally, monitoring should be done continuously while chlorine is being added. A variety of monitoring equipment is available (Culp and Culp 1974; Cheremisinoff, Cheremisinoff, and Tratner 1981). Keepers can be trained either to check monitors or to perform manual chemical tests on site, but the overall operation of a treatment system should be carried out by a person trained in water treatment. Water treatment engineers are skilled professionals, and, just as zoos would not expect a water treatment engineer to manage and care for exotic animals, they also should not expect keepers to manage and operate water treatment systems. To run a water treatment system properly is a full-time job.

Because of the known and probable negative effects of chlorine on animal health, alternatives should be considered. One option not yet seriously considered in zoos is to use chlorination but to dechlorinate the water before returning it to the exhibit pool. However, a separate treatment pool to hold a subset of the exhibit pool water may be required because chlorine does not act instantaneously in killing microorganisms.

Ozonation. The process of ozonation was described in the section on oxidation of dissolved organics. Ozone appears to be a better disinfectant than chlorine (Hettche and Ehlbeck 1955; Evans 1972; Evison 1978; Roy et al. 1981). It requires less contact time to kill microorganisms, and is effective against many organisms that are resistant to chlorine (Culp and Culp 1974). At the same time, ozone does not react with ammonia, does not appear to produce toxic compounds, is not affected by pH, and does not form carcinogens such as trihalomethanes (ozone will in fact oxidize trihalomethanes under proper pH conditions: Cheremisinoff, Cheremisinoff, and Tratner 1981). Despite all this, ozone has not been used as the final treatment in drinking water systems because bacterial regrowth can occur (Culp and Culp 1974), although more recent work indicates that an ozone residual sufficient to kill microorganisms can be obtained (Roy et al. 1981). A residual effect is particularly important in an aquatic mammal exhibit where animals are continuously reinfecting the pool water. The other drawback is that the ozone will be used up in oxidizing the organic material before serving its germicidal function if there is a heavy organic load in the water (Lohr and Gratzek 1981).

Despite the finding that ozone levels of 4 mg/l did not significantly affect TOC in a closed-loop marine mammal system (Adams and Spotte 1980), several zoos and oceanariums are using ozone treatment for both disinfection and oxidization of organics. These institutions are satisfied with its performance (J. Schneider, pers. comm.; R. Jenkins, pers. comm.; E. Asper, pers. comm.), although ozone is not the only treatment used in some of them. The Oklahoma City Zoo, for example, uses gaseous chlorination in conjunction with ozonation (Monroe 1986).

Ultraviolet Radiation. Ultraviolet radiation (UV) is another method of disinfection that is used in water and wastewater treatment and in aquariums. Ultraviolet radiant energy is generated by passing an electrical discharge through a low-pressure mercury vapor enclosed in a special glass tube. The optimal wavelength for germicidal action is between 2,500 and 2,600 Å. The absorption of these wavelengths by the cells of pathogenic organisms appears to produce lethal photochemical transformations in their DNA (Cheremisinoff, Cheremisinoff, and Tratner 1981).

The success of UV disinfection is affected by the dosage, the sizes of the pathogens, and the ability of the radiation to penetrate the water. Dosages of 40,000 uW-sec/cm^2 kill many viruses, bacteria, and smaller protozoans and fungi (Cheremisinoff, Cheremisinoff, and Tratner 1981), but larger organisms may require more than 10^6 uW-sec/cm^2 of UV (Spotte 1979). Because water penetration is critical for UV disinfection, turbidity, iron salts, and organic material will reduce its effectiveness. Microorganisms may actually be shielded from UV by large particulate matter, but this problem may be alleviated by proper mechanical filtration prior to UV treatment. Calcium, sodium, manganese, and aluminum ions are known to absorb UV and therefore reduce its effectiveness (Cheremisinoff, Cheremisinoff, and Tratner 1981). Water with high concentrations of these ions could be pretreated with GAC or ion exchangers, but this clearly adds to the cost of treatment.

Cost is one of the major drawbacks of UV disinfection. It is already the most expensive of the three methods described without considering supplemental treatments as well. Because UV has a limited ability to penetrate water (about 5 cm under ideal conditions), only a subset of the water that is being filtered at any given time is treated. When one adds to this the fact that UV produces no residual disinfecting compounds, it seems unlikely that this method alone can be used effectively in a closed-loop system. This was indeed demonstrated both theoretically (Spotte and Adams 1981) and empirically for a closed-loop marine mammal system (Spotte and Buck 1981).

TREATMENT OF UNINHABITED EXHIBIT POOLS

The discussion of water treatment thus far has focused on exhibit pools used frequently by animals. Many zoo exhibits, however, also have ponds or moats used for aesthetic purposes or as barriers, used just for drinking, or used only for an occasional swim. Such water systems are usually small compared with pools inhabited by animals. When these bodies of water accumulate organic debris from the surrounding environment or animal excreta, they require treatment. The most cost-effective treatment of small pools is to empty and refill them. If animals drink from the pools, monitoring to be certain that microorganisms are not reaching high enough concentrations to present a health hazard should be done before they are emptied. For larger pools or moats, mechanical filtration may be used to reduce particulate matter and increase the interval between changes of water. As indicated earlier, keeping the water cool will retard the growth of bacteria and algae, although this is expensive; chemical disinfection may also be appropriate. In an uninhabited moat or pool, methods of treatment can be chosen mainly on economic criteria. If it is more economical to empty and refill than to add a chemical, or to use chlorine rather than ozone, there is no animal health reason to override the cost issue.

SUMMARY AND CONCLUSIONS

The passage of the USDA animal welfare regulations for marine mammals resulted in a flourish of improvements in water quality treatment for marine mammals in zoos. As these facilities improve, so must other aquatic mammal facilities as well. The most important aspect of water quality is control of diseases and toxic substances. Our understanding of the pathogens of aquatic mammals is rapidly increasing, but little progress has been made in understanding what substances might be toxic. Removal of suspended solids is a necessary precursor to successful disinfection, and removal of dissolved organics will help alleviate at least some potentially toxic substances. Good visual clarity in aquatic exhibits should follow from this basic treatment, but if clarity is not adequate for underwater viewing, prefiltration flocculation should provide the final touches.

Standard pressure sand filters are the most suitable for large exhibit pools because of their ability to process water rapidly (see table 23.2). Even though they are designed to function at 15–20 gpm/ft^2, operating at less than that rate may result in lower costs without a reduction in the quality of filtration. Because each water system is unique, one must design as much flexibility into a system as possible to allow the most cost-effective operation and still accomplish quality treatment. For small exhibits, gravity filters are a reasonable alternative to pressure filters.

There is little reason to recommend diatomaceous earth filters for aquatic mammal exhibits. Although they remove finer particles than sand filtration does, they are relatively expensive to operate and have a high potential for fouling up. Because DE filtration must be preceded by sand filtration to prevent foul-up in most situations, flocculation appears to be a much better means of achieving lower turbidity.

The greatest controversy in water quality treatment for aquatic mammals is over disinfection. Chlorination is still clearly the dominant means of maintaining low coliform counts. The same may be true in water and wastewater treatment, but at least in these areas there is a great deal of ongoing research to determine whether a major shift in methods should be made. Such research is not being done in zoos; in fact, other than the work by Spotte and his colleagues, which has been cited throughout this chapter, systematic data on the effects of various methods of treating aquatic mammal facilities have not been published. Regardless of how little we know about the effects of chlorination on captive aquatic animals, the increasing criticism of chlorination in water and wastewater treatment (Sontheimer 1980; Jolley, Brungs, and Cumming 1980; Maugh 1981) justifies a serious effort to use alternative treatments, even at higher costs.

Ultraviolet radiation does not seem to be a viable alternative in closed-loop systems. UV's inability to penetrate more than about 5 cm of water even under ideal conditions means either that an impractical number of sterilizing units would have to be used to treat a large percentage of the water or that only a small portion of the total pool could be treated. The cost of the former approach for large pools is prohibitive, and as Spotte and colleagues have demonstrated, the latter approach does not disinfect the water (Spotte and Adams 1981; Spotte and Buck 1981).

Ozone may be the most feasible alternative to chlorine, despite some of the drawbacks outlined earlier. In addition to its direct killing action on microorganisms, some ozone residual can be obtained (Roy et al. 1981), although in a closed-loop system with animals continuously adding dissolved organic material to the water, high levels will be needed to achieve residuals because some of the ozone will be used up in the oxidation of the dissolved organics. Using activated carbon may improve the effectiveness of the ozone as a disinfectant; Adams and Spotte (1980) demonstrated the synergistic action of these two treatment methods on total organic carbon.

The effect of water temperature on maintaining good water quality should not be underestimated. Bacteria and algae grow much faster at high temperatures. Furthermore, many aquatic animals are adapted to living in cold water and are sufficiently stressed by warm water to become predisposed to disease (Montali et al. 1981).

Zoos have made great strides in the improvement of exhibits and husbandry practices in the past two decades. Much of this has been accomplished by increased research efforts, both within zoos and in collaborative efforts between zoos and universities. Most zoos have very little professional expertise in the field of water quality control and would benefit greatly from establishing collaborative efforts with universities, municipal water treatment facilities, and appropriate industries. Such collaboration will lead to a better understanding of the dynamics of water chemistry and microbiology in aquatic mammal exhibits, which is essential for the improvement of water treatment systems in zoos.

In summary, the following points should be given serious consideration, particularly by institutions developing new aquatic exhibits or renovating old ones:

1. The salinity of the water should approximate that of the animal's natural habitat. Marine mammals are adapted to living in saltwater and should not be kept in freshwater just because they do not die in it.

2. Mechanical filtration to remove suspended particles is a must. Filtration removes nutrients for microorganisms and algae and provides good water clarity. It also removes some suspended algae and bacteria, although it should not be used as the only means of controlling microorganisms.

3. Disinfection of the water is also necessary. Chlorine should not be used as a primary disinfectant unless it is removed or markedly reduced in the pool occupied by the animals; there are too many health hazards associated with it. At this point, ozonation is the most promising alternative.

4. Emptying and refilling pools in which aquatic mammals live is not a viable method of treatment for exhibits with large volumes of water. It may be economical, but it can be extremely stressful to the animals. Furthermore, the frequency with which emptying must be done during periods of warm weather, combined with the amount of time required to fill large pools, means that the exhibit is "down" much too often.

5. Water temperature is an important factor in water quality control, both because water that is either too warm or too cold stresses animals and because many harmful microorganisms flourish at high temperatures.

6. Monitoring the chemistry and biology of the water is essential. Water quality control is a dynamic process in which there are many interrelated reactions. Adjustments must constantly be made to maximize quality, but this can only be done with appropriate information about the water. Moreover, we currently have very limited knowledge of the effects of various substances on captive aquatic mammals, so the more components of the water we measure, the more likely we will be to advance our understanding.

7. Water quality treatment is a complex job and should not be performed haphazardly by untrained individuals attending to it only part-time. Zoos must hire appropriate professionals, as they do for other areas of zoo operations.

8. Aquatic exhibits are expensive to build and to operate. Many zoos do not appear to understand the extent of the commitment they make when they decide to acquire aquatic mammals, especially large ones like cetaceans and pinnipeds. Zoos must make better assessments of the costs of building and operating a proper system. If the appropriate commitment cannot be made without cutting corners, these animals should not be acquired.

REFERENCES

Adams, G., and Spotte, S. 1980. Effects of tertiary methods on total organic carbon removal in saline, closed-system marine mammal pools. *Am. J. Vet. Res.* 41:1470–74.

———. 1982. Removal of total organic carbon from marine mammal pool water by polymeric resins. *Am. J. Vet. Res.* 43: 919–21.

Baylis, J. R. 1956. Seven years of high-rate filtration. *J. Am. Water Works Assoc.* 48:585–92.

Bellhorn, R. E., Dolensek, E. P., and Flynn, W. S. 1977. Intense miosis the cause of corneal opacities in marine mammals. *Proceedings of the Annual Conference on Veterinary Ophthalmology*, 43–45.

Boness, D. J. 1985. The role of zoos and oceanariums in the conservation of marine mammals. *Proceedings of the Symposium on Endangered Marine Animals and Marine Parks* 1:429–39. Cochin, India: Marine Biological Association of India.

Briley, K. F., Williams, R. F., Longley, K. E., and Sorber, C. A. 1980. Trihalomethane production from algal precursors. In *Water chlorination: Environmental impact and health effects*, ed. R. L. Jolley, W. A. Brungs, and R. B. Cumming, 117–30. Ann Arbor: Ann Arbor Science.

Chambers, C. 1971. Chlorination for control of bacteria and viruses in treatment plant effluents. *J. Water Poll. Cont. Fed.* 43:228–41.

Cheremisinoff, N. P., Cheremisinoff, P. N., and Tratner, R. B. 1981. *Chemical and nonchemical disinfection*. Ann Arbor: Ann Arbor Science.

Cheremisinoff, P. N., and Young, R. A. 1975. *Pollution engineering practice handbook*. Ann Arbor: Ann Arbor Science.

Culp, G. L. 1978. *New concepts in water purification*. 2d ed. New York: Van Nostrand Reinhold.

Culp, G. L., and Culp, R. L. 1974. *New concepts in water purification*. New York: Van Nostrand Reinhold.

Cusick, P. K., and Bullock, B. C. 1973. Ulcerative dermatitis and pneumonia associated with *Aeromonas hydrophila* infection in the bottle-nosed dolphin. *J. Am. Vet. Med. Assoc.* 163:578–79.

Diamond, S. S., Ewing, D. E., and Cadwell, G. A. 1979. Fatal bronchopneumonia and dermatitis caused by *Pseudomonas aeruginosa* in an Atlantic bottle-nosed dolphin. *J. Am. Vet. Med. Assoc.* 175:984–87.

Dunn, J. L., Buck, J. D., and Spotte, S. 1982. Candidiasis in captive cetaceans. *J. Am. Vet. Med. Assoc.* 181:1316–21.

Evans, F. L. 1972. Ozone technology: Current status. In *Ozone in water and wastewater treatment*, ed. F. L. Evans. Ann Arbor: Ann Arbor Science.

Evison, L. M. 1978. Inactivation of enteroviruses and coliphages with ozone in water and wastewaters. *Prog. Water Technol.* 10:368.

Fowler, M. E. 1978. *Zoo and wild animal medicine*. Philadelphia: W. B. Saunders.

Friedman, S., Don Carlos, M. W., Nelson, M., and House, H. B. 1984. The beaver pond exhibit at the Minnesota Zoological Garden. *Int. Zoo Yrbk.* 21:247–57.

Hammer, M. J. 1975. *Water and wastewater technology*. New York: John Wiley.

Harwood, J. 1989. Lessons from the seal epidemic. *New Scientist*, 18 February, 38–42.

Helle, E., Hyvarinen, H., Pyysalo, H., and Wickstrom, K. 1983. Levels of organochlorine compounds in an inland seal population in eastern Finland. *Mar. Poll. Bull.* 14:256–60.

Helle, E., Olsson, M., and Jensen, S. 1976. PCB levels correlated with pathological changes in uteri. *Ambio* 5:261–63.

Hettche, O., and Ehlbeck, H. W. S. 1955. Epidemiology and prophylaxis of poliomyelitis with reference to the role of water in its transmission. *Water Poll. Abstr.* 28:145.

Hubbard, R. C. 1968. Husbandry and laboratory care of pinnipeds. In *The behavior and physiology of pinnipeds*, ed. R. J. Harrison, R. C. Hubbard, R. S. Peterson, C. E. Rice, and R. J. Schustermann, 297–358. New York: Appleton-Century-Crofts.

Jenkins, R. L. 1978. Captive husbandry of manatees at Marineland of Florida. In *The West Indian manatee in Florida*, ed. R. L. Brownell and K. Ralls, 128–30. Tallahassee: Florida Department of Natural Resources.

Johnson, P. W., and Sieburth, J. M. 1974. Ammonia removal by selective ion exchange: A backup system for microbiological filters in closed-system aquaculture. *Aquaculture* 4:61–68.

Jolley, R. L., Brungs, W. A., and Cumming, R. B., ed. 1980. *Water chlorination: Environmental impact and health effects*. Ann Arbor: Ann Arbor Science.

Kabler, P. W., Chang, S. L., Clarke, N. A., and Clark, H. F. 1963. Pathogenic bacteria and viruses in water supplies. Paper presented at the Fifth Sanitary Engineering Conference, University of Illinois.

Kovach, J. L. 1971. Activated carbon dechlorination. *Industrial Water Engineering*, Oct.–Nov, 30.

Lee, D. H. 1970. Nitrates, nitrites, and methemoglobinemia. *Environ. Res.* 3:484–511.

Lohr, A. L., and Gratzek, J. B. 1981. The effects of a new ozone-like oxidant, photozone, in a closed-loop aquatic system. Abstracts of the 12th Annual Conference of the International Association of Aquatic Animal Medicine Mystic, Conn.

Maugh, T. H. 1981. New study links chlorination and cancer. *Science* 211:694.

McCreary, J. J., and Snoeyink, V. L. 1977. Granular activated carbon in water treatment. *J. Am. Water Works Assoc.* 69:437–44.

McDevitt, A. 1986. Dolphins and whales improving. *Minn. Zoo Mag.* 1:1.

Miller, G. W., Rice, R. G., Robson, C. M., Scullen, R. L., Kuhn, W., and Wolf, H. 1978. *An assessment of ozone and chlorine dioxide technologies for treatment of municipal water supplies*. EPA Report no. 600/8-75/018. Washington, D.C.: U.S. Environmental Protection Agency.

Monroe, A. 1986. Behind the scenes. *Zoo Sounds* 22:16.

Montali, R. J., Bush, M., Strandberg, J. D., Janssen, D. L., Boness, D. J., and Whitla, J. C. 1981. Cyclic dermatitis associated with *Fusarium* sp. infection in pinnipeds. *J. Am. Vet. Med. Assoc.* 179:1198–1202.

Morris, J. C., and Weber, W. J. Jr. 1964. *Absorption of biochemically resistant materials from solution*. Public Health Service Publication no. 999-SP-11. Washington, D.C.: U.S. Public Health Service.

Nightingale, J. W. 1981. Essential elements of a successful breeding program with captive sea otters. *Proceedings of the Annual Meeting of the American Association of Zoo Veterinarians*, 84–86. Philadelphia: American Association of Zoo Veterinarians.

Oliver, B. G. 1980. Effect of temperature, pH, and bromide concentration on the trihalomethane reaction of chlorine with aquatic humic material. In *Water chlorination: Environmental impact and health effects*, ed. R. L. Jolley, W. A. Brungs, and R. B. Cumming, 141–50. Ann Arbor: Ann Arbor Science.

Reinjders, P. J. H. 1979. Organochlorine and heavy metal residues in harbor seals of Schleswig Holstein plus Denmark and the Netherlands: Their possible effects in relation to reproduction in both populations. *Int. Coun. Explor. Sea* CM 1979/N:18.

Roy, D., Engelbrecht, R. S., Wong, P. K. Y., and Chian, E. S. K. 1981. Inactivation of enteroviruses by ozone. *Water Sci. Technol.* 12:819–36.

Slanetz, L. W., Bartley, C. H., and Metcalf, T. G. 1965. Correlation of coliform and fecal streptococcal indices with the presence of Salmonellae and enteric viruses in sea water and shellfish. In *Advances in water pollution research*, ed. E. A. Pearson, 27–35.

Smith, A. W., and Skilling, D. E. 1979. Viruses and viral diseases of marine mammals. *J. Am. Vet. Med. Assoc.* 175:918–20.

Sontheimer, H. 1980. Drinking water and its treatment. *Environ. Sci. Technol.* 14:510–14.

Spotte, S. 1979. *Fish and invertebrate culture*. New York: Wiley-Interscience.

———. 1980. Seal Island: A new pinniped exhibit at Mystic Marinelife Aquarium. *Int. Zoo Yrbk.* 20:286–95.

Spotte, S., and Adams, G. 1979. Increase of total organic carbon

(TOC) in saline, closed-system marine mammal pools. *Cetology* 23:1–6.

———. 1981. Pathogen reduction in closed aquaculture systems by UV radiation: Fact or artifact? *Mar. Ecol. Prog. Ser.* 6: 295–98.

Spotte, S., and Buck, J. D. 1981. The efficacy of UV irradiation in the microbial disinfection of marine mammal water. *J. Wildl. Dis.* 17:11–16.

Standard Methods for the Examination of Water and Wastewater Treatment. 1979. 15th ed. Washington, D.C.: American Public Health Association.

Stroud, R. K., and Roelke, M. E. 1980. *Salmonella meningoence-phalomyelitis* in a northern fur seal *(Callorhinus ursinus). J. Wildl. Dis.* 16:15–18.

Sweeney, J. C. 1974. Common diseases of pinnipeds. *J. Am. Vet. Med. Assoc.* 165:805–10.

Sweeney, J. C., and Gilmartin, W. G. 1974. Survey of diseases in free-living California sea lions. *J. Wildl. Dis.* 10:370–76.

Tangredi, B. P., and Medway, W. 1980. Post-mortem isolation of *Vibrio alginolyticus* from an Atlantic white-sided dolphin *(Lagenorhynchus acutus). J. Wildl. Dis.* 16:329–31.

Tchobanoglous, G. 1972. *Wastewater engineering: Collection, treatment, disposal.* New York: McGraw-Hill.

Ulmer, F. A. Jr. 1962. The southern elephant seal in captivity. *Int. Zoo Yrbk.* 4:26–32.

Wagner, J. E., and Mann, P. C. 1978. Botulism in California sea lions *(Zalophus californianus):* A case report. *J. Zoo Anim. Med.* 9:142–45.

Watts, P. 1992. Thermal constraints on hauling out by harbor seals, *Phoca vitulina. Can. J. Zool.* 70:553–60.

Wilson, T. M., Dykes, R. W., and Tsai, K. S. 1972. Pox in young, captive harbor seals. *J. Am. Vet. Med. Assoc.* 161:611–17.

Yao, K. M. 1972. Is chlorine the only answer? *Water and Wastes Engineering,* Jan., 30.

PART FOUR

Population Management for Conservation

INTRODUCTION
DEVRA G. KLEIMAN

The 1980s saw an extraordinary increase in the orientation of zoos toward a conservation ethic. This part reviews several of the techniques and approaches that have revolutionized the management of captive animals during the past two decades.

It is clear that zoos cannot save sufficient genetic material to act as a gene bank for all animals. Hard choices must be made. Barrowclough and Flesness discuss the theory and practice behind the choice of "evolutionarily significant units" for preservation, that is, what constitutes genetic distinctness, in chapter 24. They also provide examples of the practical problems faced by zoos dealing with contaminated populations and hybridization, and especially, the choices that must be made when limited space is available.

Molecular genetics is being applied more and more in attempting to deal with such issues. In chapter 25 Ryder and Fleischer present the current techniques being used by zoo conservation biologists to determine the degree of genetic variability in populations of threatened species and subspecies, to clarify parentage for future genetic management, and to minimize the negative effects of deleterious genes. The results of molecular genetic studies are now regularly being applied to the management and reproduction of zoo species to reduce levels of inbreeding and maintain maximum levels of genetic variation and heterozygosity, the ultimate goal being gene pool preservation.

The results from molecular genetic studies are also being applied to new computer models for the demographic and population genetic analysis of zoo species. These models provide a structure within which we can make decisions about exactly which individuals to breed, when to breed them, and what to do with the offspring. This is a far cry from the "early days," when zoos would breed every individual regardless of its level of representation in a captive population. Indeed, zoos frequently bred close relatives, since shipping animals between zoos was so fraught with complications.

The importance of genetic management of captive populations became obvious in the mid-1970s when Ralls and Ballou, in a series of seminal papers based on zoo records for a number of mammalian species, demonstrated quite conclusively that inbreeding resulted in reduced survival of juveniles, and that the continued practice of mating parents and offspring and/or siblings with each other would ultimately hurt zoos' abilities to conserve species. In chapter 26, Ballou and Foose present the principles, concepts, and techniques of managing genetic diversity, from the identification of founders, to the construction of pedigrees, to the determination of effective population size, to the animal-by-animal recommendations that derive from a complete genetic and demographic analysis of a zoo species.

Pfeifer, in chapter 27, provides a review of the biological basis for dispersal behavior and then describes how such knowledge can be applied to captive mammal management.

The use of sophisticated computer models to make genetic and demographic decisions for captive populations, as well as the greater success in breeding many of the species in our care, has resulted in management programs for several species at "zero population growth" (ZPG). ZPG provides the potential for managing a population in the long term; it maintains maximum genetic diversity but does not result in the constant need for additional space that occurs with a growing population. The need to reach a given population size and then maintain ZPG for many species in zoos usually results in the problem of surplus animals, the issue that Graham discusses in chapter 28. Unquestionably, the greatest single animal rights question faced by zoos is how and when to dispose of animals declared surplus to the genetic and demographic needs of a captive population. This is not an animal welfare issue, since euthanasia need not involve any pain or suffering by an individual animal; the concept of animal rights is different. The zoo world is having to cope with the idea that what is good for an individual animal (i.e., survival) is not necessarily good for a captive population of a species faced with extinction. The survival into old age of a nonreproductive individual can reduce the genetic diversity of a population if it occupies enclosure space that otherwise could be used for genetically valuable individuals. Population, as opposed to individual, management of species is difficult for zoo staff and visitors to accept, and Graham discusses several examples of conflicts that arose from these two opposing views. Graham also presents some alternatives to euthanasia for population management and reviews the development of AZA policy for dealing with surplus animals and euthanasia.

In assuming the role of conservation organizations, zoos have looked at reintroduction of captive-bred animals as one major contribution that they can make to species survival. There are currently several ongoing reintroduction programs for rare mammals, including the Arabian oryx, *Oryx leucoryx,* golden lion tamarin, *Leontopithecus rosalia,* red wolf, *Canis rufus,* and black-footed ferret, *Mustela nigripes.* In chapter 29 Kleiman details the issues that zoos have to face when becoming involved in a reintroduction program, especially one that is international in scope. One of the main messages is that reintroduction is *not* an answer to population surpluses in zoos. Reintroduction of captive-bred specimens to the wild must be one part of a larger effort to save an endangered species, and its value must be weighed against the value of other approaches, such as purchasing land, translocating wild specimens, or supporting environmental education. Decision making about the best conservation approach requires the evaluation of a suite of factors, of which the availability of captive animals is only a small part.

The final chapter in this section, chapter 30, by Wemmer, Derrickson, and Collins discusses the role that survival or breeding centers can play in the conservation of wildlife. Such centers can maintain larger numbers of specimens than can traditional zoos, and off-exhibit facilities do not have to spend additional monies to provide what appears to the public to be a naturalistic environment for the animals. They can focus their resources on housing that provides species with critical resources for reproduction, regardless of its visual impact. Off-exhibit breeding centers, especially, can contribute greatly to zoo conservation goals at less cost. Survival centers have shown themselves to be excellent sites for research and training since they are usually far from urban centers and can accommodate students and researchers more cheaply than is possible in the city. However, they have special problems not faced by city zoos, including disease transmission from native wildlife and predation by native fauna on exotics.

24

Species, Subspecies, and Races: The Problem of Units of Management in Conservation

GEORGE F. BARROWCLOUGH AND NATHAN R. FLESNESS

THE NATURE OF THE PROBLEM

There exists limited space in the world for the captive management of animals (Soulé et al. 1986; Foose 1983). The same limitation applies, or soon will, in the wild; IUCN data indicate that only 3% of the land area of the earth is in protected areas (IUCN 1987). Other chapters in this volume and reports elsewhere (e.g., Lande and Barrowclough 1987) indicate that if our long-term goal is to maintain significant amounts of genetic variability in managed populations, then substantial numbers, at least several hundreds, of individuals will have to be maintained for each such distinct population. Given the limited space available and the substantial numbers required for each population, it is clear that only a relatively small fraction of the world's extant fauna ultimately can be maintained in intensively managed situations. Consequently, decisions will have to be made about which taxa will be actively preserved; it is not reasonable to allocate resources for minor variants of particular species at the expense of entirely omitting equally needy species from preservation programs with realistic chances of success.

Intraspecific, and to some extent, even specific taxonomy is not of a uniformly high quality. Taxonomic standards and the quality of data available for the recognition of subspecies and races have varied over time, among individual contemporaneous workers, and among higher taxonomic units. Some taxonomists, especially earlier in this century, gave formal subspecific recognition to minor geographic variation in size or color, some of which was based on inadequate sampling of numbers and localities. Some such variation may actually have been clinal, without a genetic basis, or without controls for wear or collecting methods (e.g., Mayr 1982; Wilson and Brown 1953). Thus, insignificant variation, in the sense of not representing well-differentiated genetic stocks, has often been recognized taxonomically. For instance, there are some 150 currently recognized subspecies of the pocket gopher, *Thomomys bottae,* of the western

United States. However, recent work on the genetics of the species indicates that the 11 subspecies in the Mohave Desert region of eastern California correspond to only two genetically defined units (Smith and Patton 1988). Consequently, some current subspecies do not reflect actual biological diversity.

More recently, there has been a tendency to lump geographically separate, well-differentiated populations into single species if they hybridize in restricted areas. In some cases, morphologically differentiated populations that are completely isolated geographically also have been lumped into single species because systematists *thought* the taxa might hybridize were they not allopatric (i.e., geographically isolated). Such taxa then become subspecies within the enlarged species. For example, throughout the Northern Hemisphere, there are a half dozen or so widely allopatric populations of the lynx, *Felis lynx;* all are considered members of a single species. Included in this Holarctic taxon are populations (currently recognized as subspecies) in North America and Asia that have been completely separated by the Bering Strait for many thousands of years (Tumlison 1987). Thus, some current subspecies may represent genetically distinct stocks from different geographic areas that have evolved separately for an unknown, but probably long, period of time.

A third problem is that, until recently, morphological traits were the primary data available and thus have been emphasized in the analysis of geographic variation and intraspecific systematics. Consequently, similar-appearing but genetically distinct populations frequently may not have been discovered, much less have received any taxonomic recognition. For example, recent protein studies indicate that the western flycatchers, *Empidonax difficilis,* resident on Santa Catalina Island off the coast of southern California have sufficient genetic differentiation from the mainland populations that they must have been reproductively isolated for over a hundred thousand years; hence, they are probably a distinct species (Johnson and Marten 1988). In appearance, however, they and the mainland birds are very similar, and had been considered subspecies. Species such as these have been referred to as "sibling" species (Mayr 1963).

In spite of the various difficulties listed above, it is becoming necessary to maintain substantial numbers of a variety of animals in captivity as well as in managed "natural areas." Space, time, and other resources are limiting, and so decisions must be made about which subspecies, races, and populations are worthy of inclusion in this scheme. Because of a variety of errors of commission as well as omission, the existing formal taxonomic literature is not a reliable guide for determining whether members of particular populations or groups of populations are worth managing or maintaining as separate units.

THE UNITS OF CONSERVATION MANAGEMENT

In the absence of an adequate preexisting taxonomic basis for conservation decisions, we develop a line of reasoning that will meet the objectives of first-order conservation needs. This reasoning is largely based on the approach to the "subspecies problem" developed by the American Association of Zoological Parks and Aquariums (AZA) Subcommittee on Species Survival Plans (SSP) at its July 1985 meeting (Ryder 1986b), and is in agreement with the philosophical comments of writers such as Soulé (1985), Templeton (1986), and Woodruff (1990).

For the purpose of devoting scarce or expensive resources to single-species conservation management, it is necessary to identify populations sufficiently distinct from an evolutionary and systematic point of view that they merit the investment. In the conservation literature, such populations have been termed "evolutionarily significant units" (ESUs) (Ryder 1986b; Woodruff 1990). In the systematics literature these are concordant with the "phylogenetic species" of Eldredge and Cracraft (1980), and basically the same as the "evolutionary species" of Wiley (1978) and Simpson (1961); however, they are not equivalent to the "biological species" of Mayr (1970). That is because the focus of ESUs is on the acquisition of broadly significant genetic differences, not just reproductive isolation.

The term "evolutionarily significant unit" has been adopted by some of the fraternity of captive breeding specialists to refer to populations of conservation interest. The word "significant" is problematic, and we believe that these units are generally equivalent to "phylogenetic species," a term now increasingly used by members of the systematics community. However, we recognize that phylogenetic species are unfamiliar to most workers, and that the concept may be controversial because of the present lack of consensus on precise working guidelines for their recognition. Consequently, in this chapter, we continue to refer to "evolutionarily significant units" (ESUs), but consider them to be identical to phylogenetic species.

THEORY

Isolation over time inevitably leads to the accumulation of genetic differences between the populations involved; thus,

isolation, leading to separate evolutionary histories, is the core idea of "evolutionary species." The genetic differences accumulated lead to observable differences among the isolated populations; these observable differences are the essence of the idea of "phylogenetic species." The genetic differences may be selectively neutral, they may result in external adaptation to the different local environments, or they may result in genetic, developmental, or physiological coadaptation within the individual organisms. These genetic differences may result in morphological differentiation, and hence be easily observed, or they may result in changes detectable only by sophisticated techniques (e.g., biochemical or karyological techniques or pedigree analyses). The genetic isolation may be due to geographic barriers, present or historical (e.g., Mayr 1963), or it may have arisen while the populations were contiguous due to ecological or behavioral segregation (Templeton et al. 1986; Bush 1975). In any case, reproductive isolation over evolutionary time will eventually lead to genetic distinctness.

Once it has been established (see below) that two populations have diverged and are genetically distinct, there are two lines of reasoning that argue against mixing them. These are both practical and ethical arguments. First, population genetic theory and empirical results from breeders both indicate that, if the populations are genetically quite distinct, then such mixing or hybridization will sometimes result in reduced fitness (outbreeding depression) in the hybrid population (not necessarily in the first generation) due to genetic, developmental, ecological, or behavioral incompatibilities (Templeton et al. 1986). This fitness reduction may manifest itself dramatically in the form of sterility or spontaneous abortions, or it may be more subtle, for example, taking the form of slightly decreased viability in the lineage. Second, such mixing may result in lines that differ markedly and unnecessarily from the existing natural populations of which they are intended to be exemplars. (We note that there may be occasional exceptions to this latter ethical argument; see the section below on practical problems). Consequently, it seems desirable to maintain as separate lineages those groups of populations that are genetically distinct due to an evolutionary history of genetic isolation. These are the populations that are termed phylogenetic species or ESUs.

PRACTICE

Unfortunately, there is no existing list of the phylogenetic species of the world to consult; only a very small fraction of currently threatened taxa have been studied using modern systematic techniques. As discussed above, extant lists of species and subspecies are not necessarily concordant with the ideal units for conservation and management purposes. Thus, there is no "off-the-shelf" solution to identifying ESUs; in most cases it will be necessary to go about trying to identify the proper units on a case-by-case basis.

Empirical Identification of Evolutionarily Significant Units

The above outline of what constitutes a population or set of populations of significance is based on the idea of genetic distinctness of the populations due to the accumulation of genetic differences in isolation over substantial periods of time. If the populations have been completely isolated over an evolutionarily important time span, then the differences may be expected to be discrete; that is, there will not exist a series of wild populations that blend into each other and span the range of variation among the populations in question in a gradually continuous (e.g., clinal) fashion. Hence, the observation of discrete differences in genetically determined traits between adequate samples of the populations of interest suggests that distinct taxonomic units may be involved.

General Methodology. The traits that can be expected to be particularly informative in the identification of ESUs vary among higher taxonomic levels (e.g., Chambers and Bayless 1983; White 1978). For example, in birds, long-isolated taxa often possess vocal differences or major plumage pattern and color distinctions; size differences are less diagnostic. Vocal differences also may indicate distinct units in frogs and toads. In mammals, it is not unusual for karyotypic differences to have arisen during isolation (White 1978). Electrophoretic differentiation is also indicative among mammals, as it is among salamanders. For examples of karyological and molecular techniques that have been useful in analyzing systematic problems in mammals, see Ryder (1986a) and Chambers and Bayless (1983). Modern molecular genetic techniques may be particularly useful in a wide array of taxa (Avise 1989; Hedrick and Miller 1992; see also Ryder and Fleischer, chap. 25, this volume).

The characters that traditionally have been used by systematists in diagnosing subspecies and races often have been morphological ones. Care was not always taken to ascertain that the differences were discrete rather than continuous, and there is also the real possibility that some morphological differences may simply have been the result of genetic-environmental interactions. Genetically identical individuals raised in different environments may develop into adults of different sizes and shapes. An example is the axolotl; this aquatic phase of the tiger salamander complex, *Ambystoma tigrinum*, occurs in two dramatically different morphologies depending, in some cases, upon differences in ecological conditions and the temperature of lakes (Gould 1977). For other examples of environmentally induced changes in size and shape, see Smith and Patton (1988), Ralls and Harvey (1985), and James (1983).

Consequently, the best criteria for identifying ESUs are discrete patterns of differences in characters that are frequently important in species recognition, or are associated with isolation and time of separation, in the taxonomic group being considered. However, because strong natural selection pressures and environmental differences can also occasionally lead to well-marked differences in the absence of long-term isolation, a replication of a pattern of differences across unrelated sets of characters would be particularly telling. A selective regime or environmental difference would not likely have similar effects on completely unrelated sets of characters. Hence, independent suites of characters replicating patterns of diagnostic features increase our confidence that the differences among populations are due to a long history of genetic isolation (Barrowclough 1982; Avise and Ball 1990). For example, if the natural populations of a species separate into two discrete units on the basis of vocal calls, karyotypes, electrophoretic or DNA sequence variation, and cranial morphology, then there is strong reason to believe that these units may be the product of separate evolutionary histories.

It is worth emphasizing that the search for conservation units should not be limited to tests among groups of samples representing named subspecific taxa. Rather, samples representing as much of the known species range as possible ought to be analyzed, and the results for each suite of characters should be prepared as a range-map overlay, so that possible geographic patterns of concordance of multiple characters, seen on the combined set of overlays, can be used to detect differentiated populations.

Initial Investigations. It is clear that a thorough systematic analysis of a species as outlined above will require a detailed study of geographic variation over the entire natural range of the species. For example, unless the study is a large and extensive one, restricted sample sizes alone can eliminate the distinction between qualitative (discrete) and quantitative differences among populations. Such systematic analyses are not trivial undertakings, and they are probably best left to professional systematists.

However, it may be possible to get a preliminary indication of the likelihood of the existence of multiple phylogenetic species within a traditional biological species by consulting standard taxonomic treatments such as *Mammal Species of the World* (Honacki, Kinman, and Koeppl 1982), taxonomic accounts of mammals (ASM *Mammalian Species*), or *Checklist of Birds of the World* (Paynter 1987) to see if the taxon is polytypic. If it is, then the original descriptions of the intraspecific taxa can be consulted. These should indicate how extensive a series of specimens was examined by the taxonomist writing the original description and what characteristics were cited as differing among the races. Descriptions focusing on slight size differences based on small numbers of specimens or dwelling on subtle distinctions in the shade of a color should usually not be taken as establishing separate management units.

A detailed range map will also be useful if one is available or can be constructed. Populations or named subspecific taxa occupying completely allopatric ranges or largely allopatric ranges with small regions of contiguous or touching borders (parapatry) are probably, a priori, more likely to represent separate ESUs than are races that appear from maps merely to represent arbitrary portions of a continuous range. Well-marked island races are particularly likely candidates to represent important units.

In the absence of described races, it is probably not worthwhile to conduct an extensive survey of variation in a species unless that species is very poorly known, has a fragmented range, or is a member of a higher taxon known to have a high frequency of "sibling species." The observation of *qualitative* differences in appearance among populations or a reduction in fitness in among-line matings may also indicate a need for further study. Templeton et al. (1986) give some suggestions on ways to detect fitness problems and to determine the boundaries of ESUs in cases in which doubts and questions arise.

Examples

Subspecies Do Not Correspond to ESUs: Pocket Gophers. As indicated above, Smith and Patton (1988) have compared genetic and morphometric data with the geographic distributions of the classic subspecies of pocket gophers, *Thomomys bottae*. An electrophoretic analysis of twenty-five protein loci indicated the existence of only two differentiated genetic units in an area of the northern Mohave Desert in which eleven named subspecies occur. A reanalysis of skull measurements of individuals from this area, using morphometric techniques that remove the effect of size differences, revealed two groups, based on shape, that were concordant with the geographic groups identified by electrophoresis. These two genetic units are the actual populations of interest, not the eleven described subspecies.

Subspecies Correspond to ESUs: Night Monkeys. South American night (owl) monkeys of the genus *Aotus* differ geographically in their color and pelage patterns. Several different species had been described by the beginning of the twentieth century, but by the 1950s, the prevailing taxonomic philosophy resulted in the recognition of a single widespread species with a range over most of the continent. This species included nine subspecies (Cabrera 1957).

Beginning in the 1970s, a number of allopatric chromosomal variations were discovered in these monkeys; protein electrophoresis then showed variation that was concordant with some of these races. However, taxonomic revisions based on these differences were largely ignored until, in 1983, a major taxonomic review elevated six of the former subspecies to specific rank (Hershkovitz 1983). Three additional species are also recognized based on karyotypic differences; their ranges lie within the ranges of previously recognized subspecies. In this case, subspecies based on classic taxonomic examinations of pelage eventually were shown largely to define chromosomal races that are now recognized to be the proper units for laboratory studies, conservation, and management.

Discrete and Continuous Variation and Subspecies: Spotted Owls. The spotted owl, *Strix occidentalis*, is a species of conservation concern in the western United States; it is a habitat specialist utilizing old-growth forest that is much in demand for timber harvesting. Environmentalists and various governmental agencies are debating proposed solutions to the dilemma of maintaining both viable populations of the owl and the dominant industry (lumbering) of the region. As a consequence, it has become necessary to determine the number and geographic limits of the ESUs of spotted owls.

The older taxonomic literature (AOU 1957) indicated the existence of three subspecies in a range distributed from British Columbia to central Mexico (fig. 24.1). A new examination of geographic variation in the owl involved the quantitative analysis of four independent data sets: (1) measurements of size and shape, (2) plumage color, (3) plumage pattern, and (4) electrophoresis of blood enzymes and other proteins (G. F. Barrowclough, unpub.; Barrowclough and Gutiérrez 1990). The mensural and plumage pattern data sets were each analyzed using standard multivariate methods that did not involve a priori assumptions of more than one group. The electrophoretic data set was analyzed using

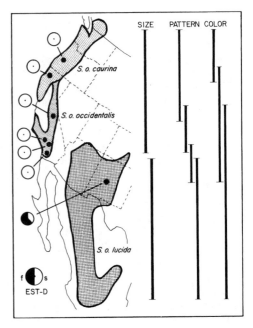

FIG. 24.1. Geographic variation and subspecies in the spotted owl, *Strix occidentalis*. Ranges of the currently recognized subspecies are indicated. An allele at the esterase-D locus not found in the coastal populations (frequency indicated by black fractions of pie diagrams) is present at a high frequency in the interior. For size, color, and feather pattern characteristics, homogeneous subsets of localities are indicated by continuous heavy lines. For size (principal component analysis of standard specimen measurements), there are two nonoverlapping subsets that correspond to the allopatric portions of the range. For plumage color (one measurement) and the pattern of spotting on feathers (principal component analysis of measurements), variation is clinal through the range, as indicated by the overlapping subsets of homogeneous localities. Data presented in this figure are for females. (After Barrowclough and Gutiérrez 1990; G. F. Barrowclough, unpub.)

standard genetic heterozygosity and F_{st} statistics. Some summary results are shown in figure 24.1. Two of the four data sets (principal component 1-"size" and electrophoresis) are congruent and indicate that the completely allopatric *S. o. lucida* subspecies is a valid phylogenetic species. We did not take the size data set by itself as definitive because of the potential problems with size measurements alluded to earlier. However, in this case, size is not clinal, but rather forms two homogeneous subsets that break where the ranges are discontinuous. Combined with the genetic results, these data indicate that it is inadvisable to treat owls from the two disjunct portions of the range as one management unit.

The relatively contiguous populations along the Pacific coast and in the Sierra and Cascade ranges are more problematic. The size and electrophoretic data sets are homogeneous in this region. Such results are agnostic with regard to numbers of genetic stocks; they are consistent with only one ESU being present, but not sufficient to reach that conclusion. Given a finite amount of time for evolutionary change, some data sets will always be relatively conservative and retain primitive similarity. The plumage pattern and color data sets are more informative, but still enigmatic. The variation in both data sets is clinal: that is, the characters continuously change; they are not abruptly different. Presumably such variation in pattern and feather color has a genetic basis; thus, the farther apart two individual owls are, the more disparate their genomes. Taxonomically, modern researchers would probably not assign formal subspecific names to parts of such a continuum, nor is it logical to assume that there is more than one ESU in this coastal range. Nevertheless, it would be inadvisable to pool individuals from distant points in a breeding scheme in situations like this. There is clearly adaptation of color and plumage to the local habitat; in fact, this is an example of Gloger's rule (Orr 1971): organisms are darker in color in areas with more humid climates.

In the case of the spotted owl, traditional taxonomy indicated three subspecies. In a new analysis, two of four suites of characters indicated that one of those classic subspecies is an ESU of its own. The other two suites of characters indicated that the second ESU (composed of the remaining two traditionally defined subspecies) is composed of clinally varying populations that must be managed with caution with regard to geography and interbreeding. Thus, any one of the four character sets would have been insufficient by itself to decipher the nature of variation in the spotted owl. The extant subspecific taxonomy only hinted at the nature of the actual variation present.

Laboratory Discovery of a Sibling Species: Tent-Making Bats. In some situations, phenotypic variation is quite conservative and more than one phylogenetic species may exist in the absence of any described subspecies or races. Such was the case of the tent-making bat, *Uroderma bilobatum*. These bats, which occur from Mexico to northern South America, are extremely similar in pelage and morphology. However, chromosomal studies indicated the existence of two karyotypic forms (Baker 1981; Baker and McDaniel 1972), which were then recognized as subspecies based on this difference. The two taxa were subsequently found to have electrophoretic differences concordant with the chromosomal cytotypes (Greenbaum 1981). Field studies have now established that the two forms are parapatric (i.e., they have geographic ranges that abut) with a quite narrow (30 km wide) hybrid zone on the Pacific slope of Honduras (fig. 24.2). Thus, molecular and cytological techniques independently confirmed the existence of a cryptic species not detectable based on either morphology or the taxonomic literature.

PRACTICAL PROBLEMS AND LIMITATIONS

Problems may arise in the course of population management that require decisions about how to proceed, in the absence of data or even when ESUs have been identified. In such cases, the views of evolutionary biologists and systematists, although not paramount, ought to be considered. Such situations may involve decisions about whether to create or maintain hybrid lines, and about the relative value of the various taxa within a single biological species or species group.

The general philosophy of the AZA Subcommittee on Species Survival Plans was that hybridization should generally be avoided. Hybridization results in the loss of future options and is justified only if populations are reduced to

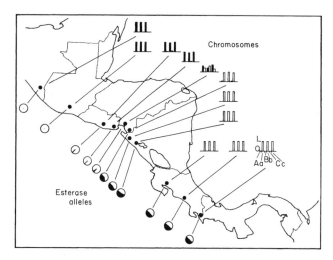

FIG. 24.2.   The geographic positions of major changes in frequencies of alternative electrophoretic alleles at an esterase locus (frequencies indicated by alternate fractions of pie diagrams) and of karyotypic forms (three different chromosomes; frequencies of alternative chromosomes indicated by black and white bars in histograms) are concordant across a narrow hybrid zone in the tent-making bat, *Uroderma bilobatum*; this strongly suggests the existence of two distinct evolutionary lineages. These Central American bats are phenotypically indistinguishable except by these molecular techniques. (Reprinted from Barrowclough 1985, courtesy of the Royal British Columbia Museum.)

one or a couple of individuals; it is used primarily as a strategy for saving a higher taxon. The application of this philosophy to particular problems is discussed below.

Stock of Unknown Provenance

Practical problems may arise if two or more phylogenetic species exist within what was once considered a single species or variety of an animal. Some or all of the existing stock being managed may be of unknown (possibly contaminated) provenance. Two alternative approaches exist. First, if sufficient pure stocks to maintain populations from the various taxa are not available, then there is no problem: maintaining a mixed line is better than maintaining no line at all and hence letting the species go extinct (see "More Taxa Than Space" below). Second, however, is the case in which known pure lines from the various ESUs as well as known hybrid or suspect lineages are available. In this situation there are two further possibilities: (1) maintaining only the pure lines and either culling the suspect and hybrid lineages or letting them die out, and (2) maintaining, separately, both pure and mixed lineages. As indicated earlier, indications of genetic coadaptation or reduced fecundity or viability, as well as aesthetic considerations, may lead some managers to prefer "pure" lineages. The existence of limited resources may also lead one to favor the first option.

Recent experience with the AZA Species Survival Plan for the Asiatic lion, *Panthera leo persica*, provides an example of this type of problem. The SSP program was initiated with existing animals in zoological collections, nearly all of captive origin. Well after the program began, circumstantial pedigree evidence emerged suggesting that almost all captive stocks in both North America and Europe were actually composed of mixed Asian and African ancestry.

The hybridization apparently occurred at the initiation of the captive pedigree. There are both molecular and some morphological results consistent with this supposition (O'Brien et al. 1987). Current plans involve reestablishing the captive population with specimens of reliable Asian provenance. It is not clear whether variation in the lion once was clinal; human extirpation of potentially intermediate lion populations began thousands of years ago in the Near East and Europe, resulting in the present dramatically disjunct remnant in India's Gir Forest.

Another case is that of the wisent or European bison, *Bison bonasus*. All individuals alive today (both in zoos and in the wild reserve in Bialowesa, Poland) descend from a very small captive population that included individuals from two named subspecies. No negative effects from the apparent hybridization have been detected (Slatis 1960). However, no alternatives to maintaining the possibly hybrid line exist.

Too Few Left

Situations may occasionally arise in which the numbers of individuals, or the numbers of one of the sexes, become so limited that the line cannot be maintained. However, great care must be exercised before reaching this conclusion. As pointed out in the genetics and conservation literature (Lande and Barrowclough 1987; Templeton and Read 1983), a short bottleneck of only a handful of individuals, perhaps even including a couple of generations of close inbreeding, is not necessarily as detrimental as often assumed.

If, though, it is clear that the stock representing a particular phylogenetic species is in immediate danger of being lost, then there are two choices available: permit the line to go extinct, or hybridize with a closely related stock to create a mixed population. If the unit is of particular value and space is available, then creating a hybrid line has the advantage of maintaining some of the genetic diversity that would otherwise be lost. However, from the viewpoint of an evolutionary biologist or a systematist, this strategy will significantly alter the gene pool, and the resultant stock will not represent any natural population or taxon. On the other hand, perhaps a hybridized population will have a better chance of survival in a world of increasing environmental variation and disturbance. From a genetic perspective, the genetic diversity represented by the original ESU will not be entirely saved through the hybridization. In fact, because of random drift and selection due to reduced population sizes, as well as the mixing of possibly coadapted gene pools, it is impossible to anticipate how much of the genetic variation will be saved or what the genetic composition of the new hybrid line ultimately will be. In some cases it will not be possible to create a viable hybrid line; this will occur if the karyotypes or gene combinations of the various units are too different (Templeton et al. 1986).

For the Galápagos tortoise from Isla Pinta, *Geochelone elephantopus abingdoni*, there are too few left to sustain the presumptive species. The remaining population consists of one male, now held in captivity at the Charles Darwin Research Station (Macfarland, Villa, and Toro 1974) at Academy Bay in the Galápagos. Hybridization is recommended to save, in part, what remains of this classic island form. A multigenerational strategy, possibly involving multiple trial crosses, some backcrosses, and certainly reintroduction of specific surplus offspring back to the island, could be developed and carried out.

A second example is that of the dusky seaside sparrow, *Ammodramus maritimus nigrescens*, in which the last pure individual died in 1987 (Avise and Nelson 1989). The last six birds were all males; they were crossed to another subspecies, then the F$_1$s were backcrossed to the surviving males to produce a group of progeny as pure as possible. A hybrid population ranging from 50% to 87.5% pure was created in captivity. This entire population subsequently went extinct because of an excess of mortality over reproduction.

More Taxa than Space

Eventually there will be insufficient space available in reserves and zoological gardens to manage sufficient numbers of all the units of conservation interest that exist, especially as natural environments become limited and fragmented. Value judgments will have to be made about which taxa, within a relatively closely related species group, are "worth" saving given the limited resources.

This is a major ethical problem, but, from the viewpoint of evolutionary biology, genetics, and systematics, we need to maintain the greatest possible diversity. In the case of distinct ESUs within a species group, for example, diversity has been partitioned by nature, due to long-term isolation, into among-ESU components rather than within-population variation. Consequently, the more divergent of these taxa will be of particular interest. Divergence in such cases is likely to track the approximate length of isolation. It may also be affected by long-term population size and the history of population bottlenecks. Thorough investigation of the various taxa ought to be performed in such cases; for example, karyotyping and molecular methods may be useful as an index of period of isolation. Also, phylogenetic species from areas that are known to have a high degree of endemism (e.g., Madagascar, the Hawaiian islands, and the Choco region of Colombia) might be sought because endemicity often reflects the period of isolation for organisms that have limited dispersal abilities.

An alternative to letting some ESUs go extinct when space becomes limited is to hybridize the taxa and try to preserve the genetic material in a single mixed line. This approach is controversial; such a choice ought to be made only after considerable study and wide discussion. Again, it involves sacrificing diverse natural gene pools for increased nonnatural individual variation. If the taxa are too divergent, it entails the danger of losing the population.

Crisis Situation with No Data

Reliable multicharacter set data are on hand for only a very small percentage of taxa of immediate conservation concern. In some cases, sound systematic results may be unavailable before wild populations are sampled to establish captive ones, or even before captive and/or wild individuals are allowed to mate to produce the next generation.

This situation should be avoided whenever possible. There is considerable interest in threatened species, and many possibilities exist for mobilizing the systematics community to assist with such problems; these approaches should be made at the earliest possible point.

Nonetheless, when unavoidable decisions must be made in the absence of sound data and within critically short time spans, we suggest that the presence of physiogeographic or other barriers sufficient to restrict gene flow within the taxon of concern over evolutionary time be used as hypothetical ESU boundaries. This should be done only while awaiting the results of analyses that will provide data to supplant the hypothetical boundaries.

SUMMARY

We consider the problem of selecting the appropriate units for conservation management. We conclude that managers of captive populations should be interested in maintaining lineages with separate evolutionary histories; these are called evolutionarily significant units, or ESUs. They are essentially identical to the phylogenetic species of systematics literature. Unfortunately, there is no existing list of these units for mammals or for any other organisms. We cannot assume that they are equivalent to either biological species or subspecies. In any case in which formal subspecies have been described, or in which there is any good reason to suspect that more than one ESU is involved, it will probably be necessary to perform a fresh, thorough study of the systematics of the taxon. ESUs are identified by searching for replicate patterns of populations occupying discrete areas of character space; the choice of character space may differ on a higher taxon-to-higher taxon basis. Karyotypes, for example, are useful in mammals but not in birds. The persons who attempt these analyses should have a background in studies of variation, evolution, biogeography, and systematics.

Several practical difficulties in captive management are discussed; these include contaminated stocks, the expediency of hybridization, and lack of data in a crisis situation.

REFERENCES

American Society of Mammalogists (ASM). 1971–present. *Mammalian Species.* Lawrence, Kans.: Allen Press.

American Ornithologists' Union (AOU). 1957. *Checklist of North American birds.* 5th ed. Baltimore: American Ornithologists' Union/Port City Press.

Avise, J. C. 1989. A role for molecular genetics in the recognition and conservation of endangered species. *Trends Ecol. Evol.* 4: 279–81.

Avise, J. C., and Ball, R. M. Jr. 1990. Principles of genealogical concordance in species concepts and biological taxonomy. In *Oxford surveys in evolutionary biology*, vol. 7, ed. D. Futuyma and J. Antonovics, 45–67. New York: Oxford University Press.

Avise, J. C., and Nelson, W. S. 1989. Molecular genetic relationships of the extinct dusky seaside sparrow. *Science* 243: 646–48.

Baker, R. J. 1981. Chromosome flow between chromosomally characterized taxa of a volant mammal, *Uroderma bilobatum* (Chiroptera: Phyllostomatidae). *Evolution* 35: 296–305.

Baker, R. J., and McDaniel, V. R. 1972. A new subspecies of *Uroderma bilobatum* (Chiroptera: Phyllostomatidae) from Middle America. *Occasional Papers of the Museum of the Texas Technological University* 7: 1–4.

Barrowclough, G. F. 1982. Geographic variation, predictiveness, and subspecies. *Auk* 99: 601–3.

———. 1985. Museum collections and molecular systematics. In *Museum collections: Their roles and future in biological research*, ed. E. H. Miller, 43–54. Victoria: British Columbia Provincial Museum.

———. Geographic variation in the spotted owl *(Strix occidentalis)*. Unpublished manuscript.

Barrowclough, G. F., and Gutiérrez, R. J. 1990. Genetic variation and differentiation in the spotted owl *(Strix occidentalis)*. *Auk* 107: 737–44.

Bush, G. L. 1975. Modes of animal speciation. *Annu. Rev. Ecol. Syst.* 6: 339–64.

Cabrera, A. 1957. Catalogo de los mamiferos de America del Sur. *Revista del Museo Argentino de Ciencias Naturales* 4: 1–732.

Chambers, S. M., and Bayless, J. W. 1983. Systematics, conservation, and the measurement of genetic diversity. In *Genetics and conservation: A reference for managing wild animal and plant populations*, ed. C. M. Schonewald-Cox, S. M. Chambers, B. MacBryde, and W. L. Thomas, 349–63. Menlo Park, Calif.: Benjamin/Cummings.

Eldredge, N., and Cracraft, J. 1980. *Phylogenetic patterns and the evolutionary process.* New York: Columbia University Press.

Foose, T. J. 1983. The relevance of captive populations to the conservation of biotic diversity. In *Genetics and conservation: A reference for managing wild animal and plant populations*, ed. C. M. Schonewald-Cox, S. M. Chambers, B. MacBryde, and W. L. Thomas, 374–401. Menlo Park, Calif.: Benjamin/Cummings.

Gould, S. J. 1977. *Ontogeny and phylogeny.* Cambridge, Mass.: Harvard University Press.

Greenbaum, I. F. 1981. Genetic interactions between hybridizing cytotypes of the tent-making bat *(Uroderma bilobatum)*. *Evolution* 35: 306–21.

Hedrick, P. W., and Miller, P. S. 1992. Conservation genetics: Techniques and fundamentals. *Ecol. Appl.* 2: 30–46.

Hershkovitz, P. 1983. Two new species of night monkeys, genus *Aotus* (Cebidae, Platyrrhini): A preliminary report on *Aotus* taxonomy. *Am. J. Primatol.* 4: 209–43.

Honacki, J. H., Kinman, K. E., and Koeppl, J. W., eds. 1982. *Mammal species of the world.* Lawrence, Kans.: Allen Press and Association of Systematic Collections.

International Union for the Conservation of Nature (IUCN). 1987. *The IUCN policy statement on captive breeding.* Gland, Switzerland: IUCN.

James, F. C. 1983. Environmental component of morphological differentiation in birds. *Science* 221: 184–86.

Johnson, N. K., and Marten, J. A. 1988. Evolutionary genetics of flycatchers. II. Differentiation in the *Empidonax difficilis* complex. *Auk* 105: 177–91.

Lande, R., and Barrowclough, G. F. 1987. Effective population size, genetic variation, and their use in population management. In *Viable Populations for Conservation*, ed. M. E. Soulé, 87–123. Cambridge: Cambridge University Press.

Macfarland, C. G., Villa, J., and Toro, B. 1974. The Galapagos giant tortoises *(Geochelone elephantopus)*. Part I: Status of the surviving populations. *Biol. Conserv.* 6: 118–33.

Mayr, E. 1963. *Animal species and evolution.* Cambridge, Mass.: Harvard University Press.

———. 1970. *Populations, species, and evolution.* Cambridge, Mass.: Harvard University Press.

———. 1982. Of what use are subspecies? *Auk* 99: 593–95.

O'Brien, S. J., Joslin, P., Smith, G. L. III, Wolfe, R., Schaffer, N., Heath, E., Ott-Joslin, J., Rawal, P. P., Bhattacharjee, K. K., and Martenson, J. S. 1987. Evidence for African origins of founders of the Asiatic lion species survival plan. *Zoo Biol.* 6: 99–116.

Orr, R. T. 1971. *Vertebrate biology.* 3d ed. Philadelphia: W. B. Saunders.

Paynter, R. A. Jr. 1987. *Checklist of birds of the world.* Vol. 16. *Comprehensive index.* Cambridge, Mass.: Museum of Comparative Zoology, Harvard University.

Ralls, K., and Harvey, P. H. 1985. Geographic variation in size and sexual dimorphism of North American weasels. *Biol. J. Linn. Soc.* 25:119–67.

Ryder, O. A. 1986a. Genetic investigations: Tools for supporting breeding programme goals. *Int. Zoo Yrbk.* 24/25:157–62.

———. 1986b. Species conservation and systematics: The dilemma of subspecies. *Trends Ecol. Evol.* 1:9–10.

Simpson, G. G. 1961. *Principles of animal taxonomy.* New York: Columbia University Press.

Slatis, H. M. 1960. An analysis of inbreeding in the European bison. *Genetics* 45:275–87.

Smith, M. F., and Patton, J. L. 1988. Subspecies of pocket gophers: Causal bases for geographic differentiation in *Thomomys bottae. Syst. Zool.* 37:163–78.

Soulé, M. E. 1985. What is conservation biology? *BioScience* 35:727–34.

Soulé, M. E., Gilpin, M., Conway, W., and Foose, T. 1986. The millennium ark: How long a voyage, how many staterooms, how many passengers? *Zoo Biol.* 5:101–13.

Templeton, A. R. 1986. Coadaptation and outbreeding depression. In *Conservation biology: The science of scarcity and diversity,* ed. M. E. Soulé, 105–16. Sunderland, Mass.: Sinauer Associates.

Templeton, A. R., Hemmer, H., Mace, G., Seal, U. S., Shields, W. M., and Woodruff, D. S. 1986. Local adaptation, coadaptation, and population boundaries. *Zoo Biol.* 5:115–25.

Templeton, A. R., and Read, B. 1983. The elimination of inbreeding depression in a captive herd of Speke's gazelle. In *Genetics and conservation: A reference for managing wild animal and plant populations,* ed. C. M. Schonewald-Cox, S. M. Chambers, B. MacBryde, and W. L. Thomas, 241–61. Menlo Park, Calif.: Benjamin/Cummings.

Tumlison, R. 1987. *Felis lynx. Mammalian Species* 269:1–8.

White, M. J. D. 1978. *Modes of speciation.* San Francisco: W. H. Freeman.

Wiley, E. O. 1978. The evolutionary species concept reconsidered. *Syst. Zool.* 27:17–26.

Wilson, E. O., and Brown, W. L. Jr. 1953. The subspecies concept and its taxonomic application. *Syst. Zool.* 2:97–111.

Woodruff, D. S. 1990. Commentary. In *The preservation and valuation of biological resources,* ed. G. H. Orians, G. M. Brown Jr., W. E. Kunin, and J. E. Swierzbinski, 119–32. Seattle: University of Washington Press.

25

Genetic Research and Its Application in Zoos

OLIVER A. RYDER AND ROBERT C. FLEISCHER

MEETING THE GOALS OF CAPTIVE PROPAGATION

One of the current goals of captive propagation programs in zoological gardens is the establishment of self-sustaining populations, particularly for threatened or endangered species. These populations may serve conservation purposes to the extent that they possess the genetic and behavioral attributes of populations of the same species in nature. Thus, in addition to providing suitable husbandry and social environments conducive to reproduction, animal managers in zoos must address the genetic well-being of populations of interbreeding individuals. Research results in the field of genetics are now frequently applied in support of zoo breeding programs. The recent proliferation of Species Survival Plans has been supported and enhanced by numerous genetic research projects.

Proper Constitution of Gene Pools

Before considerable efforts are devoted to managing gene pool resources, it is appropriate to consider whether the subjects of captive breeding efforts accurately reflect the condition of natural populations and whether all individuals may appropriately be interbred. Genetic differentiation of populations into geographic races, subspecies, and species occurs when genetic interactions (gene flow) between the populations are greatly reduced or eliminated. This may occur because of physical isolation due to geographic barriers such as rivers or oceans or because forces of natural or sexual selection act to diminish interbreeding. When gene flow between populations ceases, the populations become reproductively isolated and may then diverge genetically.

In nature, Bornean orangutans, *Pongo pygmaeus,* do not interbreed with Sumatran orangutans, nor do African and Asiatic lions, *Panthera leo,* interbreed. Neither should they be interbred in captivity unless the separation of these forms, currently considered distinct, would endanger the survival of the entire species. However, if human-induced range fragmentation was responsible for the current separa-

ration, interbreeding should be allowed, at least to estimated historical levels.

Self-Sustaining Populations

Access to wild-born specimens of many species is becoming increasingly problematic as free-living populations dwindle and receive increasing protection. Often, quarantine requirements or import regulations drafted to protect domestic livestock from the threat of disease prevent the importation of specimens, particularly artiodactyls, into zoos. For some species, free-living populations are gone, and the survival of the species depends now on the propagation of the captive stock. In such situations, the entire gene pool of a species, represented by the genetic contributions of the founder stock to subsequent generations of captive-bred individuals, is a closed system; new mutations occurring within the captive population provide the only new sources of genetic variation. This process occurs at an extremely low rate and provides significant inputs of variation only over long intervals of time or when populations are very large. For species that still have sizable wild populations that may potentially be sampled to provide migrants into captive populations, this access to new sources of variation provides the opportunity to preserve larger proportions of the wild gene pool, utilizing fewer captive individuals and animal facilities than is feasible with closed populations (Ryder 1986; Lacy 1987).

Gene Pool Preservation

Heritable variation among individuals provides the raw material upon which natural selection ultimately acts, thereby altering the frequencies of alleles in populations. A priori, we have insufficient knowledge as to which alleles are of greatest current and future benefit to reproducing generations of organisms. As a consequence, a genetic management strategy that aims to retain genetic variation in populations offers the most reasonable prospect for avoiding losses of valuable alleles and population extinction. In other words, preserving the gene pool of a population (or species)

255

is thought to maximize the chances that the population will adapt to varying environmental conditions in the future. Thus, one of the primary concerns of species conservation is the retention of genetic variation, that is, the preservation of the species' gene pool (see Soulé 1980 and Hedrick and Miller 1992 for overviews of the rationale for the above).

GENETIC RESEARCH TOOLS FOR AIDING BREEDING PROGRAMS

Genetic research activities provide useful findings that help to ensure that captive breeding programs attain their goals and may point the way for the development and application of new approaches to meeting those goals. The objects of genetic research studies may be individuals, populations, or members of diverse taxonomic categories. Conclusions derived from a variety of investigative techniques may have applications to zoological classification of animals, identification of individuals suitable for breeding and avoidance of inbreeding, construction and management of pedigrees, monitoring of genetic variability and fitness within captive populations, and identification and management of heritable diseases in a breeding group.

Chromosomal Studies

Chromosomes are structures within the nuclei of cells that contain the DNA molecules that encode nearly all the genetic information of an organism. Chromosomal investigations require access to living cells capable of dividing, usually white blood cells or skin (fibroblast) cells. The number and morphology of the chromosomes may vary among populations, subspecies, and species. Consequently, studies of chromosomes may provide insights into the classification of individuals and whether or not interbreeding is desirable.

A dramatic example exists within the Asiatic barking deer or muntjacs of the genus *Muntiacus*. The Chinese muntjac, *M. reevesi,* and the Indian muntjac, *M. muntjak,* are so similar morphologically that some authorities considered them to belong to the same species. Chromosomally, however, they are enormously divergent. The Chinese muntjac has a diploid chromosome number of 46, whereas the Indian muntjac has a diploid chromosome number of 6 in males and 7 in females (Wurster and Benirschke 1970). Orangutans, whether from Borneo or Sumatra, have 48 diploid chromosomes. However, there are structural features within the chromosomal complement of each island form that are absent in individuals from the other population. Careful chromosomal analysis of wild-caught orangutans can distinguish their geographic origin (Seuanez et al. 1979; de Boer and Seuanez 1982; Ryder and Chemnick 1993).

A detailed examination of the causes of infertility within some captive populations of one dik-dik species, *Madoqua* sp., demonstrated that several chromosomal races of dik-diks exist in East Africa that are unlikely to interbreed in nature. In captivity, interbreeding of some of the chromosomal races has produced infertile animals; their infertility clearly stems from the divergent chromosomal complements of the parental stocks (Ryder, Kumamoto et al. 1989).

In fact, based on research findings in comparative mammalian cytogenetics, there is a growing number of mammalian taxa for which chromosomal studies should be undertaken on all individuals entering conservation-oriented breeding programs (Ryder 1986). Perhaps only one-half of all mammalian species have been studied chromosomally. For a large proportion of these, relatively few individuals have been examined, and chromosomally divergent populations within the species may not have been sampled for karyotype analysis. Interestingly, the rates of chromosomal change vary among mammalian taxa. Canids and felids are conservative with respect to rates of chromosomal change compared with New World monkeys, bovids, or equids. However, a satisfactory explanation for the rate differences in karyotypic evolution among mammalian taxa has yet to be elaborated.

Only a few zoos now have the capability to perform chromosomal analyses in-house, due in part to the costs of laboratory equipment, supplies, and trained personnel. Fortunately, the blood and skin biopsy specimens necessary for establishing cell cultures for chromosomal preparations can be shipped over long distances, taking several days to reach their laboratory destination, and still provide useful results.

Protein Electrophoretic Studies

As ubiquitous components of organisms, proteins represent the major end product of DNA-encoded information. Like variation of chromosomes among species and subspecies, variation in the amino acid composition of proteins may provide information useful for meeting breeding program goals. Protein variation, which may be conveniently inferred from analyses of blood or tissue samples utilizing a variety of technical approaches, is much more extensive within populations and among taxa than is chromosomal variation. Separation of protein or enzyme moieties on the basis of their migration through a gel matrix (electrophoresis) is a commonly employed technique for demonstrating genetic variation at the protein level. The extent of protein variation, or polymorphism, itself differs among populations and species (Selander 1976; Selander and Whittam 1983).

Generally, large mammals and birds display less protein polymorphism than do invertebrates and small mammals. Past population events such as severe reductions in numbers of breeding individuals (genetic bottlenecks), migration between population subcomponents, and histories of inbreeding and catastrophic environmental changes all may affect the extent of protein polymorphism in populations. Zoo populations might be expected to show reduced amounts of protein electrophoretic variation when compared with the populations of wild animals from which they were derived due to founder effects, inbreeding, genetic drift, and selection. However, there are few studies examining protein variation in both captive populations and related wild populations. In one investigation, the genetic variation demonstrable through electrophoretic studies of remnant populations of golden lion tamarins, *Leontopithecus rosalia rosalia,* in the eastern coastal rainforests of Brazil was less than that demonstrated to be present in the captive populations of the same species (Foreman et al. 1986).

Protein variants are generally rather easy to follow through generations of individuals. With sufficient numbers of variable proteins in a population, inferences concerning parentage can be made. These inferences typically take the form of parentage exclusions, inclusion of parentage being more elusive. Thus, it is easier to determine which potential sires or dams could not be the parent of a given offspring than it is to positively identify the actual sire and/or dam. Determination of parentage typically involves either excluding all other possible parents or demonstrating that any alternative parentage assignment is an improbable event. Nonetheless, corrections of mistaken identities of individual animals, inferences of paternity and maternity, and corrections of studbooks may often be based on protein electrophoretic studies.

Analyses of heritable protein variation may help to determine whether individuals should be incorporated into a breeding program for a particular subspecies or species. As reproductively isolated populations diverge genetically, newly arising protein variants will appear over time, and eventually, at some loci, detectably different proteins will be present that can be diagnostic for specific populations. For example, although lions once ranged over much of the world, they are today found only in portions of Africa and in a single population in Gir National Forest in India. Electrophoretic studies of blood proteins from African and Asiatic lions have revealed that nearly all captive-bred Asiatic lions in Western zoos have genetic contributions from African lions. This is evidenced by the presence of protein variants normally found in African but not Asiatic lions, as well as evidence, through analysis of pedigree data, of ancestors of hybrid background (O'Brien et al. 1987). A similar investigation employing electrophoretic comparison of blood proteins from New World camelids suggested that a purported alpaca had a llama as one of its recent ancestors (Genz and Yates 1985).

Blood-Typing Studies

Genetic variation has long been known to be detectable using immunological assay methods, for example, tests for the ABO and Rh blood groups in humans. Other mammals also exhibit genetic variation at loci specifying the exterior structure of blood cells, so blood grouping may be used for parentage exclusion and population genetic purposes. Due to the expenses involved in maintaining the numbers of animals necessary for developing blood-typing tests, application of this technology has generally been limited to domestic and laboratory animals such as some monkeys, cattle, horses, poultry, and swine. The blood cells of mammal species that are closely related to domestic species for which blood-typing studies have proven useful may cross-react with the blood-typing reagents developed for those species, thereby offering the opportunity for comparative studies and parentage exclusion analyses for some exotic species. For example, blood-typing reagents developed for tests required by domestic horse breed registries cross-react with blood from other equid species. Blood-typing studies of Przewalski's horses, *Equus przewalskii*, have provided basic information concerning genetic variability and have been successfully employed to unravel problems of individual identification in this endangered species (Bowling and Ryder 1987).

Molecular Genetic Studies

Recent advances in molecular biology have resulted in the availability of a wide variety of techniques that can be used to assess kinship, patterns and levels of genetic variation, and evolutionary relationships. The two molecular techniques with the greatest potential for management of captive mammals are (1) DNA fingerprinting (including both single- and multilocus methods: reviewed by Burke 1989; Morin and Woodruff 1992; Fleischer, in press) and (2) evaluation of mitochondrial DNA sequences by restriction site analysis (reviewed by Wilson et al. 1985; Avise et al. 1987) or amplification with the polymerase chain reaction (PCR) followed by direct sequencing (Kocher et al. 1989; White, Arnheim, and Erlich 1989). Other analyses that have proven useful, mostly for systematic studies, include restriction site or sequence analysis of nuclear DNA and DNA-DNA hybridization. A new PCR-based technique, called RAPD (for "randomly amplified polymorphic DNA"), may prove useful for identifying population- or species-specific genetic markers.

DNA fingerprinting utilizes a class of repetitive DNA called variable number of tandem repeat (VNTR) DNA, or hypervariable minisatellite DNA (Jeffreys, Wilson, and Thein 1985). Both mini- and microsatellite genes are made up of small repetitive units (usually < 60 base pairs) lined up in tandem. Microsatellites, as their name implies, are small (1–5 base pairs), and generally occur in small blocks of repeats (Litt and Luty 1989; Weber and May 1989). There can be many such mini- or microsatellite arrays located on chromosomes throughout the genome, each array usually acting as an independent locus. For a given locus there may be wide variation in the number of tandem repeats, which results in a large number of alleles (often 10 or more) and heterozygosities well over 50%. Multilocus DNA fingerprinting is advantageous in that it assays variation in many of these loci simultaneously and can usually reveal variation even within severely bottlenecked populations (Fleischer, Tarr, and Pratt 1994; Rave et al. 1994). Single-locus VNTR probes and PCR-amplified microsatellites have the advantages of providing exact genotypes and allele frequencies, and the latter method requires very little DNA for analysis, but both methods usually require cloning and sequencing skills and a good deal of development time.

DNA fingerprinting can be used to exclude or assign parents (Burke 1989), to infer or correct pedigrees, to document relative degrees of kinship (Lynch 1988; Geyer et al. 1993; Rave et al. 1994), and to monitor levels of genetic variation within populations (Ryder, Chemnick et al. 1989; Gilbert et al. 1990, 1991). For example, DNA fingerprinting was used for documenting parentage in captive chimpanzees (Ely and Ferrell 1990) and wild mongooses (Keane et al. 1994), including assignment of fathers in multimale groups. Morin and Ryder (1991) used both DNA fingerprinting and restriction site analyses of mitochondrial DNA to infer a pedigree for a captive colony of lion-tailed macaques, *Macaca silenus*.

Gilbert et al. (1991) and Packer et al. (1991) have applied both multilocus and single-locus analyses to questions of parentage, kinship, and genetic variability in wild populations of African lions. DNA fingerprint data enabled them to assign parents to each cub unequivocally and revealed a strong relationship between relatedness and fingerprint similarity. Pairs of males within prides, called coalitions, were composed of either closely related or unrelated males. When the males of a coalition were close relatives, all offspring were sired by only one of the males (Packer et al. 1991), while mixed parentage was found among the offspring of unrelated male coalitions. DNA fingerprints were also used to monitor levels of genetic variation. A severely bottlenecked population of Asiatic lions (Gir Forest) showed much lower fingerprint diversity than more robust African ones, results that are consistent with theoretical expectation and previous genetic analyses. Gilbert et al. (1990) used multilocus methods to document population variation and genealogy in California Channel Island foxes, *Urocyon littoralis*. Cluster analysis of fingerprint band-sharing coefficients clearly identified a northern and a southern cluster of island populations. The small, isolated San Nicholas population showed, as would be predicted, extremely high band sharing (i.e., low genetic variability).

Mitochondrial DNA is the remnant genome of an endosymbiotic bacterium (now the mitochondrion: Gray 1989), much reduced in size and complexity (only 16,000–18,000 base pairs in a circular conformation coding for 13 proteins, 22 transfer RNAs, and 2 ribosomal RNAs in mammals: Brown 1983). Mitochondrial DNA in mammals is for the most part maternally inherited. It has been found to evolve sequence differences up to ten times faster on average than nuclear DNA, and even faster in its noncoding control region (reviewed by Brown 1983; Avise et al. 1987).

Analyses of mitochondrial DNA by restriction endonucleases have been used extensively to document patterns of genetic variation (for review see Wilson et al. 1985; Avise et al. 1987; Moritz, Dowling, and Brown 1987; Harrison 1989). Many of these studies have revealed unknown or unsuspected population structures and phylogenetic relationships. For example, Lehman et al. (1991) have identified extensive unidirectional flow of mitochondrial DNA from coyotes, *Canis latrans*, into Canadian gray wolves, *C. lupus*. This gene flow has proceeded to the point that southern wolf populations described as a separate species, the red wolf, *C. rufus*, most likely originated from recent hybridization between coyotes and gray wolves (Wayne and Jenks 1991). Obviously, strategies for breeding captive populations of wolves must now take these new relationships into account. Similar techniques have been used to determine kin relations of founder females in captive populations of Speke's gazelle, *Gazella spekei* (Templeton, Davis, and Read 1987).

The polymerase chain reaction is a recent innovation that allows small DNA sequences (mitochondrial or nuclear) to be replicated or copied literally millions of times (Saiki et al. 1988; White, Arnheim, and Erlich 1989; Vosberg 1989). This "amplification" results in sufficient genetic material for direct sequencing (Gyllensten and Erlich 1988; Kocher et al. 1989). Most studies of mammals to date do not assess variation in DNA sequence at the population level (but see Wilkinson and Chapman 1991; Taberlet and Bouvet 1994). In fact, most recent studies have used such sequence data to reconstruct the evolutionary relationships of mammals in general (Irwin, Kocher, and Wilson 1991) or of particular mammalian taxa, such as deer (Miyamoto, Kraus, and Ryder 1990), bats (Mindell, Dick, and Baker 1991; Bailey, Slightom, and Goodman 1992), rodents (Smith and Patton 1991), and primates (Brown et al. 1982). One advantage of PCR is that the mostly degraded DNA isolated from museum specimens can still yield amplified products and sequences (Pääbo, Higuchi, and Wilson 1989; Pääbo 1989, 1990). Thus, even extinct species or populations can be compared with extant ones, as shown by Higuchi et al. (1987) for the quagga and other equids, Thomas et al. (1989) for the extinct marsupial wolf, Thomas et al. (1990) for kangaroo rats, and Wayne and Jenks (1991) for the red wolf.

An additional class of molecules potentially of great importance for conservation biology (O'Brien and Evermann 1988; Hughes 1991; Schreiber and Tichy 1992) are products of the loci of the major histocompatibility complex (MHC). MHC molecules act as the "front line" of defense against disease by first binding to foreign polypeptides and then presenting them to T cells. Both balancing (Hedrick and Thomson 1983) and directional (Hughes and Nei 1988) selection have been implicated as causes for the maintenance of variation at these highly variable loci, including evidence for resistance to specific diseases such as malaria (e.g., Hill et al. 1991). Therefore, populations with greater MHC variation may have increased overall resistance to disease, and breeding plans that result in the maintenance of variation at the MHC, along with other genes, are recommended (see Ballou and Foose, chap. 26, this volume). In addition, MHC variation has been shown to play a role in kin recognition and mate choice in mice (Potts, Manning, and Wakeland 1991; Yamazaki et al. 1992), and may have a similar role in other mammalian taxa.

Pedigree Analysis

The most significant resource for the management of captive species' gene pools is a complete and accurate pedigree, which allows for the precise determination of inbreeding coefficients, probabilities of possessing alleles from founders, and retention of genetic variability in the population. However, the application of pedigree analysis to the small numbers of animals typical of captive populations in zoos often requires that new research be conducted in order to establish pedigrees, ensure their accuracy, and fully consider what possibilities exist for pedigree manipulation in a given species. The range of practical management possibilities differs among vertebrate classes, is different for species that produce multiple offspring than for those that produce single offspring, and may be influenced by reproductive seasonality and the potential for manipulating reproductive parameters through gamete and embryo collection and storage, in vitro fertilization, and gestation of embryos in surrogate dams.

RESEARCH REQUIRED FOR EFFICIENT MANAGEMENT OF GENE POOLS

Under conditions of management that allow the construction of accurate pedigrees, populations of animals may be bred and maintained over generations in a manner that optimizes the retention of genetic variation. In other words, the greatest economy in terms of investment in the animal and facilities resources necessary for meeting gene pool preservation goals necessarily involves pedigree management. The genetic research technologies discussed above may, in combination with pedigree management, provide greater opportunities for efficiently meeting conservation goals.

Parentage Exclusion and Parentage Determination

Because complete and accurate pedigrees are such important tools, the correction of inaccurate information and the filling in of missing information are worth the effort invested in the necessary research. When the sire of an offspring is listed as "either A or B," it may be possible to produce two separate analyses of the pedigree management options taking into account each possible sire assignment. With multiple unknown sires or dams, the problem expands geometrically and the predictive value of the pedigree analysis decreases. Species managers recognize these problems intuitively and make every possible effort to provide parentage assignments, although complete success is elusive. Genetic research technologies provide opportunities to correct or confirm parentage assignments. Examples include the analysis of subtle chromosomal variants, such as has been applied to a paternity analysis in *Pan paniscus* (Benirschke and Kumamoto 1983). Blood-typing and electrophoretic studies have been applied to maternity analysis in *Equus przewalskii* (Bowling and Ryder 1988), as has DNA fingerprinting in captive primates (Ely and Ferrell 1990; Morin and Ryder 1991).

Managing Inbreeding

When two reproductively capable individuals are related, there is a probability that their offspring will receive two copies of the same gene from an ancestor the parents have in common. In this case it is said that the gene is autozygous, or identical by descent. Inbreeding is said to occur when the probability of autozygosity is finite. Thus, inbreeding reduces heterozygosity and provides increased opportunities for the expression of recessive genes, generally in proportion to the value of the coefficient of inbreeding (the probability of autozygosity).

Dealing with Undesirable Genes. Inevitably, among the necessarily inbred populations that are derived from small numbers of founders, heritable traits varying from subjectively undesirable to frankly deleterious will emerge. Hairlessness in red-ruffed lemurs, *Varecia variegata ruber,* has been identified as a recessive trait thought to be carried by a single individual in the captive population. In the current pedigree of the captive population, only 7 founders have contributed genes to the 125 living individuals. Over three-quarters of the alleles present in the living population are derived from 3 individuals. One of the underrepresented founders is the carrier of the hairless trait. Pedigree management may be implemented to ensure that the genetic contribution from the carrier of the hairless trait enters the captive population, thereby increasing genetic variation, while at the same time keeping the recessive hairless condi-

tion, which can be derived through both paternal and maternal inheritance, at acceptable levels. If matings between individuals tracing their ancestry back to the carrier of the hairless trait are arranged so that, for example, the potential carrier parents both have the known carrier as a grandparent, the chance of producing hairless offspring would be only 3.75%.

Hereditary Diseases. Individual animals in all examined species of birds and mammals can carry copies of genes in a masked condition that may, under appropriate conditions, manifest themselves and produce illness or death in affected individuals. The pool of such deleterious genes in a species is referred to as genetic "load," and the conditions expressed as a result of these deleterious genes are called genetic diseases. Nearly 1,000 deleterious genes have been discovered in our human population. Many genetic diseases were first noted in individuals descended from ancestors who were part of small communities, isolated over time from other human populations by physical factors (such as people living on islands or otherwise geographically isolated) or by cultural factors (such as the Amish, Mennonites, and Ashkenazic Jews). In such small communities marriage choices are limited, and the high incidence of cousin and other consanguineous marriages produces a significantly greater chance that rare deleterious genes will be expressed in the children (Diamond and Rotter 1987).

Animal populations are no different in this regard (Ryder 1988), and when animals are intentionally inbred, the typical result is a loss of some offspring from causes that may be genetic in origin. Zoo populations typically are begun from small numbers of founder animals, and avoidance of inbreeding may not be possible. Funnel chest has been identified as a genetic condition in black-and-white ruffed lemurs, *Varecia variegata variegata.* The basis of congenital diaphragmatic hernia in *Leontopithecus rosalia rosalia* is under investigation, as is the inheritance of a coat color anomaly in *Equus przewalskii* that results in individuals lacking the typical black pigmentation on the distal extremities of the limbs and on the mane and tail.

Often it can take a number of generations of propagation before a genetic disease becomes apparent, and by then, the individual who transmitted the genetic disease (but may have been unaffected) has died. Unraveling the genetic nature of the condition and identifying which among the unaffected individuals may carry the gene for the deleterious trait is decidedly not a simple task. Medical and pathological records must be examined, potential modes of inheritance investigated, and obligate and potential carriers identified. Any conclusions reached and management options elaborated require complex calculations for all but the most simple pedigrees. In the future, linkage studies involving DNA markers may be applied to populations of endangered animals in a fashion similar to what has been done in human studies. Such studies have resulted in new diagnostic tools and opportunities for reducing the number of individuals affected with specific genetic diseases. For example, sites on DNA molecules near the location of the gene that causes Duchenne muscular dystrophy in affected individuals have been identified. These DNA marker studies allowed the development of predictive tests for the likelihood that particular individuals within a pedigree would develop the disease, and subsequently, the identification of the gene causing the disease itself (Hoffman, Brown, and Kunkel 1987). However, for such activities to be undertaken in endangered animals, appropriate samples from pedigreed individuals must be collected and saved for analysis.

Managing Selection in the Captive Environment

Differential reproduction of individuals in any generation alters the frequencies of alleles in the subsequent generation. Consequently, disproportionate reproduction by particular individuals favors the survival of genes from those ancestors and increases the chances of loss of genes from other ancestors in a fashion that depends on the structure of the pedigree. This form of selection may occur in captive breeding programs and may be a source of loss of gene pool resources over time. In captive breeding programs for animals living in herds, there has been a historic tendency to use relatively few males as sires in the herd, thereby producing an overrepresentation of genes derived from these prolific herd sires in the next generation.

Characterizing Founders and Migrants

For many species of conservation interest that have been propagated for some time in captivity, introduction of new individuals offers the possibility of increasing genetic variability and heterozygosity through the introduction of a sample of alleles from the current free-living population. In noncaptive populations the same process is accomplished by migrating individuals. Genetic migrants can have a considerable effect on the total diversity of a population, as has been shown both theoretically (Lacy 1987) and practically in the specific instance of the last wild-caught Przelwalski's horse mare, who contributed to the gene pool of the captive population in the fifth generation of breeding (MacCluer et al. 1986). However, it is necessary to ensure that any such migrants are appropriate ones; that is, that they are not from chromosomally or otherwise genetically dissimilar populations. For some species, notably orangutans or any of the gazelle species, any migrants into the captive populations will, if successful, become new founders and should be studied chromosomally (Ryder 1986, 1987).

Merging Populations

Closed breeding populations that consist of fewer reproducing individuals than are recommended for achieving gene pool conservation goals represent severe challenges to ex situ conservation efforts. The risks inherent in breeding populations constituted by very small numbers of individuals include extinction from inbreeding depression, extinction from chance events such as an unequal sex ratio or other instances of demographic stochasticity, genetic uniformity, and, through the process of genetic drift, a shift away from what may be considered typical characteristics of the species or subspecies in question so that the captive population no longer accurately reflects, phenotypically or genetically, the wild populations from which it was derived. The introduction of appropriate migrants from the wild population can

diminish these risks; however, such genetic migrants may no longer be available. Other possible strategies for preventing the extinction of small high-risk populations include artificially enhanced reproduction techniques (such as multiple clutching, superovulation and embryo transfer, and embryo splitting), selection against genetic load, as has been practiced for the Speke's gazelle (Templeton and Read 1984), and merging the population with a related form (as was undertaken with the dusky seaside sparrow).

Merging populations offers the opportunity to prevent the loss of genes encoding the unique genetic attributes of endangered populations. However, any unique genes saved may persist only in a genetic background that is different from that in which they existed prior to merging. In a merged population, after reproduction of individuals in the parent population ceases, genetic admixture may be essentially irreversible, so careful consideration of costs and benefits is required. A significant factor in the decision should be the degree to which the merging populations are genetically, behaviorally, and ecologically similar. Without research into the genetics of the populations in particular, insufficient information may be available to make an informed decision concerning merging of populations. If genetic data indicate a history of gene flow, then merging is acceptable up to the historical levels.

Reinforcing Wild Populations

Captive-bred populations, if appropriately constituted and genetically managed, offer potential sources of unrelated individuals, and thus additional genetic variation, for reinforcing small populations in natural ecosystems. Such a strategy serves conservation purposes to the extent that the potential migrants and the genetic contributions they represent are genetically appropriate. Genetic input from Bengal tigers, *Panthera tigris tigris,* might not be appropriate for reinforcing wild populations of Amur tigers, *Panthera tigris altaica,* for example. Some knowledge of the genetic, behavioral, and ecological differentiation of both the wild and captive-bred populations should exist before any such intervention is considered.

Prospects for the Future

Our understanding of the molecular organization of mammalian genomes is accelerating rapidly, due in large part to the intense effort being devoted to increasing our knowledge of the human species. Similar levels of understanding exist only for the laboratory mouse. However, the experimental approaches and, to a significant degree, the findings of recombinant DNA technology are relevant for a broad spectrum of mammalian species, provided that sufficient basic information concerning the genetics of those species is available as a base upon which to build. As numerous mammalian species become increasingly threatened with extinction, the need to collect the information essential for characterizing such basic genetic attributes of a species' genetic makeup as its chromosome number is increasing, while the time to do so dwindles. Systematic efforts to collect, catalog, and preserve samples for future genetic analyses need to be greatly expanded.

REFERENCES

Avise, J. C., Arnold, J., Ball, R. M., Bermingham, E., Lamb, T., Neigel, J. E., Reeb, C. A., and Saunders, N. C. 1987. Intraspecific phylogeography: The mitochondrial DNA bridge between population genetics and systematics. *Annu. Rev. Ecol. Syst.* 18: 489–522.

Bailey, W. J., Slightom, J. L., and Goodman, M. 1992. Rejection of the "flying primate" hypothesis by phylogenetic evidence from the e-globin gene. *Science* 256:86–89.

Benirschke, K., and Kumamoto, A. T. 1983. Paternity diagnosis in pygmy chimpanzees, *Pan paniscus. Int. Zoo Yrbk.* 23:220–22.

Bowling, A. T., and Ryder, O. A. 1987. Genetic studies of blood markers in Przewalski's horses. *J. Hered.* 78:75–80.

———. 1988. Switched identity of two Przewalski's horse mares detected by blood typing. *Zoo Biol.* 7:81–84.

Brown, W. M. 1983. Evolution of animal mitochondrial DNA. In *Evolution of genes and proteins,* ed. M. Nei and R. K. Koehn. Sunderland, Mass.: Sinauer Associates.

Brown, W. M., Prager, E. M., Wang, A., and Wilson, A. C. 1982. Mitochondrial DNA sequences of primates: Tempo and mode of evolution. *J. Mol. Evol.* 18:225–39.

Burke, T. 1989. DNA fingerprinting and other methods for the study of mating success. *Trends Ecol. Evol.* 4:139–44.

de Boer, L. E. M., and Seuanez, H. N. 1982. The chromosomes of the orangutan and their relevance to the conservation of the species. In *The orangutan: Its biology and conservation,* ed. L. E. M. de Boer. The Hague: W. Junk.

Diamond, J. M., and Rotter, J. I. 1987. Observing the founder effect in human evolution. *Nature* 329:105–6.

Ely, J., and Ferrell, R. E. 1990. DNA "fingerprints" and paternity ascertainment in chimpanzees *(Pan troglodytes). Zoo Biol.* 9:91–98.

Fleischer, R. C. In press. Application of molecular methods to the assessment of genetic mating systems in vertebrates. In *Molecular zoology: Advances, strategies and protocols,* ed. J. Ferraris and S. Palumbi. New York: Wiley-Liss.

Fleischer, R. C., Tarr, C. L., and Pratt, T. K. 1994. Genetic structure in the palila, an endangered Hawaiian honeycreeper, as assessed by DNA fingerprinting. *Mol. Ecol.* 3:383–92.

Foreman, L. M., Kleiman, D. G., Bush, R. M., Dietz, J. M., Ballou, J. D., Phillips, L. G., Coimbra-Filho, A. F., and O'Brien, S. J. 1986. Genetic variation within and among lion-tamarins. *Am. J. Phys. Anthropol.* 71:1–11.

Genz, E. J., and Yates, T. L. 1985. Genetic identification of hybrid camelids. *Zoo Biol.* 5:349–54.

Geyer, C. G., Ryder, O. A., Chemnick, L. G., and Thompson, E. A. 1993. Analysis of relatedness in the California condors from DNA fingerprints. *Mol. Biol. Evol.* 10:571–89.

Gilbert, D. A., Lehman, N., O'Brien, S. J., and Wayne, R. K. 1990. Genetic fingerprinting reflects population differentiation in the California Channel Island fox. *Nature* 344:764–66.

Gilbert, D. A., Packer, C., Pusey, A. E., Stephens, J. C., and O'Brien, S. J. 1991. Analytical DNA fingerprinting in lions: Parentage, genetic diversity, and kinship. *J. Hered.* 82:378–86.

Gray, M. W. 1989. Origin and evolution of mitochondrial DNA. *Annu. Rev. Cell Biol.* 5:25–50.

Gyllensten, U. B., and Erlich, H. A. 1988. Generation of single-stranded DNA by the polymerase chain reaction and its application to direct sequencing of the HLA-DQa locus. *Proc. Natl. Acad. Sci. USA* 85:7652–55.

Harrison, R. G. 1989. Animal mitochondrial DNA as a genetic marker in population and evolutionary biology. *Trends Ecol. Evol.* 4:6–11.

Hedrick, P. W., and Miller, P. S. 1992. Conservation genetics: Techniques and fundamentals. *Ecol. Appl.* 2:30–46.

Hedrick, P. W., and Thomson, G. 1983. Evidence for balancing selection at HLA. *Genetics* 104:449–56.

Higuchi, R. G., Wrischnik, L. A., Oakes, E., George, M., Tong, B., and Wilson, A. C. 1987. Mitochondrial DNA of the extinct quagga: Relatedness and postmortem change. *J. Mol. Evol.* 25: 283–87.

Hill, A. V. S., Allsop, C. E. M., Kwiatkowski, D., Anstey, N. M., Twumasi, P., Rowe, P. A., Bennett, S., Brewster, D., McMichael, A., and Greenwood, B. M. 1991. Common West African HLA antigens are associated with protection from severe malaria. *Nature* 352:595–600.

Hoffman, E. P., Brown, R. H., and Kunkel, L. M. 1987. Dystrophin: The protein product of the Duchenne muscular dystrophy locus. *Cell Genet.* 51:919–28.

Hughes, A. L. 1991. MHC polymorphism and the design of captive breeding programs. *Conserv. Biol.* 5:249–51.

Hughes, A. L., and Nei, M. 1988. Pattern of nucleotide substitution at major histocompatibility complex loci reveals overdominant selection. *Nature* 335:167–70.

Irwin, D. M., Kocher, T. D., and Wilson, A. C. 1991. Evolution of the cytochrome b gene of mammals. *J. Mol. Evol.* 32:128–44.

Jeffreys, A. J., Wilson, V., and Thein, S. L. 1985. Individual-specific "fingerprints" of human DNA. *Nature* 316:67–73.

Keane, B., Waser, P. M., Creel, S. R., Creel, N. M., Elliott, L. F., and Minchella, D. J. 1994. Subordinate reproduction in dwarf mongooses. *Anim. Behav.* 47:65–75.

Kocher, T. D., Thomas, W. K., Meyer, A., Edwards, S. V., Pääbo, S., Villablanca, F. S., and Wilson, A. C. 1989. Dynamics of mitochondrial DNA evolution in animals: Amplification and sequencing with conserved primers. *Proc. Natl. Acad. Sci. USA* 86:6196–6200.

Lacy, R. C. 1987. Loss of genetic diversity from managed populations: Interacting effects of drift, mutation, immigration, selection, and population subdivision. *Conserv. Biol.* 1:143–59.

Lehman, N., Clarkson, P., Mech, L. D., Meier, T. J., and Wayne, R. K. 1992. A study of the genetic relationships within and among wolf packs using DNA fingerprinting and mitochondrial DNA. *Behav. Ecol. Sociobiol.* 30:2:83–94.

Litt, M., and Luty, J. A. 1989. A hypervariable microsatellite revealed by *in vitro* amplification of a dinucleotide repeat within the cardiac muscle actin gene. *Am. J. Hum. Genet.* 44: 397–401.

Lynch, M. 1988. Estimation of relatedness by DNA fingerprinting. *Mol. Biol. Evol.* 5:584–99.

MacClure, J. W., VandeBerg, J. L., Read, B., and Ryder, O. A. 1986. Pedigree analysis by computer simulation. *Zoo Biol.* 5: 147–60.

Mindell, D. P., Dick, C. W., and Baker, R. J. 1991. Phylogenetic relationships among megabats, microbats and primates. *Proc. Natl. Acad. Sci. USA* 88:10322.

Miyamoto, M. M., Kraus, F., and Ryder, O. A. 1990. Phylogeny and evolution of antlered deer determined from mitochondrial DNA sequences. *Proc. Natl. Acad. Sci. USA* 87:6127–31.

Morin, P. A., and Ryder, O. A. 1991. Founder contribution and pedigree inference in a captive breeding colony of lion-tailed macaques, using mitochondrial DNA and DNA fingerprint analyses. *Zoo Biol.* 10:341–52.

Morin, P. A., and Woodruff, D. S. 1992. Paternity exclusion using multiple hypervariable microsatellite loci amplified from nuclear DNA of hair cells. In *Paternity in primates: Genetic tests and theories,* ed. R. D. Martin, A. F. Dixson, and E. J. Wicking, 63–81. Basel: Karger.

Moritz, C., Dowling, T. E., and Brown, W. M. 1987. Evolution of animal mitochondrial DNA: Relevance for population biology and systematics. *Annu. Rev. Ecol. Syst.* 18:269–92.

O'Brien, S. J., and Evermann, J. F. 1988. Interactive influence of infectious disease and genetic diversity in natural populations. *Trends Ecol. Evol.* 3:254–59.

O'Brien, S. J., Joslin, P., Smith, G. L. III, Wolfe, R., Schaffer, N., Heath, E., Ott-Joslin, J., Rawal, P. P., Bhattacharjee, K. K., and Martenson, J. S. 1987. Evidence for African origins of founders of the Asiatic lion species survival plan. *Zoo Biol.* 6:99–116.

Pääbo, S. 1989. Ancient DNA: Extraction, characterization, molecular cloning, and enzymatic amplification. *Proc. Natl. Acad. Sci. USA* 86:1939–43.

———. 1990. Amplifying ancient DNA. In *PCR protocols: A guide to methods and applications,* ed. M. A. Innis, D. H. Gelfand, J. J. Sninsky, and T. J. White, 159–68. San Diego, Calif.: Academic Press.

Pääbo, S., Higuchi, R. G., and Wilson, A. C. 1989. Ancient DNA and the polymerase chain reaction. *J. Biol. Chem.* 264: 9709–12.

Packer, C., Gilbert, D. A., Pusey, A. E., and O'Brien, S. J. 1991. A molecular genetic analysis of kinship and cooperation in African lions. *Nature* 351:562–65.

Potts, W. K., Manning, C. J., and Wakeland, E. K. 1991. Mating patterns in semi-natural populations of mice influenced by MHC genotype. *Nature* 352:619–21.

Rave, E. H., Fleischer, R. C., Duvall, F., and Black, J. M. 1994. Genetic analyses through DNA fingerprinting of captive populations of nene. *Conserv. Biol.* 8:744–51.

Ryder, O. A. 1986a. Genetics investigations: Tools for supporting breeding programme goals. *Int. Zoo Yrbk.* 24/25:157–162.

———. 1986b. Species conservation and systematics: The dilemma of subspecies. *Trends Ecol. Evol.* 1:9–10.

———. 1987. Conservation action for gazelles: An urgent need. *Trends Ecol. Evol.* 2:143–44.

———. 1988. Founder effects and endangered species. *Nature* 331:396.

Ryder, O. A., and Chemnick, L. G. 1993. Chromosomal and mitochondrial DNA variation in orang utans. *J. Hered.* 84:405–9.

Ryder, O. A., Chemnick, L. G., Schafer, S. F., and Shima, A. L. 1989. Individual DNA fingerprints from Galapagos tortoises. *Int. Zoo Yrbk.* 28:84–87.

Ryder, O. A., Kumamoto, A. T., Durrant, B. S., and Benirschke, K. 1989. Chromosomal divergence and reproductive isolation in dik-diks (genus *Madoqua,* Mammalia, Bovidae). In *Speciation and its consequences,* ed. D. Otte and J. A. Endler, 208–25. Sunderland, Mass.: Sinauer Associates.

Saiki, R. K., Gelfand, D. H., Stoffel, S., Scharf, S. J., Higuchi, R., Horn, G. T., Mullis, K. B., and Erlich, H. A. 1988. Primer-directed enzymatic amplification of DNA with a thermostable DNA polymerase. *Science* 239:487–91.

Schreiber, A., and Tichy, H. 1992. MHC polymorphisms and the conservation of endangered species. *Symp. Zool. Soc. Lond.* 64: 103–21.

Selander, R. K. 1976. Genic variation in natural populations. In *Molecular evolution,* ed. F. J. Ayala, 21–45. Sunderland, Mass.: Sinauer Associates.

Selander, R. K., and Whittam, T. S. 1983. Protein polymorphism and the genetic structure of populations. In *Evolution of genes and proteins,* ed. M. Nei and R. K. Koehn, 89–114. Sunderland, Mass.: Sinauer Associates.

Seuanez, H., Evans, H. J., Martin, D. E., and Fletcher, J. 1979. An inversion in chromosome 2 that distinguishes between Bornean and Sumatran orangutans. *Cytogenet. Cell Genet.* 23:137–40.

Smith, M. F., and Patton, J. L. 1991. Variation in mitochondrial cytochrome *b* sequence in natural populations of South American akodontine rodents (Muridae: Sigmodontidae). *Mol. Biol. Evol.* 8:85–103.

Soulé, M. E. 1980. Thresholds for survival: Maintaining fitness and evolutionary potential. In *Conservation biology: An evolutionary-ecological perspective,* ed. M. E. Soulé and B. A. Wilcox, 151–69. Sunderland, Mass.: Sinauer Associates.

Taberlet, P., and J. Bouvet. 1994. Mitochondrial DNA polymorphism, phylogeography, and conservation genetics of the brown bear *(Ursus arctos)* in Europe. *Proc. Royal Soc. Lond.* B255: 195–200.

Templeton, A. R., Davis, S. K., and Read, B. 1987. Genetic variability in a captive herd of Speke's gazelle *(Gazella spekei). Zoo Biol.* 6:305–13.

Templeton, A. R., and Read, B. 1984. Factors eliminating inbreeding depression in a captive herd of Speke's gazelle, *Gazella spekei. Zoo Biol.* 3:177–99.

Thomas, R. H., Schaffner, W., Wilson, A. C., and Pääbo, S. 1989. DNA phylogeny of the extinct marsupial wolf. *Nature* 340: 465–67.

Thomas, W. K., Pääbo, S., Villablanca, F. X., and Wilson, A. C. 1990. Spatial and temporal continuity of kangaroo rat populations shown by sequencing mitochondrial DNA from museum specimens. *J. Mol. Evol.* 31:101–12.

Vosberg, H.-P. 1989. The polymerase chain reaction: An improved method for the analysis of nucleic acids. *Hum. Genet.* 83:1–15.

Wayne, R. K., and Jenks, S. M. 1991. Mitochondrial DNA analysis implying extensive hybridization of the endangered red wolf *Canis rufus. Nature* 351:565–68.

Weber, J. L., and May, P. E. 1989. Abundant class of human DNA polymorphisms which can be typed using the polymerase chain reaction. *Am. J. Hum. Genet.* 44:388–96.

White, T. J., Arnheim, N., and Erlich, H. A. 1989. The polymerase chain reaction. *Trends Genet.* 5:185–89.

Wilkinson, G. S., and Chapman, A. M. 1991. Length and sequence variation in evening bat d-loop mtDNA. *Genetics* 128:608–17.

Wilson, A. C., Cann, R. L., Carr, S. M., George, M., Gyllensten, U. B., Helm-Bychowski, K. M., Higuchi, R. G., Palumbi, S. R., Prager, E. M., Sage, R. D., and Stoneking, M. 1985. Mitochondrial DNA and two perspectives on evolutionary genetics. *Biol. J. Linn. Soc.* 26:375–400.

Wurster, D. H., and Benirschke, K. 1970. Indian Muntjac, *Muntiacus muntjak:* A deer with a low diploid chromosome number. *Science* 168:1364–66.

Yamazaki, K., Beauchamp, G. K., Imai, Y., and Boyse, E. A. 1992. Expression of urinary H-2 odortypes by infant mice. *Proc. Natl. Acad. Sci. USA* 89:2756–58.

26

Demographic and Genetic Management of Captive Populations

JONATHAN D. BALLOU AND THOMAS J. FOOSE

The last fifteen years have been a time of revolutionary change in the focus and goals of zoos. This change has been motivated by a fundamental philosophical shift in the zoo community toward establishing conservation, through both captive propagation and public education, as a primary purpose. A large part of the material included in this volume has resulted as much from this shift as from the development and application of new technology.

The material discussed in this chapter has also resulted from this new conservation ethic. Two decades ago, the primary focus of zoo animal management was the exhibition, maintenance, and occasional breeding of individual specimens. Collection from the wild, rather than reproduction in captivity, was the usual means of acquiring animals for zoo exhibits. As animals became increasingly difficult to obtain from the wild, however, captive propagation became a more important means for replenishing zoo collections. At the same time, zoos began to recognize their potential contribution to wildlife conservation: the preservation of wild animal species in captivity over long periods of time and the potential to reintroduce captive-bred animals into the wild.

Significant biological problems confront this effort. Small and fragmented populations, such as those that exist in zoos and to an increasing extent in the wild, have a low probability of long-term survival. Random catastrophic demographic events, reduced vigor due to inbreeding depression, and loss of genetic diversity due to genetic drift and inbreeding all have an effect on the survival of small populations (Gilpin and Soulé 1986). Success in managing these populations ultimately rests on managing them as populations, not just as individuals.

There are also organizational problems involved in managing groups of individual zoo collections as cross-institutional biological populations. The international zoo

At the time of writing, Thomas J. Foose was with the Captive Breeding Specialist Group, Apple Valley, Minnesota.

community has responded to this additional responsibility by forming associations and programs to organize and coordinate cooperative population management efforts (Hutchins and Wiese 1991; Shoemaker and Flesness, appendix 4, this volume). The primary purpose of such programs is to contribute to the conservation of species by providing reservoirs of genetic and demographic material that can be used periodically to reinforce, revitalize, or reestablish populations in the wild. This goal requires the development of propagation programs oriented to the maintenance of genetic diversity and demographic security. It is envisioned that conservation programs for many endangered species will interactively manage both wild and captive populations for mutual support and survival.

This chapter delineates the principles, concepts, and techniques necessary to manage captive populations, concentrating on those aspects critical to the long-term maintenance of genetic diversity and demographic security. However, the scope of "population" management is broad and includes many subjects considered elsewhere in this volume: reproductive and behavioral research, data management, genetic research, program administration, and of course, basic husbandry.

The chapter begins with a discussion on establishing management goals to guide the formulation of a propagation and management plan. Genetic and demographic analyses are a critical part of this process, but can only be conducted after basic pedigree and demographic data on the current and historical population have been compiled and organized. Methods of data collection and organization are discussed in the second section, as well as by Shoemaker and Flesness (appendix 4, this volume). This is followed by a discussion of methods and techniques for both genetic and demographic analyses, using examples to illustrate various analytic procedures. The chapter concludes with a section on population management, which covers the basic strategies and concepts for combining propagation goals with the results of the demographic and genetic analyses to form the basis for the program's specific institution-by-institution and animal-by-animal breeding recommendations.

CAPTIVE MANAGEMENT GOALS

The goals of most captive management programs approach one of two extremes: individuals are either intentionally selected to be well adapted to captive environments, or they are managed to preserve genetic diversity (Foose et al. 1986; Frankham et al. 1986). Which goal is chosen depends on the managers' objective for the population. Frankham et al. (1986) distinguish among four types of captive populations of primary interest to zoos:

1. Common display species
   Population goal: Establish a tractable, easily managed population well adapted to the captive environment
   Management strategy: Select for traits adapted to captivity
   Example: Fallow deer, *Cervus dama* (Hemmer 1986)
2. Endangered species in captivity for long-term conservation
   Population goal: Long-term maintenance of a viable population and preservation of genetic diversity
   Management strategy: Maximize retention of the founders' genetic diversity and maintain a demographically stable population compatible with the limits of the captive environment's carrying capacity
   Example: Golden lion tamarin, *Leontopithecus rosalia* (Kleiman et al. 1986); Siberian tiger, *Panthera tigris altaica* (Foose and Seal 1986)
3. Rare species being propagated for immediate release into natural habitats
   Population goal: Rapid population growth and large-scale reproduction for immediate release
   Management strategy: Maximize reproduction in a captive environment as similar as possible to the natural environment
   Example: Guam rail, *Rallus owstoni* (Derrickson 1987)
4. Rare species not yet capable of self-sustaining reproduction in captivity
   Population goal: Develop husbandry techniques for achieving self-sustaining capabilities
   Management strategy: Preferentially propagate individuals capable of reproducing in the captive environment. Once the population has grown to self-sustaining status, manage the population as type 2 above
   Example: Micronesian kingfisher, *Halcyon cinnamomina* (Bahner 1991)

Adapting a species to captivity is appropriate for populations of type 1 and, initially, type 4. Frankham et al. (1986) and Foose et al. (1986) discuss basic population management strategies for these types of populations. Maintenance of genetic diversity is paramount for populations of type 2 and, eventually, type 4.

Although the intent of this chapter is to describe population management techniques specifically for populations designated for long-term conservation, many of the concepts and techniques can be appropriately applied to populations under other objectives. For example, data should be collected and demographic and genetic calculations routinely performed for *all* types of populations.

MANAGEMENT OF GENETIC DIVERSITY

Maintaining genetic diversity and demographic security are the primary population management goals for long-term conservation. Management for genetic diversity minimizes change in the genetic constitution of the population while in captivity so that if and when the opportunity arises for animals to be reintroduced into the wild, they will represent, as closely as possible, the genetic characteristics of the original founders used to establish the captive population (Hedrick et al. 1986; Lacy et al. 1995). Genetic variation is also the basis for adaptive evolution and must be retained to maintain the population's potential to adapt to changing environments. Furthermore, there are a growing number of studies that indicate a general, although not universal, positive relationship between genetic variation and both individual and population fitness (Hedrick et al. 1986; Allendorf and Leary 1986; Mitton and Grant 1984). These include a number of studies that have documented the deleterious effects of inbreeding in captive populations (Ralls, Ballou, and Templeton 1988; Lacy, Petric, and Warneke 1993) as well as the effects of low levels of variation on reproductive condition (Wildt et al. 1987; O'Brien et al. 1985). Last, maintaining genetic diversity preserves future management options, a strategy that will become increasingly important as knowledge of the genetic and demographic requirements of wild and captive populations expands.

There are several kinds of genetic variation. Animals carry many thousands of genes located on chromosomes. The exact location of a gene on the chromosome is referred to as its locus. The terms gene and locus are often used interchangeably. Each gene may occur in alternative forms, called alleles, that may produce slightly different genetic effects, such as different pelage colors, eye colors, and so forth. The number of alleles per gene or locus can vary from one (no diversity, or monomorphic locus) to many (polymorphic locus). Most vertebrate species carry two copies of each gene (they are diploid), one inherited from each parent. A few species carry only one copy of each gene (they are haploid). Both copies may represent the same allele, in which case the animal is described as homozygous for that locus, or different alleles, in which case the animal is heterozygous.

Genetic diversity comprises both allelic diversity and heterozygosity. Allelic diversity refers to the number of different alleles at any given locus in the population. Heterozygosity is the percentage of heterozygous loci in a population or individual. Thus, genetic diversity can be measured in both individuals and populations. Both allelic diversity and heterozygosity are desirable in captive populations; allelic diversity is important for a population's long-term ability to adapt, while heterozygosity is important for immediate adaptation (Allendorf 1986).

Both allelic diversity and heterozygosity are lost in small populations (numbering a few tens to a few hundreds) through the process of genetic drift. The alleles passed from parents to offspring represent only a sample of the allelic variation of the parental generation. When only a few offspring are produced, the genetic diversity of the offspring may be unrepresentative of the genetic diversity present in the parents. By chance alone, some alleles may not be passed to the offspring; others may increase or decrease in frequency. These changes in the number and frequency of alleles, as well as changes in heterozygosity due to this biased sampling process, are termed genetic drift.

The population's average heterozygosity is often used as an overall indicator of genetic diversity since it lends itself well to theoretical considerations and usually provides a simple, accurate indicator of the loss of allelic diversity (Allendorf 1986). This is not always the case, however. During bottleneck events, allelic diversity is lost much more readily than heterozygosity, and using heterozygosity alone overestimates the amount of genetic diversity retained after a bottleneck. Moreover, rare alleles (those occurring at low frequencies in the population) may also be lost faster than average heterozygosity. The genetic goals of most captive propagation programs are currently based on maintaining heterozygosity but also consider bottleneck effects in the pedigrees.

In managing genetic variation, it is important to distinguish between single-locus and multilocus, or quantitative, variation. Single-locus variation is variation in traits regulated by single genes, while quantitative variation is variation in traits regulated by many genes. Although quantitative variation is probably more important than single-locus variation for long-term evolutionary adaptation, heterozygosity and additive quantitative variation are lost at approximately the same rate. Consequently, management strategies based on maintenance of heterozygosity generally apply to maintenance of additive genetic diversity as well (Lande and Barrowclough 1987).

Selection can potentially retard or accelerate loss of genetic diversity. However, little is known about the role selection plays in captive populations (Frankham et al. 1986; Arnold 1995). Variation can be selective (influenced by selection pressures) or selectively neutral (influenced not by selection pressures but by the random process of genetic drift). The conservative approach is to assume selective neutrality, particularly in small populations in which genetic drift is likely to be a stronger force than selection. Discussions of the management and maintenance of genetic variation in this chapter refer primarily to single-locus neutral variation. (See Lacy et al. 1995; Lande and Barrowclough 1987 for further discussions of this issue.)

Loss of genetic diversity is a function of population size and time. In general, the smaller the population, the faster the loss; the longer the period of time, the greater the total loss (fig. 26.l). Therefore, those developing management plans to conserve genetic diversity must consider the questions, "How much genetic diversity is required?" and "How long should it be maintained?"

The question of how much genetic diversity is required to retain long-term fitness and evolutionary potential in captive populations is difficult to answer, since little is known

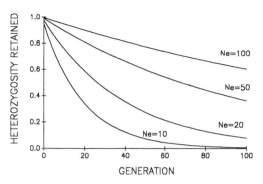

FIG. 26.1.   Percentage of original heterozygosity retained over 100 generations for effective population sizes (N_e) varying from 10 to 100.

about minimum genetic requirements of populations. One approach might be to maintain as much genetic variation as possible. This does not provide useful guidelines for the development of management programs, however, because populations would have to be "as large as possible" to achieve this result. The finite availability of captive resources strictly limits the size and number of captive populations that can be managed.

Because loss of genetic diversity is a function of time, it is also important to consider how long genetic diversity must be maintained. The time scale for management programs will vary. Some species may need the support of a captive population for a relatively short time before they can be returned to the wild. However, for many, if not most, species, captive populations will have to be maintained for the long term, often over hundreds of years. The safest approach is to initiate all programs as if they will be for the long term. They can always be concluded earlier if conditions permit.

A crude but general strategy that has been suggested in response to the questions "how much" and "for how long" is to preserve 90% of the founders' heterozygosity over a period of 200 years (Soulé et al. 1986). This "90%/200 year rule" originated from considerations of how long human population growth and development will continue to reduce wildlife habitat. Its authors estimated that this "demographic winter" will last between 500 and 1,000 years. However, they observed that some stabilization of human population growth is expected in the next 150 to 200 years. More importantly, they hypothesized that the current rapid development of biological technology, especially long-term storage of germ plasm (cryopreservation), will decrease dependence on populations of living animals for the preservation of gene pools by the end of the twenty-first century. The authors despaired of the feasibility of developing human-managed programs that would continue for hundreds of years and concluded that 200 years would be a reasonable time frame for management of captive populations. The recommendation to retain 90% of the original heterozygosity was based on the authors' consensus that the 10% loss "represents, intuitively, the zone between a potentially damaging and a tolerable loss of heterozygosity" (Soulé et al. 1986, 107).

Although this 90%/200 year rule of thumb is somewhat arbitrary, it does provide a starting point for establishing population size goals. We have chosen to use this approach to determine genetic goals for captive propagation programs and will focus our discussions on populations being managed under this goal. However, the questions "how much" and "for how long" will normally require species-specific answers (see "Demographic Analyses" below). Individual programs can modify both the time period of concern and the level of genetic diversity to be retained in response to the circumstances of the species. For example, populations that are to be reintroduced soon after a captive colony is established will require less concern about long-term maintenance of genetic diversity than populations destined to remain in captivity for many generations. In fact, more recently, population size objectives have been formulated in terms of 100 rather than 200 years, since this results in smaller, more realistic population sizes (Foose et al. 1995). Nevertheless, the general techniques for developing a plan remain the same.

Small populations are subject to demographic as well as genetic problems, and similar questions about demographic security should be considered in establishing goals for captive propagation programs. Many demographic threats are stochastic (random) in nature. They include such easily appreciated chance events as environmental variation, natural disasters, and disease epidemics (Dobson and May 1986; Goodman 1987) as well as more subtle fluctuations in birth and death rates, including distortion of sex ratios, due to simple variation among individuals.

Risks of demographic problems, like genetic risks, are functions of population size and time. The smaller the population and the longer the time period of management, the greater the risks. The relevant question is, what is the probability of a population surviving (i.e., not going extinct) for a specified period of time? Or, in other words, what population size is necessary to achieve a high probability (e.g., 95%) of survival over a long time period (e.g., 200 years) (Shaffer 1987)? In most cases, captive populations large enough to achieve the usual genetic objectives will also be large enough to insure high survival probability over the time period of concern because management in captivity will usually, though not always, be able to moderate demographic stochasticity caused by environmental variation. This is not likely to be the case for small wild populations, in which environmental variation has a tremendous effect on population survival (Goodman 1987).

DATA COMPILATION

The most important task in the development of a captive propagation plan is compiling the basic data required for population analysis and management. Data may already have been compiled in a variety of different forms if a captive population exists or has existed in the past. The best source of compiled data is a studbook, which is a chronology of a captive population listing vital information on animal identities, sexes, parentage, and birth and death dates, as well as information on animal movements between institutions (Shoemaker and Flesness, appendix 4, this volume; Glatston 1986). Currently there are approximately 250 international and regional studbooks (T. J. Foose, pers.

comm.), many of which are available as computerized data bases, and the number is growing annually.

If a studbook does not exist or is out of date, one must be compiled from original sources. Historical and current data should be collected from all institutions that have had or currently have individuals of interest. Historical data are critical for determining the ancestry of living animals and estimating certain genetic and demographic parameters (e.g., population growth rates, generation lengths, effective population sizes).

Data compilation should begin with reference to a number of sources that summarize data on captive populations. Potential sources of data are:

• **International Species Information System (ISIS).** ISIS is a computerized data base containing information on animal identities, birth and death dates, genealogies, and movements (Seal, Makey, and Murtfeldt 1976; Shoemaker and Flesness, appendix 4, this volume). ISIS collects data from institutions worldwide and is the best starting point for compiling population data if no studbook is available.

• **International Zoo Yearbook (IZY).** IZY provides an annual list of birds, mammals, reptiles, amphibians, and fishes bred in captivity (Olney 1986). Although only numbers and locations are presented, these annual listings are useful for identifying institutions that once had or currently have specimens of interest.

• **Species Registries.** Registries are single-species listings of numbers and locations of animals. They do not contain the detailed vital information necessary for population analysis, but do provide a starting point for locating institutions that once held specimens (Shoemaker and Flesness, appendix 4, this volume).

• **In-House Institutional Records.** In-house inventory records are the primary source of data. Once institutions that have had or currently have specimens of interest are identified, they can be contacted for information on the history, status, and details of their collection. Again, it is important to stress the importance of collecting historical data.

The basic data required on each animal for population analysis and management are:

• Individual identification: a simple numeric lifetime identity (i.e., studbook number). To achieve this identification, it may be necessary to link a series of different ID numbers (e.g., the local ISIS specimen numbers) the animal has had as it has moved among institutions
• Sex
• Birth date
• Death date (it is vital to record stillbirths and aborted fetuses)
• Parentage
• Whether the individual is wild-caught
  Date and site of capture
  Possible relationship to other wild-caught animals (i.e., several animals captured in a nest or herd)
  Date animal entered captivity
• Date animal left captivity or was lost to follow-up (reintroduced into the wild, escaped, lost track of)
• Institutions/facilities where it has been, with dates of shipments

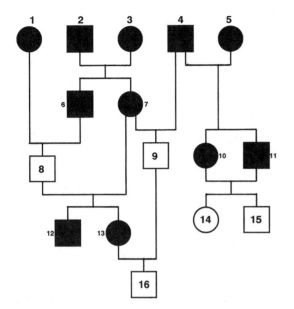

ID	Sex	Dam	Sire	Status
1	F	Wild	Wild	Dead Founder
2	M	Wild	Wild	Dead Founder
3	F	Wild	Wild	Dead Founder
4	M	Wild	Wild	Dead Founder
5	F	Wild	Wild	Dead Founder
6	M	3	2	Dead
7	F	3	2	Dead
8	M	1	6	Living
9	M	7	4	Living
10	F	5	4	Dead
11	M	5	4	Dead
12	M	7	8	Dead
13	F	7	8	Dead
14	F	10	11	Living
15	M	10	11	Living
16	M	13	9	Living

FIG. 26.2. Pedigree of a population founded with 2.3 individuals. Squares, males; circles, females; open squares and circles, living animals. Numbers are unique identifiers for each individual. The pedigree listing is presented on the right.

• Information on circumstances and cause of death
• Reproductive condition (e.g., castrated male, postreproductive female)
• Group compositions (who is housed with whom)
• Reproductive opportunities (whether animal was given opportunities to breed, and when)
• Information on past breeding experience (e.g., proven breeder?)
• Tattoo or other permanent identification marks (e.g., transponder number)
• Carcass disposition and tracer (e.g., "Sent to Univ. Kansas Museum, #12345")
• Miscellaneous comments (unusual behavior or phenotype, etc.)

When dealing with unknown or missing data, record as much information as possible. Dates or events that are partially or completely unknown should be noted as such. Unknown dates are a particular problem. Usually events are dated to the nearest day, month, or year. Uncertain parentage is also a common problem, particularly in herd situations. Record all potential parents and, if possible, indicate the likelihood (e.g., based on behavioral data) of each being the actual parent (e.g., "*Comment:* Potential Sires/Likelihood: Stbk 123/50%; Stbk 1221/25%; Stbk 1212/25%).

Most analyses require that the data be computerized for easy access and manipulation. Standard formats for pedigree data have been developed (Shoemaker and Flesness, appendix 4, this volume), and a number of computerized studbook management and analysis software packages are available, including the Single Population Animal Record Keeping System (SPARKS: ISIS 1991), and the Zoo Research Studbook Management System (Princée 1989).

GENETIC ANALYSES

The purpose of genetic analyses is to describe the genetic characteristics of a population that are important for its management. These include information on the number of founders, the distribution of their genes among living animals, the relationships among individuals in the living population, and the capacity of the population to retain genetic variation. Results of genetic analyses are used in conjunction with results of demographic analyses to arrive at a carrying capacity for the captive population and formulate recommendations for managing the population at this carrying capacity. A step-by-step procedure for calculating these genetic characteristics follows.

1. Construct the pedigree for each animal in the population.

This "pedigree" can be in the form of a standard pedigree chart and/or simply a listing of each individual with its parents (fig. 26.2) that will be used with various pedigree analysis algorithms and computer programs. Pedigree charts are particularly useful for identifying pedigree bottlenecks as well as ancestors of special interest.

2. Identify the founders of the population.

A founder is an animal that
• is from outside the population (usually the wild)
• has no known ancestors in the population at its time of entry
• has descendants in the living population or is currently living and capable of reproduction (a potential founder)

Unless it is known otherwise, founders are assumed to be unrelated to each other. When the relationships of wild-caught animals are known or suspected (e.g., several chicks captured in the same nest), it is necessary to create "hypothetical" parents (or other ancestors) to define those relationships. These hypothetical ancestors are then defined as founders. It is useful to name all hypothetical founders in an easily identifiable fashion (e.g., studbook numbers beginning with the letter H).

Figure 26.3 illustrates the identification of founders in the captive population of black-footed ferrets, *Mustela nigripes* (Ballou and Oakleaf 1989). "Willa," "Emma," "Annie,"

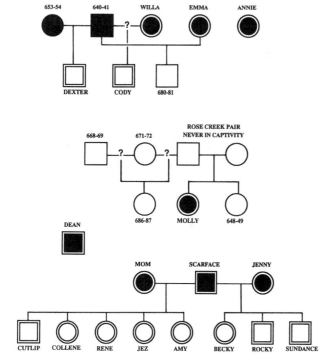

FIG. 26.3. Pedigree of the founding population of black-footed ferrets. Squares, males; circles, females; solid squares and circles, founders; double-bordered squares and circles, living animals. A question mark indicates uncertain parentage. (Reprinted with permission from U. S. Seal et al., eds., *Conservation Biology and the Black-footed Ferret* [New Haven: Yale University Press, ©1989].)

"Mom," "Jenny," "Dean," and "Scarface" are shown as founders since they are wild-caught, have no known ancestors in the captive population, and are thought not to be closely related to each other. Although "Molly" has known relatives, they were either never in captivity or died without producing offspring; she is therefore considered a founder. Female "653-54" and male "640-41" are also founders because "Dexter," who is living, is an offspring of both and "Cody" is an offspring of male "640-41."

Molecular genetic analyses (e.g., DNA fingerprinting) can be useful in examining relationships of wild-caught animals or even captive-born animals without pedigrees (Ryder and Fleischer, chap. 25, this volume; Morin and Ryder 1991; Avise et al. 1995; Ashworth and Parkin 1992; Geyer et al. 1993). However, these techniques may be useful for determining only first-order relatedness (e.g., full sibling or parent-offspring relationships).

3. Compute the genetic contribution of each founder to each living individual as well as to the living population as a whole.

Founder contribution is the percentage of an individual's or a population's genes that have descended from each founder. Calculations are based on the Mendelian premise that each parent passes (on average) 50% of its genes to its offspring, 25% to its grandoffspring, and so forth. Each founder's genetic contribution to living individuals can be calculated by constructing each individual's pedigree back to the founders and applying these Mendelian rules of segregation.

TABLE 26.1.   Founder Contributions for the Pedigree Illustrated in Figure 26.2

| Founder | Living individuals | | | | | Pop. avg. | Retentio |
	8	9	14	15	16		
1	.50	0	0	0	.13	.126	.500
2	.25	.25	0	0	.31	.162	.484
3	.25	.25	0	0	.31	.162	.487
4	0	.50	.50	.50	.25	.350	.803
5	0	0	.50	.50	0	.200	.612
Mean kinship	.150	.228	.238	.238	.244		

Note: Average proportion of each individual's genes that has descended from each founder. See text for explanation of retention and mean kinship.

The founder's genetic contribution to the current population's gene pool is its contribution averaged across all living individuals (table 26.l). Algorithms and computer programs are available for calculating founder contributions from pedigree data (Ballou 1983; Lacy 1990a).

Founder contributions in most captive populations are highly skewed, usually due to disproportionate breeding of a small proportion of the founders early in the population's history (fig. 26.4). Genetic diversity potentially contributed by the underrepresented founders is thus lost or at high risk of being lost due to genetic drift.

4. Calculate the loss of founder alleles due to genetic drift and pedigree bottlenecks.

Further loss of genetic diversity occurs when genetic drift causes founder alleles to be lost from the population. Extreme cases of genetic drift are often referred to as pedigree bottlenecks, occurring when the genetic contribution of a founder passes through only one or a few individuals. For example, only 50% of a founder's genes survive to the next generation if it produces only one offspring, 75% survive if it produces two offspring, and so forth. Bottlenecks may occur during the first generation of captive breeding if only one or two offspring of a founder live to reproduce. However, the genetic drift caused by such bottlenecks can occur at any point in the pedigree, resulting in gradual erosion of the founders' alleles. The more "pathways" a founder's genes have to the living population, the less loss will occur. Therefore, even though a large proportion of a population's gene pool may have descended from a particular founder, the population may represent only a fraction of that founder's genetic diversity.

The proportion of a founder's genes that survive to the current population is referred to as gene retention or gene survival. Although exact methods for calculating retention have been developed (Cannings, Thompson, and Skolnick 1978), it is often estimated using Monte Carlo simulation procedures ("gene dropping": MacCluer et al. 1986). "Gene drop" procedures assign two uniquely identifiable alleles to each founder. Alleles are passed, randomly, from parents to offspring according to the rules of Mendelian segregation, and the distribution and pattern of alleles among living animals are examined after each simulation (fig. 26.5). The simulations are repeated several thousand times, and the re-

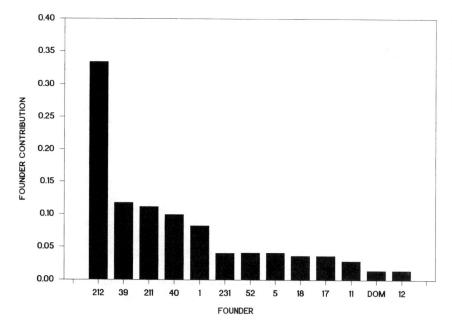

FIG. 26.4.   Founder contributions in the 1988 captive population of Przewalski's horses, *Equus przewalskii*. The distribution is heavily skewed due to disproportionate breeding among the founders early in the population's history. "DOM" is a Mongolian domestic mare that was bred to a Przewalski's horse in 1960.

GENE DROP ANALYSIS

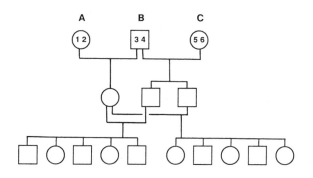

GENE DROP ANALYSIS

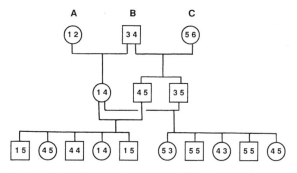

FIG. 26.5.   Gene drop analysis. *(a)* Each founder is assigned two unique alleles. *(b)* The alleles are then "dropped" through the pedigree according to the rules of Mendelian segregation; each allele has a 50% chance of being passed on to an offspring. At the end of the simulation, the pattern and distribution of alleles in the living population (bottom row) are examined. The simulation is repeated several thousand times and results are averaged across simulations to give gene retention. Note that allele 2 from founder A and allele 6 from founder C have been lost.

tention for each founder is calculated as the average percentage, across all simulations, of the founder's alleles that have survived to the living population. The retention estimates for the sample pedigree shown in figure 26.2 are listed in table 26.1. The retention for founder 1 is only 50% because she produced only one offspring, while the retention for founder 4 is higher because his genes have multiple pathways to the living population.

Gene drop analyses provide information about the distribution of founder genes in the living population that data on founder contribution do not. This is particularly true for deep, complex pedigrees, in which using founder contribution alone to determine the founders' genetic contribution to the population can be very misleading. Figure 26.6 illustrates the effects of pedigree structure on gene flow in two pedigrees that have equal levels of inbreeding and founder contribution but different levels of gene retention.

Since both skewed founder contributions and loss of alleles due to genetic drift result in the loss of founders' genetic diversity, the genetic contribution of the founders to the gene pool may be less than expected. Lacy (1989) introduced the concept of founder genome equivalent (f_g) to illustrate the combined effect skewed founder contribution and genetic drift have on the genetic diversity of a population. f_g is the number of founders that would be required to obtain the levels of genetic diversity that are observed in the current population if the founders were all equally represented and had retained all their alleles in the living population. It is calculated as

$$f_g = \frac{1}{\sum_{i=1}^{N_f} (p_i^2/r_i)} \qquad (26.1)$$

where N_f is the number of founders, p_i is the founder contribution of founder i to the population, and r_i is founder i's retention. Our sample population in figure 26.2 has 5 foun-

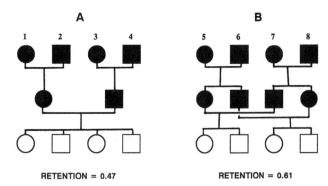

A

B

RETENTION = 0.47   RETENTION = 0.61

FIG. 26.6.   Gene drop analysis applied to two similar pedigrees. Squares, males; circles, females; open squares and circles, living animals. Pedigrees A and B each have four founders and four living animals. Founder contribution to living animals is identical for both pedigrees (25% from each founder) and all animals are non-inbred. However, genes from each founder in pedigree A pass through only one individual, creating a severe bottleneck. Genes from each founder in pedigree B pass through two individuals, creating less severe bottlenecks. As a result, more of the founder alleles in pedigree B are retained in the living population than in pedigree A.

ders, but because of retention problems and skewed founder contribution, they have an f_g of only 2.8. In essence, they behave genetically like 2.8 idealized founders.

The f_g values are often calculated with living founders excluded from the analysis. Living founders have 100% retention, and including them assumes that their alleles have been "captured" in the population, even though they may have no living descendants. Excluding living founders provides a more realistic summary of the genetic status of the population, particularly if there are many founders who are not likely to contribute offspring to the gene pool. Comparing the f_g calculated with living founders excluded with the f_g when they are included shows the contribution that genetic management can make if 100% of the living founders' genes can be retained in the population.

5. Calculate measures of genetic importance for each individual.

When selecting animals for breeding, it is useful to rank individuals according to their genetic "importance." Individuals carrying genes from overrepresented founders are not as genetically valuable as those carrying genes from underrepresented founders. A number of methods have been used to rank animals according to their genetic importance. One is the Founder Importance Coefficient (*fic*: Ballou and Lacy 1995), which is the weighted average of the founder contributions within each individual, with the population founder contribution acting as the weights. However, the *fic* does not take into consideration the effect of retention on an individual's genetic value and could potentially produce misleading results. For this reason, it has not been extensively used to measure genetic importance.

A more appropriate measure of genetic importance is mean kinship (*mk*). Mean kinship is the average of the kinship coefficients between an individual and all living individuals (including itself) in the population (Ballou and Lacy 1995; Lacy 1990a):

$$mk_i = \frac{\sum_{i=1}^{N} k_{ij}}{N} \qquad (26.2)$$

where mk_i is the mean kinship of individual i; k_{ij} is the coefficient of kinship between individuals i and j; and N is the number of living animals in the population (Ballou and Lacy 1995). The kinship coefficient is the probability that two alleles, taken at random from two individuals, are identical by descent (Crow and Kimura 1970). It is a measure of the genetic similarity of the individuals and is the same as the inbreeding coefficient of any offspring they would produce. Individuals who are carriers of rare genes will have low values of *mk* because they have few relatives in the population, whereas individuals who carry genes shared with many individuals will have a high *mk*. Ranking individuals according to their *mk* values provides a quick method for identifying genetically important animals.

Both *mk* and f_g relate directly to maintenance of genetic diversity in populations. Gene diversity, the expected level of heterozygosity of the population, can be calculated as either $1 - mk$ or $1 - 1/2f_g$; the two expressions are equivalent. Thus, breeding strategies to minimize *mk* or to maximize f_g will both maximize gene diversity (Ballou and Lacy 1995). Computer programs are available for calculating *mk* values (Lacy 1990a). Values of *mk* for the sample pedigree in figure 26.2 are shown in table 26.1.

Another measure of genetic importance is genetic uniqueness, which is the probability that a gene carried by an individual is unique (i.e., not carried by any other living animal). Genetic uniqueness is calculated using the gene drop analysis described above and can also be used to rank individuals by genetic importance (Ballou and Lacy 1995).

6. Calculate inbreeding coefficients of all individuals in the population as well as kinship coefficients between all living individuals.

Inbreeding is the mating of related individuals. If two parents are related, their offspring will be inbred, and the more closely related the parents are, the more inbred their offspring will be. The degree to which an individual is inbred is measured by its inbreeding coefficient *(f)*, which is the probability of its receiving the same allele from each parent (i.e., that the alleles are identical by descent). Offspring of father/daughter, mother/son, or full-sib matings are 25% inbred; offspring of first-cousin matings are 6.25% inbred. Inbreeding coefficients are used to examine the effects of inbreeding in the population (see below) and to determine the degree of relatedness between individuals. Algorithms and computer programs for calculating inbreeding coefficients from computerized pedigrees are available (Ballou 1983; Boyce 1983; Lacy 1990a; ISIS 1991).

7. Estimate the population's effective population size.

The extent and rate of loss of genetic diversity depends on the size of the population. However, the size of relevance is not simply the number of individuals; rather, it is the genetically effective population size (N_e). The effective size of a population is a measure of how well the population maintains genetic diversity from one generation to the next.

Genetic diversity is lost at the rate of $1/2N_e$ per generation. Populations with small effective population sizes lose genetic diversity at a faster rate than those with large effective population sizes (see fig. 26.1).

The concept of N_e is based on the genetic characteristics of a theoretical or ideal population that experiences no selection, mutations, or migration and in which all individuals are asexual and have an equal probability of contributing offspring to the next generation. Extensive population genetic models have been developed to examine the loss of genetic diversity over time in an ideal population (Kimura and Crow 1963). However, real populations differ greatly from the ideal. Estimating how rapidly a real population loses genetic diversity requires comparison of the genetic characteristics of the real population with those of the ideal population. A real population that loses genetic diversity at the same rate as an ideal population of size 50 (1% per generation) has an effective population size of 50, regardless of its actual size. Strictly defined, the effective size of a population is the size of a theoretically ideal population that loses genetic diversity at the same rate as the population of interest (Hedrick 1983). Once an effective population size is calculated, the rate at which the population loses genetic diversity can be estimated.

In general, the effective size of a population is based primarily on three characteristics: the number of breeders, their sex ratio, and the relative numbers of offspring they produce during their lifetime (their "lifetime family size"). Each of these characteristics can strongly influence a population's effective size. In general, a large number of breeders will pass on a larger proportion of the parental generation's genetic diversity than will only a few breeders. A heavily biased sex ratio in the breeders will likely result in loss of genetic diversity since the underrepresented sex will contribute an unequally large proportion of the offspring's genetic diversity. An equal sex ratio is preferable since it assures that the gene pool will receive genes from a larger number of breeders than when the sex ratio is highly skewed. Differences in family size also result in loss of genetic diversity since some individuals contribute few or no offspring to the gene pool while others producing large numbers of offspring contribute more to the gene pool. The amount of genetic diversity passed from one generation to another is, in general, maximized when all breeders produce the same number of young (i.e., family sizes are equal and the variance in family size is zero).

One method commonly used to calculate N_e is to assume that the population is not growing, has nonoverlapping generations, and that family sizes have a Poisson (random) distribution—this is the theoretically expected distribution if each individual in the population has an equal opportunity to breed. Under these assumptions the effective population size can be calculated from

$$N_e = \frac{4 * N_m * N_f}{N_m + N_f} \qquad (26.3)$$

where N_m and N_f are the total numbers of different adult males and females in the population over one generation.

Unfortunately, in captive populations, family size distributions are rarely determined by random mating and are not Poisson in form. In unmanaged populations many more adults than expected may fail to produce offspring, while in intensively managed populations fewer adults than expected may fail to produce. A more accurate method of estimating N_e incorporates information on family size. The family size of an individual is the total number of offspring it produces during its lifetime and that survive to adulthood. Ideally, only individuals who have completed their reproductive lives (are postreproductive or have died) should be used for these calculations. However, Lande and Barrowclough (1987) describe a method for estimating future reproductive performance for individuals still breeding. Both the mean family size ($\bar{k}$) and the variance in family size (V_k) need to be calculated across all individuals; individuals who fail to breed must be included, contributing family sizes of zero. These parameters can be calculated directly from studbook data.

Since $\bar{k}$ and V_k are measured over individual lifetimes, they provide accurate estimates only if the population has been stable for a relatively long time (several generations). This is unlikely for most rapidly changing captive populations, and calculations of $\bar{k}$ and V_k may not represent current population trends. Accurate estimates of current effective sizes are therefore difficult to calculate.

With estimates of $\bar{k}$ and V_k for each sex (if available), it is possible to calculate N_e separately for each sex. The effective size of males is:

$$N_{e(m)} = \frac{N_m * \bar{k}_m - 1}{\bar{k}_m + \dfrac{V_{km}}{\bar{k}_m} - 1} \qquad (26.4)$$

where $\bar{k}_m$ is the average number of young surviving to adulthood across all males; N_m is the number of adult males in the population during a generation; and $V_{k(m)}$, the variance in number of young surviving to adulthood, is defined as:

$$V_{k(m)} = \frac{\Sigma (k_m - \bar{k}_m)^2}{N_m} \qquad (26.5)$$

where the sum is over the number of adult males in the population, and k_m is the number of offspring surviving to adulthood for each male.

The effective size for females ($N_{e(f)}$) is calculated from equation (26.4) using family size data for females. The effective size for the overall population is then determined using equation (26.3), replacing N_m with $N_{e(m)}$ and N_f with $N_{e(f)}$.

The effective population size can be compared with the true population size *(N)* by calculating the ratio of N_e/N. It is theoretically possible for the effective size to be almost twice the true size if the variance in family size is zero. In reality, N_e is almost always less than the true size. Ratios of N_e/N in captive populations not genetically managed have been measured at between 0.3 and 0.5 (Flesness 1986; table 26.2).

Effective size may change radically over time. Lack of genetic management in the past may have caused N_e/N ratios to be very low. Therefore, the data used to estimate the current effective size should be relatively recent (over the last 5 years). Likewise, estimates of future effective sizes should be based on future management goals (i.e., attempts to maxi-

TABLE 26.2.   Effective Population Size for the Captive Population of Golden Lion Tamarins during a One-Generation (6-year) Period between 1981 and 1987

Variable	Males	Females
Number of adults in the population[a]	$N_m = 269$	$N_f = 275$
Mean number of offspring[b]	$\bar{k}_m = 1.7$	$\bar{k}_f = 1.6$
Variance in number of offspring[c]	$V_{km} = 12.1$	$V_{kf} = 13.5$
Effective size by sex (equation 26.4)	$N_{em} = 58.4$	$N_{ef} = 48.6$
Overall effective size (equation 26.3)	$N_e = 106$	
Actual population size[d]	$N = 357$	
Ratio of effective size to real size	$N_e/N = 0.30$	

[a] Calculated from total number of males and females that lived in the population between 1981 and 1987.
[b] Mean number of offspring surviving to age of sexual maturity (18 months) per adult.
[c] Variance in number of offspring surviving to age of sexual maturity.
[d] Harmonic mean of the population size between 1981 and 1987.

mize N_e while also aspiring to other objectives, such as zero population growth). Moreover, N_e/N ratios may be very different during the growth and carrying capacity phases of the population. Table 26.2 illustrates a calculation of the effective population size for one generation in the captive history of the golden lion tamarin.

There is an appreciable literature on effective population sizes (Lande and Barrowclough 1987; Ballou 1987a; Ryman et al. 1981; Hill 1972; Kimura and Crow 1963). Most computational methods (including those above) are derived for populations with nonoverlapping generations, rarely the case in vertebrate species. Lande and Barrowclough (1987) and Harris and Allendorf (1989) present methods for calculating effective population sizes in populations with overlapping generations. Those interested in a more detailed discussion should refer to their original articles.

8. Conduct various biochemical analyses that measure genetic variability and relationships.

Estimates of genetic variation are helpful primarily for identifying the extent of genetic differences between populations or taxa (Wayne et al. 1986; Ryder and Fleischer, chap. 25, this volume). If large differences (e.g., chromosomal differences) are found within a managed population, it may be necessary to reevaluate the goal of the program and possibly manage the population as two separate units (Templeton et al. 1986). In the words of an emerging terminology, large genetic differences may be evidence that there is more than one "evolutionarily significant unit" (ESU) within a species (see Barrowclough and Flesness, chap. 24, this volume). Interbreeding individuals from different ESUs may result in reduced survival and reproduction (outbreeding depression; see below). Unfortunately, criteria have not yet been developed to indicate what magnitude of genetic differences constitutes separate ESUs. Where different ESUs are suspected, additional analyses on morphological, behavioral, and biogeographical considerations should be conducted and considered.

Levels of genetic variation may provide information on the demographic and genetic history of the population. However, the goal of maintaining genetic diversity should not be abandoned if little or no variation is measured. It is not yet clear how representative currently measurable variation may be of the actual genetic diversity in an individual or population. There may be more diversity than can be detected by existing methods, and in the face of such uncertainty, the only prudent course of action is to manage as if diversity were present. In any case, it may be imperative to maintain what little genetic variation is present for the long-term fitness of the population.

As mentioned earlier, biochemical analyses may also be useful in resolving questions regarding parentage and in identifying relationships among founders. Long-term biochemical studies can be used to monitor the change of genetic variation in a population over time (Wayne et al. 1986). A comparison of the empirically estimated loss of variation with the theoretical loss of variation estimated from "gene drop" or similar analyses might provide insight into the types and degree of selection acting on captive populations.

It is not recommended that selection of breeding individuals be based on individual levels of heterozygosity estimated from biochemical methods. Heterozygosity at a few isozyme loci is often a poor indicator of overall individual heterozygosity (Hedrick et al. 1986; Lande and Barrowclough 1987). In addition, specific selection for known heterozygous loci (e.g., MHC loci: Hughes 1991) may select against heterozygous loci not sampled electrophoretically and decrease the overall level of genetic diversity in the population (Haig, Ballou, and Derrickson 1990; Miller and Hedrick 1991; Gilpin and Wills 1991; Vrijenhoek and Leberg 1991).

9. Adjust for uncertain parentage.

Lack of individual identification and uncertain parentage will complicate genetic analyses. This problem is common in species managed as herds, in which individual dams are often not identified, and in species in which more than one breeding male has access to females, resulting in uncertain paternity. Depending on the extent of unknown parentage, a number of different approaches can be taken.

a. Exclude individuals with unknown parentage or ancestors from the managed population. This approach is practical only if few individuals are involved and they are not otherwise important to the population. In such cases, a determining factor in the decision will be the percentage of an individual's genes that have descended from unknown ancestors. Small percentages of unknown ancestry may be acceptable. Animals who have some degree of unknown ancestry but also have ancestors whose genes are relatively rare could be kept in the population to perpetuate the contribution of underrepresented founders (see "Population Management" below). Willis (1993) points out that excluding animals of unknown parentage may result in maintaining lower levels of diversity than retaining them.

b. If questionable parentage is limited to only a few individuals, run the genetic and demographic analyses under all possible combinations to give the complete range of outcomes. If the results are insensitive to parentage possibilities, the questionable parentage should have little effect on management decisions. If the results are highly dependent on parentage, other options for analyzing the pedigree should be explored. An alternative strategy is to select the worst-case scenario as the basis for management decisions.

c. Use the potential parent most likely to be the true parent for the pedigree analysis.

d. Create hypothetical parents that represent an agglomeration of all potential parents. If the potential parents are all equally likely to be the true parent, then a new, average, "hypothetical" parent can be created. It is given a "dummy" ID number for the genetic analysis and considered as the sire (or dam) of the offspring in question. The founder contribution of the "hypothetical" parent is then calculated as the average of the founder contributions of the possible parents. Creating an "average" parent is most appropriate if the founder contributions of the potential parents are not too different. If the differences between the potential parents are very large (especially if the potential parents are founders), other options should be considered. Inbreeding coefficients are calculated by assuming that the "hypothetical" parent is unrelated to its mate and the rest of the population. In most cases, this will underestimate inbreeding coefficients for the descendants of the unknown parent(s). It is better to assume worst-case scenarios: that is, the closest relationships among putative parents.

e. When groups have been managed for several generations without individual animal identification, create hypothetical pedigrees. "Black box" populations are common in herding species kept in large groups. An example of how a worst-case strategy can be used to utilize at least some of the founder potential in such groups is the AZA Species Survival Plan for Grevy's zebra, *Equus grevyi*. With this species, there were a number of very large herds in which individual parentage was not recorded. However, considerable useful information was known: each herd had been established by a number of founder animals (usually one stallion and several mares); there had been a limited number of further immigrants of known origin to the herds; only one stallion was in each herd in any breeding season; and the dates of birth of all individual foals born into the herds were documented.

It was first assumed that a single founder female established the herd; that is, all actual founder females were amalgamated into a "hypothetical" founder female that was assigned a "dummy" ID number. All offspring born during the first few years (or a period of time equal to the age of sexual maturity for the species) were then considered to be offspring of the herd stallion and this hypothetical dam. After this first cohort, it was assumed that daughters of this pair would have matured and bred with their father. Therefore, an F_1 hypothetical female was created. The parents of this female were the herd stallion and the hypothetical founder female. Thereafter, all offspring born in the herd traced 75% of their genes to the founder stallion and only 25% to the hypothetical founder female.

Such a strategy is most useful if the herd was established by known founders. Obviously, this strategy will underestimate the actual number of founders for the herd as well as the genetic diversity involved. Inbreeding coefficients will be overestimated when a number of different breeding animals are combined under one "hypothetical" parent. However, within the herd, inbreeding coefficients will be relative, and closely related individuals will have higher coefficients than less closely related individuals.

When "hypothetical" parents or founders are created to satisfy genetic analysis requirements, individuals with unknown ancestors in their pedigree should be clearly labeled to indicate that both their founder contributions and inbreeding coefficients are based on hypothetical data.

DEMOGRAPHIC ANALYSES

The purposes of demographic analyses are to calculate basic life tables and population dynamics for the captive population; determine a carrying capacity for the captive population compatible with genetic, demographic, and resource limitations; and determine lifetime and annual reproductive objectives for each individual.

1. Demographic Characteristics of the Population
Basic demographic data of interest to the captive manager are:

a. Size of the current population and number of institutions and geographic regions over which it is distributed. This tabulation will usually be an immediate result of the data collection process (see above). It may also be useful to estimate the numbers and distribution of other taxa with similar "captive ecologies" (i.e., space and resource requirements) in order to estimate the total captive carrying capacity for the species.

b. Age and sex structure of the population. These distributions show the proportion and sex ratio of the population in each age class (fig. 26.7).

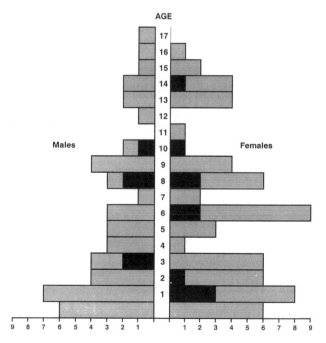

Fig. 26.7. Male and female age structures for the 1983 captive Sumatran tiger, *Panthera tigris sumatrae*, population. The solid area shows the number, sex ratio, and ages of proven breeders in the population. (From Ballou and Seidensticker 1987.)

c. Age-specific survivorship and fertility rates. Survivorship and fertility rates are calculated separately for each sex from age-specific tallies of birth and death events in the population and are usually presented in the form of a life table (Caughley 1977). A variety of different procedures have been developed to calculate life tables (Caughley 1977; Foose and Foose 1983; Foose and Ballou 1988). Table 26.3 is a life table for the captive population of golden lion tamarins.

TABLE 26.3.   Life Table Calculations for Captive Female Golden Lion Tamarins for the Period 1981–1987

Age class (years)	p_x[a]	l_x[b]	m_x[c]
0	0.61	1.00	0.00
1	0.87	0.61	0.00
2	0.90	0.53	0.32
3	0.92	0.48	0.60
4	0.92	0.44	0.74
5	0.91	0.40	0.78
6	0.90	0.37	0.72
7	0.90	0.33	0.59
8	0.89	0.30	0.53
9	0.88	0.27	0.53
10	0.86	0.23	0.53
11	0.82	0.20	0.65
12	0.76	0.17	0.89
13	0.78	0.13	0.88
14	0.88	0.10	0.52
15	0.97	0.09	0.13
16	1.00	0.08	0.00
17	1.00	0.08	0.00
18	1.00	0.08	0.00
19	0.75	0.08	0.00
20	0.25	0.06	0.00
21	0.00	0.02	0.00

[a] Proportion of females surviving from age class x to age $x + 1$.
[b] Proportion of offspring surviving to age class x.
[c] Average number of female offspring born to a female of age x.
Source: Ballou 1987b.
Note: Demographic calculations (see Caughley 1977):
Net reproductive rate (R_o)

$$R_o = \sum_{x=0}^{21} l_x m_x = 2.43$$

Exponential growth rate (r)

$$\sum_{x=0}^{21} e^{-rx} l_x m_x = 1.00$$

Solution for $r = 0.149$
$\lambda = e^r = 1.16$

Generation length (T)

$$T = \sum_{x=0}^{21} x e^{-rx} l_x m_x = 5.28$$

Growth rate per generation = $\lambda^T = 2.19$

No. female births required for zero population growth at carrying capacity of 250 females (see Keyfitz 1968)

$$= 250 * \frac{1}{\sum_{x=0}^{21} l_x} = 41$$

Because life tables derived from historical data may reflect past rather than current population trends, life tables should be based on relatively recent data (e.g., the last 5 years). However, in many populations there may not be enough recent data to construct a reliable life table, and in those cases historical data can be used to increase sample sizes.

In situations in which no data are available (e.g., because no captive population has previously existed), life table data can be estimated from basic life history data on the species (age of first reproduction, age of last reproduction, litter size) as well as from data on similar species in captivity. ISIS is a valuable source for rough survival and fecundity rates of captive populations (Shoemaker and Flesness, appendix 4, this volume).

d. Any factors that adversely affect survival and reproduction rates and patterns. Evidence of reproductive failure and high mortality rates should be investigated immediately. In addition to medical, nutritional, physiological, and behavioral causes, potential genetic causes should be examined. The deleterious effects of inbreeding on survival and reproduction (inbreeding depression) have been observed in many captive populations (Ralls and Ballou 1983; Templeton and Read 1984). Although genetic in cause, its effects are demographic and can include lower population growth rates, smaller populations, and, consequently, even higher rates of inbreeding (Gilpin and Soulé 1986). If such inbreeding depression is severe, inbreeding should be minimized.

Outbreeding depression, a reduction in fitness caused by hybridization between individuals from differently adapted or coadapted populations, can also reduce breeding success (Templeton et al. 1986). Although rarely documented in mammals or other vertebrates, outbreeding depression is most likely when ESU boundaries are transgressed (see Barrowclough and Flesness, chap. 24, this volume), either knowingly or not (e.g., owl monkeys, *Aotus trivirgatus:* Cicmanec and Campbell 1977). Templeton and Read (1984), Templeton et al. (1986), and Lynch (1991) discuss methods for examining the effects of outbreeding in captive populations. Careful consideration of the ESU status of populations should mitigate potential outbreeding problems.

2. Demographic Parameters Estimated from Life Table Data

A number of different demographic parameters are calculated directly from life tables:

a. Generation length *(T)*. Generation length is the average age at which a parent produces young (Hedrick 1983). It can be calculated directly from estimates of survival and fecundity rates (see table 26.3; Caughley 1977) and is used to estimate a minimum viable population (MVP) size for the captive population (see below). It should be calculated for each sex separately.

b. Population growth rate (λ). Life tables provide estimates of the expected growth rate of the population, assuming the estimated survival and fecundity rates remain stable over time (Caughley 1977). The growth rate is used to estimate the MVP size and the capacity of the population for self-sustainment. If it is less than 1, the population is declining; if greater than 1, the population is growing; and if equal to 1, the population size is stationary (constant).

If the growth rate is inadequate for the population to be self-sustaining, the focus of the management program should shift to research on reproductive, behavioral, and other biological and husbandry aspects of management to resolve the problems.

c. Stable age structure. The stable age structure is the eventual sex and age structure of the population if survival and fecundity rates remain stable over time (Caughley 1977).

d. Net reproductive rate (R_o). The net reproductive rate is the number of same-sex offspring produced by an average individual during its lifetime (see table 26.3). Conceptually, it is the number of same-sex animals an individual "replaces" itself with in the population. For stationary populations (zero population growth), R_o is 1: each animal exactly replaces itself in the population every generation. R_o is used to calculate animal lifetime reproductive objectives for population management.

e. Annual reproductive rates. The number of animals born each year in a stable population with growth rate λ is a function of the survival rate and the population growth rate. The annual number of female (or male) births required to achieve a population growth rate of λ for a stable population of size N is:

$$\text{Number of births} = \frac{N * \lambda}{\Sigma \lambda^{-x} \, l_x} \qquad (26.6)$$

where the summation in the denominator is over all age classes. The number of births are for the same sex from which the l_x values are calculated. For zero population growth ($\lambda = 1$), the number of births is $N/\Sigma l_x$. For example, 41 female golden lion tamarins need to be born each year to achieve zero population growth at a stable population size of 500 animals (250 females: see table 26.3). If the survival rates for males and females are the same, and if the sex ratio at birth is 1:1, the total number of births required is double the number calculated above.

f. Fertility, survival, and harvest rates necessary to maintain a stationary population. These parameters are used to develop management recommendations for designation of surplus and breeding rates, as well as to predict what effects managerial modifications of survival and fertility rates will have on the population (Beddington and Taylor 1973; see below).

* * *

Several computer programs are available to calculate these demographic parameters from life table data as well as to estimate life table data directly from computerized pedigrees (Bingaman and Ballou 1993; ISIS 1991). Table 26.3 presents calculations of values for generation length, population growth rate, and fertility rates for the captive population of golden lion tamarins.

3. Carrying Capacity Determination

For a managed population, the carrying capacity is an analytically established target size to which the program aspires. The process of establishing a carrying capacity involves reconciling the genetic and demographic goals of the population with the limited resources of zoological institutions.

Losses of both genetic diversity and demographic stochasticity are functions of population size. The smaller the population, the faster the loss of diversity, and the more unstable and susceptible to extinction it is. Thus, purely for genetic and demographic reasons, the captive population should be as large as possible. However, limited resources place severe restrictions on the sizes of captive populations. Similar species "compete" for captive habitat. Maintaining too large a population of any one taxon may deprive other needy taxa of captive resources; therefore, the carrying capacity for each taxon needs to be a compromise between maintaining some minimum viable population (MVP) size large enough for genetic and demographic goals to be realized and still allowing enough resources for other similar species' programs. While the MVP size determines the lower limit of the carrying capacity, the upper limit is determined by resource limitations.

a. Determine the lower limit of carrying capacity: minimum viable population size. The lower limit of the carrying capacity, the MVP, will be determined primarily by the long-term genetic and demographic objectives of the program and the biological characteristics of the population. As discussed above, the primary goal of most conservation-related captive propagation programs is to maintain genetic diversity and demographic security. More specifically, MVP size depends on:

- The kind and amount of genetic diversity to be preserved
- The length of time the population is to be managed
- The probability that the population will survive this time period
- The biological characteristics of the population (i.e., number of founders, generation length, effective size, and population growth rate)

The 90%/200 year rule of thumb (see "Captive Management Goals" above) is a common approach to determining how much diversity is required and for how long it should be maintained (Soulé et al. 1986). Calculating the MVP size necessary to maintain 90% of the original heterozygosity for 200 years requires modeling the population's growth from its founding number to its carrying capacity through the 200-year period. Loss of genetic diversity can be conveniently visualized as occurring during three phases: the founding event, the growth to carrying capacity, and the management of a stable population at carrying capacity (fig. 26.8; Ballou 1987c). During each phase genetic diversity is lost at a different rate, and the overall loss of heterozygosity is the cumulative loss over all three phases. Loss of heterozygosity during the founding phase is a function of the effective size of the founding population. Equation (26.1) can be used to roughly estimate the effective size of the founding population from its sex ratio. Loss of heterozygosity during the growth phase is a function of the population's growth rate and how long (measured in animal generation lengths) it remains in the growth phase. Loss of heterozygosity during the carrying capacity phase is deter-

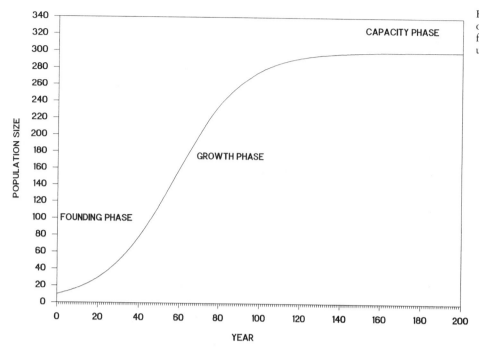

FIG. 26.8. Theoretical growth curve of a captive population showing the founding, growth, and capacity phases used to model loss of genetic diversity.

mined by the effective size of the population at carrying capacity and how long it stays at capacity, again measured in generations.

If the founder effective size, generation length, N_e/N ratio, and population growth rate are known, the carrying capacity required to maintain X% (e.g., 90%) of the variation for Y (e.g., 200) years can be calculated (Ballou 1987c). Graphs, algorithms, and computer programs have been developed for this purpose (Gilpin 1987; Ballou 1986; Soulé et al. 1986). Table 26.4 illustrates the MVP sizes required for a range of N_e/N ratios and effective founder sizes for a population growing at 8% per year.

A secondary consideration for determining the MVP size is demographic stochasticity and the susceptibility of the population to extinction due to chance or catastrophic events. Populations smaller than 50 or even 100 may be particularly vulnerable to "crashes" or extinctions due to random demographic events such as disease epidemics, natural disasters, or sex ratio distortions (Gilpin and Soulé 1986). Therefore, for demographic reasons, MVPs should be no smaller than 50 individuals (Foose et al. 1986). The MVP

based on genetic considerations will probably be large enough to insure a high probability of survival for 200 years for most captive populations, since distribution of animals among many zoos decreases the likelihood of total population extinction due to environmental stochasticity or catastrophe (Shaffer 1987). Demographic simulations can be conducted to estimate how susceptible populations with given demographic characteristics are to such chance events (Ewens et al. 1987; Goodman 1987; Lacy 1990b; Shaffer 1987). Demographic MVP models are discussed in detail in Soulé (1987).

Finally, it should be emphasized that there is no single MVP size that applies to all species or populations, nor is there a single magic-number MVP size that categorically applies to any one species all the time. Determination of MVPs depends on a number of factors. The simplistic determination of MVP described here is an example of the more general process known as population viability analysis (PVA; Soulé 1987; Gilpin and Soulé 1986).

b. Determine the upper limit of carrying capacity: captive resources. The upper limit on carrying capacity should be derived from an analysis of the amount of "captive habitat" (space and resources) currently being used by the target population and other taxa with similar "captive ecologies" (enclosure and resource requirements, exhibit value, etc.). Current population sizes and information on expansion plans can be used to estimate the captive habitat available. For example, Foose and Seal (1986) calculated the total number of enclosure spaces utilized by all large felids to determine the captive carrying capacity for Siberian tigers.

In addition, the number of different taxa in need of assistance from captive propagation programs and potentially competing for this captive space should be determined. This may require additional information on the status and trends of wild populations as well as consideration of taxonomic

TABLE 26.4. Carrying Capacities Necessary for Maintaining 90% of the Founders' Heterozygosity for 200 Years in a Population with Generation Length of 5 Years and a λ of 1.08 (8% Growth Rate per Year)

N_e/N ratio	Effective founder number				
	10	15	20	25	30
0.1	3620	2452	2084	1917	1822
0.3	1207	817	695	639	607
0.5	724	490	417	383	364
0.7	517	350	298	274	260
0.9	402	272	232	213	202
1.1	329	223	189	174	166

Source: After Soulé et al. 1986.

uniqueness. Division of the available "captive" habitat by the number of "competing" taxa will suggest the upper limit on carrying capacity for each taxon. These estimates can be refined if additional information is known about the MVP size requirements of the other "competing" taxa (Conway 1987; Foose, Seal, and Flesness 1987).

c. Establish the carrying capacity. With the lower limit of carrying capacity determined by MVP size requirements and the upper limit determined by captive resource allocation, a carrying capacity for the captive population can be established. The carrying capacity should be as large as possible within these limits. If the MVP size is larger than the population size allowed by resource allocation, then either the MVP requirements will have to be relaxed (reduce the time frame of concern and/or decrease the levels of diversity to be retained) or the biological characteristics of the population will have to be improved (acquire new founders, extend generation length, increase N_e/N ratio, and/or increase growth rate). Otherwise, it will be necessary to prioritize and select among competing taxa. The development of criteria for prioritizing taxa in need of conservation measures is complex and continues to be discussed by a number of conservation organizations (Foose, Seal, and Flesness 1987; Oates 1986; Foose 1983).

POPULATION MANAGEMENT

Genetic and demographic analyses provide the basis for formulating a captive propagation and management program, such as an AZA Species Survival Plan Masterplan (Foose and Seal 1986). Ideally, the program should provide specific recommendations for each individual in the population. More specific guidelines for population management include:

1. Attempt to obtain a sufficient number of founders to sample adequately both the heterozygosity and the allelic diversity in the source population.
Allelic diversity is lost much more rapidly than heterozygosity during bottleneck and founding events (Allendorf 1986; Fuerst and Maruyama 1986). Therefore, the primary concern is adequate sampling for allelic diversity, since this may require more founders than sampling for heterozygosity alone. Sampling for heterozygosity does, however, establish a lower limit for the effective founder size required. A sample of N effective founders retains on average $(1/2N) *$ 100% of the source population's heterozygosity. A general rule of thumb is to try to sample at least 95% of the source population's heterozygosity; this requires an effective founder size of at least ten (Denniston 1978).

The number of founders required to sample allelic diversity adequately depends on the allele frequencies in the source population. Marshall and Brown (1975), Denniston (1978), and Gregorius (1980) discuss the effective founder sizes required given various allele frequency distributions (table 26.5). Unfortunately, information on the distribution of allele frequencies in the source population is often not available. Marshall and Brown (1975) suggest that founder numbers adequate for effectively sampling allelic diversity be based on the most likely allele distributions, and con-

TABLE 26.5.   Founder Sizes Necessary to Sample All Alleles with Frequencies Equal to or Greater Than p with 95% and 99% Certainty

Allele frequency (p)	Certainty	
	95%	99%
.500	6	8
.300	11	15
.200	22	28
.100	51	66
.040	152	192
.010	754	916
.008	972	1,174

Source: After Gregorius 1980.

clude that effective founder sizes between twenty-five and fifty are sufficient in most cases. They emphasize that potential differences in genetic variation over the range of a population should be considered. Sampling strategies should attempt to compensate for and/or exploit known geographic patterns of genetic variation to optimize the levels of genetic diversity sampled, while at the same time striving to remain within the geographic boundary of the ESU.

Additional perspectives on the number of founders required will also derive from the MVP analysis described above. Specifying genetic and demographic objectives and other population characteristics will prescribe a minimum number of founders. The MVP analysis approach will also consider demographic as well as genetic factors in establishing minimum founder numbers.

It should be appreciated that founders will not necessarily or optimally enter the population only at the inception of a captive propagation project. Immigrants from the wild should periodically be incorporated into the captive population if possible. It should also be noted that failure to obtain an optimal genetic number of founders is *not* justification for cancelling plans to establish a captive propagation program. Wild-caught specimens, however, should be obtained only after extremely careful consideration of the potential effects of such removals on the wild population.

2. Expand the population size as rapidly as possible to the carrying capacity.
Genetic diversity is lost when growth rates are slow because small populations lose genetic diversity at a faster rate than large populations.

3. Stabilize the population at carrying capacity.
The current population size and growth rate determine whether the population is at, or when it will be at, carrying capacity. If the population is at or is approaching carrying capacity, demographic analysis can be used to determine how fertility and survivorship rates can be managed by "removals" of animals (harvests, culls) and/or regulation of reproduction (birth control) to stabilize the population at the desired carrying capacity (Beddington and Taylor 1973). This process may entail much "what if" analysis to determine how such managerial modifications of survivorship and fertility patterns will affect population size, growth rate, age distribution, and so forth. Table 26.6 shows how such an analysis can be applied to Siberian tigers. The ef-

TABLE 26.6.   Management Options for Stabilizing the Siberian Tiger Population at 250 Animals

Option	If reproduction is	Percentage of 0–1-year-olds to be removed	Percentage of each age class to be removed
1	Equivalent to 1956–1980 and litter size of 2.43 cubs	46	7
2	Adjusted to compensate for mortality and equally distributed over all ages	0	0
3	One litter of 2.43 cubs at any age	This level of reproduction appears insufficient to sustain the population with present mortality rates	
4	One litter of 3 cubs at age 4	0 (probably)	0 (probably)
5	Two litters of 2.43 cubs at age 5	This level of reproduction appears insufficient to sustain the population with present mortality rates	
6	Two litters of 2.43 cubs at ages 5 and 10	30	5
7	Two litters of 2.43 cubs at ages 4 and 7	35	8
8	Three litters of 2.43 cubs at ages 4, 9, and 12	53	10
9	Litters of 2.43 cubs in alternate years	72	15

Source: Foose and Seal 1986.

fects of these modifications on the effective population size should also be examined, since a reduction in the number of breeders can reduce N_e. Modifications that maintain a large effective size while still accomplishing the goal of stabilizing the population at carrying capacity should be explored (Dyke et al. 1986; Ryman et al. 1981).

4. Extend generation length as much as possible without jeopardizing demographic security.

Because genetic diversity is lost each generation, extending generation length *(T)* will reduce the amount of diversity lost during a given number of years. Alternatively, the same level of diversity can be retained with a smaller N_e if T is extended. Generation time can be lengthened by shifting the mean age of reproduction to later in life. This strategy, however, incurs greater risk of stochastic losses of animals before they can breed and may also result in reduction of fertility due to age-dependent factors.

5. Adjust representation of founder lineages to be proportional to the probable distribution of founder alleles surviving in the living population.

The most substantial part of any captive propagation program is the process of identifying which animals are to breed, how often, and with whom. The basic objective of this process is to compensate for highly skewed founder contribution distributions and loss of founder alleles by preferentially breeding descendants of underrepresented founders and restricting reproduction in those of overrepresented founders. However, this must be done within the framework of the demographic requirements of the population. The process involves four steps: (1) determining the *target founder contributions* that define the objectives for adjusting the population founder contributions; (2) determining *individual lifetime reproductive objectives* according to the genetic characteristics of each individual (i.e., how often animals are to breed); (3) determining *individual annual reproductive objectives* so that yearly population demographic needs are met (i.e., which animals are to breed each year); and (4) recommending *pairing* to accomplish all of the above (i.e., who is to breed with whom).

a. Determine the target founder contribution objectives for the population. Equalization of founder representation is usually not the optimal objective. Founder representation should not be equalized if some proportion of a founder's alleles have been lost as a result of bottlenecks in the pedigree (see "Genetic Analyses" above). With fewer genes to contribute, adjusting this founder's contribution to the same level as that of other founders not having experienced a bottleneck will overrepresent this founder's remaining genes in the population. For such founders, the founder contribution goals must be reduced according to their level of retention. For example, if a founder's retention is 50%, it could be considered only "one-half" of a founder and its contribution to the living population managed to a level of one-half that of the other founders.

Results of the gene drop and founder contribution analyses (see "Genetic Analyses" above) are used to compute a target distribution of founder representation that more accurately reflects how much of the founders' genetic diversity has survived to the living population (retention):

$$TF_i = \frac{r_i}{\sum\limits_{x=1}^{N_F} r_x} \qquad (26.7)$$

where TF_i is the target founder contribution for founder i; r_i is the proportion of founder i's alleles surviving to the living population (retention); and N_F is the number of founders in the living population. Genetic representation of founders with low retention should be managed at a lower level than that of well-represented founders. This strategy will increase the number of unique founder alleles maintained in the population. Table 26.7 shows the target founder representations for the pedigree in figure 26.2. Note that founders 2 and 3 are adequately represented according to the target founder contribution goal, whereas before they appeared to be underrepresented. The objective of genetic management then becomes attempting to shift the observed founder contributions toward the target founder contributions.

b. Combine genetic and demographic objectives to ar-

TABLE 26.7. Target Founder Contributions for Genetic Management of the Pedigree Shown in Figure 26.2

Founder	Current founder contribution	Parity[a] founder contribution	% genes surviving[b] (retention)	Target[c] founder contribution	Status of contribution[d]
1	.13	.20	.50	.17	Under
2	.16	.20	.48	.17	Adequate
3	.16	.20	.49	.17	Adequate
4	.35	.20	.80	.28	Over
5	.20	.20	.61	.21	Adequate

Note: Target founder contributions are based on the proportion of a founder's genes surviving to the living population (retention).

[a] Parity (equal representation) = 1/(number of founders).

[b] Proportion of each founder's genome surviving to the living population is based on a gene drop analysis with 5,000 simulations.

[c] See equation 26.7.

[d] Under, founder's genetic contribution is below that of its target—it is genetically underrepresented in the population; over, founder's genetic contribution is above that of its target—it is genetically overrepresented in the population; adequate, founder's genetic contribution is approximately that of its target.

rive at animal-by-animal breeding recommendations. As discussed above, demographic analyses can be used to determine the average lifetime reproductive requirements for individuals in the population (R_o). However, in order to modify current founder contributions to match target objectives, it is desirable for individuals descended from underrepresented founders to produce more than the average number of progeny, while individuals descended from overrepresented founders should produce fewer.

These individuals can be identified by examining the founder contribution within each individual. Animals with a high founder contribution from underrepresented founders (as defined by the target founder contribution) should be considered high-priority breeders (e.g., individual 8 in the sample pedigree, table 26.1). However, identifying preferred breeders by scanning founder contribution charts is often difficult. An individual may be descended from both over- and underrepresented founders, and contribution from overrepresented founders may be highly correlated with contribution from underrepresented founders. Additionally, if there are a large number of founders, the quantity of information that must be considered is formidable.

Diagnostic methods like mean kinship and genetic uniqueness simplify the process of identifying priority individuals (see "Genetic Analyses" above). Ranking of animals according to mean kinship provides a fast and simple diagnostic tool for identifying animals that are genetically valuable to the population. Furthermore, these ranking methods can be combined with the demographic requirements of the population to develop specific animal-by-animal breeding recommendations for each individual in the population. One strategy is to use the distribution of mean kinship to determine lifetime reproductive objectives for each individual. Different lifetime reproductive objectives are assigned to different levels of mean kinship: the lower the individual's *mk* value, the higher its lifetime reproductive objective. However, the scale must be established such that average lifetime reproductive objectives across all individuals achieve the overall demographic objectives. Scaling reproductive contribution according to *mk* should not

change the mean reproductive rate, only the variance across individuals.

The scaling of lifetime reproductive objectives with *mk* is dependent on how rapidly the current founder contributions are to be adjusted to match the target founder contributions. Large differences in lifetime reproductive objectives between descendants of over- and underrepresented founders will result in rapid convergence between current and target founder contributions. The range of lifetime reproductive objectives will most likely be determined by the reproductive biology of the species and how intensely the population can be managed. An example of scaling lifetime reproductive objectives according to mean kinship is shown in table 26.8.

If and when the population obtains its target distribution of founder representation, lifetime founder objectives (family sizes) should be equalized to maximize the effective size.

c. Schedule lifetime reproductive objectives to meet annual population growth objectives. Animal-by-animal breeding recommendations combine the population's yearly demographic requirements with the lifetime reproductive

TABLE 26.8. Lifetime Reproductive Recommendations for Individual Captive Golden Lion Tamarins Based on Distribution of Mean Kinship (*mk*) Values in the Population

Mean kinship range	% of population	Offspring objectives
< 0.019	12%	4
0.020 to 0.034	17%	3
0.035 to 0.050	45%	2
0.051 to 0.058	14%	1
> 0.058	12%	0
		Mean = 2.0

Note: The total number of offspring that should be produced and eventually bred per individual is a function of the individual's *mk* value. Individuals with low *mk* values carry genes that are uncommon in the population and should be bred more than individuals with common genes. Note that the mean number of births across all individuals is 2.0: each breeding pair only replaces itself and zero population growth is achieved.

goals for each individual. Demographic analyses determine the yearly number of births required to meet population growth objectives (e.g., rapid population growth or zero population growth). Given the species' litter size and breeding rates, this number can be translated into the number of pairs that need to be bred per year to accomplish the desired birth rate. For example, in golden lion tamarins, 82 births (41 female births) are needed each year for zero population growth (see table 26.3). The average litter size is 2.0, 25% of the breeding pairs fail to breed, 65% produce 1 litter per year, and 35% produce 2 litters per year. Sex ratios at birth are equal. Therefore, we need to maintain 40 breeding pairs per year to produce the 82 required births.

The animal-by-animal breeding recommendations must specify which individuals should be bred each year to meet these annual breeding requirements. The individuals selected for breeding are chosen from those who have not yet fulfilled their lifetime reproductive goals. Scheduling of which animals are to reproduce each year should take into consideration age and genetic importance so that aging, important animals are given reproductive priority. Scheduling should also take advantage of existing pairings or groups and institutions' capacities and interests. A schedule of which individuals should reproduce over the next 1–5 years is recommended.

d. Select pairings of animals among those scheduled for breeding. At this point, the specific individuals to be bred over the next several years will have been identified. The next, and final, step is to recommend pairings among those individuals. There are two principal criteria for determining who is to breed with whom. The first is to try to avoid pairing an animal from underrepresented founders with an animal from overrepresented founders. The offspring of such a pair would have founder contributions that are the average of the parents', and the underrepresented founder contribution would be linked to the overrepresented founder contribution; they could then no longer be managed independently. Therefore, when making pairing decisions, pair animals that are descended from underrepresented founders (i.e., low mean kinship) with similar animals. This strategy allows the underrepresented founder contributions to be increased in the population independently of the overrepresented founder contributions. At a later generation, when founder contributions are more evenly distributed, this is less of a concern.

It is often the case that pairings of animals with similar, underrepresented founder contributions will result in mates that are closely related to each other (a valuable brother/ sister pair will have similar, if not the same, mean kinship). Therefore, it is also important to examine relationships among potential mates and exclude pairings of closely related animals. This objective accomplishes two goals: (1) it reduces the degree of relationship within the population as a whole, therefore retaining higher levels of heterozygosity than would otherwise be retained; and (2) it reduces the potentially detrimental effects of inbreeding depression on survival and reproductive rates. Inbreeding effects are highly variable among species, and it is not possible to predict at what level inbreeding will have significant deleterious effects on the population (Brewer et al. 1990). Inbreeding

should be avoided or minimized if inbreeding depression is observed.

Unfortunately, inbreeding levels will increase in populations in which immigration is restricted. The minimum amount of inbreeding possible in a population depends on the levels of relatedness among the living animals. A rule of thumb often used in determining acceptable levels of inbreeding in a population uses the mean kinship value averaged across all living individuals. The average mk is equal to the expected inbreeding coefficient of the offspring that would be produced if all individuals in the population were bred randomly. To keep inbreeding levels low, pairings should be selected so that offspring have inbreeding coefficients no higher than the average mk.

It should be noted that minimizing inbreeding is not the primary criterion for genetic management. However, there should be an attempt to minimize inbreeding within the constraints of adjusting founder contributions toward target objectives and mating individuals to avoid linking overwith underrepresented founder contributions. There may be cases in which inbreeding is deliberately employed to purge a population of its deleterious alleles, as in the Speke's gazelle, *Gazella spekei*, program (Templeton and Read 1984). Intentional inbreeding of small populations is generally contrary to the goal of maintaining genetic diversity since it can drastically change the genetic characteristics of the population, possibly making it unsuitable for later release into the wild (Templeton and Read 1983).

6. Select against individuals with extreme outlying morphological and reproductive characteristics.

Such characteristics would include traits such as albinism and dwarfism. This stabilizing selection should help control levels of genetic load in the population (Frankham et al. 1986). Selection can and should be imposed within families by replacing individuals to be selected against with their siblings. This strategy will allow selection to be implemented while working within the constraints of equalizing family size.

7. Consider dividing the population into several subdivisions or demes among which gene flow (usually exchange of animals but also exchange of gametes or embryos) is regulated.

Subdivision of a population is advantageous for epidemiological protection (Dobson and May 1986) as well as for other practical reasons, such as reduction of shipping costs and hazards and simplification of management logistics. In addition, genetic advantages may accrue based on the theoretical argument that, without selection, random genetic drift will drive different alleles to fixation in different demes and, overall, maintain a higher level of allelic diversity (Chesser, Smith, and Brisbin 1980). However, the role of selection in captive populations is uncertain, and it is possible that similar types of selection, conscious or unconscious, will actually fix similar alleles in each deme, thereby decreasing the overall levels of genetic diversity. Furthermore, the smaller size of semi-isolated subdivisions may render them more vulnerable to demographic stochasticity. Subdivided populations with large numbers of animals in each division will benefit from the practical advantages without the consequences of some of the genetic and demographic uncertainties. It is not possible in this chapter to describe methods to determine the optimal numbers or sizes of subdivisions or the extent and rate of genetic exchange among them. More analyses are needed on the role of population subdivision in maintaining genetic diversity. The reader is referred to Lacy (1987) for discussion.

8. If possible, continually introduce new wild-caught founders into the population.

Additional genetic material will help to minimize loss of variation due to genetic drift. In some cases, it may be appropriate to devise a program of continual exchange of individuals (or genetic material) between wild and captive populations, taking care to minimize the associated epidemiological problems.

9. Utilize available reproductive technology to the fullest extent possible.

Reproductive technology (semen/ovum collection and storage, embryo transfer and freezing, etc.) should be considered a primary tool for assisting captive propagation programs in the long-term maintenance of genetic diversity. Such technology can facilitate exchange of germ plasm between wild and captive populations as well as effectively increasing the reproductive lifetimes of founders and their immediate descendants. By increasing generation length, adequate levels of genetic diversity can be maintained in smaller populations, leaving more room for populations of other needy species (Ballou and Cooper 1992).

Living founders who have not yet contributed to the population should be considered immediate candidates for germ plasm storage. Although reproductive technology is not yet available for most exotic species, it is a major focus of research by the reproductive community (Wildt 1989).

CONCLUSIONS

Zoological institutions are making a major contribution to the conservation of threatened and endangered species through captive propagation programs. Their commitment to the long-term preservation and management of captive populations is dependent upon developing cooperative captive propagation programs based on sound genetic and demographic principles. The essence of any captive propagation program is the recommendations indicating which animals are to breed, how often, and with whom. These individual-by-individual and institution-by-institution recommendations are based on the results of genetic and demographic analyses. The final result is a conservation strategy that pools the genetic and demographic potential of all the individuals in the population to satisfy the genetic and demographic needs of the population. Whenever possible, conservation strategies for wild and captive populations should be integrated to provide a comprehensive conservation plan for the species.

The technology of genetic and demographic management is growing rapidly, and experts in many areas are directing attention to the problems unique to this field. Ana-

lytic and biochemical techniques are becoming increasingly available for population managers to use in the numerous analyses required. In addition, our understanding of the genetic and demographic needs of captive populations continues to expand as more is learned about natural populations. Advances will continue to be incorporated into the procedures for developing captive propagation programs as they become available.

ACKNOWLEDGMENTS

We thank Katherine Ralls, Laurie Bingaman, Susan Haig, and Kathy Cooper as well as an anonymous reviewer for making many helpful comments on this chapter.

REFERENCES

Allendorf, F. W. 1986. Genetic drift and the loss of alleles versus heterozygosity. *Zoo Biol.* 5:181–90.

Allendorf, F. W., and Leary, R. F. 1986. Heterozygosity and fitness in natural populations of animals. In *Conservation biology: The science of scarcity and diversity*, ed. M. E. Soulé, 57–76. Sunderland, Mass.: Sinauer Associates.

Arnold, S. 1995. Monitoring quantitative genetic variation and evolution in captive populations. In *Population Management for Survival and Recovery*, ed. J. D. Ballou, M. Gilpin, and T. J. Foose, 295–317. New York: Columbia University Press.

Ashworth, D., and Parkin, D. T. 1992. Captive breeding: Can genetic fingerprinting help? *Symp. Zool. Soc. Lond.* 64:135–49.

Avise, J. C., S. M. Haig, O. A. Ryder, M. Lynch, and C. G. Geyer. 1995. Descriptive genetic studies: Applications in population management and conservation biology. In *Population Management for Survival and Recovery*, ed. J. D. Ballou, M. Gilpin, and T. J. Foose, 183–244. New York: Columbia University Press.

Bahner, B. 1991. Micronesian kingfisher SSP Program. In *AAZPA Annual Report on Conservation and Science 1990–91*, eds. M. Hutchins, R. J. Wiese, K. Willis, and S. Becker, 141–43. Wheeling, W.Va.: American Association of Zoological Parks and Aquariums.

Ballou, J. D. 1983. Calculating inbreeding coefficients from pedigrees. In *Genetics and conservation*, ed. C. M. Schonewald-Cox, S. M. Chambers, B. MacBryde, and L. Thomas, 509–20. Menlo Park, Calif.: Benjamin/Cummings.

———. 1986. *CAPACITY Lotus 1-2-3 software to calculate carrying capacities for captive populations*. Washington, D.C.: National Zoological Park.

———. 1987a. The concept of effective population size and its role in the genetic management of captive populations. *AAZPA Regional Conference Proceedings*, 43–49. Wheeling, W.Va.: American Association of Zoological Parks and Aquariums.

———. 1987b. *1986 international golden lion tamarin studbook*. Washington, D.C.: National Zoological Park.

———. 1987c. Small populations, genetic diversity, and captive carrying capacities. *AAZPA Annual Conference Proceedings*, 33–47. Wheeling, W.Va.: American Association of Zoological Parks and Aquariums.

Ballou, J. D., and Cooper, K. A. 1992. Application of biotechnology to captive breeding of endangered species. *Symp. Zool. Soc. Lond.* 64:183–296.

Ballou, J. D., and Lacy, R. C. 1995. Identifying genetically important individuals for management of genetic diversity in captive populations. In *Population management for survival and recovery*, ed. J. D. Ballou, M. Gilpin, and T. J. Foose, 76–111. New York: Columbia University Press.

Ballou, J. D., and Oakleaf, R. 1989. Demographic and genetic captive-breeding recommendations for black-footed ferrets. In *Conservation biology and the black-footed ferret*, ed. U. S. Seal, E. T. Thorne, M. A. Bogan, and S. H. Anderson, 247–67. New Haven: Yale University Press.

Ballou, J. D., and Seidensticker, J. 1987. The genetic and demographic characteristics of the 1983 captive population of Sumatran tigers *(Panthera tigris sumatrae)*. In *World conservation strategies for tigers*, ed. U. S. Seal and R. Tilson, 329–47. Park Ridge, N.J.: Noyes.

Beddington, J. R., and Taylor, D. B. 1973. Optimum age specific harvesting of a population. *Biometrics* 29:801–9.

Bingaman, L. E., and Ballou, J. D. 1993. *DEMOG 4.1: Lotus 1-2-3 spreadsheet demographic model*. Washington, D.C.: National Zoological Park.

Boyce, A. J. 1983. Computation of inbreeding and kinship coefficients on extended pedigrees. *J. Hered.* 74:400–404.

Brewer, B. A., Lacy, R. C., Foster, M. L., and Alaks, G. 1990. Inbreeding depression in insular and central populations of *Peromyscus* mice. *J. Hered.* 81:257–66.

Cannings, C., Thompson, E. S., and Skolnick, M. H. 1978. Probability functions on complex pedigrees. *Adv. Appl. Prob.* 10:26–61.

Caughley, G. 1977. *Analysis of vertebrate populations*. New York: John Wiley and Sons.

Chesser, R. K., Smith, M. H., and Brisbin, I. L. 1980. Management and maintenance of genetic variability in endangered species. *Int. Zoo Yrbk.* 20:146–54.

Cicmanec, J. C., and Campbell, A. K. 1977. Breeding the owl monkey *(Aotus trivirgatus)* in a laboratory environment. *Lab. Anim. Sci.* 27:512–17.

Conway, W. 1987. Species carrying capacity in the zoo alone. In *AAZPA Annual Conference Proceedings*, 20–32. Wheeling, W.Va.: American Association of Zoological Parks and Aquariums.

Crow, J. F., and Kimura, M. 1970. *An introduction to population genetic theory*. New York: Harper and Row.

Denniston, C. 1978. Small population size and genetic diversity: Implications for endangered species. In *Endangered birds: Management techniques for preserving threatened species*, ed. S. A. Temple, 281–89. Madison: University of Wisconsin Press.

Derrickson, S. R. 1987. Current status and captive propagation of the endangered Guam rail. In *Proceedings of the Jean Delacour/IFCB Symposium on Breeding Birds in Captivity*, ed. A. C. Risser, 187–95. North Hollywood, Calif.: IFCB.

Dobson, A. P., and May, R. M. 1986. Disease and conservation. In *Conservation biology: The science of scarcity and diversity*, ed. M. E. Soulé, 345–65. Sunderland, Mass.: Sinauer Associates.

Dyke, B., Gage, T. B., Mamelka, P. M., Goy, R. W., and Stone, W. H. 1986. A demographic analysis of the Wisconsin Regional Primate Center rhesus colony, 1962–1982. *Am. J. Primatol.* 10:257–69.

Ewens, W. J., Brockwell, P. J., Gani, J. M., and Resnick, S. I. 1987. Minimum viable population size in the presence of catastrophes. In *Viable populations for conservation*, ed. M. E. Soulé, 59–68. Cambridge: Cambridge University Press.

Flesness, N. R. 1986. Captive status and genetic considerations. In *Primates: The road to self-sustaining populations*, ed. K. Benirschke, 845–56. New York: Springer-Verlag.

Foose, T. J. 1983. The relevance of captive propagation to the conservation of biotic diversity. In *Genetics and conservation*, ed. C. M. Schonewald-Cox, S. M. Chambers, B. MacBryde, and L. Thomas, 374–401. Menlo Park, Calif.: Benjamin/Cummings.

Foose, T. J., and Ballou, J. D. 1988. Population management: Theory and practice. *Int. Zoo Yrbk.* 27:26–41.

Foose, T. J., de Boer, L., Seal, U. S., and Lande, R. 1995. Conservation management strategies based on viable populations. In *Population management for survival and recovery*, ed. J. D. Ballou, M. Gilpin, and T. J. Foose, 273–94. New York: Columbia University Press.

Foose, T. J., and Foose, E. 1983. Demographic and genetic status and management. In *The biology and management of an extinct species: Pere David's deer*, ed. B. B. Beck and C. Wemmer, 133–86. Park Ridge, N.J.: Noyes.

Foose, T. J., Lande, R., Flesness, N. R., Rabb, G., and Read, B. 1986. Propagation plans. *Zoo Biol.* 5:139–46.

Foose, T. J., and Seal, U. S. 1986. Species Survival Plans for large cats in North American zoos. In *Cats of the world*, ed. S. D. Miller and D. D. Everett, 173–98. Washington, D.C.: National Wildlife Federation.

Foose, T. J., Seal, U. S., and Flesness, N. R. 1987. Captive propagation as a component of conservation strategies for endangered primates. In *Primate conservation in the tropical rainforest*, ed. C. W. Marsh and R. A. Mittermeier, 263–99. New York: Alan R. Liss.

Frankham, R., Hemmer, H., Ryder, O. A., Cothran, E. G., Soulé, M. E., Murray, N. D., and Snyder, M. 1986. Selection in captive populations. *Zoo Biol.* 5:127–38.

Fuerst, P. A., and Maruyama, T. 1986. Considerations on the conservation of alleles and of genic heterozygosity in small managed populations. *Zoo Biol.* 5:171–80.

Geyer, C. J., Ryder, O. A., Chemnick L. G., and Thompson, E. A. 1993. Analysis of relatedness in the California condors from DNA fingerprints. *Mol. Biol. Evol.* 10:571–89.

Gilpin, M. E. 1987. *HETSIM: Basic software for simulating loss of heterozygosity in captive populations*. San Diego: University of California, San Diego.

Gilpin, M. E., and Soulé, M. E. 1986. Minimum viable populations: Processes of species extinction. In *Conservation biology: The science of scarcity and diversity*, ed. M. E. Soulé, 19–34. Sunderland, Mass.: Sinauer Associates.

Gilpin, M. E., and Wills, C. 1991. MHC and captive breeding: A rebuttal. *Conserv. Biol.* 5:554–55.

Glatston, A. R. 1986. Studbooks: The basis of breeding programs. *Int. Zoo Yrbk.* 25:162–67.

Goodman, D. 1987. The demography of chance extinction. In *Viable populations for conservation*, ed. M. E. Soulé, 11–34. Cambridge: Cambridge University Press.

Gregorius, H. 1980. The probability of losing an allele when diploid genotypes are sampled. *Biometrics* 36:643–52.

Haig, S. M., Ballou, J. D., and Derrickson, S. R. 1990. Management options for preserving genetic diversity: Reintroduction of Guam rails to the wild. *Conserv. Biol.* 4:290–300.

Harris, R. B., and Allendorf, F. W. 1989. Genetically effective population size of large mammals: An assessment of estimators. *Conserv. Biol.* 3:181–91.

Hedrick, P. W. 1983. *Genetics of populations*. Boston: Science Books International.

Hedrick, P. W., Brussard, P. F., Allendorf, F. W., Beardmore, J. A., and Orzack, S. 1986. Protein variation, fitness and captive propagation. *Zoo Biol.* 5:91–99.

Hemmer, H. 1986. Nutztier damhirsch. In *Domestikation und verhaltensgerechte Haltung des Damwildes als landwirtschaftliche Nutzart*, 71–91. Neumuhle: Herausgeben.

Hill, W. G. 1972. Effective size of populations with overlapping generations. *Theor. Popul. Biol.* 3:278–89.

Hughes, A. L. 1991. MHC polymorphism and the design of captive breeding programs. *Conserv. Biol.* 5:249–51.

Hutchins, M., and Wiese, R. J. 1991. Beyond genetic and demographic management: The future of the Species Survival Plan and related AAZPA conservation efforts. *Zoo Biol.* 10:285–92.

International Species Information System (ISIS). 1991. *SPARKS (Single Species Animal Record Keeping System)*. Apple Valley, Minn.: ISIS.

Kimura, M., and Crow, J. F. 1963. The measurement of effective population number. *Evolution* 17:279–88.

Kleiman, D. G., Beck, B. B., Dietz, J. M., Dietz, L. A., Ballou, J. D., and Coimbra-Filho. A. F. 1986. Conservation program for the golden lion tamarin: Captive research and management, ecological studies, education strategies, and reintroduction. In *Primates: The road to self-sustaining populations*, ed. K. Benirschke, 959–79. New York: Springer-Verlag.

Lacy, R. C. 1987. Loss of genetic diversity from managed populations: Interaction effects of drift, mutation, immigration, selection, and population subdivision. *Conserv. Biol.* 1:143–58.

———. 1989. Analysis of founder representation in pedigrees: Founder equivalents and founder genome equivalence. *Zoo Biol.* 8:111–24.

———. 1990a. *GENES: Pedigree analysis software*. Brookfield, Ill.: Chicago Zoological Park.

———. 1990b. *VORTEX: Population viability analysis software*. Brookfield, Ill.: Chicago Zoological Park.

Lacy, R., Ballou, J. D., Starfield, A., and Thompson, E. 1995. Pedigree analysis for population management. In *Population management for survival and recovery*, ed. J. D. Ballou, M. Gilpin, and T. J. Foose, 57–75. New York: Columbia University Press.

Lacy, R. C., Petric, A., and Warneke, M. 1993. Inbreeding and outbreeding in captive populations of wild animal species. In *The natural history of inbreeding and outbreeding*, ed. N. W. Thornhill. 352–74. Chicago: University of Chicago Press.

Lande, R., and Barrowclough, G. 1987. Effective population size, genetic variation, and their use in population management. In *Viable populations for conservation*, ed. M. E. Soulé, 87–124. Cambridge: Cambridge University Press.

Lynch, M. 1991. The genetic interpretation of inbreeding depression and outbreeding depression. *Evolution* 45:622–29.

MacCluer, J. W., VandeBerg, J. L., Read, B., and Ryder, O. A. 1986. Pedigree analysis by computer simulation. *Zoo Biol.* 5:147–60.

Marshall, D. R., and Brown, A. H. D. 1975. Optimal sampling strategies in genetic conservation. In *Crop genetic resources for today and tomorrow*, ed. O. H. Frankel and J. G. Hawkes, 53–80. Cambridge: Cambridge University Press.

Miller, P. S., and Hedrick, P. W. 1991. MHC polymorphism and the design of captive breeding programs: Simple solutions are not the answer. *Conserv. Biol.* 5:556–58.

Mitton, J. B., and Grant, M. C. 1984. Associations among protein heterozygosity, growth rate, and developmental homeostasis. *Annu. Rev. Ecol. Syst.* 15:479–500.

Morin, P. A., and Ryder, O. A. 1991. Founder contribution and pedigree inference in a captive breeding colony of lion-tailed macaques, using mitochondrial DNA and DNA fingerprint analyses. *Zoo Biol.* 10:341–52.

Oates, J. F. 1986. *SSC/IUCN action plan for African primate conservation: 1986–1990*. Morges, Switzerland: IUCN.

O'Brien, S. J., Roelke, M. E., Marker, L., Newman, A., Winkler, C. A., Meltzer, D., Colly, L., Evermann, J. F., Bush, M., and Wildt, D. E. 1985. Genetic basis for species vulnerability in the cheetah. *Science* 227:1428–34.

Olney, P. J. S. 1986. *International zoo yearbook*. London: Zoological Society of London.

Princée, F. 1989. *Zoo research studbook management*. Amsterdam: Dutch Zoo Federation.

Ralls, K., and Ballou, J. D. 1983. Extinction: Lessons from zoos. In *Genetics and conservation*, ed. C. M. Schonewald-Cox, S. M. Chambers, B. MacBryde, and L. Thomas, 164–84. Menlo Park, Calif.: Benjamin/Cummings.

Ralls, K., Ballou, J. D., and Templeton, A. R. 1988. Estimates of lethal equivalents and the cost of inbreeding in mammals. *Conserv. Biol.* 2:185–93.

Ryman, N., Baccus, R., Reuterwall, C., and Smith, M. H. 1981. Effective population size, generation interval, and potential loss of genetic variability in game species under different hunting regimes. *Oikos* 36:257–66.

Seal, U. S., Makey, D. G., and Murtfeldt, L. E. 1976. ISIS: An animal census system. *Int. Zoo Yrbk.* 16:180–84.

Shaffer, M. 1987. Minimum viable populations: Coping with uncertainty. In *Viable populations for conservation*, ed. M. E. Soulé, 69–86. Cambridge: Cambridge University Press.

Soulé, M. E. 1987. *Viable populations for conservation*. Cambridge: Cambridge University Press.

Soulé, M., Gilpin, M., Conway, W., and Foose, T. J. 1986. The millennium ark: How long a voyage, how many staterooms, how many passengers? *Zoo Biol.* 5:101–13.

Templeton, A. R., Hemmer, H., Mace, G., Seal, U. S., Shields, W. M., and Woodruff, D. S. 1986. Local adaptation, coadaptation and population boundaries. *Zoo Biol.* 5:115–25.

Templeton, A. R., and Read, B. 1983. The elimination of inbreeding depression in a captive herd of Speke's gazelle. In *Genetics and conservation*, ed. C. M. Schonewald-Cox, S. M. Chambers, B. MacBryde, and L. Thomas, 241–61. Menlo Park, Calif.: Benjamin/Cummings.

———. 1984. Factors eliminating inbreeding depression in a captive herd of Speke's gazelle. *Zoo Biol.* 3:177–99.

Vrijenhoek, R. C., and Leberg, P. L. 1991. Let's not throw the baby out with the bathwater: A comment on management for MHC diversity in captive populations. *Conserv. Biol.* 5:252–54.

Wayne, R. K., Forman, L., Newman, A. K., Simonson, J. M., and O'Brien, S. J. 1986. Genetic monitors of zoo populations: Morphological and electrophoretic assays. *Zoo Biol.* 5:215–32.

Wildt, D. E. 1989. Reproductive research in conservation biology: Priorities and avenues for support. *J. Zoo Wildl. Med.* 20:391–95.

Wildt, D. E., Bush, M., Goodrowe, K. L., Packer, C., Pusey, A. E., Brown, J. L., Joslin, P., and O'Brien, S. J. 1987. Reproductive and genetic consequences of founding isolated lion populations. *Nature* 329:328–31.

Willis, K. 1993. Use of animals with unknown ancestries in scientifically managed breeding programs. *Zoo Biol.* 12: 161–72.

27

Dispersal and Captive Mammal Management

SHARON PFEIFER

Over the last two decades, there has been a trend among zoos away from the presentation of single animal specimens caged in concrete and barred enclosures toward the exhibition of social groupings of animals displayed under quasi-naturalistic conditions. This tendency stems from increased institutional commitment to public education as well as increased public concern for animal rights, and also, in large part, from the urgent need for zoos to improve captive propagation in the face of dwindling global biodiversity. This new orientation has required that captive animal managers become reliant on sophisticated information and technology from a wide variety of disciplines. One field that has contributed significantly to improved captive animal propagation is population ecology, with its focus on the determinants of population growth and regulation. This chapter considers the adaptive function and patterns of dispersal in natural populations and the relevance of such knowledge to captive mammal management.

DISPERSAL IN NATURAL POPULATIONS OF MAMMALS

Definition

The use of the term "dispersal" in the literature lacks consistency. Dispersal has been used interchangeably with emigration, immigration, and migration, and has served to characterize not only individual animal movements between populations, but also mass movements of large populations.

With regard to movement by individuals, the term dispersal has referred to both long-distance *interpopulation* and shorter distance *intrapopulation* movement patterns (Van Valen 1971). In this chapter, "dispersal" refers to the permanent relocation of an individual, either within its own population (deme) or to a new population. It is not unreasonable to consider permanent relocation within a deme as dispersal if members of a species are fairly sedentary (i.e.,

At the time of writing, Sharon Pfeifer was with the Department of Ecology and Behavioral Biology, University of Minnesota, Minneapolis.

philopatric). In the working definition for this chapter, temporary exploratory movements by individuals are excluded from consideration. Natal dispersal occurs before onset of reproduction, while breeding dispersal occurs when individuals relocate between reproductive bouts.

Adaptive Significance of Dispersal

What advantages are conferred on dispersing individuals? Theoretically, dispersal to a new locale can have two kinds of positive effects. Dispersal can decrease inbreeding depression (genetic effects) and/or it can reduce stress and competition over limited resources (nongenetic effects). These advantages, however, bear a cost: Dispersal increases the risk of mortality and may decrease fecundity and offspring survivorship. Additionally, Shields (1984) hypothesized that breeding outside one's natal area may disrupt coadapted gene complexes, although Ralls, Harvey, and Lyles (1986) and Templeton (1986) have argued against this point. The benefits and costs of dispersal surely vary among species, but in keeping with benefit-cost theory, dispersal should evolve only if the benefits exceed the costs of dispersing. It should be noted here, however, that dispersal may bestow net benefits on individuals other than the disperser. Sedentary relatives also may benefit from the permanent departure of dispersers if those remaining gain greater access to resources, avoid the risk of dispersing themselves, and/or produce more fit offspring because of lowered inbreeding depression (Stenseth 1984). Thus, the benefits and costs of dispersal to both the disperser and its relatives must be considered to understand fully the evolution and adaptive significance of dispersal.

The majority of researchers investigating the evolution and adaptive significance of dispersal have suggested that the principal selective agent in the evolution of this behavior is inbreeding avoidance. In reviewing the literature on mammalian dispersal, however, Moore and Ali (1984) argued that it was unnecessary to invoke an ultimate causal factor such as inbreeding avoidance to explain the evolution of dispersal. Rather, they concluded that the proximate factors of competition, parental investment, and sexual selection were sufficient to explain observed dispersal patterns among mammals. Dobson and Jones (1985), in a rebuttal to Moore and Ali, argued that a more comprehensive review of the evidence on mammalian dispersal would demonstrate that competition (for mates or other resources) is inadequate to explain all observed dispersal patterns and that inbreeding avoidance cannot be excluded, based on current evidence, as a possible cause for dispersal. This disagreement merely highlights what is known to date about dispersal: its observed variation among mammal species reflects different causes and consequences, with the only generalization being that dispersal has evolved to increase individual reproductive success.

Causes of Dispersal

Just as there is much uncertainty about the ultimate cause(s) of dispersal, several proximate causes are hypothesized to trigger dispersive behavior. Early investigations of the dispersal process sought physiological mechanisms. The work of Christian (1950, 1961) and Christian and Davis (1964) revealed positive correlations between population density, hormonal imbalance, and dispersal tendency in microtine rodents. Christian's work showed that stress was density-dependent and influenced adrenopituitary secretion. Under conditions of high population density, imbalance in adrenopituitary secretion suppressed growth and reproduction in individuals and increased the probability of dispersal of less aggressive animals. Physiological research also revealed that dispersal can directly influence the disperser (Bailey 1969) as well as neighbors of dispersers (hormonal depression: Bailey 1969; pregnancy termination: Bruce 1959; territorial displacement: Healey 1967; reproduction stimulation: Lidicker 1965; Myers and Krebs 1971).

Christian's research contributed significantly to a better understanding of the proximate causes of dispersal, not only because he found physiological differences between dispersers and nondispersers, but because his findings also emphasized the relationship between population density and dispersal tendency—a concept ecologists pursued and expanded.

Howard (1966) postulated that there were two types of dispersal: density-dependent, or environmentally influenced, dispersal, as suggested by Christian, and density-independent, or innate, dispersal. Although density has been shown to influence dispersal in various vole species of the genus *Microtus* (Fairbairn 1978; Tamarin 1977), many other studies suggest that dispersal is not always a density-dependent function (Krebs et al. 1976; McClenaghan and Gaines 1976: Rose and Gaines 1976: Lidicker 1975: Mazurkiewicz and Rajska 1975). In fact, Gadgil (1971), Lomnicki (1978), Roff (1975), and Taylor and Taylor (1977) have all discussed, from a theoretical perspective, the importance of density-independent variables, including temporal and spatial environmental fluctuations, in the evolution of dispersal.

A host of other ecological factors have been studied as possible proximate mechanisms in the process of dispersal. Rates of natality and mortality, overall population growth rate, population age and sex structure, and life history patterns constitute important influences on dispersal (Tamarin

1977, 1978; Sullivan 1977). Most recently, Waser (1985) hypothesized that natal dispersal is related to rates of fecundity and juvenile/adult survivorship within demes, because these demographic factors determine the turnover rate of occupied home ranges.

An interest in the genetic and behavioral influences on dispersal was stimulated by Chitty and his behavior-genetic polymorphism hypothesis (Chitty 1958, 1960, 1967). Chitty conjectured that a relationship existed between individual genotype and the tendency to disperse, and he predicted that genetically more aggressive voles would drive away genetically less aggressive population members. Tamarin and Krebs (1969) tested this hypothesis experimentally by electrophoretically analyzing genetic markers in prairie and meadow voles, *Microtus ochrogaster* and *M. pennsylvanicus*, two species that exhibit distinct population cycles. Their findings suggested that in these species one transferrin genotype (Tf^c/Tf^c) was selected for during the increase and peak phases of population growth and was selected against during the decline phase. Further studies (Krebs et al. 1976; Gaines and Krebs 1971; Myers and Krebs 1971) strengthened the findings of Tamarin and Krebs (1969), but no clear correlation was found between the various transferrin genotypes and behavioral phenotypes in the genus *Microtus*. Electrophoretic analysis of the transferrin locus in another rodent genus, *Spermophilus*, also produced no positive correlation between genotype and dispersing ground squirrel phenotype (Michener and Michener 1977).

Despite the lack of robust evidence to support the hypothesis of a genetic component of dispersal, inferential data add a measure of support. Tamarin (1977), for example, reported that significantly more voles, *M. breweri*, with a forehead blaze (presumed to be a genetic trait) than without dispersed from his study population, and Hilborn (1975) found a nonrandom pattern of dispersal among his study litters of four different species of voles. The best supporting evidence, however, comes from an 11-year field study by Greenwood and his colleagues (Greenwood, Harvey, and Perrins 1979) on the great tit, *Parus major*. In this species, dispersal was estimated to have a heritability coefficient of roughly 60% as based on comparisons of parent and offspring dispersal distances.

Prior to 1977, environmentally unstable habitats were thought to foster dispersal (Gadgil 1971; Lomnicki 1978). Hamilton and May (1977) hypothesized that parents and offspring harbor conflicting goals and assess the benefits and costs of dispersal differently. According to their model, parents influence the timing of natal dispersal and should encourage dispersal of a portion of their offspring, even in stable environments, to increase inclusive fitness. The Hamilton-May dispersal model thus proposed that dispersal increases not only individual fitness, but inclusive fitness as well.

Investigations as to how behavior affects dispersal have produced results as inconclusive as the genetic studies. Christian's social hierarchical dispersal hypothesis (1970) predicted that an individual's rank within a group would determine the nature of its social interactions and which individuals would disperse. Amending this hypothesis somewhat, Gauthreaux (1978) predicted that high-ranking individuals should be more aggressive and, therefore, able to occupy optimal habitat areas, whereas less aggressive individuals would be forced to disperse to suboptimal habitat. Countering the evidence that aggression plays a major role in dispersal, however, are data implying that dispersal may be preceded by little or no aggression between group members, or even by complete avoidance, in some species (*Microtus*: Myers and Krebs 1971; red fox, *Vulpes vulpes*: Storm 1972; marmots, *Marmota flaviventris*: Armitage 1973; Belding's ground squirrels, *Spermophilus beldingi*: Turner 1972; Richardson's ground squirrels, *Spermophilus richardsonii*: Yeaton 1972). In light of the contradictory findings, Bekoff (1977) advised that individual behavioral ontogenies be studied in relation to subsequent dispersal patterns in order to discern more accurately the effects of social behavior on dispersal.

Patterns of Dispersal

Sex. Among mammalian species, dispersal is sex-biased in favor of males, although exceptions exist (wild dogs, *Lycaon pictus*: Frame et al. 1979; chimpanzees, *Pan troglodytes*: Pusey 1979). By contrast, most avian dispersal is female-biased. Recent interpretations of dispersal data have considered these sex-biased dispersal movements in relation to two factors: (1) type of mating system and (2) nature of resource defense.

In explanations of male-biased dispersal among mammals, it is assumed that female mammals have evolved to be the more sedentary, or philopatric, sex in order to defend those resources (e.g., nest sites) necessary for reproductive success. Male mammals presumably have not evolved to be philopatric because they increase their reproductive success by dispersing to gain breeding access to resource-defending, sedentary females. As a result of these sex differences in reproductive strategy, mammalian mating systems can be characterized as primarily polygynous with male-biased dispersal.

Relatively few mammals exhibit monogamous mating systems, a fact that may be attributable to the unique reproductive physiology of female mammals and their ability to provide most parental care alone (Kleiman 1977; see also Berger and Stevens, chap. 33, this volume). The presence of mated pairs in monogamous systems affects dispersal, with both sexes leaving. Dispersal does not necessarily occur, however, before the next generation is born. Natal dispersal in some monogamous mammal species may, in fact, be delayed for extended time periods, during which the subadult or adult offspring are reproductively suppressed by the breeding pair. Marmosets and tamarins of the family Callitrichidae, gibbons of the genus *Hylobates*, beavers, *Castor canadensis*, jackals, *Canis mesomelas*, and dwarf mongooses, *Helogale parvula*, exhibit helping behavior, in which offspring remain with the breeding pair and help tend the younger generation(s). Repressed sexual maturation and delayed dispersal produce extended social units of several generations in a small percentage of mammals.

Timing and Age. Despite the high risk of mortality associated with dispersal, almost all organisms disperse at some time during their life cycles (Shields 1984). The timing of dispersal varies with the species, but natal dispersal occurs with greatest frequency. Data on captive mammals suggest that in some species the timing of natal dispersal may be sex-dependent. Kleiman (1980) observed, for example, that young male lion tamarins, *Leontopithecus rosalia*, showing signs of sexual maturation are tolerated in the family group longer than young females exhibiting no observable signs of maturation. In two instances, the dominant, but sexually inactive, female offspring were killed, presumably by their mothers. How these data relate to dispersal timing in natural populations is unknown, but they imply that young female tamarins disperse earlier than males to avoid confrontation with the breeding female.

Life History Traits. Species with short generation times, high fecundity and mortality rates, small body sizes, rapid development, and early breeding onset are referred to as colonizing species because their life history traits enable rapid colonization of new habitats. Colonizing species typically exhibit high dispersal rates, although they do not tend to display the strongly sex-biased dispersal characteristic of longer-lived species. As mentioned by Pusey (1987), the probability of generational overlap in colonizing species such as deer mice, *Peromyscus* spp., or kangaroo rats, *Dipodomys* spp., is low, and therefore differential dispersal is not pronounced.

Among mammalian species with long generation times, low fecundity, large body sizes, slow development, and late breeding onset, sex-biased dispersal is an important component of population regulation. Waser and Jones (1983) have shown a positive correlation between longevity and sex-biased dispersal among solitary mammal species. Interpretation of the data implies that generational overlap resulting from increased longevity expands the opportunity for inbreeding in the absence of dispersal. In long-lived polygynous species it is therefore advantageous for males to disperse to decrease mate competition, ultimately reducing inbreeding.

Summary Remarks Regarding Dispersal in Natural Populations

Depending on the sex, age, and life history traits of dispersers, dispersal can have significant effects on the demographic and genetic structure of populations and, consequently, on population viability. Dispersal thus necessarily becomes a concern in captive animal management because it cannot occur without human intervention.

Studies of mammalian dispersal movements have revealed a wide degree of flexibility in this trait, precluding sweeping generalizations that can be applied to all mammal species. There are, however, some basic trends to be noted:

1. Mammalian dispersal is typically male-biased.
2. Natal dispersal appears to be more common than breeding dispersal, and should be more prevalent among long-lived species.
3. The causes for dispersal may be genetic (inbreeding avoidance) and/or nongenetic (intraspecific competition for resources).
4. The mating system and nature of resource defense are

considered to be two important factors in producing sex-biased dispersal.

As a general picture, it is young mammals that disperse, generally before their first reproductive effort. It is hypothesized that young males disperse to increase their chances for reproductive success by avoiding competition with relatives (proximate cause) or inbreeding depression (ultimate cause), and in so doing also may increase inclusive fitness. Stress, demographic factors, aggression, and genotype have been invoked as proximate factors causing dispersal, although there is also evidence to suggest that dispersal is unaffected by each of these factors.

EFFECTS OF DISPERSAL SUPPRESSION

The absence of dispersal can have profound effects on isolated (captive or fragmented) populations. Absence of dispersal or inappropriately timed dispersal (i.e., intervention and removal) can lead to neuroendocrine dysfunction as well as short- and long-term genetic consequences. Experimental fencing of natural populations has been shown to produce a "fence effect" in vole populations (Gipps and Jewell 1979; Krebs, Keller, and Tamarin 1969). Under these restricted conditions, vole numbers increased dramatically, exhausted resources, and noncompetitive individuals eventually starved.

It is more likely under natural conditions that before resources become limiting, lack of a "dispersal sink" will cause physiological dysfunction. The physiological effects of overcrowding may produce stress-induced adrenal hypertrophy and its multitude of symptoms: suppression of somatic growth, delay or prevention of sexual maturation, diminished ovulation, delayed spermatogenesis, increased intrauterine mortality, and possible curtailment of reproduction (Brown 1975). Adrenal hypertrophy also indirectly lowers disease resistance (Christian and Davis 1964).

The same physiological symptoms occur in natural social units of mammals because of intrasexual competition, and are enhanced in captivity in the absence of dispersal to reduce competition. In monogamous mammalian species such as the wolf, Canis lupus, beaver, and golden lion tamarin, typically only one male and one female of a larger social unit breed successfully. Intraspecific competition in monogamous mating systems suppresses reproduction in both sexes. In wild populations, nonreproductives of both sexes may stay and "help" their parents with younger offspring, dispersing later to breed. Dobson (1982) found natal dispersal by both sexes to occur, in fact, in eleven of twelve well-studied monogamous mammal species. In captivity, severe inhibition of future reproductive capability is possible if nonreproductive individuals are not removed when appropriate during development. In polygynous species, in which intramale competition for females is intense, young males may curtail reproduction or die from stress-related causes if unable to disperse (see Kleiman 1977).

Suppression of dispersal also can result in inbreeding, with the unmasking of deleterious recessive genes. If inbreeding is defined as breeding between closely related individuals (coefficients of relatedness equal to 0.25 or greater), its occurrence in natural populations is rare. Well-studied mammal populations exhibit frequencies of inbreeding ranging from 0% to 5.5% (Ralls, Harvey, and Lyles 1986). The apparent rarity of inbreeding among natural populations is undoubtedly related to the detrimental effects of inbreeding depression, which include decreased offspring viability, decreased fecundity, and altered sex ratios favoring an increase in males (Senner 1980). The incidence of inbreeding in zoo ungulate populations has been analyzed by Ralls, Brugger, and Ballou (1979), who found higher juvenile mortality among females. This finding is explained by the presence of two X chromosomes in female mammals, which become increasingly homozygous with repeated inbreeding. The change in sex ratio toward more males than females compounds the problem of inbreeding in uncontrolled situations (Senner 1980).

Inbreeding depression theoretically occurs at a faster rate (per generation) in small populations and those lacking immigration (Soulé 1980). Colonizing species are less likely to experience inbreeding and loss of genetic variability than are long-lived species with overlapping generations (Gilpin and Soulé 1986). A single dispersal event (or introduction) into a captive population by an unrelated individual, however, can reduce inbreeding depression substantially (Franklin 1980).

Inbreeding depression represents a short-term genetic consequence of dispersal suppression. Absence of individual movement into or out of demes can produce long-term effects on genetic variability as well.

In natural populations, dispersal is one factor influencing sex ratio. As already discussed, sex-biased dispersal produces a skewed sex ratio favoring one sex or the other (in mammals, male-biased dispersal skews the sex ratio in favor of females). Recent comparative analyses of the mating systems and social structures of selected mammal species suggested that skewed sex ratios brought about by sex-biased dispersal decreased the number of breeders of one sex and therefore reduced effective population size (N_e). Effective population size essentially defines the minimum number of randomly mating males and females in an ideal population that would produce levels of inbreeding and genetic drift equivalent to those in larger populations (see Ballou and Foose, chap. 26, this volume). Chepko-Sade et al. (1988) conjectured that many mammals live in small, semi-isolated demes and have small effective population sizes. The fact that most mammal species are polygynous, and that not all population members breed, further reduces N_e. Species-specific effective population sizes are important to successful animal management because, in the long term, a small N_e contributes to the progressive loss of genetic variability for two reasons: (1) inbreeding is inversely related to N_e, and (2) genetic drift is more prevalent as an agent of genetic change in populations with small effective population sizes.

Preventing the disruptive influences of dispersal suppression is not easy. A key objective must be to remove or introduce individuals without causing social instability that disrupts captive propagation (Kleiman 1980). Accomplishing this requires that attention be paid to what is presently known about dispersal in natural populations and to the insights into social behavior garnered from studies in captivity.

DISPERSAL AND CAPTIVE MAMMAL MANAGEMENT

"One of the least considered problems in the successful maintenance of captive populations is how and when to dispose of adults and offspring while still maintaining an optimal age and sex structure and not disrupting the social dynamics of a group" (Kleiman 1980, 257). The issue of dispersal as addressed in this chapter relates to the question of *when* to intervene in the social dynamics of captive groups. Until more reliable data are available, the following considerations may help guide decision making by animal managers.

A primary consideration must be the type of mating system known or thought to characterize a species. As in natural populations, it can be expected that young males of polygynous species will show a greater tendency to disperse than females. In captivity, removal of juvenile males to reduce intramale competition may prevent injury or death and minimize social disruption among polygynous species. The artificial removal of young males, however, reduces the possibility of female mate selection. If the mating system is monogamous, dispersal of both sexes can be expected. The difficulty lies in determining when members of each sex would disperse.

The size and composition of the social unit are also major considerations in evaluating when dispersal might occur in captivity. This is especially true for monogamous species, in which group size and composition can vary from few to many individuals of two or more generations. The social unit of beavers, for example, is the nuclear family comprising the mated pair, subadults of both sexes, and young. In this species, dispersal is delayed until the second year following birth, when both sexes disperse. Prior to dispersal, subadults play an important role in caring for the younger generation (pers. obs.). Among monogamous species with larger, extended social units, the removal of subadults and adults may not be necessary. Reproductive suppression ensures that only the alpha male and female (dominant individuals) breed, and sexual competition is minimized.

Beyond these two principal considerations of mating system and social structure, it is perhaps best to undertake detailed behavioral studies to understand how individual variation (genetic, physiological, and behavioral) influences dispersal tendency in captivity.

SUMMARY

In conclusion, dispersal is an environmentally and genetically determined trait that varies among mammalian species in terms of its proximate causation and consequences. The type of mating system and nature of resource defense appear to be fruitful constructs by which to better understand the phenomenon of dispersal. Further refinement of dispersal as a management tool will require species-specific studies both in the field and in captivity. Recognition of the significance of dispersal in captive mammal management is of vital importance to the propagation of viable populations that will enable zoos to fulfill their mission of conserving our ever-dwindling faunal diversity.

REFERENCES

Armitage, K. B. 1973. Population changes and social behavior following colonization by the yellow-bellied marmot. *J. Mammal.* 54:842–54.

Bailey, E. D. 1969. Immigration and emigration as contributory regulators of population through social disruption. *Can. J. Zool.* 47:1213–15.

Bekoff, M. 1977. Mammalian dispersal and the ontogeny of individual behavioral phenotypes. *Am. Nat.* 111:715–32.

Brown, J. 1975. *The evolution of behavior.* New York: Norton.

Bruce, H. M. 1959. An exteroceptive block to pregnancy in the mouse. *Nature* 184:105.

Chepko-Sade, B. D., and W. M. Shields, with Berger, J., Halpin, Z. T., Jones, W. T., Rogers, L. L., Rood, J. P., and Smith, A. T. 1988. The effects of dispersal and social structure on effective population size. In *Mammalian dispersal patterns,* ed. B. D. Chepko-Sade and Z. T. Halpin, 287–321. Chicago: University of Chicago Press.

Chitty, D. 1958. Self-regulation of numbers through changes in viability. *Cold Spring Harb. Symp. Quant. Biol.* 22:277–80.

———. 1960. Population processes in the vole and their relevance to general theory. *Can. J. Zool.* 38:99–113.

———. 1967. The natural selection of self-regulatory behaviour in animal populations. *Proc. Ecol. Soc. Aust.* 2:51–78.

Christian, J. J. 1950. The adreno-pituitary system and population cycles in mammals. *J. Mammal.* 31:247–59.

———. 1961. Phenomena associated with population density. *Proc. Nat. Acad. Sci. USA* 47:428–49.

———. 1970. Social subordination, population density, and mammalian evolution. *Science* 168:84–90.

Christian, J. J., and Davis, D. E. 1964. Endocrines, behavior, and population. *Science* 246:1550–60.

Dobson, F. S. 1982. Competition for mates and predominant juvenile male dispersal in mammals. *Anim. Behav.* 30:1183–92.

Dobson, F. S., and Jones, W. T. 1985. Multiple causes of dispersal. *Am. Nat.* 126:855–58.

Fairbairn, D. J. 1978. Dispersal of deer mice, *Peromyscus maniculatus. Oecologia* 32:171–94.

Frame, L. H., Malcolm, J. R., Frame, G. W., and Lawick, H. van. 1979. Social organisation of African wild dogs, *Lycaon pictus,* on the Serengeti Plains, Tanzania 1967–1978. *Z. Tierpsychol.* 50:225–49.

Franklin, I. R. 1980. Evolutionary change in small populations. In *Conservation biology: An evolutionary-ecological perspective,* ed. M. E. Soulé and B. A. Wilcox, 135–49. Sunderland, Mass.: Sinauer Associates.

Gadgil, M. 1971. Dispersal: Population consequences and evolution. *Ecology* 52:253–61.

Gaines, M. S., and Krebs, C. J. 1971. Genetic changes in fluctuating vole populations. *Evolution* 25:702–23.

Gauthreaux, S. A. Jr. 1978. The ecological significance of behavioural dominance. In *Perspectives in ethology,* vol. 3, ed. P. H. Klopfer and P. P. G. Bateson, 17–54. London: Plenum Press.

Gilpin, M. E., and Soulé, M. E. 1986. Minimum viable populations: Processes of species extinction. In *Conservation biology: The science of scarcity and diversity,* ed. M. E. Soulé, 19–34. Sunderland, Mass.: Sinauer Associates.

Gipps, J. H. W., and Jewell, P. A. 1979. Maintaining populations of bank vole, *Clethrionomys glareolus,* in large outdoor enclosures, and measuring the response of population variables to the castration of males. *J. Anim. Ecol.* 48:535–56.

Greenwood, P. J., Harvey, P. H., and Perrins, C. M. 1979. The role of dispersal in the great tit, *Parus major*: The causes, consequences, and heritability of natal dispersal. *J. Anim. Ecol.* 48:123–42.

Hamilton, W. D., and May, R. M. 1977. Dispersal in stable habitats. *Nature* 269:578–81.

Healey, M. C. 1967. Aggression and self-regulation of population size in deermice. *Ecology* 48:377–92.

Hilborn, R. 1975. Similarities in dispersal tendency among siblings in four species of voles, *Microtus. Ecology* 56:1221–25.

Howard, W. A. 1966. Innate and environmental dispersal of individual vertebrates. *Am. Midland Nat.* 63:152–61.

Kleiman, D. G. 1977. Monogamy in mammals. *Q. Rev. Biol.* 52:39–69.

———. 1980. The sociobiology of captive propagation. In *Conservation biology: An evolutionary-ecological perspective*, ed. M. E. Soulé and B. A. Wilcox, 243–61. Sunderland, Mass.: Sinauer Associates.

Krebs, C. J., Keller, B. L., and Tamarin, R. H. 1969. *Microtus* population biology: Demographic changes in fluctuating populations of *M. ochrogaster* and *M. pennsylvanicus* in southern Indiana. *Ecology* 50:587–607.

Krebs, C. J., Wingate, I., LeDuc, J., Redfield, J. A., Taitt, M., and Hilborn, R. 1976. *Microtus* population biology: Dispersal in fluctuating populations of *M. townsendii. Can. J. Zool.* 54:79–95.

Lidicker, W. Z. Jr. 1965. Comparative study of density regulation in confined populations of four species of rodents. *Res. Popul. Ecol.* 7:57–72.

———. 1975. The role of dispersal in the demography of small mammals. In *Small mammals: Their productivity and population dynamics*, ed. F. B. Golley, K. Petrusewicz, and L. Ryszkowski, 103–28. London: Cambridge University Press.

Lomnicki, A. 1978. Individual differences between animals and the natural regulation of their numbers. *J. Anim. Ecol.* 47:461–75.

Mazurkiewicz, M., and Rajska, E. 1975. Dispersion of young bank voles from their place of birth. *Acta Theriologica* 20:71–81.

McClenaghan, L. R. Jr., and Gaines, M. S. 1976. Density-dependent dispersal in *Sigmodon*: A critique. *J. Mammal.* 57:758–59.

Michener, G. R., and Michener, D. R. 1977. Population structure and dispersal in Richardson's ground squirrels. *Ecology* 58:359–68.

Moore, J., and Ali, R. 1984. Are dispersal and inbreeding avoidance related? *Anim. Behav.* 32:94–112.

Myers, J. H., and Krebs, C. J. 1971. Genetic, behavioral, and reproductive attributes of dispersing field voles *Microtus pennsylvanicus* and *M. ochrogaster. Ecol. Monogr.* 41:53–77.

Pusey, A. E. 1979. Intercommunity transfer of chimpanzees in Gombe National Park. In *The great apes*, ed. D. A. Hamburg and E. R. McCown, 465–79. Menlo Park, Calif.: Benjamin/Cummings.

Pusey, A. E. 1987. Sex-biased dispersal and inbreeding avoidance in birds and mammals. *Trends Ecol. Evol.* 2:295–99.

Ralls, K., Brugger, K., and Ballou, J. 1979. Inbreeding and juvenile mortality in small populations of ungulates. *Science* 206:1101–3.

Ralls, K., Harvey, P. H., and Lyles, A. M. 1986. Inbreeding in natural populations of birds and mammals. In *Conservation biology: The science of scarcity and diversity*, ed. M. E. Soulé, 35–56. Sunderland, Mass.: Sinauer Associates.

Roff, D. A. 1975. Population stability and the evolution of dispersal in a heterogeneous environment. *Oecologia* 19:217–37.

Rose, R. K., and Gaines, M. S. 1976. Levels of aggression in fluctuating populations of the prairie vole, *Microtus ochrogaster*, in eastern Kansas. *J. Mammal.* 57:43–57.

Senner, J. W. 1980. Inbreeding depression and the survival of zoo populations. In *Conservation biology: An evolutionary-ecological perspective*, ed. M. E. Soulé and B. A. Wilcox, 209–24. Sunderland, Mass.: Sinauer Associates.

Shields, W. M. 1984. Optimal inbreeding and the evolution of philopatry. In *The ecology of animal movement*, ed. I. R. Swingland and P. J. Greenwood, 132–59. Oxford: Clarendon Press.

Soulé, M. E. 1980. Thresholds for survival: Maintaining fitness and evolutionary potential. In *Conservation biology: An evolutionary-ecological perspective*, ed. M. E. Soulé and B. A. Wilcox, 151–69. Sunderland, Mass.: Sinauer Associates.

Stenseth, N. C. 1984. Causes and consequences of dispersal in small mammals. In *The ecology of animal movement*, ed. I. R. Swingland and P. J. Greenwood, 63–101. Oxford: Clarendon Press.

Storm, G. E. 1972. Population dynamics of red foxes in north central United States. Ph.D. thesis, University of Minnesota.

Sullivan, T. P. 1977. Demography and dispersal in island and mainland populations of the deer mouse, *Peromyscus maniculatus. Ecology* 58:964–78.

Tamarin, R. H. 1977. Dispersal in island and mainland voles. *Ecology* 58:1044–54.

———. 1978. Dispersal, population regulation, and K-selection in field mice. *Am. Nat.* 112:545–55.

Tamarin, R. H., and Krebs, C. J. 1969. *Microtus* population biology: Genetic changes at the transferrin locus in fluctuating populations of two vole species. *Evolution* 23:183–211.

Taylor, L. R., and Taylor, R. A. J. 1977. Aggregation, migration, and population mechanics. *Nature* 265:415–21.

Templeton, A. R. 1986. Coadaptation and outbreeding depression. In *Conservation biology: The science of scarcity and diversity*, ed. M. E. Soulé, 105–16. Sunderland, Mass.: Sinauer Associates.

Turner, L. W. 1972. Autoecology of the Belding ground squirrel in Oregon. Ph.D. thesis, University of Arizona.

Van Valen, L. 1971. Group selection and the evolution of dispersal. *Evolution* 25:591–98.

Waser, P. M. 1985. Does competition drive dispersal? *Ecology* 66:1170–75.

Waser, P. M., and Jones, W. T. 1983. Natal philopatry among solitary mammals. *Q. Rev. Biol.* 58:355–90.

Yeaton, R. I. 1972. Social behavior and social organization in Richardson's ground squirrel, *Spermophilus richardsonii richardsonii* in Saskatchewan. *J. Mammal.* 53:139–47.

28

Issues of Surplus Animals

STEVE GRAHAM

As the role of zoos shifts from entertainment menageries to educational/conservation facilities, all aspects of animal management are being examined and evaluated for their effectiveness and future applications. The rate of destruction of wildlife and natural habitats is accelerating. Zoos must reinforce the conservation of species in the wild and, in the worst cases, provide refuge for those species that face extinction in the wild. As zoos accept their responsibility as the major force in the conservation of animal species through captive propagation, the problem of surplus animals develops.

The captive management of animals is imprecise due to the large number of individual animals involved and the large number of participating institutions. In addition, while efforts such as the Species Survival Plan (SSP) produce overall agreement on captive management goals, the attainment of those goals cannot be programmed exactly. Thus the breeding of animals in captivity inevitably produces some animals that are not needed for the continued survival of the captive population.

It is unlikely that there is any other area of interest within the zoo profession that is more controversial than the disposition of surplus animals. It is clearly the intention of all zoo professionals to place surplus animals in the best possible situation. However, this process is sometimes subverted. There is, for instance, the "comfort of distance" (that is, "out of sight, out of mind"). In a presentation delivered at the 1987 AAZPA Annual Conference (Graham 1987), I indicated that one curatorial-level employee of a major zoo told me that the most important reason for the existence of animal dealers was to dispose of animals that curators were unwilling to euthanize. The ultimate fate of the animals is not considered.

There appears to be no simple definition of "surplus zoo animals" but I will attempt to put forth one: Surplus animals are collection individuals that do not contribute to the zoo's overall breeding management program; these may include any animal, from domestic species in a public contact area to endangered species.

In any healthy ecosystem in the wild, natural breeding results in excess numbers of animals. Every birthing season, wild populations normally produce many more young than can be accommodated within the carrying capacity of the habitat. This excess can be thought of as akin to the "surplus" seen in captive populations.

Many nonbiologists have little understanding of the concept of carrying capacity. The fact that animals face death by predation, natural catastrophe, starvation, or other unpleasant means is distressing for most nonbiologists to contemplate. While the public may demand the replication of natural habitats, zoos have largely shied away from attempts to replicate nature's inexorable population control. The carrying capacity of an individual zoo, or that of zoos in general, is a difficult issue to deal with because oftentimes the solution to limited space and resources may be unpleasant to most.

CAUSES OF SURPLUS

How do surpluses develop in zoos? One cause is indiscriminate breeding within a collection, which often leads to overrepresentation of a single bloodline and thus to high inbreeding coefficients. This practice may not only inherently weaken the total captive population (Ralls and Ballou 1983), but may also produce animals that are undesirable for placement in other facilities. Recently, however, information on the importance of avoiding inbreeding has become available to captive animal managers (see Ballou and Foose, chap. 26, this volume). Gradually, zoos are creating staff positions for geneticists and are recognizing the need for a more scientific understanding of genetic selection and management in captive populations (Flesness 1977; Foose 1977; Seal and Flesness 1978). These efforts in genetic management will eventually benefit the entire zoo community by providing guidelines that encourage the responsible breeding of captive animals (Ralls and Ballou 1986).

Another factor leading to the production of hard-to-place offspring is hand rearing, which has long been a cornerstone of many zoo breeding programs. Some zoos hand-rear neonates routinely under well-established policies and guidelines. Reasons for hand-rearing can vary greatly, however. Some species of hoofstock are hand-reared with the intention of producing more tractable adults. Zoos that have nursery exhibits may deliberately pull a neonate for hand rearing for the purpose of display. Thus, some of the surplus animal problem can be attributed to the fact that neonates are often considered a popular drawing card.

Often candidates for hand rearing are animals that are too weak to survive on their own or are rejected by their dams. While they may be inherently weak, or the dam may be inexperienced, these neonates would not have survived in the wild. It can be argued that heroic hand-rearing efforts produce individuals detrimental to the overall viability of the captive population. Such individuals also take up space that could be reserved for more fit offspring. In many cases this argument is valid; however, the issue is controversial and complicated. Some would say that hand-rearing decisions should be made on the basis of species uniqueness, rarity, and status in the wild. Others would say that endangered species should be the last ones considered for this practice because of the danger of its increasing behavioral and physical abnormalities within the limited gene pool.

The reason hand-reared animals are difficult to place is that their psychological development is often impaired. With some species, imprinting on humans can easily occur unless extraordinary efforts are made to minimize human contact and unless visual contact with conspecifics is provided. In general, imprinting can result in animals that do not recognize their own species and are unlikely to reproduce successfully (Graham, n.d.; Graham 1972; Mellen 1988).

Zoos have historically been looked upon as sanctuaries where life is to be supported at all costs. While some hand-reared young can be reproductively successful as adults (O. Oftedal, pers. comm.), it must be recognized that indiscriminate hand-rearing may result in animals that, in terms of their fitness, should not contribute to the population. As we are beginning to learn from geneticists, the quality of specimens is much more vital than is quantity in most cases.

Yet another cause of surplus in zoos is the great reduction of predation and disease and the elimination of starvation. This situation produces animals with artificially long life spans. In some zoos this problem is compounded by attempts to attain longevity records (Jones 1972; Slavens 1988, 89–159), although in most zoos, this practice is now in disfavor. Superannuated animals become a hindrance to the captive population and a drain on the resources of the zoo. Even those elderly animals that remain reproductively viable may produce weakened offspring or an abnormal sex ratio. At the Gorilla SSP Propagation Group meeting held on 8 April 1986, various participants noted that older females may produce a preponderance of male offspring.

It has been correctly stated that there is no such thing as a surplus animal, just a lack of space. Many wild animals have an approximately 1:1 sex ratio; however, because of space limitations, most collections do not reflect such natural ratios. With most hoofstock, zoos tend to keep at most two or three males with perhaps a dozen or more females.

If offspring of each sex are born in approximately equal numbers, this easily leads to a surplus of males.

It might seem that a well-managed zoo should not produce surplus, but proper management may well produce more surplus than haphazard management does. For example, demography is an important component of professional animal management. (For an illustration of an age structure in a captive population, see Ballou and Foose, chap. 26, this volume). A demographic model, quite simply, is a plan to determine the sex and age classes of the optimal breeding group within an institutional population and, in the larger sense, the total captive population. However, adherence to such demographic models may produce more surplus than otherwise. For instance, if an age class of five 3-year-old females is a goal and births do not match the need, surplus may be created that cannot be held for future inclusion in the population because of lack of space and other resources.

AVOIDING SURPLUS

An obvious method of avoiding the problem of surplus is to avoid producing it in the first place by practicing some form of birth control. However, the situation is not quite that simple. Birth control options include separation of the sexes, hormonal implants and other contraceptive drugs, and sterilization or vasectomy (see Asa et al., chap. 40, this volume). All of these are self-explanatory, and all have their hazards, the first of which is loss of reproductive ability. In most cases sterilization and vasectomy are irreversible. The effects of long-term use of implants and drugs on future reproductive viability are not sufficiently documented.

Even simple separation of the sexes may reduce reproductive ability. At the Detroit Zoo, male and female tigers, *Panthera tigris*, were separated for a number of years. After they were reunited, an 11-year-old female, an age acceptable for breeding within the guidelines of the Tiger SSP (Foose and Seal 1982), mated in three consecutive periods of heat, but no conception occurred. Upon the death of this female 3 years later, it was discovered that she was sterile. The necropsy report stated: "Both fallopian tubes were blocked, and fluid could not be forced through either of the oviducts." Separation of the sexes may also cause aberrant behaviors (Conway 1976).

When birth control is effective, the breeding group inevitably gets older and less fecund; also, a random event such as an epidemic or an error in reversible birth control could seriously damage the population's breeding potential.

DEALING WITH SURPLUS

When the problem of surplus does arise, there are various options available. A few, by their very nature, are unacceptable to AZA members, bound as they are by the AZA Code of Ethics in this regard. Pertinent sections are: "I-A: As a member of the AZA, I pledge to realize that I have moral responsibilities not only to my professional associates, my fellow employees, and the public, but also to the animals under my care." And "I-K: As a member of the AZA, I pledge to make every effort to assure that exotic animals do not find their way into the hands of those not qualified to care for them properly."

With these pledges in mind, it appears to me that the exotic pet trade, roadside "zoos," circuses, the fur trade, commercial advertising, wildlife auctions, research involving inhumane procedures, shooting preserves, petting zoos in malls or shopping centers, and zoological facilities and animal dealers not accredited by AZA should be considered unacceptable for placement of zoo animals. With a few exceptions, private individuals should also be considered unacceptable for such placement.

Foreign zoos are being considered more and more for placement of surplus animals; however, those zoos are not accredited by AZA. Acceptable zoos should be accredited by, or at least be a member in good standing of, the zoo association in their part of the world. As a practical matter, it should be pointed out that foreign zoos will eventually "fill up;" therefore, using foreign zoos as an outlet for surplus (outside of the SSP) may provide only temporary relief.

Probably the ideal option for surplus is reintroduction into the wild. This has occurred, with varying degrees of success, in a number of species, including the American bison, *Bison bison,* (Garretson 1938), Hawaiian goose, *Branta sandvicensis* (Berger 1978; Meadows 1990), Andean condor, *Vultur gryphus,* Arabian oryx, *Oryx leucoryx,* and golden lion tamarin, *Leontopithecus rosalia* (Kleiman et al. 1986). A corollary benefit of boosting wild populations is the protection afforded to the habitat, which contains many other species that receive protection along with the target species (G. Schaller, pers. comm.).

There are a number of serious logistic problems with reintroduction projects (see Kleiman, chap. 29, this volume). These problems include the dwindling availability of wilderness and, with many species, the need to train zoo-bred animals for survival in the wild. Another consideration is that reintroduction programs require long-term support and funding to insure success. The government controlling the release site area must make a long-term commitment to protect not only the animals but also the necessary habitat. The reintroduction of the Arabian oryx, for example, may hang on the fragile thread of peace in the Middle East.

Reintroduction into the wild can absorb only a minute portion of zoo surplus because of these problems of expense, logistics, and lack of suitable habitat. Therefore, this ideal option for placing zoo surplus cannot be the only one.

Although many zoo administrators have stated that none of their animals will be placed in a "research facility," I consider that to be an overly simplistic attitude toward a complex issue. Biomedical research is a necessary part of the struggle to improve the quality of life for human beings. Zoo personnel are not qualified, nor should they be, to dictate research policies; however, they must understand the need for research that benefits humans as well as animals. Research, at least in some instances, should be considered a viable option for placement of zoo surplus.

Let me describe two situations the Detroit Zoo faced in the early 1980s, one of which was handled appropriately and the other which was not.

A group of twenty-three crab-eating macaques, *Macaca*

fascicularis, had been offered to other zoos for several months and could not be relocated. They were subsequently placed in a terminal atherosclerosis research project at a university. We required that a written protocol be submitted that specifically described the research and animal manipulations. We chose to place them in terminal research because (1) we knew they would not be "recycled" to a project that we might consider unacceptable, and (2) we felt that the chosen project was a valid use of the animals, and the protocol indicated humane treatment, including anesthesia during the surgical procedure followed by additional anesthesia to kill the animals without their ever awakening. In providing our animals for this project we also protected a sizable number of wild macaques. Taking primates from the wild is highly destructive; it has been estimated that as many as ten primates die for each one that reaches the laboratory alive (Fitzgerald 1989).

The other situation involved a group of thirty-four Guinea baboons, *Papio papio,* that were placed in a research breeding facility. Although, according to the written protocol, they were not to be placed in any traumatic research, I now believe that this was an extremely short-sighted and unacceptable placement because we had no control over the fate of their offspring.

While controversial and unacceptable to some zoo administrators, feeding surplus to other zoo collection animals is another option. Laboratory animals such as mice, rats, guinea pigs, and amphibians are generally accepted by professionals and the public as food items for zoo animals. But what inherent difference exists between a surplus prairie dog, *Cynomys,* and a commercially produced guinea pig? It could also be argued that a policy of using surplus zoo-bred snakes as food should be preferred to the use of snakes commercially collected from the wild. Further, the use of humanely killed surplus hoofstock for feeding zoo carnivores may make sense from a management standpoint, especially since such a practice may provide physical and psychological benefits to the carnivores.

An obviously acceptable method of disposal of zoo surplus is to AZA-accredited zoos. However, communication, coordination, and cooperation among zoos need to be maximized. Examples of excellent zoo cooperation include ISIS (the International Species Information System) and the international and regional studbooks, which provide genetic background on individual specimens (see Shoemaker and Flesness, appendix 4, this volume). The most important example of zoo cooperation in North America is the Species Survival Plan (SSP) (Conway, Foose, and Wagner, n.d.). Started in 1981, the SSP's function is to recommend the number of institutions over which a species should be distributed as well as which animals should reproduce, be maintained, or be removed from the population. It also provides monitoring and sharing of research on animal social organization needs, reproductive physiology, and effective husbandry techniques. An elected committee of nine or more members per species makes collective decisions regarding the fate of each animal. Zoos that participate in the SSP agree to abide by the decisions of the committee and see that all that can be done for captive breeding is being done.

The SSP promotes the dictum that the total population of a species has greater importance than individual animals. For example, the tiger SSP members voted to remove white tigers from the tiger SSP (Binczik and Tilson 1990). This decision was made, in part, because of severe space limitations for tigers in zoos. Others consider the white tiger morph to be, from a conservation standpoint, undesirable (Frankham et al. 1986, 131–32).

EUTHANASIA

The most controversial method of disposing of surplus animals is euthanasia. The dictionary definition of euthanasia is simply "painless death." The American Veterinary Medical Association Panel on Euthanasia defines it as "the act of inducing painless death, specifically painlessness for the animal being subjected to euthanasia" (AVMA 1972, 1978).

The general understanding of the term, at least among pet owners, is that euthanasia is reserved for individuals that are suffering from some irreversible health problem. With regard to zoo animals, however, euthanasia may be required in other circumstances. For instance, in zoos approved for importation of hoofstock under U.S. Department of Agriculture permanent post-entry quarantine (PPEQ) regulations, placement of those animals is regulated by USDA, and the animals cannot be removed from the grounds of the importing zoo without the permission of USDA. The USDA regulation extends this requirement to domestic hoofstock housed on the zoo grounds in "farmyard" exhibits, in that they and their offspring may only be placed in other PPEQ zoos or sent directly to a USDA-approved slaughterhouse. Obviously the option of placing surplus domestics in other PPEQ zoos is all but nonexistent; euthanasia is the humane answer. An additional benefit of culling such animals is that it allows veterinarians and students to necropsy carcasses in which no apparent disease has damaged any of the working systems; it is important for veterinary personnel to be knowledgeable about healthy tissue as well as diseased tissue.

Euthanasia can also be a logical solution to the problem of physically healthy non-PPEQ animals that are surplus to a zoo's needs and cannot be placed in a suitable situation elsewhere. While euthanasia of ailing animals is controversial only in terms of timing, not final disposition, euthanasia of healthy animals to increase available space and viability of captive populations is exceedingly controversial. However, collection managers must be concerned with the viability of the species, making the individual's importance secondary.

Possibly the most difficult concept for the public to understand is that individuals of an endangered species can be considered surplus even to the point of requiring euthanasia. An article in the *New York Times* of 13 August 1984, entitled "Animal Species Rare in Wild Present a Problem as They Flourish in Zoos," presented the idea well. Sandy Friedman (then of the Chicago Zoological Park) stated in this article: "Saving endangered species to most people means breeding them." However, any breeding program produces surplus, and Thomas Foose, (formerly) AAZPA conserva-

tion coordinator, pointed out in this same article, "We can be very successful in reproducing species, but if we're going to preserve a species, we've got to make sure all the specimens are the right kind at the right time." The specimens that are not the right kind at the right time are surplus. Surplus individuals of endangered species are sometimes more easily placed, especially when attention is paid to avoiding inbreeding. However, even careful reproduction of some species is now creating surplus individuals that, due to lack of space, are often unplaceable in accredited zoos; for example, snow leopards, *Uncia uncia* (pers. obs.). Endangered species are also represented by some superannuated animals and in some instances by overrepresented bloodlines (Binczik and Tilson 1990, 3).

Thus, proper management of an endangered species is no different from proper management of an abundant species: breeding inescapably creates surplus, and this surplus must be dealt with in the best interests of the species rather than the best interests of the individuals.

AZA and the Euthanasia Issue

Any discussion of surplus and euthanasia requires a brief history of AZA's attempts to resolve this controversial matter. An early recognition of the approaching dilemma was voiced by David Zucconi, director of Tulsa Zoological Park (Zucconi 1976):

> The time may soon be upon us . . . when we will have to admit to the biological impropriety of "birth control." Certainly, such measures do limit excess population growth, but they do not provide for the same type of sound genetic management that is common to breeders of dogs, cats, and other domesticated animals. The prospect of "culling" litters of tigers, lions, or grizzly bears is not very palatable to those of us who were raised with a reverence for these magnificent species. Yet, with such small gene pools in captivity, it becomes bad animal husbandry to avoid techniques that could maintain the most natural strains possible. To paraphrase one of my colleagues, we will ultimately be pressed for a decision between the welfare of the individual and its species. Such a decision cannot be made lightly, and it is my personal opinion that a collective effort of zoos and humane societies will be necessary to resolve the problem.

At the AAZPA Annual Conference in 1976, William G. Conway of the New York Zoological Park presented a paper (Conway 1976) entitled "The Surplus Problem" containing the following insights:

> The maintenance of large numbers of superannuated animals increases crowding, depresses breeding, improves the chances for disease and generally lowers the viability of zoo populations. . . . Zoos which hope to contribute to the survival of vanishing species through propagation must deal with the surplus problem in a fashion designed to give higher priority to the welfare of species than to individuals of that species.
> . . . we cannot plan a reproductive program for most species that will not produce significant surplus unless we alter the normal behavior and physiology of the captive animals. . . . Unfortunately, it may be that parental behavior and even fertility are adversely affected by reproductive restraints in some species.
> . . . wild animal populations in zoos need to produce a surplus for many of the same reasons that they do in nature.

Prevention of reproduction will not solve the surplus problem. Removal will continue to play a significant role. . . .
A major educational contribution of zoos has been to better establish animals as individuals rather than simply indistinguishable segments of those multi-limbed mobs called herds. This sensitization is the foundation for much support for wildlife conservation. Unfortunately, it is sometimes perverted in the uneducated emotionalism of those persons and organized groups who seem to devote more of their efforts towards insuring that individual animals die well than that whole species survive at all. . . .
Despite our own emotional involvement with "our" animals, when no other humane and philosophically suitable alternative is available, zoos must not shirk from seeing that surplus animals are mercifully destroyed.

After considerable urging, an AAZPA Surplus Committee was formed in 1977 under the chairmanship of Conway. A supportive letter to Conway came from the Humane Society of the United States in 1978, written by Sue Pressman, then director of wildlife protection for HSUS: "We regard euthanizing animals by recognized humane means as being appropriate and acceptable when conditions warrant; e.g., aged, ill, infirm or surplus animals no longer capable of being housed at the zoo and suitable quarters cannot be located in other zoological institutions."

An enclosure with the Surplus Committee report by Conway dated 31 July 1978 stated: "The Committee believes that the need to euthanize surplus zoo animals (as defined elsewhere) is not a controversial issue, provided that euthanasia is accomplished by recognized humane methods."

One would think that by the time the Surplus Committee was disbanded in 1980, the unequivocal statement of 1978 would have had some beneficial effect in providing encouragement and support to zoo managers facing the problems of euthanasia. However, the prospect of euthanasia was still too difficult for some zoo directors to face. In 1982 a major AAZPA member zoo had the task of relocating an intractable elephant with such a dangerous disposition that no other zoo would accept her. The zoo director said that he was considering sending her to "a good circus." Why? "Euthanizing is against what all zoos are trained to do. . . . We are not psychologically prepared to do that."

In 1987 Robert O. Wagner, executive director of AAZPA, provided member zoos and aquariums with guidelines specifically addressing the question of euthanasia. These guidelines stated that euthanasia as a management tool is a necessary part of animal management (AAZPA 1987).

It is unrealistic to accept the concept of the SSP without also accepting the concept of culling healthy but extraneous individuals that are produced in the effort to maximize the viability of a species. The need to euthanize will be especially high at the inception of an SSP , when the species is being managed for the first time and unsuitable animals have to be culled from the existing population. Although individual SSP master plans indicate that surplus animals will be produced, recommendations for dealing with that surplus are not typically made. For instance, it is recommended that a Siberian tiger be bred only twice in its lifetime. At 12 years of age it is considered surplus to the population (Foose and Seal 1982). While such a surplus tiger may have value as an exhibit animal, so too would a tiger of

breeding age, which could also be exhibited. Guidelines for dealing with such complex situations are still clearly needed.

The Detroit Zoo and the Euthanasia Issue

Some AZA members have talked bravely among their colleagues of the need to use euthanasia as a management tool, but implementing it in their own zoos has proved more difficult. It is indeed difficult, as the Detroit Zoo learned in 1982 when zoo officials faced the issue and created a storm of controversy both locally and nationally. The zoo planned to euthanize three Siberian tigers that suffered from a variety of serious disabilities, but word filtered out into the community and a cause célèbre ensued. The zoo received hundreds of protest phone calls and letters, a national animal rights group sent representatives to Detroit to castigate the zoo, and a resident of Detroit filed suit to prevent the zoo from carrying out the euthanasia plan. The judge rendered a decision favoring the zoo on the basis that zoo officials had acted responsibly rather than capriciously in planning the euthanasia. By the time the controversy ended, the right of zoo managers to manage the animal collection (at least in Detroit) had been affirmed, and the media as well as the vast majority of the public in Detroit had accepted the validity of the zoo's action.

The turnaround in public reaction did not come easily. It required a willingness on the part of the zoo staff to face the assault squarely and firmly, explaining the rationale for the euthanasia over and over in various public forums. Stressful though it was, the strategy proved sound, and the zoo emerged stronger both in community support and in terms of its ability to manage the zoo collection.

At issue in Detroit in 1982 were three ailing tigers. In 1985, the Detroit Zoo euthanized four *healthy* tigers because they were not accepted into the Siberian tiger SSP. The rationale was that with four spaces for tigers available in the zoo, it was logical, and indeed imperative, that those spaces be occupied by individuals acceptable to the SSP. Compared with the strong public reaction of 1982, there was hardly a stir in 1985.

In 1986 a Detroit newspaper published an article on euthanasia at the zoo and emphasized the recent culling of two male lions. It appeared to be an attempt to sensationalize, but it evoked little public reaction—and attendance at the Detroit Zoo in 1986 was the highest in years. Subsequent newspaper articles in 1989 and 1990 were also basically ignored by the public.

It is of critical importance that decisions regarding disposition of animals be made by professionals and not by the media or by animal rights groups. In the early 1980s a major North American zoo planned the euthanasia of a surplus tiger. When this became known to the public through the media, an individual came forward to donate funds, and a new exhibit was built specifically for this one animal. Such an action is professionally reprehensible because it places more importance upon the individual than upon the species, it wastes funds that could be used in a more productive fashion, and it implies to the public that zoo managers should not be allowed to make decisions with regard to animal dispositions.

The history of the euthanasia controversy in Detroit may

help to alleviate future problems for other zoos. How did Detroit ride out the storm? Through education. Education begins with the staff and ends with the general public. In between, it includes the governing authority, the media, and volunteers.

It can be difficult to educate a governing authority. Such individuals cannot be expected to have a good understanding of zoo management and biological principles. Although their focus is often narrowed to the dollar value of the animals, an effort to explain the need for good animal management can be successful. One of the first actions I took as director of the Detroit Zoological Parks Department was to seek authority from Mayor Coleman A. Young concerning disposition of animals. He agreed that animals could be euthanized rather than sold if that was professionally and humanely correct. He also agreed that animals could be given away to facilities that would properly care for them, in preference to being sold to others where proper care was in question, without regard to the potential dollar value of the animals.

Understanding on the part of the keeper staff is extremely important when euthanasia is being considered. At the Detroit Zoo we have emphasized the need to face the problem of surplus animals rather than avoiding it and the need for euthanasia when this is the responsible action to take. Not all keepers have been able to accept this philosophy. Nevertheless, the effect of our efforts to instill a recognition of the realities of animal management in our keepers may be gauged by the fact that the initially high negative public reaction to the tiger euthanasia of 1982 seemed to be shared by several of our keepers, while the relative lack of negative public reaction to the tiger and lion euthanasias in 1985 and 1986 was also reflected in the keeper staff.

In regard to the public's perceptions of zoo policy, the director is probably the zoo's most visible representative. My personal efforts as director in three different zoos have included bringing the issue of euthanasia to public attention early on, beginning with mention of the probability that successful breeding programs would produce surplus that would eventually have to be culled. This strategy not only plants the seed but also provides some protection for the future, as you can honestly say, "We talked about this two years ago."

The development of direct and open communication with the media will greatly help the zoo's public image. Dealing in a straightforward manner with the media, which is the zoo's major conduit of information to the general public, is of paramount importance (Blakely 1983).

Over the years there have been efforts by various zoos to educate their supporters through their zoo publications and the media (Zucconi 1976; Krantz 1985; Applebaum, Bourne, and Latinen 1986; Ruedi 1990). It is imperative that all AZA zoos provide such educational input to their public.

Methods of Euthanasia

Possibly the most acceptable method of carrying out euthanasia is by injection, the benefit being that it is fast and, depending on the drug of choice, humane. The negative aspect is that the meat cannot be used for animal food.

Shooting is an option that is time-honored and basically accepted as humane. Such activity is feasible only in a contained area, especially in urban zoos. However, negative moral attitudes concerning firearms do cloud the issue.

The captive-bolt gun works in much the same way as a firearm but utilizes a contained bolt that produces instant death in most species when placed immediately over the brain. This method requires close proximity to the animal being euthanized and is used mainly with domestics, which are relatively easy to restrain. Meat from such carcasses can be fed to the collection carnivores (as can meat from animals culled by shooting).

CONCLUDING REMARKS

Euthanasia should be accepted as a reasonable and necessary animal management tool. To achieve such acceptance, zoo personnel must have the confidence and respect of the community. Being correct in one's implementation of sound biological principles is not enough to achieve this, however. An additional component will strongly influence the success or failure of a zoo's management program: It is absolutely essential that the program be administered by sensitive and caring individuals who share the same emotions and concerns as the public. Each time the subject is addressed, the zoo must remind the public that euthanasia decisions are difficult and even painful for those who make them. No one entered this profession for the purpose of culling animals. We must be sure that the public grasps the total concept that euthanasia is based on sound biological principles reflecting the realities of nature, *and* that such actions are not carried out by unfeeling automatons, but rather by people who are acting in the best interests of the species under their care.

SUMMARY

Surplus animals are a product of improved husbandry and management (such as SSPs). Zoos' attempts to replicate nature have grown increasingly successful; however, attempts to convince zoo professionals to accept nature's solution to the surplus problem have been much less successful.

All zoo professionals will agree that the problem is not an excess of animals but rather a lack of carrying capacity in our institutions—a situation that is unlikely to change appreciably for the better. Everyone will also agree that certain options for placement of surplus animals are fully acceptable, such as accredited zoos, legitimate foreign zoos, and the essentially limited option of reintroduction to the wild. There is also some support for placement of surplus animals in carefully chosen research projects. Less acceptable options include nonaccredited facilities, hunting preserves, the pet trade, and the entertainment industry.

Without a doubt, however, the major controversy regarding disposal of surplus animals centers on euthanasia as a management tool. Although this issue has been openly discussed since the mid-1970s, the controversy continues. The time has arrived for the zoo profession to accept the necessity of following nature's example. Considering the less acceptable options listed above, euthanasia—humane and painless death—may be the ultimate kindness.

ACKNOWLEDGMENTS

I would like to extend my thanks to Doris Applebaum, Detroit Zoological Parks Registrar, and Mary Allen, co-editor of this book, for their considerable and much-appreciated assistance in the preparation of this chapter.

REFERENCES

American Association of Zoological Parks and Aquariums (AAZPA). 1987. Euthanasia of zoo/aquarium specimens (Guidelines for AAZPA members). Wheeling, W.Va.: American Association of Zoological Parks and Aquariums.

American Veterinary Medical Association (AVMA). 1972. Report of the AVMA Panel on Euthanasia. *J. Am. Vet. Med. Assoc.* 160 (6): 761–72.

———. 1978. Report of the AVMA Panel on Euthanasia. *J. Am. Vet. Med. Assoc.* 173 (1): 59–72.

Applebaum, D., Bourne, G. R., and Latinen, K. 1986. Following Nature's rules. *Habitat* (Newsletter of the Detroit Zoological Society), Summer.

Berger, A. J. 1978. Reintroduction of Hawaiian geese. In *Endangered birds: Management techniques for preserving threatened species,* ed. S. A. Temple, 339–44. Madison: University of Wisconsin Press.

Binczik, G. A., and Tilson, R. L., eds. 1990. *Tiger Beat: The Newsletter of the Tiger SSP* 3 (1).

Blakely, R. L. 1983. The alternatives and public relations—surplus animal management: Problems and options. In *AAZPA Annual Conference Proceedings,* 292–93. Wheeling, W.Va.: American Association of Zoological Parks and Aquariums.

Conway, W. G. 1976. The surplus problem. *AAZPA National Conference Proceedings,* 20–24. Wheeling, W.Va.: American Association of Zoological Parks and Aquariums.

Conway, W. G., Foose, T. J., and Wagner, R. O. n.d. *Species Survival Plan.* Wheeling, W.Va.: American Association of Zoological Parks and Aquariums.

Fitzgerald, S. 1989. *Whose business is it?* Washington, D.C.: World Wildlife Fund.

Flesness, N. R. 1977. Gene pool conservation and computer analysis. *Int. Zoo Yrbk.* 17:77–80.

Foose, T. J. 1977. Demographic models for management of captive populations. *Int. Zoo Yrbk.* 17:70–76.

Foose, T. J., and Seal, U. S. 1982. *A Species Survival Plan for Siberian (Amur) tiger* (Panthera tigris altaica) *in North America.* Wheeling, W.Va.: American Association of Zoological Parks and Aquariums.

Frankham, R., Hemmer, H., Ryder, O. A., Cothran, E. G., Soulé, M. E., Murray, N. D., and Snyder, M. 1986. Selection in captive populations. *Zoo Biol.* 5 (2): 127–38.

Garretson, M. S. 1938. *American bison.* New York: New York Zoological Society.

Graham, Stefan H. n.d. A critique of hand-raising. In *AAZPA infant diet/care handbook,* ed. S. H. Taylor and A. D. Bietz. Wheeling, W.Va.: American Association of Zoological Parks and Aquariums.

———. 1972. The use of mirrors in imprinting chicks. *Int. Zoo News* 19 (1): 15–17 (no. 104).

Graham, Steve. 1987. The changing role of animal dealers. In *AAZPA Annual Conference Proceedings,* 646–52. Wheeling, W.Va.: American Association of Zoological Parks and Aquariums.

Jones, M. L. 1972. Longevity of mammals in captivity. *Int. Zoo News* 19 (1): 5–9 (no. 104).

Kleiman, D. G., Beck, B. B., Dietz, J. M., Dietz, L. A., Ballou, J. D., and Coimbra-Filho, A. F. 1986. Conservation program for the golden lion tamarin: Captive research and management, ecological studies, educational strategies, and reintroduction. In *Primates: The road to self-sustaining populations,* ed. K. Benirschke, 959–79. New York: Springer-Verlag.

Krantz, P. 1985. Death in the zoo. *Riverbanks* (Newsletter of the Riverbanks Zoological Park), September–October.

Meadows, R. 1990. The Hawaiian goose: Still endangered after all these years. *ZooGoer,* January–February.

Mellen, J. 1988. The effects of hand-raising on sexual behavior of captive small felids using domestic cats as a model. In *AAZPA Annual Conference Proceedings,* 253–58. Wheeling, W.Va.: American Association of Zoological Parks and Aquariums.

Ralls, K., and Ballou, J. 1983. Extinction: Lessons from zoos. In *Genetics and conservation: A reference for managing wild animal and plant populations,* ed. C. M. Schonewald-Cox, S. M. Chambers, B. MacBryde, and W. L. Thomas, 164–84. Menlo Park, Calif.: Benjamin/Cummings.

———, eds. 1986. Proceedings of the Workshop on Genetic Management of Captive Populations. *Zoo Biol.* 5(2).

Ruedi, D. 1990. Wir mussen uberzahlige Zootiere toten. *Das Tier* nr. 1/90.

Seal, U. S., and Flesness, N. R. 1978. Noah's ark: Sex and survival. In *AAZPA Annual Conference Proceedings,* 214–28. Wheeling, W.Va.: American Association of Zoological Parks and Aquariums.

Slavens, F. L. 1988. *Inventory, longevity, and breeding notes: Reptiles and amphibians in captivity, current January 1, 1988.* Seattle: Frank L. Slavens.

Zucconi, D. 1976. *Annual report of Tulsa Zoological Park, 1975–76.* Tulsa, Ok.: Tulsa Zoological Park.

29

Reintroduction Programs

DEVRA G. KLEIMAN

This chapter outlines the conditions that make a reintroduction program using captive mammals of a threatened or endangered species an appropriate conservation strategy, and presents some basic guidelines for such an effort. IUCN (1987) also provides criteria for these and related efforts.

Reintroduction is an approach that is attractive to zoo conservationists, as well as to the general public, but such a program should be undertaken only with a clear understanding of the costs and benefits. Because reintroduction is a complex endeavor that usually involves both a long-term financial commitment and active collaboration by governmental and nongovernmental agencies and institutions, it is not a viable option for the majority of endangered species held in captivity. Indeed, attempts to reintroduce a species, if poorly conceived or implemented, may actually obscure the conservation issues that led to the decline of the species in the first place—and thus may detract from, rather than add to, a species' chances of survival (IUCN 1987).

The first step in considering a reintroduction is to define the long-term conservation goals of the program and the criteria for success. Aims vary according to (1) the status of each species in captivity and in the wild and (2) the political situation within the receiving country. Generally, major goals include increasing the size of the wild population, establishing additional wild populations, and/or preserving or enhancing available habitat. Ideally, reintroduction could also be used to enhance the demographic and genetic management of both wild and captive populations. While criteria for success vary depending upon the aims of each program, a program is likely to be judged a success if the status of a species is significantly improved by the reintroduction, even if every single released individual dies. Reintroduction solely as a solution to the problem of surplus captive animals is inappropriate; an integrated plan to promote the preservation of the species in the wild is also needed.

The success of many early attempts to reintroduce mammals into natural habitats cannot be fairly evaluated since there has been limited post-release monitoring, especially for primate reintroductions (Aveling and Mitchell 1982;

Borner 1985). There have been some clear successes with ungulates, including the American bison, *Bison bison*, and the European wisent, *Bison bonasus* (Conway 1980; Campbell 1980), although those efforts also involved minimal monitoring.

In the remainder of this chapter I will concentrate on outlining those factors that should be considered in planning and implementing a reintroduction program involving the release of threatened or endangered captive mammals. There have been many more reintroduction programs for bird species (Campbell 1980), although they are neither less complicated nor less expensive than reintroduction programs for mammals. Long (1981) estimated, in a review of translocations, reintroductions, and introductions, that approximately half of the attempts failed. Cade (1986), Wemmer and Derrickson (1987), Kleiman (1989), Stanley Price (1989), Gipps (1991), and Beck et al. (1994) provide reviews and bibliographies on reintroduction programs for captive birds and mammals.

A description of a release of animals into a natural habitat needs to specify (1) whether the release occurs within the species' original geographic range, (2) whether there is a preexisting free-ranging population at the release site, and (3) the history of the specimens released (i.e., wild- or captive-born, currently in the wild or in captivity, previous experience in the wild). There are differences among authors in their use of terms (Konstant and Mittermeier 1982; IUCN 1987; Stanley Price 1989). I am defining *reintroduction* here as the release of either captive-born or wild-caught animals into an area within their original range where populations have declined or disappeared. Reintroductions may involve moving *(translocating)* wild-caught animals or releasing naive captive animals (both wild- and captive-born), and may have a conservation or an economic purpose. Goals may include improving the status of the wild population by increasing numbers (sometimes termed *restocking*) or changing the population's genetic makeup. The latter goal may be appropriate when the species exists in small groups in insular habitats that preclude outbreeding.

WHEN IS REINTRODUCTION APPROPRIATE?

Reintroduction may be appropriate when the demography and genetics of the wild population suggest that a species could go extinct and that a boost in population size or genetic diversity would protect its future. Such a judgment must be based on a thorough knowledge of the species' biology, distribution, and ecological requirements, as well as an understanding of the original factors causing the population decline.

With the condition of the wild population ascertained, there must exist a viable, self-sustaining captive population with broad genetic representation. The captive population must be sufficiently robust to sustain the loss of many animals for a prolonged period while reintroduction techniques are perfected. Animals chosen for a release program must be surplus to the future needs of the captive population and able to interbreed with animals in the wild population. There are numerous species, such as owl monkeys, *Aotus trivirgatus,* in which distinct populations appear morphologically identical, but are so different genetically that individuals cannot interbreed (Ma et al. 1976). Shields (1982) has suggested that outbreeding depression may be a more common problem than expected.

Another requirement is the existence of suitable habitat with sufficient carrying capacity (Brambell 1977) to sustain the growth of the reintroduced population. Habitat suitability can be assessed only by detailed studies of the habitat preferences, movements, shelter requirements, and foraging and feeding behavior of free-ranging wild-born animals. Critical resources may not always be self-evident. Coimbra-Filho and Mittermeier (1978) correctly identified tree holes for sleeping as a critical resource for the golden lion tamarin, *Leontopithecus rosalia.* We preceded reintroductions of this species with an evaluation of the numbers of trees with sufficient girth to provide tree holes for nocturnal nesting (J. M. Dietz, D. G. Kleiman, and B. B. Beck, unpub.). Preferred habitat should have no, or a very reduced, resident population, but be within the natural range of the species.

Since habitat loss and alteration are the paramount causes of the decline of most species, the lack of suitable protected habitat is the major ecological reason to reject proposals for a reintroduction program. Thus, a prerequisite for a reintroduction program is the existence of legally protected areas, such as national parks or equivalent reserves, with real and effective protection (Campbell 1980; U.S. Fish and Wildlife Service 1982; Aveling and Mitchell 1982; Borner 1985; Oliver 1985). There must also be the expectation that the protected areas will survive intact into the future. Without a long-term commitment, there will be a constant (and probably losing) battle to protect not only the animals but also the habitat. For example, difficulty in finding a politically safe habitat for releasing red wolves, *Canis rufus,* has been one of the major obstacles to the Red Wolf Recovery Plan (U.S. Fish and Wildlife Service 1982; Parker 1986), as it has been for the release of sea otters, *Enhydra lutris* (K. Ralls, pers. comm.).

Currently, one of the most impressive reintroduction programs involves the release of captive-born Arabian oryx, *Oryx leucoryx,* in Oman (Fitter 1984; Stanley Price 1989).

The Sultan of Oman has personally taken an interest in the program and is supporting it financially and providing equipment. Furthermore, individuals from local tribes are employed by the project, and thus directly benefit from it (Stanley Price 1986, 1989). This effort is likely to be successful, as long as the support remains at the level of government policy and the local citizenry is kept aware and involved.

While sufficient protected habitat is of paramount importance for the development of a reintroduction program, other reasons for a species' decline must also be identified and eliminated prior to the release of captive-bred animals (Brambell 1977). Hunting or poaching for food, fur, trophies, or other body parts has been a major factor in many species' decline, especially for birds and the large charismatic mammals. In other cases, species have declined or been lost due to predation, food competition, or habitat destruction caused by the introduction of nonnative species, including domestic cats, dogs, rats, rabbits, goats, and snakes. Birds and reptiles endemic to islands have suffered greatly from these causes.

Diseases that can rapidly wipe out a population (and a species, if it already exists in small numbers) may also be introduced through other carriers. Kear (1975) describes several cases in which avian species have been decimated through accidentally introduced viruses.

Free-ranging animals should not be present in an area targeted for a reintroduction if the wild population is severely endangered. It is not usually appropriate to intermix the wild and captive populations unless the species' future survival absolutely depends upon an "injection" from the captive gene pool. First, the captives may carry disease agents to which they, but not the wild individuals, are immune, a problem pointed out by many authors (Brambell 1977; Caldecott and Kavanagh 1983; Aveling and Mitchell 1982). The wild population can be protected by first releasing captives in habitats that are devoid of free-ranging animals. Alternatively, captives can be shipped to the country of destination and quarantined. Prior to release, selected free-ranging individuals can be introduced to the quarantined captives and act as "guinea pigs" to test for the presence of possible disease vectors. Prerelease screening by veterinarians of the captives' blood, urine, feces, and ectoparasites, followed by appropriate treatment, may also reduce the potential for disease transmission. However, veterinary evaluations of specimens destined for release is necessary regardless of the existence of overt health problems or the likelihood of contact between a reintroduced and a wild population.

Another reason for reducing contact between reintroduced captive-born animals and the wild population is to protect the genetic integrity of either or both populations. For example, the red wolf is currently considered extinct in the wild due to extensive crossing with the coyote, *Canis latrans* (U.S. Fish and Wildlife Service 1982, 1986; Parker 1986). To prevent further hybridization, the reintroduction program releases captives on islands or in areas known to be devoid of coyotes and hybrids.

Releasing animals into a saturated stable natural population is known to cause social disruption and stress (Brewer

TABLE 29.1.   Decision Making Concerning the Reintroduction of Lion Tamarins *(Leontopithecus):* Do the Necessary Conditions Exist?

	Leontopithecus		
	rosalia	*chrysomelas*	*chrysopygus*
1. The reasons for the reduction in species numbers have been eliminated (e.g., hunting, deforestation, commerce)	?	No	No
2. Sufficient habitat is protected and secure	Yes?	No	Yes
3. Available habitat exists with low densities of or without native animals	Yes	Yes?	?
4. It is certain that the release of animals will not jeopardize the existing wild population	No	No	No
5. Sufficient information exists about the species' biology in the wild to evaluate whether the program is a success	5	1.5	3
6. Conservation education exists	5	2	4
7. The population in captivity is secure, well managed, and has surplus animals	Yes	No	No
8. Knowledge of the techniques of reintroduction exists	3	3	3
9. Resources for postrelease monitoring are available	Yes	No	No
10. There is a need to augment the size/genetic diversity of the wild population	Yes	No	Yes?
IS REINTRODUCTION RECOMMENDED?	**YES**	**NO**	**NO**

Source: Based on material provided by C. and S. Padua, A. Rylands, C. Alves, J. and L. A. Dietz, J. Ballou, F. Simon, B. Beck, and J. Mallinson at the *Leontopithecus* Management Workshop, Belo Horizonte, Brazil, June 19–23, 1990.
Note: Scale: 5, best; 0, worst.

1978; Carter 1981; Aveling and Mitchell 1982; McGrew 1983; Borner 1985; Harcourt, in press). For newly released animals (as singletons or groups) unacquainted with an area and without established home ranges or territories, a confrontation with adapted wild animals in natural social groups may result, at best, in flight and dispersal to a marginal habitat. At worst, the native animals may attack and seriously wound or kill the newcomers (Harcourt, in press; McGrew 1983). There are several documented cases in which young chimpanzees, *Pan troglodytes,* have been attacked after release into the territory of an established group (Brewer 1978; Carter 1981; Borner 1985).

Captives may also be unacquainted with the etiquette of social interactions in natural habitats, and may overreact upon meeting a wild conspecific. For example, groups of wild golden lion tamarins regularly interact at territorial boundaries. Although the interactions have aggressive components, they rarely result in injuries (Peres 1986; pers. obs.). However, groups of newly released captive-born tamarins were very aggressive toward each other during their first conspecific encounters, resulting in the flight and loss of some individuals (D. G. Kleiman, J. M. Dietz, and B. B. Beck, unpub.).

Decision Making: A Concrete Example

This section (see also Kleiman 1990) provides a concrete example of how to decide whether the appropriate conditions exist to recommend (or argue against) reintroductions of captive-born animals or translocations of wild individuals or groups.

The lion tamarins (genus *Leontopithecus*) derive from

the Atlantic Coastal rainforests of Brazil. All species are endangered, mainly due to habitat destruction and alteration. There are captive populations of three species, each at different levels of development.

Table 29.1 lists ten conditions that should be met in order to recommend a reintroduction/translocation program. Additionally, it evaluates the position of the three lion tamarin forms with respect to each condition. Finally, a general recommendation is presented concerning whether a program of reintroduction is warranted for each of the three forms (this material was prepared in 1990).

The major reason for the decline of the lion tamarins has been deforestation. There has also been a thriving commerce in these forms because they are favored as pets. The reasons for the decline of *L. chrysopygus* and *L. chrysomelas* have not been eliminated, thus dictating against a reintroduction at this time. It is questionable whether or not the reasons for the decline of *L. rosalia* are now fully under control.

There is likely sufficient protected habitat available for *L. chrysopygus,* but not for *L. chrysomelas.* Protected habitat exists for *L. rosalia,* although in insufficient quantities for its future survival.

To prevent social disruption and disease transmission, it is preferable to use areas that have small or no populations of wild tamarins. This condition exists for *L. rosalia,* and probably for *L. chrysomelas.* There are many available confiscated *L. chrysomelas* that cannot be absorbed easily into the captive population; reintroduction may be a viable option for this small subset of wild-born animals. The situation for *L. chrysopygus* is unknown at this time.

Reintroductions should be encouraged only when there is some certainty that the release of animals from other regions (both captive and wild-born) will not jeopardize the existing native population through transmission of disease or social disruption. We do not have this confidence for the three forms of lion tamarins at this time due to our limited knowledge of their biology and status.

The evaluation of the success of a reintroduction can be accomplished only by long-term monitoring and must be based on a thorough knowledge of a species' biology, distribution, and ecological requirements. On a scale of 1–5, with 5 being the best-case scenario, I suggest that there is sufficient information available for *L. rosalia*, and totally insufficient information available for *L. chrysomelas*, with *L. chrysopygus* somewhere in between.

A conservation education program in conjunction with a reintroduction can attract and inform the local populace and may well result in greater community support for the effort. Both *L. rosalia* and *L. chrysopygus* conservation programs have strong educational components. The education program for *L. chrysomelas* is developing.

A prerequisite to the reintroduction of animals currently in captivity (whether captive or wild-born) is a secure, well-managed captive population with a long-term Masterplan and available surplus animals. This condition is met in *L. rosalia*, but not yet in *L. chrysomelas* and *L. chrysopygus*.

We have much still to learn about the methodologies of preparation, adaptation, and release of lion tamarins. With so many unanswered questions about the techniques that will ensure success—for example, for the injection of single animals into established reproductive groups—I suggest that we still consider reintroduction an experimental approach.

Access to the resources necessary to monitor the activities and survivorship of released animals is essential for a reintroduction effort, especially since we have not yet perfected our preparation and release techniques. The conservation programs for *L. chrysomelas* and *L. chrysopygus* are not yet sufficiently developed, with respect to financial support and the necessary infrastructure, to warrant a reintroduction effort. The *L. rosalia* program has a well-developed infrastructure and considerable resources to monitor the activities of released animals.

One major purpose of a reintroduction program is to augment the numbers or genetic diversity of a population. *L. rosalia* currently needs such augmentation, while the situation for *L. chrysomelas* and *L. chrysopygus* is not clear at this time.

Weighing the degree to which the necessary conditions are met for each species suggests that while reintroduction efforts may be appropriate for *L. rosalia*, they are not yet appropriate for *L. chrysomelas* or *L. chrysopygus*.

HOW DO YOU START?

Negotiations
Most reintroductions start with individual interests but ultimately involve multiple organizations, both governmental and nongovernmental, local, national, and multinational. The first step is to obtain the support and involvement of the appropriate governmental agencies, especially those that provide permits for the movements of threatened and endangered species. Collaboration should also be sought from the staffs of zoos, local universities, and conservation organizations in as well as outside the host country.

Continued success depends upon having the program eventually involve local people rather than outsiders, regardless of its location. There should be obvious benefits to the community, or support will be half-hearted or nonexistent. An abstract benefit, such as saving a species from extinction, is often not a compelling argument to a government official without resources who is under pressure from starving landless peasants. Economic benefits are obviously a strong incentive for cooperation. In Oman, local tribes are employed in the monitoring program for the Arabian oryx (Stanley Price 1986, 1989). Educational benefits (e.g., providing advanced training abroad) and the transfer of technology are additional inducements that also accelerate the transfer of the management of the program into local hands.

There must be a signed document containing the aims and objectives of the program as well as the criteria for its success. The signed agreement should also state the expectations, responsibilities, and degree of authority of each party, preferably with a preliminary schedule of work. At the outset, the responsibility for decision making at each stage of the process must be made clear, and a set of guidelines for making decisions should be provided. For example, animals may die or be born after the candidates for reintroduction are chosen, but before release. The authority for changing the list of release candidates in these circumstances must remain with a single person. Similarly, only one person should decide whether to "rescue" an animal that is doing poorly after the release. Another issue that must be included in the formal agreement is the ownership of the specimens (will they continue to be owned by the provider or be transferred to the receiver?).

Financial Support
A reintroduction program requires the long-term commitment of many individuals, including professionals living in the field for extended periods. Substantial funding is consequently required for (1) salaries; (2) field headquarters and subsistence; (3) vehicle(s), including fuel and maintenance for transport in the area of the reintroduction; (4) animal caging and shipping costs; (5) equipment and supplies for monitoring the released animals, such as binoculars, radio-telemetry equipment (receivers, antennas, and transmitters), materials for marking animals, and traps for capturing animals; (6) travel for the principals; and (7) long-distance communication. Kleiman et al. (1991) provide examples of costs for the Golden Lion Tamarin Conservation Program, which includes a reintroduction component. Expenses mount considerably when the project involves additional components, such as a conservation education effort, habitat protection, prerelease preparation and training of animals, and extensive field studies of the status and behavioral ecology of the free-ranging wild population.

Reintroduction programs for large mammals that normally range over great distances may be prohibitively expensive, since keeping track of the released animals may require the use of aircraft for radiotelemetry (Stanley Price 1986, 1989). Cost alone can prevent reintroduction programs from being used for the preservation of most species (Brambell 1977). Wildlife protection, habitat preservation, and conservation education may be more cost-effective conservation measures than reintroduction (Borner 1985).

Field Studies and Site Selection

Initial field surveys will clarify the status of the population in the wild and the availability of suitable habitat to support the reintroduced animals *and their descendants*. Releases should cease as the carrying capacity of the habitat is reached, as may soon be the case for the orangutan, *Pongo pygmaeus*, in Malaysia and Indonesia (Aveling and Mitchell 1982), where rehabilitation centers for wild-born orphans have been operating for many years.

A suitable release site should be completely protected and accessible and should have a small (or no) resident population of the target species, unless the goal of the reintroduction is to increase genetic diversity within an insular population. Planners should know whether the reserve area can sustain a genetically viable population in the future, and of what size. Field surveys may be time-consuming and complex, especially if little is known of the behavioral ecology and habitat preferences of the species. But field surveys are crucial since they may identify the causes of a species' decline in the wild and provide information necessary to eliminate the threats. If preliminary field studies indicate that there is insufficient suitable habitat or continued major threats to the species, planners must be prepared to abandon the proposed reintroduction unless they can show that the benefits of proceeding outweigh the costs.

Regular status surveys also allow for evaluation of the potential effects of the reintroduction on the native population. Similarly, information concerning behavioral ecology allows for the immediate evaluation of habitat suitability and the eventual comparison of released and wild animals. These comparisons are absolutely critical for the continued evolution of reintroduction methodology and procedures.

Choosing Animals

The choice of specimens for release derives from the project's objectives. For example, if the intent is to release only a small quantity of "genetic material" into an inbred population, then the only selection criterion might be an individual animal's genetic background. However, since most reintroductions aim to bolster the wild population's numbers significantly, the choice of animals is usually much more complicated. Biologists must also ensure that none of the selection criteria will negatively affect the genetic or demographic composition of the captive population.

The genetic characteristics of the candidates for reintroduction should be as close as possible to those of the original wild inhabitants of the region so that genetic adaptations to particular ecological characteristics of the area will be present in the released animals (Brambell 1977). For example, Stromberg and Boyce (1986) criticize the release of swift foxes, *Vulpes velox*, from Colorado stock in Canada be-

cause they believe that hybridization between the northern and southern populations will swamp the remaining fragile population of northern foxes and that the Colorado foxes will be unable to survive the cold winters of the north. Herrero, Schroeder, and Scott-Brown (1986) provide a convincing rejoinder and review the bases for their decision.

Biologists must determine the age and sex classes most appropriate for reintroduction, as well as the size and composition of groups to be reintroduced. Previous studies of the mating system, social organization, and the spatial relationships of individuals will provide guidelines for making these decisions. For example, based on such information, the groups of Jamaican hutias, *Geocapromys brownii*, golden lion tamarins, and Arabian oryx chosen for reintroduction were stable and cohesive; the hutias and tamarins were in monogamous families and the oryx in polygynous herds (Oliver 1985; Kleiman et al. 1986; Stanley Price 1986). Red wolves have been released as mated pairs (U.S. Fish and Wildlife Service 1986; Point Defiance Zoo and Aquarium 1988), and European otters, *Lutra lutra*, as trios of a single male and two females (Jeffries et al. 1985). Except for the otters, these were all reintroductions conducted in locations devoid of the species.

In saturated areas a different strategy is necessary. For example, gorilla, *Gorilla gorilla*, ecology and social behavior suggests that adult males or adult females with young are not good choices for release due to the likelihood of aggression from established groups; adolescent and adult females are probably the best candidates (Harcourt, in press). Early experiences with chimpanzee reintroductions suggested that cohesive groups should be released in already populated areas (Borner 1985). Finally, in some cases it might be best to reintroduce captive-born animals in the company of one or more wild-born individuals, rather than in a group composed only of captives.

Other decisions include the choice of season for the release, the distance between release sites, and the timing of the release(s)—that is, whether all releases will occur simultaneously or at predetermined intervals. The season chosen for release(s) should not be one in which critical resources are unavailable. Timing of releases depends in part on social organization if the animals will ultimately be occupying territories adjacent to each other.

The choice of animals and groups for reintroduction is a complex process that may require alternative strategies and considerable experimentation. Ultimately, the aim is the combination of animals that will survive best with the least preparation and cost, since a major criterion for success is a viable, free-ranging, self-sustaining population. The research and development phases of a reintroduction program may be very costly.

Cooperating Institutions

If only a single institution is holding the captive animals scheduled for reintroduction, then animals need only be moved between that institution, a halfway house quarantine facility (if necessary), and the release site. If several zoos are holding animals to be reintroduced, then coordination is more complicated, especially when substantial prerelease preparation is planned. As the individuals constituting the captive population of an endangered species are often distributed widely to minimize extinction risks, coordination will undoubtedly be complicated. In all cases, veterinary screening and treatment prior to release is necessary and is best done at a single institution for consistency.

Cooperating zoos must obtain health and import/export permits and arrange transport well in advance of the shipment itself. Institutions at the receiving site must be fully involved in the scheduling of shipments, especially if the receiving agency needs to prepare facilities or holding cages for prerelease acclimation.

Public Relations and Education

Public education and a broad base of public support are the only long-term solutions to conservation problems in both developing and developed countries. Since the local community often contributes significantly to the decline of a species through hunting or other activities that result in habitat degradation, a strategy involving the local community as collaborators rather than as obstacles to the program is the most likely to achieve success. Carley (1981) and Dietz and Nagagata (1986) describe conservation education programs acting in conjunction with the experimental release of red wolves in South Carolina and the reintroduction of the golden lion tamarin in Brazil, respectively.

Conservationists need to be sensitive to the pressures affecting the activities of local individuals, especially government officials, so that the latter are not put in impossible or compromising positions due to the activities of the reintroduction program. Although a successful conservation program clearly requires considerable basic biological knowledge, it demands public relations and political skills even more. Harcourt (in press) suggests, and I strongly agree, that the politics of reintroductions are as important as the release methodology.

A good reintroduction program involves local collaborators with a stake in its future success. In a developing country, there should be a commitment to train a future cadre of professional biologists in zoo biology, reintroduction methodology, wildlife biology, and conservation (Kleiman et al. 1986). To this end, a percentage of the project's total budget should be allocated for student support (or other forms of professional training) (see Kleiman et al. 1991).

Habitat Protection and Management

The degradation of habitats is the chief cause of species losses. A successful reintroduction requires a secure site; therefore an active program for habitat protection must exist. In some cases, habitat protection will derive from the activities of the reintroduction program (Aveling and Mitchell 1982). Additionally, reintroduction programs may need to become involved in aggressive management of land and animals or even the restoration of destroyed habitats. This need for aggressive management derives from the islandlike quality of so many reserve areas, whose ecological balance is easily upset due to their small size. The management and restoration of habitats in the Tropics are major challenges for the future (Ehrlich and Ehrlich 1981).

THE REINTRODUCTION

Preparation of Animals

We have very little experience in reintroducing captive mammals into their native habitats. No general guidelines exist for preparing species from the various taxa for reintroduction. However, there are at least six major areas of behavior to consider in the development of any preparation scheme. To survive, candidates for reintroduction must be able to (1) avoid predators; (2) acquire and process food; (3) interact socially with conspecifics; (4) find or construct shelters and nests; (5) locomote on complex terrain; and (6) orient and navigate in a complex environment. Preparation also may involve acclimatization of release candidates to the habitat and climatic conditions at the release site for some time prior to the reintroduction.

Species differences in the amount of prerelease conditioning required are likely to be significant. Herbivores may need little training in food acquisition and processing, while omnivores and carnivores may require extensive training. Species that normally live in herds or are solitary in the wild may need less preparation in the rules of social etiquette than forms that live in groups with a complex social structure. Arboreal species may need more preparation in locomotion and orientation than terrestrial forms. Migratory species or those with large home ranges may need to learn how to navigate and develop routes through natural habitats; territorial forms may need to learn how to define the limits of their ranges. We do not know which of these behaviors are learned and thus require training, and which are genetically hard-wired. Examples of different approaches to preparation (both recommended and tested) are given by Kleiman et al. (1986); Beck et al. (1991); Beck et al. (in press); Box (1991); Miller et al. (1990a, 1990b); Stanley Price (1986, 1989); Oliver (1985); Oliver et al. (1986); Parker (1986); Harcourt (in press); Rijksen (1974); Scott-Brown, Herrero, and Mamo (1986); and U.S. Fish and Wildlife Service (1982).

To prepare golden lion tamarins to forage and feed, Beck developed a feeding protocol that involved the gradual replacement of a single bowl of food with food that was distributed in different locations and hidden in "puzzle boxes," thereby forcing the animals not only to search for food, but to work to extract it. To improve locomotor ability and spatial orientation, animals were exposed to exceedingly complex three-dimensional environments that were regularly dismantled and rebuilt. The overall survival rates of prepared and unprepared tamarins did not differ (Beck et al. 1991; Beck et al., in press). Living for several months in a free-ranging condition on the zoo grounds, however, seemed to confer an advantage on tamarins after release, especially with extensive post-release support through provisioning and post-release training (Beck et al. 1991).

Red wolves have been preadapted to hunting by exposing them first to carcasses and then to live prey before reintroduction (U.S. Fish and Wildlife Service 1982). Miller et al. (1990a, 1990b) conducted one of the very few experiments to test the effects of training protocols on the behavior of captive animals with the ultimate aim of applying the techniques to the preparation of endangered black-footed ferrets, *Mustela nigripes,* for reintroduction. They used nonendangered Siberian polecats, *Mustela eversmannii,* as a model species to examine the development of predator avoidance and prey location skills in naive captives. The captives in general spent more time in surface activity than in burrows when searching for food. They also showed little evidence of a capacity for long-term memory of a negative experience with a potential predator.

For many species, social preparation is of considerable importance. Castro et al. (in press) have noted that the auditory communication skills of captive-born golden lion tamarins differ from those of wild tamarins, which could affect the ability of released captive-born individuals to interact properly with wild conspecifics.

For great ape reintroductions (and introductions), the major preparation has been social, in that candidates have been housed with conspecifics prior to release (Wilson and Elicker 1976; Pfeiffer and Koebner 1978) after being housed alone for long periods. Great ape releases have also often involved providing animals with exposure to a natural environment while still keeping them under human care. Hannah and McGrew (1991) summarize great ape rehabilitation projects, including some preparation techniques.

Incorporating preparation techniques into the normal zoo environment might result in more naturalistic and complex habitats for captive animals. At the National Zoological Park, tamarin groups scheduled for reintroduction are now released on zoo grounds during the spring and summer months. They are free-ranging for several months prior to shipment (Bronikowski, Beck, and Power 1989).

Beck (1991) points out that our attitudes toward animal welfare may be an obstacle to providing an enriched environment that would prepare captive-borns for survival in the wild. Real preparation would include exposure to food shortages, parasites and disease, predators, dramatic fluctuations in ambient conditions, and dangerous objects. To most keepers and veterinarians, such practices would simply be unacceptable.

Preparation has not generally been considered an essential element in most reintroduction programs, possibly because the training technology is not yet available. An alternative to prerelease training may be the pairing of captive-born animals with experienced wild-caught individuals prior to release, with or without post-release training.

Release and Monitoring

The reintroduction of captive-born animals into the wild signifies a change in the relationship between the animals and the animal manager, even if each specimen is outfitted with a transmitter and followed for 24 hours each day. Captive animals are the total responsibility of their caretakers; their diets, shelters, companions—indeed, most aspects of their environment—are controlled and controllable. Once the release occurs, this control is lost. Project personnel must decide whether and under what conditions to intervene if an animal begins to fail. The decision depends upon many factors, such as the political situation (can animals be allowed to die with everyone's full knowledge?); the value of the in-

dividual animal to the project because of its social, experiential, or genetic background; the perceived reason for the animal's problem (e.g., disease, predation, social conflict, human error); and the availability of captive housing for rescued individuals. If guidelines governing the rescue of reintroduced animals are clearly spelled out before the release, project personnel can avoid making a rushed decision in a confused and possibly emotionally charged climate.

The long-term monitoring of released animals is a crucial component of any reintroduction program. The zoos providing the animals for reintroduction have a special interest in the results of monitoring since it is important for them to keep their constituencies informed about the progress of individuals from their collections that have been reintroduced. Intensive monitoring can also facilitate the collection of carcasses for pathological study and thus clarify causes of death of released animals. A monitoring program will indicate how and when the behavioral repertoire of captive-born animals becomes comparable to that of wild specimens. All of this information can then be fed back into the management of the captive population.

Most reintroduction programs have included the provision of essential resources such as food, water, and shelter, both to provide support for the animals and to control their movements. Golden lion tamarins, Jamaican hutias, and Arabian oryx were all released from enclosures with shelters, with the hope that the animals would remain in the vicinity (Kleiman et al. 1986; Oliver et al. 1986; Stanley Price 1986, 1989). Sites where food and shelter are provided can be used for trapping and examining the specimens.

When to eliminate support is a major decision. It is extremely important to challenge the animals, but is also easier to control their movements if critical resources like food are provided. Achieving a wild state may mean developing fear and avoidance responses to humans, a condition that most animal managers find difficult to promote in their "charges." For each reintroduction, because of species differences and differences in goals, there will be complex decisions to be made for which there are no clear guidelines. To what extent and for how long should food supplementation continue? To what extent and for how long should humans be an important part of the lives of the released specimens? How much intensive monitoring is necessary, and how long should it continue? A common thread and a common problem will be reducing the human-animal contacts and encouraging the animals to avoid people, all while the project personnel continue to monitor the animals.

Defining Success

There are no established criteria for calling any given reintroduction a success. Griffith et al. (1989) evaluated those variables that led to the success of intentional introductions and reintroductions of native birds and mammals (not all endangered or threatened) to the wild in Australia, New Zealand, Canada, and the United States (including Hawaii) between 1973 and 1986. Greater success was associated with releasing larger numbers of individuals; extending the program duration; releasing animals into excellent habitat and into the core of their historical range; using wild-caught individuals; releasing herbivores rather than omnivores or carnivores; and releasing animals into areas without competitors. Stanley Price (1989) discusses the characteristics that make animals the most reintroducible: large animals living in cohesive groups, explorer species, nocturnal species, and species tolerant of habitat change or extreme environmental variation.

Beck et al. (1994) suggest that a reintroduction project should be counted as successful if the wild population reaches 500 individuals that are free of provisioning or other human support, or if a formal genetic/demographic analysis predicts that the population will be self-sustaining. By these stringent criteria, they found that only 16 (11%) of 145 animal reintroductions were successful. However, many of these projects are ongoing, and their success or failure cannot yet be evaluated. Also, a reintroduction attempt can have indirect, longer-term conservation benefits, such as increased public awareness, professional training, and enhanced habitat protection (Beck et al. 1994).

Beck et al. (1994) noted that the successful programs (by their definition) were longer and released more animals than the unsuccessful programs (as did Griffith et al. 1989). They also provided local employment and had community education programs. Finally, the successful projects used medical screening and post-release provisioning *less* than unsuccessful projects, a counterintuitive result.

One issue requires clarification. All reintroduced animals will eventually die, as will all captive animals. The success or failure of a program should not be measured by the mortality of the original reintroduced cohort. More important is the number and genetic variation of the surviving descendants of the released animals and the degree to which their genetic material is integrated with that of the original wild population.

ACKNOWLEDGMENTS

This chapter would not have been possible without the wise and thoughtful input of Benjamin Beck, James Dietz, and Lou Ann Dietz during the golden lion tamarin reintroduction project. Our work with golden lion tamarins has been supported by the Smithsonian Institution (International Environmental Sciences Program; Educational Outreach Program), National Zoological Park, Friends of the National Zoo, World Wildlife Fund, National Geographic Society, National Science Foundation, Wildlife Preservation Trust International, Brazilian Forestry Development Institute (IBDF—now IBAMA), Rio de Janeiro Primate Center (CPRJ-FEEMA), Brazilian Foundation for the Conservation of Nature (FBCN), Frankfurt Zoological Society, and the Roberto Marinho Foundation. We have also been supported by many of the zoos participating in the International Golden Lion Tamarin Management Program through financial contributions. Susan Lumpkin, Scott Derrickson, James Dietz, Lou Ann Dietz, and Benjamin Beck made many helpful suggestions on the manuscript, as did one anonymous reviewer.

REFERENCES

Aveling, R., and Mitchell, A. 1982. Is rehabilitating Orang Utans worth while? *Oryx* 16:263–71.

Beck, B. B. 1991. Managing zoo environments for reintroduction. *AAZPA Annual Conference Proceedings,* 436–40. Wheeling, W.Va.: American Association of Zoological Parks and Aquariums.

Beck, B. B., Kleiman, D. G., Castro, I., Rettberg-Beck, B., and Carvalho, C. In press. Preparation of captive-born golden lion tamarins for release into the wild. In *A case study in conservation biology: The golden lion tamarin,* ed. D. G. Kleiman.

Beck, B. B., Kleiman, D. G., Dietz, J. M., Castro, I., Carvalho, C., Martins, A., and Rettberg-Beck, B. 1991. Losses and reproduction in reintroduced golden lion tamarins, *Leontopithecus rosalia. Dodo* 27:50–61.

Beck, B. B., Rapaport, L. G., Stanley Price, M. R., and Wilson, A. C. 1994. Reintroduction of captive-born animals. In *Creative conservation: Interactive management of wild and captive animals.* Proceedings of the Sixth World Conference on Breeding Endangered Species, ed. G. Mace, P. Olney, and A. Feistner, 265–86. London: Chapman and Hall.

Borner, M. 1985. The rehabilitated chimpanzees of Rubondo Island. *Oryx* 19:151–54.

Box, H. O. 1991. Training for life after release: Simian primates as examples. In *Beyond captive breeding: Re-introducing endangered mammals to the wild,* ed. J. H. W. Gipps, 111–23. Oxford: Clarendon Press.

Brambell, M. R. 1977. Reintroduction. *Int. Zoo Yrbk.* 17:112–16.

Brewer, S. 1978. *The chimps of Mt. Asserik.* New York: Alfred A. Knopf.

Bronikowski, E. J. Jr., Beck, B. B., and Power, M. 1989. Innovation, exhibition, and conservation: Free-ranging tamarins at the National Zoological Park. *AAZPA Annual Conference Proceedings,* 540–46. Wheeling, W.Va.: American Association of Zoological Parks and Aquariums.

Cade, T. J. 1986. Reintroduction as a method of conservation. *Raptor Res. Rep.* no. 5: 72–84.

Caldecott, J. O., and Kavanagh, M. 1983. Can translocation help wild primates? *Oryx* 17:135–37.

Campbell, S. 1980. Is reintroduction a realistic goal? In *Conservation Biology: An Evolutionary-Ecological Perspective,* ed. M. E. Soulé and B. A. Wilcox, 263–69. Sunderland, Mass.: Sinauer Associates.

Carley, C. J. 1981. Red wolf experimental translocation summarized. *Wild Canid Survival and Research Center Bulletin,* part 1: 4–7, part 2: 8–9.

Carter, J. A. 1981. A journey to freedom. *Smithsonian* 12:90–101.

Castro, M. I., Beck, B. B., Kleiman, D. G., Ruiz-Miranda, C., and Rosenberger, A. L. In press. Environmental enrichment for golden lion tamarin *(Leontopithecus rosalia)* reintroduction. *Proceedings of the 1st Conference on Environmental Enrichment,* ed. D. Shepherdson, J. Mellen, and M. Hutchins. Washington, D.C.: Smithsonian Institution Press.

Coimbra-Filho, A. F., and Mittermeier, R. A. 1978. Reintroduction and translocation of lion tamarins: A realistic appraisal. In *Biology and behaviour of marmosets,* ed. H. Rothe, H. J. Wolters, and J. P. Hearn, 41–48. Göttingen: Eigenverlag H. Rothe.

Conway, W. G. 1980. An overview of captive propagation. In *Conservation biology: An evolutionary-ecological perspective,* ed. M. E. Soulé and B. A. Wilcox, 199–208. Sunderland, Mass.: Sinauer Associates.

Dietz, L. A., and Nagagata, E. 1986. Community conservation education program for the golden lion tamarin. In *Building support for conservation in rural areas: Workshop Proceedings,* vol. 1, ed. J. Atkinson, 8–16. Ipswich, Mass.: QLF-Atlantic Center for the Environment.

Ehrlich, P., and Ehrlich, A. 1981. *Extinction.* New York: Random House.

Fitter, R. 1984. Operation Oryx: The success continues. *Oryx* 118:136–37.

Gipps, J. H. W., ed. 1991. *Beyond captive breeding: Re-introducing endangered mammals to the wild.* Oxford: Clarendon Press.

Griffith, B., Scott, J. M., Carpenter, J. W., and Reed, C. 1989. Translocation as a species conservation tool: Status and strategy. *Science* 245:477–80.

Hannah, A. C., and McGrew, W. C. 1991. Rehabilitation of captive chimpanzees. In *Primate responses to environmental change,* ed. H. O. Box, 167–86. London: Chapman and Hall.

Harcourt, A. H. In press. Release of gorillas to the wild. In *Active management for the conservation of wild primates: Rehabilitation, reintroduction, introduction, restocking and translocation,* ed. A. H. Mitchell. IUCN-The World Conservation Union.

Herrero, S., Schroeder, C., and Scott-Brown, M. 1986. Are Canadian foxes swift enough? *Biol. Conserv.* 36:159–67.

International Union for Conservation of Nature and Natural Resources (IUCN). 1987. Translocations of living organisms: Introductions, re-introductions, and re-stocking. IUCN Council Position Statement. Gland, Switzerland: IUCN.

Jeffries, D. J., Wayre, P., Jessop, R. M., Mitchell-Jones, A. J., and Medd, R. 1985. The composition, age, size, and pre-release treatment of the groups of otters *Lutra lutra* used in the first releases of captive-bred stock in England. *Otters (J. Otter Trust)* 1984:11–16.

Kear, J. 1975. Returning the Hawaiian goose to the wild. In *Breeding endangered species in captivity,* ed. R. D. Martin, 115–23. London: Academic Press.

Kleiman, D. G. 1989. Reintroduction of captive mammals for conservation. *BioScience* 39:152–61.

———. 1990. Decision-making about a reintroduction: Do appropriate conditions exist? *Endangered Species Update* 8(1):18–19.

Kleiman, D. G., Beck, B. B., Dietz, J. M., and Dietz, L. A. 1991. Costs of a reintroduction and criteria for success: Accounting and accountability in the Golden Lion Tamarin Conservation Program. In *Beyond captive breeding: Reintroducing endangered species to the wild,* ed. J. H. W. Gipps, 125–42. Oxford: Clarendon Press.

Kleiman, D. G., Beck, B. B., Dietz, J. M., Dietz, L. A., Ballou, J. D., and Coimbra-Filho, A. F. 1986. Conservation program for the golden lion tamarin: Captive research and management, ecological studies, educational strategies, and reintroduction. In *Primates: The road to self-sustaining populations,* ed. K. Benirschke, 959–79. New York: Springer-Verlag.

Konstant, W. R., and Mittermeier, R. A. 1982. Introduction, reintroduction, and translocation of Neotropical primates: Past experiences and future possibilities. *Int. Zoo Yrbk.* 22:69–77.

Long, J. L. 1981. *Introduced birds of the world: The worldwide history, distribution, and influence of birds introduced to new environments.* New York: Universe Books.

Ma, N. S. F., Jones, T. C., Miller, A. C., Morgan, L. M., and Adams, E. A. 1976. Chromosome polymorphism and banding patterns in the owl monkey *(Aotus). Lab. Anim. Sci.* 26:1022–36.

McGrew, W. C. 1983. Chimpanzees can be rehabilitated. *Lab. Primate Newsl.* 22(2):2–3.

Miller, B., Biggins, D., Wemmer, C., Powell, R., Calvo, L., Hanebury, L., and Wharton, T. 1990a. Development of survival skills in captive-raised Siberian polecats *(Mustela eversmanni):* II. Predator avoidance. *J. Ethol.* 8:95–104.

Miller, B., Biggins, D., Wemmer, C., Powell, R., Hanebury, L., Horn, D., and Vargas, A. 1990b. Development of survival skills in captive-raised Siberian polecats *(Mustela eversmanni):* I. Locating prey. *J. Ethol.* 8:89–94.

Oliver, W. L. R. 1985. The Jamaican hutia or Indian coney *(Geocapromys brownii):* A model programme for captive breeding and re-introduction? *Proceedings, Symposium 10—Association of British Wild Animal Keepers,* 35–52.

Oliver, W. L. R., Wilkins, L., Kerr, R. H., and Kelly, D. L. 1986. The Jamaican hutia, *Geocapromys brownii:* Captive breeding and reintroduction programme history and progress. *Dodo* 23:32–58.

Parker, W. T. 1986. Proposed reintroduction of the red wolf to the Alligator River National Wildlife Refuge. Report. Asheville, N.C.: U.S. Fish and Wildlife Service, Endangered Species Field Office.

Peres, C. 1986. Costs and benefits of territorial defense in golden lion tamarins, *Leontopithecus rosalia.* M.S. thesis, University of Florida, Gainesville.

Pfeiffer, A. J., and Koebner, L. J. 1978. The resocialization of single-caged chimpanzees and the establishment of an island colony. *J. Med. Primatol.* 7:70–81.

Point Defiance Zoo and Aquarium. 1988. Restoration of red wolves in North Carolina: a summary. *Red Wolf Newsletter* 1:3. Tacoma, Wash.: Point Defiance Zoo and Aquarium.

Rijksen, H. D. 1974. Orang-utan conservation and rehabilitation in Sumatra. *Biol. Conserv.* 6:20–25.

Scott-Brown, J. M., Herrero, S., and Mamo, C. 1986. Monitoring of released swift foxes in Alberta and Saskatchewan: Final report, 1986. Report. Canadian Fish and Wildlife Service.

Shields, W. M. 1982. *Philopatry, inbreeding, and the evolution of sex.* Albany: State University of New York Press.

Stanley Price, M. 1986. The reintroduction of the Arabian oryx *(Oryx leucoryx)* into Oman. *Int. Zoo Yrbk.* 24/25:179–88.

———. 1989. *Animal re-introductions: The Arabian oryx in Oman.* New York: Cambridge University Press.

Stromberg, M. R., and Boyce, M. S. 1986. Systematics and conservation of the Swift fox, *Vulpes velox,* in North America. *Biol. Conserv.* 35:97–110.

U.S. Fish and Wildlife Service. 1982. *Red wolf recovery plan.* Atlanta, Ga.: U.S. Fish and Wildlife Service.

———. 1986. Determination of experimental population status for an introduced population of red wolves in North Carolina. *Federal Register* 51 (223):41790–97.

Wemmer, C., and Derrickson, S. 1987. Reintroduction: The zoobiologists' dream. Prospects and problems of reintroducing captive-bred wildlife. *AAZPA Annual Conference Proceedings,* 48–65. Wheeling, W.Va.: American Association of Zoological Parks and Aquariums.

Wilson, M. L., and Elicker, J. G. 1976. Establishment, maintenance, and behavior of free-ranging chimpanzees on Ossabaw Island, Georgia, U.S.A. *Primates* 17:451–73.

30

The Role of Conservation and Survival Centers in Wildlife Conservation

Christen Wemmer, Scott Derrickson, and Larry Collins

Humans have invented institutions to sustain wildlife since the beginning of urbanization and the decline of wilderness. The menagerie and the hunting preserve were among the oldest of these institutions, and the differences between them were substantial (Loisel 1912). While menageries catered to the amusement of the urban middle class, hunting preserves reserved wildlife for the elite as a symbol of aristocratic power and privilege. Menageries presented wild animals to the common people in artificial containment, whereas the hunting preserve protected wildlife in its natural environment for the exclusive use of a privileged few. National parks, biosphere reserves, wildlife refuges, conservation centers, and a variety of similar institutions have been developed more recently (cf. McNeely and Miller 1984; Carr 1989; Bildstein and Brisbin 1990; Boza 1993; Curtin 1993). Despite their diversity, their origins can all be traced to human recreation in its various manifestations. Their principal differences lie in their means of support and form of management.

This chapter deals with the role of propagation centers in the conservation of endangered wildlife. We use the adjective "propagation" rather than "breeding" to identify those centers whose management is motivated by the long-term conservation of gene pools, as opposed to production for human consumption (i.e., ranching), in which retention of wild traits is not a primary concern. This concern reflects the rapid changes taking place in zoo philosophy and objectives as a result of the present global extinction crisis. It is fair to say that zoos are in the midst of a significant reformation, and that the driving force behind this change is a growing awareness of their potential contributions to conserving wildlife through active programs in endangered species propagation, research, education, and training (Conway 1986, 1988; Seal 1988; Rudran, Wemmer, and Singh 1990; Wemmer, Pickett, and Teare 1990; Wemmer et al. 1993).

Zoos and reserves differ in many ways, but their raisons d'être are converging, and they are becoming more similar in other ways. This convergence stems primarily from the rapid and unceasing fragmentation of vast natural landscapes into an archipelago of small habitat islands whose ecological systems must be increasingly maintained by human inputs. With limited possibilities for dispersal and emigration, species inhabiting these islands exist in a situation that closely approximates that of their zoo counterparts: they are captives in a closed system that requires human intervention for its continued survival. Zoos now attempt to mimic the natural settings of the animals they keep (Hediger 1969; Hutchins, Hancocks, and Crockett 1984; Polakowski 1987), and wildlife in reserves must be managed attentively to ensure their continued survival. However, these are considerations of husbandry and management, and political factors are often more compelling determinants of institutional character. Ultimately, the survival of wildlife depends on the ability of responsible institutions to remain relevant to society and endure in a rapidly changing world.

The conservation or survival center is only one of many types of institutions that preserve wildlife. In the following paragraphs we (1) compare conservation centers and game ranches; (2) discuss some of the immediate challenges of managing wildlife in conservation centers; and (3) discuss the broader role of conservation centers in the context of mammal conservation.

THE SCOPE OF CONSERVATION CENTERS AND GAME RANCHES

Interest in wildlife management and conservation has brought about a range of methods and institutions for preserving wild animal populations. Because conservation centers and game ranches are superficially similar, it is particularly worthwhile to examine the characteristics and objectives of these institutions, and enumerate their similarities and differences.

Conservation or Survival Centers

The invention of the conservation or survival center (we use the terms interchangeably) took place in the early 1970s. These centers differ from traditional zoos in that their primary function is the breeding of rare and endangered wildlife as opposed to public exhibition and education. Consequently, their animal collections normally encompass larger populations of a smaller selection of species than those in traditional zoos. Table 30.1 summarizes pertinent information on conservation centers. Some centers specialize; examples are the Institute for Herpetological Research in Stanford, California, the Duke University Primate Center in Durham, North Carolina, and the Duiker Research and Breeding Center in Chipangali, Zimbabwe (Pinchin 1993). Breeding programs at conservation centers emphasize the preservation of genetic variability and adaptations to the natural conditions in which species evolved. These programs typically incorporate specific genetic, demographic, and behavioral management protocols in order to minimize artificial selection and progressive domestication (Foose and Ballou 1988; Frankham et al. 1986). Such programmatic objectives differ from those of most private and commercial breeders of wildlife, whose institutions might be more appropriately called game ranches or breeding farms. Conservation centers can bridge the gap between the historically artificial environment of the urban zoo and that of the national park. Often, they are closed to the public, and research and training are normally fundamental components of their programs.

Animals in conservation centers may be jointly owned by several zoos, with the ownership of offspring determined by legal documents known as breeding loan agreements (see Block and Perkins, appendix 5, this volume). In other instances, ownership may reside solely with the single institution responsible for the species' recovery and reestablishment in the wild. All black-footed ferrets, *Mustela nigripes*, for example, are owned by the state of Wyoming.

Game Ranches

In many parts of the world, native or exotic wildlife is maintained on private lands for commercial exploitation. Following Geist (1988), we use the term "game ranch" to denote those commercial enterprises that gain supplemental income through the sale of breeding stock, meat and by-products, and/or the sale of viewing or hunting privileges and associated accommodations. As currently practiced in North America, New Zealand, and southern Africa, game ranching encompasses a wide spectrum of enterprises, ranging from simple culling operations involving the harvesting of wild animals (Geist 1985) to extremely large-scale operations involving intensive husbandry and domestication (Haigh and Hudson 1993). The rapid expansion of game ranching in the past several decades is traceable to both aesthetic and financial considerations. In North America, small zoos, private breeders, seasonal amusement parks, traveling carnivals, the pet trade, and the public are all significant consumers or paying users of wildlife produced and maintained by game ranches. Private land ownership is the key

to this industry, and in countries in which most of the land is privately owned, game ranching can potentially provide economic incentives promoting both species and habitat conservation (Luxmoore 1985). Unfortunately, however, game ranching can also have a number of adverse effects on conservation, such as the elimination of predators and other species, domestication, hybridization, exposure of wildlife to exotic diseases, habitat degradation, development of illegal markets in wildlife products, the social and economic monopolization of wildlife, and the privatization of public lands (Luxmoore 1985; Geist 1985, 1988). Furthermore, because commerce in selected native or exotic species is the primary concern of game ranching, no serious effort is usually made to maintain the composition of the area's original flora and fauna unless the operation secures its principal income from the public viewing of wildlife in natural habitat.

CONSERVATION OR SURVIVAL CENTERS: GOALS AND COMMITMENT

General Goals

Sustained reproduction of wildlife is the primary objective of most conservation centers. Biological research on wildlife species in captivity and in the field is an equally important goal that is also normally pursued. Ideally, a conservation center should support multidimensional programs that promote the conservation of selected species through captive propagation and research. A well-rounded program might include several of the following elements:

1. captive propagation with participation in cooperatively organized programs
2. compilation of a detailed husbandry manual for the species
3. collection of blood or tissue for reproductive and genetic research
4. documentation of life history characteristics through research and/or collaborative compilation of data from multiple institutions
5. investigations of reintroduction methods
6. surveys of species distribution and status in the wild
7. implementation of education and training programs in the native range of the species

Though a conservation center may assume a leading role by initiating several such activities, a successful species-oriented program will kindle the desire of other zoological organizations to participate. Conservation of endangered wildlife is far more likely to succeed when it is conducted as a cooperative scientific program rather than as an independent effort, no matter how well the activity is endowed.

Conservation centers should not focus all of their resources on captive propagation of endangered species. Many taxa will disappear before their biological characteristics are known, and short-term investigations of little-known or rare taxa can make significant contributions to our biological knowledge and understanding, as well as benefiting conservation.

TABLE 30.1. A Listing of Selected Conservation Centers

Institution/address	Date established	Status and affiliations	Annual budget	No. of employees	Acres	Animal collection	Specialties
Bamberger Ranch 7714 Redbird Valley San Antonio, TX 78229	1969	Privately owned (J. David Bamberger); AAZPA-SSP participant (1 sp.)	$30K	3	640	Mammals: 1 sp. (88)	Propagation of endangered ungulates
Bell Ranch % Chicago Zoological Park 3300 Golf Rd. Brookfield, IL 60513	1987	Owned by Lane Industries; associated with Chicago Zoological Park; AAZPA-SSP participant (2 spp.)	$6K	2	1,050	Mammals: 2 spp. (10)	Propagation of large ungulates; field conservation research
St. Catherine's Island Survival Center Rt 1, Box 207-Z Midway, GA 31320	1974	Owned and managed by New York Zoological Society; AAZPA-SSP participant (10 spp.)	$400K	8	200	Mammals: 13 spp. (144) Birds: 19 spp. (154) Reptiles: 2 spp. (64)	Propagation and research on endangered mammals, birds, and reptiles
Cincinnati Zoo Breeding Center % Cincinnati Zoo 3400 Vine St. Cincinnati, OH 45220	1989	Owned and managed by the Cincinnati Zoo; AAZPA-SSP participant (5 spp.)	$40K	1	108	Mammals: 3 spp. (31) Birds: 4 spp. (19)	Off-site breeding facility for zoo
Conservation and Research Center National Zoological Park Rt. 522 South Front Royal, VA 22630	1975	Owned and managed by the Smithsonian Institution as a department of the National Zoological Park; AAZPA-SSP participant (12 spp.)	$1.1M	45	3,150	Mammals: 19 spp. (494) Birds: 22 spp. (547)	Captive propagation and research on endangered species; conservation training of developing country nationals
Duke University Primate Center 3705 Erwin Road Durham, NC 27705	1968	Owned and managed by Duke University; AAZPA-SSP participant (2 spp.)	$900K	11	55	Mammals: 24 spp. (604)	Biological studies and captive propagation of prosimian primates
Fossil Rim Wildlife Center[a] Rt. 1, Box 210 Glen Rose, TX 76043	1984	Owned by Jim Jackson and Christine Jurzykowski in cooperation with the Fossil Rim Foundation; AAZPA-SSP participant (8 spp.)	$1.1M	74	3,000	Mammals: 33 spp. (872) Birds: 4 spp. (55)	Captive propagation and research on mammals and birds; conservation education in the developing world
The Wilds 85 E. Gay St., Suite 603 Columbus, OH 43215	1984	Owned by the International Center for the Preservation of Wild Animals, Inc., a nonprofit corporation; AAZPA-SSP participant (2 spp.)	$450K	10	9,154	Mammals: 8 spp. (75)	Captive propagation and research on threatened and endangered species
International Crane Foundation E-11376 Shady Lane Road Baraboo, WI 53913	1973	Owned by the ICF, a nonprofit corporation; AAZPA-SSP participant (5 spp.)	$1.2M	5	160	Birds: 15 spp. (140)	Captive propagation and research on cranes; international training in crane conservation techniques, wetland conservation, education
Institute for Herpetological Research P.O. Box 2227 Stanford, CA 94305	1973	Owned by a nonprofit research organization; AAZPA-SSP participant (1 sp.)	$30K	2	.25	Reptiles: 32 spp. (200)	Captive propagation of reptiles; reptile husbandry and disease research

Facility	Year	Ownership	Budget			Collection	Purpose
The Lubee Foundation 18401 NW County Rd. #231 Gainesville, FL 32609	1985	A private nonprofit foundation; AAZPA-SSP participant (5 spp.)	$200K	9	90	Mammals: 32 spp. (315) Birds: 11 spp. (44)	Endangered species propagation and research (mammals and birds)
Patuxent Wildlife Research Center Laurel, MD 20708	1936	Owned and managed by the U.S. Fish and Wildlife Service; not an AAZPA-SSP participant	$2M	172	600	Birds: 13 spp. (2,188)	Captive propagation and research on selected North American mammals and birds
Point Defiance Zoo Red Wolf Facility % Point Defiance Zoo 5400 North Pearl St. Tacoma, WA 98407	1975	Owned and managed by the Point Defiance Zoo in cooperation with the U.S. Fish and Wildlife Service; AAZPA-SSP participant (1 sp.)	$175K	2	5	Mammals: 1 spp. (60)	Captive propagation and research on red wolves
San Diego Wild Animal Park[a] 15500 San Pasqual Valley Rd. Escondido, CA 92027	1972	Owned by city and managed by Zoological Society of San Diego; AAZPA-SSP participant (24 spp.)	$21.8M	415	1,840	Mammals: 127 spp. (1,644) Birds: 293 spp. (1,528) Reptiles: 3 spp. (3)	Captive propagation of birds and ungulates
Sedgwick County Zoo off-site breeding facility % Sedgwick County Zoo 5555 Zoo Blvd. Wichita, KS 67212	1976	Owned and managed by the Sedgwick County Zoological Society; AAZPA-SSP participant (1 sp.)	$70K	2	40	Mammals: 8 spp. (46) Birds: 10 spp. (40)	Off-site breeding facility for zoo
Sybille Wildlife Research Center % Wyoming Dept. of Fish & Game Box 3312 University Station Laramie, WY 82071	1952	Owned and managed by the Wyoming Dept. of Fish and Game; AAZPA-SSP participant (1 sp.)	$100K	8	15	Mammals: 11 spp. (314) Amphibs: 1 sp. (16)	Research on diseases of North American ungulates; captive propagation of black-footed ferrets
Topeka Zoo off-site breeding facility % Topeka Zoological Park 635 S.W. Gage Blvd. Topeka, KS 66606-2066	1987	Owned and managed by the Topeka Zoological Park; AAZPA-SSP participant (1 sp.)	$1.3M[b]	1	160	Mammals: 1 sp. (9)	Captive propagation of the Asian wild horse
Vogelpark Walsrode off-site breeding facility Mallorca	1985	Owned and managed by the Vogelpark Walsrode; AAZPA-SSP participant (4 spp.)	$560K	12	50	Birds: 350 spp. (2,000)	Holding and breeding facility for the bird park at Walsrode
Vogelpark Walsrode off-site facility Dominican Republic	1981	Owned and managed by the Vogelpark Walsrode; AAZPA-SSP participant (7 spp.)	$31K	3	12	Birds: 10 spp. (60)	Breeding facility for endangered South American and Caribbean parrots
White Oak Plantation 726 Owens Road Yulee, FL 32097	1975	Owned by the Gilman Paper Company; AAZPA-SSP participant (15 spp.)	$850K	16	400	Mammals: 25 spp. (350) Birds: 32 spp. (220) Reptiles: 1 sp. (8)	Research and propagation of selected endangered species
Wild Animal Habitat[a] 6300 Kings Island Drive Kings Island, OH 45034	1972	Owned by American Financial Corporation; AAZPA-SSP participant (9 spp.)	$900K	12	125	Mammals: 26 spp. (313) Birds: 8 spp. (47)	Captive propagation/reproductive research. Educational tours, Wildlife Discovery Days

[a] Facility open to the public.
[b] Not separate from zoo budget.

Range of Conservation Activities

Species Selection. The selection of species at any single conservation center is guided by several criteria, but the degree of *endangerment* is normally a primary consideration. William Conway (1974) has cogently addressed this factor: "Only one systematic method of selecting species . . . has received general attention. It is called "triage," a strategy adopted by World War I French surgeons for dealing with more casualties than they could handle. Doctors divided wounded soldiers into three groups: those who could probably recover without immediate attention, those who would probably die even with attention, and those where surgical treatment seemed likely to make the difference between life and death." Ideally, conservation centers should focus their resources primarily on species that require captive breeding. Because species conservation is best served through methods associated with habitat, community, and ecosystem preservation, the highest priority should always be given to breeding programs that are closely integrated with in situ management and recovery efforts.

The potential for cooperation with other institutions is also a critical consideration in species selection. Formally coordinated propagation programs involving several institutions have the advantage of reducing risks of loss from epidemics and accidents and of maximizing available facilities and involved personnel (Neesham 1990).

The opportunity for research is also an important factor in species selection. In some instances, nonendangered species can be used as surrogates in investigations of pertinent aspects of behavior or biology that can be directly applied to closely related endangered species. For example, at the Conservation and Research Center, the Siberian polecat, *Mustela eversmannii*, was used as a surrogate to investigate methods of maximizing the survival of captive-bred black-footed ferrets, *M. nigripes*, reintroduced into the wild (Miller et al. 1990a, 1990b).

Finally, the availability of adequate support facilities for and expertise with specific taxa is also an important selection criterion. No animals should be acquired unless proper housing and management can be provided by staff experienced in the handling and care of related taxa.

Captive Propagation. Captive propagation programs, whether in zoos or conservation centers, must include three elements to achieve their conservation objectives. First, the basic reproductive information that results from captive propagation should be maintained in the institution's record system and should also be made available to the zoological community through registration with the International Species Inventory System (ISIS) (Flesness and Mace 1988; Seal 1988; see also Shoemaker and Flesness, appendix 4, this volume). Second, every institution with long-term experience in breeding a species in captivity has an obligation to provide its results to the zoological community through publication in professional journals. Progress cannot be achieved in the absence of communication, and the preferred medium for conveying new findings on husbandry, reproductive biology, and behavior is publication in refereed journals. Third, few propagation centers have the resources to single-handedly address the genetic and demographic requirements of captive populations; significant

progress in breeding endangered species can be achieved only through active cooperation and collaboration with other zoological institutions.

While the breeding of exotic wildlife in captivity in itself is often mistakenly equated with conservation, efforts to breed wildlife independently of established cooperative programs do not usually contribute to the growing body of knowledge on which conservation practice is based. Today, successful captive propagation means gene pool preservation, which requires a combination of behavioral, genetic, and demographic management techniques (Conway 1980; Foose 1987; Kleiman 1980). Participation in cooperative programs should include membership in regional and national zoo associations and participation in their cooperative breeding programs. The Species Survival Plan (SSP) in North America and the Europäisches Erhaltungszucht Programm (EEP) in Europe are examples of such programs. Several important publications have set forth the principles and assumptions guiding these national and international efforts (Baker and George 1988; Bennett 1990; Foose 1989; Foose and Ballou 1988; IUCN 1987; Nogge 1989).

Research and Training. Conservation centers often have the potential to contribute to conservation in ways other than captive propagation. In many cases, their location and size and the absence of large-scale public visitation release them from the programmatic constraints of urban zoos. Conservation centers situated in rural settings can also devote some of their resources to research investigations both in the captive setting and in the field. Facilities that divide their resources among scientific research on the biology of endangered species, reintroductions, and training are perhaps most justified in being called "conservation or survival centers." All of these activities are vital to the accumulation and dissemination of the knowledge necessary for the long-term conservation and management of endangered species.

Many aspects of life history can be learned more quickly and economically in the captive setting than in the wild. Reproductive characteristics such as age of sexual maturity, reproductive life span, litter size, gestation period, and weaning age are easily acquired from breeding populations in captivity. Knowledge of these variables is still lacking or incomplete for many mammals. Aside from its inherent scientific value, such information remains essential for understanding population dynamics and ecology in the wild as well as for long-term management in captivity. Through routine record keeping, such information accumulates over time for any species bred in captivity. However, painstaking verification is required to ascertain the influence of captive management regimes on the resulting values. The existence of postpartum estrus, for example, will not be detected if males are separated from parturient females until weaning. Likewise, interbirth interval in captivity cannot be accurately determined unless it is known that males were available to females at all times during their periods of reproductive cycling. In the conservation center, or the rare large zoo capable of housing a number of breeding groups, data on life history parameters can be accumulated over a relatively short time, and under controlled conditions.

Many kinds of research cannot be easily conducted in a traditional zoo due to constraints imposed by sample size, facility requirements, and public access. Virtually all experimental studies demand isolation from the normal disturbances of public institutions. Behavioral, physiological, and nutritional research generally requires large sample sizes and standardized conditions and is best conducted where the influence of extraneous factors can be minimized or selectively controlled. Investigations of mammalian lactation, for example, which require weekly milk collections, demand nonstressful conditions for the maintenance of the mother-offspring relationship, and weekly handling of the animals must be carried out under predictable circumstances with minimal disturbance (Sadleir 1980). Noninvasive urinary and fecal sampling techniques for monitoring reproductive hormones are an alternative to traditional biomedical methods, which require physical or chemical restraint for blood sampling (Monfort et al. 1990; Monfort, Schwartz, and Wasser 1993; Wasser, Risler, and Steiner 1988). Long-term endocrine monitoring can now be carried out without animal handling. As previously mentioned, nonendangered surrogate species can often play an important role in comparative studies and technique development. The surrogate studies by Miller et al. (1990a, 1990b) on Siberian polecats clearly demonstrate how conservation centers can afford facilities and space for experimental work that most zoos cannot.

Large animal collections and a core research staff are invaluable resources for research and training, and conservation centers should encourage utilization of these resources by establishing close collaborative relationships with researchers and with educational and zoological institutions. At the Conservation and Research Center, mammal keepers from other zoos and a host of students and professionals from zoos and universities have used the collection for collaborative training, education, and/or research purposes. Additionally, the Center's staff has developed training courses in zoo biology/captive management and in wildlife conservation/applied ecology. These courses are aimed at students and professionals from developing nations, are conducted abroad as well as at the Center, and incorporate professionals from other zoos, museums, and universities as instructors (Rudran, Wemmer, and Singh 1990; Wemmer, Pickett, and Teare 1990; Wemmer et al. 1993).

DEALING WITH INTERACTIONS BETWEEN NATIVE WILDLIFE AND EXOTICS

Interactions between indigenous and exotic species at rural breeding centers present two potential problems: (1) the direct predation on or harassment of exotic animals by native wildlife or domestic species, and (2) the transmittal of parasites or disease organisms from indigenous to exotic species. These are also problems in the urban zoo, but the magnitude of the problem is often greater in a rural setting where animals are maintained under more natural, free-ranging conditions.

Predator Problems
Large mammalian predators, such as bobcats, *Lynx rufus*, coyotes, *Canis latrans*, and dogs, *C. familiaris*, can be excluded from pastures and other enclosures by utilizing a combination of fencing, overhangs, and "hot wires" or electric fencing (see Collins 1982, 155). One of the worst predation threats faced by rural breeding centers is that posed by dogs. Both domestic and feral dogs will form packs that can become deadly and efficient killing machines. Ungulate pastures and barns, as well as primate, carnivore, and small mammal facilities, must be rendered dog-proof. The elimination of resident dog packs should be accomplished with the cooperation and assistance of the local animal control warden.

Smaller mammalian predators such as foxes, *Vulpes* spp., raccoons, *Procyon lotor*, mink, *Mustela vison*, and cats, *Felis catus*, can be controlled using the devices mentioned above, but it may become necessary to protect small species from climbing predators by covering the tops of their enclosures with wire mesh. The same may hold true for protecting small mammals and the offspring of ungulates from avian predators. The possibility also exists of losing small mammals to snakes such as the black rat snake, *Elaphe obsoleta*. Predation by pythons (Pythoninae) and boa constrictors (Boinae) is not an uncommon problem for zoos in the Old and New World Tropics. This potential problem should be considered when selecting mesh size for outdoor enclosures of vulnerable species.

Diseases and Parasites
The direct or indirect transmission of diseases and parasites from indigenous or domestic species to exotics (and vice versa) can be a very serious problem. Rabies, tuberculosis, distemper, and a host of other diseases and parasites vectored by both wild and domestic species are a constant threat to exotic species.

A variety of lethal internal and external parasites can be transmitted to exotics from indigenous or domestic species. The meningeal worm, *Parelaphostrongylus tenuis* (Nematoda: Metastrongylidae), is a widespread parasite of white-tailed deer, *Odocoileus virginianus*, and other cervids in North America (Anderson 1963). The adult nematodes inhabit the central nervous systems of deer. Larvae are passed in deer feces and subsequently infect certain species of terrestrial slugs and snails, undergoing obligatory developmental stages within these molluscan secondary hosts (Lankester and Anderson 1968). Deer become infected by accidentally ingesting infected mollusks as they graze (Platt 1978). While this parasite causes little overt damage to white-tailed deer, many other native and exotic ungulates have been lost to meningeal worm infections, including moose, *Alces alces*, elk, *Cervus elaphus*, and caribou, *Rangifer tarandus* (Griffiths 1978), and sable antelope, *Hippotragus niger*, scimitar-horned oryx, *Oryx dammah*, and bongos, *Tragelaphus euryceros*. The proximity of free-ranging, infected white-tailed deer to exotic ungulate pastures appears to be a major factor in the transmission of *P. tenuis*. Mollusks that become infected in areas adjacent to fenced pastures can migrate into exotic hoofstock enclosures and be ingested inadvertently (Rowley et al. 1986). Where possible, perimeter fencing and other means of control should be used to maintain as great a distance as is feasible between exotic species and native wildlife or domestic animals, since it is often more practical to control the primary host via fencing and other means than to try to control the secondary host or disease vector.

All animals should undergo a strict quarantine period, which should include a complete health examination and treatment if needed, before entering the collection. Subsequent management practices for controlling parasites and diseases should include a thorough prevention program that integrates periodic physical and fecal examinations, diagnostic testing, prophylactic administration of parasiticides (Isaza, Courtney, and Kollias 1990), and vaccination (where possible). All mortalities should be carefully documented, and necropsy results should be reviewed on a regular basis by the curators, veterinarians, and pathologists. The long-term preservation of tissue samples should be employed as an integral part of the overall animal management program, as retrospective analyses could be important in detecting and analyzing causes of mortality.

Husbandry practices naturally affect the ease of controlling parasites. Ungulates that range in large enclosures under seminatural conditions present special difficulties in assessing parasitic infection because collecting fecal samples from known animals is time-consuming and individual dosages of vermicide are difficult to administer. "Barn-training" of ungulates entails considerable effort, especially in large enclosures, but its advantages often make it worth the effort. If animals are trained to feed in individual stalls, fecal collection, administration of medicines, close-hand examination, and capture for treatment or observation can be easily managed.

MAJOR CHALLENGES TO CONSERVATION CENTERS

Conservation centers have arisen to augment captive breeding of endangered species on the scale practiced by traditional zoos. The initial motivation for establishing conservation centers was to escape the typical collection limitation of maintaining only a few individuals of each species. In the following section we examine some of the factors that limit propagation programs.

Institutional Coordination

Even large survival centers can do little to preserve species by themselves because of size and economic limitations. Of course, there have been notable exceptions. The Duke of Bedford is the best-known example of an individual whose institution single-handedly saved a species—the Père David's deer, *Elaphurus davidianus*—from the brink of extinction. But most institutions lack the means for such institutional heroism, and it was this realization that led to efforts by zoos to coordinate their individual propagation programs for particular species.

Cooperation and scientific management of endangered species of mammals did not progress significantly until the beginning of the 1980s, when cooperative breeding programs, such as the North American SSP and European EEP programs, were formalized. These programs aspire to manage captive populations scientifically so as to minimize loss of genetic variability (see Ryder and Fleischer, chap. 25, and Ballou and Foose, chap. 26, this volume). Participating zoos are expected to abide by the recommendations of the species coordinator and the management group, and thus the or-

ganizational objectives of the program are expected to supersede the individual motives of member institutions. This coordination is perhaps the greatest challenge to the long-term success of any cooperative program.

In view of this, what role can propagation facilities play to enhance the survival of endangered species? In fact, conservation centers have little to offer by themselves. William Conway (1986) has remarked that all the world's zoos can deal with but a fraction of the diversity of threatened wildlife. The existence of more survival centers will not improve the odds greatly. The minimum viable size of the captive population required to maintain any single species is large, and is beyond the capacity of any single center. Like any other zoo, survival centers must participate in collaborative long-range programs.

Economic Challenges

Survival centers that exclude the public do not generate gate fees, and miss a significant source of income. Those that cater to public viewing require much larger budgets to accommodate the many requirements of visitors. At this time, it is fair to say that survival centers will almost always have to depend upon large zoos for their support, or finance their operations through gate fees and recreational services. The pure survival center generally is not a particularly satisfying experience for the family seeking an entertaining weekend at the zoo. Despite the ability of a few large zoos to support survival centers, species survival plans often require funds far in excess of a zoo's normal operating budget. Unfortunately, donor contributions to captive breeding programs are relatively uncommon, and recent changes in American tax laws make philanthropy an even less likely source of supplemental financial support in the future.

ZOOS AND SURVIVAL CENTERS: DIFFERENT INSTITUTIONS, DIFFERENT PROBLEMS

The nature of an institution determines the nature of its problems and challenges. Visitation by the public, animal management, and research are three interacting factors that differ between zoos and propagation centers.

Visitors

In traditional zoos, the visitor is a powerful determinant of priorities and economics, as the human needs associated with the educational and recreational experience must be catered to at all times (Hediger 1969). Food, toilets, human conveyance, resting stations, first aid, police, and information signage are all important concerns in a zoo that ministers to the urban population. These services are estimated to consume approximately 70% of the typical zoo's budget. In a conservation center in a rural setting the exclusion of visitors can greatly diminish costs. This is usually not an option, however, because when the paying public is excluded, the income of the conservation center is usually not sufficient to pay land taxes, salaries, and the costs of maintaining facilities and animals. This fact explains why the largest number of institutions in the United States holding exotic animals are privately owned; the exotics are, in a sense, gratuitous boarders. In Texas alone, numerous game ranches support viable breeding populations of approximately a dozen species, but the exotics produce supplemental income.

The public that visits the traditional zoo also affects its policy and practices. An animal that becomes a celebrity as a result of successful media coverage can also evoke a public hue and cry contrary to the best interests of a nationally managed breeding program. Management decisions may be viewed either as unjustified and insensitive to the animal's needs by an uninformed zoo public, or as a violation of the animal's "rights" by a minority of well-intentioned citizens. While some public reactions to zoo policy can be avoided by thoughtful publicity and planning, it is not possible to avoid crises completely. Managing well-intentioned but misguided public reaction occupies a definite but unmeasurable percentage of zoo managers' time. Such concerns are unlikely to develop to the same extent at a facility closed to the public.

Animal Management

A second set of biological problems is a consequence of the difference in the sizes of breeding groups maintained in traditional zoos and in conservation centers. It is generally easier to manage, monitor reproduction and health in, and treat problems in small groups of animals. In survival centers polygynous mammals are often managed in large mixed-sex herds for convenience and economy. Rarely is it possible, though, to monitor male parentage in large multimale breeding herds, and this problem greatly limits the value of the offspring in a propagation program managed under genetic and demographic guidelines. The preferred, but more costly and time-consuming, alternative is to maintain single males with small groups of females, which assures the identity of the sire and maintains higher levels of genetic mixing. With this method a large, productive population in a conservation center can have a far greater effect on the age and genetic composition of the cooperatively managed population as a whole. By virtue of the larger number of animals and the chance of larger "errors," conservation centers require more intensive population management than urban zoos.

Research

Biological investigation has become an important function of the modern zoo, but few zoos can afford to reserve special collections of exotic animals exclusively for research. In the traditional zoo, liberties cannot be taken with exhibit design purely for the sake of scientific research, unless the benefits to the animals and the public are appreciable. Absence of visitors and large numbers of animals are two important advantages that propagation centers offer to research. Research is increasingly becoming an important tool for improving the health, management, and productivity of wild animals in captivity. Zoos can no longer afford to neglect the scientific and conservation value of their collections.

LESSONS FROM ZOODOM

Zoos are commonly regarded as unique institutions having little in common with national parks and other natural areas. The settings and philosophies are different, but the needs for genetic and demographic management in natural

areas are often not that different from the requirements in zoos (Neesham 1990). We have made the case elsewhere that small populations of vertebrates in isolated reserves share a number of management problems with populations in zoos (Wemmer, Smith, and Mishra 1987). In either setting, small wild populations are subject to founder effects, genetic drift, and inbreeding, and manipulating wild animals to counteract these effects is usually much more difficult than in the zoo. Imagine the skills and logistics necessary to capture a prime breeding-age male tiger and transport it from one reserve to another. We now know that most tigers born into Nepal's Chitwan tiger, *Panthera tigris,* population perish before maturity, and that genetic interchange between populations is practically impossible. Tigers coming of dispersal age (18–24 months) usually die when they move into cultivated land and kill livestock or people (Smith 1984). In captive tiger populations, demography and gene flow are more easily managed.

It is fair to say that political factors can be greater obstacles in zoos and reserves than the technical challenges of manipulating individuals within a population. Given the magnitude of the global crisis in biodiversity, however, our conservation efforts must promote cooperation and incorporate a diverse spectrum of activities, institutions, and constituencies.

ACKNOWLEDGMENTS

We would like to thank Mary Allen, John Lucas, and Susan Lumpkin for helpful editorial comments on an earlier draft; Steve Monfort, John Behler, and Nate Flesness for information; and Doug Myers, Jim Jackson, Randy Caligiuri, Bob Reece, David Bamberger, Stefan Patzwahl, Hugh Quinn, Tom Thorne, Roland Smith, George Gee, Richard Ross, Claire Mirande, Elwyn Simons, Bill Conway, Steve Romo, Tim Sullivan, and Mark Reed for providing summary information on the conservation centers listed in table 30.1. We are especially grateful to Laura Walker for her secretarial assistance and patience.

REFERENCES

Anderson, R. C. 1963. The incidence, development, and experimental transmission of *Pneumostrongylus tenuis* Dougherty (Metastrongyloidea: Protostrongylidae) of the meninges of the white-tailed deer *(Odocoileus virginianus borealis)* in Ontario. *Can. J. Zool.* 41:775–91.

Baker, R. M., and George, G. G. 1988. Species management programmes in Australia and New Zealand. *Int. Zoo Yrbk.* 27:19–26.

Bennett, P. M. 1990. Establishing breeding programmes for threatened species between zoos. *J. Zool.* (Lond.) 220:513–15.

Bildstein, K. L., and Brisbin, I. L. Jr. 1990. Lands for long-term research in conservation biology. *Conserv. Biol.* 4:301–8.

Boza, M. L. 1993. Conservation in action: Past, present, and future of the National Park System in Costa Rica. *Conserv. Biol.* 7:239–47.

Carr, A. 1989. Letter to the editor. *Conserv. Biol.* 3:332–33.

Collins, L. R. 1982. Propagation and conservation centers. In *Zoological park and aquarium fundamentals,* ed. K. Sausman, 141–68. Wheeling, W.Va.: American Association of Zoological Parks and Aquariums.

Conway, W. G. 1974. Animal management models and long-term

captive propagation. *AAZPA Annual Conference Proceedings,* 141–48. Wheeling, W.Va.: American Association of Zoological Parks and Aquariums.

———. 1980. An overview of captive propagation. In *Conservation biology: An evolutionary-ecological perspective,* ed. M. E. Soulé and B. A. Wilcox, 199–208. Sunderland, Mass.: Sinauer Associates.

———. 1986. The practical difficulties and financial limitations of endangered species breeding programmes. *Int. Zoo Yrbk.* 24/25:210–19.

———. 1988. Can technology aid species preservation? In *Biodiversity,* ed. E. O. Wilson, 263–68. Washington, D.C.: National Academy Press.

Curtin, C. G. 1993. The evolution of the U.S. National Wildlife Refuge System and the doctrine of compatibility. *Conserv. Biol.* 7:29–38.

Flesness, N. R., and Mace, G. M. 1988. Population databases and zoological conservation. *Int. Zoo Yrbk.* 27:42–49.

Foose, T. J. 1987. Species Survival Plans and overall management strategies. In *Tigers of the world,* ed. R. L. Tilson and U. S. Seal, 304–16. Park Ridge, N.J.: Noyes.

———. 1989. Status of AAZPA SSP—1989. *Proceedings of the 6th EEP Conference,* ed. K. Brouwer and L. E. M. de Boer, 27–28. Amsterdam: National Foundation for Research in Zoological Gardens.

Foose, T. J., and Ballou, J. D. 1988. Management of small populations. *Int. Zoo Yrbk.* 27:26–41.

Frankham, R., Hemmer, H., Ryder, O. A., Cothran, E. G., Soulé, M. E., Murray, N. D., and Snyder, M. 1986. Selection in small populations. *Conserv. Biol.* 5:127–38.

Geist, V. 1985. Game ranching: Threat to wildlife conservation in North America. *Wildl. Soc. Bull.* 13:594–98.

———. 1988. How markets in wildlife meat and parts, and the sale of hunting privileges, jeopardize wildlife conservation. *Conserv. Biol.* 2:15–26.

Griffiths, H. J. 1978. *A handbook of veterinary parasitology: Domestic animals of North America.* Minneapolis: University of Minnesota Press.

Haigh, J. C., and Hudson, R. J. 1993. *Farming wapiti and red deer.* St. Louis, Mo.: Mosby-Year Book.

Hediger, H. 1969. *Man and animal in the zoo: Zoo biology.* London: Routledge and Kegan Paul.

Hutchins, M., Hancocks, D., and Crockett, C. 1984. Naturalistic solutions to behavioral problems of captive animals. *Der Zoologische Garten,* n.f. 54:28–42.

Isaza, R., Courtney, C. H., and Kollias, G. V. 1990. Survey of parasite control programs used in captive wild ruminants. *Zoo Biol.* 9:385–92.

International Union for Conservation of Nature and Natural Resources (IUCN). 1987. *The IUCN policy statement on captive breeding.* Gland, Switzerland: IUCN.

Kleiman, D. G. 1980. The sociobiology of captive propagation. In *Conservation biology: An evolutionary-ecological perspective,* ed. M. E. Soulé and B. Wilcox, 243–61. Sunderland, Mass.: Sinauer Associates.

Lankester, M. W., and Anderson, R. C. 1968. Gastropods as intermediate hosts of *Pneumostrongylus tenuis* Dougherty of white-tailed deer. *Can. J. Zool.* 46:373–83.

Loisel, G. 1912. *Histoire des menageries de l'antiquité à nos jours.* Antiquité Moyen Age—Renaissance, vol. 1. Paris: Octave Doin et Fils. (English translation by Saad Publications, Karachi, Pakistan.)

Luxmoore, R. 1985. Game farming in South Africa as a force in conservation. *Oryx* 19:225–31.

McNeely, J. A., and Miller, K. R., eds. 1984. *National parks, conservation, and development: The role of protected areas in sustaining society.* Washington, D.C.: Smithsonian Institution Press.

Miller, B., Biggins, D., Wemmer, C., Powell, R., Calvo, L., Hanebury, L., and Wharton, T. 1990a. Development of survival skills in captive-raised Siberian polecats *(Mustela eversmanni).* II: Predator avoidance. *J. Ethol.* 8:95–104.

Miller, B., Biggins, D., Wemmer, C., Powell, R., Hanebury, L., Horn, D., and Vargas, A. 1990b. Development of survival skills in captive-raised Siberian polecats *(Mustela eversmanni).* I: Locating prey. *J. Ethol.* 8:89–94.

Monfort, S. L., Schwartz, C. C., and Wasser, S. K. 1993. Monitoring reproduction in captive moose using urinary and fecal steroid metabolites. *J. Wildl. Mgmt.* 57:400–407.

Monfort, S. L., Wemmer, C., Kepler, T. H., Bush, M., Brown, J. L., and Wildt, D. E. 1990. Monitoring ovarian function and pregnancy in Eld's deer *(Cervus eldi thamin)* by evaluating urinary steroid metabolite secretion. *J. Reprod. Fertil.* 88:271–81.

Neesham, C. 1990. All the world's a zoo. *New Scientist* 127 (1730): 31–35.

Nogge, G. 1989. Introduction on the history and goals of EEP. In *Proceedings of the 6th EEP Conference,* ed. K. Brouwer and L. E. M. de Boer, 15–18. Amsterdam: National Foundation for Research in Zoological Gardens.

Pinchin, A. 1993. The Pan-African decade of duiker research: An integrated programme of field and captive-based conservation. *Int. Zoo News* 244:16–21.

Platt, T. R. 1978. The life cycle and systematics of *Parelaphostrongylus odocoilei* (Nematoda: Metastrongyloidea), a parasite of mule deer *(Odocoileus hemionus hemionus),* with special reference to the intermediate molluscan host. Ph.D. thesis, University of Alberta, Edmonton, 233.

Polakowski, K. J. 1987. *Zoo design: The reality of wild illusions.* Ann Arbor: University of Michigan School of Natural Resources.

Rowley, M. A., Loker, E. S., Collins, L., and Montali, R. J. 1986. *The role of terrestrial molluscs in the transmission of meningeal worm at the Conservation and Research Center in Front Royal, Virginia: A preliminary report.* Research report. Front Royal, Va.: Conservation and Research Center.

Rudran, R., Wemmer, C. M., and Singh, M. 1990. Teaching applied ecology to nationals of developing countries. In *Race to Save the Tropics,* ed. R. Goodland, 125–40. Washington, D.C.: Island Press.

Sadleir, R. M. F. S. 1980. Energy and protein intake in relation to growth of suckling black-tailed deer fawns. *Can. J. Zool.* 58:1347–54.

Seal, U. S. 1988. Intensive technology in the care of ex situ populations of vanishing species. In *Biodiversity,* ed. E. O. Wilson, 289–95. Washington, D.C.: National Academy Press.

Smith, J. L. D. 1984. Dispersal, communication, and conservation strategies for the tiger *(Panthera tigris)* in Royal Chitwan National Park, Nepal. Ph.D. thesis, University of Minnesota, St. Paul.

Wasser, S. K., Risler, L., and Steiner, R. A. 1988. Excreted steroids in primate feces over the menstrual cycle and pregnancy. *Biol. Reprod.* 39:862–72.

Wemmer, C., Smith, J. L. D., and Mishra, H. R. 1987. Tigers in the wild: The biopolitical challenges. In *Tigers of the world,* ed. R. L. Tilson and U. S. Seal, 396–405. Park Ridge, N.J.: Noyes.

Wemmer, C., Pickett, C., and Teare, J. A. 1990. Training zoo biology in tropical countries: A report on a method and progress. *Zoo Biol.* 9:461–70.

Wemmer, C., Rudran, R., Dallmeier, F., and Wilson, D. 1993. Training developing country nationals is a critical ingredient to conserving global biodiversity. *BioScience* 43:1–14.

PART FIVE

Behavior

INTRODUCTION
KATERINA V. THOMPSON

For zoos to achieve their full potential in conservation and education, ensuring the mere survival of zoo specimens is not sufficient. We must also strive to preserve behavioral diversity among the animals in our care. If captive animals fail to exhibit normal reproductive and parental behavior, then captive propagation efforts will be futile; if animals fail to develop normal behavioral repertoires, then reintroduction attempts are doomed. Preserving behavioral diversity is a challenge for zoo managers, since the captive environment differs, in ways both obvious and subtle, from the habitats in which wild mammals evolved. This section provides a theoretical overview of aspects of behavior that have particular relevance to maintaining wild mammals in captivity and discusses how behavioral diversity can be preserved.

There are few things more discomforting to a zoo visitor than watching an animal pace endlessly and fruitlessly. Despite the recent emphasis on designing naturalistic exhibits to promote behavioral well-being in captive animals, the captive environment can never fully duplicate the habitats of wild mammals. Carlstead reviews how behavior is influenced by various facets of the captive environment in chapter 31. She also discusses behavioral abnormalities that can arise in captivity and suggests approaches to minimize the negative effects of captivity on behavior.

Koontz and Roush provide an overview of animal communication in chapter 32 and explain how features of the captive environment can enhance or interfere with normal communication. They further provide insight on how animal communication signals can be exploited by animal caretakers and managers to improve animal husbandry.

Wild mammals display an astonishing diversity of social organizations, from solitary to highly gregarious. The social organization of a given species, and therefore an individual animal's tolerance of conspecifics, is somewhat flexible and is influenced by both the environment (e.g., food, space) and the social milieu (e.g., age and sex of conspecifics). Berger and Stevens describe the various types of mammalian social organizations in chapter 33 and discuss how knowledge of a species' typical social organization and mating system can be used to determine the size and composition of captive groups.

In chapter 34 Thompson reviews the general patterns of behavioral development in wild mammals so that captive managers can evaluate the progress of animals in their care. She also describes methods of recognizing and encouraging play behavior among captive mammals, both for enhancing the educational value of exhibits and for promoting the well-being of zoo animals.

Knowledge of dietary requirements (see part 2, Nutrition, this volume) is useless if animals fail to consume the diets they are offered. Wild animals differ greatly in the methods they use to seek and consume food and in their willingness to experiment with unfamiliar food types. In chapter 35 Fernandes provides an overview of foraging behavior in mammals, with special emphasis on aspects that are immediately relevant to captive husbandry.

Future conservation efforts will combine in situ and ex situ activities. It has already been shown that behavioral deficiencies exist in zoo mammals that result in reduced survivorship when they are reintroduced into the wild. It is hoped that careful attention to behavioral needs will permit the expression of more normal behavior by individuals bred for reintroduction programs, and thus a more rapid adaptation to the wild and improved survivorship.

31

Effects of Captivity on the Behavior of Wild Mammals

Kathy Carlstead

The behavior of any species of wild mammal is the product of many generations of natural selection and adaptation to specific environmental conditions. Some species' behavior has evolved for the exploitation of very specific habitats, food resources, or climatic conditions, while other species have evolved the ability to adapt their behavior to various conditions depending on the seasonal, social, or biological factors predominating at any given time. Captivity, however, imposes on wild mammals an environment that may differ vastly from that in which they have evolved. To thrive under captive conditions, a species must accommodate to these differences. A species' ability to respond to captive conditions with behavior from its normal repertoire depends on a complex interaction of developmental, experiential, and genetic factors, as well as on the degree to which the particular captive conditions resemble its natural environment. The short-term success individuals have in coping with captive conditions affects their ability to breed in captivity; this initial success therefore affects the species' ultimate ability to exist as a captive population.

An animal's daily life is affected by physical and biological factors such as social and spatial restrictions, the presence of other species, including humans, and the availability of appropriate stimuli for the development and expression of natural appetitive, defensive, and protective behaviors. Such factors vary considerably across environments depending on the degree of "captiveness" or "wildness." However, the concept of "wild" versus "captive" is a false dichotomy. Populations of animals are found ranging freely in a wide variety of habitats, from "wild" reserves to semi-wild sites where animals are provisioned. Populations termed "captive" inhabit sites ranging from large breeding corrals to complex zoo enclosures to single cages in laboratories. For simplicity, I will use "wild" and "captive" in this chapter to distinguish conditions tending more toward either extreme.

The chapter is divided into three major sections reflecting various levels of influence captivity may have on behavior: on the genetics of a captive population, on the development of behavior, and on the psychology of confined mammals. Reproduction in captivity may produce genetic changes in a captive population that distinguish it from wild populations. This would be of no consequence if captive mammal collections had constant access to new, wild-caught stock, but most zoos and propagation centers at present largely contain animals born and bred in captivity. Particularly if the desired end result is the preservation of an endangered species in a wild state, the long-term effects of captivity on behavior are important considerations (Kleiman 1980). A species' behavior derives from its genetic endowment, and because the long-term effects of captivity may act on gene frequencies in populations of captive mammals, I will begin this chapter on this theme.

LONG-TERM EFFECTS OF CAPTIVITY ON BEHAVIOR AND GENETICS

Captive populations are influenced by several random and nonrandom genetic mechanisms that may distinguish them from wild populations after a number of generations. Genetic variability is randomly reduced by inbreeding and genetic drift in small, relatively closed populations. Inbreeding increases homozygosity and may result in a lowering of fitness brought about by the expression of deleterious genes previously masked by dominant alleles. Ralls, Brugger, and Ballou (1979) present data indicating that mortality during the first 6 months of life is higher for inbred young of a number of zoo ungulate species than for noninbred young; the same has been reported for other inbred captive species (red panda, *Ailurus fulgens*: Roberts 1982; Przewalski's horse, *Equus przewalskii*: Bouwman 1977; eland, *Taurotragus oryx*: Treus and Lobanov 1971; leopard, *Panthera pardus*: Shoemaker 1982). Genetic drift, on the other hand, causes certain genes of neutral selective value to become "fixed" in a population as a result of their relative abundance in the small founding population.

Three primary selective mechanisms influence the gene frequencies of captive populations nonrandomly: artificial selection, natural selection, and relaxation of selection (Price 1984).

1. *Artificial selection* is selection for biological traits desired by humans. Such selection is goal-oriented and relatively fast when compared with the rate of change produced by natural selection in a wild population. Domesticated species have been selectively bred for biological traits of economic importance or for exaggerated morphological characteristics. Specific behavioral traits have been consciously selected in a few species, such as fighting cocks and guard dogs, but behavioral changes in domesticated populations have more often been the indirect consequence of selection for other, morphological attributes (Keeler 1975).

2. *Natural selection in captivity.* In the absence of interference by humans, the individuals possessing the phenotypes best able to adapt to captive conditions will have the highest reproductive success. This process of natural selection will be most intense in the first few generations after the transition from wild to captive environments (Price 1984).

3. *Relaxation of selection* can occur when captive conditions permit certain behavioral traits to remain in the population that would have been selected against under wild conditions. The result is an increase in genotypic and phenotypic variability for traits affecting behaviors such as food and shelter seeking, predator avoidance, and behaviors that serve to isolate populations reproductively.

Are zoo populations becoming domesticated? If the goal of zoos is to maintain wild animals in their most natural and original condition, zoo animals should not be managed like domestic animals (Hediger 1964, 1970). Price (1984) defines domestication as "that process by which a population of animals becomes adapted to man and to the captive environment by some combination of genetic changes occurring over generations and environmentally induced developmental events reoccurring during each generation." Humans have domesticated relatively few species, mostly out of economic need, and have domesticated mainly species predisposed to domestication by their social organization and reproductive behavior. Easily domesticated species generally live in large, hierarchical social groups in which the males affiliate with female groups, mating is promiscuous, and the young experience a sensitive imprinting period during development and are precocial. They are also generally adapted to a wide range of environments and dietary habits rather than to highly specialized conditions (Hale 1969; Clutton-Brock 1976). These characteristics permit easy control by humans. The mammal species found in zoological parks can be expected to be differently predisposed to domestication, and they probably differ greatly with respect to the adaptive behavioral changes that have already occurred, or may yet occur, as a result of generations in captivity. Purposeful selection for tameness or adaptation to captivity may be acceptable in cases in which the species is common in the wild and is kept in zoos only for display, or in the initial stages of establishing a captive population of a rare species that is not yet capable of self-sustaining reproduction (Frankham et al. 1986). Nevertheless,

unconscious artificial selection for traits such as docility and tractability is probably occurring in zoo animals, selection that may eventually make captive populations genotypically divergent from wild populations.

Does wild behavior degenerate in captivity? Captive breeding of endangered species has been criticized because of concerns about the possible loss of wild behavior and the turning of animals into "degenerates" that cannot survive in the wild, as is said of many domesticated species (Hediger 1968; Bendiner 1981). However, it is highly questionable whether such long-term processes will have significant effects on the species-typical behavior of captive mammals. The stability of behavior patterns is generally underestimated, and in spite of numerous reports of behavioral differences between wild and domestic species, there is little or no evidence that domestication has caused behaviors to be eliminated from a species' repertoire (Hale 1969). Locomotor components of behavior, as well as the associated sensory capacities, tend to be so evolutionarily stable that behavioral criteria are even sometimes employed taxonomically to distinguish genera or species (Mayr 1958). Even among canids, for which there are extensive comparisons of wild and domestic behavior, no behavioral traits have been observed in domestic dogs that are not observed in their wild counterparts, except for tail carriage (Scott 1954). It would appear highly unlikely that any changes in normal species-typical behaviors would have evolved in zoo mammal populations since they have not undergone the extensive artificial selection of the domestic dog.

The main behavioral differences between captive and wild populations, therefore, are quantitative rather than qualitative. They are results of changes in intensity or releasing threshold, and may be brought about by genetic changes in the population (as discussed above), by learned adjustments to the captive environment occurring during the animal's lifetime, or by the unique stimulus situations existing in captivity (Hale 1969; Price 1984). For example, reduced aggressiveness toward conspecifics and humans in laboratory rats has been shown to be largely the result of being reared in social groups in small, open cages (Price 1978; Barnett, Dickson, and Hocking 1979) rather than due to genetic differences, even after many generations of artificial selection and inbreeding. Also, the absence of certain key stimuli in the physical environment of captive animals can result in failure to express certain behavior patterns. The burrowing behavior of domestic albino rats was found to be indistinguishable from that of wild rats when they were housed in large outdoor pens; the albinos also showed a variety of other wild-type behaviors under these conditions (Boice 1977). The rarity of certain behavior patterns in the repertoire of a population may also be a consequence of selection for a particular developmental phase. In young Malamute pups, unrestrained aggression and the absence of some threat displays normally seen in adult wolves, *Canis lupus lycaon,* were concluded to be the result of selection for neoteny (retention of juvenile characteristics) rather than due to relaxation of natural selection for these behaviors (Frank and Frank 1982).

Most wild mammal species have been bred in captivity for relatively few generations, and the current long-term effects of captivity on behavior are probably minimal. To maintain captive breeding populations of animals that exhibit behavior as it evolved in the wild, conscious or unintentional selection must be minimized and an environment provided that consists of the appropriate stimuli for eliciting wild behavior. This requires a thorough knowledge of behavior in the wild state as well as consideration of environmental influences on the development of behavior.

EFFECTS OF CAPTIVITY ON BEHAVIORAL DEVELOPMENT

The dynamic, ongoing interaction between an organism and its surroundings throughout development actively implicates the environment in determining the structure and organization of the animal's response systems (Moltz 1965). Animals born and reared in captivity may, therefore, be behaviorally distinct from those born and reared in a wild environment. The extent of this difference will depend partially on the degree to which the captive environment provides the appropriate stimulation during development and partially on the phenotypic plasticity of the species, that is, the extent to which the genotype is capable of entering into different classes of relationship with the environment (Moltz 1965).

During development, periods of heightened sensitivity to certain environmental stimuli may exert lasting influences on physiology, anatomy, and behavior. These "sensitive periods" are due in part to internal changes and may occur during various developmental stages in the animal's life. What is learned during these periods serves to narrow the animal's social or object preferences to that which is familiar. The irreversibility of some early experiences, however, may have maladaptive consequences for adult behavior when the experience acquired as a result of captive rearing does not correspond sufficiently with that normally acquired in the wild.

Prenatal Experience
Interactions between the developing organism and its environment start prior to birth, for the hormonal state of the mother affects the uterine environment of the growing fetus. Various effects of stress experienced by mothers during pregnancy on the behavior of their offspring have been reported, including increases (Ader and Belfer 1962) or decreases (Thompson, Watson, and Charlsworth 1962) in emotionality in a novel environment (open field) and alterations of exploratory behavior (Archer and Blackman 1971) in rats, and reductions in attack and threat behavior in male offspring (Harvey and Chevins 1985) in mice. Behavioral dysfunctions have also been found among human children born to mothers who experienced emotional stress during pregnancy (Stott 1973). Early motor development in rat pups was retarded when the mother was experimentally stressed with flashing lights and noise on an unpredictable schedule three times per week throughout pregnancy (Fride and Weinstock 1984). Fride and Weinstock hypothesize that glucocorticoids, produced by the mother when stressed, cross the placental barrier and affect the embryonic brain. In particular, the cerebellum is affected during sensitive periods in de-

velopment. Corticosterone secreted by the mother in response to stress may also interfere with fetal testosterone production, which is necessary during fetal and early neonatal periods for the later development of masculine sexual behavior (Money and Ehrhardt 1972). The male offspring of mother rats stressed daily in the last week of gestation showed reductions in attempted copulations and ejaculation responses as adults (Ward 1972). Such studies imply that in a zoo environment, potentially stressful disturbances of pregnant mammals, such as relocation, zoo visitors, changes in management practices, social tension, or removal from a stable social group, could affect the viability and later behavior of their offspring.

The Early Social Environment
The social environment in captivity, if it deviates sufficiently from the wild situation, may deprive the young animal of specific stimulation essential for the development of normal, species-typical behavior. In mammals, rearing by the mother provides the infant with specific stimulation necessary for the normal development of emotional regulation, social interaction, and complex goal-directed behaviors, in particular, maternal and sexual behaviors. Maternal deprivation studies have demonstrated the long-term regulatory influence the parent-infant relationship may have on adult behavior, although there is a hiatus, due to a lack of systematic study, in our understanding of the processes underlying this regulatory function (Hofer 1981).

Tactile contact with the mother in rats has the immediate effect of eliciting activity in the pups, but when frequently repeated it reduces emotional reactivity later in life (Levine 1966; Hofer 1981). For rat pups, tactile contact with the mother, even if she is anesthetized and does not suckle the pups, is sufficient for suppressing emotional responses to novel stimuli at age 12–20 days (Levine 1986; Stanton, Wallstrom, and Levine 1987). Deprivation of maternal licking when pups are young has also been shown to affect the timing of sexual behavior patterns in male rats when grown; intromissions were more slowly paced and the rats took longer to ejaculate (Moore 1984).

Stimulation of the vestibular system provided by a moving mother is also important for the developing infant. Rhesus monkey *(Macaca mulatta)* infants raised with inanimate surrogate mothers that were stationary developed the self-rocking behaviors that are characteristically seen in isolation-reared monkeys, and in autistic or severely retarded children, while those raised with surrogates moving on a swing did not (Mason and Berkson 1975). The monkeys with moving surrogates did, however, retain other stereotypic patterns such as self-clasping and finger sucking. At 4 to 5 years of age they were less emotionally aroused, more responsive to partners, and benefited more from socializing experiences with peers than did the monkeys with stationary surrogates. This experiment not only illustrates the importance of vestibular stimulation as a component of parental care, but also shows some of the self-correcting behavior that developing young may perform in order to provide themselves with the necessary stimulation.

One of the main reasons for hand-rearing infant mammals in captivity is the mother's failure to provide adequate care. The reasons for such failures are diverse. Parturition is undoubtedly a stressful event for an animal, and maternal behaviors such as nest building, suckling, and retrieving are very labile (see also Hutchins, Thomas, and Asa, chap. 41, this volume). Stressful environmental events during and after parturition may disrupt these behaviors and result in rejection or harming of the infants. Parturient females may need nesting material, concealment, social isolation, silence, or temperature regulation. Failure to meet their special needs may result in a disruption of maternal behavior. The rearing strategy of a species must be carefully considered before forced isolation, forced contact with the young, or close confinement is imposed on the mother (Eisenberg and Kleiman 1977). Finally, inbreeding may account for a rise in the frequency of abnormal maternal behavior in a population, as is suggested in the case of cub killing in captive leopards (Shoemaker 1982).

Deficient maternal behavior, and even injurious behavior toward the offspring, may also be due to a lack of prior social experience with infants. Female rat pups placed postnatally with their mothers in environments with odors from other mothers with pups, or reared in groups with a large number of siblings, show superior maternal behavior in terms of pup retrieval and nest building compared with pups reared without odors or with a small number of siblings (Moretto, Paclik, and Fleming 1986). Hand-reared rhesus macaques avoid contact with their infants and are hyperaggressive toward them when they themselves become mothers ("motherless mothers": Harlow et al. 1966). Suomi (1986) points out that when Harlow started his research with rhesus macaques in the 1950s, most zoos made decisions to hand-rear captive-born primates based on health, safety, and hygienic considerations. However, once hand-rearing starts, it can become a vicious circle, producing more and more animals incapable of caring properly for their young unless compensatory experience is provided. Harlow and colleagues subsequently discovered that females who displayed aberrant infant care with their firstborn offspring could become competent mothers with later-born offspring if they remained with their firstborns for more than a week (Harlow et al. 1966; Ruppenthal et al. 1976), or if they had been given early social experience with mother-reared peers (Suomi 1986). Captive female chimpanzees, *Pan troglodytes*, are better mothers when they have social experience with nonrelated infants or mothers with infants (Hannah and Brotman 1990).

Despite the importance of the mother postnatally, social contact with peers may produce even more profound effects on later social behavior. Social deprivation studies (for a review, see Mineka and Suomi 1978) demonstrate the debilitating outcome of social deprivation. Hand-reared rhesus macaques totally isolated from conspecifics during their first few months exhibit irreversibly disturbed behavior when placed in a social group. They typically sit in a hunched position, spend large parts of their day in repetitive stereotypic motor behaviors, and are hyperaggressive, directing explosive physical attacks against their own bodies or against other monkeys. Sexual behavior is also usually aberrant (Goldfoot 1977). Laboratory rats deprived of any social contact between 22 and 70 days of age were also observed to be hyperaggressive to others when placed in a stable social group, and exhibited aberrant self-directed behaviors such as tail-chasing and manipulating the tail with the forefeet (Day et al. 1982). The excessive aggressiveness of many hand-reared zoo animals toward humans (Hediger 1964) and conspecifics, as well as some cases of self-mutilation, are analogous to these laboratory experiments; the social isolation from peers that may accompany hand-rearing can have devastating effects.

Many of the behavioral effects of isolation rearing can be overcome by providing even limited access to peers during development (see also Watts and Meder, chap. 6, this volume). Behavioral deficiencies in isolation-reared rats can be prevented by providing short periods of daily contact with peers involving rough-and-tumble play (Einon, Morgan, and Kibbler 1978). In rhesus macaques, however, adult sexual behavior remains deficient in most animals reared under conditions of limited access to peers (Goldfoot 1977). Some researchers suggest that the behavioral effects of isolation rearing on monkeys and rats are attributable to play deprivation (Einon, Morgan, and Kibbler 1978; Einon et al. 1981; Sackett 1974). Sackett theorizes that the hyperaggressiveness of isolation-reared rhesus macaques when placed in a stable social group is due to their failure to inhibit isolation-learned behaviors that are maladaptive in social settings. The function of play behavior may be to gain experience in the rapid alteration of roles and behavior patterns (Einon, Morgan, and Kibbler 1978). Isolation-reared juvenile rhesus macaques can be socially rehabilitated if they are allowed close physical contact with younger infants. The younger monkeys are less specific in their requirements for social interaction than are adults, and they provide the necessary interaction to socialize the isolates (Suomi and Harlow 1976). Hofer (1981) points out that there are many routes to the same developmental outcome in rehabilitation from the effects of aberrant early parenting; such compensatory schemes can and are being applied in zoos (i.e, in gorillas: Meder 1985).

Effects of Humans on Behavioral Development

One of the most distinctive elements of the captive environment is close contact with humans, a factor that can be expected to produce a range of behavioral characteristics not found in a wild-reared animal. Rearing in captivity may produce taming; Hediger (1964) defines tameness as "having no flight tendency with respect to man." Older wild-caught animals may be more difficult to tame than younger animals because of prior negative experience with humans or due to the absence of humans during the sensitive period for socialization. Older wild-caught moose, *Alces alces*, may never adapt to captivity and usually die of heart failure due to extreme tension (Hediger 1964).

The handling of young mother-reared mammals at an early age has been reported to have diverse effects on subsequent adult behavior, including speeding up the taming process. Generally, experiments in which mother-reared laboratory rat pups are handled at various stages of their early development produce adult animals that exhibit reduced emotional reactivity in a number of behavioral tests or in the presence of humans (Denenberg 1964, 1967). Enhanced learning in early-handled rats and primates has also been reported (Weiner et al. 1985). However, handling of young animals may also have detrimental effects, particularly if the stress of handling either the mother or the young interferes with the mother-infant relationship.

Close contact with humans at an early age, especially if it is in lieu of caregiving by the natural mother (i.e., hand rearing), leads to socialization with humans that may or may not have later consequences. Among ungulates with precocial young, filial imprinting, in which the young learn to follow the mother rather than objects and individuals that do not resemble the mother, occurs within the first day or two of life (for a review see Bateson 1966). Characteristics of filial imprinting have also been demonstrated in guinea pigs, *Cavia porcellus* (Sluckin 1968; Hess 1973). If a young animal is removed from the mother during the sensitive period for filial imprinting, following responses may come to be elicited by human caregivers, as is commonly seen in sheep and goats, but has also been reported in the American bison, *Bison bison,* zebra, *Equus* spp., African buffalo, *Syncerus caffer,* mouflon, *Ovis musimon,* and vicuña, *Vicugna vicugna* (Hediger 1968). Sexual imprinting, which leads an adult animal to direct sexual behavior preferentially to individuals resembling those it encountered when young, generally occurs during a sensitive period arising later than the sensitive period for filial imprinting. Most demonstrations of sexual imprinting, however, have been in birds; the evidence in mammals is inconclusive (Immelmann 1972). Generally, in mammals, subtle aspects of the parent-infant or juvenile-peer relationship affect later sexual preferences and competence such that one speaks of an extended period of socialization occurring during infant and juvenile stages (Bateson 1978).

Development of Learning in Captivity

Captive environments may be considerably less complex than relatively unrestricted, dynamic wild environments. Some experiments report functional variations in brain anatomy as a result of rearing in environments of varying physical complexity. Rats reared in a so-called "enriched" environment, for example, have a higher cerebral cortex weight, increased numbers of glial cells, and increased dendritic branching in the visual cortex (cf. Greenough 1976; Rosenzweig and Bennett 1976; Stein, Finger, and Hart 1983; for a review see Uphouse 1980). Behaviorally, they exhibit higher motor activity and more exploration in a standard test situation. There may also be differences in emotionality, and rearing in a physically complex environment may enhance learning to respond to a novel situation (e.g., Riittinen et al. 1986). Theories explaining the behavioral effects of experience with complex environments center on the environment-dependent development of neurons in the central nervous system that function to shape the animal's ability to cope with multiple and varied environmental challenges (Uphouse 1980).

Mental processes may develop differently in captivity than in the wild as a result of lower environmental complexity. Cognitive psychologists contend that animals possess learning mechanisms designed to detect and store information about causal relationships (Dickinson 1980). These relationships generally consist of two kinds of associations between constituent events, in which one event potentially causes another event either to happen or not to happen. In the complex and variable rearing environment of the wild, an animal learns that it can predict modifications in its environment as a result of its performing certain behaviors; it learns through experience with response-contingent stimulation that it can exert control over its environment. Without such experience, it learns that its behavior does not modify its environment in a predictable manner, and thus it may fail to respond optimally to new situations arising during its lifetime.

Mason (1978) suggested that experience with response-contingent stimulation is the essence of the mother-infant relationship; the mother provides a young animal with its first opportunities to learn that its behavior has effects on the environment and that the events around it are amenable to control. Mason reared rhesus macaque infants with surrogate mothers of two types, inanimate (a toy hobby-horse on wheels) and animate (a living dog). When he tested them at age 4, he found that monkeys raised with inanimate mothers were deficient in problem solving, often failing to respond at all to the test situation, and spent less time looking at projected photographs in a novel stimulus test. They were also unable to differentiate reliably between three levels of complexity in the slides. Mason's hypothesis is that a moving, responding mother provides her infant with stimulation that sustains interaction; even a mechanical swinging surrogate mother provides unpredictable movements that require adjusted movements from the infant (Mason and Berkson 1975). Such movements permit a young animal to learn that it can manipulate incoming stimulation by adjusting its own behavior. Deprived of experience with response-contingent stimulation, the animal is denied a motive for controlling its environment when faced with novel stimuli or problem-solving situations (Lewis and Goldberg 1969, cited in Mason 1978). (As mentioned above, Sackett [1974] proposed a similar explanation for the role of rough-and-tumble play in behavioral development, and indeed, rough-and-tumble play was three times greater in the 4-year-old monkeys in Mason's study that had been raised with animate surrogates than in those raised with inanimate surrogates.)

In another experiment, one group of rats was reared in a contingent environment in which they could control changes in lighting and presentations of food and water with lever presses. A second, noncontingent group housed in identical cages could make lever presses, but changes in their lighting, food, and water were yoked to the lever presses made by the contingent group (Joffe, Rawson, and Mulick 1973). Both groups thus received equal amounts of reward, but the contingent group had control over its onset and the noncontingent group did not. At 60 days of age, the contingent group rats, when tested in a novel, large, bare arena, were more active and explored more than rats from the noncontingent group, and were less emotional (as indicated by the number of defecations). Similarly, rhesus macaques were reared in three different environments: (1) they could control access to rewards of food, water, and treats; (2) rewards were as in (1) but were delivered randomly; and

(3) there were no rewards (daily feedings were given). When tested between the ages of 6 and 10 months, the monkeys with control over rewards were bolder in the presence of a fear-provoking toy, were more eager to enter a novel room and explored it more, and adapted better to stressful separation from peers than the monkeys without control (Mineka and Henderson 1985). Thus, lack of early experience in controlling environmental events can produce an animal that later is less able to adapt to stressful events and less likely to investigate actively and learn about novel situations. Overmeier and Seligman (1967) termed this response interference "learned helplessness," a term that has stuck despite the running debate on the actual psychological mechanisms involved.

The above examples are extremely relevant to the captive environment. Many zoo animals grow up in situations devoid of physical and social contingencies that would permit them to learn that their behavior can influence the environment. This may not matter if an animal is kept in a barren cage with no stimulation, but in a situation requiring a normal, adaptive response—for example, if it is placed in a novel environment or confined with a mate or young—its deficient experience may ultimately cause social discord, reproductive failure, disease, or even death. Fortunately, the emotional, cognitive, and anatomical deficits caused by rearing in impoverished environments, while long-lasting, may be subject to at least partial improvement by the provision of "therapy" in an enriched environment (Warren, Zerweck, and Anthony 1982; Stein, Finger, and Hart 1983). This finding is of relevance for zoo environmental enrichment programs designed to increase the activity levels of exhibit animals.

SHORT-TERM EFFECTS OF CAPTIVITY ON THE BEHAVIOR OF MAMMALS

The remainder of this chapter will discuss behavior that can be considered a direct response to the prevailing day-to-day conditions in captive environments. An animal's response to its surroundings depends on its sensory capabilities, motivational state, and previous experience with the environment. Together, these factors influence the animal's perceptions of the relevance of a given environmental stimulus and its subsequent attentional and behavioral responses. Along the continuum from captive to wild conditions, animals may use increasingly different behavioral mechanisms to adapt to their environments.

Control over the Environment

The main difference between captive and wild environments lies in the differential availability of control. Some theoretical models of behavior emphasize (1) that the degree to which an animal is stimulated by an event or situation external to itself is a function of the discrepancy between its expectations of stimulation and the actual stimulation, and (2) that the goal of a behavioral response is to control the level of stimulatory input (Sokolov 1960; Salzen 1962, 1970; Archer 1976; O'Keefe and Nadel 1978; Inglis 1983; Wiepkema 1985). A free-living animal is able to control the amount of incoming stimulation by making regulatory behavioral adjustments. It can approach, explore, attack, chase, escape, avoid, or hide from stimuli it encounters until the stimulation is brought to an acceptable level or until its expectations of stimulation are met. It can control its microclimate by moving to shade or sun, to shelter or wind, and it can satisfy appetitive motivation by actively seeking food, shelter, or a mate.

In captivity, on the other hand, an animal has a limited capacity to alter the external stimulation to which it is exposed. Many relevant stimulatory events are simply imposed on schedules that cannot be self-determined. Behavioral temperature regulation is often impossible, and appetitive motivation may have no appropriate outlet. Under these circumstances, the animal may be able to exert control over incoming stimulation only by modifying its expectations of its environment, as will be discussed below.

Evidence for the importance to developmentally nondeprived adult animals of being able to control their environment comes from experiments in which a choice is given between performing an active behavioral response to produce a biologically relevant event or having the event imposed. If rats are allowed to choose between receiving food that is delivered only upon performance of an operant behavior or receiving "free" food requiring no behavioral response, they overwhelmingly prefer to perform behavior for food (Singh 1970; review by Osborne 1977). Hungry rats trained to run down an alleyway to earn a pellet of food will even run past thousands of identical pellets to get to the goal box and obtain their reward (Stolz and Lott 1964; Overmeier, Patterson, and Weilkiewicz 1980). Deer mice, *Peromyscus maniculatus*, trained to operate levers controlling a motor-driven running wheel will run in it if they can start and stop it themselves, but they will not accept non-self-initiated motor-driven running (Kavanau 1963, 1964). Deer mice allowed to control illumination by lever presses will turn off a light each time it comes on automatically every half hour. If the light is automatically turned off every half hour, however, the mice turn it back on. Even though the mice have an aversion to bright lighting, having control over the illumination is sufficiently rewarding to override it.

The importance of behavioral control in adapting to *aversive* stimuli has also been demonstrated in many experiments, mainly with rats and mice. Weiss (1968) trained rats of one group to press a nose plate to turn off an electric shock administered to the tail. Rats of another group were "yoked" to the trained rats so that they simultaneously received the same shock as the first group, but they could not turn off the shock; it ceased only when the trained rat pressed the nose plate. Both groups thus received equal amounts of tail shock, but the trained rats had control over it and the yoked rats did not. The yoked rats eventually showed more severe physiological disturbances than the trained rats, including weight loss and gastric ulceration, indicative of severe stress. In other experiments, animals consistently able to escape shock showed fewer stress-related physiological responses than animals receiving the same amount of inescapable shock (Davis et al. 1977; Dess et al. 1983).

Captive animals may perform behaviors that provide perceptions of control rather than actual control. Some abnormal behaviors commonly observed in captive mammals may be the result of emotional arousal that has no appropriate behavioral outlet and becomes redirected to other objects or individuals. Winkelstraeter (1960) describes excessive self-scratching among primates frustrated by the failure of zoo visitors to respond to their begging for food. Sudden explosions of aggressiveness among animals that have lived together in apparent harmony may also be redirected responses to other, uncontrollable situations (Morris 1964; Meyer-Holzapfel 1968). Copulations with inanimate objects (Morris 1966) or with inappropriate partners without the normal courtship behaviors (Meyer-Holzapfel 1968) may be redirected expressions of arousal caused by unrelated, uncontrollable factors in the environment. Copulatory behaviors in laboratory animals can sometimes be induced by electric shock, handling, or novelty, or by frustration (Antelman and Caggiula 1980).

Without natural behavioral outlets, captive animals may have to rely on a conservation-withdrawal pattern of response characterized behaviorally by inactivity and submission. This response may allow the animal to obtain predictive information about the situation and thus alter its expectations of the stimulation impinging upon it. Freezing or crouching is a common response to diffuse, inescapable aversive cues that may allow the animal to monitor its situation (Blanchard and Blanchard 1969) and make preparatory physiological adjustments, as in stress-induced analgesia (for discussion, see Abbott, Schoen, and Badia 1984). The importance of predictive information for coping with aversive stimuli has been elucidated in experiments in which laboratory animals are delivered signaled or unsignaled shocks. Animals prefer conditions in which the inescapable shocks are signaled in a reliable manner (Seligman and Meyer 1968, 1970; Badia et al. 1976; for reviews, see Abbott, Schoen, and Badia 1984; Weinberg and Levine 1980). Feedback information about the cessation of the aversive stimulus may also be important because it helps the animal distinguish "safe," shock-free periods from periods in which shock is imminent (Weinberg and Levine 1980; Levine 1983).

Stress in Captivity

Threatening or aversive stimulation is experienced in wild and captive conditions alike and evokes similar physiological responses. If an animal, wild or captive, cannot cope with this stimulation, it may experience "stress." Coping is an active psychological process that alters threatening or aversive environmental conditions having stress as a major component (Levine 1983). In the previous section, I pointed out that the low controllability characteristic of captive conditions may require coping styles that tend toward reducing uncertainty. In this section, I will discuss the concept of "stress," means of assessing stress in confined animals, and the behavioral effects of chronic stress.

There is no generally accepted definition of stress, and it has many components that are not understood. The term "stress" is commonly used to refer to daily troubles and anxieties such as those experienced by human commuters or executives. With regard to nonhuman mammals, the term often refers to some unknown or intangible entity responsible for an animal's failure to behave or reproduce normally.

"Stress" may refer to different physiological and behavioral mechanisms, depending on the context. The term may be applied to an animal's physiological responses to extreme heat or cold, the social behavior of overcrowded laboratory animals, decreased productivity in farm animals, or the causes of pathology in animals or humans (Dawkins 1980). One reason for confusion is that the concept of stress is circular; diverse environmental variables elicit nonspecific autonomic and neuroendocrine responses with different time courses, as well as different behavioral responses. These behavioral reactions alter aspects of the environmental stimulation that initiated the response, subsequently influencing physiological and behavioral reactions, and so on. Discussion of "stress" thus may refer to the eliciting variables, or "stressors," to the autonomic and endocrinological changes, to behavioral adaptation, or to longer-term biological effects.

Originally, the term "stress" was used by Selye (1936, 1950) to refer to a nonspecific syndrome of physiological responses to noxious agents such as cold, heat, or physical pain. Selye's "general adaptation syndrome" is divided into three general stages. First, an alarm or emergency reaction to a stressor occurs, involving an acute activation of the sympathetic nervous system and adrenal medulla, secreting catecholamines that enable the organism to mobilize its "fight-or-flight" response (Cannon 1935). The resistance phase follows, in which activation of the neuroendocrine system, specifically, the hypothalamic-pituitary-adrenal (HPA) axis, occurs. ACTH (adrenocorticotrophic hormone) is secreted by the pituitary, stimulating the release of glucocorticoids (i.e., cortisol, corticosterone) from the adrenal cortex. Glucocorticoids amplify and extend the metabolic effects of catecholamines and help provide the body with energy in the form of glucose. Other pituitary hormones may also be released (e.g., growth hormone, prolactin, thyroid-stimulating hormone, gonadotropins) that inhibit growth and suppress reproductive function. In the final stage of the syndrome, if adaptation to the stressor does not occur or the stressor is not removed, gastric ulceration may occur and the biological defense system may become exhausted, with sequelae such as atrophy of the thymus and lowered immunological function.

Although Selye (1936, 1950) conceptualized the stress syndrome as being nonspecific because he believed the same endocrine processes to be elicited by a wide variety of noxious agents, other neuroendocrine systems have been found to respond in patterns characteristic of each stressor (Moberg 1985a). Although Selye used stressors that represented a physical insult to the animal, such as injection of foreign substances, x-rays, heat, or mechanical trauma, subsequent research has shown that the primary characteristics of stressful stimuli eliciting endocrine responses are *psychological* in nature (Selye 1956, 1974; for reviews, see Mason 1971; Hennessy and Levine 1979; Levine 1985). Mason was the first to emphasize that the apparent nonspecificity of the endocrine response lies in the psychological variables associated with the application of a noxious physical stimulus. If emotional arousal is carefully avoided when administering a treatment such as heat, cold, fasting, or exercise, the HPA axis is not activated. For instance, suddenly raising the room temperature by 15°C will increase circulating serum corticosteroid levels in rhesus macaques, but raising the temperature 1°C per hour to 15°C above normal will not (Mason 1971).

Experiments of this type have demonstrated that the complex hormonal changes that occur in conscious individuals subjected to stressful situations depend on subjective emotional experience. Levine (1985) states that "the basic cognitive process involved in stimulation of the pituitary adrenal system is one of comparison." Stress, according to his conception, is the endocrine responses to the cognitive variables of novelty and uncertainty. Mildly novel or uncertain situations may not be sufficiently aversive to activate the HPA axis, but as the degree of novelty or uncertainty increases, so does the stress response. In one example, rats normally housed in metal cages were handled only, placed in an unfamiliar metal cage with new bedding, placed in an unfamiliar metal cage with no bedding, or placed in a novel plastic container. All treatments caused increases in plasma corticosteroids, but the increases were larger for those treatments that deviated more from normal conditions in the order described above (Hennessy et al. 1979). Thus, the physiological stress response is graded according to perceptions of environmental change.

Individuals of the same species, sex, and age may differ greatly in their responses to the same environmental stimulus. There appear to be at least two different patterns of response to a perceived aversive situation: (1) an active "fight-or-flight" pattern characterized by increased activity, increased sympathetic adrenal medullary activation, and related increases in cardiac output and arterial pressure; and (2) a more passive "conservation-withdrawal" pattern characterized by decreased environment-directed activities, increased adrenocortical activation, and suppressed reproductive function (Engel 1967; Henry and Stephens 1977; Koolhaas, Schuurman, and Fokkema 1985; Moberg 1985b; Suomi 1986). Any individual may exhibit both types of response patterns; the pattern more likely to occur is dependent on rearing experience (Moberg 1985a) and genetic background (Gentsch, Vichtsteiner, and Feer 1981; Mormede et al. 1984; Suomi 1986). The idiosyncratic nature of stress responses is attributed to differences in perceptions of controllability and predictability (Dantzer and Mormede 1983; Levine 1985). There are complex interactions between the controllability and predictability components of coping responses (for reviews see Overmeier, Patterson, and Weilkiewicz 1980; Mineka and Henderson 1985). The effectiveness of predictive information in coping with aversive stimuli may be modulated by control over the situation (Davis and Levine 1982), or there may be preferences for predictability depending on the type of stressor (Badia, Harsh, and Abbott 1979; Davis and McIntire 1969). Animals thus have the capacity to develop individualistic coping styles based on their experiences with aversive stimulation, as humans are known to do (Miller 1980).

We can expect the behavioral responses of individual wild mammals in captivity to aversive stimuli to be diverse, idiosyncratic, and situation-specific. An animal crouching in the corner of its cage upon being approached may be experiencing considerably more adrenocortical activation than one that is actively bounding from wall to wall in the same situation (Duncan and Filshie 1980). When young squirrel monkeys, *Saimiri sciureus*, are separated from their mothers and placed in a novel environment, they exhibit signs of distress, such as heightened vocalization and activity, and increased plasma cortisol levels. If they are placed in a familiar environment with conspecifics when separated from their mothers, very few signs of distress are observed, but plasma cortisol levels are still very high (Levine 1983). In domestic pigs housed under five different conditions, Barnett et al. (1984) measured corticosteroid levels and recorded a number of agonistic, displacement, exploratory, manipulative, and resting behaviors. They found that only elevated frequencies of lying alone were correlated with elevated plasma corticosteroid levels. These examples demonstrate that no single behavioral variable adequately describes the response of an animal to a stressor in the environment.

It is extremely important to the health, reproduction, and welfare of an animal that it be able to inhibit or terminate adrenocortical activation. The physiological response to acute environmental change is usually of short duration. However, persistently recurring environmental events that an animal perceives as aversive and that it is unable to control or predict, or protracted aversive events such as separation, loss of attachment, or close confinement, may result in chronic elevations of adrenal hormones (Kant, Anderson, and Mougey 1987; Reichlin 1987; Rose 1987; Carlstead, Brown, and Strawn 1993) or produce adrenal hypersensitivity to ACTH (Armario et al. 1986; Friend, Dellmeier, and Gbur 1985; Mason, Brady, and Tolliver 1968; Restrepo and Armario 1987). "Chronic stress" is known to have a wide variety of deleterious, potentially fatal physiological and immunological consequences. Heightened glucocorticoid levels resulting from chronic stress result in interference with the action of insulin, loss of calcium from the bones and subsequent osteoporosis, suppression of growth, and contribution to the development of peptic ulcers. Chronically elevated steroid levels also suppress immune function by causing a reduction in T cell–mediated immune events and phagocytic function (Kelley 1985). Chronic stress may also suppress reproductive function (Eberhardt, Keverne, and Meller 1980; Moberg 1985b; Rideout et al. 1985).

One of the most obvious chronic stressors for a confined wild animal is the inability to respond to fearful situations with active avoidance or escape responses. Because most zoo animals have limited freedom of movement compared with their wild counterparts, they are often unable to withdraw effectively from aversive stimulation, whether caused by people or by cohabiting conspecifics. Siberian tigers, *Panthera tigris altaica*, at the Bucharest Zoo have been reported to develop gastroenteritis due to failing to adapt to unfamiliar quarters. A persistent high noise level lasting several months, caused by repairs in an adjacent courtyard, was also sufficient to induce gastroenteritis in some tigers (Cociu et al. 1974). The presence of zoo visitors may be underestimated as a chronic stressor for some mammalian species. Glatston et al. (1984) and Chamove, Hosey, and Schaetzel (1988) found clearly deleterious effects on the behavior of various primate species exposed to zoo visitors. Hediger (1964) describes situations in which captive animals have injured themselves or failed to breed because of their inability to escape from caretakers or visitors. He points out that the quality of the space provided for an animal may be more important for coping with escape-inducing stimulation than the quantity of space, because an animal may only need to perceive that it can retreat to safety rather than actually withdrawing (Bendiner 1981; Hediger 1964). Persistent auditory stimuli that vary in intensity, frequency, and content may be common stressors for captive animals (Stoskopf 1983). Chronic uncertainty about the actions of caretakers, workers, or veterinarians may also contribute to stress if the animal has no reliable predictive cues.

Chronic stress may lead to depression and lethargy in captive animals, as it does in humans. Fattening pigs housed in barren, overcrowded conditions often sit lethargically for long periods in a head-hanging position ("dog-sitting": van Putten 1980) and are unresponsive to their surroundings. In nonhuman primates separated from their mothers, depressive symptoms such as decreased play, decreased motor activity, severe loss of appetite, and sleep disturbances have been reported (Harlow and Zimmerman 1959; Harlow and Harlow 1965). These same symptoms can be induced in a variety of species by loss or separation from peers or mates, or by placement in an unfamiliar environment (Jesberger and Richardson 1985). Crawley (1984) observed increases in body weight and decreased social interaction and exploratory behavior in male Siberian dwarf hamsters, *Phodopus sungorus pallas*, separated from their mates for 3 weeks.

Stereotypies

A "stereotypy" is any movement pattern that (1) is performed repeatedly, (2) is relatively invariant in form, and (3) has no apparent function or goal (Odberg 1978). Stereotypies are common in zoo animals (Boorer 1972) but are rarely observed in wild, free-ranging animals. They occur in many species and have a wide variety of origins and proximate causes (see Mason 1991a for a review). Some stereotypic behaviors in zoo and farm animals occur when the animal consistently is unable to reach a particular goal by performing an appetitive behavior (Holzapfel 1938, 1939; Cronin 1985). For example, in many captive species, stereotypies occur mainly prior to feeding time, when the animal is motivated to perform food acquisition behaviors such as foraging or hunting. Winkelstraeter (1960) describes a female ocelot, *Felis pardalis*, that ran in a circular path prior to feeding. Geoffroy's cats, *Felis geoffroyi*, (K. Carlstead, unpub.) and an American black bear, *Ursus americanus*, paced for 2–4 hours before feeding time (Carlstead, Seidensticker, and Baldwin 1991). Stereotypies in ranch mink, *Mustela vison*, also peak in the hour before feeding time (K. Carlstead, pers. obs.). In tethered sows, the stereotypic movement pattern performed prior to feeding may have elements of thwarted feeding behaviors (Rushen 1984).

Physical thwarting of attempts to reach a desired place, animal, or object creates a similar appetitive situation that may cause stereotypy. A coati, *Nasua nasua*, that was locked out on exhibit away from her warm sleeping place would run back and forth repetitively for hours in front of the door to the den area (Meyer-Holzapfel 1968). Being separated from the rest of its pack resulted in a dingo, *Canis familiaris dingo*, pacing in a figure eight along a separating trellis (Meyer-Holzapfel 1968).

The inability to escape from a source of disturbance also contributes to stereotypy performance. A black bear, *Ursus americanus*, unable to withdraw from domineering conspecifics, was observed to "take little stereotyped walks" along a back wall as far away from the source of disturbance as possible (Meyer-Holzapfel 1968). Some fennec foxes, *Vulpes (=Fennecus) zerda*, ran repetitively back and forth for up to an hour after being disturbed by cage cleaning (Carlstead 1991), as did a female brown hyena, *Hyaena brunnea*, when zoo visitors were allowed too close to the cage front (Inhelder 1955).

Are stereotypies indicators of chronic stress? Stereotypic behavior in confined animals has long been considered an indication of poor welfare (e.g., Wiepkema 1983a; Broom 1983). This is because stereotypies often develop in situations known from independent behavioral and physiological evidence to be aversive and stressful, such as low stimulus input, physical restraint, or inescapable fear or frustration (Mason 1991b). Some researchers consider stereotypies to be a behavioral means of coping with a past or present aversive situation. Indeed, studies of the short-term effects of stereotypies have shown that high arousal is associated with the onset and development of stereotypies. Stereotypies seem to originate in behaviors that represent attempts by the animal to control its environment, such as escape attempts, aggressive acts against caging, and patrolling a territory (Holzapfel 1938; Cronin and Wiepkema 1985). As these actions fail to alter the animal's environment, the animal starts to organize a reduced number of behaviors into sequences that become rigidified, speeded up, repeated, and internally guided (Cronin and Wiepkema 1985; Morris 1966; Fentress 1976). However, evidence that the performance of stereotypic behavior reduces the level of stress or aversion experienced is equivocal (Rushen 1993; reviewed by Mason 1991a), suggesting that not all stereotypies may be a response to stress or aversion. In addition, individual coping styles play an important role in the expression of stereotypy in a given environment. This means that when individuals of the same species are compared, the degree of stereotypy may not necessarily reflect poorer or better welfare (Mason 1991b).

Stereotypies are sometimes thought to be caused mainly by space limitations. It is generally true that the smaller the cage, the more likely an animal is to perform a stereotypy (Paulk, Dienske, and Ribbens 1977). By increasing the size of the area available to an animal, the behavior can sometimes be eliminated or altered (Draper and Bernstein 1963; Clarke, Juno, and Maple 1982). Certainly the size and shape of an animal's cage play a role in shaping the stereotypic motor pattern an animal performs. In few cases, however, is it clear exactly how much space is needed to ensure the absence of stereotypies (Stevenson 1983). Indeed, there is evidence that cage size in some cases is not the critical factor (Berkson, Mason, and Saxon 1963). Odberg (1987) compared the behavior of voles, *Clethrionomys glareolus*, in small, rich environments and in large, sparse ones, and found less stereotypic jumping in the former. Sows kept tethered in stalls will perform considerably fewer stereotypies in the same space if they are given a handful of straw to manipulate (Fraser 1975). An American black bear virtually ceased to pace in its exhibit when provided with opportunities to forage for food (Carlstead, Seidensticker, and Baldwin 1991). Such evidence, combined with the observation that most stereotypies occur in situations in which an appetitive action fails to produce a desired endpoint, lends credence to Hediger's (1964) statements that the quality of a confined animal's space is more important than the quantity.

Stereotypies are clearly an indication of an abnormal animal-environment interaction. For most wild mammals in captivity, this probably means that the animal grew up in or is currently living in an environment suboptimal for meeting its natural, species-specific behavioral needs. Hediger (1934, 1938) long ago pointed out that we can better understand the needs of captive animals by studying their stereotypic motor reactions. Thorough studies of the development of stereotypic behavior are needed to help elucidate the deficiencies of the environments we impose on captive wild mammals.

Behavioral Effects of Low Stimulus Diversity

The term "boredom" is often used to describe the way confined mammals experience their undiversified world. Boredom is the psychological response to an environment that fails to meet the animal's needs for stimulation due to low stimulus diversity.

An animal's "needs" for stimulation are difficult both to define and to quantify. These needs are subject to great individual and species variability (Dawkins 1980). Although novelty and uncertainty may be aversive at times, not all novel or uncertain stimulation is negative. Many people experience mild stress as pleasant or as putting them in a productive state. People also seek the elevated levels of stimulation provided by the unusual or unexpected for brief periods in order to amuse themselves or when feeling bored. Certainly much of the arts and entertainment industry depends on this fact (Hebb 1949). Animals too perform exploratory, appetitive, and play behaviors that allow them to encounter novel or unexpected objects or situations, and they investigate novel stimuli presented in familiar surroundings (Glickman and Scroges 1966). In laboratory experiments giving rats a choice between novel and familiar environments, the rats, under normal circumstances, choose the novel (Hughes 1968; Montgomery 1953), and they will learn operant tasks to produce a variety of stimulus changes (for a review see Kish 1966). Animals and people therefore seem to seek changes in stimulation in similar circumstances.

In an environment low in stimulus diversity, an animal will find it difficult to exert control over the stimulation to which it is exposed. As with aversive stimuli, there may be two ways of adapting to low stimulus diversity: one response is to keep on performing the behavior necessary to find or create the desired stimulation; the alternative is to suppress or modify expectations of stimulation to fit what is available in the environment. Compared with the captive situation, appetitive and exploratory behaviors in the wild are far more likely to produce the expected stimulation; therefore, lowered expectations may be the prevailing response of animals in monotonous environments.

Chronically understimulating conditions in a captive environment may affect the behavior, psychological welfare, and health of wild mammals in two broad ways: (1) by causing decreases in stimulation-seeking behavior (lethargy), and (2) through the animals' attempts to increase stimulatory input by means of autostimulation or performance of appetitive or social behaviors in unnatural contexts.

Lethargy in confined mammals is characterized by relative inactivity and drowsiness. Animals confined in stimulus-poor, monotonous environments for prolonged periods are less likely to perform active stimulation-seeking behaviors when presented with the appropriate opportunity than are animals experienced with complex, contingent environments. I have already discussed the effects of impoverished environments on the development of normal levels of activity and emotionality in young animals. Effects of stimulatory impoverishment and enrichment have also been demonstrated in adult animals. Inglis (1975) raised rats in opaque plastic cages, then when they were adults placed half of them for 5 weeks in wire cages provided with activity wheels, toys that were changed daily, and changes in lighting and noise levels. The other rats were kept in their original plastic cages in constant dim lighting and quiet. The rats experiencing enriched conditions subsequently demonstrated an increased willingness to explore a novel maze and quicker habituation to novel surroundings. Butler (1957) deprived rhesus macaques of visual pattern stimulation for varying numbers of hours, then allowed them to seek access to visual stimulation. He found a decrease in stimulation-seeking behavior for deprivation periods longer than 4 hours.

This evidence implies that chronically understimulated captive animals depress their needs for stimulation by lowering their expectations of the level of stimulatory input from their surroundings. This also appears to be the case in humans. Experiments in which people are deprived of sensory stimulation for an extended period indicate that stimulation seeking declines and a preference develops for little or no change in environmental stimulation. Prison inmates isolated under conditions of perceptual deprivation for 7 days showed a lowered preference for high levels of visual input (Gendreau et al. 1968).

Animals chronically deprived of stimulus diversity may respond poorly when highly stimulating, novel situations arise; for example, they may overreact and fail to adapt to sudden changes, even to the point of death. Christian and Radcliffe (1952) reported on fourteen zoo animals that had been housed in small indoor cages and then died after being subjected to the acute stress of transfer to a new cage or disturbance by workers. In all these cases the adrenal cortex had atrophied, indicating an inability to sustain a response to the extreme stimulation and a failure to adapt to the new situation. Swine reared in impoverished intensive farming conditions often die during transport to the slaughterhouse due to the psychological trauma associated with the extreme change in surroundings and contact with unfamiliar pigs. Thus, chronic "boredom," although perhaps not stressful, can lead to hyperresponsiveness to stressors when they present themselves.

The second category of behavioral effects of boredom comprises attempts of animals to stimulate themselves in the face of an impoverished environment. Many cases of abnormal self-directed behaviors, such as the self-rocking and digit sucking mentioned previously in isolation-reared monkeys, have been explained as attempts by a sensorily deprived animal to stimulate its own nervous system. Other self-directed behaviors common in primates are visual fixation on or slapping of a part of the body (Paulk, Dienske, and Ribbens 1977), huddling combined with hopping or walking, rolling in a ball, and vertical circling about the cage (looping). Autostimulation is common in primates deprived of tactile stimulation during development (for a review see Mitchell 1970), but has also been observed in other mammals reared in isolation (Morris 1964; Erwin and Deni 1979). Social animals that were not deprived during development may also exhibit abnormal self-directed behaviors when housed separately from groupmates (Morris 1964; Antelman and Caggiula 1980).

Autostimulation may develop into extreme forms of self-mutilation. Self-mutilation is reportedly most common in opossums, carnivores, long-tailed monkeys, and the small South American monkeys. Meyer-Holzapfel (1968) describes several cases in which entire paws or tails were gradually gnawed away, sometimes because there was initially an injury or irritation to the appendage. Ranch mink often have damaged tails in captivity (approximately 10–20% of all individuals), although this is rare in the wild. They develop tail-biting and sucking habits that persist through molting periods, and some have been observed to run in circles in their cages, chasing the tail and biting it (de Jonge, Carlstead, and Wiepkema 1986).

Coprophagy, the eating of fecal material, and regurgitation/reingestion are also considered to be self-stimulatory responses to the boredom of captivity, particularly in the great apes (Stevenson 1983). Sixty-nine percent of 117 captive gorillas, *Gorilla gorilla*, sampled engaged in regurgitation/reingestion behaviors (Gould and Bres 1986). Hand-reared individuals, whether wild-caught or captive-born, showed a higher incidence than mother-reared individuals. Gould and Bres had some success in reducing these behaviors by feeding browse, and concluded that the time spent handling and ingesting food in captivity is too low.

Animals may also increase stimulation by performing behaviors that are natural in form, but seemingly out of context, or performed in an excessive manner because of the unavailability of the appropriate environmental stimuli as a guide. For example, excessive licking, biting, and chewing of wood, bars, fences, or hair may occur in grazing animals that are fed concentrated pelleted diets (Hintz, Sedgewick, and Schryver 1976). Morris (1964) describes cases of various carnivores copulating with objects such as bedding material, feeding dishes, or a scratching post. Animals may also create behaviors that are "occupational" in nature; Morris (1964) provides several examples of innovative visitor-oriented and object-oriented behaviors that take the place of naturally occurring behaviors. Food begging in zoo animals that are well fed and need not beg out of hunger is an example of a substitute for foraging that is adapted to the captive environment (van Keulen-Kromhout 1978). Visitor-oriented behaviors such as object throwing by great apes and elephants and urine spraying by carnivores and primates are manipulative activities that elicit pronounced responses from the human recipients (Morris 1964). Cats that throw dead prey up in the air so that they can pounce on it and "kill" it, and canids and viverrids that shake a dead prey object "to death" before eating it, provide further examples of stimulation-increasing behaviors in captive mammals.

ENVIRONMENTAL ENRICHMENT

The behavior of an animal is the principal means by which zoo personnel *and* zoo visitors assess its psychological welfare; the more its behavior resembles that of its wild counterparts, the more certain we are of an animal's general well-being. Animal exhibitors should strive for both a naturalistic setting and the performance of appropriate natural behaviors.

Providing occupation that gives confined animals some control over their environment is essential for their psychological welfare and for the display of ecologically valid behavior (Hediger 1968; Markowitz 1975). In general, "environmental enrichment" means providing a complex and diverse environment that increases the possibility that the captive animal's own behavior will produce what it needs: finding food, demarcating a territory, building a nest, maintaining its physical condition, escaping conspecifics, or hiding. An animal with more behavioral options will be better able to cope with stressful events in its surroundings or alleviate boredom. Behavioral options can be improved by increasing the complexity and variability of the environment physically, sensorily, and socially. Maple and Perkins (chap. 21, this volume) provide a review of some of the ways this can be accomplished with exhibit furnishings.

The spaces to which wild mammals are confined vary considerably in physical complexity. Behavioral improvements may be contingent upon specific components contained in the enclosure rather than larger size alone. Many zoos have found that larger, more natural-looking exhibits do not necessarily lead to greater activity or more normal behavior (Spinelli and Markowitz 1985). In a survey of gorilla and orangutan, *Pongo pygmaeus,* enclosures in forty-one zoos, Wilson (1982) found that the factors most highly correlated with activity levels were, for both species, the number of animals present; for gorillas, stationary and temporary objects available; and for orangs, stationary and movable objects available. The size and construction of the enclosure were not correlated with activity levels.

Certain behaviors may be affected more than others by increases in enclosure size and complexity. For example, moving four chimpanzees from laboratory cages to a large, naturalistic artificial island resulted in a drastic reduction in stereotypic and self-directed behaviors, but had no effect on social behaviors (Clarke, Juno, and Maple 1982).

Environmental complexity can be increased when space

is limited by providing structures that increase the surface area over which an animal can move and that make use of the vertical space of a cage or enclosure. Methods of increasing sensory complexity also should not be overlooked; for example, spraying cologne on tree stumps and branches stimulates investigation and rubbing by wolves (K. Kranz, pers. comm.). Another manner of increasing environmental complexity is to supply the enclosure with objects the animal can manipulate. Beer kegs and oil drums have proven to be suitable toys for great apes (van Hooff 1973) as well as many other large species (bears, tigers), especially when they can be used in water. Their irregular shape and buoyancy produces unpredictable movements that can sustain the animal's attention for long periods. A swinging boxing bag hung in the enclosure of a rhinoceros will elicit hours of rubbing and butting because it "responds" to the animal's actions with unpredictable movements of its own. Hanging a large dead branch from a tree in elk and deer yards provides the bull with an engaging moving surface on which to scrape his antlers (Hancocks 1980; Hutchins, Hancocks, and Crockett 1984). However, zoo staff need to consider how the qualities of toys, such as manipulability, flexibility, predictability of movement, smell, and complexity, will appeal to the skills of a particular species. Also, habituation to toys should be reduced by removing them periodically, varying the objects presented, filling them with food snacks, or placing them in novel positions or locations (Carlstead, Seidensticker, and Baldwin 1991).

Keeping mammals in appropriate social groupings is an extremely important means of creating complex environments. Social partners are an infinite source of response-contingent stimulation, allowing an individual to interact with its surroundings to a much greater degree than if it were alone. Housing gorillas and other primates in large groups is a trend that radically departs from the past and has led to a large increase in the successful breeding and natural rearing of young (Beck and Power 1988; Maple and Finlay 1989).

One important means of enriching an animal's environment is to increase greatly the time spent in food acquisition. In the wild, many species spend most of their waking hours looking for, pursuing, gathering, handling, or hiding food. Gorillas, for example, spend up to 70% of their day foraging and feeding (Maple and Finlay 1987), and black bears, 75% (Garshelis and Pelton 1980). In the vast majority of captive situations, animals are fed in one or several daily meals by human caretakers. No effort is expended to acquire the food, and it is consumed in a short time. Environmental enrichment measures that direct activity toward foraging may have beneficial effects on behavior that are preferable to the effects of merely providing toys and manipulable objects. For example, cynomolgus monkeys, *Macaca fascicularis*, normally housed in bare cages were allowed to spend an hour each day in a "playpen" cage provided with toys, manipulable materials, visual access to the neighboring animal, and deep woodchip litter sown with sunflower seeds and peanuts. Their preferred activity during this hour was to forage for the food snacks (Bryant, Pupniak, and Iverson 1988).

Naturalistic methods of feeding involve presenting food so that the animal must search for and gather it or spend time handling it; for example, by scattering small food items mixed in with a substrate or in hay (e.g., grain or mealworms in woodchips or woodwool: Chamove et al. 1982). The behavior patterns required to retrieve food fed by naturalistic delivery methods are more varied, the places of finding food more random, and the time occupied longer than with traditional feeding methods or mechanical feeders. Feeding lion-tailed macaques, *Macaca silenus*, fruits and vegetables whole rather than chopped increases dietary diversity, time spent feeding, and total amount of food consumed (Smith, Lindburg, and Vehrencamp 1989). The effects of such feeding on other behaviors may be profound: for an American black bear, hiding food throughout the exhibit virtually eliminated stereotypic pacing, whereas feeding from a mechanical feeding device did not (Carlstead, Seidensticker, and Baldwin 1991).

CONCLUSIONS

One of the major premises of this chapter is that wild mammals reared in a captive situation adapt their behavior to their environment, no matter how impoverished or enriched. The behavioral options wild mammals have for responding to captive environments have been examined, and the potential costs in terms of behavioral abnormalities, lethargy, and compromised health and reproduction have been mentioned. However, another, more general, potential cost of keeping animals in confinement must be considered: animals that do not exhibit a wide range of natural behaviors give the impression to zoo visitors of being either bored and unhappy in their enclosures or tormented by their confinement. Under these circumstances visitors will fail to develop an appreciation of biological diversity and the need to conserve it. Although the aesthetics of "naturalistic" exhibits have greatly improved in recent years, most new enclosures still fail to accommodate the animal's natural behavior. This may have been acceptable in the past, but zoo visitors today are often well-informed of animal habits through wildlife television documentaries, and zoos run the risk of provoking disappointment if they cannot exhibit active, normally behaving animals.

To maintain wild-type behavior in captivity it is necessary to fit environmental conditions to the animal, rather than expecting the animal to adapt to the conditions we impose upon it. This can be accomplished only with a thorough knowledge of an animal's long- and short-term behavioral needs. In the long term, reduced genetic variability in captive populations may have consequences for behavioral traits, but this can be determined only by comparison with wild populations, and that is often difficult or impossible, especially for rare and endangered species. Most of the effects that captivity exerts on behavior occur in the short term to the individual animal as it grows up under the specific conditions of its confinement.

The immediate psychological goal of behavior for an animal is to control the stimulation impinging upon it from its surroundings. In most cases in the wild, the animal can take a behavioral action that will increase or decrease the intensity of events happening around it. Captive conditions, being more restrictive and less diversified than the wild, may offer the animal little opportunity for behavioral control. Mammals may adapt to these circumstances by adopting passive, inactive behavioral strategies geared toward uncertainty reduction as a means of controlling aversive stimulation, or by adopting decreased expectations of stimulation as a means of coping with boredom. The low stimulus diversity of the more impoverished captive environment may cause lethargy and inactivity, hyperresponsiveness to unusual or unexpected events, or an inability to cope with stress. In an inappropriate environment, high motivation to perform a certain type of behavior may lead to abnormal self-directed behaviors, behaviors performed in an unnatural context, stereotypy, or excessive aggression.

It *is* possible, however, to provide adequate captive environments for wild mammals if their specific needs are learned and taken into consideration when designing exhibits and husbandry procedures. Recent developments in zoo research, developmental psychobiology, and animal welfare science provide an optimistic outlook for the future management of wild mammals in captivity as breeding populations. Many things can be done to enrich the environment of captive mammals, and such strategies may improve behavior even to the point of rehabilitating previously severely deprived animals. Increasing the physical and social complexity of the environment provides the animal with more behavioral options for responding to stimulation from its surroundings and gives it more opportunities to create stimulus change by manipulating its own surroundings. One of the most obvious and direct means of doing this is to devise alternatives to the standard method of feeding captive mammals in large daily meals. The large amounts of time spent in food acquisition behaviors in the wild need to be directed in captivity so that these behaviors do not find their outlet in some other, inappropriate context. Further research into the specific behavioral needs of each mammal species is necessary in order to develop appropriate environmental design and husbandry in captivity.

ACKNOWLEDGMENTS

This chapter was written while I was supported by a Smithsonian Institution Post-doctoral Fellowship.

REFERENCES

Abbott, B., Schoen, L., and Badia, P. 1984. Predictable and unpredictable shock: Behavioural measures of aversion and physiological measures of stress. *Psychol. Bull.* 96:45–71.

Ader, R., and Belfer, M. 1962. Prenatal maternal anxiety and offspring emotionality in the rat. *Psychol. Rep.* 10:711–18.

Antelman, S. M., and Caggiula, A. R. 1980. Stress-induced behavior: Chemotherapy without drugs. In *The psychobiology of consciousness,* ed. J. M. Davidson and R. J. Davidson, 65–103. New York: Plenum Press.

Archer, J. 1976. The organization of aggression and fear in vertebrates. In *Perspectives in ethology,* vol. 2, ed. P. P. G. Bateson and P. Klopfer, 231–98. London: Plenum Press.

Archer, J., and Blackman, D. 1971. Prenatal psychological stress and offspring behavior in rats and mice. *Dev. Psychobiol.* 4:193–248.

Armario, A., Lopez-Calderon, A., Jolin, T., and Balasch, J. 1986. Response of anterior pituitary hormones to chronic stress: The specificity of adaptation. *Neurosci. Biobehav. Rev.* 10:245–50.

Badia, P., Harsh, J., and Abbott, B. 1979. Choosing between predictable and unpredictable shock conditions: Data and theory. *Psychol. Bull.* 86:1107–31.

Badia, P., Harsh, J., Coker, C., and Abbott, B. 1976. Choice and the dependability of stimuli that predict shock and safety. *J. Exp. Anal. Behav.* 26:95–111.

Barnett, J. L., Cronin, G. M., Winfield, C. G., and Dewar, A. M. 1984. The welfare of adult pigs: The effects of 5 housing treatments on behavior, plasma corticosteroids, and injuries. *Appl. Anim. Behav. Sci.* 12:209–32.

Barnett, S. A., Dickson, R. G., and Hocking, W. E. 1979. Genotype and environment in the social interactions of wild and domestic Norway rats. *Aggressive Behav.* 5:105–19.

Bateson, P. P. G. 1966. The characteristics and context of imprinting. *Biol. Rev.* 41:177–220.

————. 1978. Early experience and sexual preference. In *Biological determinants of behaviour,* ed. J. B. Hutchinson, 29–53. London: Wiley.

Beck, B. B., and Power, M. L. 1988. Correlates of sexual and maternal competence in captive gorillas. *Zoo Biol.* 7:339–50.

Bendiner, R. 1981. *The fall of the wild, the rise of the zoo.* New York: E. P. Dutton.

Berkson, G., Mason, W. A., and Saxon, S. V. 1963. Situation and stimulus effects on stereotyped behaviors of chimpanzees. *J. Comp. Physiol. Psychol.* 56:786–92.

Blanchard, R. J., and Blanchard, D. C. 1969. Passive and active reactions to fear-eliciting stimuli. *J. Comp. Physiol. Psychol.* 68:129–35.

Boice, R. 1977. Burrows of wild and domestic rats: Effects of domestication, outdoor raising, age, experience, and maternal state. *J. Comp. Physiol. Psychol.* 91:649–61.

Boorer, M. 1972. Some aspects of stereotyped patterns of movement exhibited by zoo animals. *Int. Zoo Yrbk.* 12:164–66.

Bouwman, J. 1977. The future of Prezwalski horses *Equus przewalskii* in captivity. *Int. Zoo Yrbk.* 17:62–67.

Broom, D. M. 1983. Stereotypies as animal welfare indicators. In *Indicators relevant to farm animal welfare,* ed. D. Schmidt, 81–87. Current Topics in Veterinary Medical Animal Science, 23. The Hague: Martinus Nijhoff.

Bryant, C. E., Pupniak, N. M. J., and Iverson, S. D. 1988. Effects of different environmental enrichment devices on cage stereotypies and autoaggression in captive cynomolgus monkeys. *J. Med. Primatol.* 17:257–69.

Butler, R. A. 1957. The effect of deprivation of visual incentives on visual exploration motivation in monkeys. *J. Comp. Physiol. Psychol.* 50:177–79.

Cannon, W. B. 1935. Stresses and strains of homeostasis. *Am. J. Med. Sci.* 189:1–12.

Carlstead, K. 1991. Fennec fox *(Fennecus zerda)* husbandry: Environmental conditions influencing stereotypic behavior. *Int. Zoo Yrbk.* 30:202–7.

Carlstead, K., Brown, J. L., Monfort, S. L., Killens, R., and Wildt, D. E. 1992. Urinary monitoring of adrenal responses to psychological stressors in domestic and non-domestic felids. *Zoo Biol.* 11:165–76.

Carlstead, K., Brown, J. L., and Strawn, W. 1993. Behavioral and physiological correlates of stress in laboratory cats. *Appl. Anim. Behav. Sci.* 38:143–58.

Carlstead, K., Seidensticker, J. C., and Baldwin, R. 1991. Environmental enrichment for zoo bears. *Zoo Biol.* 10:3–16.

Chamove, A. S., Anderson, J. R., Morgan-Jones, S. C., and Jones, S. P. 1982. Deep woodchip litter: Hygiene, feeding and behavioral enhancement in eight primate species. *Int. J. Stud. Anim. Prob.* 3 (4):308–18.

Chamove, A. S., Hosey, G. R., and Schaetzel, P. 1988. Visitors excite primates in zoos. *Zoo Biol.* 7:359–69.

Christian, J. D., and Ratcliffe, H. L. 1952. Shock disease in captive wild animals. *Am. J. Pathol.* 28:725–37.

Clarke, A. S., Juno, C. J., and Maple, T. L. 1982. Behavioral effects of a change in the physical environment: A pilot study of captive chimpanzees. *Zoo Biol.* 1:371–80.

Clutton-Brock, J. 1976. The historical background to the domestication of animals. *Int. Zoo Yrbk.* 15:240–44.

Cociu, M., Wagner, G., Micu, N. E., and Mihaescu, G. 1974. Adaptational gastro-enteritis in Siberian tigers. *Int. Zoo Yrbk.* 14:171–74.

Crawley, J. N. 1984. Evaluation of a proposed hamster separation model of depression. *Psychiatry Res.* 11:35–47.

Cronin, G. M. 1985. The development and significance of abnormal stereotyped behaviours in tethered sows. Ph.D thesis, Agricultural University of Wageningen, Netherlands.

Cronin, G. M., and Wiepkema, P. R. 1985. An analysis of stereotyped behaviour in tethered sows. *Annales Recherche Veterinaire* 15:263–70.

Dantzer, R., and Mormede, P. 1983. Stress in farm animals: A need for reevaluation. *J. Anim. Sci.* 57:6–18.

Davis, H., and Levine, S. 1982. Predictability, control, and the pituitary-adrenal response in rats. *J. Comp. Physiol. Psychol.* 96:393–404.

Davis, H., and McIntire, R. W. 1969. Conditioned suppression under positive, negative, and no contingency between conditioned and unconditioned stimuli. *J. Exp. Anal. Behav.* 12:633–40.

Davis, H., Porter, J. W., Livingstone, T., Hermann, T., MacFadden, L., and Levine, S. 1977. Pituitary-adrenal activity and lever-press shock escape behavior. *Physiol. Behav.* 5:280–84.

Dawkins, M. S. 1980. *Animal suffering: The science of animal welfare.* London: Chapman and Hall.

Day, H. D., Seay, B. M., Hale, P., and Hendricks, D. 1982. Early social deprivation and the ontogeny of unrestricted social behavior in the laboratory rat. *Dev. Psychobiol.* 15:47–59.

de Jonge, G., Carlstead, K., and Wiepkema, P. R. 1986. *The welfare of ranch mink.* Publication 010, Centre for Poultry Research and Extension, 7361 DA Beekbergen, Netherlands.

Denenberg, V. H. 1964. Critical periods, stimulus input, and emotional reactivity: A theory of infantile stimulation. *Psychol. Rev.* 71:335–51.

———. 1967. Stimulation in infancy, emotional reactivity, and exploratory behavior. In *Biology and behavior: Neurophysiology and emotion,* ed. D. C. Glass. New York: Russell Sage Foundation and Rockefeller University Press.

Dess, N. K., Linwick, D., Patterson, J., and Overmeier, J. B. 1983. Immediate and proactive effects of controllability and predictability on plasma cortisol responses to shock in dogs. *Behav. Neurosci.* 97:1005–16.

Dickinson, A. 1980. *Contemporary animal learning.* Cambridge: Cambridge University Press.

Draper, W. A., and Bernstein, I. S. 1963. Stereotyped behaviour and cage size. *Percept. Mot. Skills* 16:231–34.

Duncan, I. J. H., and Filshie, J. H. 1980. The use of radiotelemetry devices to measure temperature and heart rate in domestic fowl. In *A handbook on biotelemetry and radio tracking,* ed. C. J. Amlaner and D. W. Macdonald, 579–88. Oxford: Pergamon Press.

Eberhardt, J. A., Keverne, E. B., and Meller, R. E. 1980. Social influences on plasma testosterone levels in male talapoin monkeys. *Horm. Behav.* 14:247–65.

Einon, D. F., Humphreys, A. P., Chivers, S. M., Field, S., and Naylor, V. 1981. Isolation has permanent effects upon the behavior of the rat but not the mouse, gerbil, or guinea pig. *Dev. Psychobiol.* 14:343–55.

Einon, D. F., Morgan, M. J., and Kibbler, C. C. 1978. Brief periods of socialization and later behaviour in the rat. *Dev. Psychobiol.* 11:213–25.

Eisenberg, J. F., and Kleiman, D. G. 1977. The usefulness of behaviour studies in developing captive breeding programmes for mammals. *Int. Zoo Yrbk.* 17:81–88.

Engel, G. L. 1967. A psychological setting of somatic disease: The giving up-given up complex. *Proc. R. Soc. Med.* 60:553–55.

Erwin, J., and Deni, R. 1979. Strangers in a strange land: Abnormal behaviors or abnormal environment? In *Captivity and behavior,* ed. J. Erwin, T. L. Maple, and G. Mitchell, 1–28. New York: Van Nostrand Reinhold.

Fentress, J. C. 1976. Dynamic boundaries of patterned behaviour: Interaction and self-organization. In *Growing points in ethology,* ed. P. P. G. Bateson and R. A. Hinde, 135–69. Cambridge: Cambridge University Press.

Frank, H., and Frank, M. G. 1982. On the effects of domestication on canine social development and behavior. *Appl. Anim. Behav. Sci.* 8:507–25.

Frankham, R., Hemmer, H., Ryder, O. A., Cothran, E. G., Soulé, M. E., Murray, N. D., and Snyder, M. 1986. Selection in captive populations. *Zoo Biol.* 5:127–38.

Fraser, D. 1975. The effect of straw on the behavior of sows in tether stalls. *Anim. Prod.* 21:59–68.

Fride, E., and Weinstock, M. 1984. The effects of prenatal exposure to predictable or unpredictable stress on early development in the rat. *Dev. Psychobiol.* 17 (6): 651–60.

Friend, T. H., Dellmeier, G. R., and Gbur, E. E. 1985. Comparison of four methods of calf confinement. I. Physiology. *J. Anim. Sci.* 60:1095–1103.

Garshelis, D. L., and Pelton, M. R. 1980. Activity of black bears in the Great Smoky Mountains National Park. *J. Mammal.* 61:8–19.

Gendreau, P. E., Freedman, N., Wilde, G. J. S., and Scott, G. D. 1968. Stimulation seeking after seven days of perceptual deprivation. *Percept. Mot. Skills* 26:547–50.

Gentsch, C., Vichtsteiner, M., and Feer, H. 1981. Locomotor activity, defecation score, and corticosterone levels during an open-field exposure: A comparison among individually and group-housed rats, and genetically selected rat lines. *Physiol. Behav.* 27:183–86.

Glatston, A. R., Geilvoet-Soeteman, E., Hora-Pecek, E., and Hooff, J. A. R. A. M. van. 1984. The influence of the zoo environment on social behavior of groups of cotton-topped tamarins, *Saguinus oedipus oedipus. Zoo Biol.* 3:241–53.

Glickman S. E., and Scroges, R. W. 1966. Curiosity in zoo animals. *Behaviour* 26:151–88.

Goldfoot, D. A. 1977. Rearing conditions which support or inhibit later sexual potential of laboratory monkeys: Hypothesis and diagnostic behavior. *Lab. Anim. Sci.* 27:548–56.

Gould, E., and Bres, M. 1986. Regurgitation and reingestion in captive gorillas: Description and intervention. *Zoo Biol.* 5:241–50.

Greenough, W. T. 1976. Enduring brain effects of differential experience and training. In *Neural mechanisms of learning and memory,* ed. M. R. Rosenzweig and E. L. Bennett, 255–78. Cambridge, Mass.: MIT Press.

Hale, E. B. 1969. Domestication and the evolution of behavior. In *The behaviour of domestic animals,* 2d ed., ed. E. S. E. Hafez, 22–42. London: Bailliere, Tindall and Cassell.

Hancocks, D. 1980. Bringing nature into the zoo: Inexpensive solutions for zoo environments. *Int. J. Stud. Anim. Prob.* 1 (3): 170–77.

Hannah, A. C., and Brotman, B. 1990. Procedures for improving maternal behavior in captive chimpanzees. *Zoo Biol.* 9:233–40.

Harlow, H. F., and Harlow, M. K. 1965. The affectional systems. In *Behavior of non-human primates,* vol. 2, ed. A. M. Schrier, 287–334. Orlando, Fla.: Academic Press.

Harlow, H. F., Harlow, M. K., Dodsworth, R. O., and Arling, G. L. 1966. Maternal behavior of rhesus monkeys deprived of mothering and peer associations in infancy. *Proc. Am. Phil. Soc.* 110: 58–66.

Harlow, H. F., and Zimmerman, R. R. 1959. Affectional responses in the infant monkey. *Science* 130:421–32.

Harvey, P. W., and Chevins, P. F. D. 1985. Crowding pregnant mice affects attack and threat behavior of male offspring. *Horm. Behav.* 19:86–97.

Hebb, D. O. 1949. *The organization of behavior.* New York: Wiley.

Hediger, H. 1934. Uber Bewegungsstereotypien bei gehaltenen Tieren. *Revue Suisse de Zoologie* 41:349–56.

———. 1938. Ergebnisse tierpsychologischer Forschung im Zirkus. *Naturwissenschaft* 26:16.

———. 1964. *Wild animals in captivity.* New York: Dover Publications.

———. 1968. *The psychology and behaviour of animals in zoos and circuses.* New York: Dover Publications.

———. 1970. *Man and animal in the zoo.* New York: Delacorte Press.

Hennessy, M. B., Heyback, J. P., Vernikos, J., and Levine, S. 1979. Plasma corticosterone concentrations sensitively reflect levels of stimulus intensity in the rat. *Physiol. Behav.* 22:821–25.

Hennessy, J. W., and Levine, S. 1979. Stress, arousal, and the pituitary-adrenal system: A psychoendocrine hypothesis. In *Prog. Psychobiol. Physiol. Psychol.* 8:133–78.

Henry, J. P., and Stephens, P. M. 1977. *Stress, health, and the social environment: A sociobiologic approach to medicine.* New York: Springer Verlag.

Hess, E. H. 1973. *Imprinting.* New York: Van Nostrand Reinhold.

Hintz, H. F., Sedgewick, C. J., and Schryver, H. F. 1976. Some observations on digestion of a pelleted diet by ruminants and nonruminants. *Int. Zoo Yrbk.* 16:54–62.

Hofer, M. A. 1981. Parental contributions to the development of their offspring. In *Parental care in mammals,* ed. D. J. Gubernick and P. H. Klopfer, 77–105. New York: Plenum Press.

Holzapfel, M. 1938. Ber Bewegungsstereotypien bei gehaltenen Säugern. I. Mitt. Bewegungsstereotypien bei Caniden und Hyaena. II. Mitt. Das "Weben" der Pferde. *Z. Tierpsychol.* 2: 46–72.

———. 1939. Die Entstehung einiger Bewegungsstereotypien bei gehaltenen Säugern und Vogeln. *Revue Suisse de Zoologie* 46: 567–80.

Hooff, J. A. R. A. M. van. 1973. The Arnhem Zoo chimpanzee consortium: An attempt to create an ecologically and socially acceptable habitat. *Int. Zoo Yrbk.* 13:195–203.

Hughes, R. N. 1968. Behaviour of male and female rats with free choice of two environments differing in novelty. *Anim. Behav.* 16:92–96.

Hutchins, M., Hancocks, D. H., and Crockett, C. 1984. Naturalistic solutions to the behavioral problems of captive animals. *Der Zoologische Garten,* n.f. Jena, 54:28–42.

Immelmann, K. 1972. Sexual and other long-term aspects of imprinting in birds and other species. In *Advances in the study of behavior,* vol. 4, ed. D. S. Lehrman, R. A. Hinde, and E. Shaw. 147–174. New York: Academic Press.

Inglis, I. R. 1975. Enriched sensory experience in adulthood increases subsequent exploratory behavior in the rat. *Anim. Behav.* 23:932–40.

———. 1983. Towards a cognitive theory of exploratory behavior. In *Exploration in animals and man,* ed. J. Archer and L. Birke, 72–103. Berkshire, U.K.: Van Nostrand Reinhold.

Inhelder, E. 1955. Zur Psychologie einiger Verhaltensweisen-besonders des Spiels- von Zootieren. *Z. Tierpsychol.* 12: 88–144.

Jesberger, J. A., and Richardson, J. S. 1985. Animal models of depression: Parallels and correlates to severe depression in humans. *Biol. Psychiatry* 20:764–84.

Joffe, J. M., Rawson, R. A., and Mulick, J. A. 1973. Control of their environment reduces emotionality in rats. *Science* 180: 1383–84.

Kant, G. J., Anderson, S. M., and Mougey, E. H. 1987. Effects of chronic stress on plasma corticosterone, ACTH, and prolactin. *Physiol. Behav.* 40:775–79.

Kavanau, J. L. 1963. Compulsory regime and control of environment in animal behavior. I. Wheel-running. *Behaviour* 20: 251–81.

———. 1964. Behavior, confinement, adaptation, and compulsory regime in laboratory studies. *Science* 143:143.

Keeler, C. E. 1975. Genetics of behavior variations in color phases of the red fox. In *The wild canids: Their systematics, behavioral ecology, and evolution,* ed. M. W. Fox, 399–413. New York: Van Nostrand Reinhold.

Kelley, K. W. 1985. Immunological consequences of changing environmental stimuli. In *Animal stress,* ed. G. P. Moberg, 193–224. Bethesda, Md.: American Physiological Society.

Keulen-Kromhout, G. van. 1978. Zoo enclosures for bears: Their influence on captive behavior and reproduction. *Int. Zoo Yrbk.* 18:177–86.

Kish, G. B. 1966. Studies of sensory reinforcement. In *Operant behavior,* ed. W. K. Honig, 10–159. New York: Appleton-Century-Crofts.

Kleiman, D. 1980. The sociobiology of captive propagation. In *Conservation biology: An evolutionary-ecological perspective,* ed. M. E. Soulé and B. A. Wilcox, 243–62. Sunderland, Mass.: Sinauer Associates.

Koolhaas, J. M., Schuurman, T., and Fokkema, D. S. 1985. Social behaviour of rats as a model for the psychophysiology of hypertension. In *Biobehavioral bases of coronary heart disease,* ed. T. M. Dembrovski, T. H. Schmidt, and G. Blumchen, 391–400. Basel: Karger.

Levine, S. 1966. Infantile stimulation and adaptation to stress. In *Endocrines and the central nervous system,* ed. R. Levine, 280–91. Baltimore: Williams and Wilkins.

———. 1983. Coping: An overview. In *Biological and psychological basis of psychosomatic disease,* ed. H. Ursin and R. Murison, 15–26. Oxford: Pergamon Press.

———. 1985. A definition of stress? In *Animal stress,* ed. G. P. Moberg, 51–70. Bethesda, Md.: American Physiological Society; Baltimore, Md.: Williams and Wilkins.

———. 1986. Maternal deprivation, stress, and development. Paper presented at the NIH Conference on the Mechanisms of Physical and Emotional Stress, 6–8 November, Bethesda, Md.

Lewis, M., and Goldberg, S. 1969. Perceptual-cognitive development in infancy: A generalized expectancy model as a function of the mother-infant interaction. *Merril-Palmer Q. Behav. Dev.* 15:81–100.

Maple, T. L., and Finlay, T. W. 1987. Post-occupancy evaluation in the zoo. *Appl. Anim. Behav. Sci.* 18:5–18.

———. 1989. Applied primatology in the modern zoo. *Zoo Biol.* suppl. 1:101–16.

Markowitz, H. 1975. New methods for increasing activity in zoo animals: Some results and proposals for the future. In *Centennial Symposium on Science and Research,* 151–62. Topeka: Hill's Division, Riviana Foods.

Mason, G. J. 1991a. Stereotypies: A critical review. *Anim. Behav.* 41:1015–37.

———. 1991b. Stereotypies and suffering. *Behav. Processes* 25: 103–15.

Mason, J. W. 1971. A reevaluation of the concept of "nonspecificity" in stress theory. *J. Psychiatr. Res.* 8:323–33.

Mason, W. A. 1978. Social experience and primate cognitive development. In *The development of behavior*, ed. G. M. Burghardt and M. Bekoff, 233–53. New York: Garland STPM.

Mason, W. A., and Berkson, G. 1975. Effects of maternal mobility on the development of rocking and other behaviors in rhesus monkeys: A study with artificial mothers. *Dev. Psychobiol.* 8: 197–211.

Mason, W. A., Brady, J. V., and Tolliver, G. A. 1968. Plasma and urinary 17-hydroxycorticosteroid responses to 72-hr avoidance sessions in the monkey. *Psychosom. Med.* 30:608–30.

Mayr, E. 1958. Behavior and systematics. In *Behavior and evolution*, ed. A. Roe and G. G. Simpson, 341–62. New Haven: Yale University Press.

Meder, A. 1985. Integration of hand-reared gorilla infants in a group. *Zoo Biol.* 4:1–12.

Meyer-Holzapfel, M. 1968. Abnormal behavior in zoo animals. In *Abnormal behavior in animals*, ed. M. W. Fox, 476–503. Philadelphia: W. B. Saunders.

Miller, S. M. 1980. When is a little information a dangerous thing? Coping with stressful events by monitoring versus blunting. In *Coping and health*, ed. S. Levine and H. Ursin, 145–69. New York: Plenum Press.

Mineka, S., and Henderson, R. W. 1985. Controllability and predictability in acquired motivation. *Annu. Rev. Psychol.* 36: 495–529.

Mineka, S., and Suomi, S. 1978. Social separation in monkeys. *Psychol. Bull.* 85:1376–1400.

Mitchell, G. 1970. Abnormal behavior in primates. *Primate Behav.* 1:195–249.

Moberg, G. P. 1985a. Biological response to stress: Key to assessment of animal well-being? In *Animal stress*, ed. G. P. Moberg, 27–50. Bethesda, Md.: American Physiological Society.

———. 1985b. Influence of stress on reproduction: Measure of well-being. In *Animal stress*, ed. G. P. Moberg, 245–67. Bethesda, Md.: American Physiological Society.

Moltz, H. 1965. Contemporary instinct theory and the fixed action pattern. *Psychol. Rev.* 72:27–47.

Money, J., and Ehrhardt, A. A. 1972. *Man and woman, boy and girl*. Baltimore: Johns Hopkins University Press.

Montgomery, K. C. 1953. Exploratory behavior as a function of "similarity" of stimulus situations. *J. Comp. Physiol. Psychol.* 46:129–33.

Moore, C. L. 1984. Maternal contributions to the development of masculine sexual behavior in laboratory rats. *Dev. Psychobiol.* 17:347–56.

Moretto, D., Paclik, L., and Fleming, A. 1986. The effects of early rearing environments on maternal behavior in adult female rats. *Dev. Psychobiol.* 19:581–91.

Mormede, P., Dantzer, R., Bluthe, R. M., and Caritez, J. C. 1984. Differences in adaptive abilities of three breeds of Chinese pigs. *Génétique, Sélection, et Evolution* 16:85–102.

Morris, D. 1964. The response of animals to a restricted environment. *Symp. Zool. Soc. Lond.* 13:99–118.

———. 1966. Abnormal rituals in stress situations: The rigidification of behavior. *Phil. Trans. R. Soc. Lond.* 251:327–30.

Odberg, F. O. 1978. *Abnormal behaviours: (stereotypies).* Proceedings of the First World Congress of Ethology Applied to Zootechnics, Madrid, 475–80.

———. 1987. The influence of cage size and environmental enrichment on the development of stereotypies in bank voles (*Clethrionomys glareolus*). *Behav. Processes* 14:155–76.

O'Keefe, J., and Nadel, L. 1978. *The hippocampus as a cognitive map.* Oxford: Clarendon Press.

Osborne, S. E. 1977. The free food (contra–freeloading) phenomenon: A review and analysis. *Anim. Learn. Behav.* 5:221–35.

Overmeier, J., Patterson, J., and Weilkiewicz, R. M. 1980. Environmental contingencies as sources of stress in animals. In *Coping and health*, ed. S. Levine and H. Ursin, 1–37. New York: Plenum Press.

Overmeier, J., and Seligman, M. E. P. 1967. Effects of inescapable shock upon subsequent escape and avoidance responding. *J. Comp. Physiol. Psychol.* 63:28.

Paulk, H. H., Dienske, H., and Ribbens, L. G. 1977. Abnormal behavior in relation to cage size in rhesus monkeys. *J. Abnorm. Psychol.* 86:87–92.

Price, E. O. 1978. Genotype versus experience effects on aggression in wild and domestic Norway rats. *Behaviour* 64:340–53.

———. 1984. Behavioral aspects of animal domestication. *Q. Rev. Biol.* 59:1–32.

Putten, G. van. 1980. Objective observations on the behaviour of fattening pigs. *Anim. Regul. Stud.* 3:105–18.

Ralls, K., Brugger, K., and Ballou, J. 1979. Inbreeding and juvenile mortality in small populations of ungulates. *Science* 206: 1101–3.

Reichlin, S. 1987. Basic research of hypothalamic-pituitary-adrenal neuroendocrinology: An overview. The physiological function of the stress response. In *Hormones and depression*, ed. U. Halbreich, 21–30. New York: Raven Press.

Restrepo, C., and Armario, A. 1987. Chronic stress alters pituitary-adrenal function in prepubertal male rats. *Psychoneuroendocrinology* 12 (5): 393–98.

Rideout, B. A., Gause, G. E., Benirschke, K., and Lasley, B. L. 1985. Stress-induced adrenal changes and their relation to reproductive failure in captive nine-banded armadillos (*Dasypus novemcinctus*). *Zoo Biol.* 4:129–37.

Riittinen, M. L., Lindroos, F., Kimanen, A., Pieninkeroinen, E., Pieninkeroinen, I., Sippola, J., Veilahti, J., Bergstrom, M., and Johansson, G. 1986. Impoverished rearing conditions increase stress-induced irritability in mice. *Dev. Psychobiol.* 19: 105–11.

Roberts, M. 1982. Demographic trends in a captive population of red pandas (*Ailurus fulgens*). *Zoo Biol.* 1:119–26.

Rose, R. M. 1987. Endocrine abnormalities in depression and stress: An overview. In *Hormones and depression*, ed. U. Halbreich, 31–47. New York: Raven Press.

Rosenzweig, M. R., and Bennett, E. L. 1976. Enriched environments: Facts, factors and fantasies. In *Knowing, thinking, and believing*, ed. L. Petrinovich and J. L. McGaugh, 179–213. New York: Plenum Press.

Ruppenthal, G. C., Arling, G. L., Harlow, H. F., Sackett, G. P., and Suomi, S. J. 1976. A 10-year perspective of motherless mother monkey behavior. *J. Abnorm. Psychol.* 85:341–49.

Rushen, J. 1984. Stereotyped behaviour, adjunctive drinking, and the feeding period of tethered sows. *Anim. Behav.* 32:1059–67.

———. 1993. The "coping" hypothesis of stereotypic behaviour. *Anim. Behav.* 45:613–15.

Sackett, G. P. 1974. Sex differences in rhesus monkeys following varied rearing experiences. In *Sex differences in behavior*, ed. R. M. Richart and R. L. Vande Wiele, 99–122. New York: John Wiley and Sons.

Salzen, E. A. 1962. Imprinting and fear. *Symp. Zool. Soc. Lond.* 8:199–218.

———. 1970. Imprinting and environmental learning. In *Development and evolution of behavior*, ed. L. R. Aronson, E. Tobach, D. S. Lehrman, and J. S. Rosenblatt. San Francisco: W. H. Freeman.

Scott, J. P. 1954. The effects of selection and domestication upon the behavior of the dog. *J. Natl. Cancer Inst.* 15:739–58.

Seligman, M. E. P., and Meyer, B. 1968. Chronic fear produced by unpredictable electric shock. *J. Comp. Physiol. Psychol.* 66:402–11.

———. 1970. Chronic fear and ulcers in rats as a function of the unpredictability of safety. *J. Comp. Physiol. Psychol.* 73:202–7.

Selye, H. 1936. A syndrome produced by diverse nocuous agents. *Nature* 138:32.

———. 1950. *Stress.* Montreal: Acta.

———. 1956. *The stress of life.* New York: McGraw Hill.

———. 1974. *Stress without distress.* London: Hodder and Stoughton.

Shoemaker, A. H. 1982. The effect of inbreeding and management on propagation of pedigree leopards. *Int. Zoo Yrbk.* 22:198–206.

Singh, D. 1970. Preference for bar pressing to obtain reward over freeloading in rats and children. *J. Comp. Physiol. Psychol.* 73:320–27.

Sluckin, W. 1968. Imprinting in guinea-pigs. *Nature* 220:1148.

Smith, A., Lindburg, D. G., and Vehrencamp, S. 1989. Effect of food preparation on feeding behavior of lion-tailed macaques. *Zoo Biol.* 8:67–75.

Sokolov, E. M. 1960. Neuronal models and the orienting reflex. In *The central nervous system and behavior,* ed. M. A. B. Brozier, New York: Josiah Macy Jr. Foundation.

Spinelli, J. S., and Markowitz, H. 1985. Prevention of cage-associated distress. *Lab Anim.* 14:19–28.

Stanton, M. E., Wallstrom, J., and Levine, S. 1987. Maternal contact inhibits pituitary-adrenal stress responses in preweanling rats. *Dev. Psychobiol.* 20:131–45.

Stein, D. G., Finger, S., and Hart, T. 1983. Brain damage and recovery: Problems and perspectives. *Behav. Neural Biol.* 37:185–222.

Stevenson, M. F. 1983. The captive environment: Its effect on exploratory and related behavioural responses in wild animals. Chap. 7 in *Exploration in animals and man,* ed. J. Archer and L. Birke, 176–97. Berkshire, U.K.: Van Nostrand Reinhold.

Stolz, S. B., and Lott, D. F. 1964. Establishment in rats of a persistent response producing a net loss of reinforcement. *J. Comp. Physiol. Psychol.* 57:147.

Stoskopf, M. K. 1983. The physiological effects of psychological stress. *Zoo Biol.* 2:179–90.

Stott, D. H. 1973. Follow-up study from birth of the effects of prenatal stress. *Dev. Med. Child Neurol.* 15:770–87.

Suomi, S. J. 1986. Behavioral aspects of successful reproduction in primates. In *Primates: The road to self-sustaining populations,* ed. K. Benirschke, 331–40. New York: Springer Verlag.

Suomi, S. J., and Harlow, H. F. 1976. Social rehabilitation of separation-induced depressive disorders in monkeys. *Am. J. Psychiatry* 133:1279–85.

Thompson, W. R., Watson, J., and Charlsworth, W. R. 1962. The effects of prenatal maternal stress on offspring behavior in rats. *Psychol. Monogr.* 76 (557):1–26.

Treus, V. D., and Lobanov, N. V. 1971. Acclimatization and domestication of the eland *Taurotragus oryx* at Askanya-Nova Zoo. *Int. Zoo Yrbk.* 11:147–56.

Uphouse, L. 1980. Reevaluation of mechanisms that mediate brain differences between enriched and impoverished animals. *Psychol. Bull.* 88:215–32.

Ward, I. L. 1972. Prenatal stress feminizes and demasculinizes the behavior of males. *Science* 175:82–84.

Warren, J. M., Zerweck, C., and Anthony, A. 1982. Effects of environmental enrichment on old mice. *Dev. Psychobiol.* 15:13–18.

Weinberg, J., and Levine, S. 1980. Psychobiology of coping in animals: The effects of predictability. In *Coping and health,* ed. S. Levine and H. Ursin, 39–60. New York: Plenum Press.

Weiner, I., Schnabel, I., Lubow, R. E., and Feldon, J. 1985. The effects of early handling on latent inhibition in male and female rats. *Dev. Psychobiol.* 18:291–97.

Weiss, J. M. 1968. Effects of coping responses on stress. *J. Comp. Physiol. Psychol.* 65:251–60.

Wiepkema, P. R. 1983a. On the significance of ethological criteria for the assessment of animal welfare. In *Indicators relevant to farm animal welfare,* ed. D. Schmidt, 69–79. Boston: M. Nijhoff.

———. 1983b. Umwelt and animal welfare. In *Farm animal housing and welfare,* ed. S. H. Baxter, M. R. Baxter, and J. A. C. MacCormack, 45–50. The Hague: Martinus Nijhoff.

Wilson, S. F. 1982. Environmental influences on the activity of captive apes. *Zoo Biol.* 1:201–9.

Winkelstraeter, K. H. 1960. Das Betteln der Zoo-Tiere (Diss.) Berlin: Hans Huber.

32

Communication and Social Behavior

FRED W. KOONTZ AND REBECCA S. ROUSH

Communication and social behavior increasingly are being considered by zoo biologists as important factors in planning management programs for captive mammals (e.g., Erwin 1986; Maple and Finlay 1986; Suomi 1986; Snowdon 1989). Educators too are quick to cite the advantages of designing zoo exhibits that promote natural communication patterns and social interactions among animals (e.g., van Hooff 1986; Maple and Finlay 1989). Our objective here is to review briefly the current theory of social communication and to illustrate the advantages of applying this knowledge to the management of captive mammals. This chapter is organized into four major sections: (1) an introductory review of communication theory, (2) a discussion of the effects of environmental design on communication, (3) a proposal for improving animal management practices by studying communication and social behavior, and (4) a brief discussion of the advantages of studying communication and social behavior in a zoo setting.

Social behavior can be defined as any action directed by an individual toward another member of its own species (Wilson 1975). The result of such an action is to influence the social relationships between conspecifics (Fentress, Fiels, and Parr 1978; Poole 1985). Social behaviors include both competitive behaviors, such as aggressive displays and fighting, and cooperative behaviors, such as predator detection, food sharing, and parental care. A necessary assumption in the study of social behavior is that individuals *do* actively affect the behavior of their conspecifics. This assumption is also the essence of animal communication theory. In fact, operationally, we can say that communication occurs when one individual's actions provide a signal that changes the behavior of another individual (Wiley 1983). Thus, communication is central to all considerations of social behavior.

MAMMALIAN COMMUNICATION: AN INTRODUCTORY REVIEW

Animal communication has been the subject of numerous reviews (Smith 1977; Green and Marler 1979; Halliday and Slater 1983; and others). The details of mammalian communication are scattered widely in the scientific literature, but introductions to the subject are provided by Ewer (1968), Sebeok (1968, 1977), Eisenberg (1981), Walther (1984), and Poole (1985).

Animal communication will be defined here as "the process in which actors use specially designed signals or displays to modify the behavior of reactors" (Krebs and Davies 1993, 349). It is assumed that the sender-receiver relationship is in some way the result of natural selection so that the sender benefits, on average, from both the signal transmission and the response of the receiver. This requirement excludes cases of information transfer that have no selective advantage. For example, a mouse rustling in the grass might transfer information to a nearby owl, but we do not consider this communication.

An animal's communication signals represent wasted energy if no other individual receives and responds to them (Smith 1977). Communication, therefore, becomes functional only when there is a response, although the response to a specific signal may or may not be immediately evident to a human observer. Also, the response to a signal is not always an overt behavioral one; many communication messages cause salient hormonal changes (e.g., responses to mouse pheromones, reviewed by Bronson and Macmillan 1983). Likewise, the response might not occur until there has been an additive effect resulting from repeated signaling (Schleidt 1973). The animal's response—immediate or delayed, behavioral or physiological—must be detected by an investigator to demonstrate that communication has occurred.

Component Analysis of Mammalian Communication

Mammalian communication has been analyzed systematically from several different theoretical perspectives. One method of analysis is to reduce the system to its four component parts: (1) the sender, (2) the communication channel and signal, (3) the receiver, and (4) noise. The communication process originates with the sender. When studying signal evolution, it is the benefit gained by the sender that is of primary importance. Benefits may be direct, as when an animal's signal attracts a potential mate, or they may be more indirect, as when an animal sounds an alarm call to warn its conspecifics. Some authors suggest that an alarm caller may promote the survival of its own genes by helping related animals who carry some of the same genes as the caller (for a discussion of such "inclusive fitness," see Wilson 1975).

Communication Channels and Signals

Collectively, the 4,100 extant mammal species possess a large and diverse repertoire of information transfer methods. Mammalian signals may be transmitted through any one of four sensory channels: optical, acoustic, chemical, or tactile. Each channel has a unique set of physical attributes that affects its use as a means of transferring information between animals. Discussions are available for optical signals (Hailman 1977), chemical signals (Eisenberg and Kleiman 1972; Albone 1984; Brown and Macdonald 1987), auditory signals (Busnel 1977; Morton 1982; Tembrock 1989), and tactile signals (Eisenberg and Golani 1977; Geldard 1977).

Optical Signals. Species possessing well-developed optical signals generally are diurnal; thus the best examples within the Mammalia are found in primates (reviewed by Oppenheimer 1977; Gautier and Gautier 1977) and in ungulates (reviewed by Walther 1984) (fig. 32.1). Visual signals do not travel around corners or through structurally complex environments, and the distance over which they can be transmitted is limited by the size of the signaler (Slater 1985). These physical limitations, together with the fact that most mammals are small and nocturnal, account for the rather limited use of long-distance visual signaling by mammals.

Virtually all species, however, practice close-range optical signaling through visual displays such as piloerection. Piloerection, an increase in the apparent body size by erection of the hair, is a widely observed optical signal. Prominently displayed genitalia are also often used as visual signals. In the pig-tailed langur, *Nasalis (=Simias) concolor* (Tenaza 1989), some other Old World monkeys (Dixson 1983), and the chimpanzee, *Pan troglodytes* (Goodall 1986), the female's anogenital area swells and becomes brightly colored during the periovulatory period. Another frequently cited example of genitalia signaling is found in the vervet monkey, *Chlorocebus (=Cercopithecus) aethiops:* adult males have a bright orange prepuce and blue scrotum, which are displayed by dominant individuals.

Evolutionary ritualization has resulted in some visual signals that appear exaggerated; such signals are associated with bright colors and are displayed through stereotypic behavioral patterns (Halliday and Slater 1983). The "open-mouthed gape," with exposure of the pink mucous membranes and teeth, is an example of a ritualized threat display that is employed by many mammals. It is noteworthy, however, that interspecific variation in signal meaning does occur. In many *Macaca* species, for example, facial expressions with baring of the teeth are exclusively shown by the *lower*-ranking of two partners; that is, they are submissive signals, not aggressive ones (de Waal 1987).

Acoustic Signals. Auditory signals travel out in all directions and bend around corners; therefore, sound is not

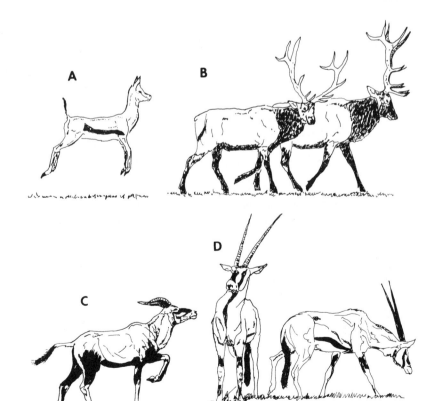

FIG. 32.1. Mammalian visual signals have many different meanings, but four especially important categories for zoo biologists to recognize are displays of alarm, aggression, courtship, and social status. *(A)* "Stotting" alarm in Thomson's gazelle, *Gazella thomsonii. (B)* "Parallel march" in an aggressive encounter of bull elk, *Cervus canadensis. (C)* "Head-up-angled-foreleg display" of a courting bull topi, *Damaliscus korrigum. (D)* "Broadside display" of a dominant bull oryx, *Oryx gazella*, to a withdrawing subordinate. (Drawings adapted from Walther 1984.)

generally a private channel of communication (see Busnel 1963, 1977). It is, however, a good means of advertising, provided that the animal is large enough to generate sufficient volume (Slater 1985). Sound communication also has the advantage that a great deal of information can be transmitted rapidly. The frequency, volume, and tonal qualities of sound can be modulated quickly, to a much greater extent than is possible with visual, chemical, or tactile signals. Vocal sound can be easily and rapidly modified by changes in the shape of the buccal cavity, and in some species (e.g., the siamang, *Hylobates syndactylus*), by special elastic vocal sacs.

Sounds produced by mammals include both vocalizations and nonvocal signals. Vocalizations, produced by vibration of the vocal cords, range in frequency from about 2 kHz in some large mammals to the ultrasound (greater than 20 kHz and as high as 100 kHz) of some bats, insectivores, and rodents (for a review of ultrasound, see Sales and Pye 1974). In general, the smaller the animal, the smaller its vocal cords, and hence the higher the frequency of its sounds.

Some gazelles and deer produce sound in their noses by vibrating cartilaginous structures, and cetaceans use their blowhole passages to create signals. In other nonvocal auditory signals, many rodents and ungulates grind their teeth (Eisenberg 1981; Walther 1984); gorillas, *Gorilla gorilla*, beat their chests (Fossey 1983); chimpanzees hit the ground with hands and sticks (Goodall 1986); rufous elephant shrews, *Elephantulus rufescens*, kangaroo rats, *Dipodomys*, and skunks, *Mephitis mephitis*, stamp the ground with their hind feet (foot-drumming is reviewed by Roeper 1981); and tenrecs, *Centetes* and *Hemicentetes*, produce sounds by rattling their quills (Eisenberg and Gould 1970). It is known that elephants, *Elephas maximus* and *Loxodonta africana*, communicate with infrasounds (frequencies less than 20 Hz, the lower limit of human hearing); the exact sound production mechanism is unclear (Payne, Langbauer, and Thomas 1986).

Chemical Signals. In recent years, it has become evident that many mammalian odors function as chemical signals that have important effects on reproduction and social behavior (Eisenberg and Kleiman 1972; Johnston 1983; Albone 1984; Brown and Macdonald 1987). Mammals are particularly rich in sources of chemical signals, which include accessory glands of the reproductive tract, feces, salivary glands, skin glands, and urine (reviewed by Adams 1980; Albone 1984). Chemical signals can either be released into the air or be dispersed by scent marking, specialized behavior patterns that function to deposit odorous substances on the ground or on environmental objects (Johnson 1973). In general, small and nocturnal species have the best-developed scent glands (reviewed by Quay 1977; Adams 1980; Sokolov 1982).

The advantages of communicating with chemical signals include their ability to be used effectively at night; the ability of air-dispersed compounds to diffuse around obstacles; energetically cheap components; minimal energy transmission requirements; a high potential range; a large information content; and persistence in time, which permits delayed communication (Wilson and Bossert 1963; Wilson 1968, 1975; Sebeok 1968, 1972). However, the relatively slow fade-out time of chemical signals can be a disadvantage because it results in rather static messages that cannot be altered abruptly (Wilson 1975). For example, the use of chemical signals usually would be disadvantageous, compared with auditory or visual signals, when conveying information about a sender's rapidly changing motivational state. Another disadvantage of the use of chemical signals is their slow transmission speed, which results in the inability to transmit messages quickly over long distances.

In the last thirty years, considerable progress has been made in describing the chemical communication systems of a variety of mammals, yet few general principles of mammalian olfactory communication have emerged. Debate also continues about the adaptive function of scent marking (Ralls 1971; Gosling 1982).

Tactile Signals. Communication by touch has been poorly studied, and its importance probably has been underestimated (Geldard 1977). Although the amount of information transferred by tactile signals is small compared with other communication modalities, it is certain that many nocturnal, highly social, and burrowing animals rely heavily on this type of signaling (Poole 1985). Allogrooming, in addition to its cleaning function (Hutchins and Barash 1976), is an important form of communication. "Snap biting" is a common warning signal practiced by rodents, carnivores, and primates. Body rubbing occurs in a sexual or affectional context in such species as tenrecs, *Hemicentetes* (Poduschka 1977), and domestic cats, *Felis catus* (Leyhausen 1979). Other examples of behaviors in which tactile information may be exchanged by mammals include nuzzling, licking, and kissing (e.g., prairie dogs, *Cynomys ludovicianus*: King 1959), huddling, and playing.

The Receiver

To a human observer, an animal's perception of a signal appears as a unitary process. However, it is wise to remember that for the vast majority of mammals, no single sensory modality is divorced from the others. The process of perception is influenced by a complex of internal and external factors that are often unknown to the observer. Each receiver enters a communication encounter with its own unique internal environment, which includes both its hormonal state and its set of previously learned experiences. These factors taken together influence an animal's specific response to any given signal.

Much has been written concerning the sensory abilities of vertebrates; recent reviews are available on vision (Levine 1985), hearing (Fay and Popper 1985), olfaction (Dodd and Squirrell 1980; Shirley 1984), and touch (Bullock, Orkand, and Grinnel 1977).

Noise

Any disturbance that alters the information content of a signal is called noise. Most communication takes place within a noisy channel. Hailman (1977) distinguished two kinds of noise: that which physically changes the signal during transmission (transmission noise) and that which overwhelms the signal with extraneous entropy (detection noise). We can expect animals to maximize efficiency by operating their communication systems as close to the ambient noise level as possible (Schleidt 1973).

Noise generated by environmental factors (e.g., wind, humidity, and temperature) has been examined for its effects on acoustic signals (Piercy and Embelton 1977; Wiley and Richards 1978), chemical signals (Wilson 1968; Regnier and Goodwin 1977), and optical signals (Hailman 1977). Noise in the acoustic channel results from both biological sources (e.g., choruses of amphibians, birds, and insects) and nonbiological sources (e.g., falling water, wind, and wind-blown vegetation). In the visual channel, background noise consists mainly of light reflections from vegetation, water, and the ground. Chemical communication is altered by the age of the scent mark, humidity, temperature, and the presence of the scent marks of other animals (Johnston and Schmidt 1979; Wellington, Beauchamp, and Wojciechowski-Metzler 1983).

ANIMAL COMMUNICATION AND THE ZOO ENVIRONMENT

The zoo environment should allow animals to express the full extent of their behavioral repertoire, or at least as much of it as is possible in captivity. The expression of natural behavior by zoo animals not only increases the welfare of the animals but also benefits education and research efforts. With regard to social behavior and communication, the issues include the provision of places to mark or display, the availability of natural spacing, visual contact between animals in different enclosures, and the reduction of noise.

Meeting the Display Needs of Captive Mammals
The display needs of mammals vary widely. Senders often position themselves, or their signals, so as to maximize the chances that their messages will be detected by conspecifics. Ewer (1973) notes that many carnivores go to considerable trouble (e.g., "hand standing" against a vertical tree) to place their anal gland scent well off the ground at the height of the receiver's nose. The rufous elephant shrew often deposits scent at conspicuous locations, for example, near well-delineated trail junctions (Koontz 1984). Some forest primates (e.g., blue monkeys, *Cercopithecus mitis*) call from characteristic heights, which apparently maximizes transmission distances by taking advantage of natural sound channels through the forest canopy (Brown 1989).

The relationship between animal communication and spatial use of enclosures remains largely unstudied for zoo mammals. A better understanding of this association would allow zoo architects to include "communication sites" in their exhibit designs, thereby enriching the environment for animal and visitor alike. In one study on enclosure use during scent marking, red pandas, *Ailurus fulgens*, were found to have significant preferences for particular marking sites, those being prominent points in the enclosure (Conover and Gittleman 1989). The objects they marked were upraised and near main travel routes. These results suggest that objects that the animals prefer to mark should be placed near food, water, latrines, and denning areas.

Natural Spacing
The availability of natural spacing is also important. Western tarsier females, *Tarsius bancanus*, are relatively solitary in captivity (Roberts and Kohn 1993). They sleep one to a nest box unless young offspring are present. (Adult males and females may be housed in pairs, but do not share nest boxes.) Females enforce these sleeping arrangements and keep the individual spacing maximized. The apparent reason for the females' behavior is that some male tarsiers are infanticidal. Whenever aggression over enclosure features (i.e., perching, resting, or eating sites) is a potential danger, several of these sites should be provided to minimize competition for them (Roberts and Kohn 1993). Enclosure size is important not only for individual spacing but also for the provision of sufficient flight distance for the animals. If sufficient flight distance is not provided so that animals may escape an aggressor or withdraw if disturbed, stereotypic behaviors such as pacing may arise (fennec fox, *Vulpes (=Fennecus) zerda*, Carlstead 1991).

Visual Contact between Animals in Different Enclosures
Visual contact between conspecific individuals or groups in separate enclosures can be beneficial, acceptable, or a source of stress. Allowing visual contact may provide beneficial social contact for individuals of a gregarious species that must be housed alone for some management reason, for example, animals recovering from injury or recently expelled from their group. In some species, visual contact between enclosures may add some stimulation. Hearn et al. (1978) reported that alternating the groups of common marmosets, *Callithrix jacchus*, housed in a centrally located exercise enclosure increased positive activity levels in the group in the central enclosure. While the change of enclosure itself aroused the central group, seeing all the other groups in the room also increased activity. This arrangement also provided excitement for the groups still in their home cages since they were able to interact with a new central group each time.

In other species, visual contact between groups or individuals has a definite negative effect. In territorial species, individuals may spend so much of their energy trying to "defend" their territories through visual and auditory displays and scent marking that they do not engage in other activities, such as eating or breeding or rearing offspring. This sort of interaction can also be a source of significant stress, causing health problems and/or a suppression of reproduction. In the Wisconsin Callitrichid Research Laboratory multiple conspecific groups of cotton-top tamarins, *Saguinus oedipus*, and pygmy marmosets, *Callithrix (=Cebuella) pygmaea*, were once housed in the same room, with most groups in visual contact. Breeding rates were low, and rates of successful rearing of offspring were even lower. When the groups were visually isolated from one another, simply by placing opaque sheets between the cages, levels of territorial displays significantly decreased and the rate of successful reproduction increased (C. T. Snowdon, pers. comm.).

Reducing Noise
The zoo environment should not only allow for the expression of natural behavior, it should also minimize disturbances (i.e., noise) that interfere with it. There are many sources of noise in the zoo, ranging from the obvious, such as other animals and zoo visitors, to the subtle, such as

cleaning solutions and enclosure materials (see above for discussion of types of noise).

Maintenance Procedures as a Source of Noise. Analyses of all types of zoo noise, and their potential effects on animal communication and social behavior, are needed. Without question, the zoo is an acoustically noisy environment. But does this change the normal rate of vocalizations? Does "noise pollution" affect behavior or reproduction? Carlstead (1991) found that vacuum cleaner noise and unexpected loud noises in the keeper area were significantly correlated with stereotypic behavior in fennec foxes. She found that manual sweeping of the enclosure, instead of vacuuming, decreased stereotypic behavior.

Humans are notably poor in their olfactory abilities, and as a result, zoo biologists have largely ignored the biological significance of the captive animal's olfactory arena and olfactory "noise." For animals that scent mark, cleaning procedures can be very disruptive; cleaning too often and using scented materials can interfere with the transmission and effects of olfactory communication signals. For common marmosets and other callitrichids, for example, daily cleaning procedures may be very disruptive. In these species, scent marking by the dominant female is part of the mechanism that suppresses the reproduction of subordinate females and thus helps maintain group stability (Epple 1972). This suggests that keepers should allow the maximum time between cleanings that still permits cage hygiene to be maintained at an acceptable level. Another possibility is to refrain from cleaning some piece of enclosure "furniture" so that scent marks on it remain undisturbed.

The enclosure itself can be a source of noise and can impede beneficial communication. The vocalizations of large animals can travel through and around walls, but those of smaller animals, especially ultrasonic vocalizations, can be impeded by the thinnest wall. Fine mesh can be substituted for solid walls, thus allowing vocal communication between neighbors.

Other sources of "noise" can be found in the enclosure itself: ceramic tiles, which are easily cleaned but are reflective of sounds and cause echoes; and glass and metal, which reflect light, a type of visual noise. Many animals are sensitive to such reflections, especially of their own images. The images may be perceived as a threat, and the animals may spend a large amount of time threatening themselves in a mirror. Animals may also injure themselves trying to get at what they perceive as an intruder encroaching on their territory. Although such agonistic behaviors are likely to decrease over time, such environments can cause animals to engage in inappropriately high levels of aggression until they have become habituated.

Zoo Visitors as a Source of Noise. Visitors can affect the social behavior and communication of zoo animals by disrupting their typical interactions. Greater numbers of visitors may increase the rate of stereotypic behavior in fennec foxes (Carlstead 1991). Zoo visitors attempting to interact with animals may also have a stimulating effect and increase animal activity levels (Hosey 1989), an effect that may be positive or negative. This type of interaction should be discouraged if it disrupts the "natural" behavior of the animals or increases rates of stereotypic behavior. Glatston et al.

(1984) found differences in the behavior of cotton-top tamarins that were on and off exhibit: the display group exhibited a lower overall rate of behavior. More importantly, the juvenile male in the display group received significantly more aggression than did the juvenile in the off-exhibit group. In all of the above cases, the larger the number of visitors, the greater the effect (Carlstead 1991; Glatston et al. 1984).

MONITORING SOCIAL DYNAMICS

Animal communication serves as an important regulator of social behavior. Signal evolution has allowed animals to influence more efficiently the actions of their conspecifics. Three typical circumstances in which communication affects social dynamics in the zoo environment are: (1) agonistic interactions, (2) affiliative interactions, and (3) maintenance of long-term social stability.

By quantifying social relationships, animal managers can establish normal behavioral baselines for exhibit groups. It is against these normal baselines that keepers can monitor their animals. By way of analogy, consider how a physician uses normal physiological values when diagnosing medical problems. Similarly, modern animal husbandry, especially for a species that cannot be routinely examined in hand because of its large size or delicate nature, requires behavioral baseline values. By periodically sampling the dynamics of an enclosure group, managers can detect significant changes in social relationships, thus allowing management intervention and the prevention of more serious problems (fig. 32.2).

Agonistic Interactions

Agonistic behavior (first defined by Scott and Fredericson 1951) refers to any activity related to fighting—aggressive, submissive, or defensive. The management of agonistic interactions among zoo animals is a critical component of all animal care programs. Situations that typically elicit aggressive behavior include antipredatory maneuvers, dominance interactions, parental disciplinary actions, sexual encounters, territorial disputes, and weaning conflicts (Wilson 1975). The most frequent situation in which aggressive behavior is shown by mammals is when they are defending assets that can be monopolized (Poole 1985). Typical assets defended are food supplies, living space, mates, offspring, resting sites, and the status that allows animals to acquire resources.

Despite the many potential resources to contest and the ample supply of anatomical weapons, life-threatening fights between mammals are infrequent in nature. This is largely due to the evolution of communication signals that function to mediate agonistic interactions between individuals. Threat, submissive, and defensive displays are used widely among the Mammalia. Ethologists define "displays" as ritualized behavioral acts that make information available to others (Smith 1977); their ritualization enhances communication by reducing message errors. Animal keepers can take advantage of these displays to obtain insight into the social dynamics of a group. It is important to note that in the wild, animals are free to escape each other, either temporarily or permanently (through dispersal); encounters that would

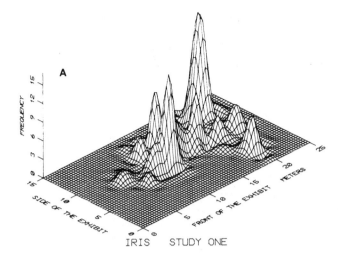

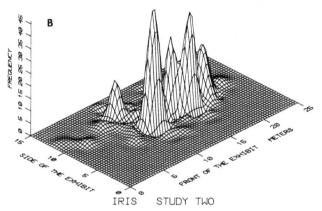

FIG. 32.2.   Spatial analyses of exhibit use is one method of gaining insights into the social dynamics of zoo mammals. At the Wildlife Conservation Park, we conducted a spatial analysis of "Iris," a 3-year-old subordinate proboscis monkey, *Nasalis larvatus*, who was kept at first with her father and his harem; her father was later replaced by an unrelated male. *(A)* In "Study One," Iris spent a large part of her time in the right rear corner of the exhibit; she was being moderately ostracized by her father. *(B)* In "Study Two," Iris spent the majority of her time in the center of the exhibit, and was well integrated within the new male's troop.

easily resolve themselves in the wild may escalate in captivity, where animals cannot disperse.

Play-fighting and play-chasing have their own set of distinct communication signals and social conventions. Certain facial expressions and postures are reserved for play situations (Fagen 1981). These signals seem to say, "what follows is play and is not serious." A familiar case is the "play face" seen in some primates, such as the chimpanzee (Goodall 1986). It is important for animal keepers to be able to recognize the differences between play and true aggression. Thompson (chapter 34, this volume) provides a more extensive discussion of play.

A recurring problem faced by animal managers is the need to introduce new animals to socially established groups, or to reintroduce individuals to their own social group after a period of separation. By closely watching the levels and types of intragroup aggression, it is possible to ascertain how successful such an introduction will be. This "tech-

nique" can be particularly useful when new pairs or groups are formed. Newly introduced animals may be targets of aggression from other group members, as was the case in a group of sable antelope, *Hippotragus niger,* observed by Thompson (1993). She found that, because the types and levels of "typical" aggression within the group were known, it was possible to determine that the levels and types of aggression directed at a new individual were distinctly different. Butting was the typical form of aggression within the group, but with the introduction of a new female, displacements and chases increased. They were nine times more common toward the new female than toward other group members. These differences in the aggression directed toward the new female indicated that she was not perceived as part of the group.

There are methods of animal introduction that can be used to reduce aggression. These include (1) placing a screen door between individuals housed in adjacent enclosures until they are thoroughly familiar with each other (e.g., Roberts et al. 1987); (2) using "creep doors" through which one animal, usually a smaller juvenile, can retreat into an adjacent area but the other animals cannot (e.g., Inglett et al. 1989); and (3) transferring an individual's odors, usually in the form of feces or soiled bedding material, before the introduction of the new animal. While these and similar methods are employed by zoo biologists, there have been no studies comparing these techniques for different species. For example, it appears that transferring individual odors before an introduction in some species reduces aggression (e.g., rufous elephant shrews), but in other cases only makes matters worse (e.g., meerkats, *Suricata suricatta*). Introduction techniques for primates and nonprimate mammals are discussed by Watts and Meder (chap. 6) and Kranz (chap. 7, this volume) respectively.

Increases in or changes in the types of intragroup aggression can also be indicative of an upheaval about to occur in a group or pair. In some species, levels of low-intensity aggression (i.e., visual threats, etc.) may increase before an outbreak of high-intensity aggression occurs, as when an older offspring is being "expelled" from a group (e.g., golden lion tamarins, *Leontopithecus rosalia:* Inglett et al. 1989). This aggression may result in severe injury or death of an animal. By being aware of baseline behaviors, it is possible to foresee these violent expulsions and remove the appropriate group member in advance.

Submissive behaviors are also good clues to social instability. Submissive displays communicate that an individual will not retaliate, even if attacked. In golden lion tamarins and other callitrichids, subordinate individuals may grimace and produce a distinctive screeching vocalization. The subordinate animal may separate itself from a family group, watch other group members, and avoid the approach of some group members but not others. There may also be bursts of one or two individuals running about the cage horizontally in a loosely circular pattern (Inglett et al. 1989). Other commonly employed submissive displays include rolling over onto the back, exposing the abdomen, as in canids, felids, and rodents; and crouching, appearing as small as possible, as in ungulates and primates. Submissive displays typically are shown by young animals toward older ones, by females toward males, and by low-ranking individuals toward higher-ranking group members.

An animal that constantly performs submissive displays even when not being threatened or challenged may be in serious danger. In at least one case in the Wisconsin Callitrichid Laboratory, a juvenile cotton-top tamarin behaved very submissively when not being threatened and was violently expelled from his family group.

A change in sleeping arrangements may also indicate impending social upheaval or a lack of group (pair) cohesion. Cotton-top tamarins sleep together in a tight bundle; if one animal sleeps by itself, it is more than likely in the process of being expelled from the group. Alternatively, if animals that are newly introduced begin to sleep together, it is often a good indication that bonding has occurred.

Certain events in the life of a group or pair are potential trouble spots, such as births, weanings, and the presence of estrous females. In the Mayotte lemur, *Eulemur (=Lemur) fulvus mayottensis*, aggression levels are higher in captivity than those reported in the wild (Hosey 1989), especially during the birthing season, apparently due to aggression by males directed at infants and the defense of infants by females. Aggression levels also rise in Western tarsiers during late pregnancy and after the birth of infants (Roberts and Kohn 1993). Males of this species are also known to be infanticidal, and females enforce increased individual distances through displacements and chases.

Males of many species compete for females that are ovulating. Male red deer, *Cervus elaphus*, have disputes over females during the rut. They first engage in roaring matches, which escalate to "parallel walks." Then, if neither contestant has retreated, they resort to lowering antlers and charging (Clutton-Brock 1979). An animal's own signals may communicate the onset of estrus; for example, some female mammals signal receptivity by exhibiting proceptive behavior, in which they demonstrate their reproductive state by actively soliciting one or more males. Female shrews, *Blarina*, *Sorex*, and *Crocidura*, rufous elephant shrews, and golden hamsters, *Mesocricetus auratus*, which normally are dominant over males, become less aggressive toward any potential mate during estrus. In other species, such as chimpanzees and orangutans, *Pongo pygmaeus*, females display the genitalia. Some Old World monkeys and apes have conspicuous swollen circumgenital areas during estrus and also release chemical and behavioral signals (reviewed by Dixson 1983).

Monitoring Animal Health

Not only is it possible to determine how well animals are getting along with other animals in their group or enclosure through social behavior observations, it is also possible to monitor the health of individuals. By knowing the normal range of behaviors, one can detect changes when they occur and use them as indicators of animal health. Certain vocalizations are usually given only in times of distress (e.g., the distress call of pygmy marmosets, Pola and Snowdon 1975). Animals may huddle more with other group members if they are physically (physiologically) stressed. In those species in which infants are carried, the young may begin to ride again, or more frequently, if ill.

Communication between Animals and Zoo Keepers

An understanding of the animal's communication system can benefit the captive animal manager. Most importantly, it can enable one to know when one is in danger. An obvious and familiar example of an animal signal giving notice of potential danger is the rattle of a rattlesnake's tail. A common sign of potential danger among mammals is piloerection, a conservative signal of arousal in all mammals. As described above, animals will defend assets they perceive as threatened; they will defend them not only from each other, but from keepers as well. Keepers should be aware that the value of any given asset, and hence the defender's behavior in protecting it, can change quickly and dramatically. For example, a bull elephant is more likely to attack his keeper when the bull is tending an estrous cow rather than a nonestrous female. The danger is that a change in the value of an asset, in this case the female elephant, may not always be noticed readily by a human observer.

In the daily lives of most mammals, optical signals are of less importance than either acoustic or chemical signals, but for the zoo biologist, optical signals are the most important means of intercepting animal messages. This is a result of our primate heritage, and consequently, our largely visual perceptual world. By accurate translation of visual signals, animal keepers can work more sagely and better care for their charges.

Animal caretakers should be aware that many visual (and acoustic) displays are graded in intensity. These variations are correlated with the signal's precise meaning and the probability of the animal's subsequent behavior (e.g., its likelihood of attacking). Careless misreading of these signs by animal keepers has resulted in needless injuries. In general, the greater the magnitude of the message to be communicated, the more prolonged and intense the signal (Lorenz 1966). For example, the aggressive display of the rhesus macaque, *Macaca mulatta*, begins simply as a hard stare, escalates gradually as the monkey rises to a standing position, and then is most intense when the mouth opens and the head bobs up and down (Wilson 1972). If the opponent, perhaps an animal keeper, has not retreated at this point, the monkey may next attack.

It is also possible to use the animals' own signals to appease or to avoid dangerous encounters with them. Direct eye contact or staring is often perceived by animals as a threat. Therefore, by simply averting one's gaze, it is possible to appear nonthreatening. Making an animal aware of one's approach and presence is also a good tactic for avoiding an agonistic interaction. Researchers and trackers in the field use the "belch vocalization" of the mountain gorilla when approaching a group or when changing position within it (M. Robbins, pers. comm.). By imitating this vocalization the researchers can communicate their presence and movement near the group (Fossey 1983).

The fact that some mammals accept trainers as part of their dominance hierarchies allows keepers to control some large and potentially dangerous animals, such as elephants. Elephant trainers exploit the fact that elephants establish social hierarchies by assuming the position of the most dominant member of the herd (fig. 32.3). We do not know, however, whether this method has any deleterious side

FIG. 32.3. Animal handlers are able to control some large mammals that follow social hierarchies by assuming the role of the dominant herd member.

effects. Some keepers have suggested that bull elephants dominated by human handlers might have lower testosterone levels, and hence suppressed reproductive potential, relative to bulls that are controlled by indirect means (e.g., via remotely operated hydraulic doors). Additionally, if the keeper who has assumed the dominant role is absent or has left the zoo, the elephant may become very difficult for its new keeper to handle. Social hierarchies, although they may be relatively stable, are still susceptible to upheaval; obviously, a keeper in the dominant role would be in very serious danger if an elephant challenged him or her.

SOCIAL BEHAVIOR AND COMMUNICATION RESEARCH IN ZOOS

Other chapters in this volume discuss the logistics of research in zoos. What we wish to mention here is what can be done in the captive setting that cannot be done in the wild. In captivity, it is possible to get close to animals that may not be approachable in the wild. Animals may be unapproachable in the field because they cannot be habituated or because they are inaccessible, as with cliff nesters or canopy dwellers. In the case of animals that are difficult to habituate, such as canopy-dwelling primates, almost everything we know, until recently, has come from captive studies. In captivity it is also possible to explore quiet vocalizations and subtle visual signals or behaviors usually performed out of a field researcher's view.

The other benefit of research in captivity is the control available. It is possible to present specific foods and objects and to manipulate the social circumstances. Maples, Haraway, and Hutto (1989) took advantage of the creation of a siamang pair to study how vocal duetting developed. The likelihood of observing such an event in the wild would be very small. With the close and constant observation possible in a zoo, Maples et al. were able to document the develop-

ment of the duet and why any particular duetting attempt failed. This is just one example of the unique contribution zoo researchers can make to the body of knowledge about animal communication and social behavior.

CONCLUSIONS

The management of wild mammals in captivity requires the consideration of a complex set of factors, including the maintenance of the proper social environment. Animal communication is a key element in the establishment of all mammalian social systems. Since many animal management problems have their origins in social behavior, it is recommended that communication mechanisms be considered when searching for answers to these problems. The animal's communication systems can also be important diagnostic tools for the captive animal manager, providing crucial information about both the animal's health and welfare and the keepers' safety.

REFERENCES

Adams, M. G. 1980. Odour-producing organs of mammals. *Symp. Zool. Soc. Lond.* 45:57–86.

Albone, E. S. 1984. *Mammalian semiochemistry: The investigation of chemical signals between mammals.* New York: John Wiley and Sons.

Bronson, F. H., and Macmillan, B. 1983. Hormonal responses to primer pheromones. In *Pheromones and reproduction in mammals,* ed. J. G. Vandenbergh, 175–97. New York: Academic Press.

Brown, C. H. 1989. The active space of blue monkey and grey-cheeked mangabey vocalizations. *Animal Behaviour* 37: 1023–34.

Brown, R. E., and Macdonald, D. W., eds. 1987. *Social odours in mammals.* 2 vols. New York: Oxford University Press.

Bullock, T., Orkand, R., and Grinnel, A. 1977. *Introduction to nervous systems.* San Francisco: W. H. Freeman.

Busnel, R. G., ed. 1963. *Acoustic behaviour of animals.* New York: Elsevier Publishing Company.

———. 1977. Acoustic communication. In *How animals communicate,* ed. T. A. Sebeok, 233–51. Bloomington: Indiana University Press.

Carlstead, K. 1991. Husbandry of the fennec fox, *Fennecus zerda:* Environmental conditions influencing stereotypic behaviour. *Int. Zoo Yrbk.* 30:202–7.

Clutton-Brock, T. H. 1979. The logical stag: Adaptive aspects of fighting in red deer (*Cervus elaphus* L.). *Anim. Behav.* 27: 211–25.

Conover, G. K., and Gittleman, J. L. 1989. Scent-marking in captive red pandas *(Ailurus fulgens). Zoo Biol.* 8:193–205.

Dixson, A. F. 1983. Observations on the evolution and behavioural significance of sexual skin in female primates. *Adv. Stud. Behav.* 13:63–106.

Dodd, G. H., and Squirrell, D. J. 1980. Structure and mechanism in the mammalian olfactory system. *Symp. Zool. Soc. Lond.* 45: 35–56.

Eisenberg, J. F. 1981. *The mammalian radiations: An analysis of trends in evolution, adaptation and behavior.* Chicago: University of Chicago Press.

Eisenberg, J. F., and Golani, I. 1977. Communication in Metatheria. In *How animals communicate,* ed. T. A. Sebeok, 575–99. Bloomington: Indiana University Press.

Eisenberg, J. F., and Gould, E. 1970. *The tenrecs: A study in mammalian behavior and evolution.* Smithsonian Contributions to Zoology, no. 27. Washington, D.C.: Smithsonian Institution Press.

Eisenberg, J. F., and Kleiman, D. G. 1972. Olfactory communication in mammals. *Annu. Rev. Ecol. Syst.* 3:1–31.

Epple, G. 1972. Social communication by olfactory signals in marmosets. *Int. Zoo Yrbk.* 13:36–42.

Erwin, J. 1986. Environments for captive propagation of primates: Interaction of social and physical factors. In *Primates: The road to self-sustaining populations,* ed. K. Benirschke, 297–306. Springer-Verlag, New York.

Ewer, R. F. 1968. *The ethology of mammals.* New York: Plenum Press.

———. 1973. *The carnivores.* Ithaca, N.Y.: Cornell University Press.

Fagen, R. 1981. *Animal play behavior.* New York: Oxford University Press.

Fay, R. R., and Popper, A. N. 1985. The octavolateralis system. In *Functional vertebrate morphology,* ed. M. Hildebrand, D. M. Bramble, K. F. Liem, and D. B. Wake, 291–316. Cambridge, Mass.: Harvard University Press.

Fentress, J. C., Fiels, R., and Parr, H. 1978. Social dynamics and communication. In *Behavior of captive wild animals,* ed. H. Markowitz and V. H. Stevens, 67–106. Chicago: Nelson-Hall.

Fossey, D. 1983. *Gorillas in the mist.* Boston: Houghton Mifflin Company.

Gautier, J. P., and Gautier, A. 1977. Communication in Old World monkeys. In *How animals communicate,* ed. T. A. Sebeok, 890–964. Bloomington: Indiana University Press.

Geldard, F. A. 1977. Tactile communication. In *How animals communicate,* ed. T. A. Sebeok, 211–32. Bloomington: Indiana University Press.

Glatston, A. R., Geilvoet-Soeteman, E., Hora-Pecek, E., and Hooff, J. A. R. A. M. van. 1984. The influence of the zoo environment on social behavior of groups of cotton-topped tamarins, *Saguinus oedipus oedipus. Zoo Biol.* 3:241–53.

Goodall, J. 1986. *The chimpanzees of Gombe: Patterns of behavior.* Cambridge Mass.: Belknap Press of Harvard University Press.

Gosling, L. M. 1982. A reassessment of the function of scent marking in territories. *Z. Tierpsychol.* 60:89–118.

Green, S., and Marler, P. 1979. The analysis of animal communication. In *Handbook of behavioral neurobiology,* vol. 3, ed. P. Marler and J. G. Vandenbergh, 73–157. New York: Plenum Press.

Hailman, J. P. 1977. *Optical signals.* Bloomington: Indiana University Press.

Halliday, T. R., and Slater, P., eds. 1983. *Animal behavior: Communication.* New York: W. H. Freeman.

Hearn, J. P., Abbott, D. H., Chambers, P. C., Hodges, J. K., and Lunn, S. F. 1978. Use of the common marmoset, *Callithrix jacchus,* in reproductive research. In *Primates in medicine,* vol. 10, 40. Basel: Karger.

Hooff, J. A. R. A. M. van. 1986. Behavioral requirements for self-sustaining primate populations: Some theoretical considerations and a closer look at social behavior. In *Primates: The road to self-sustaining populations,* ed. K. Benirschke, 307–19. New York: Springer-Verlag.

Hosey, G. R. 1989. Behavior of the Mayotte lemur, *Lemur fulvus mayottensis,* in captivity. *Zoo Biol.* 8:27–36.

Hutchins, M., and Barash, D. P. 1976. Grooming in primates: Implications for its utilitarian function. *Primates* 17:145–50.

Inglett, B. J., French, J. A., Simmons, L. G., and Vires, K. W. 1989. Dynamics of intrafamily aggression and social reintegration in lion tamarins. *Zoo Biol.* 8:67–78.

Johnson, R. P. 1973. Scent marking in mammals. *Anim. Behav.* 21:521–35.

Johnston, R. E. 1983. Chemical signals and reproduction behavior. In *Pheromones and reproduction in mammals,* ed. J. G. Vandenbergh, 3–38. New York: Academic Press.

Johnston, R. E., and Schmidt, T. 1979. Responses of hamsters to scent marks of different ages. *Behav. Neural Biol.* 26:64–75.

King, J. A. 1959. The social behavior of prairie dogs. *Sci. Am.* 10: 308–15.

Koontz, F. W. 1984. Sternal gland scent communication in the rufous elephant-shrew, *Elephantulus rufescens* Peters, with additional observations on behavior and reproduction in captivity. Ph.D. dissertation, University of Maryland.

Krebs, J. R., and Davies, N. B. 1993. *An introduction to behavioural ecology.* 3d ed. Boston: Blackwell.

Levine, J. S. 1985. The vertebrate eye. In *Functional vertebrate morphology,* ed. M. Hildebrand, D. M. Bramble, K. F. Liem, and D. B. Wake, 317–37. Cambridge Mass.: Harvard University Press.

Leyhausen, P. 1979. *Cat behavior: The predatory and social behavior of domestic and wild cats.* New York: Garland STPM Press.

Lorenz, K. Z. 1966. *On aggression.* London: Methuen.

Maple, T. L., and Finlay, T. W. 1986. Evaluation of the environment of captive nonhuman primates. In *Primates: The road to self-sustaining populations,* ed. K. Benirschke, 479–88. New York: Springer-Verlag.

———. 1989. Applied primatology in the modern zoo. *Zoo Biol.* suppl. 1:101–16.

Maples, E. G., Haraway, M. M., and Hutto, C. W. 1989. Development of coordinated singing in a newly formed siamang pair *(Hylobates syndactylus). Zoo Biol.* 8:367–78.

Morton, E. S. 1982. Grading, discreteness, redundancy, and motivation-structural rules. In *Acoustic communication in birds,* vol. 1, ed. D. E. Kroodsma, E. H. Miller, and H. Ouellet, 183–212. New York: Academic Press.

Oppenheimer, J. R. 1977. Communication in New World monkeys. In *How animals communicate*, ed. T. A. Sebeok, 851–89. Bloomington: Indiana University Press.

Payne, K. B., Langbauer, W. R., and Thomas, E. M. 1986. Infrasonic calls of the Asian elephant *(Elephas maximus). Behav. Ecol. Sociobiol.* 18:297–301.

Piercy, J. E., and Embelton, T. F. W. 1977. Review of noise propagation in the atmosphere. *J. Acoust. Soc. Am.* 61:1404–18.

Poduschka, W. 1977. Insectivore communication. In *How animals communicate*, ed. T. A.Sebeok, 600–633. Bloomington: Indiana University Press.

Pola, Y. V., and Snowdon, C. T. 1975. The vocalizations of pygmy marmosets *(Cebuella pygmaea). Anim. Behav.* 23:826–42.

Poole, T. 1985. *Social behaviour in mammals.* New York: Chapman and Hall.

Quay, W. B. 1977. Structure and function of skin glands. In *Chemical signals in vertebrates*, ed. D. Müller-Schwarze and M. M. Mozell, 1–16. New York: Plenum Press.

Ralls, K. 1971. Mammalian scent marking. *Science* 171:443–49.

Regnier, F. E., and Goodwin, M. 1977. On the chemical and environmental modulation of pheromone release from vertebrate scent markers. In *Chemical signals in vertebrates*, ed. D. Müller-Schwarze and M. M. Mozell, 115–34. New York: Plenum Press.

Roberts, M., and Kohn, F. 1993. Habitat use, foraging behavior, and activity patterns in reproducing western tarsiers, *Tarsius bancanus*, in captivity: A management synthesis. *Zoo Biol.* 12:217–32.

Roberts, M., Koontz, F., Phillips, L., and Maliniak, E. 1987. Management and biology of the prehensile-tailed porcupine, *Coendou prehensilis*, at Washington NZP and New York Zoological Park. *Int. Zoo Yrbk.* 26:265–75.

Roeper, N. J. 1981. Foot drumming in the elephant shrew, *Elephantulus rufescens*. M.S. thesis, University of Maryland.

Sales, G., and Pye, D. 1974. *Ultrasonic communication by animals.* London: Chapman and Hall.

Schleidt, W. M. 1973. Tonic communication: Continual effects of discrete signals in animal communication systems. *J. Theor. Biol.* 42:359–86.

Scott, J. P., and Fredericson, E. 1951. The causes of fighting in mice and rats. *Physiol. Zool.* 24 (4): 273–309.

Sebeok, T. A. ed. 1968. *Animal communication.* Bloomington: Indiana University Press.

———. 1972. *Perspectives in zoosemiotics.* The Hague: Mouton.

———, ed. 1977. *How animals communicate.* Bloomington: Indiana University Press.

Shirley, S. G. 1984. Mammalian chemoreception. In *Mammalian semiochemistry: The investigation of chemical signals between mammals*, ed. E. S. Albone, 243–77. New York: John Wiley and Sons.

Slater, P. J. B. 1985. *An introduction to ethology.* New York: Cambridge University Press.

Smith, W. J. 1977. *The behavior of communication.* Cambridge Mass.: Harvard University Press.

Snowdon, C. T. 1989. The criteria for successful captive propagation of endangered primates. *Zoo Biol.* suppl. 1:149–61.

Sokolov, V. E. 1982. *Mammal skin.* Berkeley: University of California Press.

Suomi, S. J. 1986. Behavioral aspects of successful reproduction in primates. In *Primates: The road to self-sustaining populations*, ed. K. Benirschke, 331–40. New York: Springer-Verlag.

Tembrock, G. 1989. Biocommunication in mammals with special references to acoustic signals. *Int. J. Mammal. Biol.* 54:65–80.

Tenaza, R. R. 1989. Female sexual swellings in the Asian colobine *Simias concolor. Am. J. Primatol.* 17:81–86.

Thompson, K. V. 1993. Aggressive behavior and dominance hierarchies in female sable antelope, *Hippotragus niger:* Implications for captive management. *Zoo Biol.* 12:189–202.

Waal, F. B. M. de. 1987. Dynamics of social relationships. In *Primate societies*, ed. B. B. Smuts, D. L. Cheney, R. M. Seyfarth, R. W. Wrangham, and T. T. Struhsaker, 421–30. Chicago: University of Chicago Press.

Walther, F. R. 1984. *Communication and expression in hoofed mammals.* Bloomington: Indiana University Press.

Wellington, J. L., Beauchamp, G. K., and Wojciechowski-Metzler, C. 1983. Stability of chemical communicants in urine: Individual identity and age of sample. *J. Chem. Ecol.* 9:235–45.

Wiley, R. H. 1983. The evolution of communication: Information and manipulation. In *Animal behaviour: Communication*, ed. T. R. Halliday and P. J. B. Slater, 156–89. New York: W. H. Freeman.

Wiley, R. H., and Richards, D. G. 1978. Physical constraints on acoustic communication in the atmosphere: Implications for the evolution of animal vocalizations. *Behav. Ecol. Sociobiol.* 3:69–94.

Wilson, E. O. 1968. Chemical systems. In *Animal communication*, ed. T. A. Sebeok, 75–102. Bloomington: Indiana University Press.

———. 1972. Animal communication. *Sci. Am.* 227 (3): 52–60.

———. 1975. *Sociobiology: The new synthesis.* Cambridge, Mass.: Harvard University Press.

Wilson, E. O., and Bossert, W. H. 1963. Chemical communication among animals. *Rec. Prog. Horm. Res.* 19:673–716.

33

Mammalian Social Organization and Mating Systems

Joel Berger and Elizabeth F. Stevens

Wild animals have been maintained in confinement for more than 5,000 years, yet study of their social organization is relatively recent (for reviews see Fisler 1969; Eisenberg 1966, 1981; Clutton-Brock and Harvey 1977; Kleiman 1977; Gosling and Petrie 1981; Smuts et al. 1987). It is now evident that the long-term maintenance of a captive population requires understanding and consideration of the species' social behavior and its mating system. Unfortunately, details about the social organization of many species are unknown. As conservation continues to emerge as a prominent theme for the twenty-first century, managers of animal populations increasingly will require knowledge of animal social organization and mating systems. The purpose of this chapter, therefore, is to summarize how knowledge of mammalian social systems can be applied to the captive situation. This chapter is organized into three sections: (1) a description of the patterns of social organization and mating systems; (2) a discussion of the ecological constraints on social organization; and (3) a discussion of the flexibility of social organization and considerations to be taken into account when forming captive social groups.

PATTERNS OF SOCIAL ORGANIZATION AND MATING SYSTEMS

Various definitions of social organization and mating systems exist (Brown and Orians 1970; Wilson 1975; Wittenberger 1981; Michener 1983; Shields 1987). One simple categorization system uses grouping patterns, the results of a species' dispersion in space and time (Eisenberg 1981). Thus, a working definition of social organization is the modal grouping pattern of a species. Social organization can be most simply categorized as either solitary or social. Examples of social organization patterns include solitary species, family groups, female kin groups, single-male groups, and multimale groups.

Definitions of mating systems use both the contributions made by the sexes to the gene pool and the breeding tactics of each sex. Mammalian mating systems can be most simply broken down into four categories: monogamous, polygynous, polyandrous, and promiscuous. The principal problem in defining these systems is identifying the extent to which males and females form bonds and the time period over which these bonds extend (Kleiman 1977; Wittenberger and Tilson 1980). The best definitions of mating systems rely on criteria related to genetic contributions (see Trivers 1972; Kleiman 1977; Emlen and Oring 1977), although data on copulation frequencies with different partners are often substituted when data on genetic contributions are lacking.

Solitary species are those in which animals are most frequently found by themselves. This is not to say that individuals never contact one another; obviously they must if reproduction occurs. But, relative to animals with other types of social organization, members of solitary species are alone most of the time. Ring-tailed cats, *Bassariscus astutus*, lesser mouse lemurs, *Microcebus murinus*, and giant pandas, *Ailuropoda melanoleuca*, are all considered solitary species.

Family groups are composed of one adult male, one adult female, and their offspring from one or more litters. The golden lion tamarin, *Leontopithecus rosalia*, is a species with a typical family group social organization. Family groups can be further subdivided into (1) pairs or temporary families, (2) nuclear families, which may include subadults, and (3) extended families, which include related but nonbreeding adults (Kleiman 1980).

Female kin groups are associations of related females not defended by males. Usually, dispersal of males from their natal groups results in groups containing only females. Males live alone or in small bachelor groups and join the female kin groups only during the breeding season. Female kin groups tend to be established along matrilines. Individual females may be somewhat spatially clumped, as in elephants and several ungulates, such as bighorn sheep, *Ovis canadensis*, and American bison, *Bison bison*; or they may be more widely dispersed but still live in proximity to one another, as in several rodents, including Belding's ground squirrels, *Spermophilus beldingi*, and white-tailed prairie dogs, *Cynomys leucurus*.

Single-male groups consist of a single adult male, two or more adult females (who can be related or unrelated), and often their young. Examples of species with single-male groups include drills, *Mandrillus leucophaeus*, and mandrills, *Mandrillus sphinx* (Schaaf 1990). In Burchell's zebras, *Equus burchellii*, Przewalski's horses, *E. przewalskii*, and feral horses, *E. caballus* (Berger 1986; Stevens 1990), these groups are called bands; in hamadryas baboons, *Papio hamadryas*, they are troops (Kummer 1968); and in black-tailed prairie dogs, *Cynomys ludovicianus*, they are coteries (King 1955; Hoogland 1982). For some species, the term "harem" is used to refer to the females in single-male groups. Males of some species defend harems year-round, as in zebras, impalas, *Aepyceros melampus*, and gorillas, *Gorilla gorilla*. Males of other species defend harems only during the breeding season, as in red deer, *Cervus elaphus*, and elephant seals, *Mirounga* spp.; in this case the sexes are segregated throughout much of the year. In species with single-male groups, juvenile males leave their natal groups and often associate with other males in bachelor groups. Adult males not associating with females are functionally bachelors, as they rarely contribute to the breeding. Adult bachelors are either loosely associated with bachelor groups or live solitarily.

Multimale groups contain two or more breeding adults of both sexes and young. This classification has been used mostly for primates such as red colobus monkeys, *Procolobus badius*, and mantled howler monkeys, *Alouatta villosa* (Struhsaker 1975; Eisenberg 1981), but other taxa (e.g., rock hyraxes, *Procavia johnstoni*) could rightfully be included in this category. African lions, *Panthera leo*, dwarf mongooses, *Helogale parvula*, and banded mongooses, *Mungos mungo*, are additional examples, although their groupings are known as prides and packs respectively (Schaller 1972; Rood 1983, 1986, 1987).

Within these different social organizations the mating system can be monogamous, polygynous, polyandrous, or promiscuous. *Monogamy* occurs when each individual mates exclusively with a single individual from the opposite sex, presumably over a substantial portion of their lifetimes (Kleiman 1977). While monogamy is practically the rule in birds, in which males participate equally in parental care, it is rare among mammals, in which males participate very little (if at all) in parental care. Monogamy occurs in about 3% of mammals, and paternal care is most common in those species that mate monogamously (Kleiman and Malcolm 1981). Two basic types of monogamy have been described: *facultative* and *obligate* (Kleiman 1977). Facultative monogamy occurs where food resources are widely distributed. The sexes coexist on one territory, sometimes protecting a common resource (e.g., rufous elephant shrews, *Elephantulus rufescens*: Rathbun 1979). Species that are facultatively monogamous may vary in their degree of association with mates, and it is suspected that in the wild they may sometimes become polygynous (Malcolm 1985; Moehlman 1986). On the other hand, species characterized by obligate monogamy are those in which two parents typically are necessary for the successful rearing of young.

Males and females are often seen together, and far less social and ecological flexibility is presumed to occur than in facultatively monogamous species (Kleiman 1977; Eisenberg 1981). Canids such as coyotes, *Canis latrans*, and silver-backed jackals, *C. mesomelas*, are examples of species in which pup survivorship is improved when males share parental responsibilities (Moehlman 1983; Bekoff and Wells 1986).

Polygyny, in which males breed with more than one female during a single breeding season and often have no parental care responsibilities, characterizes the majority of mammalian species. Polygynous systems typically involve one male defending a group of females. In contrast is *polyandry*, in which females breed with more than one male, but some males mate with only one female (Thornhill and Alcock 1983). Only a few polyandrous mammal species exist (Kleiman 1977; Wittenberger and Tilson 1980; Eisenberg 1981). Large canids such as the Asiatic wild dog, *Cuon alpinus*, African wild dog, *Lycaon pictus*, and gray wolf, *Canis lupus*, show indications of polyandry (Moehlman 1986).

Promiscuity is characterized by the absence of any pair bond or long-term relationship between the male and the female. In general, promiscuous mating systems occur in species in which males and females come together only for mating. A common promiscuous system, seen in many desert and grassland rodent species, involves a single male occupying a large range and mating with any female in estrus with which he comes in contact. The male and female part shortly after mating.

A very specialized and unusual type of mating system is *lekking*. Leks are areas where males concentrate to attract and copulate with females. Males defend very small individual territories on the lek. Females derive no material benefits from visiting leks because they are rarely, if ever, situated at or adjacent to food sources (Wittenberger 1981; Bradbury and Gibson 1983). Lekking occurs among hammer-headed bats, *Hypsignathus monstrosus* (Bradbury 1977), and several African antelopes, including the Uganda kob, *Kobus kob*, lechwe, *K. leche*, and topi, *Damaliscus korrigum*; among the latter two species, up to 100 males may congregate at a lek (Buechner and Schloeth 1965; Gosling 1986).

Table 33.1 gives selected examples of species kept in captivity, showing their different types of mating systems and social organization.

ECOLOGY AND CONSTRAINTS ON SOCIAL ORGANIZATION

Patterns of mammalian social organization have evolved in concert with, and in response to, ecological conditions. It is widely accepted that social behavior evolves as an adaptation to maximize individual fitness in the face of two main types of ecological pressures: predation pressure and resource distribution (Wrangham and Rubenstein 1986; Alexander 1974). Using a comparative approach, classic studies of ungulates (Jarman 1974; Geist 1974) and primates (Crook and Gartlan 1966; Clutton-Brock 1974) have shown that social groupings in related species vary

TABLE 33.1. Representative Species of Different Orders Varying in Social Organization and Mating Systems

Species	Social Organization	Mating System	Species	Social Organization	Mating System
Marsupials			Ground hog	SS	PO?
Antechinus	SS	PA?	(*Marmota monax*)		
(*Antechinus stuartii*)			Grasshopper mouse	FG	M?
American possum	SS	PA?	(*Onychomys leucogaster*)		
(*Didelphis virginiana*)			Deer mouse	SS, FG	PO, M?
Leadbeater's possum	FG	M	(*Peromyscus maniculatus*)		
(*Gymnobelideus leadbeateri*)			Beaver	FG	M
Tasmanian barred bandicoot	SS	PO	(*Castor canadensis*)		
(*Perameles gunnii*)			Arctic ground squirrel	FK	PO
Sugar glider	FG	PO	(*Spermophilus parryii*)		
(*Petaurus breviceps*)			Columbian ground squirrel	FK	PO
Matschie's tree kangaroo	?	PR	(*Spermophilus columbianus*)		
(*Dendrolagus matschiei*)			Mara	FG	M
Red kangaroo	?	PR	(*Dolichotis* spp.)		
(*Macropus rufus*)			**Carnivores**		
Insectivores			African wild dog	MM	M
Solenodon	SS	M?	(*Lycaon pictus*)		
(*Solenodon paradoxus*)			Gray wolf	FG	M
Hedgehog	SS	M?	(*Canis lupus*)		
(*Atelerix albiventris*)			Bat-eared fox	FG, SS	M
Microgale	SS	M?	(*Otocyon megalotis*)		
(*Microgale dobsoni*)			Dwarf mongoose	FG, OM	M
Bats			(*Helogale parvula*)		
Hammerhead bat	OM	PO, L	Spotted hyena	MM	PO
(*Hypsignathus monstrosus*)			(*Crocuta crocuta*)		
Leaf-nosed bat	OM	PO	Ring-tailed cat	SS	?
(*Phyllostomus hastatus*)			(*Bassariscus astutus*)		
Red bat	SS	?	African lion	MM, OM	PO
(*Lasiurus borealis*)			(*Panthera leo*)		
Primates			Tiger	SS	PO
Common marmoset	FG	M	(*Panthera tigris*)		
(*Callithrix jacchus*)			Jaguar	SS	PO
Golden lion tamarin	FG	M	(*Panthera onca*)		
(*Leontopithecus rosalia*)			Cheetah	SS	PO
Titi monkey	FG	M	(*Acinonyx jubatus*)		
(*Callicebus moloch*)			Grizzly bear	SS	PO
Kloss's gibbon	FG	M	(*Ursus arctos*)		
(*Hylobates klossii*)			European polecat	SS	PR
Patas monkey	OM	PO	(*Mustela putorius*)		
(*Erythrocebus patas*)			**Ungulates**		
Gorilla	MM	PO	Dik-dik	FG	M
(*Gorilla gorilla*)			(*Madoqua kirkii*)		
Orangutan	SS	PO?	Klipspringer	FG	M
(*Pongo pygmaeus*)			(*Oreotragus oreotragus*)		
Ring-tailed lemur	MM	PO?	Nilgiri tahr	SE	PO
(*Lemur catta*)			(*Hemitragus hylocrius*)		
Yellow baboon	MM	PO	African buffalo	SE	PO
(*Papio cynocephalus*)			(*Syncerus caffer*)		
Crowned guenon	OM	PO	Red deer	SE	PO
(*Cercopithecus pogonias*)			(*Cervus elaphus*)		
Red colobus	MM	PO	Collared peccary	MM	PO?
(*Procolobus badius*)			(*Pecari tajacu*)		
Rodents			Guanaco	OM	PO
Hoary marmot	FG	M	(*Lama guanicoe*)		
(*Marmota caligata*)			Burchell's zebra	OM	PO
Yellow-bellied marmot	OM	PO	(*Equus burchellii*)		
(*Marmota flaviventris*)			Grevy's zebra	?	PO
			(*Equus grevyi*)		

Source: Adapted from Clutton-Brock and Harvey 1977; Collins, Busse, and Goodall 1984; Eisenberg 1981; Kleiman 1977; Michener 1983; Smuts et al. 1987; and Macdonald 1984.

Note: Abbreviations: SS, solitary species; OM, one-male groups; MM, multimale groups; FG, family groups; FK, female kin groups; SE, sexually segregated groups; L, leks; M, monogamy; ?, classification difficult; PO, polygyny; PA, polyandry; PR, promiscuous.

according to resource distribution and predator pressure. Long-term studies have demonstrated the intricate interaction of ecological, social, demographic, and developmental constraints on social systems (Clutton-Brock 1974; Dunbar 1984; Rubenstein and Wrangham 1986; Clutton-Brock 1988).

Predation Pressure and Resource Distribution

Mammalian species have evolved a number of strategies for avoiding predators. Hiding is a practical strategy for smaller species, especially those not living in large groups. Group living can also reduce predator pressure (Hamilton 1971). By living in a large group, an individual reduces the chances that it will be the one caught by a predator, that is, it takes advantage of the difference between being one of twenty versus one of two. Predator avoidance, however, is not the only factor responsible for social organization. The distribution of resources, particularly of food, water, and shelter, plays an equally important role. It is unlikely, for example, that large groups of animals will form if food sources are widely and unevenly distributed.

Jarman's (1974) classic study of ungulates illustrates these points. Species such as duikers, *Cephalophus* spp., that live in thick vegetation and forage on leaves and berries form monogamous pair-bonds and live on exclusive territories. In antelopes that live at the forest edge and in grassland, such as impalas and Thomson's gazelles, *Gazella thomsonii*, males defend territories with lush forage that attract herds of females. These territorial males defend the females inside their territories for as long as possible and mate with any females in estrus. In contrast, African buffalo, *Syncerus caffer*, eat grass and migrate on the open savanna. Buffalo live in large mixed-sex herds in which the males have formed a dominance hierarchy. The alpha males form "tending bonds" with females in estrus. Beta males mate only when two or more females are in estrus simultaneously.

Size and Morphology

Size and morphology also influence how a species responds to ecological pressures—how it maximizes nutrient intake and avoids predators. An insectivore such as the solenodon, *Solenodon* spp., and a comparably sized herbivore like the pika, *Ochotona princeps*, might both hone their activity patterns in response to potential predation or to maximize nutrient intake, but because the morphology and nutritional demands of the two species differ dramatically, we would not expect them to exhibit similar mating systems. Pikas are apparently monogamous (Smith and Ivins 1983), while solenodons appear to be polygynous (Eisenberg and Gould 1966). In primates, several trends emerge when body size, activity patterns, grouping, and foraging patterns are considered (Clutton-Brock and Harvey 1977). Nocturnal species tend to be smaller than diurnal ones, possibly because smaller species are likely to be better concealed from predators and because they may travel more effectively over smaller branches and twigs (Clutton-Brock and Harvey 1977). Also, folivores (mature-leaf specialists) have smaller home ranges, spend more time feeding, and cover less distance per day than frugivorous primates.

Referring again to Jarman's (1974) comparative study of ungulate social organization, size and morphology patterns were also evident. The smaller species, like the duikers and Kirk's dik-dik, *Madoqua kirkii*, live in thick vegetation, avoid predators by hiding, and have a monogamous mating system. The medium-sized impalas and gazelles defend territories, find safety in numbers while foraging, and have a polygynous mating system. The very largest bovids live in large migratory herds, thereby finding safety in numbers, and have a polygynous mating system based on male dominance hierarchies.

Competition for Mates

The spatial and temporal distribution of another resource, potential mates, also influences social organization and mating systems. In the 3% of mammal species that are monogamous, the sex ratio of breeding adults is 1:1, and the competition for mates is not as keen as it is in polygynous species, in which the sex ratio of breeding adults is skewed heavily toward females.

In the majority of mammal species, males have no parental care duties. A male's reproductive success is, therefore, directly related to the number of females he can inseminate, which, in turn, is related to the distribution of females. The distribution of females is determined by the distribution of food resources and predators. Emlen and Oring (1977) formalized a model of mating systems based on these ecological constraints. They proposed two distinct types of polygynous mating systems based on the degree to which either multiple mates or resources critical to gaining multiple mates are economically defensible: (1) resource defense polygyny, in which males defend resources essential to females, and (2) female defense polygyny, in which males directly defend females. When resources are so sparsely distributed that they are not defensible, males defend females directly instead.

Examples of resource defense polygyny in mammals include species in which males defend resources attractive to females and then defend the females attracted to those territories. This is the case for most of the bovids (Owen-Smith 1977; Spinage 1986). Two camelids, the vicuña, *Vicugna vicugna* (Franklin 1974), and the guanaco, *Lama guanicoe* (Franklin 1974), defend harems on their territories year-round, as do members of the order Hyracoidea (rock hyrax, *Procavia* spp., and bush hyrax, *Heterohyrax* spp.) (Hoeck, Klein, and Hoeck 1982). Another territorial harem holder is a sciurid, the yellow-bellied marmot, *Marmota flaviventris* (Downhower and Armitage 1971; Armitage 1986), which defends a territory containing the burrows of one or more females. In all these territorial harem-holding species, changes in the abundance and distribution of resources would affect not only spacing among females but also the number of females that a male's territory could support. Elephant seals and gray seals, *Halichoerus grypus*, patrol territories on beaches where females gather to give birth and then mate (Le Boeuf 1974). In elephant seals, male reproductive success is dependent upon the ability to accumulate fat reserves during the nonbreeding season to facilitate guarding a territory and fighting with other males.

Female defense polygyny, which can be seasonal or year-round, occurs when males defend females directly and do not defend territories. Single-male units may move about together to find resources. In red deer, males defend harems only during the rut. As with elephant seals, male reproductive success is dependent upon accumulating fat reserves so that males can concentrate their efforts on defending females during the rut. In contrast, males of some of the equids and primate species defend harems year-round. In feral horses and Burchell's zebras, males defend harems during both the breeding season and the nonbreeding season. The same holds true for some of the cercopithecine primates—the hamadryas baboon, *Papio hamadryas*, the gelada baboon, *Theropithecus gelada,* and the patas monkey, *Erythrocebus patas*— as well as for gorillas. Harem stability in these species is maintained by the male's behavior toward females and intruding males.

Promiscuous mating systems can occur in both solitary and social species. In elephants, males live solitarily while females live in large female kin groups. Females are in estrus for only a few days at a time, so the distribution of sexually receptive cows is constantly changing in space and time. Bulls travel long distances to monitor the reproductive status of the cows in their home ranges. When a male finds a receptive female, he must compete with other males for the mating opportunity. Males stay with a female kin group for a few days at the most (Moss 1975).

CAPITALIZING ON THE FLEXIBILITY OF SOCIAL ORGANIZATION: CONSIDERATIONS WHEN FORMING CAPTIVE SOCIAL GROUPS

Variability from year to year, or season to season, in resource abundance and distribution, as well as in demographic parameters like population density and age structure, can affect mammal social organization. One of the best early demonstrations that the distribution of food, acting in conjunction with population density, mediates shifts in social organization stems from Kinsey's (1971) experimental work on wood rats, *Neotoma fuscipes.* Wood rats shifted from a system in which males defended territories to a strict dominance hierarchy as density increased. Other analyses of spacing have also shown that males of some territorial species will abandon resource defense when food is above or below certain threshold levels (Lott 1984).

The distribution of food is probably the key ecological constraint on species classified as facultatively monogamous. These species may vary in their degree of association with mates, and it is suspected that in the wild they may sometimes become polygynous (Malcolm 1985; Moehlman 1986). Dik-diks, for example, are probably facultatively monogamous. Males are not known to contribute any direct parental care, but because the food source is evenly, but widely, dispersed, it is likely that it would not be economically feasible for a male to defend a territory large enough to accommodate two females. In captivity, where food sources are plentiful, more than one female has been placed with a single male with no deleterious effects (Kleiman 1980).

The same concept is applicable to orangutans, *Pongo pygmaeus,* another species socially constrained by the distribution of food (Maple 1980). Due to their large size and their need to consume large quantities of food, orangutans cover a large area each day while foraging. Their solitary social organization is probably attributable to the fact that it would be impossible for males to defend food resources or females given how widely dispersed the food is. In captivity, orangutans are commonly housed in single-male social units with great success. They appear to be quite social when food sources are abundant.

Changes in demographic parameters such as age structure and sex ratio can also act as important determinants of social organization. In pronghorns, *Antilocapra americana,* traditionally a territorial species in the enclosed 20,000-acre National Bison Range, the social organization shifted to one of harem defense after a catastrophic winter die-off of older males (Byers and Kitchen 1988). In feral horses, when the sex ratio of mature males to mature females was even or weighted toward males, many single-male bands became multimale bands (Stevens 1987) as males sought different strategies for acquiring harems.

The major ecological constraints on social organization in the wild—distribution of food resources, predation pressure, and distribution of potential mates—are all regulated in the captive situation. Adequate, if not plentiful, food resources are constantly and easily available. Predators and potential prey animals are not housed together. Depending upon the breeding priorities for a particular species, individual animals are given access to potential mates under controlled circumstances. Given this control, the manager of captive animals strives to create the most appropriate social environment for each species.

What Kind of Social Group Is Appropriate in Captivity?

For those species classified as solitary, individuals are normally held in separate enclosures. Males and females are allowed access to each other only when the females are sexually receptive. This is the case for many of the solitary carnivores. In the case of giant pandas, known to be a solitary species, the male and female at the National Zoo were kept in adjacent enclosures, and for a few hours each day the door between the enclosures was opened so that they could choose to be together or to remain in their respective enclosures. Of course, if breeding is not a priority, then males and females can be kept separately year-round. Many carnivores, including tigers and bears, can be kept together in groups of the same sex, and even in pairs when contraception is available.

For social species, the first step in determining the appropriate social grouping in captivity is to find out what the species' social organization is in the wild. The next step is to decide whether or not breeding is a priority. If breeding is not desired, then either contraception has to be considered, or males cannot be kept with females. In either case, Wemmer and Fleming (1975) suggest that when developing groups of unfamiliar individuals, it is best to begin with a single pair so that social relationships can be clearly established.

Consider first the situation in which breeding is a priority. Family groups can be started by pairing a male and a female and then letting their offspring remain with them. Female kin groups and single-male groups do not differ operationally very much from one another in captivity. For those species that naturally form female kin groups, there will often not be enough kin available to form such a group in captivity, and a group will most likely have to be formed with some unrelated females mixed in. Multimale groups are less common in captivity than they are in the wild, mostly due to the fact that these groups are normally very large and occupy a tremendous amount of space, which is difficult to emulate in zoos. In general, managers have found that related males are more tolerant of each other in multimale groups than are unrelated males. Furthermore, when breeding is a priority, multimale groups may be impractical because of the need to determine and regulate paternity. Despite the fact that technological advances now make it possible to determine paternity from blood and tissue samples, most managers want to ensure that only particular males have breeding opportunities.

In situations in which breeding is not desired, the alternatives are the same for social species as for solitary species: males and females must be housed separately, or, if they are housed together, contraception must be employed. The problem of extra males is prevalent among mammals in zoos. Additional males (that is, additional to the one male housed in a single-male unit) can often be kept in bachelor groups or housed individually; bachelor groups have been formed with ruffed lemurs, *Varecia variegata*, small-clawed otters, *Amblonyx cinereus*, dwarf mongooses, meerkats, *Suricata suricatta*, cheetahs, *Acinonyx jubatus*, and gerenuks, *Litocranius walleri*. However, bachelor groups are sometimes only temporary solutions. Bachelorhood is a common phenomenon in those mammal species in which young males disperse from their natal groups (which includes most mammal species). Until males are sexually and developmentally mature, they may spend time in bachelor groups. In the wild, adult males sometimes split off from bachelor groups. Extra adult males in captivity that are not compatible with bachelor groups must be housed alone.

The formation of leks in captivity for species that naturally form leks has not yet been attempted. It would undoubtedly require considerable space and would probably involve a fair amount of aggression between males, a risk that animal managers are usually reluctant to take.

CONCLUSIONS

In recent years great strides have been made in the study of mammal social organization and mating systems, as well as in the application of such studies to the management of captive species. Understanding the patterns of social organization and the ecological pressures that influence social organization and mating systems in the wild is essential to successful captive animal management.

The beauty of animal social organization is that it is sensitive to so many environmental and ecological factors; there are not, in general, any hard-and-fast rules for each species because of these intricate links with the social and physical environment. There are, however, patterns for each species. The challenge that lies ahead for animal managers is to stay abreast of studies in natural ecosystems so that they can make better decisions about managing the social and physical environments of the animals in their care.

REFERENCES

Alexander, R. D. 1974. The evolution of social behavior. *Annu. Rev. Ecol. Syst.* 5:325–83.

Armitage, K. B. 1986. Marmot polygyny revisited: Determinants of male and female reproductive strategies. In *Ecological aspects of social evolution,* ed. D. I. Rubenstein and R. W. Wrangham, 303–31. Princeton, N.J.: Princeton University Press.

Bekoff, M., and Wells, M. C. 1986. Social ecology and behavior of coyotes. *Adv. Stud. Behav.* 16:251–338.

Berger, J. 1986. *Wild horses of the Great Basin: Social competition and population size.* Chicago: University of Chicago Press.

Bertram, B. C. R. 1975. Social factors influencing reproduction in wild lions. *J. Zool.* (Lond.) 177:463–82.

Boggess, J. 1984. Infant killing and male reproductive strategies in langurs *(Presbytis entellus).* In *Infanticide: Comparative and evolutionary perspectives,* ed. G. Hausfater, and S. B. Hrdy, 283–310. New York: Aldine.

Bradbury, J. W. 1977. Lek mating behavior in the hammerhead bat. *Z. Tierpsychol.* 45:225–55.

Bradbury, J. W., and Gibson, R. M. 1983. Leks and mate choice. In *Mate choice,* ed. P. P. G. Bateson, 109–38. Cambridge: Cambridge University Press.

Brooks, R. J. 1984. Causes and consequences of infanticide in populations of rodents. In *Infanticide: Comparative and evolutionary perspectives,* ed. G. Hausfater and S. B. Hrdy, 331–48. New York: Aldine.

Brown, J. L., and Orians, G. H. 1970. Spacing patterns in mobile animals. *Annu. Rev. Ecol. Syst.* 1:239–62.

Buechner, H. K., and Schloeth, R. 1965. Ceremonial mating behavior in Uganda kob *(Adenota kob thomasi* Neumann). *Z. Tierpsychol.* 22:209–25.

Busher, P. E., and Jenkins, S. H. 1985. Behavioral patterns of a beaver family in California. *Biol. Behav.* 10:41–54.

Byers, J. A., and Kitchen, D. 1988. Mating system shift in pronghorn. *Behav. Ecol. Sociobiol.* 22:355–60.

Clutton-Brock, T. H. 1974. Primate social organization and ecology. *Nature* 250:539–42.

———, ed. 1988. *Reproductive success: Studies of individual variation in contrasting breeding systems.* Chicago and London: University of Chicago Press.

Clutton-Brock, T. H., and Harvey, P. H. 1977. Primate ecology and social organization. *J. Zool.* (Lond.) 183:1–39.

Collins, D. A., Busse, C. D., and Goodall, J. 1984. Infanticide in two populations of savannah baboons. In *Infanticide: Comparative and evolutionary perspectives,* ed. G. Hausfater and S. B. Hrdy, 193–216. New York: Aldine.

Crook, J. H., and Gartlan, J. S. 1966. Evolution of primate societies. *Nature* 210:1200–1203.

Downhower, J. F., and Armitage, K. B. 1971. The yellow-bellied marmot and the evolution of polygyny. *Am. Nat.* 105:355–70.

Dunbar, R. I. M. 1984. *Reproductive decisions.* Princeton, N.J.: Princeton University Press.

Eisenberg, J. F. 1966. The social organization of mammals. *Handb. Zool.,* Band 8, Lieferung 39:1–92.

———. 1981. *The mammalian radiations: An analysis of trends in evolution, adaptation, and behavior.* Chicago: University of Chicago Press.

Eisenberg, J. F., and Gould, E. 1966. The behavior of *Solenodon paradoxus* in captivity with comments on the behavior of other Insectivora. *Zoologica* 51:49–58.

Elwood, R. W., and Ostermeyer, M. C. 1984. Infanticide by male and female Mongolian gerbils: Ontogeny, causation, and function. In *Infanticide: Comparative and evolutionary perspectives,* ed. G. Hausfater and S. B. Hrdy, 367–86. New York: Aldine.

Emlen, S. T., and Oring, L. W. 1977. Ecology, sexual selection, and the evolution of mating systems. *Science* 197:215–23.

Estes, R. D., and Goddard, J. 1967. Prey selection and hunting behavior of the African wild dog. *J. Wildl. Mgmt.* 31:52–69.

Fisler, G. F. 1969. Mammalian organization systems. *Los Angeles Co. Mus. Publ.* 167:1–32.

Franklin, W. L. 1974. Camels and llamas. In *The encyclopedia of mammals,* ed. D. Macdonald, 512–15. New York: Facts on File Publications.

Geist, V. 1974. On the relationship of social evolution and ecology in ungulates. *Am. Zool.* 14:205–20.

Gosling, L. M. 1986. The evolution of the mating strategies in male antelopes. In *Ecological aspects of social evolution,* ed. D. I. Rubenstein and R. W. Wrangham, 244–81. Princeton, N.J.: Princeton University Press.

Gosling, L. M., and Petrie, M. 1981. The economics of social organization. In *Physiological ecology,* ed. C. R. Townsend and P. Calow, 315–45. Oxford: Blackwell.

Hamilton, W. D. 1971. Geometry for the selfish herd. *J. Theor. Biol.* 31:295–311.

Hausfater, G., and Hrdy, S. B., eds. 1984. *Infanticide: Comparative and evolutionary perspectives.* New York: Aldine.

Hoage, R. J. 1977. Parental care in *Leontopithecus rosalia:* Sex and age differences in carrying behavior and the role of prior experience. In *Biology and conservation of the Callitrichidae,* ed. D. G. Kleiman, 293–305. Washington, D.C.: Smithsonian Institution Press.

Hoeck, H. N., Klein, H., and Hoeck, P. 1982. Flexible social organization in hyrax. *Z. Tierpsychol.* 59:265–98.

Hoogland, J. L. 1982. Prairie dogs avoid extreme inbreeding. *Science* 215:1639–41.

———. 1985. Infanticide in prairie dogs: Lactating females kill offspring of close kin. *Science* 230:1037–40.

Huck, U. W. 1984. Infanticide and the evolution of pregnancy block in rodents. In *Infanticide: Comparative and evolutionary perspectives,* ed. G. Hausfater and S. B. Hrdy, 349–66. New York: Aldine.

Jantschke, F. 1973. On the breeding and rearing of bush dogs, *Speothos venaticus,* at Frankfurt Zoo. *Int. Zoo Yrbk.* 13:141–43.

Jarman, P. J. 1974. The social organization of antelope in relation to their ecology. *Behaviour* 58:215–67.

King, J. A. 1955. *Social behavior, social organization, and population dynamics in a black-tailed prairie dog town in the Black Hills of South Dakota.* Contrib. Lab. Vert. Biol., Univ. Michigan. Ann Arbor. 67:1–123.

Kinsey, K. P. 1971. Social organization in a laboratory colony of wood rats *(Neotoma fuscipes).* In *Behavior and environment,* ed. A. H. Esser, 40–46. New York: Plenum.

Kleiman, D. G. 1977. Monogamy in mammals. *Q. Rev. Biol.* 52:39–69.

———. 1980. The sociobiology of captive propagation. In *Conservation biology: An evolutionary-ecological perspective,* ed. M. E. Soulé and B. A. Wilcox, 243–61. Sunderland, Mass.: Sinauer Associates.

Kleiman, D. G., and Malcolm, J. R. 1981. The evolution of male parental investment in mammals. In *Parental care in mammals,* ed. D. J. Gubernick and P. H. Klopfer, 347–87. New York: Plenum.

Kummer, H. 1968. *Social behavior of Hamadryas baboons.* Chicago: University of Chicago Press.

Le Boeuf, B. J. 1974. Male-male competition and reproductive success in elephant seals. *Am. Zool.* 14:163–76.

Lott, D. F. 1984. Intraspecific variation in the social systems of wild vertebrates. *Behaviour* 88:266–325.

Macdonald, D. 1984. *The encyclopedia of mammals.* New York: Facts on File Publications.

Malcolm, J. R. 1985. Paternal care in canids. *Am. Zool.* 25:853–56.

Maple, T. L. 1980. *Orang-utan behavior.* New York: Van Nostrand.

Michener, G. R. 1983. Kin identification, matriarchies, and the evolution of sociality in ground-dwelling sciurids. In *Recent advances in the study of mammalian behavior,* ed. J. F. Eisenberg and D. G. Kleiman, 528–72. Special Publication no. 7. Lawrence, Kans.: American Society of Mammalogists.

Moehlman, P. D. 1983. Socioecology of silverbacked and golden jackals *(Canis mesomelas* and *C. aureus).* In *Recent advances in the study of mammalian behavior,* ed. J. F. Eisenberg and D. G. Kleiman, 423–53. Special Publication no. 7. Lawrence, Kans.: American Society of Mammalogists.

———. 1986. Ecology of cooperation in canids. In *Ecological aspects of social evolution,* ed. D. I. Rubenstein and R. W. Wrangham, 64–86. Princeton, N.J.: Princeton University Press.

Moss, C. 1975. *Portraits in the wild.* London: Hamish Hamilton Ltd.

Owen-Smith, N. 1977. On territoriality in ungulates and an evolutionary model. *Q. Rev. Biol.* 52:1–38.

Penzhorn, B. L. 1985. Reproductive characteristics of a free-ranging population of cape mountain zebras. *J. Reprod. Fertil.* 73:51–57.

Pereira, M. E. 1983. Abortion following the immigration of an adult male baboon *(Papio cynocephalus).* *Am. J. Primatol.* 4:93–98.

Polis, G. A., Myers, C. A., and Hess, W. R. 1984. A survey of intraspecific predation within the class Mammalia. *Mammal Rev.* 4:187–98.

Rathbun, G. B. 1979. The social structure and ecology of elephant-shrews. *Beih. zur Z. Tierpsychol.* 20:1–77.

Rood, J. P. 1983. The social system of the dwarf mongoose. In *Recent advances in the study of mammalian behavior,* eds. J. F. Eisenberg, and D. G. Kleiman, 454–88. Special Publication no. 7. Lawrence, Kans.: American Society of Mammalogists.

———. 1986. Ecology and social evolution in the mongooses. I *Ecological aspects of social evolution,* eds. D. I. Rubenstein and R. W. Wrangham, 131–52. Princeton, N.J.: Princeton University Press.

———. 1987. Dispersal and intergroup transfer in the dwarf mongoose. In *Mammalian dispersal patterns: The effects of social structure on population genetics,* eds. B. D. Chepko-Sade and Z. T. Halpin, 85–103. Chicago: University of Chicago Press.

Rubenstein, D. I., and Wrangham, R. W. 1986. Socioecology: Origins and trends. In *Ecological aspects of social evolution,* ed. D. I. Rubenstein and R. W. Wrangham, 3–17. Princeton, N.J.: Princeton University Press.

Schaaf, C. D. 1990. Status of the drill *(Mandrillus leucophaeus)* in captivity and in the wild. *AAZPA Regional Conference Proceedings,* 414–20. Wheeling, W.Va.: American Association of Zoological Parks and Aquariums.

Schaller, G. B. 1972. *The Serengeti lion.* Chicago: University of Chicago Press.

Shields, W. M. 1987. Dispersal and mating systems: Investigating their causal connections. In *Mammalian dispersal patterns: The effects of social structure on population genetics,* ed. B. D.

Chepko-Sade and Z. T. Halpin, 3–26. Chicago: University of Chicago Press.

Smith, A. T., and Ivins, B. L. 1983. Spatial relationships and social organization in adult pikas: A facultatively monogamous mammal. *Z. Tierpsychol.* 66:289–308.

Smuts, B. B., Cheney, D. L., Seyfarth, R. M., Wrangham, R. W., and Struhsaker, T. T., eds. 1987. *Primate societies.* Chicago: University of Chicago Press.

Spinage, C. A. 1986. *The natural history of antelopes.* New York: Facts on File Publications.

Stevens, E. F. 1987. Ecological and demographic influences on social behavior, harem stability, and male reproductive success in feral horses *(Equus caballus).* Ph.D. dissertation, University of North Carolina, Chapel Hill.

———. 1990. Instability of harems of feral horses in relation to season and presence of subordinate stallions. *Behaviour* 112 (3–4): 149–61.

Struhsaker, T. T. 1975. *The red colobus monkey.* Chicago: University of Chicago Press.

Thornhill, R., and Alcock, J. 1983. *The evolution of insect mating systems.* Cambridge, Mass.: Harvard University Press.

Trivers, R. L. 1972. Parental investment and sexual selection. In *Sexual selection and the descent of man, 1871–1971,* ed. B. G. Campbell, 136–79. Chicago: Aldine.

Wemmer, C., and Fleming, M. J. 1975. Management of meerkats in captivity. *Int. Zoo Yrbk.* 15:74–77.

Wilson, E. O. 1975. *Sociobiology: The new synthesis.* Cambridge, Mass.: Harvard University Press.

Wittenberger, J. F. 1981. *Animal social behavior.* Boston: Duxbury Press.

Wittenberger, J. F., and Tilson, R. L. 1980. The evolution of monogamy: Hypotheses and evidence. *Annu. Rev. Ecol. Syst.* 11: 197–232.

Wolfe, J. O. 1986. Infanticide in white-footed mice, *Peromyscus leucopus. Anim. Behav.* 34:568.

Wrangham, R. W., and Rubenstein, D. I. 1986. Social evolution in birds and mammals. In *Ecological aspects of social evolution,* ed. D. I. Rubenstein and R. W. Wrangham, 452–70. Princeton, N.J.: Princeton University Press.

34

Behavioral Development and Play

KATERINA V. THOMPSON

Young mammals undergo profound physical and behavioral transformations between birth and the attainment of sexual maturity, changing from infants highly dependent on their mothers for nourishment and protection to independently functioning adults capable of dispersal or integration into the social group. During this period of maternal dependence, young mammals are buffered from the demands of the adult world, and have the opportunity for protected growth and learning. These early experiences may greatly influence adult behavior and reproductive success. Current investigations of behavioral development clearly show that immature mammals, rather than being passive recipients of experiences that modify adult behavior, are active participants in the developmental process. Young mammals display an impressive array of behavioral strategies that appear to ensure their survival and maximize their success throughout all stages of development (Bekoff 1985; Galef 1981).

Mammalian behavioral development is typically subdivided into three major periods based on the degree of maternal dependence and physical maturity (Jolly 1972). Infancy encompasses the interval from birth until weaning, and represents the period of maximal dependence on the mother. Following weaning, young animals are termed juveniles. While nutritionally independent, juveniles are frequently still dependent on their mothers (or other members of the social group) for protection from predators, physical elements, and aggressive conspecifics. The final stage of development is adulthood, the period following the attainment of sexual maturity. During the transition from the juvenile period to adulthood, animals are termed subadults. This review focuses primarily on the behavior of infant and juvenile mammals, including the general course of behavioral development in mammals as well as specific strategies adapted to various social and ecological environments.

At the time of writing, Katerina Thompson was with the Department of Zoological Research, National Zoological Park, Washington, D.C.

THE PERIOD OF DEPENDENCE

Degree of Development at Birth
Mammals vary in the extent of their physical maturation at birth, ranging from extremely undeveloped, or altricial, to well-developed, or precocial. The attributes that characterize altricial and precocial young are listed in table 34.1. The extremes of altriciality and precociality are, of course, endpoints of a continuum, and the majority of mammalian species show intermediate degrees of development (see also Kirkwood and Mace, chap. 43, this volume). Altricial young are produced by marsupials, insectivores, many rodents, rabbits, and several carnivore families, including bears, giant pandas, *Ailuropoda melanoleuca*, and weasels. Precocial young are produced by ungulates, whales, hares, and hystricomorph rodents. The young of most primate and carnivore species are intermediate, and are referred to as semialtricial or semiprecocial, depending on which traits predominate.

Some groups of mammals exhibit deviations from this basic pattern. Monotremes do not give birth to live young, but rather lay eggs. The young, when hatched, are altricial (Nowak and Paradiso 1983; Griffiths 1968). Marsupials have an extremely short gestation period and give birth to tiny young that are little more than embryos. Although rudimentary in most respects, newborn marsupials possess remarkably well developed forelimbs that are capable of grasping the mother's fur. These uniquely structured limbs allow the neonate to make its way, unassisted, from the mother's reproductive tract to her pouch or teats, where it attaches to a nipple (Ewer 1968).

Early Development of Altricial Mammals
In placental mammals, early development of altricial infants primarily involves maturation of the sensory systems and development of motor coordination (Ferron 1981; Happold 1976; Rosenblatt 1976), and has been studied extensively in domestic species such as rats, *Rattus norvegicus*, dogs,

TABLE 34.1.   Characteristics of Altricial and Precocial Infant Mammals

Altricial	Precocial
Hairless or sparsely furred	Fully furred
Sensory systems undeveloped, eyes and ears closed	Functional sensory systems
Incapable of coordinated locomotion	Capable of coordinated locomotion
Unable to maintain a stable body temperature independently	Able to thermoregulate
Complete nutritional dependence on mother	Able to eat some solid food shortly after birth
Examples	Examples
Spectacled bear, *Tremarctos ornatus*	Brindled wildebeest, *Connochaetes taurinus*
Red kangaroo, *Macropus rufus*	Common zebra, *Equus burchellii*
Oriental small-clawed otter, *Amblonyx cinereus*	Patagonian cavy, *Dolichotis patagonum*

Canis familiaris, and cats, *Felis catus*. The infant's most critical tasks at this stage are initiating and sustaining sucking and maintaining contact with nestmates. Rosenblatt (1976) has surveyed the vast body of literature on early behavioral development in altricial mammals, and much of this discussion follows his review.

At birth, altricial infants are most sensitive to thermal and tactile stimuli, which are used to locate teats and maintain contact with the mother and littermates. Infants respond to any temperature change or loss of contact with nestmates by vocalizing, which stimulates parental attentiveness (mice, *Mus musculus*: Ehret and Berndecker 1986; pikas, *Ochotona princeps*: Whitworth 1984; rodents: DeGhett 1978), and by crawling in circles, which often enables them to locate nestmates. Heightened sensitivity to olfactory cues develops within days of birth, and the infants' responses to various situations become more specific. At this stage, infant rats learn to recognize the odor of their mother (Leon 1975), littermates (Hepper 1983), and the nest site (Carr, Marasco, and Landauer 1979).

The final stage of early development begins when the eyes open. This event typically coincides with hair growth and the ability to regulate body temperature. The infants then assume an active role in initiating suckling, since they can detect the mother at a distance and approach her to nurse (Walters and Parke 1965). Vision permits greatly increased mobility, exploration, and interaction with littermates. During this period infants become better coordinated and expand their behavioral repertoire. At this point, altricial infants have reached a state of maturity comparable to that of precocial mammals at birth.

Comparative studies have indicated that the timing of the development of motor skills and sensory systems is closely associated with the demands of the environment. Ferron (1981) investigated the rates of development in four species of squirrels and found that emergence from the nest was delayed in structurally complex habitats that required well-developed locomotor skills. Red squirrels, *Tamiasciurus hudsonicus*, which inhabit complex arboreal environments, showed slower physical and behavioral development than Columbian, *Spermophilus columbianus*, and golden-mantled ground squirrels, *S. lateralis*, which inhabit relatively simple terrestrial environments. Northern flying squirrels, *Glaucomys sabrinus*, had the most complex locomotor requirements and were the slowest-developing species.

Developmental landmarks for more than 400 mammalian species are tabulated in Brainard (1985) and Eisenberg (1981).

Proximity to Caregivers

Species differ in the spatial relationships that mothers and other caregivers maintain with the young. Some species maintain constant close contact with their offspring, while others leave offspring unattended for extended periods of time. Four basic groups of species can be identified: nesters, hiders, carriers, and followers.

Nesting species leave their young in a protected den or nest, returning at intervals to feed and care for them. For example, snow leopards, *Uncia uncia*, give birth to their young in rocky, fur-lined dens; the litter remains there for the first 3 months of life (Hemmer 1972). Pikas also isolate their litters in a nest, which the mother visits twice an hour for only a few minutes (Whitworth 1984).

Hiding is the predominant infant behavioral strategy among ungulates (Estes 1976). Like nesting, hiding involves intermittent mother-offspring contact, but differs from the behavior observed in nesting species in that the hiding site is chosen by the infant (Leuthold 1977; Lent 1974) rather than being prepared by the mother. It is not uncommon for hiders to choose a fresh hiding site after each bout of activity. For example, infant Kirk's dik-diks, *Madoqua kirkii*, remain in hiding for most of their first 10 to 20 days of life, lying nearly motionless in clumps of vegetation. Calves emerge from their hiding sites for brief periods to nurse in the early morning, at dusk, and during the night (Bowker 1977).

Species in the carrier group maintain constant physical contact with their infants during early development. Most primate species adopt the carrier strategy, with infants typically clinging to the fur of the mother's back, or in some species, the belly. In marmosets and tamarins, other family members assist in carrying (Mendoza and Mason 1986; Hoage 1977; Box 1975). Marsupial infants remain constantly attached to one of the mother's nipples during the first weeks or months following birth (Nowak and Paradiso 1983; Ewer 1968). The teat swells inside the infant's mouth to provide a firm attachment. In pouched marsupials, older young continue to ride in the pouch after they become mature enough to detach from the nipple, while in pouchless species, they cling to the mother's back. Other species that carry their young include sloths, giant anteaters, *Myrmecophaga tridactyla*, and some bats.

TABLE 34.2.   Developmental, Ecological, and Social Correlates of Nesting, Hiding, Carrying, and Following Behavioral Strategies

	Nesting	Hiding	Carrying	Following	References[a]
Degree of development at birth	Altricial	Precocial	Semiprecocial (e.g., primates) or highly altricial (e.g., marsupials)	Extremely precocial	1, 2, 3
Body size	Usually small, occasionally large	Small relative to followers	No obvious trend	Large	2, 4
Habitat	Terrestrial or arboreal	Terrestrial	Arboreal, flying, or terrestrial	Terrestrial or aquatic	1, 5
Availability of nesting or hiding sites	Present	Present	Absent	Absent	2, 6
Home range stability	Stable	Stable	Stable or nomadic	Nomadic	4
Litter size	Large	Usually one young	Usually one or two	Usually one	1, 7

[a] 1, Ewer 1968; 2, Lent 1974; 3, Nowak and Paradiso 1983; 4, Lundrigan, unpub.; 5, Jolly 1972; 6, Estes 1976; 7, Rosenblatt 1976.

In follower species, infants accompany their mothers throughout their daily activities. This strategy is exhibited by several ungulate species (Leuthold 1977; Lent 1974; Walther 1965) and many aquatic mammals (Ewer 1968). The wildebeest, *Connochaetes taurinus,* a typical follower, displays the ability to follow its mother as soon as it can walk, often within minutes of birth (Estes and Estes 1979). In captive Nile hippopotamuses, *Hippopotamus amphibius,* infants spend virtually 100% of their time within one body length of their mothers for the first several weeks of life (Ralls, Lundrigan, and Kranz 1987a).

Nesting, hiding, carrying, and following can be interpreted as strategies for protecting vulnerable newborns from predators and accidents. The specific strategy used depends on a variety of ecological and social factors, as well as the degree of precociality of the infant (table 34.2). Most species adopt one strategy, but some species show a mixture of strategies, or show different strategies during different periods of development. For example, in several marsupials, young remain in the pouch and are carried throughout early development. Once they have outgrown the pouch, they are left alone in a nest while the mother forages (Ewer 1968; Beach 1939). Several prosimians that carry their young most of the time display a combined strategy incorporating a behavior pattern similar to hiding. This strategy, known as "parking," involves leaving the infant clinging to a tree branch unattended while the mother forages (Pereira, Klepper, and Simons 1987; Charles-Dominique 1977; Lekagul and McNeely 1977).

The strategies also differ in the relative responsibility of mother and infant for regulating proximity. In nesting species, the timing and duration of contact periods are largely determined by the mother (pikas: Whitworth 1984; rodents: Priestnall 1983). In hider species, mothers determine the timing of contact periods, but the infants take the active role in determining the duration of reunion periods by wandering away from their mothers and searching for hiding sites (Ralls, Lundrigan, and Kranz 1987b; Lent 1974). Constant proximity in carriers is maintained largely by the infants, which cling to their mothers' fur (African yellow-winged bat, *Lavia frons:* Vaughan and Vaughan 1987; primates: Jolly 1972). If infants become detached before they have gained motor coordination, however, they are dependent on

their mothers to retrieve them (dusky titi monkey, *Callicebus moloch:* Mendoza and Mason 1986). Infant followers assume responsibility for maintaining contact with their mothers (harbor seals, *Phoca vitulina:* Renouf and Diemand 1984; ungulates: Lent 1974), but the mothers often encourage following by vocalizing or by postural signals such as tail wagging and head bobbing (Lent 1974).

The behavioral strategy adopted by a species largely determines the daily pattern of activity shown by infants. Since infants are highly vulnerable to predation, most activity occurs under the protective watch of adults. In species that have only intermittent contact, infants may show brief bursts of concentrated activity during periods when mother and offspring are reunited. The frequency of maternal contact also affects the distribution of nursing opportunities for the infant. The constant maternal contact provided by carrier and follower strategies allows greater flexibility and often results in more frequent suckling opportunities. Mouflon, *Ovis musimon,* which are followers, are reported to nurse every 10–15 minutes during early infancy (Pfeffer 1967). Similarly, infant chimpanzees, *Pan troglodytes,* which are carried, have been observed to nurse an average of 2.7 times per hour during the first month of life (Clark 1977). In contrast, hiding and nesting species can suck only during mother-offspring reunion periods, which may be brief and infrequent. Leuthold (1977) reviewed the early development of fourteen species of hider ungulates and noted that most had two to five sucking bouts per day. The most extreme pattern is shown by the tree shrews, nesting species in which the mother approaches the nest site only once every 48 hours to nurse the young (Martin 1968; Lekagul and McNeely 1977).

These behavioral differences appear to be associated with differences in lactation physiology. Species that nurse their young at infrequent intervals tend to produce milk that contains high concentrations of fat and the protein casein; species that nurse their young very frequently produce more dilute milk (Oftedal 1980). The pattern of maternal contact exhibited by a species thus provides clues to appropriate nonmaternal milk substitutes for infants that must be hand-reared.

Familiarity with a particular species' pattern of early behavioral development and parent-offspring proximity is essential to its successful management in captivity. Such familiarity allows the detection of deviations from the normal developmental pattern that may indicate problems. Followers that do not remain close to their mothers, carrier infants that are found separated from their parents, and nester adults that constantly carry young are all cause for concern. Knowledge of a species' early developmental history allows exhibit designers to provide the necessary environmental features so that normal developmental behaviors can be expressed. For example, hider ungulates that frequently change hiding sites need to have access to multiple potential hiding areas. Similarly, nesting species should be provided with a selection of appropriate nesting sites. Tree shrews, *Tupaia belangeri*, are among the many species that require multiple nesting sites. Females rest separately from their young, and if provided with fewer than two nest boxes, often kill their offspring (Martin 1968). Knowledge of interspecific differences in early development allows informed management decisions when temporary separation of mother and young becomes necessary for medical treatment, neonatal workups, or marking of the infant. In species with intermittent contact, the normal periods of mother-infant separation are an ideal time to gain access to the infants with a minimum of trauma. Separating infants from their mothers in constant contact species is necessarily more traumatic and disruptive.

Sucking

Sucking is a universal characteristic of mammals (Vaughan 1978), and all infant mammals are initially dependent on their mothers for nutritional support. Infants take an active role in the initiation and maintenance of sucking. Characteristic odors of the mother's teat area (rabbits, *Oryctolagus cuniculus*: Hudson and Distel 1985; rats: Teicher and Blass 1977, 1976; cats: Kovach and Kling 1967), as well as its warmth (domestic sheep: Billing and Vince 1987a, 1987b) and texture (Billing and Vince 1987a, 1987b; rabbits: Hudson and Distel 1985; cats: Rosenblatt 1971), are the primary cues used by infants to locate nipples. While sucking, infant mammals use a variety of tactics to stimulate milk delivery (reviewed by Ewer 1968, 1973). For example, infants of many species exhibit kneading, massaging of the mammary gland with their forepaws, while infant ungulates commonly engage in bunting, a forceful butting of the udder. Even in highly altricial species such as rats, infants can control the amount of milk received by modulating the vigor with which they suck (Hall and Williams 1983).

In several species, each infant within a litter sucks from a particular teat and maintains this preference throughout development. This phenomenon, known as a teat order, has been described for a wide variety of exotic animals, including African civets, *Civettictis civetta* (Ewer and Wemmer 1974), binturongs, *Arctictis binturong* (Schoknecht 1984), mountain lions, *Felis concolor* (Pfeifer 1980), snow leopards (McVittie 1978), and green acouchis, *Myoprocta acouchy* (Kleiman 1972). The function of teat orders is unknown; however, it has been suggested that they may minimize potentially harmful competition among littermates for teats (Ewer 1959, 1968). Intense sibling competition for

teats was indeed observed in captive binturongs (Schoknecht 1984) and resulted in physical injuries to the cubs. In order to prevent further injury, the cubs' nails were periodically trimmed.

THE DEVELOPMENT OF INDEPENDENCE

Increasing maturity of the infant brings about changes in the quality of the mother-young relationship and a general trend toward decreased proximity. In species in which constant proximity was the rule early in development, the infant begins to wander farther away from its mother, and the mother's attempts to limit the infant's forays decrease (ungulates: Ralls, Lundrigan, and Kranz 1987a; domestic horses: Crowell-Davis 1986; cotton-top tamarins, *Saguinus o. oedipus*: Cleveland and Snowdon 1984; baboons, *Papio anubis*: Nash 1978; yellow baboons, *Papio cynocephalus*: Altmann 1978; rhesus macaques, *Macaca mulatta*: Hinde and Spencer-Booth 1967). Infants of species with intermittent contact show an increased tendency to be active in the absence of the mother (white-tailed deer, *Odocoileus virginianus*: Nelson and Woolf 1987; pika: Whitworth 1984; roe deer, *Capreolus capreolus*: Espmark 1969). In both primates (Hauser and Fairbanks 1988; Altmann 1978; Nash 1978; Hinde 1977) and ungulates (Lickliter 1984; Espmark 1969) there is a gradual shift toward greater responsibility on the part of the infant for maintaining proximity.

Sex Differences in the Development of Independence

Male and female mammals typically differ in their adult social roles. In such species, sex differences in behavior often have their roots in the earliest interactions of mother and infant. These species typically show a matrilineal social organization: females remain throughout their lives in the groups in which they were born, while males emigrate at sexual maturity (Melnick and Pearl 1987). Table 34.3 summarizes sex differences in early development in social cercopithecine primates, in which this phenomenon has been most thoroughly documented. The trend is for mothers to behave in ways that promote early independence in their sons. In contrast, immature females engage in frequent and prolonged interactions with their mothers, other adult females, and younger infants. Social grooming among primates is often interpreted as a mechanism for building and strengthening bonds between group members (Dunbar 1980, 1984; Seyfarth and Cheney 1984; Seyfarth 1977); thus these frequent grooming bouts between immature female primates and other female group members may form the matrix upon which the social group is built and maintained.

Parent-Offspring Conflict

Conflict between mother and offspring during this period of growing independence is a normal and expected feature of behavioral development. This conflict arises because an offspring shares only half of its genes with each parent, and therefore its interests cannot be expected to coincide completely with those of its parents (Trivers 1974). Clashes between parent and offspring arise over the amount and du-

TABLE 34.3. Sex Differences in Behavioral Development of Selected Cercopithecine Primates

Sex difference	Species	References
Female infants spend more time in contact with their mothers than do male infants	Rhesus macaque, *Macaca mulatta* Pigtail macaque, *Macaca nemestrina* Kra macaque, *Macaca fascicularis* Vervet monkey, *Chlorocebus aethiops* Patas monkey, *Erythrocebus patas*	White and Hinde 1975 Jensen, Bobbitt, and Gordon 1968 Thommen 1982 Fairbanks and McGuire 1985 Loy and Loy 1987
Male infants assume a greater role in maintaining proximity with their mothers	Rhesus macaque, *Macaca mulatta* Japanese macaque, *Macaca fuscata*	Berman 1984 Glick et al. 1986
Mothers reject nursing attempts of sons more than those of daughters	Rhesus macaque, *Macaca mulatta* Kra macaque, *Macaca fascicularis* Pigtail macaque, *Macaca nemestrina*	Berman 1984; White and Hinde 1975 Thommen 1982 Jensen, Bobbitt, and Gordon 1968
Grooming interactions are more frequent between mothers and daughters than between mothers and sons	Patas monkey, *Erythrocebus patas* Vervet monkey, *Chlorocebus aethiops*	Loy and Loy 1987 Fairbanks and McGuire 1985
Grooming interactions are more frequent between female infants and unrelated adult female group members	Patas monkey, *Erythrocebus patas*	Loy and Loy 1987
Female immatures are more likely to behave maternally toward infants	Patas monkey, *Erythrocebus patas* Olive baboon, *Papio anubis* Yellow baboon, *Papio cynocephalus* Chacma baboon, *Papio ursinus*	Loy and Loy 1987 Hendy 1986 Hendy 1986 Cheney 1978; Seyfarth, Cheney, and Hinde 1978

ration of parental care, with parents attempting to limit the total care provided to any particular offspring so that they are better able to care for other offspring.

Conflict may be manifested in virtually all aspects of the mother-offspring relationship, including maintenance of proximity (yellow baboons: Altmann 1978), parental comforting of distressed infants (vervet monkeys, *Chlorocebus* (=*Cercopithecus*) *aethiops:* Hauser 1986), and access to the maternal pouch in marsupials (Ewer 1968). The most widely reported manifestation of parent-offspring conflict involves disputes over suckling and is often termed weaning conflict. Infants predictably "disagree" with their mothers about the duration and frequency of individual nursing bouts and the age at which weaning occurs.

As the infant grows, its demands for care tend to increase; however, its increasing self-sufficiency allows the parent to limit the amount of care provided. Therefore, the intensity of parent-offspring conflict tends to increase with time (Trivers 1974). The proportion of the infant's attempts to initiate suckling that are successful decreases as the infant ages in many species (cervids: Gauthier and Barrette 1985; vervet monkeys: Lee 1984; pika: Whitworth 1984; bighorn sheep, *Ovis canadensis:* Berger 1979b; chimpanzees: Clark 1977). Occasionally, this decrease in sucking success is accompanied by increased maternal aggression toward her offspring (pikas: Whitworth 1984; bighorn sheep: Berger 1979b; baboons: Nash 1978). Furthermore, as the infant ages, those sucking bouts that are successful are more likely to be terminated by the mother than by the infant (cervids: Espmark 1969; Gauthier and Barrette 1985; harbor seals: Renouf and Diemand 1984), suggesting that the infant is not being permitted to drink to satiety (Berger 1979b).

Parker and McNair (1979) predicted that infants should thwart their parents' attempts to limit care by exaggerating their need. Sable antelope calves, *Hippotragus niger,* for example, display a multitude of behavioral tactics apparently aimed at increasing sucking opportunities (pers. obs.). In early infancy, the calf grasps the teats directly to initiate sucking and nurses silently. As the mother begins to resist sucking attempts and terminates sucking bouts before the calf is satiated, the calf's strategy changes. Prior to grasping a teat, the calf may spend several seconds nuzzling its mother's side until she remains still and permits sucking. If the mother attempts to walk away, the calf moves in front of her to impede her forward motion, then resumes nuzzling her. During successful sucking bouts, the infant makes a high-pitched, whimpering vocalization. If the bout is terminated by the mother, the infant continues to vocalize and makes repeated attempts to reinitiate sucking. Young commonly revert to infantile behavior, implying helplessness, in order to gain additional parental care (Trivers 1985), and this may be the reason for the sable calf's whimpering vocalizations.

More extreme tactics are occasionally employed. Clark (1977) and Van Lawick-Goodall (1968) describe temper tantrums by infant chimpanzees whose sucking attempts were rebuffed. Trivers (1985) interprets such tantrums as a form of psychological manipulation, a threat by the infant to harm itself if the parent refuses to accede to its demands.

Weaning and the Transition to Adult Feeding

The transition to adult feeding is perhaps the most critical milestone in early mammalian development. In some species, weaning is abrupt and highly predictable. For example, hooded seal pups, *Cystophora cristata,* which show the shortest period of sucking known among mammals, are completely weaned at 3–5 days of age (Bowen, Oftedal, and Boness 1985). For the vast majority of species, however, weaning is a slow, gradual process characterized by decreasing milk intake and a corresponding increase in the consumption of solid food (African elephants, *Loxodonta africana:* Lee and Moss 1986; cervids: Gauthier and Barrette 1985; baboons: Rhine et al. 1985; Nash 1978).

Weaning is ultimately achieved through the efforts of both mother and young. Mothers may discourage sucking by adopting postures that make it difficult for the young to reach the nipples (tree shrews: Martin 1968), and often actively reject sucking attempts (vervet monkeys: Hauser and Fairbanks 1988; cervids: Gauthier and Barrette 1985; cotton-top tamarins: Cleveland and Snowdon 1984; baboons: Nash 1978). Additionally, mothers may promote independent feeding by bringing food items to the young (beavers, *Castor canadensis:* Patenaude 1983; golden lion tamarins, *Leontopithecus rosalia:* Hoage 1982; dholes, *Cuon alpinus:* Johnsingh 1982; cats: Leyhausen 1979). Young of some species contribute to the weaning process by decreasing their attempts to suck as they grow increasingly able to provide for themselves (Roberts, Thompson, and Cranford 1988). Maturing juveniles apparently reach a stage at which the mother's milk cannot supply enough energy to maintain their growth, and thus independently switch to alternative food sources (Galef 1981).

Most infants are capable of adequately feeding themselves long before the complete cessation of sucking. African elephant calves, for example, normally suck for about 5 years, but calves orphaned at only 2 years of age can survive on solid food alone (Lee and Moss 1986). Additionally, the timing of weaning appears to be sensitive to the availability of solid food in the environment (vervet monkeys: Lee 1984; bighorn sheep: Berger 1979b). In captivity, where food is plentiful, weaning may occur weeks or even months earlier than in free-ranging populations (Ewer 1973). For example, free-ranging musk oxen, *Ovibos moschatus,* may continue nursing for a year or more after birth (Tener 1965), but a hand-reared individual weaned itself at only 139 days of age (Banks 1978). Thus, the time at which infants first become nutritionally independent is difficult to pinpoint using behavioral indicators and often can be determined only through anecdotes or experimental means.

Making the transition from nursing to eating solid food is far more complex than simply substituting one type of food for another. The process can involve engaging in specialized behaviors that prepare the infant's digestive system for the digestion of solid food, learning to discriminate appropriate foods from potentially harmful ones, and developing complex food acquisition skills, such as hunting (see also Fernandes, chap. 35, this volume).

In herbivores, digestion of plant material depends on microorganisms living in the animal's gut. At birth, the digestive system is virtually devoid of these essential microorganisms (Eadie and Mann 1970), and young must inoculate themselves to enable their digestive systems to assimilate plant material. Behaviors that may serve this purpose include licking the lips and tongue of the mother, which could result in the transfer of microbes in the saliva (Hungate 1968), feeding on plants that have maternal saliva remaining on them (elephants: Eltringham 1982), and eating the feces of the mother or other adults (domestic horses, *Equus caballus:* Crowell-Davis and Houpt 1985; African elephants: Guy 1977). Koalas, *Phascolarctos cinereus*, have a specialized method for transferring digestive microbes from mother to offspring. At about 5 months of age, when the infant's teeth are beginning to erupt, the mother begins producing special fecal matter composed of partially digested plant matter from the cecum, the organ in which microbial digestion occurs. The infant koala receives feedings of this material at 2- to 3-day intervals for 1–6 weeks, after which it is capable of feeding independently (Thompson 1986; Martin and Lee 1984).

Preferences for particular food items may be acquired through observation and imitation of the mother (Provenzo and Balph 1987; Leuthold 1977). Moose calves, *Alces alces,* for example, develop food preferences by first feeding simultaneously with their mothers on a single plant. Later in development, calves feed on separate plants of the same species that their mother is eating before making the final transition to selecting forage independently (Edwards 1976). In species in which adults provision the young, preferences may be learned through food sharing. At 4–5 weeks of age, golden lion tamarins regularly touch, sniff, and taste food items being consumed by their carriers (Hoage 1982). Soon after this period of investigation, the infants begin to snatch food away from family members and consume it. Preferences for certain types of solid food may be well developed long before weaning occurs at 11–15 weeks.

Learning may play an even greater role in the development of adult feeding in carnivores. The domestic cat, a solitary hunter, learns hunting skills through maternal encouragement and supervision (Leyhausen 1979). Early in development, mother cats bring prey back to the den and allow their kittens to observe its consumption. Soon after, dead prey, and later live prey, is provided for the kittens to manipulate and eat. Prey that manage to evade the kittens are recaptured by the mother and returned to the kittens. After several weeks of exposure and practice, the kittens develop sufficient hunting skills to dispatch prey independently.

Cooperative hunters, such as the social canids, show a similar dependence on learning. Dhole pups are first given regurgitated food by adults. Later, the pups are brought to the sites of kills to feed. Shortly after weaning, the pups accompany the pack on hunts, but it may be several months before the pups actually assist in making a kill (Johnsingh 1982).

Parents, particularly the mother, often play prominent roles in the acquisition of feeding skills, and premature separation of infants from their family groups may have lasting detrimental effects. Even young that are no longer nursing may be dependent on their parents for acquiring food preferences and honing feeding skills critical to their future survival and well-being. Van Lawick-Goodall (1971) reported that a 5-year-old chimpanzee juvenile, orphaned 2 years before, showed deficits in termite foraging compared with his peers, suggesting that this important feeding skill is in part developed through mother-offspring interaction.

Premature separation of mother and infant may also result in aberrant feeding behaviors. Regurgitation and reingestion of food is widespread among captive gorillas, *Gorilla gorilla,* yet absent in the wild. Wild-caught and captive-born hand-reared gorillas show much higher rates of regurgitation and reingestion than captive-born mother-reared individuals, leading Gould and Bres (1986) to speculate that this abnormal behavior results from deficits in early social development.

Predatory species in particular may be permanently affected by a lack of experience with prey items in early development. Domestic kittens separated from their mothers at an early age and with no prior exposure to live prey often show a lack of ability or inclination to hunt live prey in adulthood (Ewer 1973; Leyhausen 1965). Similarly, there are anecdotes illustrating the extreme difficulty of encouraging normal hunting behavior in captive big cats returned to the wild (Adamson 1969, 1960). The obstacles faced by Adamson's lion, *Panthera leo,* and cheetah, *Acinonyx jubatus,* could be attributed to their having passed the age at which hunting skills were most easily learned (Ewer 1973).

Interaction with conspecifics is as important in captive populations as in free-ranging ones, since such interaction may allow the learning of feeding skills specific to the captive environment. If captive-born young must be hand-reared, prompt reintroduction to adult conspecifics may allow the development of normal feeding strategies. Providing a captive environment that allows the normal development of feeding skills is critically important when reintroduction to the wild is a goal. Animals deprived of early experience may never become fully competent at foraging in a natural setting.

PLAY

As the infant becomes less dependent on its mother, it begins to interact more frequently with littermates, peers, and other members of the social group. Among the most conspicuous social activities exhibited by young mammals at this stage is play. In addition to social play, two other forms of play that may sometimes occur in a social context are locomotor play and object play.

Play is nearly ubiquitous among mammals. In his comprehensive review of the natural history of animal play behavior, Fagen (1981) found descriptions of juvenile play in all mammalian orders except the relatively poorly studied flying lemurs (order Dermoptera), aardvarks (order Tubulidentata), and hyraxes (order Hyracoidea). Play appears to be especially frequent and elaborate in the primates, carnivores, ungulates, and rodents, and it is in these taxonomic groups that play has been most thoroughly studied.

Types of Play

Play is commonly subdivided into three basic categories: object, locomotor, and social (Fagen 1981). These categories are not entirely mutually exclusive, however, since object and locomotor play frequently occur in social contexts, and elements of all three types of play frequently occur within single play bouts.

Object play involves repetitive manipulation of things in the infant's environment, and can be quite remarkable in its diversity. Goodall (1986) listed sticks, stones, dry dung, small fruits, fruit-laden twigs, and strips of skin and hair from old kills as among the favored play objects of juvenile chimpanzees. These objects were carried, thrown on the ground, used for self-tickling, rubbed on the body, rolled on the ground, thrown hand to hand, and thrown in the air to be caught or retrieved.

Object play often incorporates behaviors used in foraging or in the handling and capture of live prey, although many of the more inventive manipulations have no obvious parallel in the adult behavioral repertoire. It may occur in social as well as solitary contexts, for example, when two or more infants vie for possession of an object. Additionally, the focus of object play may itself be another animal, as when a young predator toys with a live prey item, or a juvenile playfully manipulates the body parts of its parents.

Locomotor play is composed of vigorous body movements such as running, jumping, head tossing, and body twists (Wilson and Kleiman 1974). More spectacular locomotor behaviors, such as back flips performed by rhesus macaques (Symons 1978), whirling around in the air by mountain goat kids, *Oreamnos americanus* (Dane 1977), and breaching and surf riding by infant whales (Fagen 1981), vary with the species' morphology and ecology. In general, locomotor play bears a strong resemblance to the behaviors seen in predator evasion.

Social play differs from other types of play in that it is truly interactive. It involves two or more individuals, each of whose movements are oriented toward the other and whose responses are influenced by the other's actions. Common forms of social play include play fighting, which mimics serious fighting, and approach-withdrawal play, in which individuals take turns chasing and being chased. Social play may also include elements of reproductive behavior, such as mounting.

Ontogeny of Play Behavior

Play begins early in postnatal ontogeny, shortly after infants have developed locomotor skills adequate to perform playful movements (Fagen 1976). Primates are a notable exception to this trend, with several species showing playful manipulation of objects well before they are capable of coordinated locomotion. In general, solitary forms of play (object and locomotor play) precede social forms in ontogeny (squirrel monkeys, *Saimiri sciureus:* Baldwin 1969; Nilgiri langurs, *Trachypithecus (=Presbytis) johnii:* Poirier 1968, 1970; cats: West 1974; Cuvier's gazelle, *Gazella cuvieri:* Gomendio 1988).

There is a general trend toward increasing play complexity and more interactive play as the infant matures (Baldwin 1986). For example, in domestic cats, play first appears at 4 weeks of age in the form of single play behavior patterns performed in solitary contexts. Soon after, kittens begin to create sequences of play behaviors by stringing together several repetitions of a single behavior pattern. At 5 weeks of age, these behavior patterns begin to appear in social contexts, directed at other kittens, and play bouts often involve sequences of two or three different play behaviors. Finally, during the 6th week, kittens are able to perform complex sequences containing as many as eight different play behavior patterns (West 1974).

Although play frequency, complexity, and duration peak during infancy and the juvenile period, play often persists into adulthood. The vast majority of adult play is social play with infants and juveniles. In free-ranging rhesus macaques, for example, 75% of adult play bouts involved immature individuals younger than 3 years of age, while only 25% of bouts involved two adults (Breuggeman 1978). Adults typi-

TABLE 34.4.   Characteristics Distinguishing Social Play from Aggression in the American Black Bear, *Ursus americanus*

Features distinguishing play	Examples
Some agonistic behaviors are never exhibited during play.	Components of agonistic behavior that are absent from juvenile social play include jaw snapping, swatting the ground, aggressive vocalizations, and erection of the fur on the neck and back.
Some behaviors are exhibited exclusively in the context of play.	Components of juvenile social play that are absent from agonistic interactions include head butting, muzzle seizing, hind-leg clawing, and nipping.
Some behaviors may be performed with greater frequency in play.	Biting, licking, biting intention movements, and swiping with the pad of the foot are exhibited significantly more frequently in juvenile social play than in agonistic interactions of similar duration.
Play may be less predictable and more variable.	Biting, clawing, and mounting are more variable in orientation and directed at more target areas in social play than in agonism.
Behaviors from different contexts may be interspersed during single play bouts.	Mounting, a component of adult sexual behavior, is incorporated into sequences of juvenile social play almost ten times as frequently as it appears during adult agonistic interactions.

Source: Henry and Herrero 1974.

cally do not play indiscriminately with all immatures, but rather favor playing with their offspring and younger siblings. Feral horse stallions show a remarkable ability to discriminate between their own offspring and unrelated foals, playing with their sons six times more than with unrelated, similarly aged male foals (Berger 1986). Parent-offspring play has been reported for a wide variety of taxonomic groups, including marsupials (Croft 1981; Kaufman 1975; Herrmann 1971), primates (Breuggeman 1978; Maple and Zucker 1978; Zucker, Mitchell, and Maple 1978; Sussman 1977; Hrdy 1976; Van Lawick-Goodall 1968, 1967), rodents (Wilson and Kleiman 1974), ungulates (Fagen 1981; Espmark 1971; Mohr 1968; Walther 1962), and carnivores (Kleiman and Malcolm 1981). In species that bear singleton offspring, adults rather than peers may be the primary play partners (euros, *Macropus robustus*: Croft 1981; lemurs, *Lemur* spp.: Sussman 1977; whiptail wallabies, *Macropus parryi*: Kaufmann 1975; orangutans, *Pongo pygmaeus*: MacKinnon 1974; eastern gray kangaroo, *Macropus giganteus*: Herrmann 1971).

General Characteristics of Juvenile Play

Theorists have had great difficulty formulating a comprehensive definition of play behavior because it is so diverse and so closely resembles other types of behavior, such as aggressive combat, prey catching, and predator avoidance (Martin and Caro 1985; Fagen 1981). Martin and Caro (1985), after reviewing various definitions of play, concluded that play is best characterized by the *absence* of the endpoints in which "serious" versions of the behavior patterns culminate. For example, play fighting does not result in injury or differential access to a disputed resource; likewise, predatory play does not involve killing and consuming prey.

Several additional characteristics seem to differentiate play behavior from its serious equivalents. The sequence in which behavioral components occur may be reordered (Loizos 1966) or less predictable (canids: Bekoff 1974). Play

bouts commonly incorporate behaviors usually seen in various unrelated contexts. For example, in the degu, *Octodon degus,* and the choz-choz, *Octodontomys gliroides,* two South American rodent species, elements of fighting behavior are interspersed with jumping and running, behaviors otherwise used in predator avoidance (Wilson and Kleiman 1974). Certain behaviors may be exhibited more frequently in play (American black bears, *Ursus americanus:* Henry and Herrero 1974; Loizos 1966), while others are always absent. Additionally, during play bouts, animals are more likely to alternate dominant and submissive roles than in serious fighting (squirrel monkeys: Biben 1986; baboons: Owens 1975a). Characteristics distinguishing social play from serious fighting in the American black bear are shown in table 34.4.

Possible Functions of Juvenile Play

There has been much speculation about the precise benefits young animals receive from play, but research in this area has been sparse, and the function of play remains obscure. Baldwin (1986), in his review of primate play behavior, was able to identify no fewer than thirty-two different proposed benefits of play, ranging from optimizing physiological development (Brownlee 1954) to promoting normal personality development (Harlow and Harlow 1969). Martin and Caro (1985), Fagen (1981), and Smith (1982) provide excellent reviews of the various proposed functions of play and the evidence supporting and refuting them.

Play has not lent itself to straightforward scientific investigation. The very nature of play, intermixing behavior patterns from widely divergent contexts, makes its purpose difficult to decipher. The physical appearance of play and the context in which it occurs provide few clues as to how it might improve a youngster's ability to survive or reproduce. Furthermore, researchers have found it impossible to deprive juveniles of play experimentally without simultaneously altering many other aspects of their social behavior. The behavioral deficits exhibited by animals in such play

TABLE 34.5.   Play Signals Exhibited by a Representative Sample of Species

Behavior	Species	Reference
Vocalization	Squirrel monkey, *Saimiri sciureus*	Biben and Symmes 1986
		Winter, Ploog, and Latta 1966
	Hamadryas baboon, *Papio hamadryas*	Leresche 1976
	Cotton-top tamarin, *Saguinus oedipus*	Goedeking 1985
	Vervet monkey, *Chlorocebus aethiops*	Struhsaker 1967
	Chimpanzee, *Pan troglodytes*	Van Lawick-Goodall 1968
	Gorilla, *Gorilla gorilla*	Schaller 1963
	Baboon, *Papio anubis*	Owens 1975b
	Degu, *Octodon degus*	Wilson 1982
	Dwarf mongoose, *Helogale parvula*	Rasa 1984
Play face	Mouse lemur, *Microcebus coquereli*	Pages 1983
	Tarsier, *Tarsius bancanus*	Niemitz 1974
	Common marmoset, *Callithrix jacchus*	Stevenson and Poole 1982
	Hamadryas baboon, *Papio hamadryas*	Leresche 1976
	Chimpanzee, *Pan troglodytes*	Hayaki 1985
	Japanese macaque, *Macaca fuscata*	Koyama 1985
	Rhesus macaque, *Macaca mulatta*	Symons 1978
	Yellow-bellied marmot, *Marmota flaviventris*	Jamieson and Armitage 1987
	Black bear, *Ursus americanus*	Henry and Herrero 1974
	African lion, *Panthera leo*	Schaller 1963
	Polecat, *Mustela putorius*	Poole 1978
	Collared peccary, *Pecari tajacu*	Byers 1985
	Tiger quoll, *Dasyurus maculatus*	Fagen 1981
	Choz choz, *Octodontomys gliroides*	Fagen 1981
Crescent or flattened ears	Black bear, *Ursus americanus*	Henry and Herrero 1974
Tail up	Reedbuck, *Redunca arundinum*	Jungius 1971
Gambol, stagger	Rhesus macaque, *Macaca mulatta*	Symons 1978
Odors	Short-tailed vole, *Microtus agrestis*	Wilson 1973

deprivation experiments cannot be attributed simply to the lack of opportunity to play (Bekoff 1976).

In his review of ungulate play, Byers (1984) evaluated the possible functions of play based on differences and similarities among species. Locomotor movements were common to all species and were the only form of play exhibited by some, leading Byers to suggest that play in ungulates, and perhaps other mammals as well, evolved to promote optimal physiological development. As competition among males for mates became more common, social play developed as practice for adult combat. Byers further suggested that in some species, such as the collared peccary, *Pecari (= Tayassu) tajacu*, play has assumed an additional function of maintaining group cohesion. Other species, experiencing different evolutionary selection pressures, may have developed different secondary functions for play behavior.

The form and content of juvenile play have undoubtedly been shaped by many factors that vary from species to species. It is probable that no single hypothesis will explain all types of play, and each function may not be of equal importance to all species. In spite of a recent surge of interest in play behavior, there is not a single species for which the function of play has been unambiguously determined.

Play Signals and Solicitation Behaviors
Play is frequently accompanied by the presence of play signals, communicatory behaviors that occur virtually exclusively in the context of play. These signals, typically vocalizations or facial expressions, may be displayed almost continuously throughout play bouts, and, because of their specificity, are useful indicators of the playful nature of social interactions.

Examples of behaviors from a variety of sensory modalities that have been identified as play signals are given in table 34.5. The play face (figure 34.1), characterized by a relaxed, open-mouthed expression with the lips usually covering the teeth, appears to be an almost universal mammalian play signal. Other play signals, such as play vocalizations, tend to be more species-specific. For example, degus "gurgle" during social play (Wilson 1982; Wilson and

FIG. 34.1.   Two striped hyenas, *Hyaena hyaena*, exhibiting play faces during a play bout. (Photo courtesy of Lee Miller.)

Kleiman 1974), while squirrel monkeys produce a high-pitched "peep" (Biben and Symmes 1986). In still other species, play is silent, and any vocalization emitted is an indication that play has become too rough and one of the participants is unwilling to continue the play bout (Fagen 1981). Olfactory play signals are probably more widespread than table 34.5 would suggest. It is likely that olfactory signals accompany visual and auditory indicators of play in species that depend heavily on chemical modes of communication.

In addition to play signals, certain specific behaviors, known as play solicitation behaviors, tend to be associated with the initiation of social play bouts. Representative play solicitation behaviors are given in table 34.6. While many patterns appear to be specific to certain taxonomic groups, others, denoted by asterisks in table 34.6, are common to a wide variety of mammalian species. Play solicitation behaviors appear to be of two major types: (1) locomotor movements such as head tossing, body rotation, rolling over, and bouncy gaits (termed locomotor-rotational movements by Wilson and Kleiman 1974), and (2) brief, sudden physical contact such as pouncing, nipping, nudging, and batting with the paws. Locomotor-rotational play movements are perhaps associated with the initiation of play bouts because they are unlikely to be confused with real aggressive communication signals. Play solicitations involving sudden physical contact may be more likely to be misinterpreted as actual aggression, and may therefore be restricted to play interactions among animals who are already familiar with each other.

Interspecific Differences in Play Content and Frequency

The form and content of juvenile play vary widely among species (fig. 34.2), and in general parallels the behavior and ecology of adults. Social play is structurally similar to adult fighting or sexual behavior (Fagen 1981). Examples of social play and serious aggression from three mammalian orders illustrate this point. In the punaré, *Thrichomys apereoides*, both aggression and play are characterized by upright sparring, in which the participants stand on their hind legs and push against each other's shoulders in an attempt to knock each other off balance (Thompson 1985). Escalated fighting in rhesus macaques consists of wrestling, grappling, and biting the opponent. Similar behaviors predominate in juvenile play, although bites are inhibited and inflict no damage (Symons 1978). In bighorn sheep, the principal components of both play and aggression are rearing and head butting (Berger 1979a).

Carnivorous species from a wide variety of taxonomic groups incorporate elements of predatory behavior into social play and play with objects. The lion, a carnivore, the tiger quoll, *Dasyurus maculatus*, a carnivorous marsupial, and the grasshopper mouse, *Onychomys leucogaster*, an insectivorous rodent, all show the predatory behavior pattern "pounce" as part of their play repertoire (Davies and Kemble 1983; Schaller 1972). Subtle differences among species in the structure of predatory play reflect differences in adult hunting strategies (Biben 1982a). The object play of the crab-eating fox, *Cerdocyon thous*, a solitary hunter, tends to be solitary in nature, with pups frequently attempting to monopolize objects and stealing them from littermates. In contrast, the play of the cooperatively hunting bush dog, *Speothos venaticus*, includes frequent bouts of noncompetitive group play with objects, in which several pups jointly carry sticks or stones. Biben (1982a) found a general trend among the carnivores for species that are solitary hunters to engage in solitary play with objects and for cooperative hunters that share food to participate more in group object play.

At the opposite end of the spectrum, play in species that are often the targets of predation is largely composed of locomotor behaviors that are prominent components of predator avoidance (reviewed by Byers 1984; Wilson and Kleiman 1974). Wilson and Kleiman (1974), in their broad comparative study of locomotor play, noted a general relationship between the level of predation risk and the frequency of locomotor play. In species in which predation risks were high, such as rodents and ungulates, locomotor play formed a significant portion of the entire play repertoire, while species having little predation pressure, such as seals, rarely exhibited locomotor play.

When differences in play frequency, as opposed to play content, among taxa are considered, the trends are less clear. Far too few quantitative studies of related species have been conducted to permit broad generalizations, and in most cases methodological differences among studies preclude direct comparisons. Even where detailed information exists, trends are ambiguous. Fagen (1981) reported a general tendency for juvenile social play frequency to be positively correlated with measures of sociality such as adult group size and adult tolerance of conspecifics. Groups that seem to show such an association include North American canids (Fox et al. 1976; Bekoff 1974), marmots (Barash 1976), and deer (Fagen 1981). This trend, however, may be simply a result of differences in the numbers of available playmates, rather than a reflection of a species' innate propensity to play (Fagen 1981). Even species that are solitary in nature, such as the orangutan, show high frequencies of play when play partners are available (Maple 1980; Zucker, Mitchell, and Maple 1978). Additionally, there are many taxonomic groups, such as the South American canids (Biben 1983), that show no relationship between play frequency and sociality. The relationship between play frequency and sociality remains obscure.

It has been suggested that aquatic species should show more frequent play than terrestrial species (Burghardt 1988, 1984). Since water is an energy-efficient medium in which to move, the vigorous motor patterns characteristic of play would require lower energy expenditures by aquatic species than by terrestrial ones. Play frequency data on comparable terrestrial and aquatic species are lacking, however. As Burghardt (1988) noted, many of the species commonly thought of as highly playful, such as the otter, *Lontra (=Lutra) canadensis*, are indeed aquatic.

Sex Differences in Play

There is a general trend among mammals for male juveniles to exhibit more social play than their female peers (Meaney, Stewart, and Beatty 1985). This trend appears to be correlated with the degree of sexual dimorphism in adult

TABLE 34.6. Representative Play Solicitation Behaviors

Species	Behavior patterns[a]	References
Primates		
Common marmoset	Pounce,* bat partner with hands,*	Stevenson and Poole 1982
Callithrix jacchus	stalk, bouncy approach*	
Squirrel monkey	Leap toward partner,* roll over,*	Biben 1986
Saimiri sciureus	swing from perch in front of partner	
Rhesus macaque	Transverse body rotation,* play	Symons 1978; Sade 1973
Macaca mulatta	bow,* crouch-stare, roll on back*	
Japanese macaque	Stare*	Koyama 1985
Macaca fuscata		
Chimpanzee	Stare,* play walk, sit facing away	Goodall 1986; Hayaki 1985
Pan troglodytes	from partner, finger wrestle	
Rodents		
Grasshopper mouse	Roll over on back*	Davies and Kemble 1983
Onychomys leucogaster		
Yellow-bellied marmot	Nose push,* somersault*	Jamieson and Armitage 1987
Marmota flaviventris		
Columbian ground squirrel	Jump,* nudge,* paw,* pounce*	Steiner 1971
Spermophilus columbianus		
Norway rat	Charge, pounce*	Poole and Fish 1975, 1976
Rattus norvegicus		
Choz choz	Head shake,* body twist*	Wilson and Kleiman 1974
Octodontomys gliroides		
Salt desert cavy	Head shake,* body twist*	Wilson and Kleiman 1974
Dolichotis salinicola		
Insectivores		
Hedgehog	Chase, rub against partner	Poduschka 1969
Erinaceus europaeus		
Carnivores		
European badger	Head sway*	Eibl-Eibesfeldt 1950
Meles meles		
Polecat	Pounce*	Poole 1966
Mustela putorius		
Domestic cat	Pounce,* play bow*	Martin 1984; West 1974
Felis catus		
Black bear	Rear, paw,* play bite,* head butt,	Henry and Herrero 1974
Ursus americanus	lunge	
Crab-eating raccoon	Twist body,* hop*	Lohmer 1976
Procyon cancrivorus		
African lion	Bouncy approach,* roll on back,*	Schaller 1972
Panthera leo	play bite,* nudge,* play bow*	
Wolf	Bouncy approach,* head toss,* paw	Bekoff 1972, 1974
Canis lupus	at face of partner,* play bow*	
Giant panda	Somersault*	Wilson and Kleiman 1974
Ailuropoda melanoleuca		
Odd-Toed Ungulates		
Tapir	Push with head*	Frädrich and Thenius 1972;
Tapirus indicus		Richter 1966
Square-lipped rhinoceros	Head toss,* prance*	Owen-Smith 1973, 1975
Ceratotherium simum		
Asian rhinoceros	Head toss*	Buechner et al. 1975
Rhinoceros unicornis		
Even-Toed Ungulates		
Bighorn sheep	Neck twist,* gambol,* heel kick	Berger 1980
Ovis canadensis		
Reedbuck	Head down*	Jungius 1971
Redunca arundinum		
Pygmy hippopotamus	Agitate water, lie on side, gape	Wilson and Kleiman 1974
Hexaprotodon liberiensis		
Cuvier's gazelle	Rotation of head and neck*	Gomendio 1988
Gazella cuvieri		

TABLE 34.6. *Continued*

Species	Behavior patterns[a]	References
Pinnipeds		
Stellar sea lion *Eumetopias jubatus*	Head toss,* nip*	Gentry 1974; Farentinos 1971
Harbor seal *Phoca vitulina*	Head-over-back	Wilson and Kleiman 1974
Marsupials		
Kowari *Dasycercus byrnei*	Grasp partner's head or body with forepaws	Meissner and Ganslosser 1985
Whiptail wallaby *Macropus parryi*	Paw at face of partner,* grasp partner's head	Kaufmann 1974
Sirenia		
Manatee *Trichechus manatus*	Roll on back,* rub up against partner	Hartman 1979

[a] Asterisk indicates play solicitation behaviors exhibited in a wide variety of mammalian taxonomic groups.

FIG. 34.2. Some examples of the diversity of mammalian social play. *(A)* A gray kangaroo joey, *Macropus giganteus*, sparring with its mother. (Photo courtesy of Lee Miller.) *(B)* Sable antelope calves, *Hippotragus niger*, neck wrestling. (Photo by Katerina Thompson.) *(C)* Young tiger quolls, *Dasyurus maculatus*, engaged in wrestling play. (Photograph courtesy of Lee Miller.)

aggressive behavior. Sex differences in juvenile play frequency are most common in species in which males must aggressively compete for mates and show much greater frequencies of aggression than females. In species in which frequencies of adult aggression are similar between the sexes, no sex differences have been detected in juvenile play. For example, play frequencies are equal for juvenile males and females in monogamous canids (Hill and Bekoff 1977; Bekoff 1974), monogamous primates (Stevenson and Poole 1982), solitary mustelids (Biben 1982b), and solitary felids (Barrett and Bateson 1978; Lindemann 1955). Sex differences in locomotor play are apparently uncommon. Most studies have found little difference between the sexes in locomotor play (e.g., gorillas: Brown 1988; bighorn sheep: Berger 1979a), but occasionally female juveniles exhibit more of this type of play (domestic horses: Crowell-Davis, Houpt, and Kane 1987; domestic sheep: Sachs and Harris 1978).

Where play is sexually dimorphic, differences are manifested in virtually all aspects of play, including frequency, content, ontogeny, and play partner preferences. Juvenile males of a wide variety of species have been reported to play more frequently than females (Meaney, Stewart, and Beatty 1985) and more roughly, using more play patterns involving physical contact (squirrel monkeys: Biben 1986; Siberian ibex, *Capra sibirica*: Byers 1980; rhesus macaques: Symons 1978; baboons: Owens 1975b). Males may exhibit social play earlier in ontogeny than their female siblings (punaré: Thompson 1985) and may continue playing later in development (cercopithecine primates: Bramblett and Coehlo 1987; Symons 1978). Juvenile males often seek out other juvenile males as play partners, presumably because they are more playful than females and provide opportunities to engage in more vigorous play (patas monkeys, *Erythrocebus patas*: Loy and Loy 1987; squirrel monkeys: Biben 1986; Siberian ibex: Byers 1980). Furthermore, male juveniles seem to seek out more varied play experiences, playing more often with adults (rhesus macaques: Breuggeman 1978) and unrelated individuals (Japanese macaques, *Macaca fuscata*: Koyama 1985).

Social and Environmental Factors Affecting Play

Social Factors. Group size influences play by affecting the number and proximity of potential playmates. Play is usually facilitated in large social groups since they are more likely to contain cohorts of similarly aged immature animals. Play is more frequent in large groups of squirrel monkeys than in small groups (Baldwin and Baldwin 1977, 1971). In bighorn sheep lambs, play becomes more complex with increasing group size (Berger 1979a). While increasing group size generally has a positive effect on play, overcrowding may have an inhibitory effect (cats: Leyhausen 1979).

The composition of the social group or peer group also influences juvenile play. The sex ratio of the litter or peer group may be an important factor, especially in species in which play is sexually dimorphic. For example, in the punaré, the age at which social play first appears in both male and female infants is correlated with the proportion of males in the litter: litters with more males begin to play at an earlier age (Thompson 1985). The play of domestic kittens is similarly affected by litter sex ratio, with female kittens from litters containing no males showing significantly less object play than those from mixed-sex litters (Bateson and Young 1979; Barrett and Bateson 1978). Play content may be similarly affected by cohort sex ratio. Female juveniles in cohorts containing many males may show rougher social play than females with fewer male playmates.

The particular individuals with which a juvenile initiates social play are determined by a multitude of factors, many of which have yet to be identified. Relatedness, age disparity, and dominance rank within the social group all influence a juvenile's opportunities to play and its choice of play partners. Kin generally are more likely to play together than are unrelated individuals (Japanese macaques: Glick et al. 1986; Koyama 1985; domestic pigs: Dobao, Rodriganez, and Silio 1984/85; Siberian ibex: Byers 1980; bighorn sheep: Berger 1979a). Play partners of similar ages are also strongly preferred (sable antelope: Thompson 1992; bighorn sheep: Berger 1980; Siberian ibex: Byers 1980; rhesus macaques: Breuggeman 1978;). In twin-bearing primates, play between twins, which are both closely related and identically aged, is by far the most common form of social play (Stevenson and Poole 1982; Izawa 1978; Vogt, Carlson, and Menzel 1978).

Species differ with respect to the sensitivity of social play to differences in social rank. In many primate species, offspring of high-ranking females play more often than offspring of low-ranking females (Breuggeman 1978; Cheney 1978; Gard and Meier 1977), although Symons (1978) reported that the daughter of the highest-ranking rhesus macaque in his study group seldom played and that her play solicitations were largely ignored by her peers. In coyotes, *Canis latrans*, dominance rank among pups is determined by fighting prior to the emergence of social play. Coyote pups in the middle of the dominance hierarchy play more and are more successful in soliciting play than are their high- and low-ranking siblings (Vincent and Bekoff 1978).

Environmental Factors. Food availability is known to have a profound effect on play. Baldwin and Baldwin (1973, 1974) reported that social play was virtually extinguished in a free-ranging population of squirrel monkeys during a period of extreme food scarcity. Subsequent laboratory investigations confirmed that play frequencies in this species were significantly depressed both by limited quantities and by decreased accessibility of food resources (Baldwin and Baldwin 1976). Similar effects have been documented in free-ranging rhesus macaques (Loy 1970), chacma baboons, *Papio ursinus* (Hall 1963), vervet monkeys (Lee 1984), and caribou, *Rangifer tarandus* (Müller-Schwarze and Müller-Schwarze 1982) and in captive rhesus macaques (Oakley and Reynolds 1976) and white-tailed deer (Müller-Schwarze, Stagge, and Müller-Schwarze 1982). Play also appears to be sensitive to the quality of the diet. In vervet monkeys inhabiting a seasonally fluctuating environment, play frequency was correlated with food quality: when the caloric content and the amount of protein in the diet declined, play decreased dramatically (Lee 1984).

Although play frequency is severely affected by food scarcity, this effect is only temporary. In fact, when the quality and quantity of food resources are restored to favorable levels, play rebounds, often reaching frequencies higher than exhibited prior to periods of food scarcity (vervet monkeys: Lee 1984; rhesus macaques: Oakley and Reynolds 1976). This finding suggests that juveniles may be able to compensate for brief periods of play deprivation by increasing subsequent play frequencies, in effect "making up for" lost play time.

Play is inhibited by extremes of temperature. In very cold weather, squirrel monkeys forgo play, preferring instead to bask in the sun (Baldwin 1967). Similarly, in domestic cattle, *Bos taurus*, play ceases when it is cold and wet (Brownlee 1954). Play also tends to decrease when it is very hot. An inverse relationship between the frequency of play and ambient temperature has been reported in domestic horse foals (Crowell-Davis, Houpt, and Kane 1987), northern elephant seals, *Mirounga angustirostris* (Rasa 1971), and rhesus macaques (Oakley and Reynolds 1976). Apparently, extremely cold weather causes juveniles to forgo play in order to conserve the energy needed to maintain a constant body temperature. Vigorous play in extremely hot weather may result in the production of more body heat than the juvenile can easily dissipate.

Play is often facilitated in habitats with certain specific features. Play in several species of ungulates is concentrated on grassy slopes, sandbowls, and snowfields (Berger 1980; Altmann 1956; Darling 1937). Collared peccaries play preferentially on well-worn, scent-marked "playgrounds" near bedding sites (Byers 1985), and play bouts occurring there involve more individuals and last longer than play bouts in other locations. Sandboxes, where a great deal of scent marking occurs, are the preferred sites for locomotor play in captive salt desert cavies, *Dolichotis salinicola* (Wilson and Kleiman 1974). The physical attributes that make these locations popular sites for play have yet to be identified, but perhaps they are places that are relatively safe from predation and where the risk of injury is low.

Play is sometimes inhibited in environments that present too great a risk of injury. Desert bighorn sheep frequently come into contact with the spines of the cholla cactus, *Opuntia* spp., no doubt a painful experience. Lambs in habitats where these cacti are plentiful show much lower rates of play than lambs in grassy habitats (Berger 1980, 1979a).

Not surprisingly, sick animals play less than healthy ones (Fagen 1981), and lack of play may be one of the first symptoms of illness. Gaughan (1983) reported the case of a captive snow leopard female who, in contrast to others studied, rarely played with her cubs. Her lack of play was noted by observers well before the appearance of more obvious signs of illness, such as lethargy and loss of appetite. Medical examination revealed the animal to be seriously ill. Heavy parasite infestation may similarly inhibit play (bighorn sheep: Bennett and Fewell 1987; elk, *Cervus (=canadensis) elaphus*: Altmann 1952).

Captivity. Captivity, which produces profound changes in an animal's immediate physical and social environment, often has significant effects on play. In general, play is more frequent in captive animals than in their free-ranging counterparts. For example, Stevenson and Poole (1982) observed common marmosets, *Callithrix jacchus*, in a free-ranging Brazilian population and in a laboratory colony, and noted that social play was much more frequent in captivity. The higher rates of play seen among captive animals are commonly attributed to unlimited food resources and the absence of predators (Shoemaker 1978).

Adult animals, in particular, seem to show more play in captivity (Fagen 1981). Fagen (1981) suggested that this might represent a reversion to a more infantile state, since in captivity virtually all of an animal's needs are provided for. Alternatively, he proposed that play in adult captives might provide a means of maintaining a healthy physical condition in an environment where opportunities for vigorous exercise are otherwise absent. Captive animals have no need to flee from danger and a reduced need to search actively for food; therefore play might be a captive animal's only means of staying fit and active.

Since play is sensitive to so many social and environmental factors, its presence or absence in captive individuals can be used as an index of the adequacy of the captive environment. Observations of far too little play have indeed been the impetus for reevaluation of the appropriateness of exhibit substrates, the quantity of shade, and herd parasite load in at least one zoo (Bennett and Fewell 1987).

It is desirable to provide captive animals with ample opportunities for play. Playing animals are highly visible to zoo visitors and are likely to hold a visitor's attention for a longer period of time. Also, several studies have shown that exhibit modifications that increase the amount of time captive animals spend playing often result in substantial decreases in abnormal behaviors (e.g., chimpanzees: Paquette and Prescott 1988). Play experience has further been shown to lessen the damaging effects of early social deprivation in rats (Potegal and Einon 1989; Einon, Morgan, and Kibbler 1978).

Some objects and exhibit modifications that promote play in captive animals are listed in table 34.7 (see also Maple and Perkins, chap. 21, this volume). The most important features of play objects are novelty and the ability to stimulate multiple senses (Kieber 1990; Paquette and Prescott 1988; Hutt 1967). Rotating play objects among different enclosures is a highly effective way of preserving their appeal (Kieber 1990; Paquette and Prescott 1988). If preserving the natural appearance of the exhibit is a primary objective, conspicuously man-made play objects can be restricted to off-exhibit areas (Kieber 1990).

The enigmatic nature of the function of play makes it extremely difficult to assess whether immature animals in captive environments are obtaining adequate amounts and types of play experience. Perhaps the most conservative approach to ensuring optimal juvenile development is to attempt to mimic natural social groupings and features of the native habitat such that opportunities for locomotor, object, and social play are as similar as possible to those of free-ranging animals. All captive immature animals should be provided with enough space to engage in vigorous locomotor play, a variety of objects to manipulate, and conspecifics, preferably of similar ages, with which to engage in social play. Allowing access to a wide range of play experiences may be the best way to ensure that captive animals do not suffer physiological and behavioral deficits as a result of their somewhat artificial upbringing.

CONCLUSIONS

Evidence exists that deficits in early development (most notably social development) have far-reaching and often permanent consequences. The best way to promote normal behavioral development is to allow infants to be mother-reared in a diverse and spacious physical environment and in a social environment that closely approximates that in the wild. When mother-rearing is not possible, other alternatives, in order of their desirability, are (1) using another lactating female as a foster mother, (2) hand-rearing the infant without removing it from the social group, and (3) hand-rearing the infant with conspecific peers. Hand-rearing infants in isolation should be considered a last resort, and the techniques of artificial rearing should be based on the normal developmental patterns of the species in question (Collier 1983). Understanding the natural course of development in each mammalian species is critical for ensuring that captive-born infants grow into competent adults.

TABLE 34.7.   Methods of Promoting Play Behavior in Captive Mammals

Taxonomic group	Exhibit modification or addition	Type of play promoted	References
Ungulates	Open space	Locomotor	
	Hills, sloped surfaces, rock piles	Locomotor and social	
Carnivores	Wooden balls, leather balls, sticks, stones, logs, tires, cardboard boxes, large paper bags, hanging rope, plasic jugs (with lids removed), rawhide bones, beef bones	Object	Kieber 1990; Biben 1982a; Hediger 1968
	PVC tubing	Locomotor	Biben 1982b
Rhinos and elephants	Planks, stumps, blocks of wood	Object	Hediger 1968
Aquatic mammals	Pieces of floating wood, blocks of ice with embedded fish	Object	Sanders 1987; Hediger 1968
Monkeys	Networks of branches with flexible attachment points, hanging milk crates, rope swings	Locomotor	Clark 1990; Hutchins, Hancocks, and Crockett 1978
	Nylon balls	Object	Renquist and Judge 1985
Great apes	Tire swings	Locomotor	Paquette and Prescott 1988
	Loose tires, burlap feed bags, heavy rubber feed tubs, heavy plastic drums (cut in half), straw or hay, branches, rubber balls	Object	Cole 1987; Goerke, Fleming, and Creel 1987; Cole and Ervine 1983; Sammarco 1981

REFERENCES

Adamson, J. 1960. *Born free*. London: Collins and Harvill Press.

———. 1969. *The spotted sphinx*. London: Collins and Harvill Press.

Altmann, J. 1978. Infant independence in yellow baboons. In *The development of behavior: Comparative and evolutionary aspects*, ed. G. M. Burghardt and M. Bekoff, 253–77. New York: Garland STPM Press.

Altmann, M. 1952. Social behavior of elk, *Cervus canadensis nelsoni*, in the Jackson Hole area of Wyoming. *Behaviour* 4:116–43.

———. 1956. Patterns of herd behavior in free-ranging elk of Wyoming. *Zoologica* 41:65–71.

Baldwin, J. D. 1967. A study of the social behavior of a semi-free-ranging colony of squirrel monkeys *(Saimiri sciureus)*. Ph.D. thesis, Johns Hopkins University.

———. 1969. The ontogeny of social behavior of squirrel monkeys *(Saimiri sciureus)* in a seminatural environment. *Folia Primatol.* 11:35–79.

———. 1986. Behavior in infancy: Exploration and play. In *Comparative primate biology*, vol. 2A: *Behavior, conservation, and ecology*, 295–326. New York: Alan R. Liss.

Baldwin, J. D., and Baldwin, J. I. 1971. Squirrel monkeys *(Saimiri sciureus)* in natural habitats in Panama, Colombia, Brazil, and Peru. *Primates* 12:45–61.

———. 1973. The role of play in social organization: Comparative observations on squirrel monkeys *(Saimiri)*. *Primates* 14:369–81.

———. 1974. Exploration and social play in squirrel monkeys *(Saimiri)*. *Am. Zool.* 14:303–15.

———. 1976. The effects of food ecology on social play: A laboratory simulation. *Z. Tierpsychol.* 40:1–14.

———. 1977. The role of learning phenomena in the ontogeny of exploration and play. In *Primate bio-social development*, ed. S. Chevalier-Skolnikoff and F. E. Poirier, 343–406. New York: Garland STPM Press.

Banks, D. R. 1978. Hand-rearing a musk-ox at Calgary Zoo. *Int. Zoo Yrbk.* 18:213–15.

Barash, D. P. 1976. Social behavior and individual differences in free living Alpine marmots *(Marmota marmota)*. *Anim. Behav.* 24:27–35.

Barrett, P., and Bateson, P. 1978. The development of play in cats. *Behaviour* 66:106–20.

Bateson, P., and Young, M. 1979. The influence of male kittens on the object play of their female siblings. *Behav. Neural Biol.* 27:374–78.

Beach, F. A. 1939. Maternal behavior of the pouchless marsupial *Marmosa cinerea*. *J. Mammal.* 20:315–22.

Bekoff, M. 1972. The development of social interaction, play, and metacommunication in mammals: An ethological perspective. *Q. Rev. Biol.* 47:412–34.

———. 1974. Social play and play soliciting by infant canids. *Am. Zool.* 14:323–40.

———. 1976. The social deprivation paradigm: Who's being deprived of what? *Dev. Psychobiol.* 9:497–98.

———. 1985. Evolutionary perspectives of behavioral development. *Z. Tierpsychol.* 69:166–67.

Bennett, B., and Fewell, J. H. 1987. Play frequencies in captive and free-ranging bighorn lambs *(Ovis canadensis canadensis)*. *Zoo Biol.* 6:237–41.

Berger, J. 1979a. Social ontogeny and behavioral diversity: Consequences for Bighorn sheep, *Ovis canadensis*, inhabiting desert and mountain environments. *J. Zool.* (Lond.) 188:251–66.

———. 1979b. Weaning conflict in desert and mountain bighorn sheep *(Ovis canadensis)*: An ecological interpretation. *Z. Tierpsychol.* 50:188–200.

———. 1980. The ecology, structure, and functions of social play in bighorn sheep. *J. Zool.* (Lond.) 192:531–42.

———. 1986. *Wild horses of the great basin*. Chicago: University of Chicago Press.

Berman, C. M. 1984. Variation in mother-infant relationships: Traditional and nontraditional factors. In *Female primates: Studies by women primatologists*, ed. M. F. Small, 17–36. New York: Alan R. Liss.

Biben, M. 1982a. Object play and social treatment of prey in bush dogs and crab eating foxes. *Behaviour* 79:201–11.

———. 1982b. Sex differences in the play of young ferrets. *Biol. Behav.* 7:303–8.

———. 1983. Comparative ontogeny of social behavior in three South American canids, the maned wolf, crab eating fox, and bush dog: Implications for sociality. *Anim. Behav.* 31:814–26.

———. 1986. Individual- and sex-related strategies of wrestling play in captive squirrel monkeys. *Ethology* 71:229–41.

Biben, M., and Symmes, D. 1986. Play vocalizations of squirrel monkeys *(Saimiri sciureus). Folia Primatol.* 46:173–82.

Billing, A. E., and Vince, M. A. 1987a. Teat-seeking behaviour in newborn lambs. I. Evidence for the influence of maternal skin temperature. *Appl. Anim. Behav. Sci.* 18:301–13.

———. 1987b. Teat-seeking behaviour in newborn lambs. II. Evidence for the influence of the dam's surface textures and degree of surface yield. *Appl. Anim. Behav. Sci.* 18:315–25.

Bowen, W. D., Oftedal, O. T., and Boness, D. J. 1985. Birth to weaning in four days: Remarkable growth in the hooded seal, *Cystophora cristata. Can. J. Zool.* 63:2841–46.

Bowker, M. H. 1977. Behavior of Kirk's dik-dik *(Madoqua kirki hindei)* in Kenya. Ph.D. thesis, Northern Arizona University.

Box, H. O. 1975. A social development study of young monkeys *(Callithrix jacchus)* within a captive family group. *Primates* 16:155–74.

Brainard, L. 1985. *Biological values for selected mammals.* Topeka, Kans.: American Association of Zoo Keepers.

Bramblett, C. A., and Coehlo, A. M. 1987. Development of social behavior in vervet monkeys, Syke's monkeys, and baboons. In *Comparative behavior of African monkeys,* ed. E. L. Zucker, 67–79. New York: Alan R. Liss.

Breuggeman, J. A. 1978. The function of adult play in free-ranging *Macaca mulatta.* In *Social play in primates,* ed. E. O. Smith, 169–92. New York: Academic Press.

Brown, S. G. 1988. Play behavior in lowland gorillas: Age differences, sex differences, and possible functions. *Primates* 29:219–28.

Brownlee, A. 1954. Play in domestic cattle: An analysis of its nature. *Br. Vet. J.* 110:48–68.

Buechner, H. K., Mackler, S. F., Stroman, H. R., and Xanten, W. A. 1975. Birth of an Indian rhinoceros, *Rhinoceros unicornis,* at the National Zoological Park, Washington. *Int. Zoo Yrbk.* 15:160–65.

Burghardt, G. M. 1984. On the origins of play. In *Play in animals and humans,* ed. P. K. Smith, 5–41. New York: Blackwell.

———. 1988. Precocity, play, and the ectotherm-endotherm transition: Profound reorganization or superficial adaptation? In *Handbook of behavioral neurobiology,* vol. 9, ed. E. M. Blass, 107–48. New York: Plenum.

Byers, J. A. 1980. Play partner preference in Siberian ibex, *Capra ibex siberica. Z. Tierpsychol.* 53:23–40.

———. 1984. Ungulate play behavior. In *Play in animals and humans,* ed. P. K. Smith, 43–65. New York: Blackwell.

———. 1985. Olfaction-related behavior in collared peccaries. *Z. Tierpsychol.* 70:201–10.

Carr, W. J., Marasco, E., and Landauer, M. R. 1979. Responses by rat pups to their own nest verses a strange conspecific nest. *Physiol. Behav.* 23:1149–51.

Chalmers, N. R. 1980. The ontogeny of play in feral olive baboons *(Papio anubis). Anim. Behav.* 28:570–95.

Charles-Dominique, P. 1977. *Ecology and behavior of nocturnal primates: Prosimians of equatorial West Africa.* New York: Columbia University Press.

Cheney, D. L. 1978. Play partners of immature baboons. *Anim. Behav.* 26:1038–50.

Clark, B. 1990. Environmental enrichment: An overview of theory and application for captive non-human primates. *Animal Keepers' Forum* 17:272–82.

Clark, C. B. 1977. A preliminary report on weaning among chimpanzees of the Gombe National Park, Tanzania. In *Primate biosocial development,* ed. S. Chevalier-Skolnikoff and F. E. Poirier, 235–60. New York: Garland.

Cleveland, J., and Snowdon, C. T. 1984. Social development during the first twenty weeks in the cotton-top tamarin *(Saguinus o. oedipus). Anim. Behav.* 32:432–44.

Cole, M. 1987. How we keep our gorillas occupied. *Animal Keepers' Forum* 14:401–3.

Cole, M., and Ervine, L. 1983. Maternal behavior and infant development of the lowland gorillas at Metro Toronto Zoo. *Animal Keepers' Forum* 10:387–91.

Collier, C. E. 1983. The distorted mirror: Avoiding abnormal behavior in hand reared mammals. *AAZPA Annual Conference Proceedings,* 233–34. Wheeling, W.Va.: American Association of Zoological Parks and Aquariums.

Croft, D. B. 1981. Social behaviour of the euro, *Macropus robustus,* in the Australian arid zone. *Aust. J. Wildl. Res.* 8:13–49.

Crowell-Davis, S. L. 1986. Spatial relations between mare and foals of the Welsh pony *(Equus caballus). Anim. Behav.* 34:1007–15.

Crowell-Davis, S. L., and Houpt, K. 1985. Coprophagy by foals: Effect of age and possible functions. *Equine Vet. J.* 17:17–19.

Crowell-Davis, S. L., Houpt, K. A., and Kane, L. 1987. Play development in Welsh pony *(Equus caballus)* foals. *Appl. Anim. Behav. Sci.* 18:119–31.

Dane, B. 1977. Mountain goat social behavior: Social structure and "play" behavior as affected by dominance. In *Proceedings of the First International Mountain Goat Symposium,* ed. W. M. Samuel and W. G. Macgregor, 92–106. British Columbia: Ministry of Recreation and Conservation.

Darling, F. F. 1937. *A herd of red deer.* London: Oxford University Press.

Davies, V. A., and Kemble, E. D. 1983. Social play and insect predation in northern grasshopper mice *(Onychomys leucogaster). Behav. Proc.* 8:197–204.

DeGhett, V. J. 1978. The ontogeny of ultrasound production in rodents. In *The development of behavior: Comparative and evolutionary aspects,* ed. G. M. Burghardt and M. Bekoff, 253–77. New York: Garland STPM Press.

Dobao, O. M. T., Rodriganez, J., and Silio, L. 1984/85. Choice of companions in social play in piglets. *Appl. Anim. Behav. Sci.* 13:259–66.

Dunbar, R. I. M. 1980. Determinants and evolutionary consequences of dominance among female gelada baboons. *Behav. Ecol. Sociobiol.* 7:253–65.

———. 1984. *Reproductive decisions: An economic analysis of gelada baboon social strategies.* Princeton, N.J.: Princeton University Press.

Eadie, M. J., and Mann, S. W. 1970. Development and instability of rumen microbial populations. In *Physiology of digestion and metabolism in the ruminant,* ed. A. T. Phillipson, 335–47. Newcastle-Upon-Tyne, England: Oriel Press.

Edwards, J. 1976. Learning to eat by following the mother in moose calves. *Am. Midland Nat.* 96:229–32.

Ehret, G., and Berndecker, C. 1986. Low-frequency sound communication by mouse pups *(Mus musculus):* Wriggling calls release maternal behaviour. *Anim. Behav.* 34:821–30.

Eibl-Eibesfeldt, I. 1950. On the ontogeny of behavior of a male badger *(Meles meles* L.) with particular reference to play behavior. *Z. Tierpsychol.* 7:345–51.

Einon, D. F., Morgan, M. J., and Kibbler, C. C. 1978. Brief periods of socialization and later behaviour in the rat. *Dev. Psychobiol.* 11:213–25.

Eisenberg, J. F. 1981. *The mammalian radiations: An analysis of trends in evolution, adaptation, and behavior.* Chicago: University of Chicago Press.

Eltringham, S. K. 1982. *Elephants.* Dorset, England: Blanford Press.

Espmark, Y. 1969. Mother-young relations and development of behavior in roe deer (*Capreolus capreolus* L.). *Viltrevy* 6:462–540.

———. 1971. Mother-young relationship and ontogeny of behavior in reindeer (*Rangifer tarandus,* L.). *Z. Tierpsychol.* 29:42–81.

Estes, R. D. 1976. The significance of breeding synchrony in the wildebeest. *E. Afr. Wildl. J.* 14:135–52.

Estes, R. D., and R. K. Estes. 1979. The birth and survival of wildebeest calves. *Z. Tierpsychol.* 50:45–95.

Ewer, R. F. 1959. Suckling behaviour in kittens. *Behaviour* 15:146–62.

———. 1968. *Ethology of mammals.* New York: Plenum.

———. 1973. *The carnivores.* Ithaca, N.Y.: Cornell University Press.

Ewer, R. F., and Wemmer, C. 1974. The behaviour in captivity of the African civet, *Civettictis civetta* (Schreber). *Z. Tierpsychol.* 34:359–94.

Fagen, R. 1976. Exercise, play, and physical training in animals. In *Perspectives in ethology,* ed. P. P. G. Bateson and P. H. Klopfer, 189–219. New York: Plenum.

———. 1981. *Animal play behavior.* New York: Oxford University Press.

Fairbanks, L. A., and McGuire, M. T. 1985. Relationships of vervet mothers with sons and daughters from one through three years of age. *Anim. Behav.* 33:40–50.

Farentinos, R. C. 1971. Some observations on the play behavior of the Stellar sea lion (*Eumetopias jubata*). *Z. Tierpsychol.* 28:428–38.

Ferron, J. 1981. Comparative ontogeny of behaviour in four species of squirrels (Sciuridae). *Z. Tierpsychol.* 55:192–216.

Fox, M. W., Halperin, S., Wise, A., and Kohn, E. 1976. Species and hybrid differences in frequencies of play and agonistic actions in canids. *Z. Tierpsychol.* 40:194–209.

Frädrich, H., and Thenius, E. 1972. Tapirs. In *B. Grzimek's animal life encyclopedia,* vol. 13, 17–33. New York: Van Nostrand Reinhold.

Galef, B. J. 1981. The ecology of weaning: Parasitism and the achievement of independence by altricial animals. In *Parental behavior in mammals,* ed. D. J. Gubernick and P. H. Klopfer, 211–41. New York: Plenum.

Gard, G. C., and Meier, G. W. 1977. Social and contextual factors of play behavior in sub-adult rhesus monkeys. *Primates* 18:367–77.

Gaughan, M. M. 1983. Play and infant development reflecting on mother-rearing in the captive snow leopard (*Panthera uncia*). *AAZPA Regional Conference Proceedings,* 589–98. Wheeling, W.Va.: American Association of Zoological Parks and Aquariums.

Gauthier, D., and Barrette, C. 1985. Suckling and weaning in captive white-tailed deer and fallow deer. *Behaviour* 94:128–49.

Gentry, R. L. 1974. The development of social behavior through play in the Stellar sea lion. *Am. Zool.* 14:391–403.

Glick, B. B., Eaton, G. G., Johnson, D. F., and Worlein, J. 1986. Development of partner preferences in Japanese macaques (*Macaca fuscata*): Effects of gender and kinship during the second year of life. *Int. J. Primatol.* 7:467–79.

Goedeking, P. 1985. Zur Kovariation von Lautstrukturvariabilitaten und sozialem Spiel bei Lisztaffen (*Saguinus oedipus oedipus*): Gesteuerte Lautanalysemethoden. Ph.D. thesis, Universität Bielefeld.

Goerke, B., Fleming, L., and Creel, M. 1987. Behavioral changes of a juvenile gorilla after a transfer to a more naturalistic environment. *Zoo Biol.* 8:283–95.

Gomendio, M. 1988. The development of different types of play in gazelles: Implications for the nature and functions of play. *Anim. Behav.* 36:825–36.

Goodall, J. 1986. *The chimpanzees of Gombe: Patterns of behavior.* Cambridge, Mass.: Belknap Press of Harvard University Press.

Gould, E., and Bres, M. 1986. Regurgitation and reingestion in captive gorillas: Description and intervention. *Zoo Biol.* 5:241–50.

Griffiths, M. 1968. *Echidnas.* Oxford: Pergamon Press.

Guy, P. R. 1977. Coprophagy in the African elephant (*Loxodonta africana* Blumenbach). *E. Afr. Wildl. J.* 15:174.

Hall, K. R. L. 1963. Variations in the ecology of the chacma baboon (*Papio ursinus*). *Symp. Zool. Soc. Lond.* 10:1–28.

Hall, W. G., and Williams, C. L. 1983. Suckling isn't always feeding, or is it? A search for developmental continuities. *Adv. Stud. Behav.* 13:219–54.

Happold, M. 1976. The ontogeny of social behaviour in four conilurine rodents (Muridae) of Australia. *Z. Tierpsychol.* 40:265–78.

Harlow, H. F., and Harlow, M. K. 1969. Effects of various mother-infant relationships on rhesus monkey behaviors. *Determinants of Infant Behavior* 4:15–36.

Hartman, D. 1979. *Ecology and behavior of the manatee* (Trichechus manatus) *in Florida.* Special Publication no. 5. Lawrence, Kans.: American Society of Mammalogists.

Hauser, M. D. 1986. Parent-offspring conflict: Care elicitation behaviour and the "cry-wolf" syndrome. In *Primate ontogeny, cognition, and social behaviour,* ed. J. G. Else and P. C. Lee, 193–203. Cambridge: Cambridge University Press.

Hauser, M. D., and Fairbanks, L. A. 1988. Mother-offspring conflict in vervet monkeys: Variation in response to ecological conditions. *Anim. Behav.* 36:802–13.

Hayaki, H. 1985. Social play of juvenile and adolescent chimpanzees in the Mahale Mountains National Park, Tanzania. *Primates* 26:343–60.

Hediger, H. 1968. *The psychology and behavior of animals in zoos and circuses.* New York: Dover.

Hemmer, H. 1972. *Uncia uncia. Mammal. Species* 20:1–5.

Hendy, H. 1986. Social interactions of free-ranging baboon infants. In *Primate ontogeny, cognition, and social behaviour,* ed. J. G. Else and P. C. Lee, 267–80. Cambridge: Cambridge University Press.

Henry, J. D., and Herrero, S. M. 1974. Social play in the American black bear. *Am. Zool.* 14:371–89.

Hepper, P. G. 1983. Sibling recognition in the rat. *Anim. Behav.* 31:1177–91.

Herrmann, D. 1971. Beobachtungen des Gruppenlebens ostaustralischer Graugrosskanguruhs, *Macropus giganteus* (Zimmerman, 1977) und Bennetkanguruhs, *Protemnodon rufogrisea* (Demarest, 1817). *Säugetierk. Mitt.* 19:352–62.

Hill, H. L., and Bekoff, M. 1977. The variability of some motor components of social play and agonistic behaviour in infant coyotes, *Canis latrans. Anim. Behav.* 25:907–9.

Hinde, R. A. 1977. Mother-infant separation and the nature of inter-individual relationships: Experiments with rhesus monkeys. *Proc. R. Soc. Lond.* B 196:29–50.

Hinde, R. A., and Spencer-Booth, Y. 1967. The behaviour of socially living rhesus monkeys in their first two and a half years. *Anim. Behav.* 15:183–200.

Hoage, R. J. 1977. Parental care in *Leontopithecus rosalia rosalia*:

Sex and age differences in carrying behavior and the role of prior experience. In *The biology and conservation of the Callitrichidae*, ed. D. G. Kleiman, 293–305. Washington, D.C.: Smithsonian Institution.

———. 1982. *Social and physical maturation in captive lion tamarins, Leontopithecus rosalia rosalia (Primates: Callitrichidae).* Smithsonian Contributions to Zoology, no. 354. Washington, D.C.: Smithsonian Institution Press.

Hrdy, S. B. 1976. Care and exploitation of nonhuman primate infants by conspecifics other than the mother. *Adv. Stud. Behav.* 6:101–58.

Hudson, R., and Distel, H. 1985. Nipple location by newborn rabbits: Behavioural evidence for pheromonal guidance. *Behaviour* 85:260–75.

Hungate, R. E. 1968. Ruminal fermentation. In *Handbook of physiology*, vol. 5, *Alimentary canal*, ed. C. F. Cade, 2725–45. Washington, D.C.: American Physiological Society.

Hutchins, M., Hancocks, D., and Crockett, C. 1978. Naturalistic solutions to the behavioral problems of captive animals. *AAZPA Annual Conference Proceedings*, 108–13. Wheeling, W.Va.: American Association of Zoological Parks and Aquariums.

Hutt, C. 1967. Temporal effects on response decrement and stimulus satiation in exploration. *Br. J. Psychol.* 58:365–73.

Izawa, K. 1978. A field study of the ecology and behavior of the black-mantle tamarin *(Saguinus nigricollis). Primates* 19:241–74.

Jamieson, S. H., and Armitage, K. B. 1987. Sex differences in the play behavior of yearling yellow-bellied marmots. *Ethology* 74:237–53.

Jensen, G. D., Bobbitt, R. A., and Gordon, B. N. 1968. Sex differences in development of independence of infant monkeys. *Behaviour* 30:1–14.

Johnsingh, A. J. T. 1982. Reproductive and social behaviour of the dhole, *Cuon alpinus* (Canidae). *J. Zool.* (Lond.) 198:443–63.

Jolly, A. 1972. *The evolution of primate behavior.* New York: Macmillan.

Jungius, H. 1971. *The biology and behavior of the reedbuck (Redunca arundinum Boddaert 1785) in the Kruger National Park.* Hamburg: Paul Parey.

Kaufmann, J. H. 1974. Social ethology of the whiptail wallaby, *Macropus parryi*, in northeastern New South Wales. *Anim. Behav.* 22:281–369.

———. 1975. Field observations of the social behaviour of the eastern grey kangaroo, *Macropus giganteus. Anim. Behav.* 23:214–21.

Kieber, C. 1990. Behavioral enrichment for felines in holding areas. *AAZPA Regional Conference Proceedings*, 585–89. Wheeling, W.Va.: American Association of Zoological Parks and Aquariums.

Kleiman, D. G. 1972. Maternal behavior of the green acouchi *(Myoprocta pratti)*, a South American caviomorph rodent. *Behaviour* 43:48–84.

Kleiman, D. G., and Malcolm, J. R. 1981. The evolution of male parental investment in mammals. In *Parental care in mammals*, ed. D. J. Gubernick and P. H. Klopfer, 347–87. New York: Plenum.

Kovach, J. K., and Kling, A. 1967. Mechanisms of neonate sucking behaviour in the kitten. *Anim. Behav.* 15:91–101.

Koyama, N. 1985. Playmate relationships among individuals of the Japanese monkey troop in Arashiyama. *Primates* 26:390–406.

Lawick-Goodall, J. Van. 1967. Mother-offspring relationships in free-ranging chimpanzees. In *Primate ethology*, ed. D. Morris, 287–346. Chicago: Aldine.

———. 1968. The behavior of free-living chimpanzees in the Gombe Stream Reserve. *Anim. Behav. Monogr.* 1:161–311.

———. 1971. *In the shadow of man.* Boston: Houghton Mifflin.

Lee, P. C. 1984. Ecological constraints on the social development of vervet monkeys. *Behaviour* 93:245–62.

Lee, P. C., and Moss, C. J. 1986. Early maternal investment in male and female elephant calves. *Behav. Ecol. Sociobiol.* 18:353–61.

Lekagul, B., and McNeely, J. A. 1977. *Mammals of Thailand.* Bangkok: Sahakarnbhat.

Lent, P. C. 1974. Mother-infant relationships in ungulates. In *The behavior of ungulates and its relation to management*, ed. V. Geist and F. Walther, 14–55. Morges, Switzerland: IUCN Publications.

Leon, M. 1975. Dietary control of maternal pheromone in the lactating rat. *Physiol. Behav.* 14:311–19.

Leresche, L. A. 1976. Dyadic play in hamadryas baboons. *Behaviour* 57:190–205.

Leuthold, W. 1977. *African ungulates: A comparative review of their ethology and behavioral ecology.* Berlin: Springer-Verlag.

Leyhausen, P. 1965. Über die Funktion der relativen Stimmungshierarchie (dangestellt am Beispiel der phylogenetischen und ontogenetischen Entwicklung des Beutefangs von Raubtieren). *Z. Tierpsychol.* 22:412–94.

———. 1979. *Cat behavior.* New York: Garland STPM Press.

Lickliter, R. E. 1984. Hiding behavior in domestic goat kids. *Appl. Anim. Behav. Sci.* 12:245–51.

Lindemann, W. 1955. Über die Jugendentwicklung beim Luchs *(Lynx l. lynx* Kerr) und bei der Wildkatze *(Felis s. sylvestris* Schreb.). *Behaviour* 8:1–45.

Lohmer, R. 1976. Zur Verhaltensontogenese bei *Procyon cancrivorus* (Procyonidae). *Z. Säugetierk.* 41:42–58.

Loizos, C. 1966. Play in mammals. *Symp. Zool. Soc. Lond.* 18:1–9.

Loy, J. 1970. Behavioral responses of free-ranging rhesus monkeys to food shortage. *Am. J. Phys. Anthropol.* 33:263–71.

Loy, K. M., and Loy, J. 1987. Sexual differences in early social development among captive patas monkeys. In *Comparative behavior of African monkeys*, ed. E. L. Zucker, 23–37. New York: Alan R. Liss.

MacKinnon, J. 1974. The behavior and ecology of wild orangutans *(Pongo pygmaeus). Anim. Behav.* 22:3–74.

Maple, T. 1980. *OrangUtan Behavior.* New York: Van Nostrand Reinhold.

Maple, T., and Zucker, E. L. 1978. Ethological studies of play behavior in captive great apes. In *Social play in primates*, ed. E. O. Smith, 113–42. New York: Academic Press.

Martin, P. 1984. The (four) whys and wherefores of play in cats: A review of functional, evolutionary, developmental, and causal issues. In *Play in animals and humans*, ed. P. K. Smith, 159–73. New York: Blackwell.

Martin, P., and Caro, T. M. 1985. On the functions of play and its role in behavioral development. *Adv. Stud. Behav.* 15:59–103.

Martin, R. D. 1968. Reproduction and ontogeny in tree shrews *(Tupaia belangeri)*, with reference to their general behaviour and taxonomic relationships. *Z. Tierpsychol.* 25:409–532.

Martin, R. W., and Lee, A. 1984. *Possums and gliders.* Chipping Norton, N.S.W., Australia: Surrey Beatty and Son.

McVittie, R. 1978. Nursing behaviour of snow leopard cubs. *Appl. Anim. Ethol.* 4:159–68.

Meaney, M. J., Stewart, J., and Beatty, W. W. 1985. Sex differences in social play: The socialization of sex roles. *Adv. Stud. Behav.* 15:1–58.

Meissner, K., and Ganslosser, U. 1985. Ontogeny of social behaviour of the kowari, *Dasyuroides byrnei* Spencer, 1896 (Marsupialia: Dasyuridae). I. A comparison of the behavioural repertoire of juvenile and adult kowaris. *Zool. Anz., Jena* 214:291–308.

Melnick, D. J., and Pearl, M. C. 1987. Cercopithecines in multimale groups: Genetic diversity and population structure. In *Pri-*

mate societies, ed. B. B. Smuts, D. L. Cheney, R. M. Seyfarth, R. W. Wrangham, and T. T. Struhsaker, 121–34. Chicago: University of Chicago Press.

Mendoza, S. P., and Mason, W. A. 1986. Parental division of labour and differentiation of attachments in a monogamous primate *(Callicebus moloch). Anim. Behav.* 34:1336–47.

Mohr, E. 1968. Spielbereitschaft bei Wisent. *Z. Säugetierk.* 33: 116–21.

Müller-Schwarze, D., and Müller-Schwarze, C. 1982. Play behaviour in free-ranging caribou *Rangifer tarandus. Acta Zoologica Fennica* 175:121–24.

Müller-Schwarze, D., Stagge, B., and Müller-Schwarze, C. 1982. Play behavior: Persistence, decrease, and energetic compensation during food shortage in deer fawns. *Science* 215:85–87.

Nash, L. T. 1978. The development of the mother-infant relationship in wild baboons *(Papio anubis). Anim. Behav.* 28:746–59.

Nelson, T. A., and Woolf, A. 1987. Mortality of white-tailed deer fawns in southern Illinois. *J. Wildl. Mgmt.* 51:326–29.

Niemitz, C. 1974. A contribution to the postnatal behavioral development of *Tarsius bancanus,* Horsfield, 1821, studied in two cases. *Folia Primatol.* 21:250–76.

Nowak, R. M., and Paradiso, J. L. 1983. *Walker's mammals of the world.* Baltimore: Johns Hopkins University Press.

Oakley, F. B., and Reynolds, P. C. 1976. Differing responses to social play deprivation in two species of macaque. In *The anthropological study of play: Problems and perspectives,* ed. D. F. Lancy and B. A. Tindall, 179–88. Cornwall, N.Y.: Leisure Press.

Oftedal, O. T. 1980. Milk composition and formula selection for hand-rearing young mammals. *Proceedings of the First Annual Dr. Scholl Nutrition Conference: A Conference on the Nutrition of Captive Wild Animals,* ed. E. R. Maschgan, M. E. Allen, and L. E. Fisher, 67–83. Chicago: Lincoln Park Zoological Gardens.

Owens, N. W. 1975a. A comparison of aggressive play and aggression in free living baboons, *Papio anubis. Anim. Behav.* 23: 757–65.

———. 1975b. Social play behavior in free-living baboons, *Papio anubis. Anim. Behav.* 23:387–408.

Owen-Smith, N. 1973. The behavioral ecology of the white rhinoceros. Ph.D. thesis, University of Wisconsin.

———. 1975. The social ethology of the white rhinoceros *Ceratotherium simum. Z. Tierpsychol.* 38:338–84.

Pages, E. 1983. Identification characterisation et role du jeu social chez un prosimien nocturne, *Microcebus coquereli. Biol. Behav.* 8:319–43.

Paquette, D., and Prescott, J. 1988. Use of novel objects to enhance environments of captive chimpanzees. *Zoo Biol.* 7:15–23.

Parker, G. A., and McNair, M. R. 1979. Models of parent-offspring conflict. IV. Suppression: Evolutionary retaliation by the parent. *Anim. Behav.* 27:1210–35.

Patenaude, F. 1983. Care of the young in a family of wild beavers, *Castor canadensis. Acta Zoologica Fennica* 174:121–22.

Pereira, M. E., Klepper, A., and Simons, E. L. 1987. Tactics of care for young infants by forest-living ruffed lemurs *(Varecia variegata variegata):* Ground nests, parking, and biparental guarding. *Am. J. Primatol.* 13:129–44.

Pfeffer, I. 1967. Le mouflon de Corse *(Ovis ammon musimon* Schreber 1782) position systematique ecologie et ethologie comparees. *Mammalia* (suppl.) 31:1–262.

Pfeifer, S. 1980. Role of the nursing order in social development of mountain lion kittens. *Dev. Psychobiol.* 13:47–53.

Poduschka, W. 1969. Erganzungen zum Wissen über *Erinaceus e. roumanicus* und kritische Uberlegungen zur bisherigen Literatur über europaische Igel. *Z. Tierpsychol.* 26:761–804.

Poirier, F. E. 1968. The Nilgiri langur *(Presbytis johnii)* mother-infant dyad. *Primates* 9:45–68.

———. 1970. Nilgiri langur ecology and social behavior. In *Primate behavior: Developments in field and laboratory research,* ed. L. A. Rosenblum, 251–383. New York: Academic Press.

Poole, T. B. 1966. Aggressive play in polecats. *Symp. Zool. Soc. Lond.* 18:23–44.

———. 1978. An analysis of social play in polecats (Mustelidae) with comments on the form and evolutionary history of the open mouth play face. *Anim. Behav.* 26:36–49.

Poole, T. B., and Fish, J. 1975. An investigation of playful behaviour in *Rattus norvegicus* and *Mus musculus. J. Zool. (Lond.)* 175:61–71.

———. 1976. An investigation of individual, age, and sex differences in the play of *Rattus norvegicus. J. Zool. (Lond.)* 179: 249–60.

Potegal, M., and Einon, D. 1989. Aggressive behaviors in adult rats deprived of playfighting experience as juveniles. *Dev. Psychobiol.* 22:159–72.

Priestnall, R. 1983. Postpartum changes in maternal behaviour. In *Parental behaviour of rodents,* ed. R. W. Elwood, 67–93. New York: John Wiley and Sons.

Provenzo, F. D., and Balph, D. F. 1987. Diet learning by domestic ruminants: Theory, evidence, and practical implications. *Appl. Anim. Behav. Sci.* 18:211–32.

Ralls, K., Lundrigan, B., and Kranz, K. 1987a. Mother-young relationships in captive ungulates: Behavioral changes over time. *Ethology* 75:1–14.

———. 1987b. Mother-young relationships in captive ungulates: Spatial and temporal patterns. *Zoo Biol.* 6:11–20.

Rasa, O. E. A. 1971. Social interaction and object manipulation in weaned pups of the Northern elephant seal *Mirounga angustirostris. Z. Tierpsychol.* 32:449–88.

———. 1984. A motivational analysis of object play in juvenile dwarf mongoose *(Helogale undulata rufula). Anim. Behav.* 32: 579–89.

Renouf, D., and Diemand, D. 1984. Behavioral interactions between harbour seal mothers and pups during weaning (Pinnipeds: Phocidae). *Mammalia* 48:53–58.

Renquist, D., and Judge, F. 1985. Use of nylon balls as behavioral modifier for caged primates. *Lab. Primate Newsl.* 24 (4): 4.

Rhine, R. J., Norton, G. W., Wynn, G. M., and Wayne, R. D. 1985. Weaning of free-ranging infant baboons *(Papio cynocephalus)* as indicated by one-zero and instantaneous sampling of feeding. *Int. J. Primatol.* 6:491–99.

Richter, W. von. 1966. Untersuchungen über angeborene Verhaltensweisen des Schabrackentapirs *(Tapirus indicus)* und des Flachlandtapirs *(Tapirus terrestris). Zool. Beitr.* 12:67–159.

Roberts, M. S., Thompson, K. V., and Cranford, J. A. 1988. Reproduction and growth in the punare *(Thrichomys apereoides,* Rodentia: Echimyidae) of the Brazilian Caatinga with reference to the reproductive strategies of the Echimyidae. *J. Mammal.* 69: 542–51.

Rosenblatt, J. S. 1971. Suckling and home orientation in the kitten: A comparative developmental study. In *The biopsychology of development,* ed. E. Tobach, L. R. Aronson, and E. Shaw, 345–410. New York: Academic Press.

———. 1976. Stages in the early behavioural development of altricial young of selected species of non-primate mammals. In *Growing points in ethology,* ed. P. P. G. Bateson and R. A. Hinde, 345–83. New York: Cambridge University Press.

Sachs, B. D., and Harris, V. S. 1978. Sex differences and developmental changes in selected juvenile activities (play) of domestic lambs. *Anim. Behav.* 26:678–84.

Sade, D. S. 1973. An ethogram for rhesus monkeys. I. Antithetical contrasts in posture and movement. *Am. J. Phys. Anthropol.* 38: 537–42.

Sammarco, P. 1981. Great ape keeping at Lincoln Park Zoo. *Animal Keepers' Forum* 8:323–25.

Sanders, L. 1987. And how hot was it? *Animal Keepers' Forum* 14: 345.

Schaller, G. B. 1963. *The mountain gorilla*. Chicago: University of Chicago Press.

———. 1972. *The Serengeti lion*. Chicago: University of Chicago Press.

Schoknecht, P. A. 1984. Growth and teat ownership in a litter of binturongs. *Zoo Biol.* 3:273–77.

Seyfarth, R. M. 1977. A model of social grooming among adult female monkeys. *J. Theor. Biol.* 65:671–98.

Seyfarth, R. M., and Cheney, D. L. 1984. Grooming, alliances, and reciprocal altruism in vervet monkeys. *Nature* 308:541–43.

Seyfarth, R. M., Cheney, D. L., and Hinde, R. A. 1978. Some principles relating social interactions and social structure among primates. *Recent Adv. Primatol.* 1:39–54.

Shoemaker, A. H. 1978. Observations on howler monkeys, *Alouatta caraya*, in captivity. *Der Zoologische Garten* 48:225–34.

Smith, P. K. 1982. Does play matter? Functional and evolutionary aspects of animal and human play. *Behav. Brain Sci.* 5:139–84.

Steiner, A. L. 1971. Play activity of Columbian ground squirrels. *Z. Tierpsychol.* 28:247–61.

Stevenson, M. F., and Poole, T. B. 1982. Playful interactions in family groups of the common marmoset (*Callithrix jacchus jacchus*). *Anim. Behav.* 30:886–900.

Struhsaker, T. T. 1967. *Behavior of vervet monkeys* (Cercopithecus aethiops). University of California Publications in Zoology, no. 82.

Sussman, R. W. 1977. Socialization, social structure, and ecology of two sympatric species of *Lemur*. In *Primate bio-social development*, ed. S. Chevalier-Skolnikoff and F. E. Poirier, 515–28. New York: Garland.

Symons, D. 1978. *Play and aggression: A study of rhesus monkeys*. New York: Columbia University Press.

Teicher, M. H., and Blass, E. M. 1976. Suckling in newborn rats: Elimination by nipple lavage, reinstated by pup saliva. *Science* 193:422–25.

———. 1977. First suckling response of the newborn albino rat: The role of olfaction and amniotic fluid. *Science* 198:635–38.

Tener, J. S. 1965. *Muskoxen in Canada: A biological and taxonomic review*. Monograph Series of the Canadian Wildlife Service, no. 2.

Thommen, D. R. 1982. Zur sozialentwicklung der Javaneraffen (*Macaca fascicularis*) wahrend der ersten drei lebensmonate. Ph.D. thesis, Basel University.

Thompson, K. V. 1985. Social play in the punaré (*Thrichomys apereoides*): A test of play function hypotheses. M.S. thesis, Virginia Polytechnic Institute and State University.

———. 1992. Reproductive competition, birth synchrony, and behavioral development in the sable antelope, *Hippotragus niger*. Ph.D. thesis, University of Maryland.

Thompson, V. D. 1986. Parturition and related behavior in the Queensland koala, *Phascolarctos cinereus*, at San Diego Zoo. *Int. Zoo Yrbk.* 26:217–22.

Trivers, R. L. 1974. Parent-offspring conflict. *Am. Zool.* 14:249–64.

———. 1985. *Social evolution*. Santa Cruz, Calif.: Benjamin Cummings.

Vaughan, T. A. 1978. *Mammalogy*. 2d ed. Philadelphia: Saunders College Publishing.

Vaughan, T. A., and Vaughan, R. P. 1987. Parental behavior in the African yellow-winged bat (*Lavia frons*). *J. Mammal.* 68:217–23.

Vincent, L. E., and Bekoff, M. 1978. Quantitative analyses of the ontogeny of predatory behaviour in coyotes, *Canis latrans*. *Anim. Behav.* 26:225–31.

Vogt, J. L., Carlson, H., and Menzel, E. 1978. Social behavior of a marmoset (*Saguinus fuscicollis*) group. I. Parental care and infant development. *Primates* 19:715–26.

Walters, R. H., and Parke, R. D. 1965. The role of distance receptors in the development of social responsiveness. *Adv. Child Dev. Behav.* 2:59–96.

Walther, F. 1962. Über ein Speil bei *Okapia johnstoni*. *Z. Säugetierk.* 27:245–51.

———. 1965. Verhaltensstudien an der Grantgazelle (*Gazella granti*, Brooke, 1872) im Ngorongoro-Krater. *Z. Tierpsychol.* 22:167–208.

West, M. 1974. Social play in the domestic cat. *Am. Zool.* 14:427–36.

White, L. E., and Hinde, R. A. 1975. Some factors influencing mother-infant relations in rhesus monkeys. *Anim. Behav.* 23:527–42.

Whitworth, M. R. 1984. Maternal care and behavioural development in pikas, *Ochotona princeps*. *Anim. Behav.* 32:743–52.

Wilson, S. 1973. The development of social behaviour in the vole (*Microtus agrestis*). *Zool. J. Linn. Soc.* 52:45–62.

Wilson, S. 1982. Contact-promoting behavior, social development, and relationship with parents in sibling juvenile degus (*Octodon degus*). *Dev. Psychobiol.* 15:257–68.

Wilson, S., and Kleiman, D. 1974. Eliciting play: A comparative study. *Am. Zool.* 14:331–70.

Winter, P., Ploog, D. W., and Latta, J. 1966. Vocal repertoire of the squirrel monkey (*Saimiri sciureus*), its analysis and significance. *Exp. Brain Res.* 1:359–84.

Zucker, E. L., Mitchell, G., and Maple, T. 1978. Adult male-offspring play interactions within a captive group of orangutans (*Pongo pygmaeus*). *Primates* 19:379–84.

35

Aspects of the Ecology and Psychology of Feeding and Foraging

Donna Fernandes

In nature, the lives of most mammals are dominated by a never-ending quest for food, resulting in strong selective pressures to maximize the efficiency with which they locate, subdue, or process food. These selective pressures have led to a host of morphological and physiological adaptations for feeding, from dentition and the size and shape of the tongue to the kinds of digestive enzymes produced and the structure and length of the digestive tract (Ricklefs 1979; Eisenberg 1981). The need to obtain food has led to a number of behavioral adaptations as well, which make use of various sensory mechanisms to identify edible plants or animals, spatial abilities to search efficiently for food, stalking behaviors, and even social cooperation to bring down very large prey. This chapter presents some of the basic concepts of the ecology and psychology of feeding in mammals and relates these to the management of mammals in captivity.

THE TYPE OF DIET CONSUMED

The diet of any animal species can be characterized by two related components: (1) the type of food selected and (2) the variety of foods consumed. Animals that eat only plants or their seeds and fruits are called herbivores, while animals that prey on other animals are called carnivores. Omnivores consume both plant and animal material. Still finer distinctions are sometimes made with regard to dietary type. For example, herbivores can be further broken down into folivores (leaf eaters), granivores (seed eaters), and frugivores (fruit eaters). But the utility of these distinctions is limited, since many mammals consume a combination of foodstuffs. This brings us to the second major component of diet: dietary breadth.

Animals that consume only one or a very few kinds of food are known as specialists. Classic examples of mammalian specialists include the giant panda, *Ailuropoda melanoleuca*, which feeds exclusively on bamboo; the koala, *Phas-*

colarctos cinereus, which eats only eucalyptus leaves; and the giant anteater, *Myrmecophaga tridactyla*, whose name bespeaks its rather limited diet. Specialists obtain the nutrients necessary for growth and reproduction from a very narrow range of foods. The foraging challenge facing specialists is to locate sufficient amounts of the appropriate material to sustain them. Their recognition of food is usually innate (Rozin 1976; Rozin and Schulkin 1990).

The captive management of extreme specialists can be very difficult. Regional populations of koalas, for example, are adapted to different species of eucalyptus leaves (Chinery 1992). Moreover, providing the mainstay of the specialist's diet may not be sufficient to ensure its good health. In nature, a specialist may obtain necessary nutrients from sources other than its primary food. For example, some mammals may occasionally consume soil or lick or chew mineral deposits. Very little is known about the nutrient requirements of specialists and how those requirements are met by their limited diets. Finally, temporal variation in the abundance of key food species in the specialist's native habitat may serve as a cue for reproduction. The cultivated diets fed to zoo animals may obscure these cues.

Generalists are at the opposite end of the dietary spectrum, choosing to feed on a variety of plants or animals. Since generalists consume a wide range of substances, it is unlikely that they innately recognize appropriate foods; rather, they rely on learning and experience (Rozin 1976; Rozin and Schulkin 1990). In addition, from the smorgasbord of edible substances in their environment, generalists must select a diet that is nutritionally well balanced.

Many of the mammals commonly exhibited in zoos are generalists, including bears, canids, and a host of primates. But few species rival the Norway rat, *Rattus norvegicus*, in willingness to eat almost anything. The extreme breadth of the rat's diet has endowed it with great versatility and is largely responsible for its current worldwide distribution.

The ability of rats to learn quickly to discriminate between edible and inedible substances has been the subject of considerable research, which is discussed below.

NEOPHOBIA AND FOOD AVOIDANCE

Few plants or animals passively accept their role as food for other organisms. One defense against predation that has evolved in a number of plants is the production or concentration of toxic substances known as secondary compounds (Feeney 1975; Freeland and Janzen 1974). Organisms protected by poisons or secondary compounds are generally avoided by potential consumers; however, many animals must learn to avoid these harmful species (Brower 1969).

Many animals faced with a new food are extremely suspicious of it and may avoid it for long periods of time. When they finally do ingest it, they take a very small amount. This wary response to novel foods, referred to as neophobia, has been observed in a variety of mammals and birds (Rozin 1976; Rozin and Schulkin 1990). Neophobic behavior is clearly adaptive. If the novel food turns out to be toxic, the mild effects of a low dose of poison will probably not be fatal, but the resulting discomfort will indicate that the food should be avoided in the future. Pairing of the discomfort with a clear visual cue (e.g., bright red coloration) or chemosensory cue (e.g., bitter taste) makes the learning that much faster. The readiness of animals to generalize their bad experience with one species to others that are similar in appearance has not gone unnoticed by natural selection. A multitude of edible species avoid being eaten by mimicking the appearance and behavior of distasteful species found in the same environment (Wickler 1968).

Classic studies of neophobia and poison avoidance were first conducted on wild rats by Richter (1953), Rzoska (1953), and Garcia et al. (1966). The rats were typically offered a flavored solution (e.g., vanilla) and allowed to drink it. Shortly thereafter, some of the rats were poisoned, either by exposure to x-rays or injection with lithium chloride. The rats that had been poisoned subsequently refused to drink the flavored solution when it was offered again. Surprisingly, these rats learned to associate the novel food flavor with negative consequences (i.e., the nausea induced by poisoning) after only a single pairing. Moreover, the rats learned this association even if several hours had passed between ingestion and poisoning. Subsequent studies demonstrated that wild rats are also able to distinguish between familiar and unfamiliar foods. If a rat consumes both a familiar and a novel food and then becomes sick, it will later avoid only the novel food (Shettleworth 1972).

Large generalist herbivores do not appear to possess the specialized food aversion learning mechanisms identified in the omnivorous rat. In studies of domestic cattle, sheep, ponies, and goats, Zahorik and Houpt (1981) found that although these species were able to form aversions to novel foods eaten as discrete meals when followed immediately by poisoning, they failed to learn the food aversion if there was a long delay (30 minutes or more) between ingestion and poisoning. The latter condition more accurately duplicates the situation faced by grazing animals in the wild, where they are more likely to encounter various slow-acting poi-

sons (Freeland and Janzen 1974). Nonselective grazers such as the African buffalo, *Syncerus caffer,* or Burchell's zebra, *Equus burchellii,* are particularly unlikely to evolve food avoidance mechanisms since they consume a variety of plant species within an 8–12-hour feeding period (Beekman and Prins 1989). This feeding pattern makes specific associations between a particular plant and its toxic consequences difficult. Data on plant toxin aversion by zoo herbivores are lacking. Nevertheless, toxic ornamental plants should not be used in the vicinity of large herbivore enclosures.

INTER- AND INTRASPECIFIC DIFFERENCES IN NEOPHOBIA

Recent experiments suggest that the degree of neophobia can vary, even among closely related species. Greenberg (1984) studied the wintering ecology of two insectivorous tropical migrant birds in the lowland forests of Panama. He found that the bay-breasted warbler, *Dendroica castanea,* was more of a generalist and opportunist in its foraging behavior than the chestnut-sided warbler, *D. pennsylvanica.* In laboratory studies with immature animals of both species, he found that the chestnut-sided warbler was less willing to feed in a range of unfamiliar microhabitats than the bay-breasted warbler. His results indicate that young animals respond to novel feeding situations in ways that are appropriate to the feeding ecology of their species—that is, generalists are less neophobic than specialists.

Even within a species, there are clear differences in the degree of neophobia exhibited by individuals. Some animals are much more willing to try novel foods than others. The development of neophobia and the establishment of subsequent diet preferences has been shown to be mediated by early feeding experiences. Studies of Japanese macaque, *Macaca fuscata,* troops indicate that the acquisition of food preferences by juveniles results from the young's habit of ingesting scraps dropped by their mothers (Kawamura 1959). Social transmission of diet preference has also been reported in chacma baboons, *Papio ursinus,* mantled howler monkeys, *Alouatta palliata,* and meerkats, *Suricata suricatta* (reviewed in Galef 1976). Galef and Henderson (1972) have also shown that the diet of mother rats influences the preferences found in their offspring through gustatory cues incorporated into the flavor of the mother's milk.

The acquisition and persistence of early dietary preferences can have important consequences for the management of captive mammals (see part 2, Nutrition, this volume). While all mammals need nutritious, well-balanced diets, the exposure of young animals to a wide variety of foods, particularly through the use of adults as role models, may ensure that later changes to an animal's diet, due to a change in suppliers or translocation to another facility, are readily accepted.

SELECTING A BALANCED DIET

It is not enough for a foraging mammal to learn to avoid harmful substances; the animal must also consume a sufficient range of foods to satisfy all of its quantitative nutrient requirements. Early work with captive rats suggested that these animals selected a nutritionally balanced diet when offered a choice of items containing various amounts of carbohydrates, fats, proteins, vitamins, and minerals (Richter 1955). Evidence that mammals other than rats select balanced diets is equivocal, although some field studies report correlations between preferred diets and soluble concentrations of carbohydrates, proteins, minerals, and vitamins (cf. Westoby 1974).

In earlier studies, Richter (1943) demonstrated that rats are capable of responding to certain nutritional deficiencies by selecting diets that correct the deficiencies. The term "specific hunger" was used to describe the animal's innate preference for foods that contained the deficient nutrient. Rats with an increased need for sodium due to a deficient diet or adrenalectomy consumed higher quantities of sodium-rich foods. Likewise, rats deficient in vitamin B_1 preferentially consumed thiamine-rich foods.

The typical paradigm for these studies involved raising an animal on a diet lacking some essential nutrient (sodium or thiamine). When signs of the deficiency appeared, the animal was offered a choice between the original diet and a new diet that contained the missing nutrient. Rozin (1976) has argued that the preference for the new diet is not mediated by an innate recognition that the diet contains the missing nutrient; rather, the preference for the new diet is a result of a learned aversion to the original diet (the one that caused the illness) and therefore may be explained by the rat's poison avoidance mechanism. The observation that rats will eat less and less of a nutritionally deficient diet if not offered an alternative, even to the point of starvation, is consistent with this view (Rozin 1967).

The extent to which Rozin's rat studies can provide clues to feeding or appetite problems in captive animals is uncertain, however. While some mammals may have specific appetites for specific nutrients, we have no evidence that captive mammals possess the nutritional wisdom necessary to select a balanced diet. Specific hungers (e.g., sodium: cf. Schulkin 1991) and specific receptors (e.g., polysaccharide: cf. Rozin and Schulkin 1990) are known and help to explain food selection by some animals. However, the specific mechanisms that drive nutrient regulation are complex and are beyond the scope of this chapter.

BALANCING THE GOOD AND THE EVIL

In choosing an appropriate diet from the vast array of potential foods available in nature, certain mammalian species do not completely avoid potentially toxic species. In fact, the ecological literature is replete with examples of wild mammals that consume plant material known to contain toxic secondary compounds. Animals are able to survive on such diets only if they are able to detoxify these substances in the digestive tract, liver, or kidneys. But the need to detoxify may limit the amount of material that can be eaten at one time. It has been proposed that the range of plants typically consumed by mammalian herbivores is not a consequence of nutritional wisdom due to specific nutrient needs, but rather stems from their need to avoid damaging

concentrations of any one particular toxin (Freeland and Janzen 1974).

A number of field studies have confirmed the importance of secondary plant compounds in the food selection of free-ranging primates. Oates, Swain, and Zantouske (1977) demonstrated that concentrations of tannin and alkaloids in leaves influenced the feeding behavior of black-and-white colobus monkeys, *Colobus guereza*. McKey et al. (1978) showed that secondary plant compounds affected black colobus, *C. satanas*, feeding strategies, while Glander (1981) found that mantled howler monkeys selected a diet that maximized their intake of total protein and water but minimized their intake of tannin and crude fiber.

Geophagy, or the ingestion of soil, has been observed in a variety of nonhuman primates. One explanation for this behavior is that certain soils contain compounds that help in the detoxification of secondary plant compounds (Hladik 1978; Oates 1978). A study by Gurian, O'Neill, and Price (1992) on free-ranging rhesus macaques, *Macaca mulatta*, in a large outdoor enclosure lends support to this view. The authors report that monkeys who were observed ingesting soil ate more of the vegetation growing within the enclosure than did non–soil consumers. Moreover, those monkeys who consumed the two vegetation types highest in tannin concentration—plantain leaves and yarrow roots—were all soil consumers. Previous studies have shown that kaolin, the active ingredient in Kaopectate, is found in clay soils and acts to neutralize toxins in the diet (Vermeer 1985).

In general, herbivorous mammals select from a broad spectrum of available foods. The bulk of the diet may be composed of a small subset of plants that satisfy the immediate caloric needs of the animal, while the remaining species consumed presumably satisfy other nutritional requirements (Belovsky 1978; Milton 1979; Robbins 1993).

INTRASPECIFIC DIFFERENCES IN DIET AND FORAGING BEHAVIOR

A number of field studies on primates report significant differences in the diet and foraging patterns of males and females (Clutton-Brock 1974; Gautier-Hion 1980; Pollock 1977; Rodman 1977; Waser 1977) or adults and juveniles (Van Schaik and Van Noordwijk 1986). Various explanations have been proposed to account for these differences, including sexual dimorphism, social dominance, and the changing nutritional needs of growing youngsters or reproductive females. Each of these explanations has received some empirical support, but several studies suggest that dominance interactions are primarily responsible for the observed differences in diet and foraging patterns within a species (Barton and Whiten 1993; Janson 1985; Wrangham and Waterman 1981). For example, Harrison (1983) found substantial differences between the diets of adult male and female green monkeys, *Cercopithecus sabaeus*. These differences were due to the competitive ability of males to dominate first-choice foods (fruits and flowers) as well as the tendency of lactating females to spend more time feeding on foods rich in protein (foliage, herbs, and grasses).

Social interaction also influences food selection in some

species, particularly in opportunistic species with patchy or unpredictable food resources (Lefebvre and Palameta 1988; Caraco and Giraldeau 1991). While much work in this area has been done with honeybees, Galef (1988), in a series of studies, has demonstrated that foraging efficiency in Norway rats is enhanced by social interaction and exchange of olfactory signals.

Zoo managers typically attempt to minimize feeding competition in primates by chopping foods into very small pieces so that dominant animals cannot control all of the preferred food items. Yet Smith, Lindburg, and Vehrencamp (1989) report that this practice does not prevent dominant individuals from hoarding preferred foods. In their study, ten captive lion-tailed macaques, *Macaca silenus*, were presented with fruits and vegetables in either whole or chopped form. The authors found that the dietary diversity of the group was actually higher when foods were presented whole rather than chopped. In this study, the fruits and vegetables were scattered over a bare concrete floor. An alternative way to equalize access to preferred foods is to distribute the diet over a large three-dimensional area, preferably hiding the items in a variety of nooks and crannies within the enclosure.

SPATIAL DISTRIBUTION OF FOOD

Milton (1981) has suggested that the cognitive abilities of a species may be related to the spatial distribution or patchiness of its main food source. She examined differences in brain size and mental abilities between the red spider monkey, *Ateles geoffroyi*, and the mantled howler monkey, both of which live in the tropical forests of central Panama. The more frugivorous spider monkey was found to possess superior cognitive abilities and a larger brain. Milton argued that this was due to the fact that the spider monkey requires greater spatial memory to keep track of the changing resources within its enormous home range than does the more folivorous howler monkey.

The spatial distribution of food in a species' natural habitat influences its preferred strategies for foraging in captivity as well. Roberts and Cunningham (1986) found that adult western tarsiers, *Tarsius bancanus*, are extremely reluctant to hunt for insects on the floor of their enclosure. This foraging preference is consistent with the vertical stratification of their orthopteran prey in nature. It is important for zoo managers to consider the natural foraging behavior of a species when deciding how to present the diet in a captive setting.

CONCLUDING REMARKS

Much attention is now focused on the optimum foraging strategies of animals. This is a relatively new field that embraces the disciplines of psychology and behavioral ecology (Shettleworth 1984). A species' natural mechanisms for food recognition, capture, and processing will influence how it will forage in captivity. Many natural foraging behaviors, however, will not be expressed in the captive environment due to the physical form and spatial arrangement of the zoo diet. The stalking behaviors of carnivores, for example, will not be elicited by a food pan heaped with feline diet. Maintaining such behaviors in captivity may require the occasional presentation of novel foods, live prey, or the use of appropriate enrichment devices (see Carlstead, chap. 31, this volume).

The concentration and predictability of zoo diets is also quite unlike what is found in the natural world. Edible substances are usually patchily distributed in the environment, and require extensive time to collect and consume in sufficient amounts. Moreover, most wild mammals experience great seasonal variation in the composition of their diets as populations of major prey species fluctuate and plants go through their annual cycles of leaf, fruit, or seed production (Eagle and Pelton 1983; Karasov 1985; MacCracken and Hansen 1987).

The dietary preferences exhibited by species in captivity may be different from those observed in the wild. The time or energy costs involved in handling certain food items, such as nuts with heavy shells, are often removed in the processed diets offered in captivity. This practice can result in a higher ranking for such "difficult" items in captive studies of food choice. Species in the wild may also experience considerable interspecific competition, leading to a high degree of niche separation and dietary specialization. In zoos, even in mixed-species exhibits, major ecological competitors are rarely housed together. The absence of competitors will tend to broaden the diet choices exhibited by zoo animals. Therefore, a thorough understanding of both the ecology and psychology of wild feeding behaviors is critical if the results of captive studies are to be fully understood.

REFERENCES

Barton, R. A., and Whiten, A. 1993. Feeding competition among female olive baboons, *Papio anubis. Anim. Behav.* 46:777–89.

Beekman, J. H., and Prins, H. H. T. 1989. Feeding strategies of sedentary large herbivores in East Africa with emphasis on the African buffalo, *Syncerus caffer. Afr. J. Ecol.* 27:129–47.

Belovsky, G. E. 1978. Diet optimization in a generalist herbivore: The moose. *Theor. Popul. Biol.* 14:105–34.

Brower, L. P. 1969. Ecological chemistry. *Sci. Am.* 220:22–29.

Caraco, T., and Giraldeau, L.-A. 1991. Social foraging: Producing and scrounging in a stochastic environment. *J. Theor. Biol.* 153:559–83.

Chinery, M., ed. 1992. *Illustrated encyclopedia of animals.* New York: Kingfisher Books.

Clutton-Brock, T. H. 1974. Activity patterns of red colobus *(Colobus badius tephrosceles). Folia Primatol.* 21:161–87.

Eagle, T. C., and Pelton, M. R. 1983. Seasonal nutrition of black bears in the Great Smoky Mountains National Park. *International Conference on Bear Research and Management,* 5:94–101.

Eisenberg, J. F. 1981. *The mammalian radiations: An analysis of trends in evolution, adaptation, and behavior.* Chicago: University of Chicago Press.

Feeney, P. P. 1975. Biochemical evolution between plants and their insect herbivores. In *Coevolution of animals and plants,* ed. L. E. Gilbert and P. H. Raven. Austin: University of Texas Press.

Freeland, W. J., and Janzen, D. H. 1974. Strategies in herbivory by mammals: The role of plant secondary compounds. *Am. Nat.* 108:269–89.

Galef, B. G. 1976. Social transmission of acquired behavior: A discussion of tradition and social learning in vertebrates. *Adv. Stud. Behav.* 6:77–100.

———. 1988. Communication of information concerning distant diets in a social, central place foraging species: *Rattus norvegicus*. In *Social learning: Psychological and biological perspectives,* ed. T. R. Zentall and B. G. Galef, 119–39. Hillsdale, N.J.: Lawrence Erlbaum Associates.

Galef, B. G., and Henderson, P. W. 1972. Mother's milk: A determinant of the feeding preferences of weaning rat pups. *J. Comp. Physiol. Psychol.* 78:213–19.

Garcia, J., Ervin, F. R., and Koelling, R. A. 1966. Learning with prolonged delay of reinforcement. *Psychonomic Sci.* 5:121–22.

Gautier-Hion, A. 1980. Seasonal variations of diet related to species and sex in a community of Ceropithecus monkeys. *J. Anim. Ecol.* 49:237–69.

Glander, K. E. 1981. Feeding patterns in mantled howler monkeys. In *Foraging behavior: Ecological, ethological and psychological approaches,* ed. A. C. Kamil and T. D. Sargent, 231–57. New York: Garland Press.

Greenberg, R. 1984. Differences in feeding neophobia in the tropical migrant wood warblers, *Dendroica castanea* and *D. pennsylvanica. Comp. Psychol.* 98:131–36.

Gurian, E., O'Neill, P. L., and Price, C. S. 1992. Geophagy and its relation to tannin ingestion in rhesus macaques *(Macaca mulatta). AAZPA Regional Conference Proceedings,* 152–59. Wheeling, W.Va.: American Association of Zoological Parks and Aquariums.

Harrison, M. J. S. 1983. Age and sex differences in the diet and feeding strategies of the green monkey, *Cercopithecus sabaeus. Anim. Behav.* 31:969–77.

Hladik, C. M. 1978. Adaptive strategies of primates in relation to leaf eating. In *The ecology of arboreal folivores,* ed. G. G. Montgomery, 373–95. Washington, D.C.: Smithsonian Institution Press.

Janson, C. H. 1985. Aggressive competition and food consumption in the brown capuchin monkey *(Cebus apella). Behav. Ecol. Sociobiol.* 18:125–38.

Karasov, W. H. 1985. Nutrient constraints in the feeding ecology of an omnivore in a seasonal environment. *Oecologia* 66: 280–90.

Kawamura, S. 1959. The process of sub-culture propagation among Japanese macaques. *Primates* 2:43–60.

Lefebvre, L., and Palameta, B. 1988. Mechanisms, ecology, and population diffusion of socially learned food-finding behavior in feral pigeons. In *Social learning: Psychological and biological perspectives,* ed. T. R. Zentall and B. G. Galef, 141–64. Hillsdale, N.J.: Lawrence Erlbaum Associates.

MacCracken, J. G., and Hansen, R. M. 1987. Coyote feeding strategies in southeastern Idaho: Optimal foraging by an opportunisitic predator? *J. Wildl. Mgmt.* 51 (2):278–85.

McKey, D., Waterman, P. G., Mbi, C. N., Gartlan, J. S., and Struhsaker, T. T. 1978. Phenolic content of vegetation in two African rainforests: Ecological implications. *Science* 202: 61–64.

Milton, K. 1979. Factors influencing leaf choice by howler monkeys: A test of some hypotheses of food selection by generalist herbivores. *Am. Nat.* 114:362–78.

———. 1981. Distribution of tropical plant foods as an evolutionary stimulus to primate mental development. *Am. Anthropol.* 3: 534–48.

Oates, J. 1978. Water-plant and soil consumption by guereza monkeys *(Colobus guereza):* A relationship with minerals and toxins in the diet? *Biotropica* 10:241–53.

Oates, J. F., Swain, T., and Zantouske, J. 1977. Secondary compounds and food selection by colobus monkeys. *Biochem. Syst. Ecol.* 5:317–21.

Pollock, J. I. 1977. The ecology and sociology of feeding in *Indri indri.* In *Primate ecology: Studies of feeding and ranging behavior in lemurs, monkeys, and apes,* ed. T. H. Clutton-Brock, 276–319. London: Academic Press.

Richter, C. P. 1943. Total self regulatory functions in animals and human beings. *Harvey Lect.* 38:63–103.

———. 1953. Experimentally produced reactions to food poisoning in wild and domesticated rats. *Ann. N.Y. Acad. Sci.* 56: 225–39.

———. 1955. Self-regulatory functions during gestation and lactation. *Trans Conf. Gestation,* 2d, Princeton, N.J., 11–93.

Ricklefs, R. E. 1979. *Ecology.* 2d ed. New York: Chiron Press.

Robbins, C. T. 1993. *Wildlife feeding and nutrition.* 2d ed. San Diego, Calif.: Academic Press.

Roberts, M., and Cunningham, B. 1986. Space and substrate use in captive Western tarsiers, *Tarsius bancanus. Int. J. Primatol.* 7: 113–30.

Rodman, P. S. 1977. Feeding behavior of orangutans of the Kutai Nature Reserve, East Kalimantan. In *Primate ecology: Studies of feeding and ranging behavior in lemurs, monkeys, and apes,* ed. T. H. Clutton-Brock, 384–413. London: Academic Press.

Rozin, P. 1967. Specific aversions as a component of specific hungers. *J. Comp. Physiol. Psychol.* 64:237–42.

———. 1976. The selection of foods by rats, humans, and other animals. *Adv. Stud. Behav.* 6:21–76.

Rozin, P. N., and Schulkin, J. 1990. Food selection. In *Handbook of Behavioral Neurobiology,* vol. 10, *Neurobiology of food and fluid intake,* ed. E. M. Striker. New York: Plenum Press.

Rzoska, J. 1953. Bait shyness, a study in rat behavior. *Brit. J. Anim. Behav.* 1:128–35.

Schulkin, J. 1991. *Sodium hunger: The search for a salty taste.* Cambridge: Cambridge University Press.

Shettleworth, S. 1972. Constraints on learning. *Adv. Stud. Behav.* 4:1–68.

———. 1984. Learning and behavioral ecology. In *Behavioral ecology: An evolutionary approach,* 2d ed., ed. J. R. Krebs and N. B. Davies, 170–94. Oxford: Blackwell Scientific.

Smith, A., Lindburg, D. G., and Vehrencamp, S. 1989. Effect of food preparation on feeding behavior of lion-tailed macaques. *Zoo Biol.* 8:57–65.

Van Schaik, C. P., and Van Noordwijk, M. A. 1986. The hidden costs of sociality: Intra-group variation in feeding strategies in Sumatran long-tailed macaques *(Macaca fuscata). Behaviour* 99:296–315.

Vermeer, D. E. 1985. Nigerian geophagical clay, traditional antidiarrheal pharmaceutical. *Science* 227:634–36.

Waser, P. 1977. Feeding, ranging, and group size in the mangabey *Cercocebus albigena.* In *Primate ecology: Studies of feeding and ranging behavior in lemurs, monkeys, and apes,* ed. T. H. Clutton-Brock, 183–222. London: Academic Press.

Westoby, M. 1974. An analysis of diet selection by large generalist herbivores. *Am. Nat.* 108:290–304.

Wickler, W. 1968. *Mimicry in plants and animals.* London: World University Library.

Wrangham, R. W., and Waterman, P. G. 1981. Feeding behavior of vervet monkeys on *Acacia tortilis* and *Acacia xanthophloea* with special reference to reproductive strategies and tannin production. *J. Anim. Ecol.* 50:715–31.

Zahorik, D. M., and Houpt, K. A. 1981. Species differences in feeding strategies, food hazards, and the ability to learn food aversions. In *Foraging behavior: Ecological, ethological and psychological approaches,* ed. A. C. Kamil and T. D. Sargent, 289–310. New York: Garland Press.

PART SIX

Reproduction

INTRODUCTION
Devra G. Kleiman

The management of reproduction is the key to the long-term maintenance of species in zoos or breeding centers. This section details the advances we have made in the past twenty years in our understanding of the behavior and physiology of reproduction and their application to species management.

Recognition of the occurrence of courtship and copulatory behavior is a first step toward good management. Despite the commonality of sexual behavior in mammals, there is great diversity in the expression of this behavior. In chapter 36, Estep and Dewsbury present a useful method for categorizing copulatory behaviors, developed by Dewsbury, as well as a discussion of behaviors preceding and following copulation, to help managers evaluate the behavior of animals in their care. I have often been surprised at how common it is for inexperienced (and even experienced) zoo staff to misidentify behaviors associated with courtship and copulation. Keepers may also have difficulty differentiating between a full copulation with intromission and ejaculation and a mount with or without intromission. Estep and Dewsbury's account can help zoo staff identify these behaviors and differentiate normal from abnormal behaviors.

Asa presents a thorough description of the physiological processes involved in mammalian reproduction in chapter 37, including the role played by the brain and other reproductive organs and the interactions of hormones. In chapters 38 and 39, Hodges and Wildt describe methods of assessing, controlling, and manipulating female and male reproduction respectively. Studies of the reproductive physiology of exotic zoo mammals have been thriving since the earliest attempts to store sperm and conduct artificial insemination (AI) in the mid-1960s. While cryopreservation of gametes and embryos, AI, and embryo transfer are very important potential applications for the management of reproduction of captive exotic mammals, much of the research described in the three chapters by Asa, Hodges, and Wildt is actually directed at improving our understanding of basic reproductive processes. Nonetheless, the development of genome banks to retain the genetic diversity of endangered species is seen as an important step for conserving biodiversity into the twenty-first century.

Despite the basic similarity in the physiological processes of all male and all female mammals, it is often difficult to extrapolate from one species to another, even when they are very closely related. The small but significant differences in the physiology and structure of mammalian spermatozoa from different species result in a need for species-specific recipes for the cryopreservation of male gametes. In females, species differences in the physiological and behavioral requirements for successful ovulation and implantation make the development of a standardized AI protocol, or embryo transfer protocol, exceedingly difficult. As a result, the usefulness of genome banking for direct species preservation awaits major breakthroughs in the manipulation of reproductive processes and cryopreservation of eggs, sperm, and embryos.

A major goal of any successful management program for a species maintained in zoos is the control of reproduction, especially since uncontrolled population growth is impossible in limited enclosure space. It is interesting how little attention the zoo community has given to the subject of contraception and how few options are currently available for use with exotic animals. In chapter 40, Asa et al. encourage greater standardization of techniques and record keeping in the use of contraceptives since so few guidelines are available to follow when trying to decide how to halt reproduction in a zoo species.

Chapter 41, on pregnancy and parturition, by Hutchins, Thomas, and Asa, and chapter 42, on parental care, by Baker, Baker, and Thompson, provide summaries of the physiology and behavior associated with these activities in mammals. As with sexual behavior, it is surprising how much difficulty some zoo staff have in differentiating normal from abnormal behavior. However, the more involved our zoos become in reintroduction programs, and the more impact the animal welfare community has on our management standards, the more important it will be for our zoo animals to be reared in a natural social environment and to exhibit appropriate parental, social, and reproductive behaviors. Thus, putting all of our eggs (and sperm) in one basket, that is, the "frozen zoo," is really not a final solution for the conservation of biodiversity. Ultimately, the animals we manage must exhibit some semblance of normal behavior, or the retention of genetic diversity will be meaningless. A gorilla, *Gorilla gorilla*, that cannot mate, care for its young, or socialize with other gorillas is, in fact, no gorilla at all.

In chapter 43, Kirkwood and Mace provide some theoretical underpinnings and applied data on mammalian growth. Again, the purpose is to assist zoo staff in differentiating the normal from the abnormal, that is, to provide a framework within which to evaluate the growth of any species under their care.

36

Mammalian Reproductive Behavior

Daniel Q. Estep and Donald A. Dewsbury

Reproduction refers to all those activities involved in the production of offspring. In mammals, reproduction occurs sexually, with males producing sperm and females producing eggs. The process of sexual reproduction in mammals is usually divided into three arbitrary phases: courtship, copulation, and postcopulatory activities. *Courtship* refers to those activities of males and females leading up to copulation. *Copulation* refers to those behaviors involved in the actual fertilization of egg by sperm. Postcopulatory activities include those related to pregnancy, parturition, and care of young.

The focus of this chapter will be on courtship and copulatory behavior. The diversity of courtship and copulatory patterns will be outlined, and the social and environmental factors that can influence courtship and copulation will be discussed, particularly as they relate to management of captive mammals. Postcopulatory behavior will be discussed in later chapters.

Species differences in courtship and copulatory behavior are frequently related to variations in social organization and mating systems. For example, Kleiman (1977) has hypothesized that, compared with nonmonogamous species, monogamous species display relatively little sociosexual interaction, except during pair-bond formation. This hypothesis has received general confirmation (e.g., Stribley, French, and Inglett 1987), although some exceptions have been noted, such as the Indian crested porcupine, *Hystrix indica* (Sever and Mendelssohn 1988). Therefore, to understand reproductive behavior fully and manage the breeding of wild animals in captivity properly, it is very important to understand the social organization of the animals in the wild and the variations that can occur in captivity (see Berger and Stevens, chap. 33, this volume, for a review of social organization in mammals). A more complete discussion of social influences on reproductive behavior will be given later in this chapter.

SEASONALITY AND ESTRUS

Most species of mammals breed seasonally. The proximate stimuli for the onset of breeding may include changes in rainfall, temperature, chemical stimuli, or day length. In montane voles, *Microtus montanus*, for example, reproduction is triggered by 6-methoxybenzoxazolinone, a chemical found seasonally in food resources (Berger et al. 1981). The most common proximate cue for the onset of reproductive activity is change in photoperiod, as in prairie voles, *Microtus ochrogaster* (Nelson 1985). In general, reproductive patterns have evolved so that animals breed at a time of year that allows young to be born when environmental conditions are most favorable for their growth and survival.

Estrus refers to that period of time when, behaviorally, the female is most likely to mate with the male and, physiologically, the mating is most likely to result in a successful fertilization. Within a given reproductive season females may have one or several estrous cycles. Females that are not fertilized in one cycle may show repeated estrous cycles. Some females may show a postpartum estrus within hours or days after delivering offspring. The length of estrus varies dramatically among mammalian species. It can be as short as 3 hours, as in some genera of hystricomorph rodents (Kleiman 1974), or as long as 6 days, as in clouded leopards, *Neofelis nebulosa* (Yamada and Durrant 1989). Estrus is influenced by a variety of endogenous factors, such as hormones, and external factors, including nutrition, temperature, lighting, environmental stressors, and social influences (see reviews in Hurnik 1987; Katz 1987). In some species the external factors are more important than in other species. For example, in cotton-top tamarins, *Saguinus oedipus*, regular estrous cycles are more frequent when females are removed from their natal groups and paired with unfamiliar males (Widowski et al. 1990). In captive situations it may be possible to control or induce estrus by manipulating one or several of these internal and external factors. In some domestic livestock and laboratory animals such manipulation is regularly practiced to facilitate or inhibit reproduction. Some of the social and environmental influences on reproductive behavior will be discussed later in this chapter. (For a more complete review of the domestic animal literature, see Price 1985, Hurnik 1987, and Katz 1987.)

COURTSHIP

Courtship can serve a variety of functions in animals. According to Grier and Burk (1992), those functions include mate attraction and orientation, mate assessment and mate choice, overcoming aggression from potential mates, and the synchronization of sexual and parental behavior. Not all of these functions occur in every species, and in some cases, one behavior may serve multiple functions. For example, the scent marks left by male golden hamsters, *Mesocricetus auratus*, near the burrows of females may allow the females to assess the dominance status of the males and may also act to reduce the females' aggression toward the males while increasing their receptivity (Tang-Martinez, Mueller, and Taylor 1993).

The elaborate courtship patterns characteristic of many birds, fishes, and arthropods are generally absent in mammals. Eisenberg (1981) has described the courtship and copulatory behavior of generalized terrestrial mammals. Potential mates are located and brought into close proximity through a variety of communication channels, which include visual displays, auditory signals, and olfactory signals. Chemical communication is important in the courtship and mating of many mammals, and in some species may involve a complex exchange of olfactory cues. For example, in species such as brown lemmings, *Lemmus trimucronatus*, and golden hamsters, males will scent-mark areas occupied by females before the females are sexually receptive (Coopersmith and Banks 1983; Tang-Martinez, Mueller, and Taylor 1993). It has been shown in these species that such marking familiarizes the females with the male and can facilitate later sexual behavior. In the case of golden hamsters, it reduces the females' aggression toward the male and increases their receptivity. An estrous female golden hamster will scent-mark areas occupied by dominant males who have scent-marked her home area, presumably to alert the males to her reproductive status and attract them to her (Huck et al. 1986a).

Once potential partners are located and in close proximity, the male and female typically contact each other, with one or both showing naso-nasal, naso-anogenital, or nasal contact to other glandular areas. Allogrooming by one or both partners may follow. These contacts appear to provide information about the reproductive status of the partner and result in further contact or in a cessation of contact. Further investigation and allogrooming may occur sporadically throughout the courtship and mating sequence.

If courtship continues, the male will orient toward the female and pursue her. The female may flee from the male, but not so as to escape him, and he will continue to follow her. If the male is slow in pursuing the female or in initiating copulation, she may incite him by pursuing him, grooming him, or mounting him.

Incitation of male sexual behavior by females is part of a larger category of female sexual behavior known as proceptive behavior. Beach (1976) has defined proceptive behavior as those appetitive activities by the female that increase the likelihood of mating. Beach has also delineated two other concepts relevant to female sexual behavior: attractivity and receptivity. Attractivity is the female's stimulus value to the male as a mating partner. Receptivity refers to the consummatory responses made by females that facilitate successful mating. All three of these characteristics vary with the female's reproductive state and are influenced by social and environmental factors as well as by endogenous factors. Examples of these characteristics include assumption of a standing posture that facilitates male mounting in the green acouchi, *Myoprocta acouchy pratti*, a receptive behavior (Kleiman 1970); female gorillas, *Gorilla gorilla*, backing into males and rubbing their genitals against them, a proceptive behavior (Nadler 1976); and females producing visually attractive perineal swellings in some species of primates, an example of attractivity (Beach 1976).

The delineation of these concepts and intensive study of female behavior have done much to acknowledge the important role that females play in the initiation and maintenance of sexual behavior. For too long females were thought to be largely passive recipients of male advances. This is clearly not the case in most species. Captive environmental or social conditions that do not allow females to engage in normal proceptive or receptive behavior can inhibit or prevent normal sexual behavior.

Despite the generalizations described above, there is considerable diversity among mammalian species in courtship behavior. In some species there is virtually no courtship behavior at all. For example, in northern elephant seals, *Mirounga angustirostris*, Le Boeuf (1972, 41) reports that "there is no preliminary courtship; the male does not investigate the head or anogenital region of the female." In other species, complex integrated patterns of courtship are seen. In spotted seals, *Phoca largha*, Beier and Wartzok (1979) describe patterns of ballooning, exchange breathing, jaw-clapping, and both synchronous and solitary spiraling.

For persons interested in breeding captive mammals, knowledge of estrus and/or courtship may be useful in predicting the occurrence of mating, either to promote it or to prevent it. Perhaps the most consistent indicator of ensuing copulatory activity is persistent attentions of the male toward the female. For example, in dwarf mongooses, *Helogale parvula*, estrus is signaled by an increase in male attention: "he follows her, nose to tail, for the whole of the oestrous period (which can last from one to six days)" (Rasa 1977, 347). Similar behavior has been reported in wallabies, *Macropus parma* (Maynes 1973). In male gerenuks, *Litocranius walleri*, courtship is highly ritualized, with males performing exaggerated foreleg kicks between the female's hind legs and following moving females with a peculiar goose-stepping gait (Houston, Read, and Miller 1988).

Increased attention to and even mounting of females are not infallible clues to impending mating. As Kleiman (1974) points out, the males of many hystricomorph species (and other animals as well) may show attention to and attempt mounting of females at any stage of their reproductive cycles. This is especially likely in staged encounters in which normally separated males and females are paired for short periods of time.

In many species, females show an increase in general activity coincident with estrus (Bermant and Davidson 1974; Price 1985; Hurnik 1987). This can be manifested as increased locomotion, restlessness, or increased social interactions. In dairy cattle, *Bos taurus*, and goats, *Capra hircus*, estrus has been reliably detected with activity meters or pedometers (Kiddy 1977; Doherty, Price, and Katz 1987).

Changes in female morphology signal ensuing estrus in some species. These changes include pouch development in marsupials (Lyne 1976; Bryant 1988) and the perineal swellings of some species of primates during the follicular phase (Saayman 1970). In many species, the estrous cycle can be tracked by following changes in the vaginal mucosa detected with vaginal smears (Long and Evans 1922). Females approaching estrus typically emit characteristic pheromones, chemical signals related to estrus. Although humans are relatively insensitive to these odors, domestic dogs, *Canis familiaris*, have been trained to detect estrus in domestic cattle (Kiddy, Conley, and Hawk 1978). Unfortunately, there are no simple, universal procedures for detecting estrus and predicting mating for all mammals. In some species, behavioral cues may be reliable; in others, changes in physical condition may be useful; for still others, it may take a combination of methods. A thorough study of the published literature on a given species can be helpful in suggesting ways to detect estrus and to predict mating in any captive species.

COPULATION

In contrast to taxa such as birds, mammalian copulatory patterns may be even more variable among species than are courtship patterns.

Postures

Among generalized terrestrial mammals, the basic postures of copulation are quite similar (Eisenberg 1981). The male usually mounts the female from behind, grasping her with his forepaws or forelegs between her rib cage and pelvis. In some species the male may grasp the skin of the female's neck in his teeth. There is usually shallow pelvic thrusting as the penis orients to and locates the vaginal orifice. Intromission of the penis occurs, followed by ejaculation and dismounting. The female usually stands during the mounting, deflecting her tail to the side. In many species the female may make small bodily adjustments to facilitate intromission. In some species the female may assume a lordotic posture, in which the perineal region is elevated and the back is depressed, creating a concave curvature.

There are, of course, exceptions to the above description. Ventro-ventral copulation has been reported for gorillas (Nadler 1976), orangutans, *Pongo pygmaeus* (Nadler 1977), and pygmy chimpanzees, *Pan paniscus* (de Waal 1987). In fact, considerable flexibility in copulatory postures has been shown in pygmy chimpanzees and orangutans. This is in contrast to most mammals, in which copulatory postures are usually very stereotyped. During mounting in some species, such as rhesus macaques, *Ma-*

caca mulatta, virtually all of the male's weight is supported by the female (Carpenter 1942). In others, such as white-throated wood rats, *Neotoma albigula*, there is little contact other than between the genitalia (Dewsbury 1974). In species with genital locks, such as domestic dogs, the male may dismount during copulation and orient tail-to-tail with the female while the copulatory tie remains secure (Hart 1967). In both New World and Old World tylopods (camels, llamas, guanacos, alpacas, and vicuñas), the male copulates with the female lying down in sternal recumbency rather than standing (Walther 1984).

Quantitative Aspects of Copulation

A system for classifying patterns of copulatory behavior has been proposed by Dewsbury (1972) and has been applied to mammals in general (Dewsbury 1972), muroid rodents (Dewsbury 1975), and nonhuman primates (Dewsbury and Pierce 1989). According to this schema, patterns of copulatory behavior can be characterized in relation to four diagnostic criteria: locking, thrusting, multiple intromissions, and multiple ejaculations. Although there are some intermediate cases, it is useful to treat each attribute as a dichotomy, which yields a total of sixteen possible patterns of copulatory behavior (fig. 36.1). These attributes can be assessed by asking four questions, which are considered in greater detail by Dewsbury (1972):

1. Does locking occur? In some species, such as coyotes, *Canis latrans*, there is a mechanical tie or lock that prevents—or at least offers substantial resistance to—the disengagement of male and female (Kleiman 1968). The means of locking may vary. The engorgement of the bulbus glandis

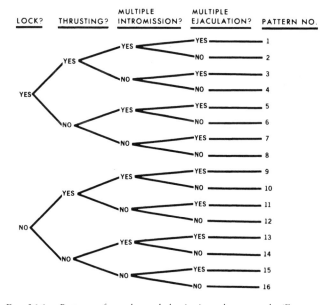

FIG. 36.1. Patterns of copulatory behavior in male mammals. (From Dewsbury 1972.)

in domestic dogs (Hart 1967), the unusual shape of the erect penis in short-tailed shrews, *Blarina brevicauda* (Gibbs 1955), and penile spines in southern grasshopper mice, *Onychomys torridus* (Horner and Taylor 1968), all assist the lock in those species.

2. Does intravaginal thrusting occur? In many species the male displays a pattern of shallow pelvic thrusting prior to insertion in order to locate the vaginal orifice. In some species, such as black-tailed deer, *Odocoileus hemionus*, there is a single, apparent, deep intravaginal thrust once insertion is achieved (Golley 1957). In contrast, other species display a pattern of repetitive pelvic thrusting after intromission. The latter pattern is characteristic of all species of nonhuman primates reported thus far (Dewsbury and Pierce 1989).

3. Are multiple intromissions prerequisite to ejaculation? In bison, *Bison bison* (Lott 1974), the male generally ejaculates the first time he gains vaginal insertion. By con-

trast, in Japanese macaques, *Macaca fuscata* (Tokuda 1961), multiple intromissions are prerequisite to ejaculation. Thus, the male mounts the female, gains insertion, and dismounts without ejaculating. It is only after several such nonejaculatory intromissions that a mount with intromission and ejaculation occurs.

4. Do multiple ejaculations occur? In pygmy mice, *Baiomys taylori* (Estep and Dewsbury 1976), copulatory activity within a mating episode generally terminates with the occurrence of the first ejaculation. In most species, however, copulation is resumed some time later, and multiple ejaculations occur within the male-female pair in a single mating episode.

With this system it is possible to classify the copulatory pattern of any species for which adequate descriptions are available. Classifications for a number of such species are presented in table 36.1.

TABLE 36.1. Patterns of Copulatory Behavior in Selected Species of Mammals

Species	Pattern no.[a]	Lock?	Thrusting?	Multiple intromissions?	Multiple ejaculations?	Reference
Order Marsupialia						
Monodelphis domestica	4	Yes	Yes	No	No	Trupin and Fadem 1982
Order Insectivora						
Elephantulus rufescens	11	No	Yes	No	Yes	Lumpkin and Koontz 1986
Suncus murinus	10	No	Yes	Yes?	No	Dryden 1969; Eisenberg and Gould 1970
Order Primates						
Galagoides demidoff (=*Galago demidovii*)	11	No?	Yes	No	Yes	Blackwell 1969
Callithrix jacchus	11	No?	Yes	No	Yes	Kendrick and Dixson 1984
Macaca arctoides	11	No?	Yes	No	Yes	Estep et al. 1984
Macaca mulatta	9	No	Yes	Yes	Yes	Carpenter 1942
Gorilla gorilla	11	No	Yes	No	Yes	Nadler 1976
Order Lagomorpha						
Oryctolagus cuniculus	15	No	No	No	Yes	Denenberg, Zarrow, and Ross 1969; Rubin and Azrin 1967
Order Rodentia						
Baiomys taylori	8	Yes	No	No	No	Estep and Dewsbury 1976
Onychomys leucogaster	7	Yes	No	No	Yes	Lanier and Dewsbury 1977
Mesocricetus auratus	13	No	No	Yes	Yes	Beach and Rabedeau 1959
Rattus norvegicus	13	No	No	Yes	Yes	Beach and Jordan 1956
Mus musculus	9	No	Yes	Yes	Yes	McGill 1962
Myoprocta acouchy	10	No	Yes	Yes	No	Kleiman 1971
Chinchilla lanigera	11	No	Yes	No	Yes	Bignami and Beach 1968
Order Carnivora						
Canis lupus	3	Yes	Yes	No	Yes	Yadav 1968
Canis latrans	3	Yes	Yes	No	Yes	Bekoff and Diamond 1976
Canis familiaris	3	Yes	Yes	No	Yes	Hart 1967
Ailuropoda melanoleuca	9	No	Yes	Yes	Yes	Kleiman 1983
Civettictis civetta	11	No	Yes?	No	Yes	Ewer and Wemmer 1974
Panthera tigris	15	No	No	No	Yes	Lanier and Dewsbury 1976
Uncia uncia	15	No	No	No	Yes	Lanier and Dewsbury 1976
Order Pinnipedia						
Mirounga angustirostris	15	No	No	No	Yes	Le Boeuf 1972
Order Proboscidea						
Elephas maximus	11	No	Yes	No	Yes	Eisenberg, McKay, and Jainudeen 1971
Order Perissodactyla						
Equus caballus	11	No	Yes	No	Yes	Hafez, Williams, and Wierzbowski 1969
Order Artiodactyla						
Cervus elaphus	11	No	Yes	No	Yes	Guinness, Lincoln, and Short 1971
Odocoileus virginianus	15	No	No	No	Yes	Warren et al. 1978
Bison bison	16	No	No	No	No	Lott 1974

[a] See figure 36.1.

Taxonomic Distribution of Copulatory Patterns

As is apparent from table 36.1, there is no simple taxonomic distribution of mammalian copulatory patterns. There are, however, a few localized concentrations. Locking patterns characterize the canids, and all species of primates reported to date display intravaginal thrusting. These regularities exist beside considerable diversity, for example, in the superfamily Muroidea of the Rodentia. Forty-five species of muroid rodents have been studied in the laboratory of one of us (Dewsbury 1975; Dewsbury and Pierce 1989). Of these, 22% display locking, 31% display thrusting, 49% require multiple intromissions, and 96% display multiple ejaculations; together the species display eight different copulatory patterns (nos. 3, 5, 7, 8, 9, 11, 13, and 15 in fig. 36.1).

It is important to recognize the diversity of copulatory patterns shown by different species of mammals. There is no "typical" mammalian pattern. Even within the same genus, closely related species may show very different patterns (e.g., genus *Macaca*: see table 36.1). Having knowledge of the copulatory pattern of a particular species may help the captive manager to discriminate between successful matings and unsuccessful matings. Identifying successful matings can help in estimating gestation periods and monitoring the reproduction of specific animals in general. If reproduction is unsuccessful, it is useful to know whether or not the animals are copulating, as the intervention procedures differ sharply depending on whether the animals fail to copulate, or copulate and fail to conceive or carry offspring to term.

Observing and Identifying Copulatory Elements

Identifying mounting of females by males is usually easy; identifying intromission is not always easy. Mounting does not always imply successful intromission. In many species there is a deep thrust and a pattern of lumbar flexure that is highly characteristic of penile insertion. In others there is no obvious correlate. In general, the occurrence of a lock can be discerned only when the male and female move (or are moved) to separate and resistance to disengagement becomes apparent. A lock may be undetected if the animals make no attempt to disengage.

It is also important to discriminate intravaginal from extravaginal thrusting. In most species males display extravaginal thrusting prior to intromission. Not all species continue to thrust intravaginally after intromission is achieved. Discrimination between the two kinds of thrusts may be difficult. In some species showing both, intravaginal thrusts are usually deeper and slower in rate than are extravaginal thrusts.

The ease of detecting ejaculation also differs across species. Again, the occurrence of mounting, with or without intromission, does not necessarily imply ejaculation. For some species there is a clear-cut behavioral indicator of ejaculation. In domestic horses, *Equus caballus*, for example, there is a characteristic series of up-and-down flexures of the tail coincident with ejaculation, known as tail flagging (Waring 1983). Unfortunately, some species (e.g., orangutans: Nadler 1977) simply have no obvious behavioral concomitants of ejaculation. When possible, it is always best to confirm the occurrence of ejaculation by taking vaginal smears from the female and checking for the presence of sperm.

The Consequences of Copulation

In many species, successful copulation does more than simply transfer sperm from male to female. It can have a variety of consequences for subsequent behavior and physiology. Copulation can lead to the termination of estrus in the female and the cessation of sexual activity in the male. Copulatory activity is sometimes reinstated in "satiated" animals, however, if a new mating partner is introduced—a phenomenon known as the "Coolidge effect" (Dewsbury 1981). Other distinctive behavioral patterns may follow copulation. In the large Felidae, for example, females often display a rolling afterreaction within a minute after mating (see Lanier and Dewsbury 1976).

Copulation can also have important physiological consequences. Whereas females of some species display complete cycles of ovulation and preparation of the uterus for implantation whether or not the female mates (spontaneous ovulators), in other species, ovulation occurs only if the female mates (induced ovulators). In yet other species, ovulation is spontaneous but the uterine changes are induced by copulatory activity. In species with these last two types of cycles, it is quite possible that sufficient numbers of spermatozoa for fertilization and pregnancy may be transferred from male to female during mating, yet the stimulation derived from the mating may be insufficient to trigger critical neuroendocrine reflexes in the female necessary for successful reproduction (Jochle 1973; Dewsbury 1978). Thus, the occurrence of a single ejaculation in some species may be insufficient to insure successful reproduction. Here again, knowing the typical courtship and copulatory pattern for a given species and then arranging the physical and social environment so as to facilitate that behavior greatly increases the probability of successful reproduction in most captive mammals.

SOCIAL FACTORS INFLUENCING COURTSHIP AND COPULATION

A variety of social factors have been found to influence the occurrence and maintenance of courtship and copulation in mammals. Knowledge of and attention to such factors may be critical to controlling the reproduction of captive mammals. A brief review of some of these factors follows; more comprehensive reviews will be cited where appropriate.

Early Experiences

Experimental studies from a variety of mammalian species show that early social isolation from conspecifics can result in deficits in adult courtship and copulatory behavior. The best-studied species are within the primates. It has been found, for example, that in rhesus macaques, total social isolation from conspecifics during the first 6 months of life can result in severe deficits in courtship and copulatory behavior (Harlow 1962, 1965). Similarly, lack of peer experience early in life produces highly abnormal reproductive behavior in chimpanzees, *Pan troglodytes* (Rogers and Davenport 1969; Riesen 1971), and is thought to produce deficits in the reproductive behavior of gorillas as well (Beck and Power 1988). Some deficits in sexual behavior also are seen in domestic Norway rats, *Rattus norvegicus,* guinea pigs, *Cavia porcellus,* and domestic dogs reared in isolation (Valenstein, Riss, and Young 1955; Gerall, Ward, and Gerall 1967; Beach 1968; Gruendel and Arnold 1969).

Rearing males in isolation from females seems to have varying effects on sexual performance, depending on the species. In domestic sheep, *Ovis aries,* rearing males only with other males produces deficits in performance (Price 1987); however, in domestic beef bulls, such rearing produces no noticeable deficits (Price, Wallach, and Silver 1990).

Hand-reared animals frequently show sexual preferences for humans and may not show normal preferences for conspecifics. This phenomenon has been reported for domestic animals such as sheep, goats, pigs, *Sus scrofa* (Kilgour 1985), and domestic cats, *Felis catus* (Mellen 1992), as well as a variety of zoo animals (Hediger 1964). Similarly, rearing males solely with members of another species can result in sexual preferences for the heterospecifics; this has been reported for domestic cattle, sheep, goats, and pigs (reviewed in Hart 1985).

Thus, the sexual behavior of mammals, and that of males in particular, is sensitive to variations in early social experience. It is always best to try to keep the social units of captives as much like those of wild animals as possible. When this is not possible, young animals should receive as much experience as possible with conspecifics.

Mate Choice and Sexual Preferences

The social and reproductive system of a species is often reflected in various aspects of its courtship and copulatory behavior. In monogamous species, since both sexes invest heavily in offspring and have much to lose if they make a mistake in mate choice, both will be choosy about their mates. In polygynous species, since females invest more in offspring and have more to lose, they will be choosier than males (Grier and Burk 1992). While polygynous males may be less particular about their mates than females, they may still show some preferences (Dewsbury 1982b). The particular characteristics that are the focus of mate choice vary considerably across species. These differences may reflect variations in social structure, the nature and intensity of mate competition, the demography of the social group, or other factors. Some of these characteristics will be reviewed here.

In a wide variety of species, closely related individuals usually do not mate with each other (see Hepper 1986). This avoidance of inbreeding can take place by one of several mechanisms, but a common one is avoidance of breeding with familiar individuals. In some species, such as gray-tailed voles, *Microtus canicaudus,* individual recognition occurs prior to weaning and inhibits breeding among familiar individuals in adulthood (Boyd and Blaustein 1985).

These results would seem to imply that the more unfamiliar the potential mate, the better; however, in some species there seems to be an optimal level of familiarity that is neither too familiar nor too unfamiliar (reviewed in Dewsbury 1988). For example, Key and McIver (1977) found that domestic sheep rams preferred ewes that were unfamiliar to them, but also preferred ewes of the same breed as their mother. Thus, managers should expect the best breeding from individuals not reared together, but not very different from each other.

In some species, males prefer females that have not mated recently (e.g., prairie voles: Ferguson et al. 1986; domestic sheep: Pepelko and Clegg 1965). Females may also prefer males without recent sexual activity (e.g., Syrian hamsters: Huck et al. 1986b). In other species, there seems to be no preference (e.g., montane voles: Ferguson et al. 1986). Finally, in yet other species, males may actually be stimulated to resume mating with a female they previously mated with if another male mates with her soon after the initial mating (e.g., bighorn sheep, *Ovis canadensis:* Hogg 1984; rhesus macaques and stump-tailed macaques, *Macaca arctoides:* Estep et al. 1986; roof rats, *Rattus rattus:* Estep 1988).

In species having dominance hierarchies, dominant individuals are frequently preferred mating partners (e.g., vervet monkeys, *Chlorocebus* (=*Cercopithecus*) *aethiops:* Keddy 1986). Among territorial species, male territory holders are frequently preferred (e.g., territorial ungulates: Leuthold 1977).

Preferences for other mate characteristics also have been noted. Female domestic sheep prefer older, larger, and sexually solicitous males (Estep et al. 1989). Female African elephants, *Loxodonta africana,* prefer males in musth to those not in musth (Poole 1989). Male domestic sheep prefer younger ewes (Lindsey and Robinson 1961) and ewes with longer wool (Tilbrook 1987).

Individual preferences unrelated to the characteristics mentioned above have been noted in domestic dogs (Beach and Le Boeuf 1967), dingoes, *Canis familiaris dingo* (Kleiman 1968), domestic horses (Asa 1986), Przewalski's horses, *Equus przewalskii* (Boyd 1986), and a variety of primate species (e.g., rhesus macaques: Herbert 1968; Phoenix 1973; bonnet macaques, *Macaca radiata:* Nadler and Rosenblum 1971; talapoin monkeys, *Miopithecus talapoin:* Dixson and Herbert 1977).

The compatibility of a mating pair or group may depend in part on some or all of these preferences, the early experiences of the animals, and their adult experiences prior to the pairing or grouping. Animals that have had previously aversive breeding experiences cannot be expected to be reliable breeders. In groups, the compatibility of nonbreeding individuals with breeding individuals can have indirect effects on breeding success. For example, in captive Przewalski's horses, anestrous mares may harass and interfere with the matings of estrous mares (Boyd 1986). In some cases, animals that are otherwise compatible in social groups must be isolated except when being bred to achieve the best reproductive success (e.g., cheetahs, *Acinonyx jubatus;* red pandas, *Ailurus fulgens:* Kleiman 1980). In other cases, it appears that compatibility is increased by extensive experience. Yamada and Durrant (1989) report that in clouded leopards, optimum breeding requires pairing potential mates by 1 year of age, prior to sexual maturity.

Social Dominance

In species in which dominance hierarchies are formed, either by males or by females, higher-ranking animals usually engage in more sexual behavior than do lower-ranking animals. Among males, there is considerable evidence that dominant members of the group are usually more sexually active than are subordinates (see reviews by Wittenberger 1981; Dewsbury 1982a; Fedigan 1983; Price 1985). The effects of female dominance rank on sexual activity have received less attention, and are less clear. In some species dominant females engage in more sexual behavior than subordinates (e.g., Przewalski's horses: Boyd 1986). In others, there is no relationship (e.g., rhesus macaques: Wilson 1981; stump-tailed macaques: Estep et al. 1984).

The mechanisms by which this difference is achieved are variable. In some species, like stump-tailed macaques, dominant males physically interfere with subordinates' copulations, and even the physical presence of dominant males can suppress the sexual behavior of subordinates (Estep et al. 1988). In others, like vervets, females may prefer dominant males as mating partners, thus conferring a dominance advantage (Keddy 1986). Kleiman (1980) has reviewed various mechanisms by which females of higher rank can achieve greater reproductive success, including physiological suppression of subordinates' ovulation in common marmosets, *Callithrix jacchus*, and behavioral interference in matings by timber wolves, *Canis lupus*. Physiological suppression of reproduction was suspected in the case of a subordinate howler monkey, *Alouatta caraya*, who bred when removed from the two higher-ranking females with whom she had lived (Shoemaker 1982). In a single-male group of Japanese macaques, it was found that the dominant female physically disrupted the matings of subordinate females (Randall and Taylor 1991).

Dominant animals are not always successful in monopolizing sexual activity in groups. The physical features of the environment sometimes make it easier or more difficult for dominant animals to engage in higher rates of sexual activity. Studies of rhesus and stump-tailed macaques have shown that subordinates engage in higher rates of copulation when there is cover present; subordinates will copulate out of sight of dominant animals when cover is available (Ruiz de Elvira and Herndon 1986; Estep et al. 1988). What is clear is that the salience of dominance effects on mating may depend on the nature of the physical environment in which the animals are housed. By manipulating the environment, managers may be able to increase or decrease the reproduction of subordinate animals.

Novelty, Audience Effects, and Overcrowding

As mentioned previously, there is a common belief that a change in sexual partners can reinstate or reinvigorate the copulatory behavior of animals (i.e., the "Coolidge effect"). As Dewsbury (1981) states, "There is no doubt that novelty plays an important role in the regulation of copulatory be-

havior under some circumstances" (478). As he goes on to point out, the effects of partner novelty are often inconsistent, difficult to replicate experimentally, usually small in magnitude, and overgeneralized. Thus caution must be used in interpreting and generalizing from different studies.

It is also important to distinguish between the initiation of sexual behavior (measured by the probability of copulation or the latency to copulate) and copulatory performance (measured by rates of mounts, intromissions, and ejaculations) when considering the effects of novelty. For example, in domestic sheep, it appears that a satiated ram's rates of ejaculation are increased if he is presented with a novel ewe, but the probability of his mating with the novel ewe is no different from that of his mating with the original ewe (Pepelko and Clegg 1965).

The difficulty of generalizing novelty effects is illustrated by the case of two closely related species of voles. In meadow voles, *Microtus pennsylvanicus,* the male was found to be more likely to resume copulation with a novel female than with the original female (Gray and Dewsbury 1975). However, in prairie voles, Gray and Dewsbury (1973) found no facilitation of sexual behavior with the introduction of a novel female.

Another manipulation that is thought to increase sexual performance is to present multiple partners simultaneously. When multiple ewes are presented to domestic sheep rams, numbers of mounts and ejaculations increase with increasing numbers of ewes (Hulet et al. 1962). In contrast, male rhesus macaques presented with two estrous females showed no more copulatory behavior than males presented with one estrous female (Herbert 1968).

In situations in which the same partners are placed together for mating repeatedly, as in some breeding centers, it is often reported that there is a decrement in sexual performance over time. There is some evidence that introducing new partners can reinstate higher levels of sexual performance (e.g., rhesus macaques: Michael and Zumpe 1978).

There is also evidence that changing the environment or moving the animals within the environment can reinstate declining sexual behavior in some animals (e.g., domestic cattle: Hale and Almquist 1960). O'Donoghue (1982) reported a resurgence of copulatory activity in a pair of orangutans when the animals were moved to a new enclosure, a new female was introduced to the pair, and the animals were put on a weight-reducing diet. It was not clear which factor or combination of factors was responsible for the increase. In other species, movements to new environments may produce fear and stress responses that interfere with normal sexual responses, at least initially (Hediger 1965).

In some species it is known that successful reproduction depends upon having a critical number of conspecific individuals present (Hediger 1965). In domestic cattle and domestic goats it has been found that males show an enhancement of sexual performance if they watch other males mount females prior to their own mating (Mader and Price 1984; Price, Smith, and Katz 1984). Such social facilitation has not always been found, however; domestic sheep, for example, show no such enhancement in sexual performance (Price 1987). As will be recalled from the discussion of dominance and sexual behavior above, the presence of higher-ranking animals can interfere with or inhibit the sexual activity of subordinates. Thus, the specific relationships between the animals can alter the potency of audience effects. Finally, it has been shown that having too many animals in a given area can decrease sexual activity and reproductive success (reviewed by Elton 1979). Boyd (1986) reported that having eighteen mares with a Przewalski's horse stallion depressed reproduction, but that when the number of mares was reduced, breeding returned to normal. Similarly, Mellen (1991) reports that captive small cats, *Felis* spp., rarely breed successfully in groups of more than two individuals.

The effects of novelty and the presence of conspecifics appear to vary widely across species. At present there is too little information on most species to identify patterns in these effects or to make generalizations. It has been hypothesized that monogamous species should not show a Coolidge effect (see Dewsbury 1981); however, the current data do not allow a fair evaluation of that hypothesis. The influence of the presence of conspecifics on mating behavior may also vary with social organization and mating system. Monogamous species or solitary species may engage in more sexual behavior in the absence of conspecifics than do polygamous species. This hypothesis also awaits confirmation. At present, the manager of captive mammals should be aware of the diversity of social factors that can influence sexual behavior and stay open to the possibility that subtle variations in these factors will produce dramatic effects on sexual behavior.

ENVIRONMENTAL INFLUENCES ON COURTSHIP AND COPULATION

A variety of environmental factors have been found to influence the sexual behavior of mammals. Chief among these are reduced food intake and inadequate nutrition. Much research has been focused on the relationship between nutrition and reproduction in captive animals. Such research has greatly improved the reproduction of many captive species (see Hediger 1965). Part 2 of this volume devotes considerable attention to nutritional issues, and they will not be reviewed here. Suffice it to say that nutritional deficits can inhibit sexual development and interfere with physiological processes and thus can retard or inhibit male and female sexual behavior (reviewed by Price 1985; Hurnik 1987).

Climatological factors such as temperature, humidity, and lighting have been implicated in breeding deficits of zoo animals and domestic farm animals (reviewed by Hediger 1965; Price 1985; Hurnik 1987). Despite this, there has been little systematic work linking these variables to specific deficits in courtship and copulatory behavior in mammals. More research is needed in this area.

Spatial factors may be important to the normal courtship and copulatory behavior of many species. As Hediger (1965) has stated, it is not only the size of the area but also the quality of the space that is important to successful breeding. Sometimes changes in the physical environment can produce interesting changes in sexual behavior. For ex-

ample, Nadler (1982) found that when he gave female orangutans access to a second room where males could not follow, the females showed less resistance to male copulatory attempts and showed higher levels of sexual solicitation. Preliminary data also suggest that an indirect effect of these spatial changes was increased reproductive success.

The presence of heterospecifics in or near the enclosures of some animals may inhibit normal reproductive behavior. Hediger (1965), for example, suggests that keeping cheetahs within sight of lions, *Panthera leo*, produces fear in the cheetahs that may inhibit breeding. Blake and Gillett (1984) report that breeders of Asian chipmunks, *Tamias sibiricus*, had poorer breeding success if other species of rodents were housed near the chipmunks. The actual mechanisms for such poor breeding have yet to be elucidated, but may be related to stress effects on reproductive physiology.

The presence of humans in or near breeding animals' enclosures can also inhibit or interfere with normal sexual behavior. Glatston et al. (1984) have shown that pairs of cotton-top tamarins on display to the public at a zoo showed lower rates of mounting as well as other kinds of social behavior than did pairs off display. Hediger (1965) has related this response to the tameness of the animals: tame animals can tolerate more human contact than can untamed animals. However, even among tame animals such as domestic pigs, relationships have been found between the responses of sows to human handlers and their reproductive success (Hemsworth, Brand, and Willems 1981). It was found that those sows showing fear of humans had smaller litters than those that were not fearful. The implication of this finding is that animals that have been poorly handled or have become fearful of humans may have poorer reproduction than those that have been handled gently or are not fearful of humans. Since many captive mammals have very frequent contact with humans, the behavior of handlers and visitors may have subtle but far-reaching effects on the sexual behavior and reproductive success of the animals. Additional research into this area is needed.

ACKNOWLEDGMENTS

Preparation of this chapter was aided by grant BNS-8904974 from the National Science Foundation to Donald A. Dewsbury.

REFERENCES

Asa, C. S. 1986. Sexual behavior of mares. In *The veterinary clinics of North America, equine practice.* vol. 2, no. 3, *Behavior*, ed. S. L. Crowell-Davis and K. A. Houpt, 653–64. Philadelphia: W. B. Saunders.

Beach, F. A. 1968. Coital behavior in dogs. III. Effects of early isolation on mating in males. *Behaviour* 30:218–38.

———. 1976. Sexual attractivity, proceptivity, and receptivity in female mammals. *Horm. Behav.* 7:105–38.

Beach, F. A., and Jordan, L. 1956. Sexual exhaustion and recovery in the male rat. *Q. J. Exp. Psychol.* 8:121–33.

Beach, F. A., and Le Boeuf, B. J. 1967. Coital behaviour in dogs. I. Preferential mating in the bitch. *Anim. Behav.* 16:546–58.

Beach, F. A., and Rabedeau, R. G. 1959. Sexual exhaustion and recovery in the male hamster. *J. Comp. Physiol. Psychol.* 52:56–61.

Beck, B. B., and Power, M. L. 1988. Correlates of sexual and maternal competence in captive gorillas. *Zoo Biol.* 7:339–50.

Beier, J. C., and Wartzok, D. 1979. Mating behaviour of captive spotted seals *(Phoca largha). Anim. Behav.* 27:772–81.

Bekoff, M., and Diamond, J. 1976. Precopulatory and copulatory behavior in coyotes. *J. Mammal.* 57:372–75.

Berger, P. J., Negus, N. C., Sanders, E. H., and Gardner, P. D. 1981. Chemical triggering of reproduction in *Microtus montanus. Science* 214:69–70.

Bermant, G., and Davidson, J. M. 1974. *Biological bases of sexual behavior.* New York: Harper and Row.

Bignami, G., and Beach, F. A. 1968. Mating behaviour in the chinchilla. *Anim. Behav.* 16:45–53.

Blackwell, K. 1969. Rearing and breeding Demidoff's galago, *Galago demidovi,* in captivity. *Int. Zoo Yrbk.* 9:74–76.

Blake, B. H., and Gillett, E. 1984. Reproduction of Asian chipmunks *(Tamias sibiricus)* in captivity. *Zoo Biol.* 3:47–63.

Boyd, L. 1986. Behavior problems of equids in zoos. In *The veterinary clinics of North America, equine practice,* vol. 2, no. 3, *Behavior,* ed. S. L. Crowell-Davis and K. A. Houpt, 653–64. Philadelphia: W. B. Saunders.

Boyd, S. K., and Blaustein, A. R. 1985. Familiarity and inbreeding avoidance in the gray-tailed vole *(Microtus canicaudus). J. Mammal.* 66:348–52.

Bryant, S. 1988. Maintenance and captive breeding of the eastern quoll *Dasyurus viverrinus. Int. Zoo Yrbk.* 27:119–24.

Carpenter, C. R. 1942. Sexual behavior of free-ranging rhesus monkeys *(Macaca mulatta). J. Comp. Psychol.* 33:113–42.

Coopersmith, C. B., and Banks, E. M. 1983. Effects of olfactory cues on sexual behavior in the brown lemming, *Lemmus trimucronatus. J. Comp. Physiol. Psychol.* 97:120–26.

Denenberg, V. H., Zarrow, M. X., and Ross, S. 1969. The behaviour of rabbits. In *The behaviour of domestic animals,* ed. E. S. E. Hafez, 417–34. Baltimore: Williams and Wilkins.

Dewsbury, D. A. 1972. Patterns of copulatory behavior in male mammals. *Q. Rev. Biol.* 47:1–33.

———. 1974. Copulatory behavior of white-throated wood rats *(Neotoma albigula)* and golden mice *(Ochrotomys nuttalli). Anim. Behav.* 22:601–10.

———. 1975. Diversity and adaptation in rodent copulatory behavior. *Science* 190:947–54.

———. 1978. The comparative method in studies of reproductive behavior. In *Sex and behavior: Status and prospectus,* ed. T. E. McGill, D. A. Dewsbury, and B. D. Sachs, 83–112. New York: Plenum Press.

———. 1981. Effects of novelty on copulatory behavior: The Coolidge effect and related phenomena. *Psychol. Bull.* 89:464–82.

———. 1982a. Dominance rank, copulatory behavior, and differential reproduction. *Q. Rev. Biol.* 57:135–59.

———. 1982b. Ejaculate cost and male choice. *Am. Nat.* 119:601–10.

———. 1988. Kin discrimination and reproductive behavior in muroid rodents. *Behav. Genet.* 18:525–36.

Dewsbury, D. A., and Pierce, J. D. Jr. 1989. Copulatory behavior of primates as viewed in broad mammalian perspective. *Am. J. Primatol.* 17:51–72.

Dixson, A. F., and Herbert, J. 1977. Gonadal hormones and sexual behavior in groups of talapoin monkeys *(Miopithecus talapoin). Horm. Behav.* 8:141–54.

Doherty, W. C., Price, E. O., and Katz, L. S. 1987. A note on activity monitoring as a supplement to estrus detection methods for dairy goats. *Appl. Anim. Behav. Sci.* 17:347–51.

Dryden, G. L. 1969. Reproduction in *Suncus murinus. J. Reprod. Fertil. Suppl.* 6:377–96.

Eisenberg, J. F. 1981. *The mammalian radiations: An analysis of trends in evolution, adaptation, and behavior.* Chicago: University of Chicago Press.

Eisenberg, J. F., and Gould, E. 1970. The tenrecs: A study in mammalian behavior and evolution. *Smithsonian Contributions to Zoology,* no. 27.

Eisenberg, J. F., McKay, G. M. , and Jainudeen, M. R. 1971. Reproductive behaviour of the Asiatic elephant. *Behaviour* 38:193–225.

Elton, R. H. 1979. Baboon behavior under crowded conditions. In *Captivity and behavior,* ed. J. Erwin, T. L. Maple, and G. Mitchell, 125–38. New York: Van Nostrand Reinhold.

Estep, D. Q. 1988. Copulations by other males shorten the postejaculatory intervals of pairs of roof rats *(Rattus rattus). Anim. Behav.* 36:299–300.

Estep, D. Q., Bruce, K. E. M., Johnston, M. E., and Gordon, T. P. 1984. Sexual behavior of group-housed stumptailed macaques *(Macaca arctoides):* Temporal, demographic, and sociosexual relationships. *Folia Primatol.* 42:115–26.

Estep, D. Q., and Dewsbury, D. A. 1976. Copulatory behavior of *Neotoma lepida* and *Baiomys taylori:* Relationships between penile morphology and behavior. *J. Mammal.* 57:570–73.

Estep, D. Q., Gordon, T. P., Wilson, M. E., and Walker, M. L. 1986. Social stimulation and the resumption of copulation in rhesus *(Macaca mulatta)* and stumptail macaques *(Macaca arctoides). Int. J. Primatol.* 7:505–15.

Estep, D. Q., Nieuwenhuijsen, K., Bruce, K. E., deNeef, K. J., Walters, P. A. III, Baker, S. C., and Slob, A. K. 1988. Inhibition of sexual behaviour among subordinate stumptail macaques, *Macaca arctoides. Anim. Behav.* 36:854–64.

Estep, D. Q., Price, E. O., Wallach, S. J. R., and Dally, M. R. 1989. Social preferences of domestic ewes for rams *(Ovis aries). Appl. Anim. Behav. Sci.* 24:287–300.

Ewer, R. F., and Wemmer, C. 1974. The behaviour in captivity of the African civet, *Civettictis civetta* (Schreber). *Z. Tierpsychol.* 34:359–94.

Fedigan, L. M. 1983. Dominance and reproductive success in primates. *Yrbk. Phys. Anthropol.* 26:91–129.

Ferguson, B., Fuentes, S. M., Sawrey, D. K., and Dewsbury, D. A. 1986. Male preferences for unmated versus mated females in two species of voles *(Microtus ochrogaster* and *M. montanus). J. Comp. Psychol.* 100:243–47.

Gerall, A. D., Ward, I. L., and Gerall, A. A. 1967. Disruption of the male rat's sexual behavior induced by social isolation. *Anim. Behav.* 15:54–58.

Gibbs, R. H. Jr. 1955. The functional anatomy of the penis of the shrew *Blarina brevicauda. Anat. Rec.* 121:298–99.

Glatston, A. R., Geilvoet-Soettman, E., Hora-Pecek, E., and van Hooff, J. A. R. A. M. 1984. The influence of the zoo environment on social behavior of groups of cotton-topped tamarins, *Saguinus o. oedipus. Zoo Biol.* 3:241–53.

Golley, F. B. 1957. Gestation period, breeding, and fawning behavior of Columbian black-tailed deer. *J. Mammal.* 38:116–20.

Gray, G. D., and Dewsbury, D. A. 1973. A quantitative description of copulatory behavior in prairie voles *(Microtus ochrogaster). Brain Behav. Evol.* 8:437–52.

———. 1975. A quantitative description of the copulatory behavior of meadow voles *(Microtus pennsylvanicus). Anim. Behav.* 23:261–67.

Grier, J., and Burk, T. 1992. *Biology of animal behavior.* 2d ed. St. Louis: Mosby.

Gruendel, A. D., and Arnold, W. J. 1969. Effects of early social deprivation on reproductive behavior of male rats. *J. Comp. Physiol. Psychol.* 67:123–28.

Guinness, F., Lincoln, G. A., and Short, R. V. 1971. The reproductive cycle of the female red deer, *Cervus elaphus* L. *J. Reprod. Fertil.* 27:427–38.

Hafez, E. S. E., Williams, N., and Wierzbowski, S. 1969. The behaviour of horses. In *The behaviour of domestic animals*, ed. E. S. E. Hafez, 391–416. Baltimore: Williams and Wilkins.

Hale, E. B., and Almquist, J. O. 1960. Relation of sexual behavior to germ cell output in farm animals. *J. Dairy Sci., Suppl.* 43: 145–69.

Harlow, H. F. 1962. The heterosexual affectional system in monkeys. *Am. Psychol.* 17:1–9.

———. 1965. Total social isolation: Effects on macaque monkey behavior. *Science* 148:666.

Hart, B. L. 1985. *The behavior of domestic animals*. New York: W. H. Freeman.

———. 1967. Sexual reflexes and mating behavior in the male dog. *J. Comp. Physiol. Psychol.* 64:388–99.

Hediger, H. 1964. *Wild animals in captivity*. New York: Dover.

———. 1965. Environmental factors influencing the reproduction of zoo animals. In *Sex and behavior*, ed. F. A. Beach, 319–54. New York: Wiley.

Hemsworth, P. H., Brand, A., and Willems, P. 1981. The behavioural response of sows to the presence of human beings and its relation to productivity. *Livestock Prod. Sci.* 8:67–74.

Hepper, P. G. 1986. Kin recognition: Functions and mechanisms. A review. *Biol. Rev.* 61:63–93.

Herbert, J. 1968. Sexual preference in the rhesus monkey *Macaca mulatta* in the laboratory. *Anim. Behav.* 16:120–28.

Hogg, J. T. 1984. Mating in bighorn sheep: Multiple creative male strategies. *Science* 225:526–29.

Horner, B. E., and Taylor, J. M. 1968. Growth and reproductive behavior in the southern grasshopper mouse. *J. Mammal.* 49: 644–60.

Houston, E. W., Read, B. W., and Miller, R. E. 1988. Captive management of the gerenuk *Litocranius walleri* at the St. Louis Zoo. *Int. Zoo Yrbk.* 27:319–26.

Huck, U. W., Lisk, R. D., Allison, J. C., and Van Dongen, C. G. 1986a. Determinants of mating success in the golden hamster *(Mesocricetus auratus)*: Social dominance and mating tactics under semi-natural conditions. *Anim. Behav.* 34:971–89.

Huck, U. W., Lisk, R. D., Parente, E. J., and Principato, D. E. 1986b. Determinants of mating success in the golden hamster *(Mesocricetus auratus)*: III. Female acceptance of multiple mating partners. *J. Comp. Psychol.* 100:128–36.

Hulet, C. V., Ercanbrack, S. K., Price, D. A., Blackwell, R. L., and Wilson, L. O. 1962. Mating behavior of the ram in the one-sire pen. *J. Anim. Sci.* 21:857–74.

Hurnik, J. F. 1987. Sexual behavior of female domestic mammals. In *The veterinary clinics of North America, food animal practice*, vol. 3, no. 2, *Farm animal behavior*, ed. E. O. Price, 423–61. Philadelphia: W. B. Saunders.

Jochle, W. 1973. Coitus-induced ovulation. *Contraception* 7: 523–64.

Katz, L. S. 1987. Endocrine systems and behavior. In *The veterinary clinics of North America, food animal practice*, vol. 3, no. 2, *Farm animal behavior*, ed. E. O. Price, 393–404. Philadelphia: W. B. Saunders.

Keddy, A. C. 1986. Female mate choice in vervet monkeys *(Cercopithecus aethiops)*. *Am. J. Primatol.* 10:125–34.

Kendrick, K. M., and Dixson, A. F. 1984. A quantitative description of copulatory and associated behaviors of captive marmosets *(Callithrix jacchus)*. *Int. J. Primatol.* 5:199–212.

Key, C., and McIver, R. M. 1977. Factors affecting sexual preferences in sheep. *Appl. Anim. Ethol.* 3:291.

Kiddy, C. A. 1977. Variation in physical activity as an indication of estrus in dairy cows. *J. Dairy Sci.* 60:235–43.

Kiddy, C. A., Conley, H. H., and Hawk, H. W. 1978. Detection of estrus-related odors in cows by trained dogs. *Biol. Reprod.* 19:389.

Kilgour, R. 1985. The behavioral background to reproduction. In *Ethology of farm animals*, ed. A. F. Fraser, 279–88. New York: Elsevier.

Kleiman, D. G. 1968. Reproduction in the Canidae. *Int. Zoo Yrbk.* 8:3–8.

———. 1970. Reproduction in the female green acouchi, *Myoprocta pratti* Pocock. *J. Reprod. Fertil.* 23:55–65.

———. 1971. The courtship and copulatory behaviour of the green acouchi, *Myoprocta pratti*. *Z. Tierpsychol.* 29:259–78.

———. 1974. Patterns of behaviour in hystricomorph rodents. *Symp. Zool. Soc. Lond.* 34:171–209.

———. 1977. Monogamy in mammals. *Q. Rev. Biol.* 52:39–69.

———. 1980. The sociobiology of captive propagation. In *Conservation biology: An evolutionary-ecological perspective*, ed. M. E. Soulé and B. A. Wilcox, 243–61. Sunderland, Mass.: Sinauer Associates.

———. 1983. Ethology and reproduction of captive giant pandas *(Ailuropoda melanoleuca)*. *Z. Tierpsychol.* 62:1–46.

Lanier, D. L., and Dewsbury, D. A. 1976. A quantitative study of copulatory behaviour of large Felidae. *Behav. Proc.* 1:327–33.

———. 1977. Studies of copulatory behaviour in northern grasshopper mice *(Onychomys leucogaster)*. *Anim. Behav.* 25: 185–92.

Le Boeuf, B. J. 1972. Sexual behavior in the northern elephant seal *Mirounga angustirostris*. *Behaviour* 41:1–26.

Leuthold, W. 1977. *African ungulates*. New York: Springer-Verlag.

Lindsey, D. R., and Robinson, T. J. 1961. Studies on the efficiency of mating in the sheep. II. The effect of freedom of rams, paddock size, and age of ewes. *J. Agric. Sci.* 57:141–45.

Long, J. A., and Evans, H. M. 1922. The oestrous cycle in the rat and its associated phenomena. *Memoirs of the University of California* 6:1–113.

Lott, D. F. 1974. Sexual and aggressive behavior of adult male American bison *(Bison bison)*. In *The behaviour of ungulates and its relation to management*, ed. V. Geist and F. Walther, 382–94. Morges, Switzerland: IUCN.

Lumpkin, S., and Koontz, F. W. 1986. Social and sexual behavior of the rufous elephant shrew *(Elephantulus rufescens)*. *J. Mammal.* 67:112–19.

Lyne, A. G. 1976. Observations on oestrus and the oestrous cycle in the marsupials *Isoodon macrourus* and *Perameles nasuta*. *Aust. J. Zool.* 24:513–21.

Mader, D. R., and Price, E. O. 1984. The effect of sexual stimulation on the sexual performance of Hereford bulls. *J. Anim. Sci.* 59:294–300.

Maynes, G. M. 1973. Reproduction in the parma wallaby, *Macropus parma* Waterhouse. *Aust. J. Zool.* 21:331–51.

McGill, T. E. 1962. Sexual behavior in three inbred strains of mice. *Behaviour* 19:341–50.

Mellen, J. D. 1991. Factors influencing reproductive success in small captive exotic felids *(Felis spp.)*: A multiple regression analysis. *Zoo Biol.* 10:95–110.

———. 1992. Effects of early rearing experience on subsequent adult sexual behavior using domestic cats *(Felis catus)* as a model for exotic small felids. *Zoo Biol.* 11:17–32.

Michael, R. P., and Zumpe, D. 1978. Potency in male rhesus monkeys: Effects of continuously receptive females. *Science* 200: 451–53.

Nadler, R. D. 1976. Sexual behavior of captive lowland gorillas. *Arch. Sex. Behav.* 5:487–502.

———. 1977. Sexual behavior of captive orangutans. *Arch. Sex. Behav.* 6:457–75.

———. 1982. Laboratory research on sexual behavior and reproduction of gorillas and orang-utans. *Am. J. Primatol. Suppl.* 1: 57–66.

Nadler, R. D., and Rosenblum, L. A. 1971. Factors influencing sexual behavior of male bonnet macaques *(Macaca radiata)*. In *Proceedings of the Third International Congress of Primatology, Zurich 1970,* vol. 3, 100–107. Basel: Karger.

Nelson, R. J. 1985. Photoperiod influences reproduction in the prairie vole *(Microtus ochrogaster)*. *Biol. Reprod.* 33:596–602.

O'Donoghue, E. R. 1982. A resurgence in reproductive behavior in a previously inactive male orangutan *(Pongo pygmaeus abelii)*. *Zoo Biol.* 1:157–59.

Pepelko, W. E., and Clegg, M. T. 1965. Studies of mating behavior and some factors influencing the sexual response in the male sheep *Ovis aries. Anim. Behav.* 13:249–58.

Phoenix, C. H. 1973. Ejaculation by male rhesus as a function of the female partner. *Horm. Behav.* 4:365–70.

Poole, J. H. 1989. Mate guarding, reproductive success, and female choice in African elephants. *Anim. Behav.* 37:842–49.

Price, E. O. 1985. Sexual behavior of large domestic farm animals: An overview. *J. Anim. Sci.* 61 (suppl. 3): 62–74.

———. 1987. Male sexual behavior. In *The veterinary clinics of North America, food animal practice,* vol. 3, no. 2, *Farm animal behavior,* ed. E. O. Price, 405–22. Philadelphia: W. B. Saunders.

Price, E. O., Smith, V. M., and Katz, L. S. 1984. Sexual stimulation of male dairy goats. *Appl. Anim. Behav. Sci.* 13:83–92.

Price, E. O., Wallach, S. J. R., and Silver, G. V. 1990. The effects of long-term individual vs. group housing on the sexual behavior of beef bulls. *Appl. Anim. Behav. Sci.* 27:277–85.

Randall, D., and Taylor, L. L. 1991. Female sexual behavior in the absence of male-male competition in captive Japanese macaques *(Macaca fuscata)*. *Zoo Biol.* 10:319–28.

Rasa, O. A. E. 1977. The ethology and sociology of the dwarf mongoose *(Helogale undulata rufula)*. *Z. Tierpsychol.* 43:337–406.

Riesen, A. H. 1971. Nissen's observations on the development of sexual behavior in captive-born, nursery-reared chimpanzees. In *The Chimpanzee,* vol. 4, ed. G. H. Bourne, 1–18, Basel: Karger.

Rogers, C. M., and Davenport, R. K. 1969. The effects of restricted rearing on sexual behavior of chimpanzees. *Dev. Psychol.* 1: 200–204.

Rubin, H. B., and Azrin, N. H. 1967. Temporal patterns of sexual behavior in rabbits as determined by an automatic recording technique. *J. Exp. Anal. Behav.* 10:219–31.

Ruiz de Elvira, M. C., and Herndon, J. G. 1986. Disruption of sexual behaviour by high ranking rhesus monkeys *(Macaca mulatta)*. *Behaviour* 96:227–40.

Saayman, G. S. 1970. The menstrual cycle and sexual behaviour in a troop of free ranging chacma baboons *(Papio ursinus)*. *Folia Primatol.* 12:81–110.

Sever, Z., and Mendelssohn, H. 1988. Copulation as a possible mechanism to maintain monogamy in porcupines, *Hystrix indica. Anim. Behav.* 36:1541–42.

Shoemaker, A. H. 1982. Fecundity in the captive howler monkey, *Alouatta caraya. Zoo Biol.* 1:149–56.

Stribley, J. A., French, J. A., and Inglett, B. J. 1987. Mating patterns in the golden lion tamarin *(Leontopithecus rosalia)*: Continuous receptivity and concealed estrus. *Folia Primatol.* 49: 137–50.

Tang-Martinez, Z., Mueller, L. L., and Taylor, G. T. 1993. Individual odours and mating success in the golden hamster, *Mesocricetus auratus. Anim. Behav.* 45:1141–51.

Tilbrook, A. J. 1987. Physical and behavioural factors affecting the sexual "attractiveness" of the ewe. *Appl. Anim. Behav. Sci.* 17:109–15.

Tokuda, K. 1961. A study on the sexual behavior in the Japanese monkey troop. *Primates* 3:1–40.

Trupin, G. L., and Fadem, B. H. 1982. Sexual behavior of the gray short-tailed opossum *(Monodelphis domestica)*. *J. Mammal.* 63:409–14.

Valenstein, E. S., Riss, W., and Young, W. C. 1955. Experiential and genetic factors in the organization of sexual behavior in male guinea pigs. *J. Comp. Physiol. Psychol.* 48:397–403.

de Waal, F. B. M. 1987. Tension regulation and nonreproductive functions of sex in captive bonobos *(Pan paniscus)*. *Natl. Geogr. Res.* 3:318–35.

Walther, F. R. 1984. *Communication and expression in hoofed ungulates.* Bloomington: Indiana University Press.

Waring, G. H. 1983. *Horse behavior.* Park Ridge, N.J.: Noyes.

Warren, R. J., Vogelsang, R. W., Kirkpatrick, R. L., and Scanlon, P. F. 1978. Reproductive behaviour of captive white-tailed deer. *Anim. Behav.* 26:179–83.

Wittenberger, J. F. 1981. *Animal social behavior.* Boston: Duxbury Press.

Widowski, T. M., Ziegler, T. E., Elowson, A. M., and Snowdon, C. T. 1990. The role of males in the stimulation of reproductive function in female cotton-top tamarins, *Saguinus o. oedipus. Anim. Behav.* 40:731–41.

Wilson, M. E. 1981. Social dominance and female reproductive behaviour in rhesus monkeys *(Macaca mulatta)*. *Anim. Behav.* 29:472–82.

Yadav, R. N. 1968. Notes on breeding the Indian wolf *Canis lupus pallipes* at the Jaipur zoo. *Int. Zoo Yrbk.* 8:17–18.

Yamada, J. K., and Durrant, B. S. 1989. Reproductive parameters of clouded leopards *(Neofelis nebulosa)*. *Zoo Biol.* 8:223–31.

37

Reproductive Physiology

CHERYL S. ASA

An understanding of reproductive processes is the only solid foundation upon which to build successful long-term captive breeding programs. Even for species that now reproduce naturally in captivity, a need has arisen for manipulations such as artificial insemination and embryo transfer for genetic reasons. These procedures are possible only as a result of years of study of reproductive phenomena in domestic and laboratory species.

This chapter will review our knowledge of the events and processes of reproductive physiology primarily from the broader base of literature on laboratory and domestic animals, supplementing each discussion with examples from exotic species when possible. A detailed compendium of basic reproductive parameters for an extensive number of mammalian species can be found in Hayssen, Van Tienhoven, and Van Tienhoven 1993.

PUBERTY

An animal's reproductive life begins with puberty, a complex, not yet fully understood process that culminates in fertility. For males, this event is marked by the first production of sperm. In nonprimate and some primate females, puberty is marked by the first ovulation, and in menstruating primate females, by first menstruation, or menarche. Important changes in hormone profiles occur that result in the activation and growth of gonads, germ cells, and often species-specific secondary sex characteristics. (Reviews of pubertal processes can be found in Ramaley 1979, Bronson and Rissman 1986, Foster 1988, Plant 1988, Kinder et al. 1987, and Ojeda 1990.)

In the male, increases in luteinizing hormone (LH), follicle-stimulating hormone (FSH), and prolactin (PRL) secreted from the anterior pituitary as well as androgens from the testicular Leydig cells are correlated with increases in testis and accessory sex organ weight (e.g., seminal vesicles and prostate) (fig. 37.1: Ramaley 1979). These changes are necessary for the stimulation of the testicular Sertoli cells, which are involved in the initiation and maintenance of normal sperm production.

An external sign of first sperm production in the male rat, *Rattus norvegicus* (Korenbrot, Huhtaniemi, and Weiner

1977), that also may occur in other species is the separation or opening of the prepuce of the penile sheath.

Many of the processes of puberty are similar in the female. Increases in the levels of pituitary LH, FSH, and PRL and ovarian progesterone and estradiol accompany an increase in ovarian weight (fig. 37.2: Ramaley 1979). A pattern of pulsatile LH release also has been shown to be important in females.

Adrenocortical hormones may play a role in pubertal onset in some species. Increases in the adrenal androgen dehydroepiandrosterone (DHA or DHEA) have been reported for the rabbit, *Oryctolagus cuniculus*, dog, *Canis familiaris*, and chimpanzee, *Pan troglodytes*, and increases in adrenal androstenedione for the dog and chimpanzee (Cutler et al. 1978). However, no adrenal androgen increase was noted at puberty for the rat, guinea pig, *Cavia porcellus*, golden hamster, *Mesocricetus auratus*, sheep, *Ovis aries*, goat, *Capra hircus*, horse, *Equus caballus*, cow, *Bos taurus*, or rhesus macaque, *Macaca mulatta* (Cutler et al. 1978), or for the crab-eating macaque, *M. fascicularis* (Meusy-Dessolle and Dang 1985). Decreases in adrenal estrogens are correlated with pubertal processes in female rats (Weisz and Gunsalus 1973; Campbell, Schwartz, and Gorski-Firlit 1977).

It appears that a minimal level of adrenal corticosterone is required for normal puberty onset (Ramaley 1973). However, excess adrenocorticotropic hormone (ACTH) (Hagino, Watanabe, and Goldzieher 1969) or glucocorticoids (Ramaley 1976) associated with what are interpreted as stressful situations, such as crowding, can cause a delay in puberty (see Moltz 1975).

Several factors affect the timing of puberty. Attainment of a critical body weight has been correlated with puberty in the Japanese macaque, *Macaca fuscata* (Mori 1979; Wolfe 1979), and squirrel monkey, *Saimiri sciureus* (Coe et al. 1981), but not in the rhesus macaque (Wilen and Naftolin 1976), bonnet macaque, *Macaca radiata* (Silk et al. 1981), or marmoset, *Callithrix jacchus* (Abbott and Hearn 1978).

Nutritional plane, rather than absolute body weight, has been shown to affect the timing of puberty. A higher level of nutrition, or its resultant increase in growth rate, advances puberty in many species (chimpanzee: Tutin 1980; stumptailed macaque, *Macaca arctoides*: Nieuwenhuijsen et

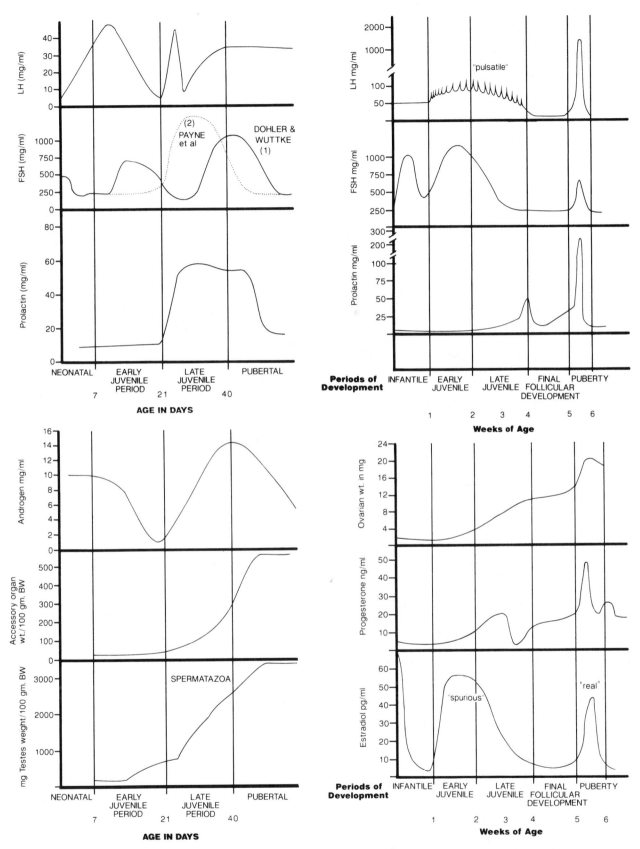

FIG. 37.1. Pubertal changes in hormone levels and in weights of the testes and accessory organs in the male rat. (From Ramaley 1979, by permission of *Biology of Reproduction*.)

FIG. 37.2. Pubertal changes in hormone levels and ovarian weight in the female rat. (From Ramaley 1979, by permission of *Biology of Reproduction*.)

al. 1985; cattle and sheep: Kinder et al. 1987; white-tailed deer, *Odocoileus virginianus:* Verme and Ullrey 1972; red deer, *Cervus elaphus:* Daniel 1963; several seal species, Phocidae: Laws 1973; California vole, *Microtus californicus:* Rissman and Johnston 1986).

Food restriction prevents reproductive development in female, but not male, house mice, *Mus musculus* (Hamilton and Bronson 1985). It is proposed that growth hormone levels, not weight gain per se, mediate this effect (Ramaley 1979). Even exposure to reduced, but not elevated, temperature can retard sexual maturation in the laboratory rat (Piacsek and Nazian 1981).

Particularly among primates, initial ovarian cycles following puberty are often infertile, a condition termed adolescent sterility (chimpanzee: Coe et al. 1979; rhesus macaque: Hartmann 1931; stump-tailed macaque: Nieuwenhuijsen et al. 1985; pig-tailed macaque, *Macaca nemestrina,* and Celebes black ape, *M. nigra:* Hadidian and Bernstein 1979). The conception rate is also low in the postpubertal period in cattle (Byerley et al. 1987). A related phenomenon, follicular development and atresia without ovulation, commonly precedes the first real ovulation of puberty in the rat (Dawson and McCabe 1951), cattle (Schams and Butz 1972), and sheep (Ryan and Foster 1978), and may well be common in other species.

MALE REPRODUCTION

In general, the male reproductive system has been studied less than that of the female, and most information that does exist comes from studies of laboratory and domestic species. (For reviews see Waites and Setchell 1990; Lamming 1990; Phillips 1974). The dearth of basic knowledge of male reproductive processes in exotic species is striking.

Anatomy

Testes function to produce spermatozoa and to synthesize and secrete androgens, especially testosterone. Spermatogenesis occurs within the densely packed seminiferous tubules, supported and sustained by the Sertoli cells. The Leydig cells, responsible for androgen production, lie in the interstitial spaces between the seminiferous tubules.

Spermatozoa are transported from the testis via the rete testis into the efferent ducts (ductuli efferentes), then into the epididymal duct. The efferent duct and head (caput) of the epididymis resorb fluid, the body (corpus) is secretory, and the tail (cauda) is relatively inactive. Spermatozoa pass from the epididymis through the vas deferens, or ductus deferens, where the accessory fluids are added, and then out via the penis (Waites and Setchell 1990; Williams-Ashman 1988).

Only in mammals do the testes descend from the abdominal cavity into a scrotum. However, the degree of descent varies among orders and families, ranging from virtually no migration (Monotremata; elephant shrews, Macroscelidea; sea cows, Sirenia; sloths and anteaters, Edentata; elephants, Proboscidea; and hyraxes, Hyracoidea), through migration to the caudal abdominal cavity (armadillos, Dasypodidae; whales and dolphins, Cetacea), migration just through the abdominal wall (hedgehogs, Er-

inaceidae; moles, Talpidae; and some seals, Otariidae), and subanal swellings (pigs, Suidae; Rodentia; Carnivora), to a pronounced swelling (Primates; Ruminants; most Marsupialia) (Carrick and Setchell 1977). The function and significance of these differences have not been satisfactorily explained (Waites and Setchell 1990).

For most species, testicular descent is permanent, but in some, descent occurs only during the breeding season (e.g., bats, Chiroptera: Eckstein and Zuckerman 1956; some rodents, *Rattus, Sciurus,* and *Tamias* spp.; and some primates, *Loris* and *Perodicticus* spp.: Prasad 1974, cited in Van Tienhoven 1983).

In species with external (i.e., scrotal) testes, failure of descent (cryptorchidism) results in reduction or absence of spermatogenesis (see Setchell 1978; Wildt, chap. 39, this volume). Testosterone production, however, may be unaffected or only moderately depressed by cryptorchidism or the resulting testicular temperature increase (Moore 1944; Glover 1955). However, although testosterone levels may not be appreciably affected by cryptorchidism, ambient temperatures high enough to result in sperm damage are typically associated with depressed concentrations of testosterone (Waites and Setchell 1990). Of further concern is the increased rate of loss of embryos fertilized by sperm that appear morphologically normal but that have been exposed to elevated ambient temperatures.

Major accessory sex glands found in male mammals include seminal vesicles and prostate and bulbourethral (Cowper's) glands, all of which secrete components of the seminal fluid. Only prostate glands have been found universally in mammals. The occurrence of the various accessory organs in a wide range of mammals is documented by Van Tienhoven (1983) and Hamilton (1990).

Two species-specific morphological features of male mammals are the penile baculum (os penis) and penile spines. The baculum, a bony core, occurs in members of five mammalian orders, Insectivora, Chiroptera, Primates, Rodentia, and Carnivora (Long and Frank 1968; Patterson and Thaeler 1982), and may facilitate intromission and prevent collapse of the urethra during copulation.

The penile spines of the rat (Beach and Levinson 1950), cat, *Felis catus* (Aronson and Cooper 1967), ferret, *Mustela putorius,* mink, *M. vison,* marten, *Martes americana,* raccoon, *Procyon lotor* (Zarrow and Clark 1968), spotted hyena, *Crocuta crocuta,* striped hyena, *Hyaena hyaena,* and aardwolf, *Proteles cristatus* (Wells 1968), may provide additional stimulation during copulation, perhaps most important in species with induced ovulation.

Endocrinology of the Testis

A hypothalamic hormone, gonadotropin-releasing hormone (GnRH, also sometimes called luteinizing hormone–releasing hormone or LHRH) stimulates pituitary secretion of follicle-stimulating hormone (FSH) and luteinizing hormone (LH), both named for their roles in the female but also active in the male. FSH is necessary for spermatogenesis via its action on the Sertoli cells, whereas LH stimulates androgen production by the Leydig cells. Circulating androgens exert negative feedback on both hypothalamic GnRH and pituitary LH production and release, helping to maintain relatively stable androgen levels. (For a more detailed review see Glover, D'Occhio, and Millar 1990). In seasonally reproducing species, the male endocrine axis is depressed, although not always totally inactive, outside the breeding season.

Testosterone is the primary androgen secreted by the adult testis. Androstenedione, although present in smaller amounts, is relatively more prominent in prepubertal and aging males. Other androgens include dehydroepiandrosterone (DHA or DHEA), dihydrotestosterone (DHT), androstenediol, and androstanediol (Setchell 1978). Androgens are necessary for the maintenance of spermatogenesis, the accessory sex organs, secondary sex characteristics (e.g., antlers), sebaceous glands, and libido.

The source of most circulating DHA is the adrenal cortex, not the testes (Gandy and Peterson 1968). Most DHT is formed by reduction of testosterone in accessory reproductive and neural tissues (Setchell 1978; Milewich and Whisenant 1982; Martini 1982). Estrogens are produced by aromatization from testosterone both in the testes and in peripheral tissues (Callard, Petro, and Ryan 1978).

Although the seminiferous tubules can convert progesterone to androgens, the interstitial Leydig cells are by far the more important source of androgens (Christensen and Mason 1965; Hall, Irby, and deKretser 1969). The pituitary gonadotropin LH (also known as interstitial cell–stimulating hormone, or ICSH) stimulates testicular androgen production (El Safoury and Bartke 1974). Each pulsatile release of LH results, in 15–30 minutes, in a pulse of testosterone (cattle: Katongole, Naftolin, and Short 1971; sheep: Schanbacher and Ford 1976; dogs: De Palatis, Moore, and Falvo 1978). When measuring circulating LH or testosterone levels, account must be taken of this pulsatile secretion in addition to possible diurnal rhythms (rhesus macaque: Perachio et al. 1977; horse: Kirkpatrick et al. 1976) or seasonal rhythms (tammar wallaby, *Macropus eugenii:* Inns 1982; rock hyrax, *Procavia capensis:* Neaves 1973; Old World mole, *Talpa europaea:* Racey 1978; bats, Vespertilionidae and Rhinolophidae: Gustafson 1979; armadillo, *Dasypus novemcinctus:* Czekala et al. 1980; horse:Kirkpatrick et al. 1977; red deer: Lincoln and Kay 1979; white-tailed deer: McMillan et al. 1974; blue fox, *Alopex lagopus:* Smith et al. 1985; rhesus macaque: Gordon, Rose, and Bernstein 1976; bonnet macaque: Glick 1979; Japanese macaque: Rostal et al. 1986; stump-tailed macaque: Nieuwenhuijsen et al. 1985).

Because changes in testosterone production are correlated with changes in testicular size, testis size measurements may be adequate for assessing reproductive status or changes when blood sampling is not practical (Willett and Ohms 1957; McMillan et al. 1974; Foote 1969; see Wildt, chap. 39, this volume).

In hibernating male bats (Vespertilionidae and Rhinolophidae) reactivation of several reproductive functions is temporally separated. Spermatogenesis precedes the rise in testosterone production by several months. Testosterone peaks to stimulate the accessory organs, epididymal sperm storage, libido, and mating late in the spermatogenic phase (Gustafson 1979; Gustafson and Shemesh 1976).

Other factors can affect testosterone secretion. Circulating levels are generally lower in aging males (Chan, Leathem, and Esashi 1977). They can also be reduced by anesthetics, with low levels sometimes continuing for days following administration (Setchell, Waites, and Lindner 1965; Cicero et al. 1977). Undernutrition also adversely affects androgen production (sheep: Setchell, Waites, and Lindner 1965; hyrax: Millar and Fairall 1976).

Spermatogenesis

A complete review of spermatogenic processes is beyond the scope of this chapter. The reader is referred to other excellent sources such as Setchell 1978, Hochereau de Rivieres et al. 1990, and Van Tienhoven 1983.

Spermatogenesis is initiated by FSH and testosterone but can be maintained by testosterone alone. Sperm pass into the epididymis, where maturation is completed and they are stored until ejaculation. Sperm that are not ejaculated may be phagocytized or leaked into the bladder (Bedford 1979). Longevity of epididymal sperm varies greatly by species (cattle, 60 days: White 1974; mole, up to 3 months: Racey 1978; bats, Chiroptera, up to 10 months: Racey 1979).

Sexual activity may enhance the rate of sperm production (rabbit: Amann 1970), whereas elevated ambient temperatures can depress spermatogenesis (red kangaroo, *Macropus rufus:* Newsome 1973; pig, *Sus scrofa:* Cameron and Blackshaw 1980).

Both whole-body and localized x-irradiation also profoundly disrupt sperm production by damaging germinal cells (Ellis 1970). Greater doses damage spermatocytes such that they are still capable of fertilization but induce genetic abnormalities that prevent complete embryonic development (Chang, Hunt, and Romanoff 1957). High-frequency sound waves (ultrasound) can cause testicular damage and sterility (Dumontier et al. 1977).

Nutrient deficiencies can depress spermatogenic function either directly or by reducing LH concentrations. The results of dietary restriction can range from no observable effect to complete cessation of spermatogenesis, depending on the species and degree of restriction (Leathem 1975; Blank and Desjardins 1984). Androgen production in these cases is relatively less affected. Overfeeding that results in overly fat males can result in an increased incidence of secondary sperm abnormalities, probably due to increased testis temperature caused by insulating scrotal fat (Skinner 1981).

Deficiencies of amino acids, essential fatty acids, zinc, and vitamins A, B, C, and E all negatively affect spermatogenesis, although at different points in the process (see Setchell 1978 for discussion). In addition, an extensive array of substances have been shown to cause chemical damage to testicular tissues (see Setchell 1978; Zaneveld, in press).

Hormones and Behavior

Androgens are generally responsible for species-specific arrays of reproductive behavior, ranging from aggression related to mate or territory defense to scent-marking, courtship, and copulation. (For descriptions of representative species, see, among others, noctule bat, *Nyctalus noctula:* Racey 1974; tree shrew, *Tupaia glis:* von Holst and Buergel-Goodwin 1975; greater galago, *Otolemur crassicaudatus:* Dixson 1976; rhesus macaque: Gordon, Rose, and

Bernstein 1976; bonnet macaque: Glick 1979; Japanese macaque: Rostal et al. 1986; stoat, *Mustela erminea*: Gulamhusein and Tam 1974; Asian elephant, *Elephas maximus*: Jainudeen, Katongole, and Short 1972; sheep: Mickelsen, Paisley, and Dahmen 1981; white-tailed deer: McMillan et al. 1974).

Not only do androgens stimulate reproductive behavior, but social factors can also cause an increase in hormone levels. Rams living with ewes have higher circulating testosterone concentrations and show more sexual and aggressive behavior than those not living with ewes (Illius, Haynes, and Lamming 1976). Likewise, territorial male impalas, *Aepyceros melampus*, have higher testosterone levels than nonterritorial males (Illius et al. 1983). Acute increases in testosterone (and in LH and prolactin when measured) are stimulated by mating activity (rabbit: Saginor and Horton 1968; rat: Kamel and Frankel 1978; giant panda, *Ailuropoda melanoleuca*: Bonney, Wood, and Kleiman 1981; rhesus macaque: Katongole, Naftolin, and Short 1971).

Sexual activity results in testosterone elevation in zebu bulls previously rated as having low libido, but not in those with high libido (Bindon, Hewetson, and Post 1976). Replacing the resident female mouse, *Mus musculus*, with a new female can cause a testosterone increase in male mice (Macrides, Bartke, and Dalterio 1975). In the male tammar wallaby, seasonal LH and testosterone increases occurred only in the presence of females (Catling and Sutherland 1980).

FEMALE REPRODUCTION

The following overview will describe the basic reproductive phenomena of the mammalian species studied to date, but, more important, will attempt to convey an appreciation for the wide array of strategies that various species have evolved to accomplish the same end, that is, production of young. Details of the endocrine and cellular events of ovarian cycles, beyond the scope of this chapter, can be found in Hansel and Convey 1983, Schneider and Leyendecker 1983, Yen and Vale 1990, Dekel 1986, and Knobil and Neill 1988.

Anatomy

The major structural components of the female reproductive system are the ovaries, oviduct, uterus, cervix, and vagina or urogenital sinus. Notable interspecies variation occurs in uterine and vaginal morphology. The Monotremata have paired uteri that open not into a vagina, but into the urogenital sinus, which terminates at the cloaca (Hughes and Carrick 1978). Marsupialia have two uteri, two cervices, and two vaginae, with several variations, such as the midline vagina of kangaroos, *Macropus* spp. (Sharman 1976).

Among Eutheria (placental mammals), four anatomical types have been described: (1) duplex uterus with two separate uterine horns connected to the vagina by two cervices (e.g., rabbit); (2) bicornuate uterus with two horns joined just anterior to the single cervix and vagina (e.g., pig); (3) bipartite uterus in which the two horns open into a promi-

nent uterine body anterior to the single cervix and vagina (e.g., cattle, sheep, and horses); and (4) simplex uterus with a single uterine body, cervix, and vagina (e.g., most primate species). Some variations on these four patterns are seen in sloths, *Bradypus* spp., which have a simplex uterus and one cervix, but a double vagina, and armadillos, *Dasypus* spp., which have a simplex uterus, but one cervix that opens into a urogenital sinus rather than a vagina (Hafez 1970; Van Tienhoven 1983).

Regarding external features, a ventral pouch is characteristic of some monotremes and marsupials. An os clitoris, homologous to the male baculum, is present in females of various rodent and carnivore species (see Long and Frank 1968; Ewer 1973). Most unusual are the genitals of the female spotted hyena. The hypertrophied clitoris is virtually indistinguishable from the male penis, and fibrous swellings resemble a scrotum (Neaves, Griffin, and Wilson 1980).

Ovarian Cycles

Of the variety of terms that have been applied to female reproductive cycles, most are restrictive. For instance, only primates are considered to have menstrual cycles; induced ovulators can have cycles of follicular growth that are not ovulatory at all, making the term ovulatory cycle inappropriate; and the term estrous cycle better describes behavioral than physiological events. The term ovarian cycle best encompasses the wide range of patterns described to date by focusing on follicular growth and development. The follicles may ovulate or may undergo regression.

The following is a description of the phases that may constitute an ovarian cycle, although its components may vary by species. Figures 37.3, 37.4, and 37.5 illustrate the major events of the ovarian cycles of the rat, horse, and gorilla, *Gorilla gorilla*, respectively.

Follicular Phase Sometimes called the proliferative phase, a term that relates to uterine development, the follicular phase is characterized by the growth and development of a follicle(s), which may subsequently rupture and

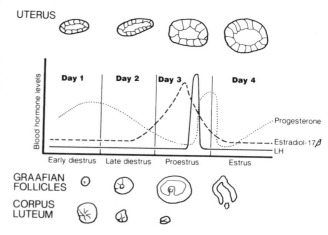

Fig. 37.3. Estrous cycle of the laboratory rat: blood hormone levels and representational changes in the uterus, Graafian follicles, and corpus luteum. (From Bentley 1976; reprinted with the permission of Cambridge University Press.)

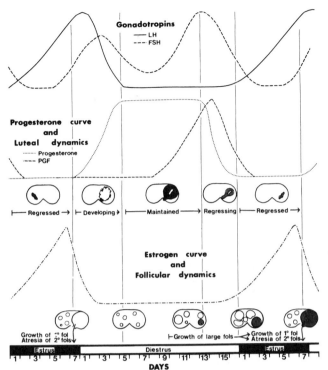

FIG. 37.4.   Estrous cycle of the horse: blood hormone levels and changes in the primary and secondary follicles and corpus luteum. (From Ginther 1979, by permission of the author.)

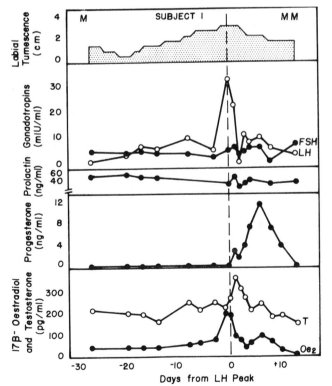

FIG. 37.5.   Menstrual cycle of the lowland gorilla: blood hormone levels, changes in labial tumescence, and occurrence of menses (solid bars at top of figure). (From Nadler 1980, by permission of the author and the *Journal of Reproduction and Fertility*.)

release an ovum (ova). Oocyte and follicular growth culminate in the mature Graafian follicle with its fluid-filled antrum. Mature follicle size is generally correlated with the animal's body size, with the notable exceptions of the vespertilionid bats and plains viscacha, *Lagostomus maximus* (Rowlands and Weir 1984), which have unusually large follicles.

Not all developing follicles are destined to ovulate. Many undergo atresia, or regression. The mechanism that determines whether a follicle ovulates or regresses is unknown. As its name suggests, the pituitary hormone FSH (follicle-stimulating hormone) stimulates follicular growth as well as the production and release of steroid hormones, primarily estrogens, by the follicle. LH (luteinizing hormone), another pituitary product, also plays a role in follicular steroid production. As with the male, hypothalamic GnRH stimulates pituitary secretion of both FSH and LH.

According to the two-cell theory of ovarian steroid synthesis, theca interna cells in preovulatory follicles, under the influence of LH, convert cholesterol to androgens, which are then transferred to the granulosa cells, where FSH enhances their aromatization to estrogens (Fortune 1981).

The estrogens secreted by the follicular granulosa cells have many effects. Unlike in the male, estrogens can exert both positive and negative feedback; that is, they suppress the secretion of FSH and enhance that of LH. Estrogens also stimulate species-specific features of estrus such as labial tumescence, perineal swelling and reddening, and proestrous sanguinous uterine discharge (table 37.1). Estrogens are also responsible for a constellation of behaviors that promote courtship and copulation.

In addition to estrogens, the ovaries have been shown to secrete androgens, primarily testosterone and androstenedione (rat: Dupon and Kim 1973; rabbit: Hilliard et al. 1974; sheep: Baird et al. 1969). A periovulatory testosterone or androstenedione peak has been measured in several species (dog: Olson et al. 1984; cattle: Kotwica and Williams 1982; goat: Homeida and Cooke 1984; horse: Noden, Oxender, and Hafs 1975; Siberian tiger, *Panthera tigris altaica*: Seal et al. 1985; baboon, *Papio cynocephalus*: Kling and Westfahl 1978; rhesus macaque: Hess and Resko 1973; chimpanzee: Nadler et al. 1985).

Although the follicular phase is primarily characteristic of nonpregnant female ovarian cycles, follicular growth can also occur both early (horse: Squires et al. 1974; cat: Schmidt, Chakraborty, and Wildt 1983; chinchilla, *Chinchilla lanigera*: Weir 1973; Asian elephant: Perry 1953) and late in pregnancy (European hare, *Lepus europaeus*: Martinet 1980; Flux 1967; black mastiff bat, *Molossus ater*: Rasweiler 1988). Ovulation early in the period of delayed implantation is typical in the mink and results in 80–90% of the embryos carried to term (Hansson 1947; Enders and Enders 1963).

Ovulation The processes that culminate in ovulation are still not fully understood. Various mechanisms that have been proposed to explain follicular rupture include increases in intrafollicular pressure and changes in enzymes, vascularity, muscular activity, and biochemical milieu (for review see Dekel 1986).

TABLE 37.1.   External Signs of the Follicular Phase

Species	Reference
Activity increase	
Cattle, *Bos taurus*	Kiddy 1977
Buffalo, *Syncerus caffer*	Williams et al. 1986
Camel, *Camelus dromedarius*	Ismail 1987
Labial or perineal swelling	
Flying squirrel, *Glaucomys volans*	Sollberger 1943
Horse, *Equus caballus*	Ginther 1979
Camel, *Camelus dromedarius*	Ismail 1987
Raccoon, *Procyon lotor*	Whitney and Underwood 1952
Martin, *Martes americana*	Enders and Leekley 1941
Stoat, *Mustela erminea*	Gulamhusein and Thawley 1972
Ferret, *M. putorius*	Hammond and Marshall 1930
Red fox, *Vulpes vulpes*	Mondain-Monval et al. 1977
Greater bushbaby, *Otolemur (Galago) crassicaudatus*	Hendrickx and Newman 1978
Red-ruffed lemur, *Varecia variegata*	Karesh et al. 1985
Ruffed lemur, *Varecia (Lemur) variegata*	Boskoff 1977
Tarsier, *Tarsius bancanus*	Wright, Izard, and Simons 1986
Talapoin monkey, *(Cercopithecus) Miopithecus*	Rowell 1977
Gelada baboon, *Theropithecus gelada*	Dunbar and Dunbar 1974
Chacma baboon, *Papio (ursinus) hamadryas*	Saayman 1972
Hamadryas baboon, *P. hamadryas*	Hendrickx 1967
Olive baboon, *P. (anubis) hamadryas*	Hendrickx and Kraemer 1969
Yellow baboon, *P. (cynocephalus) hamadryas*	Hendrickx and Kraemer 1969
Rhesus macaque, *Macaca mulatta*	Czaja et al. 1977
Crab-eating macaque, *M. fascicularis*	Nawar and Hafez 1972
Pig-tailed macaque, *M. nemestrina*	Bullock, Paris, and Goy 1972
Chimpanzee, *Pan troglodytes*	Nadler et al. 1985
Gorilla, *Gorilla gorilla*	Nadler 1980
Uterine bleeding	
Dog, *Canis familiaris*	Evans and Cole 1931
Wolf, *C. lupus*	Seal et al. 1979
Raccoon, *Procyon lotor*	Whitney and Underwood 1952
Vaginal discharge, nonsanguinous	
Elephant shrew, *Elephantulus rufescens*	Lumpkin, Koontz, and Howard 1982
Dromedary camel, *Camelus dromedarius*	Ismail 1987

The number of follicles ovulated is characteristic of each species. Larger mammals are more likely to be monovular, that is, to ovulate one ovum at each estrus, whereas medium-sized and smaller species tend to be polyovular. Among polyovular species, the number of ova is usually equivalent to the litter size. Exceptions include elephant shrews, *Macroscelidea* (Tripp 1971), and the plains viscacha (Weir 1971b), which ovulate approximately 120 and 800 ova respectively, although each gives birth to only two offspring per litter. Another anomaly is demonstrated by the tenrec, *Tenrec ecaudatus*, in which each follicle may contain more than one ovum (Nicoll and Racey 1985).

Monotremes are unique among mammals in that a shell is added to the ovulated, fertilized egg during its passage through the oviducts and uterus. The eggs are incubated in an external pouch (Hill 1933, 1941). The unusual features of marsupial reproductive cycles as they relate to gestational events are presented in the chapter on pregnancy (Hutchins, Thomas, and Asa, chap. 41, this volume).

Mammalian females are often categorized as either induced or spontaneous ovulators, terms that indicate whether the stimulation of coitus is required for ovulation to occur. However, evidence suggests that even some species

considered to be induced ovulators may at times ovulate without mating (e.g., mink: Sundqvist, Amador, and Vartke 1989; lion, *Panthera leo:* Schmidt et al. 1979; cheetah, *Acinonyx jubatus:* Asa et al. 1992). Table 37.2 lists species classed as induced ovulators.

In species that typically ovulate spontaneously, mating or artificial stimulation of the vagina and cervix can induce uterine contractions (rat: Toner and Adler 1986) or hasten ovulation (pig: Signoret, du Mesnil du Buisson, and Mauleon 1972). In the domestic cow, the ovulatory LH surge is closely related in time to the bull's ejaculation, implicating coital stimulation (Umezu et al. 1981). In the Bactrian camel, *Camelus bactrianus,* ovulation is induced not by the mechanical stimulation of copulation, as is common for other induced ovulators, but by a factor in the male's semen (Chen, Yuen, and Pan 1985).

Jochle (1973, 1975) contends that many species classed as spontaneous ovulators are sensitive to copulatory as well as other external stimuli such as cohabitation and should be termed facultative induced ovulators. However, because one or the other of these mechanisms predominates in any given species, the distinction remains useful (see Milligan 1982 for review).

TABLE 37.2. Induced Ovulators

Species	Reference
Insectivora	
Short-tailed shrew, *Blarina brevicauda*	Pearson 1944
Water shrew, *Neomys fodiens*	Price 1953
White-toothed shrew, *Crocidura russula*	Hellwing 1973
Asian musk shrew, *Suncus murinus*	Dryden 1969
European shrew, *Sorex araneus*	Brambell 1935
American mole, *Scalopus aquaticus*	Conaway 1959
Rodentia	
Thirteen-lined ground squirrel, *Spermophilus tridecemlineatus*	Foster 1934
Palm squirrel, *Funambulus pennantii*	Seth and Prasad 1969
Bank vole, *Clethrionomys glareolus*	Westlin and Nyholm 1982
Tree mouse, *Phenacomys longicaudus*	Hamilton 1962
Short-tailed vole, *Microtus agrestis*	Breed and Clarke 1970
California vole, *M. californicus*	Greenwald 1956
Montane vole, *M. montanus*	Cross 1972
Prairie vole, *M. ochrogaster*	Richmond and Conaway 1969
Meadow vole, *M. pennsylvanicus*	Clulow and Mallory 1970
Pine vole, *M. pinetorum*	Kirkpatrick and Valentine 1970
Townsend's vole, *M. townsendii*	MacFarlane and Taylor 1982
Collared lemming, *Dicrostonyx groenlandicus*	Hasler and Banks 1973
Laboratory rat, *Rattus norvegicus*	Aron, Asch, and Roos 1966
Lagomorpha	
European hare, *Lepus europaeus*	Hediger 1950
Snowshoe hare, *L. americanus*	Rowlands and Weir 1984
Jackrabbit, *L. californicus*	Rowlands and Weir 1984
Eastern cottontail, *Sylvilagus floridanus*	Rowlands and Weir 1984
Rabbit, *Oryctolagus cuniculus*	Walton and Hammond 1929
Carnivora	
Domestic cat, *Felis catus*	Dawson and Friedgood 1940
Ferret, *Mustela putorius*	Marshall 1904
Mink, *M. vison*	Hansson 1947
Weasel, *M. nivalis*	Deanesly 1944
Raccoon, *Procyon lotor*	Whitney and Underwood 1952
Artiodactyla	
Bactrian camel, *Camelus bactrianus*	Chen, Yuen, and Pan 1985
Dromedary camel, *C. dromedarius*	Marie and Anouassi 1986
Llama, *Lama glama*	England et al. 1969
Alpaca, *L. pacos*	Fernandez-Baca, Madden, and Novoa 1970

The proximate hormonal stimulus for ovulation is a surge of LH, either the result of estrogen-positive feedback (in spontaneous ovulators) or of coitus (in induced ovulators.) At least in the rat, progesterone from the adrenal cortex participates in LH induction (Mann, Korowitz, and Barraclough 1975).

Ovarian progesterone secretion begins to increase just prior to ovulation in the dog (Concannon, Hansel, and Visek 1975) and in some rodents, for example, the guinea pig (Joshi, Watson, and Labhsetwar 1973). Small amounts of preovulatory progesterone and one of its metabolites, 20-hydroxyprogesterone, secreted from ovarian interstitial, not follicular, cells, are reported in the female rhesus macaque (Resko et al. 1975). In most species, however, the progestins are characteristic of the postovulatory luteal phase, and are secreted by luteal tissue.

Mating and Insemination Female estrous or sexual behavior is stimulated by the steroid hormones present at or before ovulation. The presence and sequence of each hormone may vary by species. For example, estrogen alone stimulates sexual behavior in the collared lemming, *Dicrostonyx groenlandicus* (Hasler and Banks 1976), rabbit (Beyer and McDonald 1973), cat (Peretz 1968), ferret (Baum and Schretlen 1978), horse (Asa et al. 1984), cow (Melampy and Rakes 1958), baboon, *Papio ursinus* (Saayman 1972), talapoin monkey, *Miopithecus talapoin*, and rhesus macaque (Herbert 1970).

However, progesterone synergizes with estrogen to facilitate estrous behavior in a variety of species. In rodents (rat: Powers 1970; hamster: Ciaccio and Lisk 1971; guinea pig: Frank and Fraps 1945) and in the dog (Concannon, Hansel, and McEntree 1977), sexual receptivity is induced by estrogen followed by progesterone. Although estrogen alone produces the full complement of sexual behavior in the horse and cow, the addition of progesterone further intensifies the response (Asa et al. 1984; Melampy et al. 1957).

In much the same manner as progesterone, LHRH has been shown to synergize with estrogen to further stimulate estrous behavior in the laboratory rat (Moss and McCann 1973).

In fall-breeding ungulates such as the sheep (Robinson, Moore, and Binet 1956), fallow deer, *Cervus dama* (Asher 1985), white-tailed deer (Harder and Moorhead 1980), moose, *Alces alces* (Simkin 1965), elk, red deer (Morrison 1960), and Père David's deer, *Elaphurus davidianus* (Curlewis, Loudon, and Coleman 1988), it appears that progesterone must precede estrogen for stimulation of estrous behavior. This is accomplished in nature by the first ovulation or wave of follicular growth of the season being silent, that is, not accompanied by overt sexual behavior. This cycle with silent estrus is followed by a period of corpus luteum progesterone production that primes the female's system to respond to the estrogen of the next cycle.

Testosterone and other androgens that increase during the periovulatory period may also stimulate sexual behavior in the female (rat and cat: Whalen and Hardy 1970; rabbit: Beyer, Vidal, and Mijares 1971; cattle: Katz, Oltenacu, and Foote 1980).

Progesterone alone, or in large amounts when given with estrogen, inhibits sexual behavior in all species investigated to date (e.g., guinea pig: Zucker and Goy 1967; cattle: Melampy et al. 1957; sheep: Robinson, Moore, and Binet 1956; rabbit: Sawyer and Everett 1959; horse: Asa et al. 1984; rhesus macaque: Michael, Saayman, and Zumpe 1968).

Following copulation, a copulatory plug consisting of gelatinous seminal fluid is left in the vaginal canal of females of a wide variety of species (Virginia opossum, *Didelphis virginiana*: Hartmann 1924; some insectivores: Eadie 1948; muroid rodents, Muridae: Baumgardner et al. 1982; pocket gopher, *Geomys bursarius*: Wing 1960; ring-tailed lemur, *Lemur catta*: Evans and Goy 1968; tarsier, *Tarsius bancanus*: Wright, Izard, and Simons 1986; capuchin, *Cebus apella*: Wright and Bush 1977; rhesus macaque: Settlage and Hendrickx 1974; chimpanzee: Tinklepaugh 1930; horseshoe bat, *Rhinolophus ferrumequinum*: Oh, Mori, and Uchida 1983; noctule bat: van Heerdt and Sluiter 1965). This plug, the physical copulatory lock of canids, and the behavioral "lock" of stump-tailed macaques may all serve as forms of mate guarding as well as to stimulate sperm transport (see Adler 1978). Copulatory plugs gradually dissolve and copulatory locks end after what seem to be species-specific intervals. Oxytocin (Gwatkin 1977) and/or epinephrine (Fuchs 1972) released in response to copulation may also stimulate uterine contractions that may aid sperm transport.

Mating is typically timed to coincide with ovulation. Sperm have been reported to survive for up to 72 hours in the reproductive tract of the female rhesus macaque (Dukelow and Bruggemann 1979); 120 hours in *Lama* and *Camelus* spp. (Stekleniov 1968, cited in Thibault 1973); 5 days in the horse (Bain 1957); 12 days in the dog (Doak, Hall, and Dale 1967); 2 weeks in the Australian native cat, *Dasyurus viverrinus* (Hill and O'Donoghue 1913), and brown marsupial mouse, *Antechinus stuartii* (Selwood and McCallum 1987); and 23 days in hybrid laboratory mice (Ullmann 1976).

Sperm storage in the female reproductive tract is common among vespertilionid bats (see Racey 1979) and ranges from 16 days in *Pipistrellus ceylonicus* (Gopalakrishna and Madhavan 1971) to 198 days in *Nyctalus noctula* (Racey 1973).

Luteal Phase The period following ovulation, characterized by luteal tissue growth and secretory activity, is at times referred to as the secretory phase in primates, referring to uterine phenomena, and as the diestrous phase in domestic ungulates, indicating its occurrence between estrous periods. The term luteal phase will be used in this chapter, acknowledging the dominance of the corpus luteum among the associated features.

Following its rupture and expulsion of the oocyte, the follicle is converted into a corpus luteum (CL), or yellow body, named for its characteristic color in many species. Corpora lutea are the primary producers of the progesterone that is necessary for preparation of the uterus and mammary glands for pregnancy.

Although progesterone is the primary circulating hormone of the luteal phase, a luteal rise in estrogen has been reported in cattle and sheep (Hansel, Concannon, and Lukaszewska 1973), hanuman langurs, *Semnopithecus (=Presbytis) entellus* (Lohiya et al. 1988), chimpanzees (Graham et al. 1972), and gorillas (Nadler 1980). Luteal estrogen peaks were small or absent in the rhesus macaque (Hotchkiss, Atkinson, and Knobil 1971; Hess and Resko 1973) and hamadryas baboon, *Papio hamadryas* (Goncharov et al. 1976).

The follicular phase is typically dominated by circulating estrogens and the luteal phase by progestins. The ovulatory cycles of the owl monkey, *Aotus trivirgatus* (Bonney, Dixson, and Fleming 1979), and marmosets (Preslock, Hampton, and Hampton 1973) are unusual in that the curves of estrogen and progesterone concentrations are almost superimposed, making follicular and luteal phases indistinguishable by steroid measurement.

Corpus luteum formation spontaneously follows ovulation in most species. However, in several rodent species, CL formation requires copulatory stimulation in the same way that ovulation must be induced in the cat, ferret, and rabbit. Thus, in the rat (deGreef, Dullaart, and Zeilmaker 1977), mouse (Rowlands and Weir 1984), and hamster (Anderson 1973), for example, ovulation is spontaneous, but no luteal phase separates it from the subsequent follicular phase unless copulation occurs. Fertile mating, of course, results in pregnancy, and sterile mating is also followed by a luteal phase, sometimes called pseudopregnancy. Sustained CL function, or pseudopregnancy, lasting approximately the length of gestation, occurs spontaneously in most canids and follows sterile mating in induced ovulators. Pseudopregnancy is also common in goats (Asa et al. 1993). (See also Hutchins, Thomas, and Asa, chap. 41, this volume, on pregnancy and parturition.)

Depending on the species, LH, prolactin, or estrogen may be luteotrophic, that is, supportive of CL function. If pregnancy does not ensue, the CL regresses. CL demise is not passive, but is effected by prostaglandin $F_2\alpha$ secreted by the uterus, at least in cattle (Beal, Milvae, and Hansel 1980), sheep (Flint and Hillier 1975), horses (Douglas and Ginther 1976), guinea pigs (Illingworth and Perry 1973), and rats (Pharriss and Wyngarden 1969).

Table 37.3. External Signs of the Menstrual Phase

Species	Reference
Chiroptera	
Vampire bat, *Desmodus rotundus*	Quintero and Rasweiler 1974
Long-tongued bat, *Glossophaga soricina*	Rasweiler 1972, 1979
Fruit bat, *Carollia perspicillata*	Bonilla and Rasweiler 1974
Primates	
Capuchin, *Cebus apella*	Wright and Bush 1977
Rhesus macaque, *Macaca mulatta*	Nadler, Collins, and Blank 1984
Pig-tailed macaque, *M. nemestrina*	Krohn and Zuckerman 1937
Japanese macaque, *M. fuscata*	Nigi 1975
Celebes black ape, *M. nigra*	Mahoney 1970
Chacma baboon, *Papio (ursinus)* *hamadryas*	Gillman and Gilbert 1946
Olive baboon, *P. (anubis) hamadryas*	Zuckerman 1937
Yellow baboon, *P. (cynocephalus)* *hamadryas*	Hendrickx and Kraemer 1969
Hamadryas baboon, *P. hamadryas*	Zuckerman and Parkes 1932
Gelada baboon, *Theropithecus gelada*	Matthews 1953–1956
Woolly monkey, *Lagothrix* spp.	Hafez 1971
Orangutan, *Pongo pygmaeus*	Nadler, Collins, and Blank 1984
Chimpanzee, *Pan troglodytes*	Nadler et al. 1985
Gorilla, *Gorilla gorilla*	Nadler et al. 1979

Menstrual Phase Characteristic of many primates, the period of bloody uterine discharge called menstruation is associated with relatively low hormone levels (table 37.3). In fact, menstrual blood flow results from the withdrawal of luteal-phase estrogen and progesterone (see Shaw and Roche 1980 for review). Although menstruation traditionally has been believed to be restricted to Old World monkeys and apes, slight hemorrhage may occur during the cycles of *Cebus, Ateles,* and *Alouatta* spp. (Ioannou 1983), but not the squirrel monkey (Clewe 1969), common marmoset, or cotton-top tamarin, *Saguinus oedipus* (Hodges and Eastman 1984). Sanguinous discharge has also been reported for tarsiers, *Tarsius* spp. (Catchpole and Fulton 1943).

Even among Old World monkeys and apes, menstrual flow may be undetectable in some individuals (gorilla: Nadler 1980; stump-tailed macaque: Stenger 1972; vervet monkey, *Chlorocebus (=Cercopithecus) aethiops*: Else et al. 1986; Sykes monkey, *Cercopithecus mitis*: Rowell 1970) or detectable only by swabs (*C. aethiops*: Hess, Hendrickx, and Stabenfeldt 1979; *C. mitis*: Else et al. 1985). Neither was blood noted during the menstrual phase of the slender loris, *Loris tardigradus* (Izard and Rasmussen 1985).

As indicated in the previous section on the follicular phase, the sanguinous discharge of canids such as the domestic dog is not physiologically comparable to menstruation. Canid uterine blood flow occurs during proestrus, sometimes continuing into estrus, and is in response to estrogen stimulation, not estrogen or progesterone withdrawal (C. S. Asa, pers. obs.).

In the few bat species in which menstruation has been reported, endometrial breakdown and sloughing accompanied by blood flow occur at about the time of ovulation (vampire bat, *Desmodus rotundus*: Quintero and Rasweiler 1974; long-tongued bat, *Glossophaga soricina*: Rasweiler 1972; short-tailed fruit bat, *Carollia perspicillata*: Bonilla

and Rasweiler 1974), which may be preceded by the demise of old CL. It is unclear whether ovulation accompanied by menstruation is always preceded by CL demise, and whether withdrawal of the hormones produced by such previous CL or periovulatory estrogen stimulation is responsible for the bloody discharge.

Anovulatory Period and Lactational Anovulation The anovulatory or anestrous phase is similar to the menstrual phase in that it is characterized by relatively low levels or absence of ovarian steroids. It is, simply, a time of no overt reproductive activity. Sexual behavior does not occur regularly during the anovulatory period or following ovariectomy except in the musk shrew, *Suncus murinus* (Dryden and Anderson 1977), horse (Asa et al. 1980), and stump-tailed macaque (Slob et al. 1978).

Many species have an anovulatory season (see the section below on environmental effects). In others, anovulation results from nursing newborn young. This phenomenon is termed lactational amenorrhea in primates and lactational anovulation or anestrus in nonprimate species. Lactational amenorrhea is common in primates (gorillas: Stewart 1988; chimpanzees: Tutin 1980; rhesus macaques: Weiss et al. 1976; olive baboons, *Papio anubis*: Nicolson 1981; spider monkeys: Wolf, Harrison, and Martin 1975; howler monkeys: Glander 1980; squirrel monkeys: Travis and Holmes 1974). Likewise, lactation has been shown to suppress follicular development in laboratory rats (Taya and Greenwald 1982), hamsters (Greenwald 1965), cattle (Short et al. 1972), pigs (Peters, First, and Cassida 1969), and sheep (Kann and Martinet 1975).

Lactational anovulation is probably mediated by the ability of the high levels of prolactin that accompany lactation to suppress LHRH and/or LH (Friesen 1977). Following parturition, resumption of ovulatory cycles may be delayed even in the absence of suckling young (orangu-

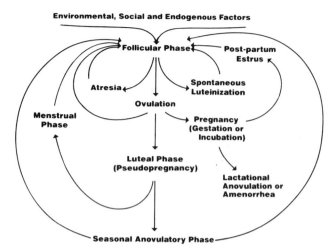

Fig. 37.6. Model incorporating the various ovarian cycle events and options found among mammalian females.

tan, *Pongo pygmaeus:* Lasley, Hodges, and Czekala 1980). Lactational anovulation is not widespread among nonprimate species, many of which experience ovulation soon after parturition, often called postpartum estrus.

Menopause Although the term menopause applies only to primate menstrual cycle suppression, there is evidence that reproductive senescence is a general occurrence in mammals (for review see vom Saal and Finch 1988). Its incidence in the wild, however, has not been established, suggesting that reproductive senescence may be an artifact of captivity attributable to extended life span. Depletion of ovarian oocytes is the major reason that females cease to ovulate, although the relative involvement of the hypothalamus, pituitary, and ovaries may differ among species (e.g., Tardif and Ziegler 1992).

The flow chart in figure 37.6 summarizes the components and options found in the ovarian cycles of various species of eutherian mammals.

Methods for Monitoring Ovarian Cycles

A wide variety of physical and physiological changes accompany ovarian changes. Some of these, such as labial swelling, perineal reddening, and sanguinous discharge, have been mentioned in previous sections. These changes, along with others such as increases in activity level and nonsanguinous vaginal discharges characteristic of the periovulatory phase, can be used to detect the follicular phase in captive mammals (see table 37.1.) These signs can be observed noninvasively, except for menstrual blood flow in some species or individuals. In such cases, either vaginal swabs or stick tests for blood in voided urine (see Nadler et al. 1979) can be used.

In most rodent species and in the Old World mole, mouse lemur, *Microcebus murinus,* and ruffed lemur, *Varecia variegata* (see table 37.4 for references), a membrane occludes the vagina except at times of breeding. In some species, the vagina is open during the entire breeding season; in others, only during estrus.

Changes in vaginal cytology, which reflect ovarian cycle stages, can be detected by smears or lavage. This technique has been verified for a very wide range of species (table 37.4). Basal body temperature (BBT) also varies with the ovulatory cycle, and these changes can be measured telemetrically. BBT decreases transiently at about the time of ovulation, then increases during the luteal phase in a variety of species (table 37.4). Although they are not useful for prediction of ovulation, BBT changes can be used to evaluate and monitor ovarian cycles.

The development of ultrasound equipment extends the range of species for which ovarian and follicular morphology can be sequentially assessed. Transducers in a variety of shapes and sizes can be inserted rectally in anesthetized or restrained animals for reproductive tract examinations (see Adams et al. 1991).

Improvements in hormone assays of urine permit noninvasive assessment of levels of LH and estrogen and progesterone metabolites in a wide variety of species (table 37.5). However, care must be taken in deciding which steroid or steroid metabolite to measure, as species differences have been noted (for example, see Klopper and Michie 1956; Romanoff et al. 1963; Goldzieher and Axelrod 1969; Plant, James, and Michael 1971; Eastman et al. 1984).

In some species, such as cats, feces are the primary excretory route for steroid hormones, making urinary hormone assays unsuitable (Shille et al. 1984). (For serum hormone results for felids, see Verhage, Beamer, and Brenner 1976 for the domestic cat, Seal et al. 1985 for the Siberian tiger, and Wildt et al. 1979 for the jaguar, *P. onca.*) Significant levels of steroid hormones have been identified in the feces of the rhesus macaque (up to 57% of excreted progesterone) and cotton-top tamarin (43% estrone; 95% progesterone), suggesting fecal sampling as an alternative to urine assays (Plant, James, and Michael 1971; Ziegler et al. 1988). Fecal measurements of estrogens and progestins have been used to monitor ovulatory cycles in a variety of species, with varying success (see Bamberg 1992 and table 37.6).

FACTORS AFFECTING REPRODUCTIVE CAPACITY

Environmental Factors

Many species inhabiting the temperate zones have evolved seasonal breeding strategies to cope with the changing environmental conditions (see Bronson 1988, 1989 for review). Negus and Berger (1972) divide these species along a facultative-obligate continuum. Facultative seasonal breeders live in unpredictable environments and respond to favorable conditions, such as plant growth due to irregular rainfall in deserts, as they occur. Obligate seasonal breeders live in predictable environments in which conditions favorable to the survival of young occur at invariant times from year to year. The most common proximate cue used by obligate seasonal breeders is change in photoperiod.

Photoperiod Photoperiod-sensitive species are typically separated into long-day and short-day breeders, meaning that they come into breeding condition in the spring, when daylight hours are increasing, or in the fall, when daylight hours are decreasing, respectively. Some examples of species

TABLE 37.4. Methods for Monitoring Ovarian Cycles

Species	Reference
Vaginal membrane open during breeding season	
Myomorph and sciuromorph rodents	Rowlands and Weir 1984
Old World mole, *Talpa europaea*	Matthews 1935
Vaginal membrane open during preovulatory period	
Hystricomorph rodents (except coypu, *Myocastor coypus*)	Weir 1974
Galago, *Galago senegalensis*	Darney and Franklin 1982
Greater galago, *Otolemur (G.) crassicaudatus*	Hendrickx and Newman 1978
Mouse lemur, *Microcebus murinus*	Perret 1986
Ruffed lemur, *Varecia (Lemur) variegata*	Boskoff 1977; Shideler, Lindburg, and Lasley 1983
Vaginal cytology	
Common wombat, *Vombatus ursinus*	Peters and Rose 1979
Potoroo, *Potorous tridactylus*	Hughes 1962
Short-nosed rat kangaroo, *Bettongia lesueuri*	Tyndale-Biscoe 1968
Hedgehog, *Hemiechinus auritus*	Munshi and Pandey 1987
Shrew, *Sorex araneus*	Brambell 1935
Musk shrew, *Suncus murinus*	Sharma and Mathur 1976 (disputed by Dryden 1969)
Rat, *Rattus norvegicus*	Long and Evans 1922
Golden hamster, *Mesocricetus auratus*	Orsini 1961
Guinea pig, *Cavia porcellus*	Stockard and Papanicolau 1917
Slender loris, *Loris tardigradus*	Ramaswami and Kumar 1962
Bushbaby, *Otolemur (Galago) crassicaudatus*	Eaton, Slob, and Resko 1973
Tarsier, *Tarsius* spp.	Catchpole and Fulton 1943
Ring-tailed lemur, *Lemur catta*	Evans and Goy 1968
Ruffed lemur, *Varecia (Lemur) variegata*	Boskoff 1977
Squirrel monkey, *Saimiri sciureus*	Gould, Cline, and Williams 1973
Capuchin, *Cebus apella*	Wright and Bush 1977
Langur, *Semnopithecus (=Presbytis) entellus*	Lohiya et al. 1988
Bonnet macaque, *Macaca radiata*	Kanagawa et al. 1973
Rhesus macaque, *M. mulatta*	Parakkal and Gregoire 1972
Crab-eating macaque, *M. fascicularis*	Mehta et al. 1986
Olive baboon, *Papio (anubis) hamadryas*	Hendrickx 1967
Hamadryas baboon, *P. hamadryas*	Zuckerman and Parkes 1932
Long-tongued bat, *Glossophaga soricina*	Rasweiler 1972
Domestic cat, *Felis catus*	Shille, Lundstrom, and Stabenfeldt 1979
Cheetah, *Acinonyx jubatus*	Asa et al. 1992
Domestic dog, *Canis familiaris*	Gier 1960
Wolf, *Canis lupus*	Seal et al. 1979
Red fox, *Vulpes vulpes*	Bassett and Leekley 1942
Brown hyena, *Hyaena brunnea*	Ensley et al. 1982
Vaginal pH	
Cattle, *Bos taurus*	Schilling and Zust 1968
Horse, *Equus caballus*	Polak and Kammlade 1981
Ultrasound	
Rhesus macaque, *Macaca mulatta*	Morgan et al. 1987
Brown hyena, *Hyaena brunnea*	Ensley et al. 1982
Horse, *Equus caballus*	Ginther 1986
Cattle, *Bos taurus*	Pierson and Ginther 1988
Basal body temperature	
Common wombat, *Vombatus ursinus*	Peters and Rose 1979
Langur, *Semnopithecus (=Presbytis) entellus*	Lohiya et al. 1988
Rhesus macaque, *Macaca mulatta*	Balin and Wan 1968
Chimpanzee, *Pan troglodytes*	Graham et al. 1977
Orangutan, *Pongo pygmaeus*	Asa et al. 1994
Pig-tailed macaque, *Macaca nemestrina*	White, Blaine, and Blakeley 1973
Gibbon, *Hylobates lar*	Carpenter 1941
Cattle, *Bos taurus*	Fallon 1959

TABLE 37.5. Use of Urinary Hormone Measurements to Monitor Ovarian Cycles

Species	Reference
Progesterone metabolites	
Crab-eating macaque, *Macaca fascicularis*	Mehta et al. 1986
Vervet monkey, *Chlorocebus (=Cercopithecus) aethiops*	Andelman et al. 1985
Baboon, *Papio* spp.	Goldzieher and Axelrod 1969
Giant panda, *Ailuropoda melanoleuca*	Hodges et al. 1984
Domestic pig, *Sus scrofa*	Schomberg et al. 1966
Blackbuck, *Antilope cervicapra*	Holt et al. 1988
Okapi, *Okapia johnstoni*	Loskutoff, Ott, and Lasley 1982
Giraffe, *Giraffa camelopardalis*	Loskutoff et al. 1986
Progesterone and estrogen metabolites	
Common marmoset, *Callithrix jacchus*	Eastman et al. 1984
Golden lion tamarin, *Leontopithecus rosalia*	French and Stribley 1985
Baboon, *Papio (anubis) hamadryas*	Hodges et al. 1986
Domestic cat, *Felis catus*	Shille et al. 1984
Brown hyena, *Hyaena brunnea*	Ensley et al. 1982
Giant panda, *Ailuropoda melanoleuca*	Bonney, Wood, and Kleiman 1981
Asian elephant, *Elephas maximus*	Ramsay, Lasley, and Stabenfeldt 1980
Indian rhinoceros, *Rhinoceros unicornis*	Kassam and Lasley 1981
Pig, *Sus scrofa*	Lunaas 1962
Horse, *Equus caballus*	Palmer and Jousset 1975
Cattle, *Bos taurus*	Mellin and Erb 1966
Owl monkey, *Aotus trivirgatus*	Bonney and Setchell 1980
Orangutan, *Pongo pygmaeus*	Collins, Graham, and Preedy 1975
Chimpanzee, *Pan troglodytes*	Graham et al. 1972
Gorilla, *Gorilla gorilla*	Mitchell et al. 1982
Estrone and luteinizing hormone	
Douc langur, *Pygathrix nemaeus*	Hodges, Czekala, and Lasley 1979
Capuchin, *Cebus albifrons*	Hodges, Czekala, and Lasley 1979
Rhesus macaque, *Macaca mulatta*	Hodges, Czekala, and Lasley 1979
Orangutan, *Pongo pygmaeus*	Lasley, Hodges, and Czekala 1980
Pygmy chimpanzee, *Pan paniscus*	Lasley, Hodges, and Czekala 1980
Chimpanzee, *Pan troglodytes*	Hodges, Czekala, and Lasley 1979
Gorilla, *Gorilla gorilla*	Hodges, Czekala, and Lasley 1979
Estrogen metabolites	
Lion-tailed macaque, *Macaca silenus*	Shideler et al. 1983
Okapi, *Okapia johnstoni*	Loskutoff et al. 1987
Cotton-top tamarin, *Saguinus oedipus*	Brand 1981

TABLE 37.6. Use of Fecal Hormone Measurements to Monitor Ovarian Cycles

Species	Reference
Estrogens and progestins	
Cotton-top tamarin, *Saguinus oedipus*	Ziegler et al. 1988
Pig-tailed macaque, *Macaca nemestrina*	Wasser, Risler, and Steiner 1988
Yellow baboon, *Papio (cynocephalus) hamadryas*	Wasser, Risler, and Steiner 1988
Cheetah, *Acinonyx jubatus*	Gross 1992
Maned wolf, *Chrysocyon brachyurus*	Gross 1992
Black-footed ferret, *Mustela nigripes*	Gross 1992
Asian small-clawed otter, *Amblonyx (=Aonyx) cinereus*	Gross 1992
North American river otter, *Lutra canadensis*	Gross 1992
Siberian tiger, *Panthera tigris altaica*	Gross 1992
Bengal tiger, *P. t. tigris*	Gross 1992
Cattle, *Bos taurus*	Desaulniers et al. 1989
Musk ox, *Ovibus moschatus*	Desaulniers et al. 1989
Horse, *Equus caballus*	Kirkpatrick et al. 1992
Scimitar-horned oryx, *Oryx dammah*	Shaw et al. 1992
Progestins	
American bison, *Bison bison*	Kirkpatrick et al. 1992
Estrogens	
Common marmoset, *Callithrix jacchus*	Hodges, Tari, and Heistermann 1992; Pryce and Döbeli 1992
Goeldi's monkey, *Callimico goeldii*	Hodges, Tari, and Heistermann 1992; Pryce and Döbeli 1992

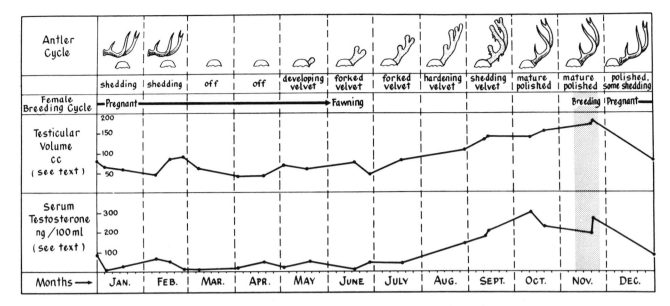

FIG. 37.7.   Seasonal changes in antlers, testis size, and serum testosterone in the white-tailed deer. (From McMillan et al. 1974, by permission of the authors.)

that respond to the long days of spring are the pallid bat, *Antrozous pallidus* (Beasley and Zucker 1984), ferret (Bissonette 1932), and horse (Sharp and Ginther 1975). The rock hyrax, *Procavia capensis* (Millar and Glover 1973), white-tailed deer (Plotka et al. 1979; see fig. 37.7), and sheep (Yeates 1949) are examples of short-day breeders.

Photic information is processed by the pineal gland via the superior cervical ganglion (see Legan and Winans 1981; Goldman and Darrow 1983; Reiter 1983 for reviews). However, these structures are not involved in the timing of reproduction in the apparently photoperiod-sensitive wolf (Asa et al. 1987).

Photoperiod effects are considered to be mediated by changes in exposure to sunlight. However, the impala (Murray 1982) and wildebeest, *Connochaetes taurinus* (Sinclair 1977), appear to respond to phases of the moon, with estrus and ovulation occurring between full moons. It is unclear how this effect is mediated, whether by changes in light intensity or perhaps in gravitational forces.

Rainfall The breeding seasons of many species coincide with periods of rainfall, particularly in tropical areas where photoperiod varies little. These species include both facultative (desert jerboa, *Jaculus jaculus*: Ghobrial and Hodieb 1973) and obligate (rhesus macaque: Eckstein and Kelly 1966) seasonal breeders. However, the true stimulus is likely to be the nutritional content of the resultant vegetation, not the rainfall itself.

Temperature Elevated temperatures have been associated with reductions in sperm quality and testosterone concentrations in males (see discussion above and Waites and Setchell 1990). In females, high ambient temperatures are followed by decreases in gonadotropin levels and follicular growth, a higher incidence of abnormal ova, and lower conception rates (Dutt 1963; Badinga et al. 1985; Flowers and

Day 1990). Even the conceptus is susceptible to temperature elevations, as seen in the resulting high embryonic mortality and teratology (Dutt 1963; Hendrickx et al. 1979; Mieusset et al. 1992).

Nutrition Most studies of the effects of nutrition on reproductive parameters have focused primarily on caloric or protein levels in the diet or assessment of body condition. As with the study of other aspects of reproduction, domestic species have received the most attention. In general, the nutritional requirements for reproduction are not different from those for health maintenance.

A reduced plane of nutrition can affect reproductive potential. Although food restriction can result in decreased testis size (ground squirrel, *Spermophilus lateralis*: Forger et al. 1986; little brown bat, *Myotis lucifugus*: Damassa and Gustafson 1985), nutritional deprivation probably has a more profound effect on female than on male reproduction (see Gerloff and Morrow 1980; Ghafoorunissa 1980).

Fertility depression, probably in the form of a decreased ovulation rate, occurs in underfed cattle (Wiltbank et al. 1962), sheep (Gunn and Doney 1973), goats (Henniawati and Fletcher 1986), pigs (Armstrong and Britt 1987), eland, *Taurotragus oryx* (Skinner and van Zyl 1969), white-tailed deer (Ozoga and Verme 1982), collared peccaries, *Pecari* (=*Tayassu*) *tajacu* (Hellgren et al. 1985; Lochmiller, Hellgren, and Grant 1986), horses (Van Niekerk and Van Heerden 1972), red kangaroos (Newsome 1966), rabbits (Kirkpatrick and Kibbe 1971), rats (Widdowson and Cowen 1972), and mice (Gangrade and Dominic 1985). Chacma baboons, *Papio ursinus*, become acyclic on an inadequate diet (Gillman and Gilbert 1946).

Ovulation rate can be increased in some ungulates by giving extra feed just prior to ovulation, a practice called "flushing" (white-tailed deer: Ransom 1967; pig and sheep: Hafez and Jainudeen 1974). However, the increased number of ovulated follicles that may follow flushing does not necessarily result in an increased number of viable embryos.

Data on the effects of specific nutrients are limited. However, in female domestic ungulates, deficiencies in phosphorus or magnesium can result in ovarian dysfunction, a decreased incidence of estrus, or even anestrus. Likewise, vitamin A or E deficiencies can cause irregular cycles or anestrus (Hafez and Jainudeen 1974). In the male, vitamins A (in the form of dietary retinol) and E are required for proper development and functioning of the testis (Waites and Setchell 1990).

The interaction of nutrition and reproduction is especially evident in many seasonally breeding species. Supplemental food, either offered by humans or naturally occurring, can extend the breeding season in various mice and voles (*Peromyscus* spp.: Jameson 1953; Fordham 1971; short-tailed vole, *Microtus agrestis:* Smyth 1968; woodland mouse, *Apodemus sylvaticus,* and bank vole, *Clethrionomys glareolus:* Flowerdew 1973).

Level of nutrition has been implicated in reproductive capacity in some herbivores by the observation that breeding activity may be associated with the availability of green vegetation, often the result of local rainfall (California vole: Nelson, Dark, and Zucker 1983; black-tailed jackrabbit, *Lepus californicus:* Lechleitner 1959; African buffalo, *Syncerus caffer:* Grimsdell 1973; zebra, *Equus zebra:* Penzhorn 1985). In some cases, simple increases in protein or caloric intake may be responsible for the initiation of breeding. However, 6-methoxy-2-benzoxazolinone (6-MBOA), which is present in sprouting vegetation, stimulates reproduction in a variety of species (e.g., vole, *Microtus montanus:* Berger, Negus, and Rowsemitt 1987; rabbit: Gooding and Long 1957; mouse, rat, horse, and mink: Ginther et al. 1985). 6-MBOA may work via activation of the thyroid (Vaughn et al. 1988).

In contrast, coumestrol, a plant compound with estrogenic effects that is present in clover and other leguminous plants, can inhibit reproduction by blocking gonadotropin release (Leavitt and Wright 1965). Compounds with estrogenic activity, and presumably the potential to interrupt ovarian events if present in large quantities, also have been identified in barley grain, *Hordeum vulgare,* oat grain, *Avena sativa,* apples, *Pyrus malus,* cherries, *Prunus avium,* potatoes, *Solanum tuberosum,* and Bengal gram, *Cicer arietinum* (Hafez and Jainudeen 1974).

Food restriction can inhibit gonadotropic hormones (rat: Campbell et al. 1977; cattle: Gauthier and Coulaud 1986), stimulate progesterone release in sheep (Chesworth and Easdon 1983), or cause hypothalamic-pituitary hypersensitivity to estrogen or testosterone negative feedback (Howland and Ibrahim 1973; Pirke and Spyra 1981). Water restriction can also deleteriously affect reproduction (Nelson and Desjardins 1987; Lidicker 1973).

Social Factors

Social interactions can either stimulate or suppress reproductive function. Many of these effects are mediated by olfactory communication. Reproductive suppression resulting from dominance interactions or from changes in population density has been related to changes in the adrenal cortex, although the proximate sensory modality has not been identified in most cases.

Priming Pheromones Mammalian chemical communication may produce both behavioral and physiological responses. Only the latter will be considered in this discussion. Primer pheromones regulate reproductive processes in various ways.

Female reproductive activity can be suppressed by stimuli from other females or group members in many rodent species, pigs, marmosets, tamarins, *Saguinus fuscicollis* (Vandenbergh 1988), and sugar gliders, *Petaurus breviceps* (Schultze-Westrum 1969).

In contrast, the onset of ovarian cycles at puberty or at the beginning of the breeding season can be advanced by stimuli from adult males in various rodents, cattle, sheep, pigs, tamarins (Vandenbergh 1988), and mouse lemurs (Perret 1985). An increased incidence of ovulation has also been demonstrated in nonseasonally breeding goats exposed to males (Chemineau 1983).

Induction of ovarian synchrony and changes in cycle length by stimuli from either the same or the opposite sex has been demonstrated in various rodent species, cattle, goats, sheep (Vandenbergh 1988), and mouse lemurs (Perret 1986).

Termination of pregnancy in response to exposure to strange males or their urine occurs in pine voles, *Microtus pinetorum* (Schadler 1981), and mice (Parkes and Bruce 1962).

In the female gray opossum, *Monodelphis domestica* (Fadem 1987), cuis, *Galea musteloides* (Weir 1971a), and Cape porcupine, *Hystrix africaeaustralis* (Van Aarde 1985), the inception of estrous behavior and ovarian activity is induced, not merely enhanced, by the presence of males.

Dominance Effects Subordinate status can result in suppression of ovulation via increased circulating prolactin and cortisol in talapoin monkeys (Bowman, Dilley, and Keverne 1978); this effect is probably mediated by aggressive attacks from more dominant females. In male vervet monkeys (McGuire, Brammer, and Raleigh 1986), talapoin monkeys (Eberhart, Keverne, and Meller 1983), and olive baboons, *Papio (=anubis) hamadryas* (Sapolsky 1982), cortisol levels are related to social status and aggressive interactions. The relationship of the pituitary-adrenocortical system to dominance has also been demonstrated in a pheromonal signal found in the urine of pigs injected with ACTH (adrenocorticotropic hormone) that induces submissive behavior in others (McGlone 1985). What is less clear is why relatively high adrenocortical activity is correlated with dominance in some species and with subordinate status in others. The explanation may lie in the dynamics, not the absolute levels, of adrenal hormones.

The lower reproductive contribution of subordinate female rabbits (Mykytowycz and Fullagar 1973) has not been explained, and could result from differential access to resources, primer pheromones, stress-related adrenocortical changes, or some combination of these. In the wild, it is likely that all these factors contribute to status-related differential reproduction.

Density-Dependent Effects Primarily in experiments with rodents (*Mus musculus:* Christian 1980; *Peromyscus* *maniculatus:* Terman 1973), increased population density has been shown to result in decreased fertility. The mechanism that translates density into physiological response may be increased levels of aggression and adrenocortical responses proportional to the degree of crowding.

Housing solitary species such as the mouse lemur in social groups results in high cortisol levels and poor reproductive success, even in the absence of crowding (Perret and Predine 1984). Interestingly, social isolation, as well as high densities, can depress reproductive potential in the normally gregarious house mouse (Rastogi, Milone, and Chieffi 1981). Similarly, in both olive and chacma baboons, social isolation resulted in longer follicular phases, and thus longer cycles, than did social contact with other female baboons. However, the period of perineal tumescence was longer in the chacma (Howard-Tripp and Bielert 1978) but shorter in the olive baboon (Rowell 1969) females that were isolated than in those socially housed.

Stress Regardless of the definition of stress, factors that stimulate the hypothalamic-pituitary-adrenocortical axis can interfere with reproduction (Rivier, Rivier, and Vale 1986). Both natural and synthetic glucocorticoids negatively affect reproductive parameters (male and female rat: Hagino, Watanabe, and Goldzieher 1969; Bambino and Hseuh 1981; female armadillo, *Dasypus novemcinctus:* Rideout et al. 1985; female horse: Asa, Robinson, and Ginther 1983; Asa and Ginther 1982; male and female pig: Liptrap 1970; Liptrap and Raeside 1968; male and female cattle: Thibier and Rollando 1976; Edwards et al. 1987; female baboon species: Hagino 1972).

An unusual relationship between adrenal stress response and reproduction is found in male dasyurid marsupials, *Antechinus* spp., in which adrenal weight and corticosteroid levels increase just after mating and appear to lead to death (Lee, Bradley, and Braithwaite 1977). A strong relationship between stress, measured as sympathetic nervous system stimulation, and reproductive failure has been described for the tree shrew (von Holst 1969 in Van Tienhoven 1983).

Glucocorticoids have been shown to fluctuate during estrous cycles of the mouse (Nichols and Chevins 1981), rat (Buckingham, Dohler, and Wilson 1978), and horse (Asa, Robinson, and Ginther 1983). In the rodents, corticosterone levels are positively correlated with those of estrogen, whereas in the horse, cortisol has a negative correlation with estradiol and with follicular size.

CONCLUSIONS

Although an enormous amount of work is represented by the studies cited in this chapter, we are only beginning to understand the reproductive processes of a very few species. Our successes in manipulating reproductive function in domestic and laboratory species are built on decades of research. The farther from these species our studies venture, the more variability on the theme of reproduction we find. If we are to attain the goal of effectively managing the reproduction of exotic species in captivity, this variability must be recognized, and a commitment of time and resources must be made toward building a foundation of biological knowledge upon which to base such management programs.

REFERENCES

Abbott, D. H., and J. P. Hearn. 1978. Physical, hormonal and behavioural aspects of sexual development in the marmoset monkey, *Callithrix jacchus. J. Reprod. Fertil.* 53:155–66.

Adams, G. P., Plotka, E. D., Asa, C. S., and Ginther, O. J. 1991. Feasibility of characterizing reproductive events in large nondomestic species by transrectal ultrasonic imaging. *Zoo Biol.* 10:247–59.

Adler, N. T. 1978. Social and environmental control of reproductive processes in animals. In *Sex and behavior,* ed. T. E. McGill, D. A. Dewsbury, and B. D. Sachs, 115–60. New York: Plenum Press.

Amann, R. P. 1970. Sperm production rates. In *The testis I,* ed. A. D. Johnson, W. R. Gomes, and N. L. Vandemark, 433–82. New York: Academic Press.

Andelman, S., Else, J. G., Hearn, J. P., and Hodges, J. K. 1985. The non-invasive monitoring of reproductive events in the wild vervet monkey *(Cercopithecus aethiops)* using urinary pregnanediol-3a-glucuronide and its correlation with behavioural observations. *J. Zool.* (Lond.) (A) 205:467–77.

Anderson, L. L. 1973. Effects of hysterectomy and other factors on luteal function. In *Handbook of physiology,* sec. 7, vol. 2, part 2, ed. R. O. Greep, 69–86. Washington, D.C.: American Physiological Society.

Armstrong, J. D., and Britt, J. H. 1987. Nutritionally induced anestrus in gilts: Metabolic and endocrine changes associated with cessation and resumption of estrous cycles. *J. Anim. Sci.* 65:508–23.

Aron, C., Asch, G., and Roos, J. 1966. Triggering ovulation by coitus in the rat. *Int. Rev. Cytol.* 20:139–72.

Aronson, L. R., and Cooper, M. L. 1967. Penile spines of the domestic cat: Their endocrine-behavior relations. *Anat. Rec.* 157:71–78.

Asa, C. S., Fischer, F., Carrasco, E., and Puricelli, C. 1994. Correlation between urinary pregnanediol glucuronide and basal body temperature in female orangutans, *Pongo pygmaeus. Am. J. Primatol.* 33:275–81.

Asa, C. S., and Ginther, O. J. 1982. Glucocorticoid suppression of oestrus, follicles, LH, and ovulation in the mare. *J. Reprod. Fertil., Suppl.* 32:247–51.

Asa, C. S., Goldfoot, D. A., Garcia, M. C., and Ginther, O. J. 1980. Sexual behavior in ovariectomized and seasonally anovulatory mares. *Horm. Behav.* 14:46–54.

———. 1984. The effect of estradiol and progesterone on the sexual behavior of ovariectomized mares. *Physiol. Behav.* 33:681–86.

Asa, C. S., Houston, E. W., Plotka, E. D., Jenness, B., and Lynch, M. 1993. Patterns of serum estradiol and progesterone during the ovulatory cycle and possible pseudopregnancy in Rocky Mountain goats *(Oreamnos americanus). J. Zoo Wildl. Med.* 24:190–95.

Asa, C. S., Junge, R. E., Bircher, J. S., Noble, G. A., Sarri, K. J., and Plotka, E. D. 1992. Assessing reproductive cycles and pregnancy in cheetahs *(Acinonyx jubatus)* by vaginal cytology. *Zoo Biol.* 11:139–51.

Asa, C. S., Robinson, J. A., and Ginther, O. J. 1983. Changes in plasma cortisol concentrations during the ovulatory cycle of the mare. *J. Endocrinol.* 99:329–34.

Asa, C. S., Seal, U. S., Letellier, M., Plotka, E. D., and Peterson, E. K. 1987. Pinealectomy or superior-cervical ganglionectomy do not alter reproduction in the wolf *(Canis lupus). Biol. Reprod.* 37:14–21.

Asher, G. W. 1985. Oestrous cycle and breeding season of farmed fallow deer, *Dama dama. J. Reprod. Fertil.* 75:521–29.

Badinga, L., Collier, R. J., Thatcher, W. W., and Wilcox, C. J.

1985. Effects of climatic and management factors on conception rate of dairy cattle in subtropical environment. *J. Dairy Sci.* 68: 78–85.

Bain, A. M. 1957. Estrus and infertility of the Thoroughbred mare in Australia. *J. Am. Vet. Med. Assoc.* 131:179–85.

Baird, D., Horton, T. R., Longcope, C., and Tait, F. 1969. Steroid dynamics under steady-state conditions. *Recent Prog. Horm. Res.* 25:611–64.

Balin, H., and Wan, L. S. 1968. The significance of circadian rhythms in the search for the moment of ovulation in primates. *Fertil. Steril.* 19:228–43.

Bamberg, E., ed. 1992. *The First International Symposium on Faecal Steroid Monitoring in Zoo Animals.* Rotterdam: Royal Rotterdam Zoological and Botanical Gardens.

Bambino, T. H., and Hsueh, A. J. W. 1981. Direct inhibitory effect of glucocorticoids upon testicular luteinizing hormone receptor and steroidogenesis *in vivo* and *in vitro. Endocrinology* 108: 2142–48.

Bassett, C. F., and Leekley, J. R. 1942. Determination of estrum in the fox vixen. *N. Am. Vet.* 23:454–57.

Baum, M. J., and Schretlen, P. J. M. 1978. Oestrogenic induction of sexual behaviour in ovariectomized ferrets housed under short or long photoperiods. *J. Endocrinol.* 78:295–96.

Baumgardner, D. J., Hartung, T. G., Sawrey, D. K., Webster, D. G., and Dewsbury, D. A. 1982. Muroid copulatory plugs and female reproductive tracts: A comparative investigation. *J. Mammal.* 63:110–17.

Beach, F. A., and Levinson, G. 1950. Effects of androgen on the glans penis and mating behavior of male rats. *J. Exp. Zool.* 114: 159–68.

Beal, W. E., Milvae, R. A., and Hansel, W. 1980. Oestrous length and plasma progesterone concentrations following administration of prostaglandin F$_2\alpha$ early in the bovine oestrous cycle. *J. Reprod. Fertil.* 59:393–96.

Beasley, L. J., and Zucker, I. 1984. Photoperiod influences the annual reproductive cycle of the male pallid bat *(Antrozous pallidus). J. Reprod. Fertil.* 70:567–73.

Bedford, J. M. 1979. Evolution of sperm maturation and sperm storage function of the epididymis. In *The spermatozoon,* ed. D. W. Fawcett and J. M. Bedford, 7–21. Baltimore and Munich: Urban and Schwarzenberg.

Bentley, P. J. 1976. *Comparative vertebrate endocrinology.* Cambridge: Cambridge University Press.

Berger, P. J., Negus, N. C., and Rowsemitt, C. N. 1987. Effect of 6-methoxybenzoxazolinone on sex ratio and breeding performance in *Microtus montanus. Biol. Reprod.* 36:255–60.

Beyer, C., and McDonald, P. 1973. Hormonal control of sexual behavior in the female rabbit. *Adv. Reprod. Physiol.* 6:185–219.

Beyer, C., Vidal, N., and Mijares, A. 1971. Probable role of aromatization in the induction of estrous behavior by androgen in the ovariectomized rabbit. *Endocrinology* 87:1386–89.

Bindon, B. M., Hewetson, R. W., and Post, T. B. 1976. Plasma LH and testosterone in zebu crossbred bulls after exposure to an estrous cow and injection of synthetic GnRH. *Theriogenology* 5: 45–60.

Bissonette, R. H. 1932. Modification of mammalian sexual cycles: Reactions of ferrets *(Putorius vulgaris)* of both sexes to electric light after dark in November and December. *Proc. R. Soc. Lond.* B 110:322–36.

Blank, J. L., and Desjardins, C. 1984. Spermatogenesis is modified by food intake in mice. *Biol. Reprod.* 30:410–15.

Bonilla, H., and Rasweiler, J. J. 1974. Breeding activity, preimplantation development, and oviduct histology of the short-tailed fruit bat, *Carollia,* in captivity. *Anat. Rec.* 179:385–404.

Bonney, R. C., Dixson, A. F., and Fleming, D. 1979. Cyclic changes in the circulating and urinary levels of ovarian steroids in the adult female owl monkey *(Aotus trivirgatus). J. Reprod. Fertil.* 56:271–80.

Bonney, R. C., and Setchell, K. D. R. 1980. The excretion of gonadal steroids during the reproductive cycle of the owl monkey *(Aotus trivirgatus). J. Steroid Biochem.* 12:417–21.

Bonney, R. C., Wood, D. J., and Kleiman, D. G. 1981. Endocrine correlates of behavioural oestrus in the female giant panda *(Ailuropoda melanoleuca)* and associated hormonal changes in the male. *J. Reprod. Fertil.* 64:209–15.

Boskoff, K. J. 1977. Aspects of reproduction in ruffed lemurs *(Lemur variegatus). Folia Primatol.* 28:241–50.

Bowman, L. A., Dilley, S. R., and Keverne, E. B. 1978. Suppression of oestrogen-induced LH surges by social subordination in talapoin monkeys. *Nature* 275:56–58.

Brambell, F. W. R. 1935. Reproduction in the common shrew *(Sorex araneus* Linnaeus). 1.The oestrous cycle of the female. *Phil. Trans. R. Soc. Lond.* B 225:1–50.

Brand, H. M. 1981. Urinary oestrogen excretion in the female cotton-topped tamarin *(Saguinus oedipus oedipus). J. Reprod. Fertil.* 62:467–73.

Breed, W. G., and Clarke, J. R. 1970. Ovulation and associated histological changes in the ovary following coitus in the vole *(Microtus agrestis). J. Reprod. Fertil.* 22:173–75.

Bronson, F. H. 1988. Seasonal regulation of reproduction in mammals. In *The physiology of reproduction,* vol. 1, ed. E. Knobil and J. D. Neill, 1831–71. New York: Raven Press.

———. 1989. *Mammalian reproductive biology.* Chicago: University of Chicago Press.

Bronson, F. H., and Rissman, E. 1986. Biology of puberty. *Biol. Rev.* 61:157–95.

Buckingham, J. C., Dohler, K. D., and Wilson, C. A. 1978. Activity of the pituitary-adrenocortical system and thyroid gland during the oestrous cycle of the rat. *J. Endocrinol.* 78:359–66.

Bullock, D. W., Paris, C. A., and Goy, R. W. 1972. Sexual behaviour, swelling of sex skin, and plasma progesterone in the pigtail macaque. *J. Reprod. Fertil.* 31:225–36.

Byerley, D. J., Stargmiller, R. B., Berardinelli, J. G., and Short, R. E. 1987. Pregnancy rates of beef heifers bred either on pubertal or third estrus. *J. Anim. Sci.* 65:645–50.

Callard, G. V., Petro, Z., and Ryan, K. J. 1978. Conversion of androgen to estrogen and other steroids in the vertebrate brain. *Am. Zool.* 18:511–23.

Cameron, R. D. A., and Blackshaw, A. W. 1980. The effect of elevated ambient temperature on spermatogenesis in the boar. *J. Reprod. Fertil.* 59:173–79.

Campbell, C. S., Schwartz, N. B., and Gorski-Firlit, M. 1977. The role of adrenal and ovarian steroids in the control of serum LH and FSH. *Endocrinology* 101:162–72.

Campbell, G. A., Kurcz, M., Marshall, S., and Meites, J. 1977. Effects of starvation in rats on serum levels of follicle-stimulating hormone, luteinizing hormone, thyrotropin, growth hormone, and prolactin: Response to LH-releasing hormone and thyrotropin-releasing hormone. *Endocrinology* 100:580–87.

Carpenter, C. R. 1941. The menstrual cycle and body temperature in two gibbons *(Hylobates lar). Anat. Rec.* 79:291–96.

Carrick, F. N., and Setchell, B. P. 1977. The evolution of the scrotum. In *Reproduction and evolution,* ed. J. N. Calaby and C. H. Tyndale-Biscoe, 165–70. Canberra: Australian Academy of Science.

Catchpole, H. R., and Fulton, J. F. 1943. The oestrous cycle in *Tarsius:* Observations on a captive pair. *J. Mammal.* 24:90–93.

Catling, P. C., and Sutherland, R. L. 1980. Effect of gonadectomy, season, and the presence of female tammar wallabies *(Macropus eugenii)* on concentrations of testosterone, luteinizing hormone, and follicle-stimulating hormone in the plasma of male tammar wallabies. *J. Endocrinol.* 86:25–33.

Chan, S. W. C., Leathem, J. H., and Esashi, T. 1977. Testicular metabolism and serum testosterone in aging male rats. *Endocrinology* 101:128–33.

Chang, M. C., Hunt, D. M., and Romanoff, E. B. 1957. Effects of radiocobalt irradiation of rabbit spermatozoa in vitro on fertilization and early development. *Anat. Rec.* 129:211–29.

Chemineau, P. 1983. Effect on oestrus and ovulation of exposing creole goats to the male at three times of the year. *J. Reprod. Fertil.* 67:65–72.

Chen, B. X., Yuen, Z. X., and Pan, G. W. 1985. Semen-induced ovulation in the Bactrian camel *(Camelus bactrianus). J. Reprod. Fertil.* 74:335–39.

Chesworth, J. M., and Easdon, M. P. 1983. Effect of diet and season on steroid hormones in the ruminant. *J. Steroid Biochem.* 19:715–24.

Christensen, A. K., and Mason, N. R. 1965. Comparative ability of seminiferous tubules and interstitial tissue of rat testes to synthesize androgens from progesterone-4-C in vitro. *Endocrinology* 76:646–56.

Christian, J. J. 1980. Endocrine factors in population regulation. In *Biosocial mechanisms of population regulation,* ed. M. Cohen, R. Malpass, and H. Klein, 55–116. New Haven: Yale University Press.

Ciaccio, L. A., and Lisk, R. D. 1971. The role of progesterone in regulating the period of sexual receptivity in the female hamster. *J. Endocrinol.* 50:201–7.

Cicero, T. J., Bell, R. D., Meyer, E. R., and Schweitzer, J. 1977. Narcotics and the hypothalamic-pituitary-gonadal axis: Acute effects on luteinizing hormone, testosterone, and androgen-dependent systems. *J. Pharmacol. Exp. Ther.* 210:76–83.

Clewe, T. H. 1969. Observations on reproduction of squirrel monkeys in captivity. *J. Reprod. Fertil., Suppl.* 6:151–56.

Clulow, F. V., and Mallory, F. F. 1970. Oestrus and induced ovulation in the vole, *Microtus pennsylvanicus. J. Reprod. Fertil.* 23:341–43.

Coe, C. L., Chen, J., Lowe, E. L., Davidson, J. M., and Levine, S. 1981. Hormonal and behavioral changes at puberty in the squirrel monkey. *Horm. Behav.* 15:36–53.

Coe, C. L., Connolly, A. C., Kraemer, H. C., and Levine, S. 1979. Reproductive development and behavior of captive female chimpanzees. *Primates* 20:571–82.

Collins, D. C., Graham, C. E., and Preedy, J. R. K. 1975. Identification and measurement of urinary estrone, estradiol-17, estriol, pregnanediol, and androsterone during the menstrual cycle of the orangutan. *Endocrinology* 96:93–101.

Conaway, C. H. 1959. The reproductive cycle of the eastern mole. *J. Mammal.* 40:180–94.

Concannon, P., Hansel, W., and McEntree, K. 1977. Changes in LH, progesterone, and sexual behavior associated with preovulatory luteinization in the bitch. *Biol. Reprod.* 17:604–13.

Concannon, P. W., Hansel, W., and Visek, W. J. 1975. The ovarian cycle of the bitch: Plasma estrogen, LH, and progesterone. *Biol. Reprod.* 13:112–21.

Cross, P. C. 1972. Observations on the induction of ovulation in *Microtus montanus. J. Mammal.* 53:210–12.

Curlewis, J. D., Loudon, A. S. I., and Coleman, P. M. 1988. Oestrous cycles and the breeding season of the Père David's deer hind *(Elaphurus davidianus). J. Reprod. Fertil.* 82:119–26.

Cutler, G. B. Jr., Glenn, M., Bush, M., Hodgen, G. D., Graham, C. E., and Loriaux, D. L. 1978. Adrenarche: A survey of rodents, domestic animals, and primates. *Endocrinology* 103:2112–18.

Czaja, J. A., Robinson, J. A., Eisele, S. G., Scheffler, G., and Goy, R. W. 1977. Relationship between sexual skin colour of female rhesus monkeys and midcycle plasma levels of oestradiol and progesterone. *J. Reprod. Fertil.* 49:147–50.

Czekala, N. M., Hodges, J. K., Gause, G. E., and Lasley, B. L. 1980. Annual circulating testosterone levels in captive and free-ranging male armadillos *(Dasypus novemcinctus). J. Reprod. Fertil.* 59:199–204.

Damassa, D. A., and Gustafson, A. W. 1985. Relationship of food intake to the induction of plasma sex steroid–binding protein and testicular activity in immature male little brown bats *(Myotis lucifugus lucifugus). J. Reprod. Fertil.* 74:701–8.

Daniel, M. J. 1963. Early fertility of red deer hinds in New Zealand. *Nature* 200:380–82.

Darney, K. J. Jr., and Franklin, L. E. 1982. Analysis of the estrous cycle of the laboratory-housed Senegal galago *(Galago senegalensis senegalensis):* Natural and induced cycles. *Folia Primatol.* 37:106–26.

Dawson, A. B., and Friedgood, H. B. 1940. The time and sequence of the preovulatory changes in the cat ovary after mating or mechanical stimulation of the cervix uteri. *Anat. Rec.* 76:411–29.

Dawson, A. B., and McCabe, M. 1951. Interstitial tissue of the ovary in infantile and juvenile rats. *J. Morphol.* 88:543–64.

Deanesly, R. 1944. The reproductive cycle of the female weasel *(Mustela nivalis). Proc. Zool. Soc. Lond.* 114:339–49.

deGreef, W. J., Dullaart, J., and Zeilmaker, G. H. 1977. Serum concentrations of progesterone, luteinizing hormone, follicle stimulating hormone, and prolactin in pseudopregnant rats: Effect of decidualization. *Endocrinology* 101:1054–63.

Dekel, N. 1986. Hormonal control of ovulation. *Biochem. Act. Horm.* 13:57–90.

De Palatis, L., Moore, J., and Falvo, R. E. 1978. Plasma concentrations of testosterone and LH in the male dog. *J. Reprod. Fertil.* 52:201–7.

Desaulniers, D. M., Goff, A. K., Betteridge, K. J., Rowell, J. E., and Flood, P. F. 1989. Reproductive hormone concentrations in faeces during the oestrous cycle and pregnancy in cattle *(Bos taurus)* and musk oxen *(Ovibus moschatus). Can. J. Zool.* 67:1148–54.

Dixson, A. F. 1976. Effects of testosterone on the sternal cutaneous glands and genitalia of the male greater galago *(Galago crassicaudatus crassicaudatus). Folia Primatol.* 26:207–13.

Doak, R. L., Hall, A., and Dale, H. E. 1967. Longevity of spermatozoa in the reproductive tract of the bitch. *J. Reprod. Fertil.* 13:51–58.

Douglas, R. H., and Ginther, O. J. 1976. Concentration of prostaglandins F in uterine venous plasma of anesthetized mares during the estrous cycle and early pregnancy. *Prostaglandins* 11:251–60.

Dryden, G. L. 1969. Reproduction in *Suncus murinus. J. Reprod. Fertil., Suppl.* 6:377–96.

Dryden, G. L., and Anderson, J. N. 1977. Ovarian hormone: Lack of effect on reproductive structures of female Asian musk shrews. *Science* 197:782–84.

Dukelow, W. R., and Bruggemann, S. 1979. Characteristics of the menstrual cycle in non-human primates. II. Ovulation and optimal mating time in macaques. *J. Med. Primatol.* 8:79–90.

Dumontier, A., Burdick, A., Ewigman, B., and Fahim, M. S. 1977. Effects of sonication on mature rat testes. *Fertil. Steril.* 28:195–204.

Dunbar, R. I. M., and Dunbar, P. 1974. The reproductive cycle of the gelada baboon. *Anim. Behav.* 22:203–10.

Dupon, C., and Kim, M. H. 1973. Peripheral plasma levels of testosterone, androstenedione, and oestradiol during the rat oestrous cycle. *J. Endocrinol.* 59:653–54.

Dutt, R. H. 1963. Critical period for early embryo mortality in ewes exposed to high ambient temperature. *J. Anim. Sci.* 22: 713–19.

Eadie, W. R. 1948. Corpora amylacea in the prostatic secretion and experiments on the formation of a copulatory plug in some insectivores. *Anat. Rec.* 102:259–67.

Eastman, S. A. K., Makawiti, D. W., Collins, W. P., and Hodges, J. K. 1984. Pattern of excretion of urinary steroid metabolites in the marmoset monkey. *J. Endocrinol.* 102:19–26.

Eaton, G. G., Slob, A., and Resko, J. A. 1973. Cycles of mating behaviour, oestrogen, and progesterone in the thick-tailed bush-baby *(Galago crassicaudatus crassicaudatus)* under laboratory conditions. *Anim. Behav.* 21:309–15.

Eberhart, J. A., Keverne, E. B., and Meller, R. E. 1983. Social influences on circulating levels of cortisol and prolactin in male talapoin monkeys. *Physiol. Behav.* 30:361–70.

Eckstein, P., and Kelly, W. A. 1966. A survey of the breeding performance of rhesus monkeys in the laboratory. *Symp. Zool. Soc. Lond.* 17:91–112.

Eckstein, P., and Zuckerman, S. 1956. Morphology of the reproductive tract. In *Marshall's physiology of reproduction,* 3d ed., vol. 1, part 1, ed. A. S. Parkes, 43–155. London: Longmans, Green and Company.

Edwards, L. M., Rahe, C. H., Griffin, J. L., Wolfe, D. F., Marple, D. N., Cummins, K. A., and Pitchett, J. F. 1987. Effect of transportation stress on ovarian function in superovulated Hereford heifers. *Theriogenology* 28:291–99.

Ellis, L. C. 1970. Radiation effects. In *The testes III,* ed. A. D. Johnson, W. R. Gomes, and N. L. VanDemark, 333–76. New York: Academic Press.

El Safoury, S., and Bartke, A. 1974. Effects of follicle-stimulating hormone and luteinizing hormone on plasma testosterone levels in hypophysectomized and in intact immature and adult rats. *J. Endocrinol.* 61:193–98.

Else, J. G., Eley, R. M., Suleman, M. A., and Lequin, R. M. 1985. Reproductive biology of Sykes and blue monkeys *(Cercopithecus mitis). Am. J. Primatol.* 9:189–96.

Else, J. G., Eley, R. M., Wangula, C., Worthman, C., and Lequin, R. M. 1986. Reproduction in the vervet monkey *(Cercopithecus aethiops)*: II. Annual menstrual patterns and seasonality. *Am. J. Primatol.* 11:333–42.

Enders, R. K., and Enders, A. C. 1963. Morphology of the female reproductive tract during delayed implantation in the mink. In *Delayed implantation,* ed. A. C. Enders, 129–39. Chicago: University of Chicago Press.

Enders, R. K., and Leekley, J. R. 1941. Cyclic changes in the vulva of the marten *(Martes americana). Anat. Rec.* 79:1–5.

England, B. G., Foote, W. C., Matthews, D. H., Cardozo, A. G., and Riera, S. 1969. Ovulation and corpus luteum function in the llama *(Lama glama). J. Endocrinol.* 45:505–13.

Ensley, P. K., Wing, A. E., Gosink, B. B., Lasley, B. L., and Durrant, B. 1982. Application of noninvasive techniques to monitor reproductive function in a brown hyena *(Hyaena brunnea). Zoo Biol.* 1:333–43.

Evans, H. M., and Cole, H. H. 1931. An introduction to the study of the oestrous cycle in the dog. *Memoirs of the University of California* 9:65–118.

Evans, C. S., and Goy, R. W. 1968. Social behaviour and reproductive cycles in captive ring-tailed lemurs *(Lemur catta). J. Zool.* (Lond.) 156:181–97.

Ewer, R. F. 1973. *The carnivores.* Ithaca, N.Y.: Cornell University Press.

Fadem, B. H. 1987. Activation of estrus by pheromones in a marsupial: Stimulus control and endocrine factors. *Biol. Reprod.* 36:328–32.

Fallon, G. R. 1959. Some aspects of oestrus in cattle with reference

to fertility on artificial insemination. 3. Body temperature and the oestrous cycle. *Queensland J. Agric. Sci.* 16:439–47.

Fernandez-Baca, S., Madden, D. H. L., and Novoa, C. 1970. Effect of different mating stimuli on induction of ovulation in the alpaca. *J. Reprod. Fertil.* 22:261–67.

Flint, A. P. F., and Hillier, K. 1975. Prostaglandins and reproductive processes in female sheep and goats. In *Prostaglandins and reproduction,* ed. S. M. M. Karim, 271–308. Lancaster, U.K.: MTP Press.

Flowerdew, J. R. 1973. The effect of natural and artificial changes in food supply on breeding in woodland mice and voles. *J. Reprod. Fertil., Suppl.* 19:259–69.

Flowers, B., and Day, B. N. 1990. Alterations in gonadotropin secretion and ovarian function in prepubertal gilts by elevated environmental temperature. *Biol. Reprod.* 42:465–71.

Flux, E. C. 1967. Reproduction and body weights of the hare, *Lepus europaeus pallus,* in New Zealand. *N.Z. J. Sci.* 10: 357–401.

Foote, R. H. 1969. Research techniques to study reproductive physiology in the male. In *Techniques and procedures in animal science research,* 80–101. Champaign, Ill.: American Society of Animal Science.

Fordham, R. A. 1971. Field populations of deer mice with supplemental food. *Ecology* 52:138–45.

Forger, N. G., Dark, J., Barnes, B. M., and Zucker, I. 1986. Fat ablation and food restriction influence reproductive development and hibernation in ground squirrels. *Biol. Reprod.* 34: 831–40.

Fortune, J. 1981. Bovine theca and granulosa cells interact to promote androgen and progestin production. *Biol. Reprod.* 24: 39A.

Foster, D. L. 1988. Puberty in the female sheep. In *The physiology of reproduction,* vol. 1, ed. E. Knobil and J. D. Neill, 1739–62. New York: Raven Press.

Foster, M. 1934. The reproductive cycle in the female ground squirrel *Citellus tridecemlineatus* M. *Am. J. Anat.* 54:487–511.

Frank, A. H., and Fraps, R. M. 1945. Induction of estrus in the ovariectomized golden hamster. *Endocrinology* 37:357–61.

French, J. A., and Stribley, J. A. 1985. Patterns of urinary oestrogen excretion in female golden lion tamarins *(Leontopithecus rosalia). J. Reprod. Fertil.* 75:537–46.

Friesen, H. G. 1977. Prolactin. In *Frontiers in reproduction and fertility control,* part 2, ed. R. O. Greep and M. A. Koblinsky, 25–32. Cambridge, Mass.: MIT Press.

Fuchs, A. R. 1972. Uterine activity during and after mating in the rabbit. *Fertil. Steril.* 23:915–23.

Gandy, H. M., and Peterson, R. E. 1968. Measurement of testosterone and 17-ketosteroids in plasma by the double isotope dilution derivative technique. *J. Clin. Endocrinol.* 28:949–77.

Gangrade, B. K., and Dominic, C. J. 1985. Influence of conspecific males on the oestrous cycle of underfed female mice. *Exp. Clin. Endocrinol.* 86:35–40.

Gauthier, D., and Coulaud, G. 1986. Effect of underfeeding on testosterone-LH feedback in the bull. *J. Endocrinol.* 110:233–38.

Gerloff, B. J., and Morrow, D. A. 1980. Effect of nutrition on reproduction in dairy cattle. In *Current therapy in theriogenology,* ed. D. A. Morrow, 310–20. Philadelphia: W. B. Saunders.

Ghafoorunissa 1980. Undernutrition and fertility in male rats. *J. Reprod. Fertil.* 59:317–20.

Ghobrial, L. I., and Hodieb, A. S. K. 1973. Climate and seasonal variations in the breeding of the desert jerboa, *Jaculus jaculus,* in the Sudan. *J. Reprod. Fertil., Suppl.* 19:221–33.

Gier, H. T. 1960. Estrous cycle in the bitch, vaginal fluids. *Vet. Scope* 5:2–9.

Gillman, J., and Gilbert, C. 1946. The reproductive cycle of the chacma baboon with special reference to the problems of menstrual irregularities as assessed by the behaviour of the sex skin. *S. Afr. J. Med. Sci.* 11:1–54.

Ginther, O. J. 1979. *Reproductive biology of the mare: Basic and applied aspects.* Cross Plains, Wisc.: Equiservices.

———. 1986. Ultrasonic imaging and reproductive events in the mare. Cross Plains, Wisc.: Equiservices.

Ginther, O. J., Bergfelt, D. R., Scraba, S. T., Pivonka, P. R., and Nuti, L. C. 1985. Effects of 6-MBOA on reproductive function in ponies, mice, rats, and mink. *Theriogenology* 24:587–95.

Glander, K. E. 1980. Reproduction and population growth in free-ranging mantled howler monkeys. *Am. J. Phys. Anthropol.* 53:25–36.

Glick, B. B. 1979. Testicular size, testosterone level, and body weight in male *Macaca radiata*, maturational and seasonal effects. *Folia Primatol.* 32:268–89.

Glover, T. D. 1955. Some effects of scrotal insulation on the semen of rams. *Proceedings of the Society for the Study of Fertility* 7:66–75.

Glover, T. D., D'Occhio, M. J., and Millar, R. P. 1990. Male life cycle and seasonality. In *Marshall's physiology of reproduction,* 4th ed., vol. 2, *Reproduction in the male,* ed. G. E. Lamming, 213–78. London: Churchill Livingstone.

Goldman, B. D., and Darrow, J. M. 1983. The pineal gland and mammalian photoperiodism. *Neuroendocrinology* 37:386–96.

Goldzieher, J. W., and Axelrod, L. R. 1969. Urinary metabolites of [4-14C] progesterone in the baboon (*Papio* spp.). *Gen. Comp. Endocrinol.* 13:201–5.

Goncharov, N., Aso, T., Cekan, Z., Pachalia, N., and Dicfalusy, E. 1976. Hormonal changes during the menstrual cycle of the baboon *(Papio hamadryas). Acta Endocrinol.* 82:396–412.

Gooding, C. D., and Long, J. L. 1957. Some fluctuations within rabbit populations in Western Australia. *J. Aust. Inst. Agric. Sci.* 23:334–45.

Gopalakrishna, A., and Madhavan, A. 1971. Survival of spermatozoa in the female genital tract of the Indian vespertilionid bat, *Pipistrellus ceylonicus chrysothrix* (Wroughton). *Proceedings of the Indian Academy of Science* B 73:43–49.

Gordon, T. P., Rose, R. M., and Bernstein, I. S. 1976. Seasonal rhythms in plasma testosterone levels in the rhesus monkey *(Macaca mulatta):* A three year study. *Horm. Behav.* 7:229–43.

Gould, K. G., Cline, E. M., and Williams, W. L. 1973. Observations on the induction of ovulation and fertilization in vitro in the squirrel monkey *(Saimiri sciureus). Fertil. Steril.* 24:260–68.

Graham, C. E., Collins, D. C., Robinson, H., and Preedy, J. R. K. 1972. Urinary levels of estrogen and pregnanediol and plasma levels of progesterone during the menstrual cycle of the chimpanzee: Relationship to the sexual swelling. *Endocrinology* 91:13–24.

Graham, C. E., Warren, H., Misner, J., Collins, D. C., and Preedy, J. R. K. 1977. The association between basal body temperature, sexual swelling, and urinary gonadal hormone levels in the menstrual cycle of the chimpanzee. *J. Reprod. Fertil.* 50:23–28.

Greenwald, G. S. 1956. The reproductive cycle of the field mouse, *Microtus californicus. J. Mammal.* 37:213–22.

———. 1965. Histological transformation of the ovary of the lactating hamster. *Endocrinology* 77:641–50.

Grimsdell, J. J. R. 1973. Reproduction in the African buffalo, *Syncerus caffer,* in western Uganda. *J. Reprod. Fertil., Suppl.* 19:303–18.

Gross, T. S. 1992. Faecal steroid measurements in several carnivores. In *The First International Symposium on Faecal Steroid Monitoring in Zoo Animals,* ed. E. Bamberg, 55–61. Rotterdam: Royal Rotterdam Zoological and Botanical Gardens.

Gulamhusein, A. P., and Tam, W. H. 1974. Reproduction in the male stoat. *J. Reprod. Fertil.* 36:405–8.

Gulamhusein, A. P., and Thawley, A. R. 1972. Plasma progesterone levels in the stoat. *J. Reprod. Fertil.* 31:492–93.

Gunn, R. G., and Doney, J. M. 1973. The effects of nutrition and rainfall at the time of mating on the reproductive performance of ewes. *J. Reprod. Fertil., Suppl.* 19:253–58.

Gustafson, A. W. 1979. Male reproductive patterns in hibernating bats. *J. Reprod. Fertil.* 56:317–31.

Gustafson, A. W., and Shemesh, M. 1976. Changes in testosterone levels during the annual reproductive cycle of the hibernating bat *Myotis lucifugus lucifugus* with a survey of plasma testosterone levels in adult male vertebrates. *Biol. Reprod.* 15:9–24.

Gwatkin, R. B. L. 1977. *Fertilization mechanisms in man and mammals.* New York: Plenum Press.

Hadidian, J., and Bernstein, I. S. 1979. Female reproductive cycles and birth data from an Old World monkey colony. *Primates* 20:429–42.

Hafez, E. S. E. 1970. Female reproductive organs. In *Reproduction and breeding techniques for laboratory animals,* ed. E. S. E. Hafez, 74–106. Philadelphia: Lea and Febiger.

———. 1971. Reproductive cycles. In *Comparative reproduction of nonhuman primates,* ed. E. S. E. Hafez, 160–204. Springfield, Ill.: C. C. Thomas.

Hafez, E. S. E., and Jainudeen, M. R. 1974. Reproductive failure in females. In *Reproduction in farm animals,* 3d ed., ed. E. S. E. Hafez, 351–72. Philadelphia: Lea and Febiger.

Hagino, N. 1972. The effect of synthetic corticosteroids on ovarian function in the baboon. *J. Clin. Endocrinol. Metab.* 35:716–21.

Hagino, N., Watanabe, M., and Goldzieher, J. W. 1969. Inhibition by adrenocorticotrophin of gonadotrophin-induced ovulation in immature female rats. *Endocrinology* 84:308–14.

Hall, P. F., Irby, D. C., and deKretser, D. M. 1969. Conversion of cholesterol to androgens by rat testes: Comparison of interstitial cells and seminiferous tubules. *Endocrinology* 84:488–96.

Hamilton, D. W. 1990. Anatomy of mammalian male accessory reproductive organs. In *Marshall's physiology of reproduction,* 4th ed., vol. 2, *Reproduction in the male,* ed. G. E. Lamming, 691–746. London: Churchill Livingstone.

Hamilton, G. D., and Bronson, F. H. 1985. Food restriction and reproductive development in wild house mice. *Biol. Reprod.* 32:773–78.

Hamilton, W. J. III. 1962. Reproductive adaptations of the red tree mouse. *J. Mammal.* 43:486–504.

Hammond, J., and Marshall, F. H. A. 1930. Oestrus and pseudopregnancy in the ferret. *Proc. R. Soc. Lond.* B 105:607–30.

Hansel, W., Concannon, P. W., and Lukaszewska, J. H. 1973. Corpora lutea of the large domestic mammals. *Biol. Reprod.* 8:222–45.

Hansel, W., and Convey, E. M. 1983. Physiology of the estrous cycle. *J. Anim. Sci.* 57:404–24.

Hansson, A. 1947. The physiology of reproduction in mink (*Mustela vison* Schreb.). *Acta Zool.* 28:1–136.

Harder, J. D., and Moorhead, D. L. 1980. The development of corpora lutea and plasma progesterone levels associated with the onset of the breeding season in the white-tailed deer *(Odocoileus virginianus). Biol. Reprod.* 22:185–91.

Hartmann, C. G. 1924. Observations on the motility of the opossum genital tract and the vaginal plug. *Anat. Rec.* 27:293–303.

———. 1931. On the relative sterility of the adolescent organism. *Science* 74:226–27.

Hasler, J. F., and Banks, E. M. 1973. Ovulation and ovum maturation in the collared lemming *(Dicrostonyx groenlandicus). Biol. Reprod.* 9:88–98.

———. 1976. The behavioral and somatic effects of ovariectomy and replacement therapy in female collared lemmings (Dicrostonyx groenlandicus). Horm. Behav. 7:59–74.

Hayssen, V., van Tienhoven, A., and van Tienhoven, A. 1993. Asdell's patterns of mammalian reproduction. Ithaca, N.Y.: Cornell University Press.

Hediger, H. 1950. Wild animals in captivity. Trans. G. Sircom. London: Butterworths.

Hellgren, E. C., Lochmiller, R. L., Amoss, M. A., and Grant, W. E. 1985. Serum progesterone, estradiol-17B, and glucocorticoids in the collared peccary during gestation and lactation as influenced by dietary protein and energy. Gen. Comp. Endocrinol. 59:358–68.

Hellwing, S. 1973. Husbandry and breeding of white-toothed shrews. Int. Zoo Yrbk. 13:127–34.

Hendrickx, A. G. 1967. The menstrual cycle of the baboon as determined by the vaginal smear, vaginal biopsy, and perineal swelling. In The baboon in medical research, vol. 2, ed. H. Vagtborg, 437–59. Austin: University of Texas Press.

Hendrickx, A. G., and Kraemer, D. C. 1969. Observations on the menstrual cycle, optimal mating time, and pre-implantation embryos of the baboon, Papio anubis and Papio cynocephalus. J. Reprod. Fertil., Suppl. 6:119–28.

Hendrickx, A. G., and Newman, L. M. 1978. Reproduction of the greater bushbaby (Galago crassicaudatus panganiensis) under laboratory conditions. J. Med. Primatol. 7:26–43.

Hendrickx, A. G., Stone, G. W., Hendrickson, R. V., and Mayayoshi, K. 1979. Teratogenic effects of hyperthermia in the bonnet monkey (Macaca radiata). Teratology 19:177–82.

Henniawati, and Fletcher, I. C. 1986. Reproduction in Indonesian sheep and goats at two levels of nutrition. Anim. Reprod. Sci. 12:77–84.

Herbert, J. 1970. Hormones and reproductive behaviour in rhesus and talapoin monkeys. J. Reprod. Fertil., Suppl. 11:119–40.

Hess, D. L., Hendrickx, A. G., and Stabenfeldt, G. H. 1979. Reproductive and hormonal patterns in the African green monkey (Cercopithecus aethiops). J. Med. Primatol. 8:237–81.

Hess, D. L., and Resko, J. A. 1973. The effects of progesterone on the pattern of testosterone and estradiol concentrations in the systemic plasma of the female rhesus monkey during the intermenstrual period. Endocrinology 92:446–53.

Hill, J. P. 1933. The development of Monotremata. II. The structure of the egg-shell. Trans. Zool. Soc. Lond. 21:443–76.

———. 1941. The development of the Monotremata. V. Further observations on the histology and secretory activities of the oviduct prior to and during gestation. Trans. Zool. Soc. Lond. 25:1–31.

Hill, J. P., and O'Donoghue, C. H. 1913. The reproductive cycle in the marsupial Dasyurus viverrinus. Q. J. Microsc. Sci. 59:133–74.

Hilliard, J., Scaramuzzi, R. J., Pang, C., Penardi, R., and Sawyer, C. H. 1974. Testosterone secretion by the rabbit ovary in vivo. Endocrinology 94:267–71.

Hochereau de Riviers, M.-T., Courtens, J.-L., Courot, M., and de Reviers, M. 1990. Spermatogenesis in mammals and birds. In Marshall's physiology of reproduction, 4th ed., vol. 2, Reproduction in the male, ed. G. E. Lamming, 106–82. London: Churchill Livingstone.

Hodges, J. K., Bevan, D. J., Celma, M., Hearn, J. P., Jones, D. M., Kleiman, D. G., Knight, J. A., and Moore, H. D. M. 1984. Aspects of the reproductive endocrinology of the female giant panda (Ailuropoda melanoleuca) in captivity with special reference to the detection of ovulation and pregnancy. J. Zool. (Lond.) 203:253–67.

Hodges, J. K., Czekala, N. M., and Lasley, B. L. 1979. Estro-

gen and luteinizing hormone secretion in diverse primate species from simplified urinary analysis. J. Med. Primatol. 3:349–64.

Hodges, J. K., and Eastman, S. A. K. 1984. Monitoring ovarian function in marmosets and tamarins by the measurement of urinary estrogen metabolites. Am. J. Primatol. 6:187–97.

Hodges, J. K., Tarara, R., Hearn, J. P., and Else, J. G. 1986. The detection of ovulation and early pregnancy in the baboon by direct measurement of conjugated steroids in urine. Am. J. Primatol. 10:329–38.

Hodges, J. K., Tari, S., and Heistermann, M. 1992. Faecal steroid excretion of sex steroids in Neotropical monkeys: Coping with different metabolic strategies. In The First International Symposium on Faecal Steroid Monitoring in Zoo Animals, ed. E. Bamberg, 47–48. Rotterdam: Royal Rotterdam Zoological and Botanical Gardens.

Holt, W. V., Moore, H. D. M., North, R. D., Hartman, T. D., and Hodges, J. K. 1988. Hormonal and behavioural detection of oestrus in blackbuck, Antilope cervicapra, and successful artificial insemination with fresh and frozen semen. J. Reprod. Fertil. 82:717–25.

Homeida, A. M., and Cooke, R. G. 1984. Plasma concentrations of testosterone and 5-dihydrotestosterone around luteolysis in goats and their behavioral effects after ovariectomy. J. Steroid Biochem. 20:1357–60.

Hotchkiss, J., Atkinson, L. E., and Knobil, E. 1971. Time course of serum estrogen and luteinizing hormone (LH) concentrations during the menstrual cycle of the rhesus monkey. Endocrinology 89:177–83.

Howard-Tripp, M. E., and Bielert, C. 1978. Social contact influences on the menstrual cycle of the female chacma baboon (Papio ursinus). J. S. Afr. Vet. Assoc. 49:191–92.

Howland, B. E., and Ibrahim, E. A. 1973. Increased LH-suppressing effect of oestrogen in ovariectomized rats as a result of underfeeding. J. Reprod. Fertil. 35:545–48.

Hughes, R. L. 1962. Reproduction in the macropod marsupial Potorous tridactylus (Kerr). Aust. J. Zool. 10:193–224.

Hughes, R. L., and Carrick, F. N. 1978. Reproduction in female monotremes. Aust. Zool. 20:233–53.

Illingworth, D. V., and Perry, J. S. 1973. Effects of oestrogen administered early or late in the oestrous cycle, upon the survival and regression of the corpus luteum of the guinea pig. J. Reprod. Fertil. 33:457–67.

Illius, A. W., Haynes, N. B., and Lamming, G. E. 1976. Effects of ewe proximity on peripheral plasma testosterone levels and behavior in the ram. J. Reprod. Fertil. 48:25–32.

Illius, A. W., Haynes, N. B., Lamming, G. E., Howles, C. M., Fairall, N., and Millar, R. P. 1983. Evaluation of LH–RH stimulation of testosterone as an index of reproductive status in rams and its application in wild antelope. J. Reprod. Fertil. 68:105–12.

Inns, R. W. 1982. Seasonal changes in the accessory reproductive system and plasma testosterone levels in the male tammar wallaby, Macropus eugenii, in the wild. J. Reprod. Fertil. 66:745–57.

Ioannou, J. M. 1983. Female reproductive organs. In Reproduction in New World Primates, ed. J. Hearn, 131–59. Lancaster, England: MTP Press.

Ismail, S. T., 1987. A review of reproduction in the female camel (Camelus dromedarius). Theriogenology 28:363–71.

Izard, M. K., and Rasmussen, D. T. 1985. Reproduction in the slender loris (Loris tardigradus malabaricus). Am. J. Primatol. 8:153–65.

Jainudeen, M. R., Katongole, C. B., and Short, R. V. 1972. Plasma testosterone levels in relation to musth and sexual activity in the male Asiatic elephant *(Elephas maximus)*. *J. Reprod. Fertil.* 29: 99–103.

Jameson, E. W. 1953. Reproduction of deermice *(Peromyscus maniculatus* and *P. boylii)* in Sierra Nevada, California. *J. Mammal.* 34:44–58.

Jochle, W. 1973. Coitus induced ovulation. *Contraception* 7: 523–64.

———. 1975. Current research in coitus-induced ovulation: A review. *J. Reprod. Fertil., Suppl.* 22:165–207.

Joshi, H. S., Watson, D. J., and Labhsetwar, A. P. 1973. Ovarian secretion of oestradiol, oestrone, and 20-dihydroprogesterone and progesterone during the oestrous cycle of the guinea pig. *J. Reprod. Fertil.* 35:177–81.

Kamel, F., and Frankel, A. I. 1978. Hormone release during mating in the male rat: Time course, relation to sexual behavior, and interaction with handling procedures. *Endocrinology* 103: 2172–79.

Kanagawa, H., Hafez, E. S. E., Mori, J., Kurosawa, T., and Kothari, L. 1973. Cyclic changes in cervical mucus and LH levels in the bonnet macaque *(Macaca radiata)*. *Folia Primatol.* 19: 208–17.

Kann, G., and Martinet, J. 1975. Prolactin levels and duration of postpartum anestrus in lactating ewes. *Nature* 257:63–64.

Karesh, W. B., Willis, M. S., Czekala, N. M., and Lasley, B. L. 1985. Induction of fertile mating in a red ruffed lemur *(Varecia variegata rubra)* using pregnant mare serum gonadotropin. *Zoo Biol.* 4:147–52.

Kassam, A. A. H., and Lasley, B. L. 1981. Estrogen excretory patterns in the Indian rhinoceros *(Rhinoceros unicornis)*, determined by simplified urinary analysis. *Am. J. Vet. Res.* 42: 251–55.

Katongole, C. B., Naftolin, F., and Short, R. V. 1971. Relation between blood levels of luteinizing hormone and testosterone in bulls and the effects of sexual stimulation. *J. Endocrinol.* 50: 456–66.

Katz, L. S., Oltenacu, E. A. B., and Foote, R. H. 1980. The behavioral responses in ovariectomized cattle to either estradiol, testosterone, androstenedione, or dihydrotestosterone. *Horm. Behav.* 14:224–35.

Kiddy, C. A. 1977. Variation in physical activity as an indication of estrus in dairy cows. *J. Dairy Sci.* 60:235–43.

Kinder, J. E., Day, M. L., and Kittok, R. J. 1987. Endocrine regulation of puberty in cows and ewes. *J. Reprod. Fertil., Suppl.* 34: 167–87.

Kirkpatrick, J. F., Shideler, S. E., Lasley, B. L., Turner, J. W. Jr., and Czekala, N. M. 1992. Field application of faecal steroid monitoring to free-ranging wildlife. In *The First International Symposium on Faecal Steroid Monitoring in Zoo Animals*, ed. E. Bamberg, 25–34. Rotterdam: Royal Rotterdam Zoological and Botanical Gardens.

Kirkpatrick, J. F., Vail, R., Devous, S., Schwend, S., Baker, C. B., and Wiesner, L. 1976. Diurnal variation of plasma testosterone in wild stallions. *Biol. Reprod.* 15:98–101.

Kirkpatrick, J. F., Wiesner, L., Kenney, R. M., Ganjam, V. K., and Turner, J. W. Jr. 1977. Seasonal variation in plasma androgens and testosterone in the North American wild horse. *J. Endocrinol.* 72:237–38.

Kirkpatrick, R. L., and Kibbe, D. P. 1971. Nutritive restriction and reproductive characteristics of captive cottontail rabbits. *J. Wildl. Mgmt.* 35:332–38.

Kirkpatrick, R. L., and Valentine, G. L. 1970. Reproduction in captive pine voles, *Microtus pinetorum*. *J. Mammal.* 51: 779–85.

Kling, D. R., and Westfahl, P. K. 1978. Steroid changes during the menstrual cycle of the baboon *(Papio cynocephalus)* and human. *Biol. Reprod.* 18:392–400.

Klopper, A., and Michie, E. A. 1956. The excretion of urinary pregnanediol after administration of progesterone. *J. Endocrinol.* 13:360–64.

Knobil, E., and Neill, J. D. 1988. *The physiology of reproduction*, vol. 1. New York: Raven Press.

Korenbrot, C. C., Huhtaniemi, I. T., and Weiner, I. 1977. Preputial separation as an external sign of pubertal development in the male rat. *Biol. Reprod.* 17:298–303.

Kotwica, J., and Williams, G. L. 1982. Relationship of plasma testosterone concentrations to pituitary-ovarian hormone secretion during the bovine estrous cycle and the effects of testosterone propionate administered during luteal regression. *Biol. Reprod.* 27:790–801.

Krohn, P. L., and Zuckerman, S. 1937. Water metabolism in relation to the menstrual cycle. *J. Physiol.* 88:369–87.

Lamming, G. E., ed. 1990. *Marshall's physiology of reproduction*, 4th ed., vol. 2, *Reproduction in the male*. London: Churchill Livingstone.

Lasley, B. L., Hodges, J. K., and Czekala, N. M. 1980. Monitoring the female reproductive cycle of great apes and other primate species by determination of oestrogen and LH in small volumes of urine. *J. Reprod. Fertil., Suppl.* 28:121–29.

Laws, R. M. 1973. Effects of human activities on reproduction in the wild. *J. Reprod. Fertil., Suppl.* 19:523–32.

Leathem, J. H. 1975. Nutritional influences on testicular composition and function in mammals. In *Handbook of physiology*, sec. 7, *Endocrinology*, vol. 5, *Male reproductive system*, ed. R. O. Greep and E. B. Astwood, 225–32. Washington, D.C.: American Physiological Society.

Leavitt, W. W., and Wright, P. A. 1965. The plant estrogen, coumestrol, as an agent affecting hypophyseal gonadotropic function. *J. Exp. Zool.* 160:319–28.

Lechleitner, R. R. 1959. Sex ratio, age class, and reproduction of the black-tailed jack rabbit. *J. Mammal.* 40:63–81.

Lee, A. K., Bradley, A. J., and Braithwaite, R. W. 1977. Corticosteroid levels and male mortality in *Antechinus stuartii*. In *The biology of marsupials*, ed. B. Stonehouse and D. Gilmore, 209–20. Baltimore: University Park Press.

Legan, S. J., and Winans, S. S. 1981. The photoneuroendocrine control of seasonal breeding in the ewe. *Gen. Comp. Endocrinol.* 45:317–28.

Lidicker, W. Z. Jr. 1973. Regulation of numbers in an island population of the California vole, a problem in community dynamics. *Ecol. Monogr.* 43:271–302.

Lincoln, G. A., and Kay, R. N. B. 1979. Effects of season on the secretion of LH and testosterone in intact and castrated red deer stags. *J. Reprod. Fertil.* 55:75–80.

Liptrap, R. M. 1970. Effect of corticotrophin and corticosteroids on oestrus, ovulation, and oestrogen excretion in the sow. *J. Endocrinol.* 47:197–205.

Liptrap, R. M., and Raeside, J. I. 1968. Effect of corticotrophin and corticosteroids on plasma interstitial cell-stimulating hormone and the urinary steroids in the boar. *J. Endocrinol.* 42:33–43.

Lochmiller, R. L., Hellgren, E. C., and Grant, W. E. 1986. Reproductive responses to nutritional stress in adult female collared peccaries. *J. Wildl. Mgmt.* 50:295–300.

Lohiya, N. K., Sharma, R. S. M., Puri, C. P., David, G. F. X., and Anand Kumar, T. C. 1988. Reproductive exocrine and endocrine profile of female langur monkeys, *Presbytis entellus*. *J. Reprod. Fertil.* 82:485–92.

Long, C. A., and Frank, T. 1968. Morphometric variation and function in the baculum, with comments on correlation of parts. *J. Mammal.* 49:32–43.

Long, J. A., and Evans, H. M. 1922. The oestrous cycle of the rat and its associated phenomena. *Memoirs of the University of California* 6:1–148.

Loskutoff, N. M., Kasman, L. H., Raphael, B. L., Ott-Joslin, J. E., and Lasley, B. L. 1987. Urinary steroid evaluations to monitor ovarian function in exotic ungulates: IV. Estrogen metabolism in the okapi (Okapia johnstoni). Zoo Biol. 6:213–18.

Loskutoff, N. M., Ott, J. E., and Lasley, B. L. 1982. Urinary steroid evaluation to monitor ovarian function in exotic ungulates: I. Pregnanediol-3-glucuronide immunoreactivity in the okapi (Okapia johnstoni). Zoo Biol. 1:45–53.

Loskutoff, N. M., Walker, L., Ott-Joslin, J. E., Raphael, B. L., and Lasley, B. L. 1986. Urinary steroid evaluations to monitor ovarian function in exotic ungulates: II. Comparison between the giraffe (Giraffa camelopardalis) and the okapi (Okapia johnstoni). Zoo Biol. 5:331–38.

Lumpkin, S., Koontz, F., and Howard, J. G. 1982. The oestrous cycle of the rufous elephant-shrew, Elephantulus rufescens. J. Reprod. Fertil. 66:671–74.

Lunaas, T. 1962. Urinary oestrogen levels in the sow during oestrous cycle and early pregnancy. J. Reprod. Fertil. 4:13–20.

MacFarlane, J. D., and Taylor, J. M. 1982. Nature of estrus and ovulation in Microtus townsendii (Bachman). J. Mammal. 63:104–9.

Macrides, F., Bartke, A., and Dalterio, S. 1975. Strange females increase plasma testosterone levels in male mice. Science 189:1104–6.

Mahoney, C. J. 1970. Study of the menstrual cycle in Macaca irus with special reference to the detection of ovulation. J. Reprod. Fertil. 21:153–63.

Mann, D. R., Korowitz, C. D., and Barraclough, C. A. 1975. Adrenal gland involvement in synchronizing the preovulatory release of LH in rats. Proc. Soc. Exp. Biol. Med. 150:115–20.

Marie, M., and Anouassi, A. 1986. Mating-induced luteinizing hormone surge and ovulation in the female camel (Camelus dromedarius). Biol. Reprod. 35:792–98.

Marshall, F. H. A. 1904. The oestrous cycle of the common ferret. Q. J. Microsc. Sci. 48:323–45.

Martinet, L. 1980. Oestrous behaviour, follicular growth, and ovulation during pregnancy in the hare (Lepus europaeus). J. Reprod. Fertil. 59:441–45.

Martini, L. 1982. The 5α-reductase of testosterone in the neuroendocrine structures: Biological and physiological implications. Endocrinol. Rev. 3:1–25.

Matthews, L. H. 1935. The oestrous cycle and intersexuality in the female mole, T. europaea. Proc. Zool. Soc. Lond. 347–83.

———. 1953–1956. The sexual skin of the gelada baboon (Theropithecus gelada). Trans. Zool. Soc. Lond. 28:543–52.

McGlone, J. J. 1985. Olfactory cues and pig agonistic behavior: Evidence for a submissive pheromone. Physiol. Behav. 34:195–98.

McGuire, M. T., Brammer, G. L., and Raleigh, M. J. 1986. Resting cortisol levels and the emergence of dominant status among male vervet monkeys. Horm. Behav. 20:106–17.

McMillan, J. M., Seal, U. S., Keenlyne, K. D., Erickson, A. W., and Jones, J. E. 1974. Annual testosterone rhythm in the adult white-tailed deer (Odocoileus virginianus borealis). Endocrinology 94:1034–40.

Mehta, R. R., Jenco, J. M., Gaynor, L. V., and Chatterton, R. T. Jr. 1986. Relationships between ovarian morphology, vaginal cytology, serum progesterone, and urinary immunoreactive pregnanediol during the menstrual cycle of the cynomolgus monkey. Biol. Reprod. 35:981–86.

Melampy, R. M., Emmerson, M. A., Rakes, J. M., Hanka, L. J., and Eness, P. G. 1957. The effect of progesterone on the estrous response of estrogen-conditioned ovariectomized cows. J. Anim. Sci. 16:967–75.

Melampy, R. M., and Rakes, J. M. 1958. Induced estrus in ovariectomized cows. Iowa State Coll. J. Sci. 33:85–90.

Mellin, T. N., and Erb, R. E. 1966. Estrogen metabolism and excretion during the bovine estrous cycle. Steroids 7:589–606.

Meusy-Dessolle, N., and Dang, D. C. 1985. Plasma concentrations of testosterone, dihydrotestosterone, 4-androstenedione, dehydroepiandrosterone, and oestradiol-17B in the crab-eating monkey (Macaca fascicularis) from birth to adulthood. J. Reprod. Fertil. 74:347–59.

Michael, R. P., Saayman, G. S., and Zumpe, D. 1968. The suppression of mounting behavior and ejaculation in male rhesus monkeys (Macaca mulatta) by administration of progesterone to their female partners. J. Endocrinol. 41:421–31.

Mickelsen, W. D., Paisley, L. G., and Dahmen, J. J. 1981. Seasonal variations in scrotal circumference, sperm quality, and sexual ability in rams. J. Am. Vet. Med. Assoc. 181:376–80.

Mieusset, R., Casares, P. Q., Partica, L. G. S., Sowerbutts, S. F., Zupp, J. L., and Setchell, B. P. 1992. Effects of heating the testes and epididymides of rams by scrotal insulation on fertility and embryonic mortality in ewes inseminated with frozen semen. J. Reprod. Fertil. 94:337–43.

Milewich, L., and Whisenant, M. G. 1982. Metabolism of androstenedione by human platelets: A source of potent androgens. J. Clin. Endocrinol. Metab. 54:969–74.

Millar, R., and Fairall, N. 1976. Hypothalamic, pituitary, and gonadal hormone production in relation to nutrition in the male hyrax (Procavia capensis). J. Reprod. Fertil. 47:339–41.

Millar, R. P., and Glover, T. D. 1973. Regulation of seasonal sexual activity in an ascrotal mammal, the rock hyrax, Procavia capensis. J. Reprod. Fertil., Suppl. 19:203–20.

Milligan, S. R. 1982. Induced ovulation in mammals. Oxf. Rev. Reprod. Biol. 4:1–46.

Mitchell, W. R., Presley, S., Czekala, N. M., and Lasley, B. L. 1982. Urinary immunoreactive oestrogen and pregnanediol-3-glucuronide during the normal menstrual cycle of the female lowland gorilla (Gorilla gorilla). Am. J. Primatol. 2:167–75.

Moltz, H. 1975. The search for the determinants of puberty in the rat. In Hormonal correlates of behavior, vol. 1, ed. B. E. Eleftheriou and R. L. Sprott, 35–154. New York: Plenum Press.

Mondain-Monval, M., Dutourne, B., Bonnin-Laffargue, M., Canivenc, R., and Scholler, R. 1977. Ovarian activity during the anoestrus and the reproductive season of the red fox (Vulpes vulpes L.). J. Steroid Biochem. 8:761–69.

Moore, C. R. 1944. Hormone secretion by experimental cryptorchid testes. Yale J. Biol. Med. 17:203–16.

Morgan, P. M., Hutz, R. J., Kraus, E. M., Cormie, J. A., Dierschke, D. J., and Bavister, B. D. 1987. Evaluation of ultrasonography for monitoring follicular growth in rhesus monkeys. Theriogenology 27:769–80.

Mori, A. 1979. Analysis of population changes by measurement of body weight in the Koshima troop of Japanese monkeys. Primates 20:371–97.

Morrison, J. A. 1960. Ovarian characteristics of elk of known breeding history. J. Wildl. Mgmt. 24:297–307.

Moss, R. L., and McCann, S. M. 1973. Induction of mating behavior in rats by luteinizing hormone-releasing factor. Science 181:177–79.

Munshi, S., and Pandey, S. D. 1987. The oestrous cycle in the large-eared hedgehog, Hemiechinus auritus Gmelin. Anim. Reprod. Sci. 13:157–60.

Murray, M. G. 1982. The rut of impala: Aspects of seasonal mating under tropical condition. Z. Tierpsychol. 59:319–37.

Mykytowycz, R., and Fullagar, P. J. 1973. Effect of social environment on reproduction in the rabbit, Oryctolagus cuniculus. J. Reprod. Fertil., Suppl. 19:503–22.

Nadler, R. D. 1980. Reproductive physiology and behaviour of gorillas. J. Reprod. Fertil., Suppl. 28:79–89.

Nadler, R. D., Collins, D. C., and Blank, M. S. 1984. Luteinizing hormone and gonadal steroid levels during the menstrual cycle of orangutans. *J. Med. Primatol.* 13:305–14.

Nadler, R. D., Graham, C. E., Collins, D. C., and Gould, K. G. 1979. Plasma gonadotropins, prolactin, gonadal steroids, and genital swelling during the menstrual cycle of lowland gorillas. *Endocrinology* 105:290–96.

Nadler, R. D., Graham, C. E., Gosselin, R. E., and Collins, D. C. 1985. Serum levels of gonadotropins and gonadal steroids, including testosterone, during the menstrual cycle of the chimpanzee *(Pan troglodytes). Am. J. Primatol.* 9:273–84.

Nawar, N. M., and Hafez, E. S. E. 1972. Reproductive cycle of the crab-eating macaque *(Macaca fascicularis). Primates* 13:43–56.

Neaves, W. B. 1973. Changes in testicular Leydig cells and in plasma testosterone levels among seasonally breeding rock hyrax. *Biol. Reprod.* 8:451–66.

Neaves, W. B., Griffin, J. E., and Wilson, J. D. 1980. Sexual dimorphism of the phallus in spotted hyaena *(Crocuta crocuta). J. Reprod. Fertil.* 59:509–13.

Negus, N. C., and Berger, P. J. 1972. Environmental factors and reproductive processes in mammalian populations. In *Biology of reproduction: Basic and clinical studies*, ed. J. T. Velardo and B. Kaspoons, 89–98. Third American Congress on Anatomy, New Orleans.

Nelson, R. J., Dark, J., and Zucker, I. 1983. Influence of photoperiod, nutrition, and water availability on reproduction of male California voles *(Microtus californicus). J. Reprod. Fertil.* 69:473–77.

Nelson, R. J., and Desjardins, C. 1987. Water availability affects reproduction in deer mice. *Biol. Reprod.* 37:257–60.

Newsome, A. E. 1966. The influence of food on breeding in the red kangaroo in central Australia. *CSIRO Wildl. Res.* 11:187–96.

———. 1973. Cellular degeneration in the testis of red kangaroos during hot weather and drought in central Australia. *J. Reprod. Fertil., Suppl.* 19:191–201.

Nichols, D. J., and Chevins, P. F. D. 1981. Plasma corticosterone fluctuations during the oestrous cycle of the house mouse. *Experientia* 37:319–20.

Nicoll, M. E., and Racey, P. A. 1985. Follicular development, ovulation, fertilization, and fetal development in tenrecs *(Tenrec ecaudatus). J. Reprod. Fertil.* 74:47–55.

Nicolson, N. A. 1981. Suckling patterns, postpartum amenorrhea, and birth intervals in wild baboons *(Papio anubis).* Ph.D. thesis, Harvard University.

Nieuwenhuijsen, K., deNeef, K. J., van der Werff ten Bosch, J. J., and Slob, A. K. 1987. Testosterone, testis size, seasonality, and behavior in group-living stumptail macaques *(Macaca arctoides). Horm. Behav.* 21:153–69.

Nieuwenhuijsen, K., Lammers, A. J. J. C., deNeef, K. J., and Slob, A. K. 1985. Reproduction and social rank in female stumptail macaques *(Macaca arctoides). Int. J. Primatol.* 6:77–100.

Nigi, H. 1975. Menstrual cycle and some other related aspects of Japanese monkeys *(Macaca fuscata). Primates* 16:207–16.

Noden, P. A., Oxender, W. D., and Hafs, H. D. 1975. The cycle of oestrus, ovulation, and plasma levels of hormones in the mare. *J. Reprod. Fertil., Suppl.* 23:189–92.

Oh, Y. K., Mori, T., and Uchida, T. A. 1983. Studies on the vaginal plug of the Japanese greater horseshoe bat, *Rhinolophus ferrumequinum nippon. J. Reprod. Fertil.* 68:365–69.

Ojeda, S. R. 1990. Involvement of neuronotrophic factors in female reproductive development. In *Neuroendocrine regulation of reproduction*, ed. S. S. C. Yen and W. W. Vale, 63–70. Norwell, Mass.: Serono Symposia.

Olson, P. N., Bowen, R. A., Behrendt, M. D., Olson, J. D., and Nett, T. M. 1984. Concentrations of testosterone in canine serum during late anestrus, proestrus, and early diestrus. *Am. J. Vet. Res.* 45:145–48.

Orsini, M. W. 1961. The external vaginal phenomena characterizing the stages of the estrous cycle, pregnancy, pseudopregnancy, and lactation in the anestrous hamster, *Mesocricetus auratus* Waterhouse. *Proc. Anim. Care Panel* 11:193–206.

Ozoga, J. J., and Verme, L. J. 1982. Physical and reproductive characteristics of a supplementally fed white-tailed deer herd. *J. Wildl. Mgmt.* 46:281–301.

Palmer, E., and Jousset, B. 1975. Urinary oestrogen and plasma progesterone levels in non-pregnant mares. *J. Reprod. Fertil., Suppl.* 23:213–21.

Parakkal, P. F., and Gregoire, A. T. 1972. Differentiation of vaginal epithelium in the normal and hormone-treated rhesus monkey. *Biol. Reprod.* 6:117–30.

Parkes, A. S., and Bruce, H. M. 1962. Pregnancy-block in female mice placed in boxes soiled by males. *J. Reprod. Fertil.* 4:303–8.

Patterson, B. D., and Thaeler, C. S. 1982. The mammalian baculum: Hypotheses on the nature of bacular variability. *J. Mammal.* 63:1–15.

Pearson, O. P. 1944. Reproduction in the shrew *(Blarina brevicauda* Say). *Am. J. Anat.* 75:39–93.

Penzhorn, B. L. 1985. Reproductive characteristics of a free-ranging population of Cape Mountain Zebra *(Equus zebra zebra). J. Reprod. Fertil.* 73:51–57.

Perachio, A. A., Alexander, M., Marr, L. D., and Collins, D. C. 1977. Diurnal variations of serum testosterone levels in intact and gonadectomized male and female rhesus monkeys. *Steroids* 29:21–33.

Peretz, E. 1968. Estrogen dose and duration of the mating period in cats. *Physiol. Behav.* 3:41–43.

Perret, M. 1985. Influence of social factors on seasonal variations in plasma testosterone levels of *Microcebus murinus. Z. Tierpsychol.* 69:265–80.

———. 1986. Social influences on oestrous cycle length and plasma progesterone concentrations in the female lesser mouse lemur *(Microcebus murinus). J. Reprod. Fertil.* 77:303–11.

Perret, M., and Predine, J. 1984. Effects of long–term grouping on serum cortisol levels in *Microcebus murinus* (Prosimi). *Horm. Behav.* 18:346–58.

Perry, J. S. 1953. The reproduction of the African elephant, *Loxodonta africana. Phil. Trans. R. Soc. Lond.* B 237:93–149.

Peters, D. G., and Rose, R. W. 1979. The oestrous cycle and basal body temperature in the common wombat *(Vombatus ursinus). J. Reprod. Fertil.* 57:453–60.

Peters, J. B., First, N. L., and Cassida, L. E. 1969. Effects of pig removal and oxytocin injections on ovarian and pituitary changes in mammilectomized postpartum sows. *J. Anim. Sci.* 28:537–41.

Pharriss, B. B., and Wyngarden, L. J. 1969. The effect of prostaglandin $F_2\alpha$ on the progesterone content of ovaries from pseudopregnant rats. *Proc. Soc. Exp. Biol. Med.* 130:92–94.

Phillips, D. M. 1974. *Spermiogenesis.* New York: Academic Press.

Piacsek, B. E., and Nazian, S. J. 1981. Thermal influences on sexual maturation in the rat. In *Environmental factors in mammal reproduction*, ed. D. Gilmore and B. Cook, 214–31. Baltimore: University Park Press.

Pierson, R. A., and Ginther, O. J. 1988. Ultrasonic imaging of the ovaries and uterus in cattle. *Theriogenology* 29:21–37.

Pirke, K. M., and Spyra, B. 1981. Influence of starvation on testosterone-luteinizing hormone feedback in the rat. *Acta Endocrinol.* 96:413–21.

Plant, T. M. 1988. Puberty in primates. In *The physiology of reproduction*, vol. 1, ed. E. Knobil and J. D. Neill, 1763–88. New York: Raven Press.

Plant, T. M., James, V. H. T., and Michael, R. P. 1971. Conversion of {3-14C}-progesterone to androsterone by female rhesus monkeys *(Macaca mulatta). J. Endocrinol.* 51:751–61.

Plotka, E. D., Seal, U. S., Letellier, M. A., Verme, L. J., and Ozoga, J. J. 1979. Endocrine and morphologic effects of pinealectomy in white-tailed deer. In *Animal models for research on contraception and fertility,* ed. M. J. Alexander, 452–66. Hagerstown, Md.: Harper and Row.

Polak, K. L., and Kammlade, W. G. 1981. Vaginal pH during estrus in mares. *Theriogenology* 15:271–76.

Powers, J. B. 1970. Hormonal control of sexual receptivity during the estrous cycle of the rat. *Physiol. Behav.* 5:95–97.

Prasad, M. R. N. 1974. Mannliche geschlechtsorgane. In *Handbuch der zoologie,* vol. 8, no. 51, ed. J. G. Helmcke, D. Stark, and H. Wermuth, 1–150. Berlin: Walter de Gruyter.

Preslock, J. P., Hampton, S. H., and Hampton, J. K. Jr. 1973. Cyclic variations of serum progestins and immuno-reactive estrogens in marmosets. *Endocrinology* 92:1096–1101.

Price, M. 1953. The reproductive cycle of the water shrew, *Neomys fodiens bicolor. Proc. Zool. Soc. Lond.* 123:599–621.

Pryce, C. R., and Döbeli, M. 1992. Coping with different metabolic strategies. In *The First International Symposium on Faecal Steroid Monitoring in Zoo Animals,* ed. E. Bamberg, 35–46. Rotterdam: Royal Rotterdam Zoological and Botanical Gardens.

Quintero, F., and Rasweiler, J. J. 1974. Ovulation and early embryonic development in the captive vampire bat, *Desmodus rotundus. J. Reprod. Fertil.* 41:265–73.

Racey, P. A. 1973. The viability of spermatozoa after prolonged storage by male and female European bats. *Periodicum Biologorum* 75:201–5.

———. 1974. The reproductive cycle in male noctule bats, *Nyctalus noctula. J. Reprod. Fertil.* 41:169–82.

———. 1978. Seasonal changes in testosterone levels and androgen-dependent organs in male moles *(Talpa europaea). J. Reprod. Fertil.* 52:195–200.

———. 1979. The prolonged storage and survival of spermatozoa in Chiroptera. *J. Reprod. Fertil.* 56:391–402.

Ramaley, J. A. 1973. Role of the adrenal in PMS-induced ovulation before puberty: Effect of adrenalectomy. *Endocrinology* 92:881–87.

———. 1976. Effects of corticosterone treatment on puberty in female rats. *Proc. Soc. Exp. Biol. Med.* 153:514–17.

———. 1979. Development of gonadotropin regulation in the prepubertal mammal. *Biol. Reprod.* 20:1–31.

Ramaswami, L. S., and Kumar, T. C. 1962. Reproductive cycle of the slender loris. *Naturwissenschaften* 49:115–16.

Ramsay, E. C., Lasley, B. L., and Stabenfeldt, G. H. 1980. Monitoring the estrous cycle of the Asian elephant *(Elephas maximus),* using urinary estrogens. *Am. J. Vet. Res.* 42:256–60.

Ransom, A. B. 1967. Reproductive biology of white-tailed deer in Manitoba. *J. Wildl. Mgmt.* 31:114–22.

Rastogi, R. K., Milone, M., and Chieffi, G. 1981. Impact of sociosexual conditions on the epididymis and fertility in the male mouse. *J. Reprod. Fertil.* 63:331–34.

Rasweiler, J. J. 1972. Reproduction in the long-tongued bat, *Glossophaga soricina.* I. Preimplantation development and history of the oviduct. *J. Reprod. Fertil.* 31:249–62.

———. 1979. Early embryonic development and implantation in bats. *J. Reprod. Fertil.* 56:403–16.

———. 1988. Ovarian function in the captive black mastiff bat, *Molossus ater. J. Reprod. Fertil.* 82:97–111.

Reiter, R. J. 1983. The pineal gland: An intermediary between the environment and the endocrine system. *Psychoneuroendocrinology* 8:31–40.

Resko, J. A., Koering, M. J., Goy, R. W., and Phoenix, C. H. 1975.

Preovulatory progestins: Observations on their source in rhesus monkeys. *J. Clin. Endocrinol. Metab.* 41:120–25.

Richmond, M., and Conaway, C. H. 1969. Induced ovulation and oestrus in *Microtus ochrogaster. J. Reprod. Fertil., Suppl.* 6:357–76.

Rideout, B. A., Gause, G. E., Benirschke, K., and Lasley, B. L. 1985. Stress-induced adrenal changes and their relation to reproductive failure in captive nine-banded armadillos *(Dasypus novemcinctus). Zoo Biol.* 4:129–37.

Rissman, E. R., and Johnston, R. E. 1986. Nutritional and social cues influence the onset of puberty in California voles. *Physiol. Behav.* 36:343–47.

Rivier, C., Rivier, J., and Vale, W. 1986. Stress-induced inhibition of reproductive function: Role of endogenous corticotropin-releasing factor. *Science* 231:607–9.

Robinson, T. J., Moore, N. W., and Binet, F. E. 1956. The effect of the duration of progesterone pretreatment on the response of the spayed ewe to oestrogen. *J. Endocrinol.* 14:1–7.

Romanoff, L. P., Grace, M. P., Sugarman, E. M., and Pincus, G. 1963. Metabolism of progesterone-4-C14 in immature chimpanzees. *Gen. Comp. Endocrinol.* 3:649–54.

Rostal, D. C., Glick, B. B., Eaton, G. G., and Resko, J. A. 1986. Seasonality of adult male Japanese macaques *(Macaca fuscata)*: Androgens and behavior in a confined troop. *Horm. Behav.* 20:452–62.

Rowell, T. E. 1969. Effect of social environment on the menstrual cycles of baboons. *J. Reprod. Fertil., Suppl.* 6:117–18.

———. 1970. Reproductive cycle of two *Cercopithecus* monkeys. *J. Reprod. Fertil.* 22:321–38.

———. 1977. Reproductive cycles of the talapoin monkey *(Miopithecus talapoin). Folia Primatol.* 28:188–202.

Rowlands, I. W., and Weir, B. J. 1984. Mammals: Non-primate eutherians. In *Marshall's physiology of reproduction,* 4th ed., vol. 1, *Reproductive cycles of vertebrates,* ed. G. E. Lamming, 455–658. Edinburgh: Churchill Livingstone.

Ryan, K. D., and Foster, D. L. 1978. Two LH surges at puberty in the female lamb: Possible role of progesterone. Eleventh annual meeting, Society for the Study of Reproduction, Abstract 118.

Saayman, G. S. 1972. Effects of ovarian hormones upon the sexual skin and mounting behaviour in the free-ranging chacma baboon *(Papio ursinus). Folia Primatol.* 17:297–303.

Saginor, M., and Horton, R. 1968. Reflex release of gonadotropin and increased plasma testosterone concentration in male rabbits during copulation. *Endocrinology* 82:627–30.

Sapolsky, R. M. 1982. The endocrine stress-response and social status in the wild baboon. *Horm. Behav.* 16:279–92.

Sawyer, C. H., and Everett, J. W. 1959. Stimulatory and inhibitory effects of progesterone on the release of pituitary ovulating hormone in the rabbit. *Endocrinology* 65:644–51.

Schadler, M. H. 1981. Postimplantation abortion in pine voles *(Microtus pinetorum)* induced by strange males and pheromones of strange males. *Biol. Reprod.* 25:295–97.

Schams, D., and Butz, H. D. 1972. Plasma levels of luteinizing hormone in female and male calves from birth until puberty. Seventh International Congress on Animal Reproduction, Munich, 2175–78.

Schanbacher, B. D., and Ford, J. J. 1976. Seasonal profiles of plasma luteinizing hormone, testosterone, and estradiol in the ram. *Endocrinology* 99:752–57.

Schilling, E., and Zust, J. 1968. Diagnosis of oestrus and ovulation in cows by pH measurements intro vaginam and by apparent viscosity of vaginal mucus. *J. Reprod. Fertil.* 15:307–11.

Schmidt, A. M., Nadal, L. A., Schmidt, M. J., and Beamer, N. B. 1979. Serum concentrations of oestradiol and progesterone during the normal oestrous cycle and early pregnancy in the lion *(Panthera leo). J. Reprod. Fertil.* 57:267–72.

Schmidt, P. M., Chakraborty, P. K., and Wildt, D. E. 1983. Ovarian activity, circulating hormones, and sexual behavior in the cat. II. Relationships during pregnancy, parturition, lactation, and the postpartum estrus. *Biol. Reprod.* 28:657–71.

Schneider, H. P. G., and Leyendecker, G. 1983. Physiology of the ovarian cycle. In *The ovary,* ed. G. B. Serra, 191–215. New York: Raven Press.

Schomberg, D. W., Jones, P. H., Erb, R. E., and Gomes, W. R. 1966. Metabolites of progesterone in urine compared with progesterone in ovarian venous plasma of the cycling domestic sow. *J. Anim. Sci.* 25:1181–89.

Schultze-Westrum, T. G. 1969. Social communication by chemical signals in flying phalangers *(Petaurus breviceps papua).* In *Olfaction and taste: Proceedings of the Third International Symposium,* ed. C. Pfaffmann, 268–77. New York: Rockefeller University Press.

Seal, U. S., Plotka, E. D., Packard, J. M., and Mech, L. D. 1979. Endocrine correlates of reproduction in the wolf. I. Serum progesterone, estradiol, and LH during the estrous cycle. *Biol. Reprod.* 21:1057–66.

Seal, U. S., Plotka, E. D., Smith, J. D., Wright, F. H., Reindl, N. J., Taylor, R. S., and Seal, M. F. 1985. Immunoreactive luteinizing hormone, estradiol, progesterone, testosterone, and androstenedione levels during the breeding season and anestrus in Siberian tigers. *Biol. Reprod.* 32:361–68.

Selwood, L., and McCallum, F. 1987. Relationship between longevity of spermatozoa after insemination and the percentage of normal embryos in brown marsupial mice *(Antechinus stuartii).* *J. Reprod. Fertil., Suppl.* 79:495–503.

Setchell, B. P. 1978. *The mammalian testis.* Ithaca, N.Y.: Cornell University Press.

Setchell, B. P., Waites, G. M. H., and Lindner, H. R. 1965. Effect of undernutrition on testicular blood flow and metabolism and the output of testosterone in the ram. *J. Reprod. Fertil.* 9:149–62.

Seth, P., and Prasad, M. R. N. 1969. Reproductive cycle of the female five-striped Indian palm squirrel, *Funambulus pennanti* (Wroughton). *J. Reprod. Fertil.* 20:211–22.

Settlage, D. S. F., and Hendrickx, A. G. 1974. Observations on coagulum characteristics of the rhesus monkey electroejaculate. *Biol. Reprod.* 11:619–23.

Sharma, A., and Mathur, R. S. 1976. Histomorphological changes in the female reproductive tract of *Suncus murinus sindensis* (Anderson) during the oestrus cycle. *Folia Biol.* 24:277–84.

Sharman, G. B. 1976. Evolution of viviparity in mammals. In *Reproduction in mammals,* vol. 6, ed. C. R. Austin and R. V. Short, 32–70. Cambridge: Cambridge University Press.

Sharp, D. C., and Ginther, O. J. 1975. Stimulation of follicular activity and estrous behavior in anestrous mares with light and temperature. *J. Anim. Sci.* 41:1368–72.

Shaw, H. J., Green, D. I., Sainsbury, A. W., and Holt, W. V. 1992. Monitoring ovarian function in scimitar-horned oryx *(Oryx dammah)* by faecal analysis. In *The First International Symposium on Faecal Steroid Monitoring in Zoo Animals,* ed. E. Bamberg, 68–70. Rotterdam: Royal Rotterdam Zoological and Botanical Gardens.

Shaw, S. T. Jr., and Roche, P. C. 1980. Menstruation. *Oxf. Rev. Reprod. Biol.* 2:41–96.

Shideler, S. E., Czekala, M. N., Kasman, L. H., Lindburg, D. G., and Lasley, B. L. 1983. Monitoring ovulation and implantation in the lion-tailed macaque *(Macaca silenus)* through urinary estrone conjugate evaluations. *Biol. Reprod.* 29:905–11.

Shideler, S. E., Lindburg, D. G., and Lasley, B. L. 1983. Estrogen-behavior correlates in the reproductive physiology and behavior of the ruffed lemur *(Lemur variegatus).* *Horm. Behav.* 17:249–63.

Shille, V. M., Lundstrom, K. E., and Stabenfeldt, G. H. 1979. Follicular function in the domestic cat as determined by estradiol-17B concentrations in plasma: Relation to estrous behaviour and cornification of exfoliated vaginal epithelium. *Biol. Reprod.* 21:953–63.

Shille, V. M., Wing, A. E., Lasley, B. L., and Banks, J. A. 1984. Excretion of radiolabeled estradiol in the cat *(Felis catus,* L.): A preliminary report. *Zoo Biol.* 3:201–9.

Short, R. E., Bellows, R. A., Moody, E. L., and Howland, B. E. 1972. Effects of suckling and mastectomy on bovine postpartum reproduction. *J. Anim. Sci.* 34:70–74.

Signoret, J. P., du Mesnil du Buisson, F., and Mauleon, P. 1972. Effect of mating on the onset and duration of ovulation in the sow. *J. Reprod. Fertil.* 31:327–30.

Silk, J. B., Clark-Wheatley, C. B., Rodman, P. S., and Samuels, A. 1981. Differential reproductive success and facultative adjustment of sex ratios among captive female bonnet macaques *(Macaca radiata).* *Anim. Behav.* 29:1106–20.

Simkin, D. W. 1965. Reproduction and productivity of moose in northwestern Ontario. *J. Wildl. Mgmt.* 30:121–30.

Sinclair, A. R. E. 1977. Lunar cycle and timing of mating season in Serengeti wildebeest. *Nature* 267:832–33.

Skinner, J. D. 1981. Nutrition and fertility in pedigree bulls. In *Environmental factors in mammal reproduction,* ed. D. Gilmore and B. Cook, 160–68. Baltimore: University Park Press.

Skinner, J. D., and van Zyl, J. H. M. 1969. Reproductive performance of the common eland, *Taurotragus oryx,* in two environments. *J. Reprod. Fertil., Suppl.* 6:319–22.

Slob, A. K., Wiegand, S. J., Goy, R. W., and Robinson, J. A. 1978. Heterosexual interactions in laboratory-housed stump-tail macaques *(Macaca arctoides).* Observations during the menstrual cycle and after ovariectomy. *Horm. Behav.* 10:193–211.

Smith, A. J., Mondain-Monval, M., Møller, O. M., Scholler, R., and Hansson, V. 1985. Seasonal variations of LH, prolactin, androstenedione, testosterone, and testicular FSH binding in the male blue fox *(Alopex lagopus).* *J. Reprod. Fertil.* 74:449–58.

Smyth, M. 1968. Winter breeding in woodland mice, *Apodemus sylvaticus,* and voles, *Clethrionomys glareolus* and *Microtus agrestis,* near Oxford. *J. Anim. Ecol.* 35:471–85.

Sollberger, D. E. 1943. Notes on the breeding habits of the Eastern flying squirrel *(Glaucomys volans volans).* *J. Mammal.* 24:163–73.

Squires, E. L., Douglas, R. H., Steffenhagen, W. P., and Ginther, O. J. 1974. Ovarian changes during the estrous cycle and pregnancy in mares. *J. Anim. Sci.* 38:330–38.

Stekleniov, E. P. 1968. Des particularités anatomo-morpologiques de la structure et des fonctions physiologiques des trompes de Fallope chez camelides (genaes *Lama* et *Camelus).* In *6ème Congress Internationale Insemination Artificiale,* Paris, vol. 1, 17.

Stenger, V. G. 1972. Studies on reproduction in the stump-tailed macaque. In *Breeding primates,* ed. W. I. B. Beveridge, 100–104. Basel: Karger.

Stewart, K. J. 1988. Suckling and lactational anoestrus in wild gorillas *(Gorilla gorilla).* *J. Reprod. Fertil.* 83:627–34.

Stockard, C. R., and Papanicolau, C. N. 1917. The existence of a typical oestrous cycle in the guinea pig with a study of its histological and physiological changes. *Am. J. Anat.* 22:225–83.

Sundqvist, C., Amador, A. G., and Vartke, A. 1989. Reproduction and fertility in the mink *(Mustela vison).* *J. Reprod. Fertil.* 85:413–41.

Tardif, S. D., and Ziegler, T. E. 1992. Features of female reproductive senescence in tamarins *(Saguinus* spp.), a New World primate. *J. Reprod. Fertil.* 94:411–21.

Taya, K., and Greenwald, G. S. 1982. Mechanism of suppression of ovarian follicular development during lactation in the rat. *Biol. Reprod.* 27:1090–1101.

Terman, C. R. 1973. Reproductive inhibition in asymptotic population of prairie deermice. *J. Reprod. Fertil., Suppl.* 19:457–64.

Thibault, C. 1973. Sperm transport and storage in vertebrates. *J. Reprod. Fertil., Suppl.* 18:39–53.

Thibier, M., and Rollando, O. 1976. The effect of dexamethasone (DXM) on circulating testosterone and luteinizing hormone (LH) in young post-pubertal bulls. *Theriogenology* 5:53–60.

Tinklepaugh, O. L. 1930. Occurrence of a vaginal plug in the chimpanzee. *Anat. Rec.* 46:329–32.

Toner, J. P., and Adler, N. T. 1986. Influence of mating and vaginocervical stimulation on rat uterine activity. *J. Reprod. Fertil.* 78:239–49.

Travis, J. C., and Holmes, W. N. 1974. Some physiological and behavioural changes associated with oestrus and pregnancy in the squirrel monkey *(Saimiri sciureus). J. Zool.* (Lond.) 174:41–66.

Tripp, H. R. H. 1971. Reproduction in elephant shrews (Macroscelididae) with special reference to ovulation and implantation. *J. Reprod. Fertil.* 26:149–59.

Tutin, C. E. G. 1980. Reproductive behaviour of wild chimpanzees in the Gombe National Park, Tanzania. *J. Reprod. Fertil., Suppl.* 28:43–57.

Tyndale-Biscoe, C. H. 1968. Reproduction and post-natal development in the marsupial, *Bettongia lesseur* (Quay and Gaimard). *Aust. J. Zool.* 16:577–602.

Ullmann, S. L. 1976. Anomalous litters of hybrid mice and the retention of spermatozoa in the female tract. *J. Reprod. Fertil.* 47:13–18.

Umezu, M., Masaki, J., Sasada, H., and Ohta, M. 1981. Mating behaviour of a bull and its relationship with serum LH levels in a group of oestrous cows. *J. Reprod. Fertil.* 63:467–70.

Van Aarde, R. J. 1985. Reproduction in captive female cape porcupines *(Hystrix africae-australis). J. Reprod. Fertil.* 75:577–82.

Vandenbergh, J. G. 1988. Pheromones and mammalian reproduction. In *The physiology of reproduction,* vol. 3, ed. E. Knobil and J. Neill, 1679–96. New York: Raven Press.

van Heerdt, P. F., and Sluiter, J. W. 1965. Notes on the distribution and behaviour of the noctule bat *(Nyctalus noctula)* in the Netherlands. *Mammalia* 29:463–77.

Van Niekerk, C. H., and Van Heerden, J. S. 1972. Nutritional and ovarian activity of mares early in the breeding season. *J. S. Afr. Vet. Assoc.* 43:351–52.

Van Tienhoven, A. 1983. *Reproductive physiology of vertebrates.* 2d ed. Ithaca, N.Y.: Cornell University Press.

Vaughn, M. K., Little, J. C., Vaughn, G. M., and Reiter, R. J. 1988. Hormonal consequences of subcutaneous 6-methoxy-2-benzoxazolinone pellets or injections in prepubertal male and female rats. *J. Reprod. Fertil.* 83:859–66.

Verhage, H. G., Beamer, N. B., and Brenner, R. M. 1976. Plasma levels of estradiol and progesterone in the cat during polyestrus, pregnancy, and pseudopregnancy. *Biol. Reprod.* 14:579–85.

Verme, L. J., and Ullrey, D. E. 1972. Feeding and nutrition of deer. In *Digestive physiology and nutrition of ruminants,* vol. 3, *Practical nutrition,* ed. D. C. Church. Corvallis: D. C. Church, Department of Animal Science, Oregon State University.

vom Saal, F. S., and Finch, C. E. 1988. Reproductive senescence: Phenomena and mechanisms in mammals and selected vertebrates. In *The physiology of reproduction,* vol. 2, ed. E. Knobil and J. Neill, 2351–2413. New York: Raven Press.

von Holst, D. 1969. Sozialer stress bei Tupajas *(Tupaia belangeri). Z. Vergl. Physiol.* 63:1–58.

von Holst, D., and Buergel-Goodwin, U. 1975. The influence of sex hormones on chinning by male *Tupaia belangeri. J. Comp. Physiol.* 103:123–51.

Waites, G. M. H., and Setchell, B. P. 1990. Physiology of the mammalian testis. In *Marshall's physiology of reproduction,* 4th ed., vol. 2, *Reproduction in the male,* ed. G. E. Lamming, 1–105. London: Churchill Livingstone.

Walton, A., and Hammond, J. 1929. Observation of ovulation in the rabbit. *Br. J. Exp. Biol.* 6:190–204.

Wasser, S. K., Risler, L., and Steiner, R. A. 1988. Excreted steroids in primate feces over the menstrual cycle and pregnancy. *Biol. Reprod.* 39:862–72.

Weir, B. J. 1971a. Evocation of oestrus in the cuis, *Galea musteloides. J. Reprod. Fertil.* 26:405–8.

———. 1971b. The reproductive organs of the plains viscacha, *Lagostomus maximus. J. Reprod. Fertil.* 25:365–73.

———. 1973. The induction of ovulation and oestrus in the chinchilla. *J. Reprod. Fertil.* 33:61–68.

———. 1974. Reproductive characteristics of hystricomorph rodents. *Symp. Zool. Soc. Lond.* 34:265–301.

Weiss, G., Butler, W. R., Dierschke, D. J., and Knobil, E. 1976. Influence of suckling on gonadotropin secretion in the postpartum rhesus monkey. *Proc. Soc. Exp. Biol. Med.* 153:330–31.

Weisz, J., and Gunsalus, P. 1973. Estrogen levels in immature female rats: True or spurious—ovarian or adrenal? *Endocrinology* 93:1057–65.

Wells, M. E. 1968. A comparison of the reproductive tracts of *Crocuta crocuta, Hyaena hyaena,* and *Proteles cristatus. E. Afr. Wildl. J.* 6:63–70.

Westlin, L. M., and Nyholm, E. 1982. Sterile matings initiate the breeding season in the bank vole, *Clethrionomys glareolus:* A field and laboratory study. *Can. J. Zool.* 60:387–416.

Whalen, R. E., and Hardy, D. F. 1970. Induction of receptivity in female rats and cats with estrogen and testosterone. *Physiol. Behav.* 5:529–33.

White, I. G. 1974. Mammalian semen. In *Reproduction in farm animals,* ed. E. S. E. Hafez, 101–22. Philadelphia: Lea and Febiger.

White, R. J., Blaine, C. R., and Blakley, G. A. 1973. Detecting ovulation in *Macaca nemestrina* by correlation of vaginal cytology, body temperature, and perineal tumescence with laparoscopy. *Am. J. Phys. Anthropol.* 38:189–94.

Whitney, L. F., and Underwood, A. B. 1952. *The raccoon.* Orange, Conn.: Practical Science Publishing Company.

Widdowson, E. M., and Cowen, J. 1972. The effect of protein deficiency and calorie deficiency on the reproduction of rats. *Br. J. Nutr.* 27:85–95.

Wildt, D. E., Platz, C. C., Chakraborty, P. K., and Seager, S. W. J. 1979. Estrous and ovarian activity in a female jaguar *(Panthera onca). J. Reprod. Fertil.* 56:555–58.

Wilen, R., and Naftolin, F. 1976. Age, weight, and weight gain in the individual rhesus monkey *(Macaca mulatta). Biol. Reprod.* 15:356–60.

Willett, E. L., and Ohms, J. I. 1957. Measurement of testicular size and its relation to production of spermatozoa by bulls. *J. Dairy Sci.* 40:1559–70.

Williams, W. F., Osman, A. M., Shehata, S. H. M., and Gross, T. S. 1986. Pedometer detection of prostaglandin F$_2\alpha$-induced luteolysis and estrus in the Egyptian buffalo. *Anim. Reprod. Sci.* 11:237–41.

Williams-Ashman, H. G. 1988. Perspectives in the male sexual physiology of eutherian mammals. In *The physiology of reproduction,* vol. 1., E. Knobil and J. D. Neill, 727–52. New York: Raven Press.

Wiltbank, J. N., Rowden, W. W., Ingalls, J. E., Gregory, K. E., and Koch, R. M. 1962. Effect of energy level on reproductive phenomena of mature Hereford cows. *J. Anim. Sci.* 21:219–25.

Wing, E. S. 1960. Reproduction in the pocket gopher in north-central Florida. *J. Mammal.* 41:35–43.

Wolf, R. H., Harrison, R. M., and Martin, T. W. 1975. A review of reproductive patterns in New World monkeys. *Lab. Anim. Sci.* 25:814–25.

Wolfe, L. 1979. Sexual maturation among members of a transported troop of Japanese macaques *(Macaca fuscata)*. *Primates* 20:411–18.

Wright, E. M. Jr., and Bush, D. E. 1977. The reproductive cycle of the capuchin *(Cebus apella)*. *Lab. Anim. Sci.* 27:651–54.

Wright, P. C., Izard, M. K., and Simons, E. L. 1986. Reproductive cycles in *Tarsius bancanus*. *Am. J. Primatol.* 11:207–15.

Yeates, N. T. M. 1949. The breeding season of the sheep with particular reference to its modification by artificial means using light. *J. Agric. Sci.* 39:1–43.

Yen, S. S. C., and Vale, W. W. 1990. *Neuroendocrine regulation of reproduction.* Norwell, Mass.: Serono Symposia.

Zaneveld, L. J. D. In press. Male contraception: Nonhormonal approaches. In *Contraception in wildlife,* ed. U. S. Seal and E. D. Plotka. Lewiston, N.Y.: Edwin Mellen Press.

Zarrow, M. X., and Clark, J. H. 1968. Ovulation following vaginal stimulation in a spontaneous ovulator and its implications. *J. Endocrinol.* 40:343–52.

Ziegler, T. E., Sholl, S. A., Scheffler, G., Haggerty, M. A., and Lasley, B. L. 1988. Excretion of estrone, estradiol, and progesterone in the urine and feces in the female cotton-top tamarin *(Saguinus oedipus oedipus)*. *Am. J. Primatol.* 17:185–95.

Zucker, I., and Goy, R. W. 1967. Sexual receptivity in the guinea pig: Inhibitory and facilitatory actions of progesterone and related compounds. *J. Comp. Physiol. Psychol.* 64:378–83.

Zuckerman, S. 1937. The duration and phases of the menstrual cycle in primates. *Proc. Zool. Soc. Lond.* 107a:315–29.

Zuckerman, S., and Parkes, A. S. 1932. The menstrual cycle of the primates. 5. The cycle of the baboon. *Proc. Zool. Soc. Lond.* 1932:139–91.

38

Determining and Manipulating
Female Reproductive Parameters

J. Keith Hodges

Most wild mammals kept in captivity are intensively managed. Under these conditions the ability to determine and, when necessary, manipulate female reproductive status can greatly facilitate any attempt to enhance the captive breeding of rare or endangered species. More specifically, objective and reliable methods for monitoring key reproductive events such as ovulation and pregnancy not only find widespread application in the management of natural breeding but also provide the basis for studies designed to accelerate reproduction by artificial means.

This chapter outlines the development and application of some of the methods available for assessing reproductive status in female exotic mammals, with emphasis on the detection of ovulation and pregnancy. The potential for manipulating the natural control of reproduction to enhance fertility in endangered species is also discussed.

METHODS FOR DETERMINING FEMALE REPRODUCTIVE STATUS

General Considerations
There are a variety of methods that can, at least in theory, provide useful information about female reproductive status (see also Asa, chap. 37, this volume). In practice, the choice of a particular method depends largely on the type of information required, the species in question, and the circumstances under which the study is to be carried out. The importance of accuracy and reliability, together with the need for versatility in multispecies application, have been discussed previously (Hodges 1985; Hodges et al. 1986). Practicality is also essential from the dual standpoint of avoiding the physical problems of handling and working with wild animals and avoiding techniques that are restricted in use by expense or need for complex laboratory backup.

A list of some of the methods currently available for monitoring changes in reproductive status in female exotic mammals is given in table 38.1 (see also Asa, chap. 37, this volume). No single method is ideal, although, in general, noninvasive procedures involving no animal contact are preferable to those requiring capture and restraint whenever frequent application over long periods of time is necessary.

Assessment of Changes in Vaginal Contents
The detection of estrus and ovulation by measurement of changes in vaginal contents is well described for laboratory animals and, to a lesser extent, humans (D'Souza 1978; Bonnar 1983). Cellular and electrical changes in the vaginal epithelium as well as changes in the physical and chemical characteristics of cervical mucus have been shown to reflect ovarian function to different degrees in different species. There are, however, problems in applying this approach to estrus detection in exotic mammals, and consequently there is little recent literature on the subject. The main limitations, as outlined by D'Souza (1978), are the need for restraint or sedation coupled with daily sampling, difficulties in standardizing the methods of sample collection and interpretation of results, and limited predictive value. Thus, useful information may be generated by these methods when combined with other techniques; on their own, they are of limited value.

Laparotomy and Laparoscopy
Laparotomy and laparoscopy are both surgical procedures requiring immobilization and anesthesia. As such, their potential for routine application in the same individual is somewhat restricted. Of the two, laparoscopy is preferable because it causes less surgical trauma, adds a magnification capability to enhance viewing of the target organ, and is more applicable to animals of small size. It has now largely superseded laparotomy as a method for assessing reproductive status in exotic animals.

The main advantage of laparoscopy over most other techniques is that it permits direct visualization of the repro-

TABLE 38.1. Methods for assessing reproductive status in female exotic mammals

	Noninvasive	
Invasive	Capture and/or restraint required	No animal contact required
Laparotomy	Vaginal smear	Observation/behavior
Laparoscopy	Ultrasonography	Urine sample[a]
Blood sample[a]	Saliva sample[a]	Fecal sample[a]

[a] Methods involving hormone analysis

ductive organs and thus reduces any potential problems of interpreting information on reproductive status obtained by more indirect means. Its principal disadvantage is that, as with any surgical procedure, there is a certain risk involved in the use of anesthesia, and in most cases, frequent and repeated application is impractical. Nevertheless, the laparoscope has in recent years become a valuable diagnostic aid and research tool in several areas of zoological medicine (Harrison and Wildt 1980).

One area in which laparoscopy has been particularly useful is the monitoring of ovarian function in carnivores, in which there has been limited success in the development of less invasive procedures. The use of laparoscopy for monitoring ovarian function and timing of ovulation in natural and induced cycles in domestic dogs and cats has been widely reported by Wildt and co-workers (Wildt, Kinney, and Seager 1977; Wildt and Seager 1979; Wildt 1980). Similar techniques have been applied to obtaining basic reproductive information and as an aid to studies on induction of ovulation and artificial insemination (AI) in various exotic carnivores, including the jaguar, *Panthera onca*, lion, *P. leo*, cheetah, *Acinonyx jubatus*, tiger, *P. tigris*, puma, *Felis concolor*, and Kodiak bear, *Ursus arctos* (Wildt et al. 1979; Bush, Seager, and Wildt 1980; Bonney, Moore, and Jones 1981). In such situations of intensive study, particularly those in which precise timing of ovulation is essential for successful AI, laparoscopy has been and will continue to be an extremely useful tool. It is also of considerable diagnostic value in helping to identify abnormal or pathological reproductive conditions contributing to infertility and in suspected clinical complications of pregnancy (e.g., Bush, Seager, and Wildt 1980).

Ultrasound

Real-time ultrasound represents one of the more promising recent developments in noninvasive technology for assessing reproductive status in exotic species. Although there are drawbacks in that restraint and often sedation are needed, the main advantage of ultrasound is that it allows direct observation of the reproductive organs without surgical intervention. In many cases, it also allows immediate diagnosis from a single observation. Yet, despite the established success of ultrasound as a diagnostic tool in humans and domestic animals, its potential in exotic species is only now beginning to be realized. The use of ultrasound for early pregnancy detection and fetal monitoring in various laboratory primates, including common marmosets, *Callithix jacchus*, rhesus macaques, *Macaca mulatta*, cynomolgus macaques, *M. fascicularis*, and baboons, *Papio* spp., has recently been reported (Tarantal and Hendrickx 1988, 1989;

Farine et al. 1988; Oerke et al. 1995). The advantages of real-time ultrasound for the detection of pregnancy in a wide variety of other exotic species have also been demonstrated by du Boulay and Wilson (1988), Hildebrandt and Göritz (in press), and Adams et al. (1991). Their papers describe the application and results of real-time ultrasonic investigation of pregnancy in over twenty species of zoo animals, including great apes, monkeys, elephants, ungulates, marine mammals, lizards, and snakes. A single scan is usually sufficient to visualize the gestation sac at an early stage of development, while repeated observations enable fetal development and the course of pregnancy to be followed. Direct observation of the ovaries and even individual follicles is also possible, and although frequent scanning to determine the time of ovulation is often impractical, ultrasound may be helpful in assessing ovarian response to hormonal stimulation during ovulation induction therapy. Another area in which ultrasound offers considerable potential is that of sexing monomorphic species, especially birds and reptiles but also beavers, *Castor* sp. (Wilson and du Boulay 1988), which are difficult to sex from their outward appearance.

Hormone Measurement

Hormone analysis is undoubtedly the most precise indirect method of monitoring reproductive function. However, since correct interpretation of hormonal data requires a knowledge of the reproductive physiology of each species, monitoring methods based on hormonal analysis first need to provide the basic physiological information (hormone metabolism, patterns of secretion and excretion) on which their subsequent application depends. Although certain basic commonalities exist among mammal species in their reproductive endocrinology, marked differences (in both the pattern and levels of hormones produced) make extrapolation of findings from one species to another difficult and potentially misleading. Hormones are present and can be measured in various biological fluids, including blood, saliva, and urine, as well as in feces. The choice of which to use depends on various factors, including the type of information required, the assay techniques involved, species differences in steroid metabolism and route of excretion, and the practicality of sample collection, particularly when frequent sampling over extended periods is necessary.

Blood Measurement of hormones in blood is probably the most informative and widely used method for assessing reproductive function in laboratory and domestic animals. In most zoo animals, however, the problems associated with the collection of samples make this procedure impractical for routine application. A single blood sample is usually insufficient to provide useful information, and serial sampling, which requires repeated capture and restraint, causes unnecessary stress to the animal, which in itself can inhibit reproduction. With the recent development of simplified procedures for urinary hormone analysis, blood sampling is no longer necessary, and for the majority of species is simply unacceptable. There are, however, circumstances in which the use of blood sampling can be justified by the lack of suitable alternatives. For instance, the only reliable method of monitoring ovarian function in elephants has until recently been the measurement of progesterone in serum or plasma (Hess, Schmidt, and Schmidt 1983; Plotka et al. 1988; Brannian et al. 1988). Similarly, the measurement of circulating hormones (progesterone or prolactin) provides the most reliable test for pregnancy in these species (Hess, Schmidt, and Schmidt 1983, McNeilly et al. 1983; Hodges, McNeilly, and Hess 1987). The prolactin test is particularly useful since a diagnosis can often be made from a single value; since frequent sampling is not required, the information obtained clearly justifies the use of the procedure. Additionally, since most Asian elephants, *Elephas maximus,* in captivity are well trained and intensively managed, collection of blood samples without sedation or stress is relatively straightforward.

Urine Over recent years considerable advances have been made in the development of techniques for urinary hormone analysis and in their application to the assessment of reproductive status in exotic species. The main advantage of this approach is that sample collection is noninvasive, thus avoiding the need for animal capture or restraint. At present, urinary hormone analysis provides the most practical approach to long-term physiological studies on most exotic mammals (see also Asa, chap. 37, this volume).

Methods for the collection of urine samples have been described in a number of studies (see Hodges 1985; Lasley 1985 for references). Since most samples are either single voidings or incomplete 24-hour collections, creatinine determination is used to compensate for differences in urine concentration and volume (Taussky 1954; Brand 1981). Despite certain limitations involved in the use of creatinine measurements, good correlations between hormone/creatinine index and 24-hour excretion rates have been demonstrated for a number of species (Metcalf and Hunt 1976; Shideler and Lasley 1982; Hodges and Eastman 1984).

Since comparative studies require multispecies application of assays, validation of hormone measurements in each species is essential. Different species vary not only in their reproductive patterns but also in the qualitative nature of the metabolites excreted in their urine, particularly those of the steroid hormones. Identification of those excreted metabolites that best reflect key reproductive events is therefore essential and often requires the use of chromatography or other purification steps prior to routine assay (Hodges 1985).

The majority of steroids in urine are present in the conjugated form. Early analyses of steroids in urine involved the laborious process of hydrolysis and solvent extraction prior to assay; however, the introduction of nonextraction assays allowing direct measurement of steroid conjugates has now greatly simplified procedures. By avoiding the need

for hydrolysis, a process that itself can be inefficient, direct assays for steroid conjugates have the additional advantage of often generating a more informative hormone profile than previously possible with extraction methods (Shideler et al. 1983b; Hodges and Eastman 1984; Lasley et al. 1985).

Even simpler assays based on the use of enzymatic procedures are now available as an alternative to conventional assays using radioisotopes. The advantages of these enzyme immunoassays (EIAs), including low cost, ease of performance, and convenience, as well as avoidance of the problems associated with the use and disposal of radioactive materials, make them particularly suitable for institutions with limited laboratory facilities such as zoos and other animal collections. Furthermore, the endpoint of these tests is a color change that is simple to quantify. The tests require minimal instrumentation and are therefore amenable to use under field conditions. The application of EIAs to reproductive monitoring in exotic mammals has recently been described (Hodges 1985; Czekala et al. 1988; Hodges and Green 1989; Hindle, Mostl, and Hodges 1992; Shideler et al. 1993).

Urinary hormone analysis is now the predominant method for monitoring reproductive function in exotic mammals. To date, this approach has been successfully applied to the detection of ovulation and pregnancy in a wide range of species, including great apes, Old and New World monkeys, ungulates, some carnivores, giant pandas, *Ailuropoda melanoleuca,* and even marine mammals (see table 38.2; see also Asa, chap. 37, this volume). In addition to providing results of practical value, these studies have also provided a great deal of physiological information about reproductive cycles in exotic species, many of them being studied for the first time. Although the studies referred to (see table 38.2) are limited to animals in zoos and other captive situations, collection of urine samples in the wild is possible, and noninvasive endocrine monitoring of free-ranging animals has been reported for the vervet monkey, *Chlorocebus* (=*Cercopithecus*) *aethiops* (Andelman et al. 1985), African elephant, *Loxodonta africana* (Poole et al. 1984), black rhinoceros, *Diceros bicornis* (Brett, Hodges, and Wanjohi 1989), and various ungulate species (Lasley and Kirkpatrick 1991).

Although the foregoing discussion has concentrated on the measurement of urinary steroid metabolites, gonadotropic hormones such as pituitary LH and FSH are also excreted in urine. The major drawback to their measurement by immunoassay methods is that species specificity in the immunological activity of these hormones usually makes multispecies application of assays difficult. A recently characterized monoclonal antibody against bovine LH that is reported to cross-react with LH from diverse mammalian species (Matteri et al. 1987) is therefore of interest as a potential immunological LH assay suitable for use in a wide range of mammals. In contrast, biological activity is less species-specific, and in vitro bioassays have been established for urinary LH (Hodges, McNeilly, and Hess 1979; Harlow, Hearn, and Hodges 1984) and more recently FSH (Dahl et al. 1987) that have been successfully applied to a variety of exotic species (see also Czekala, Hodges, and Lasley 1981; Dahl, Czekala, and Hseuh 1987; Monfort

TABLE 38.2.   Some studies in which urinary hormone analysis has yielded information on endocrine profiles in exotic mammals helpful in the detection of ovulation and pregnancy

Species	Ovarian cycle/ovulation	Pregnancy
Primates		
Lemur spp.	Shideler and Lasley 1982	Shideler et al. 1983a
Saddleback tamarin, *Saguinus fuscicollis*	Hodges et al. 1981; Heistermann and Hodges 1995	
Cotton-top tamarin, *Saguinus oedipus*	Brand 1981; Ziegler et al. 1987; Hodges and Eastman 1984	Ziegler et al. 1987
Common marmoset, *Callithrix jacchus*	Eastman et al. 1984	Eastman et al. 1984
Goeldi's monkey, *Callimico goeldii*	Christen et al. 1989; Carroll et al. 1990	Carroll et al. 1990
Squirrel monkey, *Saimiri sciureus*	Hodges et al. 1981	
Spider monkey, *Ateles fusciceps*	Hodges et al. 1981	
Owl monkey, *Aotus trivirgatus*	Bonney and Setchell 1980	
Capuchin monkey, *Cebus apella*	Hodges, Czekala, and Lasley 1979	Czekala, Hodges, and Lasley, 1981
Macaque spp.	Shideler et al. 1983b, 1985; Monfort et al. 1986, 1987	Shideler et al. 1983b; Monfort et al. 1986, 1987
Vervet, *Chlorocebus* (= *Cercopithecus*) *aethiops*	Hodges 1985	Andelman et al. 1985
Baboon, *Papio cynocephalus*	Hodges et al. 1986	
Douc langur, *Pygathrix nemaeus*	Czekala, Hodges, and Lasley 1981	
Chimpanzee, *Pan troglodytes*	Graham et al. 1977; Hodges, Czekala, and Lasley 1979	
Orangutan, *Pongo pygmaeus*	Collins, Graham, and Preedy 1975; Bonney and Kingsley 1982	Czekala, Hodges, and Lasley 1981; Czekala et al. 1983
Gorilla, *Gorilla gorilla*	Hodges, Czekala, and Lasley 1979; Mitchell et al. 1983; Czekala, Mitchell and Lasley, 1986; Czekala et al. 1988	Martin, Seaton, and Lusty 1975; Czekala et al. 1983; Hodges and Green 1989
Artiodactyla		
Okapi, *Okapia johnstoni*	Loskutoff, Ott, and Lasley 1982, 1983	
Giraffe, *Giraffa camelopardalis*	Loskutoff et al. 1986	
Scimitar-horned oryx, *Oryx dammah*	Durrant 1983	
Bison, *Bison bison*	Kirkpatrick et al. 1991	
Blackbuck, *Antilope cervicapra*	Hodges and Hearn 1983; Holt et al. 1988	Holt et al. 1988
Suni antelope, *Neotragus moschatus*	Loskutoff et al. 1990	
White-tailed deer, *Odocoileus virginianus*	Knox et al. 1992	
Eld's deer, *Cervus eldii thamin*	Monfort et al. 1990	
Perissodactyla		
Indian rhinoceros, *Rhinoceros unicornis*	Kassam and Lasley 1980; Kasman, McCowan, and Lasley 1985	Kasman, McCowan, and Lasley 1985
Black rhinoceros, *Diceros bicornis*	Hindle, Mostl, and Hodges 1992; Hodges and Green 1989	Ramsay, Kasman, and Lasley 1987
White rhinoceros, *Ceratotherium simum*	Hindle, Mostl, and Hodges 1992	Hodges and Green 1989
Malayan tapir, *Tapirus indicus*	Kasman, McCowan, and Lasley 1985	
Brazilian tapir, *Tapirus terrestris*	Kasman, McCowan, and Lasley 1985	
Carnivora		
Brown hyena, *Hyaena brunnea*	Ensley et al. 1982	
Giant panda, *Ailuropoda melanoleuca*	Bonney, Wood, and Kleiman 1982; Hodges et al. 1984	Hodges et al. 1984; Monfort et al. 1989
Proboscidea		
Asian elephant, *Elephas maximus*	Dahl, Czekala, and Hseuh 1987; Czekala, Roocroft, and Bates 1989; Niemuller, Shaw, and Hodges 1993	Niemuller, Shaw, and Hodges 1993
Cetacea		
Killer whale, *Orcinus orca*	Walker et al. 1987	Walker et al. 1987

et al. 1989). However, biological assays are laborious and time-consuming and, while useful in a research context, are unsuitable for routine application as a monitoring procedure.

Certain species, primarily primates, also produce a gonadotropin of placental (or chorionic) origin that is excreted in large quantities in the urine. Although the patterns and amounts of chorionic gonadotropin (CG) production vary considerably among species (see Findlay 1980 for references), its measurement by a hemagglutination inhibition assay (HIA) has proved of enormous practical value as a quick and simple method of pregnancy diagnosis in primates. The HIA assay for pregnancy in nonhuman primates (NHPPT) distributed by the National Institutes for Arthritis, Metabolic and Digestive Diseases (NIAMDD), U.S.A., allowed diagnosis of pregnancy from within 2 to 5 weeks of conception and for variable periods thereafter depending on the species. The main disadvantage of the test is that, being qualitative, it detects only the presence or absence of CG without providing information on levels or patterns of production. Unfortunately, this test is no longer being distributed, and an equivalent cross-species primate pregnancy test kit is not yet available.

Other species known to secrete a pregnancy-specific (chorionic) gonadotropin are members of the Equidae. However, while plasma profiles of eCG are well characterized, it is only very recently that a method of measuring urinary eCG has been established (Roser and Lofstedt 1989). A semiquantitative enzyme-linked immunosorbent dipstick assay (Marechek) has now been developed (Monoclonal Antibodies, Inc., Mountain View, Calif.) and provides the first simple and convenient equine pregnancy test based on the detection of urinary eCG.

Feces In addition to urinary excretion, large amounts of steroid hormones are also excreted in feces. In fact, in several mammalian species, fecal excretion predominates. Based on the development of methodology for fecal steroid analysis and its use in monitoring aspects of reproductive status in women (Adlercreutz and Jarvenpaa 1982) and domestic animals (Bamberg et al. 1984; Mostl et al. 1984), there has been considerable recent interest in the application of similar techniques to reproductive monitoring in exotic species. The measurement of ovarian steroids in feces has now been reported for various species, including New and Old World primates (Risler, Wasser, and Sackett 1987; Wasser, Risler, and Steiner 1988; Ziegler et al. 1987; Heistermann, Tari, and Hodges 1992), carnivores (Shille et al. 1985), and ungulates (Safar-Hermann et al. 1987; Lasley and Kirkpatrick 1991; Bamberg et al. 1991; Schwarzenberger et al. 1993; Shideler et al. 1994). However, relatively little is known about which metabolites best reflect gonadal function. Consequently, reports describing the application of fecal steroid analysis to the monitoring of reproductive events are still limited (Safar-Hermann et al. 1987; Wasser, Monfort, and Wildt 1991; Heistermann et al. 1993). The extent to which fecal analysis will be exploited probably depends more on the particular circumstances and species involved than on any intrinsic advantage it has over other approaches (especially urine analysis). One situation in which an advantage does exist is the study of animals in the wild. Although sequential urine collection in the wild is feasible and has been demonstrated for a number of species, opportunities for long-term studies can be greatly increased if fecal samples can be utilized. In some species, fecal analysis may be necessary due to a lack of alternatives, either because of the nature of the excreted metabolites or the fact that an insignificant amount of hormone excretion occurs through the urinary route (e.g., slow loris, *Nycticebus coucang:* Perez et al. 1988). Work on the domestic cat provides a good example of the latter situation and suggests that fecal analysis may be necessary for noninvasive endocrine monitoring of exotic Felidae in general (Shille et al. 1985). Recent observations on the measurement of excreted steroid

metabolites in several felid species support this view (Brown et al. 1995). Despite these specific situations in which fecal analysis is advantageous, the approach in general has major disadvantages in that the laboratory procedures currently required are complex, laborious, and expensive compared with those involved in urinary analysis.

Saliva Minute quantities of steroid hormones are also present in saliva, and can be measured using highly sensitive immunoassay procedures. While the collection of saliva can under certain circumstances be considered a noninvasive procedure and as such has proved useful for monitoring reproductive status in women, its advantages for studies on exotic species are less obvious. Compared with the collection of urine, obtaining saliva samples from large, intractable animals poses greater practical problems, making widespread application of the technique unlikely. While progress to date has been limited, findings by N. M. Czekala (unpub.) suggest that measurement of salivary progestagens may be useful for diagnosing pregnancy in the black rhinoceros.

METHODS FOR MANIPULATING FEMALE REPRODUCTIVE STATUS

The ability to monitor reproductive function in exotic animals is not only essential for more efficient natural breeding programs, but also forms the basis for studies designed to accelerate captive breeding by artificial means. Knowledge gained through studies on laboratory and domestic animals has led to the development of a variety of techniques by which the natural mechanisms regulating fertility can be manipulated. Although many of these are now in widespread use throughout the livestock industry, little progress has been made in extending this technology to endangered species, largely due to a lack of understanding of their reproductive physiology. Nevertheless, there are a number of basic approaches that, if developed on a proper scientific basis, could be of considerable practical benefit in increasing reproductive output in a variety of captive endangered species.

Modification of the Ovarian Cycle

One of the more obvious approaches is the modification of the estrous cycle in order to control the time at which ovulation occurs. Since the accurate prediction and detection of ovulation is essential to the success of procedures such as artificial insemination and embryo recovery and transfer, the use of physiological and pharmacological treatment to manipulate the natural timing of the estrous cycle is an important component of any such artificial breeding attempt. Most of the technology required for estrus manipulation has been developed in domestic livestock, in which the estrous cycle is characterized by a relatively long luteal phase and a much shorter preovulatory or follicular phase. In these species (and presumably in those nondomesticated ungulates with similar cycle characteristics), modification of the functional life span of the corpus luteum, either by inducing premature luteal regression or by artificially extending the luteal phase, provides the most effective method of controlling the time of ovulation (Hunter 1980). Synchronization of ovulation (e.g., for embryo transfer) can be achieved by performing one or both procedures concurrently in different individuals. In contrast, this approach is generally not practical for those species (notably Old World monkeys and apes) with an extended interval from luteal regression to ovulation.

The principles underlying estrous synchronization treatments and the various techniques available (as applied to domestic species) have been well described (e.g., see Hunter 1980; Gordon 1983 for references). In brief, there are two basic approaches: (1) progesterone or synthetic progestagen treatment to prolong the luteal phase, followed by abrupt withdrawal of treatment to allow (synchronous) resumption of the follicular phase; and (2) administration of a luteolytic agent (usually synthetic prostaglandin $F_2\alpha$) to terminate corpus luteum function, allowing (synchronous) resumption of the follicular phase.

Both approaches, either alone or in combination, have been applied routinely in domestic livestock, especially sheep and cattle, for many years (e.g., Roche 1976; Haresign 1978). More recently, their use has been extended to a variety of nondomesticated ungulates, including gaur, *Bos gaurus* (Stover, Evans, and Dolensek 1981), bongo, *Tragelaphus eurycerus,* and eland, *Taurotragus oryx* (Dresser et al. 1984; Dresser 1986), blackbuck, *Antilope cervicapra* (Hodges 1985; Holt et al. 1988), addax, *Addax nasomaculatus* (Densmore et al. 1987), zebra, *Equus* sp. (Summers et al. 1987a), and deer (Curlewis, Loudon, and Coleman 1988), and more recently, to the gorilla, *Gorilla gorilla* (Goodrowe, Wildt, and Monfort 1992). These techniques have contributed to the success of both embryo transfer and artificial insemination procedures in many of these species (see Hodges 1992). A single injection of prostaglandin $F_2\alpha$ is also luteolytic in certain New World monkeys, including the common marmoset, *Callithrix jacchus* (Summers, Wennink, and Hodges 1985), in which (unusually for primates) it allows synchronization of ovulation for embryo transfer studies (Summers et al. 1987b). The authors' preliminary observations indicate that estrumate causes luteal regression in the Asian elephant, although the practical value of this effect in terms of ovulation control is probably limited.

Induction of Ovulation

Since many endangered species are seasonal breeders, another way in which reproduction can be manipulated is to regulate the timing of the annual onset of ovarian cyclicity. Induction of ovulation during seasonal anestrus could be used to regulate the time of year at which breeding occurs or possibly even to extend the natural period of seasonal reproductive activity. One approach to manipulating the onset of seasonal breeding is the exogenous administration of the pineal hormone melatonin. Originally developed as a means of overcoming seasonal inhibition of breeding in domestic species, particularly sheep (Kennaway, Gilmore, and Seamark 1982; Arendt et al. 1983), the administration of melatonin by implant or by feeding offers the potential for manipulating the onset of ovarian cyclicity (i.e., ovulation) in a variety of seasonally breeding exotic species and

has already shown practical usage in the management and breeding of deer (Bubenik 1983; Adam and Atkinson 1984) and wallabies (Loudon 1985). The advantage of using melatonin is that it is easy to administer (by simple implants or by addition to feed pellets of ruminants) and so can be used in a large number of individuals at the same time; the major disadvantage is that since there is normally a delay of several weeks from the beginning of treatment to response, precise "control" over the timing of ovulation cannot be achieved. Although melatonin provides a convenient method of stimulating reproductive activity in short-day breeders (animals that respond to decreasing day length), unfortunately there is no simple way as yet of achieving this in species that respond to long days.

An alternative approach that gives a greater degree of control over the timing of ovulation is the use of the hypothalamic decapeptide gonadotropin-releasing hormone (GnRH). The response to chronic administration of low doses of GnRH is more rapid and consistent than with melatonin, with ovulation usually occurring within 2 to 3 days during seasonal and postpartum anestrus in cattle, sheep, and deer (Riley, Peters, and Lamming 1981; McLeod, Haresign, and Lamming 1982; Fisher et al. 1986). Initially, a pulsatile mode of delivery of GnRH was thought to be necessary, making long-term administration potentially difficult. More recent research, showing that continuous administration is at least partially effective in domestic hoofstock, has greatly improved the prospects for routine application, and a number of GnRH-impregnated, biodegradable implants are already under trial (McLeod, Haresign, and Lamming 1983; Jagger, Peters, and Lamming 1987). In other species, however, particularly primates (Knobil 1980) and species for which GnRH dose response characteristics are not known, a pulsatile mode of delivery may continue to be necessary. With this in mind, simplified implantable devices for pulsatile administration of GnRH have been developed, and their suitability for long-term use in endangered species has been demonstrated (Lasley and Wing 1983).

An obvious extension of the use of GnRH is its potential application to the treatment of certain types of infertility. Hypothalamic or pituitary disorders resulting in anovulation in women can be effectively treated with GnRH (Leyendecker and Wildt 1983), and many similar applications can be considered in endangered species. In wild animals, in which seasonal constraints on reproduction are common and the "stress" of captivity may itself contribute to reproductive failure, there is considerable potential in the application of GnRH treatment to the management of both natural and artificial breeding.

GnRH acts by stimulating the natural ovulation rate for any given species. This is often the most acceptable form of ovulation induction, since it avoids the potential problems of ovarian hyperstimulation and superfetation associated with more traditional methods of ovulation induction. Occasionally, however, it is desirable to induce superovulation, whereby the ovary is stimulated to increase its normal ovulatory quota, thus producing larger numbers of oocytes in any given cycle. In addition to controlling the time of numbers of embryos from a single animal. Once fertilization is achieved, either by natural mating or artificial insemination, recovery of the preimplantation embryos from either the oviducts or uterus is necessary. The embryos are then available for transfer to synchronized recipients, either immediately or after a period of storage in liquid nitrogen.

Superovulation is achieved by inducing multiple follicular development, usually with an exogenous FSH-rich gonadotropin preparation, with or without subsequent LH/hCG treatment to induce follicular rupture. Protocols vary widely according to species. Among the ungulates, pregnant mares' serum gonadotropin (PMSG), porcine FSH, and to a lesser degree, human menopausal gonadotropin (HMG) have been widely used for inducing superovulation in domestic livestock (see Hunter 1980; Gordon 1983, for references), although poor predictability of response (particularly to PMSG) raises concerns about the use of such treatments in endangered species, which are generally available only in limited numbers in captivity. Various factors are thought to influence the ovarian (ovulatory) response to exogenous gonadotropins, including timing of the injection in relation to stage of cycle, dose of hormone and hormonal content of the preparation, age and nutritional status of the animal, and season. Another consideration is that the use of large quantities of species-nonspecific gonadotropins carries a risk of stimulating antibody production that, after repeated use, may impair responsiveness to further treatment or even lead to infertility (e.g., Bavister, Dees, and Schultz 1986).

For these reasons, superovulation with exogenous gonadotropins has not been used to any great extent in exotic species to date, although some success has been achieved in Bovidae (due to their similarity to domestic cattle) (e.g., Stover, Evans, and Dolensek 1981; Dresser et al. 1982, 1984) and in Felidae (e.g., Rowlands and Sadleir 1968; Bonney, Moore, and Jones 1981). Among nonhuman primates, exogenous gonadotropins have been used to induce multiple follicular development and ovulation in a number of laboratory species such as rhesus macaques (e.g., Abbasi et al. 1987; Bavister and Boatman 1989), pig-tailed macaques, *Macaca nemestrina* (Cranfield et al. 1989), and gorillas (Loskutoff et al. 1991). Success in terms of ovulation rate and oocyte fertilizability tends to be variable, and certainly, outside the laboratory, little has been achieved so far. The recent developments in ovarian stimulation protocols for use in human in vitro fertilization and embryo transfer (e.g., Hillier et al. 1985) should, however, improve our understanding of the physiological requirements for controlled ovarian stimulation in nonhuman primates and lead to greater success in the application of superovulation procedures.

Induction of multiple follicular development with FSH-rich preparations must often be followed by the (somewhat species-dependent) additional administration of hCG or GnRH to induce follicular rupture and ovulation. hCG can also be used alone to control the timing of ovulation without necessarily affecting ovulation rate. This method has many practical applications, including induction of reproductive cyclicity in reflex ovulators such as cats (Wildt, Kinney, and Seager 1978; Wildt et al. 1981; Brown et al.

1995) and timing of ovulation for artificial insemination in primates (Gould, Martin, and Warner 1985). Careful timing of the hCG injection is itself important, since premature administration may impair follicular and oocyte function and even suppress ovulation (Williams and Hodgen 1980).

CONCLUSION

Much progress has been made the last ten years in establishing appropriate methodology for determining reproductive parameters in wild mammals. The need for a noninvasive approach to reproductive assessment has led to the development of greatly improved, simplified immunoassay techniques for the measurement of excreted hormones and their metabolites. While most information to date derives from the measurement of hormones in urine, there is now also considerable interest in fecal hormone analysis due to the relative ease of sample collection, particularly under field conditions. Among the nonendocrine techniques, the recent advances in the use of real-time ultrasonography in a wide variety of zoo species have already emphasized the value of this technique.

In contrast, there has been relatively little progress in the application of techniques for manipulating reproductive functions in wild mammals. While the technology exists for regulating fertility in domestic animals, its application to exotic species so far has been limited. At the same time, the importance of reproductive technologies to the long-term genetic management of captive populations of wild mammals is becoming increasingly apparent, and progress in both their development and application is now urgently required.

REFERENCES

Abbasi, R., Kenigsberg, D., Danforth, D., Falk, R., and Hodgen, G. D. 1987. Cumulative ovulation rate in human menopausal/human chorionic gonadotropin-treated monkeys: "Step-up" versus "step-down" dose regimens. *Fertil. Steril.* 47:1019–24.

Adam, C. L., and Atkinson, T. 1984. Effect of feeding melatonin to red deer *(Cervus elaphus)* on the onset of the breeding season. *J. Reprod. Fertil.* 72:463–66.

Adams, G. P., Plotka, E. D., Asa, C. S., and Ginther, O. J. 1991. Feasibility of characterizing reproductive events in large nondomestic species by transrectal ultrasonic imaging. *Zoo Biol.* 10:247–59.

Adlercreutz, H., and Jarvenpaa, P. 1982. Assay of estrogens in human feces. *J. Steroid Biochem.* 17:639–45.

Andelman, S., Else, J. G., Hearn, J. P., and Hodges, J. K. 1985. The non-invasive monitoring of reproductive events in wild vervet monkeys *(Cercopithecus aethiops)* using pregnanediol-3-glucuronide and its correlation with behavioural observations. *J. Zool.* (Lond.) 205:467–77.

Arendt, J., Symons, A. M., Laud, C. A., and Pryde, S. J. 1983. Melatonin can induce early onset of the breeding season in ewes. *J. Endocrinol.* 97:397–400.

Bamberg, E., Choi, H. S., Mostl, E., Wurm, W., Lorin, D., and Arbeiter, K. 1984. Enzymatic determination of unconjugated oestrogens in feces for pregnancy diagnosis in mares. *Equine Vet. J.* 16:537–39.

Bamberg, E., Möstl, E., Patzl, M., and King, G. J. 1991. Pregnancy diagnosis by enzyme immunoassay of estrogens in feces from nondomestic species. *J. Zoo Wildl. Med.* 22:73–77.

Bavister, B. D., and Boatman, D. E. 1989. In vitro fertilization and embryo transfer technology as an aid to the conservation of endangered primates. *Zoo Biol., Suppl.* 1:21–31.

Bavister, B. D., Dees, C., and Schultz, R. D. 1986. Refractoriness of rhesus monkeys to repeated ovarian stimulation by exogenous gonadotrophins is caused by non-precipitating antibodies. *Am. J. Reprod. Immunol. Microbiol.* 11:11–16.

Bonnar, J. 1983. Biological approaches to ovulation detection. In: *Ovulation: Methods for its prediction and detection*, ed. S. L. Jeffcoate, 33–47. New York: John Wiley and Sons.

Bonney, R. C., and Kingsley, S. 1982. Endocrinology of pregnancy in the Orangutan *(Pongo pygmaeus)* and its evolutionary significance. *Int. J. Primatol.* 3:431–44.

Bonney, R. C., Moore, H. D. M., and Jones, D. M. 1981. Plasma concentrations of oestradiol-17β and progesterone, and laparoscopic observations of the ovary in the puma *(Felis concolor)* during estrus, pseudopregnancy, and pregnancy. *J. Reprod. Fertil.* 63:523–31.

Bonney, R. C., and Setchell, K. D. R. 1980. The excretion of gonadal steroids during the reproductive cycle of the owl monkey *(Aotus trivirgatus)*. *J. Steroid Biochem.* 12:417–21.

Bonney, R. C., Wood, D. J., and Kleiman, D. G. 1982. Endocrine correlates of behavioural estrus in the female Giant Panda *(Ailuropoda melanoleuca)* and associated hormonal changes in the male. *J. Reprod. Fertil.* 64:209–15.

Brand, H. M. 1981. Urinary oestrogen excretion in the female cotton-topped tamarin *(Saguinus oedipus oedipus)*. *J. Reprod. Fertil.* 62:467–73.

Brannian, J. D., Griffin, F., Papkoff, M., and Terranova, P. F. 1988. Short and long phases of progesterone secretion during the oestrous cycle of the African elephant. *J. Reprod. Fertil.* 84:357–65.

Brett, R. A., Hodges, J. K., and Wanjohi, E. 1989. The assessment of reproductive status and its effect in the bionomics of the black rhinoceros. *Symp. Zool. Soc. Lond.* 61:147–63.

Brown, J. L., Wasser, S. K., Wildt, D. E., and Graham, L. H. 1994. Comparative aspects of steroid hormone metabolism and ovarian activity in felids, measured noninvasively in feces. *Biol. Reprod.* 51:776–86.

Brown, J. L., Wildt, D. E., Graham, L. H., Byers, A. P., Collins, L., Barrett, S., and Howard, J. 1995. Natural versus chorionic gonadotropin-induced ovarian responses in the clouded leopard *(Neofelis nebulosa)* assessed by fecal steroid analysis. *Biol. Reprod.* 53:93–102.

Bubenik, G. A. 1983. Shift of seasonal cycle in white-tailed deer by oral administration of melatonin. *J. Exp. Zool.* 235:155–56.

Bush, M., Seager, S. W. J., and Wildt, D. E. 1980. Laparoscopy in zoo mammals. In *Animal laparoscopy*, ed. R. M. Harrison and D. E. Wildt, 183–97. Baltimore: Williams and Wilkins.

Carroll, J. B., Abbott, D. H., George, L. M., Hindle, J. E., and Martin, R. D. 1990. Urinary endocrine monitoring of the ovarian cycle and pregnancy in Goeldi's monkey. *J. Reprod. Fertil.* 89:149–61.

Christen, A., Döbeli, M., Kempken, B., Zachmann, M., and Martin, R. D. 1989. Urinary excretion of oestradiol-17β in the female cycle of Goeldi's monkeys *(Callimico goeldii)*. *Folia Primatol.* 52:191–200.

Collins, D. C., Graham, C. E., and Preedy, J. R. K. 1975. Identification and measurement of urinary estrone, estradiol-17β, estriol and pregnanediol and androsterone during the menstrual cycle of the orang-utan. *Endocrinology* 96:93–101.

Cranfield, M. R., Schaffer, N., Bavister, B. D., Berger, N., Boat-man, D. E., Kempske, S., Miner, N., Panos, M., Adams, J., and Morgan, P. M. 1989. Assessment of oocytes retrieved from stimulated and unstimulated ovaries of pig-tailed macaques *(Macaca nemestrina)* as a model to enhance the genetic diversity of captive lion-tailed macaques *(Macaca silenus)*. *Zoo Biol., Suppl.* 1:33–46.

Curlewis, J. D., Loudon, A. S. I., and Coleman, A. P. M. 1988. Estrous cycles and the breeding season of the Père David's deer hind *(Elaphurus davidianus)*. *J. Reprod. Fertil.* 82:119–26.

Czekala, N. M., Benirschke, K., McClure, H., and Lasley, B. L. 1983. Urinary estrogen excretion during pregnancy in the gorilla *(Gorilla gorilla)*, orangutan *(Pongo pygmaeus)*, and the human *(Homo sapiens)*. *Biol. Reprod.* 28:289–94.

Czekala, N. M., Hodges, J. K., and Lasley, B. L. 1981. Pregnancy monitoring in diverse primate species by estrogen and bioactive luteinizing hormone determinations in small volumes of urine. *J. Med. Primatol.* 10:1–15.

Czekala, N. M., Mitchell, W. R., and Lasley, B. L. 1986. Direct measurement of urinary estrone conjugates during the normal menstrual cycle of the gorilla *(Gorilla gorilla)*. *Am. J. Primatol.* 68:1988–93.

Czekala, N. M., Roocroft, A., and Bates, M. 1989. Estrogen metabolism in the Asian elephant *(Elephas maximus)*. *Biol. Reprod.* 40 (suppl. 1), abs. no. 214.

Czekala, N. M., Roser, J. F., Mortensen, R. B., Reichard, T., and Lasley, B. L. 1988. Urinary hormone analysis as a diagnostic tool to evaluate the ovarian function of female gorillas *(Gorilla gorilla)* *J. Reprod. Fertil.* 82:255–61.

Dahl, K. D., Czekala, N. M., and Hseuh, A. J. W. 1987. Measurement of urinary bioactive follicle-stimulating hormone during reproductive cycles in diverse mammalian species. *Biol. Reprod.* 36 (suppl. 1), 168.

Dahl, K. D., Czekala, N. M., Lim, P., and Hseuh, A. J. W. 1987. Monitoring the menstrual cycle of humans and lowland gorillas based on urinary profiles of bioactive follicle stimulating hormone and steroid metabolites. *J. Clin. Endocrinol. Metab.* 6:486–92.

Densmore, M. A., Bowen, M. J., Magyar, S. J., Amoss, M. S., Robinson, R. M., Harns, P. G., and Kraemer, D. C. 1987. Artificial insemination with frozen, thawed semen and pregnancy diagnosis in Addax *(Addax nasomaculatus)*. *Zoo Biol.* 6:21–29.

Dresser, B. L. 1986. Embryo transfer in exotic bovids. *Int. Zoo Yrbk.* 24/25:138–42.

Dresser, B. L., Kramer, L., Pope, C. E., Dahlhausen, R. D., and Blauser, C. 1982. Superovulation of African eland *(Taurotragus oryx)* and interspecies embryo transfer to Holstein cattle. *Theriogenology* 21:232–40.

Dresser, B. L., Pope, C. E., Kraemer, L., Kuehn, G., Dahlhausen, R. D., and Thomas, W. D. 1984. Superovulation of bongo antelope *(Tragelaphus eurycerus)* and interspecies embryo transfer to African eland *(Tragelaphus oryx)*. *Theriogenology* 21:232–39.

D'Souza, F. 1978. Detection of estrus. *Symp. Zool. Soc. Lond.* 43:175–93.

du Boulay, G. H., and Wilson, O. L. 1988. Diagnosis of pregnancy and disease by ultrasound in exotic species. *Symp. Zool. Soc. Lond.* 60:135–50.

Durrant, B. S. 1983. Reproductive studies of the Oryx. *Zoo Biol.* 2:191–97.

Eastman, S. A., Makawiti, D. W., Collins, W. P., and Hodges, J. K. 1984. Pattern of excretion of urinary steroid metabolites during the ovarian cycle and pregnancy in the marmoset monkey. *J. Endocrinol.* 102:19–26.

Ensley, P. K., Wing, A. E., Gosink, B. B., Lasley, B. L., and Durrant, B. 1982. Application of non-invasive techniques to monitor reproductive function in a Brown Hyena *(Hyaena brunnea)*. *Zoo Biol.* 1:333–43.

Farine, D., MacCarter, G. D., Timor-Tritch, I. E., Yeh, M. N., and Stark, J. R. I. 1988. Real-time ultrasonic evaluation of the baboon-pregnancy: Biometric measurements. *J. Med. Primatol.* 17:215–22.

Findlay, J. K. 1980. Immunological diagnosis of early pregnancy. In *Immunological approaches to fertility control,* ed. J. P. Hearn, 63–81. Lancaster: MTP Press.

Fisher, M. W., Fennessy, P. F., Suttie, J. M., Corson, I. D., Pearse, A. J. T., Davis, G. H., and Johnstone, P. D. 1986. Early induction of ovulation in yearling red deer hinds. *Proc. N.Z. Soc. Anim. Prod.* 43.

Goodrowe, K. L., Wildt, D. E., and Monfort, S. L. 1992. Effective suppression of ovarian cyclicity in the Lowland Gorilla with an oral contraceptive. *Zoo Biol.* 11:261–69.

Gordon, I. 1983. *Controlled breeding in farm animals.* New York: Pergamon Press.

Gould, K. G., Martin, D. E., and Warner, H. 1985. Improved method for artificial insemination in the Great Apes. *Am. J. Primatol.* 8:61–67.

Graham, C. E., Warner, H., Misener, J., Collins, D. C., and Preedy, J. R. K. 1977. The association between basal body temperature, sexual swelling, and urinary gonadal hormone levels in the menstrual cycle of the chimpanzee. *J. Reprod. Fertil.* 50:23–28.

Haresign, W. 1978. Ovulation control in the sheep. In *Control of ovulation,* ed. D. B. Crighton, G. R. Foxcroft, W. B. Haynes, and G. E. Lamming, 435–51. Boston: Butterworths.

Harlow, C. R., Hearn, J. P., and Hodges, J. K. 1984. Ovulation in the marmoset monkey: Endocrinology, prediction, and detection. *J. Endocrinol.* 103:17–24.

Harrison, R. M., and Wildt, D. E., ed. 1980. *Animal laparoscopy.* Baltimore: Williams and Wilkins.

Heistermann, M., and Hodges, J. K. 1995. Endocrine monitoring of the ovarian cycle and pregnancy in the saddle back tamarin *(Saguinus fuscicollis)* by measurement of steroid conjugates in urine. *Am. J. Primatol.* 35:117–27.

Heistermann, M., Tari, S., and Hodges, J. K. 1992. Monitoring ovarian function in Callitrichidae by faecal steroid analysis. *J. Reprod. Fertil.* Abs. Ser. 9, no. 46.

Hess, D. L., Schmidt, A. M., and Schmidt, M. J. 1983. Reproductive cycle of the Asian elephant *(Elephas maximus)* in captivity. *Biol. Reprod.* 28:767–73.

Hildebrandt, T., and Göritz, F. In press. Ultrasonography as a tool in zoo management. In *Research and captive propagation,* ed. U. Ganslosser, J. K. Hodges, and W. Kaumanns. Erlangen: Filander.

Hillier, S. G., Afnan, A. M. M., Margara, R. A., and Winston, R. M. L. 1985. Superovulation strategy before in vitro fertilization. *Clin. Obstet. Gynecol.* 12:687–723.

Hindle, J. E., Mostl, E., and Hodges, J. K. 1992. Measurement of urinary oestrogens and 20-dihydroprogesterone during ovarian cycles of black *(Diceros bicornis)* and white *(Ceratotherium simum)* rhinoceroses. *J. Reprod. Fertil.* 94:237–49.

Hodges, J. K. 1985. The endocrine control of reproduction. *Symp. Zool. Soc. Lond.* 54:149–68.

———. 1992. Detection of oestrous cycles and timing of ovulation. *Symp. Zool. Soc. Lond.* 64:73–88.

Hodges, J. K., Bevan, D. J., Celma, M., Hearn, J. P., Jones, D. M., Kleiman, D. G., Knight, J. A., and Moore, H. D. M. 1984. Aspects of the reproductive endocrinology of the female Giant Panda *(Ailuropoda melanoleuca)* in captivity with special reference to the detection of ovulation and pregnancy. *J. Zool.* (Lond.) 203:253–68.

Hodges, J. K., Czekala, N. M., and Lasley, B. L. 1979. Estrogen

and luteinizing hormone secretion in diverse primate species from simplified urinary analysis. *J. Med. Primatol.* 3:349–64.

Hodges, J. K., and Eastman, S. A. K. 1984. Monitoring ovarian function in marmosets and tamarins by the measurement of urinary oestrogen metabolites. *Am. J. Primatol.* 6:187–97.

Hodges, J. K., and Green, D. G. 1989. A simplified enzyme immunoassay for urinary pregnanediol-3-glucuronide: Applications to reproductive assessment of exotic species. *J. Zool.* (Lond.) 219:89–99.

Hodges, J. K., Gulick, B. A., Czekala, N. M., and Lasley, B. L. 1981. Comparison of urinary oestrogen excretion in South American primates. *J. Reprod. Fertil.* 61:83–90.

Hodges, J. K., and Hearn, J. P. 1983. The prediction and detection of ovulation: Applications to comparative medicine and conservation. In *Ovulation: Methods for its prediction and detection,* ed. S. L. Jeffcoate, 103–22. New York: John Wiley and Sons.

Hodges, J. K., McNeilly, A. S., and Hess, D. L. 1987. Circulating hormones during pregnancy in the Asian and African elephants: A diagnostic test based on the measurement of prolactin. *Int. Zoo Yrbk.* 26:285–89.

Hodges, J. K., Tarara, R., Hearn, J. P., and Else, J. G. 1986. The detection of ovulation and early pregnancy in the baboon by direct measurement of conjugated steroids in urine. *Am. J. Primatol.* 10:329–38.

Holt, W. V., Moore, H. D. M., North, R. D., Hartman, T. D., and Hodges, J. K. 1988. Hormonal and behavioural detection of estrus in blackbuck *(Antilope cervicapra)* and successful artificial insemination with fresh and frozen semen. *J. Reprod. Fertil.* 82:717–25.

Hunter, R. F. H. 1980. *Physiology and technology of reproduction in female domestic animals.* London: Academic Press.

Jagger, J. P., Peters, A. R., and Lamming, G. E. 1987. Hormone responses to low dose GnRH treatment in postpartum beef cows. *J. Reprod. Fertil.* 80:263–69.

Kasman, L. H., McCowan, B., and Lasley, B. L. 1985. Pregnancy detection in tapirs by direct urinary estrone sulfate analysis. *Zoo Biol.* 4:301–6.

Kassam, A. A. H., and Lasley, B. L. 1980. Estrogen excretory patterns in the Indian rhinoceros *(Rhinoceros unicornis)* determined by simplified urinary analysis. *Am. J. Vet. Res.* 42:251–56.

Kennaway, D. J., Gilmore, T. A., and Seamark, R. F. 1982. Effect of melatonin feeding on serum prolactin and gonadotropin levels and the onset of seasonal estrous cyclicity in sheep. *Endocrinology* 110:1766–72.

Kirkpatrick, J. F., Kiney, V., Bancroft, K., Shideler, S. E., and Lasley, B. L. 1991. Oestrous cycle of the North American bison *(Bison bison)* characterized by urinary pregnanediol-3-glucuronide. *J. Reprod. Fertil.* 93:541–47.

Knobil, E. 1980. The neuroendocrine control of the menstrual cycle. *Recent Prog. Horm. Res.* 36:53–88.

Knox, W. M., Miller, K. V., Collins, D. C., Bush, P. B., Kiser, T. E., and Marchington, R. L. 1992. Serum and urinary levels of reproductive hormones associated with the estrous cycle in white-tailed deer *(Odocoileus virginianus)*. *Zoo Biol.* 11:121–31.

Lasley, B. L. 1985. Methods for evaluating reproductive function in exotic species. *Adv. Vet. Sci. Comp. Med.* 30:209–28.

Lasley, B. L., and Kirkpatrick, J. F. 1991. Monitoring ovarian function in captive and free-ranging wildlife by means of urinary and faecal steroids. *J. Zoo Wildl. Med.* 22:23–31.

Lasley, B. L., Stabenfeldt, G. H., Overstreet, J. W., Hanson, F. W., Czekala, N. M., and Munro, C. 1985. Urinary hormone levels at the time of ovulation and implantation. *Fertil. Steril.* 43:861–67.

Lasley, B. L., and Wing, A. 1983. Stimulating ovarian function in exotic carnivores with pulses of GnRH. *Proceedings of the Annual Meeting of the American Association of Zoo Veterinarians*, 14–15. Philadelphia: American Association of Zoo Veterinarians.

Leyendecker, G., and Wildt, L. 1983. Induction of ovulation with chronic intermittent (pulsatile) administration of GnRH in women with hypothalamic amenorrhoea. *J. Reprod. Fertil.* 69: 397–409.

Loskutoff, N. M., Huntress, S. L., Putman, J. M., Yee, B., Bowsher, T. R., Chacon, R. R., Calle, P. P., Cambre, R. C., Rosen, G. F., Kraemer, D. C., Czekala, N. M., and Raphael, B. L. 1991. Stimulation of ovarian activity for oocyte retrieval in nonreproductive Western Lowland gorillas *(Gorilla gorilla gorilla)*. *J. Zoo Wildl. Med.* 22: 32–41.

Loskutoff, N. M., Ott, J. E., and Lasley, B. L. 1982. Urinary steroid evaluations to monitor ovarian function in exotic ungulates. I. Pregnanediol-3-glucuronide immunoreactivity in the okapi *(Okapia johnstoni)*. *Zoo Biol.* 1: 45–54.

———. 1983. Strategies for assessing ovarian function in exotic species. *J. Zoo Anim. Med.* 14: 3–12.

Loskutoff, N. M., Raphael, B. L., Nemec, L. A., Wolfe, B. A., Howard, J. G., and Kraemer, D. C. 1990. Reproductive physiology of suni *(Neotragus moschatus zuluensis)*. I. Female anatomical traits, manipulation of ovarian activity, and non-surgical embryo recovery. *J. Reprod. Fertil.* 88: 533–42.

Loskutoff, N. M., Walker, L., Ott-Joslin, J. E., Raphael, B. L., and Lasley, B. L. 1986. Urinary steroid evaluations to monitor ovarian function in exotic ungulates: II. Comparison between the giraffe *(Giraffa camelopardalis)* and the okapi *(Okapia johnstoni)*. *Zoo Biol.* 5: 331–38.

Loudon, A. S. I. 1985. Lactation and neonatal survival. *Symp. Zool. Soc. Lond.* 54: 183–207.

Martin, R. D., Seaton, B., and Lusty, J. A. 1975. Application of urinary hormone determinations in the management of gorillas. *Rep. Jersey Wildl. Pres. Trust* 12: 61–70.

Matteri, R. L., Roser, J. F., Baldwin, D. M., Lipovetsky, V., and Papkoff, H. 1987. Characterization of a monoclonal antibody which detects luteinizing hormone from diverse mammalian species. *Dom. Anim. Endocrinol.* 4 (3): 157–65.

McLeod, B. J., Haresign, W., and Lamming, G. E. 1982. The induction of ovulation and luteal function in seasonally anoestrous ewes treated with small-dose multiple injections of GnRH. *J. Reprod. Fertil.* 65: 215–21.

———. 1983. Induction of ovulation in seasonally anoestrous ewes by continuous infusion of low doses of GnRH. *J. Reprod. Fertil.* 68: 489–95.

McNeilly, A. S., Martin, R. D., Hodges, J. K., and Smutts, G. L. 1983. Blood concentrations of gonadotrophins, prolactin, and gonadal steroids in males and non-pregnant and pregnant female African elephants *(Loxodonta africana)*. *J. Reprod. Fertil.* 67: 113–20.

Metcalf, M. G., and Hunt, E. G. 1976. Calculation of estrogen excretion rates from urinary estrogen to creatinine ratios. *Clin. Biochem.* 9: 75–77.

Mitchell, W. R., Presley, S., Czekala, N. M., and Lasley, B. L. 1983. Urinary immunoreactive estrogen and pregnanediol-3-glucuronide during the normal menstrual cycle of the female lowland gorilla *(Gorilla gorilla)*. *Am. J. Primatol.* 2: 167–75.

Monfort, S. L., Dahl, K. D., Czekala, N. M., Stevens, L., Bush, M., and Wildt, D. E. 1989. Monitoring ovarian function in the giant panda *(Ailuropoda melanoleuca)* by evaluating urinary bioactive FSH and steroid metabolites. *J. Reprod. Fertil.* 85: 203–12.

Monfort, S. L., Hess, D. L., Shideler, S. E., Samuels, S. J., Hendrickx, A. G., and Lasley, B. L. 1987. Comparison of serum estradiol to urinary estrone conjugates in the rhesus macaque *(Macaca mulatta)*. *Biol. Reprod.* 37: 832–37.

Monfort, S. L., Jayaraman, S., Shideler, S. E., Lasley, B. L., and Hendrickx, A. G. 1986. Monitoring ovulation and implantation in the cynomolgus macaque *(Macaca fascicularis)* through evaluations of urinary estrone conjugates and progesterone metabolites: A technique for routine evaluation of reproductive parameters. *J. Med. Primatol.* 15: 17–26.

Monfort, S. L., Wemmer, C., Kepler, T. H., Bush, M., Brown, J. L., and Wildt, D. E. 1990. Monitoring ovarian function and pregnancy in Eld's deer *(Cervus eldi thamin)* by evaluating urinary steroid metabolite secretion. *J. Reprod. Fertil.* 88: 271–81.

Mostl, E., Choi, H. S., Wurm, W., Ismail, M. N., and Bamberg, E. 1984. Pregnancy diagnosis in cows and heifers by determination of oestradiol-17 α in feces. *Br. Vet. J.* 140: 287–91.

Niemüller, C. A., Shaw, H. J., and Hodges, J. K. 1993. Noninvasive monitoring of ovarian function in Asian elephants *(Elephas maximus)* by measurement of urinary 5β-pregnantriol. *J. Reprod. Fertil.* 99: 617–25.

———. 1993. Monitoring pregnancy in the Asian elephant *(Elephas maximus)* by urinary and plasma progestin analysis. *J. Reprod. Fertil.* Abs. Ser. 11, no. 103.

Oerke, A.-K., Einspanier, A., and Hodges, J. K. 1995. Detection of pregnancy and monitoring patterns of uterine and fetal growth in the marmoset monkey *(Callithrix jacchus)* by real-time ultrasonography. *Am. J. Primatol.* 36: 1–13.

Paul-Murphy, J., Tell, L. A., Bravo, W., Fowler, M. E., and Lasley, B. L. 1991. Urinary steroid evaluations to monitor ovarian function in exotic ungulates: VIII. Correspondence of urinary and plasma steroids in the llama *(Lama glama)* during nonconceptive and conceptive cycles. *Zoo Biol.* 10: 225–36.

Perez, L., Czekala, N. M., Weisenseel, A., and Lasley, B. L. 1988. Excretion of radiolabeled estradiol metabolites in the slow loris *(Nycticebus coucang)*. *Am. J. Primatol.* 16: 321–30.

Phillips, J. A., Alexander, N., Karesh, B., Millar, R., and Lasley, B. L. 1985. Stimulating male sexual behaviour with repetitive pulses of GnRH in female green iguanas *(Iguana iguana)*. *J. Exp. Zool.* 234: 481–84.

Plotka, E. D., Seal, U. S., Zarembka, F. R., Simmons, L. G., Teare, A., Phillips, L. G., Hinshaw, K. C., and Wood, D. G. 1988. Ovarian function in the elephant: Luteinizing hormone and progesterone cycles in African and Asian elephants. *Biol. Reprod.* 38: 309–14.

Poole, J. H., Kasman, L. H., Ramsay, E. C., and Lasley, B. L. 1984. Musth and urinary testosterone concentrations in the African elephant *(Loxodonta africana)* *J. Reprod. Fertil.* 70: 255–60.

Ramsay, E. C., Kasman, L. H., and Lasley, B. L. 1987. Urinary steroid evaluations to monitor ovarian function in exotic ungulates: V. Estrogen and pregnanediol-3-glucuronide excretion in the black rhinoceros *(Diceros bicornis)*. *Zoo Biol.* 6: 275–82.

Riley, G. M., Peters, A. R., and Lamming, G. E. 1981. Induction of pulsatile LH release, FSH release, and ovulation in postpartum beef cows by repeated small doses of GnRH. *J. Reprod. Fertil.* 63: 559–65.

Risler, L., Wasser, S. K., and Sackett, G. P. 1987. Measurement of excreted steroids in *Macaca nemestrina*. *Am. J. Primatol.* 12: 91–100.

Roche, J. F. 1976. Fertility in cows after treatment with a prostaglandin analogue with or without progesterone. *J. Reprod. Fertil.* 46: 341–45.

Roser, J. F., and Lofstedt, R. M. 1989. Urinary and CG patterns in the mare during pregnancy. *Theriogenology* 32: 607–22.

Rowlands, I. W., and Sadleir, R. M. F. S. 1968. Induction of ovulation in the lion, *Panthera leo*. *J. Reprod. Fertil.* 16: 105–11.

Safar-Hermann, N., Ismail, M. N., Choi, H. S., Mostl, E., and Bamberg, E. 1987. Pregnancy diagnosis in zoo animals by estrogen determination in feces. *Zoo Biol.* 6: 189–93.

Schwarzenberger, F., Francke, R., and Göltenboth, R. 1993. Concentrations of faecal immunoreactive progestagen metabolites during the oestrous cycle and pregnancy in the black rhinoceros (*Diceros bicornis michaeli*) *J. Reprod. Fert.* 98:285–91.

Shideler, S. E., Czekala, N. M., Benirschke, K., and Lasley, B. L. 1983a. Urinary estrogens during pregnancy of the ruffed lemur (*Lemur variegatus*). *Biol. Reprod.* 28:263–69.

Shideler, S. E., Czekala, N. M., Kasman, L. H., Lindburg, D. G., and Lasley, B. L. 1983b. Monitoring ovulation and implantation in the lion-tailed macaque *(Macaca silenus)* through urinary estrone conjugate evaluations. *Biol. Reprod.* 29:905–11.

Shideler, S. E., and Lasley, B. L. 1982. A comparison of primate ovarian cycles. *Am. J. Primatol.* 1 (Suppl.): 171–80.

Shideler, S. E., Mitchell, W. R., Lindburg, D. G., and Lasley, B. L. 1985. Monitoring luteal function in the lion-tailed macaque *(Macaca silenus)* through measurement of urinary progesterone metabolites. *Zoo Biol.* 4:65–73.

Shideler, S. E., Savage, A., Ortuno, A. M., Moorman, E. A., and Lasley, B. L. 1994. Monitoring female reproductive function by measurement of fecal estrogen and progesterone metabolites in the white-faced saki (*Pithecia pithecia*). *Am. J. Primatol.* 32: 95–108.

Shideler, S. E., Shackleton, C. H. L., Moran, F. M., Stauffer, P., Lohstroh, P. N., and Lasley, B. L. 1993. Enzyme immunoassays for ovarian steroid metabolites in the urine of *Macaca fascicularis. J. Med. Primatol.* 22:301–12.

Shille, V. M., Wing, A. E., Lasley, B. L., and Banks, J. A. 1985. Excretion of radiolabeled estradiol in the cat (*Felis catus*, L.): A preliminary report. *Zoo Biol.* 3:201–9.

Stavy, M., Gilbert, D., and Martin, R. D. 1979. Routine determination of sex in monomorphic bird species using fecal steroid analysis. *Int. Zoo Yrbk.* 19:209–14.

Stover, J., Evans, J., and Dolensek, E. P. 1981. Interspecies embryo transfer from the Gaur to domestic Holstein. *Proceedings of the Annual Meeting of the American Association of Zoo Veterinarians,* 122–24. Philadelphia: American Association of Zoo Veterinarians.

Summers, P. M., Shepherd, A. M., Hodges, J. K., Kydd, J., Boyle, M. S., and Allen, W. R. 1987a. Successful transfer of the embryos of Przewalski's horses *(Equus przewalskii)* and Grant zebras *(Equus burchelli)* to domestic mares *(Equus caballus). J. Reprod. Fertil.* 80:13–20.

Summers, P. M., Shepherd, A. M., Taylor, C. T., and Hearn, J. P. 1987b. The effects of cryopreservation and transfer on embryonic development in the common marmoset, *Callithrix jacchus. J. Reprod. Fertil.* 79:241–50.

Summers, P. M., Wennink, C. J., and Hodges, J. K. 1985. Cloprostenol-induced luteolysis on the marmoset monkey, *Callithrix jacchus. J. Reprod. Fertil.* 73:133–38.

Tarantal, A. F., and Hendrickx, A. G. 1988. Use of ultrasound for early pregnancy detection in the rhesus and cynomolgus ma-

caques *(Macaca mulatta* and *Macaca fascicularis). J. Med. Primatol.* 17:105–12.

———. 1989. The use of ultrasonography for evaluating pregnancy in macaques. In *Non-human primates: Developmental biology and toxicology,* ed. D. Neubert, H. J. Merker, and A. G. Hendrickx, 91–100. Berlin: Ueberreuter Wissenschaft.

Taussky, H. H. 1954. A microcoloruinetric determination of creatinine in urine by the Jaffe reaction. *J. Biol. Chem.* 208:853–61.

Walker, L. A., Czekala, N. M., Cornell, L. H., Joseph, B. E., Dahl, K. D., and Lasley, B. L. 1987. Analysis of the ovarian cycle and pregnancy of the killer whale by urinary hormone measurement. *Biol. Reprod.* 36, suppl. 1., abs. 250.

Wasser, S. K., Monfort, S. L., and Wildt, D. E. 1991. Rapid extraction of faecal steroids for measuring reproductive cyclicity and early pregnancy in free-ranging yellow baboons (*Papio cynocephalus cynocephalus). J. Reprod. Fertil.* 92:415–23.

Wasser, S. K., Risler, L., and Steiner, R. A. 1988. Excreted steroids in primate feces over the menstrual cycle and pregnancy. *Biol. Reprod.* 39:862–72.

Wildt, D. E. 1980. Laparoscopy in the dog and cat. In *Animal laparoscopy,* ed. R. M. Harrison and D. E. Wildt, 31–72. Baltimore: Williams and Wilkins.

Wildt, D. E., Bush, M., Whitlock, B., and Seager, S. W. J. 1978. Laparoscopy: A method for direct examination of internal organs in zoo veterinary medicine and research. *Int. Zoo Yrbk.* 18: 194–97.

Wildt, D. E., Kinney, G. M., and Seager, S. W. J. 1977. Laparoscopy for direct observation of internal organs of the domestic cat and dog. *Am. J. Vet. Res.* 38:1429–32.

———. 1978. Gonadotropin induced reproductive cyclicity in the domestic cat. *Lab. Anim. Sci.* 28:301–7.

Wildt, D. E., Platz, C. C., Chakraborty, P. K., and Seager, S. W. J. 1979. Estrus and ovarian activity in a female jaguar *(Panthera onca). J. Reprod. Fertil.* 56:555–58.

Wildt, D. E., Platz, C. C., Seager, S. W. J., and Bush, M. 1981. Induction of ovarian activity in the cheetah (*Acinonyx jubatus). Biol. Reprod.* 24:217–22.

Wildt, D. E., and Seager, S. W. J. 1979. Laparoscopic determination of ovarian and uterine morphology during the reproductive cycle of the cat. In *Current therapy in theriogenology,* ed. D. Horrow, 38–72. Philadelphia: W. B. Saunders.

Williams, R. F., and Hodgen, G. D. 1980. Disparate effects of human chorionic gonadotrophin during the late follicular phase in monkeys: Normal ovulation, follicular atresia, ovarian acyclicity, and hypersecretion of follicle-stimulating hormone. *Fertil. Steril.* 33:64–71.

Ziegler, T. E., Bridson, W. E., Snowdon, C. T., and Eman, S. 1987. Urinary gonadotropin and estrogen excretion during the postpartum estrus, conception, and pregnancy in the cotton-top tamarin. *Am. J. Primatol.* 12:127–40.

39

Male Reproduction: Assessment, Management, and Control of Fertility

David E. Wildt

An understanding of the male's contribution to reproductive performance is critical for optimizing captive propagation of wildlife species. In domestic animals and humans, the study of the physiology of male reproduction (andrology) has been facilitated by an arsenal of techniques ranging from simple microscopic assessments of sperm concentration to integrated computerized systems for measuring sperm velocity and linearity. A general data base has been established for interrelating hypothalamic-pituitary-testicular function in the normal male of many common species. In contrast, understanding the reproductively abnormal or subfertile male has been more challenging and historically less successful because the etiology of infertility often is obscure. In domestic livestock and laboratory animals, eliminating or culling suspect males usually is more economical than attempting to improve reproductive performance therapeutically. Consequently, most of our information on theoretical and applied techniques for studying male reproduction originates from human clinical investigations. This data base, although largely empirical, provides a massive resource of ideas for generating strategies to study reproductive processes in males of various wildlife species.

The scientific literature detailing approaches for manipulating male reproductive activity in zoo mammals is extremely limited. Most efforts have focused on evaluations of semen from a few animals of a selected species or rudimentary attempts to establish baseline concentrations of circulating hormones, predominantly testosterone and luteinizing hormone (LH). There is an urgent need to expand such studies for two major reasons. First, male infertility contributes significantly to reproductive failure in many zoo-maintained species. An understanding of the reproductive characteristics of the "normal" male of any given species is a prerequisite for identifying and attempting to treat subfertile or suspect individuals. Second, assisted reproductive technology, including artificial insemination, embryo transfer, in vitro fertilization, and embryo/gamete cryopreserva-

tion, has considerable potential for propagating as well as improving the genetic diversity of captive wildlife populations (Wildt 1989a, 1989b, 1990; Wildt et al. 1992). The success of all of these approaches is dependent on an understanding of male physiology as well as on the ability to collect, evaluate, and sustain the viability of spermatozoa.

This chapter details the factors known to influence male reproduction and describes strategies for assessing and manipulating male reproductive activity. Although some of the approaches described have been applied to captive wildlife, many originate from human and domestic animal studies. There is no doubt that mammals (even those closely related taxonomically) exhibit species-specific and even population-specific reproductive and endocrine norms. Therefore, a successful approach to studying or manipulating male fertility in one species may require modification or may fail completely in another species. Within reason, however, these evaluative and therapeutic concepts should have valid, generalized application to many zoo animals.

THE CONTROL OF MALE REPRODUCTIVE FUNCTION

An accurate andrologic evaluation requires an understanding of the hypothalamic-pituitary-testicular axis (Amann 1986). The two basic functions of the testes are production of spermatozoa and secretion of hormones; these functions are segregated anatomically within the testes. The interstitial or Leydig cells (a minor contributor to overall testicular mass) are under the influence of the pituitary hormone LH and produce testosterone, estradiol, and other hormones. The majority (usually 90%) of the testis mass consists of seminiferous tubules, the site of spermatogenesis. Within the seminiferous tubules, diffuse Sertoli cells extend from the lamina propria of the tubule to the tubular lumen. Closely adjacent to the Sertoli cells, spermatogonia divide by mitosis and then meiosis to form primary and then secondary spermatocytes before eventually forming spermatids. The Sertoli cells contain the binding sites for another pituitary hormone, follicle-stimulating hormone (FSH), and play a pivotal role in hormonal control of spermatogenesis, providing the microenvironment optimal for normal germ cell development. Actual spermatogenesis is controlled by FSH and testosterone acting directly on the seminiferous tubular epithelium.

The control of testicular function is a complex feedback system involving the hypothalamus (which secretes gonadotropin-releasing hormone, GnRH), the pituitary (which releases FSH and LH, collectively known as gonadotropins), and the testes themselves. GnRH is released from the hypothalamus in discrete pulses, inducing the pituitary to secrete both FSH and LH. LH production is immediate and pulsatile (in response to GnRH stimulation), while FSH release is more attenuated, with few marked fluctuations in blood concentrations. Circulating gonadal steroids, primarily testosterone but also estradiol, regulate FSH and LH by influencing the amount of GnRH secreted as well as the sensitivity of the pituitary cells to GnRH. Therefore, if testicular activity wanes, the resulting depressed levels of gonadal steroids exert less negative feedback on the hypothalamus and pituitary, allowing greater GnRH, FSH, and LH secretion, thereby increasing both gonadal steroid production and spermatogenesis. A testis-secreted glycoprotein known as inhibin appears to suppress pituitary FSH release. Inhibin's effect has been demonstrated in a variety of species (Scott and Burger 1981; Wickings, Marshall, and Nieschlag 1986), but its precise mechanism of action remains unknown. The classic endocrine concept of a dual feedback control of FSH by steroids and inhibin has been challenged by suggestions that the α-subunit of inhibin may exert FSH-inhibitory effects whereas the ß-subunit may be stimulatory. Therefore, inhibin may regulate FSH biosynthesis by a "push-pull" mechanism (Tsonis and Sharpe 1986; Vale et al. 1986).

This feedback system is not a closed loop. Many external events, including olfactory, auditory, and visual signals, nutrition, psychic stress, and seasonality, influence male reproduction. Although there are exceptions, most of these external events exert their influence at the level of the hypothalamus. Because the reproductive patterns of wild mammals are susceptible to environmental conditions, it is essential that factors such as captivity stress and alterations in photoperiod be considered in securing an accurate andrologic evaluation.

THE LIMITATIONS OF MALE FERTILITY ASSESSMENT

In assessing the reproductive competence of a male of any species, the criteria for determining that fertility or infertility exists are crucial. Standard semen characteristics alone are an indirect measure of sperm function and do not provide a reliably predictive index of fertility. A more accurate and consistent approach involves a multifactorial analysis not only of seminal traits but also of reproductive history and physical health, as well as a battery of laboratory tests ranging from blood concentrations of hormones to the functional capacity of sperm in vitro. A major determinant of reproductive soundness is the comparative similarity of the suspect male to fertile conspecifics of about the same age maintained in a comparable environment. Because so few baseline data are available, this criterion is difficult to apply to wildlife species. *A single evaluation of an individual animal with no definitive reproductive history is of limited value* unless compared with data from a large normal population. A proven breeder male that produces an ejaculate containing high numbers of motile sperm with few abnormal forms generally can be categorized as a satisfactory potential breeder. In contrast, *a single azoospermic (no living sperm) or oligospermic (few sperm) ejaculate from a proven or unproven male does not warrant a diagnosis of infertility.*

EVALUATION OF THE MALE

History and Physical Examination

Animal history and general physical health can provide direction for subsequent evaluation or therapy. Collection of information on (1) age, (2) reproductive seasonality, (3) disease, illness, or injury, (4) the captive environment, (5) number of pregnancies and offspring produced, (6) estimates of libido, (7) reproductive performance of close relatives, and (8) records of exposure to toxic agents such as pesticides or heavy metals is an important first step in the assessment process. This information should be studied in the context of the spermatogenic cycle, since the sperm present in the epididymis on any given day began development many days earlier. Consequently, many testicular insults exert no effect on semen quality until weeks later. Retrospectively identifying the precise timing of the trauma in a subfertile male or, conversely, estimating the onset of subfertility from a known traumatic event is difficult, in part because of variations in the intensity of the insult as well as variations among individuals in their ability to compensate for disease or injury. Additionally, the duration of the seminiferous epithelial cycle, which dictates the number of sperm produced per day, is species-specific (Ortavant, Courot, and Hocherean de Reviers 1977) and largely unknown for most nondomestic species.

A detailed physical examination with particular attention to the genitalia may reveal the cause of infertility. Reproductive health includes sound structural conformation, particularly of the hind legs, which usually support the male's weight during copulation. Testicular integrity, size, and tonicity are the single most important elements in the physical examination. Displacing or manipulating each testis within the scrotal sac can reveal the presence of adhesions. Length and width measures of each testis (using laboratory calipers) can be converted to testicular volume with the formula $V = 0.524 \times L \times W^2$, where V = volume (cm³), L = length (cm), and W = width (cm) (Howard et al. 1983). Alternatively, in species with a pendulous scrotum, scrotal circumference (SC) can be determined by looping a flexible tape around the greatest diameter of the scrotal contents (Ott 1986). Testicular volume correlates well with sperm production and fertility in humans (Sherins and Howards 1985). In domestic bulls SC is highly heritable, providing a predictive index of sperm production and testicular pathology and a more accurate estimator of puberty than either age or body weight (Larsen 1986; Ott 1986). An SC value more than one standard deviation below the population mean suggests a deficiency in testicular mass, whereas at two standard deviations below the mean a diagnosis of severe testicular hypoplasia is indicated (Larsen 1986).

Based on the available mammalian data, testicular size appears to fluctuate markedly in most seasonal breeders (see Lincoln 1981 for review), a factor that must be considered in the timing of fertility examinations. For example, maximal testicular volume in European ferrets, *Mustela putorius*, and black-footed ferrets, *Mustela nigripes*, appears to be sustained for only 6 to 12 weeks during the seasonal estrous period of the female (Neal et al. 1977). During the breeding season, testicular volume in rhesus macaques, *Macaca mulatta,* is double that observed during the inactive season (Wickings, Marshall, and Nieschlag 1986). In a circannual study of red deer, *Cervus elaphus*, the male with the greatest SC value also produced the highest-quality ejaculate when compared with herdmates (Haigh et al. 1984). In other species, changes in testicular volume may be subtle or the results difficult to interpret. An evaluation of twenty-one species of wild felids indicated no statistical correlation between combined testicular volume and electroejaculate quality among individual fertile males within each species (J. G. Howard and D. E. Wildt, unpub.). In contrast, when electroejaculate quality appeared to be compromised by a loss of genetic diversity in a geographically isolated population of East African lions, *Panthera leo*, a concomitant depression in testicular volume was observed (Wildt et al. 1987a). From a diagnostic perspective, males with hypoplastic (small) or extremely flaccid testes (evaluated during periods of seasonal female sexual activity) likely are experiencing poor gonadal function. Because Leydig cell activity is almost always preserved in cases of testicular atrophy, libido or virilization characteristics are rarely affected (Sherins and Howards 1985).

Unilateral cryptorchidism (a single testis retained in the abdominal cavity) has been reported in a variety of mammals, including captive maned wolves, *Chrysocyon brachyurus* (M. Rodden, pers. comm.), and free-ranging Florida panthers, *Felis concolor coryi* (Miller et al. 1990; Barone et al. 1994). Bilateral cryptorchidism, which invariably causes sterility, is less common than the unilateral condition. Males with a single descended testicle frequently mature normally in body conformation and sexual behavior. In most species, one scrotal testis is adequate for fertility, although men with unilateral cryptorchidism have higher than normal rates of infertility (Lipshultz 1976). Hormonal or surgical treatment to remedy cryptorchidism is not recommended due to the high heritability of the condition and, for this reason, *cryptorchid males should not be used* for breeding.

In some species (particularly those with a pendulous scrotal sac), the caput (head), corpus (body), and cauda (tail) regions of the epididymides can be palpated. Segmental aplasia, a developmental defect, can cause azoospermia with normal ejaculatory reflexes. Hyperplasia of the epididymis caused by inflammation, fibrosis, tumors, abscesses, or sperm granulomas essentially occludes sperm outflow from the testes, severely depressing fertility. No treatment is available.

The anatomy of some species allows direct observation or palpation of the penis and adjacent external genitalia. Abnormal development of the penis and associated preputial sheath can result in a persistent frenulum (or adhesion), a genetic defect preventing normal vaginal penetration. This abnormality has been observed in the Florida panther (M. E. Roelke, pers. comm.). Penile papillofibromatas or hematomas likewise can interfere with copulation. Phimosis is an abnormal constriction of the sheath inhibiting penile extrusion. Although sometimes induced by physical trauma, phimosis, like persistent frenulum, usually has genetic origins, suggesting that males with these conditions should not be used for breeding.

In larger species, rectal palpation provides an approach for indirect examination of the accessory glands and other tissues associated with the male reproductive tract. Abnormalities of the ampullae of the ductus deferens, vesicular glands, and prostate often have a chronic inflammatory etiology and can result in varying degrees of infertility.

Endocrine Diagnostic Procedures

Radioimmunoassay (RIA) technology permits the analysis of many aspects of endocrine function. Commercially available RIA kits allow reasonably accurate measurement of circulating steroids, including testosterone, estradiol, progesterone, and cortisol. In contrast, because of species-specific hormonal moieties, measurement of protein hormones (i.e., gonadotropins) is more difficult, requiring highly technical (and often heterologous) systems developed through laborious validation procedures. Several zoological parks have established referral laboratories, thereby providing a centralized facility to serve many zoos. Research continues into novel evaluative approaches, including the enzyme-linked immunosorbent assay (ELISA), enzyme immunoassays (EIA), and fluorescence immunoassays (FIA), methods that eventually will be inexpensive and easily conducted in most zoos.

Hormonal analysis of body fluids or waste products can offer a wealth of information on endocrine status. The evaluation of blood usually is an opportunistic strategy employed at the time of a general physical or reproductive evaluation. Monitoring of hormonal metabolites in urine or feces is a relatively new approach and ensures that endocrine data are uncompromised by restraint or anesthesia stress. This approach, which has been used largely in the monitoring of females (Monfort et al. 1990; see Lasley and Kirkpatrick 1991 for review), has great potential for males of a wide range of wildlife species, primarily because the technology is noninvasive and atraumatic. Although there are few data available on urinary or fecal hormone metabolites in males of any species, there is no doubt that this approach now is the method of choice for assessing endocrine function in zoo and free-living animals. Regardless of the approach used, it is imperative that serial blood, urine, or fecal aliquots be evaluated, as a single sample is of little or no use in assessing endocrine condition. Studies in both domestic and nondomestic species have confirmed that steroid and protein hormone secretion is a dynamic process;

circulating and excreted concentrations can vary markedly over days, hours, or even minutes. Little effort has been made to correlate the endocrine status of wild species with reproductive capacity; this field deserves additional attention. In the overall analysis of male fertility potential, assessing endocrine condition alone is only moderately informative. Endocrine values appear more valuable when studied in the context of ejaculate characteristics or when used to establish baseline physiological norms for a particular species.

Testosterone The assay of testosterone is useful for identifying male sexual maturity (puberty), pituitary gonadotropin deficiency, and profound dysfunction in Leydig cell activity. There are many ways in which testosterone measurements are useful for studying wild mammals. Circulating testosterone has been found to (1) be greater in territorial than nonterritorial free-ranging impala, *Aepyceros melampus* (Illius et al. 1983); (2) be elevated significantly in male elephants, *Elephas maximus,* exhibiting musth (Jainudeen, Katongole, and Short 1972); (3) correlate with testicular size in wild blesbok, *Damaliscus dorcas* (Illius et al. 1983); (4) be similar between free-ranging and zoo-maintained cheetahs, *Acinonyx jubatus* (Wildt et al. 1987b); (5) correlate with puberty in the tiger, *Panthera tigris* (Wildt et al. 1987c); (6) be similar in male and female free-ranging spotted hyenas, *Crocuta crocuta* (Racey and Skinner 1979; Frank, Smith, and Davidson 1985; Lindeque, Skinner, and Millar 1986); (7) vary markedly among taxonomically related felids (Wildt et al. 1988; Brown et al. 1989); and (8) vary with season in many species (Resko 1967; Miller and Glover 1973; Whitehead and McEwan 1973; McMillin et al. 1974, 1976; Robinson et al. 1975; West and Nordan 1976; Mirarchi et al. 1978; Lincoln and Kay 1979; Slob, Ocms, and Ureeburg 1979; Stokkan, Hove, and Carr 1980; Mossing and Damber 1981; Bubenik et al. 1982; Schams and Barth 1982; Sempere and Lacroix 1982; Haigh et al. 1984; Brown et al. 1991b, 1991c; Monfort et al. 1993a, 1993b).

Infertility, hypofunction of the Leydig cells, and severely depressed or nonexistent libido are all associated with abnormally low testosterone production. Aberrantly high circulating testosterone concentrations can indicate the presence of an interstitial cell tumor. It has been possible to correlate circulating testosterone with semen quality in domestic animals, humans, cheetahs, lions, and gorillas, *Gorilla gorilla,* but males with higher testosterone concentrations do not necessarily produce higher-quality ejaculates (Lincoln 1979; Malak and Thibier 1982; Resko 1982; Gould 1983; Wildt et al. 1984; Noci et al. 1985b; Brown et al. 1991a). However, when multiple testosterone values are measured in blood over time among and within even closely related species, interesting comparative and evolutionary differences are revealed. For example, baseline testosterone concentrations within the Felidae, although relatively consistent within a given species, vary significantly among species and usually are unrelated to most individual seminal quality characteristics (Wildt et al. 1987b, 1988; Brown et al. 1991a). One exception is a possible inverse relationship between chronically depressed testosterone levels and increased production of pleiomorphic or structurally abnormal spermatozoa. Frequently, feline species, subspecies, or populations that produce comparatively low circulating testosterone concentrations also ejaculate comparatively high numbers of malformed sperm (Wildt et al. 1988). At present, the most convincing argument that there is an indirect relationship between testosterone and sperm pleiomorphisms comes from the work of Howard et al. (1990, 1993; Howard, Bush, and Wildt 1991) on the domestic cat. These investigators determined that certain cats classified as teratospermic (producing more than 60% abnormal sperm) consistently produce lower circulating testosterone levels than their normospermic counterparts. Furthermore, compared with sperm from the latter "normal" males, sperm from the teratospermic males are less capable of penetrating zona-intact domestic cat oocytes in an in vitro fertilization system.

Baseline testosterone in many species, including primates and African elephants, *Loxodonta africana,* is secreted on a diurnal schedule (Resko 1982; Gould 1983; Howard et al. 1984; see Wickings, Marshall, and Nieschlag 1986 for review). Therefore, for comparative evaluations among individuals, all blood samples should be taken at a similar time of day. Testosterone can be evaluated by challenging the male with commercially available synthetic GnRH. After induction of anesthesia, blood samples are collected before and then at 15–30-minute intervals (for 2–3 hours) after an intravenous or intramuscular injection of 25–100 μg GnRH. In normal males, GnRH stimulates pituitary LH release, causing assayable increases in serum testosterone levels within 15–90 minutes. A failure of testosterone levels to rise indicates a pituitary or Leydig cell abnormality. GnRH has been shown to induce acute elevations in serum testosterone in the male cheetah, lion, leopard, *Panthera pardus,* tiger, clouded leopard, *Neofelis nebulosa,* spotted hyena, African elephant, impala, Cape buffalo, *Syncerus caffer,* and a variety of nonhuman primates (Wildt et al. 1983b, 1986a, 1987c; Blank 1986; Lindeque et al. 1986; Wickings, Marshall, and Nieschlag 1986; Brown et al. 1988, 1989, 1991a, 1991b, 1991c). An alternative and more direct way of measuring testicular testosterone secretion involves the injection of human chorionic gonadotropin (hCG) followed by serial evaluations of blood androgens; hCG stimulation testing has been conducted in free-living Cape buffalo and impala (Brown et al. 1991b, 1991c). It has been suggested that testicular steroidogenesis may be abnormal in certain species for up to 10 days after hCG treatment (Amann 1986). For this reason, and because it is not antigenic, GnRH may be preferable to hCG for challenging testosterone production.

FSH and LH In human males, some laboratory animals, and the gorilla, elevated serum FSH assists in identifying individuals with isolated germ cell depletion or complete germinal aplasia (Gould and Kling 1982; Freischem et al. 1984; Stanwell-Smith et al. 1985). Few comparable studies have been conducted in other species because historically there has been little interest in FSH. However, FSH heterologous radioimmunoassays have been developed recently for the leopard (Brown et al. 1988, 1989), lion (Brown et al. 1991a), leopard cat, *Felis bengalensis* (Howard and Wildt 1990), Cape buffalo (Brown et al. 1991b), impala (Brown et al. 1991c), and Eld's deer, *Cervus eldii* (Monfort et al. 1993b). Although primarily useful for establishing endocrine norms for a specific species or population, these immunologic FSH assessments have not been as informative as LH measured by the same approaches. This has been the general trend in domestic and laboratory animals, and, in part, is related to the "noisy" or extremely dynamic secretory nature of this particular hormone from the pituitary. There are indications that "bioactive" FSH assays (like the in vitro granulosa cell aromatase bioassay, or GAB) may provide a more realistic and accurate picture of physiological FSH patterns in wildlife species (Dahl et al. 1987; S. L. Monfort and D. E. Wildt, unpub.). The long-term usefulness of these labor-intensive bioassays for understanding pituitary function remains to be proven.

Studies relating circulating LH to testicular exocrine function have been limited and often equivocal. Most results suggest that LH levels are not related to testicular size or activity; however, there are exceptions. In studies of reproductive seasonality in the ram, testicular size and spermatogenesis have been correlated positively with LH as well as FSH levels (Courot and Ortavant 1981). In selected studies in human males, LH concentrations were greater in cases of oligo- or azoospermia than in normospermic men (Christiansen 1975; Fossati et al. 1979; Vasquez et al. 1986). Likewise, peripheral concentrations of LH were twice as high in azoospermic cheetahs as in their normal counterparts (Wildt et al. 1984).

The usefulness of LH in andrologic assessments is confounded by the pulsatile secretory pattern characteristic of the hormone (reported in monkeys, wild hoofstock, and felids as well as most domestic and laboratory animals), which varies markedly from species to species (Knobil 1974; Lincoln and Kay 1979; Wickings, Marshall, and Nieschlag 1986; Brown et al. 1988, 1989, 1991a, 1991b). Even blood sampling as frequent as every 15 minutes may miss a low-amplitude LH pulse. It also is possible that anesthetics used during reproductive-endocrine evaluations compromise hypothalamic-pituitary activity, significantly altering or impairing normal FSH/LH patterns. The limited data from wildlife species tend to support both possibilities. LH profiles derived from blood samples taken at 15-minute intervals from anesthetized cheetahs, lions, tigers, leopards, clouded leopards, and African elephants show little or no evidence of an episodic release pattern (Wildt et al. 1984, 1986a, 1987a, 1987b, 1988). However, when the sampling frequency is increased in male tigers, leopards, lions, Cape buffalo, and impala to once every 5–10 minutes for 2–3 hours, distinct LH pulses are evident in some males (Brown et al. 1988, 1989, 1991a, 1991b, 1991c). The failure of other males to exhibit a pulsatile pattern suggests that the sampling should be even more frequent or that the hypothalamic-pituitary axis in certain individuals is influenced by the anesthetic event. Assessing the latter possibility should be a high research priority. This, of course, would require obtaining serial blood samples from unanesthetized, fully conscious individuals. Although such practices would be dangerous to animal handlers, certain species or individuals may be amenable to such manipulations. For example, Monfort and associates trained adult Eld's deer males to

tolerate a jugular cannula device, which allowed blood samples to be collected every 10 minutes for 8 consecutive hours, even during periods of rut (Monfort et al. 1993a, 1993b).

The assay of circulating FSH and LH after injection of GnRH is a classic approach to evaluating pituitary function. Gonadotropin profiles from serial blood samples taken before and after an exogenous GnRH challenge (similar to testing for testosterone responsiveness) can effectively diagnose pituitary anomalies. GnRH stimulates a sharp rise and fall in serum LH in males from a wide variety of species, including the cheetah, tiger, leopard, clouded leopard, African elephant, lion, Cape buffalo, impala, Eld's deer, and various nonhuman primates (Wildt et al. 1983b, 1986a, 1987c; see Wickings, Marshall, and Nieschlag 1986 for review; Brown et al. 1988, 1989, 1991a, 1991b, 1991c; Monfort et al. 1993b; D. E. Wildt, M. Bush, and J. G. Howard, unpub.). If serum LH fails to rise within 60 minutes of a 25–100 μg injection of GnRH, then a pituitary anomaly may be suspected.

Estrogens The monitoring of blood or urinary estrogen levels may be of value in diagnosing certain pathological conditions, including Sertoli cell tumors or seminomas. Estradiol-17ß concentrations in male dogs affected with this neoplasm often are 2–5 times greater than normal (Nachreiner 1986). However, not all Sertoli cell tumors are estrogenic, and others secrete estrogens other than estradiol-17ß.

Glucocorticoid Hormones Measuring adrenal glucocorticoid or "stress" hormones may be a helpful indirect approach for assessing male reproductive ability. Some wildlife species, including certain felids and the gorilla, produce high proportions of pleiomorphic spermatozoa in the ejaculate. It is possible that hyperadrenal activity, as determined by elevated glucocorticoid concentrations, is common in stressed wildlife and could influence male reproductive characteristics. Increased adrenal function has been shown to have detrimental effects on hypothalamic, pituitary, and gonadal function in humans and a variety of domestic species (see Wildt et al. 1984 for review). At least three species of felids (clouded leopard, leopard, puma, *Felis concolor*) ejaculate relatively high proportions of structurally defective spermatozoa in the presence of extraordinarily elevated circulating concentrations of cortisol, a major glucocorticoid (Wildt et al. 1986a, 1986b, 1988; Miller et al. 1990). During anesthesia of leopards, high basal levels of cortisol are accompanied by a significant 2-hour decline in circulating testosterone, a finding not evident in the lion, tiger, puma, or cheetah (Wildt et al. 1984, 1987c, 1988; Brown et al. 1991a).

Further endocrine studies are warranted to determine whether environmental factors or the stresses associated with manipulations (i.e., anesthesia, electroejaculation) significantly influence male reproductive performance. One confirmatory approach is to measure circulating cortisol concentrations in males during a manipulatory episode and then contrast this profile with one collected after an exogenous bolus of synthetic adrenocorticotropic hormone (ACTH). The synthetic hormone mimics the pituitary's naturally produced ACTH and acts directly to provoke adrenal gland release of glucocorticoids. Given that the ACTH dose is adequate, maximal adrenal responsiveness can be quantified over time and compared with the manipulatory event. For example, in wildebeests, *Connochaetes taurinus*, greater kudu, *Tragelaphus strepsiceros*, and lions, ACTH challenge tests have been used to demonstrate that electroejaculation fails to elicit an adrenal response even close to the marked rise measured after exogenous ACTH (Schiewe et al. 1991; J. L. Brown, D. E. Wildt, and M. Bush, unpub.). These investigators have used such evidence to support their assertion that electroejaculation is a safe manipulatory technique.

Thyroid Hormones The effect of thyroid activity on male reproductive function is controversial. Hyperthyroidism, as deduced by serum assays of thyroxine and triiodothyronine, can influence spermatogenesis adversely through arrested testicular growth caused by decreases in LH pulsatility (Chandrasekhar et al. 1985). Hypothyroidism appears unrelated to infertility in human males (Sherins and Howards 1985). In animals, decreased thyroid function tends to be expressed as general lethargy and loss of libido rather than influencing specific seminal characteristics (Chandrasekhar et al. 1985). In one report, approximately 45% of subfertile male dogs had depressed serum levels of thyroid hormones (Nachreiner 1986). However, definitive studies demonstrating that thyroid hormone supplementation can improve male fertility have not been done, and in general, it appears that most hypothyroid males continue to reproduce.

INFERTILITY AS RELATED TO MALE REPRODUCTIVE BEHAVIOR

Reproductive performance can be compromised not only by anomalies in the hypothalamic-pituitary-gonadal axis, but also by behavioral abnormalities that prevent the male from copulating with the female. Such defects may have a hormonal origin, although the task of isolating the endocrine components of abnormal male sexual behavior is formidable. Evidence exists that testosterone profiles vary among captive animal populations that differ in their patterns of copulatory behavior. Rhesus macaques recently collected from the wild and demonstrating vigorous reproductive behavior have more consistent diurnal fluctuations in circulating testosterone than age-matched, laboratory-reared males (Resko 1982). Additionally, old rhesus males that refuse to copulate have a greater proportion of testosterone bound to plasma proteins than do sexually active males (Resko 1982). These data suggest that the sexual behavior of the male is associated with endogenous and probably very complicated hormonal mechanisms.

Additionally, the possibility of psychoendocrine disease as expressed by captivity stress is germane to assessments of infertility. The altered adrenal function and interrupted LH secretory patterns found in mammals exposed to severe psychological stress often are reversible in the event of habituation or elimination of the stressor. Behaviorally infertile males should be provided with housing facilities conducive to reproduction. An environment with behavioral enrichment opportunities may be the easiest and most logical first

line of attack in alleviating severe cases of male reproductive failure. It is noteworthy that male gorillas previously considered infertile have become proven breeders after exposure to a novel environment and a change in diet (Gould 1983).

TECHNIQUES OF SEMEN COLLECTION

Semen quality is affected by current sexual activity. Therefore, males scheduled for evaluation should be isolated from estrous females for 3–7 days before semen collection. It is also prudent to avoid assessing males after recent stresses, such as captive transport, vaccination, or parasite treatment. The semen collection approach chosen should be minimally stressful to the animal. Methods of collection for wildlife species include electroejaculation, manual stimulation, the use of an artificial vagina, and postmortem retrieval. Because it can be employed while an animal is under anesthesia, electroejaculation is the most consistently useful approach. In exceptional circumstances semen has been collected from unanesthetized zoo animals either by manual massage or with an artificial vagina. Viable spermatozoa also may be obtained invasively from the caudae epididymides and ductus deferentia shortly after an animal's death.

Electroejaculation

Electroejaculation has been used to collect semen from species as diverse as the mouse and the elephant. Ejaculates from more than ninety different mammalian species have been collected by the research staff at the National Zoo. Most species respond to electroejaculation by producing seminal fluid containing spermatozoa. Detailing the electroejaculate characteristics of the vast number of species studied to date is beyond the scope of this chapter. However, this information is available from referenced material for such species as the Malayan tapir, *Tapirus indicus*, lesser kudu, *Tragelaphus imberbis*, greater kudu, Cape buffalo, banteng, *Bos javanicus*, sable antelope, *Hippotragus niger*, white-tailed gnu, *Connochaetes gnou*, blesbok, *Damaliscus dorcas phillipsi*, Mongolian wild ass, *Equus hemionus onager*, Przewalski's horse, *Equus przewalskii*, springbok, *Antidorcas marsupialis*, Speke's gazelle, *Gazella spekei*, Dorcas gazelle, *Gazella dorcas*, impala, black-footed ferret, koala, *Phascolarctos cinereus*, brushtail possum, *Trichosurus vulpecula*, dolphin, *Tursiops truncatus*, elephants, and various species of cervids, felids, and nonhuman primates (Rodger 1978; Harrison 1980; Howard et al. 1981, 1983, 1984; Merilan, Read, and Boever 1982; Wildt et al. 1983a, 1986b, 1987a, 1987b, 1987c, 1988, 1992; Wildt 1985, 1986; Schiewe et al. 1991; Curry et al. 1989; Schroeder and Keller 1989, 1990; Durrant 1990; Brown et al. 1991a, 1991b, 1991c; Howard and Wildt 1990; Monfort et al. 1993a).

Electrical stimulators manufactured for domestic animal semen collection generally are adaptable for use in zoo species. Unfortunately, comparative evaluations of stimulation requirements are often confounded because stimulation current, frequency, voltage, and waveform have not been standardized among laboratories. Various models of ejaculators delivering either alternating current (AC) or direct current (DC) are effective. The electrostimulator should be equipped with gauges that accurately monitor voltage and amperage.

The use of anesthesia with electroejaculation requires that food be withheld for 12–24 hours in monogastric species and up to 72 hours in ruminants. Certain sedatives, including xylazine (Rompun), diazepam (Valium), and phenothiazine derivatives such as acetylpromazine (acepromazine), relax the urethral musculature and may cause urine contamination of the electroejaculate. This problem can be particularly prevalent in carnivores, but many species of ungulates tolerate a low sedative dosage (in combination with a general anesthetic drug) to smooth anesthesia.

Two types of electroejaculation techniques have been adapted to zoo species. A penile electrode procedure in which the unanesthetized male is restrained and an ejaculatory response induced by direct electrical stimulation of the penis has been used in various nonhuman primates. Although effective in monkeys, this approach is neither humane nor practical for zoological specimens.

The preferred method is rectal probe electroejaculation, performed on animals in a surgical plane of anesthesia. The probe is made of plastic or Teflon, and copper or stainless steel electrodes are mounted on the probe surface in either a ring or a longitudinal configuration. The use of longitudinal electrodes is preferable because only moderate somatic stimulation results. Optimal rectal probe diameter generally conforms with the size of a normal excreted stool and permits adequate contact between the electrodes and the adjacent rectal mucosa.

The anesthetized male is placed in lateral recumbency or another position that facilitates access to the anus and the glans penis. Feces are removed manually from the rectum, and the lubricated probe is inserted so that the electrodes are positioned over the expected orientation of the male accessory organs. Usually longitudinal electrodes are mounted on only a portion of the probe circumference, allowing the electrodes to be positioned ventrally (against the accessory organs). Standardizing the electroejaculation protocol so that all males of a particular species receive the same number of electrical stimuli at the same voltage increments is beneficial for comparing males. The National Zoo protocol involves repeating sets of ten stimulations applied at increasing increments of voltage and amperage. Generally, the total 20-minute sequence is divided into three series of 30–40 stimuli per series. Stimuli are given in a 3-second-on and 3-second-off pattern with a continuous rise in voltage from 0 volts to the desired peak, then returning to 0 volts. For the majority of species tested, initial voltages range from 2 to 5 volts, and at the end of collection, rarely exceed 10 volts.

Most zoo mammals respond to electroejaculation with a spermic ejaculate, which is collected in a prewarmed, sterile plastic vial to prevent temperature shock and contamination. Erection may or may not accompany ejaculation, but in most cases the penis becomes erect. Inexplicably, ease of collection and semen quality varies among even closely related species. For example, high-quality semen has been obtained more easily from certain equids, such as the Mongolian wild ass and Przewalski's horse, than from others such as the zebra, *Equus burchellii*, and domestic horse

(Howard, Bush, and Wildt 1986; Durrant 1990). Similarly, although electroejaculates have been obtained from the timber wolf, *Canis lupus*, and various foxes (Graham et al. 1978), the domestic dog generally is resistant to this collection method. Other species difficult to electroejaculate include the giraffe, *Giraffa camelopardalis*, white rhinoceros, *Ceratotherium simum*, and certain marsupials (red kangaroo, *Macropus rufus*, potoroo, *Potorous apicalis*, bandicoots, *Isoodon macrourus*, dasyurids: Rodger and Pollitt 1981; Howard, Bush, and Wildt 1986). Undoubtedly the unique anatomical configuration of the male reproductive tract in each species contributes to some of the difficulties in using conventional electroejaculation equipment originally designed for farm livestock. It also is possible that certain anesthetics in some species may inhibit ejaculation.

Rectal probe electroejaculation is safe when used correctly. Although there is little specific information on the libido or breeding ability of animals subjected to such treatment, testosterone levels are unaffected (see Wickings, Marshall, and Nieschlag 1986 for review), and males have been known to copulate readily with females within days of electroejaculation (Wildt et al. 1993). Fertility is normal, as electroejaculated males subsequently produce offspring. The author is aware of two examples worthy of note. On one occasion a free-living Florida panther was discovered consorting and mating with a female only days after "field" electroejaculation. This female subsequently produced cubs. On another occasion, a captive cheetah was observed copulating 14 days after electroejaculation, an event that resulted in the birth of seven healthy cubs (Wildt et al. 1993). Electroejaculation has been found to elicit an adrenal response (increased serum cortisol) in a variety of species, including felids, hoofstock, and elephants (Wildt et al. 1984, 1986a, 1987c, 1988; Brown et al. 1988, 1989; Schiewe et al. 1991; D. E. Wildt, J. L. Brown, and M. Bush, unpub.). In all species studied to date, the response is acute, with cortisol concentrations either declining coincident with the termination of the semen collection procedure or being no greater than that observed under general anesthesia alone.

Artificial Vagina and Manual Stimulation

The artificial vagina (AV) technique, commonly used in farm livestock, involves the male mounting either a "teaser" female or a fabricated dummy and directing the penis into an AV containing a collection vial. Although the AV is a "natural approach," the male requires training, and there always is the danger of injury to the animal handler. Nevertheless, semen has been collected with an AV from the camel, *Camelus bactrianus*, reindeer, *Rangifer tarandus*, red deer, alpaca, *Lama pacos*, chimpanzee, *Pan troglodytes*, Eld's deer, Père David's deer, *Elaphurus davidianus*, and cheetah (see Watson 1978 for review; Durrant, Schuerman, and Millard 1985; Marson et al. 1989). Manual stimulation of the penis to produce reflex erection and ejaculation also has been successful in certain canids, including both blue, *Alopex lagopus*, and silver-black, *Vulpes vulpes*, foxes as well as timber wolves. The temperament and training required of the animals limit the practicality of this approach for conducting routine semen evaluations for most wildlife species. Nonetheless, in situations in which (1) large quantities of semen are required over time from an extremely valuable male or (2) novel approaches can be developed to avoid personnel injury, developing AV techniques for selected individuals may be worthwhile. Compared with electroejaculation, semen samples collected using an AV usually are smaller in volume but contain more sperm per unit volume.

Postmortem Sperm Recovery

Mature spermatozoa can be collected postmortem by flushing the ductus deferentia and caudae epididymides with air or warmed saline. The success of recovery can be increased significantly by either flushing these portions of the tract immediately after death or by maintaining the tissues at 5°C until flushing can be performed. In the latter case, ice can be used to maintain a cool temperature, but only if the tissues are not exposed directly to the ice surface. The initial motility of epididymal spermatozoa often is poor but can be improved by dilution with an appropriate tissue culture medium or semen extender followed by incubation at 21°–37°C. Spermatozoa of wild African elephants collected within 15 minutes after death by flushing the excurrent testicular duct became motile immediately after dilution with buffered saline (Jones, Bailey, and Skinner 1975). The reproductive tracts of male Florida panthers killed in car accidents have been cold-shipped to the National Zoo, where motile sperm have been recovered by flushing (J. G. Howard and M. E. Roelke, unpub.). After freezing and thawing, these sperm have demonstrated progressive forward motility.

SEMEN ANALYSIS

Establishing the precise minimal ejaculate criteria for a given species is an advantage for identifying subfertile individuals or for preparing for artificial breeding. Unfortunately, the minimum ejaculate characteristics required to produce a pregnancy are unknown or, at best, are general estimates for most mammals, including humans. However, the range in ejaculate factors for proven breeders is being determined gradually for many species, including zoo animals. If the population size is large, then comparing an individual with his conspecifics provides information on his potential for being "fertile."

The semen analysis process must be thorough. Ejaculate volume and pH are evaluated immediately after collection of the sample. Aliquots of the ejaculate are assessed microscopically at 37°C for sperm motility (percentage) and progressive sperm status (a subjective evaluation of speed of forward progression based on a scale of 0–5: 0, no motility or movement; 1, slight side-to-side movement with no forward progression; 2, moderate side-to-side movement with occasional slow forward progression; 3, side-to-side movement with slow forward progression; 4, steady forward progression; 5, rapid, steady forward progression). A minimum of four microscopic fields (400×) are examined and an average motility and progressive status rating estimated.

A variety of environmental insults, including heat, cold, and chemical contamination of the collection vessel, can compromise the motility estimate. When sperm concentration exceeds one billion sperm/ml, it is essential to dilute the

semen with saline or a suitable culture medium (37°C) before assessing cell motility. Swirling masses of motile sperm may be evident in undiluted semen, but because individual cells cannot be identified, it is impossible to accurately determine the motility or velocity of sperm. Certain taxa, especially the marsupials, produce semen containing densely packed globular cells (prostatic bodies) (Rodger and Hughes 1973; Rodger and White 1975, 1978; Wildt et al. 1991). These cells clearly present special problems in making motility estimates, necessitating seminal dilution with a tissue culture medium. The semen of most primates and rodents coagulates immediately after ejaculation, posing difficulties in handling and evaluation. The coagulum from some of these species has been digested by incubating the ejaculate in normal saline at 37°C or by adding a 1–2% solution of the enzymes trypsin or pronase (Howard, Bush, and Wildt 1986; see Wildt 1986 for review).

Multiple estimates of sperm viability over time (for example, at 30–60-minute intervals for several hours) also are useful because rapid loss of motility has been associated with infertility (Soderberg 1986). At least a portion of the cases of short-lived motility in vitro are attributable to urine contamination of the ejaculate, which can be detected macroscopically by observing a yellow color or by detecting an abnormal pH. For ungulates, urine contamination increases (alkalinizes) seminal pH above normal. For carnivores, inadvertent urine excretion causes the sample to become unusually acidic. Regardless of taxon, urine destroys or rapidly depresses sperm motility. Likewise, seminal fluid constituents suppress sperm movement.

Undiluted raw sperm, particularly from wild felids, generally maintain in vitro motility for 5 hours or less. The motility of fresh sperm from these and other species can be improved markedly by diluting the semen with a tissue culture medium, by removing seminal fluid by means of low-speed centrifugation (300 Xg for 10 minutes) (Howard et al. 1983), or by allowing washed and centrifuged spermatozoa to migrate or "swim up" into a culture medium layered onto the sperm pellet (Makler et al. 1984; Howard and Wildt 1990; Howard et al. 1990). Such treatment greatly increases the motility longevity of sperm (as much as fivefold), including those collected from wild felid ejaculates. Alternatively, semen samples have been passed through bovine serum albumin gradients, columns that trap immotile and structurally abnormal sperm (Ericsson, Langevin, and Nishino 1973; Tang and Chan 1983). Depending on the density of the gradient substrates, motility and normality percentages of recovered sperm can be improved markedly, although sperm concentration usually is depressed in the recovered fraction.

More sophisticated, objective methods for evaluating sperm motility also are available. Most of these procedures have been developed for assessing human reproductive potential, and few have been tested in animal models. The technique of multiple-exposure photography (in which 1- or 2-second time-exposure negatives are prepared by darkfield exposure) allows tracking of the motility and velocity of individual sperm (Albertsen et al. 1983; Kamidono et al. 1984). More expensive methods using laser-Doppler spectroscopy and computer-aided analysis of motion pictures or videomicrographs offer useful approaches for detailing sperm motility percentage, swimming curvature/speed, and linear progression (see Sherins and Howards 1985 for review). These latter factors may be important, as studies of infertile men indicate that sperm swimming speed is related to fertility.

Sperm concentration is determined by filling a 10 μl capillary pipette with semen, which is then mixed with the reservoir solution of a commercially available erythrocyte assay kit (1:200 dilution ratio). Both chambers of a hemacytometer are filled with diluted semen, and the numbers of sperm in the four large (1 mm^2) corner squares of each chamber are counted under phase-contrast microscopy. Sperm concentration/ml of ejaculate ($\times$ 10^6) is the total number of sperm cells counted in each chamber divided by 2. An average of the two chambers provides the overall sperm concentration. Multiplying by the volume and then by the motility percentage rating provides the index *motile sperm/ejaculate,* which is a more reliable measure of sperm output than sperm concentration alone. Automated counting systems, including the Coulter Counter and spectrophotometry, have been used for assessing sperm concentration, but are imprecise, particularly when sperm numbers are less than 10 million/ml or when the ejaculate contains extraneous cells and other debris. Multiple-exposure photography systems used for quantifying sperm motility also have been adapted effectively for determining sperm concentration (Kamidono et al. 1984).

Sperm morphology is a sensitive index of germinal epithelial integrity and is an accurate predictor of fertility in some species (Bostofte, Serup, and Rebbe 1982; Freischem et al. 1984). Sperm morphology is evaluated by fixing ejaculate aliquots in 1% glutaraldehyde and then examining in detail 100 or more sperm. Analysis can be facilitated by the use of an eosin-nigrosin stain, but currently the most accurate observations are achieved with high-resolution phase-contrast or differential interference microscopy (1,000$\times$). The classification system for sperm morphology historically categorized cells affected with various structural defects (pleiomorphisms). Initially, sperm were subdivided into normal, primary, or secondary categories. Primary abnormalities included an abnormal head shape, including a defective acrosome; a missing section of the midpiece; a tightly coiled flagellum; or bicephalic, biflagellate, macrocephalic, or microcephalic features. Primary abnormalities were thought to originate in the testes during spermatogenesis, whereas secondary abnormalities were thought to arise as the sperm moved through the excurrent duct system. However, these ideas about the exact origins of specific abnormalities have been challenged (Ott 1986). Conventional wisdom now suggests that some primary sperm defects may occur during sperm transport, whereas some secondary anomalies may occur during spermatogenesis. This lack of consistency probably argues for eliminating the primary versus secondary classification scheme. Regardless, because the spermatozoan's sole function is to deliver its DNA load into the oocyte, any structural abnormality that interferes with this objective should be cause for concern. Therefore, animals producing high proportions of sperm with anomalies in head size or mitochondrial sheath, flagellar derangement, or

acrosomal abnormalities should be viewed with suspicion. The acrosome, which is integral to the fertilization process, should be closely adhered to the nucleus. Defects in the acrosomal region usually are expressed as vesiculations or irregularities in the cell border.

Often a wide range in ejaculate values is reported for a given species. Much of this variation can be attributed to differences among laboratories in technique and subjective criteria. However, it is not unusual for ejaculate volume, sperm concentration, and sperm motility percentage to vary profoundly within a species or even between ejaculates from a single individual. Therefore, when assessing male fertility, it is important to accumulate semen data on each male over time. Males suspected of reproductive dysfunction should be electroejaculated on at least three occasions at 3- to 4-week intervals before final judgement of fertility status is made.

No single seminal trait should be used exclusively to assess ejaculate status. Sperm motility percentage is probably the most critical criterion in establishing potential infertility (Freischem et al. 1984), although the correlation between motility estimates and overall fertility is relatively low. Traditionally, however, insufficient emphasis has been placed on progressive sperm status and sperm morphology. High motility estimates are trivial if sperm cells show circular or backward movement or no forward progression. Likewise, sperm may exhibit good forward progression but a high incidence of pleiomorphisms. A high prevalence of abnormal cells may be indicative of sexual immaturity, endocrine aberrations, or degenerative changes in the testicular seminiferous epithelium. However, the interpretation of sperm morphology is complicated by the striking heterogeneity of sperm integrity within species. Vast ranges in sperm morphology are observed in the ejaculates of many species, including the gorilla, koala, and most species of Felidae. Although the etiology is unknown, sperm pleiomorphisms have been associated indirectly with captivity stress and more directly related to loss of genetic variability (inbreeding) (Wyrobek 1979; Wildt et al. 1983a, 1987a, 1988; O'Brien et al. 1983, 1985). Two prominent examples include the geographically isolated and genetically compromised African lions of the Ngorongoro Crater in Tanzania (Wildt et al. 1987a; O'Brien et al. 1987) and the Florida panther (Miller et al. 1990). The ejaculates of the latter puma subspecies are unique, as 50% of all sperm are afflicted with an abnormal acrosome (Barone et al. 1994).

More important is the effect of abnormal sperm on reproductive performance. The fertilization potential of an aberrant spermatozoon is likely to be impaired because of severely compromised cell motility or acrosomal integrity, or perhaps even altered DNA content in instances of micro- or macrocephaly. The most convincing evidence supporting this assertion comes from the recent work of Howard et al. (1993; Howard, Bush, and Wildt 1991), who demonstrated that sperm collected from teratospermic domestic cats (producing high proportions of structurally abnormal sperm) are less capable of binding, penetrating, and fertilizing conspecific oocytes in vitro compared with those from normospermic males. These sperm now are known to be filtered by the oocyte's zona pellucida (Howard et al. 1993). The Asian lions of India, another genetically restricted population, are known to produce many pleiomorphic sperm, low conception rates, and a high incidence of stillborn cubs (Wildt et al. 1987a). Likewise, at least one Florida panther male producing an extraordinary number of pleiomorphic sperm (>90% per ejaculate) is known to have repeatedly copulated with estrous females who failed to conceive (Miller et al. 1990).

Functional Assessment of Sperm Viability

Functional tests of sperm viability add dimension, accuracy, and a certain degree of assurance to evaluations of male reproductive competence. One such measure has been the movement of sperm cells through cervical mucus, a valuable index of fertilizing ability in humans (Alexander 1981; Takemoto et al. 1985). Because cervical mucus is not readily available, a synthetic, homogeneous medium of polyacrylamide gel, which exhibits rheologic properties similar to those of cervical mucus, has been tested in a variety of species, including some zoo animals (Hall et al. 1985). The assay consists of measuring the distance of sperm migration in a capillary tube filled with the synthetic gel; greater penetration distances indicate more robust sperm motility. The sperm migration assay may be a useful adjunct to evaluations of reproductive potential. However, the approach is specific in interpretive merit, as sperm penetration distance varies markedly among species and, in some species, depends on sperm concentration.

The functional assay receiving the most attention in recent years has been the sperm penetration assay, which is based on the ability of sperm to penetrate heterologous ova. The ova used most frequently have been collected from hormonally stimulated golden hamsters, a species that appears unique in that these ova accept sperm from many different mammalian taxa. The protective covering of the ovum, the zona pellucida, is removed enzymatically, resulting in a "zona-free" hamster ovum. Numerous studies have demonstrated a relationship between the rate of fertilization in this heterologous in vitro system and fertility in human males (e.g., sperm from fertile men are capable of penetrating zona-free hamster oocytes at a higher rate than those from subfertile or infertile men) (Yanagimachi, Yanagimachi, and Rogers 1976; Rogers et al. 1979; Albertsen et al. 1983). This test is labor-intensive and relatively complex. Collected sperm are washed and incubated in culture medium for 4–18 hours to permit sperm capacitation. The sperm and ova are then incubated together in a specially controlled environmental chamber for 2–4 hours, after which the ova are microscopically scored for the number penetrated and the number of sperm penetrating per ovum. The most common endpoint for a positive score is decondensation of the sperm nucleus in the ovum cytoplasm. This particular assay has been applied to the tiger (Post et al. 1987; Byers et al. 1987, 1989a), leopard cat (Howard and Wildt 1990), and nonhuman primates (Durrant 1987).

The zona-free hamster ovum assay is not without its critics. Perhaps its most serious limitation is its inability to measure the sperm's capacity for binding and penetrating the protective investment of the ovum (i.e., the zona pellucida itself). Howard, Bush, and Wildt (1991) recently have circumvented this problem in felids by developing a heterologous evaluation system that measures penetration of zona pellucida–intact domestic cat oocytes. The latter are readily available from ovariohysterectomy material collected from veterinary clinics and can be used fresh or after long-term storage in a high-salt solution (Andrews et al. 1992). Leopard cat, puma, and cheetah sperm are capable of penetrating domestic cat oocytes (Howard and Wildt 1990; Wildt et al. 1993), and this assay has been used effectively to discriminate among individual males that produce distinctly different ejaculate characteristics (Howard and Wildt 1990).

These tests examine the ability of sperm to capacitate, undergo the acrosomal reaction, penetrate the zona pellucida, and generate a fusogenic equatorial segment, information critical for assessing the functional competence of the spermatozoon. Negative results, however, deserve a second evaluation, because with such a complex bioassay, spuriously low fertilization rates might easily result from numerous technical problems arising during the in vitro handling of the gametes. For example, capacitation requirements for sperm vary widely among and within species. Whereas human sperm are incubated 8–15 hours before insemination, felid sperm require only 1–3 hours of preinsemination culture (Byers et al. 1987, 1989a; Howard and Wildt 1990; Howard et al. 1991, 1993).

Sperm penetration assays, although as yet applied to few mammalian systems, soon may be valuable for routinely assessing male reproductive potential. These assays will be particularly useful for evaluating the fertilization potential of sperm from rare species in which few females are available for pregnancy testing. Likewise, these tests could serve a valuable role in assessing freeze-thawing technology in the development of sperm cryobanking programs (Wildt 1992).

Testicular Biopsy

Testicular biopsy is a direct approach to evaluating spermatogenic function that is particularly valuable for animals from which a semen sample cannot be collected or species for which FSH and LH assays are unavailable. A microscopic analysis of testicular tissue can establish the presence of all necessary cellular elements as well as discriminating between an aspermatogenic testis and one producing sperm. The main purposes of testicular biopsy of oligospermic males are to identify the etiology of acquired infertility, assess the severity and hereditary complications of severe subfertility, and formulate an appropriate prognosis. Histological assessments alone are subjective and therefore provide little basis for quantifying the normalcy of sperm production. Additionally, degeneration of developing sperm cells commonly occurs even in the seminiferous tubules of normal testes. Morphometric techniques are available for quantifying spermatogenesis from testicular biopsies. The spherical nuclei of young spermatids in tubular cross-sections can be counted per unit volume of testis to provide an estimate of the efficiency of sperm production (Amann 1986).

In wildlife species, the tissue sample is obtained after inducing anesthesia and surgically preparing the scrotal area. Needle biopsies have been reported (Cohen et al. 1984), although a common problem is that insufficient tissue is retrieved for evaluation. A more direct technique involves using an ultrafine surgical blade to make an incision through the scrotum, tunica vaginalis, tunica albuginea, and 2–3 mm into the testicular parenchyma. Moderate constriction maintained at the neck of the scrotum suppresses the testes tightly against the scrotal wall, everting tissue on the testis surface through the incision. This sample is shaved from the testicle with a sharp surgical blade and immersed in glutaraldehyde, Karnovsky's, Bouin's, or Zenker's fixative (Amann 1986). Formalin distorts the walls of the seminiferous tubules as well as chromatin patterns, and is not used as a testicular tissue fixative. All layers of the biopsy site are sutured, and prophylactic antibiotic is administered systemically. At the National Zoo, we have used this approach successfully in the lion, Cape buffalo, and impala.

In animals with acquired infertility, histological evaluations of testicular tissue suggest the severity of testicular degeneration. For example, examination of gorilla testicular tissue in independent laboratories has revealed marked testicular atrophy, degeneration, and fibrosis of the seminiferous tubules (Dixson, Moore, and Holt 1980; Foster and Rowley 1982). The exact causes of abnormal cellular structure induced by other variables are complex and include hypogonadotropism, neoplasms, inflammatory or vascular diseases, cryptorchidism, drugs, and genetic disorders.

Temporary decreases in sperm concentration and motility have been reported in human males and dogs after bilateral testicular biopsy, possibly as the result of the formation of sperm antibodies (Burke 1986). Other studies have detected no circulating sperm-immobilizing or sperm-agglutinating antibodies in biopsied men or dogs (Burke 1986). Generally, histological sampling of the male gonad is not contraindicated if the procedure is performed carefully, minimal tissue is retrieved, and the epididymal region is avoided to prevent accidental intrusion and consequent ductal obstruction.

Biochemical Characteristics of Semen

The biochemical components of semen do not reflect testicular function but rather the relative contributions of the epididymides and accessory glands to the semen. The composition of the biochemical components of seminal plasma is sensitive to the interval of ejaculatory abstinence, the degree of sexual excitement, sperm concentration, and the relative amounts of degradatory enzymes. Because of the potential effects of these variables, simply measuring the concentration of a compound in the semen has limited diagnostic value.

CLASSIFICATION AND ETIOLOGY OF MALE INFERTILITY DISORDERS

Comprehensive descriptions of the etiology of male infertility are beyond the scope of this text. For more details and references, the reader is referred to the excellent review by Sherins and Howards (1985) and the text of Morrow (1986).

Heat

Warming the testes to internal body temperature rapidly damages primary spermatocytes and causes subsequent decreases in sperm concentration and motility. Even acute heat insults (as brief as 30 minutes) can result in oligospermia for as long as 5 weeks. Increased intratesticular temperatures may result from high fever, scrotal dermatitis, or inflammation of the testis and epididymis. The physical attributes of some species (e.g., the small scrotal sac and hairy physique of the gorilla) and sitting or lying on heated floors have been suggested as potential sources of temperature-induced testicular damage (Gould 1983). Usually temperature damage is reversible; testes maintained at typical external body temperatures eventually return to normal function.

Nutritional Deficits

There are no published data demonstrating that nutritional deficiencies influence the reproductive performance of male zoo animals. However, there is a definite relationship between a lack of certain minerals and fertility dysfunction in some domestic species and humans (see Mertz 1986 for review), which suggests that similar deficiencies might provoke similar conditions in wild animal species. Perhaps the most marked effects of a deficit occur when zinc is lacking in the diet because this mineral plays a key role in reproductive function in both the male and the female. The seminiferous tubules of rats fed a zinc-deficient diet become atrophic, which results in a marked decrease in the number of spermatids present. The reversibility of the degeneration is highly dependent on the duration of the deficiency; however, most of the germinal tissue usually regenerates after prolonged exposure to a proper diet. Similar types of hypogonadism have been observed in zinc-deficient bull calves and human males, in which the abnormality also is manifested by smaller testes and lower testosterone concentrations. All of these effects appear to originate at the level of the gonad rather than at the hypothalamus or pituitary. Males exposed to zinc deficits in utero generally display abnormally low birth weights, a higher than normal number of congenital anomalies, and often abnormal behaviors.

A dietary manganese deficiency also results in testicular degeneration in rats and rabbits, which leads to sterility and lack of libido. A low-selenium diet in mice and rats results in aspermic ejaculates or semen containing high proportions of immotile sperm or sperm in which the head is separated from the cellular midpiece. Selenium appears to play a role in the normal development of the spermatozoon, especially in the stabilization of the mitochondrial sheath during spermiogenesis. Ejaculates from mice and rats fed a selenium-deficient diet have a high incidence of sperm midpiece and flagellar abnormalities, with a simultaneous decline in fertility.

Finally, there is recent, unpublished evidence that felids fed strictly muscle meat (which is low in minerals and vitamins) produce poor-quality ejaculates (J. G. Howard, M. E. Roelke, W. F. Swanson, and D. E. Wildt, unpub.). In most cases, semen quality improves markedly when the diet is improved by feeding bones, whole carcasses, and vitamin/mineral supplements.

Endocrine Disorders

The primary endocrine cause of male infertility is gonadotropin deficiency resulting in hypogonadotropic hypogonadism. This disorder, common in human males (Sherins and Howards 1985), also has been identified in the mink, *Mustela vison* (Tung et al. 1984), and probably exists in other mammalian species. Hypogonadotropic hypogonadism can occur as an isolated deficiency in pituitary LH and FSH secretion, likely caused by the absence of hypothalamic GnRH release. The absence of LH and FSH leads to failure of sexual maturation in the prepubertal male and to decreased libido, loss of male sex characteristics, and aspermatogenesis in the adult. A gonadotropin deficiency also can occur as the result of pituitary tumors or damage resulting from cranial trauma. Diabetes mellitus and hyperandrogenism have been shown to decrease spermatogenesis and result in testicular atrophy. Excessive glucocorticoid production, as a consequence of stress or adrenal dysfunction, can influence male reproductive performance adversely at the level of the hypothalamus, pituitary, or gonad.

Karyotype Abnormalities

A variety of testicular disorders in humans are associated with karyotype abnormalities. Genetic conditions resulting in an additional X chromosome (Klinefelter's syndrome, XXY) or Y chromosome (XYY syndrome) have been related to the presence of small, fibrous testes and primary failure of both the seminiferous tubules and the Leydig cells (Sherins and Howards 1985). Males with the XXY syndrome normally are azoospermic (with elevated FSH and LH levels and low testosterone concentrations: Resko 1982), whereas males with the XYY condition are either azoospermic or severely oligospermic. It is also notable that human males with a normal peripheral karyotype may be infertile as a consequence of abnormalities of only the meiotic chromosomes of the testicular germ cells.

In zoo animals, little attention has been directed to the relationship between chromosomal anomalies and reproductive performance. However, the potential adverse effects of either natural aberrations or those induced by mismanagement are best illustrated by studies of the Kirk's dik-dik, *Madoqua kirkii* (Howard et al. 1989). Kirk's dik-dik populations maintained in North American zoos exhibit two distinct karyotypes designated as cytotype *a* and cytotype *b*. Pedigree surveys indicate that animals with the two cytotypes originated from different geographic regions of Kenya. Cytotype *a* animals have a diploid number of 46 chromosomes, whereas the males and females of cytotype *b* have 47 and 46 chromosomes respectively. These differences are not due to classic Robertsonian chromosomal fusion/fission, but rather are related to multiple rearrangements including inversions, X autosome translocation, and tandem fusions (Ryder et al. 1989). The two genotypes will hybridize to produce F_1 offspring, which traditionally experience fertility problems. Howard et al. (1989) examined the electroejaculate characteristics of cytotype *a*, *b*, and *ab* males. Cytotype *a* and *b* males produce high-quality and comparable spermic semen samples, whereas the ejaculates of the cytohybrids are composed entirely of immature spermatozoa. Histological analyses indicate the presence of meiotic activity, but no spermiogenesis (sperm maturation) and no mature sperm within the seminiferous tubules or the epididymis. These results demonstrate how the interbreeding of two phenotypically similar yet chromosomally different genotypes can adversely affect male reproductive performance and, in this particular case, result in sterility. These observations also illustrate the importance of understanding the fundamental genetics of wild species populations before the onset of large-scale captive propagation programs.

Varicocele

A varicocele is an abnormal dilation of the veins of the spermatic cord caused by the incompetency of valves in the internal spermatic vein. This condition results in (1) downward reflux of blood into the spermatic cord veins, which causes elevations of intrascrotal temperature, (2) decreases in testicular blood flow, and (3) greater exposure of the testes to adrenal steroids and catecholamines. Sperm concentration depression, germinal cell hypoplasia, maturation arrest, and even azoospermia or germinal aplasia may result.

Ductal Occlusion

Transport of sperm and seminal fluid into the ejaculate requires that the efferent and epididymal ducts, ductus deferens, prostatic ducts, and urethra be patent. Ductal occlusion is a likely cause of infertility in males with normal testicular size, libido, secondary sex characteristics, and circulating hormone profiles. Obstruction within the excretory network, with the exception of urethral occlusion, is a difficult diagnosis and is usually attempted by contrast studies of the outflow tract. Lesions are commonly focal, and often result from congenital abnormalities or ductal stricture after infection. The former are not treatable; however, in some cases epididymal occlusion results from epididymitis, and prompt antibiotic therapy may decrease the severity of the occlusion. Conditions contributing to duct occlusion include bilateral tuberculous epididymitis, gonorrheal urethritis, smallpox, and filariasis. A variety of microsurgical procedures have been developed to bypass occlusions of the epididymis and ductus deferens in human males, but to date they have not been used on a practical basis in animals.

Ejaculatory Dysfunction

Animals may copulate normally but have abnormal seminal emission. For example, altered smooth muscle integrity at the neck of the bladder can allow retrograde ejaculation into the bladder. Retrograde ejaculation can be confirmed by the presence of numerous sperm cells in a postejaculatory urine specimen. The administration of sympathomimetic drugs and certain antihistamines has been effective in treating humans with retrograde ejaculation (Sherins and Howards 1985).

Ischemia

Severe, rapid, and permanent spermatogenic damage can result from testicular ischemia (deficient blood supply); testicular torsion for as little as 1–2 hours may lead to such damage (Soderberg 1986). Interstitial cells are less susceptible to such an acute insult, but may be adversely affected if blood flow is critically impaired. A unilateral condition can be treated by hemicastration of the affected gonad.

Drugs and Radiation

Chemotherapeutic agents for controlling malignancies have profound and chronic effects on germ cell production and endocrine function. The severity of these effects is dependent on drug class, drug dosage, and the age of the individual. Likewise, the testes are highly radiosensitive, probably because of rapid cell division within the germinal epithelium. Few quantitative studies have been published, but techniques for shielding the testes should be considered seriously whenever high dosages of radiation are directed toward the genital region. Most drugs commonly used in wildlife medical management do not compromise male reproductive function. Anesthetic drugs have the potential for depressing hypothalamic-pituitary-gonadal activity, but the effect generally is acute and reversible with recovery from the anesthesia. Prolonged therapeutic use of steroids can arrest spermatogenesis, and high doses of the nitrofurantoin antibiotics may inhibit spermatogenesis. Antimetabolite and other cancer chemotherapeutic drugs, antithyrogenic drugs, and certain classes of tranquilizers also can interfere with spermatogenesis. These disruptive effects usually are reversible depending on the dose and duration of exposure.

Orchitis/Epididymitis

Inflammation of the testis and epididymis may result from infection, immune-mediated disorders, or trauma. The reproductive organs can be infected by bacteria, viruses, or fungi, which can be introduced via the bloodstream or ascending routes or by penetrating scrotal trauma. Prostatic disease may be a primary focus of infection or may contribute to retrograde transport of infectious material from the urinary tract into the epididymis and testis. Chronic or recurrent acute cases of epididymitis can obstruct, distend, or scar the tubules as well as causing microabscesses and sperm granulomas. Orchitis results in depressed sperm production, poor sperm motility, and increasing numbers of cellular pleiomorphisms. Severe inflammatory responses interrupt the integrity of the seminiferous tubules and epididymal duct, thereby exposing sperm to the peripheral circulation. Antibodies and sensitized lymphocytes against sperm can result from the immune response. Simultaneous rupture of the intercellular union between Sertoli and germinal cells can expose these antibodies to the antigens on developing sperm cells. Lymphocytic orchitis is characterized by lymphocytic infiltration of the testes, focal degeneration, and segmental or diffuse testicular atrophy. Allergic orchitis has been induced experimentally in the rat, guinea pig, *Cavia porcellus*, rhesus macaque, and human.

A strain of mink has been discovered that develops a high incidence of orchitis coincident with the period from peak seasonal sexual activity (March) to the onset of testicular regression (April) (Tung et al. 1984). Antisperm antibodies also increase during this period, suggesting that testicular autoimmunity most likely develops during testicular regression.

Brucella abortus, *Corynebacterium*, and some bacterial opportunists are among the important etiological agents inducing orchitis. *Brucella* infection, in particular, leads to chronic gonadal inflammation and eventually to infertility. Serologic testing or semen culture may aid in the diagnosis, but at present there is no effective treatment, and males with brucellosis should not be used for breeding. If an infectious agent is involved in orchitis/epididymitis, prognosis for fertility recovery is guarded, particularly when testicular edema occurs and body temperature is elevated.

Systemic Disease

There is little specific information available for any species on the effects of systemic illness on testicular function. Relevant factors include the potentially toxic effects of therapeutic drugs, protein catabolism, the influence of the disease itself, and fever. A febrile state alters spermatogenesis, and the proportion of defective sperm forms is increased by viral and bacterial illnesses. Seminal characteristics may not recover for weeks or even months after the insult.

Systemic diseases associated with renal failure, liver cirrhosis, diabetes mellitus, metastatic neoplasia, and hyperadrenocorticism as well as certain infectious diseases such as canine distemper markedly alter hormone metabolism and suppress fertility (Levitan et al. 1984). Bacterial organisms frequently associated with testicular inflammation and cellular degeneration include *Brucella*, *Mycobacterium*, *Salmonella*, *Corynebacterium*, *Pasteurella*, *Escherichia*, and *Proteus*. Other organisms to be considered include mycoplasmas, cytomegaloviruses, myxoviruses (mumps), and trichomonads (Keeling 1982). Less subtle infectious disease conditions that could influence male fertility are leptospirosis and shigellosis (Gould 1983). There is a need to clarify the effects of syphilis, gonorrhea, chlamydial urethritis, and genital herpes on male reproductive performance (Keeling 1982). Additionally, many of these conditions may not have as great an effect on male fertility as on the general health and reproductive performance of exposed females. Acute infections can be addressed in some cases by appropriate and usually long-term antibiotic therapy of infected and exposed individuals. In selected species in which systemic infections persistently affect fertility, vaccination protocols, when available, should be considered.

HORMONAL TREATMENT OF MALE INFERTILITY

Traditionally, hormonal therapies are used to combat two types of male infertility: (1) hypogonadotropic hypogonadism (i.e., suboptimal endogenous gonadotropin levels causing poor gonadal function) and (2) idiopathic infertility (i.e., reproductive failure of unknown origin).

Hypogonadotropic Hypogonadism

Gonadotropins. Exogenous gonadotropins have been effective in stimulating spermatogenesis in males with hypogonadotropic hypogonadism (Sherins and Howards 1985). Therapies have been tested predominantly in human males and a very few species of domestic animals. The gonadotropins of choice for stimulating seminiferous tubule function are commercially available FSH, human menopausal gonadotropin (hMG), and pregnant mares' serum gonadotropin (PMSG). Direct stimulation of Leydig cell function is accomplished by administering human chorionic gonadotropin (hCG). The FSH and hMG compounds, glycoproteins with a relatively short half-life (t 1/2), require injection at 24- to 48-hour intervals. Because of its greater t 1/2, PMSG theoretically can be administered at 4- to 7-day intervals. The repeated administration of PMSG in female mammals has been associated with the formation of antibodies to gonadotropins. Few similar data are available for PMSG-treated males, although repeated subcutaneous injections of hCG stimulate antibody production in nonhuman primates (see Wickings, Marshall, and Nieschlag 1986 for review).

Multiple intramuscular doses of hCG stimulate testosterone secretion and cause virilization in primates (Wickings, Marshall, and Nieschlag 1986). Similar treatment stimulates testosterone secretion in a strain of mink with normally low pituitary LH release patterns (Tung et al. 1984). Additionally, the administration of hCG to intact rhesus macaques significantly increases sexual activity, as measured by greater mount frequencies and decreases in ejaculatory latency (Herndon, Allen, and Blakely 1980). A combination of hCG with FSH-like gonadotropins (given three times weekly) stimulates spermatogenesis in most hypogonadotropic men (Sherins and Howards 1985). The few studies employing PMSG have focused on laboratory animals and suggest that oligospermic males may benefit from serial PMSG injection protocols (Soderberg 1986). Azoospermic males do not respond to PMSG therapy. Whereas FSH and hMG therapy require simultaneous use of hCG, PMSG treatment, due to natural LH contaminants, does not require a secondary drug source.

Gonadotropin-Releasing Hormone. In individuals with a congenital absence of hypothalamic GnRH, synthetic sources of GnRH or GnRH agonists ("super" GnRH sources) appear effective in alleviating hypogonadal function. Intermittent pulsatile delivery of GnRH is necessary to stimulate pituitary gonadotropin release, the administration interval probably being species-specific. The requirement for frequent administration makes it difficult to ensure consistent and repeated stimulation. Several laboratories are currently testing the efficacy of implantable osmotic minipumps capable of providing either low-dose pulsatile or continuous release of GnRH. Because of its simple biochemical structure (10 amino acids), GnRH appears to be non-species-specific and nonimmunogenic. The action of GnRH is manifested through its stimulation of FSH and LH release; hence, the gonad is affected indirectly rather than directly by the exogenous treatment. Of the hormones available, GnRH and its chemical derivatives hold the most promise for developing reliable protocols to combat endocrine deficiencies contributing to infertility.

Idiopathic Infertility

Hormonal therapy for the treatment of idiopathic infertility is highly controversial, speculative, and usually unsuccessful (Resko 1982; Sherins and Howards 1985; Swerdloff et al. 1985). In human males, reproductive failures of unknown origin have been treated for decades using a variety of hormonal treatment protocols. The highly variable responses reported by laboratories testing similar treatments often are attributed to poor experimental design, including the lack of comparative control data. Poorly understood conditions such as oligospermia may have a genetic basis, as suggested by evaluations of identical twins with this disorder (Smallridge et al. 1984), and thus may not be susceptible to treatment. Nonetheless, we should not exclude trying any reasonable treatment on other animal species. But unpredictability is to be expected, and it is imperative to adhere to certain therapeutic criteria. First, *male fertility should be evaluated repeatedly over a period of at least 3 months before and 3 months after pharmacological treatment*. Second, *therapeutic compounds for stimulating spermatogenesis must be given for at least 3 months*. Third, every effort must be made to *compare the reproductive performance of the treated individual with that of a normal, conspecific male population*. However, virtually *no azoospermic male will improve as a result of conventional hormonal therapy*.

Androgens. The administration of testosterone to an intact male inhibits, rather than stimulates, spermatogenesis by exerting excessive negative feedback on hypothalamic and pituitary hormone release. Realizing that the maturation of epididymal sperm requires androgens, some investigators have treated oligospermic, infertile men with low oral doses of testosterone derivatives (see Nieschlag, Michel, and Knuth 1985 for review). The results are inconclusive, although sperm motility was improved in one study. One potential strategy is the testosterone rebound approach, which involves a parenteral injection of androgens three times a week for 10 weeks. During therapy, gonadotropic hormone release is depressed severely, and azoospermia results. Withdrawing the testosterone treatment causes a sharp rebound in pituitary FSH and LH release, with sperm concentrations increasing significantly above pretreatment levels in some studies.

Gonadotropins. The literature concerning the efficacy of gonadotropin therapy in cases of idiopathic infertility is largely empirical and frequently equivocal. Reviews indicate that administering hMG in some studies improves semen quality in as many as 50% of oligospermic males, yet pregnancy rate is not improved significantly (Sherins and Howards 1985). Other efforts in which males have been treated for up to 30 weeks have failed to consistently alter either sperm production or pregnancy rate (Sherins and Howards 1985).

Gonadotropin-Releasing Hormone. The increased FSH levels found in some human males with idiopathic oligospermia or azoospermia can be selectively reduced by pulsatile GnRH treatment (Gross et al. 1986; Hönigl, Knuth, and Nieschlag 1986). However, there is no evidence to suggest that the serial administration of GnRH to oligospermic males with an intact pituitary-gonadal axis results in increased fertility (Fauser et al. 1985).

Antiestrogens. Two compounds, commonly called antiestrogens, have been tested in cases of male infertility. The first, clomiphene citrate (CC), is a synthetic nonsteroidal compound closely related to diethylstilbestrol. In normal human males, CC increases circulating levels of FSH, LH, and testosterone. In men with idiopathic oligospermia, numerous studies have reported increased sperm concentrations and, occasionally, increased motility ratings after CC treatment (Mićić and Dotlić 1985). However, under rigidly controlled experimental conditions, many individuals fail to respond (Resko 1982; Sherins and Howards 1985). Of particular interest is the finding that the incidence of pregnancy in the mates of CC-treated males generally does not improve. The CC protocol used frequently in men has failed to improve sperm concentration or motility ratings in oligospermic gorillas (D. E. Wildt, J. G. Howard, and M. Bush, unpub.).

The second compound, tamoxifen, reportedly increases sperm concentration, but the data are confounded by a lack of suitable controls (Dony et al. 1985; Noci et al. 1985a). The wide use of this approach should be restricted until more information is available.

SEASONAL INFLUENCES ON MALE REPRODUCTION

In most wild species, essential activities of the life cycle (feeding, migration, and reproduction) are regulated by season. Reproductive performance usually is associated with season, thereby ensuring that young are born at times maximizing their chances for survival. Often photoperiod acts as the proximate factor modulating onset and cessation of reproductive activity. Definitive conclusions about the effects of seasonality on physiological patterns are difficult to establish in many wildlife species, especially those maintained in captive conditions. Some species are not only seasonal but nocturnal, presenting particular challenges in collecting data that will allow the accurate plotting of the ebb and flow of endogenous endocrine patterns. Certain primates may be seasonal (e.g., *Macaca mulatta*), whereas their close relatives (e.g., *Macaca fascicularis*) are not (see Wickings, Marshall, and Nieschlag 1986 for review). Free-ranging males in their native habitats may exhibit more profound variations in the hypothalamic-pituitary-testicular axis than their counterparts in captivity, where the environment is influenced by artificial photoperiods and diets.

Lincoln (1981) offers an excellent summary of the seasonal aspects of testicular function in both domestic and wildlife species. Among wild mammals there are numerous examples of seasonal testicular activity, with seasonal regression of the testes often rendering the male infertile for part of the year. To understand the significance of the seasonal cycle in the male of any species, it is necessary to consider the ecology of the animal in its natural habitat. In the most typical pattern, full sexual competence in the male is achieved some weeks before receptive females are available, and this fertility extends over the full period when successful mating may occur (Lincoln 1981).

In species studied to date, it is apparent that the seasonal onset of gonadal activity is a consequence of an increased pulsatility of GnRH, which results in greater secretion of LH and testosterone (Hansen 1985). In certain species, male seasonality is controlled primarily by the length of the photoperiod, with species classified as "long-day" or "short-day" breeders. This is a somewhat misleading classification because some species appear to alter reproductive function

as a result of refractoriness to short or long days (rather than being stimulated directly by changing photoperiod: Lincoln and Short 1980). Photoperiod mediates endocrine response by (1) directly affecting GnRH and LH pulsatility; (2) varying the GnRH storage capabilities of the hypothalamus; (3) altering the responsiveness of the hypothalamic-pituitary axis to the negative feedback actions of gonadal steroids; and (4) possibly influencing the ability of GnRH to stimulate gonadotropin secretion (see Hansen 1985 for review).

In many species the pineal gland also appears to play an active role, transducing neural input from the eye into production of the hormone melatonin. The pineal and its secretions may stimulate, inhibit, or have no effect on reproduction; the influence is species-specific as well as seasonally dependent within species. In male primates such as the rhesus macaque, the mechanism for regulating seasonality is unknown, but apparently it is unrelated to photoperiod-induced alterations in melatonin activity (Wickings, Marshall, and Nieschlag 1986). However, administering exogenous melatonin hastens the onset of estrus in anestrous ferrets, while estrous ferrets become anestrous after melatonin treatment (Thorpe and Herbert 1976). In white-tailed deer, *Odocoileus virginianus*, removing the pineal gland in March, when males are at their sexual nadir, increases basal LH and testosterone concentrations, enhances LH and testosterone response to GnRH, and accelerates testicular growth (Plotka et al. 1984). Therefore, it appears that pinealectomy eliminates melatonin, which normally inhibits the synthesis and release of hypothalamic GnRH.

In contrast, exogenous melatonin has been used in several species of Cervidae (including white-tailed deer) to shorten the period of male sexual inactivity. A subcutaneous implant of melatonin in a sealed envelope of Silastic sheeting was tested in male roe deer, *Capreolus capreolus*, beginning in May, approximately 4 to 5 months before the normal onset of rut (Lincoln et al. 1984). Compared with untreated controls, precocious sexual development (including the premature shedding of antler velvet, swelling of the neck musculature, growth of the neck mane, and rutting odor of urine) occurred in all the melatonin-treated stags. The treated males demonstrated rutting behavior in late July and early August, at least 6 weeks before the control stags. The rutting phase for the melatonin-treated animals ended in early October, 6 weeks earlier than normal, indicating an apparent refractoriness to the stimulatory effects of constant melatonin. Oral treatment of male white-tailed deer or red deer with melatonin, given daily in the afternoon during the early summer (at the nadir of the sexual cycle), also induces early testicular development and rutting behavior (Bubenik 1983; Adam and Atkinson 1984; Adam, Moir, and Atkinson 1986). The fertility of melatonin-treated red deer stags is no different from that of naturally rutting males (Adam, Moir, and Atkinson 1986).

The reasons for the different effects of melatonin among species have not been examined. To understand why species respond to melatonin differently, it will be necessary to identify the target tissues for the hormone as well as the mechanism by which melatonin alters cellular function (Hansen 1985).

Lincoln (1981) has reviewed the known physiological characteristics and testicular morphology/histology associated with seasonality in wild mammals. Functional changes in the testes attributable to season have been studied in such diverse species as the vole, *Microtus agrestis* (Grocock and Clarke 1975), mole, *Talpa europaea* (Racey 1978), mongoose, *Herpestes auropunctatus* (Gorman 1976), brown hare, *Lepus europaeus* (Lincoln 1974), rock hyrax, *Procavia capensis* (Miller and Glover 1970), clouded leopard (Wildt et al. 1986a), tiger (Byers et al. 1989b), blesbok, kudu, springbok, and impala (Skinner 1971; Brown et al. 1991c), hartebeest, *Alcelaphus buselaphus* (Skinner, Van Zyl, and Van Heerden 1973), Cape buffalo (Brown et al. 1991b), and rhesus macaque (Zamboni, Conaway, and Van Pelt 1974). The influence of seasonal changes on reproductive-endocrine function has been most intensely examined in the Cervidae (Lincoln, Guinness, and Short 1972; Whitehead and McEwan 1973; McMillin et al. 1974; West and Nordan 1976; Mirarchi et al. 1978; Stokkan, Hove, and Carr 1980; Mossing and Damber 1981; Bubenik et al. 1982; Schams and Barth 1982; Sempere and Lacroix 1982; Snyder et al. 1983; Haigh et al. 1984; Bubenik and Smith 1987; Loudon and Curlewis 1988; Monfort et al. 1993a, 1993b). Efforts have focused on the relationship of hormonal fluctuations to the onset of rutting behavior and the growth and casting of antlers. Seasonal elevations in testosterone have been associated with increases in sexual activity, aggressiveness, and testicular size, these factors being maximally coincident with the onset of female cyclicity. More recent studies have established seasonal patterns in FSH, LH, and prolactin secretion as well as reproductive-endocrine differences among black-tailed deer, *Odocoileus hemionus columbianus*, white-tailed deer, red deer, roe deer, reindeer/caribou, and Eld's deer. Few investigations have simultaneously monitored ejaculate characteristics, although red deer and Eld's deer males produce greater numbers of morphologically normal spermatozoa during the breeding season than during periods of female acyclicity (Haigh et al. 1984; Monfort et al. 1993a). Most evidence indicates that hypothalamic-derived GnRH drives the annual testicular cycle in deer (Fennessy et al. 1988). Recently, Lincoln (1987) reported that continuous infusion of a potent GnRH agonist, Buserelin, administered during the nonbreeding season stimulated testicular activity in red deer stags. Increased plasma LH and testosterone concentrations, testicular growth, a rutting odor, and increased aggressive behavior were observed.

From a practical perspective, although bears, felids, and ungulates can be seasonal breeders in nature, viable-appearing sperm usually can be collected (by electroejaculation) from captive males in North America throughout the year. In contrast, sperm cannot be retrieved during the inactive seasons of any rodents or mustelids. The captive environment may affect the synchrony of male and female peak reproductive performance. An analysis of breeding records for captive clouded leopards demonstrated that maximal female estrous activity is observed from late December through February (Wildt et al. 1986a, 1986b). The greatest number of motile sperm per ejaculate measured in males evaluated throughout the year is detected in June or July. The data suggest that a physiological asymmetry may exist in peak reproductive performance between the male and female clouded leopard, perhaps as a result of differing adaptations to the captive environment.

INHIBITION OF MALE REPRODUCTION

Most reproductive research is oriented toward improving, rather than inhibiting, male fertility. However, zoo management programs require that reproductive control methods be applied to species that overpropagate in captivity. As captive breeding techniques improve and animal space becomes more limited, dealing with "excess" animals, especially males, will be a continuing challenge. This particular issue already has served as the incentive for a workshop addressing contraception techniques for zoo animals, and the reader is referred to those proceedings for more details (Seal 1990; see also Asa et al., chap. 40, this volume). In brief, there are two basic approaches to male contraception: (1) blocking testicular function and (2) preventing gamete transport.

The most effective method for blocking male reproduction, castration, is unacceptable for most captive wildlife species. Gonadectomy (i.e., castration) eliminates the source of androgen responsible for virilization and for maintaining the majestic appearance of many exhibit animals (e.g., the manes of male lions). Scrotal vasectomy, the ligation or severing of the ductus deferens, inhibits sperm transport without altering normal endocrine function. A scrotal vasectomy generally is not a simple procedure, and considerable care must be exercised to avoid damaging the spermatic artery-vein plexus. In contrast, a laparoscopic vasectomy technique has been described and applied to a variety of domestic as well as zoo species (Bush, Seager, and Wildt 1980; Wildt, Seager, and Bridges 1981). Each ductus deferens is identified intra-abdominally using a laparoscope and coagulated or severed using an ancillary forceps. Sperm concentration generally is reduced to zero within 5 days of this simple procedure.

Because androgens suppress pituitary release of FSH and LH, it would appear logical that testosterone or its derivatives could be used for chronic suppression of testicular function. However, all research efforts to date have shown that testosterone esters (including testosterone propionate, enanthate, cypionate, and cyclohexanecarboxylate) must be injected either daily or at least weekly to be effective (see Nieschlag, Michel, and Knuth 1985 for review), an impractical requirement in the management of most zoo species. Certain androgenic derivatives also may induce unacceptable side effects, including weight gain, decreased testicular size, and alterations in blood chemistries. Oral androgens (testosterone undecanoate, fluoxymesterone, mesterelone) also have been tested but are ineffective because, although spermatogenesis is depressed, ejaculates do not achieve aspermia. Testosterone also has been injected in combination with other hormones, including cyproterone acetate (an antiandrogen), progestogens (norethindrone, medroxyprogesterone acetate, megestrol acetate), and danazol (a derivative of ethinyltestosterone). In most cases, sperm concentration decreases after treatment, but aspermia is not universally achieved. The primary advantage of the steroidal contraceptive approach is that fertility returns when treatment stops. The major disadvantages are the required frequency and route of administration and the inconsistency in reaching an aspermic condition during treatment.

Since the biochemical elucidation of GnRH, amino acid substitutions have permitted the synthesis of GnRH superacting agonists and antagonists (blockers to pituitary gonadotropin release). Both of these types of GnRH analogues have been considered as potential male antifertility drugs. Implantable osmotic mini-pumps have been used to deliver a constant infusion of GnRH agonist or antagonist in fertility trials involving macaque monkeys (Akhtar et al. 1983; Weinbauer et al. 1984; Mann et al. 1985; Wickings, Marshall, and Nieschlag 1986). Consistent findings of aspermia and reversibility after hormone withdrawal suggest that this approach may be of eventual value in controlling fertility in certain species.

A related strategy is the active immunization of males against GnRH. The peptide, conjugated to human serum albumin and emulsified in Freund's adjuvant, is injected into the animal at 2- to 3-month intervals, stimulating an immune response. The antibodies thus formed neutralize endogenously produced GnRH. Although this is still an experimental procedure, red deer stags have been successfully immunized against GnRH (Lincoln, Fraser, and Fletcher 1982). Three of four treated males cast their antlers prematurely in autumn instead of spring. When the deer had peak circulating titers of GnRH antibodies, the testes were at minimal size and testosterone levels were at nadir concentrations. The immunized stags demonstrated no rutting behavior in the autumn.

THE FUTURE

The key to the successful breeding of wildlife species in zoos is both fundamental and applied knowledge of reproduction. Since the mid-1970s, there has been gradually increasing support for the view that the reproductive physiology of wildlife species can be studied and understood using research approaches similar to those used for decades with farm livestock and common laboratory animals. This chapter more often than not has outlined what is not yet known about regulating or manipulating male reproductive activity and dealing with instances of subfertility or infertility. Experience tells us that before we can deal with abnormal reproductive performance, we must first understand what best can be termed as "normal." This observation alone mandates the need for much more basic research with most zoo species, and most of this should be descriptive, that is, characterizing such functions as normal semen and hormonal characteristics as well as the influence of environmental factors (i.e., season, nutrition, stress). Given the conservation biology crisis and the number of species requiring assistance, one quickly could become discouraged by the overwhelming challenges and work yet required.

To avoid this pitfall, perhaps a more enlightened and positive approach is to focus on the considerable progress that has been and is being made in the field of zoo animal reproductive science. These accomplishments, which have been alluded to throughout this chapter, are rather remarkable given that (1) few zoos have organized reproductive research programs and (2) federal funding for such efforts is so dismally poor. A review of the chapter indicates that information on fundamental semen characteristics and endogenous hormone profiles is now available for a wide range of species. There is also sufficient evidence demonstrating that the technical laboratory procedures used for assessing the reproductive status of humans and domestic animals are relatively effective for many wildlife species. Particularly exciting are new strategies for measuring endocrine products in voided urine and feces, which provide an accurate and atraumatic approach for evaluating physiological status while eliminating the need for animal restraint and anesthesia. These advances are complemented by the usually reliable ability to collect semen samples routinely and safely, especially by electroejaculation. The ability to evaluate, process, and use these semen samples has improved exponentially, and advances, especially in sperm function bioassays, allow more accurate estimates of fertility potential.

The extent of infertility in captive wildlife species remains unknown, and we understand even less about how to identify the causes or provide treatment for poor reproductive performance. However, there is little doubt that this area of research will receive more attention and will be bolstered by the gradually developing data base on what is normal, as well as by continued related efforts in human medicine.

Finally, more research is warranted because the conservation community is rapidly developing an interest in the practical potential of reproductive biotechnology. There have been a number of symposia, review articles, and reports detailing the potential and problems of using techniques such as artificial insemination, embryo transfer, and in vitro fertilization for studying and propagating rare animal species (see Holt and Moore 1988; Wildt 1989a, 1989b, 1990, 1992; Wildt and Seal 1988; Wildt et al. 1992 for review). There are an ever-increasing number of reports documenting the births of live offspring to a variety of wild species as a result of each of these biotechniques. These "assisted" breeding approaches pose unique challenges, and often the precise techniques required vary considerably, primarily because of profound or subtle physiological differences among related species (Wildt et al. 1992). The ultimate utility of reproductive biotechnology will be based largely on a comprehensive understanding of basic reproductive processes in the male as well as the female. Therefore, as this science proceeds, it will always be important to emphasize the value of fundamental norms. This information will serve as the framework for effectively assessing, managing, and controlling fertility in wildlife species.

ACKNOWLEDGMENTS

The author is indebted to M. Bush, J. G. Howard, R. J. Montali, S. Monfort, J. Brown, K. L. Goodrowe, M. C. Schiewe, and A. P. Byers for reviewing and offering helpful criticism of the manuscript. The author's cited research is supported, in part, by the Friends of the National Zoo, the

National Geographic Society, the New Opportunities in Animal Health Sciences (NOAHS) Center, the U.S. Fish and Wildlife Service, and the National Institutes of Health.

REFERENCES

Adam, C. L., and Atkinson, T. 1984. Effect of feeding melatonin to red deer *(Cervus elaphus)* on the onset of the breeding season. *J. Reprod. Fertil.* 72:463–66.

Adam, C. L., Moir, C. E., and Atkinson, T. 1986. Induction of early breeding in red deer *(Cervus elaphus)* by melatonin. *J. Reprod. Fertil.* 76:569–73.

Akhtar, F. B., Marshall, G. R., Wickings, E. J., and Nieschlag, E. 1983. Reversible induction of azoospermia in rhesus monkeys by constant infusion of a gonadotropin-releasing hormone using osmotic mini-pumps. *J. Clin. Endocrinol. Metab.* 56:534–40.

Albertsen, P. L., Chang, T. S. K., Vindivich, D., Robinson, J. C., and Smyth, J. W. 1983. A critical method of evaluating tests for male infertility. *J. Urol.* 130:467–75.

Alexander, N. J. 1981. Evaluation of male infertility with an in vitro cervical mucus penetration test. *Fertil. Steril.* 36:201–8.

Amann, R. P. 1986. Reproductive physiology and endocrinology of the dog. In *Current therapy in theriogenology,* ed. D. Morrow, 532–38. Philadelphia: W. B. Saunders.

Andrews, J. C., Howard, J. G., Bavister, B. D., and Wildt, D. E. 1992. Sperm capacitation in the domestic cat *(Felis catus)* and leopard cat *(Felis bengalensis)* studied with a salt-stored zona pellucida assay. *Mol. Reprod. Dev.* 31:200–207.

Barone, M. H., Roelke, M. E., Howard, J. G., Anderson, A. E., and Wildt, D. E. 1994. Reproductive characteristics of male Florida panthers: Comparative studies from Florida, Texas, Colorado, Chile, and North American zoos. *J. Mammal.* 75:150–62.

Blank, M. S. 1986. Pituitary gonadotropins and prolactin. In *Reproduction and development,* vol. 3, *Comparative primate biology,* ed. W. R. Dukelow and J. Erwin, 17–61. New York: Alan R. Liss.

Bostofte, E., Serup, J., and Rebbe, H. 1982. Relation between morphologically abnormal spermatozoa and pregnancies obtained during a 20-year follow-up period. *Int. J. Androl.* 5:379–86.

Brown, J. L., Bush, M., Packer, C., Pusey, A. E., Monfort, S. L., O'Brien, S. J., Janssen, D. L., and Wildt, D. E. 1991a. Developmental changes in pituitary-gonadal function in free-ranging lions *(Panthera leo)* of the Serengeti Plains and Ngorongoro Crater. *J. Reprod. Fertil.* 91:29–40.

Brown, J. L., Goodrowe, K. L., Simmons, L. G., Armstrong, D. L., and Wildt, D. E. 1988. Evaluation of pituitary-gonadal response to GnRH, and adrenal status, in the leopard *(Panthera pardus japonesis)* and tiger *(Panthera tigris)*. *J. Reprod. Fertil.* 82:227–36.

Brown, J. L., Wildt, D. E., Phillips, L. G., Seidensticker, J., Fernando, S. B. U., Miththapala, S., and Goodrowe, K. L. 1989. Ejaculate characteristic, and adrenal-pituitary-gonadal interrelationships in captive leopards *(Panthera pardus kotiya)* isolated on the island of Sri Lanka. *J. Reprod. Fertil.* 85:605–13.

Brown, J. L., Wildt, D. E., Raath, C. R., de Vos, V., Howard, J. G., Janssen, D., Citino, S., and Bush, M. 1991b. Impact of season on seminal characteristics and endocrine status of adult free-living African buffalo *(Syncerus caffer caffer)* *J. Reprod. Fertil.* 92:47–57.

Brown, J. L., Wildt, D. E., Raath, C. R., de Vos, V., Janssen, D. L., Citino, S., Howard, J. G., and Bush, M. 1991c. Seasonal variation in pituitary-gonadal function in free-ranging impala *(Aepyceros melampus)* *J. Reprod. Fertil.* 93:497–505.

Bubenik, G. A. 1983. Shift of seasonal cycle in white-tailed deer by oral administration of melatonin. *J. Exp. Zool.* 225:155–56.

Bubenik, G. A., Morris, J. M., Schams, D., and Claus, A. 1982. Photoperiodicity and circannual levels of LH, FSH, and testosterone in normal and castrated male white-tailed deer. *Can. J. Physiol. Pharmacol.* 60:788–93.

Bubenik, G. A., and Smith, P. S. 1987. Circadian and circannual rhythms of melatonin in plasma of male white-tailed deer and the effect of oral administration of melatonin. *J. Exp. Zool.* 241:81–89.

Burke, T. J. 1986. Testicular biopsy. In *Small animal reproduction and infertility: A clinical approach to diagnosis and treatment,* ed. T. J. Burke, 140–46. Philadelphia: Lea & Febiger.

Bush, M., Seager, S. W. J., and Wildt, D. E. 1980. Laparoscopy in zoo mammals. In *Animal laparoscopy,* ed. R. M. Harrison and D. E. Wildt, 169–82. Baltimore: Williams and Wilkins.

Byers, A. P., Hunter, A. G., Hensleigh, H. C., Kreeger, T. J., Binczik, G., Reindl, N. J., Seal, U. S., and Tilson, R. L. 1987. In vitro capacitation of Siberian tiger spermatozoa. *Zoo Biol.* 6:297–304.

Byers, A. P., Hunter, A. G., Seal, U. S., Binczik, G. A., Graham, E. F., Reindl, N. J., and Tilson, R. L. 1989a. In vitro induction of capacitation of fresh and frozen spermatozoa of the Siberian tiger *(Panthera tigris)*. *J. Reprod. Fertil.* 86:599–607.

Byers, A. P., Hunter, A. G., Seal, U. S., Graham, E. F., and Tilson, R. L. 1989b. Effect of season on semen quality, seminal plasma chemistry, and hormone levels in male Siberian tigers. *Biol. Reprod. Suppl.* 40 (1): 156.

Chandrasekhar, Y., D'Occhio, M. J., Holland, M. K., and Setchell, B. P. 1985. Activity of the hypothalamo-pituitary axis and testicular development in prepubertal ram lambs with induced hypothyroidism or hyperthyroidism. *Endocrinology* 117:1645–51.

Christiansen, P. 1975. Studies on the relationship between spermatogenesis and urinary levels of follicle stimulating hormone and luteinizing hormone in oligospermic men. *Acta Endocrinol.* 78:192–208.

Cohen, M. S., Frye, S., Warner, R. S., and Leiter, E. 1984. Testicular needle biopsy in the diagnosis of infertility. *Urology* 24:439–42.

Courot, M., and Ortavant, R. 1981. Endocrine control of spermatogenesis in rams. *J. Reprod. Fertil., Suppl.* 30:47–60.

Curry, P. T., Ziemer, T., Van der Horst, G., Burgess, W., Straley, M., Atherton, R. W., and Kitchin, R. M. 1989. A comparison of sperm morphology and silver nitrate staining characteristics in the domestic ferret and the black-footed ferret. *Gamete Res.* 22:27–36.

Dahl, D. K., Czekala, N. M., Lim, P., and Hsueh, A. J. W. 1987. Monitoring the menstrual cycle of humans and lowland gorillas based on urinary profiles of bioactive follicle stimulating hormone and steroid metabolites. *J. Clin. Endocrin. Metab.* 64:486–93.

Dixson, A. F., Moore, H. D. M., and Holt, W. V. 1980. Testicular atrophy in captive gorillas *(Gorilla gorilla)*. *J. Zool.* (Lond.) 191:315–22.

Dony, J. M., Smals, A. G., Rolland, R., Fauser, B. C., and Thomas, C. M. 1985. Effect of lower versus higher doses of tamoxifen on pituitary-gonadal function and sperm indices in oligozoospermic men. *Andrologia* 17:369–78.

Durrant, B. S. 1987. Penetration of hamster ova by non-human primate spermatozoa. *J. Androl.* 8:27.

———. 1990. Semen characteristics of the Przewalski's stallion *(Equus przewalskii)*. *Theriogenology* 33:221.

Durrant, B. S., Schuerman, T., and Millard, S. 1985. Noninvasive semen collection in the cheetah. *AAZPA Annual Conference Proceedings,* 564–67. Wheeling, W.Va.: American Association of Zoological Parks and Aquariums.

Ericsson, R. J., Langevin, C. N., and Nishino, M. 1973. Isolation of fractions rich in human Y sperm. *Nature* 246:421–24.

Fauser, B. C., Rolland, R., Dony, J. M., and Corbey, R. S. 1985. Long-term, pulsatile, low dose, subcutaneous luteinizing hormone-releasing hormone administration in men with idiopathic oligozoospermia: Failure of therapeutic and hormonal response. *Andrologia* 17:143–49.

Fennessy, P. F., Suttie, J. M., Crosbie, S. F., Corson, I. D., Elgar, H. J., and Lapwood, D. R. 1988. Plasma LH and testosterone responses to gonadotrophin-releasing hormone in adult red deer (*Cervus elaphus*) stags during the annual antler cycle. *J. Endocrin.* 117:35–41.

Fossati, P., Asfour, M., Blacker, C., Bouteny, J. J., and Hermand, E. 1979. Serum and seminal gonadotropins in normal and infertile men: Correlations with sperm count, prolactinemia, and seminal prolactin. *Arch. Androl.* 2:247–52.

Foster, J. W., and Rowley, M. J. 1982. Testicular biopsy in the study of gorilla infertility. *Am. J. Primatol., Suppl.* 1:121–25.

Frank, L. G., Smith, E. R., and Davidson, J. M. 1985. Testicular origin of circulating androgens in spotted hyaena, *Crocuta crocuta*. *J. Zool.* (Lond.) 207:613–15.

Freischem, C. W., Knuth, U. A., Langer, K., Schneider, H. P., and Nieschlag, E. 1984. The lack of discriminant seminal and endocrine variables in the partners of fertile and infertile women. *Arch. Gynecol.* 236:1–12.

Gorman, M. L. 1976. Seasonal changes in the reproductive pattern of feral *Herpestes auropunctatus* (Carnivora: Viverridae) in the Fijian Islands. *J. Zool.* (Lond.) 178:237–46.

Gould, K. G. 1983. Diagnosis and treatment of infertility in male great apes. *Zoo Biol.* 2:281–93.

Gould, K. G., and Kling, O. R. 1982. Fertility in the male gorilla: Relationship to semen parameters and serum hormones. *Am. J. Primatol.* 2:311–16.

Graham, E. F., Schmehl, M. K. L., Evenson, B. F., and Nelson, D. S. 1978. Semen preservation in non-domestic mammals. *Symp. Zool. Soc. Lond.* 43:153–73.

Grocock, C. A., and Clarke, J. R. 1975. Spermatogenesis in mature and regressed testes of the vole, *Microtus agrestis*. *J. Reprod. Fertil.* 43:461–70.

Gross, K. M., Matsumoto, A. M., Berger, R. E., and Bremner, W. J. 1986. Increased frequency of pulsatile luteinizing hormone-releasing hormone administration selectively decreases follicle-stimulating hormone levels in men with idiopathic azoospermia. *Fertil. Steril.* 45:392–96.

Haigh, J. C., Cates, W. F., Glover, G. J., and Rawlings, N. C. 1984. Relationships between seasonal changes in serum testosterone concentrations, scrotal circumference, and sperm morphology of male wapiti (*Cervus elaphus*). *J. Reprod. Fertil.* 70:413–18.

Hall, L. L., Bush, M., Howard, J. G., and Wildt, D. E. 1985. Intra- and interspecies comparison of sperm migration through polyacrylamide gel as an index of spermatozoal viability. *Zoo Biol.* 4:329–37.

Hansen, P. J. 1985. Photoperiodic regulation of reproduction in mammals breeding during long days versus mammals breeding during short days. *Anim. Reprod. Sci.* 9:301–5.

Harrison, R. M. 1980. Semen parameters in *Macaca mulatta*: Ejaculates from random and selected monkeys. *J. Med. Primatol.* 9:265–73.

Herndon, J. G., Allen, W. C., and Blakely, R. D. 1980. Increases in testosterone levels and in copulatory behavior of male rhesus monkeys following treatment with human chorionic gonadotropin. *Horm. Behav.* 14:337–47.

Hönigl, W., Knuth, U. A., and Nieschlag, E. 1986. Selective reduction of elevated FSH levels in infertile men by pulsatile LHRH treatment. *Clin. Endocrinol.* 24:177–82.

Holt, W. V., and Moore, H. D. M. 1988. Semen banking: Is it now feasible for captive endangered species? *Oryx* 22:172–78.

Howard, J. G., Brown, J. L., Bush, M., and Wildt, D. E. 1990. Teratospermic and normospermic domestic cats: Ejaculate traits, pituitary-gonadal hormones, and improvement of sperm viability and morphology after swim-up processing. *J. Androl.* 11:204–15.

Howard, J. G., Bush, M., de Vos, V., and Wildt, D. E. 1984. Electroejaculation, semen characteristics, and testosterone concentrations of free-ranging African elephants (*Loxodonta africana*). *J. Reprod. Fertil.* 72:187–95.

Howard, J. G., Bush, M., and Wildt, D. E. 1986. Semen collection, analysis, and cryopreservation in non-domestic mammals. In *Current therapy in theriogenology,* ed. D. A. Morrow, 1047–53. Philadelphia: W. B. Saunders.

Howard, J. G., Bush, M., and Wildt, D. E. 1991. Teratospermia in domestic cats compromises penetration of zona-free hamster ova and cat zona pellucidae. *J. Androl.* 12:36–45.

Howard, J. G., Donoghue, A. M., Johnston, L. A., and Wildt, D. E. 1993. Zona pellucida filtration of structural abnormal spermatozoa and reduced fertilization in teratospermic cats. *Biol. Reprod.* 49:131–39.

Howard, J. G., Pursel, V. G., Wildt, D. E., and Bush, M. 1981. Comparison of various extenders for freeze preservation of semen from selected captive wild ungulates. *J. Am. Vet. Med. Assoc.* 179:1157–61.

Howard, J. G., Raphael, B. L., Brown, J. L., Citino, S., Schiewe, M. C., and Bush, M. 1989. Male sterility associated with karyotypic hybridization in Kirk's dik-dik. *Proceedings of the Annual Meeting of the American Association of Zoo Veterinarians,* 58–60. Philadelphia: American Association of Zoo Veterinarians.

Howard, J. G., and Wildt, D. E. 1990. Ejaculate and hormonal characteristics in the leopard cat (*Felis bengalensis*) and sperm function as measured by in vitro penetration of zona-free hamster ova and zona-intact domestic cat oocytes. *Mol. Reprod. Dev.* 26:163–74.

Howard, J. G., Wildt, D. E., Chakraborty, P. K., and Bush, M. 1983. Reproductive traits including seasonal observations on semen quality and serum hormone concentrations in the Dorcas gazelle. *Theriogenology* 20:221–29.

Illius, A. W., Haynes, N. B., Lamming, G. E., Howles, C. M., Fairall, N., and Millar, R. P. 1983. Evaluation of LH-RH stimulation of testosterone as an index of reproductive status in rams and its application in wild antelope. *J. Reprod. Fertil.* 68:105–12.

Jainudeen, M. R., Katongole, C. B., and Short, R. V. 1972. Plasma testosterone in relation to musth and sexual activity in the male Asian elephant, *Elephas maximus*. *J. Reprod. Fertil.* 29:99–103.

Jones, R. C., Bailey, D. W., and Skinner, J. D. 1975. Studies on the collection and storage of semen from the African elephant, *Loxodonta africana*. *Koedoe* 18:147–64.

Kamidono, S., Hamaguchi, T., Okada, H., Hazama, M., Matsumoto, O., and Ishigami, J. 1984. A new method for rapid spermatozoal concentration and motility: A multiple-exposure photography system using the Polaroid camera. *Fertil. Steril.* 41:620–24.

Keeling, M. E. 1982. Veterinary perspectives of infertility in male great apes. *Am. J. Primatol., Suppl.* 1:87–95.

Knobil, E. 1974. On the control of gonadotropin secretion in the rhesus monkey. *Recent Prog. Horm. Res.* 30:1–46.

Larsen, L. L. 1986. Examination of the reproductive system of the bull. In *Current therapy in theriogenology,* ed. D. A. Morrow, 101–16. Philadelphia: W. B. Saunders.

Lasley, B. L., and Kirkpatrick, J. F. 1991. Ovarian function in captive and free-ranging wildlife by means of urinary and fecal steroids. *J. Zoo Wildl. Med.* 22:23–31.

Levitan, D., Moser, S. A., Goldstein, D. A., Kletzky, O. A., Lobo, R. A., and Massry, S. G. 1984. Disturbances in the hypothalamic-pituitary-gonadal axis in male patients with acute renal failure. *Am. J. Nephrol.* 4:99–106.

Lincoln, G. A. 1974. Reproduction and "March madness" in the brown hare, *Lepus europaeus. J. Zool.* (Lond.) 174:1–14.

———. 1979. Use of a pulsed infusion of luteinizing hormone-releasing hormone to mimic seasonally induced endocrine changes in the ram. *J. Endocrinol.* 83:251–60.

———. 1981. Seasonal aspects of testicular function. In *The testis,* ed. H. Burger and D. de Kretser, 255–302. New York: Raven Press.

———. 1987. Long-term stimulatory effects of a continuous infusion of LHRH agonist on testicular function in male red deer *(Cervus elaphus). J. Reprod. Fertil.* 80:257–61.

Lincoln, G. A., Fraser, H. M., and Fletcher, T. J. 1982. Antler growth in male red deer *(Cervus elaphus)* after active immunization against LH-RH. *J. Reprod. Fertil.* 66:703–8.

———. 1984. Induction of early rutting in male red deer *(Cervus elaphus)* by melatonin and its dependence on LHRH. *J. Reprod. Fertil.* 72:339–43.

Lincoln, G. A., Guinness, F., and Short, R. V. 1972. The way in which testosterone controls the social and sexual behavior of the red deer stag *(Cervus elaphus). Horm. Behav.* 3:375–96.

Lincoln, G. A., and Kay, R. N. B. 1979. Effects of season on the secretion of LH and testosterone in intact and castrated red deer stags *(Cervus elaphus). J. Reprod. Fertil.* 55:75–80.

Lincoln, G. A., and Short, R. V. 1980. Seasonal breeding: Nature's contraceptive. *Recent Prog. Horm. Res.* 36:1–52.

Lindeque, M., Skinner, J. D., and Millar, R. P. 1986. Adrenal and gonadal contribution to circulating androgens in spotted hyaenas *(Crocuta crocuta)* as revealed by LHRH, hCG, and ACTH stimulation. *J. Reprod. Fertil.* 78:211–17.

Lipshultz, L. I. 1976. Cryptorchidism in the subfertile male. *Fertil. Steril.* 27:609–12.

Loudon, A. S. I., and Curlewis, J. D. 1988. Cycles of antler and testicular growth in an aseasonal tropical deer *(Axis axis). J. Reprod. Fertil.* 83:729–38.

Makler, A., Murillo, O., Huszar, G., Tarlatzis, B., DeCherney, A., and Naftolin, F. 1984. Improved techniques for separating motile spermatozoa from human semen. II. An atraumatic centrifugation method. *Int. J. Androl.* 7:71–78.

Malak, G. A., and Thibier, M. 1982. Plasma LH and testosterone responses to synthetic gonadotropin-releasing hormone (GnRH) or dexamethasone-GnRH combined treatment and their relationship to semen output of bulls. *J. Reprod. Fertil.* 64:107–13.

Mann, D. R., Smith, M. M., Gould, K. G., and Collins, D. C. 1985. Effect of a gonadotropin-releasing hormone agonist on luteinizing hormone and testosterone secretion and testicular histology in male rhesus monkeys. *Fertil. Steril.* 43:115–21.

Marson, J., Gervais, D., Meuris, S., Cooper, R. W., and Jouannet, P. 1989. Influence of ejaculation frequency on semen characteristics in chimpanzees *(Pan troglodytes). J. Reprod. Fertil.* 85:43–50.

McMillin, J. M., Seal, U. S., Keenlyne, K. D., Erickson, A. W., and Jones, J. E. 1974. Annual testosterone rhythm in the adult white-tailed deer *(Odocoileus virginianus borealis). Endocrinology* 94:1034–40.

McMillin, J. M., Seal, U. S., Rodgers, L., and Erickson, A. W. 1976. Annual testosterone rhythm in the black bear *(Ursus americanus). Biol. Reprod.* 15:163–67.

Merilan, C. P., Read, B. W., and Boever, W. J. 1982. Semen collection procedures for captive wild animals. *Int. Zoo Yrbk.* 22:241–44.

Mertz, W. 1986. *Trace elements in human and animal nutrition.* 5th ed. 2 vols. New York: Academic Press.

Mićić, S., and Dotlić, R. 1985. Evaluation of sperm parameters in clinical trial with clomiphene citrate of oligospermic men. *J. Urol.* 133:221–22.

Miller, A. M., Roelke, M. E., Goodrowe, K. L., Howard, J. G., and Wildt, D. E. 1990. Oocyte recovery, maturation and fertilization in vitro in the puma *(Felis concolor). J. Reprod. Fertil.* 88:249–58.

Miller, R. P., and Glover, T. D. 1970. Seasonal changes in the reproductive tract of the male rock hyrax, *Procavia capensis. J. Reprod. Fertil.* 23:497–99.

———. 1973. Regulation of seasonal sexual activity in an ascrotal mammal, the rock hyrax, *Procavia capensis. J. Reprod. Fertil., Suppl.* 19:203–20.

Mirarchi, R. E., Howland, B. E., Scanlon, P. F., Kirkpatrick, R. L., and Sanford, L. M. 1978. Seasonal variation in plasma LH, FSH, prolactin, and testosterone concentrations in adult male white-tailed deer. *Can. J. Zool.* 56:121–27.

Monfort, S. L., Brown, J. L., Bush, M., Wood, T. C., Wemmer, C., Vargus, A., Williamson, L. R., Montali, R., and Wildt, D. E. 1993a. Circannual interrelationships among reproductive hormones, gross morphometry, behaviour, ejaculate characteristics, and testicular histology in Eld's deer stags *(Cervus eldi thamin). J. Reprod. Fertil.* 98:471–80.

Monfort, S. L., Brown, J. L., Wood, T. C., Wemmer, C., Vargus, A., Williamson, L. R., and Wildt, D. E. 1993b. Seasonal secretory patterns of basal and GnRH-induced LH, FSH, and testosterone in Eld's deer *(Cervus eldi thamin). J. Reprod. Fertil.* 98:481–88.

Monfort, S. L., Wemmer, C., Kepler, T. H., Bush, M., Brown, J. L., and Wildt, D. E. 1990. Monitoring ovarian function and pregnancy in the Eld's deer *(Cervus eldi)* by evaluating urinary steroid metabolite excretion. *J. Reprod. Fertil.* 88:271–81.

Morrow, D. A. 1986. *Current therapy in theriogenology.* Philadelphia: W. B. Saunders.

Mossing, T., and Damber, J. E. 1981. Rutting behavior and androgen variation in reindeer *(Rangifer tarandus* L.). *J. Chem. Ecol.* 7:377–89.

Nachreiner, R. F. 1986. Laboratory endocrine diagnostic procedures in theriogenology. In *Current therapy in theriogenology,* ed. D. A. Morrow, 17–20. Philadelphia: W. B. Saunders.

Neal, J., Murphy, B. D., Moger, W. H., and Oliphant, L. W. 1977. Reproduction in the male ferret: Gonadal activity during the annual cycle; recrudescence and maturation. *Biol Reprod.* 17:380–85.

Nieschlag, E., Michel, E., and Knuth, U. A. 1985. Endocrine approach to male fertility regulation. *Proceedings of the Third International Conference on Andrology,* 9–23.

Noci, I., Chelo, E., Sattarelli, O., Donati Cori, G., and Scarselli, G. 1985a. Tamoxifen and oligospermia. *Arch. Androl.* 15:83–88.

Noci, I., Saltarelli, O., Dubini, V., Tantini, C., Chelo, E., Messori, A., and Scarselli, G. 1985b. Plasma concentrations of FSH and testosterone in male infertile patients. *Acta Eur. Fertil.* 16:175–78.

O'Brien, S. J., Martenson, J. S., Packer, C., Herbst, L., de Vos, V., Joslin, P., Ott-Joslin, J., Wildt, D. E., and Bush, M. 1987. Biochemical genetic variation in zoogeographic isolates of African and Asiatic lions. *Natl. Geogr. Res.* 3:114–24.

O'Brien, S. J., Roelke, M. E., Marker, L., Newman, A., Winkler, C. W., Meltzer, D., Colly, L., Evermann, J., Bush, M., and Wildt, D. E. 1985. Genetic basis for species vulnerability in the cheetah. *Science* 227:1428–34.

O'Brien, S. J., Wildt, D. E., Goldman, D., Merril, C. R., and Bush, M. 1983. The cheetah is depauperate in genetic variation. *Science* 221:459–62.

Ortavant, R., Courot, M., and Hocherean de Reviers, M. T. 1977. Spermatogenesis in domestic mammals. In *Reproduction in domestic animals,* ed. H. H. Cole and P. T. Cupps, 203–56. New York: Academic Press.

Ott, R. S. 1986. Breeding soundness examination of bulls. In *Current therapy in theriogenology*, ed. D. A. Morrow, 125–36. Philadelphia: W. B. Saunders.

Plotka, E. D., Seal, U. S., Letellier, M. A., Verme, L. J., and Ozoga, J. J. 1984. Early effects of pinealectomy on LH and testosterone secretion in white-tailed deer. *J. Endocrinol.* 103:1–7.

Post, G. S., Hensleigh, H. C., Byers, A. P., Seal, U. S., Kreeger, T. J., Reindl, N. J., and Tilson, R. L. 1987. Penetration of zona-free hamster ova by Siberian tiger sperm. *Zoo Biol.* 6:183–87.

Racey, P. A. 1978. Seasonal changes in testosterone and androgen-dependent organs in male moles *(Talpa europaea)*. *J. Reprod. Fertil.* 52:195–200.

Racey, P. A., and Skinner, J. D. 1979. Endocrine aspects of sexual mimicry in spotted hyaenas, *Crocuta crocuta*. *J. Reprod. Fertil.* 187:315–26.

Resko, J. A. 1967. Plasma androgen levels of the rhesus monkey: Effects of age and season. *Endocrinology* 81:1203–12.

———. 1982. Endocrine correlates of infertility in male primates. *Am. J. Primatol., Suppl.* 1:37–42.

Robinson, J. A., Scheffler, G., Eisele, S. G., and Goy, R. W. 1975. Effects of age and season on sexual behavior and plasma testosterone and dihydrotestosterone concentration of laboratory-housed rhesus monkeys *(Macaca mulatta)*. *Biol. Reprod.* 13:203–10.

Rodger, J. C. 1978. Male reproduction: Its usefulness in discussions of Macropodidae evolution. *Aust. Mammal.* 2:73–80.

Rodger, J. C., and Hughes, R. L. 1973. Studies of the accessory glands of male marsupials. *Aust. J. Zool.* 21:303–20.

Rodger, J. C., and Pollitt, C. C. 1981. Radiographic examination of electroejaculation in marsupials. *Biol. Reprod.* 24:1125–34.

Rodger, J. C., and White, I. G. 1975. Electroejaculation of Australian marsupials and analyses of the sugars in the seminal plasma from three macropod species. *J. Reprod. Fertil.* 43:233–39.

———. 1978. The collection, handling, and some properties of marsupial semen. In *Artificial breeding of non-domestic species*, ed. P. F. Watson, 289–301. London: Academic Press.

Rogers, B. J., Van Campen, H., Ueno, M., Lambert, H., Bronson, R., and Hale, R. 1979. Analysis of human spermatozoal fertilizing ability using zona-free ova. *Fertil. Steril.* 32:664–70.

Ryder, O. A., Kumamoto, A. R., Durrant, B. S., and Benirschke, K. 1989. Chromosomal divergence and reproductive isolation in dik-diks. In *Speciation and its consequences*, ed. D. Otte and J. A. Endler, 208–25. Sunderland, Mass.: Sinauer Associates.

Schams, D., and Barth, D. 1982. Annual profiles of reproductive hormones in peripheral plasma of the male roe deer *(Capreolus capreolus)*. *J. Reprod. Fertil.* 66:463–68.

Schiewe, M. C., Bush, M., de Vos, V., Brown, J. L., and Wildt, D. E. 1991. Semen characteristics, sperm freezing, and endocrine profiles in free-ranging wildebeest *(Connochaetes taurinus)* and greater kudu *(Tragelaphus strepsiceros)*. *J. Zoo Wildl. Med.* 22:58–72.

Schroeder, J. P., and Keller, K. V. 1989. Seasonality of serum testosterone levels and sperm density in *Tursiops truncatus*. *J. Exp. Zool.* 249:316–21.

———. 1990. Artificial insemination of bottlenose dolphins. In *The bottlenose dolphin*, ed. S. Leatherwood and R. R. Reeves, 447–60. San Diego: Academic Press.

Scott, R. S., and Burger, H. G. 1981. Mechanism of action of inhibin. *Biol. Reprod.* 24:541–50.

Seal, U. S. 1990. *Fertility control in wildlife*. New Haven: Yale University Press.

Sempere, A. J., and Lacroix, A. 1982. Temporal and seasonal relationships between LH, testosterone, and antlers in fawn and adult male roe deer *(Capreolus capreolus* L.): A longitudinal study from birth to 4 years of age. *Acta Endocrinol.* 99:295–301.

Sherins, R. J., and Howards, S. S. 1985. Male infertility. In *Campbell's urology*, 5th ed., ed. P. C. Walsh, R. E. Gittes, A. D. Perlmutter, and T. A. Stamey, 640–97. Philadelphia: W. B. Saunders.

Skinner, J. D. 1971. The effect of season on spermatogenesis in some ungulates. *J. Reprod. Fertil., Suppl.* 13:29–37.

Skinner, J. D., Van Zyl, J. H. M., and Van Heerden, J. A. H. 1973. The effect of season on reproduction in the black wildebeest and red hartebeest in South Africa. *J. Reprod. Fertil., Suppl.* 19:101–10.

Slob, A. K., Ocms, M. P., and Ureeburg, J. T. M. 1979. Annual changes in serum testosterone in laboratory housed male stump-tailed macaques *(Macaca arctoides)*. *Biol. Reprod.* 20:981–84.

Smallridge, R. C., Vigersky, R., Glass, A. R., Griffin, J. E., White, B. J., and Eil, C. 1984. Androgen receptor abnormalities in identical twins with oligospermia: Clinical and biochemical studies. *Am. J. Med.* 77:1049–54.

Snyder, D. C., Cowan, R. L., Hagen, D. R., and Schanbacher, B. D. 1983. Effect of pinealectomy on seasonal changes in antler growth and concentrations of testosterone and prolactin in white–tailed deer. *Biol. Reprod.* 29:63–71.

Soderberg, S. F. 1986. Infertility in the male dog. In *Current therapy in theriogenology*, ed. D. A. Morrow, 544–48. Philadelphia: W. B. Saunders.

Stanwell–Smith, R., Thompson, S. G., Haines, A. P., Jeffcoate, S. L., and Hendry, W. F. 1985. Plasma concentrations of pituitary and testicular hormones of fertile and infertile men. *Clin. Reprod. Fertil.* 3:37–48.

Stokkan, K. A., Hove, K., and Carr, W. R. 1980. Plasma concentrations of testosterone and luteinizing hormone in rutting reindeer bulls *(Rangifer tarandus)*. *Can. J. Zool.* 58:2081–83.

Swerdloff, R. S., Overstreet, J. W., Sokol, R. Z., and Rajfer, J. 1985. Infertility in the male. *Ann. Intern. Med.* 103:906–19.

Takemoto, F. S., Rogers, B. J., Wiltbank, M. C., Soderdahl, D. W., Vaughn, W. K., and Hale, R. W. 1985. Comparison of the penetration ability of hamster spermatozoa into bovine cervical mucus and zona-free hamster eggs. *J. Androl.* 6:162–70.

Tang, L. C. H., and Chan, S. Y. W. 1983. Use of albumin gradients for isolation of progressively motile human spermatozoa. *Singapore J. Obstet. Gynecol.* 14:138–42.

Thorpe, D. A., and Herbert, J. 1976. Studies on the duration of the breeding season and photorefractoriness in female ferrets pinealectomized or treated with melatonin. *J. Endocrinol.* 70:255–62.

Tsonis, C. G., and Sharpe, R. M. 1986. Dual gonadal control of follicle-stimulating hormone. *Nature* 321:724–25.

Tung, K. S., Ellis, L. E., Childs, G. V., and Dufau, M. 1984. The dark mink: A model of male infertility. *Endocrinology* 114:922–29.

Vale, W., Rivier, J., Vaugham, J., McClintock, R., Corrigan, A., Woo, W., Karr, D., and Spies, J. 1986. Purification and characterization of an FSH releasing protein from porcine ovarian follicular fluid. *Nature* 321:776–78.

Vasquez, J. M., Ben-Nun, I., Greenblatt, R. B., Mahesh, V. B., and Keel, B. A. 1986. Correlation between follicle-stimulating hormone, luteinizing hormone, prolactin, and testosterone with sperm cell concentration and motility. *Obstet. Gynecol.* 67:86–90.

Watson, P. F. 1978. A review of techniques of semen collection in mammals. *Symp. Zool. Soc. Lond.* 43:97–126.

Weinbauer, G. F., Surmann, F. J., Akhtar, F. B., Shah, G. V., Vickery, B. H., and Nieschlag, E. 1984. Reversible inhibition of testicular function by a gonadotropin-releasing hormone antagonist in monkeys *(Macaca fascicularis)*. *Fertil. Steril.* 42:906–11.

West, N. O., and Nordan, H. C. 1976. Hormonal regulation of reproduction and the antler cycle in the male Columbian black-tailed deer. Part 1. Seasonal changes in the histology of the reproductive organs, serum testosterone, sperm production, and the antler cycle. *Can. J. Zool.* 54:1617–36.

Whitehead, P. E., and McEwan, E. H. 1973. Seasonal variation in the plasma testosterone concentration of reindeer and caribou. *Can. J. Zool.* 51:651–58.

Wickings, E. J., Marshall, G. R., and Nieschlag, E. 1986. Endocrine regulation of male reproduction. In *Reproduction and development: Comparative primate biology,* vol. 3, ed. W. R. Dukelow and J. Erwin, 149–70. New York: Alan R. Liss.

Wildt, D. E. 1985. Reproductive techniques of potential use in the artificial propagation of nonhuman primates. In *The lion-tailed macaque: Status and conservation,* ed. P. G. Heltne, 161–94. New York: Alan R. Liss.

———. 1986. Spermatozoa: Collection, evaluation, metabolism, freezing, and artificial insemination. In *Reproduction and development: Comparative primate biology,* vol. 3, ed. W. R. Dukelow and J. Erwin, 171–94. New York: Alan R. Liss.

———. 1989a. Reproductive research in conservation biology: Priorities and avenues for support. *J. Zoo Wildl. Med.* 20: 391–95.

———. 1989b. Strategies for the practical application of reproductive technologies to endangered species. *Zoo Biol. Suppl.* 1: 17–20.

———. 1990. Potential applications of IVF technology for species conservation. In *Fertilization in mammals,* ed. B. D. Bavister, E. Roldan, and J. Cummins, 349–64. Boston: Serono Publishing.

———. 1992. Genetic resource banking for conserving wildlife species: Justification, examples, and becoming organized on a global basis. *Anim. Reprod. Sci.* 28:247–57.

Wildt, D. E., Brown, J. L., Bush, M., Barone, M. H., Cooper, K. A., Grisham, J., and Howard, J. G. 1993. Reproductive status of cheetahs *(Acinonyx jubatus)* in North American zoos: The benefits of physiological surveys for strategic planning. *Zoo Biol.* 12: 45–80.

Wildt, D. E., Bush, M., Goodrowe, K. L., Packer, C., Pusey, A. E., Brown, J. L., Joslin, P., and O'Brien, S. J. 1987a. Reproductive and genetic consequences of founding isolated lion populations. *Nature* 329:328–31.

Wildt, D. E., Bush, M., Howard, J. G., O'Brien, S. J., Meltzer, D., van Dyk, A., Ebedes, H., and Brand, D. J. 1983a. Unique seminal quality in the South African cheetah and a comparative evaluation in the domestic cat. *Biol. Reprod.* 29:1019–25.

Wildt, D. E., Bush, M., O'Brien, S. J., Murray, N. D., Taylor, A., and Marshall-Graves, J. A. 1991. Semen characteristics in free-living koalas *(Phascolarctos cinereus). J. Reprod. Fertil.* 92: 99–107.

Wildt, D. E., Chakraborty, P. K., Meltzer, D., and Bush, M. 1983b.

Pituitary and gonadal response to luteinizing hormone-releasing hormone administration in the female and male cheetah. *J. Endocrinol.* 101:51–56.

Wildt, D. E., Donoghue, A. M., Johnston, L. A., Schmidt, P. M., and Howard, J. G. 1992. Species and genetic effects on the utility of biotechnology for conservation. *Symp. Zool. Soc. Lond.* 64: 45–59.

Wildt, D. E., Howard, J. G., Chakraborty, P. K., and Bush, M. 1986a. Reproductive physiology of the clouded leopard: II. A circannual analysis of adrenal-pituitary-testicular relationships during electroejaculation or after an adrenocorticotropin hormone challenge. *Biol. Reprod.* 34:949–59.

Wildt, D. E., Howard, J. G., Hall, L. L., and Bush, M. 1986b. Reproductive physiology of the clouded leopard. I. Ejaculates contain high proportions of pleiomorphic spermatozoa throughout the year. *Biol. Reprod.* 34:937–47.

Wildt, D. E., Meltzer, D., Chakraborty, P. K., and Bush, M. 1984. Adrenal-testicular-pituitary relationships in the cheetah subjected to anesthesia/electroejaculation. *Biol. Reprod.* 30: 665–72.

Wildt, D. E., O'Brien, S. J., Howard, J. G., Caro, T. M., Roelke, M. E., Brown, J. L., and Bush, M. 1987b. Similarity in ejaculate-endocrine characteristics in captive versus free-ranging cheetahs of two subspecies. *Biol. Reprod.* 36:351–60.

Wildt, D. E., Phillips, L. G., Simmons, L. G., Chakraborty, P. K., Brown, J. L., Howard, J. G., Teare, A., and Bush, M. 1988. A comparative analysis of ejaculate and hormonal characteristics of the captive male cheetah, tiger, leopard and puma. *Biol. Reprod.* 38:245–55.

Wildt, D. E., Phillips, L. G., Simmons, L. G., Goodrowe, K. G., Howard, J. G., Brown, J. L., and Bush, M. 1987c. Seminal-endocrine characteristics of the tiger and the potential for artificial breeding. In *Tigers of the world: The biology, biopolitics, management and conservation of an endangered species,* ed. R. L. Tilson and U. S. Seal, 255–79. Park Ridge, N.J.: Noyes.

Wildt, D. E., Seager, S. W. J., and Bridges, C. H. 1981. Sterilization of the male dog and cat by laparoscopic occlusion of the ductus deferens. *Am. J. Vet. Res.* 42:1888–97.

Wildt, D. E., and Seal, U. S. 1988. *Research priorities for single species conservation biology.* Washington, D.C.: Smithsonian Institution.

Wyrobek, A. J. 1979. Changes in mammalian sperm morphology after x-ray and chemical exposures. *Genetics* 92:105–19.

Yanagimachi, R., Yanagimachi, H., and Rogers, B. J. 1976. The use of zona-free animal ova as a test system for the assessment of the fertilizing capacity of human spermatozoa. *Biol. Reprod.* 15: 471–76.

Zamboni, L., Conaway, C. H., and Van Pelt, L. 1974. Seasonal changes in production of semen in free-ranging rhesus monkeys. *Biol. Reprod.* 11:251–67.

40

Contraception as a Management Tool for Controlling Surplus Animals

CHERYL S. ASA, INGRID PORTON, ANNE M. BAKER, AND EDWARD D. PLOTKA

The concept of zoos as a collective ark is now a familiar one. The continuing explosion of the human population and the consequent shrinking of wildlife habitat make the zoo's role as a reserve for endangered species essential. The emergence of well-organized national and international captive breeding programs has focused attention on the limited carrying capacity of zoos. A 1986 analysis (Soulé et al. 1986) suggested that the space available for mammals, birds, reptiles, and amphibians in North American zoos could accommodate a total of only 925 species. Allowing for 300 individuals per species, only 275 mammal species could be maintained in self-sustaining populations. The same authors suggested that, at the very least, 815 species of mammals would require captive habitat. Clearly, even if additional zoo space becomes available, severe space restrictions will remain a reality. The realization that excess numbers of one species will deprive another species of captive habitat underscores the importance of planned breeding programs. Such programs require the ability to prevent as well as enhance reproduction.

The need for well-designed, scientifically based breeding programs stimulated the development of the AZA (American Zoo and Aquarium Association) Species Survival Plans (SSP). These programs now number approximately 60 and are based on the principle of maintaining each captive population at a minimum size while preserving genetic diversity (see Ballou and Foose, chap. 26, this volume). Typically, the number of offspring required from each individual is substantially below the number that individual could produce in a lifetime. Consequently, the very structure of the SSP demands that the captive animal manager have available an array of birth control options that will permit adherence to recommendations that exclude reproduction in any given period.

Not all species exhibited in zoos are endangered or part of a planned breeding program. Uncontrolled breeding of other species reduces the space available for species in cooperative breeding programs and creates a number of animals that are surplus to maintaining the genetic health of the population. The disposition of surplus animals to unqualified individuals or institutions violates the moral and ethical code of conduct expected of zoo professionals. The best solution to the surplus problem is to prevent it. Managers can no longer take a laissez-faire attitude toward the procreation of any species in their care. The manager's goal should be for every birth to be a planned birth. Although honest accidents, an excess of one sex, and other factors preclude the possibility of totally eliminating the surplus animal problem, responsible animal management can substantially reduce it. The availability of a variety of birth control options is essential if such goals are to be realized.

SURVEY OF CONTRACEPTIVE METHODS CURRENTLY IN USE

Most contraceptive research and development has been for human or pet applications or for wildlife or feral population management (table 40.1). In contrast, reproduction in captive animals has traditionally been viewed by zoo biologists as the ultimate indication of the health and well-being of the animals (Hediger 1964; Curtis 1982). Prevention of reproduction has been viewed not as a management tool, but as the antithesis of a breeding program; the solution to the surplus animal problem was more space (Perry, Bridgwater, and Horsemen 1975) and less prohibitive legislation (Curtis 1982). However, the importance of reversible contraception as a method to aid in the establishment of genetically variable captive populations within the constraints of limited captive habitat was recognized early on by Seal et al. (1976). By the late 1980s, the need to delay or space the breeding of individuals to accomplish the goals set by many of the SSPs led to an increasing awareness of the value of birth control.

In response to the dearth of knowledge concerning the options available to captive wildlife managers (Knowles 1986), the AZA formed its Contraceptive Task Force in

TABLE 40.1.   Contraceptive Use in Wild and Captive Populations

Species	Hormone[a]	Reference
Microtus spp.	Mestranol	Howard and Marsh 1969
Cynomys ludovicianus	DES	Pfeiffer 1972; Garrett and Franklin 1983
Oryctolagus cuniculus	Chlormadinone	Vickery and Bennett 1969; Vickery et al. 1970; Erickson, Vickery, and Bennett 1970; Glass and Morris 1972
	Progesterone	Chang 1967; Nutting and Mares 1970; Vickery et al. 1970; Hudson, Hemphill, and Tillson 1978
Callithrix jacchus	GnRH analogue	Hodges and Hearn 1979
Macaca mulatta	Norethindrone	Nygren et al. 1974
	Megestrol	Cuadros, Brinson, and Sundaram 1970; Cuadros and Sundaram 1976
	GnRH analogue	Chappel et al. 1980; Balmaceda et al. 1984
M. arctoides	GnRH analogue	Fraser, Laird, and Blakeley 1980; Fraser et al. 1987
M. fascicularis	GnRH analogue	Corbin et al. 1978
	GnRH + norgestimate	Danforth et al. 1990
Papio spp.	Norgestrel	Humpel et al. 1977
	Norethisterone	Beck et al. 1979
Papio anubis	Progesterone	Tillson et al. 1976
	hCG	Stevens et al. 1981
Papio papio	GnRH analogue	Vickery and McRae 1980
Saimiri sciureus	Megestrol	Harrison and Dukelow 1971
Mustela vison	DES	Travis and Schaible 1962
Mephitis mephitis	DES	Storm and Sanderson 1969b
Vulpes vulpes	DES	Linhart and Enders 1964; Oleyar and McGinnes 1974; Allen 1982
	Clomiphene	Cheatum and Hansel 1967
	Chlormadinone	Cheatum and Hansel 1967
	Mestranol	Cheatum and Hansel 1967
	MPA	Storm and Sanderson 1969a
Urocyon cinereoargenteus	DES	Oleyar and McGinnes 1974
Canis familiaris	Testosterone	Simmons and Hamner 1973
	Melengestrol	Sokolowski and Van Ravenswaay 1976; Wildt and Seager 1977
	Proligesterone	Van Os and Oldenkamp 1978
	Mibolerone	Sokolowski and Zimbelman 1976
	GnRH agonist	Vickery et al. 1984
C. lupus	Mibolerone	Gardner, Hueston, and Donovan 1985
C. latrans	DES	Balser 1964; Brushman et al. 1967
Felis catus	Megestrol	Burke 1977; Remfry 1978; McDonald 1980; Kirkpatrick 1986
	MPA	Kirkpatrick 1986
Panthera tigris	MPA	Seal et al. 1975, 1976
	Melengestrol	Seal et al. 1975, 1976
P. pardus	MPA	Seal et al. 1975, 1976
	Melengestrol	Seal et al. 1975, 1976
	Mibolerone	Gardner, Hueston, and Donovan 1985
P. onca	MPA	Seal et al. 1975, 1976
	Melengestrol	Seal et al. 1975, 1976
	Mibolerone	Gardner, Hueston, and Donovan 1985
P. leo	MPA	Seal et al. 1975, 1976
	Melengestrol	Seal et al. 1975, 1976
	Mibolerone	Gardner, Hueston, and Donovan 1985
Cervus canadensis	DES	Greer, Hawkins, and Catlin 1968
Odocoileus virginianus	DES	Harder 1971; Harder and Peterle 1974; Bell and Peterle 1975; Matschke 1977b, 1980
	Melengestrol	Bell and Peterle 1975; Matschke 1977a
Capra hircus	Melengestrol	Hoffman and Wright 1990
Ovis aries	GnRH analogue	Clarke, Fraser, and McNeilly 1978
Oreamnos americanus	Melengestrol	Hoffman and Moorhead 1990
Bos taurus	Melengestrol	Hansel, Malven, and Black 1961; Zimbelman 1963; Hill et al. 1971
	MPA	Zimbelman 1963
Equus caballus	Estradiol + progesterone ethinyl	Plotka et al. 1988
	Estradiol	Plotka et al. 1988
	Norethistrone	Kirkpatrick and Turner 1987

[a] DES, diethylstilbestrol; MPA, medroxyprogesterone acetate.

TABLE 40.2.   Commercially Available, Reversible Contraceptive Methods Used in Zoo Carnivores, Primates, and Ungulates

Method	Carnivores			Primates			Ungulates		
	No. of species	No. of entries	% failure	No. of species	No. of entries	% failure	No. of species	No. of entries	% failure
MGA implant	31	438	1.1	38	600	3.0	22	79	1.3
Norplant	0	0	—	2	16	0	0	0	—
Birth control pills	0	0	—	6	55	9.1	0	0	—
Depo-Provera	4	5	0	6	64	0	2	4	0
Ovaban/Megace	8	10	0	2	2	0	1	1	0
Mibolerone	1	2	0	0	0	—	0	0	—

Note: Summary of survey data base compiled by the AZA Contraception Advisory Group.

mid-1989, later given permanent status as the Contraception Advisory Group. Two of its goals were to compile and disseminate information on the efficacy and safety of contraceptive methods and to coordinate and recommend research into alternative techniques (Wemmer 1989).

To accomplish the first goal, the Contraception Advisory Group developed a data base compiled from information gathered through detailed questionnaires. Surveys designed to obtain historical data on the use of birth control methods in zoo mammals were distributed by taxonomic group. New and follow-up data are collected annually. Between 1989 and 1993 one ungulate, two carnivore, and three primate surveys were sent to 149 North American zoos, and had response rates varying from 57% to 82%.

Survey data revealed that the most frequently used reversible contraceptive method for all taxonomic groups was the melengestrol acetate (MGA) implant (table 40.2). The most significant problem reported with its use was implant loss, 6% and 16% of carnivore and primate implants respectively (Porton, Asa, and Baker 1990), due to infection, social grooming, and intramuscular migration. In many cases implant loss was not immediately detected, and it resulted in three carnivore and seventeen primate pregnancies. The loss rate can be reduced by gas sterilization of the implant, preferably with ethylene oxide, followed by degassing for 1 week, and strict adherence to sterile procedures during implant insertion. In social species, isolation of the female for 4–6 days or use of steel sutures (in callitrichids) to prevent allogrooming of the incision site is also recommended. Identification microchip transponders (see Rice and Kalk, chap. 5, this volume) can be placed in implants prior to their insertion in the animals to facilitate confirmation that the implant is in place or location in the event that it migrates.

The MGA implant has proved to be very effective (table 40.2). The reported failure rate was based solely on those cases in which the implant was confirmed to be in place at conception. The primate data were particularly revealing in that 83% of the species that conceived while implanted were cebids. Analyzed by species, the failure rate was 42% for squirrel monkeys, Saimiri sciureus, 100% for the black-capped capuchin, Cebus apella, and 56% for spider monkeys, Ateles geoffroyi. The failures can perhaps be explained by the differences in steroid dynamics, binding proteins, or receptors that underlie the unusually high levels of endogenous steroids in some New World monkeys (e.g., Nagle et al. 1989; Torii et al. 1987).

Mating was observed in most MGA-implanted carnivore and primate species for which there was an adequate sample size. The effects of MGA implants on perineal tumescence in Old World monkeys varied between genera and even between species. Irregular or reduced sexual swellings were reported to occur in Tonkean macaques, Macaca tonkeana, Barbary macaques, M. sylvanus, and sooty mangabeys, Cercocebus torquatus, whereas complete suppression occurred in lion-tailed macaques, M. silenus, agile mangabeys, Cercocebus galeritus, mandrills, Mandrillus sphinx, and patas monkeys, Erythrocebus patas. Variations in expression of cycling are probably due to species differences in response thresholds to the hormone treatment. Thresholds for suppression of behavioral and peripheral signs of cycling (e.g., perineal swelling) appear to be higher than for contraceptive efficacy.

In the only study of the effects of MGA implants on behavior (Portugal and Asa 1995), the behavior of treated hamadryas baboon females, Papio hamadryas, most resembled that of females that were pregnant or in the luteal phase of the menstrual cycle. Affiliative interactions were lower than in control females, but there was no increase in aggression.

Systematically collected vaginal cytology data from two brown lemurs, Eulemur fulvus, and one black lemur, E. macaco, confirmed that the MGA implants suppressed cycling. Observations of three implanted ruffed lemurs, Varecia variegata, revealed that the vaginal orifice remained sealed throughout the breeding season.

The following data were reported by Porton, Asa, and Baker (1990). Twelve primates were unknowingly implanted while pregnant; of these, eight gave birth to live young. One patas monkey and four golden lion tamarins, Leontopithecus rosalia, were implanted during the first trimester, and one black-and-white colobus monkey, Colobus guereza, and two golden lion tamarins were implanted during the third trimester. The four golden lion tamarins implanted in their first trimester aborted. It was not known whether the MGA implant or the procedure contributed to the abortions. (For further discussion see "Reversible Female-Directed Techniques," below.)

Four ungulate species were implanted while pregnant. A Nile hippopotamus, Hippopotamus amphibius, and a collared peccary, Pecari (=Tayassu) tajacu, gave birth without complications, while a gaur, Bos gaurus, aborted 3 months after implant insertion, and a Siberian ibex, Capra ibex, implanted in her third trimester had to undergo a cesarian delivery (Porton and Hornbeck 1993).

Eleven of nineteen primates that had MGA implants removed to allow reproduction became pregnant. Of the eight females that did not conceive, two died 7 months post–implant removal, two were transferred to new locations and placed in unfamiliar social groups, and the implant from one female was never recovered and may in fact still have been functioning. Three *Varecia* whose implants were removed between 1 and 3 months prior to the breeding season failed to conceive, but were prevented from breeding the following year by separation from males.

Discounting two females whose implants had only recently been removed at the time of the survey, thirteen of nineteen carnivores conceived following implant removal. Of the remaining six females, four were nulliparous prior to implant use and at least two had previously experienced reproductive problems. Taking the above considerations into account, the survey results suggest that reversibility in reproductively sound individuals is actually quite high.

The time between implant removal and return to fertility did not appear to be correlated with duration of implant use. Four carnivores and seven primates that conceived within 3 months of implant removal had been implanted for 11–44 months, with the majority (ten) implanted for 18 months or longer.

Injectable medroxyprogesterone acetate (Depo-Provera) was the second most frequently used reversible method. The only confirmed failure, in a Nile hippopotamus, was dose-related. The same female was successfully contracepted with an increased and more frequently administered dose (Porton and Hornbeck 1993). Three female black lemurs, *Eulemur macaco macaco*, treated with Depo-Provera while pregnant gave birth to live offspring.

Nine orangutans, *Pongo pygmaeus*, were each implanted with two 70 mg capsules of levonorgestrel (Norplant), supplied by The Population Council. Prior to elective removal of the capsules, five females were successfully contracepted for 1–2 years, and two for approximately 4 years. One female conceived after 14 months, but implant presence was never confirmed; a second conceived after 51 months. Seven chimpanzees, *Pan troglodytes*, were implanted with the Norplant commercially available to women (six 36 mg levonorgestrel capsules, 216 mg total). Data are not yet available to confirm whether the 5-year period of efficacy shown for humans applies to great apes.

Birth control pills have been administered to four ape species, a mandrill, and a spider monkey. Four failures were reported in orangutans (two on Norinyl 1+35, two on Ortho-Novum 1/50) and two in chimpanzees (the same female on Modicon 28 and on Ortho-Novum 1/50). One orangutan conceived during a period of several days when pills were not taken. Identifying the cause of the other failures is difficult because an ape can hold the food or liquid containing a pill in its mouth for long periods and later spit it out.

Four other methods reported were involved exclusively in research trials: zona pellucida vaccine, the vas plug, Lupron Depot, and MGA in feed. Because these methods were still experimental, evaluation would be premature.

Concerns regarding the long-term safety of MGA in felids (Kollias 1988) were supported by a recent retrospective study (Munson and Mason 1991). Histological examination of reproductive tracts revealed an association between MGA use and uterine pathology. It is hoped that further analysis can determine the importance of variables such as species, length of use, and age during use. Meanwhile, because no other contraceptive methods have been shown to be safe and effective in felids, Munson and Mason (1991) recommend that MGA treatment be interrupted periodically to give the uterus time for recuperation and that permanent surgical sterilization be considered. Based on studies of progestin treatment of domestic dogs and cats, these problems are not completely unexpected (for reviews see Asa and Porton 1991; Lein and Concannon 1983). The even larger body of literature on laboratory primates indicates that progestins do not induce similar pathology in primates. Too little data exist for other taxonomic groups, such as the ungulates, to be predictive. The need for development of alternative methods of contraception should be obvious.

PERMANENT STERILIZATION

Although prevention of reproduction most frequently must be temporary and reversible, in some cases permanent contraception, or sterilization, is appropriate. Surgical gonadectomy removes the sources of sex steroids as well as gametes in both males and females. Alternatively, chemical sterilization can be performed, either to avoid surgery or, with some agents, to preserve steroidogenesis (Carter 1990; Wiebe, Barr, and Buckingham 1989).

Duct ligation in either the male or the female should be considered permanent. Both techniques effectively prevent conception without suppressing hormone production and thus do not affect social or sexual behavior. As with gonadectomy, vasectomy or tubal ligation can be accomplished surgically, but sclerosing agents injected into the ducts or epididymis offer alternative approaches (e.g., Carter 1990).

REVERSIBLE CONTRACEPTION

Choosing the most suitable contraceptive for each animal and situation is facilitated by understanding not only the methods available, but the points of action of each contraceptive in the sequence of reproductive events. To provide such a framework, the following sections include brief descriptions of male and female reproductive processes.

Hormonal Control of Reproduction

Ovulation, spermatogenesis, and the production of male (androgens) and female (estrogens and progesterone) gonadal steroid hormones are dependent on appropriate stimulation from luteinizing hormone (LH) and follicle-stimulating hormone (FSH; originally called interstitial cell–stimulating hormone in the male) secreted by the anterior pituitary. These hormones, in turn, are controlled by the decapeptide gonadotropin-releasing hormone (GnRH; also called luteinizing hormone–releasing hormone, LHRH), which is released from the hypothalamus in pulses. The pituitary and hypothalamic hormones are subject to both positive and negative feedback control by the same gonadal hormones whose secretion they stimulate, resulting in a tightly orchestrated feedback loop. Thus, the gonadal hormones as well as other agents that suppress the production or release of gonadotropins can effectively prevent follicle growth, ovulation, or spermatogenesis. In the female, the dynamics of progesterone and estrogen levels can be critical for implantation. Furthermore, progesterone, secreted by corpora lutea on the ovary or by the placenta, is necessary for the support of pregnancy. Therefore, interfering with production of progesterone and estrogen may prevent implantation or pregnancy maintenance.

Reversible Male-Directed Techniques

Steroid Hormones. Testosterone administration disrupts spermatogenesis in the male via negative feedback effects on GnRH and LH and FSH. Without stimulation from the gonadotropins, spermatogenesis does not occur. Microencapsulated testosterone propionate injected into feral stallions achieved contraception (Kirkpatrick, Turner, and Perkins 1982; Turner and Kirkpatrick 1982). Booster injections of this slow-release, microencapsulated formulation were required once per year in this seasonal breeder; continuous breeders might require more frequent treatment. At present, microencapsulated testosterone is not commercially available. Free testosterone and testosterone cypionate, although readily available, would require administration daily or weekly. Possible long-term effects, such as hypermasculinization, including increased aggression or hypersexuality, have not been assessed.

The antiandrogen cyproterone acetate has been successful in disrupting epididymal sperm maturation (Kaur, Ramakrishnan, and Rajalakshmi 1990). However, its long-term efficacy and safety as a contraceptive have not been established.

Hormone Antagonists and Agonists. Analogues of GnRH include both antagonists and agonists. Pure antagonists bind receptors of the native hormone and thus block its action. Current-generation antagonists are much less potent than agonists and so are required in much higher doses, making them less practical and more costly for chronic use.

Agonists share at least some of the biological action of their native hormone and achieve contraception through negative feedback, not by direct blockage. As mentioned above, pituitary hormones respond to pulsatile, not tonic, GnRH stimulation. Thus, after an initial stimulatory phase, agonists suppress LH and FSH production when administered continuously. Leuprolide acetate (Lupron) is an agonist presently marketed in the United States.

In the male, analogues of GnRH can interfere with the stimulatory effect of GnRH on LH and FSH secretion and thus suppress spermatogenesis (Vickery 1981). However, because testosterone production also is disrupted, testosterone-supported male behavior and secondary sex characteristics are diminished (Davis-daSilva and Wallen 1989; Doering et al. 1980). For some species, suppression of male aggression may be desirable. Where male-typical characteristics and behavior are desired, testosterone administration combined with a higher dose of agonist successfully preserves these features while maintaining azoospermia (Nestor and Vickery 1988).

Subcutaneously implantable devices are being developed to provide sustained release of peptide hormones such as GnRH analogues (Deghenghi 1989; Furr and Hutchinson 1989; Davidson et al. 1988; Burns, McRae, and Sanders 1988), which will make their application to contraception more feasible.

Occlusion of the Vas Deferens. Although vasectomy is an attractive option in many situations, the difficulties attendant on microsurgical reversal have stimulated the search for reversible vas occlusion methods (see review by Zaneveld et al. 1986). The approaches being investigated include extravasal as well as intravasal devices. Extravasal devices such as vas clips can successfully block sperm passage but also produce local tissue necrosis. A wide variety of intravasal devices, including injectable silicone, cylindrical plugs, spherical beads, threads of silicone or suture material, and series of polypropylene beads, have been designed. However, none that were adequately evaluated sustained effective sperm obstruction without also generating fibrosis or perforation. The valve, which lies both in and alongside the vas, showed promise of true reversibility, allowing sperm flow to be turned both off and on. Unfortunately, despite experimentation with several designs and materials, problems with sperm passage and perforation have not been solved (see Zaneveld et al. 1986 for a review).

One of the most promising vas occlusion devices now being tested (Zaneveld et al. 1986, 1988) consists of two silicone plugs that are inserted in opposite directions along the vas through a single incision. Each is connected via surgical-grade thread to a button of silicone that lies outside the vas to facilitate retrieval. This device has proved effective in trials with rhesus macaques, *Macaca mulatta*. However, in early trials with several primate and felid species in zoos, the extent of species diversity in vas morphology precluded general use of the preformed plugs. This problem may be solved by injectable materials that solidify in situ. In ongoing tests with a variety of primates, felids, ungulates, and marsupials, injectable plugs have blocked passage of sperm (L. J. D. Zaneveld and C. S. Asa, unpub.).

As with vasectomy, vas plugs may result in the induction of antisperm antibodies that can compromise subsequent fertility. Following vasectomy reversal by vasovasostomy in one study of human males, 86% had developed antisperm antibodies (Gupta et al. 1975). Forty to ninety percent of human and rhesus macaque males may still have normal sperm counts, but the subsequent pregnancy rates of partners range from 20% to 25% (Alexander 1977). Although improving microsurgical techniques may improve the pregnancy rate, some of the fertilization failure has been traced to the presence of sperm antibodies.

Immunocontraception. As discussed in the preceding section, antibodies to sperm can effect contraception. Several vaccines against hypothalamic and pituitary hormones show promise for treatment of males. Immunization against LH or GnRH not only blocks spermatogenesis but also interferes with the production of testosterone and thus suppresses male-typical behavior (Esbenshade and Johnson 1987; Hodges and Hearn 1979). This suppression of androgen secretion along with spermatogenesis makes this treatment functionally equivalent to castration.

A vaccine against FSH, the other pituitary gonadotropin,

may preferentially obstruct spermatogenesis while sparing androgen production (Moudgal et al. 1986). FSH supports spermatogenesis, but not steroidogenesis, a role that is filled by LH.

Because permanent damage is more likely to result when these vaccines are administered to males than to females, most research on vaccine contraception has been directed toward females (Alexander and Ackerman 1988).

Chemosterilants. Gossypol, isolated from cottonseed, has received much attention for its contraceptive potential (Waller, Zaneveld, and Farnsworth 1985). Unfortunately, extreme variability among species in its effectiveness and deleterious effects on the liver and kidneys (Nomeir and Abou-Donia 1985; WHO 1985) severely limit its applicability.

Another class of compounds, which came close to being marketed for humans, shows encouraging potential for nonhuman species. Bisdiamines reversibly inhibit spermatogenesis without affecting hormone levels (Beyler et al. 1961), but also inhibit alcohol dehydrogenase activity (Heller, Moore, and Paulsen 1961). However, for treatment of captive animals with no access to alcohol, this side effect presents no concern. In a trial with male wolves (*Canis lupus*), bisdiamine fed daily in meat successfully suppressed spermatogenesis but not mating behavior (Asa et al. 1995).

Reversible Female-Directed Techniques

Most contraceptive research and development has targeted the female. In general, female-directed contraception often is more effective because it can be more specific—that is, because females produce fewer gametes at more discrete intervals than males. Perhaps more important, virtually all contraceptives have been developed originally for humans, in which cultural factors favor contracepting females.

Possible Points of Intervention. The female reproduction sequence begins in the hypothalamus with the production of GnRH or LHRH and ends with embryo implantation and gestation. The stages at which contraceptives can be targeted include ovulation, fertilization, implantation, and gestation. If the animal is pregnant at the time of contraceptive administration, special considerations apply.

Approaches to contraception fall into four basic categories: hormonal, immunological, mechanical, and surgical. The greatest experience and success in female contraception to date has occurred with compounds possessing gonadal hormone–like activity. These include both naturally occurring and synthetic steroids (estrogens, progestins, and androgens) as well as synthetic nonsteroidal compounds possessing steroidlike activity, such as diethylstilbestrol (DES). Synthetic steroids were developed to be active when given orally or to exhibit greater biological potency per gram than natural steroids, thus requiring smaller amounts or doses. Steroids act at more than one stage of the reproductive cycle.

Most of the studies listed in table 40.1 used methods that rely on blocking ovulation for effective contraception. Pharmacological doses of steroids or gonadotropin agonists and antagonists suppress the hypothalamic-pituitary-gonadal axis and thus prevent ovum maturation, estrogen production, ovulation, corpus luteum formation, and all subsequent events. A sequela of ovulatory cycle suppression is the absence of estrous periods, normally supported by circulating estradiol.

Since the union of the egg and the sperm occurs at the junction of the oviduct and uterus in most species, if ovulation does occur, contraceptives can block fertilization by (1) altering the rate of migration of the sperm or egg so that both do not reach the junction at the same time or (2) impeding the ability of the sperm to penetrate the egg by blocking either capacitation or enzyme action at the egg surface. Both estrogens and progestins have been reported either to delay or accelerate tubal ovum transport, depending on the time of administration and dose (Holst and Braden 1972). In addition, progestins can inhibit sperm capacitation in the female tract (Bedford 1970; Gwatkin and Williams 1970), a process necessary for fertilization.

If events to this point occur unimpeded, contraception still can be achieved by preventing implantation. By altering the typical release sequence and concentrations of gonadal steroids, hormone administration is thought to interfere with implantation. RU 486, the synthetic antiprogestin best known as an abortifacient, also prevents implantation by competing with progesterone for its own receptors (Swahn et al. 1990).

Finally, steroid effects on pregnancy and parturition must be considered. In general, progestins, as the name implies, support gestation and circulate at relatively high levels throughout pregnancy, falling just prior to parturition. Estrogens play a role in some species, typically being notable in the early phases of pregnancy and then again at parturition, when a sharp increase may be seen (see Hutchins, Thomas, and Asa, chap. 41, this volume). Therefore, altering the species-typical estrogen/progestin balance may compromise the pregnancy. For example, the synthetic progestin melengestrol acetate (MGA), successfully used for contraception in white-tailed deer, *Odocoileus virginianus* (Bell and Peterle 1975; Matschke 1977a), prevented parturition in pregnant deer (Plotka and Seal 1989). Removal of implants resulted in delivery. In contrast, MGA implanted early in pregnancy was associated with abortion in golden lion tamarins. However, females implanted during later stages gave birth without complications (J. Ballou, pers. comm.). Of further concern is the possible risk of congenital abnormalities in infants exposed to steroids during the early stages of development (Nora and Nora 1973). Obviously, the responses of a wider range of species require study before broad recommendations can be made regarding the safety of hormone administration during pregnancy.

Additional caution is warranted when considering hormone treatment of lactating females. Estrogens, in particular, can suppress the production and release of prolactin, the pituitary hormone necessary for stimulation and maintenance of lactation. For this reason, birth control pills containing estrogen are not recommended for use in lactating females (Rinehart 1975). Progestin-only contraception is preferable during lactation. MGA-implanted golden lion tamarins, for example, apparently nursed infants successfully (J. Ballou, pers. comm.). Nevertheless, because steroid hor-

TABLE 40.3.   Deaths per Year Associated with Parturition per 100,000 Noncontracepted Women Compared with Deaths per Year per 100,000 Women Using Contraception

	Age group					
	15–19 years	20–24 years	25–29 years	30–34 years	35–39 years	40–44 years
Parturition	7.0	7.4	9.1	14.8	25.7	28.2
Contraception						
Birth control pills (nonsmokers)	0.3	0.5	0.9	1.9	13.8	31.6
IUD	0.8	0.8	1.0	1.0	1.4	1.4

Source: Adapted from Ory 1983

mones can pass through the milk to the developing infant (Nilsson, Nygren, and Johansson 1977, 1978), other forms of contraception might be advisable for lactating females.

Steroid Hormones. The formulations of most commercially available birth control pills include a synthetic estrogen (usually ethinyl estradiol or mestranol) plus a synthetic progestin (norethindrone, norgestrel, or levonorgestrel). Although estrogens are more potent ovulation blockers at lower doses than progestins, they carry more risks, including tumorigenesis, blood clotting, hypertension, and endometrial hyperplasia (Crane, Harris, and Winsor 1971; Sartwell, Arthes, and Tonaschia 1977; Whitehead 1978; Zador 1976). Adding the progestin to the estrogen regimen seems to counter many of estrogen's risks without compromising its efficacy. More important, however, in most species, the risks associated with pregnancy and parturition are much greater than the risks associated with contraception (see table 40.3).

Some combination pills, as they are called, blend estrogen and progestin in each pill; some are supplied as sequential pills with different formulations. In humans, hormone-containing pills are administered for 21 days, then either an inert pill or nothing is given for 7 days before repeating the 28-day cycle. For zoo applications, continuous treatment may be preferable. Among species that exhibit external signs of estrus, the complete absence of such signs is a reliable indicator that the pills are indeed being consumed and are effective.

Provera (medroxyprogesterone acetate, The Upjohn Company) is an injectable synthetic progestin now available for contraceptive use in the United States. In its slower-release formulation (Depo-Provera), a single injection can be effective for 2–3 months, making it an attractive alternative to orally administered pills for some species. In particular, species with a relatively short breeding season are likely candidates for this treatment. Although it has been approved for use in human females as a contraceptive, a study conducted with lions, *Panthera leo,* revealed somewhat reduced cortisol levels in Provera-treated females (Seal et al. 1976). However, cortisol levels did not differ between Depo-Provera–treated and control black lemurs (I. Porton and C. S. Asa, unpub.). The dynamics of weight gain in black lemurs associated with Depo-Provera treatment is now being investigated. Studies of Depo-Provera also are currently under way with harbor seals, *Phoca vitulina*, sea lions (B. Raphael, pers. comm.), and gray seals, *Halichoerus grypus* (Seely and Ronald 1991).

Melengestrol acetate (MGA), a synthetic progestin very similar in structure to medroxyprogesterone, has been successfully used by zoos for more than a decade. Supplied in a silicone matrix by U. S. Seal and now by E. Plotka, MGA implants can effectively block reproduction in carnivores, primates, and hoofstock for at least 2 years. Replacement at 2-year intervals can provide continuous, long-term contraception. However, as indicated earlier, implant use should be interrupted periodically in felids, and possibly other carnivores, as a precaution against possible overstimulation of the uterus. As described in the survey results above, rates for efficacy and return to fertility are quite high.

MGA also is active orally and can be given with food. Such an approach has proved successful in treating hoofstock herds (B. Raphael and P. P. Calle, pers. comm.). Drawbacks include the failure of some subordinate individuals to acquire an adequate dose and the possibility that the male antler cycle may be interrupted in species that grow and cast antlers each year.

An additional caution regarding steroid use relates to the lipophilic nature of steroids. Determining proper dose is complicated by the tendency of the administered steroid to diffuse into fat until equilibration with blood levels is reached, then slowly to leach back out as blood levels drop. Therefore, in treatment of animals that are overweight or that naturally have substantial fat deposits (e.g., seals and bears), care must be taken in calculating the dose and in monitoring for side effects.

Another implantable progestin, levonorgestrel (Norplant), has been approved for use in human females. Six matchstick-sized implants placed subcutaneously provide contraception for up to 5 years. Reversal before that time can be achieved simply by removal. Although Norplant is considered safe for long-term use, irregular uterine bleeding during the early months of use is an undesirable side effect in some individuals (Sivin 1988; Faundes, Sivin, and Stern 1978)

RU 486, the synthetic antiprogesterone, also may be used to interfere with normal ovulatory cycles by hindering the hypothalamic and pituitary feedback effects of progesterone (Baulieu 1989). As with its effect on the uterus discussed above, it functions by competing with progesterone for binding to its own receptors throughout the reproductive tract (Swahn et al. 1990). However, the current political climate has delayed commercial availability of RU 486 in the United States.

Androgens have been used to suppress hypothalamic and pituitary hormone secretion, most notably in female beagles, *Canis familiaris*. Both testosterone and androstenedione (a biologically less potent androgen), administered via silicone implants, successfully suppress estrus for more than 2 years (Simmons and Hamner 1973). Normal fertility follows implant removal. However, androgen treatment is invariably associated with masculinization. Although male-like behavior subsides with cessation of treatment, morphological changes typically remain.

Hormone Antagonists and Agonists. As described for the male, GnRH analogues can effectively arrest reproduction in the female (Fraser, Bergquist, and Gudmundson 1989; Nestor and Vickery 1988). Initial administration of an agonist, such as Lupron, may stimulate estrus and ovulation, but continued treatment prevents further cycles. However, in induced ovulators such as felids and mustelids, agonist treatment that results in estrus and ovulation will likely be followed by a period of pseudopregnancy, making assessment of efficacy problematic. Also, the elevation in progesterone levels that accompanies pseudopregnancy contraindicates short-term use of GnRH agonists in these species because of the risks of progestin exposure. Long-term continuous suppression, however, is an acceptable alternative, as only one pseudopregnancy would be experienced. As with males, treatment with antagonists is less practical due to the need for larger doses and the greater cost.

Immunocontraception. Immunization against antigens involved in reproductive processes could offer reversible contraception without surgery or alterations in normal reproductive cycles. Research on several such antigens is being actively pursued, but all are still considered experimental. Vaccines against embryonic and placental antigens work postconception, those against hypothalamic and pituitary hormones prevent ovulation, and gamete antigens block conception. Brief summaries of the current status of these vaccines follow (see review by Covey, O'Brien, and Moore 1985).

Embryonic antigens include alloantigens controlled by histocompatibility genes (Searle et al. 1976), oncofetal antigens (Hamilton et al. 1979), and structural trophoblastic antigens (Billington 1978). All have proved to be poor candidates for vaccines. Alloantigens are present only during the preimplantation period and are highly polymorphic; oncofetal antigens may result in birth defects or retardation when contraception fails; and trophoblastic antigens can presently be produced only in small quantities and may not be tissue-specific.

Vaccines against LH and GnRH prevent ovulation, but, as in the male, steroid hormone levels also decline (Fraser 1983; Hodges and Hearn 1979). Investigators are searching for a dose that might prevent the ovulatory LH surge without substantially suppressing steroid output. However, the functional ovariectomy that these vaccines accomplish would be appropriate in carnivores to eliminate exposure to both exogenous and endogenous progestins. Combined with their reversibility, this factor could make these vaccines an ideal female carnivore contraceptive.

The specificity of placental proteins to pregnancy makes them suitable candidates for contraceptive vaccines. However, for the pregnancy-specific glycoproteins that have so far been evaluated for vaccine production, results have been mixed (Bahl and Muralidhar 1980). The physiological roles of these proteins must be better defined before they can be seriously considered as contraceptive targets.

Vaccines against placental lactogen can disrupt pregnancy in the rat, mouse, and baboon, *Papio* spp. (Bahl and Muralidhar 1980). However, although placental lactogen is secreted only during pregnancy, it is immunologically similar to pituitary growth hormone. Before such vaccines could be put to contraceptive use, molecular modifications would be needed to avoid blocking pituitary action.

Chorionic gonadotropin, another protein specific to pregnancy in many species (rodents: Wide, Hobson, and Wide 1980; primates: Hobson and Wide 1981; Hodgen et al. 1973; equids: Roser and Lofstedt 1989), has been the focus of much research. Because of its similarity to pituitary LH, several approaches have been attempted to increase its specificity (Bahl and Muralidhar 1980; Ramakrishnan et al. 1979; Matsura et al. 1979; Talwar 1974). Unfortunately, because increasing its specificity also seems to decrease its antigenicity and thus its effectiveness, broader trials are not yet indicated.

Despite encouraging results from early trials, immunization of females with hyaluronidase or acrosin, sperm enzymes involved in penetration of oocyte vestments, does not reliably reduce fertility (Syner, Kuros, and Moghissi 1979; Morton 1976). Vaccines against germ-cell antigens (GA-1) in female rabbits and mice (Naz, Poffenberger, and Menge 1986) have been more successful, but are less attractive because they act postfertilization.

Fertilization antigen (FA-1), which blocks fertilization in immunized female rabbits, and a vaccine against lactate dehydrogenase-C4 (LDH-C4), an enzyme unique to sperm cells that probably results in sperm agglutination in the oviduct, given to female rabbits (Goldberg 1973) and baboons (Goldberg 1979), both reduced conception rates (Naz et al. 1984). Nonetheless, because there are millions of sperm in each ejaculate, achieving sufficiently high titers to affect enough sperm cells to prevent most conceptions may not be feasible.

To date, the vaccines that show the most promise for captive wildlife contraception are directed at the zona pellucida (ZP) (see reviews by Sacco and Yurewicz 1989; Aitken, Richardson, and Hulme 1984). The ZP is an acellular glycoprotein layer that surrounds the oocyte and preimplantation embryo. Synthesized by the oocyte during early follicular growth, it protects the oocyte and provides the block to polyspermy by regulating the number of spermatozoa that can enter at the time of fertilization. Several features of the ZP make it attractive as a target for immunological contraception: (1) it is a unique structure, so immunization should not broadly affect the organism; (2) the primary block to fertility occurs before conception at the point of sperm entry; and (3) ZP antigens are both specific and highly immunogenic.

Nearly 20 years ago, Ownby and Shivers (1972) first demonstrated that zona antiserum prevented sperm attachment in vitro in the hamster. Since that time, zona antiserum also has been raised in the rat, mouse, rabbit, cow, pig, marmoset, *Callithrix jacchus*, and human, and has been used to block fertilization of ova in the hamster, rat, mouse, rabbit, dog, marmoset, squirrel monkey, rhesus macaque, bonnet macaque, *Macaca radiata*, cynomolgus macaque, *Macaca fascicularis*, baboon, chimpanzee, human, and horse (Kirkpatrick, Turner, and Perkins 1992; Liu, Bernoco, and Feldman 1989; Stevens 1986; Bamezai et al. 1986; Gulyas, Gwatkin, and Yuan 1983; Wood and Dunbar 1981; Sacco, Subramanian, and Yurewicz 1981; Sacco et al. 1981; Mahi and Yanagimachi 1979; Gwatkin, Williams, and Meyerhofer 1979; Shivers et al. 1978; Gwatkin and Williams 1978; Sacco 1977; Gwatkin, Williams, and Carlo 1977; Tsunoda and Chang 1976a, 1976b, 1976c).

Treatment typically consists of several (usually three to four) injections of vaccine, which can be delivered by dart. Adjuvants, which are added to the vaccine to enhance the immune response, may induce inflammation or granulation at the injection site. In general, the adjuvants that are the most immunogenic, and thus provoke the strongest immune response, also generate the most severe reaction at the injection site. Freund's complete adjuvant, the most effective, causes animals subsequently to test positive for TB. Booster doses are required at approximately yearly intervals. Fertility is expected to return gradually over several months if booster injections are not given.

Unfortunately, in most in vivo tests that assessed ovarian physiology, successful obstruction of fertilization has been accompanied by undesirable side effects ranging from altered hormone patterns to complete cessation of ovarian function (e.g., Sehgal, Gupta, and Bhatnagar 1989; Mahi-Brown et al. 1988; Skinner et al. 1984; Sacco et al. 1983; Wood, Lie, and Dunbar 1981). It has become apparent that a normal ZP is necessary not only for sperm penetration but for oocyte development and for communication between the oocyte and the surrounding follicle (Sehgal, Gupta, and Bhatnagar 1989).

Manifestation of side effects has varied by species, so far being most profound in the rabbit (Skinner et al. 1984) and least apparent in the horse (Liu, Bernoco, and Feldman 1989). Even in the horse, however, long-term treatment results in cycle alteration (Kirkpatrick et al. 1992). The severity of deleterious effects in other species appears to lie between these two extremes. Although cessation of cycles might be acceptable in some cases, the original hope for this technique that made it more attractive than available alternatives was that it would block only entry of sperm into the ovum; thus hormone production would not be altered, and the sociosexual dynamics of group-living animals need not be disrupted.

Of further concern are the prospects for reversibility after long-term treatment. To date, no investigation of ZP vaccines has been carried beyond 2 years, and most are considerably shorter in duration. Longer treatment might well result in permanent deficits in ovarian function (Aitken, Richardson, and Hulme 1984; Bousquet et al. 1981). Several lines of investigation provide hope for refining the technique to minimize its untoward effects. The simplest approach is to try minimizing the more generalized effects by determining the minimum effective dose for blocking fertilization (Sacco, Yurewicz, and Subramanian 1989). Another strategy is the use of less potent adjuvants (Upadhyay et al. 1989; Sacco, Yurewicz, and Subramanian 1989; Hender-son, Hulme, and Aitken 1988; Mahi-Brown et al. 1985; Gulyas, Gwatkin, and Yuan 1983; Gwatkin, Anderson, and Williams 1980), which may result in less generalized immune responses. Alternatively, purer forms of the antigen may be formulated for a more precisely directed immune reaction (Millar et al. 1989; Sacco, Yurewicz, and Subramanian 1989; Sacco et al. 1987; Skinner and Dunbar 1984).

All immunocontraceptive techniques share problems regarding not only species differences in immune response but also individual variability. Such variability may be manifested both in initial antibody production and in duration of response. Although it is thought that boosters will be necessary only once per year, antibody titers may wane sooner in some animals and last much longer in others (Fraser 1980).

Intrauterine Devices. Only two intrauterine devices (IUDs) are currently available in the United States: the copper T380A, which is effective for at least 4 years, and a progesterone-releasing T-shaped device, which must be replaced annually (Mishell 1989). Although IUDs have been associated with pelvic inflammatory disease, the risk of such infection is statistically increased only during the first 4 months postinsertion (Lee et al. 1983). Monofilament tail strings have not been found to increase that risk (Triman and Liskin 1988). Rather, attention to aseptic technique during insertion, with or without prophylactic systemic antibiotics, is critical to preventing infection.

In humans, the chance for infection with consequent infertility is higher for females who have a history of salpingitis (tubal infection), are nulliparous and under 25 years of age, or who have multiple sexual partners (Lee, Rubin, and Borucki 1988; Zhang 1993; Cramer et al. 1985). However, the IUD is considered safe and very effective when used by parous females in monogamous relationships. The IUD may be suitable for use in apes if such cautions are heeded.

Abortion and Abortifacients. For first-trimester abortion in humans (Kaunitz and Grimes 1985), suction alone and suction plus curettage are the techniques most commonly used. Such procedures are generally applicable to nonhuman species as well. In both methods, the cervix is dilated for passage of a cannula and suction is applied to remove uterine contents. Curettage may be incorporated to ensure complete evacuation.

Cervical dilation can be accomplished mechanically, with cannulas or specially designed dilators, or chemically, with prostaglandins (E or F series) given by injection or pessary, or by cervical insertion of laminaria, hydroscopic seaweed (Kaunitz and Grimes 1985). Laminaria, which resemble sticks when dry, swell within the cervix and appear to cause dilation either via direct drying or by stimulating endogenous prostaglandin secretion. Mechanical methods carry the risk of cervical or uterine puncture, whereas prostaglandins commonly are accompanied by uterine cramping, nausea, and vomiting.

Higher doses of prostaglandins can be used to induce abortion, but are not recommended for humans or nonhuman primates because of their side effects and their 5–15% failure rate (Gail 1980). Analogues with fewer side effects are being evaluated. Prostaglandins can be used safely in early pregnancy in hoofstock.

For mid-trimester abortion in humans, cervical dilation and aspiration are followed by forceps extraction. Uterotonic agents such as oxytocin or prostaglandins are typically administered either during or after extraction (Stubblefield 1985).

Several nonsurgical alternatives are available for postcoital induction of abortion. The synthetic estrogens diethylstilbestrol (DES) and ethinyl estradiol block implantation when administered for 1 and 5 days respectively, beginning within 72 hours after mating (Fasoli et al. 1989). However, estrogens can be associated with severe side effects in canids (Bowen, Olson, and Behrendt 1985). Insertion of an IUD within 10 days of mating also can terminate pregnancy (Fasoli et al. 1989).

Progesterone antagonists, such as the much-publicized RU 486, can effectively terminate pregnancy by obstructing the binding of progesterone necessary for pregnancy maintenance. However, RU 486 alone has only a 60% success rate at inducing complete abortion. Combining RU 486 with a low dose of prostaglandin E results in maximum efficacy (95%) while minimizing the side effects that accompany prostaglandins (Swahn et al. 1990). Adding Anordrin, a luteolytic synthetic steroid that interferes with pregnancy maintenance by a separate pathway, also increases the effectiveness of RU 486 (Chang, Wang, and Bardin 1993).

Methods of Delivery

The development of long-acting preparations and sustained delivery methods has improved the effectiveness, safety, and acceptability of hormonal contraceptives. Because many side effects of steroid hormones are dose-dependent, the degree of risk can be proportional to the amount of hormone delivered. The blood level of the hormone necessary for contraception is represented by a narrow zone. Oral administration results in immediate high blood levels that decrease with time. Treatment must be repeated daily to maintain concentrations above the minimum effective level. The injectable controlled-release system meters the steroid into the blood at a rate designed to sustain the optimal level for a longer period (weeks or months: e.g., Depo-Provera and Noristat). Subcutaneous or intramuscular implants in the form of Silastic rods or capsules provide slow diffusion of the hormone for an even longer period (years). Devices that release steroids by diffusion or erosion of a biodegradable polymer also maintain blood levels of the hormone in the appropriate range for relatively long periods (months or years).

As with oral preparations, the most significant shortcoming of the injectable progestins is their nonlinear release profile. Immediately after injection, blood levels of hormone far exceed what is necessary for effective contraception (Howard, Warren, and Fotherby 1975). Thereafter, serum levels gradually decline until, between 2 and 4 months later, they fall below the threshold of effectiveness. The search for new formulations with more linear release profiles shows promise for the near future.

The use of contraceptive implants that utilize an inert carrier to control the rate and duration of drug release began in 1964 with the discovery that silicone rubber could be used for prolonged drug therapy (Folkman and Long 1964). Shortly thereafter, Segal and Croxatto (1969) proposed using silicone rubber implants for delivery of contraceptive steroids. Implantable contraceptives have been used effectively for almost 20 years in a wide range of species.

Long-acting steroid contraceptives can be designed for either systemic or local delivery. Implants and injectables are designed for delivery into the general circulatory system. Hormone-impregnated intrauterine and intracervical devices can secrete steroids locally, and effectively reduce the concentrations of circulating hormones by direct delivery to the target organ, the reproductive tract.

Peptide hormones such as GnRH require different vehicles for sustained release (Pitt 1987). Various approaches that show promise include biodegradable polymers (Deghenghi 1989), nondegradable polymers (Furr and Hutchinson 1989), silicone elastomer matrices (Burns, McRae, and Sanders 1988), and reservoir systems (Davidson et al. 1988). The use of biodegradable polymers for the programmed delivery of contraceptives represents a major advance in technology that allows considerable flexibility in system design (Baker and Lonsdale 1974). Although field tests of biodegradable polymers are limited, this form of contraceptive delivery has considerable potential (Langer 1990).

CHOOSING THE APPROPRIATE CONTRACEPTIVE METHOD

No contraceptive method is 100% effective and without risk. However, when compared with the risks of pregnancy and parturition, most contraceptives have been shown to be surprisingly safe (see table 40.3). Still, when selecting a method, many factors must be weighed to achieve the appropriate balance of efficacy and risk for the situation.

Sterilization is a viable method of birth control when an animal has been determined to have reached the end of its reproductive life. This may occur for a number of reasons. Future pregnancies may no longer be medically desirable for old females. Individuals may be overrepresented genetically or may exhibit a heritable defect. Managers may wish not to produce hybrids of two species or subspecies. Sterilizing such animals allows managers to meet reproductive goals without removing the animals from their social group. More frequently, however, managers will wish to curtail breeding for some definable period, with the option of breeding again at the end of that period. In such instances reversible contraception is indicated.

Of the contraceptives described in this chapter, only a few presently are easily obtainable, and all of those target the female. They include the MGA implant, birth control pills, and Depo-Provera. Other methods that are still in the experimental stages may become available over the next several years. As new forms of contraception are developed, managers will have an increasingly wide variety of methods from which to choose and will be able to select a contraceptive method to suit the specifics of the situation. Physiology, behavior, and management objectives are all important considerations in selecting the best contraceptive method. Because these variables, and thus the contraceptive of choice, may change over time, situations should be reevaluated periodically.

One of the first choices facing the manager will be whether to separate the male(s) and the female(s) or to use contraception in one sex or the other. For species that are solitary except during the breeding season, physical separation (which may mean nothing more than not putting the male and female together) is the simplest, least invasive, and most reliable way to prevent pregnancy. For more social species, separation may be reasonable if there is a short, distinct breeding season, as is the case for lemurs, or if estrus is readily identifiable so that periodic short-term separation is possible. Separating social species into all-male and all-female groups, as is common practice in the management of many ungulates, is another possibility if such an arrangement is consistent with the normal social organization of the species.

Separation is not a feasible option for many social species. Periodically removing an animal from its group may affect its social status and result in group instability. For some species, separation from conspecifics is extremely stressful and will have a negative effect on the health of the separated individual. When separation of an animal from its social group is not advisable, the decision becomes one of which sex to contracept. When a single male is kept with multiple females and no reproduction at all is desirable, contracepting the male would be the simplest choice, assuming that ease of administration, duration of contraception, and efficacy are comparable for the male and female contraceptives being considered. For monogamous animals or for groups with multiple males and multiple females, the choice becomes more complicated, and each of the following factors needs to be weighed before the final choice is made.

Ease of administration may influence the choice of contraceptive and of the sex to contracept. Birth control pills can be effectively administered orally if dissolved in juice or crushed in a favorite food. Injectables, such as Depo-Provera or immunocontraceptives, can be administered via blowdart or via direct injection of a restrained animal. Other methods, such as implants, IUDs, and vas plugs, require anesthesia. In some situations it is simpler to give birth control pills to females or to implant several females than to use vas plugs in the male(s). The desired duration of contraception also is important to consider. Although a birth control pill is easier to administer than an implant, the pill must be given daily, whereas the implant need only be replaced every 2 years. Vaccines require several initial injections but may need booster injections only once per year thereafter. Although insertions of IUDs and vas plugs require relatively precise surgical skills, these contraceptives can be effective indefinitely. For seasonal breeders, one or two injections of Depo-Provera per year may suffice and may be preferable to the 12 months of continuous exogenous hormone therapy provided by an implant.

A contraceptive's failure rate may in some situations be of paramount importance. When production of unwanted young would be extremely problematic, efficacy may override all other considerations. In other cases, an occasional failure may be acceptable, allowing more latitude in choice. The ability of the manager to determine whether the contraceptive device is in place may influence the selection of a method, particularly in instances in which maximum efficacy is necessary. For example, females of some primate species exhibit perineal swellings that serve to advertise their estrous condition. The MGA implant eliminates these swellings in some populations of some species (e.g., lion-tailed macaques), and in these populations the appearance of a perineal swelling is a reliable indicator that the implant is no longer in place.

In addition to the question of whether to isolate animals briefly during estrus, there may be other behavioral considerations. The expression of normal sexual behavior may be altered by some contraceptive methods, and in certain instances this may not be desirable. For example, males in multimale primate groups often actively compete for access to estrous females. If the chosen contraceptive eliminates the estrous condition, contracepting all but a few females can intensify male-male competition for access to those few females that still display estrus.

In other instances, altering normal sexual behavior may be desirable. For example, females of some primate species compete for the attention of the male, and an estrous female may be the target of aggression from other females in the group. In this situation, suppressing estrus in females that need to be contracepted could reduce levels of aggression within the social group.

An animal's age may influence the choice of a contraceptive method. Some management situations make it impossible for managers to administer contraception more than once a year. This may necessitate contracepting individuals that may become sexually mature during the subsequent year. Due to the dearth of data relating hormone manipulation before or during puberty to subsequent fertility, it is not possible to predict the effects on such individuals of any of the contraceptive methods that alter the hormonal milieu. These include all of the methods discussed in this chapter except IUDs, vas plugs, and possibly short-term zona pellucida vaccine.

Different forms of contraception may be appropriate to different stages in an animal's life span and to different management situations and objectives. Reversible forms of birth control provide the manager with a variety of options as well as with the ability to review the situation periodically and choose a different option in response to changing conditions.

THE NEED FOR RESEARCH

From the material presented in this chapter, there may appear to be many contraceptive options available. Unfortunately, most of these methods are still considered experimental, even for humans, the species for which most are being developed. Add to this the probable species differences in dose, efficacy, and safety, and it should be obvious that considerable research effort will be required before routine recommendations can be made for their use in wildlife.

The AZA Contraception Advisory Group is coordinating research trials among zoos for several of the techniques discussed. We cannot stress too strongly the need for zoos to participate in such research. The popular press often gives the mistaken impression that new discoveries are immediately applicable and marketable, a situation that virtually never occurs.

REFERENCES

Aitken, R. J., Richardson, D. W., and Hulme, M. 1984. Immunological interference with the properties of the zona pellucida. In *Immunological aspects of reproduction in mammals,* ed. D. B. Crighton, 305–25. London: Butterworths.

Alexander, N. J. 1977. Vasectomy and vasovasostomy in rhesus monkeys: The effect of circulating antisperm antibodies on fertility. *Fertil. Steril.* 28:562–69.

Alexander, N. J., and Ackerman, S. 1988. Sperm antigens and antibodies. In *Female contraception,* ed. B. Runnebaum, T. Rabe, and L. Kiesel, 356–67. Berlin: Springer-Verlag.

Allen, S. H. 1982. Bait consumption and diethylstilbestrol influence on North Dakota red fox reproductive performance. *Wildl. Soc. Bull.* 10:370–74.

Asa, C. S., and Porton, I. 1991. Concerns and prospects for contraception in carnivores. *Proceedings of the Annual Meeting of the American Association of Zoo Veterinarians,* 298–303. Philadelphia: American Association of Zoo Veterinarians.

Asa, C. S., Zaneveld, L. J. D., Munson, L., Callahan, M., and Byers, A. P. 1995. Efficacy, safety, and reversibility of bisdiamine as a male-directed oral contraceptive in gray wolves (*Canis lupus*). *Proceedings of the Annual Meeting of the American Association of Zoo Veterinarians,* 396–97. Philadelphia: American Association of Zoo Veterinarians.

Bahl, O. P., and Muralidhar, K. 1980. Current status of antifertility vaccine. In *Immunological aspects of infertility and fertility regulation,* ed. D. S. Dhindsa and G. F. B. Schumacher, 224–57. New York: Elsevier/North Holland.

Baker, R. W., and Lonsdale, H. K. 1974. Controlled release: Mechanisms and rate. In *Controlled release of biologically active agents,* ed. A. C. Tanquary and R. E. Lacey, 15–72. Advances in Experimental Medicine and Biology, vol. 47. New York: Plenum Press.

Balmaceda, J. P., Borghi, M. R., Burgos, L., Pauerstein, C. V., Schally, A. V., and Asch, R. H. 1984. The effects of chronic administration of LH-RH agonists and antagonists on the menstrual cycle and endometrium of the rhesus monkey. *Contraception* 29:83–90.

Balser, D. S. 1964. Management of predator populations with antifertility agents. *J. Wildl. Mgmt.* 28:352–58.

Bamezai, A. K., Suman, A., Das, C., and Talwar, G. P. 1986. Effect of immunization against porcine zona pellucida (PZP) on steroid hormone profiles and fertility in primates. *J. Reprod. Immunol., Suppl.* 9:85.

Baulieu, E. E. 1989. Contragestion and other clinical applications of RU 486, an antiprogesterone at the receptor. *Science* 245:1351–57.

Beck, R. A., Cowsar, D. R., Lewis, D. H., Gibson, J. W., and Flowers, C. E. Jr. 1979. New long-acting injectable microcapsule contraception system. *Am. J. Obstet. Gynecol.* 135:419–26

Bedford, J. M. 1970. The influence of oestrogen and progesterone on sperm capacitation in the reproductive tract of the female rabbit. *J. Endocrinol.* 46:191–200.

Bell, R. L., and Peterle, T. J. 1975. Hormone implants control reproduction in white-tailed deer. *Wildl. Soc. Bull.* 3:152–56.

Beyler, A. L., Poots, G. O., Coulston, F., and Surrey, A. R. 1961. The selective testicular effects of certain bis(dichloroacetyl)diamines. *Endocrinology* 69:819–33.

Billington, W. D. 1978. Immunological interference with implantation. *Ups. J. Med. Sci., Suppl.* 22:51–58.

Bousquet, D., Leveille, M. C., Roberts, K. D., Chapdelaine, A., and Bleau, G. 1981. The cellular origin of the zona pellucida antigen in the human and hamster. *J. Exp. Zool.* 215:215–18.

Bowen, R. A., Olson, P. N., and Behrendt, M. D. 1985. Efficacy and toxicity of estrogens commonly used to terminate canine pregnancy. *J. Am. Vet. Med. Assoc.* 186:783–88.

Brushman, H. H., Linhart, S. B., Balser, D. S., and Sparks, L. W. 1967. A technique for producing antifertility tallow baits for predatory mammals. *J. Wildl. Mgmt.* 32:183–84.

Burke T. 1977. Fertility control in the cat. *Vet. Clin. N. Am.* 7:699–703.

Burns, R., McRae, G. I., and Sanders, L. 1988. A one year controlled release system for the LHRH agonist RS-49947. *Proceedings of the 15th International Conference on Controlled Release Bioactive Materials,* 19–26. Basel: Controlled Release Society.

Carter, C. N. 1990. Pet population control: Another decade without solutions? *J. Am. Vet. Med. Assoc.* 197:192–95.

Chang, C. C., Wang, W.-C., and Bardin, C. W. 1993. Termination of early pregnancy in the rat, rabbit, and hamster with RU 486 and Anordrin. *Contraception* 47:597–608.

Chang, M. C. 1967. Effects of progesterone and related compounds on fertilization, transportation, and development of rabbit eggs. *Endocrinology* 81:1251–60.

Chappel, S. C., Ellinwood, W. E., Huckins, C., Herbert, D. C., and Spies, H. G. 1980. Active immunization of male rhesus monkeys against luteinizing hormone releasing hormone. *Biol. Reprod.* 22:333–42.

Cheatum, E. L., and Hansel, W. 1967. Rabies control by inhibition of fox reproduction. Cornell University, Ithaca, N.Y. Manuscript.

Clarke, I. J., Fraser, H. M., and McNeilly, A. S. 1978. Active immunization of ewes against luteinizing hormone releasing hormone and its effects on ovulation and gonadotrophin, prolactin, and ovarian steroid secretion. *J. Endocrinol.* 78:39–47.

Corbin, A., Beattie, C. W., Tracy, J., Jones, R., Foell, T. J., Yardley, J., and Rees, R. W. 1978. Effect of LH-RH peptide antagonist on serum LH, ovulation, and menstrual cycle of crab-eating macaque. *Contraception* 18:105–20.

Covey, D. C., O'Brien, K. D., and Moore, D. E. 1985. Current trends in antifertility vaccine research. *West. J. Med.* 142:197–202.

Cramer, D. W., Schiff, I., Schoenbaum, S. C., Gibson, M., Belisle, S., Albrecht, B., Stillman, R. J., Berger, M. J., Wilson, E., Stadel, B. V., and Seibel, M. 1985. Tubal infertility and the intrauterine device. *New Engl. J. Med.* 312:941–47.

Crane, M. G., Harris, J. J., and Winsor, W. III. 1971. Hypertension, oral contraceptive agents, and conjugated estrogens. *Ann. Intern. Med.* 74:13–21.

Cuadros, A., Brinson, A., and Sundaram, K. 1970. Progestational activity of megestrol acetate polydimethylsiloxane (PDS) capsules in rhesus monkeys. *Contraception* 2:29.

Cuadros, A., and Sundaram, K. 1976. Reversible inhibition of ovulation in the rhesus monkey by polydimethylsiloxane subdermal capsules of megestrol acetate. *Fertil. Steril.* 27:171–77.

Curtis, L. 1982. Husbandry of mammals. In *Zoological park and aquarium fundamentals,* ed. K. Sausman, 245–55. Wheeling, W.Va: American Association of Zoological Parks and Aquariums.

Danforth, D. R., Williams, R. F., Hsiu, J. C., Roh, S. I., Hahn, D., McGuire, J. L., and Hodgen, G. D. 1990. Intermittent GnRH antagonist plus progestin contraception conserving tonic ovarian estrogen secretion and reducing progestin exposure. *Contraception* 41:623–31.

Davidson, G. W. III., Domg, A., Sanders, L. M., and McRae, G. 1988. Hydrogels for controlled release of peptides. *Proceedings of the 15th International Conference on Controlled Release Bioactive Materials,* 54–60. Basel: Controlled Release Society.

Davis-daSilva, M., and Wallen, K. 1989. Suppression of male rhesus testicular function and sexual behavior by a gonadotropin releasing-hormone agonist. *Physiol. Behav.* 45:963–68.

Deghenghi, R. 1989. Kinetics of sustained release delivery systems. In *GnRH analogues in cancer and human reproduction,* vol. 1, *Basic aspects,* ed. B. H. Vickery and B. Lunenfeld, 137–41. Dordrecht: Kluwer.

Doering, C. H., McGinnis, P. R., Kraemer, H. C., and Hamburg, D. A. 1980. Hormonal and behavioral response of male chimpanzees to a long-acting analog of gonadotropin-releasing hormone. *Arch. Sex. Behav.* 9:441–50.

Eckert, R., and Randall, D. 1983. *Animal physiology: Mechanisms and adaptations.* San Francisco: W. H. Freeman.

Erickson, G. I., Vickery, B. H., and Bennett, J. P. 1970. Studies on the antifertility mechanisms of low doses of chlormadinone acetate using egg transfer in the rabbit. *Biol. Reprod.* 2:279–83.

Esbenshade, K. L., and Johnson, B. H. 1987. Active immunization of boars against gonadotropin releasing hormone. II. Effects on libido and response to testosterone propionate. *Theriogenology* 27:581–85.

Fasoli, M., Parazzini, F., Cecchetti, G., and LaVecchia, C. 1989. Post-coital contraception: An overview of published studies. *Contraception* 39:459–68.

Faundes, A., Sivin, I., and Stern, J. 1978. Long-acting contraceptive implants: An analysis of menstrual bleeding patterns. *Contraception* 18:335–65.

Folkman, J., and Long, D. M. 1964. The rise of silicone rubber as a carrier for prolonged drug therapy. *J. Surg. Res.* 4:139–41.

Fraser, H. M. 1980. Inhibition of reproductive function by antibodies to luteinizing hormone releasing hormone. In *Immunological aspects of reproduction and fertility control,* ed. J. P. Hearn, 143–71. Baltimore: University Park Press.

———. 1983. Active immunization of stump tailed macaque monkeys against luteinizing hormone releasing hormone, and its effects on menstrual cycles, ovarian steroids, and positive feedback. *J. Reprod. Immunol.* 5:173–83.

Fraser, H. M., Bergquist, C., and Gudmundson, J. A. 1989. LHRH analogues for female contraception. In *LHRH and its analogues,* ed. R. W. Shaw and J. C. Marshall, 214–32. London: Wright.

Fraser, H. M., Laird, N. C., and Blakeley, D. M. 1980. Decreased pituitary responsiveness and inhibition of the luteinizing hormone surge and ovulation in the stumptailed monkey *(Macaca arctoides)* by chronic treatment with an agonist of luteinizing hormone-releasing hormone. *Endocrinology* 106:452–57.

Fraser, H. M., Sandow, J., Seidel, H., and von Rechenberg, W. 1987. An implant of a gonadotropin releasing hormone agonist (buserelin) which suppresses ovarian function in the macaque for 3–5 months. *Acta Endocrinol.* 115:521–27.

Furr, B. J. A., and Hutchinson, F. G. 1989. Formulation of luteinizing hormone releasing hormone analogues. In *LHRH and its analogues,* ed. R. W. Shaw and J. C. Marshall, 49–63. London: Wright.

Gail, L. J. 1980. The use of prostaglandins in human reproduction. *Popul. Rep.* [G], no. 8.

Gardner, H. M., Hueston, W. D., and Donovan, E. F. 1985. Use of mibolerone in wolves and three *Panthera* species. *J. Am. Vet. Med. Assoc.* 187:1193–94.

Garrett, M. G., and Franklin, W. L. 1983. Diethylstilbestrol as a temporary chemosterilant to control black-tailed prairie dog populations. *J. Range Mgmt.* 36:753–56.

Glass, R. H., and McL. Morris, J. 1972. Antifertility effects of an intracervical progestational device. *Biol. Reprod.* 7:160–65.

Goldberg, E. 1973. Infertility in female rabbits immunized with lactate dehydrogenase-X. *Science* 181:458–59.

———. 1979. Sperm specific antigens and immunological approaches for control of fertility. In *Recent advances in reproduction and regulation of fertility,* 281–90. Amsterdam: Elsevier/North Holland.

Greer, K. R., Hawkins, W. H., and Catlin, J. E. 1968. Experimental studies of controlled reproduction in elk (Wapiti). *J. Wildl. Mgmt.* 32:368–76.

Gulyas, B. J., Gwatkin, R. B. L., and Yuan, L. C. 1983. Active immunization of cynomolgus monkeys *(Macaca fascicularis)* with porcine zonae pellucidae. *Gamete Res.* 4:299–307.

Gupta, I., Dhawan, S., Goel, G. D., and Saha, K. 1975. Low fertility rate in vasovasostomized males and its possible immunologic mechanism. *Int. J. Fertil.* 20:183–91.

Gwatkin, R. B. L., Anderson, O. F., and Williams, D. T. 1980. Large-scale isolation of bovine and pig zonae pellucidae: Chemical, immunological, and receptor properties. *Gamete Res.* 3:217–31.

Gwatkin, R. B. L., and Williams, D. T. 1970. Inhibition of sperm capacitation in vitro by contraceptive steroids. *Nature* 227:182–83.

———. 1978. Immunization of female rabbits with heat-solubilized bovine zonae: Production of anti-zona antibody and inhibition of fertility. *Gamete Res.* 1:19–26.

Gwatkin, R. B. L., Williams, D. T., and Carlo, D. J. 1977. Immunization of mice with heat-solubilized hamster zonae: Production of anti-zona antibody and inhibition of fertility. *Fertil. Steril.* 28:871–77.

Gwatkin, R. B. L., Williams, D. T., and Meyerhofer, M. 1979. Isolation of bovine zona pellucida from ovaries with collagenase: Antigenic and sperm receptor properties. *Gamete Res.* 2:187–92.

Hamilton, M. S., Beer, A. E., May, R. D., and Vitetta, E. S. 1979. The influence of immunization of female mice with F-9 teratocarcinoma cells on the reproductive performance. *Transplant. Proc.* 11:1069–72.

Hansel, W., Malven, P. V., and Black, D. L. 1961. Estrous cycle regulation in the bovine. *J. Anim. Sci.* 20:621–25.

Harder, J. D. 1971. The application of an antifertility agent in the control of a white-tailed deer population. Ph.D. thesis, Ohio State University, Columbus.

Harder, J. D., and Peterle, T. J. 1974. Effects of diethylstilbestrol on reproductive performance in white-tailed deer. *J. Wildl. Mgmt.* 38:183–96.

Harrison, R. M., and Dukelow, W. R. 1971. Megestrol acetate: Its effect on inhibition of ovulation in squirrel monkeys, *Saimiri sciureus. J. Reprod. Fertil.* 25:99–101.

Hediger, H. 1964. *Wild animals in captivity.* New York: Dover.

Heller, C. G., Moore, D. J., and Paulsen, C. A. 1961. Suppression of spermatogenesis and chronic toxicity in man of a new series of bis(dichloroacetyl)diamines. *Toxicol. Appl. Pharmacol.* 3:1–11.

Henderson, C. J., Hulme, M. J., and Aitken, R. J. 1988. Contraceptive potential of antibodies to the zona pellucida. *J. Reprod. Fertil.* 83:325–43.

Hill, J. R. Jr., Lamond, D. R., Henricks, D. M., Dickey, J. F., and Niswender, G. D. 1971. The effect of melengestrol acetate (MGA) on ovarian function and fertilization in beef heifers. *Biol. Reprod.* 4:16–22.

Hobson, B. M., and Wide, L. 1981. The similarity of chorionic gonadotrophin and its subunits in term placentae from man, apes, Old and New World monkeys, and a prosimian. *Folia Primatol.* 35:51–64.

Hodgen, G. D., Nixon, W. E., Vaitukaitus, J. L., Tullner, W. W., and Ross, G. T. 1973. Neutralization of primate chorionic gonadotropin activities by antisera against the subunits of human chorionic gonadotropin in radioimmunoassay and bioassay. *Endocrinology* 92:705–9.

Hodges, J. K., and Hearn, J. P. 1979. Long-term suppression of fertility by immunisation against LHRH and its reversibility in female and male marmoset monkeys. In *Recent advances in reproduction and regulation of fertility*, ed. G. P. Talwar, 87–96. Amsterdam: Elsevier/North Holland Biomedical Press.

Hoffman, R., and Moorhead, B. In press. Biological methods for regulation of population growth in mountain goats. In *Contraception in wildlife*, ed. U. S. Seal and E. D. Plotka. Lewiston, N.Y.: Edwin Mellen Press.

Hoffman, R. A., and Wright, R. G. 1990. Fertility control in a nonnative population of mountain goat. *Northwest Sci.* 64:1–6.

Holst, P. J., and Braden, A. W. H. 1972. Ovum transport in the ewe. *Aust. J. Biol. Sci.* 25:167–73.

Howard, G., Warren, R. J., and Fotherby, K. 1975. Plasma levels of norethistrone in women receiving norethistrone oenanthate intramuscularly. *Contraception* 12:45–50.

Howard, W. E., and Marsh, R. E. 1969. Mestranol as a reproductive inhibitor in rats and voles. *J. Wildl. Mgmt.* 33:403–8.

Hudson, R., Hemphill, P., and Tillson, S. A. 1978. Preclinical evaluation of intrauterine progesterone as a contraceptive agent. I. Local contraceptive effects and their reversal. *Contraception* 17:465–73.

Humpel, M., Kuhne, G., Schulze, P. E., and Speck, U. 1977. Injectable depot contraceptives on d-norgestrel basis. I. Pharmacokinetic studies in dog and baboons. *Contraception* 15:401–12.

Kaunitz, A. M., and Grimes, D. A. 1985. First-trimester abortion technology. In *Fertility control*, ed. S. L. Corson, R. J. Derman, and L. B. Tyrer, 63–76. Boston: Little, Brown.

Kaur, J., Ramakrishnan, P. R., and Rajalakshmi, M. 1990. Inhibition of spermatozoa maturation in rhesus monkey by cyproterone acetate. *Contraception* 42:349–59.

Kirkpatrick, J. F. 1986. Chemical fertility control in feral cats. Final Report, Contract no. 316505-3590, Department of Animal Control, Billings, Mont.

Kirkpatrick, J. F., Liu, I. M. K., Turner, J. W. Jr., Naugle, R., and Keiper, R. 1992. Long-term effects of porcine zonae pellucidae immunocontraception on ovarian function in feral horses *(Equus caballus)*. *J. Reprod. Fertil.* 94:437–44.

Kirkpatrick, J. F., and Turner, J. W. Jr. 1987. Chemical fertility control and the management of the Assateague feral ponies. Final Report, NPS Contract CA 1600-3-0005, Assateague Island National Seashore, Berlin, Md.

Kirkpatrick, J. F., Turner, J. W. Jr., and Perkins, A. 1982. Reversible fertility control in feral horses. *J. Equine Vet. Sci.* 2:114–18.

Knowles, J. M. 1986. Wild and captive populations: Triage, contraception, and culling. *Int. Zoo Yrbk.* 24/25:206–10.

Kollias, G. V. Jr. 1988. Complications of progestogen contraception in exotic felids. *Proceedings of the Joint Conference of the American Association of Zoo Veterinarians and the American Association of Wildlife Veterinarians*, 249.

Langer, R. 1990. New methods of drug delivery. *Science* 249:1527–33.

Lee, N. C., Rubin, G. L., and Borucki, R. 1988. The intrauterine device and pelvic inflammatory disease revisited: New results from the Women's Health Study. *Obstet. Gynecol.* 72:1–6.

Lee, N. C., Rubin, G. L., Ory, H. W., and Burkman, R. T. 1983. Type of intrauterine device and the risk of pelvic inflammatory disease. *Obstet. Gynecol.* 62:1–6.

Lein, D. H., and Concannon, P. W. 1983. Infertility and fertility treatments and management in the queen and tomcat. In *Current veterinary therapy 7: Small animal practice*, ed. R. W. Kirk, 936. Philadelphia: W. B. Saunders.

Linhart, S. B., and Enders, R. K. 1964. Some effects of diethylstilbestrol on reproduction in captive red fox. *J. Wildl. Mgmt.* 28:358–63.

Liu, I. K. M., Bernoco, M., and Feldman, M. 1989. Contraception in mares heteroimmunized with pig zonae pellucidae. *J. Reprod. Fertil.* 85:19–28.

Mahi, C. A., and Yanagimachi, R. 1979. Prevention of in vitro fertilization of canine oocytes by antiovary antisera: A potential approach to fertility control in the bitch. *J. Exp. Zool.* 210:129–35.

Mahi-Brown, C. A., Yanagimachi, R., Hoffman, J. C., and Huang, T. T. F. Jr. 1985. Fertility control in bitches by active immunization with porcine zonae pellucidae: Use of different adjuvants and patterns of estradiol and progesterone levels in estrous cycles. *Biol. Reprod.* 32:761–72.

Mahi-Brown, C. A., Yanagimachi, R., Nelson, M. L., Yanagimachi, H., and Palumbro, N. 1988. Ovarian histopathology of bitches immunized with porcine zonae pellucidae. *Am. J. Reprod. Immunol. Microbiol.* 18:94–103.

Matschke, G. H. 1977a. Antifertility action of two synthetic progestins in female white-tailed deer. *J. Wildl. Mgmt.* 41:194–96.

———. 1977b. Microencapsulated diethylstilbestrol as an oral contraceptive in white-tailed deer. *J. Wildl. Mgmt.* 41:87–91.

———. 1980. Efficacy of steroid implants in preventing pregnancy in white-tailed deer. *J. Wildl. Mgmt.* 44:756–58.

Matsura, S., Ohashi, M., Chen, H. C., and Hodgen, G. D. 1979. An hCG specific antiserum against synthetic peptide analogs to the C-terminal peptide of its Beta-subunit. *Endocrinology* 104:396–401.

McDonald, M. 1980. Population control of feral cats using megestrol acetate. *Vet. Rec.* 106:129.

Millar, S. E., Chamow, S. M., Baur, A. W., Oliver, C., Robey, F., and Dean, J. 1989. Vaccination with a synthetic zona pellucida peptide produces long-term contraception in female mice. *Science* 246:935–38.

Mishell, D. R. Jr. 1989. Contraception. *N. Engl. J. Med.* 320:777–87.

Morton, D. B. 1976. Lysosomal enzymes in mammalian spermatozoa. In *Lysosomes in biology and pathology*, vol. 5, ed. T. T. Dingle and R. T. Dean, 203–55. Amsterdam: Elsevier.

Moudgal, N. R., Murthy, G. S., Rao, A. V., Ravindranath, N., Sairam, M. R., Kotagi, S. G., and Martin, F. 1986. Immunization against FSH as a method of male contraception. In *Immunological approaches to contraception and promotion of fertility*, ed. G. P. Talwar, 103–13. New York: Plenum Press.

Munson, L., and Mason, R. J. 1991. Pathological findings in the uteri of progestogen-implanted exotic felids. *Proceedings of the Annual Meeting of the American Association of Zoo Veterinarians*, 311–12. Philadelphia: American Association of Zoo Veterinarians.

Nagle, C. A., Paul, N., Mazzoni, I., Quiroga, S., Torres, M., Mendizabel, A. F., and Farinati, Z. 1989. Interovarian relationship in the secretion of progesterone during the luteal phase of the capuchin monkey *(Cebus apella)*. *J. Reprod. Fertil.* 85:389–96.

Naz, R. K., Alexander, N. J., Isahakia, M., and Hamilton, M. 1984. Monoclonal antibody against human germ cell membrane glycoprotein that inhibits fertilization. *Science* 225:342–44.

Naz, R. K., Poffenberger, R. J., and Menge, A. C. 1986. Reduction of fertility in female rabbits and mice actively immunized with a germ cell antigen (GA-1) from the rabbit. *J. Reprod. Immunol.* 9:163–73.

Nestor, J. J. Jr., and Vickery, B. H. 1988. LHRH analogues in control of fertility and gonadal hormone dependent disease. *Annu. Rep. Med. Chem.* 23:211–20.

Nilsson, S., Nygren, K., and Johansson, E. 1977. D-norgestrel concentration in maternal plasma, milk, and child plasma during administration of oral contraceptive to nursing women. *Am. J. Obstet. Gynecol.* 129:178.

———. 1978. Ethinyl estradiol in human milk and plasma after oral administration. *Contraception* 17:131–39.

Nomeir, A. A., and Abou-Donia, M. B. 1985. Toxicological effects of gossypol. In *Male fertility and its regulation*, ed. T. J. Lobl and E. S. E. Hafez, 111–33.

Nora, J. J., and Nora, A. H. 1973. Birth defects and oral contraceptives. *Lancet* 1:941–42.

Nutting, E. F., and Mares, S. E. 1970. Inhibition of fertilization in rabbits during treatment with progesterone. *Biol. Reprod.* 2:230–38.

Nygren, K. G., Lindberg, P., Martinsson, K., Bosu, W. T. K., and Johansson, E. D. B. 1974. Radioimmunoassay of norethindrone: Peripheral plasma after oral administration to humans and rhesus monkeys. *Contraception* 9:265.

Oleyar, C. M., and McGinnes, G. S. 1974. Field evaluation of diethylstilbestrol for suppressing reproduction in foxes. *J. Wildl. Mgmt.* 38:101–6.

Ory, H. W. 1983. Mortality associated with fertility and fertility control. *Fam. Plann. Perspect.* 15:50–56.

Ownby, C. L., and Shivers, C. A. 1972. Antigens of the hamster ovary and effects of anti-ovary serum on eggs. *Biol. Reprod.* 6:310–18.

Perry, J., Bridgwater, D. D., and Horsemen, D. L. 1975. Captive propagation: A progress report. In *Breeding endangered species in captivity*, ed. R. D. Martin, 361–77. London: Academic Press.

Pfeiffer, D. G. 1972. Effects of diethylstilbestrol on reproduction in the black-tailed prairie dog. M.S. thesis, South Dakota State University, Brookings.

Pitt, C. G. 1987. The controlled delivery of polypeptides including LHRH analogs. In *LHRH and its analogs: Contraceptive and therapeutic applications*, part 2, ed. B. H. Vickery and J. J. Nestor Jr., 557–75. Lancaster, England: MTP Press Ltd.

Plotka, E. D., Eagle, T. C., Vevea, D. N., Koller, A. L., Siniff, D. B., Tester, J. R., and Seal, U. S. 1988. Effects of hormone implants on estrus and ovulation in feral mares. *J. Wildl. Dis.* 24:507–14.

Plotka, E. D., and Seal, U. S. 1989. Fertility control in deer. *J. Wildl. Dis.* 25:643–46.

Population Reports. 1983. *Long-acting progestins: Promise and prospects.* Population Reports, series K, no. 2. Baltimore: Population Information Program, Johns Hopkins University.

Porton, I., Asa, C., and Baker, A. 1990. Survey results on the use of birth control methods in primates and carnivores in North American zoos. *AAZPA Annual Conference Proceedings*, 489–97. Wheeling, W.Va.: American Association of Zoological Parks and Aquariums.

Porton, I., and Hornbeck, B. 1993. A North American contraceptive database for ungulates. *Int. Zoo Yrbk.* 32:155–59.

Portugal, M. M., and Asa, C. S. 1995. Effects of chronic melengestrol acetate contraceptive treatment on perineal tumescence, body weight, and sociosexual behavior of hamadryas baboons *(Papio hamadryas)*. *Zoo Biol.* 14:251–59.

Ramakrishnan, S., Das, C., Dubey, S. K., Solahuddin, M., and Tolwar, G. P. 1979. Immunogenicity of three C-terminal synthetic peptides of the beta-subunit of human chorionic gonadotropin

and properties of the antibodies raised against 45 amino acid C-terminal peptide. *J. Reprod. Immunol.* 1:249–61.

Remfry, J. 1978. Control of feral cat populations by long-term administration of megestrol acetate. *Vet. Rec.* 103:403–4.

Rinehart, W. 1975. The Minipill: A limited alternative for certain women. *Popul. Rep.* 3:A53–A67.

Roser, J. F., and Lofstedt, R. M. 1989. Urinary eCG patterns in the mare during pregnancy. *Theriogenology* 32:607–22.

Sacco, A. G. 1977. Antigenic cross-reactivity between human and pig zona pellucida. *Biol. Reprod.* 16:164–73.

Sacco, A. G., Pierce, D. L., Subramanian, M. G., Yurewicz, E. C., and Dukelow, W. R. 1987. Ovaries remain functional in squirrel monkeys *(Saimiri sciureus)* immunized with porcine zona pellucida 55,000 macromolecule. *Biol. Reprod.* 36:481–90.

Sacco, A. G., Subramanian, M. G., and Yurewicz, E. C. 1981. Passage of zona antibodies via placenta and milk following active immunization of female mice with porcine zona pellucidae. *J. Reprod. Immunol.* 3:313–22.

Sacco, A. G., Subramanian, M. G., Yurewicz, E. C., DeMayo, F. J., and Dukelow, W. R. 1983. Heteroimmunization of squirrel monkeys *(Saimiri sciureus)* with a purified porcine zona antigen (PPZA): Immune response and biologic activity of antiserum. *Fertil. Steril.* 39:350–58.

Sacco, A. G., and Yurewicz, E. C. 1989. Use of the zona pellucida as an immunocontraceptive target antigen. In *The mammalian egg coat: Structure and function*, ed. J. Dietl, 128–53. Berlin: Springer-Verlag.

Sacco, A. G., Yurewicz, E. C., and Subramanian, M. G. 1989. Effect of varying dosages and adjustments on antibody response in squirrel monkeys *(Saimiri sciureus)* immunized with the porcine zona pellucida $M_r = 55,000$ glycoprotein (ZP3). *Am. J. Reprod. Immunol.* 21:1–8.

Sacco, A. G., Yurewicz, E. C., Subramanian, M. G., and DeMayo, F. J. 1981. Zona pellucida composition: Species cross reactivity and contraceptive potential of antiserum to a purified pig zona antigen (PPZA). *Biol. Reprod.* 25:997–1008.

Sartwell, P. E., Arthes, F. G., and Tonaschia, J. A. 1977. Exogenous hormones, reproductive history, and breast cancer. *J. Natl. Cancer Inst.* 59:1589–92.

Seal, U. S., Barton, R., Mather, L., Gray, C. W., and Plotka, E. D. 1975. Long-term control of reproduction in female lions *(Panthera leo)* with implanted contraceptives. *Proceedings of the Annual Meeting of the American Association of Zoo Veterinarians*, 66–80. Philadelphia: American Association of Zoo Veterinarians.

Seal, U. S., Barton, R., Mather, L., Oberding, K., Plotka, E. D., and Gray, C. W. 1976. Hormonal contraception in captive female lions *(Panthera leo)*. *J. Zoo Anim. Med.* 7:1–17.

Searle, R. F., Sellens, M. H., Elson, J., Jenkinson, E. J., and Billington, W. D. 1976. Detection of alloantigens during preimplantation development and early trophoblast differentiation in the mouse by immunoperoxidase labeling. *J. Exp. Med.* 143:348–59.

Seely, A. J., and Ronald, K. 1991. The effect of Depo-Provera on reproduction in the grey seal *(Halichoerus grypus)*. *Proceedings of the Annual Meeting of the American Association of Zoo Veterinarians*, 304–10. Philadelphia: American Association of Zoo Veterinarians.

Segal, S. J., and Croxatto, H. B. 1969. Single administration of hormones for longer term control of reproductive function. *13th Annual Meeting, American Fertility Society*, Abstract.

Sehgal, S., Gupta, S. K., and Bhatnagar, P. 1989. Long-term effects of immunization with porcine zona pellucida on rabbit ovaries. *Pathology* 21:105–10.

Shivers, C. A., Gengozian, N., Franklin, S., and McLaughlin, C. L. 1978. Antigenic cross-reactivity between human and marmoset zonae pellucidae, a potential target for immuno-contraception. *J. Med. Primatol.* 7:242–48.

Simmons, J. G., and Hamner, C. E. 1973. Inhibition of estrus in the dog with testosterone implants. *Am. J. Vet. Res.* 34:1409–19.

Sivin, I. 1988. International experience with Norplant and Norplant-2 contraceptives. *Stud. Fam. Plann.* 11:227–37.

Skinner, S. M., and Dunbar, B. S. 1984. Comparison of immunization using a purified zona pellucida (ZP) protein or total ZP protein on ovarian follicular development. *Biol. Reprod.* 30 (suppl. 1): 73.

Skinner, S. M., Mills, T., Kirchick, H. J., and Dunbar, B. S. 1984. Immunization with zona pellucida proteins results in abnormal ovarian follicular differentiation and inhibition of gonadotropin-induced steroid secretion. *Endocrinology* 115:2418–32.

Sokolowski, J. H., and Van Ravenswaay, F. 1976. Effects of melengestrol acetate on reproduction in the Beagle bitch. *Am. J. Vet. Res.* 37:943–45.

Sokolowski, J. H., and Zimbelman, R. G. 1976. Evaluation of selected compounds for estrus control in the bitch. *Am. J. Vet. Res.* 37:939–41.

Soulé, M., Gilpin, M., Conway, W., and Foose, T. 1986. The millennium ark: How long a voyage, how many staterooms, how many passengers? *Zoo Biol.* 5:101–13.

Stevens, V. C. 1986. Development of a vaccine against human chorionic gonadotropin using a synthetic peptide as the immunogen. In *Reproductive immunology,* ed. D. A. Clark and B. A. Croy, 162–69. Amsterdam: Elsevier Scientific.

Stevens, V. C., Powell, J. E., Lee, A. C., and Griffin, D. 1981. Antifertility effects of immunization of female baboons with C-terminal peptides of the ß-subunit of human chorionic gonadotropin. *Fertil. Steril.* 36:98–105.

Storm, G. L., and Sanderson, G. C. 1969a. Effect of medroxyprogesterone acetate (Provera) on productivity in captive foxes. *J. Mammal.* 50:147–49.

———. 1969b. Results of a field test to control striped skunks with diethylstilbestrol. *Trans. Ill. State Acad. Sci.* 62:193–97.

Stubblefield, P. G. 1985. Induced abortion in the mid-trimester. In *Fertility control,* ed. S. L. Corson, R. J. Derman, and L. B. Tyrer, 77–87. Boston: Little, Brown.

Swahn, M. L., Gottleib, C., Green, K., and Bygdeman, M. 1990. Oral administration of RU 486 and 9-methylene PGE(2) for termination of early pregnancy. *Contraception* 41:461–74.

Syner, F. N., Kuros, B. S., and Moghissi, K. S. 1979. Active immunization of female rabbits with purified rabbit acrosin and effect on fertility. *Fertil. Steril.* 32:468–73.

Talwar, G. P. 1974. Immunological approaches to fertility control. In *7th Karolinska symposium,* ed. E. Diczfalusy, 370. Stockholm: Karolinska Institute.

Tillson, S. A., Swisher, D. A., Pharriss, B. B., Erickson, R. E., and Neill, J. D. 1976. Interrelationships between pituitary gonadotrophins and ovarian steroids in baboons during continuous intrauterine progesterone treatment. *Biol. Reprod.* 15:291–96.

Torii, R., Koizumi, H., Tanioka, Y., Inaba, T., and Mori, J. 1987. Serum LH, progesterone, and estradiol–17 levels throughout the ovarian cycle during the early stage of pregnancy and after the parturition and abortion in the common marmoset, *Callithrix jacchus. Primates* 28:229–38.

Travis, H. G., and Schaible, P. J. 1962. Effect of diethylstilbestrol fed periodically during gestation of female mink upon reproduction and kit performance. *Am. J. Vet. Res.* 23:359–61.

Triman, K., and Liskin, L. 1988. Intrauterine devices. *Popul. Rep.* 16:1–31.

Tsunoda, Y., and Chang, M. C. 1976a. Effect of anti-rat ovary antiserum on the fertilization of rat, mouse, and hamster eggs in vivo and vitro. *Biol. Reprod.* 14:354–61.

———. 1976b. The effect of passive immunization with hetero- and iso-immune anti-ovary antiserum on the fertilization of mouse, rat, and hamster eggs. *Biol. Reprod.* 15:361–65.

———. 1976c. In vivo and in vitro fertilization of hamster, rat, and mouse eggs after treatment with anti-hamster ovary antiserum. *J. Exp. Zool.* 195:409–13.

Turner, J. W. Jr., and Kirkpatrick, J. F. 1982. Androgens, behavior and fertility control in feral stallions. *J. Reprod. Fertil., Suppl.* 32:79–87.

Upadhyay, S. N., Thillaikoothan, P., Bamezai, A., Gayaraman, S., and Talwar, G. P. 1989. Role of adjuvants in inhibitory influence of immunization with porcine zona pellucida antigen (ZP-3) on ovarian folliculogenesis in bonnet monkeys: A morphological study. *Biol. Reprod.* 41:665–73.

Van Os, J. L., and Oldenkamp, E. P. 1978. Oestrus control in bitches with proligestone, a new progestational steroid. *J. Small Anim. Pract.* 19:521–29.

Vickery, B. H. 1981. Physiology and antifertility effects of LHRH and agonistic analogs in male animals. In *LHRH and agonistic analogs in male animals,* ed. J. J. Sciarra, 275. Philadelphia: Harper and Row.

Vickery, B. H., and Bennett, J. B. 1969. Mechanisms of antifertility action of chlormadinone acetate in the rabbit. *Biol. Reprod.* 1: 372–77.

Vickery, B. H., Erickson, G. I., Bennett, J. P., Mueller, N. S., and Haleblian, J. K. 1970. Antifertility effects in the rabbit by continuous low release of progestin from an intrauterine device. *Biol. Reprod.* 3:154–62.

Vickery, B. H., and McRae, G. I. 1980. Effects of continuous treatment with superagonists of LHRH when initiated at different times of the menstrual cycle in female baboons. *Int. J. Fertil.* 25: 171–78.

Vickery, B. H., McRae, G. I., Briones, W., Worden, A., Seidenberg, R., Shanbacher, B. D., and Falvo, R. 1984. Effects of an LHRH agonist analog upon sexual function in male dogs. *J. Androl.* 5: 28–42.

Waller, D. P., Zaneveld, L. D., and Farnsworth, N. R. 1985. Gossypol: Pharmacology and current status as a male contraceptive. In *Economic and medicinal plant research,* vol. 1, ed. H. Wagner, H. Hilkins, and N. Farnsworth, 87–99. London: Academic Press.

Wemmer, C. 1989. Animal contraceptive task force formed. *AAZPA Newsl.* 30 (9): 16.

Whitehead, M. I. 1978. The effects of oestrogens and progestogens on the post-menopausal endometrium. *Maturitas* 1:87–98.

Wide, L., Hobson, B., and Wide, M. 1980. Chorionic gonadotropin in rodents. In *Chorionic gonadotropin,* ed. S. J. Siegal, 1–15. New York: Plenum Press.

Wiebe, J. P., Barr, K. J., and Buckingham, K. D. 1989. Sustained azoospermia in squirrel monkey, *Saimiri sciureus,* resulting from a single intratesticular glycerol injection. *Contraception* 39: 447–57.

Wildt, D. E., and Seager, S. W. J. 1977. Reproduction control in dogs. *Vet. Clin. N. Am.* 7:775–87.

Wood, D. M., and Dunbar, B. S. 1981. Direct detection of two cross-reactive antigens between porcine and rabbit zonae pellucidae by radioimmunoassay and immunoelectrophoresis. *J. Exp. Zool.* 217:423–33.

Wood, D. M., Lie, C., and Dunbar, B. S. 1981. Effect of alloimmunization and heteroimmunization with zonae pellucidae on fertility in rabbits. *Biol. Reprod.* 25:439–50.

World Health Organization (WHO). 1985. Fourteenth annual report of the special programme of research, development, and research training in human reproduction. Geneva, Switzerland: World Health Organization.

Zador, G. 1976. Estrogens and thromboembolic diseases. *Acta Obstet. Gynecol. Scand. Suppl.* 54:13–28.

Zaneveld, L. J. D., Burns, J. W., Beyler, S. A., Depel, W., and Shapiro, S. W. 1986. Development of a new reversible vas deferens occlusion device. In *Male contraception: Advances and future prospects,* ed. G. I. Zatuchni, A. Goldsmith, J. M. Spieler, and J. J. Sciarra, 201–8. Philadelphia: Harper and Row.

———. 1988. Development of a potentially reversible vas deferens occlusion device and evaluation in primates. *Fertil. Steril.* 49: 527–33.

Zhang, J. 1993. Factors associated with Copper T IUD removal for bleeding/pain: A multivariate analysis. *Contraception* 48: 13–22.

Zimbelman, R. G. 1963. Determination of the minimum effective dose of 6-methyl-17-acetoxyprogesterone for control of the estrual cycle of cattle. *J. Anim. Sci.* 22:1051.

41

Pregnancy and Parturition in Captive Mammals

MICHAEL HUTCHINS, PATRICK THOMAS, AND CHERYL S. ASA

Detailed knowledge of a species' reproductive biology and behavior is essential to the development of a successful captive breeding program (Kleiman 1975, 1980; Lasley 1980; Eisenberg and Kleiman 1977). One of the most critical periods in mammalian reproduction extends from conception to birth. The purpose of this chapter is to review physiological and behavioral factors related to pregnancy and parturition in mammals. Rather than attempting to review these processes in the entire class, we will describe some of the similarities and differences that exist among its various members. In addition, we will focus on issues relevant to zoo animal management and propagation.

PHYSIOLOGY OF PREGNANCY AND PARTURITION

A knowledge of the physiological aspects of pregnancy can be useful in captive animal management (Kleiman 1975; Lasley 1980). Unfortunately, previous studies have focused primarily on humans, laboratory rodents, and domestic ungulates and carnivores. Detailed data on the physiological aspects of pregnancy in a wide variety of mammals are provided by Hayssen, Van Tienhoven, and Van Tienhoven (1993), Lamming (1984), and Knobil and Neill (1988).

For the purposes of this discussion, conception, or fertilization of the ovum, constitutes the initiation of pregnancy. In most mammals, the major events that follow fertilization include transport of the fertilized ovum, or zygote, to the uterus; maternal recognition of pregnancy, with ensuing maintenance of the corpora lutea (CL); implantation of the zygote in the uterine lining; and placentation. Following a species-typical period of development, gestation ends with parturition, or expulsion of the fetus from its uterine environment.

Among mammals, the most divergent reproductive pattern is found in the Monotremata. The duck-billed platypus, *Ornithorhynchus anatinus*, lays eggs that are incubated in a nest. Another monotreme, the echidna, *Tachyglossus acu-*

leatus, incubates its eggs first for 2–4 weeks in utero, then in an external pouch (Griffiths 1984).

Marsupials differ from both monotremes and eutherian mammals in that the embryo spends a relatively short time in utero (e.g., marsupial mouse, *Sminthopsis larapinta*, 12.5 days: Godfrey 1969; red kangaroo, *Macropus rufus*, 33 days: Sharman 1963). The extremely small neonate (range 5 mg–1 g), which is born at an early stage of development relative to eutherian mammals, climbs into the pouch and attaches itself to a teat without maternal assistance (Tyndale-Biscoe 1973, 1984).

Maternal Recognition of Pregnancy

If conception does not occur at the time of ovulation, most female mammals begin another ovulatory cycle or enter a quiescent phase. The CL that form as a result of ovulation may regress spontaneously, or, in some species, transient prostaglandin $F_2\alpha$ ($PGF_2\alpha$) may cause CL demise (Hendricks and Mayer 1977). If conception does occur, CL production of steroid hormones, particularly progesterone, must continue to maintain pregnancy. Thus the maternal system must receive a signal that fertilization has occurred, and the obvious source of such a signal is the newly formed zygote.

Although investigations into maternal recognition of pregnancy are ongoing, it appears that the zygotes or embryos of most species do communicate with the maternal system. The earliest message yet detected appears in maternal blood serum as little as 1 hour after fertilization (Nancarrow, Wallace, and Grewal 1981). A substance released by the zygote (Orozco, Perkins, and Clarke 1986; Nancarrow, Wallace, and Grewal 1981) stimulates production of this early pregnancy factor (EPF) by the maternal oviduct and ovaries (Morton et al. 1980). Although the function of EPF is still uncertain, it is specific to pregnancy, and its presence at other times indicates pathology. Not only does the presence of EPF in maternal serum confirm fertilization, but its subsequent disappearance during the first half of pregnancy signals embryonic or fetal loss (Morton, Rolfe, and Cavanagh 1982). EPF has been found in all species studied to date, including the mouse, *Mus musculus* (Morton, Hegh, and Clunie 1976), domestic sheep, *Ovis aries* (Nancarrow, Wallace, and Grewal 1981; Morton et al. 1979), domestic cow, *Bos taurus* (Nancarrow, Wallace, and Grewal 1981), domestic pig, *Sus scrofa* (Morton, Morton, and Ellendorf 1983), domestic horse, *Equus caballus*, wallaby (species not given) (Morton, Rolfe, and Cavanagh 1982), and human (Morton et al. 1977).

A number of gonadotropic hormones may be responsible for maintaining the CL, including luteinizing hormone (LH), follicle-stimulating hormone (FSH), prolactin (PRL), chorionic gonadotropin (CG), and perhaps pregnant mare's serum gonadotropin (PMSG). However, there is great variation among species (Josimovich 1967). For example, LH may be the primary luteotroph in the cow (Hansel 1971). In sheep, a combination of LH and PRL may be involved. In the laboratory mouse, PRL induced by copulation is sufficient for CL maintenance prior to implantation, after which LH is necessary (Robson, Sullivan, and Wilson 1971). In the rabbit, *Oryctolagus cuniculus*, both LH and FSH are required for CL secretion of progesterone, whereas in the hamster, *Mesocricetus auratus*, the necessary combination is FSH and PRL (Greenwald 1967).

PMSG, the pregnancy-specific gonadotropin of the horse, is probably unique to equids. PMSG is produced by the fetal chorionic girdle cells, which invade the uterine lining (Allen 1969). It first appears in maternal serum between days 35 and 41 of gestation, but is never excreted in urine.

Implantation

The time of implantation varies greatly by species, but it commonly occurs between 1 and 4 weeks postfertilization. In many species gonadotropic hormones increase or first appear at or near the time of implantation. Chorionic gonadotropin (CG), produced by the trophoblast or cell layer that becomes the placenta (Wislocki and Streeter 1938), is responsible for maintaining functional CL, and thus for progesterone secretion, in many species. CG has been found in the placentas of prosimians, New and Old World monkeys, great apes, and humans throughout gestation (Hobson and Wide 1981). The discovery of CG in the laboratory rat, mouse, hamster, guinea pig, *Cavia porcellus*, and horse suggests that it may be more prevalent among mammals than previously believed (Wide, Hobson, and Wide 1980; Roser and Lofstedt 1989). Its levels decrease throughout pregnancy in all primates studied, and it becomes undetectable in the urine of rhesus macaques, *Macaca mulatta*, by late gestation (Hobson et al. 1975). In sheep and cows, trophoblastin, a protein present in the trophoblast cells of the conceptus 2 weeks after ovulation, acts to prevent CL demise (Martal et al. 1979; Findlay 1983). A variety of other pregnancy-specific or pregnancy-associated hormones have been reported, although their roles have not been well established. These hormones include uteroglobin or blastokinin (rabbit: Beier 1968), lactoferrin or uteroferrin (pig and horse: Bazer and First 1983), placental lactogen or chorionic somatomammotropin (primates: Walsh et al.

1977; Chard 1983), Schwangerschraft's protein 1 (SP₁), pregnancy-associated proteins A (PAPP-A) and B (PAPP-B), placental protein 5 (PP5) (Klopper 1983), and an unnamed progesterone-dependent protein (domestic cat, *Felis catus*: Boomsma and Verhage 1987). The development of a radioimmunoassay for detection of PAPP-B in the cow permits pregnancy diagnosis 24 days postconception (Sasser et al. 1986). Unfortunately, measurement of the other pregnancy proteins by routine assay procedures is not yet possible.

Most species require only progesterone for implantation, but estradiol enhances the survival rate of embryos (Hodgen and Itskovitch 1988). Some rodents and perhaps the bonnet macaque, *Macaca radiata*, require estrogen as well as progesterone for implantation (Levasseur 1984; Ravindranath and Moudgal 1987).

Gestation

The estrogens and progestins that support pregnancy are supplied by the ovaries. There is a great deal of species variation in patterns of steroid secretion and excretion throughout pregnancy; progestins typically dominate in early pregnancy and estrogens in later stages. In species with relatively short gestation periods (20–60 days), only the ovarian CL are necessary for steroid production. In those with longer gestations, however, the feto-placental unit supplements—or in some cases replaces—the ovaries as a source of steroid hormones (see Ryan 1973; Amoroso and Finn 1962). In the white-tailed deer, *Odocoileus virginianus* (Plotka et al. 1983), and the cow (Wendorf, Lawyer, and First 1983), the adrenal glands produce progesterone, which may contribute to pregnancy maintenance. Although androgens have been detected in maternal serum (e.g., domestic dog, *Canis familiaris*: Concannon and Castracane 1985), their role in pregnancy and fetal development is unknown.

Although ovarian activity during pregnancy is commonly restricted to CL function, some species show follicular growth during this period. These follicles may ovulate before forming accessory CL or may luteinize spontaneously (e.g., cat: Schmidt, Chakraborty, and Wildt 1983; horse: Squires et al. 1974; chinchilla, *Chinchilla lanigera*: Weir 1973; Asian elephant, *Elephas maximus*: Perry 1953). The European hare, *Lepus europaeus*, shows continued follicular growth during pregnancy; ovulation and fertile matings have been recorded 1–5 days before parturition (Martinet 1980; Flux 1967). Superfetation, the fertilization of another ovum or set of ova during pregnancy, also has been described for the mouse (Rollhauser 1949) and the sheep (Scanlon 1972).

Parturition

Gestation ends with parturition, a series of events that is probably initiated by a signal from the fetus, although this signal has not been identified in most species. Perhaps most thoroughly investigated in the rhesus macaque, sheep, and goat, *Capra hircus*, a fetal pituitary release of adrenocorticotropic hormone (ACTH) stimulates the release of adrenal cortisol, which acts on placental steroid metabolism to suppress the production of progesterone and enhance that of estrogen. This estrogen, passing into the uterus, stimulates

PGF$_2\alpha$ release, which causes secretion of posterior pituitary oxytocin. Together with oxytocin, PGF$_2\alpha$ stimulates contractions of the uterine muscles (First 1979; Challis and Olson 1988; Fuchs 1983). Relaxin, a hormone isolated from the ovaries and placentas of many species, has been implicated along with estrogen and prostaglandins in cervical softening (Weiss 1984). In marsupials, a transient elevation of prolactin, and perhaps PGF$_2\alpha$, precedes the decline in progesterone necessary for the initiation of labor (Tyndale-Biscoe, Hinds, and Horn 1988).

LENGTH OF GESTATION

Gestation length is species-specific (Holm 1966) and thus is largely determined genetically. Even within a given species, breeds may have slightly different gestation lengths (e.g., cow: Jainudeen and Hafez 1980; sheep: Smith 1967; pig: Cox 1964; horse: Howell and Rollins 1951). Among kangaroos, *Macropus* spp., interspecific hybrids have pregnancy durations that are intermediate to the mean lengths of the two parental species, which also implies a strong genetic component (Poole 1975).

Forces other than genotype, however, can act to modify the inherent pattern (Kiltie 1982; Racey 1981). Time of conception during the breeding season, for example, can affect pregnancy duration. In sheep, early breeding results in longer pregnancies, and in horses, spring breeding results in longer pregnancies than does fall breeding (Van Tienhoven 1983; Campitelli, Carenzi, and Verga 1982). Male fetuses tend to be carried longer than female fetuses in some species (e.g., cow: Jainudeen and Hafez 1980; sheep: Terrill 1974). In others, older dams tend to have longer pregnancies than younger dams (e.g., sheep: Terrill 1974).

Increasing litter size is correlated with shorter gestation length in some mammals (e.g., cow: Jainudeen and Hafez 1980; brown bandicoot, *Isoodon obesulus*: Stoddart and Braithewaite 1979; hystricomorph rodents: Weir 1974; mice: Dewar 1968; canids: Naaktgeboren 1968; sheep: Terrill 1974). Experiments with laboratory rabbits suggest that the effect of litter size on gestation length is a function of uterine volume (Csapo and Lloyd-Jacobs 1962).

A reduced level of nutrition has been associated with both shorter (e.g., sheep: Terrill 1974) and longer pregnancies (e.g., rhesus macaque: Riopelle and Hale 1975; common eland, *Taurotragus oryx*: Skinner and van Zyl 1969; white-tailed deer: Verme and Ullrey 1984; hamster: Labov et al. 1986), whereas an enriched diet resulted in shorter pregnancies in the horse (Howell and Rollins 1951) and yellow baboon, *Papio cynocephalus* (Silk 1986). In some heterothermic bats (e.g., *Miniopterus schreibersi fuliginosus*: Uchida, Inoue, and Kimura 1984; *Pipistrellus pipistrellus*: Racey 1973) warmer temperatures accelerate and colder temperatures retard embryonic growth and thus advance or delay parturition respectively.

The most commonly recognized phenomenon that influences gestation length is delayed implantation (embryonic diapause). Obligate diapause, the type most often found in higher mammals, is a quiescent period of blastocyst development that occurs in every pregnancy (e.g., in some bats, Chiroptera; armadillos, Edentata; mustelids and ur-

sids, Carnivora; and pinnipeds, Pinnipedia: Van Tienhoven 1983; Oxberry 1979; Wimsatt 1975; Enders 1963). In contrast, facultative diapause is a quiescent period that may occur under certain stressful conditions, such as during lactation (e.g., in rodents, Myomorpha, and shrews, Soricidae: Van Tienhoven 1983; Renfree and Calaby 1981; Wimsatt 1975).

Embryonic diapause is especially prevalent in macropod marsupials, in which it can be either obligate or facultative (Renfree 1981). In most kangaroos, fertilization occurs at a postpartum estrus, although estrus may be prepartum in some species (Sharman, Calaby, and Poole 1966). Following conception, development of the embryo is delayed by the suckling stimulus of the newborn. Its development resumes late in the pouch life of the older sibling. Birth is accompanied by yet another ovulation and potential conception. This new embryo will then undergo facultative lactational diapause in turn. Thus, a female can have three offspring at one time: one that is becoming independent of the pouch, but may continue to suckle for several months; one that is firmly attached to a teat in the pouch; and one in embryonic diapause. Each mammary gland produces milk of the proper composition for the needs of the suckling young at various stages of growth. If pouch young are lost at any time, embryonic development proceeds without further delay (Stewart and Tyndale-Biscoe 1983; Renfree 1981).

There are several variations on this theme. Some marsupials experience an additional obligate seasonal diapause. In others, ovulation is suppressed during gestation until late in the pouch life of the most recent offspring, and diapause of the embryo continues during suckling. Embryonic diapause is known to be absent in only one macropod species, the western grey kangaroo, *Macropus fuliginosus* (Poole 1975). However, Tyndale-Biscoe (1968) contends that the embryos of all marsupials experience diapause, but that in nonmacropods the period is very brief. Furthermore, Renfree (1981) and Vogel (1981) suggest that all mammalian embryos are capable of some degree of diapause. Vogel considers diapause characteristic of ancestral insectivores in which lactation lasted longer than gestation; thus, diapause prevents the need to suckle two litters simultaneously. Diapause may also allow some marsupials to respond more quickly to favorable conditions in an unpredictable environment (Low 1978).

Another form of pregnancy prolongation is delayed or retarded development, described most extensively in heterothermic bats (e.g., Mexican fruit bat, *Artibeus jamaicensis*: Fleming 1971; California leaf-nosed bat, *Macrotus californicus*: Bradshaw 1962; lump-nosed bat, *Plecotus rafinesquii*: Pearson, Koford, and Pearson 1952). In these species, the lowered metabolic rate associated with hibernation results in slower embryonic or fetal growth. Bernard (1989) suggested that the principal effect of this phenomenon is to lengthen the reproductive cycle so that gametogenesis is initiated in the middle of summer and parturition and lactation occur in the following summer, when food is abundant. Retarded development may also occur in the hedgehog, *Erinaceus europaeus* (Herter 1965).

It should be noted that female mammals maintain considerable control over the actual timing of birth by being able to prolong the initial stage of parturition if disturbed. Thus, behavioral factors can have minor influences on pregnancy duration (see "Timing of Birth" and "Prepartus Phase" below).

INTERBIRTH INTERVALS

The reproductive potential of many captive mammals is determined not only by gestation length but also by interbirth interval (IBI). A species' life history strategy places some constraints on its reproductive potential (Pianka 1970). The IBI of some species is also influenced by seasonal factors. For example, parturition in temperate or alpine species is mediated by photoperiodic cues and timed to coincide with favorable weather or the peak availability of food resources (e.g., mountain goat, *Oreamnos americanus*: Hutchins 1984; beaver, *Castor canadensis*: Patenaude and Bovet 1983). Thus, interspecific differences in reproductive strategies can be expected to influence the frequency with which litters are produced. However, within-species variation can occur as the result of many factors, including age at first breeding, presence of suckling offspring, and sex of previous offspring. Poor physical condition of the dam can prolong the IBI, as has been documented in red deer, *Cervus elaphus* (Clutton-Brock, Guinness, and Albon 1982), and horses (Howell and Rollins 1951), but Berger (1986) noted shorter IBIs in feral horses that were in poor physical condition.

Although lactational anovulation has been documented in a variety of mammals (e.g., red deer: Loudon, McNeilly, and Milne 1983), primatological studies provide the best data on the effect that suckling offspring have on IBIs. According to Altmann, Altmann, and Hausfater (1978), primate IBIs consist of three major phases: (1) a period of postpartum amenorrhea, (2) a period of cycling, which consists of one or more estrous cycles, and (3) a period of gestation. In macaques, *Macaca* spp., the postpartum anovulatory phase is apparently due to both the residual effects of pregnancy and the suckling stimulus. Under laboratory conditions, rhesus macaques and crab-eating macaques, *Macaca fascicularis*, have a postpartum anovulatory interval of about 3 months if nursing does not occur; this is extended if the mother nurses an infant. By the 4th month, however, the suckling stimulus appears to be totally responsible for suppressing ovulation, although the hormonal mechanisms involved remain enigmatic (Williams 1986). Female yellow baboons that lose young infants begin cycling within 1 month and typically conceive by the second estrus. In contrast, females with surviving offspring experience 12 months of postpartum amenorrhea, and typically do not conceive until their fourth estrous cycle (Altmann 1980). Similar phenomena have been documented in a variety of Old World monkeys, apes, and prosimians (mountain gorilla, *Gorilla gorilla beringei*: Stewart 1988; lesser galago, *Galago senegalensis*: Izard and Simons 1987; hanuman langur, *Semnopithecus* (=*Presbytis*) *entellus*: Harley 1985; stump-tailed macaque, *Macaca arctoides*: Nieuwenhuijsen et al. 1985; rhesus macaque: Simpson et al. 1981; Gomendio 1989; lowland gorilla, *G. g. gorilla*: Nadler et. al. 1981; chimpanzee, *Pan troglodytes*: Nadler et al. 1981; Tutin 1980; Japanese macaque, *M. fuscata*: Tanaka, Tokuda, and

Kotera 1970). It should be noted, however, that Burton and Sawchuk (1982) found no relationship between infant loss and IBI in Barbary macaques, *M. sylvanus*.

In New World monkeys the relationship between IBI and lactation is even more equivocal. Howler monkeys, *Alouatta* spp., show an effect of lactation on IBI similar to that in Old World monkeys (Crockett and Sekulic 1984; Glander 1980). In contrast, the owl monkey, *Aotus trivirgatus*, appears to be unaffected by lactation and has an IBI similar to its length of gestation (Hunter et al. 1979). Reproductive function in marmosets also appears to be unaffected by lactation (Poole and Evans 1982; Lunn and McNeilly 1982); however, French (1983) reported an effect for cotton-top tamarins, *Saguinus oedipus*. In squirrel monkeys, *Saimiri sciureus*, lactation coincides with the nonbreeding season, making it difficult to discern what effect—if any—it may have on IBI (Coe and Rosenblum 1978; Williams 1987).

Bercovitch (1987) found that reproductive success in female olive baboons, *Papio anubis*, was related to weight; furthermore, lactating females weighed less and pregnant females weighed more than cycling females. He argued that post-lactating females must surpass a minimum weight threshold before normal cycling is resumed. Thus, suckling offspring impose an energetic cost on females, which in turn affects the interval between the births of present and subsequent offspring. In contrast, female white-tailed shrews, *Crocidura russula* (=*suaveolens*) *monacha*, are often simultaneously pregnant and lactating. No delayed implantation has been observed in this species, however, and there is no difference in gestation length when females are lactating versus when they are not (Hellwing 1973). In this case the energy requirements of lactation and simultaneous pregnancy are partitioned in time: early in gestation, the female lactates heavily and the young grow rapidly; embryonic growth rates increase at or about the time of weaning (Mover, Ar, and Hellwing 1989).

Loss of an infant is known to shorten IBIs in other mammals. For example, Wemmer and Murtaugh (1981) showed that IBIs in binturongs, *Arctictis binturong*, averaged 317.6 days when the female reared her infant and 271.9 days when the infant died or was removed. Laurie (1979) observed a greater one-horned rhinoceros cow, *Rhinoceros unicornis*, mating shortly after the death of her newborn calf. Her next calf was born in 17 months, about half the length of a normal IBI for this species (Laurie 1982). However, captive female rhinoceroses are known to resume cycling before their calves are 1 year old (J. Doherty, pers. comm.). Thus, in relatively asocial species, at least a portion of the IBI may be due to female avoidance of males, especially when females are accompanied by small infants.

In the case of highly endangered species, early removal of infants can be used as a management strategy to reduce IBIs and increase reproductive output. For example, Williams (1987, 383) suggested that "intervention to reduce the amount of suckling during the breeding season" could be used to increase fecundity in harem groups of captive rhesus macaques. However, he also cautioned that early removal of offspring is not a viable strategy if it deprives infants of learning experiences necessary for their own reproductive success (i.e., socialization). French (1983) reported a relationship between IBI and lactation in cotton-top tamarins, which would make them potential candidates for early infant removal. However, experience in assisting with the rearing of younger siblings appears to be an important determinant of future reproductive success in callitrichids (Tardif, Richter, and Carson 1984).

There is some evidence that sex of previous offspring may affect IBIs, although the reason for this phenomenon is still unknown. For example, Kranz, Xanten, and Lumpkin (1983) determined that female Dorcas gazelles, *Gazella dorcas,* had significantly longer IBIs after giving birth to males as opposed to females. Similarly, Clutton-Brock, Guinness, and Albon (1982) noted that red deer were more likely to be barren the year after raising a male fawn than after raising a female fawn, a phenomenon that could be attributed to the relative cost of producing sons versus daughters (Trivers 1972). However, Simpson et al. (1981) found that female rhesus macaques tended to have longer IBIs after producing daughters than after producing sons.

Age at first breeding appears to influence IBIs in some species. For example, once they reach sexual maturity, Dall sheep, *Ovis dalli,* ewes are capable of producing offspring on an annual basis. However, Heimer and Watson (1982) found that early breeding by ewes (i.e., breeding as yearlings) was followed by alternate-year reproduction. The energetic costs of reproduction exact a toll on females, and younger individuals may require more than a year of recovery before their next pregnancy.

MATERNAL AND FETAL NUTRITION

The most comprehensive information available on the nutritional and metabolic aspects of pregnancy comes from domestic ungulates, laboratory rodents, and humans (Metcalfe, Stock, and Barron 1988). In general, gestation requires a larger quantity or quality of the normal ration, particularly during the last trimester. Indeed, in sheep, 70% of fetal weight gain and 80% of energy and protein deposition to the fetus occur during this time (Pryor 1980). In this species, the additional requirement has been calculated as 100 g digestible organic matter per kg of fetal body weight per day (Russell, Doney, and Reid 1967), or 56% more feed intake and 65% more energy intake, during the last 6 weeks of pregnancy (Pope 1972). A review of the energy costs of pregnancy in selected mammals is provided by Randolph et al. (1977, table 3, 40).

Deficiencies of particular vitamins and minerals can affect pregnancy maintenance and fetal development as well. For example, too little vitamin A, beta-carotene, iodine, or manganese may result in abortion or fetal deformities in domestic cattle (Gerloff and Morrow 1980). Similarly, low reproductive success in felids has been attributed to deficiencies in dietary taurine, an essential amino acid (Sturman et al. 1986). Supplementation of folic acid has resulted in increased birth weight in squirrel monkey neonates (Rasmussen, Thenen, and Hayes 1980).

Undernourishment during pregnancy is known to lead to fetal resorption or abortion in many species, including the horse (Van Niekerk 1965), elk, *Cervus canadensis* (Thorne,

Dean, and Hepworth 1976), squirrel monkey (Manocha 1976), and rabbit (Stodart and Myers 1966). For sheep and goats, in particular, undernourishment in late pregnancy, especially with twins, often results in ketosis or pregnancy toxemia (Pope 1972; Lindahl 1972; Church and Lloyd 1972). In contrast, a high plane of nutrition, as reflected in maternal body weight, has been correlated with larger litters or larger neonates in many species (e.g., red deer: Clutton-Brock, Guinness, and Albon 1982; bandicoot: Stoddart and Braithewaite 1979; rhesus macaque: Kohrs, Harper, and Kerr 1976; Norway rat, *Rattus norvegicus:* Leslie, Venables, and Venables 1952–1953; Perry 1945–1946).

It should be noted, however, that overfeeding can have detrimental effects, including a suppression of reproduction. Although a high caloric intake or continuous, unlimited feeding increases ovulation rates among sheep and swine (Flowers et al. 1989; Pryor 1980), embryonic mortality prior to implantation also increases (Hafez and Jainudeen 1974). This effect may be related to the decrease in progesterone levels and resulting embryonic mortality that have been causally linked to high postmating food rations (Parr et al. 1987). In addition, pregnant female bovids and caprids, especially those with multiple fetuses, that are overfed in early pregnancy are subsequently susceptible to pregnancy toxemia in late pregnancy, characterized by a lack of appetite and neurological disorders (Bruere 1980; Pryor 1980; Hafez and Jainudeen 1974). The apparent paradox of the deleterious effects of both high and low planes of nutrition can perhaps be explained by the finding that maximum conception rates are associated with moderate progesterone levels. Because progesterone concentration is inversely related to nutrition level, only a moderate feeding level will optimize conception (Parr et al. 1987).

Insufficient water intake can result in decreased food intake and undernutrition. In addition, limited water intake can suppress gametogenesis independently from food intake (Nelson and Desjardins 1987).

PREGNANCY DIAGNOSIS

The ability to predict whether and when an animal will give birth is often important to zoo managers. For example, in those cases in which females should be isolated from the rest of the social group before parturition (see "Social Factors and Pregnancy Outcome" below), it is desirable to know precisely when births are going to occur. For important births (i.e., those involving highly endangered or valuable animals), it is also helpful to be ready to provide medical support or shelter if necessary. Provision of shelter may be important because captive mammals do not always give birth at opportune times. This is especially true of subtropical or tropical species that lack strong seasonal peaks in reproduction. When these animals are transported to more temperate climates, births may occur at any time of year, including midwinter (e.g., gray brocket deer, *Mazama gouazoubira,* and pampas deer, *Ozotoceros bezoarticus:* Frädrich 1987). Since many mammals lack thermoregulatory mechanisms at birth, death can result from hypothermia. Early detection of pregnancies also makes it possible for curators and keepers to anticipate the need for dietary changes associated with pregnancy (see "Maternal and Fetal Nutrition," above).

The methods available for pregnancy detection in mammals have been reviewed by Hodges (1986). Capture and restraint are generally required for laparoscopy, palpation, ultrasound imaging of fetuses, and collection of blood for hormone assays. The use of urine and feces as sources of hormone metabolites for assays is often more practical in the zoo setting. A list of some hormone-based assays used for pregnancy diagnosis is given in table 41.1.

Estrogens and progestins have been measured in the urine of a wide variety of mammals (Hodges, Czekala, and Lasley 1979). Monfort et al. (1987) have confirmed that urinary estrone conjugates parallel the levels of estradiol in serum, making urinary assays an excellent method of early pregnancy detection. However, even among the primates, the proportions of the three classic estrogens (estrone, E_1, estradiol, E_2, and estriol, E_3) found during pregnancy vary greatly (Lasley et al. 1981). Enzyme immunoassays for urinary estrone conjugates (Czekala et al. 1986) and progesterone (Munro and Stabenfeldt 1984), unlike radioimmunoassays, do not require the handling of radioactive substances; this requirement was previously a problem for zoos and small laboratories.

Similarly, the presence of CG, which may be detected as early as 11 days postfertilization (Atkinson et al. 1975) in urine as well as in blood, is a reliable indicator of early pregnancy. Unfortunately, EPF, which increases on the first day of conception, can be measured only in blood.

In species such as the domestic cat, and possibly other felids, in which feces, not urine, are the major excretory route for estrogens (Shille et al. 1984), and in circumstances in which collection of feces is less problematic than collection of urine, estrogens still can be measured. Pregnancy has been diagnosed successfully in a variety of ungulates by assay of fecal estrogens (Mostl et al. 1984; Bamberg et al. 1984; Choi et al. 1987; Safar-Hermann et al. 1987) and in the pig-tailed macaque, *Macaca nemestrina,* by fecal progestin (Wasser, Risler, and Steiner 1988). Pregnancy-related increases in estrone sulfate (Heap and Hamon 1979) and progesterone (Batra et al. 1983; Chang and Estergreen 1983) also can be measured in the milk of lactating bovids (see table 41.1).

In some species, serum-based or urine-based pregnancy diagnosis is confounded by a hormonal condition known as false pregnancy or pseudopregnancy (Johnston 1980a); diagnosis of this condition is made on the basis of breeding history and physical examination. In lagomorphs, felids, and mustelids, which have induced ovulation, and in some rodents, which have induced CL function, pseudopregnancy follows infertile matings. Ovulation in most canids and at least two marsupials results in persistent CL function whether or not fertilization, or even copulation, has occurred. In some species, pseudopregnancy is equal in length to pregnancy (e.g., wolf, *Canis lupus:* Seal et al. 1979; coyote, *Canis latrans:* Gier 1975; ferret, *Mustela putorius furo:* Heap and Hamon 1974; arctic fox, *Alopex lagopus:* Møller 1973a; mink, *Mustela vison:* Møller 1973b; Virginia opossum, *Didelphis virginiana:* Hartman 1925; Australian native cat, *Dasyurus viverrinus:* O'Donoghue 1911). In oth-

ers, however, the duration of pseudopregnancy is about half that of pregnancy (e.g., cat: Paape et al. 1975; Norway rat: Hilliard 1973; puma, *Felis concolor:* Bonney, Moore, and Jones 1981; rabbit: Hilliard, Spies, and Sawyer 1968).

Hormonal changes offer some of the best early indicators of pregnancy in mammals, but sample collection or laboratory testing may not always be possible. In such cases, zoo managers may have to rely on other cues. In some instances, changes in the dam's external appearance can be used to detect pregnancy. For example, swelling of the labia or changes in labial pigmentation indicate pregnancy in some primates (Wasser, Risler, and Steiner 1988). Orangutans, *Pongo pygmaeus,* show an abrupt swelling of the labia majora within 2–4 weeks after conception (Graham 1981; van der Werff ten Bosch 1982).

Other physical signs of pregnancy in its later stages include a swollen and distended abdomen and an increase in maternal body weight (e.g., lowland gorilla: Meder 1986; common marmoset, *Callithrix jacchus:* Rothe 1977; European weasel, *Mustela nivalis:* Hartman 1964; dog: Harrop 1960; bottle-nosed dolphin, *Tursiops truncatus:* Tavolga and Essapian 1957). In some cases, various portions of the fetus may be visible as they press against the uterine walls (e.g., impala, *Aepyceros melampus:* Jarman 1976; common marmoset: Rothe 1977; European weasel: Hartman 1964; dog: Harrop 1960; bottle-nosed dolphin: Tavolga and Essapian 1957). Fetal movement is sometimes also detectable by visual examination (e.g., wildebeest, *Connochaetes taurinus:* Estes and Estes 1979; bottle-nosed dolphin: Tavolga and Essapian 1957; cotton mouse, *Peromyscus gossypinus:* Pournelle 1952). When animals can be handled or restrained, pregnancy can sometimes be confirmed by rectal or abdominal palpation (dog: Sokolowski 1980; mountain tapir, *Tapirus pinchaque:* Bonney and Crotty 1979; common marmoset: Rothe 1977; cow, horse: Zemjanis 1974; elk: Greer and Hawkins 1967). Occasionally, the various stages of fetal growth can also be determined through palpation techniques, but these require practice (macaques, *Macaca* spp.: Mahoney and Eisele 1978; saddleback tamarins, *Saguinus fuscicollis:* Gengozian, Smith, and Gosslee 1974; dog: Harrop 1960).

Some technological advances in pregnancy detection have proved useful to zoo managers (see also "Physiology of Pregnancy and Parturition" above). Notable among these are ultrasound and laparoscopy (Harrison and Wildt 1980; Adams et al. 1991). In the former, ultrasonic waves are directed into the body by a transducer; as the waves encounter changes in tissue density, echoes are reflected back into the transducer, then transmitted to a detection device, such as a television monitor (Shimizu 1988; Smith and Lindzey 1982). Other devices make use of the Doppler shift principle to detect tissue movement, such as blood flow (Harper and Cohen 1985; Barrett 1981). Pregnancy is confirmed if a fetal pulse is detected, and in some cases it is also possible to detect multiple fetuses (Fukui and Too 1978). Fetal pulse rate decreases linearly with gestational age, and the relationship between fetal age and pulse rate has been determined for several species (e.g., primates: Murata et al. 1978; pig: Too et al. 1974; cow, horse: Mitchell 1973). In dogs, the earliest ultrasonic evidence of fetal heartbeat is found about

TABLE 41.1.   Assays Used for Pregnancy Diagnosis in Selected Mammals

Substance	Source	Species	Reference
Anuclear cells	Vaginal smear	Cheetah, *Acinonyx jubatus*	Asa et al. 1992
Early pregnancy factor (EPF)	Blood	Sheep, *Ovis aries*	Morton et al. 1979
		Cow, *Bos taurus*	Nancarrow, Wallace, and Grewal 1981
		Mouse, *Mus musculus*	Morton, Hegh, and Clunie 1976
		Horse, *Equus caballus*	Morton, Rolfe, and Cavanagh 1982
		Wallaby	Morton, Rolfe, and Cavanagh 1982
		Pig, *Sus scrofa*	Morton, Morton, and Ellendorf 1983
		Rabbit, *Oryctolagus cuniculus*	Sueoka et al. 1988
Pregnancy-associated protein B	Blood	Cow	Sasser et al. 1986
		Red deer, *Cervus elaphus*	Haigh, Cranfield, and Sasser 1988
		Horse	Lea and Bolton 1988
		Mountain goat, *Oreamnos americanus*	Houston et al. 1986
		Mule deer, *Odocoileus hemionus*	Wood et al. 1986
		White-tailed deer, *O. virginianus*	Wood et al. 1986
Chorionic gonadotropin (CG)	Blood	Rat, *Rattus norvegicus*	Wide, Hobson, and Wide 1980
		Mouse	Wide, Hobson, and Wide 1980
		Guinea pig, *Cavia porcellus*	Wide, Hobson, and Wide 1980
		Hamster, *Mesocricetus auratus*	Wide, Hobson, and Wide 1980
		Bonnet macaque, *Macaca radiata*	Chakraborti and Jagannadha Rao 1987
		Rhesus macaque, *M. mulatta*	Atkinson et al. 1975
	Urine	Olive baboon, *Papio anubis*	Hodgen and Neimann 1975
		Yellow baboon, *Papio cynocephalus*	Hodgen and Neimann 1975
		Marmoset, *Callithrix jacchus*	Hobson et al. 1977; Heger, Merker, and Neubert 1988
		Owl monkey, *Aotus trivirgatus*	Hall and Hodgen 1979
		Rhesus macaque	Hodgen and Ross 1974
		Crab-eating macaque, *M. fascicularis*	Hodgen and Ross 1974
		Orangutan, *Pongo pygmaeus*	Hodgen et al. 1977
		Gorilla, *Gorilla gorilla*	Tullner and Gray 1968
		Chimpanzee, *Pan troglodytes*	Clegg and Weaver 1972
		Squirrel monkey, *Saimiri sciureus*	Hodgen et al. 1978
		Horse	Roser and Lofstedt 1989
		Giant panda, *Ailuropoda melanoleuca*	Monfort et al. 1989
Prolactin	Blood	Elephant, *Loxodonta africana*	McNeilly et al. 1983
Estrogens	Blood	Alaskan fur seal, *Callorhinus ursinus*	Daniel 1974
		Mongoose lemur, *Lemur mongoz*	Perry, Izard, and Fail 1992
	Urine	Asian wild horse, *E. przewalskii*	Czekala et al. 1990
		Horse	Evans et al. 1984
		Gorilla	Hopper, Tullner, and Gray 1968
		Orangutan, *Pongo pygmaeus*	Masters and Markham 1991
		Babirusa, *Babyrousa babyrussa*	Chaudhuri et al. 1990
		Malayan tapir, *Tapirus indicus*	Kasman, McCowan, and Lasley 1985
		Okapi, *Okapia johnstoni*	Loskutoff, Ott, and Lasley 1982
		Ruffed lemur, *Varecia variegata*	Shideler et al. 1983a
		Tamarin, *Saguinus bicolor*	Heistermann et al. 1987
		Vervet monkey, *Chlorocebus (=Cacopithecus) aethiops*	Andelman et al. 1985
		Lion-tailed macaque, *M. silenus*	Shideler et al. 1983b
		Pig	Choi et al. 1987
	Milk	Cow	Chang and Estergreen 1983
		Murrah buffalo (spp?)	Batra et al. 1983

TABLE 41.1. *Continued*

Substance	Source	Species	Reference
	Feces	Cow	Mostl et al. 1984
		Horse	Sist, Youngblood, and Williams 1987
		Cape buffalo, *Syncerus caffer*	Safar-Hermann et al. 1987
		Yak, *Bos mutus*	Safar-Hermann et al. 1987
		Nubian ibex, *Capra nubiana*	Safar-Hermann et al. 1987
		Grevy's zebra, *E. grevyi*	Safar-Hermann et al. 1987
		Pig	Choi et al. 1987
		Goeldi's monkey, *Callimico goeldii*	Pryce and Döbeli 1992
		Goat, *Capra hircus*	Holtz 1992
Progestins	Blood	Little brown bat, *Myotis lucifugus*	Buchanan and Younglai 1986
		Squirrel monkey	Diamond et al. 1987
		Bighorn sheep, *Ovis canadensis*	Brundige, Layne, and McCabe 1988
		Sheep	Gadsby et al. 1976
	Urine	Gorilla	Hodges and Green 1989
		Indian rhino, *Rhinoceros unicornis*	Kasman, Ramsay, and Lasley 1986; Hodges and Green 1989
		Black rhino, *Diceros bicornis*	Ramsay, Kasman, and Lasley 1987
		Giant panda	Hodges et al. 1984
		Rhesus macaque	Liskowski and Wolfe 1972
		Blackbuck, *Antilope cervicapra*	Holt et al. 1988
		Mountain zebra, *E. zebra*	Kirkpatrick, Lasley, and Shideler 1990
		Eld's deer, *Cervus eldii*	Monfort et al. 1990
		Llama, *Lama glama*	Paul-Murphy et al. 1991
	Feces	Pig-tailed macaque, *Macaca nemestrina*	Wasser, Risler, and Steiner 1988
		White rhino, *Ceratotherium simum*	Hodges and Green 1989
		Yellow baboon	Wasser, Monfort, and Wildt 1991
		Caribou, *Rangifer tarandus*	Messier et al. 1990
		Musk oxen, *Ovibos moschatus*	Desaulniers et al. 1989
		American bison, *Bison bison*	Kirkpatrick et al. 1992
		Cheetah	Gross 1992
		Black-footed ferret, *Mustela nigripes*	Gross 1992
		Maned wolf, *Chrysocyon brachyurus*	Gross 1992
		Siberian tiger, *Panthera tigris altaica*	Gross 1992
		Bengal tiger, *P. t. tigris*	Gross 1992

28 days after conception (Shille and Gontara 1985). Among primates, age of the fetus has also been ascertained by measuring the widest diameter between the fetal temporal bones (i.e., the biparietal diameter) when the skull is scanned at right angles (rhesus macaque: Sabbagha 1975) and by other indices of skeletal growth, such as femur length (human: O'Brien, Queenan, and Campbell 1981).

Laparoscopy involves direct examination of the peritoneal cavity with an endoscope. In many cases, laparoscopy has been used successfully to diagnose pregnancy, to determine litter size, to differentiate between pregnancy and pseudopregnancy, and to identify and treat medical problems associated with reproductive failure (e.g., dog and cat: Wildt 1980; pig: Wildt, Morcom, and Dukelow 1975; rodents: Dukelow 1980; primates: Harrison 1980; sheep: Phillippo et al. 1971). Similarly, the imminence of parturition can sometimes be determined through vaginoscopic examination of the cervix (e.g., rhesus macaque: Mahoney and Eisele 1978).

X-rays are another potential method of pregnancy diagnosis. In humans, chromosomal aberrations can result from repeated long-term exposure to x-rays during medical and dental procedures. Lasley (1980) argues that they should therefore be avoided as a diagnostic tool for animals. Radiographs have, however, been used successfully for pregnancy detection in dogs (Sokolowski 1980), cats (Boyd 1971), white-tailed deer (Verme, Fay, and Mostosky 1962), and tigers, *Panthera tigris* (U. S. Seal, pers. comm.), and these methods may prove to be useful for other species as well. In some cases, fetal age and weight can also be determined by using radiographic techniques (white-tailed deer: Ozoga and Verme 1985; rhesus macaque: Ferron, Miller, and McNulty 1976).

A major drawback to the above techniques is that they generally require that the dam be immobilized or restrained, especially when one is dealing with large or dangerous species. Chemical immobilization and physical restraint entail risks to both the fetus and the dam; however, some managers have avoided this problem by training animals to submit to regular ultrasonic testing (e.g., bottle-nosed dolphins: Cornell et al. 1987).

PHYSICAL SIGNS OF IMPENDING BIRTH

As a dam nears term, additional physical changes may allow a more accurate estimate of parturition time. For example, in many mammals, the mammary glands or nipples may become swollen or distended near the end of pregnancy (e.g., bats: Racey 1988; lowland gorilla: Meder 1986; giant panda, *Ailuropoda melanoleuca*: Kleiman 1985; horse: Waring 1983; Asian elephant: Mainka and Lothrop 1980; cow: Sloss and Duffy 1980; impala: Jarman 1976; white-tailed deer: Townsend and Baily 1975; canids: Naaktgeboren 1968; pig: Jones 1966; European weasel: Hartman 1964; bottle-nosed dolphin: Tavolga and Essapian 1957). In some species, mammary engorgement is accompanied by changes in pigmentation (e.g., dik-dik, *Madoqua kirkii*: Hendrichs and Hendrichs 1971) or by free-flowing milk (e.g., African elephant, *Loxodonta africana*: Styles 1982; mountain tapir: Bonney and Crotty 1979). The appearance of a waxy material at the end of the milk canal (i.e., "waxing" of the nipples) is also characteristic of some species. For example, in mares, waxing of the two enlarged nipples occurs several days before parturition (Rossdale 1967).

Enlargement of the mammary glands or nipples is not always a reliable indicator of pregnancy or impending birth, especially in females that previously have had young. Among common marmosets (Rothe 1977), for example, only primiparas show a slight change in mammary and nipple size prior to parturition; thus, for multiparas, enlargement of the glands and nipples is of little predictive value. Furthermore, nonpregnant females and even males may exhibit irregular but spontaneous breast enlargement, and males sometimes exceed lactating females in this regard. However, in some cases, clear secretions can be expressed from the nipples up to a week before parturition; such secretions are a reliable indicator of impending delivery in this species (Phillips and Grist 1975). Similar prepartum secretions have been noted in other species, including cattle (Sloss and Duffy 1980), mountain tapirs (Bonney and Crotty 1979), African elephants (Lang 1967), and dogs (Harrop 1960). Wild and domestic canids reportedly shed the hair on their abdomens for up to a week prior to parturition, thus exposing the nipples; Naaktgeboren (1968) suggested that this characteristic could be used to predict impending parturition. Such shedding can, however, occur during pseudopregnancy as well.

In some species, the vulvar region of the dam may become swollen and distended, or the vulva itself may become dilated, as parturition approaches; this is sometimes accompanied by a mucous discharge (e.g., African elephant: Styles 1982; vampire bat, *Desmodus rotundus*: Mills 1980; cow: Sloss and Duffy 1980; mountain tapir: Bonney and Crotty 1979; Coke's hartebeest, *Alcelaphus buselaphus*: Gosling 1969; horse: Rossdale 1967; dog: Harrop 1960; bottle-nosed dolphin: Tavolga and Essapian 1957). However, there is much variation in this regard, and some species (e.g.,

common marmosets: Rothe 1977) show little or no swelling until immediately before parturition. In vampire bats, the skin around the vulva becomes darkly pigmented in the last months before parturition (Schmidt and Manske 1973, cited in Fowler 1986). Just prior to parturition, the hindquarters of the bitch, cow, and mare may take on a noticeable "sunken" appearance, due primarily to a relaxation of the pelvic ligaments (Waring 1983; Sloss and Duffy 1980; Harrop 1960). Female elephants, chimpanzees, and baboons, *Papio* spp., reportedly expel mucous plugs from the aperture of the cervix within 24 hours of parturition (Lang 1967; Mitchell and Brandt 1975). In some rodents, onset of parturition can be predicted by a separation of the pubic symphysis, which commonly occurs about a week before parturition in the guinea pig (Naaktgeboren and Vandendriessche 1962, cited in Kleiman 1972).

In a variety of species, the amniotic sac may be seen protruding from the vulva shortly before parturition. Similarly, the sudden rupture of the allantochorion and passage of large quantities of fluid from the vulva (i.e., "breaking water") is a good indication that parturition is imminent (e.g., dog and cat: Hart 1985; African elephant: Styles 1982; wildebeest: Estes and Estes 1979; Weddell seal, *Leptonychotes weddellii*: Stirling 1969; horse: Rossdale 1967). A decrease in basal body temperature within 24 hours before parturition has been documented for the pig-tailed macaque (Ruppenthal and Goodlin 1982), dog (Concannon et al. 1977), horse (Cross, Threlfall, and Kline 1992), cow (Ewbank 1963), and sheep (Ewbank 1969). Interestingly, a temperature elevation has been reported for the pig (Elmore et al. 1979).

TIMING OF BIRTH

Little is known about the factors influencing the actual times when births occur. Whereas some mammals (e.g., wildebeest: Estes and Estes 1979; impala: Jarman 1976; deer mice, *Peromyscus* spp.: Layne 1968) tend to give birth in the daytime, many others have a tendency to give birth at night or in the early morning—times when light levels are low and disturbances are greatly reduced (e.g., horse: Campitelli, Carenzi, and Verga 1982; pig: Alexander, Signoret, and Hafez 1974; elephant seal, *Mirounga angustirostris*: Le Boeuf, Whiting, and Gantt 1972; many Old World monkeys: Brandt and Mitchell 1971). Although the peak hours of births in sheep are highly variable, they are known to be affected by genetic factors (George 1969) and are probably affected by weather, illumination, and behavioral stress as well (Alexander, Signoret, and Hafez 1974; see "Prepartus Phase" below). Time of parturition in laboratory rats is affected by both photoperiod and feeding schedules (Bosc, Nicolle, and Ducelliez 1986; Bosc and Nicolle 1985). The photic influence on time of birth in rats can be modified by adrenalectomy; parturition occurs earlier in adrenalectomized than in normal rats exposed to the same light regime (Bosc and Nicolle 1980). Recent evidence suggests that the effect of photoperiod on time of parturition may be mediated by melatonin, a substance produced by the pineal gland. Bosc (1987) found that injections of melatonin modified time of birth in the rat in a manner analogous to that of photoperiod manipulation.

Nocturnal births present logistic problems for zoo managers in that personnel are not always available to monitor the animals. Jensen and Bobbitt (1967) describe methods for shifting parturition time from night to day in a laboratory colony of pig-tailed macaques by reversing the light cycle and altering environmental noise levels and maintenance routines. Similar techniques might be applicable to off-exhibit breeding facilities in zoos. In addition, several studies have shown that daytime births in livestock can be increased by manipulating feeding regimes. For example, nighttime feedings increased the percentage of daytime births in cattle (Clark, Spearow, and Owens 1983; Lowman et al. 1981), whereas morning feedings had a similar effect in sheep (Gonyou and Cobb 1986).

BEHAVIORAL SIGNS OF IMPENDING BIRTH

Parturition can sometimes be predicted on the basis of known gestation lengths or physical changes in the dam (see "Physical Signs of Impending Birth" above). However, copulations are not always observed, and gestation lengths may vary, not only among species but also among individuals of the same species (Kiltie 1982). Similarly, physical indications of impending birth are not always present, or may be evident only during the latter stages of the process. Fortunately, many female mammals exhibit characteristic prepartum behavior, thus allowing managers to predict impending births with reasonable exactness (Fraser 1968). The form and frequency of these behaviors vary, however, depending on the species and sometimes on the individual in question. Table 41.2 lists some common behaviors associated with imminent parturition in mammals.

Some species may exhibit nest-building behavior in preparation for the infant's arrival (e.g., canids: Hart 1985; Naaktgeboren 1968; giant panda: Kleiman 1985; hamster: Daly 1972; pig: Jones 1966; ruffed lemur, *Varecia variegata*: Petter-Rousseaux 1964; rabbit: Ross et al. 1963), and, in captivity, should be provided with suitable materials for this activity. It is extremely difficult to predict impending birth in marsupials. However, the females of some species exhibit frequent pouch grooming just prior to or shortly after parturition (e.g., kowari, *Dasycercus (=Dasyuroides) byrnei*: Hutson 1976; tammar wallaby, *Macropus eugenii*: Russell and Giles 1974).

The accuracy of time of birth estimations depends on a knowledge of the range of behavioral variation possible in a given species. For example, when a sow suddenly becomes inactive, lies on her side, and shows signs of abdominal contractions, she is likely to give birth within 10 to 90 minutes (Signoret et al. 1975). In contrast, pregnant bottle-nosed dolphins may strain and flex their bodies as if they were experiencing contractions for up to 3 months before parturition (Tavolga and Essapian 1957).

Unfortunately, some species appear to lack any overt signs of impending birth, and the process itself may be very rapid (e.g., ring-tailed mongoose, *Galidia elegans*: Larkin and Roberts 1983; harp seal, *Phoca groenlandica*: Stewart,

Lightfoot, and Innes 1981). In such cases, prediction must be based on other cues.

EVENTS OF PARTURITION

Several authors have attempted to classify the events that characterize parturition into different stages or phases, but the literature is far from being standardized. This discussion follows the classification of Kemps and Timmermans (1982), who divide parturition into three distinct phases: prepartus, partus, and postpartus. The prepartus phase includes the period extending from the first contractions to immediately before birth. The partus phase encompasses the birth itself, and the postpartus phase extends from birth to the severing of the umbilical cord and expulsion of the placenta.

Prepartum Phase

During labor, dams may adopt a variety of postures (e.g., lying, sitting, hanging, or standing) depending on the species or individual. For example, female Atlantic harbor seals, *Phoca vitulina concolor*, characteristically lie on their bellies during labor, with the vaginal slit and hind flipper slightly raised. The head is held close to the ground, and the front flippers are pressed closely against the body (Lawson and Renouf 1985).

Abdominal straining is often evident during labor, and dams of many species may assume a "squatting" or "crouching" posture similar to that used for urination or defecation (e.g., rhesus macaque: Adachi, Saito, and Tanioka 1982; impala: Jarman 1976; horse: Rossdale 1967; hamster: Rowell 1961; agouti, *Dasyprocta punctata*: Enders 1931). There is great variation in the frequency and strength of uterine contractions experienced by dams, but both frequency and intensity generally increase as labor progresses. In bats, the contractions are arrhythmic, occurring in a series of three to six or more rapid spasms, followed by a variable rest interval of a few seconds to several minutes (Tamsitt and Valdivieso 1966; Wimsatt 1960). Contractions are sometimes accompanied by vocalizations suggestive of pain and by labored or rapid breathing (e.g., harbor seal: Lawson and Renouf 1985; mountain goat: Hutchins 1984; hamster: Rowell 1961; various bats: Wimsatt 1960).

Length of labor is highly variable among mammals and can be influenced by many factors, including parity, the number of young in a litter, complications during delivery (see "Abnormalities of Pregnancy and Parturition" below), and environmental factors. For example, with a few exceptions (e.g., elephant seals: Le Boeuf, Whiting, and Gantt 1972), birth in phocid seals is a comparatively rapid process, perhaps owing to the shape of the fetus, which is fusiform or sausage-shaped (Stewart, Lightfoot, and Innes 1981). Average time to delivery in harbor seals from the onset of obvious contractions is only 3.5 minutes (Lawson and Renouf 1985). In contrast, normal labor can be a long process in polytocous species (i.e., those that typically give birth to multiple offspring). In dogs, for example, the time between the first and last deliveries may be as much as 16

TABLE 41.2. Behavioral Signs of Imminent Parturition in Selected Mammals

Behavior	Species	Reference
Restlessness or pacing		
	African elephant, *Loxodonta africana*	Styles 1982; Lang 1967
	Bats, various species	Wimsatt 1960
	Beaver, *Castor canadensis*	Patenaude and Bovet 1983
	Common marmoset, *Callithrix jacchus*	Rothe 1977
	Domestic dog, *Canis familiaris*	Hart 1985
	Giant panda, *Ailuropoda melanoleuca*	Kleiman 1985
	Hamster, *Mesocricetus auratus*	Rowell 1961
	Horses, *Equus* spp.	Waring 1983
	Lowland gorilla, *Gorilla g. gorilla*	Nadler 1974
	Mountain tapir, *Tapirus pinchaque*	Bonney and Crotty 1979
	White-tailed deer, *Odocoileus virginianus*	Schwede, Hendrichs, and McShea 1993
Lethargy		
	Deer mouse, *Peromyscus* spp.	Layne 1968
	Bottle-nosed dolphin, *Tursiops truncatus*	Tavolga and Essapian 1957
	Giant panda	Kleiman 1985
	Tree shrew, *Tupaia belangeri*	Martin 1968
Frequent genital grooming or rubbing		
	Coke's hartebeest, *Alcelaphus buselaphus*	Gosling 1969
	Common marmoset	Rothe 1977
	Domestic cat, *Felis catus*	Hart 1985
	Domestic dog	Hart 1985
	Giant panda	Kleiman 1985
	Indri, *Propithecus verreauxi*	Richard 1976
	Laboratory rat, *Rattus norvegicus*	Rosenblatt and Lehrman 1963
	Red kangaroo, *Macropus rufus*	Tyndale-Biscoe 1973
	White-tailed deer	Townsend and Baily 1975
Increased aggression toward and/or isolation from conspecifics		
	Black lemur, *Eulemur m. macaco*	Frueh 1979
	Bottle-nosed dolphin	Tavolga and Essapian 1957
	Coke's hartebeest	Gosling 1969
	Hamster	Wise 1974
	Horses	Waring 1983
	Mountain goat, *Oreamnos americanus*	Hutchins 1984
	White-tailed deer	Townsend and Baily 1975
Frequent urination and/or defecation		
	Bottle-nosed dolphin	Tavolga and Essapian 1957
	White-tailed deer	Townsend and Baily 1975
Depressed appetite		
	Giant panda	Kleiman 1985
Labored, irregular, or rapid breathing		
	Black-footed ferret, *Mustela nigripes*	Hillman and Carpenter 1983
	Bottle-nosed dolphin	Tavolga and Essapian 1957
	Hamster	Rowell 1961
	Mountain goat	Hutchins 1984

hours, and in pigs, 24 hours (Pond and Houpt 1978; Hart 1985). Primiparous females may experience more difficult deliveries than multiparous females, perhaps owing to the relative size of the birth canal.

Labor can also be affected by environmental factors. In many mammalian species, environmental disturbances causing fright or anxiety can interfere with the birth process (Bontekoe et al. 1977). For example, the presence of a strange conspecific during labor inhibits uterine contractions in some female canids (Bleicher 1962; Naaktgeboren 1968). Similarly, Newton, Foshee, and Newton (1966) found that time between second and third births was 64%

to 72% longer in laboratory mice when dams were forced to give birth in an unfamiliar environment.

Bontekoe et al. (1977) showed that stress associated with environmental disturbances may either stimulate or inhibit uterine activity in sheep and rabbits, depending upon the stage of gestation. These authors concluded that an increase in epinephrine levels (due to stress) was responsible for blocking or activating uterine motility. The direction of the effect was dependent on the ratio of sex steroid concentrations (especially estradiol-17β and progesterone) in the blood. The authors speculated that inhibition of labor contractions in a stressful situation is adaptive in that it offers the mother a chance to move to a more favorable environment before giving birth.

Females of many species seek out a secluded, quiet, sheltered place in which to give birth and should be provided with suitable locations in captivity (e.g., nest boxes or dens). To reduce behavioral stress, changes in feeding procedures, cleaning routines, and keeper staff should be avoided at this time. Closed-circuit television is recommended as a means for observing pregnant, parturient, or immediately postparturient females without having to disturb them (e.g., snow leopards, *Uncia uncia*: Freeman and Hutchins 1978).

Partus Phase

The dam may adopt a variety of postures during parturition, depending on the species and individual in question. Many ungulates (fig. 41.1), such as elephants and giraffes, *Giraffa camelopardalis,* typically give birth while standing (Robinson et al. 1965; Styles 1982), whereas others expel the fetus while reclining (e.g., pig: Jones 1966), or may adopt either posture (e.g., mountain goat: Hutchins 1984). Domestic dogs and cats typically give birth while lying on their sides, usually with the head oriented toward the hindquarters (Fox 1966; Hart 1985). Vespertilionid bats, which normally hang upside down, reverse their normal position during parturition; the tail is recurved ventrally so that the uropatagial membrane forms a pouchlike receptacle into which the young is received (Wimsatt 1960). However, other bat species are known to give birth in their typical resting position (e.g., Mills 1980; Tamsitt and Valdivieso 1966; Ramakrishna 1950; West and Redshaw 1987). Some kangaroos give birth with the tail pulled forward between the legs and with the back propped up against a vertical support (e.g., red kangaroo: Tyndale-Biscoe 1973). Many primates deliver in a squatting or sitting position (e.g., lowland gorilla: Beck 1984; crab-eating macaque: Kemps and Timmermans 1982; common marmoset: Rothe 1977). Rodents typically assume a quadrupedal or bipedal crouching or "hunched over" position as the fetus emerges (e.g., beaver: Patenaude and Bovet 1983; acouchi, *Myoprocta acouchy*: Kleiman 1972; deer mice: Pournelle 1952; Clark 1937; agouti: Enders 1931).

The amount of assistance the dam gives to the emerging young also varies among species. Among kangaroos, for instance, the female offers no assistance to the infant as it leaves the birth canal and makes its journey to the pouch (Tyndale-Biscoe 1973). In some other mammals, the mother licks her infant vigorously, thus helping to free it from the amniotic sac (e.g., agouti: Enders 1931; dog and cat: Hart 1985; Rodrigues fruit bat, *Pteropus rodricensis*: West and Redshaw 1987). Furthermore, a mother may help her neonate during emergence either by removing the amniotic membranes or by actually pulling the infant from the birth canal with her teeth or forelegs (e.g., dog and cat: Hart 1985; black lemur, *Eulemur macaco*: Frueh 1979; deer mice: Clark 1937; bats: Sherman 1930; bonobo, *Pan paniscus*: Bolser and Savage-Rumbaugh 1989). In some cases, the infant assists in its own birth by grasping portions of the mother's body and pulling itself out (e.g., squirrel monkey: Hopf 1967; bats: Wimsatt 1960). Newborn kangaroos emerge fully enclosed in the fluid-filled amnion; they free

FIG. 41.1.   Many ungulates typically give birth while standing. (Photo Jessie Cohen, National Zoological Park.)

themselves from the membranes with the well-developed claws on their forelegs (Tyndale-Biscoe 1973).

Postpartum Phase

As it passes from the birth canal, the fetus begins its life outside the womb. It is not physically separated from the mother, however, until the umbilical cord is detached. In many cases, the umbilical cord is broken as part of the normal birth process; as the fetus leaves the birth canal or as the female pivots to orient herself toward her offspring, the cord becomes taut and eventually snaps as a result of tension (e.g., mountain goat: Hutchins 1984; beaver: Patenaude and Bovet 1983; various seals: Stewart, Lightfoot, and Innes 1981; bottle-nosed dolphin: Tavolga and Essapian 1957). In other cases, the dam may actively sever the cord, usually by chewing through it with her teeth or by consuming it along with the placenta (e.g., dog: Hart 1985; Bleicher 1962; common marmoset: Rothe 1977; acouchi: Kleiman 1972; bats: Wimsatt 1960; agouti: Enders 1931; see below).

A female mammal's initial reaction to her newborn is generally dependent on the behavior of the newborn: active, healthy newborns tend to stimulate maternal care, while stillborn, relatively inactive, or physically unhealthy infants are frequently ignored (see Rothe 1977). The vocalizations of infants may be particularly important in some species. Indeed, playbacks of recorded infant distress calls have been

FIG. 41.2. Female mammals typically begin licking their infants during or shortly after parturition. This stimulation may serve several functions for the neonate. (Photo Jessie Cohen, National Zoological Park.)

effective in eliciting maternal behavior in some species (e.g., black-footed cats, *Felis nigripes*: Leyhausen and Tonkin 1966; common marmosets: Rothe 1975). This approach deserves further exploration as a management tool.

During or shortly after parturition, female mammals typically orient toward their infants and begin licking them thoroughly (fig. 41.2) (e.g., many carnivores: Ewer 1973; many ungulates: Lent 1974; many primates: Brandt and Mitchell 1971; many bats: Wimsatt 1960; rodents: Patenaude and Bovet 1983; Clark 1937; Enders 1931). Maternal licking of neonates generally does not occur in aquatic mammals, such as cetaceans and pinnipeds (Ewer 1973). It is also reportedly absent in some terrestrial mammals (Lent 1974; Packard et al. 1987). Several functions have been proposed for this behavior. Maternal licking may be responsible for stimulating movement and initiating respiration in the newborn (Townsend and Baily 1975; Blauvelt 1955), and it may also help to keep the neonate clean and dry, thus resulting in more efficient thermoregulation (Lent 1974; Ewer 1973). Furthermore, maternal licking, in conjunction with olfaction, is thought to be important in the development of the mother-offspring bond (Gubernick 1981; Ewer

1973), although evidence suggests that vaginal stimulation during birth may also contribute to the bonding process (Keverne et al. 1983). In some species, perineal grooming by the mother stimulates urination and defecation in the newborn (Lent 1974; Ewer 1973). The female consumes her offspring's wastes, a behavior that may help to eliminate odors, thus reducing the probability of predation, or prevent fouling of the nest (Lent 1974; Ewer 1973).

With the possible exception of the monotremes, which lay eggs rather than giving birth to live young, most mammals pass birth fluids, fetal membranes, and the placenta during or after the expulsion of the fetus. Time from birth to passage of the placenta varies greatly. In some eutherian mammals, the afterbirth is largely ignored, whereas in others, it may be consumed. Eating of the placenta, or placentophagy, has been reported in a wide variety of species, including rodents (e.g., beaver: Patenaude and Bovet 1983; hamster: Rowell 1961), artiodactyls (Lent 1974), carnivores (Ewer 1973), bats (Wimsatt 1960; West and Redshaw 1987), and most primates (Brandt and Mitchell 1971). Placentophagy generally does not occur in aquatic mammals, such as pinnipeds and cetaceans (Ewer 1973; Tavolga and Essapian 1957), although partial ingestion of a placenta has been reported in Hooker's sea lion, *Phocarctos hookeri* (Marlow 1974).

Several functions have been proposed for placentophagy (Kristal 1980). Consumption of the placenta, fetal membranes, and birth fluids removes olfactory cues that might result in predation on the newborn (Lent 1974; Ewer 1973).

FIG. 41.3. In some species, care of offspring involves constant cradling of young. (Photo Jessie Cohen, National Zoological Park.)

Being a large organ, the placenta may also have some nutritional value (Ewer 1973). In addition, when expelled, the organ is filled with hormones, and there is some evidence that these may contribute to the production or letdown of milk in rats and cows (Kristal 1980; Zarrow, Denenberg, and Sachs 1972). Furthermore, Kristal (1980) suggests that the placenta contains factors that prevent a mother from forming antibodies against fetal antigens that might act to inhibit subsequent pregnancies. It should be noted, however, that failure to consume the placenta does not seem to have any adverse effects on the mother. Indeed, Zarrow, Denenberg, and Sachs (1972) have proposed that placentophagy may be physiologically significant only if environmental conditions are marginal.

Behavior of Conspecifics toward Pregnant and Parturient Females and Their Infants

Many behavioral factors associated with parturition can influence reproductive success. The first consideration is whether or not the female is caring for her infant properly (fig. 41.3). However, success can also be influenced by social interactions with other conspecifics. Indeed, as a result of their altered behavior, appearance, and odor, pregnant and parturient females may elicit different responses from other group members than do nonpregnant females. Of course, the range of responses is largely dependent on a species' social organization, as this will determine the number and types of conspecifics present during both pregnancy and parturition (see Eisenberg 1966; Spencer-Booth 1970; Caine and Mitchell 1979; see also Baker, Baker, and Thompson, chap. 42, this volume). For example, relatively solitary, territorial species, such as ursids, many felids, and many mustelids, do not typically interact with conspecifics at or near the time of birth (Ewer 1973), and encounters that do occur are likely to be antagonistic. Among social species, however, a pregnant female or newborn infant can stimulate a variety of responses, ranging from aggression to caregiving.

Among some social mammals, conspecifics are simply benign—though curious—bystanders, whereas in others, they may aid the pregnant female during labor or birth. Direct aid during the birth process appears to be rare, but it has been documented in several orders, including the Chiroptera, Edentata, Primates, and Rodentia. Among rodents, for example, female spiny mice, *Acomys* sp., are known to exhibit "midwifery" behavior (Piechocki 1975). During parturition, other females gather around the mother, licking the infant as it emerges and helping to free it from the amniotic membranes. Similarly, in the monogamous beaver, the male and yearling offspring gather closely around the female and newborn, presumably aiding in thermoregulation, and also lick the infant shortly after birth (Patenaude and Bovet 1983). Among primates, male marmosets and tamarins (Callitrichidae) have been known to assist with the births of their offspring (see Langford 1963; Blakely and Curtis, cited in Caine and Mitchell 1979). Ullrich (1970) described a captive male orangutan that exhibited similar behavior; however, orangutans are relatively asocial animals (MacKinnon 1971), and this behavior was probably an artifact of captivity. Among edentates, McCrane (1966) describes several instances in which captive two-toed sloths,

Choloepus didactylus, actively assisted during births, both by helping the infant to reach the mother's abdomen and by preventing it from falling (i.e., by blocking it with their bodies). Other colony members clustered around a parturient female vampire bat, licking fluids from her vagina and from the emerging fetus (Mills 1980).

In many social species, females seek isolation just prior to parturition, as seen, for example, in many herd-forming ungulates. It has been suggested that isolation helps to reduce the incidence of accidental "adoptions" that could occur when females give birth in close proximity to one another. Newborn ungulates will approach any nearby female, and the potential for confusion is high (Lent 1974). The risk of predation may also be minimized by withdrawing from the herd so that birth can occur in a concealed or inaccessible area (Hutchins 1984; Jarman 1976; Lent 1974). While both of these factors are likely to be important, predation appears to have the strongest effect. Indeed, Lott and Galland (1985) found that female bison, *Bison bison,* inhabiting open terrain usually gave birth within the herd, whereas cows in habitat with cover usually gave birth alone. Alternatively, Hutchins (1984) suggested that females and infants are especially vulnerable to aggressive attacks by other conspecifics during and shortly after the birth process, and that by seeking isolation, dams may minimize this risk. Attacks by conspecifics on females and neonates have been documented among several ungulate species, both in captivity and in the wild (e.g., mountain goat: Hutchins 1984; African elephant: Styles 1982; Coke's hartebeest: Gosling 1969; collared peccary, *Pecari tajacu:* Packard et al. 1990).

Among primates, females and juveniles generally exhibit greater interest in newborns than do adult males (Caine and Mitchell 1979). Attempts to kidnap infants have been documented in a wide variety of species (e.g., bonnet macaque: Silk 1980; rhesus macaque: Mitchell and Brandt 1975; squirrel monkey: Bowden, Winter, and Ploog 1967). Similar behavior has been observed among other mammals and can result in aggressive interactions as females attempt to protect their newborns (e.g., Dall sheep: Bullerman 1976; domestic sheep: Alexander, Signoret, and Hafez 1974; elephant seal: Le Boeuf, Whiting, and Gantt 1972). The outcome of such interactions depends largely on the size and dominance status of the mother; the infants of subordinate females are at greatest risk. In some instances kidnappings may result in infants being left without maternal care (e.g., sheep: Alexander, Signoret, and Hafez 1974).

In some species, pregnant, parturient, and immediately postparturient females are harassed by males, and this can affect breeding success. Among ungulates (Hutchins 1984; Manski 1982; Jarman 1976; Townsend and Baily 1975), cetaceans (Amunden 1986; Tavolga and Essapian 1957; McBride and Kritzler 1951), and primates (Wallis and Lemmon 1986; Rothe 1977; Gouzoules 1974; Rowell, Hinde, and Spencer-Booth 1964; Doyle, Pelletier, and Bekker 1967), males court parturient or immediately postparturient females aggressively; this behavior may be triggered as a result of olfactory and visual cues resembling those of estrus (Wallis and Lemmon 1986; Hutchins 1984; Manski 1982; Gouzoules 1974). In some instances, the associated stress results in the female abandoning her offspring. The infant can also be injured by the male; for example, Mc-Bride and Kritzler (1951) describe an infant bottle-nosed dolphin that sustained bruises and lacerations as a result of aggressive courtship of its mother by males. In such cases, it is advisable to isolate the female before parturition. It should be noted, however, that the females of some species have an immediate postpartum estrus (e.g., large Malayan mouse deer, *Tragulus napu*: Davis 1965; pika, *Ochotona princeps*: Severaid 1950; vole, *Microtus ochrogaster*: Richmond and Conaway 1969), and mating within a few hours after parturition is normal. Sexual behavior during early pregnancy has been reported for the horse (Tomasgard and Benjaminsen 1975), rhesus macaque (Bielert et al. 1976), and gorilla (Hess 1973), during the 10 days before parturition in the coyote (Gier 1975), and throughout gestation in an Old World porcupine, *Hystrix indica* (Sever and Mendelssohn 1988), and the house shrew, *Suncus murinus* (Dryden 1969).

An important decision for the zoo manager is whether to isolate the pregnant female before parturition or allow her to remain in the social group. In the case of relatively solitary species, it is probably best to isolate the female before parturition, as the presence of conspecifics may either disrupt the birth process or interfere with early postpartum maternal care. Similarly, the females of social species may require isolation to prevent aggression, harassment, or interference by other group members. For example, Izard and Simons (1986) showed that isolation prior to parturition significantly decreased neonatal mortality in three galago species. In the wild, female galagos normally sleep in groups during the day; however, they seek social isolation prior to parturition and for some time after their infants are born. Infanticide is relatively common among some mammals (Hausfater and Hrdy 1984), and newborns are always at some risk, especially under captive conditions where there is little opportunity for hiding or escape (see Baker, Baker, and Thompson, chap. 42, this volume).

Whenever possible, zoo managers should attempt to simulate a natural social milieu at the time of birth (Kleiman 1980). For example, at the Bronx Zoo/Wildlife Conservation Park, adult male and female snow leopards are maintained separately except during the breeding season. Free-ranging snow leopards are relatively asocial, or at least do not form permanent social relationships with other adults (Schaller 1977). Thus, a male would not typically be present during parturition, nor during the rearing of cubs. Some zoo managers, fearful for the survival of important infants (e.g., those born to highly endangered species), might argue that, whenever possible, all pregnant females should be isolated before giving birth. It should be noted, however, that pregnant females of highly social species may be stressed by isolation, and that this may have a detrimental effect on breeding success (e.g., social primates: Kaplan 1972; Wolfheim, Jensen, and Bobbitt 1970).

ABNORMALITIES OF PREGNANCY AND PARTURITION

Although most mammals commonly held in zoos go through pregnancy and parturition without difficulty, com-plications do occasionally arise. Not all of the elements influencing a dam and fetus during pregnancy are well understood; however, it is clear that certain factors, such as improper nutrition, overcrowding, stress, inadequate cage design, injury, and illness, can have adverse effects on both mother and offspring (Hafez and Jainudeen 1974; Benirschke 1967). The following section outlines some of the more common problems associated with pregnancy and parturition and briefly summarizes management and clinical techniques used to avoid or correct such conditions.

Breech Birth or Faulty Positioning of the Fetus
One of the more commonly encountered disorders of parturition is the "breech birth," or posterior presentation of the fetus. With the notable exception of certain species of insectivorous bats (Wimsatt 1960) and cetaceans (Tavolga and Essapian 1957; Essapian 1963), mammals normally give birth with the fetus in an anterior, longitudinal presentation, with the body fully extended in the birth canal. Among seals (Stewart, Lightfoot, and Innes 1981) and some other mammals (e.g., slender loris, *Loris tardigradus*: Kadam and Swayaamprabha 1980; deer mice: Layne 1968; hamster: Rowell 1961), cephalic and caudal (i.e., breech) presentations appear to be equally common. "Abnormal" breech births have been recorded in a wide variety of mammals (e.g., primates: Brandt and Mitchell 1971; ungulates: Norment 1980; Sloss and Duffy 1980; Lent 1974; carnivores: Law and Boyle 1983; Fox 1966).

Several factors can affect the positioning and delivery of the fetus and thus lead to a breech birth. Deformities in either the dam's birth canal or the fetus itself can hinder proper alignment (Hafez and Jainudeen 1974); so can excessive fetal movement just prior to parturition, or the death of the fetus prior to the onset of parturition (Sloss and Duffy 1980).

In most breech births, the dam is able to expel the fetus on her own, although the delivery may be protracted in comparison with normal births. For example, Bowden, Winter, and Ploog (1967) observed an abnormal breech presentation in a squirrel monkey in which the female experienced more than 900 contractions over a period of 3 days before the fetus emerged; this can be compared with 1–1.5 hours and 300–350 contractions during normal parturitions. In cases in which a dystocia results from faulty positioning (see "Dystocia" below), human intervention may be required. In large mammals, the clinical procedures used in the removal of a fetus usually involve sedation or anesthesia. The easiest and safest method of delivering the fetus is by manual removal. With smaller mammals, this method is often impractical, and a cesarean section is the best alternative. If the fetus is already dead, a fetotomy (i.e., surgical sectioning and removal of the fetus) can sometimes be performed in lieu of a cesarean section.

Dystocia
Dystocia is a prolonged or difficult labor, usually characterized by some functional defect or physical blockage of the birth canal. Along with breech births, it is among the most frequent complications of parturition, and is known to occur in a wide variety of mammals (e.g., giraffe: Citino, Bush, and Phillips 1984; Asian elephant and California sea lion,

Zalophus californianus: Klös and Lang 1982; cow: Sloss and Duffy 1980; chinchilla: Paterson 1967; dog: Bennett 1980; gelada baboon, *Theropithecus gelada:* Hubbell 1962).

Several factors may be responsible for dystocia. As mentioned earlier, faulty positioning of the fetus in the birth canal can result in a blockage that prevents normal birth (e.g., Grevy's zebra, *Equus grevyi:* Smith 1982). Another frequent cause of dystocia is fetopelvic disproportion, which occurs when the fetus is too large to pass through the pelvic girdle of the dam (e.g., cow: Sloss and Duffy 1980; dog: Bennett 1980; gelada baboon: Hubbell 1962). One indication of fetopelvic disproportion is an expectant dam continuously straining with little or no sign of fetal expulsion. Often the vaginal area will be dry. The perineum can be palpated for the presence of a fetus; digital examination of the birth canal is generally also recommended to assess the degree of cervical dilation and to identify any congenital abnormalities that might be present (Bennett 1980). If the dam's condition is not differentiated from a typical labor, fetal death can occur, usually from suffocation or trauma. In cases of fetopelvic disproportion, removal of the fetus typically requires a cesarean section or fetotomy (Sloss and Duffy 1980; Hubbell 1962). Ultrasonography and x-rays (see "Pregnancy Diagnosis" above) have proved useful in the detection of fetal death in small domestic animals (e.g., cat: Biller and Haibel 1987; dog: Farrow, Morgan, and Story 1976).

Ruptured uteri during late pregnancy can cause, or be the result of, dystocia (e.g., puma, *Felis concolor:* Peters 1963). Uterine ruptures may result from trauma, fetal malformations, intrauterine pressure during parturition, or a variety of other factors (Sloss and Duffy 1980). If the uterus ruptures during labor, straining by the dam typically ceases. If the initial signs of labor are not detected, it is difficult to recognize signs of trouble.

Another cause of dystocia is ineffective labor. This can result from a variety of factors, including nutritional deficiencies, toxemia, multiple offspring, excessive uterine load, or an abnormally large fetus (see Sloss and Duffy 1980). It is often difficult to distinguish between ineffective labor and fetopelvic disproportion, but in most instances the dam would be treated in the same manner.

Multiple offspring, especially in species that normally have a single offspring, can result in ineffective labor and dystocia. Uterine contractions may weaken or stop after the expulsion of one fetus, or two fetuses may be presented simultaneously (e.g., sea otters, *Enhydra lutris:* Williams, Mattison, and Ames 1980). As with other types of dystocia, large mammals need to be sedated or anesthetized before the fetuses can be delivered. In many instances, at least one fetus can be manually removed from the birth canal. Oxytocin can be administered to the dam after the birth of the first fetus to help stimulate uterine contractions. Occasionally, a cesarean section is necessary.

Resorption or Retention of the Fetus or Placenta

Pregnancy may continue indefinitely when a fetus dies and is not expelled by the dam. Depending on gestational age, the embryo or fetus may undergo resorption, mummification, or maceration.

Prenatal mortality can result from a variety of factors, including nutritional deficiencies, endocrine abnormalities, large litter sizes, thermal stress, lactation, immunological incompatibility, chromosomal aberrations, and inbreeding (Hafez and Jainudeen 1974; see also "Abortion" below). When an embryo or fetus dies, intrauterine liquids are quickly absorbed into the dam's body. The fetal tissues begin to decompose, and the process is considered to be enzymatic if no infection occurs. Among cattle and swine, if the fetus dies prior to the 6th week of gestation, resorption is nearly complete (Sloss and Duffy 1980; Hafez and Jainudeen 1974).

Fetal mummification has been documented in a variety of ungulates (e.g., Bactrian camel, *Camelus bactrianus:* Maberry and Ditterbrandt 1971; horse: Roberts and Myhre 1983; cow: Sloss and Duffy 1980; pig: Pond and Houpt 1978; Hafez and Jainudeen 1974) and primates (King and Chalifoux 1986). Mummification involves retention of a dead fetus, resorption of the placental fluids, and subsequent dehydration of the fetal tissues. Usually there are no obvious signs of maternal illness, and in some species, mummified fetuses are frequently carried for many months beyond the normal gestation period without apparent harm to the dam (Hafez and Jainudeen 1974).

Fetal maceration is a more serious condition than mummification because it involves a massive uterine infection. Maceration can be suspected when the condition of a pregnant female deteriorates rapidly and she has a fetid, bloody vaginal discharge (Gahlot et al. 1983; Sloss and Duffy 1980). Following the diagnosis of maceration, the entire uterus should be evacuated, thoroughly cleaned, and intrauterine medication administered. Long-acting antibiotics should be administered to lessen the risk of further infection.

In a formal sense, parturition is not completed until the fetal membranes, including the placenta, have been expelled from the dam's body. Placental retention occurs in a wide variety of mammals and can lead to infection or death (Sloss and Duffy 1980; Jordan 1965). There is a general tendency for membranes to be retained in older females and in instances in which gestation terminates prematurely or is abnormally prolonged. The retention of fetal membranes can sometimes be detected by observing a small portion of tissue hanging from the vulva. More frequently, however, there are no overt signs, as the tissue is retained entirely within the vagina or uterus, and diagnosis can be made only when the condition of the dam begins to deteriorate. When practical, manual removal of the membranes is the best solution. If this is not feasible, the administration of oxytocin can help promote expulsion (Sloss and Duffy 1980; Fox 1966).

Abortion

The premature expulsion from the uterus of a dead fetus or of a living fetus before it has reached a viable age is termed spontaneous abortion. Abortions may result from a variety of factors, including genetic abnormalities, developmental malformations, hormonal aberrations, infections, fatigue, trauma, drugs, litter size, behavioral stress, overcrowding, and inadequate nutrition (see Johnston 1980b; Kendrick and Howarth 1974; Medearis 1967; Hafez and Jainudeen

1974; see also "Social Factors and Pregnancy Outcome" below and "Maternal and Fetal Nutrition" above). For example, Thurman, Morton, and Stair (1983) described a white-handed gibbon, *Hylobates lar,* that apparently aborted due to a *Salmonella* infection, and Wimsatt (1960) noted that little brown bats, *Myotis lucifugus,* tended to abort fetuses shortly after they were handled. Roberts and Myhre (1983) found that mares aborted much more frequently when carrying twins than when carrying only one fetus. Furthermore, Lloyd and Christian (1969) found a relationship between abortion frequency and population density in laboratory mice, with higher frequencies occurring in the more densely populated colonies.

A phenomenon known as abrupto placentae, the premature separation of the placenta from the uterus, is known to cause fetal death and result in abortion in primates (e.g., chimpanzee: Soma 1990; lowland gorilla: Benirschke and Miller 1982; lion-tailed macaque: Calle and Ensley 1985). The factors surrounding the spontaneous expulsion of a fetus are still not well understood, even for domestic animals. Interestingly, Herrenkohl (1979) found that female rats subjected to prenatal stress had more spontaneous abortions upon reaching adulthood than did nonstressed rats. She speculated that prenatal stress may lead to imbalances in fetal hormones at a critical stage in hypothalamic differentiation, thereby producing reproductive dysfunctions in adulthood. Other scientists have argued that abortions may be an adaptive response to unfavorable environmental conditions or to embryonic malformation (see Bernds and Barash 1979; Carr 1967). Still others have argued that social factors, especially those related to reproductive competition, may be involved (see "Social Factors and Pregnancy Outcome" below; Wasser and Barash 1983). Detection of early abortion in many mammals is difficult because the embryo is often eaten by the dam (e.g., primates: King and Chalifoux 1986). During the last trimester of pregnancy, however, abortions can sometimes be predicted in cattle by the appearance of a bloody vaginal discharge (Sloss and Duffy 1980). Since many cases of abortion also involve the retention of fetal membranes, it is important to treat the dam with antibiotics, although practical considerations may prevent this in some cases.

Stillbirth

Because most births are not actually witnessed, the term stillbirth (also called perinatal mortality) will be used here to describe any fetus that is found dead (having died before, during, or shortly after parturition). A wide range of internal and external factors acting on the dam or fetus at any time during pregnancy can lead to a stillbirth.

The occurrence of multiple births in species that typically have one offspring can result in stillbirths (e.g., horse: Nishikawa and Hafez 1974; sea otter: Williams, Mattison, and Ames 1980). In certain polytocous species (i.e., those that typically have multiple fetuses), there is a positive correlation between the incidence of stillbirths and litter size (e.g., pig: Pond and Houpt 1978). Stillbirths have also been attributed to nutritional deficiencies (e.g., white-tailed deer: Verme and Ullrey 1984; cat: Sturman et al. 1986); genetic

factors, including inbreeding and congenital defects (e.g., cattle: Sloss and Duffy 1980); difficulties during parturition, including dystocia and abnormal fetal presentation (e.g., bottle-nosed dolphin: Amunden 1986; Essapian 1963; lowland gorilla: Randall, Taylor, and Banks 1984; Geoffroy's cat, *Felis geoffroyi:* Law and Boyle 1983; elephant seal: Le Boeuf, Whiting, and Gantt 1972); premature expulsion of the fetus (e.g., Northern fur seals, *Callorhinus ursinus:* Bigg 1984); ruptured umbilical cords (e.g., pig: Day 1980); placental lesions caused by infarcts (i.e., areas of dead tissue caused by an obstruction of blood vessels) or premature separation (e.g., primates: King and Chalifoux 1986); and maternal and fetal infections (primates: King and Chalifoux 1986; ungulates: Medearis 1967; Kendrick and Howarth 1974). In some species, the incidence of stillbirths is related to the sex of the fetus, with male fetuses being stillborn more often than female fetuses (e.g., cattle: Sloss and Duffy 1980). Birth order has some effect on the incidence of stillbirths in pigs, with the frequency being highest in the latter third of the young born (Randall 1972). Thus, intrauterine location of the fetus may be a factor in polytocous species, since the last individuals born must travel the length of the uterine horn during the birth process. This, in turn, may increase the probability of death from suffocation (Day 1980).

Fetal Malformation

Malformations are usually caused by abnormal development of the fetus during the embryonic period, and can be attributed to genetic and developmental aberrations, nutritional deficiencies, infections, trauma, or exposure to toxic substances (Fox 1966; Hutt 1967; Sloss and Duffy 1980). Many types of congenital defects have been identified in domestic, zoo, and wild animals (see Hutt 1967 and Leipold 1980 for a comprehensive review). In most instances, malformed fetuses do not survive, although minor deformities may not seriously hamper a young animal's development. One of the goals of the modern zoo, however, is the long-term maintenance of animal populations in captivity (Foose 1983). In some cases this requires the systematic elimination of traits deemed undesirable or potentially hazardous. Thus, malformed offspring may be euthanized if the malformation is serious enough to hamper normal function.

Prolapsed Uterus or Vagina

Eversion or prolapse of the vagina or prolapse of the cervix through the vagina is a fairly common occurrence in domestic livestock (Fielden 1980; Sloss and Duffy 1980) and has been documented in a variety of mammals, including rodents, lagomorphs, and various ungulates (Wallach and Boever 1983). Diagnosis is readily made by visual examination: the prolapsed mass, sometimes including the bowel or bladder, can be seen protruding from the lips of the vulva (Fielden 1980). Although this condition usually occurs in multiparous females during the later stages of pregnancy, there is some evidence that the tendency to prolapse can be inherited, so it has also been observed in primiparas (Sloss and Duffy 1980). Risk of recurrence in the affected animal is very high (Fielden 1980). Because most prolapses are experienced by multiparas, frequent stretching of the vagina may predispose it to eversion.

Prolapses usually require veterinary intervention because they seldom involute properly. In most cases, large mammals will need to be sedated or anesthetized prior to handling (e.g., pygmy hippopotamus, *Hexaprotodon (=Choeropsis) liberiensis:* Bush, Lemken, and Moore 1972). All prolapsed tissues must be thoroughly cleaned before being repositioned. Antibiotics are administered, and the vagina is sutured into its correct position (Fielden 1980).

Additional Problems

Environmental factors, such as temperature and humidity, are known to affect conception and pregnancy at several levels. Transient infertility due to heat stress has been most extensively documented in domestic cattle (Ingraham, Gillette, and Wagner 1974; Thatcher 1974). Postfertilization hypothermia can also affect fetal development adversely and results in increased embryonic mortality in many species (cattle: Biggers et al. 1987; sheep: Alliston and Ulberg 1961; Dutt 1963; pig: Trujano and Wrathall 1985; rabbit: Alliston, Howarth, and Ulberg 1965; mouse: Elliot and Ulberg 1971). Captive mammals should therefore be maintained at temperature ranges that are tolerable for the species. Deviations from the norm may result in reproductive failure.

SOCIAL FACTORS AND PREGNANCY OUTCOME

Many social factors can influence pregnancy outcome (Wasser and Barash 1983). For example, among some social mammals, only the dominant female breeds, while subordinate females, which are reproductively suppressed, help to raise her offspring. Wasser and Barash (1983) suggest the term "reproductive despotism" for this phenomenon. It has been reported in several group-living species, including golden lion tamarins, *Leontopithecus rosalia* (Kleiman 1980), cotton-top tamarins (Savage, Ziegler, and Snowdon 1988), common marmosets (Carroll 1986), dwarf mongooses, *Helogale parvula* (Rood 1980), African wild dogs, *Lycaon pictus* (Frame et al. 1979), wolves (Rabb, Woolpy, and Ginsburg 1967), and naked mole rats, *Heterocephalus glaber* (Jarvis 1981, 1991). There are also many social species in which dominant females tend to have higher reproductive rates than subordinates (e.g., gelada baboons: Dunbar 1980). Such differences are thought to be due to female-female competition (Dunbar and Sharman 1983).

Dominant females can suppress reproduction in subordinates through a variety of mechanisms, including estrous cycle disruption (Huck, Bracken, and Lisk 1983; Bowman, Dilley, and Keverne 1978), mating interference, and infanticide (see Kleiman 1980; Hrdy 1979). However, there is some evidence that dominant females may also interfere with normal pregnancies. It has been suggested, for instance, that the stress of living with dominant females can lead to fetal resorptions, abortions, and stillbirths in subordinate females (Wasser and Barash 1983). For example, Nash (1974) described a case in which a pregnant female

olive baboon was attacked by two other females; she subsequently aborted her fetus (also see Wasser and Starling 1988; Wasser 1983).

The presence of strange males can also have a deleterious effect on pregnancy. In some mammals, such as rodents, implantation is inhibited and pregnancy is blocked when recently mated females are exposed to unfamiliar males (Bruce 1960). The effect is strongest when the male is dominant in his own social group (Huck 1982). Postimplantation termination of pregnancy after exposure to strange males has also been documented (e.g., voles, *Microtus* spp.: Kenny, Evans, and Dewsbury 1977). Similarly, Pereira (1983) and Mohnot, Agoramoorthy, and Pajpurohit (1986) observed several cases of abortion in free-ranging troops of yellow baboons and hanuman langurs, respectively, in which circumstantial evidence suggested that the losses were due to the recent immigrations of aggressive, top-ranking males. Furthermore, Berger (1983) found a correlation between abortion frequency and male takeovers in feral horses. Pregnant females were forced to copulate with the new males, and their abortions were attributed to harassment or "stress imposed by changing social environments." Pregnancy block and inducement of abortion have been interpreted as male reproductive tactics; a female that loses her fetus prematurely ovulates and becomes sexually receptive much sooner than one that carries her fetus to term (see Berger 1983; Pereira 1983; Schwagmeyer 1979). In contrast, pair-bond disruption immediately after mating can cause implantation failure in some rodents (e.g., Mongolian gerbil, *Meriones unguiculatus:* Norris 1985; montane vole, *Microtus montanus:* Berger and Negus 1982). The implications of these findings for zoo animal management are clear: care should be taken when introducing new animals into established groups, especially when one or more females may be pregnant (see also Berger and Stevens, chap. 33, this volume).

In some cases, social factors have been shown to be important in stimulating or delaying parturition, and thus can have a bearing on pregnancy outcome. Among Northern fur seals, for instance, parturition may be triggered by the social stimulus of large numbers of conspecifics. Such concentrations occur when females and males gather on their traditional breeding beaches (Bigg 1984). Bigg (1984) suggests that the high incidence of stillbirths and abortions seen in captive pinnipeds may be related to social factors. Indeed, the social milieu of captive animals rarely changes. Thus, the lack of appropriate cues to trigger parturition may result in premature births or abnormally long gestations—problems that are frequently exhibited by these species under captive conditions.

SUMMARY AND CONCLUSIONS

We have shown how a knowledge of both the physiological and behavioral aspects of pregnancy can contribute to the development of successful captive breeding programs. Of particular importance to zoo managers are (1) the use of hormonal, physical, and behavioral cues to detect pregnancy and estimate the time of birth, (2) the special nutritional and housing needs of pregnant females and neonates, (3) the possible influence of social factors and behavioral stresses on pregnancy outcome, and (4) the recognition and treatment of various abnormalities of pregnancy and parturition.

It is our hope that the information contained here will aid zoo managers in their efforts to propagate endangered wildlife. As Poole and Trefethen (1978, 344) have stated, "Knowledge is the essential prerequisite to making a management decision respecting a species, population, or group of wildlife. A decision made in the absence of information about a species or population, depending on the result, is, at worst, an act of ignorance, or, at best, a stroke of good fortune." Unfortunately, in reviewing our current state of knowledge, it is evident that there are glaring deficiencies in our understanding of mammalian reproduction. Indeed, many of the general principles outlined in this chapter are based on studies of domestic species and therefore may not be applicable to exotic mammals. There is a clear and urgent need for detailed information on the reproductive biology of a variety of species. We encourage zoos to become more involved in scientific research, both by instituting their own research programs and by cooperating with interested colleges and universities.

ACKNOWLEDGMENTS

The authors would like to express their appreciation to C. Crockett, E. Dierenfeld, J. G. Doherty, E. Dolensek, B. Durant, D. G. Kleiman, E. Paul, and S. Lumpkin for reading and commenting on the manuscript.

REFERENCES

Adachi, M., Saito, R., and Tanioka, Y. 1982. Observation of delivery behavior in the rhesus monkey. *Primates* 24(4): 583–86.

Adams, G. P., Plotka, E. D., Asa, C. S., and Ginther, O. J. 1991. Feasibility of characterizing reproductive events in large nondomestic species by transrectal ultrasonic imaging. *Zoo Biol.* 10:247–59.

Alexander, G., Signoret, J. P., and Hafez, E. S. E. 1974. Sexual and maternal behavior. In *Reproduction in farm animals,* ed. E. S. E. Hafez, 222–54. Philadelphia: Lea and Febiger.

Allen, W. R. 1969. The immunological measurement of pregnant mares serum gonadotropin. *J. Endocrinol.* 43:593–98.

Alliston, C. W., Howarth, B., and Ulberg, L. C. 1965. Embryonic mortality following culture in vitro of one- and two-cell rabbit eggs at elevated temperatures. *J. Reprod. Fertil.* 9:337–41.

Alliston, C. W., and Ulberg, L. C. 1961. Early pregnancy loss in sheep at ambient temperatures of 70° and 90° F as determined by embryo transfer. *J. Anim. Sci.* 20:608–13.

Altmann, J. 1980. *Baboon mothers and infants.* Cambridge, Mass.: Harvard University Press.

Altmann, J., Altmann, S. A., and Hausfater, G. 1978. Primate infant's effects on mother's future reproduction. *Science* 201: 1028–30.

Amoroso, E. C., and Finn, C. A. 1962. Ovarian activity during gestation, ovum transport, and implantation. In *The ovary,* 1st ed., ed. S. Zuckerman, 451–537. New York: Academic Press.

Amunden, M. 1986. Breeding the bottle-nosed dolphin at the Kolmarden Dolphinarium. *Int. Zoo Yrbk.* 24/25:263–71.

Andelman, S. J., Else, J. G., Hearn, J. P., and Hodges, J. K. 1985. The non-invasive monitoring of reproductive events in wild vervet monkeys *(Cercopithecus aethiops)* using urinary pregnanediol-3δ-glucuronide and its correlation with behavioural observations. *J. Zool.* (Lond.) 205:467–77.

Asa, C. S., Junge, R. E., Bircher, J. S., Noble, G. A., Sarri, K. J., and Plotka, E. D. 1992. Assessing reproductive cycles of pregnancy in cheetahs *(Acinonyx jubatus).* *Zoo Biol.* 11:139–51.

Atkinson, L. E., Hotchkiss, J., Fritz, G. R., Surve, A. H., Neill, J. D., and Knobil, E. 1975. Circulating levels of steroids and chorionic gonadotrophin during pregnancy in the rhesus monkey with special attention to the rescue of the corpus luteum in early pregnancy. *Biol. Reprod.* 12:335–45.

Bamberg, E., Choi, H. S., Mostl, E., Wurm, W., Lorin, D., and Arbeiter, K. 1984. Enzymatic determination of unconjugated oestrogens in feces for pregnancy diagnosis in mares. *Equine Vet. J.* 16:537–39.

Barrett, R. H. 1981. Pregnancy diagnosis with Doppler ultrasonic fetal pulse detectors. *Wildl. Soc. Bull.* 9 (1): 60–63.

Batra, S. K., Arora, R. C., Bachlaus, N. K., and Paudey, R. S. 1983. Blood and milk progesterone in pregnant and nonpregnant buffalo. *J. Dairy Sci.* 62:1390–93.

Bazer, F. W., and First, N. 1983. Pregnancy and parturition. *J. Anim. Sci.* 57:425–60.

Beck, B. 1984. The birth of a lowland gorilla in captivity. *Primates* 25 (3): 378–83.

Beier, H. M. 1968. Uteroglobin: A hormone-sensitive endometrial protein involved in blastocyst development. *Biochem. Biophys. Acta* 160:289–91.

Benirschke, K., ed. 1967. *Comparative aspects of reproductive failure.* Berlin: Springer-Verlag.

Benirschke, K., and Miller, C. J. 1982. Anatomical and functional differences in the placenta of primates. *Biol. Reprod.* 26:29–53.

Bennett, D. 1980. Normal and abnormal parturition. In *Current therapy in theriogenology,* ed. D. Morrow, 595–606. Philadelphia: W. B. Saunders.

Bercovitch, F. B. 1987. Female weight and reproductive condition in a population of olive baboons *(Papio anubis).* *Am. J. Primatol.* 12:189–95.

Berger, J. 1983. Induced abortion and social factors in wild horses. *Nature* 303:59–61.

———. 1986. *Wild horses of the Great Basin.* Chicago: University of Chicago Press.

Berger, P. J., and Negus, N. C. 1982. Stud male maintenance of pregnancy in *Microtus montanus.* *J. Mammal.* 63:148–51.

Bernard, R. T. F. 1989. The adaptive significance of reproductive delay phenomena in some South African Microchiroptera. *Mammal Rev.* 19 (1): 27–34.

Bernds, W., and Barash, D. P. 1979. Early termination of parental investment in mammals, including humans. In *Evolutionary biology and human social behavior,* ed. N. Chagnon and W. Irons, 487–506. North Scituate, Mass.: Duxbury.

Bielert, C., Czaja, J. A., Eisele, S., Scheffler, G., Robinson, J. A., and Goy, R. W. 1976. Mating in the rhesus monkey *(Macaca mulatta)* after conception and its relationship to oestradiol and progesterone levels throughout pregnancy. *J. Reprod. Fertil.* 46: 179–87.

Bigg, M. A. 1984. Stimuli for parturition in Northern fur seals *(Callorhinus ursinus).* *J. Mammal.* 65 (2): 333–36.

Biggers, B. G., Geisert, R. D., Wetteman, R. P., and Buchanan, D. S. 1987. Effect of heat stress on early embryonic development in the beef cow. *J. Anim. Sci.* 64:1512–18.

Biller, D. S., and Haibel, G. K. 1987. Torsion of the uterus in a cat. *J. Am. Vet. Assoc.* 191 (9): 1128–29.

Blauvelt, H. 1955. Dynamics of the mother-newborn relationship in goats. *Group Processes* 1:211–58.

Bleicher, N. 1962. Behavior of the bitch during parturition. *J. Am. Vet. Med. Assoc.* 140:1076–79.

Bolser, L., and Savage-Rumbaugh, S. 1989. Periparturitional behavior of a bonobo *(Pan paniscus)*. *Am. J. Primatol.* 17:93–103.

Bonney, R. C., Moore, H. D. M., and Jones, D. M. 1981. Plasma concentrations of oestradiol-17β and progesterone and laparoscopic observations of the ovary in the puma *(Felis concolor)* during oestrus, pseudopregnancy, and pregnancy. *J. Reprod. Fertil.* 63:523–31.

Bonney, S., and Crotty, M. J. 1979. Breeding the mountain tapir at the Los Angeles Zoo. *Int. Zoo Yrbk.* 19:198–200.

Bontekoe, E. H. M., Blacquiere, J. F., Naaktgeboren, C., Dieleman, S. J., and Williams, P. P. M. 1977. Influence of environmental disturbances on uterine motility during pregnancy and parturition in rabbit and sheep. *Behav. Processes* 2:41–73.

Boomsma, R. A., and Verhage, H. G. 1987. Detection of a progesterone-dependent secretory protein synthesized by cat endometrium. *Biol. Reprod.* 37:117–26.

Bosc, M. J. 1987. Time of parturition in rats after melatonin administration or change of photoperiod. *J. Reprod. Fertil.* 80:563–68.

Bosc, M. J., and Nicolle, A. 1980. Influence of photoperiod on the time of parturition in the rat. I. Effect of the length of daily illumination on normal or adrenalectomized animals. *Reprod. Nutr. Dev.* 20:735–45.

———. 1985. Influence of photoperiod on the time of birth in the rat. IV. Effects of an imposed feeding rhythm. *Reprod. Nutr. Dev.* 25:39–48.

Bosc, M. J., Nicolle, A., and Ducelliez, D. 1986. Time of birth and daily activity mediated by feeding rhythms in the pregnant rat. *Reprod. Nutr. Dev.* 26:777–89.

Bowden, D., Winter, P., and Ploog, D. 1967. Pregnancy and delivery behavior in the squirrel monkey and other animals. *Folia Primatol.* 5:1–42.

Bowman, L. A., Dilley, S. R., and Keverne, E. B. 1978. Suppression of oestrogen-induced LH surges by social subordination in talapoin monkeys. *Nature* 275:56–58.

Boyd, J. S. 1971. The radiographic identification of various stages of pregnancy in the domestic cat. *J. Small Anim. Pract.* 12:501.

Bradshaw, G. V. R. 1962. Reproductive cycle of the California leaf-nosed bat, *Macrotus californicus*. *Science* 136:645–46.

Brandt, E. M., and Mitchell, G. 1971. Parturition in primates. In *Primate behaviour: Developments in field and laboratory research,* ed. L. A. Rosenblum, 178–223. New York: Academic Press.

Bruce, H. M. 1960. A block to pregnancy in the mouse caused by proximity of strange males. *J. Reprod. Fertil.* 1:96–103.

Bruere, A. N. 1980. Pregnancy toxemia. In *Current therapy in theriogenology,* ed. D. A. Morrow, 903–7. Philadelphia: W. B. Saunders.

Brundige, G. C., Layne, L. J., and McCabe, T. R. 1988. Early pregnancy determination using serum progesterone concentration in bighorn sheep. *J. Wildl. Mgmt.* 52 (4): 610–12.

Buchanan, G. D., and Younglai, E. V. 1986. Plasma progesterone levels during pregnancy in the little brown bat, *Myotis lucifugus* (Vespertilionidae). *Biol. Reprod.* 34:878–84.

Bullerman, R. 1976. Breeding Dall sheep at Milwaukee Zoo. *Int. Zoo Yrbk.* 16:126–29.

Burton, F. D., and Sawchuk, L. A. 1982. Birth intervals in *M. sylvanus* of Gibraltar. *Primates* 23 (1): 140–44.

Bush, M., Lemken, R., and Moore, J. A. 1972. Prolapsed uterus in a pygmy hippopotamus. *J. Am. Vet. Med. Assoc.* 161:651.

Caine, N., and Mitchell, G. 1979. Behavior of primates present during parturition. In *Captivity and behavior,* ed. J. Erwin, T. L. Maple, and G. Mitchell, 112–24. New York: Van Nostrand Reinhold.

Calle, P. P., and Ensley, P. K. 1985. Abrupto placentae in a lion-tailed macaque. *J. Am. Vet. Med. Assoc.* 187:1275–76.

Campitelli, S., Carenzi, C., and Verga, M. 1982. Factors which influence parturition in the mare and development in the foal. *Appl. Anim. Ethol.* 9:7–14.

Carr, D. H. 1967. Cytogenetics of abortions. In *Comparative aspects of reproductive failure,* ed. K. Benirschke, 96–117. Berlin: Springer-Verlag.

Carroll, J. B. 1986. Social correlates of reproductive suppression in captive callitrichid family groups. *Dodo* 23:80–85.

Chakraborti, R., and Jagannadha Rao, R. A. 1987. An avidin-biotin micro-enzyme immunoassay for monkey chorionic gonadotrophin. *J. Reprod. Fertil.* 80:151–58.

Challis, J. R. G., and Olson, D. M. 1988. Parturition. In *The physiology of reproduction,* vol. 1, ed. E. Knobil and J. D. Neill, 2177–2234. New York: Raven Press.

Chang, C. F., and Estergreen, V. L. 1983. Development of a direct enzyme immunoassay of milk progesterone and its application to pregnancy diagnosis in cows. *Steroids* 41:173–95.

Chard, T. 1983. Human placental lactogen. In *Current topics in experimental endocrinology,* vol. 4, *The endocrinology of pregnancy and parturition,* ed. L. Martini and V. H. T. James, 167–91. New York: Academic Press.

Choi, H. S., Kiesenhofer, E., Gantner, H., Hois, J., and Bamberg, E. 1987. Pregnancy diagnosis in sows by estimation of oestrogens in blood, urine, or faeces. *Anim. Reprod. Sci.* 15:209–16.

Chaudhuri, M., Carrasco, E., Kalk, P., and Thau, R. B. 1990. Urinary oestrogen excretion during oestrus and pregnancy in the babirusa *Babyrousa babyrussa*. *Int. Zoo Yrbk.* 29:188–92.

Church, D. C., and Lloyd, W. E. 1972. Veterinary dietetics and therapeutic nutrition. In *Digestive physiology and nutrition of ruminants,* vol. 3, *Practical nutrition,* ed. D. C. Church. Corvallis: D. C. Church, Department of Animal Sciences, Oregon State University.

Citino, S. B., Bush, M., and Phillips, L. G. 1984. Dystocia and fatal hyperthermic episode in a giraffe. *J. Am. Vet. Med. Assoc.* 185 (11): 1440–42.

Clark, A. K., Spearow, A. C., and Owens, M. J. 1983. Relationship of feeding time to time of parturition for dry Holstein cows. *J. Dairy Sci.* 66 (suppl. 1): 138.

Clark, F. H. 1937. Parturition in the deer mouse. *J. Mammal.* 18:85–87.

Clegg, M. T., and Weaver, M. 1972. Chorionic gonadotropin secretion during pregnancy in the chimpanzee *(Pan troglodytes)*. *Proc. Soc. Exp. Biol. Med.* 139:1170–74.

Clutton-Brock, T. H., Guinness, F. E., and Albon, S. D. 1982. *Red deer: Behavior and ecology of two sexes.* Chicago: University of Chicago Press.

Coe, C. L., and Rosenblum, L. A. 1978. Annual reproductive strategy of the squirrel monkey *(Saimiri sciureus)*. *Folia Primatol.* 29:19–42.

Concannon, P. W., and Castracane, V. D. 1985. Serum androgen and testosterone concentrations during pregnancy and nonpregnant cycles in dogs. *Biol. Reprod.* 33:1078–83.

Concannon, P. W., Powers, M. E., Holder, W., and Hansel, W. 1977. Pregnancy and parturition in the bitch. *Biol. Reprod.* 16:517–26.

Cornell, L., Asper, E. D., Antrim, J. E., Searles, S. S., Young, W. G., and Goff, T. 1987. Progress report: Results of a long-range captive breeding program for the bottle-nosed dolphin, *Tursiops truncatus* and *Tursiops truncatus gillii*. *Zoo Biol.* 6:41–53.

Cox, D. F. 1964. Genetic variation in the gestation period of swine. *J. Anim. Sci.* 23:746–51.

Crockett, C., and Sekulic, R. 1984. Infanticide in red howler monkeys *(Alouatta seniculus)*. In *Infanticide: Comparative and evolutionary perspectives,* ed. G. Hausfater and S. B. Hrdy, 173–91. New York: Aldine.

Cross, D. T., Threlfall, W. R., and Kline, R. C. 1992. Body temperature fluctuations in the periparturient horse mare. *Theriogenology* 37:1041–48.

Csapo, A. F., and Lloyd-Jacobs, M. A. 1962. Placenta, uterus volume, and the control of the pregnant uterus in rabbits. *Am. J. Obstet. Gynecol.* 83:1073–82.

Czekala, N. M., Gallusser, S., Meier, J. E., and Lasley, B. L. 1986. The development and application of an enzyme immunoassay for urinary estrone conjugates. *Zoo Biol.* 5:1–6.

Czekala, N. M., Kasman, L., Allen, J., Oosterhuis, J., and Lasley, B. L. 1990. Urinary steroid evaluations to monitor ovarian functions in exotic ungulates: VI. Pregnancy detection in exotic Equidae. *Zoo Biol.* 9:43–48.

Daly, M. 1972. The maternal behaviour cycle in golden hamsters. *Z. Tierpsychologie* 31:289–99.

Daniel, J. C. 1974. Circulating levels of oestradiol-17β during early pregnancy in the Alaskan fur seal showing an estrogen surge preceding implantation. *J. Reprod. Fertil.* 37:425–28.

Davis, J. 1965. A preliminary report on the reproductive behaviour of the small Malayan chevrotain, *Tragulus javanicus* at New York Zoo. *Int. Zoo Yrbk.* 5:42–44.

Day, B. N. 1980. Parturition. In *Current therapy in theriogenology*, ed. D. Morrow, 1064–67. Philadelphia: W. B. Saunders.

Desaulniers, D. M., Goff, A. K., Betteridge, K. J., Rowell, J. E., and Flood, P. F. 1989. Reproductive hormone concentrations in faeces during the oestrous cycle and pregnancy in cattle *(Bos taurus)* and musk oxen *(Ovibos moschatus)*. *Can. J. Zool.* 67:1148–54.

Dewar, A. D. 1968. Litter size and the duration of pregnancy in mice. *Q. J. Exp. Physiol.* 53:155–63.

Diamond, E. J., Aksel, S., Hazelton, J. M., Wiebe, R. H., and Abee, C. R. 1987. Serum oestradiol, progesterone, chorionic gonadotrophin and prolactin concentrations during pregnancy in the Bolivian squirrel monkey *(Saimiri sciureus)*. *J. Reprod. Fertil.* 80:373–81.

Doyle, G. A., Pelletier, A., and Bekker, T. 1967. Courtship, mating, and parturition in the Lesser bushbaby *(Galago senegalensis moholi)* under semi-natural conditions. *Folia Primatol.* 7:169–97.

Dryden, G. 1969. Reproduction in *Suncus murinus*. *J. Reprod. Fertil. Suppl.* 6:377–96.

Dukelow, W. R. 1980. Laparoscopy in small animals and ancillary techniques. In *Animal laparoscopy*, ed. R. M. Harrison and D. E. Wildt, 95–106. Baltimore: Williams and Wilkins.

Dunbar, R. I. M. 1980. Determinants and evolutionary consequences of dominance among female gelada baboons. *Behav. Ecol. Sociobiol.* 7:253–65.

Dunbar, R. I. M., and Sharman, M. 1983. Female competition for access to males affects birth rates in baboons. *Behav. Ecol. Sociobiol.* 13:157–59.

Dutt, R. H. 1963. Critical period for early embryo mortality in ewes exposed to high ambient temperature. *J. Anim. Sci.* 22:713–19.

Eisenberg, J. F. 1966. The social organization of mammals. *Handbuch der Zoologie* 10:1–92.

Eisenberg, J. F., and Kleiman, D. G. 1977. The usefulness of behaviour studies in developing captive breeding programmes for mammals. *Int. Zoo Yrbk.* 17:81–88.

Elliot, D. S., and Ulberg, L. C. 1971. Early embryo development in the mammal. I. Effects of experimental alterations during first cell division in the mouse. *J. Anim. Sci.* 33:86–95.

Elmore, R. G., Martin, C. E., Riley, J. L., and Littledike, T. 1979. Body temperature of farrowing swine. *J. Am. Vet. Med. Assoc.* 174:620–22.

Enders, A. C. 1963. *Delayed implantation*. Chicago: University of Chicago Press.

Enders, R. K. 1931. Parturition in the agouti, with notes on several pregnant uteri. *J. Mammal.* 12:390–96.

Essapian, F. S. 1963. Observations on abnormalities of parturition in captive bottle-nosed dolphins, *Tursiops truncatus*, and concurrent behavior of other porpoises. *J. Mammal.* 44 (3):405–14.

Estes, R. D., and Estes, R. K. 1979. The birth and survival of wildebeest calves. *Z. Tierpsychologie* 50:45–95.

Evans, K. L., Hughes, J. P., Couto, M., Kasman, L. H., and Lasley, B. L. 1984. Pregnancy diagnosis in the domestic horse through direct urinary estrone conjugate analysis. *Theriogenology* 22:615–20.

Ewbank, R. 1963. Predicting the time of parturition in the normal cow: A study of the pre-calving drop in body temperature in relation to the external signs of imminent calving. *Vet. Rec.* 75:367–71.

————. 1969. The fall in rectal temperature seen before parturition in sheep. *J. Reprod. Fertil.* 19:569–71.

Ewer, R. F. 1973. *The carnivores*. Ithaca, N.Y.: Cornell University Press.

Farrow, C. S., Morgan, J. P., and Story, E. D. 1976. Late term fetal death in the dog: Early radiographic diagnosis. *J. Am. Vet. Radiol. Soc.* 17:11–17.

Ferron, R. R., Miller, R. S., and McNulty, W. P. 1976. Estimation of fetal age and weight from radiographic skull diameters on the rhesus monkey. *J. Med. Primatol.* 5:41–48.

Fielden, E. D. 1980. Vaginal prolapse. In *Current therapy in theriogenology*, ed. D. A. Morrow, 914–16. Philadelphia: W. B. Saunders.

Findlay, J. K. 1983. The endocrinology of the preimplantation period. In *Current topics in experimental endocrinology*, vol. 4, *The endocrinology of pregnancy and parturition*, ed. L. Martini and V. H. T. James, 36–61. New York: Academic Press.

First, N. L. 1979. Mechanisms controlling parturition in farm animals. In *Animal production*, ed. H. Hawk, 215–57. Montclair, N.J.: Allanheld Osmun.

Fleming, T. H. 1971. *Artibeus jamaicensis:* Delayed embryonic development in a Neotropical bat. *Science* 171:402–4.

Flowers, B., Martin, M. J., Cantley, T. C., and Day, B. N. 1989. Endocrine changes associated with dietary-induced increase in ovulation rate (flushing) in gilts. *J. Anim. Sci.* 67:771–78.

Flux, E. C. 1967. Reproduction and body weights of the hare, *Lepus europaeus pallas*, in New Zealand. *N. Z. J. Sci.* 10:357–401.

Foose, T. J. 1983. The relevance of captive populations to the conservation of biological diversity. In *Genetics and conservation*, ed. C. M. Schonewald-Cox, S. M. Chambers, B. MacBryde, and W. L. Thomas, 374–401. Menlo Park, Calif.: Benjamin/Cummings.

Fowler, M. E., ed. 1986. *Zoo and wild animal medicine*. Philadelphia: W. B. Saunders.

Fox, M. W. 1966. *Canine pediatrics, development, neonatal and congenital diseases*. Springfield: Charles C. Thomas.

Frädrich, H. 1987. The husbandry of tropical and temperate cervids in the West Berlin Zoo. In *Biology and management of the Cervidae*, ed. C. Wemmer, 422–27. Washington, D.C.: Smithsonian Institution Press.

Frame, L. H., Malcolm, J. R., Frame, G. W., and Lawick, H. van. 1979. Social organization of African wild dogs *Lycaon pictus* on the Serengeti Plains, Tanzania (1967–1978). *Z. Tierpsychol.* 50:225–49.

Fraser, A. F. 1968. *Reproductive behaviour in ungulates*. New York: Academic Press.

Freeman, H., and Hutchins, M. 1978. Captive management of snow leopard cubs *(Uncia uncia)*: An overview. *Der Zoologische Garten* 50 (6):377–92.

French, J. A. 1983. Lactation and fertility: An examination of nursing and interbirth intervals in cotton-top tamarins *(Saguinus o. oedipus)*. *Folia Primatol.* 40:276–82.

Frueh, R. J. 1979. The breeding and management of black lemurs at St. Louis Zoo. *Int. Zoo Yrbk.* 19:214–17.

Fuchs, A. R. 1983. The role of oxytocin in parturition. In *Current topics in experimental endocrinology*, vol. 4, *The endocrinology of pregnancy and parturition*, ed. L. Martini and V. H. T. James, 231–65. New York: Academic Press.

Fukui, Y., and Too, K. 1978. Studies on pregnancy diagnosis in domestic animals by an ultrasonic Doppler method. II. An evaluation for predicting the litter size in utero in the pig. *Jpn. J. Anim. Reprod.* 24:174–80.

Gadsby, J. E., Burton, R. D., Heap, R. B., and Perry, J. S. 1976. Steroid metabolism and synthesis in early embryonic tissue of the pig, sheep, and cow. *J. Endocrinol.* 71:45–65P.

Gahlot, T. K., Chouhan, D. S., Khatri, S. K., Bishnoi, B. L., and Chowdhury, B. R. 1983. Macerated fetus in a camel. *Vet. Med. Small Anim. Clin.* 78:429–30.

Gengozian, N., Smith, T. A., and Gosslee, D. G. 1974. External uterine palpation to identify stages of pregnancy in the marmoset, *Saguinus fuscicollis. J. Med. Primatol.* 3:236–43.

George, J. M. 1969. Variation in the time of parturition of Merino and Dorset Horn ewes. *J. Agric. Sci.* 73:295–99.

Gerloff, B. J., and Morrow, D. A. 1980. Effect of nutrition on reproduction in dairy cattle. In *Current therapy in theriogenology,* ed. D. A. Morrow, 310–20. Philadelphia: W. B. Saunders.

Gier, H. T. 1975. Ecology and behavior of the coyote *(Canis latrans)*. In *The wild canids,* ed. M. W. Fox, 247–62. New York: Van Nostrand Reinhold.

Glander, K. E. 1980. Reproduction and population growth in free-ranging mantled howler monkeys. *Am. J. Phys. Anthropol.* 53:25–36.

Godfrey, G. K. 1969. Reproduction in a laboratory colony of the marsupial mouse, *Sminthopsis larapinta* (Marsupialia: Dasyuridae). *Aust. J. Zool.* 17:637–54.

Gomendio, M. 1989. Suckling behaviour and fertility in rhesus macaques *(Macaca mulatta). J. Zool.* 217:449–67.

Gonyou, H. W., and Cobb, A. R. 1986. The influence of time of feeding on the time of parturition in ewes. *Can. J. Anim. Sci.* 66:569–74.

Gosling, L. M. 1969. Parturition and related behaviour in Coke's hartebeest, *Alcelaphus buselaphus cokei* Gunther. *J. Reprod. Fertil. Suppl.* 6:265–86.

Gouzoules, H. T. 1974. Group responses to parturition in *Macaca arctoides. Primates* 15 (2–3): 287–92.

Graham, C. E. 1981. Menstrual cycle of the great apes. In *Reproductive biology of the great apes: Comparative and biomedical perspectives,* ed. C. E. Graham, 1–43. New York: Academic Press.

Greenwald, G. S. 1967. Luteotrophic complex of the hamsters. *J. Endocrinol.* 80:118–30.

Greer, K. R., and Hawkins, J. R. 1967. Determining pregnancy in elk by rectal palpation. *J. Wildl. Mgmt.* 31:145–49.

Griffiths, M. 1984. Mammals: Monotremes. In *Marshall's physiology of reproduction*, 4th ed., vol. 1, *Reproductive cycles of vertebrates*, ed. G. E. Lamming, 351–85. Edinburgh: Churchill-Livingstone.

Gross, T. S. 1992. Faecal steroid measurements in several carnivores. In *The First International Symposium on Faecal Steroid Monitoring in Zoo Animals*, ed. E. Bamberg, 55–61. Royal Rotterdam Zoological and Botanical Gardens.

Gubernick, D. J. 1981. Parent and infant attachment in mammals. In *Parental care in mammals*, ed. D. J. Gubernick and P. H. Klopfer, 243–305. New York: Plenum Press.

Hafez, E. S. E., and Jainudeen, M. R. 1974. Reproductive failure in females. In *Reproduction in farm animals*, ed. E. S. E. Hafez, 351–72. Philadelphia: Lea and Febiger.

Haigh, J. C., Cranfield, M., and Sasser, R. G. 1988. Estrus synchronization and pregnancy diagnosis in red deer. *J. Zoo Anim. Med.* 19 (4): 202–7.

Hall, R. D., and Hodgen, G. D. 1979. Pregnancy diagnosis in owl monkeys *(Aotus trivirgatus)*: Evaluation of the hemagglutination inhibition test for urinary chorionic gonadotropin. *Lab. Anim. Sci.* 29:345–48.

Hansel, W. 1971. Survival and gonadotropin responsiveness of luteal cells in vitro. In *Karolinska symposia on research methods in reproductive endocrinology, third symposium: In vitro methods in reproductive cell biology*, 295–317. Stockholm: Karolinska Institute.

Harley, D. 1985. Birth spacing in langur monkeys, *Presbytis entellus. Int. J. Primatol.* 6:227–42.

Harper, W. L., and Cohen, R. D. H. 1985. Accuracy of Doppler ultrasound in diagnosing pregnancy in bighorn sheep. *J. Wildl. Mgmt.* 49:793–96.

Harrison, R. M. 1980. Laparoscopy in monkeys and apes. In *Animal laparoscopy*, ed. R. M. Harrison and D. E. Wildt, 73–93. Baltimore: Williams and Wilkins.

Harrison, R. M., and Wildt, D. E., eds. 1980. *Animal laparoscopy*. Baltimore: Williams and Wilkins.

Harrop, A. E. 1960. *Reproduction in the dog*. Baltimore: Williams and Wilkins.

Hart, B. L. 1985. *The behavior of domestic animals*. New York: W. H. Freeman.

Hartman, C. G. 1925. Interruption of pregnancy by ovariectomy in the placental opossum: Study in physiology of implantation. *Am. J. Physiol.* 71:436–54.

Hartman, L. 1964. The behaviour and breeding of captive weasels *(Mustela nivalis* L.). *N. Z. J. Sci.* 7:147–56.

Hausfater, G., and Hrdy, S. B. 1984. *Infanticide: Comparative and evolutionary perspectives*. New York: Aldine.

Hayssen, V., Van Tienhoven, A., and Van Tienhoven, A. 1993. *Asdell's patterns of mammalian reproduction*. Ithaca, N.Y.: Cornell University Press.

Heap, R.B., and Hamon, H. 1974. Plasma progesterone levels in pregnant and pseudopregnant ferrets. *J. Reprod. Fertil.* 39:149–52.

———. 1979. Oestrone sulfate in milk as an indicator of a viable conceptus in cows. *Br. Vet. J.* 135:355–63.

Heger, W., Merker, H. J., and Neubert, D. 1988. Evaluation of seven test kits for the detection of pregnancies in the common marmoset, *Callithrix jacchus. Folia Primatol.* 51:106–11.

Heimer, W. E., and Watson, S. M. 1982. Differing reproductive patterns in Dall sheep: Population strategy or management artifact? *Proceedings of the Biennial Symposium of the Northern Wild Sheep and Goat Council* 2:288–306. Fort Collins, Colo.: Northern Wild Sheep and Goat Council.

Heistermann, M., Prove, E., Wolters, H. J., and Mika, G. 1987. Urinary oestrogen and progesterone excretion before and during pregnancy in a pied bare-faced tamarin *(Saguinus bicolor bicolor). J. Reprod. Fertil.* 80:635–40.

Hellwing, S. 1973. The postnatal development of the white-toothed shrew *Crocidura russula monacha* in captivity. *Z. Säugetierkunde* 38:257–70.

Hendrichs, H., and Hendrichs, U. 1971. *Dikdik und elefanten*. Munich: Piper Verlag.

Hendricks, D. M., and Mayer, D. T. 1977. Gonadal hormones and uterine factors. In *Reproduction in domestic animals*, 3d ed., ed. H. H. Cole and P. T. Cupps, 79–117. New York: Academic Press.

Herrenkohl, L. R. 1979. Prenatal stress reduces fertility and fecundity in female offspring. *Science* 206:1097–99.

Herter, K. 1965. *Hedgehogs*. London: Phoenix House.

Hess, J. P. 1973. Some observations on the sexual behavior of captive lowland gorillas. In *Comparative ecology and behavior of primates*, ed. R. P. Michael and J. H. Crook, 508–81. New York: Academic Press.

Hilliard, J. 1973. Corpus luteum function in guinea pigs, hamsters, rats, mice, and rabbits. *Biol. Reprod.* 8:203–21.

Hilliard, J., Spies, H. G., and Sawyer, C. H. 1968. Cholesterol storage and progestin secretion during pregnancy and pseudopregnancy in the rabbit. *J. Endocrinol.* 82:157–65.

Hillman, C. N., and Carpenter, J. W. 1983. Breeding biology and behavior of captive black-footed ferrets, *Mustela nigripes*. *Int. Zoo Yrbk.* 23:186–91.

Hobson, B. M., Hearn, J. P., Lunn, S. F., and Flockhart, J. H. 1977. Urinary excretion of biologically active chorionic gonadotrophin by the pregnant marmoset *(Callithrix jacchus jacchus)*. *Folia Primatol.* 28:251–58.

Hobson, B. M., and Wide, L. 1981. The similarity of chorionic gonadotropin and its subunits in term placentae from man, apes, Old and New World monkeys, and a prosimian. *Folia Primatol.* 35:51–64.

Hobson, W., Faiman, C., Dougherty, W. D., Reyes, F. I., and Winter, J. S. D. 1975. Radioimmunoassay of rhesus monkey chorionic gonadotropin. *Fertil. Steril.* 26:93–97.

Hodgen, G. D., and Itskovitch, J. 1988. Recognition and maintenance of pregnancy. In *The physiology of reproduction*, vol. 1, ed. E. Knobil and J. D. Neill, 1995–2022. New York: Raven Press.

Hodgen, G. D., and Neimann, W. H. 1975. Application of the subhuman primate pregnancy test kit to pregnancy diagnosis in baboons. *Lab. Anim. Sci.* 25:757–58.

Hodgen, G. D., and Ross, G. T. 1974. Pregnancy diagnosis by a hemagglutination inhibition test for urinary macaque chorionic gonadotropin (mCG). *J. Clin. Endocrinol. Metab.* 38:927–30.

Hodgen, G. D., Stolzenberg, S. J., Jones, D. C. L., Hildebrand, D. F., and Turner, C. K. 1978. Pregnancy diagnosis in squirrel monkeys: Hemagglutination test, radioimmunoassay, and bioassay of chorionic gonadotropin. *J. Med. Primatol.* 7:59–64.

Hodgen, G. D., Turner, C. K., Smith, E. E., and Bush, R. M. 1977. Pregnancy diagnosis in the orangutan *(Pongo pygmaeus)* using the subhuman primate pregnancy test kit. *Lab. Anim. Sci.* 27:99–101.

Hodges, J. K. 1986. Monitoring changes in reproductive status. *Int. Zoo Yrbk.* 24/25:126–30.

Hodges, J. K., Bevan, D. J., Celma, M., Hearn, J. P., Jones, D. M., Kleiman, D. G., Knight, J. A., and Moore, H. D. M. 1984. Aspects of the reproductive endocrinology of the female giant panda *(Ailuropoda melanoleuca)* in captivity with special reference to the detection of ovulation and pregnancy. *J. Zool.* (Lond.) 203:253–67.

Hodges, J. K., Czekala, N. M., and Lasley, B. L. 1979. Estrogen and luteinizing hormone secretion in diverse primate species from simplified urinary analysis. *J. Med. Primatol.* 3:359–64.

Hodges, J. K., and Green, D. I. 1989. The development of an enzyme-immunoassay for urinary pregnanediol-3-glucuronide and its application to reproductive assessment in exotic mammals. *J. Zool.* (Lond.) 219:89–99.

Holm, L. W. 1966. The gestation period of mammals. *Symp. Zool. Soc. Lond.* 15:403–18.

Holt, W. V., Moore, H. D. M., North, R. D., Hartman, T. D., and Hodges, J. K. 1988. Hormonal and behavioural detection of oestrus in blackbuck, *Antilope cervicapra,* and successful artificial insemination with fresh and frozen semen. *J. Reprod. Fertil.* 82:717–25.

Holtz, W. 1992. Pregnancy diagnosis through faecal estrogens in goats. In *The First International Symposium on Faecal Steroid Monitoring in Zoo Animals,* ed. E. Bamberg, 62–67. Royal Rotterdam Zoological and Botanical Gardens.

Hopf, S. 1967. Notes on pregnancy, delivery, and infant survival in captive squirrel monkeys. *Primates* 8:323–32.

Hopper, B. R., Tullner, W. W., and Gray, C. W. 1968. Urinary estrogen excretion during pregnancy in a gorilla. *Proc. Soc. Exp. Biol. Med.* 129:213–14.

Houston, D. B., Robbins, C. T., Ruder, C. A., and Sasser, R. G. 1986. Pregnancy detection in mountain goats by assay for pregnancy-specific protein. *J. Wildl. Mgmt.* 50:740–42.

Howell, C., and Rollins, W. 1951. Environmental sources of variation in the gestation length of the horse. *J. Anim. Sci.* 10:789–96.

Hrdy, S. 1979. Infanticide among mammals: A review, classification, and examination of the implications for reproductive strategies of females. *Ethol. Sociobiol.* 1:13–40.

Hubbell, G. 1962. Birth of a gelada baboon, *Theropithecus gelada,* by cesarean section. *Int. Zoo Yrbk.* 4:142.

Huck, U. W. 1982. Pregnancy block in laboratory mice as a function of male social status. *J. Reprod. Fertil.* 66:181–84.

Huck, U. W., Bracken, A. C., and Lisk, R. D. 1983. Female-induced pregnancy block in the golden hamster. *Behav. Neurobiol.* 38:190–93.

Hunter, J., Martin, R. D., Dixson, A. F., and Rudder, B. C. C. 1979. Gestation and interbirth intervals in owl monkey *(Aotus trivirgatus griseimembra)*. *Folia Primatol.* 31:165–75.

Hutchins, M. 1984. The mother-offspring relationship in mountain goats *(Oreamnos americanus)*. Ph.D. thesis, University of Washington.

Hutson, G. D. 1976. Grooming behaviour and birth in the Dasyurid marsupial, *Dasyuroides byrnei. Aust. J. Zool.* 24:277–82.

Hutt, F. B. 1967. Malformations and defects of genetic origin in domestic animals. In *Comparative aspects of reproductive failure,* ed. K. Benirschke, 256–67. Berlin: Springer-Verlag.

Ingraham, R. M., Gillette, D. D., and Wagner, W. E. 1974. Relationship of temperature and humidity to conception rate of Holstein cows in subtropical climate. *J. Dairy Sci.* 57:476–81.

Izard, M. K., and Simons, E. L. 1986. Isolation of females prior to parturition reduces neonatal mortality in *Galago. Am. J. Primatol.* 10:249–55.

———. 1987. Lactation and interbirth interval in the Senegal Galago *(Galago senegalensis moholi). J. Med. Primatol.* 16:323–32.

Jainudeen, M. R., and Hafez, E. S. E. 1980. Gestation, prenatal physiology, and parturition. In *Reproduction in farm animals,* ed. E. S. E. Hafez, 247–383. Philadelphia: Lea and Febiger.

Jarman, M. V. 1976. Impala social behaviour: Birth behaviour. *E. Afr. Wildl. J.* 14:153–67.

Jarvis, J. U. M. 1981. Eusociality in a mammal: Cooperative breeding in naked mole rat colonies. *Science* 212:571–73.

———. 1991. Reproduction of naked mole-rats. In *The biology of the naked mole-rat,* ed. P. W. Sherman, J. U. M. Jarvis, and R. D. Alexander. Princeton, N.J.: Princeton University Press.

Jensen, G. D., and Bobbitt, R. A. 1967. Changing parturition time in monkeys *(Macaca nemestrina)* from night to day. *Lab. Anim. Care* 17 (4): 379–81.

Johnston, S. D. 1980a. False pregnancy. In *Current therapy in theriogenology,* ed. D. Morrow, 623–24. Philadelphia: W. B. Saunders.

———. 1980b. Spontaneous abortion. In *Current therapy in theriogenology,* ed. D. Morrow, 606–14. Philadelphia: W. B. Saunders.

Jones, J. E. T. 1966. Observations on parturition in the sow. *Br. Vet. J.* 122:420–26, 471–78.

Jordan, W. J. 1965. Retention of the placenta in some zoo animals. In *Proceedings of the Seventh International Symposium on Diseases of Zoo Animals,* 7–13. Zurich and Basel: German Academy of Science Institute for Comparative Pathology.

Josimovich, J. B. 1967. Protein hormones and gestation. In *Comparative aspects of reproductive failure*, ed. K. Benirschke, 170–93. Berlin: Springer-Verlag.

Kadam, K. M., and Swayaamprabha, M. S. 1980. Parturition in the slender loris *(Loris tardigradus lydekkerianus)*. *Primates* 21 (4): 567–71.

Kaplan, J. 1972. Differences in the mother-infant relations of squirrel monkeys housed in social and restricted environments. *Dev. Psychobiol.* 5:43–52.

Kasman, L. H., McCowan, B., and Lasley, B. L. 1985. Pregnancy detection in tapirs by direct urinary sulfate analysis. *Zoo Biol.* 4:301–6.

Kasman, L. H., Ramsay, E. C., and Lasley, B. L. 1986. Urinary steroid evaluations to monitor ovarian function in exotic ungulates. III: Estrone sulfate and pregnanediol-3-glucuronide excretion in the Indian rhinoceros *(Rhinoceros unicornis)*. *Zoo Biol.* 5:355–61.

Kemps, A., and Timmermans, P. 1982. Parturition behaviour in pluriparous Java-macaques *(Macaca fascicularis)*. *Primates* 23 (1): 75–88.

Kendrick, J. W., and Howarth, J. A. 1974. Reproductive infection. In *Reproduction in farm animals*, 3d ed., ed. E. S. E. Hafez, 394–406. Philadelphia: Lea and Febiger.

Kenny, A. M., Evans, R. L., and Dewsbury, D. A. 1977. Postimplantation pregnancy disruption in *Microtus ochrogaster, M. pennsylvanicus*, and *Peromyscus maniculatus*. *J. Reprod. Fertil.* 49:365–67.

Keverne, E. B., Levy, F., Poindron, P., and Lindsay, D. R. 1983. Vaginal stimulation: An important determinant of maternal bonding in sheep. *Science* 219:81–83.

Kiltie, R. A. 1982. Intraspecific variation in the mammalian gestation period. *J. Mammal.* 63 (4): 646–52.

King, N. W., and Chalifoux, L. V. 1986. Prenatal and neonatal pathology of captive nonhuman primates. In *Primates: The road to self-sustaining populations*, ed. K. Benirschke. New York: Springer-Verlag.

Kirkpatrick, J. F., Lasley, B. L., and Shideler, S. E. 1990. Urinary steroid evaluations to monitor ovarian function in exotic ungulates. VII. Urinary progesterone metabolites in the Equidae as assessed by immunoassay. *Zoo Biol.* 9:341–48.

Kirkpatrick, J. F., Shideler, S. E., Lasley, B. L., Turner, J. W., and Czekala, N. M. 1992. Field application of faecal steroid monitoring to free-ranging wildlife. In *The First International Symposium on Faecal Steroid Monitoring in Zoo Animals*, ed. E. Bamberg, 25–34. Rotterdam: Royal Rotterdam Zoological and Botanical Gardens.

Kleiman, D. G. 1972. Maternal behaviour of the green acouchi *(Myoprocta pratti Pocock)*, a South American caviomorph rodent. *Behaviour* 43:48–84.

———. 1975. Management of breeding programs in zoos. In *Research in zoos and aquariums*, 157–77. Washington, D.C.: National Academy of Sciences.

———. 1980. The sociobiology of captive propagation. In *Conservation biology: An evolutionary-ecological perspective*, ed. M. E. Soulé and B. A. Wilcox, 243–61. Sunderland, Mass.: Sinauer Associates.

———. 1985. Social and reproductive behavior of the giant panda *(Ailuropoda melanoleuca)*. *Bongo* (Berlin) 10, *Proceedings of the International Symposium on the Giant Panda*: 45–58.

Klopper, A. 1983. Specific pregnancy proteins. In *Current topics in experimental endocrinology*, vol. 4, *The endocrinology of pregnancy and parturition*, ed. L. Martini and V. H. T. James, 127–65. New York: Academic Press.

Klös, H. G., and Lang, E. M. 1982. *Handbook of zoo medicine: Diseases and treatment of wild animals in zoos, game parks,* circuses, and private collections. New York: Van Nostrand Reinhold.

Knobil, E., and Neill, J. D. 1988. *The physiology of reproduction.* Vol. 1. New York: Raven Press.

Kohrs, M. B., Harper, A. E., and Kerr, G. R. 1976. Effects of a low protein diet during pregnancy of the rhesus monkey. I. Reproductive efficiency. *Am. J. Clin. Nutr.* 29:1149–57.

Kranz, K. R., Xanten, W. A., and Lumpkin, S. 1983. Breeding history of the Dorcas gazelles at the National Zoological Park, 1961–1981. *Int. Zoo Yrbk.* 23:195–203.

Kristal, M. B. 1980. Placentophagia: A biobehavioral enigma. *Neurosci. Biobehav. Rev.* 4:141–50.

Labov, J. B., Huck, U. W., Vaswani, P., and Lisk, R. D. 1986. Sex ratio manipulation and decreased growth of male offspring of undernourished golden hamsters. *Behav. Ecol. Sociobiol.* 18: 241–49.

Lamming, G. E., ed. 1984. *Marshall's physiology of reproduction*, 4th ed., vol. 1, *Reproductive cycles of vertebrates*. Edinburgh: Churchill Livingstone.

Lang, E. M. 1967. The birth of an African elephant at Basle Zoo. *Int. Zoo Yrbk.* 7:154–57.

Langford, J. B. 1963. Breeding behavior of *Hapale jacchus* (common marmoset). *S. Afr. J. Sci.* 59:299–300.

Larkin, P., and Roberts, M. 1983. Reproduction in the ring-tailed mongoose. *Int. Zoo Yrbk.* 22:188–93.

Lasley, B. L. 1980. Endocrine research advances in breeding endangered species. *Int. Zoo Yrbk.* 20:166–70.

Lasley, B. L., Monfort, S. L., Hodges, J. K., and Czekala, N. M. 1981. Comparison of urinary estrogens during pregnancy in diverse species. In *Fetal endocrinology*, 111–26. New York: Academic Press.

Laurie, A. 1979. The ecology and behavior of the greater one-horned rhinoceros, *Rhinoceros unicornis*. Ph.D. thesis, Cambridge University.

———. 1982. Behavioral ecology of the greater one-horned rhinoceros, *Rhinoceros unicornis*. *J. Zool.* (Lond.) 196:307–41.

Law, G., and Boyle, H. 1983. Breeding the Geoffroy's cat at Glasgow Zoo. *Int. Zoo Yrbk.* 22:191–95.

Lawson, J. W., and Renouf, D. 1985. Parturition in the Atlantic harbor seal *Phoca vitulina concolor*. *J. Mammal.* 66 (2): 395–98.

Layne, J. N. 1968. Ontogeny. In *Biology of Peromyscus (Rodentia)*, ed. J. A. King, 148–53. Special Publication no. 2. Lawrence, Kans.: American Society of Mammalogists.

Lea, R. G., and Bolton, A. E. 1988. An immunological demonstration of a pregnancy-specific protein in the horse and its use in the serological detection of early pregnancy. *J. Reprod. Fertil.* 84: 431–36.

Le Boeuf, B. J., Whiting, R. J., and Gantt, F. 1972. Perinatal behavior of Northern elephant seal females and their young. *Behaviour* 43:121–56.

Leipold, H. W. 1980. Congenital defects of zoo and wild mammals: A review. In *The comparative pathology of zoo animals*, ed. R. J. Montali and G. Migaki, 457–70. Washington, D.C., Smithsonian Institution Press.

Lent, P. C. 1974. Mother-infant relationships in ungulates. In *The behaviour of ungulates and its relation to management*, vol. 1, ed. V. Geist and F. Walther, 14–55. Morges, Switzerland: IUCN.

Leslie, P. H., Venables, U. M., and Venables, L. S. V. 1952–1953. The fertility and population structure of the brown rat *(Rattus norvegicus)* in corn ricks and some other habitats. *Proc. Zool. Soc. Lond.* 122:187–238.

Levasseur, M. C. 1984. An involvement of estradiol at the time of implantation in placental mammals. *Anim. Reprod. Sci.* 7: 467–88.

Leyhausen, P., and Tonkin, B. 1966. Breeding the black-footed cat, *Felis nigripes,* in captivity. *Int. Zoo Yrbk.* 6:176–82.

Lindahl, I. L. 1972. Nutrition and feeding of goats. In *Digestive physiology and nutrition of ruminants,* vol. 3, *Practical nutrition,* ed. D. C. Church. Corvallis: D. C. Church, Department of Animal Science, Oregon State University.

Liskowski, L., and Wolfe, R. C. 1972. Urinary excretion of progesterone metabolites in pregnant rhesus monkeys. *Proc. Soc. Exp. Biol. Med.* 139:1123–26.

Lloyd, J. A., and Christian, J. J. 1969. Reproductive activity of individual females in three experimental freely growing populations of house mice *Mus musculus. J. Mammal.* 50:49–59.

Loskutoff, N. M., Ott, J. E., and Lasley, B. L. 1982. Urinary steroid evaluations to monitor ovarian function in exotic ungulates: I. Pregnanediol-3-glucuronide immunoreactivity in the okapi *(Okapia johnstoni). Zoo Biol.* 1:45–53.

Lott, D. F., and Galland, J. C. 1985. Parturition in American bison: Precocity and systematic variation in cow isolation. *Z. Tierpsychol.* 69:66–71.

Loudon, A. S. L., McNeilly, A. S., and Milne, J. A. 1983. Nutrition and lactational control of fertility in red deer. *Nature* 302:145–47.

Low, B. S. 1978. Environmental uncertainty and the parental strategies of marsupials and placentals. *Am. Nat.* 112:197–213.

Lowman, B. G., Hankley, M. S., Scott, N. A., Deas, D. W., and Hunter, E. A. 1981. Influence of time of feeding on time of parturition in beef cows. *Vet. Rec.* 109:557–59.

Lunn, S. F., and McNeilly, A. S. 1982. Failure of lactation to have a consistent effect on interbirth interval in the common marmoset, *Callithrix jacchus jacchus. Folia Primatol.* 37:99–105.

Maberry, A. B., and Ditterbrandt, M. 1971. Note on mummified foetuses in a Bactrian camel at Portland Zoo. *Int. Zoo Yrbk.* 11:126–27.

MacKinnon, J. 1971. The orang-utan in Sabah today. *Oryx* 11:141–91.

Mahoney, C. J., and Eisele, S. 1978. A programme of prepartum care for the rhesus monkey, *Macaca mulatta:* Results of the first two years of study. In *Recent advances in primatology,* vol. 2, *Conservation,* ed. D. J. Chivers and W. Lane-Petter, 265–67. New York: Academic Press.

Mainka, S. A., and Lothrop, C. D. 1980. Reproductive and hormonal changes during the estrous cycle and pregnancy in Asian elephants *(Elephas maximus). Zoo Biol.* 9:411–19.

Manocha, S. 1976. Abortion and cannibalism in squirrel monkeys associated with experimental protein deficiency during gestation. *Lab. Anim. Sci.* 26:649–50.

Manski, D. A. 1982. Herding and sexual advances toward females in late stages of pregnancy in addax antelope. *Der Zoologische Garten* 52:106–12.

Marlow, B. J. 1974. Ingestion of placenta in Hooker's sea lion. *N. Z. J. Mar. Freshwater Res.* 8 (1): 233–38.

Martal, J., Lacroix, M.-C., Loudes, C., Saunier, M., and Winterberger-Torres, S. 1979. Trophoblastin, an antiluteolytic protein present in early pregnancy in sheep. *J. Reprod. Fertil.* 56:63–73.

Martin, R. D. 1968. Reproduction and ontogeny in tree shrews with reference to their general behavior and taxonomic relationships. *Z. Tierpsychol.* 25:409–532.

Martinet, L. 1980. Oestrus behaviour, follicular growth, and ovulation during pregnancy in the hare *(Lepus europaeus). J. Reprod. Fertil.* 59:441–45.

Masters, A. M., and Markham, R. J. 1991. Assessing reproductive status in orang-utans by using urinary estrone. *Zoo Biol.* 10:197–207.

McBride, A. F., and Kritzler, H. 1951. Observations on pregnancy, parturition, and postnatal behavior in the bottle-nosed dolphin. *J. Mammal.* 32 (8): 251–66.

McCrane, M. P. 1966. Birth, behaviour, and development of a hand-reared two-toed sloth. *Int. Zoo Yrbk.* 6:153–163.

McNeilly, A. S., Martin, R. D., Hodges, J. K., and Smuts, G. L. 1983. Blood concentrations of gonadotrophins, prolactin, and gonadal steroids in males and in nonpregnant and pregnant female African elephants *(Loxodonta africana). J. Reprod. Fertil.* 67:113–20.

Medearis, D. N. 1967. Comparative aspects of reproductive failure induced in mammals by viruses. In *Comparative aspects of reproductive failure,* ed. K. Benirschke, 333–49. Berlin: Springer-Verlag.

Meder, A. 1986. Physical and activity changes associated with pregnancy in captive lowland gorillas *(Gorilla gorilla gorilla). Am. J. Primatol.* 11:111–16.

Messier, F., Desaulniers, D. M., Goff, A. K., Nault, R., Patenaude, R., and Crete, M. 1990. Caribou pregnancy diagnosis from immunoreactive progestins and estrogens excreted in feces. *J. Wildl. Mgmt.* 54:279–83.

Metcalfe, J., Stock, M. K., and Barron, D. H. 1988. Maternal physiology during gestation. In *The physiology of reproduction,* vol. 1, ed. E. Knobil and J. D. Neill, 2145–76. New York: Raven Press.

Mills, R. S. 1980. Parturition and social interaction among captive vampire bats *Desmodus rotundus. J. Mammal.* 61 (2): 336–37.

Mitchell, D. 1973. Detection of foetal circulation in the mare and cow by Doppler ultra-sound. *Vet. Rec.* 93:365–68.

Mitchell, G., and Brandt, E. M. 1975. Behavior of the female rhesus monkey during birth. In *The rhesus monkey,* vol. 2, ed. G. H. Bourne, 232–45. New York: Academic Press.

Mohnot, S. M., Agoramoorthy, G., and Pajpurohit, L. S. 1986. Male takeovers inducing abortions in Hanuman langur, *Presbytis entellus. Primate Rep.* 14:208.

Møller, O. M. 1973a. Progesterone concentrations in the peripheral plasma of the blue fox *(Alopex lagopus)* during pregnancy and the oestrous cycle. *J. Endocrinol.* 59:429–38.

———. 1973b. The progesterone concentrations in the peripheral plasma of the mink *(Mustela vison)* during pregnancy. *J. Endocrinol.* 56:121–32.

Monfort, S. L., Dahl, K. D., Czekala, N. M., Stevens, L., Bush, M., and Wildt, D. E. 1989. Monitoring ovarian function and pregnancy in the giant panda *(Ailuropoda melanoleuca)* by evaluating urinary bioactive FSH and steroid metabolites. *J. Reprod. Fertil.* 85:203–12.

Monfort, S. L., Hess, D. L., Shideler, S. E., Samuels, S. J., Hendrickx, A. G., and Lasley, B. L. 1987. Comparison of serum estradiol to urinary estrone conjugates in the rhesus macaque *(Macaca mulatta). Biol. Reprod.* 37:832–37.

Monfort, S. L., Wemmer, C., Kepler, T. H., Bush, M., Brown, J. L., and Wildt, D. E. 1990. Monitoring ovarian function in pregnancy in Eld's deer *(Cervus eldi)* by evaluating urinary steroid metabolite excretion. *J. Reprod. Fertil.* 88:271–81.

Morton, H., Hegh, V., and Clunie, G. J. A. 1976. Studies of the rosette inhibition test in pregnant mice: Evidence of immunosuppression? *Proc. R. Soc. Lond.* B 193:413–19.

Morton, H., Morton, D. J., and Ellendorf, F. 1983. The appearance and characteristics of early pregnancy factor in the pig. *J. Reprod. Fertil.* 68:437–46.

Morton, H., Nancarrow, C. D., Scaramuzzi, R. J., Evison, B. M., and Clunie, G. J. A. 1979. Detection of early pregnancy in sheep by the rosette inhibition test. *J. Reprod. Fertil.* 56:75–80.

Morton, H., Rolfe, B., and Cavanagh, A. 1982. Early pregnancy factor: Biology and clinical significance. In *Pregnancy proteins: Biology, chemistry, and clinical application,* ed. J. G. Grundzinskas, 391–405. Sydney: Academic Press.

Morton, H., Rolfe, B., Clunie, G. J. A., Anderson, M. J., and Morrison, J. 1977. An early pregnancy factor detected in human serum by the rosette inhibition test. *Lancet* 1:394–97.

Morton, H., Rolfe, B. E., McNeill, L., Clarke, P., Clarke, F. M., and Clunie, G. J. A. 1980. Early pregnancy factor: Tissues involved in its production in the mouse. *J. Reprod. Immunol.* 2: 73–82.

Mostl, E., Choi, H. S., Wurm, W., Ismail, M. N., and Bamberg, E. 1984. Pregnancy diagnosis in cows and heifers by determination of oestradiol-17β in faeces. *Br. Vet. J.* 140:287–91.

Mover, H., Ar, A., and Hellwing, S. 1989. Energetic costs of lactation with and without simultaneous pregnancy in the white-toothed shrew, *Crocidura russula monacha. Physiol. Zool.* 62 (4): 919–36.

Munro, C., and Stabenfeldt, G. 1984. Development of a microtitre plate enzyme immunoassay for the determination of progesterone. *J. Endocrinol.* 101:41–49.

Murata, Y., Martin, C. B. Jr., Ikennoue, T., and Petrie, R. N. 1978. Cardiac systolic time intervals in fetal monkeys: Preinjection period. *Am. J. Obstet. Gynecol.* 132:285–93.

Naaktgeboren, C. 1968. Some aspects of parturition in wild and domestic Canidae. *Int. Zoo Yrbk.* 8:8–13.

Nadler, R. D. 1974. Periparturitional behavior of a primiparous lowland gorilla. *Primates* 15 (1): 55–73.

Nadler, R. D., Graham, C. E., Collins, D. C., and Kling, O. R. 1981. Postpartum amenorrhea and behavior of great apes. In *Reproductive biology of the great apes*, ed. C. E. Graham, 69–81. New York: Academic Press.

Nancarrow, C. D., Wallace, A. L. C., and Grewal, A. S. 1981. The early pregnancy factor of sheep and cattle. *J. Reprod. Fertil. Suppl.* 30:191–99.

Nash, L. T. 1974. Parturition in a feral baboon. *Primates* 15 (2–3): 279–85.

Nelson, R. J., and Desjardins, C. 1987. Water availability affects reproduction in deer mice. *Biol. Reprod.* 37:257–60.

Newton, N., Foshee, D., and Newton, M. 1966. Parturient mice: Effect of environment on labor. *Science* 151:1560–61.

Nieuwenhuijsen, K., Lammers, A. J. J. C., de Neef, K. J., and Slob, A. K. 1985. Reproduction and social rank in female stumptail macaques *(Macaca arctoides). Int. J. Primatol.* 6:77–99.

Nishikawa, Y., and Hafez, E. S. E. 1974. Horses. In *Reproduction in farm animals*, ed. E. S. E. Hafez, 288–300. Philadelphia: Lea and Febiger.

Norment, C. J. 1980. Breech presentation of the fetus in a pregnant musk oxen. *J. Mammal.* 61 (4): 776–77.

Norris, M. L. 1985. Disruption of pairbonding induces pregnancy failure in newly mated Mongolian gerbils *(Meriones unguiculatus). J. Reprod. Fertil.* 75:43–47.

O'Brien, G. D., Queenan, J. T., and Campbell, S. 1981. Assessment of gestational age in the second trimester by real-time ultrasound measurement of femur length. *Am. J. Obstet. Gynecol.* 139: 540–45.

O'Donoghue, C. H. 1911. The growth changes in the mammary apparatus of *Dasyurus* and the relation of the corpora lutea thereto. *Q. J. Microsc. Sci.* 57:187–235.

Orozco, C., Perkins, T., and Clarke, F. M. 1986. Platelet activating factor induces the expression of early pregnancy factor activity in female mice. *J. Reprod. Fertil.* 78:549–55.

Oxberry, B. A. 1979. Female reproductive patterns in hibernating bats. *J. Reprod. Fertil.* 56:359–67.

Ozoga, J. J., and Verme, L. J. 1985. Determining fetus age in live white-tailed does by x-ray. *J. Wildl. Mgmt.* 49:372–74.

Paape, S. R., Schille, V. M., Seto, H., and Stabenfeldt, G. H. 1975. Luteal activity in the pseudopregnant cat. *Biol. Reprod.* 13: 470–74.

Packard, J. M., Babbitt, K. J., Hannon, P. G., and Grant, W. E. 1990. Infanticide in captive collared peccaries *(Tayassu tajacu). Zoo Biol.* 9:49–53.

Packard, J. M., Dowdell, D. M., Grant, W. E., Hellgren, E. C., and Lochmiller, R. L. 1987. Parturition and related behavior of the collared peccary *(Tayassu tajacu). J. Mammal.* 68 (3): 679–81.

Parr, R. A., Davis, I. F., Fairclough, R. J., and Miles, M. A. 1987. Overfeeding during early pregnancy reduces peripheral progesterone concentration and pregnancy rate in sheep. *J. Reprod. Fertil.* 80:317–20.

Patenaude, F., and Bovet, J. 1983. Parturition related behavior in wild American beavers *Castor canadensis. Z. Säugetierkunde* 48:136–45.

Paterson, J. F. 1967. The guinea pig or cavy *(Cavia porcellus).* In *The U.F.A.W. handbook on the care and management of laboratory animals.* Baltimore: Williams and Wilkins.

Paul-Murphy, J., Tell, L. A., Bravo, W., Fowler, M. E., and Lasley, B. L. 1991. Urinary steroid evaluations to monitor ovarian function in exotic ungulates: VIII. Correspondence of urinary and plasma steroids in the llama *(Lama glama)* during nonconceptive and conceptive cycles. *Zoo Biol.* 10:225–36.

Pearson, O. P., Koford, M. R., and Pearson, A. K. 1952. Reproduction in the lump-nosed bat *(Corynorhinus rafinesquei)* in California. *J. Mammal.* 33:273–320.

Pereira, M. E. 1983. Abortion following the immigration of an adult male baboon *(Papio cynocephalus). Am. J. Primatol.* 4: 93–98.

Perry, J. M., Izard, M. K., and Fail, P. A. 1992. Observations on reproduction, hormones, copulatory behavior, and neonatal mortality in captive *Lemur mongoz* (Mongoose lemur). *Zoo Biol.* 11:81–97.

Perry, J. S. 1945–1946. The reproduction of the brown rat (*Rattus norvegicus* Erxleben). *Proc. Zool. Soc. Lond.* B 115:19–46.

Perry, J. S. 1953. The reproduction of the African elephant, *Loxodonta africana. Phil. Trans. R. Soc. Lond.* B 237:93–149.

Peters, J. C. 1963. Ruptured uterus in a puma. In *Proceedings of the Fifth International Symposium on Diseases of Zoo Animals,* 80–81. Amsterdam: Royal Netherlands Veterinary Association.

Petter-Rousseaux, A. 1964. Reproductive physiology and behavior of the Lemuroidea. In *Evolutionary and genetic biology of the primates,* vol. 2, ed. J. Buettner-Janusch, 91–132. New York: Academic Press.

Phillippo, M., Swapp, G. H., Robinson, J. J., and Gill, J. C. 1971. The diagnosis of pregnancy and estimation of fetal numbers in sheep by laparoscopy. *J. Reprod. Fertil.* 27:129–32.

Phillips, I. R., and Grist, S. M. 1975. The use of transabdominal palpation to determine the course of pregnancy in the marmoset *(Callithrix jacchus). J. Reprod. Fertil.* 43:103–8.

Pianka, E. R. 1970. On r- and K-selection. *Am. Nat.* 104:292–97.

Piechocki, R. 1975. The cricetid rodents. In *Grzimek's animal life encyclopedia,* vol. 2, *Mammals,* ed. B. Grzimek, 296–406. New York: Van Nostrand Reinhold.

Plotka, E. D., Seal, U. S., Verme, L. J., and Ozoga, J. J. 1983. The adrenal gland in white-tailed deer: A significant source of progesterone. *J. Wildl. Mgmt.* 47:38–44.

Pond, W. G., and Houpt, K. A. 1978. *The biology of the pig.* Ithaca, N.Y.: Cornell University Press.

Poole, D. A., and Trefethen, J. B. 1978. The maintenance of wildlife populations. In *Wildlife and America,* ed. H. P. Brokaw, 339–49. Washington, D.C.: Council on Environmental Quality.

Poole, T. B., and Evans, R. B. 1982. Reproduction, infant survival, and productivity of a colony of common marmosets *(Callithrix jacchus jacchus). Lab. Anim.* 16:88–94.

Poole, W. E. 1975. Reproduction in two species of grey kangaroos, *Macropus giganteus* Shaw and *M. fuliginosus* (Desmarest). II. Gestation, parturition, and pouch life. *Aust. J. Zool.* 23:333–53.

Pope, A. L. 1972. Feeding and nutrition of ewes and rams. In *Di-

gestive physiology and nutrition of ruminants, vol. 3, *Practical nutrition,* ed. D. C. Church. Corvallis: D. C. Church, Department of Animal Sciences, Oregon State University.

Pournelle, G. H. 1952. Reproduction and early postnatal development of the cotton mouse, *Peromyscus gossypinus gossypinus. J. Mammal.* 33:1–20.

Pryce, C. R., and Döbeli, M. 1992. Coping with different metabolic strategies. In *The First International Symposium on Faecal Steroid Monitoring in Zoo Animals,* ed. E. Bamberg, 35–46. Royal Rotterdam Zoological and Botanical Gardens.

Pryor, W. J. 1980. Feeding sheep for high reproductive performance. In *Current therapy in theriogenology,* ed. D. Morrow, 882–88. Philadelphia: W. B. Saunders.

Rabb, G. B., Woolpy, J. H., and Ginsburg, B. E. 1967. Social relationships in a group of captive wolves. *Am. Zool.* 7:305–12.

Racey, P. A. 1973. Environmental factors affecting the length of gestation in heterothermic bats. *J. Reprod. Fertil. Suppl.* 19:175–89.

———. 1981. Environmental factors affecting the length of gestation in mammals. In *Environmental factors in mammalian reproduction,* ed. D. Gilmore and B. Cook, 197–213. Baltimore: University Park Press.

———. 1988. Reproductive assessment in bats. In *Ecological and behavioral methods for the study of bats,* ed. T. H. Kunz, 31–44. Washington, D.C.: Smithsonian Institution Press.

Ramakrishna, P. A. 1950. Parturition in certain Indian bats. *J. Mammal.* 31:274–78.

Ramsay, E. C., Kasman, L. H., and Lasley, B. L. 1987. Urinary steroid evaluations to monitor ovarian function in exotic ungulates: V. Estrogen and pregnanediol-3-glucuronide excretion in the black rhinoceros *(Diceros bicornis). Zoo Biol.* 6:275–82.

Randall, G. C. B. 1972. Observations on parturition in the sow. II. Factors influencing stillbirth and perinatal mortality. *Vet. Rec.* 90:183.

Randall, P., Taylor, P., and Banks, D. 1984. Pregnancy and stillbirth in a lowland gorilla. *Int. Zoo Yrbk.* 23:183–85.

Randolph, P. A., Randolph, J. C., Mattingly, K., and Foster, M. M. 1977. Energy costs of reproduction in the cotton rat, *Sigmodon hispidus. Ecology* 58:31–45.

Rasmussen, K. M., Thenen, S. W., and Hayes, K. C. 1980. Effect of folic acid supplementation on pregnancy in the squirrel monkey. *J. Med. Primatol.* 9:169–84.

Ravindranath, N., and Moudgal, N. 1987. Use of tamoxifen, an antioestrogen, in establishing a need for oestrogen in early pregnancy in the bonnet monkey *(Macaca radiata). J. Reprod. Fertil.* 81:327–36.

Renfree, M. B. 1981. Embryonic diapause in marsupials. *J. Reprod. Fertil. Suppl.* 29:67–78.

Renfree, M. B., and Calaby, J. M. 1981. Background to delayed implantation and embryonic diapause. *J. Reprod. Fertil. Suppl.* 29:1–9.

Richard, A. F. 1976. Preliminary observations on the birth and development of *Propithecus verreauxi* to the age of six months. *Primates* 17 (3): 357–66.

Richmond, M. E., and Conaway, C. H. 1969. Management, breeding, and reproductive performance of the vole, *Microtus ochrogaster,* in a laboratory colony. *Lab. Anim. Care* 19:80–87.

Riopelle, A. J., and Hale, P. A. 1975. Nutritional and environmental factors affecting gestation lengths in mammals. *Am. J. Clin. Nutr.* 28:1170–76.

Roberts, S. J., and Myhre, G. 1983. A review of twinning in horses and the possible therapeutic value of supplemental progesterone to prevent abortion of equine twin fetuses the latter half of the gestation period. *Cornell Vet* 73:257–64.

Robinson, H. G. N., Gribble, W. D., Page, W. G., and Jones, G. W. 1965. Notes on the birth of a reticulated giraffe. *Int. Zoo Yrbk.* 5:49–52.

Robson, J. M., Sullivan, F. M., and Wilson, C. 1971. The maintenance of pregnancy during the preimplantation period in mice treated with phenelzine derivatives. *J. Endocrinol.* 49:635–48.

Rollhauser, H. 1949. Superfetation in the mouse. *Anat. Rec.* 105:657–63.

Rood, J. P. 1980. Mating relations and breeding suppression in the dwarf mongoose. *Anim. Behav.* 28:143–50.

Rosenblatt, J. S., and Lehrman, D. S. 1963. Maternal behavior in the laboratory rat. In *Maternal behavior in mammals,* ed. H. L. Rheingold, 8–57. New York: John Wiley and Sons.

Roser, J. F., and Lofstedt, R. M. 1989. Urinary eCG patterns in the mare during pregnancy. *Theriogenology* 32:607–22.

Ross, S., Sawin, P. B., Zarrow, M. X., and Denenberg, V. H. 1963. Maternal behavior in the rabbit. In *Maternal behavior in mammals,* ed. H. L. Rheingold, 94–121. New York: John Wiley.

Rossdale, P. D. 1967. Clinical studies on the newborn thoroughbred foal. I. Perinatal behaviour. *Br. Vet. J.* 123:470–81.

Rothe, H. 1975. Influence of newborn marmoset's *(Callithrix jacchus)* behaviour on expression and efficiency of maternal and paternal care. *Proceedings of the Fifth International Congress of Primatology,* ed. S. Kondo, M. Kawai, A. Ehara and K. Kawamura, 315–20. Basel: S. Karger.

———. 1977. Parturition and related behavior in *Callithrix jacchus* (Ceboidea, Callitrichidae). In *The biology and conservation of the Callitrichidae,* ed. D. G. Kleiman, 193–206. Washington, D.C.: Smithsonian Institution Press.

Rowell, T. E. 1961. The family group in golden hamsters: Its formation and break-up. *Behaviour* 17:81–93.

Rowell, T. E., Hinde, R. A., and Spencer-Booth, Y. 1964. Aunt-infant interactions in captive rhesus monkeys. *Anim. Behav.* 12:219–26.

Ruppenthal, G. C., and Goodlin, B. L. 1982. Monitoring temperature of pigtail macaques *(Macaca nemestrina)* during pregnancy and parturition. *Am. J. Obstet. Gynecol.* 143:971–73.

Russell, A. J. F., Doney, J. M., and Reid, R. L. 1967. Energy requirements of the pregnant ewe. *J. Agric. Sci. Cambridge* 68:359–63.

Russell, E. M., and Giles, D. C. 1974. The effects of young in the pouch on pouch-cleaning in the tammar wallaby *Macropus eugenii* Desmarest (Marsupialia). *Behaviour* 51:19–37.

Ryan, K. J. 1973. Steroid hormones in mammalian pregnancy. In *Handbook of physiology,* sec. 7, *Endocrinology,* vol. 2, *Female reproductive system,* part 2, ed. R. O. Greep and E. B. Astwood, 285–93. Washington, D.C.: American Philosophical Society.

Sabbagha, R. 1975. Sonar biparietal growth standards in the rhesus monkey. *Am. J. Obstet. Gynecol.* 121:371–74.

Safar-Hermann, N., Ismail, M. N., Choi, H. S., Mostl, E., and Bamberg, E. 1987. Pregnancy diagnosis in zoo animals by estrogen determination in feces. *Zoo Biol.* 6:189–93.

Sasser, R. G., Ruder, C. A., Ivani, K. A., Butler, J. E., and Hamilton, W. C. 1986. Detection of pregnancy by radioimmunoassay of a novel pregnancy-specific protein in serum of cows and a profile of serum concentrations during gestation. *Biol. Reprod.* 35:936–42.

Savage, A., Ziegler, T. E., and Snowdon, C. T. 1988. Sociosexual development, pair bond formation, and mechanisms of fertility suppression in female cotton-top tamarins *(Saguinus oedipus oedipus). Am. J. Primatol.* 14:345–59.

Scanlon, P. F. 1972. An apparent case of superfoetation in a ewe. *Aust. Vet. J.* 48:74–79.

Schaller, G. B. 1977. *Mountain monarchs.* Chicago: University of Chicago Press.

Schmidt, P. M., Chakraborty, P. K., and Wildt, D. E. 1983. Ovarian activity, circulating hormones, and sexual behavior in the cat. II. Relationships during pregnancy, parturition, and lactation, and the postpartum estrus. *Biol. Reprod.* 28:657–71.

Schwagmeyer, P. L. 1979. The Bruce effect: An evaluation of male/female advantages. *Am. Nat.* 114:932–38.

Schwede, G., Hendrichs, H., and McShea, W. 1993. Social and spatial organization of female white-tailed deer, *Odocoileus virginianus*, during the fawning season. *Anim. Behav.* 45:1007–17.

Seal, U. S., Plotka, E. D., Packard, J. M., and Mech, L. D. 1979. Endocrine correlates of reproduction in the wolf. I. Serum progesterone, estradiol, and LH during the estrous cycle. *Biol. Reprod.* 21:1057–66.

Sever, Z., and Mendelssohn, H. 1988. Copulation as a possible mechanism to maintain monogamy in porcupines, *Hystrix indica. Anim. Behav.* 36:1541–42.

Severaid, J. H. 1950. The gestation period of the pika, *Ochotona princeps. J. Mammal.* 31:356–57.

Sharman, G. B. 1963. Delayed implantation in marsupials. In *Delayed implantation*, ed. A. C. Enders, 3–14. Chicago: University of Chicago Press.

Sharman, G. B., Calaby, J. H., and Poole, W. E. 1966. Patterns of reproduction in female diprotodont marsupials. *Symp. Zool. Soc. Lond.* 15:205–32.

Sherman, H. B. 1930. Birth of the young *Myotis austroriparius. J. Mammal.* 11:495–503.

Shideler, S. E., Czekala, N. M., Benirschke, K., and Lasley, B. L. 1983a. Urinary estrogens during pregnancy in the ruffed lemur *(Lemur variegatus). Biol. Reprod.* 28:963–69.

Shideler, S. E., Czekala, N. M., Kasman, L. H., Lindburg, D. G., and Lasley, B. L. 1983b. Monitoring ovulation and implantation in the lion-tailed macaque *(Macaca silenus)* through urinary estrone conjugate evaluations. *Biol. Reprod.* 29:905–11.

Shille, V. M., and Gontara, K. J. 1985. The use of ultrasonography for pregnancy diagnosis in the bitch. *J. Am. Vet. Med. Assoc.* 187:1021–25.

Shille, V. M., Wing, A. E., Lasley, B. L., and Banks, J. A. 1984. Excretion of radiolabelled estradiol in the cat (*Felis catus* L.): A preliminary report. *Zoo Biol.* 3:201–9.

Shimizu, K. 1988. Ultrasonic assessment of pregnancy and fetal development in three species of macaque. *J. Med. Primatol.* 17:247–56.

Signoret, J. P., Baldwin, B. A., Fraser, D., and Hafez, E. S. E. 1975. The behaviour of swine. In *The behaviour of domestic animals*, ed. E. S. E. Hafez, 295–329. London: Bailliere-Tindall.

Silk, J. B. 1980. Kidnapping and female competition among captive bonnet macaques. *Primates* 21:100–110.

———. 1986. Eating for two: Behavioral and environmental correlates of gestation length among free-ranging baboons *(Papio cynocephalus). Int. J. Primatol.* 7:583–602.

Simpson, M. J. A., Simpson, A. F., Hooley, J., and Zunz, M. 1981. Infant-related influences on birth intervals in rhesus monkeys. *Nature* 290:49–51.

Sist, M. D., Youngblood, M. A., and Williams, J. F. 1987. Using fecal estrone sulfate concentrations to detect pregnancies. *Vet. Med.* 14:1036–43.

Skinner, J. D., and van Zyl, J. N. M. 1969. Reproductive performance of the common eland, *Taurotragus oryx*, in two environments. *J. Reprod. Fertil. Suppl.* 6:319–22.

Sloss, V., and Duffy, J. H. 1980. *Handbook of bovine obstetrics.* Baltimore: Williams and Wilkins.

Smith, J. A. 1982. Cesarean section in a zebra. In *Proceedings of the Annual Meeting of the American Association of Zoo Veterinarians*, ed. M. E. Fowler, 71–73. New Orleans: American Association of Zoo Veterinarians.

Smith, J. D. 1967. Breed differences in the duration of gestation in sheep. *Aust. Vet. J.* 43:63–64.

Smith, R. B., and Lindzey, F. G. 1982. Use of ultrasound for detecting pregnancy in mule deer. *J. Wildl. Mgmt.* 46 (4): 1089–92.

Sokolowski, J. H. 1980. Normal events of gestation in the bitch and methods of pregnancy diagnosis. In *Current therapy in theriogenology*, ed. D. A. Morrow, 590–95. Philadelphia: W. B. Saunders.

Soma, H. 1990. Placental implications for pregnancy complications in the chimpanzee *(Pan troglodytes). Zoo Biol.* 9:141–47.

Spencer-Booth, Y. 1970. The relationships between mammalian young and conspecifics other than mothers and peers. In *Advances in the study of behavior*, vol. 3, ed. D. S. Lehrman and E. Shaw, 120–94. New York: Academic Press.

Squires, E. L., Douglas, R. N., Steffenhagen, W. P., and Ginther, O. J. 1974. Ovarian changes during the estrous cycle and pregnancy in mares. *J. Anim. Sci.* 38:330–38.

Stewart, F., and Tyndale-Biscoe, C. H. 1983. Pregnancy and parturition in marsupials. In *Current topics in experimental endocrinology*, vol. 4, *The endocrinology of pregnancy and parturition*, ed. L. Martini and V. H. T. James, 1–33. New York: Academic Press.

Stewart, K. J. 1988. Suckling and lactational anoestrus in wild gorillas *(Gorilla gorilla). J. Reprod. Fertil.* 83:627–34.

Stewart, R. E. A., Lightfoot, N., and Innes, S. 1981. Parturition in harp seals. *J. Mammal.* 62 (4): 845–50.

Stirling, I. 1969. Birth of a Weddell seal pup. *J. Mammal.* 50 (1): 155–56.

Stodart, E., and Myers, K. 1966. The effect of different foods on confined populations of wild rabbits, *Oryctolagus cuniculus* (L.). *CSIRO Wildl. Res.* 11:111–18.

Stoddart, D. M., and Braithewaite, R. W. 1979. A strategy for utilization of regenerating heathland habitat by the brown bandicoot *(Isoodon obesulus*, Marsupialia: Peramelidae). *J. Anim. Ecol.* 48:168–79.

Sturman, J. A., Gargano, A. D., Messing, J. M., and Imaki, H. 1986. Feline maternal taurine deficiency: Effect on mother and offspring. *J. Nutr.* 116:655–67.

Styles, T. E. 1982. The birth and early development of an African elephant at the Metro Toronto Zoo. *Int. Zoo Yrbk.* 22:215–17.

Sueoka, K., Dharmarajan, A. M., Michael, E., Atlas, S. J., and Wallach, E. E. 1988. Detection of early pregnancy factor (EPF) using the rabbit ovary and oviduct profused in vitro. *J. Reprod. Fertil.* 84:325–31.

Tamsitt, J. R., and Valdivieso, D. 1966. Parturition in the red fig-eating bat, *Stenoderma rufum. J. Mammal.* 47 (2): 352–53.

Tanaka, T., Tokuda, K., and Kotera, S. 1970. Effects of infant loss on the interbirth interval of Japanese monkeys. *Primates* 11:113–17.

Tardif, S. D., Richter, C. B., and Carson, R. L. 1984. Effects of sibling rearing experience on future reproductive success in two species of Callitrichidae. *Am. J. Primatol.* 6:377–80.

Tavolga, M. C., and Essapian, F. S. 1957. The behavior of the bottle-nosed dolphin *(Tursiops truncatus)*: Mating, pregnancy, parturition, and mother-infant behavior. *Zoologica* 42:11–31.

Terrill, C. E. 1974. Reproduction in sheep. In *Reproduction in farm animals*, 3d ed., ed. E. S. E. Hafez, 265–74. Philadelphia: Lea and Febiger.

Thatcher, W. W. 1974. Effects of season, climate, and temperature on reproduction and lactation. *J. Dairy Sci.* 57:360–68.

Thorne, E. T., Dean, R. E., and Hepworth, W. G. 1976. Nutrition during gestation in relation to successful reproduction. *J. Wildl. Mgmt.* 40:330–35.

Thurman, J. D., Morton, R. J., and Stair, E. L. 1983. Septic abortion caused by *Salmonella heidelberg* in a white-handed gibbon. *J. Am. Vet. Med. Assoc.* 183 (11): 1325–26.

Tomasgard, G., and Benjaminsen, E. 1975. Plasma progesterone in mares showing estrus during pregnancy. *Nord. Vet. Med.* 27:570–74.

Too, K., Kawata, K., Fukui, Y., Sato, K., Kagota, K., and Kawabe,

K. 1974. Studies on pregnancy diagnosis in domestic animals by an ultrasonic Doppler method. I. Pregnancy diagnosis in the pig and fetal heart rate changes during pregnancy. *Jpn. J. Vet. Res.* 22:61–71.

Townsend, T. W., and Baily, E. D. 1975. Parturitional, early maternal, and neonatal behavior in penned white-tailed deer: *J. Mammal.* 56 (2): 347–62.

Trivers, R. L. 1972. Parental investment and sexual selection. In *Sexual selection and the descent of man,* ed. B. Campbell, 136–79. Chicago: Aldine.

Trujano, M., and Wrathall, A. E. 1985. Developmental abnormalities in cultured early porcine embryos induced by hypothermia. *Br. Vet. J.* 141:603–10.

Tullner, W. W., and Gray, C. W. 1968. Chorionic gonadotropin excretion during pregnancy in a gorilla. *Proc. Soc. Exp. Biol. Med.* 128:954–56.

Tutin, C. E. G. 1980. Reproductive behavior of wild chimpanzees in the Gombe National Park, Tanzania. *J. Reprod. Fertil. Suppl.* 28:43–57.

Tyndale-Biscoe, C. H. 1968. Reproduction and postnatal development in the marsupial, *Bettongia lesueuri* (Quoy and Gaimard). *Aust. J. Zool.* 16:577–602.

———. 1973. *Life of marsupials.* Melbourne: Edward Arnold (Australia).

———. 1984. Mammals: Marsupials. In *Marshall's physiology of reproduction,* 4th ed., vol. 1, *Reproductive cycles of vertebrates,* 386–454. Edinburgh: Churchill Livingstone.

Tyndale-Biscoe, C. H., Hinds, L. A., and Horn, C. A. 1988. Fetal role in the control of parturition in the tammar, *Macropus eugenii. J. Reprod. Fertil.* 82:419–28.

Uchida, T. A., Inoue, C., and Kimura, K. 1984. Effects of elevated temperatures on the embryonic development and corpus luteum activity in the Japanese long-fingered bat, *Miniopterus schreibersi fuliginosus. J. Reprod. Fertil.* 71:439–44.

Ullrich, W. 1970. Geburt und natürliche Geburtshilfe beim Orangutan. *Der Zoologische Garten* 39:284–89.

van der Werff ten Bosch, J. J. 1982. The physiology of reproduction of the orangutan. In *The orangutan: Its biology and conservation,* ed. L. E. M. de Boer, 201–14. The Hague: W. Junk.

Van Niekerk, C. N. 1965. Early embryonic resorption in mares. *J. S. Afr. Vet. Med. Assoc.* 36:61–69.

Van Tienhoven, A. 1983. *Reproductive physiology of vertebrates.* 2d ed. Ithaca, N.Y.: Cornell University Press.

Verme, L. J., Fay, L. D., and Mostosky, U. V. 1962. Use of x-ray in determining pregnancy in deer. *J. Wildl. Mgmt.* 45:972–75.

Verme, L. J., and Ullrey, D. E. 1984. Physiology and nutrition. In *White-tailed deer: Ecology and management,* ed. L. K. Halls, 91–118. Harrisburg, Pa.: Stackpole Books.

Vogel, P. 1981. Occurrence of delayed implantation in insectivores. *J. Reprod. Fertil. Suppl.* 29:51–60.

Wallach, J. D., and Boever, W. S. 1983. *Diseases of exotic animals: Medical and surgical management.* Philadelphia: W. B. Saunders.

Wallis, J., and Lemmon, W. B. 1986. Social behavior and genital swelling in pregnant chimpanzees *(Pan troglodytes). Am. J. Primatol.* 10:171–83.

Walsh, S. W., Wolf, R. C., Meyer, R. K., Aubert, M. L., and Friesen, H. 1977. Chorionic gonadotropin, chorionic somatomammotropin, and prolactin in the uterine vein and peripheral plasma of pregnant rhesus monkeys. *Endocrinology* 100: 851–55.

Waring, G. H. 1983. *Horse behavior.* Park Ridge, N.J.: Noyes.

Wasser, S. K., ed. 1983. *Social behavior of female vertebrates.* New York: Academic Press.

Wasser, S. K., and Barash, D. P. 1983. Reproductive suppression among female mammals: Implications for biomedicine and sexual selection theory. *Q. Rev. Biol.* 58:513–38.

Wasser, S. K., Monfort, S. L., and Wildt, D. E. 1991. Rapid extraction of faecal steroids for measuring reproductive cyclicity and early pregnancy in free-ranging yellow baboons *(Papio cynocephalus cynocephalus). J. Reprod. Fertil.* 92:415–23.

Wasser, S. K., Risler, L., and Steiner, R. A. 1988. Excreted steroids in primate feces over the menstrual cycle and pregnancy. *Biol. Reprod.* 39:862–72.

Wasser, S. K., and Starling, A. K. 1988. Proximate and ultimate causes of reproductive suppression among female yellow baboons at Mikumi National Park, Tanzania. *Am. J. Primatol.* 16: 97–121.

Weir, B. J. 1973. The induction of ovulation and oestrus in the chinchilla. *J. Reprod. Fertil.* 33:61–68.

———. 1974. Reproductive characteristics of hystricomorph rodents. *Symp. Zool. Soc. Lond.* 34:265–301.

Weiss, G. 1984. Relaxin. *Annu. Rev. Physiol.* 46:43–52.

Wemmer, C., and Murtaugh, J. 1981. Copulatory behavior and reproduction in the binturong, *Arctictis binturong. J. Mammal.* 62:342–52.

Wendorf, G. L., Lawyer, M. S., and First, N. L. 1983. Role of the adrenals in the maintenance of pregnancy in cows. *J. Reprod. Fertil.* 68:281–87.

West, C. C., and Redshaw, M. E. 1987. Maternal behaviour in the Rodriguez fruit bat, *Pteropus rodricensis. Dodo* 24:68–81.

Wide, L., Hobson, B., and Wide, M. 1980. Chorionic gonadotropin in rodents. In *Chorionic gonadotropin,* ed. S. J. Siegal, 1–15. New York: Plenum Press.

Wildt, D. E. 1980. Laparoscopy in the dog and cat. In *Animal laparoscopy,* ed. R. M. Harrison and D. E. Wildt, 31–72. Baltimore: Williams and Wilkins.

Wildt, D. E., Morcom, C. B., and Dukelow, W. R. 1975. Laparoscopic pregnancy diagnosis and uterine fluid recovery in swine. *J. Reprod. Fertil.* 44:301–4.

Williams, R. F. 1986. The interbirth interval in primates: Effects of pregnancy and nursing. In *Primates: The road to self-sustaining populations,* ed. K. Benirschke, 375–85. New York: Springer-Verlag.

Williams, T. D., Mattison, J. A., and Ames, J. A. 1980. Twinning in a California sea otter. *J. Mammal.* 61 (3): 575–76.

Wimsatt, W. A. 1960. An analysis of parturition in Chiroptera, including new observations on *Myotis l. lucifugus. J. Mammal.* 41 (2): 183–200.

———. 1975. Some comparative aspects of implantation. *Biol. Reprod.* 12:1–40.

Wise, D. A. 1974. Aggression in the female golden hamster: Effects of reproductive state and social isolation. *Horm. Behav.* 5: 235–50.

Wislocki, G. B., and Streeter, G. L. 1938. On the placentation of the macaque *(Macaca mulatta)* from the time of implantation until formation of the definitive placenta. *Carnegie Contrib. Embryol.* 27:1–66.

Wolfheim, J. H., Jensen, G. D., and Bobbitt, R. A. 1970. Effects of group environment on the mother-infant relationship in pigtailed monkeys *(Macaca nemestrina). Primates* 11:119–24.

Wood, A. K., Short, R. E., Darling, A., Dusek, G. L., Sasser, R. G., and Ruder, C. A. 1986. Serum assays for detecting pregnancy in mule and white-tailed deer. *J. Wildl. Mgmt.* 50:684–87.

Zarrow, M. X., Denenberg, V. H., and Sachs, B. W. 1972. Hormones and maternal behavior in mammals. In *Hormones and behavior,* ed. S. Levine, 105–34. New York: Academic Press.

Zemjanis, R. 1974. Pregnancy diagnosis. In *Reproduction in farm animals,* 3d ed., ed. E. S. E. Hafez, 437–43. Philadelphia: Lea and Febiger.

42

Parental Care in Captive Mammals

ANDREW J. BAKER, ANNE M. BAKER, AND KATERINA V. THOMPSON

THE ADAPTIVE SIGNIFICANCE
OF PARENTAL CARE

All mammal infants must receive some care in order to survive. How much care an infant receives, and from whom, is largely determined by (1) the certainty and degree of relatedness between the infant and the caregiver and (2) the cost to the caregiver relative to the benefit to the recipient (Hamilton 1964). In turn, these factors are influenced by a multitude of environmental factors. Ultimately, the seasonal and spatial distribution of resources and the presence or absence of predators affect the social organization and reproductive strategy of every species (Packer 1986; Wrangham and Rubenstein 1986; Alexander 1974). Clutton-Brock (1991) provides an excellent review of the environmental and social factors influencing the evolution of parental care.

Maternal care is universal among the mammals. All mothers provide milk as nourishment for their young, but other maternal care behaviors, such as nest building, grooming, and carrying, vary greatly among species. Also highly variable are the extent of postweaning care and the participation of males and other group members in the care of young. For example, tree shrew, *Tupaia* spp., mothers leave their young in rudimentary nests, visiting them only infrequently to nurse (Martin 1975a), while callitrichid young are cared for extensively by their mother, father, and siblings (Hoage 1977; Box 1975; Epple 1975).

The extent to which the male assists the female can often be predicted from the species' mating system (see Berger and Stevens, chap. 33, this volume). The more certain a male is of his paternity, the more likely he is to invest in caring for the young of a particular female (Zeveloff and Boyce 1980; Trivers 1972) rather than jeopardizing the survival of his offspring by abandoning the female and seeking new mates.

Males in many monogamous species, having a high certainty of paternity, provide high levels of parental care. In some instances they assume the primary responsibility for all forms of care except nursing. For species that live in polygynous social groups, the more males there are in the group, the less likely that any one male can control the mating opportunities of females within the group. Therefore females often mate with more than one male, and a male's certainty of paternity for the young of any particular female is low. However, because a male potentially has fathered some young in the group, he may provide indirect care for all young in the group (Kleiman and Malcolm 1981) instead of caring directly for any one female's young. Males of solitary species are with a female for only a brief time during mating, have little ability to control her access to other males, and are not around to provide care when young are born. Thus, in the wild, there is almost no paternal care in solitary species.

The degree and duration of parental care are closely related to how developed the young are at birth (see Thompson, chap. 34, this volume). Details of the general patterns of parental care found in individual species are given by Hayssen, Van Tienhoven, and Van Tienhoven (1993), Elwood (1983, rodents only) and Eisenberg (1981).

Behaviors that confer reproductive or survival advantages in one environment may not do so in another, and this may result in great diversity in parental care among closely related species. This diversity underscores the need for managers to be familiar with the natural social structure of each species that they manage, to evaluate behaviors seen in captivity in the framework in which they evolved, and to adjust management practices accordingly.

GENERAL PATTERNS OF PARENTAL CARE

Maternal Care

In most mammalian species mothers are the primary caregivers (Clutton-Brock 1991). Mothers build nests, nurse and clean young, huddle with young to provide warmth,

At the time of writing, Anne M. Baker was with the Chicago Zoological Park in Brookfield, Illinois and Katerina V. Thompson was with the Department of Zoological Research, National Zoological Park, Smithsonian Institution, Washington, D.C.

and transport and protect young. In a number of species mothers continue to provide care far beyond the time of weaning. They may provision weaned young with food, protect them from conspecifics, and defend them against predators. For animals that live in stable social groups, mothers may play an important role in establishing their offspring's social position in the group (Cheney 1977).

Although many of the obvious needs of infants can be met in captivity when mothers are absent, there are subtle, sometimes overlooked, components of maternal care that play important roles in producing healthy infants and, ultimately, healthy adults. There is evidence that mother-infant interactions regulate biochemical and physiological sequences that are important in growth and development (Levine 1982; Butler, Suskind, and Schonberg 1978; Kuhn, Butler, and Schonberg 1978); for example, experimental studies on rats have shown that early separation from the mother results in hyperactive young (Hofer 1981).

In an energetic sense maternal care begins at the time of conception. Pregnancy and lactation are energetically demanding, and adequate nutrition is especially important during pregnancy (Oftedal 1985; Sadleir 1969). Isolating pregnant females from stress is important not only for maintaining the pregnancy but also for the production of healthy offspring.

Shortly before birth, distinct hormonal changes occur. In most mammals progesterone levels begin to fall several days prior to parturition, and levels of estradiol and prolactin begin to rise (Rosenblatt and Siegel 1981). These changes may trigger nest building, and they eventually initiate parturition and lactation. They also stimulate maternal behavior by "priming" the pregnant female to respond to the appearance of young. In many mammals this priming results in an increase in female aggression toward anything other than young. The defense of young is common to almost all mothers; keepers and other individuals dealing with mothers and newborns should exercise special caution. Even normally tractable females can become unpredictable when an infant is present.

Evidence from rodents suggests that the factors that maintain maternal behavior following parturition are very different from those that initiate it (Rosenblatt 1967). While the onset of maternal care is governed by endocrine processes, its maintenance is dependent on sensory stimulation provided by the young. The time of transition between these two phases roughly corresponds to the time of birth. Females show rapid postpartum declines in the hormones that stimulated maternal behavior prior to and during parturition. Levels of estrogen drop sharply, except during the postpartum estrus found in some species, and remain low throughout lactation. Progesterone levels remain low, while prolactin levels remain high (Rosenblatt and Siegel 1981). The stimuli provided by young play a dominant role in postpartum maternal behavior. The presence of the young immediately postpartum appears to be crucial in maintaining maternal responsiveness to young (Harper 1981).

In most terrestrial placental mammals, mothers lick the neonate clean (Ewer 1968). Licking dries the neonate's coat, thus aiding in thermoregulation, and provides tactile stimulation that initiates the onset of breathing (Ewer 1968), urination, and defecation (see Hutchins, Thomas, and Asa, chap. 41, this volume). For ungulates, it has been proposed that the licking increases neuroexcitability, thereby promoting more rapid motor development of young (Lent 1974).

One of the most important functions of licking may be to provide the mother with gustatory and olfactory input that will aid her in identifying her infant, and in some instances reduce her aggressiveness toward young (Hepper 1987; Levy and Poindron 1987). Maternal-offspring recognition has been documented in a variety of species, including rodents (Elwood and McCauley 1983), bats (Yalden and Morris 1975; Kleiman 1969), pinnipeds (Marlow 1975), and ungulates (Carson and Wood-Gush 1983; Lent 1974). It generally develops within hours or days of parturition, during a period of intensive mother-infant contact. In social species, parturient females may seek seclusion from conspecifics and may remain apart from the social group for several days. In ungulates, the postpartum mother-infant contact period ranges from 40 minutes in Grant's gazelle, *Gazella granti*, to 20 hours in kudu, *Tragelaphus* spp. This period of intensive contact appears to be essential for mother-infant bonding (Pohle 1987; Spinage 1986; Levy and Poindron 1987; Dagg and Foster 1976). Once this bond has formed, a mother will usually drive strange young away (Lent 1974). In captivity, failure to isolate females that normally would leave the herd may result in attempted adoption or nursing interference by other females (Read and Frueh 1980; Lent 1974). Prolonged intervention between mother and young may prevent the mother-infant bond from forming and ultimately result in female rejection of young.

Nursing begins any time from minutes to hours after birth, depending on the species. In species with multiple offspring per birth, the female sometimes will not suckle the first infant until the entire litter has been born, even though the interval may be a long one.

Because of their high surface area-to-body weight ratio, many neonates do not have sufficient energy to maintain a constant body temperature and require an external source of heat. In most altricial mammals, and some precocial ones, frequent contact with one or both parents provides this heat. The prolonged contact necessary for thermoregulation may also function in establishing the bond between mother and infant. Contact with other young in the nest may serve to conserve body heat when parents are absent.

The initially strong bond between a mother and her infant weakens as the infant matures and begins to take an active interest in its surroundings. To a great degree the freedom an infant has to explore its surroundings is dependent on its mother's willingness to allow it this freedom. A mother's attitude toward her infant can be affected by both her parity and, in social species, her social rank (Altmann 1980). In general, primiparous mothers, once they have accepted and begun to take care of an infant, are much more protective of that infant than are multiparous mothers (Amundin 1986; Shoemaker 1979; Carlier and Noirot 1965). Primate mothers of low social rank are more restrictive of their infants than are mothers of high social rank, possibly because they have little control over how an interaction between their infant and other members of the social group will progress (Altmann 1980).

Paternal Care

With the exception of lactation, all infant care behaviors characteristic of mothers can also be exhibited by fathers. Kleiman and Malcolm (1981) have defined direct and indirect forms of paternal care. Direct care includes those behaviors that have an immediate physical influence on young: feeding, carrying, grooming, protecting, and playing with infants. Indirect care consists of acts performed in the absence of young that may nevertheless increase their survivorship: acquisition, defense, and maintenance of resources; shelter construction and maintenance; sentinel and other antipredator behavior; and provisioning of pregnant or lactating females.

While direct care by mothers is universal among mammals, direct paternal care is rare, occurring regularly in fewer than 5% of mammalian species (Kleiman and Malcolm 1981). In most orders, direct male care is unreported or reported for only a few species (Kleiman and Malcolm 1981). The major exceptions occur among the primates and carnivores. In the callitrichids and in some cebids, such as titi monkeys (*Callicebus* spp.) and owl monkeys (*Aotus* spp.), fathers play a major role in carrying infants (Epple 1975; Cebul and Epple 1984; Robinson, Wright, and Kinzey 1986; see Whitten 1986 for a review of the primates). In a number of carnivore species, fathers are actively involved in guarding the young and providing food (dwarf mongoose, *Helogale parvula*: Rood 1986; jackals, *Canis mesomelas* and *C. aureus*: Moehlman 1986; African wild dog, *Lycaon pictus*: Malcolm and Marten 1982; bush dog, *Speothos venaticus*: Jantschke 1973; bat-eared fox, *Otocyon megalotis*: Malcolm 1986; see Malcolm 1985 for review of the canids). Direct paternal care is also reported from some rodent genera (*Mus, Rattus, Microtus, Baiomys, Onychomys, Peromyscus, Meriones, Dicrostonyx*: Elwood 1983).

The characteristic low level or absence of male parental care among mammals is largely attributed to two factors. First, male mammals can generally achieve greater reproductive success by maximizing the number of offspring they father (i.e., maximizing their number of effective copulations) than they can by increasing investment in specific offspring. Therefore, males expend energy on territory acquisition and defense, mate acquisition, and mate defense rather than on direct care of infants. Second, direct male care, especially of precocial young, may have a negligible effect on offspring survivorship. These two factors are not independent: males may benefit by maximizing the number of offspring they sire precisely because investment in the care of specific offspring has little or no effect on their survival.

Species with extensive paternal care of infants exhibit several common characteristics. First, most are monogamous. Monogamy has several implications relevant to paternal investment in infants. The very fact that a male remains with only one female likely reflects some ecological limitation on his ability to be effectively polygynous (i.e., resource distribution prevents his defense of sufficient space to support more than one female). Also, certainty of paternity is likely to be higher in a monogamous mating system than in mating systems in which males cannot monitor female sexual behavior (e.g., solitary or multimale polygynous systems: for further discussion see Kleiman 1977; Werren, Gross, and Shine 1980; Wittenberger and Tilson 1980). Second, most species exhibiting extensive direct male care bear altricial young, so male involvement in infant care can have a substantial effect on infant and maternal well-being. Among most primates, infants must be transported, and males can contribute by sharing this duty. For some carnivores, food comes in large, difficult, and sometimes dangerous units, so males can contribute by providing food. Monogamous species bearing relatively precocial young (e.g., elephant shrews, *Elephantulus rufescens* and *Rhynchocyon chrysopygus*: Rathbun 1979; dik-dik, *Madoqua* spp.: K. R. Kranz, pers. comm.) tend not to exhibit extensive paternal care.

Care by Other Group Members

In many social mammals, individuals other than parents also care for neonates and infants (alloparenting: Spencer-Booth 1970). Alloparenting has been reported in callitrichid primates (Epple 1975; Box 1977; Hoage 1977), colobine primates (Hrdy 1977; McKenna 1981), elephants (McKay 1973; Lee 1987), a number of canids (Mech 1970; Malcolm and Marten 1982; Moehlman 1986), and some bats (McCracken 1984), rodents (Sherman 1980; Hoogland 1981), cetaceans (Caldwell and Caldwell 1977), non-callitrichid/colobine primates (Fairbanks 1990), and non-canid carnivores (Owens and Owens 1984; Rasa 1977; Rood 1978; Packer and Pusey 1983). Alloparenting is less characteristic or unreported among monotremes, marsupials, edentates, elephant shrews, tree shrews, lagomorphs, insectivores, most rodent groups, pinnipeds, and ungulates (for reviews see Riedman 1982; Gittleman 1985).

The most extensive alloparenting is observed in species whose social organization consists of a single breeding pair and their offspring from one or more previous litters (callitrichids: Box 1977; Epple 1975; Hoage 1977; dwarf mongoose: Rasa 1977; Rood 1978; African wild dog: Malcolm and Marten 1982). In these species, nonreproductive males and females ("helpers": Emlen 1984) may participate in all infant care behaviors shown by mothers, including carrying, guarding, food sharing, and nursing.

In species characterized by groups containing multiple breeding females, reproductive individuals may also act as alloparents. In these species, alloparenting is typically a female activity (e.g., African elephants, *Loxodonta africana*: Lee 1987; vervet monkeys, *Chlorocebus (=Cercopithecus) aethiops*: Fairbanks 1990) and is less extensive than in the callitrichids and the previously mentioned carnivores, but may involve communal nursing (e.g., some bats: McCracken 1984; lions, *Panthera leo*: Schaller 1972; Packer and Pusey 1983).

There are several reasons why nonparents might care for young. First, alloparents often are related to the young with which they interact; by caring for a younger relative, the alloparent may increase the probability that genes it shares with the infant will be passed on to future generations (Hamilton 1964). Second, alloparenting may provide "practice" that will increase the alloparent's chances of successfully rearing its own young in the future (Spencer-Booth 1970). Third, individuals may care for young from whom (or from whose mother) they may receive help in the future (reciprocal altruism: Trivers 1972). Finally, in some colonial species, nursing of nonoffspring young may reflect the difficulties a mother has in locating and recognizing her own offspring (e.g., bats: McCracken 1984; northern elephant seals, *Mirounga angustirostris:* Riedman 1982; Riedman and Le Boeuf 1982).

Apparent care behaviors are not necessarily beneficial to young. Inexperienced "helpers" may handle young incorrectly. Other behaviors may be deliberately detrimental to infants. Among some ungulates and primates, "kidnapping" by adult females may be a form of competitive interference (Lent 1974; Mohnot 1980; Silk 1980) that decreases the probability that young will survive. Adult male cercopithecid primates may use infants as "buffers" against aggression from other males (Deag and Crook 1971; Packer 1980).

Infanticide

In nature, animals often behave in ways that increase their individual reproductive success at the expense of that of conspecifics. Infanticide, the killing of immature conspecifics, may be a dramatic example of such a selfish reproductive tactic (Hausfater and Hrdy 1984). Cases of infanticide in captivity must therefore be interpreted with caution, since they do not necessarily reflect problems with the physical environment per se, but rather may be a predictable consequence of alterations in the social environment.

Infanticide in Nature. Maternal infanticide in nature usually takes the form of mothers abandoning their dependent offspring. Evolutionary theory predicts that maternal abandonment should occur when the current offspring are unlikely to survive or when continuing to provide parental care for those offspring would jeopardize the survival of the mother (Packer and Pusey 1984). Abandonment enables the female to devote her limited resources to future offspring with potentially higher chances of survival. For example, in lions (Packer and Pusey 1984) and brown bears, *Ursus arctos* (Tait 1980), mothers have been known to abandon their young when only one offspring of a litter remains. Similarly, in some species that typically have multiple offspring, mothers cease to lactate if litter size drops to one young (Hunsaker and Shupe 1977).

Infanticide by females other than the mother may serve to eliminate individuals that might compete with the infanticidal female's own offspring in the future. In Belding's ground squirrels, *Spermophilus beldingi* (Sherman 1981), and black-tailed prairie dogs, *Cynomys ludovicianus* (Hoogland 1985), immigrant females attempt to usurp occupied territories by killing the pups of the residents. The death of a litter may precipitate abandonment of the territory, allowing the immigrant to establish herself there. Dominant females kill the offspring of subordinate females in a variety of social carnivores, including African wild dogs, wolves, *Canis lupus,* dwarf mongooses, and brown hyenas, *Hyaena brunnea* (reviewed by Packer and Pusey 1984). In several of these species the mother of the dead

pups subsequently helps to care for the dominant female's young. Thus the benefits to the dominant female are twofold: more resources are available for her litter, and an additional female is available to assist with their care. Other species in which females have been reported to kill nondescendant offspring include vampire bats, *Desmodus rotundus* (Wimsatt and Guerriere 1961), and hamsters, *Mesocricetus* spp. (Rowell 1961).

Infanticide by males has been documented in a number of species in the wild, and often occurs when an intruder male ousts a resident male (Packer and Pusey 1984). Since females often do not return to estrus until their offspring are weaned, the killing of her dependent young may hasten a female's return to estrus and allow the immigrant male to mate with her more quickly. In hanuman langurs, *Semnopithecus (=Presbytis) entellus,* for example, when the breeding male in a harem is replaced, the incoming male kills the recent offspring of the previous male (Hrdy 1977). Male infanticide has been reported in many mammalian species, including rodents (Labov 1984; Hrdy 1979), equids (Hrdy 1979), carnivores (Packer and Pusey 1984), and primates (Crockett and Sekulic 1984; Leland, Struhsaker, and Butynski 1984; Butynski 1982; Collins, Busse, and Goodall 1984; Hrdy 1977). Male infanticide can be easily averted in captivity by postponing introductions of new males until infants are past their period of vulnerability. In primates, for example, new males should not be introduced to groups with infants until the infants have outgrown their natal coats, and care should be taken in the process.

Infanticide in Captivity. Instances of infanticide in captivity can often be traced to inadequacies of the captive social or physical environment. In some cases, its cause may be obvious (e.g., extreme overcrowding: Rasa 1979), but often infanticide appears to result from more subtle alterations in the social environment. In species that are solitary or live in single-sex groups in the wild, males maintained in the enclosure during infant rearing may become infanticidal (white rhino, *Ceratotherium simum:* Lindemann 1982; Syrian hyrax, *Procavia capensis syriaca:* Mendelssohn 1965). In some species, the mere presence of a male in a nearby (but separate) enclosure may cause females to become infanticidal. In several instances female spectacled bears, *Tremarctos ornatus,* have abandoned or eaten cubs when a male was in close physical proximity (Aquilina 1981; Peel, Price, and Karsten 1979). In monogamous species, *removal* of the male may predispose the female to maternal neglect or infanticide. Female bush dogs, for example, fail to rear young in the absence of the male (Jantschke 1973; I. Porton, pers. comm.).

Maternal infanticide may occur in response to disturbance in the physical environment. Captive female maned wolves, *Chrysocyon brachyurus,* often move young between dens when disturbed, and if alternative dens are not available, may kill young (Faust and Scherpner 1967; Brady and Ditton 1979). Other sources of disturbance that may provoke maternal infanticide include moving the parturient female to a new enclosure, excessive noise, and disturbance by human caretakers. Maternal infanticide or abandonment in response to postpartum disturbance appears to be espe-

osa: Blomquist, Muuronen, and Rantanen 1981; brown hyena: Eaton 1981; giant otter, *Pteronura brasiliensis:* Hagenbeck and Wünnemann 1992; small spotted genet, *Genetta servalina:* Flint 1975; polar bear, *Ursus maritimus:* J. Seidensticker, pers. comm.).

FACILITATING APPROPRIATE PARENTAL BEHAVIOR IN CAPTIVITY

Competent parental behavior is a nearly universal goal of zoo managers and caretakers. Mother rearing is thought to be crucial in the development of behaviorally competent individuals able to reproduce and rear their own offspring (e.g., Kleiman 1975), and these capabilities have become increasingly important with the growing focus on the maintenance of self-sustaining captive populations that are potential sources for reintroduction programs. Maternal competence appears, unsurprisingly, to be characteristic in the wild; abuse, unprovoked abandonment, and neglect by mothers are not reported as major causes of infant mortality (e.g., cheetah, *Acinonyx jubatus:* Laurenson 1993; common chimpanzee, *Pan troglodytes:* Goodall 1986). However, rearing failures resulting from maternal neglect, abuse, or cannibalism are common in zoos for a variety of species (e.g., gorilla, *Gorilla g. gorilla:* Nadler 1975; cheetah: McKeown, cited in Lee 1992; Laurenson 1993; aardvark, *Orycteropus afer:* Goldman 1986). Encouraging appropriate maternal behavior, especially in "difficult" species or individuals, can be one of the most challenging aspects of zoo animal husbandry.

There are anecdotal reports of husbandry and management procedures associated with successful infant rearing for a wide variety of mammalian species. In some cases, these reports document an initial failure, implementation of procedural or environmental changes, and subsequent success. However, most such reports do not conclusively demonstrate a cause-and-effect relationship between these changes and successful rearing. Few institutions work with sufficient numbers of a species or work with the species under the controlled variety of conditions required to reach firm conclusions on factors associated with appropriate maternal behavior (for exceptions, see Ruppenthal et al. 1976; Suomi and Ripp 1983 for rhesus macaques, *Macaca mulatta;* Hannah and Brotman 1990 for chimpanzees). Even in the most rigorous investigations, a limited set of variables has been studied (e.g., degree of social isolation during rearing for rhesus macaques; prereproductive exposure to infants for chimpanzees). For some species, surveys have resulted in data on a wider array of variables hypothesized to affect maternal behavior, including physical and social environment at parturition and individual history (e.g., striped hyena, *Hyaena hyaena:* Rieger 1979; gorilla: Miller-Schroeder and Paterson 1989). For most species, such data are totally lacking, and we advocate well-designed efforts in this direction, particularly for species that traditionally have exhibited infant-rearing difficulties in captivity.

Psychological stress as a major cause of maternal failure in the captive environment is an underlying assumption of this section, and suggestions for stress reduction will be a primary focus. It should be remembered that typical behav-

ioral mechanisms for stress reduction are usually unavailable to zoo animals (flight) or generally undesirable and ineffective in the captive context (aggression). The level of stress experienced by an individual will depend on the physical and social environment and on the individual's reaction to those conditions. Two individuals of the same species may experience different levels of stress in the same situation because of genetic or developmental differences (e.g., Joffe 1965; Suomi and Ripp 1983; see also Carlstead, chap. 31, this volume). Zoo managers can maximize the probability of appropriate parental behavior by (1) providing each individual with the optimal social and physical environment at parturition and (2) providing each individual with a developmental environment that prepares it to deliver appropriate parental care and enables it to cope with the stressors routinely associated with zoo facilities.

ENVIRONMENT AT PARTURITION

Stability in both the social and physical environment is crucial at parturition. Changes in either, even if viewed as positive by zoo staff, can be experienced as at least transiently stressful by the animal. An African civet, *Civettictis civetta,* at the Philadelphia Zoo began frantically pacing following the introduction of a small pile of wood mulch into her tile-floored cage and did not stop until the mulch was removed (K. R. Kranz, pers. comm.). Moseley and Carroll (1992) noted extreme maternal agitation and subsequent rearing failure after the attempted periparturitional separation of a female spectacled bear and her 23-month-old male offspring. Changes in social groupings, husbandry procedures, and the physical environment—in particular, those changes required specifically for the birth (e.g., new nest boxes, removal of the male)—should be anticipated and implemented sufficiently prior to parturition to allow adjustment on the part of the expectant mother.

Physical Environment at Parturition

All aspects of the physical environment should be considered in preparation for a birth and reevaluated following any failure in maternal care.

It is important to provide materials that will allow for the expression of maternal behaviors. This is generally of greatest concern for species bearing altricial young that are not carried by the mother. For most of these species nest boxes or dens must be provided. Groups for which nest boxes or dens appear to be important include monotremes and some marsupials, which leave young in a nest after they leave the pouch (Beach 1939; Collins 1973; Aslin 1974; Hunsaker 1977; Thomas 1982; Meissner and Ganslosser 1985; Boisvert and Grisham 1988; Bryant 1988; Conway 1988), armadillos (Eisenberg 1981), carnivores (Roberts 1975; Aquilina and Beyer 1979; Brady and Ditton 1979; Parker 1979; Peel, Price, and Karsten 1979; Rieger 1979; Aquilina 1981; Poglayen-Neuwall 1987; Blomquist and Larsson 1990; Williams et al. 1991; Hagenbeck and Wünnemann 1992), insectivores (Gould and Eisenberg 1966; Dryden 1975; Brodie, Brodie, and Johnson 1982; Michalak 1987), lagomorphs (Ross et al. 1963; Eisenberg 1981), myomorph and sciuromorph rodents (Xanten, Kessler, and Grumm

1988; Wharton 1986), tree shrews (Martin 1975a, 1975b), pigs (Kranz 1990), aardvarks (Dulaney 1987a; Wilson 1993), and some prosimian primates (Klopfer and Klopfer 1970; Martin 1975a, 1975b; Brockman, Willis, and Karesh 1987; Wright et al. 1989).

Den or nest box size and shape are probably important for many species, but preferred or successful designs have been described for only a few. Rieger's (1979) survey suggested that striped hyenas would not use dens that were too large. For polar bears, success has been achieved using small dens with rounded perimeters (Wemmer 1974; van Keulen-Kromhout 1978). Richardson (1991b) recommends that nest boxes for wild cat species contain a main chamber slightly longer than body length, slightly taller than shoulder height, and wide enough to allow the female to lie on her side with legs outstretched, preceded by a small entry chamber with an entrance at the corner diagonal to the opening between the two chambers to create a tunnel effect. For many species, a lip will prevent infants from leaving the nest box or den prematurely.

Multiple boxes or dens are recommended or required for some species because adults sleep separately from infants (e.g., tree shrews: Martin 1975a, 1975b), because mothers move infants between nesting sites (e.g., maned wolf: Faust and Scherpner 1967; Brady and Ditton 1979; red panda, *Ailurus fulgens*: Roberts 1975; marsh mongoose, *Atilax paludinosus*: Freese 1981; black-footed cat, *Felis nigripes*: Leyhausen 1979; giant otter: Hagenbeck and Wünnemann 1992), or to allow the female to separate herself from the male (binturong, *Arctictis binturong*: Aquilina and Beyer 1979; streaked tenrec, *Hemicentetes semispinosus*: Eisenberg and Muckenhirn 1968; Prevost's squirrel, *Callosciurus prevostii*: Edwards 1978; Malayan giant squirrel, *Ratufa bicolor*: Willis 1980). Providing multiple nest boxes or dens is the conservative approach. Multiple designs and locations can allow for choice by individuals and thus can guide future changes in design (overall dimensions, compartmentalization, entrance size, number of entrances, entrance tunnel) and placement (height, lighting, microclimate).

Species that build nests must also be provided with the appropriate raw materials, such as leaves, straw, grasses, branches or twigs, paper towels, tissue, woodwool, or wood shavings (see Eisenberg 1981 for an overview by order and many of the references cited above for details by species; also, bears: Partridge 1992; European harvest mouse, *Micromys minutus*: Trautman, Smythe, and Glogowski 1989; babirusa, *Babyrousa babyrussa*: MacLaughlin and Thomas 1991). Again, the conservative approach with a new individual or new species is to provide large quantities and a variety of nesting materials.

Other aspects of the physical environment, such as exhibit size and complexity, are not as exclusively linked to maternal care but can affect the probability of successful rearing. Amundin (1986) noted that in small pools, bottlenosed dolphin, *Tursiops truncatus*, mothers frequently had to push calves away from walls. Rieger (1979), in a survey of nine zoos, found indications of a positive correlation between exhibit size and rearing success for striped hyenas. Miller-Schroeder and Paterson (1989) concluded from their survey on gorillas that more complex and larger exhibits fa-

vored mother rearing and reduced the chances of infant abuse.

Outside the exhibit itself, care should be taken to avoid unnecessary stressors such as loud noises or unusual activity. Martin (1975b) reported that a single testing of a 30-second alarm bell disrupted nursing patterns of tree shrews in his laboratory for a week and, in an adjacent laboratory, was associated with fivefold and ninefold increases in infant mortality for domestic rats and mice respectively (see also Carlstead, chap. 31, this volume).

Human presence and activities are the most characteristic external stressors in the zoo environment. Several studies have demonstrated negative effects of visitor presence on the behavior of zoo primates, including reduced affiliation and increased agonism between cagemates (Chamove, Hosey, and Schaetzel 1988; Fa 1989). Cotton-top tamarins, *Saguinus oedipus*, on exhibit displayed higher levels of mother-young agonism and greater avoidance of offspring by parents than did individuals not on exhibit (Glatston et al. 1984).

Zoo animals are likely to be less than normally tolerant of visitor disturbance after parturition (e.g., giraffe, *Giraffa camelopardalis*: Kristal and Noonan 1979). Substantial anecdotal evidence suggests that carnivores, in particular, are prone to exhibit excessive carrying behavior, neglect, and cannibalism if not offered a higher level of privacy than experienced at other times (Faust and Scherpner 1967; Roberts 1975; Poglayen-Neuwall 1987; Brady and Ditton 1979; Peel, Price, and Karsten 1979; Paintiff and Anderson 1980; Aquilina 1981; Blomquist and Larsson 1990; Hagenbeck and Wünnemann 1992). If secluded off-exhibit denning areas are not available, exhibits or buildings may have to be temporarily closed to the public after parturition (e.g., Roberts 1975). A pair of fennec foxes, *Vulpes (=Fennecus) zerda*, at the Philadelphia Zoo failed to rear three litters despite being completely visually isolated from the public, but succeeded with two subsequent litters when the wing of the building they occupied was closed postpartum.

In addition to visitor presence, animals must cope with the presence in off-exhibit areas of their regular caretakers, other staff such as veterinarians, curators, directors, and service personnel, and nonemployees. Frequently, staff members that are rarely in off-exhibit areas visit shortly after a birth to see a new baby, especially in the case of high-profile species such as gorillas. Such visits can be a source of stress, especially since they fall outside the routine to which the animal has become accustomed (e.g., Martin 1975b). In addition, the usual caretaking routine is often disrupted in the excitement of the new birth. The following guidelines for the postpartum period can reduce the potential for stress caused by caretakers and other zoo personnel: (1) avoid changing caretaker routines in the period following parturition, except to increase the seclusion afforded the new mother; (2) avoid personnel changes in the caretaker staff; (3) restrict or eliminate access to off-exhibit areas by nonessential personnel, especially those that are not regular visitors.

Social Environment at Parturition

As a general rule, captive social environments should approximate those in the wild. Three basic aspects of social

TABLE 42.1. Social Organization in the Wild and Extent of Paternal Care in Captivity

Social organization type	Representative species	Extent of paternal care in captivity [a]
Association of males and females throughout period of infant rearing	Most primates	1
	Pinnipeds	2
	Capybara	1
Female aggregaton with little or intermittent male-female contact	Coati	4
	Elephants	3
	Vampire bats	4
Females solitary, with little or intermittent male-female contact	Tree kangaroo	3
	Maned wolf	3
	Aardvark	4

[a] 1, male actively involved in infant care; 2, male tolerant but not involved in infant care; 3, male behavior variable, unpredictable; 4, male frequently intolerant and/or infanticidal

organization in the wild must be considered when planning captive breeding groups: (1) Do females associate with other females during infant rearing? (2) Do males and females associate during infant rearing? (3) In social species, do parturient females seek isolation?

Sociality of Females. In species in which females are generally solitary or monogamous, housing multiple females together may result in infanticide or poor reproductive success. For example, Demidoff's galagos, *Galagoídes demidoff*, showed normal maternal care only when maintained as monogamous pairs; when housed in multifemale groups, females competed intensely for access to infants and the infants had to be hand-reared (Dulaney 1987b). However, females of some species that are monogamous in the wild have bred successfully in multifemale groups when food and nesting sites were provided in abundance (e.g., dik-diks, *Madoqua kirkii:* Kleiman 1980). Females of social species may show inadequate maternal behavior when housed alone. This has been documented in a variety of captive primates, including gorillas (Nadler 1980), pig-tailed macaques, *Macaca nemestrina* (Wolfheim, Jensen, and Bobbitt 1970) and squirrel monkeys, *Saimiri sciureus* (Kaplan 1972). Separation of new mothers and infants from their social group does not have the same negative effects in chimpanzees and orangutans, *Pongo pygmaeus*, species that typically give birth in isolation (Miller and Nadler 1980).

Extent of Male-Female Association. In general, if males and females are normally in close physical proximity during infant rearing in the wild, the father can be safely left in the captive social group. If females are solitary or live in single-sex groups in the wild, males should be removed from the captive group prior to parturition (table 42.1).

Closely related species may show very different social organizations, thus dictating different breeding group compositions. The order Carnivora provides a useful example, since many species are commonly exhibited and bred in zoos. Within the family Procyonidae, all three types listed in table 42.1 exist. Wild red pandas live in pairs or small family groups; in captivity they breed successfully as year-round pairs (Roberts 1975). Raccoons, *Procyon lotor*, are solitary in the wild, with some degree of home range overlap between the sexes. Coatis, *Nasua* spp., form sexually segregated social groups, with males and females associating only for mating (Russell 1981). In the latter two species, males should be removed prior to parturition.

Unfortunately, for many species, social organization in the wild is poorly known or ambiguous. Many of these species are small and nocturnal, which makes determination of the degree of association difficult. Many mammalian species exhibit social organizations in which males and females have independent, but largely overlapping, home ranges.

In deciding whether the father should be permitted to remain in a captive family group during infant rearing, both the temporal and spatial aspects of association in nature are of critical importance. Animals may share a home range while rarely coming into close contact (as is common in felids and ursids). In these species males are typically intolerant of young, even their own. In other species, animals may generally move independently but may encounter one another frequently. Males of these species may show a high degree of tolerance for infants in the wild, but may show inconsistent and unpredictable paternal reactions to infants in captivity. In some such species, individual males may be tolerant of (or may behave affiliatively toward) infants, but the literature abounds with anecdotes of male infanticide and inadequate maternal care in the presence of the male (Matschie's tree kangaroo, *Dendrolagus matschiei:* Hutchins et al. 1991; vampire bat: Wimsatt and Guerriere 1961; hamsters: Rowell 1961; Eurasian water shrew, *Neomys fodiens:* Michalak 1987; Asian elephants, *Elephas maximus:* Anghi 1962; Syrian hyrax: Mendelssohn 1965; mountain tapir, *Tapirus pinchaque:* Bonney and Crotty 1979; white rhino: Lindemann 1982; serow, *Naemorhedus* spp.: Meckvichai and Mahannop 1987; ring-tailed cat, *Bassariscus astutus:* Poglayen-Neuwall and Poglayen-Neuwall 1993; spectacled bear: Aquilina 1981; African golden cat, *Profelis aurata:* Tonkin and Kohler 1981). No general pattern has emerged from published accounts that enables prediction of whether an attempt at leaving the male in will be successful. Unfortunately, the reported instances of infant survival seem to encourage attempts at allowing fathers to remain with mothers and new infants. We recommend that, in the absence of compelling evidence that males are tolerant of infants, males be removed prior to parturition and reintroduced, if necessary, only when infants are large enough to be less vulnerable. Captive managers have an obligation to allocate sufficient space for separating males and females during infant rearing rather than forcing animals to cope with an unnatural and potentially stressful social situation.

As with any informal rule, notable exceptions exist.

Orangutans are solitary in the wild but breed successfully in captive groups consisting of a single male and multiple females (see Berger and Stevens, chap. 33, this volume). Conversely, free-ranging bottle-nosed dolphins are highly social, but males are intolerant of infants in captivity (Amundin 1986; Caldwell and Caldwell 1977), possibly as a result of severe space restrictions. When resources (e.g., space, resting areas, nesting areas) are much more limited in captivity than in the wild, it may be necessary, even for social species, to separate males from their mates and offspring, especially in those species in which males normally do not participate in parental care.

Seclusion of Parturient Females. If females normally isolate themselves from conspecifics for the period of time during and shortly after parturition, managers should consider short-term separation of expectant mothers. Mothers and new infants are routinely separated from conspecifics in many ungulate species (Miller, Read, and Boever 1985; Nilgiri tahr, *Hemitragus hylocrius:* Swengel and Pichner 1987; lesser kudu, *Tragelaphus imberbis:* Houston, Kelly, and Read 1987; Grevy's zebra, *Equus grevyi:* Fischer and Read 1989; Rocky Mountain goats, *Oreamnos americanus:* Hutchins et al. 1987). Extreme interference by conspecifics is unusual in social ungulates, and in most cases it is sufficient to monitor the behavior of conspecifics during the days immediately following parturition, removing the mother-infant pair only if harassment is persistent.

Management Strategies. Several things can be done to increase the likelihood that infants and other conspecifics (whether male or female) will be able to coexist peacefully. If a male is to be left in, it should be the father only. As described above, unrelated males are likely to be infanticidal, even in highly social species. Enclosures should be sufficiently large so that infants and new mothers are not forced into contact with other animals. For the same reason, enclosures should offer extra nest boxes (if appropriate for the species), visual barriers, and refuges for harassed animals. In all cases, the mother-infant pair should be watched closely for any signs of distress.

DEVELOPMENTAL EFFECTS ON PARENTAL CARE

Prenatal Experience
Laboratory studies on domestic rodents have shown that stressors (e.g., repeated electric shocks) experienced by a female can affect the behavior of her in utero offspring and even of offspring not yet conceived (Thompson 1957; Joffe 1965). Offspring of these stressed females may show high frequencies of stress-related behaviors such as "freezing," defecation, and urination when placed in a novel environment. This phenomenon is thought to be the result of changes in the hormonal environment experienced by the fetus. Only some rodent strains demonstrate these effects, indicating genetically based variation in vulnerability to such manipulations (Weir and De Fries 1964). We found no reports on the subsequent maternal behavior of the offspring of stressed mothers, but the heightened "emotionality" exhibited by such individuals in novel situations suggests that as adults they may have more difficulty dealing

with stresses experienced postparturition. No comparable studies have been conducted on nondomestic species, but the steps for maternal stress reduction suggested above should have the additional benefit of reducing any negative effects on the behavioral development of in utero offspring.

Early Postnatal Experience
Mother Rearing versus Hand Rearing. It is accepted as near-doctrine that mother-reared animals are more likely to exhibit competent parental behavior themselves than are individuals reared by human foster parents (e.g., Kleiman 1980). Negative effects of hand rearing on adult maternal behavior have been documented for several primate and laboratory species (rhesus macaques: Harlow, Harlow, and Suomi 1971; Ruppenthal et al. 1976; chimpanzees: Davenport 1979; domestic rats: Thoman and Arnold 1968). On the other hand, Martin (1975b) reported that hand-reared tree shrews, *Tupaia belangeri,* and lesser mouse lemurs, *Microcebus murinus,* were as successful as mother-reared individuals, and indicated that under certain circumstances hand-reared individuals could be more successful because they are less reactive to human disturbance.

For most species, however, data are distressingly lacking. While there are literally hundreds of reports of hand rearing in the literature, information on the subsequent parental behavior of the hand-reared individuals is almost never published. In general, single institutions do not have sufficient sample sizes for valid comparisons of mother-reared versus hand-reared individuals, but the information is often obtainable through multi-institutional surveys or studbooks. We suspect that the paucity of reports is partially due to the fact that hand-reared individuals of some species are unlikely to reproduce at all, making evaluation of their parental behavior difficult at best (e.g., red pandas: M. S. Roberts, pers. comm.). We encourage all studbook keepers to analyze their data bases for any differences in reproductive and rearing success between hand-reared and mother-reared individuals and to include these results in their studbooks (e.g., Rettberg-Beck and Ballou 1988 for golden lion tamarins, *Leontopithecus rosalia*).

The following section is written with the assumption that mother rearing is preferable to hand rearing, recognizing that hand rearing is sometimes suggested to produce more tractable adults (e.g., ungulates: Kranz and Lumpkin 1982; Moore 1982; Kranz, Xanten, and Lumpkin 1984) or because of the lower infant mortality rate of hand rearing versus mother rearing for certain species or individuals.

Alternatives to Hand Rearing. Some degree of human intervention is often unavoidable for infants whose mothers have died or who have had to be removed from mothers because of maternal abuse, neglect, or illness. A number of methods have been developed to avoid birth-to-weaning rearing by a human caretaker (see also Watts and Meder, chap. 6, this volume).

In some cases, infants can be returned to biological mothers that were initially unresponsive or incompetent after a short period of hand rearing (e.g., orangutan: Cole et al. 1979; Keiter, Reichard, and Simmons 1983; aardvark: Wilson 1993). Tranquilization of the mother to facilitate acceptance has been reported occasionally (giraffe, camel,

Camelus dromedarius: Gandal 1961; orangutan: Cole et al. 1979; margay, *Leopardus (=Felis) wiedii:* Paintiff and Anderson 1980), as has confinement of the mother in a small space with her litter (lemurs: Katz 1980; red-ruffed lemur, *Varecia variegata ruber:* Knobbe 1991; cheetah: Laurenson 1993; golden lion tamarin: A. J. Baker, pers. obs.), although the latter technique may provoke abuse or cannibalism. In any reintroduction of an infant, the risk of injury to the infant and the ability of zoo staff to intervene if necessary must be assessed in advance. Both factors will vary depending on the facilities and the species in question (e.g., it will probably be easier to remove an abused infant from an aardvark than from an orangutan).

Alternatively, infants can be fostered to conspecific females (rhesus macaque: Suomi and Ripp 1983; pygmy hedgehog tenrec, *Echinops telfairi:* Coker 1981; red panda: Roberts 1982; red kangaroo, *Macropus rufus:* Houston, Knobbe, and Read 1989; other macropods: Merchant and Sharman 1966; rodents: Huck and Banks 1980; McGuire 1988; domestic pigs, *Sus scrofa:* Dellmeier and Friend 1991; but see Qiu 1990 for giant panda, *Ailuropoda melanoleuca*) or to females of related species (ocelot, *Felis pardalis,* to domestic cat: Dunn 1974; black bear, *Ursus americanus,* to domestic dog: Haigh and Latour 1982; between macropods: Merchant and Sharman 1966; Johnson 1981; between rodents: Huck and Banks 1980; McGuire 1988). This technique is most likely to work in species that bear altricial young and in which mothers lack strong infant identification mechanisms. Among species that bear precocial young and have strong and early bonding mechanisms (e.g., ungulates), fostering can potentially be accomplished if the foster mother has had little or no contact with her own infant and the infant to be fostered is presented shortly after parturition (domestic sheep: Smith, Van-Toller, and Boyes 1966; domestic cattle: Hudson 1977; domestic goats: Klopfer and Klopfer 1968), or if feces or birth fluids from the biological offspring are rubbed on the neonate to be fostered (Hart 1985). Prolonged contact between a neonate and an intended foster mother may also eventually lead to acceptance, but poses a risk of infant injury (domestic sheep and goats: Herscher, Richmond, and Moore 1963) or starvation. Tranquilizers have been used to facilitate acceptance of foster neonates in domestic sheep (Neathery 1971), and might be considered in attempts to foster an exotic neonate to a female of a domestic species.

It is sometimes possible to provide supplementary feeding to infants that remain with their mothers, for example, in cases in which primate mothers will support and otherwise care for their infants but will not nurse them, or in which females cannot provide sufficient milk because of physiological problems or large litter size. Mothers can be trained to tolerate this feeding while the infant is being carried (e.g., orangutan: Fontaine 1979), or the infant can be removed for feeding (golden lion tamarin: Dumond, Hoover, and Norconk 1979; common marmoset, *Callithrix jacchus:* Stevenson and Sutcliffe 1978; red panda: Conway 1981; tree shrews, *Tupaia tana* and *T. minor:* M. S. Roberts, pers. comm.). Infants themselves have also been trained to approach a caretaker for feeding, which allows them to be reintroduced to a social group before weaning is complete (ungulates: Read 1982; Mayor 1984; stump-tailed macaque, *Macaca arctoides:* Chamove and Anderson 1982; Celebes macaque, *Macaca nigra:* Hawes et al. 1991).

Managing Hand-Reared Infants. The most extensive information on the maternal competence of hand-reared females comes from work on rhesus macaques (Ruppenthal et al. 1976; Suomi and Ripp 1983). Suomi and Ripp reported that early integration of hand-reared infants into a peer group and the housing of such animals in stable conspecific social groups through maturation and parturition greatly reduced the rate of neglect and abuse by "motherless mothers." This result is probably broadly applicable for mammals, especially primates (e.g., gorilla: Beck and Power 1988; ruffed lemur: Shideler and Lindburg 1982), and suggests the following conservative guidelines for mammalian hand rearing. Infants should be reared with a peer (preferably a conspecific or, alternatively, of a closely related species) whenever possible, even if transfer of individuals between institutions is necessary. With some species, it may be necessary to isolate infants initially to prevent injurious sucking (mouse lemurs: Glatston 1981; cats: Richardson 1991a; red pandas: Glatston 1992; gazelles: Lindsay and Wood 1992). For solitary species, conspecific contact should be continued through the age at which the individual might disperse from its littermates and/or mother. For social species, integration into a stable social unit, ideally one mirroring a "natural" group, should be effected as early as possible (see also Watts and Meder, chap. 6, this volume).

Managing Environmental Effects on Mother-Reared Infants. Contrary to the general theme of this section, laboratory evidence suggests that for altricial species, a certain amount of disturbance (e.g., periodic handling or other mechanical disturbances, or exposure to brief temperature changes) can have a positive effect on subsequent behavioral development that may be relevant to adult parental behavior. Domestic cats, rabbits, and rodents subjected to such neonatal disturbance showed greater activity and reduced "emotional reactivity" when placed in novel environments (Wilson, Warren, and Abbot 1965; Denenberg et al. 1973; but see Daly 1973 for discussion of interpretation of these results). As argued above in regard to prenatal effects, individuals that are less disturbed by novelty may also be more likely to cope successfully with the stresses associated with parturition and infant rearing. We do not suggest here that infants be disturbed specifically for this purpose, but these data should perhaps relieve anxiety about periodic handling of altricial neonates (e.g., for weighing and medical examination) if this can be done without unduly disturbing the mother.

Later Postnatal Experience

As described above for captive rhesus macaques (Suomi and Ripp 1983), postweaning socialization can be very important in the development of appropriate maternal behavior, especially for individuals that experience social deficits prior to weaning. Rogers and Davenport (1970) found that common chimpanzees that had remained with their mothers for more than 18 months were more successful in rearing their own infants than were individuals separated from their mothers prior to this age. Wild Japanese macaques, *Macaca fuscata,* orphaned prior to 4 years of age were more likely to mishandle and less likely to rear their first infants than were nonorphaned females, although they were as successful as nonorphans with subsequent infants (Hasegawa and Hiraiwa 1980). In general, it is advisable to provide juvenile and subadult animals the same opportunities to interact with infants, peers, parents, and other elders that they would have in a typical natural social group.

In the wild, females of many group-living species are exposed to infants prior to their own first parturition, which gives them the opportunity to become accustomed to (or perhaps lose fear of) the visual, olfactory, and auditory stimuli presented by neonates. Among cooperatively breeding species, mostly primates and carnivores (callitrichids: Epple 1975; Box 1977; Hoage 1977; dwarf mongoose: Rood 1980; African wild dog: Malcolm and Marten 1982), prereproductive subadults and adults are not only exposed to neonates but also participate in all facets of infant care except nursing. Studies on captive vervets (Fairbanks 1990) and callitrichids (e.g., Hoage 1977; Tardif, Richter, and Carson 1984; but see Baker and Woods 1992) suggest that individuals with prereproductive infant-carrying experience have greater rearing success with their own offspring (see also Salo and French 1989 for paternal experience effects on infant growth rates in Mongolian gerbils, *Meriones unguiculatus*). Hannah and Brotman (1990) reported that ten nulliparous common chimpanzees provided with infant exposure each successfully reared their own first infants, while eight females without such experience were unsuccessful. There are also a number of anecdotal reports on the exposure of nulliparous or previously unsuccessful primate females to infants or nursing demonstrations (Littlewood and Smith 1979; Schildkraut 1982). Cornell et al. (1987) suggest that nulliparous bottle-nosed dolphins also benefit by being housed with females that are rearing calves.

Adjustment to human presence during infancy can reduce the stress that a captive individual experiences as a reproductive adult. The caretaker-animal relationship developed during this time probably affects the individual's perception of the threat represented by humans in general. Mellen (1988) advocates daily handling of mother-reared small cats as a technique for reducing adult fearfulness, and Petter (1975) suggests a similar procedure for mouse lemurs.

Data on rhesus macaques (Suomi and Ripp 1983) provide an interesting perspective on the importance of individual differences and the potential effects of postweaning experience on future parental behavior. "Motherless" peer-raised rhesus macaques showed widely varying reactions to repeated experimental separations from their social groups (see also Dolhinow 1980 on reactions of captive infant hanuman langurs to separation from their mothers and Goodall 1986 on orphaned wild chimpanzees). Most female youngsters appeared to "cope" with these separations, but approximately a quarter to a third exhibited signs of extreme depression. These reactive females were much more likely to show inadequate maternal care of their firstborns than were the nonreactive females or females that had not experienced repeated separations. This result suggests that individual susceptibility to emotionality, perhaps genetically

based (Suomi 1981), and stressful environmental conditions during maturation can combine to have a major effect on adult parental behavior. This should be kept in mind in cases in which individuals from social species have to be separated from groups repeatedly or for long periods (e.g., for medical treatment).

Experience as a Mother

Experience relevant to successful infant rearing does not end at first parturition; maternal behavior can be affected by a female's experience with previous young. In general, a female's performance is likely to improve with experience. In making decisions regarding removal of infants from primiparous females or previously unsuccessful multiparous females, several points should be considered.

First, rearing failure with first infants or litters is common in zoos and is not necessarily predictive of failure with subsequent young. Published information indicates relatively low rearing success among primiparas for a number of species, with a suspiciously (spuriously?) high representation of primates and carnivores (gorilla: Nadler 1975, 1983; chimpanzee: Rogers and Davenport 1970; rhesus macaque: Ruppenthal et al. 1976; squirrel monkey: Taub, Adams, and Auerbach 1978; cotton-top tamarin: Kirkwood et al. 1985; Snowdon, Savage, and McConnell 1985; black lemur, *Eulemur macaco:* Frueh 1979; red panda: Glatston and Roberts 1988; giant panda: Liu 1988; striped hyena: Rieger 1979; paca, *Agouti paca:* Meritt 1989). The few available data suggest a similar pattern for at least some species in the wild (gorilla, *Gorilla g. berengei:* Harcourt 1987; rhesus macaque: Drickamer 1974; (orphaned) Japanese macaque: Hasegawa and Hiraiwa 1980; sea otter, *Enhydra lutris:* Kenyon, cited in Antrim and Cornell 1980; elephant seal: Reiter, Panken, and Le Boeuf 1981). In some species, captive individuals may experience first parturitions at an earlier age than do their wild counterparts (e.g., gorillas: Harcourt 1987); psychosocial immaturity (i.e., age effects independent of parity effects) may therefore be an additional factor in the high rate of failure among primiparous females in captivity. For example, primiparous "motherless mother" rhesus macaques are more likely to provide adequate care and less likely to abuse their infants if they are more than 8 years old at the time of their first viable delivery (Ruppenthal et al. 1976). Analyses of available records (e.g., by studbook keepers) to separate age and parity effects, clarify any systematic taxonomic variation in such effects, and elucidate potential interactions between parity, age, and hand rearing versus mother rearing would be useful for shaping managers' expectations and guiding their actions.

Second, variation in maternal behavior is to be expected, and apparently aberrant behaviors that are not directly threatening to infants often should be tolerated (e.g., Maple and Warren-Leubecker 1983), especially with primiparous females.

Finally, experience with one offspring, whether ultimately successful or not, can increase the probability of appropriate behavior toward subsequent offspring. "Motherless mother" rhesus macaques allowed to keep an infant for at least 2 days, even if they were abusive, were more likely to rear their next infants than were females who had less than 2 days of infant contact (Ruppenthal et al. 1976).

In conclusion, before removing infants for hand rearing, zoo staff must weigh the value of the experience the female might gain along with the perceived risk to the infant, the likelihood of successful hand rearing, and the relative value of the infant hand-reared versus mother-reared. These factors, in turn, will depend on such variables as the previous history of the female, the age of the female, the sex of the infant(s), the species-specific value of maternal experience, and the species-specific effects of hand rearing on behavior. Long-term gain in maternal competence often may outweigh the short-term loss of a single infant or litter, but for many species, we are lacking the data necessary to make informed decisions.

ACKNOWLEDGMENTS

We thank Devra Kleiman, Robert Lacy, Karl Kranz, and two anonymous reviewers for their thorough and constructive reviews of the manuscript.

REFERENCES

Alexander, R. A. 1974. The evolution of social behavior. *Annu. Rev. Ecol. Syst.* 5:325–83.

Altmann, J. 1980. *Baboon mothers and infants.* Cambridge, Mass.: Harvard University Press.

Amundin, M. 1986. Breeding the bottle-nosed dolphin *(Tursiops truncatus)* at the Komarden Dolphinarium. *Int. Zoo Yrbk.* 24/25:263–71.

Anghi, Cs. G. 1962. Breeding Indian elephants *(Elephas maximus)* at the Budapest Zoo. *Int. Zoo Yrbk.* 4:83–86.

Antrim, J. E., and Cornell, L. H. 1980. Reproduction of the sea otter *Enhydra lutris* in captivity. *Int. Zoo Yrbk.* 20:76–80.

Aquilina, G. D. 1981. Stimulation of maternal behavior in the spectacled bear *(Tremarctos ornatus)* at the Buffalo Zoo. *Int. Zoo Yrbk.* 21:143–45.

Aquilina, G. D., and Beyer, R. H. 1979. The exhibition and breeding of binturongs *(Arctictis binturong)* as a family group at Buffalo Zoo. *Int. Zoo Yrbk.* 19:185–88.

Aslin, H. J. 1974. The behaviour of *Dasyuroides byrnei* in captivity. *Z. Tierpsychol.* 35:187–208.

Baker, A. J., and Woods, F. 1992. Reproduction of the emperor tamarin *(Saguinus imperator)* in captivity, with comparisons to cotton-top and golden lion tamarins. *Am. J. Primatol.* 26:1–10.

Beach, F. A. 1939. Maternal behavior of the pouchless marsupial *(Marmosa cinerea).* *J. Mammal.* 20:315–21.

Beck, B. B., and Power, M. L. 1988. Correlates of sexual and maternal competence in captive gorillas. *Zoo Biol.* 7:339–50.

Blomquist, L., and Larsson, H. O. 1990. Breeding the wolverine *Gulo gulo* in Scandinavian zoos. *Int. Zoo Yrbk.* 29:156–63.

Blomquist, L., Muuronen, P., and Rantanen, V. 1981. Breeding the least weasel *(Mustela rixosa)* in Helsinki Zoo. *Der Zoologische Garten* 51:363–68.

Boisvert, M., and Grisham, J. 1988. Reproduction of the short-nosed echidna *Tachyglossus aculeatus* at the Oklahoma City Zoo. *Int. Zoo Yrbk.* 27:103–8.

Bonney, S., and Crotty, M. J. 1979. Breeding the mountain tapir *(Tapirus pinchaque)* at the Los Angeles Zoo. *Int. Zoo Yrbk.* 19:198–200.

Box, H. O. 1975. Quantitative studies of behavior within captive groups of marmoset monkeys *(Callithrix jacchus).* *Primates* 16:155–74.

———. 1977. Quantitative data on the carrying of young captive monkeys *(Callithrix jacchus)* by other members of their family groups. *Primates* 18:475–84.

Brady, C. A., and Ditton, M. K. 1979. Management and breeding of maned wolves *(Chrysocyon brachyurus)* at the National Zoological Park, Washington. *Int. Zoo Yrbk.* 19:171–76.

Brockman, D. K., Willis, M. S., and Karesh, W. B. 1987. Management and husbandry of ruffed lemurs, *Varecia variegata,* at the San Diego Zoo. II. Reproduction, pregnancy, parturition, litter size, infant care, and reintroduction of hand-raised infants. *Zoo Biol.* 6:349–63.

Brodie, E. D. III, Brodie, E. D. Jr., and Johnson, J. A. 1982. Breeding the African hedgehog *Atelerix pruneri* in captivity. *Int. Zoo Yrbk.* 22:195–97.

Bryant, S. 1988. Maintenance and captive breeding of the Eastern quoll *Dasyurus viverrinus.* *Int. Zoo Yrbk.* 27:119–24.

Butler, S. R., Suskind, M. R., and Schonberg, S. M. 1978. Maternal behavior as a regulator of polymine biosynthesis in brain and heart of the developing rat pup. *Science* 199:445–47.

Butynski, T. M. 1982. Harem male replacement and infanticide in the blue monkey *(Cercopithecus ascanius schmidti)* in the Kibale Forest, Uganda. *Am. J. Primatol.* 3:1–22.

Caldwell, M. C., and Caldwell, D. K. 1977. Social interactions and reproduction in the Atlantic bottle-nosed dolphin. In *Breeding dolphins: Present status, suggestions for the future,* ed. S. H. Ridgeway and K. Benirschke, 133–42. Marine Mammal Commission Report no. MMC-76/07, Washington, D.C.

Carlier, C., and Noirot, E. 1965. Effects of previous experience on maternal retrieving in rats. *Anim. Behav.* 13:423–26.

Carson, K., and Wood-Gush, D. G. M. 1983. Equine behaviour: I. A review of the literature on social and dam-foal behaviour. *Appl. Anim. Ethol.* 10:165–79.

Cebul, M. S., and Epple, G. 1984. Father-offspring relationships in laboratory families of saddle-back tamarins *(Saguinus fuscicollis).* In *Primate paternalism,* ed. D. M. Taub, 1–19. New York: Van Nostrand Reinhold.

Chamove, A. S., and Anderson, J. R. 1982. Hand-rearing infant stump-tailed macaques. *Zoo Biol.* 1:323–31.

Chamove, A. S., Hosey, G. R., and Schaetzel, P. 1988. Visitors excite primates in zoos. *Zoo Biol.* 7:359–69.

Cheney, D. L. 1977. The acquisition of rank and development of reciprocal alliances among free-ranging baboons. *Behav. Ecol. Sociobiol.* 2:303–18.

Clutton-Brock, T. H. 1991. *The evolution of parental care.* Princeton, N.J.: Princeton University Press.

Coker, M. 1981. Raising infant pygmy hedgehog tenrecs *(Echinops telfairi)* in captivity. *Animal Keepers' Forum* 8 (2): 42–44.

Cole, M., Devison, D., Eldridge, P. T., Mehren, K. G., and Rapley, W. A. 1979. Notes on the early hand-rearing of an orang-utan *Pongo pygmaeus* and its subsequent reintroduction to the mother. *Int. Zoo Yrbk.* 19:263–64.

Collins, D. A., Busse, C. D., and Goodall, J. 1984. Infanticide in two populations of savanna baboons. In *Infanticide,* ed. G. Hausfater and S. Hrdy, 193–215. New York: Aldine.

Collins, L. R. 1973. *Monotremes and marsupials: A reference for zoological institutions.* Washington, D.C.: Smithsonian Institution Press.

Conway, K. 1981. Supplementary feeding of maternally reared red pandas *Ailurus fulgens.* *Int. Zoo Yrbk.* 21:236–40.

———. 1988. Captive management of the tiger quoll *Dasyurus maculatus.* *Int. Zoo Yrbk.* 27:108–19.

Cornell, L. H., Asper, E. D., Antrim, J. E., Searles, S. S., Young, W. G., and Goff, T. 1987. Progress report: Results of a long-range captive breeding program for the bottlenose dolphin, *Tursiops truncatus* and *Tursiops truncatus gilli.* *Zoo Biol.* 6:41–53.

Crockett, C. M., and Sekulic, R. 1984. Infanticide in red howler monkeys *(Alouatta seniculus).* In *Infanticide,* ed. G. Hausfater and S. Hrdy, 173–215. New York: Aldine.

Dagg, A. I., and Foster, J. B. 1976. *The giraffe: Its biology, behavior, and ecology.* New York: Van Nostrand Reinhold.

Daly, M. 1973. Early stimulation of rodents: A critical review of present interpretations. *Br. J. Psychol.* 64:435–60.

Davenport, R. K. 1979. Some behavioral disturbances of great apes in captivity. In *The great apes,* ed. D. A. Hamburg and E. R. McCown, 341–57. Menlo Park, Calif.: Benjamin/Cummings.

Deag, J. M., and Crook, J. H. 1971. Social behavior and agonistic buffering in the wild Barbary macaque, *Macaca sylvanus. Folia Primatol.* 15:183–200.

Dellmeier, G. R., and Friend, T. H. 1991. Behavior and extensive management of domestic sows *(Sus scrofa)* and litters. In *Ungulate behavior and management,* ed. E. C. Mungall, 327–41. Amsterdam: Elsevier.

Denenberg, V. H., Wyly, M. V., Burns, J. K., and Zarrow, M. X. 1973. Behavioral effects of handling rabbits in infancy. *Physiol. Behav.* 10:1001–4.

Dolhinow, P. 1980. An experimental study of mother loss in the Indian langur monkey *Presbytis entellus. Folia Primatol.* 33: 77–128.

Drickamer, L. 1974. A ten-year summary of reproductive data for free-ranging *Macaca mulatta. Folia Primatol.* 21:61–80.

Dryden, G. 1975. Establishment and maintenance of shrew colonies. *Int. Zoo Yrbk.* 15:12–18.

Dulaney, M. W. 1987a. A mother-reared second-captive-generation aardvark *Orycteropus afer* at the Cincinnati Zoo. *Int. Zoo Yrbk.* 26:281–85.

———. 1987b. Successful breeding of Demidoff's galagos at the Cincinnati Zoo. *Int. Zoo Yrbk.* 26:229–31.

Dumond, F. V., Hoover, B. L., and Norconk, M. A. 1979. Hand-feeding parent-reared golden lion tamarins *Leontopithecus rosalia rosalia* at Monkey Jungle. *Int. Zoo Yrbk.* 19:155–58.

Dunn, G. L. 1974. Use of a domestic cat as a foster mother for an ocelot *Felis pardalis. Int. Zoo Yrbk.* 14:218–19.

Eaton, R. L. 1981. The ethology, propagation, and husbandry of the brown hyena *(Hyaena brunnea). Der Zoologische Garten* 51:123–49.

Edwards, T. J. 1978. Breeding Prevost's squirrel *(Callosciurus prevosti)* in captivity. *Int. Zoo Yrbk.* 18:124.

Eisenberg, J. F. 1981. *The mammalian radiations: An analysis of trends in evolution, adaptation, and behavior.* Chicago: University of Chicago Press.

Eisenberg, J. F., and Muckenhirn, N. 1968. The reproduction and rearing of Tenrecoid insectivores in captivity. *Int. Zoo Yrbk.* 8: 106–10.

Elwood, R. W. 1983. Paternal care in rodents. In *Parental behavior of rodents,* ed. R. W. Elwood, 235–57. New York: John Wiley and Sons.

Elwood, R. W., and McCauley, P. J. 1983. Communication in rodents: Infants to adults. In *Parental behavior of rodents,* ed. R. W. Elwood, 127–49. New York: John Wiley and Sons.

Emlen, S. T. 1984. Cooperative breeding in birds and mammals. In *Behavioral ecology: An evolutionary approach,* ed. J. R. Krebs and N. B. Davies, 305–39. Oxford: Blackwell Scientific Publications.

Epple, G. 1975. Parental behavior in *Saguinus fuscicollis* sp. (Callithricidae). *Folia Primatol.* 24:221–38.

Ewer, R. F. 1968. *Ethology of mammals.* London: Logos Press.

Fa, J. E. 1989. Influence of people on the behavior of display primates. In *Housing, care and psychological well-being of captive and laboratory primates,* ed. E. F. Segal, 270–90. Park Ridge, N.J.: Noyes.

Fairbanks, L. A. 1990. Reciprocal benefits of allomothering for female vervet monkeys. *Anim. Behav.* 40:553–62.

Faust, R., and Scherpner, C. 1967. A note on breeding of the maned wolf *(Chrysocyon brachyurus)* at Frankfurt Zoo. *Int. Zoo Yrbk.* 7:119.

Fischer, M. T., and Read, B. W. 1989. The captive management of Grevy's zebra *(Equus grevyi)* at the St. Louis Zoological Park. *AAZPA Regional Conference Proceedings,* 61–69. Wheeling, W.Va.: American Association of Zoological Parks and Aquariums.

Flint, M. 1975. Hand-rearing the small-spotted genet, *Genetta genetta,* at Randolph Park Zoo, Tucson. *Int. Zoo Yrbk.* 15: 244–45.

Fontaine, R. 1979. Training an unrestrained orang-utan mother *Pongo pygmaeus* to permit supplemental feeding of her infant. *Int. Zoo Yrbk.* 19:168–70.

Freese, R. 1981. Notes on breeding the marsh mongoose *(Atilax paludinosus)* at the Berlin Zoo. *Int. Zoo Yrbk.* 21:147–51.

Frueh, R. J. 1979. The breeding and management of black lemurs *Lemur macaco macaco* at St. Louis Zoo. *Int. Zoo Yrbk.* 19: 214–17.

Gandal, C. P. 1961. The use of a tranquilizer and diuretic in the successful management of two "reluctant zoo mothers." *Int. Zoo Yrbk.* 3:119–20.

Gittleman, J. L. 1985. Functions of communal care in mammals. In *Evolution: Essays in honor of John Maynard Smith,* ed. P. J. Greenwood and M. Slatkin, 187–205. Cambridge: Cambridge University Press.

Glatston, A. R. 1981. The husbandry, breeding and hand-rearing of the lesser mouse lemur *Microcebus murinus* at Rotterdam Zoo. *Int. Zoo Yrbk.* 21:131–37.

———. 1992. *The red or lesser panda studbook,* no. 7. Rotterdam: Royal Rotterdam Zoological and Botanical Gardens.

Glatston, A. R., Geilvoet-Soeteman, E., Hora-Pecek, E., and Hooff, J. A. R. A. M. van. 1984. The influence of the zoo environment on social behavior of groups of cotton-topped tamarins, *Saguinus oedipus oedipus. Zoo Biol.* 3:241–53.

Glatston, A. R., and Roberts, M. 1988. The current status and future prospects of the red panda *(Ailurus fulgens)* studbook population. *Zoo Biol.* 7:47–59.

Goldman, C. A. 1986. A review of the management of the aardvark *(Orycteropus afer)* in captivity. *Int. Zoo Yrbk.* 24/25:286–94.

Goodall, J. 1986. *The chimpanzees of Gombe: Patterns of behavior.* Cambridge, Mass.: Belknap Press of Harvard University Press.

Gould, E., and Eisenberg, J. F. 1966. Notes on the biology of the Tenrecidae. *J. Mammal.* 47:660–86.

Hagenbeck, C., and Wünnemann, K. 1992. Breeding the giant otter *Pteronura brasiliensis* at Carl Hagenbeck's Tierpark. *Int. Zoo Yrbk.* 31:240–45.

Haigh, J. C., and Latour, S. 1982. A domestic dog as a foster mother for an American black bear cub *Ursus (Euarctos) americanus. Int. Zoo Yrbk.* 22:262–63.

Hamilton, W. D. 1964. The genetical evolution of social behaviour. *J. Theor. Biol.* 7:1–51.

Hannah, A. C., and Brotman, B. 1990. Procedures for improving maternal behavior in captive chimpanzees. *Zoo Biol.* 9:233–40.

Harcourt, A. H. 1987. Behaviour of wild gorillas *Gorilla gorilla* and their management in captivity. *Int. Zoo Yrbk.* 26:248–55.

Harlow, H. F., Harlow, M. K., and Suomi, S. T. 1971. From thought to therapy: Lessons from a primate laboratory. *Am. Sci.* 59:538–49.

Harper, L. V. 1981. Offspring effects upon parents. In *Parental care in mammals,* ed. D. J. Gubernick and P. H. Klopfer, 117–77. New York: Plenum Press.

Hart, B. L. 1985. *The behavior of domestic animals*. New York: W. H. Freeman.

Hasegawa, T., and Hiraiwa, M. 1980. Social interactions of orphans observed in a free-ranging troop of Japanese monkeys. *Folia Primatol.* 33:129–58.

Hausfater, G., and Hrdy, S. B., eds. 1984. *Infanticide*. New York: Aldine.

Hawes, J., Maxwell, J., Priest, G., Feroz, L., Turnage, J., and Loomis, M. 1991. Protocols in hand-rearing a Celebes macaque (*Macaca nigra*) at the San Diego Zoo. *Animal Keepers' Forum* 18(3):95–96.

Hayssen, V., Van Tienhoven, A., and Van Tienhoven, A., eds. 1993. *Asdell's patterns of mammalian reproduction*. Ithaca, N.Y.: Cornell University Press.

Hepper, P. G. 1987. The amniotic fluid: An important priming role in kin recognition. *Anim. Behav.* 35:1343–46.

Herscher, L., Richmond, J. B., and Moore, A. U. 1963. Maternal behavior in sheep and goats. In *Maternal behavior in mammals*, ed. H. L. Rheingold, 203–32. New York: John Wiley.

Hoage, R. J. 1977. Parental care in *Leontopithecus rosalia rosalia*: Sex and age differences and the role of prior experience. In *The biology and conservation of the Callitrichidae*, ed. D. G. Kleiman, 293–305. Washington, D.C.: Smithsonian Institution Press.

Hofer, M. A. 1981. Parental contributions to the development of offspring. In *Parental care in mammals*, ed. D. J. Gubernick and P. H. Klopfer, 77–116. New York: Plenum Press.

Hoogland, J. L. 1981. Nepotism and cooperative breeding in the black-tailed prairie dog (Sciuridae: *Cynomys ludovicianus*). In *Natural selection and social behavior*, ed. R. D. Alexander and D. W. Tinkle, 283–310. New York: Chiron Press.

———. 1985. Infanticide in prairie dogs: Lactating females kill offspring of close kin. *Science* 230:1037–40.

Houston, B. W., Kelly, C. M., and Read, B. W. 1987. The captive management of lesser kudu (*Tragelaphus imberbis*) at the St. Louis Zoo. *AAZPA Regional Conference Proceedings*, 572–83. Wheeling, W.Va.: American Association of Zoological Parks and Aquariums.

Houston, B. W., Knobbe, C. M., and Read, B. W. 1989. A preliminary report on the use of cross-fostering as a tool in the captive management of red kangaroos (*Megaleia rufa*) at the St. Louis Zoo. *AAZPA Regional Conference Proceedings*, 77–81. Wheeling, W.Va.: American Association of Zoological Parks and Aquariums.

Hrdy, S. B. 1977. *The langurs of Abu: Female and male strategies of reproduction*. Cambridge, Mass.: Harvard University Press.

———. 1979. Infanticide among animals: A review, classification, and examination of the implications for the reproductive strategies of females. *Ethol. Sociobiol.* 1:13–40.

Huck, U. W., and Banks, E. M. 1980. The effects of cross-fostering on the behaviour of two species of North American lemmings, *Dicrostonyx groenlandicus* and *Lemmus trimucronatus*: I. Olfactory preferences. *Anim. Behav.* 28:1046–52.

Hudson, S. J. 1977. Multiple fostering of calves onto nurse cows at birth. *Appl. Anim. Ethol.* 3:57–63.

Hunsaker, D. II. 1977. Ecology of New World marsupials. In *The biology of marsupials*, ed. D. Hunsaker II, 95–156. New York: Academic Press.

Hunsaker, D. II, and Shupe, D. 1977. Behavior of New World marsupials. In *The biology of marsupials*, ed. D. Hunsaker II, 279–347. New York: Academic Press.

Hutchins, M., Smith, G. M., Mead, D. C., Elbin, S., and Steenberg, J. 1991. Social behavior of Matschie's tree kangaroo (*Dendrolagus matschiei*) and its implications for captive management. *Zoo Biol.* 10:147–64.

Hutchins, M., Thompson, G., Sleeper, B., and Foster, J. W. 1987. Management and breeding of the Rocky Mountain goat *Oreamnos americanus* at Woodland Park Zoo. *Int. Zoo Yrbk.* 26:297–308.

Jantschke, F. 1973. On the breeding and rearing of bush dogs (*Speothos venaticus*) at Frankfurt Zoo. *Int. Zoo Yrbk.* 13:141–43.

Joffe, J. M. 1965. Genotype and prenatal and premating stress interact to affect adult behavior in rats. *Science* 150:1844–45.

Johnson, P. M. 1981. The rearing of marsupial pouch young by foster mothers of different species. *Int. Zoo Yrbk.* 21:173–76.

Kaplan, J. 1972. Differences in the mother-infant relations of squirrel monkeys housed in social and restricted environments. *Dev. Psychobiol.* 5:43–52.

Katz, A. S. 1980. Management techniques to reduce perinatal loss in a lemur colony. *AAZPA Regional Conference Proceedings*, 137–40. Wheeling, W.Va.: American Association of Zoological Parks and Aquariums.

Keiter, M. D., Reichard, T., and Simmons, J. 1983. Removal, early hand rearing, and successful reintroduction of an orangutan (*Pongo pygmaeus pygmaeus* × *abelii*) to her mother. *Zoo Biol.* 2:55–59.

Kirkwood, J. K., Epstein, M. A., Terlecki, A. J., and Underwood, S. J. 1985. Rearing a second generation of cotton-top tamarins (*Saguinus oedipus oedipus*) in captivity. *Lab. Anim.* 19:269–72.

Kleiman, D. G. 1969. Maternal care, growth rate, and development in the noctule (*Nyctalus noctula*), pipistrelle (*Pipistrellus pipistrellus*), and serotine (*Eptesicus serotinus*) bats. *J. Zool.* (Lond.) 157:187–211.

———. 1975. Management of breeding programs in zoos. In *Research in zoos and aquariums*, 157–77. Washington, D.C.: National Academy of Sciences.

———. 1977. Monogamy in mammals. *Q. Rev. Biol.* 52:39–69.

———. 1980. The sociobiology of captive propagation. In *Conservation biology: An evolutionary-ecological perspective*, ed. M. Soulé and B. Wilcox, 243–61. Sunderland, Mass.: Sinauer Associates.

Kleiman, D. G., and Malcolm, J. R. 1981. The evolution of male parental investment in mammals. In *Parental care in mammals*, ed. D. J. Gubernick and P. H. Klopfer, 347–87. New York: Plenum Press.

Klopfer, P. H., and Klopfer, M. S. 1968. Maternal imprinting in goats: Fostering of alien young. *Z. Tierpsychol.* 25:862–66.

———. 1970. Patterns of maternal care in lemurs. *Z. Tierpsychol.* 27:984–96.

Knobbe, J. 1991. Early resocialization of hand-reared primates. *AAZPA Regional Conference Proceedings*, 763–70. Wheeling, W.Va.: American Association of Zoological Parks and Aquariums.

Kranz, K. R. 1990. The history of warthogs at the Philadelphia Zoo. *Phila. Zoo Rev.* 3 (2): 1–8.

Kranz, K. R., and Lumpkin, S. 1982. Notes on the yellow-backed duiker in captivity with some comments on its natural history. *Int. Zoo Yrbk.* 22:232–40.

Kranz, K. R., Xanten, W. A., and Lumpkin, S. 1984. Breeding history of the dorcas gazelles *Gazella dorcas* at the National Zoological Park, 1961–1981. *Int. Zoo Yrbk.* 23:195–203.

Kristal, M. B., and Noonan, M. 1979. Perinatal maternal and neonatal behaviour in the captive reticulated giraffe. *S. Afr. J. Zool.* 14:103–7.

Kuhn, C. M., Butler, S. R., and Schonberg, S. M. 1978. Selective depression of serum growth hormone during maternal deprivation in rat pups. *Science* 201:1036.

Labov, J. B. 1984. Infanticidal behavior in male and female rodents: Sectional introduction and directions for future research.

In *Infanticide,* ed. G. Hausfater and S. Hrdy, 323–29. New York: Aldine.

Laurenson, M. K. 1993. Early maternal behavior of wild cheetahs: Implications for captive husbandry. *Zoo Biol.* 12:31–43.

Lee, A. R. 1992. *Management guidelines for the welfare of zoo animals: Cheetah.* London: The Federation of Zoological Gardens of Great Britain and Ireland.

Lee, P. C. 1987. Allomothering among African elephants. *Anim. Behav.* 35:278–91.

Leland, L., Struhsaker, T. T., and Butynski, T. M. 1984. Infanticide by adult males in three primate species of Kibale National Forest, Uganda: A test of hypotheses. In *Infanticide,* ed. G. Hausfater and S. Hrdy, 151–72. New York: Aldine.

Lent, P. C. 1974. Mother-infant relationships in ungulates. In *The behaviour of ungulates and its relation to management,* vol. 1, ed. V. Geist and F. Walther, 14–55. Morges, Switzerland: IUCN.

Levine, S. 1982. Mother-infant relationships: Stress and coping. *Ann. Ist. Super. Sanita.* 18:223–30.

Levy, F., and Poindron, P. 1987. The importance of amniotic fluids for the establishment of maternal behaviour in experienced and inexperienced ewes. *Anim. Behav.* 35:1188–1192.

Leyhausen, P. 1979. *Cat Behavior.* Trans. B. A. Tonkin. New York: Garland STPM Press.

Lindemann, H. 1982. *African rhinoceroses in captivity.* Copenhagen: University of Copenhagen.

Lindsay, N., and Wood, J. 1992. Hand-rearing three species of gazelle *Gazella* spp. in the Kingdom of Saudi Arabia. *Int. Zoo Yrbk.* 31:250–55.

Littlewood, A., and Smith, J. 1979. Breeding and hand-rearing mandrills *Mandrillus sphinx* at Portland Zoo. *Int. Zoo Yrbk.* 19:161–65.

Liu, W. 1988. Litter size and survival rate in captive giant pandas. *Int. Zoo Yrbk.* 27:304–7.

MacLaughlin, K. A., and Thomas, P. R. 1991. The management of babirusa *(Babyrousa babyrussa)* at the New York Zoological Park. *AAZPA Regional Conference Proceedings,* 650–57. Wheeling, W.Va.: American Association of Zoological Parks and Aquariums.

Malcolm, J. R. 1985. Paternal care in canids. *Am. Zool.* 25:853–56.

———. 1986. Socio-ecology of bat-eared foxes *(Otocyon megalotis). J. Zool.* (Lond.) 208:457–67.

Malcolm, J. R., and Marten, K. 1982. Natural selection and the communal rearing of pups in African wild dogs *(Lycaon pictus). Behav. Ecol. Sociobiol.* 10:1–13.

Maple, T. L., and Warren-Leubecker, A. 1983. Variability in the parental conduct of captive great apes and some generalizations to humankind. In *Child abuse: The nonhuman primate data,* ed. M. Reite and N. G. Caine, 119–37. New York: Alan R. Liss.

Marlow, B. J. 1975. The comparative behavior of the Australasian sea lions *(Neophoca cinerea* and *Phocarctos hookeri)* (Pinnipedia: Otariidae). *Mammalia* 39 (2):159–230.

Martin, R. D. 1975a. Breeding tree-shrews *(Tupaia belangeri)* and mouse lemurs *(Microcebus murinus)* in captivity. *Int. Zoo Yrbk.* 15:35–41.

———. 1975b. General principles for breeding small mammals in captivity. In *Breeding endangered species in captivity,* ed. R. D. Martin, 143–66. London: Academic Press.

Mayor, J. 1984. Hand-feeding an orphaned scimitar-horned oryx *Oryx dammah* calf after its integration with the herd. *Int. Zoo Yrbk.* 23:243–48.

McCracken, G. F. 1984. Communal nursing in Mexican free-tailed bat maternity communities. *Science* 223:1090–91.

McGuire, B. 1988. Effects of cross-fostering on parental behavior of meadow voles *(Microtus pennsylvanicus). J. Mammal.* 69:332–41.

McKay, G. M. 1973. The ecology and behavior of the Asiatic elephant in southeastern Ceylon. *Smithsonian Contributions to Zoology,* no. 125.

McKenna, J. J. 1981. Primate infant caregiving: Origins, consequences, and variability, with emphasis on the common langur monkey. In *Parental care in mammals,* ed. D. J. Gubernick and P. H. Klopfer, 389–416. New York: Plenum Press.

Mech, L. D. 1970. *The wolf: The ecology of an endangered species.* New York: American Museum of Natural History.

Meckvichai, C., and Mahannop, A. 1987. Breeding of Sumatran serow at Dusit Zoo. In *The biology and management of* Capricornis *and related mountain antelopes,* ed. H. Soma, 147–53. London: Croom Helm.

Meissner, K., and Ganslosser, V. 1985. Development of young in the kowari *Dasyuroides byrnei* Spencer, 1896. *Zoo Biol.* 4:351–59.

Mellen, J. D. 1988. The effects of hand-raising on sexual behavior of captive small felids using domestic cats as a model. *AAZPA Annual Conference Proceedings,* 253–59. Wheeling, W.Va.: American Association of Zoological Parks and Aquariums.

Mendelssohn, H. 1965. Breeding Syrian hyrax *(Procavia capensis syriaca)* Schreber 1784. *Int. Zoo Yrbk.* 5:116–25.

Merchant, J. C., and Sharman, G. B. 1966. Observations on the attachment of marsupial young by foster mothers of the same or different species. *Aust. J. Zool.* 14:593–609.

Meritt, D. 1989. The husbandry and management of the paca *Cuniculus paca* at Lincoln Park Zoo, Chicago. *Int. Zoo Yrbk.* 28:264–67.

Michalak, I. 1987. Keeping and breeding the Eurasian water shrew *Neomys fodiens* under laboratory conditions. *Int. Zoo Yrbk.* 26:223–28.

Miller, L. C., and Nadler, R. D. 1980. Mother-infant relations and infant development in captive chimpanzees and orang-utans. *Int. J. Primatol.* 2:247–61.

Miller, R. E., Read, B. W., and Boever, W. T. 1985. Neonatal artiodactylid care at the St. Louis Zoological Park. *AAZPA Annual Conference Proceedings,* 492–97. Wheeling, W.Va.: American Association of Zoological Parks and Aquariums.

Miller-Schroeder, P., and Paterson, J. D. 1989. Environmental influences on reproduction and maternal behavior in captive gorillas: Results of a survey. In *Housing, care, and psychological well-being of captive and laboratory primates,* ed. E. F. Segal, 389–415. Park Ridge, N.J.: Noyes.

Moehlman, P. D. 1986. Ecology of cooperation in canids. In *Ecological aspects of social evolution,* ed. D. I. Rubenstein and R. W. Wrangham, 64–86. Princeton, N.J.: Princeton University Press.

Mohnot, S. M. 1980. Intergroup infant kidnapping in hanuman langurs. *Folia Primatol.* 34:259–77.

Moore, D. 1982. History and assessment of future management of pronghorn *(Antilocapra americana)* in captivity "East of the Mississippi." *AAZPA Regional Conference Proceedings,* 35–48. Wheeling, W.Va.: American Association of Zoological Parks and Aquariums.

Moseley, D. J., and Carroll, J. B. 1992. The maintenance and breeding of spectacled bears at Jersey Zoo. In *Management guidelines for bears and raccoons,* ed. J Partridge, 87–93. Bristol, U.K.: Association of British Wild Animal Keepers.

Nadler, R. D. 1975. Determinants of variability in maternal behavior of captive female gorillas. *Symp. Int. Primatol. Soc.* 5:207–16.

———. 1980. Child abuse: Evidence from non-human primates. *Dev. Psychobiol.* 13:507–12.

———. 1983. Experiential influences on infant abuse of gorillas and some other nonhuman primates. In *Child abuse: The nonhuman primate data,* ed. M. Reite and N. G. Caine, 139–49. New York: Alan R. Liss.

Neathery, M. W. 1971. Acceptance of orphan lambs by tranquilized ewes *(Ovis aries). Anim. Behav.* 19:75–79.

Oftedal, O. T. 1985. Pregnancy and lactation. In *Bioenergetics of wild herbivores,* ed. R. J. Hudson and R. J. White, 215–38. Boca Raton, Fla.: CRC Press.

Owens, D. D., and Owens, M. J. 1984. Helping behavior in brown hyenas. *Nature* 308:843–45.

Packer, C. 1980. Male care and exploitation of infants in *Papio anubis. Anim. Behav.* 28:512–20.

———. 1986. The ecology of sociality in felids. In *Ecological aspects of social evolution,* ed. D. I. Rubenstein and R. W. Wrangham, 429–51. Princeton: Princeton University Press.

Packer, C., and Pusey, A. E. 1983. Male takeovers and female reproductive parameters: A simulation of oestrous synchrony in lions *(Panthera leo). Anim. Behav.* 31:334–40.

———. 1984. Infanticide in carnivores. In *Infanticide,* ed. G. Hausfater and S. Hrdy, 31–42. New York: Aldine.

Paintiff, J. A., and Anderson, D. E. 1980. Breeding the margay *Felis wiedi* at New Orleans Zoo. *Int. Zoo Yrbk.* 20:223–24.

Parker, C. 1979. Birth, care, and development of Chinese hog badgers *(Arctonyx collaris)* at Metro Toronto Zoo. *Int. Zoo Yrbk.* 19:182–85.

Partridge, J., ed. 1992. *Management guidelines for bears and raccoons.* Bristol, U.K.: Association of British Wild Animal Keepers.

Peel, R. R., Price, J., and Karsten, P. 1979. Mother-rearing of a spectacled bear cub *(Tremarctos ornatus)* at Calgary Zoo. *Int. Zoo Yrbk.* 19:177–82.

Petter, J. J. 1975. Breeding of Malagasy lemurs in captivity. In *Breeding endangered species in captivity,* ed. R. D. Martin, 187–202. London: Academic Press.

Poglayen-Neuwall, I. 1987. Management and breeding of the ringtail or cacomistle *Bassariscus astutus* in captivity. *Int. Zoo Yrbk.* 26:276–80.

Poglayen-Neuwall, I., and Poglayen-Neuwall, I. 1993. Behavior, reproduction, and postnatal development of *Bassariscus astutus* (Carnivora, Procyonidae) in captivity. *Der Zoologische Garten* 63:73–125.

Pohle, C. 1987. Experiences of keeping and breeding Saiga antelope at Tierpark, Berlin. In *The biology and management of Capricornis and related mountain antelopes,* ed. H. Soma, 191–204. London: Croom Helm.

Qiu, B. 1990. A review of giant panda, *Ailuropoda melanoleuca,* births during 1989. *Int. Zoo Yrbk.* 29:153–55.

Rasa, O. A. E. 1977. The ethology and sociology of the dwarf mongoose. *Z. Tierpsychol.* 43:337–406.

———. 1979. The effects of crowding on the social relationships and behaviour of the dwarf mongoose *(Helogale undulata rufula). Z. Tierpsychol.* 49:317–29.

Rathbun, G. B. 1979. The social structure and ecology of elephant shrews. *Z. Tierpsychol.,* Suppl. 20:1–76.

Read, B. 1982. Successful reintroduction of bottle-raised calves to antelope herds at St. Louis Zoo. *Int. Zoo Yrbk.* 22:269–70.

Read, B., and Frueh, R. J. 1980. Management and breeding of Speke's gazelle *(Gazella spekei)* at the St. Louis Zoo, with a note on artificial insemination. *Int. Zoo Yrbk.* 20:99–105.

Reiter, J., Panken, K., and Le Boeuf, B. J. 1981. Female competition and reproductive success in northern elephant seals. *Anim. Behav.* 29:670–87.

Rettberg-Beck, B., and Ballou, J. D. 1988. Survival and reproduction of hand-reared golden lion tamarins. In *1987 golden lion tamarin studbook,* ed. J. D. Ballou, 10–14. Washington, D.C.: National Zoological Park.

Richardson, D. M. 1991a. Guidelines for handrearing exotic felids. In *Management guidelines for exotic cats,* ed. J. Partridge, 116–17. Bristol, U.K.: Association of British Wild Animal Keepers.

———. 1991b. Housing exotic felids. In *Management guidelines for exotic cats,* ed. J. Partridge, 113–15. Bristol, U.K.: Association of British Wild Animal Keepers.

Riedman, M. L. 1982. The evolution of alloparental care and adoption in mammals and birds. *Q. Rev. Biol.* 57:405–35.

Riedman, M. L., and Le Boeuf, B. J. 1982. Mother-pup separation and adoption in northern elephant seals. *Behav. Ecol. Sociobiol.* 11:203–15.

Rieger, I. 1979. Breeding the striped hyena *(Hyaena hyaena)* in captivity. *Int. Zoo Yrbk.* 19:193–98.

Roberts, M. S. 1975. Growth and development of mother-reared red pandas *(Ailurus fulgens). Int. Zoo Yrbk.* 15:57–63.

———. 1982. Demographic trends in a captive population of red pandas *(Ailurus fulgens). Zoo Biol.* 1:119–26.

Robinson, J. G., Wright, P. C., and Kinzey, W. G. 1986. Monogamous cebids and their relatives: Intergroup calls and spacing. In *Primate societies,* ed. B. B. Smuts, D. L. Cheney, R. M. Seyfarth, R. W. Wrangham, and T. T. Struhsaker, 44–53. Chicago: University of Chicago Press.

Rogers, C. M., and Davenport, R. K. 1970. Chimpanzee maternal behaviour. In *The chimpanzee,* vol. 3, ed. G. H. Bourne, 361–68. Baltimore: University Park Press.

Rood, J. P. 1978. Dwarf mongoose helpers at the den. *Z. Tierpsychol.* 48:277–87.

———. 1980. Mating relationships and breeding suppression in the dwarf mongoose. *Anim. Behav.* 28:143–50.

———. 1986. Ecology and social evolution in the mongooses. In *Ecological aspects of social evolution,* ed. D. I. Rubenstein and R. W. Wrangham, 131–52. Princeton: Princeton University Press.

Rosenblatt, J. S. 1967. Non-hormonal basis of maternal behavior. *Science* 156:1512–14.

Rosenblatt, J. S., and Siegel, H. I. 1981. Factors governing the onset and maintenance of maternal behavior among non-primate mammals: The role of hormonal and non-hormonal factors. In *Parental care in mammals,* ed. D. J. Gubernick and P. J. Klopfer, 14–76. New York: Plenum Press.

Ross, S., Sawin, P. B., Zarrow, M. X., and Denenberg, V. H. 1963. Maternal behavior in the rabbit. In *Maternal behavior in mammals,* ed. H. Rheingold, 94–121. New York: John Wiley and Sons.

Rowell, T. E. 1961. Maternal behaviour in non-maternal golden hamsters *(Mesocricetus auratus). Anim. Behav.* 9:11–15.

Ruppenthal, G. C., Arling, G. L., Harlow, H. F., Sackett, G. P., and Suomi, S. J. 1976. A ten-year perspective of motherless mother monkey behavior. *J. Abnorm. Psychol.* 85:341–49.

Russell, J. K. 1981. Exclusion of adult male coatis from social groups: Protection from predation. *J. Mammal.* 62:206–8.

Sadleir, R. M. F. S. 1969. *The ecology of reproduction in wild and domestic mammals.* London: Methuen.

Salo, A. L., and French, J. A. 1989. Early experience, reproductive success, and development of parental behaviour in Mongolian gerbils. *Anim. Behav.* 38:693–702.

Schaller, G. B. 1972. *The Serengeti lion.* Chicago: University of Chicago Press.

Schildkraut, D. S. 1982. Labor in vain: The problem of inadequate mothering in captive gorillas. *AAZPA Regional Conference Proceedings,* 138–40. Wheeling, W.Va.: American Association of Zoological Parks and Aquariums.

Sherman, P. W. 1980. The limits of ground squirrel nepotism. In *Sociobiology: Beyond nature/nurture,* ed. G. W. Barlow and J. Silverberg, 505–44. Boulder, Colo.: Westview Press.

————. 1981. Reproductive competition and infanticide in Belding's ground squirrels and other animals. In *Natural selection and social behavior: Recent research and new theory*, ed. R. D. Alexander and D. W. Tinkle, 311–31. New York: Chiron Press.

Shideler, S. E., and Lindburg, D. G. 1982. Selected aspects of *Lemur variegatus* reproductive biology. *Zoo Biol.* 1:127–34.

Shoemaker, A. 1979. Reproduction and development of the black howler monkey *(Alouatta caraya)* at Columbia Zoo. *Int. Zoo Yrbk.* 19:150–55.

Silk, J. B. 1980. Kidnapping and female competition among female bonnet macaques. *Primates* 21:100–110.

Smith, F. V., Van-Toller, L., and Boyes, T. 1966. The critical period in the attachment of lambs and ewes. *Anim. Behav.* 14:120–25.

Snowdon, C. T., Savage, A., and McConnell, P. B. 1985. A breeding colony of cotton-top tamarins *(Saguinus oedipus)*. *Lab. Anim. Sci.* 35:477–80.

Spencer-Booth, Y. 1970. The relationships between mammalian young and conspecifics other than mothers and peers: A review. *Adv. Stud. Behav.* 3:119–94.

Spinage, C. A. 1986. *The natural history of antelopes*. New York: Facts on File.

Stevenson, M. F., and Sutcliffe, A. G. 1978. Breeding a second generation of common marmosets *Callithrix jacchus* in captivity. *Int. Zoo Yrbk.* 18:109–14.

Suomi, S. J. 1981. Genetic, maternal, and environmental influences on social development in rhesus monkeys. In *Primate behavior and sociobiology*, ed. B. Chiarelli, 81–87. New York: Springer-Verlag.

Suomi, S. J., and Ripp, C. 1983. A history of motherless mother monkey mothering at the University of Wisconsin primate laboratory. In *Child abuse: The nonhuman primate data*, ed. M. Reite and N. G. Caine, 49–78. New York: Alan R. Liss.

Swengel, F. B., and Pichner, J. 1987. Status and management of the Nilgiri tahr in captivity. *AAZPA Regional Conference Proceedings*, 584–89. Wheeling, W.Va.: American Association of Zoological Parks and Aquariums.

Tait, D. E. N. 1980. Abandonment as a tactic in grizzly bears. *Am. Nat.* 115:800–808.

Tardif, S. D., Richter, C. B., and Carson, R. L. 1984. Effects of sibling-rearing experience on future reproductive success in two species of Callitrichidae. *Am. J. Primatol.* 6:377–80.

Taub, D. M., Adams, M., and Auerbach, K. G. 1978. Reproductive performance in a breeding colony of Brazilian squirrel monkeys *(Saimiri sciureus)*. *Lab. Anim. Sci.* 28:562–66.

Thoman, E. B., and Arnold, W. J. 1968. Effects of incubator rearing with social deprivation on maternal behavior in rats. *J. Comp. Physiol. Psychol.* 65:441–46.

Thomas, E. E. 1982. Notes on the behaviour of the mountain pygmy-possum *(Burramys parvus)* in captivity. In *The management of Australian mammals in captivity*, ed. D. D. Evans, 85–86. Victoria, Australia: The Zoological Board of Victoria.

Thompson, W. R. 1957. Influence of prenatal maternal anxiety on emotionality in young rats. *Science* 125:698–99.

Tonkin, B. A., and Kohler, E. 1981. Observations on the Indian desert cat *(Felis silvestris ornata)* in captivity. *Int. Zoo Yrbk.* 21:151–54.

Trautman, K., Smythe, A., and Glogowski, B. 1989. The exhibition and captive management of the European harvest mouse *(Micro-mys minutus)* at the Philadelphia Zoological Garden. *AAZPA Regional Conference Proceedings*, 902–9. Wheeling, W.Va.: American Association of Zoological Parks and Aquariums.

Trivers, R. L. 1972. Parental investment and sexual selection. In *Sexual selection and the descent of man 1871–1971*, ed. B. Campbell, 136–70. Chicago: Aldine.

van Keulen-Kromhout, G. 1978. Zoo enclosures for bears *Ursidae:* Their influence on captive behavior and reproduction. *Int. Zoo Yrbk.* 18:177–86.

Weir, M. W., and De Fries, J. C. 1964. Prenatal maternal influence on behavior in mice: Evidence of a genetic basis. *J. Comp. Physiol. Psychol.* 58:412–17.

Wemmer, C. 1974. Design for polar bear maternity dens. *Int. Zoo Yrbk.* 14:222–23.

Werren, J. H., Gross, M. R., and Shine, R. 1980. Paternity and the evolution of male parental care. *J. Theor. Biol.* 82:619–31.

Wharton, D. C. 1986. Management procedures for the successful breeding of the striped grass mouse *Lemniscomys striatus*. *Int. Zoo Yrbk.* 24/25:260–65.

Whitten, P. L. 1986. Infants and adult males. In *Primate societies*, ed. B. B. Smuts, D. L. Cheney, R. M. Seyfarth, R. W. Wrangham, and T. T. Struhsaker, 343–57. Chicago: University of Chicago Press.

Williams, E. S., Thorne, E. T., Kwiatkowski, D. R., Anderson, S. L., and Lutz, K. 1991. Reproductive biology and management of captive black-footed ferrets *(Mustela nigripes)*. *Zoo Biol.* 10:383–98.

Willis, R. B. 1980. Breeding the Malayan giant squirrel *(Ratufa bicolor)* at London Zoo. *Int. Zoo Yrbk.* 20:218–20.

Wilson, G. L. 1993. Exhibition and breeding of aardvarks at the Philadelphia Zoological Garden. *Animal Keepers' Forum* 20:209–15.

Wilson, M., Warren, J. M., and Abbot, L. 1965. Infantile stimulation, activity, and learning by cats. *Child Dev.* 36:843–53.

Wimsatt, W. A., and Guerriere, A. 1961. Care and maintenance of the common vampire in captivity. *J. Mammal.* 42:449–55.

Wittenberger, J. F., and Tilson, R. L. 1980. The evolution of monogamy: Hypotheses and evidence. *Annu. Rev. Ecol. Syst.* 11:197–232.

Wolfheim, J. H., Jensen, G. D., and Bobbitt, R. A. 1970. Effects of the group environment on the mother-infant relationship in pig-tailed monkey *(Macaca nemestrina)*. *Primates* 11:119–24.

Wrangham, R. W., and Rubenstein, D. I. 1986. Social evolution in birds and mammals. In *Ecological aspects of social evolution* ed. D. I. Rubenstein and R. W. Wrangham, 452–70. Princeton, N.J.: Princeton University Press.

Wright, P. C., Haring, D. M., Izard, M. K., and Simons, E. L. 1989. Psychological well-being of nocturnal primates in captivity. In *Housing, care, and psychological well-being of captive and laboratory primates*, ed. E. F. Segal, 61–74. Park Ridge, N.J.: Noyes.

Xanten, W., Kessler, D. S., and Grumm, J. 1988. Breeding and management of Prevost's squirrel *Callosciurus prevosti* at the National Zoological Park. *Int. Zoo Yrbk.* 27:283–86.

Yalden, D. W., and Morris, P. A. 1975. *The lives of bats*. New York: Demeter Press.

Zeveloff, S. I., and Boyce, M. S. 1980. Parental investment and mating systems in mammals. *Evolution* 34:973–82.

43

Patterns of Growth in Mammals

JAMES K. KIRKWOOD AND GEORGINA M. MACE

Managers of zoological collections are now placing greater emphasis on captive breeding. Along with techniques that improve reproductive rates, an understanding of normal growth patterns (and the management regimes that contribute to them) can greatly enhance the prospect of rearing animals that will go on to become successful breeders themselves. In this chapter we will give a broad description of the growth of mammals, discuss factors that may affect it, and end with recommendations for future research that should be undertaken in zoos and records that should be kept on growing animals. We will concentrate upon practical aspects of the growth process that are relevant to the maintenance of wild animals in captivity.

"Growth" at its simplest means an increase in size, but this process occurs with concomitant changes in the shape (morphology), structure (anatomy), chemical composition, and function of the organism as it develops from a fertilized egg into an adult. These changes are generally described by the term "development." The selective forces acting on growth and on development may be quite different, so that the two often are not closely correlated across species. This taxonomic variation in growth and development is important from two different viewpoints. On a practical level, this variation needs to be considered when attempting to extrapolate findings from one species to another, or across broader taxonomic groups. For example, figure 43.1 shows the different rates of development in six species representing six major mammalian groups. The six species have similar adult body weights (about 1,300 g), but different developmental patterns. Clearly, findings from one species will not help in predicting the timing of key developmental stages in others. Second, differential growth and development have been widely discussed as key factors in the origins and evolution of species diversity (Gould 1977; Huxley 1932; Thompson 1917), and therefore there is some interest in understanding different growth patterns, their origins, and their implications.

Some information is available on patterns of postnatal weight gain for about 10% of the approximately 4,000 spe-

cies of mammals (see Zullinger et al. 1984 for a review). However, for most of these, the data are restricted to a few body weight measurements; our knowledge of other aspects of growth and development is limited. A vast amount of research, however, has been undertaken on the growth of humans, domestic farm animals, and some laboratory species from a variety of different perspectives (e.g., biochemical and morphological). As is often the case, the knowledge gained by such intensive studies on domestic and laboratory species has provided an invaluable basis from which to make inferences about other species, and we will refer to these data where appropriate.

THE PATTERN OF WEIGHT GAIN

When body weight is plotted against age from conception, mammals, like most other forms of life, show an S-shaped, or sigmoid, growth curve. For example, figure 43.2a shows the pattern of weight increase from conception in the common marmoset, *Callithrix jacchus*. This curve describes the *cumulative growth*. The *velocity of growth* (or instantaneous or absolute growth rate), which is usually measured in grams (g) or kilograms (kg) gained per day, is initially slow but accelerates until reaching a peak or plateau, usually when the mammal is about one-third to one-half grown, and then decelerates until adult body mass is approached (fig. 43.2b). The velocity of growth in relation to the body weight already achieved is known as the *relative growth rate* and is generally expressed in terms of g or kg gained per day per g or kg of body weight. It rises to a peak at an early stage of growth and then declines gradually (fig. 43.2c).

Apart from the obvious differences among species in the adult size achieved and the time taken to do so (which we will consider later), there is considerable variation among species in the shape of the cumulative growth curve. The shape of a growth curve (e.g., fig. 43.2a) can often be described quite closely by relatively simple mathematical equations. Three commonly applied equations are shown

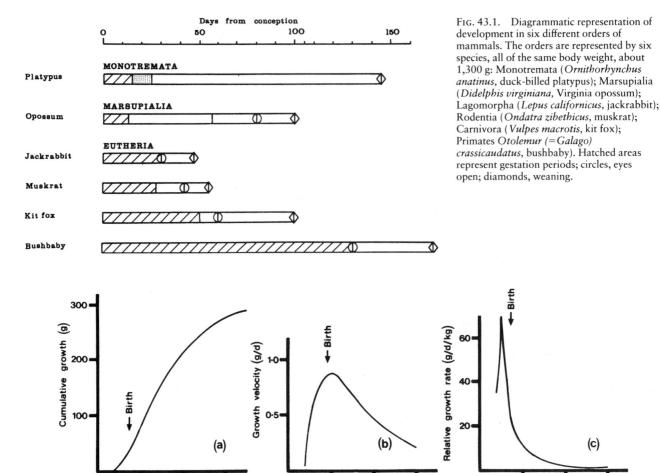

FIG. 43.1. Diagrammatic representation of development in six different orders of mammals. The orders are represented by six species, all of the same body weight, about 1,300 g: Monotremata (*Ornithorhynchus anatinus*, duck-billed platypus); Marsupialia (*Didelphis virginiana*, Virginia opossum); Lagomorpha (*Lepus californicus*, jackrabbit); Rodentia (*Ondatra zibethicus*, muskrat); Carnivora (*Vulpes macrotis*, kit fox); Primates *Otolemur (=Galago) crassicaudatus*, bushbaby). Hatched areas represent gestation periods; circles, eyes open; diamonds, weaning.

FIG. 43.2.   Three ways of describing the growth of the common marmoset, *Callithrix jacchus: (a)* cumulative growth; *(b)* velocity of growth; *(c)* relative growth rate. (Data from Hearn 1982; Chambers and Hearn 1985.)

plotted in figure 43.3. These equations can be used to summarize otherwise complex growth data in terms of a few parameters, or to facilitate comparison of patterns or rates of growth among a number of different species (Zullinger et al. 1984; Wilson 1977; Ricklefs 1968). The three equations all describe broadly S-shaped curves, but with slightly differing properties. The logistic curve (fig. 43.3b) has its inflection point where 50% asymptotic weight is reached, the Gompertz curve (fig. 43.3a) at 37%, and the Von Bertalanffy curve (fig. 43.3c) at 30%. From a practical standpoint, the differences are slight, and a curve drawn by eye is as useful as a statistically fitted curve for most purposes.

All these equations describe curves in which a plateau is effectively reached, representing the attainment of adult mass. In reality, such clearly defined plateaus are rarely seen. A few species continue to show a gradual weight increase well into middle age or beyond (e.g., laboratory rats, *Rattus norvegicus*, fig. 43.4). Generally, this prolonged growth is due to the deposition of body fat rather than to

any increase in skeletal size. Growth of the long bones ceases after the epiphyses close, and the timing of closure varies among sites. In male rhesus macaques, *Macaca mulatta*, the sequence of epiphyseal closure is: distal humerus (24 months), distal fibula (33 months), proximal femur (45 months), proximal radius (48 months), proximal ulna and distal tibia (52 months), proximal fibula (54 months), distal radius (60 months), distal ulna and femur and proximal tibia (69 months), and proximal humerus (72 months) (Watts 1986). In some species (e.g., the rat), some epiphyses never completely close (see McCance 1962).

Another way in which some growth curves deviate from the classic sigmoid form is in showing oscillations due to seasonal influences. For example, many large ungulates inhabiting temperate zones probably show seasonal fluctuations in growth rate similar to those measured in the red deer, *Cervus elaphus* (fig. 43.5), in which growth slows during the winter months. These fluctuations are extreme in the Svalbard reindeer, *Rangifer tarandus platyrhynchus*, in its

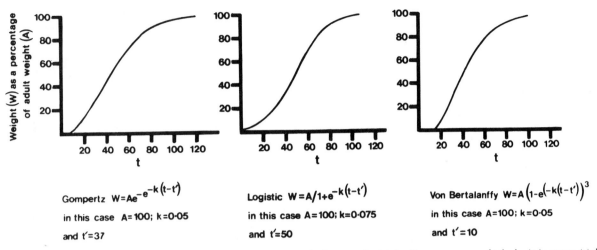

FIG. 43.3.   The shapes of three curves that approximate patterns of growth of mammals: (a) the Gompertz curve; (b) the logistic curve; (c) the von Bertalanffy curve.

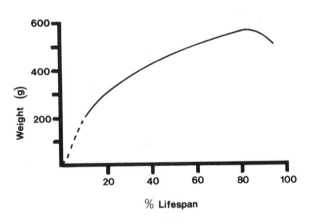

FIG. 43.4.   Body weight changes throughout the life span in male laboratory rats, *Rattus norvegicus*. (After Yu et al. 1982.)

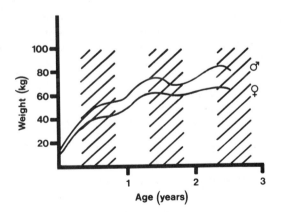

FIG. 43.5.   Seasonal fluctuations in the growth curves of male and female red deer, *Cervus elaphus*. The hatched areas indicate the winter months, from November to April inclusive. (From Blaxter et al. 1974.)

natural habitat (Tyler 1987); this species gains about 30 kg each summer but loses at least half of that each winter, finally reaching adult weight at about 4 years of age.

These general effects, as well as a number of factors that influence individual growth rates (discussed below), may make it difficult to define precisely a species' adult weight or the exact age at which it is attained. However, unlike that of other animal groups such as the fishes and reptiles, in which individuals continue to grow throughout their lives (Goss 1974), the growth of mammals is quite clearly determinate; it follows some regular pattern throughout early life and then ceases. Possible exceptions to this rule are some large ungulates (e.g., elephants: Hanks 1972; bovids: Jarman 1983) and cetaceans (Goss 1974).

THE PATTERN OF DEVELOPMENT

Early Embryonic Development

In all mammals, the diameter of the fertilized egg is about 0.1 mm, and its mass is about 5×10^{-7} g (one-half of one millionth of a gram). The differences among species in adult shape and size arise largely through variation in the timing of onset and duration of body development and variation in growth rates (see "Morphological Development and Allometry" below). In the first few days after fertilization, cell division results in a solid ball of cells without any increase in overall mass. This ball of cells then develops into a blastocyst, a fluid-filled sphere lined with cells. The blastocyst stage is reached 3–10 days after fertilization in most mammals, shortly after the conceptus has completed its descent of the oviduct and has entered the uterus. Implantation into or onto the wall of the uterus usually follows this within a few days, but in some species this process and further development of the blastocyst is delayed. This delay, known as embryonic diapause, is seen in species of many different families, and can last for up to a year in some marsupials (see Hutchins, Thomas, and Asa, chap. 41, this volume). Reactivation and implantation of the blastocyst after embryonic diapause is influenced by environmental factors, notably by changes in photoperiod (Renfree 1982).

The embryo develops from the cells at one pole of the blastocyst, while the rest of the blastocyst develops into the fetal membranes that constitute the placenta. Initially, placental growth is considerably greater than that of the embryo. The form of the placenta and its attachment to maternal tissues varies among taxonomic groups (Renfree 1982), and this variation may influence the rate and form of intrauterine development (see below).

After implantation, the embryo undergoes a phase of organogenesis in which the rudiments of the organs and tissues of the body are established. A detailed account of this process is beyond the scope of the chapter, but it occurs rapidly, in a matter of days rather than weeks, and more rapidly in smaller species than in larger ones. Details of the embryonic development of eutherian mammals and marsupials are given by Phillips (1975).

Morphological Development and Allometry

The cumulative growth curves of individual organs usually show a sigmoid pattern with time, similar to that describing the growth of the whole body (e.g., fig. 43.2a), but the relationships among different organs are complex. When some are half-grown, others have already reached maximum size, and still others may be just starting to grow. Thus, at the time of birth, although all the organs are present, their relative proportions are unlike those in the adult. The brain, the eyes, and the digestive system are examples of organs that approach their adult mass early compared with the body as a whole, while the locomotor and sexual organs exemplify those that approach their adult size at a late stage. The relationships of stage of growth of some organs to stage of growth of the body as a whole are shown in figure 43.6.

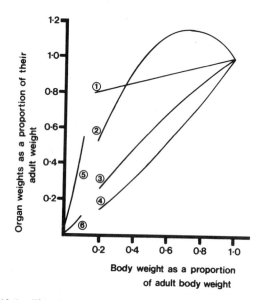

FIG. 43.6.   The relationship of the growth of some organs to the growth of the whole body. Curves 1, 2, 3, and 4 represent the brain, empty alimentary tract, spleen, and muscles of neck and thorax of the sheep respectively (Butterfield et al. 1983); curves 5 and 6 represent the brain and liver of the common marmoset, *Callithrix jacchus.* (From Chambers and Hearn 1985.)

The pattern of growth of the internal organs has been studied in detail in only a few mammalian species; namely, humans, domestic farm animals, and laboratory animals. Since the measurements can be made only at postmortem, this is not surprising. However, there are measurements on quite a wide range of species for external characters such as tail length, body length, and foot length during the period of growth. The relationship of head and body length to body weight during growth in squirrel monkeys, *Saimiri sciureus*, is shown in figure 43.7. If these data (length in cm and body weight in kg) are plotted on logarithmic scales, it is found that the relationship is described by the formula

$$\log \text{length} = -1.425 + 0.33 \cdot \log \text{weight} \quad (43.1)$$

in which the value -1.425 is the intercept, the point at which the line crosses the y-axis, and the value 0.33 is the slope or gradient of the line. This is equivalent to

$$\text{length} = 0.038 \cdot \text{weight}^{0.33} \quad (43.2)$$

This form of equation, which has been widely used to describe the growth of one part of the body in relation to another, or in relation to the growth of the body as a whole, is called the allometric equation (see Huxley 1932; Schmidt-Nielsen 1984). A plot of sitting height against weight during growth of the rhesus macaque has a similar form (Hartman and Straus 1933), such that, like length, sitting height is proportional to the 0.33 or $\frac{1}{3}$ power of body weight; or conversely, height is proportional to weight cubed (kg^3), which is the expected relationship between measures of length and volume (weight) in objects that are of similar shape. In such relationships the values of the exponent and the constant may differ among taxonomic groups. These relationships have significance for the study of growth processes and their contribution to the evolution of morphological differences among species (Gould 1977; Huxley 1932). They are also of direct practical value in three ways. First, a knowledge of the relationship of, for example, body length to age can help in estimating the birth date of an individual whose age is unknown. Second, if the data are extensive, it may be possible to assess condition by examining body weight in relation to some linear measure of body size, and in humans such weight/height curves are commonly used to check that growth is proceeding normally. Third, the normal weights of individual organs in relation to body weight can be described in this way, and such relationships can be used as standards against which to judge abnormality.

Body Composition during Growth

The major components of the bodies of mammals are water, protein, fat, and minerals. In the adult laboratory mouse, *Mus musculus*, these constituents contribute about 71%, 18%, 9%, and 4% respectively. However, there is considerable variation in the adult fat content both among species and among individuals within the same species. Larger species tend to have a higher proportion of body fat than smaller ones (Pitts and Bullard 1968), but there is also a great deal of variation associated with factors other than body size.

At birth, mammals typically have a higher water content (about 80%), a lower fat content (usually about 2%, but it

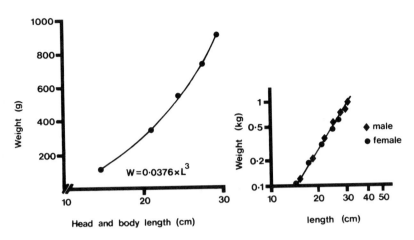

FIG. 43.7. *(a)* The relationship of head and body length to weight during postnatal growth in squirrel monkeys, *Saimiri sciureus*. *(b)* The same data plotted on a logarithmic scale. (Data from Long and Cooper 1968.)

can be much higher than this in some species, such as guinea pigs, *Cavia porcellus*, humans, and seals: Robbins 1983), and a slightly lower protein and mineral content than adults. The proportion of fat to protein deposited during postnatal growth varies among species, and also varies within species according to the plane of nutrition. Generally, in the early stages of postnatal growth the tissue deposited consists mainly of protein, and the proportion of fat increases as adult size is approached. Some species (e.g., seals) do, however, deposit more fat at an early stage.

When offered a high-quality diet ad libitum, individuals of some species will eat more than required to sustain normal growth. When this occurs, the extra energy is largely deposited as fat. Rosenblum and Smiley (1980) found that about 20% of bonnet macaques, *Macaca radiata*, became obese when offered food ad libitum. Adult laboratory rats, when offered a rich, varied, and highly palatable "cafeteria" diet of items such as potato chips, chocolate, cake, and cookies, were found to ingest more energy per day than those fed on standard pellet diets, and to deposit fat as a result (Rothwell and Stock 1982). Although the intake of growing rats on a "cafeteria" diet also increased, growth rate was not altered, nor did the animals appear to deposit more fat.

Age and Size at Birth and Sexual Maturity

Across species, body size, neonatal weight, gestation length, and age at sexual maturity are all strongly correlated, and the details of these relationships have been published for a variety of taxonomic groups (Harvey and Clutton-Brock 1985; Gittleman 1986; Eisenberg 1981; Millar 1981; Blueweiss et al. 1978; Sacher and Staffeldt 1974). Gestation period tends to increase with increasing adult body weight across species (e.g., Martin and MacLarnon 1985), but there are large differences among taxa. Similarly, weight at birth as a proportion of adult weight varies among broad taxonomic groups. Marsupials never weigh more than 1 g at birth (Lee and Cockburn 1985) and are therefore born at about 0.02% of adult weight. Eutherians are generally born at between 1% and 20% of adult weight, although neonatal bears are only 0.1% of adult weight (Sacher and Staffeldt 1974). In marsupials, the gestation period is variable due to differences among species in the preimplantation phase, and

ranges from about 15 days in the long-nosed bandicoot, *Perameles nasuta*, to about 28 days in the tammar wallaby, *Macropus eugenii* (Lee and Cockburn 1985).

The time of sexual maturation can be hard to define because in many species the physiological maturation of reproductive organs does not necessarily coincide with the first successful breeding attempt. Individuals may be prevented from breeding by hormonal changes influenced environmentally (e.g., breeding seasons) or behaviorally (e.g., social suppression in marmoset monkeys: Abbott 1987), or by being excluded from access to breeding individuals of the opposite sex (e.g., young males in bachelor herds). It is quite common for sexual maturation to precede adult body size by a considerable margin. For example, male bighorn sheep, *Ovis canadensis*, are sexually mature at 1.5 to 2.5 years of age, but body growth and particularly horn development continue for another 5-6 years (Geist 1971). In fact, prolongation of body growth relative to sexual maturation among males seems to be common in polygynous species of ungulates (Ralls 1977; Jarman 1983) and primates (Shea 1986). In nonpolygynous species, males and females tend to mature at approximately the same age and stage of growth, but this varies widely. In some species, individuals can attain sexual maturity when only one-half grown, and in general, it is rare for sexual maturation to coincide with or occur after the attainment of adult size.

THE RATE OF GROWTH

Comparing Growth Rates

As we have already seen (see fig. 43.2b), the velocity of growth depends upon the stage of growth, and this has to be taken into account when comparing growth rates between species. Valid comparisons can be made by examining the growth velocity at a given stage of growth (for example, at 20% of adult size), by comparing average weight gain over a defined part of the growth curve (e.g., between 20% and 80% of adult size), or by comparing the rate constants of curves of the kind illustrated in figure 43.3 when these equations are fitted to actual growth data.

Such comparisons have revealed some of the factors influencing the rate of growth in mammals. These factors can be divided into two types: genetic and environmental.

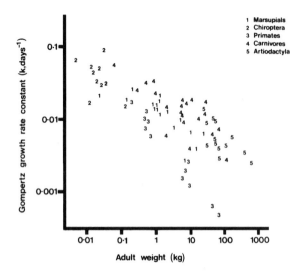

FIG. 43.8.   The relationship of growth rate (the Gompertz growth rate constant, days^{-1}) to adult weight in species from five mammalian orders. (Data from Zullinger et al. 1984.)

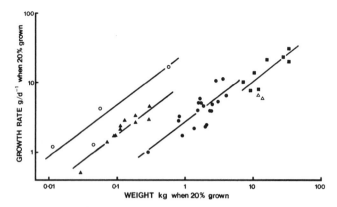

FIG. 43.9.   The relationship between growth rate and body weight at 20% of adult weight. Open circles, prosimians; solid triangles, New World monkeys; solid circles, Old World monkeys; solid squares, great apes; open triangles, humans. The lines represent the mean growth rate per kg$^{3/4}$ (g/d · kg$^{3/4}$) for each of the groups, excluding humans. (Data from Kirkwood 1985.)

Genetic Factors Influencing Growth Rate

The Influence of Adult Size on Growth Rate. The influence of adult size on growth rate and on the time taken to grow to adulthood has received considerable attention (Zullinger et al. 1984; Case 1978; Taylor 1965, 1980). Figure 43.8 shows the growth constant K of the Gompertz curve (see fig. 43.3) fitted to growth data from Zullinger et al. (1984) and plotted against body weight for seventy species from five mammalian orders. This plot shows that K (d^{-1}), an index of relative growth rate (Ricklefs 1968), tends to decrease with increasing body weight. In such comparisons among species with a wide range in adult weights, when the logarithm of K is plotted against the logarithm of body weight, the points typically fall about a line whose slope is close to $-\frac{1}{4}$. The precise value of the gradient depends upon the species included in the sample and on the statistical method used in its calculation.

If the absolute growth rate (g/day) at a given stage of growth is plotted against adult weight (again using logarithmic scales) for a wide range of mammals, the slope of the relationship is typically found to be close to $\frac{3}{4}$. This finding implies that with each doubling in size at a particular stage of growth (e.g., when 50% grown) between species, there tends to be about a 68% greater rate of weight gain. It is not precisely understood why growth velocity is related to weight between species in this way, but it may be a consequence of the capacity for energy intake, which, like metabolic rate (Kleiber 1975), scales with approximately the $\frac{3}{4}$ power of body weight (Kirkwood and Webster 1984; Kirkwood 1983).

In figure 43.9, the growth rates and weights of some primate species when 20% grown are shown. Kirkwood (1985) interpreted these data as indicating that within the groups prosimians, New World primates, Old World primates, and apes, growth rates tend to increase with about the $\frac{3}{4}$ power of weight, but that there are marked differences in growth rate among these groups that are not related to size. The value of the gradient in such comparisons, al-though often close to $\frac{3}{4}$, has been found to vary among orders (for example, Gittleman and Oftedal [1987] found a slope of 0.56 in carnivores, and Russell [1982] found a slope of 0.82 in marsupials) and may also be dependent on the taxonomic level of the analysis, that is, whether species within the entire class Mammalia or within an order or family are examined.

While considering the influence of adult weight on growth rate, we should also point out the associated relationship between adult size and time taken to grow to adulthood. Small mammals tend to reach adult size, or a given proportion of it, sooner than larger ones. Taking prosimians as an example, the lesser mouse lemur, *Microcebus murinus* (adult weight 0.1 kg), reaches 20% of adult weight about 10 days after birth (Glatston 1981), while the ruffed lemur, *Varecia (=Lemur) variegata* (adult weight 3 kg) reaches 20% of adult weight about 35 days after birth (Cartmill et al. 1979). Likewise, among ungulates, the Chinese water deer, *Hydropotes inermis*, reaches 20% of its adult weight in about 25 days (Kirkwood et al. 1988), while the addax, *Addax nasomaculatus*, which is about 7 times heavier when full grown, was found to reach 20% of its adult weight in 50 days (Markham and Kirkwood 1988). To be more specific, time taken to grow to adulthood is proportional to adult weight raised to about the $\frac{1}{4}$ power (Taylor 1965). The durations of many other physiological and life history events tend to scale in this way (Calder 1984). Taylor (1965, 1980) advocated the use of a "metabolic age" scale for comparing patterns of growth among species, defining "metabolic age" as age in days divided by the $\frac{1}{4}$ power of adult weight. (In fact, he recommended the exponent 0.27, and we use $\frac{1}{4}$ here to imply less precision.) The patterns of postnatal growth for eight species in relation to metabolic age, including the rapidly growing masked shrew, *Sorex cinereus*, and humans, which grow very slowly, are shown in figure 43.10. The pattern of growth of the ruffed lemur in figure 43.10 is probably close to the average mammalian pattern.

Phylogeny. It is apparent in figures 43.8 and 43.9 that

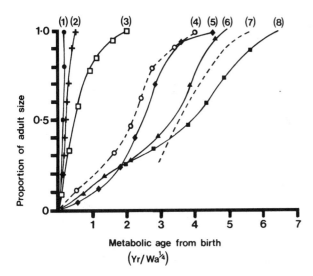

FIG. 43.10.   Patterns of growth in some mammals in relation to metabolic age (a body size–independent index of age: see text). 1, masked shrew, *Sorex cinereus* (Forsyth 1976); 2, ruffed lemur, *Varecia* (=*Lemur*) *variegata* (Cartmill et al. 1979); 3, cotton-top tamarin, *Saguinus oedipus* (Kirkwood 1983); 4, rhesus macaque, *Macaca mulatta* (Bourne 1975); 5, gorilla, *Gorilla gorilla* (Gijzen and Tijskens 1971); 6, chimpanzee, *Pan troglodytes* (Smith, Butler, and Pace 1975); 7, gibbon, *Hylobates lar* (Schultz 1944); human, *Homo sapiens* (Altman and Dittmer 1962).

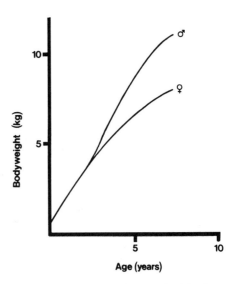

FIG. 43.11.   Sexual dimorphism in the growth of the rhesus macaque, *Macaca mulatta*. (After Bourne 1975.)

some of the variation in growth rate among species of similar adult weight is associated with phylogeny, or the taxonomic position of the species (see also fig. 43.10). On a broad scale, the primates tend to have slower growth rates than the other orders, and the carnivores and artiodactyls tend to grow faster. These kinds of differences persist at lower taxonomic levels; for example, the marmosets and tamarins (Callitrichidae) grow more slowly than the prosimians (Prosimii) but more rapidly than the Old World monkeys (Cercopithecidae) (Kirkwood 1985). The reasons for these differences are not well understood. Some may be associated with major functional differences among the various taxonomic groups. For example, species with relatively low body temperatures tend to grow more slowly, and there may be an association between basal metabolic rate and growth rate (McNab 1986b).

Variation in growth rate among species of birds has been found to be associated with differences in the pattern of development: altricial species (those that are reared by the parents in the nest) grow more rapidly than precocial ones (those that feed themselves from hatching) (Ricklefs 1973, 1979). Among eutherian mammals there is also considerable variation in the degree of development at birth. For example, the canids are generally born blind, helpless, and completely dependent on the parents for food, while many deer and antelope neonates stand and walk within minutes of birth. However, the distinction between altricial and precocial young is less clear-cut than in birds, and most authors have devised a simple scoring system for the state of the neonate at birth (e.g., by scoring for whether hair or teeth are present at birth and whether the eyes and ears are open), which actually leads to an altricial/precocial continuum rather than a dichotomy (Case 1978; Portmann 1962).

E. M. Zullinger (pers. comm.) has shown that the more precocial species tend to have slower growth rates, at least in rodents as a group and across orders of mammals, although Case (1978), using a different method of measuring growth rate, found no association. The gestation period tends to be relatively long in precocial species (Martin and MacLarnon 1985; Sacher and Staffeldt 1974), although there are exceptions, such as the hares, *Lepus* spp., whose highly precocial young are born after a relatively short gestation (Mace 1979; Sacher and Staffeldt 1974).

Sex. In most mammalian species, adult males are larger than adult females. On average, the ratio of male size to female size is about 1.1–1.5, but in some species the ratio is much higher (e.g., 2.5 in southern elephant seals, *Mirounga leonina;* 1.7 in hamadryas baboons, *Papio hamadryas*). Adult size dimorphism can be a result of variation between the sexes in growth rate and in the period of growth. The growth processes resulting in size dimorphism have been reviewed for ungulates (Jarman 1983) and primates (Shea 1986). In general, sexual size dimorphism is a result of both increases in growth rate and prolongation of the growth period, though species differ in the relative contribution of each (Leigh 1992). The difference in growth rates between male and female rhesus macaques is shown in figure 43.11. In some mammalian species, sexual size dimorphism is present at birth, which, in the absence of sex differences in gestation length, indicates sex differences in prenatal growth rates. In some highly dimorphic species, gestation may be slightly longer for the larger sex (e.g., red deer: Clutton-Brock, Guinness, and Albon 1982).

Environmental Factors Influencing Prenatal Growth

Maternal Size. Neonatal weight is closely related to adult weight, and thus to maternal weight, across species. In general, eutherian neonates weigh between about 1% and 20% of adult weight (see above). However, across species, there is a tendency for neonate size to become relatively smaller with increasing maternal size; neonatal weight is

TABLE 43.1.   Variation in Birth Weights of Cotton-Top Tamarins, *Saguinus oedipus*, between Colonies

	Colony 1		Colony 2	
	Mean birth weight (g)	n	Mean birth weight (g)	n
Singles	44.0	2	37.0	4
Twins	43.2	32	36.0	20
Triplets	36.2	8	34.0	3

Sources: Colony 1, Wolfe et al. 1975; Colony 2, Hampton, Hampton, and Levy 1971.

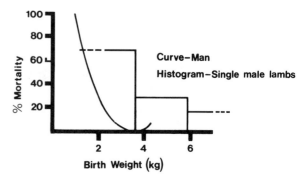

FIG. 43.12.   Neonatal mortality in relation to birth weight in sheep and humans. (Data on humans from Record, Gibson, and McKeown 1952; on sheep, from Huffman, Kluk, and Pappaioanou 1985.)

related to adult weight raised to about the 0.9 power (Harvey and Clutton-Brock 1985; Blueweiss et al. 1978; Millar 1977). Within species, larger mothers tend to produce larger babies; this may be an effect of the intrauterine environment rather than a genetic effect.

Maternal Nutrition. The plane of nutrition of the mother has been shown to influence birth weight, and thus fetal growth rate, in humans (Habicht et al. 1974) and sheep (Thompson and Aitken 1959). It is quite possible that differences in mean birth weight reported between two colonies of cotton-top tamarins, *Saguinus oedipus* (table 43.1), were also due to differences in the nutritional status of the breeding females (although other factors could be involved).

It would in fact be surprising if the fetal growth rate were entirely independent of the mother's condition, especially in those species in which the total litter mass is relatively large. However, the fetus is often remarkably well buffered from the effects of suboptimal maternal nutrition. It is usually in the later stages of pregnancy, when the fetus's growth makes significant demands on maternal resources, that poor maternal nutrition may constrain fetal growth.

Total litter mass typically ranges from 20%–40% of the mother's mass in the smallest species of eutherian mammals to 1%–2% in species with adult weights of 10–1,000 kg (Tuomi 1980). Using the logic described below (see "Food Requirements during Growth" below) to estimate the energy requirements of growing mammals based on their weight and daily growth rate, it can be calculated that the extra energy needed per fetus near full term is unlikely to exceed 10% of the mother's maintenance requirement. In rats, peak intake during pregnancy is increased by 65% over that required for maintenance (Cripps and Williams 1975). In cattle, current recommendations suggest providing 1.3 times the maintenance ration in late pregnancy (Simms and Hand 1986). In women, however, even though it is estimated that requirements in late pregnancy should exceed maintenance by about 14%, in practice this increase does not always occur (Prentice and Whitehead 1986).

Of course, it is not just inadequate maternal energy intake that can compromise fetal growth and viability; deficiencies of specific nutrients may also have this effect. For example, inadequate protein intake was shown to lead to a high incidence of abortion in squirrel monkeys (Manocha and Long 1977).

Consequences of Low Birth Weight. Restricted maternal nutrition does not affect all fetal organs to the same extent. Some will be more retarded than others (Hafez and

Dyer 1969), and since it is in the later stages of pregnancy that maternal food restriction is most likely to affect the fetus, those organs whose growth is greatest in late pregnancy are most likely to be affected (Alexander 1974). Generally, babies born smaller than average remain relatively small throughout the period of growth (Widdowson 1974).

Neonatal mortality rates are highly dependent upon body weight at birth (fig. 43.12). Individuals of low birth weight will tend to have reduced energy reserves, and because body surface area becomes greater relative to mass as body size decreases, they are also more prone to chilling and hypothermia in cold conditions. Furthermore, they may lack the strength to compete successfully with larger siblings for opportunities to suck at the teat.

Litter Size. Single lambs, *Ovis aries,* are on average 0.5 kg heavier than twins at birth (Starke, Smith, and Joubert 1958). Litter size also has a striking effect on birth weight in humans, cattle, *Bos taurus,* pigs, *Sus scrofa,* laboratory rodents (Hafez and Dyer 1969), and the cotton-top tamarin (see table 43.1).

Litter size is itself dependent upon maternal nutrition in some species (e.g., sheep), and differences in maternal nutrition may underlie differences in average litter size observed among colonies of common marmosets (table 43.2), although other factors could be involved.

Thermal Environment of the Mother. In those bats that enter a state of torpor, or lethargy, in cold temperatures (e.g., the pipistrelle, *Pipistrellus pipistrellus*), fetal growth rate is reduced and gestation period is prolonged as the temperature drops (Racey 1969). Conversely, too high a temperature has been found to result in low birth weights in lambs (Alexander and Williams 1971).

Infectious Diseases. A variety of infectious diseases, such as cytomegalovirus and rubella infections in pregnant

TABLE 43.2.   Variation in Average Litter Size among Colonies of Common Marmosets, *Callithrix jacchus*

Colony described by	Average litter size
Hampton et al. (1978)	1.86
Hiddleston (1976)	2.23
Abbott and Hearn (1978)	2.10
Poole and Evans (1982)	2.69

Source: After Poole and Evans 1982.

women and bovine virus diarrheal infections in cattle, can cause a reduction in fetal growth rate and result in low birth weight (Blood, Radostits, and Henderson 1983).

Environmental Factors Influencing Postnatal Growth

The growth curve and pattern of development of an individual is dictated by the interaction of genetic and environmental influences. Within a species, growth curves often vary among captive individuals kept in different colonies or between captive and wild individuals (e.g., Faucheaux, Bertrand, and Bourliere 1978), and adult sizes may also differ as a result. Adult captive-born cotton-top tamarins were found to be heavier on average than adult wild-caught specimens kept in identical conditions (Kirkwood 1983), and differences in adult weights of common marmosets kept in different colonies have been reported by Poole and Evans (1982). A great deal of the variation in growth rate and adult size in wild individuals can also be attributed to prevailing environmental conditions (e.g., mountain brushtail possum, *Trichosurus caninus*: Barnett, How, and Humphreys 1982).

If there is such a thing as an optimum growth curve, then we are still some way from being able to define it for any species, except possibly humans. A precise optimum environment for growing animals (e.g., in terms of temperature, nutrition, housing, and social structure) is rarely possible. However, this should not deter successful breeders of certain species from making precise recommendations available to others. Such recommendations will help to encourage better management directly, and will also help indirectly because it is only through the trial-and-error testing of precise recommendations that improvements will be made.

Nutrition. The pattern of postnatal growth is dependent upon the quantity and quality of the food eaten. There is an extensive literature on the effects of nutrient imbalances on the growth of laboratory animals and livestock (e.g., the National Research Council publications on the nutrient requirements of domestic and laboratory animals; see table 10.1 in Oftedal and Allen, chap. 10, this volume), and it would be inappropriate to attempt any kind of review here. Suffice it to say that specific deficiencies of any of the essential amino acids, fats, vitamins, and minerals will impair or prevent growth and predispose the individual to disease or death.

All mammals are dependent on their mothers' milk for a short period after birth. From cross-species comparisons it is clear that the milk production of the mother is geared to match the demands of the young for "normal" growth. A baboon, *Papio* spp., whose single infant grows relatively slowly (Kirkwood 1985), provides relatively little energy in her milk each day (about 160 kJ/d · kg$^{3/4}$), while the brown rat, whose numerous babies all grow rather rapidly, has a much greater milk energy output (about 1,000 kJ/d · kg$^{3/4}$) (Oftedal 1984).

If we look at the situation within a species, however, it is apparent that to some extent the opposite is true: the growth rate of the infant is dependent upon the milk production rate of the dam. In species with variable litter sizes,

preweaning growth rates are often lower in large litters than in small ones. In marmosets and tamarins, although triplets are quite common in captivity (Stevenson and Sutcliffe 1978; Hearn and Burden 1979; Kirkwood et al. 1985), mothers are only very rarely able to rear all three infants, and one usually dies from lack of food soon after birth. It is not clear whether this is due to an inability of the mother to produce enough food to support triplets or to competition among the infants for access to her two teats.

The energy expended by a mother each day is much greater during lactation than during pregnancy, because during lactation the infants are both bigger and growing more rapidly. Although mothers can sustain their milk production for a while by using stored reserves if food intake is inadequate, their capacity to do this is limited. The growth rate of the suckling infants is ultimately dependent upon the nutrition of the mother. While in the most slowly growing of all mammals, humans, the energy requirements of lactation exceed maintenance by 24% or less (Prentice and Whitehead 1986), the energy requirements of lactation in those species that have large litters of rapidly growing young (e.g., dogs, *Canis familiaris*, rats, rabbits, *Oryctolagus cuniculus*, and pigs) may be two to three times the maintenance level (Oftedal 1984).

The effects of undernutrition on growing mammals were demonstrated dramatically by McCance and Widdowson (1974). By restricting energy intake, they stopped the growth of piglets at about 10 kg body weight (about 3% of adult weight) for periods of up to 3 years. They then provided a normal ration. As soon as the pigs were able to eat as much as they wished, their growth rate became roughly normal for pigs of their body weight. However, they did not attain full adult size, and the longer their growth had been held back, the smaller they were as adults (fig. 43.13). This and other experiments by McCance and Widdowson (reviewed in McCance and Widdowson 1974) showed that the long-term effects of periods of undernutrition during growth are dependent on the duration and the severity of the undernutrition, and particularly on the stage of growth at which it occurs: generally, the earlier it occurs, the more likely it is to lead to reduced adult size.

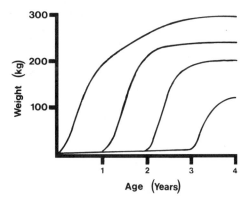

FIG. 43.13.   The effect of severe energy restriction for 1, 2, or 3 years on the growth of the pig, compared with controls fed ad libitum, whose growth is shown by the curve on the left. (After McCance and Widdowson 1974.)

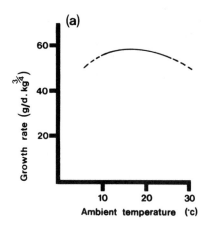

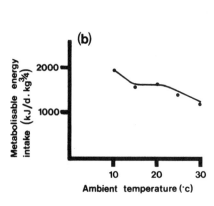

FIG. 43.14.   The effect of ambient temperature on *(a)* growth rate and *(b)* metabolizable energy intake in young pigs fed ad libitum. (After Close, Mount, and Brown 1978.)

Some developmental events are more dependent on age than on weight. For example, eruption and development of the teeth in McCance and Widdowson's pigs tended to proceed roughly on schedule, in spite of the fact that the jaws were not growing. This resulted in crowding of the teeth and abnormalities in their location, position, and shape. These abnormalities did not resolve when the dietary restriction was lifted.

Reduced adult size resulting from inadequate nutrition during growth also tends to be accompanied by slightly abnormal morphology, since the growth of the late-developing organs (e.g., limbs) is usually more severely compromised than that of the early-developing organs (e.g., brain).

Excess food during growth has been shown to predispose rats and hamsters, *Mesocricetus auratus,* to certain diseases, especially neoplasia, in later life (Yu et al. 1982; Feldman, McConnell, and Knapka 1982). It may also lead to obesity. As mentioned earlier, Rosenblum and Smiley (1980) reported that about 20% of bonnet macaques fed ad libitum became markedly obese. Robbins (1983) has drawn attention to the evidence that young animals may not be able to moderate their intake of milk and that excesses can lead to digestive disturbances. Great Dane dogs fed ad libitum on high-quality diets were found to develop a high incidence of skeletal abnormalities (Hedhammar et al. 1974). Spencer and Hull (1984) allowed infant rabbits to suckle another lactating doe in addition to their own mother and found that they would typically take in twice the normal amount of milk. As a result, the double-fed babies weighed 65% more than a single-fed control group by 21 days postpartum; the extra weight gained was due to fat deposition. Even when full grown, those rabbits that had been double-fed remained 12.5% fatter on average than the control group.

There is evidence that human infants fed via nasogastric tubes with artificial milk can grow more rapidly than normally fed infants (Calvert et al. 1983), and force-fed rats certainly do so as well (Widdowson and McCance 1960). In the rabbit, human, and rat, it appears that fat infants tend to become fat adults. This capacity to ingest excess energy and deposit abnormal amounts of fat may be a general property of mammals and should be kept in mind when hand-rearing young.

The Thermal Environment. Infant mammals often do not have a fully developed capacity for maintaining body temperature. They may depend on the proximity of one or more parents or siblings to keep warm.

As the ambient temperature drops below the comfortable range for the individual, it must start expending energy in order to maintain body temperature. Heat is generated in response to cold either by shivering or by the metabolism of brown adipose tissue (Bligh 1985). The colder the conditions, the greater the heat production must be. At the other end of the scale, as environmental temperature begins to exceed the comfortable limit, most mammals have some capacity to keep cool by panting.

Environmental temperature can have an effect on food intake and growth rate. Studies by Close, Mount, and Brown (1978) showed that in the temperature range of 10°–30°C, growth rate remained fairly constant in pigs offered food ad libitum, although there was some evidence for a decline in growth rate at the top end of this temperature range (fig. 43.14). At the lower temperature, the pigs maintained growth rate, in spite of their increased energy expenditure in keeping warm by increasing food intake (fig. 43.14).

While the pigs in this study were able to maintain growth rate across a wide range of ambient temperatures, there is likely to be great variation among species in their abilities to do this. There are upper and lower limits to the temperature range that can be withstood; growth rate will become increasingly compromised at temperatures outside this range.

Social and Other Environmental Factors. Growth rate may be compromised in gang-caged animals when low-ranking individuals are unable to gain access to a food hopper. For example, Tasse (1986) found that rock cavies, *Kerodon rupestris,* reared with one adult female weighed significantly more than those reared with a pair of adults. It has also been found that early environmental enrichment and stimulation leads to accelerated growth in rats, primates, and humans (Fritz and Fritz 1985).

FOOD REQUIREMENTS DURING GROWTH

Estimation of the quantities of nutrients needed by growing animals is a complex task. We are not yet at a stage at which this can be done with great confidence for species other than domestic farm animals. However, enough is known to enable the rough prediction of energy requirements during growth (Kirkwood 1991; Kirkwood and Bennett 1992). These estimates are given in terms of metabolizable energy, or the fraction of the gross energy intake remaining after the proportions lost in feces, urine, and gases produced by fermentation have been subtracted.

During growth, the energy requirement can be artificially but usefully divided into two components: first, the requirement to maintain the animal at the size it has attained, and second, the requirement for growth. The maintenance component, E_m (kJ/day), is largely dependent upon body weight, and therefore increases as growth proceeds. Among adults of different species E_m is typically about 500 kJ/d · kg$^{3/4}$. There is variation about this mean, however, as adult marsupials tend to have lower metabolic rates than eutherians, for example (Dawson and Hulbert 1970). Weight-independent variation in metabolic rate has been reviewed by McNab (1986a). Although E_m is an abstract concept for growing animals, it is useful to assume that a value for E_m of about 500 kJ/d · kg$^{3/4}$ is typical, at least for some eutherian mammals in comfortable environments and with low activity costs. The energy requirement for weight gain, E_g (kJ/d), is dependent upon three factors: the daily weight gain (g/d), which as we have seen reaches a peak when the animal is one-third to one-half grown, the chemical composition of the tissue deposited, and the efficiency with which this tissue is synthesized from absorbed nutrients.

As discussed above, the daily weight gain depends on the species, its size, and its stage of growth. The composition of the tissue deposited changes throughout growth. In general, the later the stage of growth, the greater the proportion of fat deposited. Each gram of fat deposited has an energy content of about 39 kJ, while each gram of lean tissue (protein and water) has an energy content of 6 kJ (Webster 1977). Obviously, therefore, more energy is needed to increase body weight by 1 gram if the tissue deposited is fat than if it is lean. Tissue deposited is rarely, if ever, purely fat or lean, and its energy value is typically found to increase from about 7 kJ/g to 15 kJ/g in wild animals as growth proceeds, although different patterns are seen in some species (Robbins 1983). In captivity, when high-quality diets are provided ad libitum, a higher proportion of fat may be deposited, and the energy density of the tissue may considerably exceed 15 kJ/g in the later stages of growth (e.g., cattle: Webster 1978).

In addition to the energy stored as fat or lean, some energy is needed to fuel the process of tissue deposition (the transport of the materials and their metabolism into structural or storage compounds). The cost of tissue deposition varies among species and according to the composition of the tissue deposited and the composition of the diet (Blaxter 1971; Millward, Garlick, and Reeds 1976). Pullar and Webster (1977) measured the metabolizable energy costs of deposition of protein and fat in rats fed on a standard pellet diet as 2.25 kJ/kJ and 1.36 kJ/kJ respectively. Since the energy densities of protein and fat are 24 kJ/g and 39 kJ/g respectively, the cost of deposition of either of these substances works out to be 53 kJ/g dry matter. Protein is associated with about three times its own weight of water in liv-

ing tissue, so the energy cost of depositing 1 g of wet protein (lean tissue) is about 13 kJ. These figures pertain to a monogastric animal whose dietary energy source is largely carbohydrate. The cost of fat and lean deposition in carnivores fed on flesh may be less than this, and the cost of deposition in ruminants fed on roughage may be more (Millward, Garlick, and Reeds 1976; Blaxter 1971).

For the purpose of producing a rough estimate of the energy requirements for growth, we assume that the cost of depositing 1 kJ of tissue is 1.25 kJ, and that the energy content of tissue deposited is constant at 12 kJ/g. Under these circumstances, the cost of each gram of weight gained will be 15 kJ. If the body weight of a young animal is known and growth curves are available to give an indication of its growth rate (g/d), a rough estimate of its energy requirements can be made. Kirkwood (1985) described the way in which energy requirements are predicted to change during growth and to vary with size and phylogenetic differences in growth rate among species.

This approach has proved useful in the estimation of the energy requirements of growing domestic livestock, in which enough is known about the underlying assumptions (E_m, the energy density of tissue deposited, and the cost of tissue deposition) to allow quite accurate predictions to be made. The same data are not available for most exotic species, so only rough estimates of the magnitude of the energy requirement and the way in which it is likely to change throughout the period of growth can be made. Once the energy requirement has been estimated, calculation of the amount of food needed to provide this energy is relatively straightforward. Metabolizable energy values of foods for monogastric or ruminant animals can be looked up in standard tables of the nutrient composition of foods (e.g., Paul and Southgate 1978).

FURTHER RESEARCH: THE INFORMATION NEEDED

As we have pointed out, even the most basic information about growth, namely, how weight increases with age, is available for only about 10% of mammalian species. Furthermore, such data as are available are often based on studies of very few individuals, and it is difficult to judge whether the patterns reported are normal (which, for want of a better description, we can define as like those of wild individuals reared under favorable conditions) or not.

When faced with the task of, for example, hand-rearing an individual of a species for which no previous growth data are available, it is possible to use the general principles we have described to make rough predictions about the rate and duration of growth. However, it would be better if growth curves were available for each species, and the zoo community could make rapid progress toward this goal by taking every opportunity to record the growth of the animals in its care. In addition to contributing to our knowledge of the basic biology of wild animals, regular measurement of weight and other parameters (see below) provides an excellent way of checking the progress of an individual, and can reveal fluctuations that give an early indication of disease or suboptimal management. As more data become available, it will be possible to compare growth rates of individuals reared at different zoos and to relate variation to differences in management practices, and thus to provide criteria with which to evaluate management.

We recommend that the following basic information be recorded and that the parameters listed be measured at regular intervals throughout growth, or for as long as practical constraints allow.

Background information
1. Species and subspecies
2. Individual identification number
3. Identification numbers of parents
4. Sex
5. Date of birth
6. Birth weight
7. Notes on management system (mother-reared, hand-reared, etc.)
8. Diet provided

Preventive medicine
1. If colostrum is fed, from what species, and how much
2. Vaccinations
3. Other (e.g., prophylactic antibiotics, hyperimmune sera)

Quantitative measurements of growth
1. Body weight in relation to age
2. Some linear measure of size in relation to age, for example, standing height at shoulder in ungulates; length from nose to tip of tail

Development
1. Age at eyes opening (if appropriate)
2. Age at leaving nest (if appropriate)
3. Eruption of teeth in relation to age
4. Age at which first solid food is taken
5. Age at which weaning is complete
6. Age at first mating
7. Age at first birth
8. Other records of physical development

Food consumption
1. Amount of milk consumed per day
2. Amount of solid food consumed per day
3. Frequency of feedings

The frequency with which measurements of growth and food consumption are made depends on practical constraints, but also on the duration of growth of the animal under study. Once weekly or once monthly would be appropriate for description of the growth and food requirements of large ungulates or great apes, which take years to reach adult size, but almost daily measurements are more appropriate for small mammals that reach adult size in a few weeks.

This list could be extended enormously (to include, for example, the age at first scratching the left ear), but unless some significance can be attached to the observations and measurements, or they are required for some specific study, they just clutter the field.

Finally, it is important that, when such studies are undertaken, they are written up and published in the scientific press (this applies to both successful and unsuccessful rearing attempts). Publication requires careful thought and assimilation of the data collected, and takes a lot of time, but it should be seen as part of the job. Unless such reports are published, the experiences and knowledge gained are not handed down, disseminated, or subjected to wide scrutiny, application, or criticism, and without this no real progress can be made.

CONCLUDING REMARKS

The neonatal and early juvenile periods are known to be times of high risk of mortality in zoo-born and other animals. Knowledge of growth, development, and food requirements in relation to management regime are vital for sensible attempts to improve the survival of young. Much of the information on growth and development of wild mammals that is available to us comes from studies performed in zoos.

When rearing wild animals, it is helpful to monitor growth and development and to judge them against standards for the species in order to prevent deviations and correct health or management problems. We have shown here that although the growth patterns of only about 10% of mammalian species have been described as yet, it is possible, using allometric scaling techniques, to make some estimates of how growth is likely to proceed in many other species. Nevertheless, the more exact our knowledge of the growth and development of individuals of each species, the better. Opportunities to record these processes should be taken whenever possible.

REFERENCES

Abbott, D. H. 1987. Behaviourally mediated suppression of reproduction in female marmosets. *J. Zool.* (Lond.) 213:455–70.

Abbott, D. H., and Hearn, J. P. 1978. Sexual dimorphism in the marmoset monkey: Aspects of physical, hormonal, and behavioural development. *J. Reprod. Fertil.* 53:153–66.

Alexander, G. 1974. Birth weight of lambs: Influences and consequences. In *Size at birth*. Ciba Foundation Symposium no. 27. Amsterdam: Associated Scientific Publishers.

Alexander, G., and Williams, D. 1971. Heat stress and the development of the conceptus in domestic sheep. *Journal of Agricultural Science* 76:53–72.

Altman, P. S., and Dittmer, D. S., eds. 1962. *Growth.* Washington, D.C.: Federation of American Sciences for Experimental Biology.

Barnett, J. L., How, R. A., and Humphreys, W. F. 1982. Habitat effects on organ weights, longevity, and reproduction in the mountain brushtail possum, *Trichosurus caninus* (Ogilvy). *Aust. J. Zool.* 30:23–32.

Blaxter, K. L. 1971. Methods of measuring the energy metabolism of animals and interpretation of results obtained. *Fed. Proc.* 30:1436–43.

Blaxter, K. L., Kay, R. N. B., Sharman, G. A. M., and Hamilton, W. J. 1974. *Farming the red deer.* London: HMSO.

Bligh, J. 1985. Temperature regulation. In *Stress physiology in livestock,* vol. 1, *Basic principles,* ed. M. K. Yousef, 75–96. Boca Raton, Fla.: CRC Press.

Blood, D. C., Radostits, O. M., and Henderson, J. A. 1983. *Veterinary medicine.* 6th ed. London: Bailliere Tindall.

Blueweiss, L., Fox, H., Kudzuma, V., Nakashima, D., Peters, R., and Sams, S. 1978. Relationship between body size and some life history parameters. *Oecologia* 37:257–72.

Bourne, G. H., ed. 1975. *The rhesus monkey.* Vol. 1. New York, London: Academic Press.

Butterfield, R. M., Zamara, J., James, A. M., Thompson, J. M., and

Reddacliff, K. J. 1983. Changes in body composition relative to weight and maturity in large and small strains of Australian merino rams. 3. Body organs. *Animal Production* 36:461–70.

Calder, W. A. III. 1984. *Size, function, and life history.* Cambridge, Mass.: Harvard University Press.

Calvert, S. A., Aynsley-Green, A., Jenkins, P. A., and Newman, C. 1983. *British Paediatric Association 55th Annual Meeting.* (Abstracts G39: 86.)

Cartmill, M., Brown, K., Eaglen, R., and Anderson, D. E. 1979. Hand-rearing twin ruffed lemurs, *Lemur variegatus,* at the Duke University Primate Centre. *Int. Zoo Yrbk.* 19:258–61.

Case, T. J. 1978. On the evolution and adaptive significance of postnatal growth rates in the terrestrial vertebrates. *Q. Rev. Biol.* 53:243–82.

Chambers, P. L., and Hearn, J. P. 1985. Embryonic, fetal, and placental development in the common marmoset monkey *(Callithrix jacchus). J. Zool.* (Lond.) A 207:545–61.

Close, W. H., Mount, L. E., and Brown, D. 1978. The effects of plane of nutrition and environmental temperature on the energy metabolism of the growing pig. 2. Growth rate, including protein and fat deposition. *Br. J. Nutr.* 40:423–31.

Clutton-Brock, T. H., Guinness, F. E., and Albon, S. D. 1982. *Red deer: Behavior and ecology of two sexes.* Chicago: University of Chicago Press.

Cripps, A. W., and Williams, V. J. 1975. The effect of pregnancy and lactation on food intake, gastro-intestinal anatomy, and the absorptive capacity of the small intestine in the albino rat. *Br. J. Nutr.* 33:17–32.

Dawson, T. J., and Hulbert, A. J. 1970. Standard metabolism, body temperature, and surface area of Australian marsupials. *Am. J. Physiol.* 218:1233–38.

Eisenberg, J. F. 1981. *The mammalian radiations.* London: Athlone Press.

Faucheaux, B., Bertrand, M., and Bourliere, F. 1978. Some effects of living conditions upon pattern of growth in the stumptail macaque *(Macaca arctoides). Folia Primatol.* 30:220–36.

Feldman, D. B., McConnell, E. E., and Knapka, J. J. 1982. Growth, kidney disease, and longevity of Syrian hamsters *(Mesocricetus auratus)* fed varying levels of protein. *Lab. Anim. Sci.* 32:613–18.

Forsyth, D. J. 1976. A field study of growth and development of nestling masked shrews *(Sorex cinereus). J. Mammal.* 57:708–21.

Fritz, J., and Fritz, P. 1985. The hand-rearing unit, management decisions that may affect chimpanzee development. In *Clinical management of infant great apes,* ed. C. E. Graham and J. A. Bowen, 1–34. New York: Alan R. Liss.

Geist, V. 1971. *Mountain sheep: A study in behavior and evolution.* Chicago: University of Chicago Press.

Gijzen, A., and Tijskens, J. 1971. Growth in weight of the lowland gorilla, *Gorilla g. gorilla,* and of the mountain gorilla, *Gorilla g. beringei. Int. Zoo Yrbk.* 21:131–37.

Gittleman, J. 1986. Carnivore life history patterns: Allometric, phylogenetic, and ecological associations. *Am. Nat.* 127:744–76.

Gittleman, J. L., and Oftedal, O. T. 1987. Comparative growth and lactation energetics in carnivores. In *Reproductive energetics in mammals,* ed. A. S. I. Loudon and P. A. Racey, 41–77. Symposium of the Zoological Society of London no. 57.

Glatston, A. R. 1981. The husbandry, breeding, and hand-rearing of the lesser mouse lemur, *Microcebus murinus,* at Rotterdam Zoo. *Int. Zoo Yrbk.* 21:131–37.

Goss, R. J. 1974. Ageing versus growth. *Perspect. Biol. Med.* 17:485–94.

Gould, S. J. 1977. *Ontogeny and phylogeny.* Cambridge, Mass.: Belknap Press of Harvard University Press.

Habicht, J. P., Lechtig, A., Yarbrough, C., and Klein, R. E. 1974. Maternal nutrition, birth weight, and infant mortality. In *Size at birth,* 353–77. Ciba Foundation Symposium no. 27. Amsterdam: Associated Scientific Publishers.

Hafez, E. S. E., and Dyer, I. A. 1969. *Animal growth and nutrition.* Philadelphia: Lea and Febiger.

Hampton, J. K., Hampton, S. H., and Levy, B. M. 1971. Reproductive physiology and pregnancy in marmosets. In *Medical primatology,* ed. E. I. Goldsmith and J. Moor-Jankowski, 527–34. Basel: Karger.

Hampton, S. H., Gross, M. J., and Hampton, J. K. Jr. 1978. A comparison of captive breeding performance and offspring survival in the family Callitrichidae. *Primates Med.* 10:88–95.

Hanks, J. 1972. Growth of the African elephant *(Loxodonta africana). E. Afr. Wildl. J.* 10:251–72.

Hartman, C. G., and Straus, W. L. Jr. 1933. *The anatomy of the rhesus macaque* (Macaca mulatta). New York: Hafner Publishing Co.

Harvey, P. H., and Clutton-Brock, T. H. 1985. Life history variation in primates. *Evolution* 39:559–81.

Hearn, J. P. 1982. The reproductive physiology of the common marmoset *Callithrix jacchus* in captivity. *Int. Zoo Yrbk.* 22:138–43.

Hearn, J. P., and Burden, F. J. 1979. Collaborative rearing of marmoset triplets. *Lab. Anim.* 13:131–33.

Hedhammar, A., Wu, F., Krook, L., Schryver, H. F., Lahunta, A., de Whalen, J. P., Kaufez, F. A., Nunez, E. A., Hintz, H. F., Sheffy, B. E., and Ryan, G. E. 1974. Over-nutrition and skeletal disease: an experimental study in growing Great Dane dogs. *Cornell Vet. Suppl.* 5:1–160.

Hiddleston, W. A. 1976. Large scale production of a small laboratory primate, *Callithrix jacchus.* In *The laboratory animal in the study of reproduction,* ed. T. Antikatzades, S. Ericksen, and A. Spiegel, 51–57. New York: Fisher.

———. 1978. The production of the common marmoset, *Callithrix jacchus* as a laboratory animal. In *Recent advances in primatology,* vol. 1., ed. D. J. Chivers and J. Herbert. London: Academic Press.

Hill Farming Research Organisation (HFRO). 1979. *Science and hill farming.* Edinburgh: HFRO.

Huffman, E. M., Kluk, J. H., and Pappaioanou, M. 1985. Factors associated with neonatal lamb mortality. *Theriogenology* 24:163–71.

Huxley, J. 1932. *Problems of relative growth.* London: Methuen.

Jarman, P. 1983. Mating system and sexual dimorphism in large, terrestrial mammalian herbivores. *Biol. Rev.* 58:485–520.

Kihlstrom, J. E. 1972. Period of gestation and body weight in some placental mammals. *Comp. Biochem. Physiol.* 43:673–79.

Kirkwood, J. K. 1983. Effects of diet on health, weight, and litter size in captive cotton-top tamarins *Saguinus o. oedipus. Primates* 24:515–20.

———. 1985. Patterns of growth in primates. *J. Zool.* (Lond.) A 205:123–36.

———. 1991. Energy requirements for maintenance and growth of wild mammals, birds, and reptiles in captivity. *J. Nutr.* 121:S29–S34.

Kirkwood, J. K., and Bennett, P. M. 1992. Approaches and limitations to the prediction of energy requirements in wild animal husbandry and veterinary care. *Proc. Nutr. Soc.* 51:117–24.

Kirkwood, J. K., Epstein, M. A., Terlecki, A. J., and Underwood, S. J. 1985. Rearing a second generation of cotton-top tamarins *(Saguinus o. oedipus)* in captivity. *Lab. Anim.* 19:269–72.

Kirkwood, J. K., and Webster, A. J. F. 1984. Energy budget strategies for growth in mammals and birds. *Anim. Prod.* 38:147–55.

Kirkwood, J. K., Williams, P., Moxey, T., Wallbank, M., Stadler,

S. G., Howlett, J., Markham, J., Dean, C., Watts, E., and Eva, J. 1988. Management and milk intake of young artificially reared Chinese water deer *Hydropotes inermis* and their growth compared to mother-reared fawns. *Int. Zoo Yrbk.* 27:308–16.

Kleiber, M. 1975. *The fire of life.* New York: Kviegar.

Lee, A. K., and Cockburn, A. 1985. *Evolutionary ecology of marsupials.* Cambridge: Cambridge University Press.

Leigh, S. R. 1992. Patterns of variation in the ontogeny of primate body size dimorphism. *J. Hum. Evol.* 23:27–50.

Leutenegger, W. 1973. Maternal-fetal relationships in primates. *Folia Primatol.* 20:283–90.

———. 1976. Allometry of neonatal size in eutherian mammals. *Nature* 263:229–30.

Linstedt, S. C., and Calder, W. A. 1981. Body size, physiological time, and longevity of homeothermic animals. *Q. Rev. Biol.* 56:1–16.

Long, J. O., and Cooper, R. W. 1968. Physical growth and dental eruption in captive-born squirrel monkeys *Saimiri sciureus* (Letitia, Columbia). In *The squirrel monkey,* ed. L. A. Rosenblum and R. W. Cooper, 193–205. New York, London: Academic Press.

MacArthur, R. W., and Wilson, E. O. 1967. *The theory of island biogeography.* Princeton N.J.: Princeton University Press.

Mace, G. M. 1979. The evolutionary ecology of small mammals. D.Phil. thesis, University of Sussex, England.

Manocha, S. L., and Long, J. 1977. Experimental protein malnutrition during gestation and breeding performance of squirrel monkeys, *Saimiri sciureus. Primates* 18:923–30.

Markham, J., and Kirkwood, J. K. 1988. Formula intake and growth of an addax, *Addax nasomaculatus,* hand-reared at the London Zoo. *Int. Zoo Yrbk.* 27:316–19.

Martin, R. D., and MacLarnon, A. M. 1985. Gestation period, neonatal size, and maternal investment in placental mammals. *Nature* 313:220–23.

McCance, R. A. 1962. Food, growth, and time. *Lancet* ii:671–76.

McCance, R. A., and Widdowson, E. M. 1974. The determinants of growth and form. *Proc. R. Soc. Lond.* B. 185:1–17.

McLaren, A. 1982. The embryo. In *Embryonic and fetal development,* ed. C. R. Austin and R. V. Short, 1–25. Cambridge: Cambridge University Press.

McNab, B. K. 1986a. The influence of food habits on the energetics of eutherian mammals. *Ecol. Monogr.* 56:1–19.

———. 1986b. The reproduction of marsupial and eutherian mammals in relation to energy expenditure. In *Reproductive energetics of mammals,* ed. A. S. I. Loudon and P. A. Racey, 29–40. Symposium of the Zoological Society of London no. 57. New York: Oxford University Press.

Millar, J. S. 1977. Adaptive features of mammalian reproduction. *Evolution* 31:370–86.

———. 1981. Prepartum reproductive characteristics of eutherian mammals. *Evolution* 35:1149–63.

Millward, D. J., Garlick, P. J., and Reeds, P. J. 1976. The energy cost of growth. *Proc. Nutr. Soc.* 35:339–49.

Oftedal, O. 1984. Milk composition, milk yield, and energy output at peak lactation: A comparative review. *Symp. Zool. Soc. Lond.* 51:33–85.

Paul, A. A., and Southgate, D. A. T. 1978. *McCance and Widdowson's The composition of foods.* London: HMSO.

Phillips, J. B. 1975. *Development of vertebrate anatomy.* St. Louis: C. V. Mosby Co.

Pitts, G. C., and Bullard, T. R. 1968. Some interspecific aspects of body composition in mammals. In *Body composition in animals and man.* Washington. D.C.: National Academy of Sciences.

Poole, T. B., and Evans, R. G. 1982. Reproduction, infant survival, and productivity of a colony of common marmosets *(Callithrix jacchus jacchus). Lab. Anim.* 16:88–97.

Portmann, A. 1962. Cerebralisation und ontogenese. *Medezin. Grundlagenforsch.* 4:1–62.

Prentice, A. M., and Whitehead, R. G. 1986. The energetics of human reproduction. In *Reproductive energetics in mammals,* ed. A. S. I. Loudon and P. A. Racey, 275–304. Symposium of the Zoological Society of London no. 57.

Pullar, J. D., and Webster, A. J. F. 1977. The energy cost of fat and protein deposition in the rat. *Br. J. Nutr.* 37:355–63.

Racey, P. A. 1969. Diagnosis of pregnancy and experimental extension of gestation in the pipistrelle bat, *Pipistrellus pipistrellus. J. Reprod. Fertil.* 19:465–74.

Ralls, K. 1977. Sexual dimorphism in mammals: Avian models and unanswered questions. *Am. Nat.* 111:917–38.

Record, R. G., Gibson, J. R., and McKeown, T. 1952. Fetal and infant mortality in multiple pregnancy. *J. Obstet. Gynaecol. Br. Emp.* 59:471–82.

Renfree, M. B. 1982. Implantation and placentation. In *Embryonic and fetal development,* ed. C. R. Austin and R. V. Short, 26–69. Cambridge: Cambridge University Press.

Ricklefs, R. E. 1968. Patterns of growth in birds. *Ibis* 110:419–51.

———. 1973. Patterns of growth in birds. II. Growth rate and mode of development. *Ibis* 115:117–201.

———. 1979. Adaptation, constraint, and compromise in avian postnatal development. *Biol. Rev.* 54:269–90.

Robbins, C. T. 1983. *Wildlife feeding and nutrition.* New York, London: Academic Press.

Rosenblum, L. A., and Smiley, J. 1980. Weight gain in bonnet and pig–tail macaques. *J. Med. Primatol.* 9:247–53.

Rothwell, M. J., and Stock, N. J. 1982. Effects of feeding a palatable "cafeteria" diet on energy balance in young and adult lean Zucker rats. *Br. J. Nutr.* 47:461–71.

Russell, E. M. 1982. Patterns of parental care and parental investment in marsupials. *Biol. Rev.* 57:1423–86.

Sacher, G. A., and Staffeldt, E. F. 1974. Relation of gestation time to brain weight for placental mammals: Implications for the theory of vertebrate growth. *Am. Nat.* 108:593–615.

Schmidt-Nielsen, K. 1984. *Scaling: Why is animal size so important?* Cambridge: Cambridge University Press.

Schultz, A. H. 1944. Age changes and variability in gibbons: A morphological study on a population sample of man-like apes. *Am. J. Phys. Anthropol.* 2:1–129.

Shea, B. T. 1986. Ontogenetic approaches to sexual dimorphism in primates. *Hum. Evol.* 1:97–110.

Simms, J. C., and Hand, M. S. 1986. Special dietary management in lactation and gestation. In *Current veterinary therapy: Food animal practice,* 2d ed., ed. J. L. Howard, 218–39. Philadelphia: W. B. Saunders.

Smith, A. H., Butler, T. M., and Pace, N. 1975. Weight growth of colony-reared chimpanzees. *Folia Primatol.* 24:29–59.

Spencer, A. S., and Hull, D. 1984. The effect of over-feeding newborn rabbits on somatic and visceral growth, body composition, and long-term growth potential. *Br. J. Nutr.* 51:389–402.

Starke, J. S., Smith, J. B., and Joubert, D. M. 1958. *The birth weight of lambs.* South African Department of Agriculture Technical Services Bulletin no. 382.

Stevenson, M. F., and Sutcliffe, A. G. 1978. Breeding a second generation of common marmosets *Callithrix jacchus* in captivity. *Int. Zoo Yrbk.* 18:109–14.

Tasse, J. 1986. Maternal and paternal care in the rock cavy, *Kerodon rupestris,* a South American hystricomorph rodent. *Zoo Biol.* 5:27–43.

Taylor, St. C. S. 1965. A relation between mature weight and time taken to mature in mammals. *Anim. Prod.* 7:203–20.

———. 1980. Live weight growth from embryo to adult in domesticated mammals. *Anim. Prod.* 31:223–35.

Thompson, D. W. 1917. *On growth and form.* Cambridge: Cambridge University Press.

Thompson, W., and Aitken, F. C. 1959. *Diet in relation to reproduction and viability of the young.* Part 2. *Sheep: World survey of reproduction and review of feeding experiments.* Technical Communication of the Commonwealth Bureau of Animal Nutrition no. 20.

Tuomi, J. 1980. Mammalian reproductive strategies: A generalized relation of litter size to body size. *Oecologia* 45:39–44.

Tyler, N. J. C. 1987. Body composition and energy balance of pregnant and non-pregnant Svalbard reindeer during winter. In *Reproductive energetics in mammals,* ed. A. S. I. Loudon and P. A. Racey, 203–29. Symposium of the Zoological Society of London no. 57.

Watts, E. S. 1986. Skeletal development. In *Comparative primate biology,* vol. 3, ed. W. R. Dukelow and J. Erwin. New York: Alan R. Liss.

Webster, A. J. F. 1977. Selection for leanness and the energetic efficiency of growth in meat animals. *Proc. Nutr. Soc.* 36:53–59.

———. 1978. Prediction of the energy requirements for growth in beef cattle. *World Rev. Nutr. Diet.* 30:189–226.

Weiner, J. 1987. Limits to energy budget and tactics in energy investments during reproduction in the Djungarian hamster (*Phodopus sungorus sungorus* Pallas 1970). In *Reproductive energetics in mammals,* ed. A. S. I. Loudon and P. A. Racey, 167–87. Symposium of the Zoological Society of London no. 57.

Western, D. 1979. Size, life history, and ecology in mammals. *Afr. J. Ecol.* 17:185–204.

Widdowson, E. M. 1974. Immediate and long-term consequences of being large or small at birth: A comparative approach. In *Size at birth,* 65–82. Ciba Foundation Symposium no. 27. Amsterdam: Associated Scientific Publishers.

Widdowson, E. M., and McCance, R. A. 1960. Some effects of accelerating growth. 1. General somatic development. *Proc. R. Soc. Lond.* B 152:188–206.

Wilson, B. J. 1977. Growth curves: Their analysis and use. In *Growth and poultry meat production,* ed. K. N. Boorman and B. J. Wilson, 89–15. Edinburgh: British Poultry Science Ltd.

Wolfe, L. G., Deinhart, F., Ogden, J. D., Adams, M. R., and Fisher, L. E. 1975. Reproduction of wild-caught and laboratory-born marmoset species used in biomedical research *(Saguinus* spp.; *Callithrix jacchus). Lab. Anim. Sci.* 25:802–13.

Yu, B. P., Masoro, E. J., Murata, I., Bertrand, H. A., and Lynd, F. T. 1982. Lifespan study of SPF Fischer 344 male rats fed ad libitum on restricted diets: Longevity, growth, lean body mass, and disease. *J. Gerontol.* 37:130–41.

Zullinger, E. M., Ricklefs, R. E., Redford, K. H., and Mace, G. M. 1984. Fitting sigmoidal equations to mammalian growth curves. *J. Mammal.* 65:607–36.

PART SEVEN

Captive Mammal Research

INTRODUCTION
DEVRA G. KLEIMAN

The material presented throughout this book on animal husbandry and exhibitry, nutrition, population management, behavior, and reproduction represents the actual results of both basic and applied research projects (conducted both in and outside of zoos). Indeed, without the immense amount of research completed over the past three decades, much of it in zoos, there would have been no need to revise Crandall's original volume on the management of wild mammals in captivity. It is curious that zoo staff so often forget the origins of the advances in management techniques derived from research.

In chapter 44, Hardy describes the history of research in zoos and then provides several summaries of the disciplines that are currently represented in zoo research, using surveys, publications, and the new C.A.U.Z. (Consortium of Aquariums, Universities, and Zoos) data base. She also reviews the distribution of taxon preferences. Clearly, the listed disciplines are those that survive well in a zoo context; certain areas of research are definitely not suited to zoos.

Benirschke argues powerfully for separate research units in zoos in chapter 45 and provides numerous examples in which basic research has provided the key information necessary to breed certain species. He emphasizes the importance of timely publication of results and of ensuring that information gets back to the zoo community, especially when researchers are from academic institutions that are oriented toward basic research. He acknowledges the different "styles" of academically inclined researchers and zoo managers, and the potential for conflict, but suggests that zoo managers be flexible with their scientists. Benirschke stresses that in most industries, research and development account for 3–5% of the annual budget, a level not reached by the zoo community. He also emphasizes that the broader academic community is not exploiting the opportunities provided by zoos.

There is a perception that zoos do not do "good science," and indeed, many zoo studies are not sufficiently rigorous. But research in zoos does pose special problems since there are so many variables outside the control of the researcher, especially when working with exhibit animals. Doing good science requires training, but doing good science in zoos also requires a special temperament that tolerates and can adapt to constant changes.

While emphasizing behavioral research, Crockett's chapter on data collection and analytic techniques (chapter 46) provides a recipe that can be applied to any discipline. It emphasizes the importance of formulating the problem, developing a research design, setting out alternative hypotheses, devising appropriate sampling and data recording techniques, and conducting statistical analyses. All too often zoos do not test alternative hypotheses when trying to find the basis for a given behavior pattern or biological characteristic; such a lack of scientific rigor nullifies the results of many research projects within zoos.

Zoos are wonderful resources for scientists interested in evolutionary biology because of the numbers of exotic animals demonstrating different adaptations that are housed at one site. A number of important advances have been made in our understanding of mammalian evolution that derived from research on the life history characteristics of mammals being held in zoos, for example, through correlations between phylogeny, morphology, and ecology. Some of the data are simple and straightforward to collect, such as weights and measurements, and in chapter 47, Lundrigan presents the methods to follow in collecting these data correctly.

In chapter 48, the final chapter of the section, Grand emphasizes how the study of dead animals can actually extend the useful lives of specimens held in zoos, and how much more information on life histories could be collected through the study of animals that die in the zoo (as all eventually will). Most of our zoos do not support the research of comparative anatomists, despite the contribution to evolutionary biology such scientists can make.

44

Current Research Activities in Zoos

DONNA FITZROY HARDY

As the mission of modern zoos and aquariums has come to focus on conservation of endangered animals, scientific research has become more acceptable in zoological facilities. Indeed, in their survey of American zoos nearly ten years before this writing, Finlay and Maple (1986) found that most of their respondents reported that research had taken place in their institutions between 1981 and 1983. While the exact nature of these research efforts was not reported, it is clear that research studies were fairly common at zoos in the early 1980s. Most of the research projects involved mammals, with reptiles, birds, fishes, and people (in that order) also being studied at these institutions.

During the ten years since Finlay and Maple distributed their survey, research programs have assumed more prominence at many zoos. Many factors have contributed to the increasing acceptance of research by the zoo community, perhaps the most important being the establishment and rapid expansion of the Species Survival Plans (SSP) of the American Zoo and Aquarium Association (AZA) during the 1980s. The primary objective of these programs is management of viable populations of endangered species in captivity to assist with their conservation in the wild. The biological aspects of the SSP for each species involve compilation of husbandry standards and promotion of conservation-relevant research. At about the same time that SSP programs were beginning to promote zoo-based research, the journal *Zoo Biology* was founded. In its first eleven years, this journal has established itself as an important vehicle for publication and dissemination of the results of scientific studies at zoos. And in 1985, the Consortium of Aquariums, Universities, and Zoos (C.A.U.Z.) was created for the express purpose of establishing communication links between university-based scientists and educators and their counterparts at zoos and aquariums (Hardy 1992). As connections have grown between university and zoo professionals, research committees, research guidelines, affiliations with local universities, and collaborative studies have proliferated at many zoos. The status of zoo research in 1993 is presented here.

THE IMPORTANCE OF ZOO RESEARCH

Successful management of animals in captivity requires a thorough understanding of their species-specific behavior in order to meet their housing and breeding requirements. Successful breeding of endangered species in captivity may also depend upon understanding their patterns of social and reproductive behavior; such knowledge may be crucial in addressing problems associated with social isolation of young animals or maternal rejection of young, in managing medical problems, and in developing realistic and humane exhibits (Moran and Sorensen 1984). Traditionally, however, the study of animal behavior by psychologists has been confined to relatively few species, with few cross-species comparisons (Beach 1950; Porter, Johnson, and Granger 1981), and relatively little interest has been shown by university researchers in the study of captive exotic animals.

In her recent paper on behavioral research at zoos, Kleiman (1992) pointed out that zoos offer many advantages to behavioral researchers, including opportunities for longitudinal studies as well as for collection of precise life history information for a wide variety of animals, including secretive and nocturnal species. She pointed out that zoo research has been dominated by behavioral research, partly because such studies have immediate application to captive management. In her view, behavioral research is potentially more appropriate for small and medium-sized zoos than is high-technology research in reproductive physiology because the study of animal behavior does not usually require expensive equipment. She noted an increasing focus on rare and endangered species and on applied questions in zoo research as well as a shift of emphasis from classic comparative ethology to evolutionary biology and physiology.

While there is increasing interest among zoo professionals in the return of captive-bred animals to their native habitats, there has been little systematic research directed at the problems involved in this challenging enterprise. And far more effort has been expended on reintroductions of birds than on reintroductions of mammals. In an interesting discussion of reintroductions, Wemmer and Derrickson (1987) documented reintroduction efforts for 2 species of amphibians, 5 species of reptiles, 33 species of birds, and 18 species of mammals. They documented 7 captive breeding programs targeted for reintroductions of birds and 3 programs for mammals. Of the 71 references on reintroductions that accompanied this paper, 63% pertained to bird reintroductions and only 25% to mammal reintroductions. The importance of zoo-based studies of captive-reared mammals (like those of the black-footed ferret, *Mustela nigripes*, and golden lion tamarin, *Leontopithecus rosalia*) to successful reintroduction efforts has been pointed out by Kleiman (1992) and many other authors.

THE HISTORY OF ZOO RESEARCH

The Beginning of Research in the Zoo
In their analysis of the history of zoo research, Wemmer and Thompson (1995) provided the background for current research efforts in zoos. They reported that, during the nineteenth century, research at zoos centered on taxonomic and anatomical descriptions and was conducted by a staff member known as the prosector, the forerunner of the modern veterinarian and pathologist. Most prosectors had a broad understanding of contemporary zoology and a prolific record of publication. By about the time of World War I, zoo research came to involve fieldwork and the collection of natural history information, but by that time, academic scientists had lost interest in zoos and aquariums as laboratories or settings for research. Zoo research became more diversified in the 1960s and led to the current studies in environmental enrichment and behavioral biology, to the use of molecular biology in the study of systematics and genetic variation, and to the emerging field of conservation biology. And with decreases in funding for academic research, university scientists in North America are now beginning to turn to zoos and aquariums as resources for scientific investigation. Wemmer and Thompson also pointed out that even though zoos and aquariums are not recognized by the public as scientific institutions, research programs at zoos are becoming more and more common—partly out of the increasing need of zoos to justify their existence with scientific data.

Zoo Research during the 1980s
Finlay and Maple (1986) sent questionnaires to 153 zoos and aquariums in 1983–1984 and learned that research was being conducted at 70% of the 120 zoos that responded. Although what was considered to be research probably varied widely among these institutions, the research projects reported fell into a number of categories. For example, of those institutions that conducted research, 72% reported conducting research involving reproduction, 72% behavior research, 43% other biomedical research, 42% conservation research, 42% husbandry research, 30% physiological research, 28% research in pathology, and 20% genetic research. Nonprimate mammals were being studied by 70% of these institutions, great apes by 38%, other primates by 45%, and marine mammals by 22%, while reptiles were being studied by 44%, birds by 43%, fishes by 19%, and people by 14% of them. Finlay and Maple noted that while research activities were relatively common in zoos at that time, only 39% of the institutions conducting research had appointed research committees, and only 57% typically published their research. Research was more commonly conducted at large than at small zoos, and zoos with university affiliations were the most likely to conduct research. In addition, zoos and aquariums with academic affiliations were more likely to publish the results of their research (75%) than were institutions not affiliated with universities (41%).

Zoo Research Funded by IMS Grants (1984–1993)
Each year, the federal Institute of Museum Services (IMS) funds projects in a wide variety of institutions, including art history, natural history, science, and children's museums as well as zoos, botanical gardens, aquariums, historic sites, and nature centers. Over a ten-year period from 1984 to 1993, 156 IMS grants were given to zoos and aquariums for projects involving invertebrates (0.6%), fishes (5.8%), amphibians (0.6%), reptiles (4.5%), birds (9.0%), and mammals (51.3%). A significant percentage of the grants to zoos (28.2%) funded projects other than research (e.g., facility renovation). Between 4 and 11 projects with mammals have been funded each year, and there seems to be no special trend in the kinds of projects that were funded throughout this period. Of the 80 projects with mammals funded by the IMS, most (58.8%) involved captive management and propagation of endangered species; projects of this type were funded every year. Projects involving reproductive physiology (20.0%) and veterinary medicine, pathology, and parasitology (10.0%) received funding in at least half of the years. Projects in some areas, such as animal behavior and behavioral ecology (5.0%), genetics and population biology (2.5%), behavioral/environmental enrichment (1.3%), and nutrition and diet (1.3%), are rarely funded by the IMS. No projects in design and evaluation of mammal exhibits or systematics and taxonomy have ever been funded by the IMS. Projects in ecology, natural history, fieldwork, reintroductions, rehabilitation, and wildlife management are probably not considered appropriate for funding by this governmental agency.

Articles Published in *Zoo Biology* (1982–1992)
An analysis of the contents of the first eleven years of *Zoo Biology* suggests that most published zoo research is based on the study of mammals. Of the 353 research papers published during this period by this journal, 1.4% are on invertebrates, 1.7% on fishes, 0.6% on amphibians, 4.2% on reptiles, 10.2% on birds, 0.6% on visitor studies, and 81.3% on nonhuman mammals. And of the 287 papers based on mammal research, 29.6% are in the area of animal behavior and behavioral ecology, with an additional 5.9% on behavioral/environmental enrichment for zoo animals. Articles on reproductive physiology are also numerous (20.2% of mammal articles) in the journal. Less frequent are articles on morphology and development (5.6%), genetics and population biology (3.8%), and wildlife management (2.3%). Since this journal concentrates on

zoo-based studies, it is not surprising that it has published no articles in the areas of ecology, natural history, fieldwork, reintroductions, rehabilitation, or systematics. *Zoo Biology* publishes applied as well as basic research papers, and many of its articles on mammals (24.0%) involve some aspect of captive management. And if one includes research articles on veterinary medicine, pathology, and parasitology (5.6%), nutrition and diet (3.5%), and design and evaluation of exhibits for mammals (1.2%) with the captive management studies, more than half (54.7%) of the articles in *Zoo Biology* involve some aspect of the management of wild mammals in captivity.

CURRENT RESEARCH PROJECTS IN ZOOS

Research Projects Reported by Zoos and Publications by Zoo Staff (1991–1992)

In its *Annual Report on Conservation and Science* for 1991–1992 (Wiese et al. 1992), the American Association of Zoological Parks and Aquariums (AAZPA) listed the current activities of zoo and aquarium staff reported by its member zoos. Included in this list were the titles of many zoo research projects, most of which involved mammals. An analysis of 478 research projects listed by 40 zoos reveals that 2.9% of the research involved invertebrates, 2.9% fishes, 1.7% amphibians, 10.3% reptiles, 18.6% birds, and 63.2% mammals. Visitor studies accounted for an additional 0.4% of these projects. While one would expect that captive management would be the prime focus of research studies conducted by the staff of zoos and aquariums, only 4.3% of the mammal projects involved research in this area. Most of the 302 projects with mammals were studies of animal behavior or behavioral ecology (22.8%), reproductive physiology (19.5%), ecology, natural history, or fieldwork (16.6%), or wildlife management (12.9%). Other research areas included behavioral/environmental enrichment (1.7%), design and evaluation of mammal exhibits (1.7%), genetics and population biology (4.3%), morphology and development (4.0%), nutrition and diet (3.3%), reintroductions (2.0%), rehabilitation (3.0%), systematics and taxonomy (1.3%), and veterinary medicine, pathology, and parasitology (2.6%).

The AAZPA report also included a bibliography of the papers published by zoo staff during the same period. In addition to being published as books and chapters in books and in the Conference Proceedings of the AZA, the American Association of Zoo Veterinarians, and other organizations, these papers appeared in a wide range of journals: *Zoo Biology, International Zoo Yearbook, Applied Animal Behavior Science, The Zooculturist, Journal of Zoo and Wildlife Medicine, Mammalia, Journal of Mammalogy, American Naturalist, Primates, Behaviour, Wildlife Conservation, Journal of Wildlife Diseases, Hormones and Behavior, American Journal of Primatology, International Journal of Primatology, Natural History, Theriogenology, Biology of Reproduction, Journal of Medical Primatology, Oryx, Diseases of Aquatic Organisms, Molecular Reproduction and Development, Dodo, Journal of Reproduction and Fertility, Behavioural Processes, Animal Behaviour, Nature, Journal of Wildlife Management, National Geographic Research, Marine Mammal Science, Journal of Experimental Zoology,* and many others. An analysis of 247 papers published by staff at 35 zoos during 1991–1992 showed a distribution among the major taxonomic groups similar to that of the research activities of zoo staff: invertebrates 2.0%, fishes 1.6%, amphibians 2.0%, reptiles 6.5%, birds 19.4%, and mammals 68.4%.

When one compares the kinds of research activity reported by zoos during 1991–1992 with the nature of publications by zoo staff for the same period, some surprises emerge. The largest percentage of research projects reported in zoos for 1991–1992 (22.8%), as well as a relatively large percentage of the papers published in *Zoo Biology* (29.6%), involved the study of animal behavior or behavioral ecology. This concentration of effort might lead one to expect an equally large percentage of papers published by zoo staff in this area. However, relatively few (5.3%) of the articles published by zoo staff in 1991–1992 were on animal behavior or behavioral ecology. It seems that the great emphasis on behavioral research in zoos is not reflected in this list of published articles. Indeed, two other important areas of zoo research are more likely to be published than behavioral research: 30.8% of the articles were in the area of reproductive physiology and 23.1% were based on studies of ecology, natural history, or fieldwork. Comparison of the list of current projects with the list of articles published by zoo staff produced another unexpected result: in contrast to the relatively rare mention (4.3%) of captive management projects among the research activities of zoos, 10.1% of the published articles were in this area. And while only 2.6% of the projects reported were in veterinary medicine, pathology, or parasitology, papers in these areas accounted for 11.2% of the articles published by zoo staff during 1991–1992. Few articles were published in the fields of wildlife management (3.6%), behavioral/environmental enrichment (3.6%), mammal exhibit design or evaluation (0.6%), genetics or population biology (4.7%), or reintroductions (2.4%). And not surprisingly, the analysis found no papers published in areas in which few zoo research projects were being conducted (morphology and development, rehabilitation, and systematics and taxonomy).

Current Projects of C.A.U.Z. Network Members (1993)

The Consortium of Aquariums, Universities, and Zoos grew from the recognition by many people of the need to bring about closer working relationships between zoos and aquariums and the college and university community in Southern California (Hardy 1992). An alliance was formed by university, aquarium, and zoo professionals in 1985 with the goal of opening communication among scientists and educators in American universities, zoos, and aquariums. Soon after the founding of C.A.U.Z., however, it became evident that educators and scientists from all over the world shared an interest in disseminating ideas and collaborating on research projects. In 1992, a major effort was made to extend the network to Great Britain (Hardy 1993). By 1993, C.A.U.Z. had developed an international data base, with about a third of the network members having addresses outside of the United States.

In response to the widely perceived need to share information, the current function of C.A.U.Z. is to facilitate communication through the publication of annual directories and the maintenance of a data base of information submitted by members. C.A.U.Z. members include zoo, university, and aquarium people who are specialists in a wide range of fields. These fields include animal behavior, captive management, conservation biology, ecology and natural history, exhibit design and evaluation, genetics and population biology, morphology and development, nutrition and diet, parasitology, rehabilitation, reintroductions, reproductive physiology, restoration ecology, systematics and taxonomy, veterinary medicine and pathology, and wildlife management. The 1993–1994 C.A.U.Z. directory provides information submitted by 632 people from 332 institutions in 19 countries.

The C.A.U.Z. directories and data base are widely regarded as valuable resources by the conservation community. In spring 1993, information in the data base was analyzed for the purpose of learning about current research. (Projects involving animal training, genetic management of captive populations, collections management, and keeping of animal records were not considered to be research for the purposes of this analysis.) Research projects were reported by 370 (54%) of the 695 people in the C.A.U.Z. data base, and most (60%) of the projects involved the study of mammals (including humans) (fig. 44.1). Of the studies on nonhuman mammals, 42% involved animal behavior (i.e., animal behavior and behavioral ecology; behavioral and environmental enrichment) (fig. 44.2). Projects were also

TABLE 44.1.   Distribution of Research Projects in the C.A.U.Z. Data Base among the Mammalian Orders

Mammalian order	Percentage of projects
Order Monotremata (monotremes)	0.4
Order Marsupialia (marsupials)	1.9
Order Insectivora (insectivores)	0.2
Order Dermoptera (flying lemurs)	0
Order Chiroptera (bats)	2.2
Order Primates (primates)	43.7
Order Edentata (edentates)	1.5
Order Pholidota (pangolins)	0
Order Lagomorpha (lagomorphs)	0
Order Rodentia (rodents)	3.0
Order Cetacea (cetaceans)	2.4
Order Carnivora (carnivores)	16.1
Order Pinnipedia (pinnipeds)	3.0
Order Tubulidentata (aardvarks)	0
Order Proboscidea (elephants)	6.2
Order Hyracoidea (hyraxes)	0
Order Sirenia (manatees, dugongs)	0.6
Order Perissodactyla (horses, asses)	2.8
Order Artiodactyla (other hoofed mammals)	15.9

concentrated in the areas of ecology, natural history, field studies, reproductive physiology, veterinary medicine, pathology, parasitology, genetics, population biology, and the design and evaluation of mammal exhibits. Although the largest percentage of research projects involved behavior, there was a broad range of research on mammals in all research categories.

Mammal research in zoos encompasses most of the mammalian orders, with the greatest concentration being on primates, carnivores, and hoofed mammals (table 44.1). Research projects are also conducted on marsupials, bats, edentates, rodents, cetaceans, pinnipeds, elephants, and equids, although to a much lesser degree. Few projects are conducted on monotremes, insectivores, or manatees, and none are reported for flying lemurs, pangolins, lagomorphs, aardvarks, or hyraxes.

The amount of interest directed at the various taxonomic groups is at least partly determined by their relative representation in zoo collections, as representatives of the orders Primates, Carnivora, and Artiodactyla are exhibited by most zoos. Analysis of the research on these three orders reveals that attention is focused on only a few families within each order (table 44.2). Among the primates, most research is concentrated on Old World monkeys and great apes. Among carnivores, most effort is directed to felids. And among the hoofed mammals, research is focused on the cervids and bovids. These five families (Cercopithecidae, Pongidae, Felidae, Cervidae, and Bovidae) are very well represented in zoo collections.

An analysis of the subject areas of the projects conducted on the three mammalian orders receiving the greatest attention reveals that research is concentrated in only a few areas. Among the primates, carnivores, and artiodactyls, the largest proportion of research projects involves the study of behavior, and the second largest is in the area of reproductive physiology. The third largest proportion of research on these three orders is in the area of ecology, natural history,

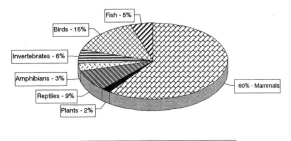

Research in C.A.U.Z. Database

FIG. 44.1.   Distribution among taxonomic groups of the research projects reported in the C.A.U.Z. data base in spring 1993.

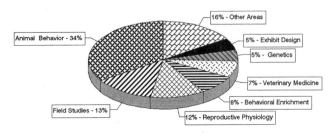

Research with Mammals in C.A.U.Z. Database

FIG. 44.2.   Distribution by subject area of the research projects involving nonhuman mammals reported in the C.A.U.Z. data base in spring 1993.

TABLE 44.2. Distribution of Research Projects in the C.A.U.Z. Data Base among the Families of the Orders Primates, Carnivora, and Artiodactyla

Order	Family	Percentage of projects
Primates (203 projects)		
	Lemuridae (lemurs)	7.4
	Indriidae (indris, sifaka)	0
	Daubentoniidae (aye-ayes)	0.5
	Lorisidae (lorises, pottos, galagos)	1.0
	Tarsiidae (tarsiers)	0
	Cebidae (New World monkeys)	13.8
	Callitrichidae (marmosets, tamarins)	14.3
	Cercopithecidae (Old World monkeys)	22.7
	Hylobatidae (lesser apes)	5.9
	Pongidae (great apes)	34.5
Carnivora (75 projects)		
	Canidae (foxes, dogs, jackals)	17.3
	Ursidae (giant pandas, bears)	14.7
	Procyonidae (red pandas, raccoons)	10.7
	Mustelidae (weasels, otters, minks)	12.0
	Viverridae (civets, genets, meerkats)	1.3
	Hyaenidae (hyenas, aardwolves)	1.3
	Felidae (cats, leopards, cheetahs)	42.7
Artiodactyla (74 projects)		
	Suidae (babirusa, warthogs, pigs)	10.8
	Tayassuidae (peccaries)	2.7
	Hippopotamidae (hippopotamuses)	0
	Camelidae (camels, llamas, alpaca)	1.4
	Tragulidae (chevrotains)	1.4
	Cervidae (deer, caribou, reindeer)	24.3
	Giraffidae (giraffes, okapi)	2.7
	Antilocapridae (pronghorns)	0
	Bovidae (cattle, bison, sheep, gazelles)	56.8

and field studies. Considering the focus of zoo people on the management of animals in captivity, surprisingly little research is reported in veterinary medicine, pathology, and parasitology, nutrition and diet, or mammal exhibit design and evaluation.

When the families of the three most commonly studied mammalian orders are examined with respect to the kinds of research being conducted, other facts emerge. As might be expected, the greatest concentration of research in the primate families involves behavior, with behavioral and environmental enrichment studies being conducted almost exclusively with the great apes. Research in reproductive physiology is also focused on the great apes. Genetic research, ecology, natural history, and field studies, and studies in veterinary medicine, pathology, and parasitology are fewer in number but are more evenly distributed among the primate families. As table 44.2 shows, research on carnivores is concentrated in the family Felidae; this concentration is probably related to the prominence of both large and small cats in zoo collections. Compared with studies on primates, however, research on carnivores is not concentrated in the area of animal behavior and behavioral ecology, but is more uniformly distributed among the various areas. Research within the order Artiodactyla is concentrated in the family Bovidae, a group that is widely represented in zoo collections. Behavioral studies and research on bovid reproductive physiology are most common. Little research is

conducted on mammalian orders other than Primates, Carnivora, and Artiodactyla, with the exception of elephants. When research is conducted on the other mammalian orders, it is most likely to be in the area of behavior and behavioral ecology.

CONCLUSIONS

The annual directories of C.A.U.Z. provide insight into the kinds of research being conducted by its network members, about half of whom are zoo and aquarium professionals. Although much of the activity of this group of people revolves around the day-to-day requirements of managing wild animals in captivity, many of them find time to engage in research activities. Some of their projects probably entail data collection for the kind of research that might be considered "applied" or "problem-driven" (e.g., enclosure utilization studies, enrichment studies, diet studies, methods of wildlife rehabilitation and techniques of release), but many important "question-driven" basic research studies are also being conducted at zoos.

Most research reported by those submitting information to C.A.U.Z. is with mammals, and most of this research is in three areas: animal behavior and behavioral ecology; ecology, natural history and field studies; and reproductive physiology. Current research with mammals is concentrated in only a few orders (Primates, Carnivora, Artiodactyla); interest in these groups is probably greatly affected by their representation in zoo collections. Indeed, some little-exhibited mammalian orders (Dermoptera, Pholidota, Lagomorpha, Tubulidentata, Hyracoidea) are not reported to be subjects of current research. It is not surprising that the most commonly studied animals are those most closely related to ourselves, members of the family Pongidae, and that by far the most common kind of research with this group is behavioral. Many studies on the captive propagation and management of mammals are focused on exhibit design and evaluation, reproductive physiology, veterinary medicine, pathology, and parasitology. Relatively few systematic studies, however, are reported on nutrition and diet.

The current emphasis on captive breeding of endangered species for eventual return to the wild is reflected by the interest of people in the C.A.U.Z. data base in engaging in research in the areas of ecology and natural history and by the relatively large numbers of field studies they conduct. This interest of zoo-based scientists in the ecology and behavior of animals in their natural habitat is not yet reflected in many studies of reintroduction of captive-reared mammals, however. Future successful releases of captive-reared animals will require a great deal more emphasis in this area of research. And while the importance of field studies has been recognized by zoo researchers, few of them are conducting projects in wildlife management, a research area that would seem to have great relevance to successful long-term reintroductions. The relatively new fields of conservation biology and restoration ecology will also play an important role in future reintroduction programs, but since research in those fields is more likely to be university-based than zoo-based, increased cooperation and collaboration between zoo and university scientists are crucial.

The results of well-designed, thoroughly conducted research studies deserve to be shared with the zoo as well as the academic community. While presentation of research papers at professional conferences serves the function of disseminating the information to those in attendance (or who later read the proceedings of the meetings), this method restricts the information flow to a limited group of people. And since relatively few university scientists attend the conferences of the American Zoo and Aquarium Association, limiting research reports to their paper or poster sessions precludes dispersal to the scientific community at large. And while publication of research reports in proceedings is convenient, the relative lack of scientific scrutiny for material in these publications may make them a less reliable source of information than some other publications. Good research should also be published in scientific journals that are widely read by the zoo as well as the academic community. Fortunately, a lot of zoo research finds its way into such publications.

It is important to recognize that while behavioral research with mammals is widely conducted at zoos, it is not as likely to be published in scientific journals as are studies in other areas of zoo research. An explanation for this apparent discrepancy between research activity and publication may be that many behavioral studies in the zoo are long-term ones; lengthy projects may result in fewer publications. Or perhaps most behavioral studies at the zoo involve too few individuals to make a meaningful contribution to the literature. Or the nature of zoo research may be too applied for many journals. However, while it is true that some journals (*Journal of Experimental Zoology, Journal of Mammalogy, Hormones and Behavior*) are probably not likely to accept zoo-based behavioral research, other journals do (*Zoo Biology, International Zoo Yearbook, Applied Animal Behavior Science, The Zooculturist, Behaviour, Animal Behaviour*).

The reasons why many behavioral studies of mammals do not get published are complex and varied. It is possible that many behavioral projects considered to be research studies do not involve the collection of the kind of empirical data that produces published articles in refereed journals. It seems unlikely, however, that fewer journals accept papers based on research with captive animals than papers based on field studies. Kleiman (1992) addresses some of the problems encountered by researchers in her excellent article on behavioral research at zoos. Finlay and Maple (1986) point out that there are few trained scientists at most zoos, and that many scientists who do work at zoos are likely to be involved in data collection for the purpose of solving management problems rather than contributing to the scientific literature. If this were the entire explanation, however, then one might wonder why zoo veterinarians and others involved in zoo medicine and reproductive physiology have a better record of publication than do behavioral researchers. But rather than dwelling on possible problems with conducting zoo research, we should place our emphasis on solutions. If the scientific staff at zoos is otherwise engaged, or the rest of the zoo staff is inadequately trained to design and conduct scientific studies, the obvious solution may be to turn to the scientists and graduate students at local universities. As Finlay and Maple point out, zoos and aquariums can be extraordinary resources for academics, and affiliation with universities has clear advantages for zoos and aquariums. Collaboration with a university not only provides access to a wide range of expertise, but often results in an improvement in the quality of research and a greater likelihood of publication of zoo/aquarium studies.

While some American zoos have had long-standing relationships with local universities, such relationships were not common in the past. More British zoos appear to have university affiliations than do zoos in the United States, a fact that probably contributes to their research productivity (Hardy 1993). Before the establishment of C.A.U.Z., it was difficult for zoo people in the United States to contact university scientists for the purpose of collaboration on research projects. Such joint research efforts have been made considerably easier for both zoo and university researchers through the listing of research interests and current research projects in the annual C.A.U.Z. directories. Scientific studies of mammals and other animals are benefiting from such shared efforts. As productive research becomes a common undertaking of more and more zoos, many of them will establish research programs and form research committees with zoo and university members. Cooperation and sharing of information between those studying mammals in captivity and those studying mammals in the wild will play an important role in the future conservation efforts of both university and zoo scientists.

REFERENCES

Beach, F. A. 1950. The snark was a boojum. *Am. Psychol.* 5: 115–24.

Finlay, T. W., and Maple, T. L. 1986. A survey of research in American zoos and aquariums. *Zoo Biol.* 5:261–68.

Hardy, D. F. 1992. The Consortium of Aquariums, Universities, and Zoos. *Int. Zoo News* 39/8 (241): 17–20.

———. 1993. Research in British zoos. *Int. Zoo News* 40/3 (244): 5–14.

Kleiman, D. G. 1992. Behavioral research in zoos: Past, present, and future. *Zoo Biol.* 11:301–12.

Moran, G., and Sorensen, L. 1984. The behavioral researcher and the zoological park. *Appl. Anim. Behav. Sci.* 13:143–55.

Porter, J. H., Johnson, S. B., and Granger, R. G. 1981. The snark is still a boojum. *Comp. Psychol. Newsl.* 1:1–3.

Wemmer, C., and Derrickson, S. 1987. Reintroduction: The zoobiologist's dream. *AAZPA Annual Conference Proceedings*, Portland, Oregon, 48–65. Wheeling, W.Va.: American Association of Zoological Parks and Aquariums.

Wemmer, C., and Thompson, S. D. 1995. Short history of scientific research in zoological gardens. In *The ark evolving: Zoos and aquariums in transition*, ed. C. Wemmer, 70–94. Front Royal, Va.: Conservation and Research Center (Smithsonian Institution).

Wiese, R. J., Hutchins, M., Willis, K., and Becker, S. eds. 1992. *AAZPA Annual Report on Conservation and Science*. Bethesda, Md.: American Association of Zoological Parks and Aquariums.

45

The Need for Multidisciplinary Research Units in the Zoo

Kurt Benirschke

In this chapter I wish to persuade the reader that zoological gardens must be convinced to undertake serious investigations of a broad variety if they wish to remain competitive in the future. "The cost of not doing research" is high (Gibson 1980). This is an accepted dictum in medicine. Physicians have accepted the notion that if we wish to free ourselves of the scourge of major illnesses, the latest of which is AIDS, then investigative efforts are an absolute necessity. We accept the fact that without a clear understanding of the nature of the virus that causes AIDS, without knowledge of its receptor sites, its DNA composition, the body's immune system mechanisms, and other aspects of this complex disease, no meaningful therapy, let alone a vaccine, will ever come about. Through research we have eliminated dreaded diseases such as rickets, childbed fever, and poliomyelitis. Zoos are remiss in not having made similar progress commensurate with their needs, and it is high time that they caught up (Benirschke 1987). If we are really intent on preserving zoo animals for our descendants, it is now urgent that research on them, particularly the endangered species, be more widely undertaken. Zoos simply must begin independent research efforts on a broad scale, now!

To be sure, some investigative efforts in zoos have been going on for a long time. They have sometimes been undertaken by the personnel of zoological parks, but more often by students from associated universities. Such studies have been primarily of an observational nature, and have usually focused on behavior. They do not suffice to fill the needs of the future. Finlay and Maples (1986) used a questionnaire to examine formally what research was under way in U.S. zoos. The questionnaire was sent to 153 zoos and addressed such aspects as the current status of research, types of studies being undertaken, and anticipated needs. The findings from this survey indicated that almost all zoos encourage research activities. Most zoos also believe that their participation is expanding in the direction of additional research. While this may be true, a much broader panoply of research than is evident from this survey is now urgently needed. It is especially important, of course, that this research be carried out to the benefit of endangered species kept in zoos. This seems to me to be an essential requirement, for without the knowledge gained from such studies, it is unlikely that we will overcome the many deficiencies in our ability to care for them properly. We will not manage them adequately genetically, behaviorally, or nutritionally, let alone reproduce them at will, without more knowledge. As the wilderness shrinks, zoos will be the only refuges for many species, at least for some time to come.

One might ask whether the knowledge acquired in the study of human diseases and in veterinary research on domestic animals would not suffice for the task of caring for endangered animals. While it is true that many known regimens are applicable to zoo animals, such as the treatment of tuberculosis, this sort of technology transfer is not so readily accomplished in other cases. Take, for example, the prevention of rickets in exotic species. In humans and many other mammals, when sunlight is not available, the regular intake of vitamin D_2 is sufficient to prevent rickets; however, this has been found to be inadequate for South American primates, which must be medicated with vitamin D_3 because their steroid metabolism differs substantially from that of humans (Hunt et al. 1967). Numerous other examples can be cited to support the argument that investigative efforts on exotics are needed. Indeed, one may justifiably ask why it is that so little is known about the biology of most exotic animals, since many of them have been kept in zoological gardens for over a century. Why did it take us so long to recognize the essential need for basic biological research on the great variety of zoo animals?

One reason may be that it was once easier to purchase new animals from foreign lands than it is now. The replacement of lost specimens was faster and less expensive than the acquisition of the detailed biological knowledge necessary for successful animal management. However, new laws (e.g., CITES) now govern traffic in many species and often prohibit new acquisitions. Also, social and political instability in foreign lands and the decline in numbers of professional trappers make animal acquisition difficult. Most significant of all, however, has been the dramatic decline in wild populations of many of the favorite zoo species, so that future importation is limited by a lack of supply. Soon importation will cease altogether.

This problem is best appreciated when one considers the reduction of the five rhinoceros species, favorite zoo exhibits. No Javan rhinoceros, *Rhinoceros sondaicus*, is ever likely to be shown in a zoo again, and only with the greatest of efforts are a few specimens of the Sumatran rhinoceros, *Dicerorhinus sumatrensis*, now coming into the best-equipped zoos, which hope to breed a backup captive stock. The main obstacle to this goal is that virtually nothing of their reproductive behavior and nothing of their reproductive biology is known. The other three species (white rhinoceros, *Ceratotherium simum*; black rhinoceros, *Diceros bicornis*; Indian rhinoceros, *Rhinoceros unicornis*) fare only slightly better in the wild (Bradley Martin and Bradley Martin 1982), although the zoo stock in the United States is probably large enough to allow for captive maintenance without the need for future importation. The same can be said for many other mammals, as well as many bird and reptile species.

Like the medical profession, veterinarians have long recognized the need for research. Research on farm animals was needed for better milk production, better weight gain of cattle, avoidance of parasitism in swine, and so on. Extensive research on these commercially valuable species has proceeded in veterinary schools and in private laboratories. In the past, however, veterinarians were generally unable to study exotic species, since most were not introduced to them in veterinary school. Most veterinary schools were not located near zoos, and there was little "demand" for veterinary services for zoo animals. It is only in the last three decades that veterinarians have become established professionally in zoos, and they have had their hands full putting out brushfires.

Why has research not been an obligation of zoo curators in the past? This is also a complex issue. Curators were generally not laboratory scientists; indeed, often they were not scientists at all, a situation that is now changing rapidly. In most cases, they were oriented primarily toward taxonomy and preoccupied with the mere acquisition of animals for exhibition and with the management of the collection. Often they did not see the need for investigative efforts on a broad scale.

What about the zoo managers? They were concerned mainly with budgets and often knew too little of the essence of scientific research to defend the need for it. Consequently, zoo budgets did not include provisions for a research staff to conduct "basic research." And, it must be emphasized, it is *basic research* that is especially badly needed at this time, as has been argued for many years with reference to human medicine. Basic research has had its ups and downs over the years, even in its justification during congressional budget reviews. But it is safe to say that all serious reviewers agree that the ultimate rewards of basic research outweigh those of applied research activity.

As it was difficult to defend basic research in general, it is not really surprising that true basic research did not exist in zoological gardens and aquariums until very recently. For this reason the zoo community sponsored a special symposium to explore the wisdom of conducting zoo research (ILAR 1975). It was found that research was difficult to conduct in zoos because research budgets came into competition with the needs of curators and veterinarians, and because laboratories for bench scientists did not exist. Furthermore, animal protection societies of all kinds found it necessary to demonstrate against the establishment of zoo research activities, to the probable detriment of the very animals they believed they were protecting. Nevertheless, it was generally acknowledged at this meeting that research in zoos should be fostered.

With this as background, I will next discuss some of the current needs for biomedical research on exotic species. These needs can be best met by conducting research within the confines of the zoo. Modern zoological parks will simply have to establish departments whose sole purpose is to conduct research, and they will benefit from building research facilities. Moreover, zoos need to create a congenial working environment for scientists. I will then briefly review the history of research in zoos and describe the current distribution of zoo research units in the United States. Finally, I will analyze the likely future trends in this field, some possible funding avenues, and the problem of personnel resources.

CURRENT NEEDS FOR RESEARCH

The increasing difficulty of obtaining additional wild animals for exhibition means that zoos must manage their animals in a manner consistent with the new principle of modern zoos: they must create "self-sustaining populations" (Lang 1964; Benirschke 1986). Zoos have a moral obligation to participate actively in the conservation of species, and the various chapters of this book are testimony to that obligation. The general lack of precise knowledge about the species to be managed hampers successful execution of this task.

In particular, too little is known of the genetic makeup of wild animals for zoo managers to avoid the effects of inbreeding in captive populations; the creation of studbooks is only a first step in the direction of adequate genetic management. Clearly, genetic studies of all sorts need to be conducted, and foremost among these is the chromosomal delineation of captive animals. It must be learned which of the many species kept in zoos vary in their cytogenetic complements, as breeding chromosomally divergent animals may have serious consequences. The differences between Bornean, *Pongo p. pygmaeus*, and Sumatran orangutans, *Pongo p. abelii* (Seuanez et al. 1976), are a familiar example of chromosomal divergence, but spider monkeys, *Ateles* spp., owl monkeys, *Aotus* spp., gazelles of different kinds, and many more wild animals have chromosomal complements requiring study prior to the establishment of breeding groups (Benirschke and Kumamoto 1987). Most managers would decry the fact that, sometime in the past, a domestic mare found access to the breeding group of Przewalski's horses, *Equus przewalskii*. Such accidents should be avoided at all costs in the future. Without the delineation of the chromosomal complements of animals, this is impossible, as there are too many "look-alikes."

One can make a similar point about the need to understand better the reasons for the genetic homogeneity of the cheetah, *Acinonyx jubatus* (O'Brien et al. 1983), and to ascertain whether a similar situation exists for other species with poor reproductive performance. The most modern genetic studies now include the delineation of the genome by ever more refined DNA analysis, and the applications of the polymerase chain reaction (PCR) in the exploration of wildlife genetics have been amply demonstrated by the studies of Garner and Ryder (1992). Infinitesimal quantities of DNA (e.g., from hair) can now be used to do sophisticated analyses. Genetic studies in human medicine are now culminating in the ongoing Human Genome Project, whose goal is to identify every gene on the human genome. To understand human descent better, it would be logical to study primates; such studies are most practical when done on zoo specimens. One may argue that it is difficult to defend the use of zoo primates for research on human evolution, but the results of much genetic research on primates have in the past contributed to the study and elimination of human diseases. It is likely that such studies will ultimately benefit zoo populations as well.

Hand in hand with this need goes the need to store samples from the remains of dead specimens for future DNA study or other sophisticated work. The creation of banks of frozen tissues—the so-called frozen zoo—is essential (Benirschke 1984). While there is currently wide recognition of the need to conserve genomes, the conservation of botanic species is far advanced over that of animals. On the other hand, many sophisticated national research laboratories formerly engaged in defense work are currently refocusing their missions. They are superbly equipped for computerization, storage of sophisticated information, pattern recognition, and many of the other chores that must be done in genetic research. In the long run, collaboration between these research laboratories and zoos would be less expensive than the establishment of numerous specialized genetic laboratories in zoos.

Research on reproductive physiology is equally important, and the abundance of ongoing research efforts in this field (Finlay and Maple 1986) shows that many zoos are cognizant of this need. The precise understanding of reproductive hormones and their routine analysis by sophisticated tests have allowed physicians to manage human patients infinitely better than is currently possible with wild animals in captivity. To achieve an understanding of exotics equal to that of human reproduction will require study of the wide variety of reproductive mechanisms among the vertebrates in captivity, the differences in their hormonal makeup, seasonality, placental function and morphology, and so forth. Lasley and Anderson (1991) discuss just where modern biotechnology might fit in with the breeding of exotic species. It is much easier to talk loosely about interspecific embryo transfer, surrogate mothers, pregnancy surveillance, and other technological methods from which humans and domestic animal production have benefited than to exe-

cute such techniques on pandas, *Ailuropoda melanoleuca*, giraffes, *Giraffa camelopardalis*, okapis, *Okapia johnstoni*, and other exotic species. On the other hand, the successful manipulation of infertile animals, such as reptiles, with modern technological methods such as GnRH pumps (Phillips et al. 1985) clearly shows that such exploration has great promise. With this new knowledge, iguana species, rarely bred after importation in the past, can now be successfully bred. Basic research in reproductive biology will have broad application in the future management of zoo species.

Infectious diseases continue to haunt large zoo collections, particularly when different species are housed together. A good example is the malignant catarrhal fever, presumably originating from imperceptibly infected gnus, *Connochaetes* spp., that has wreaked havoc on a number of collections of exotic hoofstock (Heuschele, Oosterhuis, et al. 1984). Parasitism in animals continues to be a problem, and despite the availability of many drugs for the control of worms, greater efforts must be made in the study and prevention of such infections. There are a wide variety of host-specific infections for which comparative knowledge will be of little assistance. Direct study of these diseases is imperative.

Behavioral studies have been conducted in the zoo environment perhaps for a longer time than any other type. Their results are discussed in other chapters in this volume. Behavioral research is popular, probably because it is noninvasive and can be conducted readily by outsiders, such as students and professionals from nearby universities. Regrettably, the findings of university research have rarely had a significant effect on the management of the animals studied. One reason is that there has often been only minimal contact between students and the professional staff of zoos. Also, much of this work has not been published, or has been undertaken with insufficient rigor. I believe that there is clearly a need for "in-house" behavioral studies. When such efforts have in fact been carried out—and examples from the National Zoological Park in Washington are shining testimony to this—the results have had a major effect on animal collection management. Before the behavior of golden lion tamarins, *Leontopithecus rosalia*, was understood, these rare animals did not reproduce well in captivity, and nobody could have dreamed that one day they would be released into the land of their origin. Behavioral studies have laid the foundation for making this possible.

There are, however, numerous future needs for behavioral research; for instance, many more studies on such aspects as maternal behavior, sexual incompatibilities, and social relations in many species are needed. Why is it, for instance, that white rhinoceroses have been so difficult to breed in pairs, while the opposite is true of black rhinos? Are larger social groups of white rhinos needed, or is space the important issue? What are the circumstances that have led to the dramatic population expansion of the white rhino herd at the San Diego Wild Animal Park, while before their placement in that environment no reproduction occurred in the same specimens?

Physiological research is a type of research for which the

need may not be so obvious; nevertheless, it is important for better management of animals in the future. For instance, we must better comprehend the seasonality of animal reproduction and the dependence of many species on the cyclicity of light, mediated through the cyclicity of the secretion of hormones such as melatonin. Perhaps animals have a much greater dependence on specific dietary items than is currently appreciated. Not only would such information make it possible to manage the animals better with regard to their own preferences (e.g., providing a means to get away from too much constant light) and thereby improve their well-being, but it might also be useful for more intensive management (e.g., more rapid breeding). It is likely that precise physiological information will have significant consequences for the survival and reproductive success of exotic animals in captivity.

Adequate nutritional support for wild animals in captivity is crucial (see part 2 of this volume). This has long been recognized, of course, and numerous papers and books have been published on the nutrition of exotic animals. Nevertheless, most zoos still prefer to feed cheap and processed materials, such as ground horsemeat for carnivores or standardized monkey pellets for all monkeys, rather than study the precise needs of each species. The example of adding vitamin D$_3$ to the diets of South American primates has already been mentioned. One must wonder why it took so long for zoos to realize that leaf-eating primates have very special dietary needs. Until this requirement was finally recognized by an investigator from a university, colobine species fared poorly in zoos because they possess such complex and poorly studied stomachs (Kuhn 1964).

It will be impossible for all zoos to meet all special nutritional requirements, but recognizing them is the first step. This can come only from in-depth study of the dietary needs and feeding behavior of animals in the wild. The neonate and its need for specific milk support for a prolonged period, including antibodies (Heuschele, Halligan et al. 1984), is a prime subject for such a detailed approach.

Similarly, it has been shown recently that better control of ambient temperature (sufficient shade; heat from floor devices rather than the ubiquitous red heat lamps used in zoos) has a beneficial effect on animal health (Phillips 1986). A better understanding of such simple parameters makes management easier and, at times, even less expensive. Of course, many other aspects of physiology need to be studied, including endocrinology (see part 6 of this volume). While these may not necessarily be "popular" research endeavors, they need to be taken more seriously. In any case, they may be the most challenging undertakings in terms of staff selection.

Pathology studies on all deceased animals should be mandatory. Only by this means has it been possible to recognize the true nature of most human diseases and consequently to diagnose and treat them. Autopsies are considered to be a basic element of proper management, so it may be presumptuous to list pathology as a research need; however, not all zoological gardens perform autopsies, and they should be encouraged to do so. Further, postmortem examinations make available tissue samples for genetic, virologic, and other studies, creating a surveillance mechanism that facilitates supervision of the health of an animal colony. Pathologists also could be materially helpful by collecting and studying the placentas of the wide variety of mammals kept in zoos, as knowledge of comparative placentation is seriously deficient (Mossman 1987), and such knowledge will be helpful in predicting the success of interspecies embryo transfers (Durrant and Benirschke 1981). It will also aid in a better understanding of perinatal deaths and abortions. Computerization of data, ideally with interzoo transfer capability, is highly desirable.

It is certainly impossible for the zoo community to take on all aspects of relevant scientific research at once, and some hard and difficult choices will have to be made. It is impossible to write a prescription for how to make them or which are applicable to a given zoo. Some institutions have already made some choices and, having laid a foundation, are beginning to expand their research activities. For instance, the Wildlife Conservation Society has had a longstanding tradition of obtaining vital information through sponsored field research. This is perhaps best exemplified by the publications that have come from investigations of the gorilla, *Gorilla gorilla*, jaguar, *Felis onca*, tiger, *Panthera tigris*, and most recently the giant panda, *Ailuropoda melanoleuca*, by George Schaller and colleagues (e.g., Schaller et al. 1989). It is unquestionable that all zoos as well as the wider scientific community have benefited from these studies. At the Cincinnati Zoo, an intensive effort has been focused on interspecies embryo transfer and breeding by artificial insemination, while the San Diego Zoo has opted to focus on laboratory research.

Often the choice of research activities will be dictated by the needs of a specific resident group of animals. This is clearly shown by the intensive golden lion tamarin investigations that have gone on at the National Zoological Park for many years. The immediate demands were for husbandry and disease control. Work then expanded to include behavioral and genetic studies, resulting in a field research program that eventuated in the reintroduction of the animals into the wild. In other cases, the direction of research will follow the interests or particular competence of individuals; for instance, I have espoused a laboratory presence in zoos, based on my familiarity with biomedical research and the benefits that have derived from it for human medicine. Such activity has wide application to many species and has been attractive to potential financial donors.

Zoo research programs should be guided by the needs perceived locally as most urgent. Often zoos must choose between applied and basic research. Not all scientists are willing to work toward applied goals, and basic research is often not immediately applicable to captive management. It would not be logical, for instance, for zoos to begin by employing scientists who are primarily engaged in *Drosophila* genetics; while they may have received their degrees in this subdiscipline, one would hope and anticipate that scientists would not be attracted to working in a zoo if this remained their focus of research. Zoo scientists should not be deaf to the needs that are pervasive in the zoo community. Here, more erudite animal management through better genetics, conservation of species, and behavioral, nutritional, and other studies is now an urgent need. Investigators with an applied bent may be the first choice for employment since not all of these needs can be met through basic research activities. Once research in general has taken a firm foothold in zoos, basic research activities will naturally evolve.

WHY SEPARATE RESEARCH UNITS?

It is impossible for any scientist to embrace all of the different disciplines' techniques or the breadth of their developmental progress. Consequently, it is important to bring expertise in many disciplines into zoological parks, whether in laboratories or other scientific settings. Zoo research units provide a unique opportunity for collaborative efforts among scientists of different disciplines. Traditionally there have been few true research laboratories in zoological gardens, although in many European zoos scientists carry on some laboratory efforts. In general, however, these efforts relate more directly to the health and maintenance of the collections than to independent basic research. Thus, for instance, in the Tierpark Berlin, Germany, several scientists engage in research on the pathology and microbiology of collection animals. This group, however, has been severely understaffed, and its ability to stretch beyond immediate diagnostic needs is limited. Now a new direction has taken hold, with more fundamental studies gaining ground. Only at the London Zoo has there been a true laboratory research effort in a variety of scientific disciplines in past years. There, the Institute of Zoology, originally the Nuffield and Wellcome Institutes, has been directly associated with the zoo. Its research in genetics, endocrinology, biochemistry, and other topics is well known and has led to significant advances. Moreover, under the aegis of the Zoological Society of London, many important scientific meetings have been sponsored and the proceedings published.

In the United States, the Philadelphia Zoo has established the Penrose Laboratory, a major research laboratory in which much nutritional, microbiological, and other research has been undertaken. As mentioned earlier, the Wildlife Conservation Society has focused on field research and has made very many extremely important studies of the ecology and general biology of endangered animals in situ. It continues to undertake this work and has recently expanded its in-house investigations as well. At the San Diego Zoo, where autopsies have been systematically done on all animals since 1956, a complete research department was formally established in 1975, employing scientists from several different disciplines with good results. At the National Zoological Park in Washington, D.C., the Smithsonian Institution has long fostered active research on animals both in its own collection and in the field. The results of this activity have profoundly influenced the maintenance of animals in other zoos. Smithsonian-sponsored scientists have had a meaningful and fruitful collaboration with sophisticated scientists from outside the zoo environment; moreover, their investigative efforts have played a key role in our understanding of the biology of insectivores and South American primates. More recently, other zoos (Brookfield, Cincinnati, Columbus, Los Angeles, and Minnesota, to name a few) have also established departments that are solely devoted to investigative efforts.

Many zoos have encouraged some type of research by inviting scientists from nearby universities to use their collections for education or research. More often, however, zoos have been approached by scientists with requests to make available to them tissues from necropsies, blood from animals incidentally handled, and other materials for research on, for example, the mechanisms of aging (Jones 1982), taxonomy (Sibley and Ahlquist 1983, 1984), and biochemical studies (Doellgast and Benirschke 1979). The results of such studies have been mixed. Good publications have been issued, but the knowledge often does not reach the zoo. These studies have often led to conflicts, as the scientists do not understand the difficulties of specimen collection and have often been remiss in making available the research results. Also, their scientific studies have frequently had little immediate relation to animal maintenance and have been of little interest to the zoo community. Thus, in trying to acquire important specimens, scientists have met with difficulty. Once these problems are understood, they can be rapidly rectified, assuming good will on both sides. Such studies, however, are not a permanent solution to the need for zoo research. It is truly rare that the zoological community has asked scientists in universities to solve some of zoos' immediate problems. In a few instances of parasitism or microbiological problems, universities have materially helped out, but at other times, the needs of zoos have been of little interest to and have not met with a positive response from university scientists. For all these reasons it is clearly important that independent research units be established in zoological gardens.

An analogy can be made between zoo research and medical research: major advances in therapy for and prevention of diseases have come about through systematic basic research, but practicing physicians cannot be directly involved in making these breakthroughs, since they are too busy with clinical diagnosis and therapy to embrace the multitude of modern, state-of-the-art research tools. Likewise, in the zoo community, curators and veterinarians should not be expected to make major advances in the understanding of basic biological facts about their charges. To be sure, they can aid in advancing our general knowledge by exploring better methods of husbandry, seeking to prevent and cure diseases, doing training and behavior modification, studying taxonomy, and so on. Often, however, the task of acquiring breakthrough knowledge will fall to individuals who do not also have the constant obligation of management and therapy. It will require dedicated investigators working in a variety of disciplines. Curators and veterinarians need not fear replacement by such scientists and should aid them as much as possible.

THE NATURE OF A RESEARCH DEPARTMENT

In the best of all possible worlds, scientists will work in a separate unit within the zoo, have close affiliations with university departments corresponding to their disciplines, have continuous interaction with other zoo staff, be responsive to the needs of the curators, veterinarians, and animals, and be funded by a special zoo budget as well as by grants. Such a world does not exist as yet, in part because we, all those concerned with this area of endeavor, have not spoken up loudly enough in favor of it. For instance, few zoos have earmarked budgets for facilities in which to do serious laboratory investigations, and hardly any have facilities in place. In part for this reason, it is difficult to find dedicated scientists willing to undertake zoo research.

The task of finding appropriate research staff is more difficult than it would appear at first glance. While it may be possible to find a first-rate scientist, say, a geneticist, who is interested in wildlife research, he will have his own idea of what is important. For instance, he may decide that DNA-DNA hybridization is the most fruitful avenue for his research. He may not be willing to undertake the time-consuming but vitally important task of studbook analysis, or to study the cytogenetics of orangutans. Scenarios of this kind are abundant, and from them comes the occasional hostility that develops between various segments of the zoo community. In large measure this happens because research is still so new, an orphan child in zoos. This situation is bound to change, however, and the writing of this chapter is testimony to the recognition that change is needed. Curiously, little has changed since Hediger expressed the problem so well in 1969. Said he: "However galling it may be . . . it has to be admitted that scientific research is usually placed last in zoological gardens, if indeed it has any place at all."

Hediger (1969) also strongly advocated that zoos be associated closely with universities, as a "pressing need of our times," and suggested then that such affiliations would make zoologists and other scientists available for zoo research. It is my strong opinion that we, the zoo community, cannot wait for university scientists to carry out the research necessary for the management of our stocks. It will have to come from in-house efforts. Dathe (1985) saw this problem in a similar light. He also argued for the usage of modern technology, "biotechnology" as he called it, in the management of zoo animals and gave many pertinent examples of its benefits.

Colleagues of mine in the medical community are astonished to learn of the paucity of research on the vast and interesting problems seen in zoos. They also suggest (and this is not a bad analogy) that they would not invest their money in the stock of a company that did not have at least 3–5% of its budget devoted to research and development. Clearly, initiating and funding research is a significant challenge for all zoos and one of the most important ones to be faced straight on. The administrative staffs of all zoos, large or small, must make the difficult decision to set aside money for serious research efforts. The research budget should be a set percentage of the operating cost and be immune from cuts to meet other needs. Only then can we confidently say that we have done our part to rectify our long-standing neglect of research. The first priority is to marshal the political will for this undertaking. Then each zoo must decide which research is most suitable for itself and how scientific staff can be integrated into its community.

In order to attract serious scientists to modern zoos, we will have to do much educating, probably beginning at the college level. Aspiring young scientists will have to be coaxed into our community by its challenges, needs, and developing opportunities. When I see the enormous number of medical and allied scientists who have been lured into cancer research and, more recently, into AIDS research, however, I must admit that it is not so much the challenges as it is the availability of research funds and some sort of stable outlook for future development that attracts qualified people. Of great importance are salaries of appropriate size and a congenial research environment.

It seems to me highly desirable that zoo-employed scientists have firm appointments in a university department. Such appointments would help them to remain credible because publication of investigative results would be necessary for promotion, contact with students would keep them current in research techniques and scientific knowledge, and they would have access to graduate students and other help. Most importantly, they would "rub shoulders" with fellow scientists and learn by this association of new technology, potential collaborators, and so forth. Zoo administrators, in turn, would have to accept somewhat different behavior from scientists than they are accustomed to from other staff. In their quest to succeed, scientists will be very much more irregular in their hours at work, they will need to be given time to teach, and they will also be critical of some traditions of zoos that have long been held inviolable. But all this will be for the betterment of the modern zoo, even though it will require adjustments and perhaps more generous salaries than zoos have customarily paid.

In this chapter much emphasis has been placed on in-house laboratory units, primarily because of my familiarity with them. Scientists cannot work in a vacuum; a critical mass of them is needed to interact, and that can happen only in groups. Having the zoo's investigative needs met in an independent unit or department provides unique advantages. It will cement relationships among scientists and often lead to fuller professional development. At the same time, zoos will have to engage much more actively in field research, for instance, in the long-held tradition of the Wildlife Conservation Society. Field studies are not only important in the overall context of zoo-sponsored research, but also keep researchers in touch with the natural world. This contact is important to both basic and applied research scientists. It provides the basis for enlightened animal maintenance and is enormously stimulating and gratifying to the researchers as well.

It is essential that the significant findings made through the basic research activities of zoo research departments be translated into management practices, for nothing is more frustrating to motivated scientists than to see all their labor go for naught. Another difficulty is the complexity of the personal needs of an investigator working in a zoo. He or she may be used to a university environment and find a zoo very different. Similarly, zoo administrators will find personalities in such scientists very different from their own, and clashes must be avoided if productive interaction is to proceed. There are generally no "up-and-out" policies in zoos for research scientists, nor standards established by which to measure their progress.

And what is the director to do when an excellent scientist veers from his or her avowed original interest to an esoteric area of study, say, the pheromones of bumblebees? Such events may be rare, and it is of course impossible to write prescriptions for them. It is my opinion that such incidents will have to be handled on a case-by-case basis and that they should be considered in the hiring discussion with the new scientist. The director of research will have to establish firm policies and take overall charge of the crew. The tougher the director of research is, the better the research endeavor will turn out to be. Much more immediate will be the difficulties that arise from misconceptions that other staff, longtime employees of the zoo, may have when scientists come aboard. Perhaps scientists command larger salaries and seem to have more freedom. These are problems that universities and medical schools also face, and their solutions may be emulated, at least in part.

With all these needs, there remains the urgent quest for research funds. The plight of endangered animals has been sufficiently publicized to be readily understood by the public. The allocation of national funding, however, has been extremely slow and the appropriated monies minuscule, especially in comparison with the largesse aimed at human medical research and in light of the enormous research needs. It must be a priority of the zoo community at large to seek, through Congress, the National Science Foundation, and private foundations, allocation of funding comparable to that earmarked for other research endeavors. We must also be cautioned that much of the needed research for zoos, when compared with the molecular biological investigations currently being undertaken at universities, may seem antiquated or even trivial. A rapid catch-up is needed, and may be possible, given enough financial support. If national agencies such as NSF are to consider supporting research on endangered species, it should be made clear to their reviewers that the scientific nature of the intended work must not be judged exclusively by molecular biologists, as they would see little merit in the pursuit of some of this essential zoo work.

Much of the badly needed research could be undertaken by staff at biomedical laboratories on the side, as is done in medicine. An example would be chromosomal studies of gazelles or orangutans. For instance, a laboratory responsible for the routine performance of diagnostic chromosome studies from amniocentesis could also investigate the chromosomal site of the fragile X syndrome, and other questions. It is argued that biomedical laboratories are either the service type or the research type, but that is not so. In a large number of institutions with which I am familiar, service work proceeds and is often well funded, while the supervisor uses the same facility and staff to explore research goals. To be sure, the research is often supported by a separate grant, but there is no reason why a similar approach cannot be taken in the zoo community. It is equally possible that human cytogenetic laboratories could be persuaded to do the occasional chromosome study on important species, such as spider monkeys, whose taxonomy is of special concern to zoos. It would not then be necessary to have a cytogenetic laboratory in every zoo for this purpose. Likewise, a zoo's general laboratory in which hematology studies are undertaken for "routine" purposes can readily participate in parasitological or other investigations that aid in the general scientific effort. Such is frequently the case already; it merely needs to be propagated.

It should be possible to obtain from benevolent donors and large foundations endowments specifically dedicated to creating research "chairs." For the important field research carried out by the Wildlife Conservation Society, such support has been notably successful. A beginning has also been made in this direction by the establishment of the Kleberg Chair in Genetics at the San Diego Zoo's Center for Research in Endangered Species (CRES). Greater effort needs to be made in this direction. I am only too familiar with the many needs that exist in the daily affairs of the zoo; nevertheless, some donors want to support research of this specific type, and they should be befriended.

One often-asked question is just how a small zoo with an earnest desire to contribute should commence with a research effort when its budget is so much smaller than that of the zoos that have so far been cited. It might begin with an analysis of the national picture, ascertained from the annual American Zoo and Aquarium Association (AZA) meetings, *International Zoo Yearbook*, *Zoo Biology*, and other publications. In addition, it should weigh its own unanswered needs and review its collection. For instance, it may well be that a small zoo has a unique collection of a particular species not widely represented in zoos—armadillos, for example. A careful analysis might show that little is known of the animal's reproduction, feeding habits, temperature control, dependence on light cycles, and other characteristics, and that the zoo would therefore be in a unique position to add to the body of scientific knowledge. It might team up with a nearby university or employ an interested scientist to take on this challenge. Another zoo may find that its horticultural collection should be the main focus, and yet another, the behavior of certain "problem" animals in its collection. Most zoological gardens have abundant subjects for investigative efforts. As long as they acknowledge the facts that they cannot take on all aspects of research and that all research ultimately will advance knowledge of animals in captivity, their contribution will be valuable. Some zoos will have superior relations with a foreign country and may be able to establish field stations. The possibilities are endless. The main point I wish to make is that, as already emphasized by Hediger, the total amount of research currently proceeding is puny given the very large number of species in our care. Moreover, for many of them, there is not much time to conduct even current projects. The animals will be gone before we have even fathomed their chromosome sets, let alone the intricacies of their total physiology.

Can zoos catch up with other scientific institutions? This rhetorical question assumes, of course, that zoo science stands alone, which it does not. It, like other disciplines, is part of all scientific endeavor. It now employs the medicine, the techniques and instruments, indeed, the entire body of knowledge of many other disciplines. Its computer programs, behavioral studies, and hematologic and parasitological background have all come from multidisciplinary studies, some of which have been done in zoos or, in the case of field studies, based in zoo communities.

The way in which zoos differ from other scientific institutions is that they have collections of animals that are generally inaccessible to members of the broader scientific community, unless they themselves undertake field trips. At the same time, some of the needed research could not possibly be undertaken in the field, and yet the potentially valuable research materials and opportunities in zoos are not currently being exploited. In the case of endangered animals, such opportunities could be forever lost. The Przewalski's horse is a relevant example. Its genetics, its differences from domestic horses, its placentation, and many other biological parameters could never be studied in the wild. Thus, zoos have not only unique opportunities for research, but also, in my opinion, the obligation to conduct it.

Of course zoos cannot possibly "catch up" with all of the scientific arena, but a strong beginning should be made. Often a sound collaboration of outside scientists with zoos has gone a long way. I recall the remarkable insight gained in the genetic study of the cheetah and other carnivores by genetics experts from the National Cancer Institute and scientists from the National Zoo. Such collaboration does not fall precisely into the arena of "The Need for Multidisciplinary Research Units in the Zoo," the title of this chapter; nevertheless, without it, this scientific study probably would not have been conducted. Its results have had very important ramifications for zoo animal management as well as for inquiries into taxonomy and other biological questions. Being an optimist, I believe that zoos will catch up, not by doing all of the research themselves, but by becoming an integral part of the entire research community.

Finally, we should be cautioned that animal protection societies will keep an eager eye on such research establishments, since many shudder reflexively when they hear the words "animal research." Education in that direction is also needed, as is meticulous attention to animal welfare, a topic that is hardly in need of defense in the context of this book.

REFERENCES

Benirschke, K. 1984. The frozen zoo concept. *Zoo Biol.* 3:325–28.
———. ed. 1986. *Primates: The road to self-sustaining populations.* New York: Springer-Verlag.
———. 1987. The mandate for research in zoos. *Interdiscipl. Sci. Rev.* 12:10–22.
Benirschke, K., and Kumamoto, A. T. 1987. Challenges of artiodactyl cytogenetics. *La Kromosomo* II.45.
Bradley Martin, E., and Bradley Martin, C. 1982. *Run rhino run.* London: Chatto & Windus.
Dathe, H. H. 1985. Zur Anwendbarkeit biotechnischer Methoden in Zoologischen Gärten. *Milu* (Berlin) 6:325–35.
Doellgast, G. J., and Benirschke, K. 1979. Placental alkaline phosphatase in Hominidae. *Nature* 280:601–2.
Durrant, B., and Benirschke, K. 1981. Embryo transfer in exotic animals. *Theriogenology* 15:77–83.
Finlay, T. W., and Maple, T. L. 1986. A survey of research in American zoos and aquariums. *Zoo Biol.* 5:261–68.
Garner, K. J., and Ryder, O. A. 1992. Some applications of PCR to studies in wildlife genetics. *Symp. Zool. Soc. Lond.* 64:167–81.

Gibson, W. C. 1980. The cost of not doing medical research. *JAMA* 244:1817–19.
Hediger, H. 1969. *Man and animal in the zoo.* London: Routledge and Kegan Paul.
Heuschele, W. P., Halligan, K., Janssen, D. L., Oosterhuis, J. O., and Schofield, S. 1984. Etiology and prevention of neonatal diarrhea in hand-raised exotic ruminants. In *Proceedings of the 4th Annual Meeting of the American Association of Zoo Veterinarians,* Louisville, Kentucky, 80–81. Philadelphia: American Association of Zoo Veterinarians.
Heuschele, W. P., Oosterhuis, J., Anderson, M. P., Swansen, M., and Fletcher, H. R. 1984. Malignant catarrhal fever in wild ruminants. In *One medicine,* ed. O. A. Ryder and M. L. Byrd, 296–308. New York: Springer-Verlag.
Hunt, R. D., Garcia, F. G., Hegsted, D. M., and Kaplinsky, N. 1967. Vitamin D_2 and D_3 in New World primates: Influence on calcium absorption. *Science* 157:943–45.
Institute of Laboratory Animal Resources (ILAR). 1975. *Research in zoos and aquariums.* Washington, D.C.: National Academy of Sciences.
Jones, M. L. 1982. Longevity of captive mammals. *Der Zoologische Garten* 52:113–38.
Kuhn, J. J. 1964. Zur Kenntnis von Bau und Funktion des Magens der Schlankaffen (Colobinae). *Folia Primatol.* 2:193–221.
Lang, E. 1964. Survival in zoos. *Symp. Zool. Soc. Lond.* 13:129–32.
Lasley, B. L., and Anderson, G. B. 1991. Where does biotechnology fit in captive breeding programs? Guest editorial. *Zoo Biol.* 10:195–96.
Mossman, H. W. 1987. *Vertebrate fetal membranes: Comparative ontogeny and morphology; evolution; phylogenetic significance; basic functions; research opportunities.* London: Macmillan.
O'Brien, S. J., Wildt, D. E., Goldman, D., Merril, C. R., and Bush, M. 1983. The cheetah is depauperate in genetic variation. *Science* 221:459–62.
Phillips, J. A. 1986. A biologically relevant heating module for animal enclosures. *Int. Zoo Yrbk.* 24/25:311–15.
Phillips, J. A., Alexander, N., Karesh, W. B., Miller, R., and Lasley, B. L. 1985. Stimulating male sexual behavior with repetitive pulses of GnRH in female green iguana, *Iguana iguana. J. Exp. Zool.* 234:481–84.
Schaller, G., Hu, J., Pan, W., and Zhu, J. 1985. *The giant pandas of Wolong.* Chicago: University of Chicago Press.
Schaller, G. B., Teng, Q., Johnson, K., Wang, X., Shen, H., and Hu Jinchu. 1989. Feeding ecology of giant pandas and Asiatic black bears in Tangjiahe reserve, China. In *Carnivore behavior, ecology, and evolution,* ed. J. Gittleman, 212–41. Ithaca, N.Y.: Cornell University Press.
Seuanez, H. N., Fletcher, J., Evans, H. J., and Martin, D. E. 1976. A polymorphic structural rearrangement in two populations of orangutan. *Cytogenet. Cell Genet.* 17:327–37.
Sibley, C. G., and Ahlquist, J. E. 1983. The phylogeny and classification of birds based on the data of DNA-DNA hybridization. *Curr. Ornithol.* 1:245–92.
———. 1984. The phylogeny of the hominoid primates, as indicated by DNA-DNA hybridization. *J. Mol. Evol.* 20:2–15.

46

Data Collection in the Zoo Setting, Emphasizing Behavior

CAROLYN M. CROCKETT

Systematic observations and record keeping are essential for consistent advances in the management of zoos and related facilities. Casual observations of the outcomes of innovative exhibit modifications are of much greater value when supplemented by data collected using appropriate quantitative methods. Quantification is important because qualitative observations may provide inaccurate estimates of what is really occurring. A great deal of "success" in zoo exhibitry may be serendipity—the right combination of individual animals that happen to be of a species able to thrive in marginal conditions. Only systematic data collection can lead to the conclusion that particular management decisions had anything to do with success. Just because "we did this and it worked" does not mean that it is the best approach to captive management. It may have been coincidence.

This chapter evolved from an earlier paper (Crockett Wilson 1978) and a revision prepared for a workshop on applied behavioral research in zoos. My original motivation for writing the 1978 version was to provide a simpler and more zoo-oriented description of methodology than Altmann's (1974) excellent landmark paper. Although I have drawn considerably from both Altmann (1974) and Sackett (1978b), this synthesis has been particularly influenced by my own observational research on primates and by my experience in assisting dozens of students in the design of zoo research projects. This chapter provides an overview of techniques sufficient to allow an inexperienced researcher to design and conduct a quantified study of zoo animals. Observational research on behavior is emphasized, but I suggest ways these methods can be applied to the systematic collection of other data pertinent to zoo management. For further details on methodology, serious researchers should consult Bakeman and Gottman (1986), Martin and Bateson (1986, 1993), Altmann (1974, 1984), Lehner (1979), and Sackett (1978b).

RESEARCH DESIGN: PRELIMINARY CONSIDERATIONS

Most research in zoos is nonexperimental. For example, the researcher usually is unable to manipulate environmental conditions or group composition in a well-controlled manner. Collection of physical information (e.g., measurements, urine specimens) may be too invasive to perform on a regular basis. Thus, many studies are primarily descriptive and based on observational data. Information is collected, and after some period of time, an effort is made to determine what it means. Such studies frequently remain unpublished because of their unfocused and possibly ungeneralizable conclusions. This fate can be avoided by clearly identifying research questions before beginning data collection.

Formulation of a Problem

Data collection methods are designed with respect to the question being asked, and therefore, an appropriately formulated problem is the first step in research design (Altmann 1974). In a zoo setting, possible research questions might include:

1. What is the relative use of different locations in the enclosure, and what behaviors are displayed there? For example, Byers (1977) asked whether Siberian ibex kids, *Capra sibirica*, played more on the sloped or on the flat surfaces of their naturalistic zoo enclosure.

2. Are the animals most active during hours that the zoo is open to the public? For example, Conway et al. (1978) and Oswald and Kuyk (1978) investigated the effects of public presence and artificial daylight reversal on the activity levels of animals housed in Woodland Park Zoo's Nocturnal House.

3. Does the addition of floor covering material such as straw or woodchips reduce aggression and inactivity (e.g., An-

FIG. 46.1.   Zoo research might focus on the behavioral indicators of pregnancy and impending birth. Lowland gorilla Nina supports 1-hour-old infant Zuri, still attached by the umbilical cord. (Photo by Carol Beach, Woodland Park Zoo.)

derson and Chamove 1984; Chamove et al. 1982; Chamove and Anderson 1979)? Anderson and Chamove (1984) provided a succinct list of questions they hoped to answer through their research on this topic, which is a good idea for any zoo research project.

4. What behavioral indicators of pregnancy can be identified, and are they correlated with physical characteristics (e.g., lowland gorillas, *Gorilla gorilla gorilla*: Meder 1986) (fig. 46.1)?

Independent and Dependent Variables. After determining the research question, the next step is to identify the relevant dependent and independent variables. This is especially important because the independent variables may be more or less out of one's control, and the best that can be done may be to record them systematically.

The *dependent variables* are the effects that the researcher is primarily interested in quantifying. These can include behavioral variables such as rates of aggression, sexual behavior, or play. They can also be physical measurements such as food intake or weight. Occurrence of injuries, interbirth interval length, and infant survival rate are some dependent variables that can be derived from daily reports.

The *independent variables* are the factors that the researcher believes affect the dependent variables of interest. Some independent variables are continuous-interval variables, such as temperature or time of day. Others are categorical or nominal variables, such as gender (male or female), enclosure type (naturalistic or bare concrete), or physical condition (pregnant or not pregnant). It is important to consider that continuous-interval variables can be grouped into categories (e.g., morning and afternoon; hot, warm, cool, cold), and that an independent variable in one study may be a dependent variable in another (e.g., food intake). Independent variables can also include age/sex composition of groups, the rearing conditions of individuals whose behavior serves as dependent variables, food delivery schedule, size of enclosure, and many others. Thus, the importance of having accurate and systematic records available to draw upon becomes obvious. Furthermore, when independent variables of particular interest are identified in advance, they can be specified and filled in on each data collection sheet.

Alternative Hypotheses, Confounding, and Bias. Much research in zoos is descriptive in nature (we don't know what is going on and want to find out). However, research data are most amenable to statistical analysis and interpretation when null and alternative hypotheses are specified beforehand (see "Data Analysis" below). Whether or not a specific hypothesis is formulated, the methodology must be appropriate for ruling out alternative hypotheses. For example, the researcher may hypothesize that males use the top branches in an enclosure more than females do. Suppose that data are collected on males in the morning and on females in the afternoon. Further suppose that these data suggest that males do use the top branches a greater percentage of the time. Under these circumstances, one cannot rule out the alternative hypothesis that animals, regardless of gender, spend more time in the top branches in the morning. (In this example, the independent variables are sex and time of day, while the dependent variable is the percentage of time spent in the top branches.)

A common goal of zoo research is to identify changes in behavior occurring as a result of a change in the zoo environment, such as the addition of "furniture" or the introduction or loss of a group member. To assess unambiguously the effects of such a change, all other factors must be held constant. Since such control is often difficult or impossible in a zoo setting, the interpretation of results must take into account the possible effects of any extraneous, uncontrolled events. For example, if a new branch were introduced into a cage and a few days later a new infant were born, one might not be able to conclude unequivocally that changes in activity or enclosure utilization (dependent variables) were a result of one and only one of these factors (independent variables)—that is, they are "confounded." To resolve this confounding, the branch would have to be removed and reintroduced, replicating the experimental manipulation. Seasonal and weather changes may also influence the behavior of one's subjects in a manner that can confound interpretation of a project's results. These factors must be recorded systematically if their effects are to be assessed. Thus, the researcher not only needs to take into account changes that were intentionally brought about, but also must characterize factors that may represent environmental changes from the animals' point of view.

It is usually impractical and expensive to collect data 24 hours a day, every day. For this reason, sampling methods have been devised to ensure unbiased estimates of behavior based on a subset of total time. *Unbiased* means that the observations are representative of what is going on when observations are not being made, and that, when data are being collected, researchers do not inadvertently record data supporting their hypotheses at the expense of data refuting them. Sampling methods (see table 46.1) and observer bias will be discussed below.

When and How Often to Collect Data. Another preliminary consideration in research design is *when* to observe. If the research question focuses on diurnal variation in behavior, then all time periods of interest must be sampled (e.g., Brannian and Cloak 1985; Bradley and Johnson 1978; Conway et al. 1978; Oswald and Kuyk 1978). It may be practical to eliminate the hours of darkness from the sample if preliminary observations indicate that the animals are mostly inactive then. Around-the-clock observations are essential for studies of parturition and other events whose exact timing may be impossible to predict (e.g., Fitch 1986).

To study day-to-day changes in behavior, such as correlates of estrous cycles or infant development, daily or almost daily records are necessary. If the amount of time available for data collection is limited, making observations at the same time each day will eliminate the confounding factor of time of day. However, this will also sacrifice generalizability to other time periods unless diurnal variation in behavior has been ruled out first. If specific behaviors are of interest, preliminary observations will determine the best times to record them. For example, Byers (1977) made 50 hours of preliminary observations to determine when ibex play was most common. It turned out that 95% of play occurred between 0500 and 0700 and between 1900 and 2115, so Byers's systematic data collection was done at those times.

Longitudinal studies (e.g., developmental) raise the question of how often observations must be made in order to provide valid estimates and yet be practical from a time and resource point of view. Kraemer et al. (1977) suggest a method for evaluating the spacing and timing of observations in order to minimize sample error and cost of data collection. For their research project, a "saturation sample" pilot study determined that the optimal sampling strategy was to observe each chimpanzee, *Pan troglodytes*, mother-infant pair for three 30-minute periods per week on three different days at different times (morning, midday, afternoon). For physical data (e.g., weight) that cannot be taken daily, records at approximately equal intervals are desirable (e.g., once a week). All weighings should be done at approximately the same interval since last feeding (e.g., Kawata and Elsen 1984).

Determining What Information Is Important. Determining what types of information are needed to answer a research question requires a reading of the relevant literature (e.g., past research on the topic or species in question) as well as preliminary observations. Knowing what has been done before may suggest useful techniques and avoid unnecessary duplication. If the project is observational, decide what behaviors are of interest and what parameters are of biological importance (Altmann 1984). For example, is it more relevant to know how often the behaviors occur (e.g., hourly rate), how much of the time is spent in particular activities (percentage of observation time), or how long the animals tend to engage in a behavior once it begins (bout duration) (see tables 46.2 and 46.3.)? Determine whether sequences of behavior are important (e.g., in courtship interactions), as their recording and analysis greatly complicate a research design (see Bakeman and Gottman 1986; Lehner 1979; Bakeman 1978).

Decide whether identification of individual animals is essential, for example, in order to record actors and recipients of social interactions. In some cases, subjects can be lumped into age and sex classes without loss of essential information. If identification is necessary, marking of individuals may be required (see Rice and Kalk, chap. 5, this volume). If enclosure use is a subject of study, obtain accurate maps or blueprints of the exhibit.

Keep in mind that the time required for data analysis increases with the types of information that are gathered. To be useful for addressing specific management questions or for student projects of a few months' duration, data must be collected, analyzed, and interpreted quickly. Therefore it is advisable to keep data collection simple.

Preliminary Analyses. As a final preliminary consideration, data collection methods should be planned with some thought to subsequent data analysis. As elaborated below, this may involve providing space on checksheets for summing data. A good rule is to try some preliminary analyses after some initial data collection. Determine whether all of the research questions posed are indeed answerable with the method chosen. *Preliminary analyses are important.*

Defining Recording Categories

In order to record data systematically, appropriate categories must be defined. A precise definition for each category must be written out, both to ensure that observers do not "drift" from the original definition and to enable other researchers to understand fully and use the same recording system. Part of this task follows from the identification of independent and dependent variables as described previously. In general, defining recording categories for non-behavioral data is more straightforward than developing ethograms.

The project's objectives and constraints will affect the types of categories selected. For example, for management and research purposes it may be desirable to record the reproductive states of female monkeys each day. Hausfater (1975) categorized estrous cycles of wild baboons, *Papio cynocephalus*, by days before and after the day of onset of rapid deturgescence of the sex skin. For captive lion-tailed macaques, *Macaca silenus*, Lindburg, Shideler, and Fitch (1985) used estrogen content of daily urine samples to categorize estrous cycles; the day after peak estrogen was day 0, the most likely day of ovulation, and other cycle days were categorized by number of days before or after day 0. During analysis such categories are sometimes collapsed; for example, Wasser (1983) used sex-skin characteristics to identify four cycling and three pregnant categories in *P. cynocephalus*.

For behavioral and nonbehavioral categories, a thorough literature search will reveal whether adequate categories have already been defined. When preexisting categories are used, not only does the researcher avoid "reinventing the wheel," but the previous literature can also be cited, thus shortening a manuscript prepared for publication. This practice also facilitates direct comparisons with the results of prior research.

Ethograms. In the early days of ethology, an ethogram (a catalog of an animal's behavioral repertoire, also known as a behavioral inventory or a behavior taxonomy) was always the first step and was sometimes itself the objective of many years' study. Defining behaviors is still an essential step, but the extensiveness and detail with which this needs to be done depend on the specific question at hand. A project's objective may be the detailed comparison of two or more related species with respect to qualitative and quantitative aspects of their behavior. Such interspecific comparisons are the core of the comparative method, which originated in comparative morphology and was extended to behavior by the classical ethologists (Lorenz 1958; Tinbergen 1951). A similar project goal would be to describe behavioral development in detail, both qualitatively and quantitatively.

In general, one of the first tasks of a project is to formulate a list of well-named, carefully defined behaviors relevant to the research objectives. Generally, one must select the behaviors essential to a study to avoid being swamped during data collection (Hinde 1973). Often during data analysis, behaviors are collapsed into larger categories anyway (e.g., Stanley and Aspey 1984, 103). There is a certain amount of arbitrariness about observational data collection: abstraction always occurs, and information is always lost (G. P. Sackett, pers. comm.).

Several ways of describing behavior may be included in a single taxonomy (Hinde 1973). The *physical description* of behavior can be "molecular" (including minute details of muscle and skeletal action), or it can be "molar" (Sackett, Ruppenthal, and Gluck 1978); a molar description of "walk" might be "slow, quadrupedal locomotion." Or, using what Hinde (1973) calls *description by consequence,* behaviors can be defined in terms of their effects. For example, "approach" behavior has the effect of decreasing distance between two animals, regardless of the mode of locomotion; "supplanting" might be defined as the approach of one animal followed by the immediate departure of another.

In formulating an ethogram, it is advisable to use objective names and operational definitions whenever possible; try to avoid subjective inference regarding function. Several physically distinct behaviors could be inferred to have the same function, whereas one behavior could be inferred to have several functions. For this reason, objectively defined behaviors are the best starting point. For example, in describing a facial expression common to many monkeys, "open mouth stare" is more objective than "open mouth threat (fig. 46.2)."

Functionally organized taxonomies do have their advantages, however (Rosenblum 1978). Researchers often find, after some experience, that it is appropriate to lump behaviors into a larger functional category such as "threat" or "aggression." This may occur during, or as a result of, data analysis. Another example is "protective interference," a subjective description by consequence that includes several distinct behaviors that mother macaques use to protect their infants (Kaufman and Rosenblum 1966). If several types of behavior are eventually included within one scored category, each type should be described in the ethogram. For some types of behavior, observer judgment is very important. For example, in discriminating between play and aggression, the ability to make reliable judgments may require many hours of observation to develop.

A behavior taxonomy might be restricted to discrete

FIG. 46.2.   In formulating an ethogram, use objective names and operational definitions. The function of this open mouth expression given by an adult male lion-tailed macaque should be verified from quantitative observations. (Photo by Joy Spurr, Woodland Park Zoo.)

categories of behavior. On the other hand, researchers not especially concerned with sequences of behavior might record fairly predictable sequences, such as "copulation" and "rough and tumble play," as single units of behavior (G. P. Sackett, pers. comm.). Disputes have arisen regarding the use of "catchy" behavior names such as "rape," "cuckoldry," and so on because they have special connotations for humans. The term "forced copulation" may be preferable to "rape," although the latter has the virtue of simplicity. Simply be aware that a controversy exists; it may be one that a researcher prefers to avoid by using conservative behavior names.

Examples of ethograms published for studies conducted in zoos and similar facilities are given by Macedonia (1987, 58), Nash and Chilton (1986, 40), Tasse (1986, 119), Traylor-Holzer and Fritz (1985, 119, including definitions for recording spatial locations for evaluating enclosure use), Stanley and Aspey (1984, 91, 94–95, 103), Freeman (1983, 7), Kleiman (1983), and Byers (1977, 201–2).

Exhaustive and Mutually Exclusive Recording Categories. For purposes of data recording and analysis, it is often advantageous (and for some sampling methods, necessary) to define categories that are both exhaustive and mutually exclusive. *Exhaustive* means that the subject ("S") is always recorded as doing something, even if "inactive," "other," or "not visible." *Mutually exclusive* means that the subject is never recorded as doing more than one thing simultaneously; that is, S can be "sitting" or "grooming," but not both. The recording system should include rules for establishing priorities or precedence, such as recording the "action" rather than the "posture" (Sackett 1978a).

Within a particular scoring system (e.g., a checksheet), more than one set of mutually exclusive and exhaustive categories can be included: for example, the subject could

TABLE 46.1.   Summary of Sampling Methods

Sampling method	Scoring basis	Mutually exclusive	Exhaustive	Comments and uses
Ad libitum	Behavior change	No	No	Longhand field notes. Preliminary observations; ethogram development.
Continuous	Behavior change	Yes	No	For frequencies (onsets) of selected behaviors, especially infrequent behaviors of short duration.
		Yes	Yes	When relative frequencies are to be calculated.
		Yes	Yes	For transition times (to calculate durations).
Scan/instantaneous	Time-point	Yes[a]	Yes	Especially useful for time budgets, activity patterns, group behavioral synchrony; usually produces high interobserver reliability.
One/zero	Time-interval	Yes[b]	Yes	Not recommended except for special circumstances (see text).

Note: See tables 46.2 and 46.3 for definitions of terms.
[a] Simultaneous behaviors can be scored and later combined into mutually exclusive categories.
[b] More than one mutually exclusive category can be scored per interval.

be scored, simultaneously, for one behavior, one location, and one proximity relationship (e.g., nearest neighbor identity and distance). Examples are given below (see "Data Recording Systems").

In some cases a behavior may occur simultaneously with many other behaviors, and its importance relative to the concomitant behaviors may be unknown. Using clearly specified recording methods (e.g., carefully designed checksheets to be described below), two behaviors can be recorded and later analyzed separately and in combination. For example, a subject might spend 10% of the time standing and 10% of the time chewing; by recording both behaviors, it could be calculated that 5% of the time is spent chewing while standing (and 5% chewing in other postures). If chewing were given precedence over standing when both occurred simultaneously, it would not be possible to quantify gross activity patterns into the mutually exclusive and exhaustive categories of "lying," "standing," and "locomotion."

An exhaustive set of categories is not necessary if the observer is interested only in recording the frequency of selected behaviors.

Choosing Sampling Methods

Sampling methods are used to make estimates about an entire population (e.g., all lions in captivity) based on a subset, or sample, of that population (e.g., the lions in one zoo observed for 200 hours). Certain methods of sampling have been devised to ensure that the estimate obtained is unbiased (Altmann 1974). Even though a research project usually has predefined categories of all the possible things to record, some behaviors, individuals, or locations might be momentarily more interesting than others. If who, what, or when to observe were entirely up to the observer's whims, his or her interest—and data recording—might focus on certain events to the exclusion of others that also had been predetermined to be important. This is the essence of observer bias.

Table 46.1 summarizes the major sampling methods, table 46.2 gives some pertinent definitions, and table 46.3 presents some useful calculations.

"Focus" of Observations. In zoo situations (and most other settings where behavioral observations are made), the

observer cannot pay attention to everything at the same time. Thus, during a sampling period, the observer restricts his or her focus. The focus should never be greater than the space, number of behaviors, and number of individuals that can be scored completely (Altmann 1984). The most common focus is on a single individual ("focal animal") such that all behaviors of interest initiated by that animal are

TABLE 46.2.   Terms Pertinent to Behavioral Data Collection

Term	Definition
Event	The onset or the single defining instant of any behavior; instantaneous behavior; momentary behavior (Sackett 1978a).
State	Behavior with appreciable duration (durational behavior), or any behavior at a given instant in time.
Duration	Time spent in a state.
Transition time	Time of onset or termination of behavior; changing from one state to another.
Frequency	Number of occurrences; can refer to events or states (see "bout"). Try not to be confused by the fact that in genetics gene "frequency" refers to the proportion of an allele in the population, and that in other contexts "frequency" is a "rate" (occurrence per unit time; see below), such as radio frequency.
Bout	One occurrence of a durational behavior or a behavior sequence (e.g., a play bout).
Rate	Frequency (number of occurrences) per unit time; requires knowledge of sample duration. Rates are most useful and interpretable when translated to a common time base, e.g., frequency per hour (see table 46.3).
Exhaustive	Behavior taxonomy is all-encompassing; subject is always recorded as doing something, even if "not visible" or "other."
Mutually exclusive	Recording categories do not overlap; within a given set of categories, the subject is never recorded as doing more than one thing simultaneously.

Note: Several definitions are paraphrased from Altmann 1974.

TABLE 46.3.   Useful Calculations for Analyzing Behavioral Data

Calculation	Definition
Raw scores	Unadjusted totals per observation (or focal sample) period (e.g., total occurrences per behavior, recorded with any sampling method); can be used in statistical tests if all observation periods are of equal duration.
Adjusted or corrected scores	Raw scores weighted so that all scores are equivalent (e.g., to adjust when observation periods are unequal across subjects or days).
Proportion	A fraction expressed in decimals, e.g., 5/8 = .63.
Probability	Expressed by a proportion; for example, if a study's results show that during the full moon an average of 5 of 8 females in a group are in estrus, one may conclude that the probability of any female being in estrus during the full moon is .63.
Percentage	Same calculation as proportion but multiplied by 100 so that unity = 100% (unity for proportions and probabilities = 1.0).
Range	Highest and lowest score (e.g., of frequencies, durations, rates, percentages).
Mean	The sum of the scores / sample size or number of scores (N).
Median	The midpoint of the scores (half are greater and half are smaller).
Variability	Measures of variation in scores about the mean; see any general statistics book for calculating standard deviations and other variability (error) measures.
Rate (e.g., of occurrence of solitary behavior or social interaction)	Frequency / observation time.
Hourly rate (frequency per hour)	Frequency / hours of observation, in decimals.
Relative frequency	Frequency of one behavior / total behavior changes (total number of behaviors); indicates probability of a particular behavior being observed at a randomly selected behavior change (Sackett, Ruppenthal, and Gluck 1978).
Mean duration per bout	Total duration of a behavior / its frequency.
Mean duration per hour (mean minutes per hour in a state)	Total duration in minutes / hours of observation, in decimals.
Mean rate (or duration or percentage) per individual (e.g., averaged across the entire group or within age/sex classes)	Sum of mean rates (or durations or percentages) for all individuals / total number of individuals in group (or subgroup).
Percentage of time (continuous sampling)[a]	(Total duration of behavior / total duration of observation) × 100.
Percentage of time (scan sampling)[a]	(Number of point samples when behavior was scored / total number of point samples) × 100.

[a] When these percentages are expressed as proportions, they indicate the probability that a given behavior will be seen during any randomly selected moment.

recorded. In some sampling systems all interactions in which S is the recipient are also recorded. Although recording S as both actor and recipient allows one to collect more complete information about interactions, this protocol requires special consideration during data analysis (described below). If one chooses to focus on one animal at a time, then total observation time may have to be increased if each focal subject is to occur often enough in the sample to be adequately characterized.

The focus, which should be predefined in the methodology, could be any one of the following:

1. Focal animal: selected from the total group or a subset of it. Note that what Altmann (1974) called "focal-animal sampling," I call "continuous sampling" (see below and Altmann 1984).
2. Focal subgroup: for example, "mother-infant pair" or "all females."
3. Group or subgroup, one individual at a time (see "Instantaneous and Scan Sampling" below) (Martin and Bateson 1986, 1993).
4. All occurrences of certain behaviors (Altmann 1974): note that this is equivalent to focusing on the total group while restricting attention to certain behaviors, such as aggression or sexual behavior.

5. Sequences of behavior (sequence sampling: Altmann 1974): The interest here is behavior sequences, such as those that occur during interactions. Individual identities and rates of occurrence may be sacrificed unless devices such as audio or video recorders are used (see "Data Recording Systems" below). Sequence sampling was effectively used by Byers (1977).
6. Location: focusing of attention on a particular place in the enclosure, such as a nest box or feeding trough, and recording what events occur there.

Random Sampling and Balanced Observations. To avoid observer bias, the order in which focal subjects or locations are sampled during each observation period should be randomized (fig. 46.3). Random sampling can be accomplished by using the table of random numbers found at the end of most statistics textbooks. However, an easier way to sample randomly at the zoo is the following: Label two envelopes, one "To Do" and the other "Done." Write each subject's (or location's) name on a 3-by-5-inch index card. Shuffle the cards, put them in the "To Do" envelope, and select one. List the name on the card as the first subject (or location) to be sampled, place the card in the "Done" envelope, and repeat until all the cards have been drawn and their order recorded. This is random sampling without re-

placement, which ensures that each subject is observed only once during an observation period. Random sampling should be repeated for each observation period.

It is important to remember that if subject A's card is drawn and A is not visible, data must still be recorded on this individual under the "not visible" category. Subject A may appear sometime during the sample period. As described in the section on data analysis below, adjustments for nonvisible time depend on what the subject might be doing while out of sight.

A methodology in which observation times were selected at random rather than being prescheduled would reduce other sources of bias. However, interobservation variability might swamp any meaningful results unless a large number of observations were made at each time of day to eliminate the potential error introduced by diurnal variation in behavior.

Given the nature of the zoo setting and the schedules of observers, many of whom are zoo staff or students, observation times are unlikely to be randomized. Under such circumstances it is more important for them to be "balanced," that is, to schedule the same number of observation periods during each of several selected time blocks. If several time blocks are being sampled and observations occur only once a day, some effort should be made to avoid scheduling consecutive days' observations during the same time block; this will reduce bias imposed by abnormal streaks of weather or other factors (i.e., confounding of weather and time-of-day effects). Such potential bias is not a problem if all subjects are observed daily during all time blocks sampled. If daily observations are not possible, evenly spaced observations (e.g., every third day) provide "balance" (as long as there are no behavioral cycles coinciding with the same interval). If at all possible, a pilot study should be conducted to determine the optimal observation schedule (Thiemann and Kraemer 1984; Kraemer et al. 1977). Scheduling observation periods well in advance will allow the project to run more smoothly, especially if arrangements for after-hours admission must be made.

Bases for Recording a Score. Essentially, there are two kinds of events that activate the observer to record a score: a change in behavior or the passage of time (Sackett 1978a). A *behavior change* scoring system, as the name implies, usually involves recording the onset of a new behavior but may also include recording the termination of the current behavior or the transition time between two behaviors. Behavior-change scoring is usually associated with continuous sampling systems. For some behaviors the transition from one to another "bout" (see table 46.2) can be ambiguous. In such cases, the behavior taxonomy should include defining events that signal when a new behavior should be recorded: for example, a certain number of seconds of inactivity that must elapse before a new behavior bout is recorded, or a certain critical distance that must be reached before "approach" is scored.

A *time sampling* scoring system is time-based rather than behavior change–based. At the end of a predetermined time interval, the observer either scores the behavior occurring at the moment of the transition between intervals (scan, instantaneous, or point sampling), or scores the occurrence or nonoccurrence of each behavior during the interval (one-zero sampling). These methods and the factors contributing to choice of time interval length are discussed below (see "Sampling Methods: Uses and Limitations").

Sample Period. For a variety of reasons having to do with checksheet format and ease of data analysis, it is useful to divide observation periods into equal-length sample periods. There are several types of sample periods, but generally the primary or focal sample period is considered to be the length of time during which a particular individual, behavior, or location is the focus of observation. Since individual subjects are the most common focus, I will elaborate using that example. Generally, the more individual subjects there are to be observed during the observation period, the shorter the focal sample period will be. (However, increasing focal sample duration will reduce between-sample variability, which is desirable for some kinds of analysis.)

A simple system is to define a *basic observation period*

that includes a complete replication of data collection; that is, each subject is observed once and only once in random order. Let's say that the basic observation period is 1 hour. If five subjects are to be observed, then the *focal sample period* ought to be 10 minutes, providing an additional 10 minutes during the basic observation period to shuffle papers and to deal with unexpected events (or to record different kinds of data between focal samples, as described below). Within each focal sample period, smaller *time intervals* may be employed, for example, as in all time sampling scoring systems, or to keep a time base in continuous sampling. When methodology dictates collecting more than one kind of data, define the basic observation period to allow for this. When there is only one subject, or when the whole group is observed at once, the basic observation period is synonymous with the focal sample period. The length of the basic observation period should be shorter than the "fatigue threshold," which is likely to be reached faster when a noisy public is present to distract the researcher.

Although projects by zoo staff and students may be constrained by other schedules, or by the nature of the project itself, for the sake of data analysis and statistical tests it is best for each observation day to be uniform in terms of total observation duration and the number of focal samples taken. These concerns will be described further in the section on data analysis below.

SAMPLING METHODS: USES AND LIMITATIONS

Ad Libitum Sampling. Ad lib sampling (Altmann 1974) is equivalent to traditional field notes and generally involves nonsystematic, informal observations preliminary to quantified study. This technique is useful for recording rare, unusual events. Hinde (1973) notes that a "comment" column is useful on checksheets for recording this sort of information (although the observer must be careful not to overuse it and thus neglect systematic data recording). Sade (1975) describes a method for transcription of handwritten field notes for computer analysis and mentions ways of correcting for observability bias in a field study of free-ranging monkeys.

Continuous Sampling. In continuous sampling (focal-animal sampling: Altmann 1974; continuous real-time measurement: Sackett 1978a), all occurrences of specified behaviors and interactions are recorded. This behavior-change method usually records behavior initiated by (and in some protocols, directed toward) focal subject(s), but can be modified to record focal behaviors, sequences, or locations, as noted previously.

Continuous sampling always allows for the calculation of frequency and rates of behavior. If behavior termination or transition times are recorded, then durations also can be calculated. Continuous sampling of a focal animal potentially allows for the most complete record of behavior and is the only way to collect data on sequences without missing anything. Analyzing continuous data can be very time-consuming if many behaviors or subjects are involved, especially if the analysis is done by hand. If sequences are not important, and a computer is not to be used, a checksheet

can be designed to simplify data collation and analysis (as described below). If the behaviors of the most interest are momentary or relatively infrequent, continuous sampling is the method of choice.

Instantaneous and Scan Sampling. Instantaneous and scan sampling (Altmann 1974) (point sampling: Dunbar 1976; discontinuous probe sampling: Sackett 1978a) are time-sampling-based systems in which the observer records the behavioral *state* (see table 46.2) at the instant ending a predefined interval—for example, on the minute—which is usually signaled by an auditory device of some sort. To avoid bias, the observer must record only what the subject is doing at that instant, whether an ongoing behavior, the onset of a new behavior of some duration, or a brief behavior that happens to coincide with the sampling instant.

One potential problem with these methods is the difficulty of identifying a particular behavior or subject at a single glance. An effective solution is to observe the subject for, say, 5 seconds after the signal and then record the behavior observed *at the last instant* (e.g., on the count of five) (Sackett 1978a). This "count-to-five" method worked very well in a field study of red howler monkeys, *Alouatta seniculus*, scanned at 15-minute intervals (C. M. Crockett, unpub.). When the time intervals are short (e.g., 30 seconds or less), the observer is likely to anticipate the next time signal so that behavior determination can be made without the counting method. Some researchers record the first behavior that lasts for a defined duration, such as 5 seconds ("sustained" behavior: Mahler 1984), but this leads to underrepresentation of instantaneous behaviors and should be avoided (Clutton-Brock 1977).

Instantaneous sampling refers to methods in which the focus is a single individual (this is why I avoid using Altmann's [1974] term "focal-animal sampling" to refer to the continuous sampling method). Scan sampling involves scoring an entire group (or subgroup), and hence the observer must visually "scan" to record the behavior of all individuals. Although it takes more than an "instant" to scan a group, the observer records only the behavioral state occurring when each individual is first seen (or after 5 seconds of observation using the "count-to-five" method). To avoid bias, scans should be performed in a systematic manner; for example, always from the left to the right of the enclosure. In principle and in common usage, "instantaneous" and "scan" sampling are equivalent, and I will hereafter use "scan sampling" to refer to both unless specifically noted. However, Martin and Bateson (1993) have made the distinction that "scanning" is a "sampling rule" for "focusing" on the whole group, one individual at a time, whereas the term "instantaneous" should be reserved for the "recording rule" (the basis for recording a score; see above).

Scan sampling provides the easiest method for estimating the percentage of time spent in specific activities (or percentage usage of different enclosure locations): simply divide the number of samples (scans) in which the behavior of interest occurred (or location was occupied) by the total number of samples and multiply by 100 (see table 46.3). Scan sampling is thus particularly well suited to studies of activity cycles (variation in behavior as a function of time of day). It is less suitable for collecting data on specific social interactions, since they often occur in sequences that cannot be recorded using a scan sample. Infrequent behaviors of short duration are generally missed unless the interval between scan samples is very short or the total duration of observation is long. Rates and bout durations cannot be calculated with this method (techniques for estimating approximations of rates and durations, e.g., Griffin and Adams 1983, seem more work than designing a "mixed sampling strategy" as described below). The great advantage of scan sampling is its relative simplicity: naive observers can quickly learn to discriminate among behaviors to score if the number to choose from is relatively small. Thus, inter- and intraobserver reliability is usually high (see the discussion of reliability below).

The interval length chosen for scan sampling depends on various factors, such as the subject's activity level (how often it changes behavior, and how long the behaviors scored typically last), group size (how many individuals are to be scanned per interval), whether a single or a mixed sampling strategy (see below) is to be used, and whether temporal autocorrelation is an issue in statistical analysis (see below). In general, the shorter the interval, the closer data collection approximates what can be recorded with continuous sampling. Shorter intervals, however, mean more data to analyze, since data are scored for each interval. Longer scan intervals are more practical for relatively inactive animals, especially when combined with continuous sampling of selected behaviors of brief duration (i.e., a mixed sampling strategy). Some types of information, such as food intake or animals' locations plotted on a map of the enclosure, can be recorded only once a day and can still be treated as a scan sample. For all practical purposes, once-a-day records avoid the problem of temporal autocorrelation.

The timing of scan sampling intervals, especially short ones (60 seconds or less), is best achieved with an auditory signal so that the observer does not have to take his or her eyes off the subject. Stopwatches with circular countdown timing options are ideal for this purpose, although few models have this feature.

One-Zero Sampling. In one-zero (or 1-0) sampling (Altmann 1974) (modified frequency: Sackett 1978a; Hansen frequency, named after Hansen 1966) time intervals are established just as in scan sampling. However, each behavior category occurring during the interval is given an arbitrary score of "1" regardless of its true frequency. For example, a behavior observed five times during an interval is still scored as "1," and a behavior of longer duration is given a score of "1" for every interval in which it occurs, regardless of onset. Thus, more than one behavior category can be scored per interval. Because true durations, true frequencies, and true percentages of observation time spent in different activities cannot be calculated with this method, Altmann (1974) advised that it not be used.

In response, a number of studies were published comparing how estimates of rates, durations, and percentages of time varied depending on the sampling method used to score the same series of events (e.g., Suen 1986; Suen and Ary 1984; Rhine and Ender 1983; Rhine and Linville 1980;

Kraemer 1979; Tyler 1979; Rhine and Flanigon 1978; Sackett 1978a; Chow and Rosenblum 1977; Leger 1977; Dunbar 1976). Although the two time-sampling-based methods provide results that are generally positively correlated with one another, the degree to which they reflect the true occurrence of behavior depends a lot upon the sampling interval length relative to behavior rate and bout duration (e.g., Suen and Ary 1984); of course, average rate and duration will vary from behavior to behavior.

One-zero sampling systematically overestimates the true percentage of time spent in activities, hence its estimates of duration cannot be directly compared with those obtained by continuous or scan sampling techniques. Thus, *one-zero sampling should be avoided when estimates are to be compared with those of other studies using other methods.* However, because one-zero is easy to score and analyze and produces high interobserver reliability, it can be employed when many observers are to be used and direct comparison with other studies is not important. Nevertheless, proper training and data collection design can achieve equally high interobserver reliability in studies using scan sampling. One-zero sampling can also be used to quantify past daily reports in which the information recorded is accurate only to that level. For example, occurrence or nonoccurrence (1-0) in the written record can be scored for sexual behavior, consumption of particular foods, use of a new cage furnishing, fresh injuries, and so on for each individual present that day. Some events tend to be biologically important at the one-zero level; for example, whether a female mates at least once during estrus or whether an animal eats at least once during a day. Such one-zero scoring of keepers' records was used effectively to supplement systematic data on proceptive calling by female lion-tailed macaques, *Macaca silenus* (Lindburg 1990). My personal recommendation is to avoid one-zero sampling except in cases such as the above.

DATA RECORDING SYSTEMS

There are many ways to record data, and they vary in their reliability, ease of use, cost, and time required for transcription and analysis. Audio- and videotape-recorded data, for example, require at least twice as much time to transcribe as to record. However, tape-recording an ongoing event that is unpredictable, such as the introduction of a new animal, may be the most successful way to preserve rapidly occurring interactions. Transcription is easier if the observer narrates ongoing behavior using memorized codes (see "Codes" below). Recent advances in microcomputer technology have made personal computers a new option for data recording. Small computers can be programmed to accept coded data (entered by keyboard or barcode reader) that can then be analyzed by the computer itself or transferred via modem to a mainframe for analysis (e.g., Bonsall, Zumpe, and Michael 1983; Flowers 1982; Flowers and Leger 1982; Forney, Leete, and Lindburg 1991). Commercially available products such as The Observer (Noldus 1991) and EVENT (Ha 1991) can turn a personal computer into a behavior coding and tabulating system. Computer technology seems to be the method of choice when large amounts of data are to be collected. However, for many projects, paper and pencil data sheets are perfectly adequate.

Codes

Codes are useful for recording behavior in a variety of sampling schemes. Depending on the number of behaviors to be scored, one may simply code each behavior with one to three letters or numbers. When there are many behaviors to record (and memorize codes for), reliability is improved by use of mnemonic abbreviations (e.g., "GR" = groom, "AP" = approach) or a dimensionalized coding scheme in which the first letter or number designates a general category and the second, the specific behavior (e.g., "LW" = locomotion-walk, "LC" = locomotion-climb, "HG" = handle-groom, "HH" = handle-hit; see Bobbitt, Jensen, and Gordon 1964; Astley et al. 1991).

Codes can be used to record more than behavior. Depending on the sampling method and scoring system used, codes can identify individuals and discriminate between actors and recipients. Codes for locations may also be useful. When developing codes that eventually will be analyzed by computer, keep in mind what the available computer system or existing programs can handle to avoid having to write a program to translate an inappropriate coding scheme. For example, some programs can handle only numeric data, or take longer to analyze alphanumeric data, increasing the cost. However, since conversion from alphanumeric data to numbers is usually easy, the increased accuracy gained by memorizing letter codes may make it worthwhile.

Paper and Pencil Methods

For many zoo research projects, a photocopied *data sheet* is a suitable and inexpensive method of recording data. Experiment with preliminary versions before a final version is adopted. Professionally printed NCR (no carbon required) paper is a good choice if duplicate data records are important. Leaving large margins on the data sheet master ensures that important information is not lost during reproduction; wide left-hand margins are useful if the filled data sheets are to be stored in three-ring binders.

Hinde (1973) gives a number of useful suggestions regarding the format of data sheets. Published papers rarely include samples of the data sheet used, but examples can be found in works by Lehner (1979), Crockett and Hutchins (1978), Bramblett (1976), Price and Stokes (1975), Kleiman (1974, 1975), and Hinde (1973). Figures 46.4 through 46.7 present "generic" data sheets suitable for different sampling methods and purposes. The data sheet format that a researcher selects will be a function of sampling method, information to be recorded, number of subjects, duration of sample period, and method of analysis (by hand vs. by computer). Each sheet should include the project name (or species) and spaces to enter date, time, weather (if relevant), observer, focal subject, location in zoo, and other information that is pertinent to the project and may serve as independent variables (e.g., phase or conditions of study). A space for comments may appear at the bottom of the sheet or in a separate column (e.g., one space per time interval).

Recall that mutually exclusive and exhaustive scoring systems require separate columns, categories, or codes to record when the subject is (1) out of sight (and where, if that is possible to determine) or (2) doing something undefined.

Several data sheet formats may have to be tried before arriving at one that is well suited to the perceptual-motor skills of the observer. For example, in a checksheet format, relatively frequent behaviors might be placed toward the left-hand side of the page and less frequent ones toward the right. Or coded behavior names might be arranged in alphabetical order. Summary columns and rows can be included in the data sheet to aid in collation (compilation) and analysis (e.g., figs. 46.4 and 46.5). When codes are to be written rather than columns checked, make sure that the data sheet cells are large enough to accommodate legible entries.

A common data sheet format lists behaviors as column headings and time intervals as row headings (fig. 46.4). Behaviors are recorded by making a check mark in the appropriate cell or by entering the code of the interactee (recipient of social behavior) or location of the focal animal. This format is suitable for time sampling (fig. 46.4a) and for continuous sampling of behavior frequencies (fig. 46.4b) when sequence is not important (durations of selected behaviors might be timed with a stopwatch and recorded in the Comments space). When a format such as that shown in figure 46.4a is used to scan more than one individual per interval, each individual's ID code could be entered in the appropriate cell. Additional columns for non-mutually-exclusive concurrent behaviors can be included on scan checksheets (fig. 46.5).

To record continuous sequences, codes for actors, behaviors, and recipients can be written in the order in which they occur, using the first column of each row to enter time of onset (fig. 46.6a). Alternatively, time intervals can be prelabeled such that behavior is recorded in the row indicating the minute period (or other time interval length) in which it occurred (fig. 46.6b). Durations can be calculated or estimated if a mutually exclusive and exhaustive set of behaviors is recorded, and it is predetermined which ones are "events" (e.g., ca. 1 second duration) and which are "states" (variable duration). The onset of the next behavior is assumed to terminate the previous one. Transcription of data recorded with this method is tedious and time-consuming unless a computer is used (see below), although tally sheets can be designed to make tabulation easier (see "Data Analysis" below).

Another method of recording continuous sampling data is to number columns labeled with behavior names in the sequence that the behaviors occur. This protocol must include a way to identify actors and recipients if this information is important. Behavior frequencies can be calculated easily as column sums (each sequence number is equivalent to a check mark). Durations cannot be determined with this method unless columns to record time of onset and termination are included.

Maps can be used to record various kinds of data. On a scale map of the enclosure one can code each animal's location, using a scan sampling technique. Later, interindividual distances and location preferences can be calculated from map plots (e.g., Kirkevold and Crockett 1987). It may also

GENERIC TIME SAMPLING DATA SHEET

Date: 10/2/86 Species: *LTM* Subject: *Fred* Observer: *CMC*
Enclosure: *Out* Weather: *Sun, 75*
Start Time: 0900 h

Interval	Beh.1	Beh.2	Beh.3	Beh.4	Beh.5	Beh.6	Other	NotVis	Comments
0:00:15	1								
0:00:30	1								
0:00:45		1							
0:01:00						1			
0:01:15								1	
0:01:30								1	
0:01:45								1	
0:02:00				1					
0:02:15	1								
0:02:30	1								
0:02:45							1		
0:03:00			1						
0:03:15			1						
0:03:30			1						
0:03:45	1								
0:04:00	1								
0:04:15	1								
0:04:30		1							
0:04:45		1							
0:05:00	1								
TOTAL:	8	3	3	1	0	1	1	3	20
PERCENT:	40	15	15	5	0	5	5	15	100

Comments: *Data sheet filled in is example of scan sampling.*

GENERIC BEHAVIOR FREQUENCY DATA SHEET

Date: 10/7/86 Species: *LTM* Subject: *Fred* Observer: *CMC*
Enclosure: *Out* Weather: *Cloudy, 65*
Start Time: 1000 h

Minutes	Beh.1	Beh.2	Beh.3	Beh.4	Beh.5	Beh.6	Beh.7	Beh.8	Comments
1									
2									
3	1 1			1					
4		1							
5									
6					1 1				
7							1		
8						111			
9	1		1						
10									
11									
12			1 1						
13				1					
14									
15						1			
16	1								
17	111			1					
18							1		
19								1 1	
20	1		1 1						
TOTAL:	8	1	5	3	2	3	1	4	= 27 onsets

Comments: *Only intervals with behavior onsets have tallies.*

FIG. 46.4. *(a)* Time sampling data sheet for eight mutually exclusive and exhaustive behavior categories. For scan sampling, the behavior occurring at the instant of the interval marker is checked; there is only one tally per row (interval), as shown here. For one-zero sampling, all behaviors occurring during the interval would be checked once. *(b)* Data sheet for recording behavior frequency. Behavior onsets are recorded by checking the cell corresponding to the time interval of occurrence. Multiple tallies may occur in one cell, and some rows (intervals) may have no tallies because no new behavior onsets occurred.

SCAN SAMPLE DATA SHEET WITH CONCURRENT CATEGORIES

Date: 10/6/86 Species: *Llama* Subject: *B* Observer: *CMC*
Enclosure: *North* Weather: *Sun, 85*
Start Time: 0800 h

Interval	BASIC POSTURE LIE	SIT	STAND	MOVE	NOT VISIBLE	CONCURRENT CHEW	VOCAL.	SOCIAL	OTHER	Comments
0:00:15	1					1				
0:00:30	1					1				
0:00:45			1							
0:01:00			1							
0:01:15			1							
0:01:30				1						
0:01:45					1					Behind rock
0:02:00				1						
0:02:15			1					1		Nuzzle A
0:02:30			1						1	Eat grass
0:02:45				1		1				
0:03:00			1			1				
0:03:15			1							
0:03:30		1								
0:03:45	1									
0:04:00	1									
0:04:15	1									
0:04:30	1									
0:04:45	1									
0:05:00	1									
TOTAL:	8	1	7	3	1	4	0	1	1	20 scans
PERCENT:	40	5	35	15	5	20	0	5	5	

FIG. 46.5. Scan sampling data sheet for scoring non-mutually-exclusive scan categories. At each interval, one of the basic postures *or* "not visible" *must* be checked. One of the concurrent categories may also be checked.

be possible to record simple behavior categories next to the individual's identification code. The map technique is a good method to use when it is not clear from the outset of the project which location divisions might be important for analysis.

Another format for recording data is a matrix table, for example, with columns labeled with behavior names and rows labeled with locations. Each matrix could be for a single subject for a specified observation duration, or one matrix could be used for all animals in the enclosure if their ID codes were recorded. Column totals of tally marks would produce behavior totals, and row totals would produce location totals. A matrix tally sheet could be used for scan sample data, using one tally mark per scan, or for continuous recording of frequency data (behavior by location). For recording all occurrences of one interactive behavior, a matrix could list actors as row headings and recipients as column headings; using continuous sampling, a tally mark would be made in the proper cell whenever the specified interaction occurred (e.g., supplanting: Lehner 1979, 151).

DATA SHEET FOR RECORDING SEQUENCES (CONTINUOUS SAMPLING)

Date: 10/7/86
Species: *LTM*
Subject: *A*
Observer: *CMC*
Enclosure: *Indoor*
Weather: *Not applicable*
Start Time: *0900 h*

Time:	Behaviors coded in sequence	Comments
9:00:05	A GR A	A grooms self
9:00:45	A WK	A walks
9:01:00	A AP B	A approaches B
9:01:05	A GR B	A grooms B
9:03:10	A LV B	A leaves B
9:03:15	A SI	A sits
9:06:05	A HH	A handles hay
9:07:30	A SI	
9:09:10	A AP B	
9:09:15	A GR B	

DATA SHEET FOR RECORDING SEQUENCES (CONTINUOUS SAMPLING)

Date: 10/7/86
Species: *LTM*
Subject: *A*
Observer: *CMC*
Enclosure: *Indoor*
Weather: *Not applicable*
Start Time: *0900 h*

Minutes:	Behaviors coded in sequence	Comments
1	A GR A, A WK	
2	A AP B, A GR B	
3		
4	A LV B, A SI	
5		
6		
7	A HH	
8	A SI	
9		
10	A AP B, A GR B	

FIG. 46.6. Data sheets for recording sequences of behavior using continuous sampling. *(a)* Data sheet for recording onset time. *(b)* Data sheet for recording within time intervals.

Mixed Sampling Methods

For many projects conducted in the zoo setting, more than one type of data must be recorded. As described above, location and behavior data can be recorded at the same time using either continuous or scan sampling. However, in many cases a mixed sampling strategy is most appropriate. In such cases, scan data can be recorded in columns at the left of the page and continuous data on the right (fig. 46.7). Generally, mixed sampling strategies record location, nearest neighbor, and general behavior category on the scan, and frequency or interaction data using continuous sampling. For example, one scan sample category might be "social behavior," whereas specific behavior, actor, and re-

cipient would be recorded continuously. Another possibility is to observe focal subjects in random order, recording data using continuous sampling; then, between focal samples, record scan data on all subjects (e.g., their locations and general activity). This method was used by Stanley and Aspey (1984).

Standard Forms

In addition to its use in specific research projects, systematic data collection can be applied to the day-to-day management of animals. Systematic records are facilitated by using standard forms for recording information. Such forms may be a part of daily reports, or they may be designed for special events. For example, Lindburg and Robinson (1986) developed a form for systematically recording the conditions and outcome of animal introductions.

Data Sheets and Computer Analysis

In some cases, data may be recorded with pencil and paper methods but with computer tabulation in mind. If the researcher has a microcomputer with a spreadsheet program, the data sheet can be designed and printed using the program (figs. 46.4–46.7 were all made using Microsoft Excel). Create the data sheet with column and row formulas for summing data, calculating percentages, or whatever calculations are appropriate (see table 46.3). Penciled entries can then be copied into a spreadsheet file, and the computer can automatically calculate the sums and other statistics for the sample period. Often it is faster to tally by hand and enter only the sums into the spreadsheet, which then calculates the percentages, rates, and other desired statistics.

When data recorded by hand are to be analyzed by a mainframe package such as SPSS or SAS (see Tabachnick and Fidell 1989), it is most appropriate for the data sheet to resemble figure 46.6a rather than checksheet column formats like figures 46.4, 46.5, and 46.7. This is because the computer program can use routines such as cross-tabulation to count frequencies of, for example, coded behaviors per coded actor. Some microcomputer statistical programs have limits on the number of columns and rows that can be analyzed by cross-tabulation—for example, 10 rows (behaviors) by 10 columns (actors)—so recoding or analyzing in subsets may be required. New programs with more features

MIXED SAMPLING DATA SHEET WITH CONCURRENT CATEGORIES

Date: 10/8/86
Species: *Red panda*
Enclosure: *South*
Observer: *CMC*
Weather: *Cloudy, 55*
Start Time: 0800 h

Interval	Subject	LOCA-TION (Scan)	NEAR NEIGH. (Scan)	N.V.	SOC	STAT	MOVE	EAT	OTHER	GROOM	SEX	OTHER	Comments
0:00	A	1	B		1					B	BB		2 mounts
	B	1	A		1								
	C	4	D	1									In den
	D	4	C	1									In den
0:05	A	2	B				1						
	B	1	A			1							
	C	3	B				1					1	Climbs tree
	D	4	B	1									Den
0:10	A	2	D		1							1	Bites D
	B	2	A			1				A		1	Plays w/D
	C	?	?	1									
	D	2	A		1								
0:15	A	1	B		1								
	B	3	D			1							Still play
	C	?	?	1									
	D	3	B		1								same bout

FIG. 46.7. Mixed sampling data sheet for scoring three concurrent scan categories as well as continuous data. Scan data are recorded at the beginning of each interval, and continuous data are recorded throughout the interval. Observation period duration for the sheet shown here is 20 minutes. NEAR NEIGH., nearest neighbor; N.V., not visible; SOC, social; STAT, stationary.

are being released regularly, and it is worth the effort to evaluate a program's capabilities for the price prior to purchase. Some powerful programs are available inexpensively through site licenses to universities (e.g., SYSTAT: Wilkinson 1989). My personal favorite for the Macintosh is Data Desk (Velleman 1993), but I usually enter data and prepare the data file in Microsoft Excel beforehand.

Replication and Inter- and Intraobserver Reliability

The methods used in a research project should be defined clearly enough so that another researcher could use the same technique based on the written description provided in the final report or publication. Unequivocal behavior definitions are thus especially important. Given the variation in terminology, it is also advisable to *describe* as well as name the sampling method used.

An observer should be consistent in data collection from day to day (intraobserver reliability). Thus, if at all possible, preliminary data collection should be used as "practice" and either not be analyzed or be analyzed selectively (the least equivocal data being used). When more than one observer is to be used in a project, formal interobserver reliability testing is recommended. A common method involves having two or more persons collect data on the same subject simultaneously. The recorded data are then compared and the percentage of agreement calculated. A common calculation of agreement is:

$$\% \text{ Agreement} = \frac{\text{Agreements}}{\text{Agreements} + \text{Disagreements}} \times 100$$

Errors can be made regarding identifications of individuals, behaviors, sequence of interaction, and so on. Percentage of agreement on individual occurrences of behavior is a more suitable test for time sampling than for continuous sampling (Caro et al. 1979). Depending on the methodology, reliability should be 85–95% before a new observer's data are used in analysis.

Percentage of agreement is the easiest way to calculate reliability but is considered to be the poorest index of reliability from a statistician's point of view: "Observer agreement does not by itself assess observer accuracy unless it is compared with some previously established standard" (Hollenbeck 1978, 81). On the other hand, any measure of reliability is better than none at all: Kent, O'Leary, and Kanowitz (1974, cited in Hollenbeck 1978) found that observers who knew that they were being assessed showed significantly higher observer agreement scores than did uninformed observers. Ralls, Lundrigan, and Kranz (1983) found the prospect of establishing interobserver reliability among 50 volunteer observers daunting. Instead, these authors assessed the variability of the behavioral data the volunteers recorded and determined that interobserver variability was low compared with the intrinsic variability of the behavior recorded, which indirectly suggested adequately high reliability. The authors attributed this low variability to a well-designed checksheet and to time spent training and supervising the observers.

Large projects with many observers could use videotaped "real" sequences as a "standard" by which to measure

agreement. Ideally, observers should be assessed repeatedly over time. Generally, many zoo projects are conducted by a single observer who improves in reliability over time through practice. An additional factor to consider is degree of interest in the research. A person collecting data for a project conceived and designed by himself or herself is likely to be inherently more reliable, although the danger of observer bias—recording "predicted" behavior in ambiguous situations—may be increased. Martin and Bateson (1993) and Caro et al. (1979) discuss various factors affecting reliability and techniques for evaluating reliability. The Observer 3.0 data coding system includes a reliability calculation.

DATA ANALYSIS

The purpose of this section is to introduce the reader to some considerations and techniques that are useful in the analysis of data collected in the zoo setting. It is not intended to provide all of the skills needed and should be used in conjunction with the more thorough references cited. Some aspects of data analysis should be considered *before* a data recording method is adopted. As indicated previously, preliminary analyses *are* important: they may suggest a revision to the data sheet, data collection schedule, or collation protocol.

Statistical Tests

All behavioral research projects will involve some descriptive statistics (e.g., table 46.3). Behavioral researchers should also use statistical tests in order to test hypotheses and draw conclusions (Lehner 1979, 226). Otherwise, the conclusions may be unjustified. The purpose of statistical tests is to "determine how large the observed differences must be before we can have confidence that they represent real differences in the larger group from which only a few events were sampled" (Siegel 1956, 2). Statistical tests are posed in such a manner that, given a large enough difference, the *null hypothesis* can be rejected and therefore the *alternative hypothesis* (the one we predict or hope to be true) can be accepted. For example, a null hypothesis might be that the means (averages) of two samples, such as mean aggression rates in two enclosures, do not differ. Rejection of the null hypothesis indicates that we can accept the alternative hypothesis that the two sample means are statistically significantly different.

If the results of a research project are to be applied to management decisions in a zoo or aquarium, it is doubly important that the conclusions of the study have some statistical basis. However, statistical significance alone should not dictate decisions because the magnitude of the effect ("effect size": Martin and Bateson 1986) is really more important. Even if expensive enclosure modifications resulted in statistically significantly reduced aggression, they might not be worth applying throughout the zoo if the behavior change was small and no reduction in injuries could be demonstrated. On the other hand, behavior might be altered dramatically in some individuals but not in others, resulting in marginal statistical significance but a large average-effect size.

"Significant" differences usually cannot be eyeballed from graphed data unless error (variability) measures are included. For example, one can compare Byers's (1977) figures 4 and 5: All types of social play by female ibex kids were significantly more frequent on sloped than on flat surfaces, even though the magnitude of the differences seems small; on the other hand, males' social play types — especially rear and butt — seem more frequent on flat than on sloped surfaces, yet none of the differences was statistically significant. Why this is so is related to the variability of the males' data: Some males showed high frequencies of rear and butt play on flat surfaces, while other males did not (Byers 1977, 204). This example points out the dangers of concluding "significance" without doing the proper statistical tests.

Parametric versus Nonparametric Tests. Parametric statistics are based on assumptions about "parameters," such as the mean (average) and variability measures (variance or its square root, the standard deviation), that describe the "population" from which the sample data have been selected. These parameters define mathematical distributions such as "the normal distribution" upon which statistical equations for particular tests are based. Nonparametric tests are generally more appropriate for behavioral research because they are "distribution free" and do not require many assumptions about the "population" from which the data were drawn (Lehner 1979). Furthermore, high observer reliability is needed only at the measurement level of analysis: if only rank orders are analyzed in statistical tests (true of most nonparametric tests), then observers' accuracy in recording behavior needs to be precise only at the level of rank order (Sackett, Ruppenthal, and Gluck 1978). For example, as long as the observer accurately records that male A is aggressive more often than male B, and B is aggressive more often than C, the outcome of a rank-order statistical test will not be changed if a few aggressive acts are missed.

For the beginning statistician, the best strategy is to become familiar with the most common nonparametric statistical tests. Learn which ones are appropriate for which comparisons or kinds of data. Gradually expand the statistical repertoire with experience (learning about statistics is much like becoming fluent in a foreign language—familiarity comes with use). Siegel (1956) and Conover (1980) describe most nonparametric tests in detail, and Lehner (1979) provides an adequate and usable summary of the most common ones. Furthermore, Lehner (1979) uses examples that are more relevant to zoo studies (also see Brown and Downhower 1988). Some readers may be unfamiliar with some of the statistical terminology used in this chapter. Inman and Conover's (1983) textbook is a good general introduction to descriptive, parametric, and nonparametric statistics. More advanced statistics books with an emphasis on biological examples include Zar (1984), Sokal and Rohlf (1969, 1981, 1987), and Snedecor and Cochran (1980). Tabachnick and Fidell (1989) describe multivariate statistics and computer programs that calculate them. Martin and Bateson (1993) list other statistics books and articles in their useful annotated bibliography. I have found the manuals to two statistical software packages to be particularly helpful in improving my understanding of statistics and data analysis (Wilkinson 1989; Velleman 1993).

Table 46.4 lists a variety of nonparametric tests. Most can be done rather easily by hand and pocket calculator. To become familiar with these tests, it can be useful to look at published research and see which tests were used in which situations. Try to determine what the unit of analysis was, or exactly how the data might have been set up to do the test. Be warned, however, that inappropriately applied statistics sometimes do get published.

Parametric tests can be used if certain assumptions, such as homogeneity of variance, are met (the importance of the "normality" assumption has been overemphasized: Kraemer 1981). Parametric tests can be preferable to nonparametric tests because they generally have greater "power"; that is, smaller differences are required to reject the null hypothesis. In some cases, a parametric test is necessary for multivariate analysis, or when unequal sample sizes make use of the Friedman ANOVA inappropriate. Whenever percentages or proportions are to be used in parametric statistics, it is recommended that the data first be arcsine-transformed to normalize the distribution ($q = \arcsin \sqrt{p}$, where p is a proportion: Sokal and Rohlf 1969, 386). This transformation was used by Stanley and Aspey (1984, 95).

TABLE 46.4. Summary of Common Nonparametric Tests

Type of data	Statistical test	Examples of use
Nominal—frequency	Chi-square (association and goodness-of-fit)	Izard and Simons 1986; Gaspari and Crockett 1984; Ralls, Brugger, and Ballou 1979; Byers 1977
	G-test (multiway contingency)	Crockett and Sekulic 1984; Sokal and Rohlf 1969, 1981
	Binomial	Izard and Simons 1986
Ordinal—rank order		
Two samples		
Independent	Mann-Whitney U	Macedonia 1987; Ralls, Lundrigan, and Kranz 1987; Freeman 1983; Kleiman 1983; Byers 1977
Correlated (paired)	Wilcoxon signed ranks	Freeman 1983; Kleiman 1980, 1983; Byers 1977
	Sign test	Ralls, Lundrigan, and Kranz 1987; Ralls, Brugger, and Ballou 1979
Correlation	Spearman's correlation	Macedonia 1987; Gaspari and Crockett 1984; Freeman 1983
Three or more samples		
Independent	Kruskal-Wallis one-way ANOVA	
Correlated	Friedman two-way ANOVA	Nash and Chilton 1986; Vestal and Vander Stoep 1978

Note: Conover 1980 and Siegel 1956 may be consulted for details and more tests.

No Statistical Tests. In some cases, no statistical tests are necessary. For example, McGrew, Brennan, and Russell (1986) reported the rate of opening of gum reservoirs in an artificial gum tree by three groups of marmosets, *Callithrix jacchus*. A simple graph was sufficient to show that all three groups succeeded in tapping the gum reservoirs. However, statistical tests could have been used to determine whether the three groups differed in rate of opening and whether this difference was related to group size.

When no comparisons are being made nor hypotheses tested, purely descriptive statistics (mean or median, and perhaps range and standard deviation) may be adequate (e.g., Mahler 1984). Sample sizes upon which descriptive statistics are based should always be stated.

The Unit of Analysis. In order to do statistical tests, one has to decide what the unit of analysis will be. In experimental studies, this is usually obvious: for example, the number of trials before a rat learns a task. In studies of observed behaviors in which the researcher defines the behaviors, the issue is more complicated. The unit of analysis might be the total number of occurrences (frequency) of a behavior, its hourly rate of occurrence, the percentage of time spent performing the behavior, the total duration of the behavior, or mean bout duration. Furthermore, the researcher must determine whether each animal's overall "score" (total frequency, mean rate, duration, or whatever) will be a data point, or whether each animal will contribute one score per observation period or designated time (e.g., age) block (but beware of "the pooling fallacy": Machlis, Dodd, and Fentress 1985). Perhaps individuals cannot be distinguished, and each observation period contributes one score that is the average or total of all individuals. The appropriate unit of analysis will depend in part on the statistical test to be used.

In some instances, the choice of unit of analysis depends on maximizing statistical "power": the likelihood of rejecting the null hypothesis when the alternative hypothesis (the one that the researcher proposes) is true (Lehner 1979, 230). One way of increasing power is to use a parametric test rather than its nonparametric equivalent. Another way is to increase the sample size: for a given magnitude of difference (e.g., between two means), the difference is more likely to be statistically significant when the means are based on more individual data points. For some statistical tests, minimum sample sizes are required in order to demonstrate significance (e.g., Mann-Whitney *U*; Siegel 1956). Freeman (1983) used the Mann-Whitney *U* to test differences between successfully and unsuccessfully breeding snow leopard, *Uncia uncia*, pairs, analyzing data for each sex separately (fig. 46.8). For the sample sizes in that study (three successful and five unsuccessful pairs), in order to achieve a two-tailed level of significance (a probability of 0.05 or less), there could be no reversals. In other words, significant differences could be demonstrated only if all three successful pairs ranked above (or below) the five unsuccessful pairs.

Many studies of captive animals involve small groups, in some cases too few individuals to use one data point per subject for some kinds of statistical tests. In such cases, the sample size (and statistical power) can be increased by using one score per subject per observation period or time block.

FIG. 46.8. The Mann-Whitney *U* nonparametric statistic was used to test for behavioral differences between successfully and unsuccessfully breeding snow leopard pairs. Boris is the cub of a successful pair. (Photo by Cathy Shelton, Woodland Park Zoo.)

However, one cannot simply lump multiple scores from one individual with those of others without the possibility of committing a type I error—that is, rejecting the null hypothesis when it is in fact true ("the pooling fallacy": Machlis, Dodd, and Fentress 1985). Such an error can occur when within-individual variance (i.e., between observations of the same animal) is less than between-individual variance (Leger and Didrichsons 1994). Some ways to avoid this problem while maximizing statistical power include (1) using a more complex design (e.g., a repeated measures test), (2) examining the sources of variance in detail, using the results to determine the grouping into units of analysis (e.g., see Thiemann and Kraemer 1984; Kraemer et al. 1982), (3) using the mean or sum across all individuals within a basic observation period (so that each individual contributes equally), and (4) testing each subject's data separately (this might be done if each individual's response to a change was of interest).

Some examples from the literature illustrate different units of analysis. Byers (1977, figures 4 and 5) used a Wilcoxon matched pairs test to determine whether play events occurred at different rates on different substrates. For example, for each individual ibex kid, the total number of "butt" play events that occurred on sloped surfaces was paired (matched) with the same kid's total number of "butt" play events on flat surfaces. (Sloped and flat areas each made up about half of the enclosure; otherwise the play events per *S* would have been multiplied by the proportion of the enclosure made up of the surface type on which they occurred to correct for differences in "available" area.) To compare sex differences in behavior, Freeman (1983)

FIG. 46.9.   *Galago senegalensis* at Woodland Park Zoo's Nocturnal House. (Photo by Karen Anderson, Woodland Park Zoo.)

matched male and female percentages of time spent in selected behaviors (calculated from scan samples) for members of eight mated snow leopard pairs. Since pairs were studied for different numbers of years, "cat-mean" data (mean percentage per leopard across years of study) were used in statistical tests. In Kleiman's (1980) figure 50.4, the total amount of time that the sexually active male golden lion tamarin, *Leontopithecus rosalia,* spent grooming the female was matched with the total duration of grooming by the sexually inactive male for each observation period. Thus, each observation session contributed one score per male, and the data from each trio (two males and one female housed together) were statistically tested separately. In Nash and Chilton's (1986) study, each galago, *Galago senegalensis* (fig. 46.9) was observed for the same amount of time for each of three "phases," except that infants' observation sessions were twice as long. The analyzed data for each behavior scored consisted of total frequency per individual per phase (i.e., "raw" scores), except for infants, whose frequencies were halved ("corrected" or "adjusted") to make them equivalent. (Alternatively, raw frequencies could have been converted into hourly rates.) In a longitudinal study of chimpanzee development, all observations (made 3 days a week) over a 3-month seasonal period for a single subject were combined "to yield a single data point for purposes of analysis" (Kraemer et al. 1982).

The Problem of Independence
Theoretically, for purposes of statistical analysis, data points (e.g., the units of analysis described above) should be

independent. For example, one individual's rate of performing a given behavior should be unrelated to another individual's rate, or the occurrence of one behavior type should not influence the probability of occurrence of another. In reality, the independence assumption is often violated by social, interactive behaviors, which usually influence the behavior of other group members and thus may be inherently correlated (G. P. Sackett, pers. comm.). Furthermore, when more than one of a mutually exclusive and exhaustive set of behaviors is tested, the outcome of one statistical test is not independent of the outcome of the other: if behaviors are categorized as either "social" or "nonsocial," rejecting the null hypothesis that social behaviors did not differ between conditions guarantees that the difference in nonsocial behaviors will also be statistically significant (Sackett et al. 1978). For this reason, adjustments to probability levels are sometimes applied to make tests more conservative (e.g., Stanley and Aspey 1984, 99).

Temporal Autocorrelation
Another aspect of independence is temporal autocorrelation, or the probability that the occurrence of a behavior at one point in time will affect its likelihood of being observed at the next point in time. Obviously, the shorter the time interval between successive "points," the more likely that temporal autocorrelation will occur. For scan or instantaneous samples that are converted to percentages, this poses no problem; shorter intervals generally produce more accurate estimates of true percentages of time spent performing the behavior in question. However, contingency analyses (chi-square, goodness-of-fit tests) require independent data points (Siegel 1956). If, for example, one wanted to compare the use of several different enclosure locations, one possibility would be to count the number of times that the subject was scored in each location. However, these counts could not be used in a chi-square test if the points in time were temporally autocorrelated—that is, if the animal's location on a particular branch was not independent of the fact that it was found there at the last interval.

The interval at which independence can be assumed varies with behavior, species, and so forth, so no general rule can be stated; the appropriate interval must be determined from the data. Janson (1984) found that nearest neighbors of wild brown capuchins, *Cebus apella,* usually were temporally autocorrelated at 5-minute intervals, rarely were at 10-minute intervals, and never were at 15-minute intervals. Thus, only records at 15-minute intervals were used for analyses requiring independence. Stanley and Aspey (1984) recorded scan samples of interindividual distances of ungulates at 10-minute intervals and treated them as independent measures. A pilot study using continuous sampling could be used to choose the appropriate scan interval. For example, Slatkin (1975) computed the autocorrelation time for adult male geladas, *Theropithecus gelada,* and yellow baboons, *Papio cynocephalus,* in this manner; the correlation time was about 1 minute for the geladas and 4–5 minutes for the yellow baboons.

Ketchum (1985) studied enclosure utilization in snow leopards at Woodland Park Zoo. Scan samples were taken every 20 seconds, an interval likely to be highly autocorrelated. The enclosure was divided into four location categories (based on visibility to the public and distance that the cats could see), and the percentage of scan samples spent in each area was calculated. In order to analyze these data with a chi-square goodness-of-fit test, which requires independence as well as frequency (i.e., not percentage) data, the percentages were multiplied by *the number of focal sample periods*. This calculation produces adjusted frequencies approximately equivalent to randomly sampling the location of the subject once per period. Since the sample periods were at least 2 hours apart, and often more than a day apart, these adjusted frequencies were accepted as independent. The *expected frequencies* were calculated by multiplying the number of sample periods by the percentage of the enclosure area that each location category constituted. (Expected frequencies in this test are the values that we would "expect" if the snow leopards were using the locations in proportion to their availability, that is, showing no preference.)

Sokal and Rohlf (1969, 607) present a test for comparing two percentages; however, if this test is used on scan sample data, the scan intervals must not be temporally autocorrelated. If there is reason to believe that they are, a simple but statistically conservative solution is to use the number of observation periods as *n* in the equation.

The logic of the independence requirement is simple: Recall that the power of the statistical test improves with sample size. Obviously, the closer the scan samples, the more samples there will be in a given observation period. An inflated sample size will increase the likelihood of refuting the null hypothesis (and committing a type I error), and scan sample interval length will be inversely related to achieving statistical significance. Clearly it is not valid to pick a sampling interval that would guarantee significance. On the other hand, using the technique of multiplying percentages by the number of observation periods makes the test unnecessarily conservative when the true interval of independence is less than the sample duration.

Whenever each focal sample period contributes a data point, the underlying assumption is that each session is an independent estimate of the animal's behavior. This further stresses the importance of scheduling balanced or randomized observation periods so as not to introduce systematic bias.

The violation of the independence assumption restricts the number of conventional statistical tests that can be applied to certain behavioral data. Dunbar and Dunbar (1975, appendix C) describe some considerations and solutions with respect to the independence assumption.

Data Collation

General Considerations and Techniques. During data collation (e.g., when the observer is totaling up a data sheet), two important considerations ought to be taken into account.

1. Data for each subject and/or observation session should be equivalent, that is, based on the same amount of observation time. If observation times differ, equivalence can be achieved by converting raw scores to rates or per-

centages. The researcher must also decide whether to use total observation time (or total number of scans) as a base, or the amount of time (or number of scans) during which the subject is visible as a base (see "The Problem of Visibility" below).

2. Data summaries should not be collapsed across all observation sessions until it is determined whether scores per focal sample period or some other time block will be used in statistical tests. In any event, when observation periods are not of equal length, it is often advisable for each session or day to contribute equally. (If temperatures were unusually low on the day that the observation session was especially long, for example, behavior during cold weather would be overrepresented.) Observation schedules in which each subject is observed for the same amount of time (per time block, if relevant) avoid many problems. However, time "not visible" may vary across subjects and observation days, complicating analysis (see below).

To facilitate the collating and transcribing of data from the original data sheets, some attention should be paid to the design of summary or tabulation sheets. Where possible, include summary rows on the data sheets themselves (e.g., figs. 46.4 and 46.5). When data on more than one animal are recorded at once (typical scan sample, e.g., fig. 46.7), unless each subject has its own column, summary rows within subjects are not possible. In such cases, and for continuous data recorded in sequence (e.g., fig. 46.6), tabulation sheets should be designed. Some tabulation sheets may be in the form of matrices. For data recorded in equal-height rows, as in figure 46.7, a "mask" sheet can be made such that only one subject's rows are revealed at a time, facilitating the addition of columns. Another idea is to make a transparency of the data sheet master, overlay it sequentially upon filled data sheets, and make tally marks with washable pen (this works only if the cells are big enough to hold numerous tallies—enough for one observation session).

Estimates Based on Continuous Focal-Animal Sampling. When recording the interactive behaviors of a focal animal, one may decide to record all behaviors directed toward the subject, S, as well as those initiated by the subject. This method allows efficient use of observation time but requires special considerations in some data analyses. Thus, in samples in which S_i is the focal animal and in samples in which S_j is the focal animal, all of their interactions will be recorded. Each of the samples (i or j) or both (i + j) will give an *estimate* of their *rate of interaction* (Altmann 1974) as shown in table 46.5.

Consider the interaction data summarized in table 46.6. When the *sum* of observation time for subject I and subject J is used as a time base, each cell in the frequency matrix can be used to calculate a valid estimate of *that dyad's* hourly rate of interaction. In this example, subject I was observed to groom J a total of 9 times while they were focal subjects, and I groomed K once while K was the focal subject, totaling 10 grooms by I. Although I, J, and K were each focal animals for 1 hour of observation, one cannot divide 10 grooms by 3 hours to yield a grooming rate of 3.3 for I because focal sampling of J does not reveal interactions be-

TABLE 46.5. Estimates of Interaction Rates

Subject	Sample duration	Number of interactions$_{i,j}$	Rate
i	20 min (1/3 hr)	5	15/hr
j	10 min (1/6 hr)	3	18/hr
i + j	30 min (1/2 hr)	8	16/hr

TABLE 46.6. Social Grooming Interactions for Subjects I, J, and K

Sample duration	Focal subject	Interaction	Frequency
60 min	I	I grooms J	5
		J grooms I	3
60 min	J	J grooms I	6
		I grooms J	4
60 min	K	K grooms I	5
		I grooms K	1
180 min = 3 hr			24

Frequency matrix

Groomer	Groomee I	Groomee J	Groomee K	Total
I		9	1	10
J	9		0	9
K	5	0		5
Total	14	9	1	24

Hourly rate

Groomer	Groomee I	Groomee J	Groomee K	Total
I		4.5	.5	5.0
J	4.5		0	4.5
K	2.5	0		2.5
Mean grooming rate per individual:				4.0

tween I and K (e.g., during the hour that J was the focal subject, I could have groomed K 5 times). To calculate a mean rate per individual, rates per dyad must be calculated, then summed and divided by the number of individuals (table 46.6). See Michener (1980) and Shapiro and Altham (1978) for other considerations in estimating interaction rates.

The Problem of Visibility

When estimates of behavioral rates or percentages are based only on the duration of the sample when the subject is visible (e.g., as done by Ralls, Kranz, and Lundrigan 1986), it is important to consider that the animal's behavior when visible may not be a random sample of total behavior. In other words, the animal may be performing the same behaviors at different rates or may be engaging in different behaviors when out of sight. Many zoo enclosures have indoor and outdoor sections. The observer should sample both sections before concluding that behavior inside is the same as (or different from) behavior outside. If behavior is the same inside and out, then rates can be calculated using time observable as the divisor. In other situations, a subject may be unobservable because it has entered a den or nest box, where perhaps only a few behaviors are likely to occur. In such cases, total sample time should probably be the divisor, and "in den" should be considered a behavior. Similarly, some animals in naturalistic enclosures may be scored as "not visible" primarily when they are lying down, concealed by tall vegetation; in this case using observation time while "visible" as the divisor would overestimate the actual percentage of "active" behavior. The results of such a study might therefore include a category for "percentage of time not visible," which would be combined with "percentage of time inactive" for some analyses. The important point here is that if a large percentage of observation time occurs when the subjects are out of sight, results should be interpreted with this consideration in mind. This is especially important if a management decision rests upon the outcome of the study. Adjustments to the data may or may not be appropriate (Sackett 1978a).

CONCLUSION

Data collection in the zoo setting can provide answers to management questions as well as basic information about the biology of captive animals. Research is now being recognized as important and is expanding in many zoos (Finlay and Maple 1986). To be most useful, data should be quantified in a manner amenable to statistical analysis, whether it be statistical testing or straightforward description. Furthermore, proper sampling methods should be used so as to avoid observer bias and other sorts of sampling error. This chapter has summarized the major sampling methods and has provided some hints for data analysis.

Systematic data collection is not difficult and mostly requires *systematic thinking* ahead of time. A project is more likely to be successful if these guidelines are followed:

1. Formulate a *specific* research question.
2. Keep data collection *simple.*
3. Perform *preliminary analyses* on some sample data before finalizing the data collection design.
4. *Collate* and begin to analyze data while data collection is in progress.
5. Finally, if the results of the study seem to be of general interest, *publish* them.

ACKNOWLEDGMENTS

This chapter was revised from a manuscript prepared for a workshop, "Applying Behavioral Research to Zoo Animal Management," held at Woodland Park Zoo in 1986 and partially funded by a Conservation Grant from the Institute of Museum Services. I thank C. Kline for assisting with the literature search and M. Hutchins for having the inspiration to develop the workshop. This chapter has been greatly improved by numerous constructive comments from J. Altmann, S. Lumpkin, and R. Baldwin, and conversations with G. Sackett and C. Janson. The Regional Primate Research Center at the University of Washington (funded by NIH grant no. RR00166) provided support during final revisions.

REFERENCES

Altmann, J. 1974. Observational study of behavior. *Behaviour* 49: 227–67.

———. 1984. Observational sampling methods for insect behavioral ecology. *Florida Entomologist* 67 (1): 50–56.

Anderson, J. R., and Chamove, A. S. 1984. Allowing captive primates to forage. In *Standards in laboratory management*, part 2, 253–56. Potters Bar, U.K.: Universities Federation for Animal Welfare.

Astley, C. A., Smith, O. A., Ray, R. D., Golanov, E. V., Chesney, M. A., Chalyan, V. G., Taylor, D. J., and Bowden, D. M. 1991. Integrating behavior and cardiovascular responses: The code. *Am. J. Physiol.* 261:R172–81.

Bakeman, R. 1978. Untangling streams of behavior: Sequential analyses of behavioral data. In *Observing behavior*, vol. 2, *Data collection and analysis methods*, ed. G. P. Sackett, 63–78. Baltimore: University Park Press.

Bakeman, R., and Gottman, J. M. 1986. *Observing interaction.* Cambridge: Cambridge University Press.

Bobbitt, R. A., Jensen, G. D., and Gordon, B. N. 1964. Behavioral elements (taxonomy) for observing mother-infant-peer interaction in *Macaca nemestrina*. *Primates* 5:71–80.

Bonsall, R. W., Zumpe, D., and Michael, R. P. 1983. A computerized system for scoring primate behavior using standard keyboards. *Am. J. Primatol.* 4:273–80.

Bradley, W. P., and Johnson, L. A. 1978. Preliminary observations on the spring activity patterns and spatial utilization patterns in a captive group of elk. In *Applied behavioral research at the Woodland Park Zoological Gardens*, ed. C. Crockett and M. Hutchins, 311–30. Seattle: Pika Press.

Bramblett, C. A. 1976. *Patterns of primate behavior.* Palo Alto, Calif.: Mayfield.

Brannian, J., and Cloak, C. 1985. Observations of daily activity patterns in two captive short-nosed echidnas, *Tachyglossus aculeatus*. *Zoo Biol.* 4:75–81.

Brown, L., and Downhower, J. F. 1988. *Analyses in behavioral ecology: A manual for lab and field.* Sunderland, Mass.: Sinauer Associates.

Byers, J. A. 1977. Terrain preferences in the play behavior of Siberian ibex kids *(Capra ibex sibirica)*. *Z. Tierpsychol.* 45: 199–209.

Caro, T. M., Roper, R., Young, M., and Dank, G. R. 1979. Interobserver reliability. *Behaviour* 69:303–15.

Chamove, A. S., and Anderson, J. R. 1979. Woodchip litter in macaque groups. *J. Inst. Anim. Tech.* 30:69–72.

Chamove, A. S., Anderson, J. R., Morgan-Jones, S. C., and Jones, S. P. 1982. Deep woodchip litter: Hygiene, feeding, and behavioral enhancement in eight primate species. *Int. J. Stud. Anim. Prob.* 3 (4): 308–18.

Chow, I. A., and Rosenblum, L. A. 1977. A statistical investigation of the time-sampling methods in studying primate behavior. *Primates* 18:555–63.

Clutton-Brock, T. H. 1977. Appendix I: Methodology and measurement. In *Primate ecology*, ed. T. H. Clutton-Brock, 585–90. London: Academic Press.

Conover, W. J. 1980. *Practical nonparametric statistics.* New York: Wiley.

Conway, K. J., Shaw, L. J., Micklesen, S., and Crouse, D. W. 1978. Activity rhythms of ten species of nocturnal animals as a function of light intensity. In *Applied behavioral research at the Woodland Park Zoological Gardens*, ed. C. Crockett and M. Hutchins, 102–40. Seattle: Pika Press.

Crockett, C., and Hutchins, M., eds. 1978. *Applied behavioral research at the Woodland Park Zoological Gardens.* Seattle: Pika Press.

Crockett, C. M., and Sekulic, R. 1984. Infanticide in red howler monkeys *(Alouatta seniculus)*. *Infanticide: Comparative and evolutionary perspectives*, ed. G. Hausfater and S. B. Hrdy, 173–91. New York: Aldine.

Crockett Wilson, C. 1978. Methods of observational research in the zoo setting. In *Applied behavioral research at the Woodland Park Zoological Gardens*, ed. C. Crockett and M. Hutchins, 51–73. Seattle: Pika Press.

Dunbar, R. I. M. 1976. Some aspects of research design and their implications in the observational study of behavior. *Behaviour* 58:78–98.

Dunbar, R. I. M., and Dunbar, P. 1975. *Social dynamics of gelada baboons.* Contributions to Primatology, no. 6. Basel: Karger.

Finlay, T. W., and Maple, T. L. 1986. A survey of research in American zoos and aquariums. *Zoo Biol.* 5:261–68.

Fitch, H. 1986. Birth observations of lion-tailed macaques. Paper presented at Second Lion-Tailed Macaque Symposium, Woodland Park Zoo, Seattle.

Flowers, J. H. 1982. Some simple Apple II software for the collection and analysis of behavioral data. *Behav. Res. Methods Instrumentation* 14 (2): 241–49.

Flowers, J. H., and Leger, D. W. 1982. Personal computers and behavioral observation: An introduction. *Behav. Res. Methods Instrumentation* 14 (2): 227–30.

Forney, K. A., Leete, A. J., and Lindburg, D. G. 1991. A bar code scoring system for behavioral research. *Am. J. Primatol.* 23: 127–35.

Freeman, H. 1983. Behavior in adult pairs of captive snow leopards *(Panthera uncia)*. *Zoo Biol.* 2:1–22.

Gaspari, M. K., and Crockett, C. M. 1984. The role of scent marking in *Lemur catta* agonistic behavior. *Zoo Biol.* 3:123–32.

Griffin, B., and Adams, R. 1983. A parametric model for estimating prevalence, incidence, and mean bout duration from point sampling. *Am. J. Primatol.* 4:261–71.

Ha, J. C. 1991. EVENT-PC and EVENT-MAC Software. Regional Primate Research Center, University of Washington, Seattle.

Hansen, E. W. 1966. The development of maternal and infant behavior in the rhesus monkey. *Behaviour* 27:107–49.

Hausfater, G. 1975. *Dominance and reproduction in baboons* (Papio cynocephalus). Contributions to Primatology, no. 7. Basel: Karger.

Hinde, R. A. 1973. On the design of check sheets. *Primates* 14: 393–406.

Hollenbeck, A. R. 1978. Problems of reliability in observational research. In *Observing behavior*, vol. 2, *Data collection and analysis methods*, ed. G. P. Sackett, 79–98. Baltimore: University Park Press.

Inman, R. L., and Conover, W. J. 1983. *A modern approach to statistics.* New York: Wiley.

Izard, M. K., and Simons, E. L. 1986. Isolation of females prior to parturition reduces neonatal mortality in *Galago*. *Am. J. Primatol.* 10:249–55.

Janson, C. H. 1984. Female choice and mating system of the brown capuchin monkey *Cebus apella* (Primates: Cebidae). *Z. Tierpsychol.* 65:177–200.

Kaufman, I. C., and Rosenblum, L. A. 1966. A behavioral taxonomy for *Macaca nemestrina* and *Macaca radiata*: Based on longitudinal observations of family groups in the laboratory. *Primates* 7:205–58.

Kawata, K., and Elsen, K. M. 1984. Growth and feeding relationships of a hand-reared lowland gorilla infant *(Gorilla g. gorilla)*. *Zoo Biol.* 3:151–57.

Kent, R. N., O'Leary, D. D., and Kanowitz, J. 1974. Observer reliability as a function of circumstances of assessment. Paper presented to the Annual Convention of the Western Psychological Association, San Francisco.

Ketchum, M. H. 1985. Activity patterns and enclosure utilization in the snow leopard, *Panthera uncia*. Master's thesis, Teaching Biology, Department of Biology, University of Washington.

Kirkevold, B. C., and Crockett, C. M. 1987. Behavioral development and proximity patterns in captive DeBrazza's monkeys. In *Comparative behavior of African monkeys*, ed. E. L. Zucker, 39–65. New York: Alan R. Liss.

Kleiman, D. G. 1974. Activity rhythms in the giant panda. *Int. Zoo Yrbk.* 14:165–69.

———. 1975. Management of breeding programs in zoos. In *Research in zoos and aquariums: A symposium*, 157–77. Washington, D.C.: National Academy of Sciences.

———. 1980. The sociobiology of captive propagation. In *Conservation biology: An evolutionary-ecological perspective*, ed. M. E. Soulé & B. A. Wilcox, 243–61. Sunderland, Mass: Sinauer Associates.

———. 1983. Ethology and reproduction of captive giant pandas *(Ailuropoda melanoleuca)*. *Z. Tierpsychol.* 62:1–46.

Kraemer, H. C. 1979. One-zero sampling in the study of primate behavior. *Primates* 20:237–44.

———. 1981. Coping strategies in psychiatric clinical research. *J. Consult. Clin. Psychol.* 49:309–19.

Kraemer, H. C., Alexander, B., Clark, C., Busse, C., and Riss, D. 1977. Empirical choice of sampling procedures for optimal research design in the longitudinal study of primate behavior. *Primates* 18:825–33.

Kraemer, H. C., Horvat, J. R., Doering, C., and McGinnis, P. R. 1982. Male chimpanzee development focusing on adolescence: Integration of behavioral with physiological changes. *Primates* 23 (3): 393–405.

Leger, D. W. 1977. An empirical evaluation of instantaneous and one-zero sampling of chimpanzee behavior. *Primates* 18:387–93.

Leger, D. W., and Didrichsons, I. A. 1994. An assessment of data pooling and some alternatives. *Anim. Behav.* 48 (4): 823–32.

Lehner, P. N. 1979. *Handbook of ethological methods.* New York: Garland STPM.

Lindburg, D. G. 1990. Proceptive calling by female lion-tailed macaques. *Zoo Biol.* 9:437–46.

Lindburg, D. G., and Robinson, P. 1986. Animal introductions: Some suggestions for easing the trauma. *Animal Keepers' Forum*, January, 8–11.

Lindburg, D. G., Shideler, S., and Fitch, H. 1985. Sexual behavior in relation to time of ovulation in the lion-tailed macaque. In *The lion-tailed macaque: Status and conservation*, ed. P. G. Heltne, 131–48. New York: Alan R. Liss.

Lorenz, K. 1958. The evolution of behavior. *Sci. Am.*, December.

Macedonia, J. M. 1987. Effects of housing differences upon activity budgets in captive sifakas *(Propithecus verreauxi)*. *Zoo Biol.* 6:55–67.

Machlis, L., Dodd, P. W. D., and Fentress, J. C. 1985. The pooling fallacy: Problems arising when individuals contribute more than one observation to the data set. *Z. Tierpsychol.* 68:201–14.

Mahler, A. E. 1984. Activity budgets and use of space by South American tapir *(Tapiris terrestris)* in a zoological park setting. *Zoo Biol.* 3:35–46.

Martin, P., and Bateson, P. 1986. *Measuring behaviour: An introductory guide.* New Rochelle, N.Y.: Cambridge University Press.

———. 1993. *Measuring behaviour: An introductory guide.* 2d ed. Cambridge: Cambridge University Press.

McGrew, W. C., Brennan, J. A., and Russell, J. 1986. An artificial "gum tree" for marmosets *(Callithrix j. jacchus)*. *Zoo Biol.* 5:45–50.

Meder, A. 1986. Physical and activity changes associated with pregnancy in captive lowland gorillas *(Gorilla gorilla gorilla)*. *Am. J. Primatol.* 11:111–16.

Michener, G. R. 1980. The measurement and interpretation of interaction rates: An example with adult Richardson's ground squirrels. *Biol. Behav.* 5:371–84.

Nash, L. T., and Chilton, S.-M. 1986. Space or novelty?: Effects of altered cage size on *Galago* behavior. *Am. J. Primatol.* 10:37–49.

Noldus, L. P. J. 1991. The Observer: A software system for collection and analysis of observational data. *Behav. Res. Methods, Instruments, and Computers* 23:415–29.

Oswald, M., and Kuyk, K. 1978. The behavior of three lorisoid primate species before and after the public opening of the Nocturnal House. In *Applied behavioral research at the Woodland Park Zoological Gardens*, ed. C. Crockett and M. Hutchins, 81–101. Seattle: Pika Press.

Price, E. O., and Stokes, A. W. 1975. *Animal behavior in laboratory and field.* 2d ed. San Francisco: W. H. Freeman.

Ralls, K., Brugger, K., and Ballou, J. 1979. Inbreeding and juvenile mortality in small populations of ungulates. *Science* 206:1101–3.

Ralls, K., Kranz, K., and Lundrigan, B. 1986. Mother-young relationships in captive ungulates: Variability and clustering. *Anim. Behav.* 34:134–45.

Ralls, K., Lundrigan, B., and Kranz, K. 1983. Variability of behavioural data recorded by volunteer observers. *Int. Zoo Yrbk.* 22:244–49.

———. 1987. Mother-young relationships in captive ungulates: Spatial and temporal patterns. *Zoo Biol.* 6:11–20.

Rhine, R. J., and Ender, P. B. 1983. Comparability of methods used in the sampling of primate behavior. *Am. J. Primatol.* 5:1–15.

Rhine, R. J., and Flanigon, M. 1978. An empirical comparison of one-zero, focal animal, and instantaneous methods of sampling spontaneous primate social behavior. *Primates* 19:353–61.

Rhine, R. J., and Linville, A. K. 1980. Properties of one-zero scores in observational studies of primate social behavior: The effect of assumptions on empirical analyses. *Primates* 21:111–22.

Rosenblum, L. A. 1978. The creation of a behavioral taxonomy. In *Observing behavior*, vol. 2, *Data collection and analysis methods*, ed. G. P. Sackett, 15–24. Baltimore: University Park Press.

Sackett, G. P. 1978a. Measurement in observational research. In *Observing behavior*, vol. 2, *Data collection and analysis methods*, ed. G. P. Sackett, 25–43. Baltimore: University Park Press.

———, ed. 1978b. *Observing behavior.* Vol. 2, *Data collection and analysis methods.* Baltimore: University Park Press.

Sackett, G. P., Ruppenthal, G. C., and Gluck, J. 1978. Introduction: An overview of methodological and statistical problems in observational research. In *Observing behavior*, vol. 2, *Data collection and analysis methods*, ed. G. P. Sackett, 1–14. Baltimore: University Park Press.

Sade, D. S. 1975. Management of data on social behavior of free-ranging rhesus monkeys. In *Personalized data base systems*, ed. B. Mittman and L. Borman, 95–110. New York: John Wiley and Sons.

Shapiro, D. Y., and Altham, P. M. E. 1978. Testing assumptions of data selection in focal animal sampling. *Behaviour* 67:115–33.

Siegel, S. 1956. *Nonparametric statistics for the behavioral sciences.* New York: McGraw-Hill.

Slatkin, M. 1975. A report on the feeding behavior of two East African baboon species. In *Contemporary primatology*, 418–22. Basel: Karger.

Snedecor, G. W., and Cochran, W. G. 1980. *Statistical methods.* 7th ed. Ames, Iowa: Iowa State University Press.

Sokal, R. R., and Rohlf, F. J. 1969, 1981. *Biometry.* San Francisco and New York: W. H. Freeman.

———. 1987. *Introduction to biostatistics.* 2d ed. New York: W. H. Freeman.

Stanley, M. E., and Aspey, W. P. 1984. An ethometric analysis in a zoological garden: Modification of ungulate behavior by the visual presence of a predator. *Zoo Biol.* 3:89–109.

Suen, H. K. 1986. On the utility of a post hoc correction procedure for one-zero sampling duration estimates. *Primates* 27 (2): 237–44.

Suen, H. K., and Ary, D. 1984. Variables influencing one-zero and instantaneous time sampling outcomes. *Primates* 25:89–94.

Tabachnick, G. G., and Fidell, L. S. 1989. *Using multivariate statistics.* New York: Harper and Row.

Tasse, J. 1986. Maternal and paternal care in the rock cavy, *Kerodon rupestris,* a South American hystricomorph rodent. *Zoo Biol.* 3:89–109.

Thiemann, S., and Kraemer, H. C. 1984. Sources of behavioral variance: Implications for sample size decisions. *Am. J. Primatol.* 7 (4): 367–75.

Tinbergen, N. 1951. *The study of instinct.* Oxford: Oxford University Press.

Traylor-Holtzer, K., and Fritz, P. 1985. Utilization of space by adult and juvenile groups of captive chimpanzees *(Pan troglodytes). Zoo Biol.* 4:115–27.

Tyler, S. 1979. Time-sampling: A matter of convention. *Anim. Behav.* 27:801–10.

Velleman, P. F. 1993. *Data desk.* Ithaca, N.Y.: Data Descriptions, Inc.

Vestal, B. M., and Vander Stoep, A. 1978. Effect of distance between feeders on aggression in captive chamois *(Rupicapra rupicapra). Appl. Anim. Ethol.* 4:253–60.

Wasser, S. K. 1983. Reproductive competition and cooperation among female yellow baboons. In *Social behavior of female vertebrates,* ed. S. K. Wasser, 349–90. New York: Academic Press.

Wilkinson, L. 1989. *SYSTAT: The system for statistics.* Evanston, IL: Systat, Inc.

Zar, J. H. 1984. *Biostatistical analysis.* 2d ed. Englewood Cliffs, N.J.: Prentice-Hall.

47

Standard Methods for Measuring Mammals

BARBARA LUNDRIGAN

Zoos and other captive animal facilities have an unparalleled opportunity to obtain valuable measurement data from animals— data that in many instances are impossible to obtain from their free-ranging wild conspecifics. Yet this important opportunity is often lost because zoo management personnel are unwilling to collect such data, or because they do not use standardized techniques so that their data can be usefully compared with other data sets and made accessible to other researchers.

Field biologists typically collect a series of standard size measurements that are used in identification, in monitoring the effects of environmental or genetic changes on body size and shape, and as baseline information for studies of the relationship between body size parameters and other aspects of biology, such as diet, reproductive rate, metabolic rate, home range size, and longevity.

With captive animals, the goals are much the same. Standard size measurements can be used to corroborate identifications, to monitor the effects of environmental or genetic changes (in this case, particularly changes associated with captive management such as adjustments in diet, enclosure size, or breeding regime), and as baseline information for evolutionary and wildlife biologists. Although captivity may have a confounding effect on some body size parameters, the value of these data to evolutionary and wildlife biologists cannot be overemphasized. In many instances, measurements from wild conspecifics are simply not available. Moreover, captivity permits repeated measurements of the same individual over time, which is rarely possible in the field. Such longitudinal data can be used to assess changes in management practices, and are essential for establishing norms for growth and development.

This chapter describes the standard methods used by North American mammalogists for taking simple external measurements from small and large mammals; the same methods should be used when captive mammals are measured so that the data can be used for subsequent reference and comparison. I include only the relatively few measurements that mammalogists consider most important, and

whenever possible provide references to more detailed information.

MEASURING MAMMALS

All measurements should be recorded in metric units. There are no rules regarding level of precision; however, suggested standards for mammals of various sizes are given by Ansell (1965). In general, weights of small mammals are given to the nearest gram or tenth of a kilogram and linear measurements to the nearest millimeter. Weights of large mammals are given to the nearest kilogram and linear measurements to the nearest millimeter or centimeter.

The following information should be recorded with the measurements: scientific name, sex, identifying number (i.e., zoo number and/or collector number), date of measurement, date of death (where applicable), reproductive condition (e.g., pregnant or lactating), general condition of the specimen (e.g., alive, recently killed, moderately decomposed), and any damage that might affect the accuracy of a measurement (e.g., a broken tail or torn ear). For captive animals, include the date of birth or date and locality of capture if possible.

Measuring Small Terrestrial Mammals

There are many excellent sources of information on measuring small mammals (i.e., less than 15 kg). These include works by Skinner and Smithers (1990), Handley (1988, bats only), DeBlase and Martin (1981), Hall (1981), Nagorsen and Peterson (1980), and Peterson (1965, bats only). The basic equipment needed includes a metric ruler, calipers or dividers, and a metric weighing device.

The five standard external measurements for small mammals are total length (TL), tail length (T), hind foot length (HF), ear length (E), and weight (wt) (fig. 47.1). Two additional measurements, tragus length (Tr) and forearm length (FA), are taken from bats (fig. 47.2). European mammalogists usually measure head plus body length (HB) instead of total length.

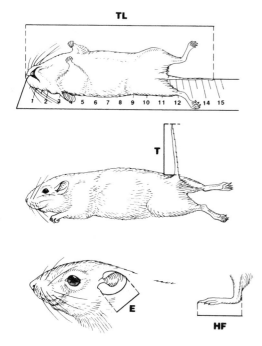

FIG. 47.1.   Standard external measurements for small mammals: total length (TL), tail length (T), hind foot length cum unguis (HF), and ear length (E). (Adapted from DeBlase and Martin 1981.)

Nagorson & Peterson (1980)

Ansell (1965)

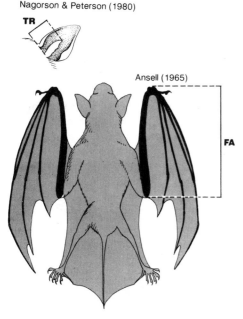

FIG. 47.2.   Additional standard external measurements for bats: forearm length (FA) and tragus length (Tr). (Adapted from Ansell 1965; Nagorsen and Peterson 1980.)

To record measurement data, most collectors use abbreviations, with dashes to separate one measure from the next (e.g., TL 102—T 45—HF 11 (c.u.)—E 35—Tr 14—FA 44.) The weight measurement follows the linear measurements (e.g., wt = 15 g).

Total Length. Lay the animal on its back against the flat side of a ruler. The nose should extend forward and the

body and tail should lie flat against the ruler but should not be stretched. Measure from the tip of the nose to the tip of the tail, excluding tail hair that extends beyond the tip. Alternatively, place the body on a soft board, insert pins to mark the tip of the nose and the tip of the tail, remove the body, and measure the distance between pins. If the animal is conscious or for other reasons cannot be placed in a relaxed position, measure middorsally following the curves of the body from the tip of the nose to the tip of the tail and label "along curves."

Tail Length. Lay the animal on its belly and hold the tail up at a 90° angle from the body. Using a ruler, measure along the dorsal (upper) surface of the tail from its junction with the body (root) to its tip, excluding hair that extends beyond the tip. In species for which it is difficult to locate the root of the tail (e.g., Canadian river otter, *Lontra* [=*Lutra*] *canadensis*), measure from the middle of the anus and label "T M/A."

Hind Foot Length. Press the sole of the hind foot gently against the flat side of a ruler so that the toes are straightened. Measure from the calcaneum (heel) to the end of the claw on the longest toe. European mammalogists do not include the claw in this measurement. Therefore, it is essential to indicate the method used: cum unguis (c.u.) for with claw, or sine unguis (s.u.) for without claw.

Ear Length. Using calipers, dividers, or a ruler, measure from the base of the notch below the ear opening to the most distant point on the margin of the pinna (external ear), excluding ear hair that extends beyond this point.

Tragus Length. The tragus is a leaflike structure projecting from the base of the ear in most bats. Using calipers, dividers, or a ruler, measure from the base of the tragus (where it joins the ear) to its tip, excluding hair that extends beyond the tip.

Forearm Length. Fold the wing, and using calipers, dividers, or a ruler, measure on the dorsal surface of the wing from the tip of the ulna (elbow) to the most distant point on the carpus (wrist).

Weight. Most field collectors use a Pesola spring-balance scale to weigh small mammals because it is light, inexpensive, and easy to handle. Pesola scales range in maximum capacity from 5 grams to 20 kilograms. A triple-beam balance is more cumbersome, but may be preferable for weighing small mammals because of its greater accuracy (maximum capacity 2,610 g). The abbreviation "ca." (*circa*) is used to designate an approximate weight.

Measuring Large Terrestrial Mammals

Information on measuring large terrestrial mammals (i.e., 15 kg or more) can be found in works by Nagorsen and Peterson (1980), Sachs (1967, ungulates only), and Ansell (1965). The basic equipment needed includes two straight, stiff rods, a flexible metal tape measure, a ball of heavy string (for distances greater than the length of the tape measure), large calipers or dividers, and a metric weighing device.

The same standard external measurements recorded for small mammals (total length, tail length, hind foot length, ear length, and weight) are recorded for large mammals (fig. 47.3). Two additional measurements, shoulder height

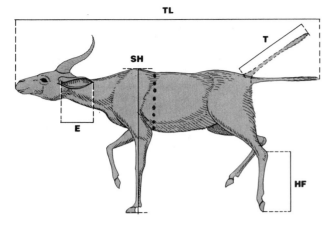

FIG. 47.3.   Standard external measurements for large mammals: total length point to point (TL), tail length (T), hind foot length cum unguis (HF), ear length (E), shoulder height (SH), and axillary girth (dotted line). (Adapted from Ansell 1965.)

(SH) and axillary girth, are usually taken for ungulates and sometimes for other large mammals (fig. 47.3).

Total Length. Lay the animal on its back or side with the nose pointed forward, the backbone in a natural, relaxed position, and the tail extended in line with the backbone. Place one rod perpendicular to the long axis of the body touching the tip of the nose, and a second rod perpendicular to the long axis of the body touching the tip of the tail (excluding tail hair that extends beyond the tip). Measure in a straight line by running a tape measure from rod to rod just above the body. If the animal is conscious or for other reasons cannot be placed in a relaxed position, measure mid-dorsally following the curves of the body from the tip of the nose, across the back of the head and along the backbone, to the tip of the tail. Always indicate the method of measurement: "point to point" or "along curves."

Tail Length. Hold the tail at a 90° angle above the dorsal surface of the body (or 30–45° for ungulates: Ansell 1965), and, using a tape measure, measure from the root of the tail to the tip of the tail, excluding hair that extends beyond the tip. In species for which it is difficult to locate the root of the tail (e.g., aardvark, *Orycteropus afer*), measure from the middle of the anus and label "T M/A."

Hind Foot. Hold the hind foot so that the toes are straightened, and, using large calipers or dividers, measure from the calcaneum (heel) to the tip of the claw on the longest toe. For ungulates, extend the lower leg and measure from the calcaneum (hock or heel) to the tip of the hoof (synonymous with the claw). European mammalogists do not include the claw (or hoof) in this measurement. Therefore, it is essential to indicate the method used: cum unguis (c.u.) for with claw (or hoof), or sine unguis (s.u.) for without claw (or hoof).

Ear. The ear is measured as in small mammals.

Shoulder Height. In a standing animal, shoulder height is the distance from the highest point on the withers (or shoulder) to the sole of the foreleg hoof (or foot). If the animal is lying on its side, hold the limb in its natural position, place one rod perpendicular to the long axis of the body touching the highest point on the withers (or shoulder), and place a second rod perpendicular to the long axis of the body touching the sole of the hoof (or foot). Measure in a straight line by running a tape measure from rod to rod just above the body.

Axillary Girth. Axillary girth measurements should be taken only from live animals and fresh carcasses, as the body may become distended shortly after death. Using a flexible tape measure, measure the circumference of the body immediately behind the forelegs. If the tape cannot be passed around the body, measure from dorsal to pectoral midline and label "Half Axillary Girth."

Weight. Weights of large mammals are particularly valuable because they are recorded so infrequently. Some captive mammals (e.g., many primates and some carnivores) can be enticed or trained to stand on a floor scale. Special equipment may be needed for weighing extremely large mammals (e.g., the National Zoological Park borrows truck scales to weigh elephants). Large carcasses can be weighed in pieces, but an allowance should be made for fluid loss. For a discussion of techniques for weighing large mammals, see Schemnitz and Giles (1980).

MEASURING MARINE MAMMALS

Marine mammals (pinnipeds, cetaceans, and sirenians) differ in basic body structure from terrestrial mammals and therefore demand a somewhat different set of external measurements. The equipment needed is the same as for large terrestrial mammals.

Measuring Pinnipeds

The best source of information on measuring pinnipeds (seals, sea lions, and walruses) is the recommendations of the American Society of Mammalogists Committee on Marine Mammals (1967). There are five standard external measurements for pinnipeds (fig. 47.4).

Standard Length. Standard length in pinnipeds is equivalent to total length in large terrestrial mammals and is mea-

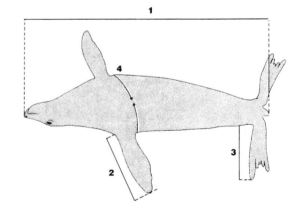

FIG. 47.4.   Standard external measurements for pinnipeds recommended by the American Society of Mammalogists Committee on Marine Mammals: standard length (1), anterior length of front flipper (2), anterior length of hind flipper (3), and axillary girth (4). (Adapted from Committee on Marine Mammals 1967.)

sured in the same manner. If the animal is conscious or for other reasons cannot be placed in a relaxed, belly-up position, measure the shortest surface distance from the tip of the nose to the tip of the tail by following the curves of the body along the back, side, or belly, and label "Curvilinear Length."

Anterior Length of Front Flipper. Hold the flipper at right angles to the body and, using a tape measure, large calipers, or dividers, measure in a straight line from the anterior insertion of the flipper to the tip of the first claw or fleshy extension.

Anterior Length of Hind Flipper. Hold the flipper at right angles to the body and, using a tape measure, large calipers, or dividers, measure in a straight line from the anterior insertion of the flipper to the tip of the first claw or fleshy extension.

Axillary Girth. Axillary girth in pinnipeds is equivalent to axillary girth in large terrestrial mammals and is measured in the same manner.

Weight. Many captive pinnipeds can be trained to stand on a floor scale. Large carcasses can be weighed in pieces; the Committee on Marine Mammals (1967) suggests a 10% allowance for loss of body fluids.

Measuring Cetaceans

The best source of information on measuring cetaceans (whales, dolphins, and porpoises) is the recommendations of the American Society of Mammalogists Committee on Marine Mammals (1961). Thirteen of the most important external measurements recommended by that body are briefly described below (fig. 47.5).

The first seven measurements should be taken in a straight line parallel to the long axis of the body and labeled "axial."

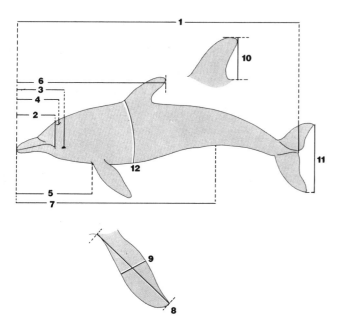

FIG. 47.5.   Standard external measurements for cetaceans recommended by the American Society of Mammalogists Committee on Marine Mammals. (Adapted from Committee on Marine Mammals 1961.)

For each measurement, place a rod perpendicular to the long axis of the body at each of the two reference points. Adjust the rods laterally so that the line between them is parallel to the body axis, and measure the straight-line distance between the two rods.

The primary reference point for the first seven measurements is the anteriormost point on the head, excluding the lower jaw. This is almost always the anterior tip of the upper jaw; thus, "tip of the upper jaw" is used below. In species in which the two are not equivalent (e.g., dwarf sperm whale, *Kogia simus*), use the anteriormost point on the head, excluding the lower jaw, as the primary reference point.

1. (Total length): Tip of the upper jaw to notch between the tail flukes (or the midpoint of the fluke margin if no notch is present)
2. Tip of the upper jaw to corner of the mouth
3. Tip of the upper jaw to center of the eye
4. Tip of the upper jaw to center of the blowhole (or midpoint between the two blowholes if two are present)
5. Tip of the upper jaw to anterior insertion of the flipper
6. Tip of the upper jaw to tip of the dorsal fin
7. Tip of the upper jaw to center of the anus

The remaining measurements (except girth and weight) are straight-line distances measured from point to point (using a tape measure, calipers, or dividers):

8. Length of flipper: from the anterior insertion of the flipper to its tip
9. Width of flipper: the maximum width of the flipper, perpendicular to its long axis
10. Height of dorsal fin: from the base of the dorsal fin to its tip
11. Width of flukes: the width across the flukes, from tip to tip
12. Maximum girth: the circumference of the body at its widest point. Indicate the (axial) distance from that point to the tip of the upper jaw. If the tape measure cannot be passed under the body, measure from dorsal to ventral midline and label "Half Maximum Girth."
13. Weight: measured as for pinnipeds

Measuring Sirenians

There is very little information on measuring sirenians (dugongs and manatees). Domning (1977) provides a long list of the external measurements he used to describe a dugong, *Dugong dugon*, and Murie (1874, 1885) provides a similar list for the American manatee, *Trichechus manatus*.

Many of the standard external measurements taken from cetaceans are also appropriate for sirenians. Measurements of sirenians should (minimally) include total length, length and width of flipper, maximum girth, width of tail, and body weight.

MEASURING TEETH

Although toothrow measurements are not considered standard external measurements, they are useful indicators of size. The most commonly taken toothrow measurements are of the upper (maxillary) toothrow.

Alveolar Length of Maxillary Toothrow. Using calipers or dividers, measure on one side of the upper toothrow from the anterior surface of the canine near its junction with the jawbone to the posterior surface of the last molar near its junction with the jawbone.

Alveolar Length of Molar Toothrow. This measurement is the same as alveolar length of maxillary toothrow except that the canine tooth is not included in the measurement; the first reference point is the first premolar (or first molar if there are no premolars).

DISCUSSION

Data Availability

Measurement data are useful only if they are accessible for analysis. Data should be stored in an easily retrievable form, and large amounts of data on the same species should be published or otherwise compiled.

Animals collected by field biologists are usually accessioned to a museum, where they and the data associated with them are maintained for future study. In contrast, zoological parks and other captive facilities often have no formal ties with museums. Animals that die in captivity are usually incinerated, and the associated data are placed in files that are not available to most researchers. Three primary goals of research-oriented captive facilities should be to collect standard measurement data, to maintain data files that are easily accessible to researchers both within and outside the facility, and to initiate the transfer of valuable specimens to museum collections.

Using Measurement Data

Morphological measurements taken from captive mammals may differ considerably from those of wild-caught conspecifics. These differences may reflect increased inbreeding in captivity, nutritional differences between captive and wild populations, or the effects of differences in the physical environment. Whatever their causes, the source of a specimen should be considered in any application of the data. For management purposes, the differences themselves are of interest, as they can be used in assessing the effects of the captive environment. However, for those using data from captive mammals as estimates for wild conspecifics, these differences represent a potential source of error. A better un-

derstanding of phenotypic plasticity and the influence of captivity on body size would be useful in this context.

ACKNOWLEDGMENTS

I thank Stephen Dobson, Susan Lumpkin, and Philip Myers for helpful suggestions on an earlier draft of the manuscript.

REFERENCES

Ansell, W. F. H. 1965. Standardisation of field data on mammals. *Zool. Afr.* 1 (1): 97–113.

Committee on Marine Mammals, American Society of Mammalogists. 1961. Standardized methods for measuring and recording data on the smaller cetaceans. *J. Mammal.* 42:471–76.

Committee on Marine Mammals, American Society of Mammalogists. 1967. Standard measurements of seals. *J. Mammal.* 48: 459–62.

DeBlase, A. F., and Martin, R. E. 1981. *A manual of mammalogy with keys to families of the world.* Dubuque, Iowa: Wm. C. Brown.

Domning, D. 1977. *Observations on the myology of* Dugong dugon *(Muller).* Smithsonian Contributions to Zoology, no. 226. Washington, D.C.: Smithsonian Institution Press.

Hall, E. R. 1981. *The mammals of North America.* New York: John Wiley and Sons.

Handley, C. O. 1988. Specimen preparation. In *Ecological and behavioral methods for the study of bats,* ed. T. H. Kunz, 437–57. Washington, D.C.: Smithsonian Institution Press.

Murie, J. 1874. On the form and structure of the manatee *(Manatus americanus). Trans. Zool. Soc. Lond.* 8 (3): 127–202.

Murie, J. 1885. Further observations on the manatee. *Trans. Zool. Soc. Lond.* 11 (2): 19–48.

Nagorsen, D. W., and Peterson, R. L. 1980. *Mammal collectors' manual: A guide for collecting, documenting and preparing mammal specimens for scientific research.* Life Sciences Miscellaneous Publications. Toronto: Royal Ontario Museum.

Peterson, R. L. 1965. *Collecting bat specimens for scientific purposes.* Toronto: Royal Ontario Museum.

Sachs, R. 1967. Liveweights and body measurements of Serengeti game animals. *E. Afr. Wildl. J.* 5:24–27.

Schemnitz, S. D., and Giles, R. H. Jr. 1980. Instrumentation. In *Wildlife Management Techniques Manual,* ed. S. D. Schemnitz, 449–505. Washington, D.C.: The Wildlife Society.

Skinner, J. D., and Smithers, R. H. N. 1990. *The mammals of the southern African subregion.* Pretoria: University of Pretoria Press.

48

Disposal versus Disposition: The Role of a Comparative Anatomist in a Zoological Park

THEODORE I. GRAND

When Sir Arthur Conan Doyle tried to kill off Sherlock Holmes, he entitled that story "The Final Problem." As subsequent literary history shows, Doyle's disposal was so thoughtless and poorly conceived that he had to bring Holmes back in *The Return of Sherlock Holmes* and explain that the great detective had not died at Reichenbach Falls after all. By definition, though certainly not by design, several "final problems" complete the management of any captive animal. Why did it die? What can we do to prevent another such death? How can we improve husbandry? What are we to do with the animal's remains?

The word "disposal" implies "quick and efficient," but as Conan Doyle learned, it may also imply "inadequate and unsatisfactory"; on the other hand, "disposition" projects a sense of thought and planning. For those of us who work with exotic species, the pride and concern that we exercise during their lives on exhibition should also be applied at their termini.

The magnitude of the problem of optimal disposition is barely acknowledged. In reference to this problem, Benirschke (chap. 45, this volume) writes, "Pathologic studies on all deceased animals should be mandatory." For several years the American Society of Mammalogists had a standing committee (now extinct) to explore the needs of the research community in relation to the remains of captive exotics. Hardy (1986; chap. 44, this volume) established a national network, a clearinghouse as it were: the Consortium of Aquariums, Universities, and Zoos (C.A.U.Z.), whose purpose is to facilitate communication within the university-aquarium-zoo community. Even the National Park Service has initiated a newsletter, *Clearing House Classifieds,* to dispose of surplus objects in its collections: weapons, military prints, photographic equipment.

At the National Zoological Park (NZP), the annual inventory for 1991 showed roughly 3,500 animals, with increases and decreases through trades, importing, and breeding. For the years 1991 and 1992 the inventory recorded 579 and 767 deaths respectively; 45% and 57% of the deceased were mammals. Approximately one-quarter to one-third of these animals were small mammals, while the remaining individuals were carnivores, ungulates, primates, and other large exotics. Thus, the disposition problem at the National Zoo for mammals alone encompasses approximately 200 animals per year. Similar statistics might be applied to losses in the bird collection. What should be done? Disposal or disposition, that is the question.

THE PROBLEM OF MEASUREMENT

The time of death may be the only point in the life span when some animals are immobile and physically accessible—a last opportunity to take measurements. Roberts and Kohn (1991) not only discuss various measurements to be taken at death, but argue forcefully for regular weighings (where possible) of small animals as a method of monitoring health and reproductive state. Lundrigan (chap. 47, this volume) presents, with rigor, the techniques of measuring mammals of various sizes and body configurations. I am in favor of measurement and strict protocol, but it is appropriate to offer a cautionary comment on the inherent problems of postmortem as well as antemortem measurement. The people assigned to measure an animal may not be the same people who chose the measurement; therefore, without practice and care, the values may not be comparable each time they are taken. At the NZP, several pairs of individuals took the "same" measurements on three short-lived giant panda, *Ailuropoda melanoleuca,* cubs. This change of personnel is to be avoided whenever possible.

Pooled data on the lengths and weights of individuals fall into a difficult-to-evaluate statistical class: the cross-sectional sample, in which individuals of a given sex class or age class are clustered together. By contrast, longitudinal data follow the same individual throughout a specified period. The value of such data is debated among its potential users. At best, scientists are leery of cross-sectional information taken by others; at their most critical, they avoid it altogether because of the possibility of differential environmental effects (see discussion below on abnormal musculoskeletal development and increased adiposity in captive individuals).

During each postmortem examination the veterinary pathologist automatically makes size judgments: are the kidneys normal? is the spleen (or the liver) too large? The *Handbook of Biological Data* (Spector 1956) is filled with such data for many species, though not representative of the diversity that fills zoos and aquaria. Again, most scientists do not rely upon such data because of variations in measurement technique, which are frequently not reported: was the kidney weighed with or without its capsule? was the brain weighed with or without its meninges? was the heart exsanguinated? was gut weight taken with or without its contents?

As a practicing scientist, I must state categorically that *numbers* per se (body masses, organ weights, lengths of body segments) *are not automatically useful to anyone.* In fact, in the hands of number-crunching nonbiologists, these data are downright dangerous. Important conclusions about the biology of exotic species do not miraculously emerge from pools of numbers. Why? Because the research goal is the primary framework from which measurements should be designed and applied. Question first, measure second. In other words, one makes a hypothesis, determines what the sample population is to be (such as living or postmortem animals), and then decides on the most feasible techniques for gathering the data (that is, the measurements). Measurements are not neutral philosophical items, and the measurement of deceased animals suggests the first contribution the comparative anatomist can make to the zoological collection: he or she can help select those measures most appropriate to the investigation.

DEATH AS INCONVENIENCE

Sometimes death comes suddenly; sometimes, after prolonged exercise of clinical skills. Sometimes euthanasia will be scheduled, as when an animal has an irreparably broken leg, the one time when zoo personnel can project a disposition plan. Unfortunately, only a fraction of zoo deaths come about in this way. The remainder are unpredictable and may have catastrophic effects.

The moment of death is a stressful time for those involved in management (the curator, the keeper staff) and for the individual who must make some public announcement. However, removed from the emotionality of the event, two classic end users with complementary goals are well adapted to deal objectively with the cause of death and the disposition of the remains.

THE PATHOLOGIST

The first priority of the pathologist is diagnosis of the cause of death. This information may suggest alterations in husbandry, increased alertness on the part of the keepers, or perhaps a change in the exhibit or holding area. Within the confines of public health, safety, and the law, the pathologist also determines which tissues should be saved and which sent off to laboratories or museum collections. Ideally, he or she will have the technological capability to freeze and store tissues and blood for investigators not resident at the zoological park. A few researchers, both within zoos and at universities, have standing requests for blood or organs of certain species.

THE COMPARATIVE ANATOMIST

The comparative anatomist's interests are nonclinical and are devoted to the preservation of gross materials (skin, skulls and teeth, postcranial parts, whole organs, rather than fluids or cells). He or she is aware of the zoological and ecological significance of the deceased animal, its research potential, adaptations that might interest zoology teachers, and researchers who could make further use of the animal (Doolittle and Grand, in press).

Let us take as examples three actual cases that I worked on. Three South American rodents died at NZP within a few weeks of one another: a prehensile-tailed porcupine, *Coendou prehensilis*, a Patagonian mara, *Dolichotis patagonum*, and a Cuban hutia, *Capromys pilorides*. The porcupine died suddenly on exhibit and was brought to the Department of Pathology for postmortem examination. An acute infection of *Salmonella* was the probable cause of death. Its cage was sanitized, and its mate examined. The mara kicked backward violently with its hind legs and shattered several bones in one foot. Surgical repair was judged impossible, and the animal was euthanized. The Cuban hutia died from a malignant neoplasm growing around its trachea. The cause of death was determined in each of these cases. Then, the question became: *What could be done to extend the educational and research value of these animals beyond their lifetimes?*

Research gives some direction to the disposition problem, and here is the way I answered the question at NZP; it is not necessarily "The Way" other institutions could or should do it.

Research in Functional Anatomy

Coendou prehensilis is a prehensile-tailed, arboreal, slow-climbing relative of our North American porcupine species; it is arguably also a relative of the Ecuadorean pacarana *Dinomys branickii* (Grand and Eisenberg 1982). The data available to test certain hypotheses about these relationships were few, so I wanted to take advantage of this rare opportunity. The animal weighed nearly 3 kilograms, and my dissection began by plucking its 300 grams of quills! It possessed, in addition, 150 grams of epidermis. The skin, which was quite thin, did not hold my attention, but the pile of quills certainly did (fig. 48.1). In evolutionary terms the animal had invested 10% of its body weight in antipredator protection.

Next, I wanted to know how much muscle the animal possessed and where (by region of the body) the muscle groups were concentrated. The animal was about 35% muscle, and its distribution between forelimbs and hindlimbs was almost 1:1. This is the usual distribution for moderately sized arboreal climbers, regardless of lineage. In

FIG. 48.1.   The quills from an adult *Coendou*.

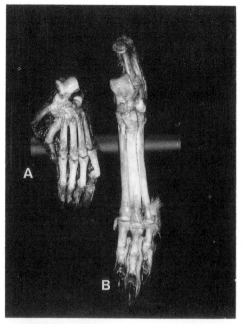

FIG. 48.2.   The feet of *(A) Coendou* and *(B) Dolichotis*, and *(C)* the hand of *Colobus*.

equal measure, such climbers use their forelimbs to pull and their hindlimbs to push the body mass along a branch. The muscularity in the back extensors was low and balanced from neck and thorax to lumbar region, the arrangement found in other climbers (Grand 1978). These muscles produce sinusoidal motion rather than explosive forward thrust. By contrast, the quantity and organization of the tail muscles are spectacular (10% of all the muscle in the body). The porcupine invested its musculature in suspensory ability and agility at slender branch ends, a convergence with howler monkeys, *Alouatta,* the binturong, *Arctictis,* the kinkajou, *Potos,* the tamandua, *Tamandua,* the ring-tailed possum, *Pseudocheirus,* and climbers of a few other lineages.

The feet and forepaws of *Coendou* were also instructive as to function. Early in their evolutionary history the porcupines lost both the thumb and big toe; however, when they colonized the forest canopy, they had to evolve alternative mechanisms for grasping (Grand and Eisenberg 1982). Bony extensions of the carpus (similar to the giant panda's "thumb") and tarsus replaced the lost digits (fig. 48.2a). My preparations of skin and skeleton (modified from Hildebrand 1968) demonstrate the structural mechanisms of bone, skin, and muscle by which the porcupine can grasp a curved linear support surface (Doolittle and Grand, in press). In contrast, the black-and-white colobus monkey, *Colobus guereza,* has also lost its thumb, but compensates for the loss with long, curved metacarpals and phalanges (Figure 48.2c).

The Patagonian mara is a lovely, jackrabbit-like South American rodent. In the mid-1970s, through the foresight of Dr. John Eisenberg, I had the privilege of dissecting a pair of mara from the NZP (Grand 1978). Such is the unpredictability of life, however, that I had no further opportunity to verify or expand those data until the animal described above "appeared at my doorstep." The animal weighed about 6 kilograms, and skin represented less than 6% of its body mass. It was 50% muscle, and the muscle was quite distinct in its regional distribution: the hindlimb had four times as much muscle as the forelimb, 25% of all the muscle in the

body was in the back, and over half of that muscle was in the lumbar region. Since the animal's explosive acceleration (in effect, the kick backward that shattered its leg) originates in these massive lumbar extensors and recruits, in sequence, the hip, knee, and ankle, we can appreciate how much force the mara put into his ricochet-style locomotion. The conventional image of gross anatomy is the meticulous (some might say slavish) description of the origin and insertion of particular muscles. By contrast, this functional analysis offers an extremely sophisticated biomechanical picture of locomotor adaptation: a muscular (kinetic) chain that links the lower back to the elongated foot. And, as fig. 48.2b also shows, the foot converges with that of the dog, rather than that of its South American relative, the porcupine. *Dolichotis*, from my perspective, invests in muscularity and skeletal proportions for high-speed escape on the ground just as clearly as *Coendou* invests in quills, climbing ability, and agility within the forest canopy.

Since my long-term research deals with body composition and functional anatomy, these data went into my data bank. I was able to confirm the accuracy of my earlier dissections and add to my range of species variability, and I kept the quills and skeletons for teaching demonstrations.

The Cuban hutia was an aged animal and could not be compared with normal adult animals of other species. Nevertheless, I could not pass up the opportunity to dissect it. Osteoarthritic erosion was evident around several joints (shoulder, hip, and knee, in particular) and the menisci and capsule over the knee joint (fig. 48.3a) were ossified (something I do not recall ever seeing with such severity). The pad on the sole of the foot (fig. 48.3b) had been displaced laterally, and the epithelium, no longer being sloughed off by normal wear, had become hyperkeratotic (an abnormal increase in the thickness of the keratinized epithelium); in fact, it had had to be trimmed regularly. This hyperkeratosis is the epidermal equivalent of ever-growing rodent incisors, which do not wear down if they malocclude and must be trimmed or clipped back.

I also noted severe asymmetry in the planes of the right and left molar rows. One plane was tilted with reference to the other (see lines in fig. 48.3c) and showed that the animal had been favoring the dental row on one side of his mouth. The right and left maxillary incisors also showed asymmetrical wear. Further observation showed erosion of the maxillary bone (the hole labeled *x* in fig. 48.3c) and suggested that the neoplasm began in the nasal turbinates or sinuses and progressively disrupted the animal's ability to chew. This was the site of the tumor origin; the growth around the trachea, which killed the animal, was secondary. The keeper staff had noticed an occasional bloody nose, but until the postmortem reconstruction, the picture was incomplete.

Perspectives for the Pathologist and Animal Keeper

I continue to learn from my colleagues in the Department of Pathology at NZP. I see variations and anomalies in the gastrointestinal and urogenital tracts, cardiovascular pathology, parasites, and the interactions of diseases with the glands and organs. With my perspective on the hutia, I returned to them my observations on the long-term effects of caging: fatty inclusions in muscle, arthritic wear of the joints, and skeletal abnormalities. Such factors do not cause death, but they constitute a background stress that erodes health. Demonstrations of musculoskeletal abnormality help to sensitize the staff to the effects of reduced activity. (And, as with human beings, they remind us that the stimulus to physical activity helps, rather than hinders, life).

A Resource for Graphics, Exhibition, and Education

An exhibit was developed for the Primate House at the NZP. One phase of the exhibit concentrated on the adaptations of hands and feet that permit monkeys to climb and to

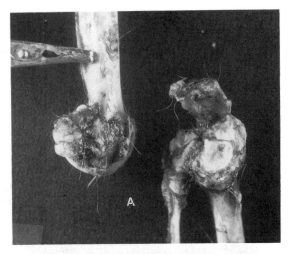

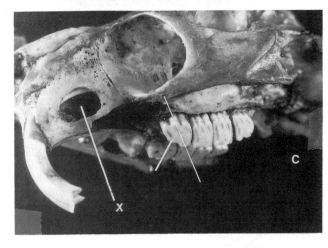

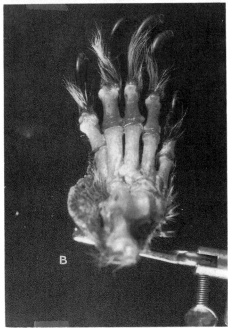

FIG. 48.3.   *Capromys pilorides. (A)* Osteoarthritic erosion of the knee joint; ossified semilunar cartilages. *(B)* Hyperkeratosis of plantar pad and its lateral displacement. *(C)* Abnormal shift of the occlusal plane; naso-maxillary erosion and the primary tumor site.

hang suspended from branches, and pointed out differences between monkey hands and feet and the claws and hooves of other mammals. The hands and feet of the *Colobus*, in comparison with those of the porcupine and the mara, illustrate still other adaptations: the palmar and volar skin, the musculature, the proportions of fingers and toes, nails rather than claws (the comparative anatomist can specify precisely what distinguishes them). Preparations of actual animals have a greater impact on students than pictures in a book. When I meet science students (in the zoo or classroom), these materials make for exciting, hands-on demonstrations. The retractile claw mechanisms of a cat might seem passé, but the same adaptation in an ocelot, *Felis pardalis*, certainly "stirs 'em up."

A Conduit and Liaison

When I work on an animal that duplicates a preparation I already have, I contact a teacher from a high school or university to determine whether he or she would be interested in using the animal as part of a zoo-teaching module. I meet the teacher and student(s), give them an overview of the animal's natural history, some guidance into its functional anatomy, and a brief list of references. The teacher and students take the roughly flensed (cleaned) skeleton to prepare on their own schedule, and follow their own learning goals.

Ultimate disposition, however, is related to institutional policy and commitment. In the case of the NZP, federal ownership comes first, and we first determine the requirements of the departments of the NZP and the Smithsonian: the Animal Departments, Education Department, the National Museum of Natural History (NMNH), and the Friends of the National Zoo (FONZ). If the specimen is loaned, transferred, or donated, some formal record is essential.

Of course, disposition must be consistent with the pathologist's judgment of public health and safety requirements. For example, bovids of African origin, which may carry foot-and-mouth disease, must be incinerated according to U.S. Department of Agriculture (USDA) regulations.

My own research in anatomy and growth requires that I dissect, as opportunity presents itself, most marsupials, insectivores, carnivores, bats, primates, and edentates. I average about 110 dissections per year, approximately one-third of the mammals lost per year to our collection. I dissect some birds (upon request) and no reptiles. This disparity between the annual number lost and my capacities serves to emphasize the magnitude of the loss to research and educational programs nationwide and worldwide.

I want to return to the point about unpredictability to which I previously alluded. One must be in residence virtually full-time at a place like NZP to take advantage of the collection. One never knows from day to day what will happen. This is exciting and challenging, but it is not for the impatient. One must maintain several research lines: if a bat turns up, that animal fits into one series; a red panda, *Ailurus fulgens*, is placed in a study series that includes raccoons and bears; a dorcas gazelle, *Gazella dorcas*, goes into still another study. Thus, it takes years and patience to build one's research on a given lineage. It took me about ten years to complete one study of kangaroos (Grand 1990), another study of growth in the African Bovidae (Grand 1991), a model of brain and muscle development in altricial and precocial mammals (Grand 1992), and still another of the proboscis and rays of the star-nosed mole, *Condylura cristata* (Gould, McShea, and Grand 1993).

As to opportunism in the comparisons of the Patagonian mara and the prehensile-tailed porcupine, I could equally have compared the rat kangaroo, *Potorous*, with the tree kangaroo, *Dendrolagus*, and the wallabies, or *Macropus*, the red kangaroo, with the dorcas gazelle. In a zoological collection, instructive comparisons are infinite, and the mind of the comparative anatomist is energized by the diversity we happily accept as natural. Who else, for example, could see giraffe, *Giraffa camelopardalis*, knees on one day and a star-nosed mole proboscis the next?

Many hypokinetic (reduced activity) disorders of animals and humans (increased incidences of arthritis, fatty inclusion in muscle, excess adipose stores, bad teeth, abnormal calcium in bone) could be understood through the study of captive species.

The comparative anatomist is comfortable with the transition from research to education through the preservation of quills, skulls, postcrania, paws, and feet. One might emphasize birds, so that one would preserve the feet of raptors, swimmers, and passerines; the wings of flapping and soaring birds; the bills and beaks of grain, fruit, and insect eaters. Gross anatomists *automatically* save adaptations, for museum use and for the visitors to our facilities. An explanation of these adaptations when we were young probably led some of us to enter biology in college. Neither the pathologist nor geneticist nor cell biologist preserves materials in similar ways for similar reasons (nor should they).

THE DISPOSITION PROBLEM: SOLUTION AND RESOLUTION

Comparative anatomists, or prosectors, were associated with zoos into the early twentieth century, but few of us survive. Nonetheless, the anatomist continues to serve research, educational, and conduit-liaison functions as these integrate with the goals of the modern zoological garden.

National networks of exchange have been explored and proposed by a committee of the American Society of Mammalogists, and more successfully by Donna FitzRoy Hardy of California State University (Northridge): data on tissue and species needs and availability now go into the C.A.U.Z. data base. Interested investigators (within an institution as well as outsiders) contact the pathology personnel and describe what they want, and zoo staff save and coordinate distribution of the materials (soft tissues, fluids, etc). Unfortunately, this vision of a national network throws the entire burden upon local personnel. Several individuals may want the same parts preserved differently, or they may want different tissues preserved in several ways. Hours are spent during the postmortem examination trying to satisfy those requests. Where will we store the tissues? Who will package and ship the tissues? Who will pay for the time spent?

There is an alternative resolution to the disposition problem: the development of a reliable, regional network of high school, private school, and college teachers and researchers who will respond rapidly and personally (Doolittle and Grand, in press). Zoo staff may feel put upon by the semi-anonymous individual requests that come in by mail, phone, or fax. If one negotiates face-to-face, creative attention and thoughtful preservation are easier and more effective. When we send out specimens along a huge network, we receive minimal feedback, and we may store materials that never get picked up or paid for ("the check is in the mail"). If one knows the investigator, one can call immediately and he or she will arrive right away, or have a valid reason why not. If one knows what is needed, one can save something that never made the original want list. And the local investigator's feedback is more likely to be useful than a long-distance phone call complaining that tissue preservation was unsatisfactory. Two appreciative locals can contribute far more to the institution than ten or more anonymous colleagues at a distance. If you call someone you know, it fuels enthusiasm on both sides. You will then *be more likely to call* that familiar someone *when something is not on the list,* but looks interesting.

How to balance the two solutions? The C. of C.A.U.Z. stands for "Consortium," which means partners, and partners, in turn, means understanding as well as collaboration. If both sides of the communication network appreciate this, the national system and the computer hookup among the zoo-aquarium-university community will work. Where the zoo possesses sufficient resources for the comparative anatomist (laboratory space, partial equipment support, partial salary), the decision for disposition can be equitably divided by pathologist and anatomist between the preservation of tissues and fluids and that of body parts such as skulls and skeletons. The network is thus more likely to be successful (read: efficient).

The history of comparative anatomy is recapitulated each time a student appreciates the adaptation of a tooth, claw, or paw. What better way to use these marvelous creatures who have lived under our care than to keep them for further study? What better way to extend their lives?

ACKNOWLEDGMENTS

My zoo collaboration began at the Portland (Oregon)—now, Washington Park—Zoo, through my friendship with Matt Maberry. When I began working at the NZP twenty years ago, it was through the encouragement and vision of John Eisenberg and Theodore H. Reed. I owe them the combined debts of science and friendship. Since I work in the Department of Pathology as well as in the Department of Zoological Research, I acknowledge the continued support and cooperation of Dick Montali, Head of the DOP, Richard Freeman (now at NMNH), and a succession of residents: Peter Mann, Don Nichols, Bruce Rideout, and Chris Schiller. In the development of this chapter I have benefited from the critical commentary of Judith Block, Devra Kleiman, Susan Lumpkin, Dick Montali, Mary Duncan, José Dias of the NZP; Karl Kranz and Robert Snyder of the Philadelphia Zoological Gardens; Bruce Rideout of the San Diego Zoo; Richard Doolittle of the Rochester Institute of Technology; and Donna FitzRoy Hardy of California State University (Northridge).

Financial support has come from the Friends of the National Zoo, (Paul) Newman's Own Foods, a senior postdoctoral fellowship from the Smithsonian Institution, and a senior postdoctoral award from the Wenner-Gren Foundation for Anthropological Research. While each award came to me for my research, each was sufficiently flexible that I could pursue some of the educational experiments I have discussed here, and for that I owe each institution a considerable debt.

REFERENCES

Doolittle, R. L., and Grand, T. I. In press. The benefits of the zoological park to the teaching of comparative vertebrate anatomy. *Zoo Biol.*

Gould, E., McShea, W., and Grand, T. 1993. Function of the star in the star-nosed mole, *Condylura cristata. J. Mammal.* 74: 108–16.

Grand, T. I. 1978. Adaptations of tissue and limb segments to facilitate moving and feeding in arboreal folivores. In *The ecology of arboreal folivores,* ed. G. G. Montgomery, 231–41. Washington, D.C.: Smithsonian Institution Press.

———. 1990. Body composition and the evolution of the Macropodidae *(Potorous, Dendrolagus,* and *Macropus). Anat. Embryol.* 182:85–92.

———. 1991. Patterns of muscular growth in the African Bovidae. *Appl. Anim. Behav. Sci.* 29:471–82.

———. 1992. Altricial and precocial mammals: A model of neural and muscular development. *Zoo Biol.* 11:3–15.

Grand, T. I., and J. F. Eisenberg. 1982. On the affinities of the Dinomyidae. *Säugetierkundliche Mitteilungen* 30:151–57.

Hardy, D. F. 1986. The role of the Consortium of Aquariums, Universities, and Zoos in promoting research in zoos. AAZPA Conference Proceedings, Minneapolis, Minnesota, 14–18 September. Wheeling, W.Va.: American Association of Zoological Parks and Aquariums.

Hildebrand, M. 1968. *Anatomical preparations.* Berkeley: University of California Press.

Roberts, M., and Kohn, F. B. 1991. A technique for obtaining early life history data in pouched marsupials. *Zoo Biol.* 10:81–86.

Spector, H. S., ed. 1956. *Handbook of biological data.* Philadelphia: W. B. Saunders.

APPENDIXES

Appendix 1
Mammalian Phylogeny

John F. Eisenberg

The Early History of Mammals

One may well ask, What is a mammal? All living mammals represent endpoints of natural selection, and the class Mammalia has had a very long evolutionary history. All mammals possess hair at some stage in their life cycles, and in most species hair persists throughout life, although in some aquatic forms the hairs have been reduced to remnant bristles or are lost in adults. All female mammals possess functional mammary glands that produce milk, which serves as nourishment for the newborn. In males, these glands are present but rudimentary. The thoracic and abdominal cavities are separated by a muscular diaphragm. The mammalian brain shows considerable enlargement over that of a comparably sized reptile, and the top of the forebrain, or the neopallium, is proportionally larger in mammals than in other vertebrates.

In skeletal anatomy, all recent mammals are defined by the fact that the lower jaw is composed of only a single pair of bones, the dentaries, which articulate directly with the cranium. Most species are also characterized by a heterodont dentition; that is, the teeth are differentiated into functional types: incisors, canines, premolars, and molars. Some extant mammalian species have secondarily lost their teeth (e.g., anteaters and pangolins), while others (e.g., dolphins) have reverted to a homodont condition, in which all teeth are similar. In contrast to the reptilian condition of continual tooth replacement, in mammals teeth are replaced only once (diphydonty). The skull possesses two occipital condyles to articulate it with the spinal column, instead of one as in reptiles.

Living mammals descended from reptiles. During the Paleozoic, in the Pennsylvanian period, approximately 320 million years before the present, the Synapsida exhibited several different lines of descent. One of these was the Cotylosauria, which were characterized by moderate size, and in some forms, possessed a large sail-like dorsal fin. This fin may have been a device to capture radiant energy; thus an evolutionary tendency toward higher body temperatures, or endothermy, may already have been under way. In any event, the Cotylosauria eventually gave rise to the Therapsida, in which we observe the beginnings of the evolution of the heterodont dentition. These mammal-like reptiles also developed two occipital condyles on the skull that articulated with the first vertebra.

In the fossil record of the Triassic, approximately 200 million years ago, the oldest known fossil mammals appear. These are grouped into the family Morganucodontidae. One such form, *Eozostrodon*, is known from a nearly complete skeleton as well as a skull. The articulation of the dentary with the cranium is nearly complete, thus setting the stage for the typical mammalian jaw articulation. This family can be referred to the order Triconodonta because of the distinctive molar cusps, which are arranged in linear series of three. None of these forms survived beyond the Jurassic, and they ranged in size from approximately 15 g to 2 kg.

Toward the end of the Jurassic, the Triconodonta were contemporaries with two other mammalian orders whose exact origin is unknown: the Multituberculata and the Docodonta. The latter group appeared very briefly in time and had a four-cusp molar. The Multituberculata were an exceedingly diverse group and are well represented to the Eocene. Their molar specializations indicate that they may well have been herbivores, and one family is characterized by a large, shearing third premolar that has a distinctive shape termed plagiaulacoid. About 150 million years ago, the Pantotheria appeared. Their teeth exhibit a basic three-cusp triangular pattern, and they are believed to be the stem group that gave rise to modern marsupials and placentals. The Multituberculata and the Pantotheria both appear in the fossil record of the late Cretaceous, perhaps 100 million years before the present (Lillegraven, Kielan-Jaworowska, and Clemans 1979).

As we pass from the Therapsida to the earliest mammals, the morganucodontids, we observe the following trends. First of all, there is a separation of hearing and mastication. In the mammal-like reptiles, the jawbone was composed of several components: the dentary, the angular, the articular, and the quadrate. The quadrate and the articular not only formed part of the jaw joint but also conducted sonic vibrations to the tympanum, supported by the angular. In turn, the stapes conducted sound from the tympanum to the cochlea. Clearly, bone conduction was involved in the hearing process. But as mammals underwent their evolution, the hearing function was separated completely from the jaw such that the quadrate became the incus, the angular became the tympanic bone, and the articular became the malleus. Thus, the classic three ear ossicles of mammals came to be enclosed in their own skull chamber away from direct contact with the jaw, and the dentary itself began to articulate with the squamosal, thereby freeing the inner ear to evolve independently of the masticatory apparatus. Apparently, hearing and its refinements went hand in hand with the evolution of nocturnality, in which both audition and olfaction became primary senses in locating prey (Crompton and Jenkins 1979).

The evolution of the cuspidate form of teeth and the differentiation of teeth into different functional types is tied to increasing efficiency both in grasping prey and in mastication. Traditionally the haplodont reptilian condition is considered primitive. The cusps are simple and the teeth conical, upper and lower teeth alternate, and the chewing movements are by and large up and down, with little movement horizontally. As one proceeds from this condition to the Mammalia, one finds a trend toward increasing lateral jaw movement by development of the muscles that attach the jaw to the pterygoid bones. This capacity for lateral movement offers two types of chewing: (1) chewing involving a crushing effect, and (2) shearing on one side or the other if the cusps are allowed to slide past one another as the jaw is moved laterally. Alternate movements of the jaw also involve forward and backward motion. Finally, the evolution of the so-called therian level of cusp development allows a mortar and pestle effect when the protocone of the trigon grinds against the talonid. Thus, the teeth ceased to be simply instruments for grasping and crushing and became instruments for the fine mastication of prey. Probably such evolution of cusps went hand in hand with the evolution of more efficient prey capture and digestion. Greater masticatory efficiency led to an overall ability to raise the metabolic rate. Hence the evolution of endothermy probably accompanied the adoption of a nocturnal habitus and specializations in food processing. It would appear, then, that as mammals began to evolve, they were specializing for feeding upon insects and for feeding at night, when competition with the coexisting, smaller therapsid reptiles was reduced (Eisenberg 1981; Lillegraven, Kielan-Jaworowska, and Clemans 1979).

Concomitant with the above morphological syndrome was evidently selection favoring a smaller body size. This change may have been the result of increasing specialization for insect prey of certain sizes, in which case a smaller body size would have increased foraging efficiency. No doubt at some point in this sequence of adaptation for nocturnality and insectivory, hair evolved, although the therapsids themselves may have had hair and may have already been on their way toward the evolution of endothermy.

The evolutionary trend away from multiple tooth replacements toward the restriction of two sets of teeth may have accompanied the evolution of lactation. Lactation by females could have resulted in the very rapid growth of young to near-adult proportions, thus relieving the necessity for multiple tooth replacements and in effect confining the tooth replacement to shortly after weaning and the attainment of adult size. Modern manatees, *Trichechus*, and elephants, Proboscidea, do replace teeth throughout life, but this phenomenon involves delayed eruption of molars. The loss of milk teeth in the extant marsupials may have been a secondary adaptation to the condition of obligate teat attachment, which accompanies the development of a pouch and a departure on the part of marsupials from producing eggs. This assumes that egg-laying, a condition still retained by the extant Monotremata, was characteristic of all earlier mammals prior to the marsupial-eutherian split (Eisenberg 1981).

The great diversification of the Mammalia began at the close of the Cretaceous and the beginning of the Paleocene period, which commenced some 70 million years ago, and concluded at the close of the Eocene some 50 million years ago. The adaptive radiations of the Mammalia at the close of the Cretaceous undoubtedly resulted from new genetic mutations and drastic alterations in selective pressures deriving from a major environmental perturbation (Lillegraven, Kielan-Jaworowska, and Clemans 1979; Eisenberg 1981).

At some point in the Cretaceous, marsupials and eutherians went their separate evolutionary ways. The next great branching occurred when the ancestors of the Edentata began their own separate course of evolution. They are recognizable in the Paleocene of South America. The South American edentates have had such a long evolutionary history that the contemporary forms bear little superficial resemblance to one another. Sloths, anteaters, and armadillos, however, clearly had a common ancestor. The African pangolins are sometimes considered closely related to the edentates, but most workers now feel that they had a quite dif-

ferent evolutionary history; nevertheless, their lineage is ancient (McKenna 1975; Eisenberg 1981).

The rest of the eutherian mammals show again a profound and ancient split, with the elephant shrews, rabbits, and hares branching off quite early; subsequently, the rodents appeared. The next great branching occurred when the Deltatheridia began a radiation into a carnivorous way of life. In fact, they were the earliest carnivorous mammals, but are not at all related to the true carnivores, which appear much later in time. By the time of the Eocene, four additional major stocks of eutherians were evolving. One would lead eventually to the modern-day carnivores; the second, to the insectivores; the third, to the tree shrews, bats, flying lemurs, and primates; and the fourth would begin to radiate into the herbivorous niches ultimately leading to the extant ungulates, proboscideans, and perissodactyls (Eisenberg 1981).

The cetaceans are believed to be closely allied to the so-called ungulate radiation, but their origin is still somewhat obscure. One can see that by the close of the Eocene all of the ordinal taxa of mammals had established lineages. Isolation due to continental drift had set the stage for independent evolutionary trends among the mammals of South America, Australia, and Madagascar. Continued continental drift was the major cause of the early distinctive continental faunas (Eisenberg 1981).

The Influence of Continental Drift

About 200 million years before the present, all the continents were united. A separation into northern and southern continents, namely, Laurasia and Gondwanaland, occurred approximately 180 million years ago. South America, Africa, Antarctica, and Australia made up the more or less contiguous southern landmass. South America and Africa then separated from this landmass 135 million years ago, and the separation of Antarctica from Australia and that of Africa from Madagascar occurred about 65 million years ago. Thus, Antarctica and Australia became isolated early on from the contiguous continental landmasses, as did South America. Africa, to some extent, was isolated until the Oligocene, and then became more firmly connected to Eurasia, with greater transfers of fauna between Africa and Eurasia in the Miocene. Although there were some sporadic contacts between South America and North America in the Paleocene and Miocene, the completion of the Panamanian land bridge in the Pliocene allowed for major continental faunal interchanges. There were intermittent connections between North America and northeastern Asia in the Eocene and Miocene, but the major connections and disconnections occurred in the Pliocene (Eisenberg 1981).

This early separation of the continental landmasses allowed distinctive faunas to evolve, especially on island continents such as South America and Australia. Indeed, Australia has served as a refugium for some of the earliest lines of phylogenetic descent among the mammals. In Australia we still find the order Monotremata, including the platypus, *Ornithorhynchus anatinus*, and the spiny anteaters or echidnas, Tachyglossidae, as well as a stunning adaptive radiation of marsupials. Marsupials were also distinctive elements of the old South American fauna, and some sixty-four species of small marsupials persist in South America to the present day.

Although early mammals were small, insectivorous, and probably nocturnal, once the dinosaurs became extinct at the close of the Cretaceous, many new opportunities for resource exploitation were opened for the endothermic mammals. From humble beginnings, mammals became specialized for an aquatic life, for a volant life, for feeding upon vegetation, for diurnal life, for arboreality, and all the other wonderful forms of adaptation that we see today. Even so, the more than four thousand species of extant mammals still show traces of their origins. For example, most mammals are small. A frequency distribution of mammalian total lengths, based on species averages, shows a strongly biased distribution toward the small end of the size scale. Considering the great diversity among rodents and bats, and recognizing that these constitute together 70% of all living species of mammals, it is no wonder that our mammals' average size tends to be small. In short, large mammals are represented by a relatively small number of species (Eisenberg 1981).

The Mammalian Trichotomy

The extant mammals represent three major subclasses defined by profound differences in their modes of reproduction. The Prototheria, represented by the platypus and spiny anteaters (echidnas), reproduce by means of laying eggs. In the case of the echidna, the egg is deposited in a pouch, where the female incubates it and the young is hatched. The platypus, on the other hand, digs a burrow in a streamside bank, lines a nesting chamber with vegetation, lays the egg in this nest, and then incubates it until hatching. Both platypus and echidna mothers nurse their young, but the milk is secreted from a series of small pores; the milk ducts are not organized in a common duct terminating in a nipple, as is characteristic of other mammalian taxa. It is believed that this egg-laying condition is a primitive character and may represent the condition shown by early mammals in the Jurassic.

The Metatheria, or marsupials, retain the egg within the uterus, where early embryonic development proceeds. The shell membrane remains intact, but nutrient exchange between the embryo and the mother can occur mediated by a yolk sac placenta, or in the case of bandicoots, *Peramelidae*, a chorioallantoic placenta that is functional for a brief time (Eisenberg 1981). Marsupials are lactation specialists in that intrauterine development is brief. At birth the young attach to a teat, and lactation is quite a long process. In most marsupials the teat area is enclosed in a pouch, but this character is not universal.

The eutherians, in general, have reduced the relative duration of lactation in favor of retaining the embryo for a longer period in the uterus. The elaboration of the embryonic trophoblast and the development of a chorioallantoic placenta with a long functional duration in eutherians means that a great deal of nutrient exchange can take place between the mother and the young. From this standpoint, eutherians may be viewed as gestational specialists. In any event, all three forms of reproduction have persisted for millions of years and appear equally efficient in the production of the next generation (Eisenberg 1981).

Conservative (Primitive) and Derived Mammals

Members of the various mammalian orders that have survived to the present exhibit an astonishing array of adaptations. Some species are carrying forward into the present time a conservative morphology and occupy ecological niches that probably do not differ very much from those of their original stock. On the other hand, the forces of natural selection have molded many taxa through time for increasing specializations for the exploitation of particular habitats. The modern toothed whales represent such an extreme specialization. They are entirely aquatic, have evolved sophisticated sonar systems used to locate prey under water, and some of the smaller dolphins exhibit astonishing cognitive abilities. Similarly, many of the modern pinnipeds are almost independent of land, have developed sophisticated communication systems, and again, show advanced cognitive abilities. These developments in aquatic mammals are paralleled by those in the higher primates. Since humans are members of this order, it is not surprising that in recent years increasing attention has been devoted to the ecology and behavioral capacities of the great apes, in particular, the orangutan, *Pongo pygmaeus*, chimpanzees, *Pan* spp., and gorilla, *Gorilla gorilla*. The anthropoid apes have attained a relatively large brain size and have been the subject of recent investigations concerning their ability to learn, and in general, manifest higher mental processes (Schusterman, Thomas, and Wood 1986).

While investigations of animal intelligence seem to center on those orders mentioned in the previous paragraph, many fruitful lines of research could be developed with other ordinal taxa. The flexibility of social organization in many mammals suggests an astonishing degree of adaptability based on individually acquired experience. The adaptive advantages of the wide variety of mating and rearing systems displayed by the Mammalia offer inviting arenas for investigation by biologists. Above all, however, mammals may be viewed by professional and amateur alike as marvelous products of the process of natural selection. A true aesthetic appreciation can develop when one views the individual behavior patterns of mammalian species as external manifestations of their highly perfected morphologies. As we come to know our fellow mammals better through increasing study, a sense of wonderment develops in all of us.

The Management of Mammalian Populations

Mammals have been important to humankind since the dawn of the human lineage. After all, we are mammals, and the sense of kinship has manifested itself in many ways. Some mammals have been predators on humans, and humans have been a predator on other mammals. We share many diseases with our kin. We have placed our fellow mammals in useful categories, useless categories, and even deified them in some cultures. As our technical abilities developed, we reached a stage during the Pleistocene when our ancestors were accomplished hunters. About 10,000 years ago, however, vast climatic changes, and perhaps our own activities, had reduced many other mammalian species, especially those that were used by us as food, to small relictual populations, and major extinction events began to occur.

Humans might not have been totally responsible for these events; nevertheless, in response to these dwindling resources, a great revolution occurred in human technology, namely, the domestication of plants and animals as food resources. Gathering activities had led to intimate knowledge of plant productivity cycles, and no doubt human hunters had often taken young animals into their camps as pets. The same phenomena can still be witnessed in the cultures of some indigenous South American Indians. While we will probably never understand the exact sequence of events in the domestication process, models have been proposed for describing domestication where archaeological evidence allows inferences concerning its stages.

Pires-Ferreria, Pires-Ferreria, and Kaulice (1976) propose the following sequence of events for the New World camelids: A generalized hunting culture of about 7,500 years ago began to hunt wild camelids. They gradually increased their knowledge of camelid territorial and social behavior and went on to become specialists in hunting camelids. Because of the territorial behavior of the vicuña, *Vicugna vicugna*, and guanaco, *Lama guanicöe*, the hunters were able to use this knowledge to develop a cropping scheme. This set the stage for control over breeding, and finally the herding of domestic camelids. From the wild guanaco this culture derived a pack animal, and through selective breeding, developed the alpaca, *Lama pacos*, as a special wool-producing variant of the guanaco stock. Domestication was apparently complete about 4,300 years ago.

Forestry and agronomy derive from Neolithic knowledge of plants. Modern-day wildlife management and animal husbandry derive from our ancestors' knowledge of natural history and the application of that knowledge to wild and, subsequently, domestic populations of animals. The maintenance of large collections of exotic animals that have no direct utility as food or as providers of any related economic function has occurred whenever human cultures have reached an advanced, urban state. The ancient Egyptians maintained collections of exotics, as did the Aztecs. In Europe, zoos, or menageries, sprang up in the eighteenth century in association with royalty and served as a means of displaying exotic creatures from lands that were being incorporated into a colonial system by the European powers. The first truly modern zoological parks were created in London and Paris during the early nineteenth century. Here, the object of exhibiting exotics was not just the entertainment and education of the public with respect to the products of the empire, but also a systematic attempt to study the biology of animals, living and dead. When an animal died at the London Zoo it was autopsied and ultimately transferred to the British Museum (Natural History). This system led not only to the description of new species, but also to detailed treatises on anatomy, and finally, to the preservation of museum specimens for future study. Thus the concept of the zoological park as a multifunctional institution became established in Western culture. The first modern zoological park in the United States opened in the city of Philadelphia in 1878 (Eisenberg 1979).

In North America, the problem of extinction of vast herds of big game with the opening of the West was readily appreciated at the close of the nineteenth century. At that time our first national park, Yellowstone, was established as a refuge for indigenous species that once had been widespread but now were extremely restricted. In particular, the plight of the American bison, *Bison bison,* was used to illustrate the need for propagation of endangered species in captivity (Hornaday 1913).

Forestry as a method of habitat manipulation and the practice of sustained-yield harvest of timber were imported from Europe and implemented in the United States at the turn of the century. Wildlife management, under the guidance of Aldo Leopold, developed into a full-blown science in the 1930s. Professionals trained in these two disciplines have primary oversight of the maintenance of natural diversity in North America and Europe. But as the wilderness areas of the world dwindle, humankind has been increasingly occupied with the preservation of a representative sample of the earth's biota. While the restoration and preservation of intact ecosystems may be an ideal goal, in some cases the situation has deteriorated to the point at which captive propagation of species seems to be the only effective means of preserving them (Leopold 1933; Osborn 1962).

The National Zoological Park in Washington, D.C., was established in 1889, in part to assist in conserving in captivity the vanishing wildlife of the western territories and states of the United States. The plight of the bison had highlighted similar problems faced by the bighorn sheep, *Ovis canadensis,* and the pronghorn antelope, *Antilocapra americana.* Although it was to be some years before the National Zoological Park achieved its potential, parallel developments were occurring in New York. The New York Zoological Society (now the Wildlife Conservation Society) secured a tract of land in the borough of the Bronx in 1896. William T. Hornaday had originally helped to establish the National Zoological Park, but a quarrel with Samuel Pierpont Langley, then secretary of the Smithsonian Institution, led Hornaday to resign in 1890, only to be appointed by Henry Fairfield Osborn as director of the Bronx Zoo some six years following his resignation in Washington. Both institutions through the years have contributed significantly to wildlife conservation programs (Osborn 1962; Hamlet 1985).

Thus, the lines between zoological parks, seminaturalistic breeding farms, and wildlife preserves have become somewhat blurred and their goals intertwined. The maintenance of captive populations has taken a new twist, and the definition of a zoological park is now a moot point. Mammals are now kept in captivity for a variety of reasons: to protect endangered species; to further the study of the biology of species that are difficult to study in the wild; to elucidate basic information on nutritional needs and reproductive physiology in a wide variety of species; and, finally, to establish new stocks of animals for laboratory purposes in full recognition of the extreme importance of mammals to the biomedical profession. Much is still to be learned, and the time is short.

In some sectors of our society, the ethics of maintaining mammals in captivity are being questioned. Aside from theoretical considerations that lie within the domain of philosophy, those of us that have entered the profession of zoological park management have in fact inherited captive populations from other generations of curators. The mammals over which we have custody in many cases can be maintained only in a captive state. In my mind there is no doubt that we must continue perpetuating these specimens to the best of our ability.

The second part of the question concerns whether we should introduce new specimens from the wild into extant collections. In the case of threatened and endangered species, this may be the only alternative to standing by and letting them become extinct.

There are many circumstances in which new species may need to be brought into captivity with the aim of future reintroductions into the wild. This is especially true for island species and continental species whose habitat has been fragmented to the point of extreme vulnerability. Smaller forms (less than 1 kg in weight) are good candidates for captive maintenance at relatively low cost. For example, the marsupial rabbit-eared bandicoot, *Macrotis lagotis,* and the barred bandicoot, *Perameles gunnii,* are recent success stories in Australia (J. Beck and R. Southgate, ITC VI, Sydney, pers. comm.). With a greater effort, the golden lion tamarin, *Leontopithecus rosalia,* was reintroduced into its original habitat (Kleiman et al. 1991). In the case of species already represented in collections, it may be necessary to import or introduce new specimens to maintain genetic heterozygosity at a healthy level in the confined populations. Decisions of this nature must, of course, be made on a case-by-case basis.

A balance must be maintained when opposing viewpoints become polarized. Those attempting to maintain a balance are truly the "peacemakers." This is certainly not the time to take an extremist position; rather, we are in the midst of an environmental crisis that demands a pragmatic approach. Above all, however, we owe it to those specimens in our care to provide the highest standard of maintenance and the best quality of life that we can offer.

References

Crompton, A. W., and Jenkins, F. A. Jr. 1979. Origin of mammals. In *Mesozoic mammals,* ed. J. A. Lillegraven, Z. Kielan-Jaworowska, and W. A. Clemans, 59–73. Berkeley: University of California Press.

Eisenberg, J. F. 1979. Different climates—Different zoos. In *A zoo for all seasons,* 154–69. Washington, D.C.: Smithsonian Exposition Books.

———. 1981. *The mammalian radiations.* Chicago: University of Chicago Press.

Hamlet, S. E. 1985. The National Zoological Park from its beginnings to 1973. Mimeographed.

Hornaday, W. T. 1913. *Our vanishing wildlife.* New York: Charles Scribner's Sons.

Kleiman, D. G., Beck, B. B., Dietz, J. M., and Dietz, L. A. 1991. Costs of a reintroduction and criteria for success: Accounting and accountability in the Golden Lion Tamarin Conservation Program. In *Beyond captive breeding: Re-introducing endangered species to the wild,* ed. J. H. W. Gipps. Oxford: Oxford University Press.

Leopold, A. 1933. *Game management.* New York: Charles Scribner's Sons.

Lillegraven, J. A., Kielan-Jaworowska, Z., and Clemans, W. A., eds. 1979. *Mesozoic mammals.* Berkeley: University of California Press.

McKenna, M. C. 1975. Toward a phylogenetic classification of the Mammalia. In *The phylogeny of primates,* ed. W. P. Luckett and F. S. Szalay, 21–46. New York: Plenum.

Osborn, H. F. 1962. *Our crowded planet.* Garden City, N.Y.: Doubleday.

Pires-Ferreria, J. W., Pires-Ferreria, E., and Kaulice, P. 1976. Preceramic animal utilization in the central Peruvian Andes. *Science* 197:483–90.

Schusterman, R. J., Thomas, J. A., and Wood, F. G., eds. 1986. *Dolphin cognition and behavior: A comparative approach.* Hillsdale, N.J.: Lawrence Erlbaum Associates.

Appendix 2
Annotated Bibliography and Journals of Captive Management

KAY A. KENYON AND MICHAELE M. ROBINSON

This appendix contains an annotated bibliography of books and a list of serials relevant to the subjects covered in this volume. It is organized into the following subject categories: General Reference, Basic Husbandry, Nutrition, Exhibitry, Population Management for Conservation, Behavior, Reproduction, and Captive Mammal Research, plus a list of relevant periodicals. Many of the books in each section overlap in subject matter with those in other sections, so it is advisable to look at the entire list.

This bibliography is intended for zoo staff, researchers, mammalogists, students, and zoo librarians. It is by no means complete, but should serve as a basic list of information sources on captive wild mammals. A more extensive list entitled *Recommended List of Books and Other Information Sources for Zoo and Aquarium Libraries* (3d ed., 1995) is maintained by Kay Kenyon with contributions from other zoo and aquarium librarians.

GENERAL REFERENCE

Allen, G. A. 1938–40. *The Mammals of China and Mongolia.* 2 vols. (Natural History of Central Asia, vol. 11.) New York: The American Museum of Natural History.

   The only authoritative and complete treatment of the mammalian fauna of this region published in English to date.

AZA (formerly *AAZPA*) *Annual Conference Proceedings* and *AZA Regional Conference Proceedings.* 19–. (Published annually.) Wheeling, W.Va.: American Zoo and Aquarium Association.

   Each volume contains papers presented by zoo and aquarium personnel at regional and annual conferences. Topics include mammals, zoo management, conservation, research, and education. One of the few publications that deals exclusively with zoos and aquariums.

Bjarvall, A., and S. Ullstrom. 1986. *Mammals of Britain and Europe.* London: Croom Helm. 240 pp.

   Comprehensive summaries of the indigenous and introduced land and sea mammal species of Britain and Europe. The text provides information for identification as well as discussing the biology, ecology, conservation, and aspects of the economic importance of each species. Beautifully illustrated with accurate and clear drawings and distribution maps.

Chapman, J. A., and G. A. Feldhamer, eds. 1982. *Wild Mammals of North America: Biology, Management, and Economics.* Baltimore, Md.: Johns Hopkins University Press. 1,147 pp.

   This volume addresses species' biology and ecology for wild-

At the time of writing, Michaele M. Robinson was with the Ernst Schwarz Library, Zoological Society of San Diego.

life management. Provides information for each species on nomenclature, distribution, description, physiology, genetics, reproduction, development, ecology, food habits, behavior, economic status and management, and a bibliography.

Corbet, G. B., and J. E. Hill. 1992. *The Mammals of the Indomalayan Region: A Systematic Review.* New York: Oxford University Press. 488 pp.

   Updates Chasen's (1940) *Handlist of Malaysian Mammals* and Ellerman and Morrison-Scott's (1951) *Checklist of Palearctic and Indian Mammals 1758–1946.* Covers 1,041 species in the Indomalayan (or Oriental) region. Diagnostic characteristics and distributions for each genus, species, and subspecies are given with references to appropriate works. A working tool that every mammalian systematist should have.

Eisenberg, J. F. 1981. *The Mammalian Radiations: An Analysis of Trends in Evolution, Adaptation, and Behavior.* Chicago: University of Chicago Press. 610 pp.

   The evolution, adaptations, and behavior of mammals. The section on behavior is especially useful for the zoo professional. It covers such topics as social interactions, courtship and sexual behavior, parental care, and play behavior.

Eisenberg, J. F. 1989. *Mammals of the Neotropics.* Vol. 1. 449 pp. Redford, K. H., and Eisenberg, J. F. 1992. Vol. 2. 430 pp. Chicago: University of Chicago Press.

   A comprehensive guide to the mammals of South America and the Republic of Panama. Species accounts include description, distribution, natural history, measurements, range, and habitat. Drawings and maps are included. A monumental and thorough reference work on a topic never fully covered before in the literature.

Estes, R. D. 1991. *The Behavior Guide to African Mammals.* Berkeley: University of California Press. 611 pp.

   A unique, comprehensive survey of the taxonomy, distribution, and description as well as the ecology and behavior of large African mammals. The section on ungulates is particularly thorough.

Ewer, R. F. 1973. *The Carnivores.* Ithaca, N.Y.: Cornell University Press. 494 pp.

   A classic work on the functional anatomy and behavior of the large cats, bears, and other carnivore groups. For both the general and the professional reader.

Genoways, H. H., ed. 1987–. v. 1–. *Current Mammalogy.* New York: Plenum Press.

   Two volumes of this series have been published so far. Contains research papers on topics ranging from genetics to systematics, physiology, ecology, and behavior.

Gittleman, J. L., ed. 1989. *Carnivore Behavior, Ecology, and Evolution.* Ithaca, N.Y.: Comstock. 620 pp.

A comprehensive volume on carnivore biology. Papers discuss such topics as the role of odor in the social lives of carnivores, mating tactics and spacing patterns of solitary carnivores, adaptations for aquatic living, and the physiology and evolution of delayed implantation.

Grzimek, B. 1990. *Grzimek's Encyclopedia of Mammals.* 5 vols. New York: McGraw-Hill. (Translation of *Grzimeks Enzyklopädie Säugetiere,* Kindler Verlag, 1988.)

These five volumes replace *Grzimek's Animal Life Encyclopedia,* vols. 11–13, *Mammals.* Packed full of excellent color photos, maps, diagrams, and summary boxes. Useful for anyone interested in mammals at any level.

International Zoo Yearbook. 1959–. Vol. 1–. London: Zoological Society of London.

This is an annual collection of articles on captive management and new developments in the zoo world (husbandry, breeding, buildings, exhibits, etc). Appendices list captive animals bred, rare animals in captivity, and studbooks. Periodically a volume will also include a world directory of zoos and aquariums. A very important resource for the animal manager. A listing of the special subjects featured in *International Zoo Yearbook* between 1959 and 1993 is given in table A2.1.

Kingdon, J. 1971–1982. *East African Mammals: An Atlas of Evolution in Africa.* 7 vols. Chicago: University of Chicago Press.

This seven-volume work provides a natural history account of each species of mammal living in East Africa. Distribution maps and many excellent drawings are included.

Lever, C. 1985. *Naturalized Mammals of the World.* New York: Longman. 487 pp.

Contains species accounts of mammal introductions and their effects on native biota. Old and new range maps are included for each species. One of the few books on this neglected but important topic.

MacDonald, D., ed. 1984. *The Encyclopedia of Mammals.* New York: Facts on File. 895 pp.

Written by internationally acclaimed experts, this work contains facts on animal behavior, conservation, ecology, and the latest fieldwork for over 700 species representing all orders of mammals. Beautiful color photographs and drawings supplement the text.

Mammalian Species. 1969–. no. 1–. New York: American Society of Mammalogists.

A continuing series of brief but comprehensive species accounts prepared by recognized experts in the field. Information on each species includes classification, characteristics, distribution, form and function, ontogeny and reproduction, ecology, genetics, behavior, a bibliography, and comments. An invaluable reference for researchers.

Napier, J. R., and P. H. Napier. 1985. *The Natural History of Primates.* Cambridge, Mass.: MIT Press. 200 pp.

General survey of primate morphology, evolution, and ethology with brief descriptive accounts for each genus.

Nowak, R. M. 1991. *Walker's Mammals of the World.* 5th ed. 2 vols. Baltimore, Md.: Johns Hopkins University Press.

Provides basic natural history facts and descriptions for over 1,000 living mammalian genera and 4,000 species. In this fifth revised and expanded edition, all new information includes citations of specific references. Photographs or drawings are provided for each species.

Prater, S. H. 1980. *The Book of Indian Animals.* 3d rev. ed. Bombay: Bombay Natural History Society. 324 pp.

The mammalian fauna of India, Pakistan, Sri Lanka, and the surrounding border regions. An introduction to each family covered includes its natural history, physical characteristics, behav-

TABLE A2.1. Special Subjects Featured in *International Zoo Yearbook* between 1959 and 1993

Volume	Subject
1	Apes in captivity*
2	Elephants, hippopotamuses, and rhinoceroses in captivity*
3	Small mammals in captivity*
4	Aquatic exhibits in zoos and aquaria*
5	Ungulates in captivity*
6	Nutrition of animals in captivity*
7	Penguins in captivity*
8	(reprint): Canids and felids in captivity
9	(reprint): Amphibians and reptiles in captivity
10	Birds of prey in captivity*
11	Marsupials in captivity*
12	South American primates in captivity
13	Waterfowl in captivity*
14	Animal trade and transport
15	Small mammals in captivity
16	Principles of zoo animal feeding
17	Breeding endangered species in captivity (second conference)
18	Penguins
19	Reptiles
20	Breeding endangered species in captivity (third conference)
21	Zoo display and information techniques
22	New World primates
23	Birds of prey
24/25	Breeding endangered species in captivity (fourth conference)
26	Aquatic exhibits
27	Conservation science and zoos
28	Reptiles and amphibians
29	Horticulture in zoos
30	Invertebrates
31	Australasian fauna
32	Ungulates

* Out of print

ior and habitats, and interactions with conspecifics and other species. Well illustrated.

Ridgeway, S. H., and Sir R. J. Harrison, eds. 1981–1989. *Handbook of Marine Mammals.* 4 vols. New York: Academic Press.

This well-illustrated series is meant for field and laboratory use as a practical aid to identification and to provide basic information. Volumes published to date include Vol. 1, *The Walrus, Sea Lions, Fur Seals, and Sea Otter;* Vol. 2, *Seals;* Vol. 3, *Sirenians and Baleen Whales;* and Vol. 4, *River Dolphins and Larger Toothed Whales.* Includes chapters on taxonomy, evolution, external and internal characteristics, distribution and abundance, behavior, life history and reproduction, diseases, and exploitation and protection.

Smithers, R. H. N. 1983. *The Mammals of the Southern African Subregion.* Pretoria, South Africa: University of Pretoria. 736 pp.

Covers the mammals of Namibia, Botswana, Zimbabwe, Mozambique, and the Republic of South Africa. Each entry is provided with complete natural history information and a color illustration. An excellent companion to Kingdon's *East African Mammals.*

Smuts, B. B., D. L. Cheney, R. M. Seyfarth, R. W. Wrangham, and T. T. Struhsaker, eds. 1987. *Primate Societies.* Chicago: University of Chicago Press. 578 pp.

A review of field studies on nonhuman primates. General descriptions of taxonomic groups with emphasis on social behavior are followed by essays on socioecology and communication in primates.

Strahan, R., ed. 1983. *The Australian Museum Complete Book of Australian Mammals*. Sydney: Agus & Robertson. 530 pp.

A basic reference on native and introduced mammals of Australia and Tasmania. Range maps and excellent color photographs are provided.

Walton, D. W., and B. J. Richardson, eds. 1989. *Fauna of Australia*. Vol. 1B. *Mammalia*. Canberra: Australian Government Publishing Service. 1,224 pp.

A comprehensive description of the morphology, physiology, and ethology of the Australian mammal families, with extensive bibliographies.

Wilson, D. E., and D. M. Reeder. 1993. *Mammal Species of the World: A Taxonomic and Geographic Reference*. 2d ed. Washington, D.C.: Smithsonian Institution Press. 1,206 pp.

A checklist of the world's mammal species. Each species account provides scientific name and authority, type locality, distribution, comments, and protected status (for some). A valuable tool for researchers.

BASIC HUSBANDRY

American Association of Zoo Keepers. 1992. *Biological Values for Selected Mammals*. 3d ed. Topeka, Kans.: American Association of Zoo Keepers, Inc.

This handy and informative publication contains biological data on 457 species of mammals. Included are common name, scientific name, geographic range, normal adult size and weight, estrous cycle, gestation period, number of young, weaning, sexual maturity, pulse and respiration rate, and names used for the male, female, and young of each species. Ideal for quick reference.

American Association of Zoo Veterinarians. 1976–. *Proceedings of the Annual Meeting of the American Association of Zoo Veterinarians*. Atlanta, Ga.: AAZV.

Papers from the annual meetings of the AAZV. One of the few sources of information on zoo animal medicine.

Cheville, N. F. 1988. *Introduction to Veterinary Pathology*. Ames: Iowa State University Press. 537 pp.

Although this book is intended for the beginning student of veterinary pathology, it is also of value to curators and managers. Its focus is on pathophysiology of diseases, and it includes discussions of commonly used pathology terms. It is clearly written and exceptionally well illustrated.

Crandall, L. S. 1964. *The Management of Wild Mammals in Captivity*. Chicago: University of Chicago Press. 761 pp.

A comprehensive guide to mammal husbandry. Provides information on general care, diet, history in captivity, exhibit techniques, and propagation.

Davis, J. W., L. H. Karstad, and D. O. Trainer, eds. 1981. *Infectious Diseases of Wild Mammals*. 2d ed. Ames: Iowa State University Press. 446 pp.

Contributions from forty-seven authors. Part 1 covers viral diseases; part 2, bacterial, rickettsial, and mycotic diseases; and part 3, neoplastic diseases. Discussion of each disease includes information on synonyms, distribution and hosts, etiology, transmission, signs, pathogenesis, pathology, diagnosis, prognosis, treatment and control, and an extensive bibliography. Well supplemented with descriptive material.

Diersauf, L. A., ed. 1990. *Handbook of Marine Mammal Medicine*. Boca Raton, Fla.: CRC Press.

Wide in scope, this book covers information on medicine, surgery, pathology, physiology, husbandry, feeding, housing, and strandings and rehabilitation of marine mammals. Includes polar bears, otters, and whales. An excellent reference for the veterinarian as well as the animal caretaker.

Erkrankungen der Zootiere (International Symposium on Diseases in Zoo Animals). 1959–. Berlin: Akademie Verlag.

Proceedings from the annual international symposia held in Europe. Papers are primarily in English and German. Covers diseases affecting animals in captive collections. One of the few available sources on this specialized topic.

Ettinger, S. J., ed. 1989. *Textbook of Veterinary Internal Medicine: Diseases of the Dog and Cat*. 3d ed. 2 vols. Philadelphia: W. B. Saunders. 2,400 pp.

Although intended for the practicing veterinarian, this classic textbook will be useful to all professionals concerned with diseases of mammals. This completely rewritten edition includes sections on manifestations of clinical disease, infectious diseases, therapeutic considerations, cancer neoplasia, and diseases of the various organ systems.

Flecknell, P. A. 1987. *Laboratory Animal Anesthesia: An Introduction for Research Workers and Technicians*. San Diego, Calif.: Academic Press. 156 pp.

This handbook provides a basic guide to anesthesia and is intended for research workers and animal technicians. Sections deal with preoperative care, anesthetic techniques, anesthetic management, and postoperative management. Appendices include anesthetic techniques and physiological data, and drug dose rates.

Fowler, M. E., ed. 1986. *Zoo and Wild Animal Medicine*. 2d ed. Philadelphia: W. B. Saunders. 1,127 pp.

A complete revision of the first edition, this is the most up-to-date, authoritative text on veterinary medicine of captive exotic animals. More than eighty authors have contributed their knowledge and expertise on diseases, nutrition, parasites, husbandry, reproduction, restraint, pathology, and preventive medicine. Highly recommended for veterinarians who work with exotics.

Fowler, M. E. 1993. *Zoo and Wild Animal Medicine: Current Therapy 3*. Philadelphia: W. B. Saunders. 635 pp.

A complementary volume to *Zoo and Wild Animal Medicine* (2d ed). Recent clinical developments are discussed, and there are new chapters on game farming and animal welfare. Special attention is given to elephants and reproductive problems of camelids.

Fox, J. G., ed. 1988. *Biology and Diseases of the Ferret*. Philadelphia: Lea & Febiger. 345 pp.

Although this work contains data applicable to the biology, management, and diseases of ferrets, it should be considered a text on the entire family Mustelidae. Sections on biology and husbandry (with emphasis on anatomy and nutrition), diseases and clinical applications, and research applications are included. Well illustrated, with many anatomical drawings.

Griner, L. A. 1983. *Pathology of Zoo Animals: A Review of Necropsies Conducted over a Fourteen-Year Period at the San Diego Zoo and San Diego Wild Animal Park*. San Diego, Calif.: Zoological Society of San Diego. 608 pp.

A brief description of each particular order and family is followed by a chart listing the species and number of specimens necropsied. This is followed by discussion of various examinations according to disease type. A good cross-section of pathology data on a large zoo animal collection.

Hand, S. J., ed. 1990. *Care and Handling of Australian Native Animals*. Chipping Norton, N.S.W., Australia: Surrey Beatty and Sons. 210 pp.

A practical guide to animal care, including emergency first aid, caging and enclosure requirements, diets, breeding, handling, marking, and diseases and parasites. Nicely illustrated with numerous drawings and photos.

Harkness, J. E., and J. E. Wagner. 1989. *The Biology and Medicine of Rabbits and Rodents.* 3d ed. Philadelphia: Lea & Febiger. 230 pp.

A basic text for laboratory medicine. Coverage includes rabbits, guinea pigs, mice, rats, hamsters, and gerbils. Intended to bridge the gap between monographs on various laboratory species and periodical articles. Emphasis is on practical aspects of rabbit and rodent care and health. Substantial detail is provided on biology and husbandry, clinical signs and procedures, specific diseases, and their diagnoses.

Hediger, H. 1964. *Wild Animals in Captivity.* New York: Dover. 207 pp.

This classic provides the foundation for the study of zoo biology. Discusses animal behavior and the basic principles of managing captive wild animals in terms of space requirements, diet, and animal-human relationships. Though old, still useful today.

Hediger, H. 1968. *The Psychology and Behaviour of Animals in Zoos and Circuses.* New York: Dover. 166 pp.

This collection of essays on animal psychology is based on the author's own experiences and observations. Included is the daily behavior of animals in the wild as well as that of animals in zoos and circuses. Useful for anyone dealing with exotic animals.

Hediger, H. 1969. *Man and Animal in the Zoo: Zoo Biology.* London: Routledge & Kegan Paul. 303 pp.

A supplement to the author's previous book, *Wild Animals in Captivity.* Discusses animal behavior and the basic principles of managing captive animals.

Klös, H. G., and E. M. Lang. 1982. *Handbook of Zoo Medicine: Diseases and Treatment of Wild Animals in Zoos, Game Parks, Circuses, and Private Collections.* New York: Van Nostrand Reinhold. 453 pp.

This is a translation of *Zootierkrankheiten,* originally published by Verlag Paul Parey, Berlin, in 1976. It includes contributions from twenty-two European veterinarians. A general section discusses the role of the zoo veterinarian, veterinary facilities and equipment, immobilization and injection, and nutrition. The remainder of the book is divided into special sections by taxon, under which are headings for special comments, chemical restraint, parasites, infections, organic and deficiency diseases, hand rearing and diseases of the young, and surgical procedures and obstetrics.

Markowitz, H. 1982. *Behavioral Enrichment in the Zoo.* New York: Van Nostrand Reinhold. 210 pp.

Describes innovative programs that encourage activity in captive animals. Should challenge zoos to use these programs as well as find other methods to enrich the lives of animals in zoos.

Montali, R. J., and G. Migaki, eds. 1980. *The Comparative Pathology of Zoo Animals.* (Proceedings of a symposium held at the National Zoological Park, Smithsonian Institution, 2–4 October 1978.) Washington, D.C.: Smithsonian Institution Press. 684 pp.

A collection of eighty-eight papers presented by leading researchers at a symposium on zoo animal diseases and disease mechanisms. Good reference lists are included with each chapter. A welcome addition to the scattered literature of zoo animal medicine.

Morrow, D. A., ed. 1986. *Current Therapy in Theriogenology: Diagnosis, Treatment, and Prevention of Reproductive Diseases in Small and Large Animals.* 2d ed. Philadelphia: W. B. Saunders. 1,143 pp.

This 1,143-page volume is the most authoritative and informative reference source available on the reproductive conditions of animals. It also supplements existing publications on theriogenology. Included are sections on hormone and antibiotic therapy, embryo transfer, cytogenetics, reproductive problems of animal species, and diagnostic procedures.

Paddleford, R. R., ed. 1988. *Manual of Small Animal Anesthesia.* New York: Churchill Livingstone. 344 pp.

This practical guide for the clinician is presented in an outline format to provide information in an easily retrievable form. Some of the topics covered include controlled ventilation and mechanical ventilators, emergencies and complications (with a pharmacology of emergency drugs), and fluid, electrolyte, and acid-base anesthesia for reptiles, birds, primates, and small exotic mammals.

Pedersen, N. C. 1988. *Feline Infectious Diseases.* Goleta, Calif.: American Veterinary Publications. 404 pp.

The first textbook devoted exclusively to this subject. Five well-illustrated sections cover viral diseases; bacterial diseases; mycoplasmal, rickettsial, chlamydial, and L-form diseases; fungal diseases (mycoses); and parasitic diseases.

Schmidt, R. E., and G. B. Hubbard. 1987. *Atlas of Zoo Animal Pathology.* 2 vols. Boca Raton, Fla: CRC Press.

This atlas focuses on the histology of lesions of zoo animals. It is organized according to organ systems and is designed as a pictorial reference for the zoo animal veterinarian or pathologist. Volume 1 covers mammals, and volume 2 covers avian, reptilian, and miscellaneous species.

Segal, E. F., ed. 1989. *Housing, Care, and Psychological Well-Being of Captive and Laboratory Primates.* Park Ridge, N.J.: Noyes. 544 pp.

Details the maintenance of captive primates, describing practical solutions to problems and methods for providing environmental enrichment. Discusses specifics for each family, including natural history, social grouping patterns, reproductive behavior, diet and growth, medical problems, and individual case studies.

Slijper, E. J. 1976. *Whales and Dolphins.* Ann Arbor, Mich.: University of Michigan Press. 170 pp.

A good general book on whales and dolphins. Information is provided on breathing and diving, blood circulation, behavior, nutrition and digestion, and reproduction. Photos and illustrations are included. Could still be considered one of the best on this topic for the zoo professional.

Wallach, J. D., and J. B. Williams. 1983. *Diseases of Exotic Animals: Medical and Surgical Management.* Philadelphia: W. B. Saunders. 1,159 pp.

An extensive review of the diseases of mammals, birds, reptiles and amphibians, and tropical fishes, arranged by taxonomic order. Covers anatomy, physiology, and diagnosis and treatment, with a heavy emphasis on nutrition. Each chapter contains a brief description of the genera of the order and a classification table, charts of biological normals, housing requirements, diseases, reproduction, specialized surgical procedures, and an extensive bibliography.

NUTRITION

Bunn, S., ed. 1988. *American Association of Zoo Keepers, Inc. Diet Notebook.* Vol. 1. *Mammals.* Topeka, Kans.: American Association of Zoo Keepers, Inc.

A compilation of diets for captive exotic mammals written by staff of North American zoos. Includes contributor and institution, ISIS number, diet, preparation instructions, notes and remarks, and (for some) nutritional analysis. A handy manual for zoos, even though the diets are not screened and no judgment of nutritional quality has been made.

Burger, I. H., and J. P. W. Rivers, eds. 1989. *Nutrition of the Dog and Cat.* New York: Cambridge University Press. 417 pp.

A compilation of papers on the principles of feeding these domestic animals, including studies of clinical nutrition.

Church, D. C. 1991. *Livestock Feeds and Feeding.* 3d ed. Englewood Cliffs, N.J.: Prentice Hall. 546 pp.

A good introduction to the nutrition and feeding of livestock, including the chemical composition and animal utilization of feedstuffs, and nutrient needs of animals as affected by genetic and environmental factors.

Dr. Scholl Nutrition Conference. 1980–. *Proceedings of the Dr. Scholl Conference on the Nutrition of Captive Wild Animals.* Chicago: Lincoln Park Zoological Society.

Subjects covered in these biannual proceedings range from general nutrition of exotic animals to requirements of individual species and families. One of the few sources of information about nutrition of exotic animals.

Hacker, J. B., and J. H. Ternouth, eds. 1987. *Nutrition of Herbivores.* San Diego, Calif.: Academic Press. 552 pp.

A series of reviews on factors affecting digestion and metabolism in a wide range of wild and domestic herbivores.

Hofmann, R. R. 1973. *The Ruminant Stomach: Stomach Structure and Feeding Habits of East African Game Ruminants.* Nairobi, Kenya: East African Literature Bureau. 354 pp.

Contains information on the anatomy and physiology of the digestive systems and the feeding habits of twenty-six species of East African wild ruminants. Good illustrations.

Hume, I. D. 1982. *Digestive Physiology and Nutrition of Marsupials.* New York: Cambridge University Press. 256 pp.

Organized into the various groups of marsupials by their dietary habits (carnivores, omnivores, herbivores). Topics include fermentation, metabolism, minerals, and vitamins.

Langer, P. 1988. *Mammalian Herbivore Stomach: Comparative Anatomy, Function, and Evolution.* New York: G. Fischer. 557 pp.

A highly technical and detailed account of the functional anatomy of the stomachs of large mammals. Included are even-toed ungulates, sirenians, tree sloths, leaf-eating monkeys, and kangaroos. Good functional diagrams and black-and-white photographs of stomach anatomy.

Montgomery, G. G., ed. 1978. *The Ecology of Arboreal Folivores.* (A symposium held at the Conservation and Research Center, National Zoological Park, Smithsonian Institution, 29–31 May 1975.) Washington, D.C.: Smithsonian Institution Press. 574 pp.

Papers given at a symposium that addressed plant ecology and animal adaptations for feeding on leaves. A guide to the captive management of mammals such as monkeys and koalas.

Robbins, C. T. 1993. *Wildlife Feeding and Nutrition.* 2d ed. San Diego, Calif.: Academic Press. 352 pp.

Reviews the basic principles of nutrition for free-ranging and captive wild animals.

Stevens, C. E. 1988. *Comparative Physiology of the Vertebrate Digestive System.* New York: Cambridge University Press. 300 pp.

Describes characteristics of the digestive system for major groups of vertebrates and various adaptations for ingestion and digestion of food and absorption of nutrients.

Van Soest, P. J. 1988. *Nutritional Ecology of the Ruminant.* Ithaca, N.Y.: Cornell University Press. 384 pp.

A basic text on chemical analysis of forages and the digestion and metabolism of ruminants.

EXHIBITRY

Hancocks, D. 1971. *Animals and Architecture.* New York: Praeger. 200 pp.

A history of zoological garden architecture. Well illustrated with drawings and photographs of exhibits, from old farm buildings and menageries to state-of-the-art exhibits of our time. Includes a chapter on animal architecture. Stresses naturalistic enclosures. Though older, it is a classic in this small field of literature.

International Symposium on Zoo Design and Construction. 1975, 1976, 1980, 1992. *Zoo Design 1, 2,* and *3* and *Zoo Design and Construction.* (Proceedings of the International Symposium on Zoo Design and Construction held at Paignton Zoological and Botanical Gardens and Oldway Mansion, Paignton, Devon, England.)

These four volumes contain papers given and a summary of the discussions at four international symposia attended by zoo directors, curators, architects, and other zoo staff. Papers address such topics as general principles of zoo design, quarters for large aquatic mammals, indoor exhibits, the use of glass, facilities for visitors, the use of plants, building zoos in regions of extreme temperatures, and redesigning old zoos.

Polakowski, K. J. 1987. *Zoo Design: The Reality of Wild Illusions.* Ann Arbor: University of Michigan, School of Natural Resources. 193 pp.

A compendium of design concepts for zoos from professionals who participated in a landscape architecture design course. Discussed are such topics as design philosophies in the past and present, carrying out the goals of the zoo through the design of exhibits, long-range development planning, presenting themes in exhibits, and using plants for both animals and people. One of the few books on this topic.

Sausman, K., ed. 1982. *Zoological Park and Aquarium Fundamentals.* Wheeling, W.Va.: American Association of Zoological Parks and Aquariums. 356 pp.

Contributors to this volume provide basic information for the successful design, development, and overall operation of the modern zoo and aquarium.

POPULATION MANAGEMENT FOR CONSERVATION

AZA Manual of Federal Wildlife Regulations. 1994. Bethesda, Md.: American Zoo and Aquarium Association.

This two-volume set is a guide to all federally and internationally protected wildlife species. It includes laws and regulations applicable to their exhibition or holding, transportation, and trade. Volume 1 contains all protected species listed at national or international levels. Volume 2, parts A and B contain the text of the laws and regulations governing the species listed in volume 1.

Bean, M. J. 1983. *The Evolution of National Wildlife Law.* Rev. and expanded ed. New York: Praeger. 449 pp.

This revised and expanded edition provides the layperson as well as the lawyer with a comprehensive account of the development of wildlife conservation law in the United States. It discusses such subjects as the Endangered Species Act, regulations on the taking of wildlife, and the protection of marine mammals.

Benirschke, K., ed. 1986. *Primates: The Road to Self-Sustaining Populations.* New York: Springer-Verlag. 1,044 pp.

The published proceedings of a conference, this book brings together current knowledge of the status of primates in nature and their reproductive needs in captivity. A solid basis for future conservation actions, it should be of interest to scientists, students, conservationists, and managers of zoos.

Captive Breeding Specialist Group. 1988. *Proceedings of the Annual Meeting.* (Held 10–11 September 1988 in Stuttgart.) Apple Valley, Minn.: Captive Breeding Specialist Group, Species Survival Commission, IUCN.

Contains a collection of letters, article reprints, status reports, statements, survival plans, laws, and programs relating to selected endangered species and geographic areas. Loose-leaf format.

Convention on International Trade in Endangered Species of Wild Fauna and Flora. 1980. *Guidelines for Transport and Preparation for Shipment of Live Wild Animals and Plants.* New York: United Nations Environment Programme. 109 pp.

A practical manual for the transportation of wild animals and plants, with particular reference to CITES-protected species. It includes transport information for animals often restricted by air carriers (e. g., large terrestrial mammals and reptiles) and even illustrates the placement of the animal within the container.

Ester, C., and K. W. Sessions, eds. 1992 (vol. 1, 2d ed.), 1983 (vol. 2–3). *Controlled Wildlife: A Three-Volume Guide to U.S. Wildlife Laws and Permit Procedures.* Lawrence, Kans.: Association of Systematics Collections, Museum of Natural History.

This three-volume guide provides simple explanations of U.S. wildlife laws. Volume 1 discusses the general requirements and permits, such as quarantine, customs clearance, and welfare, needed to conduct specific animal transactions. Volume 2 lists federally controlled animals and the laws that govern their use. Volume 3 summarizes major state wildlife laws and regulations. It also lists key contact people and legal sources for each state. An important set of volumes for those involved in transporting animals.

Gipps, J. H. W., ed. 1991. *Beyond Captive Breeding: Reintroducing Endangered Mammals to the Wild.* (Symposia of the Zoological Society of London, no. 62.) Oxford: Clarendon Press. 284 pp.

An examination of the theory and practice of reintroduction with detailed case studies of the Arabian oryx, red wolf, and black-footed ferret. One of the few books on this expanding field.

Goodwin, H., and C. Holloway. 1966 edition, completely revised in 1971 with new and revised sheets in 1973, 1974, and 1976. *IUCN Red Data Book.* Vol. 1. *Mammalia.* Morges, Switzerland: IUCN.

Short reports on the status of threatened species of mammals. Each sheet provides data on status, distribution, population, habitat, and conservation measures taken and proposed for each species. Although still the international authority for threatened species, much of this edition is outdated.

Hearn, J. P., and J. K. Hodges, eds. 1985. *Advances in Animal Conservation.* (Symposia of the Zoological Society of London, no. 54.) New York: Oxford University Press. 282 pp.

Proceedings of a symposium sponsored by the Zoological Society of London. The volume is divided into four major sections: conservation in the wild, conservation in captivity, conservation and comparative medicine, and government and conservation.

Hoage, R. J., ed. 1985. *Animal Extinctions: What Everyone Should Know.* Washington, D.C.: Smithsonian Institution Press. 192 pp.

A series of twelve papers presented at a public symposium at the National Zoological Park. Discussion focuses on the complex issues surrounding the extinction of species in the wild. Some interesting solutions are suggested. The role of zoos in preserving wildlife is also discussed.

International Air Transport Association. 1973–. *Live Animal Regulations.* Montreal: International Air Transport Association.

An annual guide to shipping live animals on international and intranational airlines. Specific requirements and types of shipping containers for each species are listed. The remaining sections contain general information on behavior, sedation, and accompanying personnel; shipping procedures and samples of required forms; requirements for cleaning, feeding, and loading; and individual carrier regulations and restrictions.

Lee, P. C., J. Thornback, and E. L. Bennett. 1988. *Threatened Primates of Africa: The IUCN Red Data Book.* Cambridge: IUCN Conservation Monitoring Centre. 153 pp.

Another volume in the IUCN Red Data Book series. Provides the most up-to-date information available on the conservation status of African primates. Detailed species accounts are provided for thirty threatened primates along with a summary of captive breeding efforts and a list of references.

Lyster, Simon. 1985. *International Wildlife Law: An Analysis of International Treaties Concerned with the Conservation of Wildlife.* Cambridge: Grotius. 470 pp.

An in-depth study that details the purposes and provisions of the major international and regional treaties relating to wildlife conservation. The first half of the book analyzes the individual treaties and the second half contains the actual texts.

Moore, H. D. M., W. V. Holt, and G. M. Mace. 1992. *Biotechnology and the Conservation of Genetic Diversity.* Oxford: Clarendon Press. 240 pp.

Recent advances in reproductive techniques such as artificial insemination, cryopreservation, and DNA fingerprinting are discussed in relation to management of captive populations.

Pringle, J. A. 1983. *The Conservationists and the Killers: The Story of Game Protection and the Wildlife Society of Southern Africa.* Cape Town: T. V. Bulpin and Books of Africa, Ltd. 319 pp.

This book tells of the struggle between conservationists and hunters to determine the fate of southern Africa's wildlife. It begins with the arrival of white settlers at the Cape in 1652, and chronicles the development of game laws, and the nearly impossible task of enforcing them, through the formation of game protection associations, to current conservation policies. Beautifully illustrated with paintings and historical photographs.

Ralls, K., and J. Ballou, eds. 1986. *Proceedings of the Workshop on Genetic Management of Captive Populations.* (*Zoo Biology,* vol. 5, no. 2.) New York: Alan R. Liss.

In the first five papers of this special issue of *Zoo Biology,* a panel of experts discusses current topics of genetic management and breeding of captive populations, protein and genetic variation, inbreeding, problems of selection in captive populations, and captive breeding plans. In the remaining papers, other workshop participants present recent findings and techniques of captive population management.

Schonewald-Cox, C., ed. 1983. *Genetics and Conservation: A Reference for Managing Wild Animal and Plant Populations.* Menlo Park, Calif: Benjamin/Cummings. 722 pp.

Basic genetic principles and technologies relevant to the management of zoological gardens and nature reserves. The authors focus on the maintenance of genetic diversity and discuss isolation, extinction, population bottlenecks, founding of new populations, and merging of naturally disjunct populations.

Soulé, M. E., ed. 1986. *Conservation Biology: The Science of Scarcity and Diversity.* Sunderland, Mass: Sinauer Associates. 584 pp.

The latest synthesis of conservation biology, with contributions from forty-five authors. The first five sections focus on core areas of conservation such as biogeography, ecology, systematics, genetics, behavior, and habitats. The last section examines the relationships between conservation biology and society and between conservation biology and ethics.

Soulé, M. E., ed. 1987. *Viable Populations for Conservation.* Cambridge: Cambridge University Press. 189 pp.

One newly recognized aspect of conservation biology today is the problem of determining the viable population size for a species. This technical volume brings together for the first time information on topics such as effective population sizes, genetic variation, extinction, and minimum viable populations.

Soulé, M. E., and B. A. Wilcox, eds. 1980. *Conservation Biology: An Evolutionary-Ecological Perspective.* Sunderland, Mass: Sinauer Associates. 395 pp.

Covers the practical and theoretical aspects of conservation biology. Of particular interest to zoo biologists is the section on captive propagation and conservation, which provides a forum for discussing the pros and cons, technology, and theory of captive breeding of endangered species.

Stanley Price, M. R. 1989. *Animal Re-introduction: The Arabian Oryx in Oman.* New York: Cambridge University Press. 291 pp.

A scientific account of the planning, problems, and successes of the first seven years of the Arabian oryx reintroduction project in Oman. Maps, drawings, graphs, and references are included. An important example for future reintroductions.

Thornback, J., and M. Jenkins. 1982–. *The IUCN Mammal Red Data Book*. Part 1: *Threatened Mammalian Taxa of the Americas and the Australian Zoogeographic Region (Excluding Cetacea)*. Cambridge: IUCN Conservation Monitoring Centre.

This volume continues where the previous volume, *Mammalia* (by Goodwin and Holloway), ended. This newer 1982 edition, however, covers only 155 mammals (excluding Cetacea) inhabiting North America, Central America, South America, Australia, New Zealand, and the island of New Guinea. Each short report includes information on status, distribution, population, habitat and ecology, threats to survival, conservation measures taken and proposed, and captive breeding for each species.

United States. Office of the Federal Register. Annual. *Code of Federal Regulations*. Title 8: *Animals and Animal Products*. 2 vols. Title 50: *Wildlife and Fisheries*. 2 vols. Washington, D.C.: U.S. Government Printing Office.

The primary source for current government regulations dealing with animals. Title 8 contains regulations on animal health, interstate transportation, quarantine, and animal welfare. Title 50 is the current list of regulations on wildlife possession, selling, trapping, importing, and exporting.

Western, D., and M. C. Pearl. 1989. *Conservation for the Twenty-First Century*. New York: Oxford University Press. 365 pp.

Centering on the subject of wildlife and its habitat, this book is organized around four themes: tomorrow's world, conservation biology, conservation management, and conservation realities.

Wolfheim, J. H. 1983. *Primates of the World: Distribution, Abundance, and Conservation*. Seattle: University of Washington Press. 831 pp.

Provides information on the natural history and conservation of primate species around the world. Maps are included.

BEHAVIOR

Eisenberg, J. F., and D. G. Kleiman, eds. 1983. *Advances in the Study of Mammalian Behavior*. (Special Publication of the American Society of Mammalogists, no. 7.) Stillwater, Okla: American Society of Mammalogists. 753 pp.

A collection of papers delivered at a conference held in 1980 at the National Zoological Park's Conservation and Research Center. A good introduction to the many subdisciplines of behavioral studies and their applications.

Ewer, R. F. 1968. *Ethology of Mammals*. New York: Plenum. 418 pp.

Discusses basic principles of mammalian behavior based on structure and relationship to the environment. Chapter topics include expression and communication, courtship and mating, parent and offspring, and play.

Fagen, R. 1981. *Animal Play Behavior*. New York: Oxford University Press. 684 pp.

An in-depth look into the biology of animal play. Some chapters are very theoretical, while others require no technical background in biology.

Geist, V., and F. Walther, eds. 1974. *The Behaviour of Ungulates and Its Relation to Management*. 2 vols. Morges, Switzerland: IUCN. (IUCN Publications, New Series, no. 24.)

A series of papers presented at an international symposium held at the University of Calgary, Alberta, Canada, in November 1971. Volume 1 deals primarily with social behavior and ecology, classification, and taxonomy. Volume 2 focuses on ecology and management. A technical treatment, well illustrated, aimed at managers of captive and wild ungulates.

Krebs, J. R., and N. B. Davies, eds. 1984. *Behavioural Ecology: An Evolutionary Approach*. 2d ed. Oxford: Blackwell Scientific Publications. 493 pp.

Contributors discuss such topics as kin and group selection, learning, mate choice, behavioral adaptation, and animal signals. An important reference for researchers and students of animal behavior, animal ecology, and evolutionary biology.

Leuthold, W., ed. 1977. *African Ungulates: A Comparative Review of Their Ethology and Behavioral Ecology*. New York: Springer-Verlag. 307 pp.

Thoroughly covers the behavior, ecology, and conservation of African ungulates. Primarily concerned with East African species.

Poole, T. B. 1985. *Social Behaviour in Mammals*. New York: Chapman & Hall. 248 pp.

A good summary of research on mammalian behavior in natural environments. Discusses competitive behaviors such as fighting, threat, and submission, and cooperative interactions such as mating and parental care. Illustrations and a good bibliography are included.

Tuttle, R. H. 1986. *Apes of the World: Their Social Behavior, Communication, Mentality, and Ecology*. Park Ridge, N.J.: Noyes. 421 pp.

A comprehensive text on ape behavior and ecology. Topics range from taxonomy and distribution to tool use and communication. More than 1,360 journals, monographs, and symposia are referenced in the text.

REPRODUCTION

Brackett, B. G., G. E. Seidel Jr., and S. M. Seidel, eds. 1981. *New Technologies in Animal Breeding*. New York: Academic Press. 268 pp.

Provides valuable information on current and future technologies in the field of domestic animal breeding such as artificial insemination, embryo transfer, sex selection, cloning, and gene transfer.

Daly, M., and M. Wilson. 1983. *Sex, Evolution, and Behavior*. 2d ed. Boston: Willard Grant Press.

An evolutionary approach to the subject of sexual and reproductive behavior among animals. This textbook-like monograph provides a good introduction to sociobiology.

Graham, C. E., ed. 1981. *Reproductive Biology of the Great Apes: Comparative and Biomedical Perspectives*. New York: Academic Press. 437 pp.

A review of the physiology, morphology, endocrinology, and sexual behavior of great apes, both in captivity and in the wild. Most of the documentation on captive animals comes from primate centers.

Gubernick, D. J., and P. H. Klopfer, eds. 1981. *Parental Care in Mammals*. New York: Plenum. 459 pp.

The evolution of parental care, mother-infant relationships, and the social network of the infant are discussed.

Hayssen, V. 1993. *Asdell's Patterns of Mammalian Reproduction: A Compendium of Species-Specific Data*. Ithaca, N.Y.: Comstock. 1,023 pp.

Information such as breeding season, gestation period, litter size, physiology of reproduction, and age of puberty is provided for each species. The list of literature cited is quite extensive.

Martin, R. D., ed. 1975. *Breeding Endangered Species in Captivity*. (Proceedings of the First International Conference on Breeding Endangered Species in Captivity held in Jersey, Great Britain, May 1972.) New York: Academic Press. 420 pp.

This collection of papers is devoted specifically to techniques of captive breeding of endangered species. Some of the animals discussed are the marmoset, river otter, sloth bear, pygmy chimpanzee, Indian rhino, and orangutan.

Perry, J. S., and I. W. Rowlands, eds. 1969. *Biology of Reproduction in Mammals.* (Proceedings of the Symposium of the Society for the Study of Fertility held in Nairobi, Kenya, April 1968.) Oxford: Blackwell. 531 pp. (*Journal of Reproduction and Fertility,* supplement no. 6.)

   Proceedings of a symposium on the biology of reproduction in African mammals. Topics range from menstrual cycles of baboons to the breeding season and litter size of African mole rats.

Rowlands, I. W., ed. 1966. *Comparative Biology of Reproduction in Mammals.* (Proceedings of an international symposium held at the Zoological Society of London on 24–26 November 1964.) (Symposia of the Zoological Society of London, no. 15.) New York: Academic Press. 559 pp.

   A collection of twenty-eight papers on the reproductive processes of mammals. Each chapter discusses in detail the reproduction of a single species or group of animals. Topics include gestation period, chromosome studies, litter size, breeding season and mating, and reproductive anatomy. Dated, but still cited in current literature.

Smith, G. R., and J. P. Hearn, eds. 1988. *Reproduction and Disease in Captive and Wild Animals.* (Symposia of the Zoological Society of London, no. 60.) Oxford: Clarendon Press. 209 pp.

   A series of papers presenting current research on reproduction and diseases of wild and captive animals. Topics include natural suppression of fertility, effects of chemicals on gamete production, and disease transmission between wild and domestic animals.

Tyndale-Biscoe, H., and M. Renfree. 1987. *Reproductive Physiology of Marsupials.* (Monographs on Marsupial Biology.) Cambridge: Cambridge University Press. 476 pp.

   A summary of current knowledge of marsupial reproduction. Discusses breeding biology by family and then by subject, such as reproductive anatomy, lactation, and so forth.

Watson, P. F., ed. 1978. *Artificial Breeding of Non-Domestic Animals.* (Proceedings of a symposium held at the Zoological Society of London on 7 and 8 September 1977.) (Symposia of the Zoological Society of London, no. 43.) New York: Academic Press. 376 pp.

   Contains proceedings of a symposium on artificial breeding of wild animals in captivity. Semen collection and preservation are emphasized. Although more current research is available, this is still a useful book for captive breeders.

CAPTIVE MAMMAL RESEARCH

Crockett, C., and M. Hutchins, eds. 1977. *Applied Behavioral Research at the Woodland Park Zoological Gardens.* Seattle, Wash.: Pika Press. 407 pp.

   This volume contains a collection of research papers done by students of zoo biology and animal behavior. Topics include cage utilization by the white-handed gibbon and behavioral adaptation of the wolf family to three types of zoo habitats. A good example of the kinds of research that can be done in a zoo.

Lehner, P. N. 1979. *Handbook of Ethological Methods.* New York: Garland STPM Press. 403 pp.

   Clearly written, well illustrated, and presents a logical, meaningful, and practical approach to studying animal behavior. Topics include the design of research, data collection methods and equipment (advantages and disadvantages of each type), statistical tests, experimental manipulation, and presentation and interpretation of results.

Markowitz, H., and V. J. Stevens, eds. 1978. *Behavior of Captive Wild Animals.* Chicago: Nelson-Hall. 315 pp.

   The authors discuss behavioral research on animals in zoos and other captive environments. Subjects covered include predation, communication, group behavior, and applying knowledge of natural behavior to the captive habitat.

Martin, P., and P. Bateson. 1993. *Measuring Behaviour: An Introductory Guide.* 2d ed. Cambridge: Cambridge University Press. 222 pp.

   This book provides a comprehensive review of the principles and techniques used for measuring animal and human behavior. It discusses how to record direct observations and analyze data.

Research in Zoos and Aquariums. 1975. (A symposium held at the 49th Conference of the AAZPA, Houston, Texas, 6–11 October 1973.) Washington, D.C.: National Academy of Sciences. 215 pp.

   Papers from a symposium sponsored by the Institute of Laboratory Animal Resources in cooperation with the American Association of Zoological Parks and Aquariums. Contributions are grouped under four main topics: general aspects of administration, funding, and research opportunities; behavioral research; reproductive biology research; and special applications.

White, G. C., and R. A. Garrott. 1990. *Analysis of Wildlife Radio-Tracking Data.* San Diego, Calif.: Academic Press. 383 pp.

   Discusses the principles of designing radio-tracking studies. Describes methods of estimating measurements of animal movement (home range, habitat use, migration). Reviews some current software programs.

PERIODICALS

African Journal of Ecology. Quarterly. 1963–. Oxford, U.K.: Blackwell Scientific Publications.

American Journal of Primatology. 12/year. 1981–. New York: Alan R. Liss.

Animal Behaviour. 12/year. 1953–. A publication of the Association for the Study of Animal Behaviour and Animal Behavior Society. London: Bailliere Tindall.

Australian Wildlife Research. Quarterly. 1974–. East Melbourne, Victoria: CSIRO.

Behaviour. Bimonthly. 1947–. Leiden, The Netherlands: E. J. Brill.

Behavioural Ecology and Sociobiology. 12/yr. 1976–. New York: Springer-Verlag.

Conservation Biology. Quarterly. 1986–. Cambridge, Mass.: Blackwell Scientific Publications.

Ethology (formerly *Zeitschrift für Tierpsychologie*). 16/year. 1937–. Berlin: Verlag Paul Parey.

Folia Primatologica. Quarterly. 1963–. Basel, Switzerland: S. Karger.

International Journal of Primatology. Bimonthly. 1980–. New York: Plenum Press.

Journal of Mammalogy. Quarterly. 1919–. A publication of the American Society of Mammalogists. Provo, Utah: Brigham Young University Press.

Journal of Medical Primatology. Bimonthly. 1984–. New York: Alan R. Liss.

Journal of Reproduction and Fertility. Bimonthly. 1960–. Cambridge: Journal of Reproduction and Fertility, Ltd.

Journal of the American Veterinary Medical Association. Biweekly. 1915–. Shaumburg, Ill.: American Veterinary Medical Association.

Journal of Wildlife Diseases. 1965–. Ames, Iowa: Wildlife Disease Association. Distributed by Allen Press, Lawrence, Kans.

Journal of Wildlife Management. Quarterly. 1937–. Bethesda, Md.: Wildlife Society.

Journal of Zoo and Wild Animal Medicine (formerly *Journal of Zoo Animal Medicine*). Quarterly. 1970–. Atlanta, Ga.: American Association of Zoo Veterinarians.

Journal of Zoology. 12/year. 1830–. London: Published for the Zoological Society of London by Oxford University Press.

Mammalia. Quarterly. 1936–. (Text in French and English, summaries in both languages.) Paris: Musée Nationale D'Histoire Naturelle.

Mammal Review. Quarterly. 1970–. Oxford: Blackwell Scientific Publications.

Marine Mammal Science. Quarterly. 1985–. Lawrence, Kans.: Allen Press.

Oryx. Quarterly. 1903–. Oxford: Blackwell Scientific Publications.

Primates. Quarterly. 1957–. (Text in English, French, or German.) Japan: Japan Monkey Centre.

Trends in Ecology and Evolution. 12/year. 1986–. Cambridge: Elsevier.

Zeitschrift für Säugetierkunde. 6/year. 1926–. (Text in English and German.) Hamburg: Paul Parey.

Zoo Biology. Bimonthly. 1982–. New York: Alan R. Liss.

Der Zoologische Garten. 6/year. 1929–. (Text in English, French, German, and Russian; summaries in English.) Jena: G. Fischer.

Appendix 3
Summary of United States Wildlife Regulations Applicable to Zoos

KRISTIN L. VEHRS

This appendix is an overview of the major United States federal regulations affecting zoological parks and aquariums and those mammals normally displayed in such facilities. In many instances, the regulations are broad, and only those sections relevant to zoological parks and aquariums have been included. This summary is a general description and is not intended to be definitive; therefore, the specific laws and regulations should be reviewed prior to undertaking covered transactions.

Legislation is written very broadly: it authorizes a program, specifies its general aim and conduct, and usually puts a ceiling on monies that can be used to finance it. The enacting legislation authorizes the promulgation of regulations to implement the program. In some instances, the purpose of the legislation is to implement international agreements. For example, a section of the Endangered Species Act implements the Convention on International Trade in Endangered Species.

The purpose of regulations is to implement the legislation; therefore, regulations are very specific. They provide the nuts and bolts of the program outlined by the enacting legislation. Regulations are issued by the federal agency with jurisdiction over the issue covered by the legislation. For example, the Public Health Service Act is administered by the Department of Health and Human Services (HHS). HHS issues the regulations that implement the Public Health Service Act.

Federal legislation affecting U.S. zoos is not generally directed at zoos per se but has been enacted for other purposes, such as to control the spread of infectious or contagious diseases that might affect agricultural livestock or to protect endangered species and marine mammals. Zoos are included, however, in the specific programs outlined by the general legislation.

This summary includes only federal legislation and regulations. There are no references to state laws and regulations, which should also be consulted prior to animal transactions. State laws address many of the same topics as federal laws, but there is generally a narrower focus on items of particular interest to the individual state. In most cases, federal law overrides state law when there are inconsistencies between the two. The federal laws, enacted by the U.S. Congress, are cited as Volume number *U.S. Code* (U.S.C.) Page number. The regulations, issued by the federal agency with jurisdiction to implement the laws, are cited as Volume number *Code of Federal Regulations* (C.F.R.) Part number. Regulations often have separate sections of definitions; these should be consulted because they may list items or species that are specifically included or excluded in the regulations.

Regulations are revised frequently, and revisions are published in the *Federal Register*. New regulations are incorporated into biennial volumes of the *Code of Federal Regulations*. Copies of the laws and the regulations are available in the *AZA Manual of Federal Wildlife Regulations* or from the U.S. Government Printing Office.

ANIMAL WELFARE ACT

The Animal Welfare Act (AWA) (7 U.S.C. 2131 et. seq.) was enacted in 1966 to ensure that animals used in research facilities, for exhibition purposes, and as pets are provided with humane care and treatment. The AWA regulates aspects of animal transportation, purchase, sale, housing, care, handling, and treatment. The U.S. Department of Agriculture (USDA) Animal and Plant Health Inspection Service (APHIS) is the agency responsible for administering this act.

Under the AWA, zoological parks and aquariums that display certain mammals must be licensed as exhibitors by APHIS. The AWA regulations do not apply to cold-blooded animals, fishes, birds, horses and farm animals, or rats and mice. Current regulations cover dogs, cats, monkeys, guinea pigs, hamsters, rabbits, and most other warm-blooded mammals.

The regulations pertaining to exotic animals are divided into three categories:

1. Nonhuman primates
2. Marine mammals
3. Warm-blooded animals other than dogs, cats, rabbits, hamsters, guinea pigs, nonhuman primates, and marine mammals

Each of the categories includes facilities and operating standards, animal health and husbandry standards, and transportation standards.

Applications for licensing must be submitted to the Veterinarian in Charge in the state where the applicant operates. The applicant will be charged a licensing fee. In addition, the facility must be inspected to ensure that it meets minimum standards (see below). APHIS personnel will inspect the facility's equipment, business records, and animal holdings. The AWA requires that facilities be inspected at least once annually.

If APHIS believes that an applicant has committed violations within the previous 2 years that demonstrate lack of fitness for a license, USDA may call a hearing to give the applicant the opportunity to show cause why the application should not be denied.

Maintenance of the license is subject to acknowledgment of the care standards and agreement to abide by them, payment of the annual licensing fee, and the filing of an annual report. The report form (VS Form 18-3) is provided by the Veterinarian in Charge and must be filed every year within 30 days of the anniversary date of the license. The exhibitor must report the number of animals on hand, identifying species and sex. Animals that have been bought or sold, transported, traded, or donated must also be reported.

The AWA requires that minimum standards be issued covering humane handling, housing, feeding, watering, transportation, sanitation, ventilation, shelter from extremes of weather and temperature, adequate veterinary care, and separation of incompatible animals. The facilities themselves are inspected to ascertain that they meet certain requirements, including those covering structural strength of the enclosure, sources of water and power, available storage for food and bedding, adequate systems for the disposal of wastes, facilities for employees, including washroom sinks and showers, and control of ambient temperatures and ventilation.

The regulations establish specific space requirements for marine mammals and nonhuman primates. For all other mammals, the AWA regulations state that animal enclosures shall be constructed and maintained so as to provide sufficient space to allow each animal to make normal postural and social adjustments with adequate freedom of movement. APHIS plans to institute specific space requirements for other mammals covered by the Animal Welfare Act in the future.

The transportation section of the regulations contains requirements for both the structural strength and size of the primary shipping container used. There are requirements regarding ventilation and the minimum air circulation space between the primary container and any adjacent cargo. Furthermore, the regulations address other factors that must be considered, including compatibility of species shipped together, ages and sexes of species, sanitation, food and water, and care in transit and terminal facilities.

Records must be kept of all transactions involving animals covered by the AWA (VS Form 18-20). The origin of the animal and date of acquisition are the key information. The record must accompany the animal at all times. If animals are shipped for sale, given away, or disposed of, new records must be prepared listing the animals involved and the name and address of the recipient. Shipping containers must be marked and accompanied by a description of each animal, corresponding to the shipping records.

The penalties for violating APHIS standards are administrative suspensions, revocations of licenses, and cease-and-desist orders. To provide immediate relief for animals in extreme cases, a license can be suspended for up to 21 days without a hearing or other preliminaries. A cease-and-desist order requires an exhibitor to cease specific practices of which he is accused. If the order is violated, courts may levy fines for each day the violation continues.

Regulations are found in 9 C.F.R. parts 1 through 4. The Animal Welfare Act was amended in December 1985 (Public Law 99-198: Food Security Act). Two of the amendments directly affect zoological parks. The first requires APHIS to issue standards of care to promote the psychological well-being of primates. Each institution must have on file an enrichment plan for their primates.

Second, any zoological park that receives federal grants for conducting research, experimentation, or testing involving the use of animals must register as a research facility. As in licensing, registrants must agree to abide by the USDA standards of care and must file an annual report each calendar year with the Veterinarian in Charge. Every research facility is required to consider alternatives to using animals and to ensure that animal pain and distress are minimized. Moreover, every research facility is required to establish an Institutional Animal Committee composed of at least three members. One member must be a veterinarian, and at least one member must not be affiliated with the facility—this individual is intended to represent the general community's interest. These individuals should possess sufficient ability to assess animal care, treatment, and experimental practices in experimental research.

The Institutional Animal Committee must inspect all animal study areas and animal facilities of the research institution at least twice a year. The Committee must file a report with APHIS twice a year. If APHIS determines that conditions of animal care, treatment, or practice have not been in compliance with the Animal Welfare Act, they will notify the federal funding agency to suspend the research facility's federal support.

The regulations implementing these amendments have now been published and are important additions to the federal regulations affecting zoological parks and aquariums. The regulations can be found in 9 C.F.R, part 3, subpart D.

APHIS AUTHORIZATION ACT: USDA QUARANTINE/IMPORTATION REQUIREMENTS

USDA/APHIS regulates the importation and exportation of ruminants, swine, poultry, birds, pigeons, horses, animal semen, blood, and serum under the USDA/APHIS Authorization Act (21 U.S.C. 101-111 & 134). The act gives USDA the authority to protect the United States against the introduction of infectious or contagious diseases. The act also prohibits or regulates movement into the United States of animals that are or have been infected with or exposed to any communicable disease.

Zoological parks desiring to import ruminants, swine, poultry, birds, pigeons, horses, or animal semen must meet APHIS quarantine requirements in addition to securing any other necessary permits or authorizations. Animal semen is defined as semen from cattle, sheep, goats, other ruminants, swine, horses, asses, mules, zebras, dogs, and poultry.

Generally, shipments must enter the United States through an APHIS-designated port: Los Angeles, Miami, Honolulu, or New York. During quarantine, the importer is responsible for all expenses, including transportation to the quarantine facility, feed, handling, and any expenses incurred as a result of the quarantine being extended. No visitors are allowed in quarantine facilities, except the importer or his agent with the authorization of the importer. If a disease outbreak occurs in the animals during quarantine, all may be euthanized, depending on the nature of the disease. A reservation fee is required for each lot of animals to be quarantined in APHIS facilities; this fee will be applied to the overall quarantine service fees.

Ruminants and swine must be accompanied by a health certificate signed by a salaried veterinary officer of the national government of the exporting country. The certificate must state that the animals were in the country of export for 60 days before shipment and have been found to be free of certain diseases. Ruminants and swine must be quarantined for at least 15 days. During their quarantine, they will be subject to testing to determine their disease-free status.

Horses (including asses, mules, and zebras) must be accompanied by a health certificate signed by a salaried veterinary officer of the national government of the exporting country. The certificate must state that the animals were in the country of export for 60 days before shipment and have been found to be free of certain diseases.

Horses imported from the Western Hemisphere must be quarantined for at least 7 days. Horses imported from any country on the continent of Africa or that have transited Africa must enter the United States only at the port of New York and must be quarantined for at least 60 days. They must test negative for dourine, glanders, equine piroplasmosis, equine infectious anemia, and any other disease for which USDA considers testing necessary.

USDA requires that horses, cattle, swine, sheep, or goats intended for exportation to a foreign country be accompanied from the state of origin to the port of embarkation by an original health certificate, which should certify that the animals were inspected within 30 days before the date of export and were found to be sound, healthy, and free from evidence of communicable disease. The results of tests conducted prior to export are also recorded on the health certificate. Applications for export permits should be sent to the Administrator of Veterinary Services, APHIS.

Zoological parks desiring to import and display ruminants or swine originating in a country where foot-and-mouth disease or rinderpest is known to exist are subject to more stringent restrictions by USDA. There are separate regulations for the importation of animal semen from countries where rinderpest or foot-and-mouth disease is known to exist. Entry of such ruminants and wild swine will be only at the port of New York. The animals must be quarantined overseas in a USDA-approved embarkation quarantine facility for 60 days before shipment and must have passed two successive negative blood tests for foot-and-mouth disease and rinderpest during that preembarkation quarantine. A health certificate signed by a salaried veterinary officer of the national government of the exporting country must accompany the animals. The certificate must state that the animals were in the country of export for 60 days before shipment and that they have been found to be free of certain diseases. The animals must be shipped directly from the embarkation port to New York, unaccompanied by any other ruminants or swine, and be quarantined at that port.

To receive and display ruminants or swine from countries where foot-and-mouth disease or rinderpest is known to exist, the recipient facility must apply to USDA to become a Permanent Post Entry Quarantine (PPEQ) facility. Approval is based on inspection of the physical facilities of the establishment and its methods of operation by APHIS personnel. Requirements include satisfactory pens, cages, or enclosures. Disposition of waste, sewage, and specimens that die must be within the zoological park or at preapproved burial sites. All PPEQ animal carcasses must be incinerated. The facility must maintain the enclosures so as to ensure that PPEQ display animals do not come into physical contact with the general public or with domestic livestock. Fencing for the enclosures must meet USDA requirements.

The site is an important factor for a PPEQ facility. The requirements for a facility located in an urban area are different from those for a facility located in a rural area in close proximity to domestic farm animals. Once ruminants enter a PPEQ facility, they (including their parts or carcasses) cannot be moved to another location without USDA's approval. PPEQ animals can be moved only among PPEQ facilities. However, the progeny of PPEQ animals may be transferred without restriction.

The APHIS has separate regulations on the importation of elephants, hippopotamuses, rhinoceroses, and tapirs. Elephants, hippopotamuses, rhinoceroses, and tapirs cannot be imported without an import permit issued by APHIS Veterinary Services. The importation must take place within 30 days of the date of arrival proposed on the permit. The port veterinarian must be notified of the arrival date at least 72 hours before arrival.

A health certificate must accompany the animals. The certificate must be signed by a salaried veterinarian of the national veterinary service of the country where inspection and treatment occurred or by a veterinarian authorized by the national veterinary service. The certificate must certify:

1. that the animals were inspected and found free of any ectoparasites not more than 72 hours before loading;
2. that the animals were treated for ectoparasites at least 3 but not more than 14 days prior to loading; treatment must have been by thoroughly wetting with a pesticide applied with a hand-held nozzle sprayer, a spray-dip machine, or a dip vat;
3. that the animals, after being treated, did not have physical contact with or share a pen or bedding materials with any elephant, hippopotamus, rhinoceros, or tapir not in the same shipment to the United States; and

4. the name and concentration of the pesticide; both must be adequate to kill the types of ectoparasites likely to infest the animals.

The animals must be imported into the United States at Los Angeles, Miami, Honolulu, or New York. Other ports of entry may be permitted on a case-by-case basis if certain conditions are met, including inspection and treatment of the animals at a facility provided by the importer that is adequate for inspection, treatment, and incineration. Prior to moving the animals to the facility provided by the importer, the animals must be inspected at the port and sprayed and dipped, as is feasible.

Hay, straw, feed, bedding, and other material that accompanied the animals from the country of export must be removed, as is feasible, sealed in plastic bags, and incinerated by the importer. The shipping container or vehicle containing the animals must be sealed by an inspector with an official seal of USDA. Plastic sheeting must be fastened around the shipping container.

The animals must be inspected within 24 hours of being unloaded at the port of entry or at the facility provided by the importer. Each animal shall be removed from its shipping container, placed on a concrete or nonporous surface, and physically inspected for ectoparasites by an inspector. If no ectoparasites are found, the animal must be sprayed or dipped one time. If ectoparasites are found, the animal must be sprayed or dipped as many times as necessary until no ectoparasites are found.

All hay, straw, feed, and bedding and the plastic sheet used to wrap the shipping container must be sealed in plastic bags and incinerated. Shipping containers must be cleaned and disinfected or incinerated.

Elephants, hippopotamuses, rhinoceroses, and tapirs imported from Canada are exempt from these requirements if accompanied by a document signed by a salaried veterinarian of the Canadian government stating that they were not imported into Canada during the preceding year and that they did not have physical contact with or share a pen or bedding materials with an elephant, hippopotamus, rhinoceros, or tapir imported into Canada during that year.

Regulations are located in 9 C.F.R. parts 75, 82, 92, 93 and 94.

ENDANGERED SPECIES ACT

The Endangered Species Act (ESA) (16 U.S.C. 1531 et. seq.), enacted in 1973, places restrictions on a wide range of activities involving endangered and threatened animals and plants to help ensure their continued survival. The ESA prohibits the use of these protected species unless authorized by a permit from the U.S. Fish and Wildlife Service (FWS) of the Department of the Interior. FWS is the primary agency that administers the ESA; the National Marine Fisheries Service (NMFS) of the Department of Commerce has shared responsibility for those marine mammals under its jurisdiction that are endangered species.

The ESA defines an endangered species as any animal or plant listed by regulation as being in danger of extinction. A threatened species is defined as any animal or plant listed by regulation as being likely to become endangered within the foreseeable future. The ESA defines fish and wildlife to include any part, product, egg, or offspring thereof, or the dead body or parts thereof. The U.S. List of Endangered and Threatened Wildlife and Plants includes both native and foreign species.

It is unlawful for any person subject to the jurisdiction of the United States, without a permit, to commit, attempt to commit, solicit another to commit, or cause to be committed any of the following activities with regard to endangered or threatened wildlife: import or export; deliver, receive, carry, transport, or ship in interstate or foreign commerce in the course of a commercial activity; sell or offer for sale in interstate or foreign commerce;

take, which means harm, harass, pursue, hunt, shoot, wound, trap, kill, capture, or collect, or attempt to engage in any such conduct; possess, ship, deliver, carry, transport, sell, or receive unlawfully taken wildlife; or violate any federal regulation pertaining to listed species.

The Fish and Wildlife Service's Wildlife Permit Office may issue permits for prohibited activities for certain purposes.

Endangered species permits: These permits allow activities related to scientific research or enhancement of propagation or survival of the species.

Threatened species permits: These permits allow activities related to scientific research; enhancement of propagation or survival of the species; zoological, horticultural or botanical exhibition; educational purposes, and special purposes that are consistent with the ESA.

Captive-bred wildlife: Qualified persons may register with the FWS under the captive-bred wildlife regulation. The regulation covers only living exotic animals of species listed under the ESA that are born in captivity from parents that mated in captivity in the United States. To transport, deliver, receive, sell, or offer captive-bred specimens for sale in interstate commerce, both the buyer and seller must be registered for the families of wildlife involved. Registrants must still comply with state laws.

Economic hardship: If a facility is likely to face undue economic hardship as a result of the listing of a species on the endangered species list, the facility may apply for an economic hardship permit within a year of the date when the species is first proposed as endangered. FWS will consider criteria listed in the regulations, including the severity of the economic hardship and the effect of the permit on wild populations.

Listed specimens that were held in captivity on 28 December 1973, for purposes not contrary to the ESA and not in the course of a commercial activity, are exempt from the ESA's prohibitions. These specimens are covered by a grandfather clause. If the specimens are to be sold in interstate or foreign commerce, the exemption does not apply. FWS or Customs officers may refuse to clear endangered or threatened wildlife for importation or exportation until the importer or exporter has demonstrated that the animals qualify for the exemption.

Commercial activities involving legally acquired endangered or threatened species that take place entirely within one state are not prohibited by the ESA. However, many states regulate activities involving protected species, and therefore, state fish and wildlife personnel should be contacted regarding their regulations.

Endangered and threatened species may be shipped interstate as a bona fide gift or loan if there is no barter, credit, or other form of compensation involved, provided there are no other prohibitions involved.

In considering whether to issue an endangered species permit or a threatened species permit, the issuing agency (either FWS or NMFS) must consider, among other criteria: (1) whether the intended purpose is adequate to justify removing individual specimens from the wild; (2) the probable direct and indirect effects on wild populations; (3) whether the permit would conflict with any known program intended to enhance the survival probabilities of the population; (4) whether the intended purpose would likely reduce the threat of extinction facing the species; (5) the opinions of scientists or other experts concerning the species; and (6) whether the expertise, facilities, or other resources available to the applicant appear adequate for successful accomplishment of the stated objective.

Permit applications may be obtained from the FWS Federal Wildlife Permit Office. Applicants should allow at least 60 days for processing of these applications. Summaries of all applications for endangered species permits will be published in the *Federal Register* and the public will be allowed 30 days to comment.

While FWS has primary jurisdiction over the ESA, NMFS enforces the ESA with regard to many marine species (for the list of species, see "Marine Mammal Protection Act" below). Unlike FWS, NMFS has no prescribed permit application form. Applications are submitted in the form of a letter. All applications for endangered species permits will be published in the *Federal Register* and the public will be allowed 30 days to comment.

Unless an exception is obtained (from the FWS Regional Law Enforcement Office), all endangered wildlife imported or exported must enter at one of the following designated ports: Los Angeles, San Francisco, Miami, Honolulu, Chicago, New Orleans, New York, Seattle, and Dallas/Fort Worth.

Regulations are found in 50 C.F.R. parts 1, 2, 3, 10, 13, 14, 16, 17, 219, 220, 221, 222, 226, 227, and 424.

CONVENTION ON INTERNATIONAL TRADE IN ENDANGERED SPECIES OF WILD FAUNA AND FLORA (CITES)

CITES is an international treaty that is implemented in the United States by the Endangered Species Act. CITES establishes procedures to regulate the import and export of species threatened by trade.

The treaty covers animals and plants, whether alive or dead, or any readily recognizable part or derivative of an animal or plant. CITES imposes no restrictions or controls on shipments between U.S. states or territories, including Guam, the Commonwealth of Puerto Rico, the Trust Territories, the U.S. Virgin Islands, and American Samoa. Regulations to enforce CITES became effective in May 1977. The ESA designated the Secretary of the Interior as both the Management and Scientific Authority for CITES.

U.S. regulations require that imports of species listed in any of the three appendices of CITES be accompanied by proper permits or certificates of exception. The FWS Federal Wildlife Permit Office acts as the U.S. Management Authority for CITES. This office accepts permit applications, coordinates their review, and determines whether a permit or certificate should be issued.

The FWS Office of Scientific Authority acts as the U.S. Scientific Authority for CITES. This office is responsible for the issuance of findings of no detriment to the survival of the species involved, as required by CITES permitting procedures. The approval of the Scientific Authority is necessary before the Management Authority can issue a permit. (If a species is also covered by the Endangered Species Act or the Marine Mammal Protection Act, fulfilling the requirements of those acts will also fulfill CITES requirements.)

CITES Appendix I includes species threatened with extinction. Shipments of Appendix I species require two permits: an export permit from the exporting country stating that the specimen has been taken in accordance with treaty requirements, and an import permit from the importing country. The import permit must be obtained first. Appendix I permits can be issued only if the import is not primarily for commercial purposes and will not be detrimental to the survival of the species.

Appendix II includes species that are not presently threatened with extinction but may become so unless their trade is regulated. CITES controls are less stringent for Appendix II species than for Appendix I species; import permits are not required. An export permit or reexport certificate must accompany each shipment. Export permits can be issued for any purpose as long as the export will not be detrimental to the survival of the species. Reexport certificates are required for specimens previously imported.

Appendix III includes species not covered by Appendices I or II but which are regulated by a CITES party nation for conservation purposes. International shipments of these species require either an export permit from the country that listed the species or a reexport certificate or certificate of origin from any other country.

Pre-Convention animals, animals acquired prior to the date the species was listed by CITES, do not require a CITES permit, but a certificate of pre-Convention status is required.

If a country is a CITES party nation, only documents issued by the country's Management Authority can be used. Wildlife imported from a non-CITES nation must be accompanied by documents containing all the information normally required in CITES export permits.

All CITES wildlife shipments must enter and leave the United States through Customs ports designated by FWS (Los Angeles, San Francisco, Miami, Honolulu, Chicago, New Orleans, New York, Seattle, Dallas/Fort Worth) unless an exception is obtained. Shipment containers must be marked on the outside with the names and addresses of the sender and receiver and an accurate statement of the species. The sender must comply with the International Air Transport Association Live Animal Regulations (IATA) and the CITES Transport Guidelines. Regulations implementing CITES are found in 50 C.F.R. part 23.

MARINE MAMMAL PROTECTION ACT

The Marine Mammal Protection Act (MMPA) (16 U.S.C. 1361 et. seq.) was enacted in 1972 to protect all species of whales, dolphins, seals, polar bears, walrus, manatees, and sea otters. It is administered by both the U.S. Fish and Wildlife Service of the Department of the Interior and the National Marine Fisheries Service of the Department of Commerce. Polar bears, sea otters, walrus, dugongs, and manatees are under the jurisdiction of FWS. Cetaceans (whales and porpoises) and pinnipeds (other than walrus but including seals and sea lions) are under the jurisdiction of NMFS. The MMPA makes it illegal to take or import any marine mammal without a permit; to import a marine mammal taken in violation of the MMPA or foreign law; or to use, possess, transport, or sell an illegally taken marine mammal. Except for purposes of scientific research, it is also illegal to import a marine mammal that was pregnant, nursing, or less than 8 months old at the time of taking or is listed as a depleted species in the wild under the MMPA.

The MMPA provides for the issuance of public display and scientific research permits authorizing the taking or importation of marine mammals. This provision is a specific exemption to the moratorium against the taking of marine mammals. Public display permits cannot be issued for species designated as depleted—below their optimum sustainable population—or listed as either endangered or threatened under the Endangered Species Act.

The 1994 amendments to the MMPA made significant changes to the requirements for public display permits. The MMPA requires that an applicant (facility) for public display, import, or export permits meet the following criteria.

• Offer a program for educational or conservation purposes that is based on professionally recognized standards of the public display community;
• Be registered or hold a license issued by APHIS;
• Maintain facilities for the display of marine mammals that are open to the public on a regularly scheduled basis, access to which is not limited or restricted other than by the charging of an admission fee.

The amendments specify that a public display permit will grant the permittee the right to take, import, purchase, offer to purchase, possess, or transport the marine mammals covered by the permit and to sell, export, or otherwise transfer possession of the marine mammals to another facility that meets the requirements for a public display permit. Recipients of transferred marine mammals will have the same rights and responsibilities as the original permittee.

The American Zoo and Aquarium Association (AZA) and the Alliance of Marine Mammal Parks and Aquariums have both submitted education standards for the public display community to NMFS at its request.

The Secretary of the Interior or the Secretary of Commerce may continue to impose permit conditions pertaining to the methods of capture, supervision, care, and transportation as they apply to the authorized taking or importation, but may not impose conditions once the taking or importation has been accomplished. The 1994 amendments codified the 1979 Memorandum of Understanding between the APHIS, NMFS, and FWS affirming APHIS as the sole agency to administer and enforce standards for humane handling, care, treatment, and transportation of marine mammals under the Animal Welfare Act.

Anyone selling, purchasing, exporting, or transporting a marine mammal under an MMPA permit must notify the Secretary of the Interior or Commerce at least 15 days before taking such action.

If the Secretary of the Interior or Commerce finds that a facility no longer satisfies the requirements pertaining to educational or conservation programs or public accessibility, or, with the concurrence of the Secretary of Agriculture, finds that a facility no longer meets the registration or licensing requirements established pursuant to the Animal Welfare Act, the Secretary may take steps to revoke the applicable permit, seize the animals, and provide for their disposition. The Secretary is authorized to recover from the noncompliant facility any costs incurred as a result of any such seizure.

Regulations implementing the 1994 amendments have not yet been proposed.

Applications should be submitted to FWS or NMFS, as appropriate. All applications for marine mammal permits will be published in the *Federal Register*. The public will be allowed 30 days to comment.

All marine mammal permits are reviewed by the Marine Mammal Commission. The commission is an independent body made up of three members appointed by the President of the United States and governed by an executive director. There is also a nine-member Committee of Scientific Advisors on Marine Mammals that assists the commission in making recommendations. The commission, among other duties, is charged with reviewing (1) U.S. laws as they pertain to international treaties on marine mammals; (2) the condition of marine mammal stocks in the wild; and (3) all marine mammal applications for public display or scientific research.

FUR SEAL ACT OF 1966

Northern fur seals, *Callorhinus ursinus*, are regulated by NMFS under the Fur Seal Act of 1966 (16 U.S.C. 1153) and not the Marine Mammal Protection Act.

Permits may be issued for the taking, transportation, or possession of fur seals for (among other things) educational, scientific, or exhibition purposes. The permit requirements are similar to those of the MMPA. Fur seals taken for educational, scientific, or exhibition purposes may be taken only from the Pribilof Islands by NMFS personnel on behalf of a permit holder.

Applications should be made by letter to NMFS. Permit applications will be published in the *Federal Register* and the public will be allowed 30 days to comment. The applications will then be reviewed by the Marine Mammal Commission.

NMFS will consider, among other criteria: (1) whether the taking will be consistent with the Fur Seal Act, (2) whether a substantial public benefit will be gained from public display, taking into account the kind of display and the anticipated audience and the effect on the fur seal population and the marine ecosystem; (3) the applicant's qualifications for the proper care and maintenance of the species; and (4) the adequacy of the facilities. NMFS may impose conditions such as transportation, care, and maintenance methods, reporting and inspection requirements, transfer or assignability of the permit, and the disposition of the fur seal and its progeny.

The permit is subject to modification, suspension, or revocation by NMFS. The permittee is entitled to written notification specifying the action taken and reasons therefor and necessary corrections for alleged deficiencies. Regulations are found in 50 C.F.R., part 215.

PUBLIC HEALTH SERVICE ACT

The Public Health Service Act (42 U.S.C. 264) was enacted to prevent the introduction, transmission, or spread of communicable diseases from foreign countries into the United States. Its restrictions apply to importations of turtles, psittacine birds, rodents, bats, and primates. The Department of Health and Human Services is responsible for implementing the act.

Live nonhuman primates may be imported into the United States and sold, resold, or distributed for bona fide scientific, educational, or exhibition purposes.

Presently, there are interim guidelines for handling nonhuman primates during transit and transport. The Centers for Disease Control (CDC) are developing technical standards for importation and quarantine of nonhuman primates as well as new regulations. This whole area is in a state of flux; therefore, importers should contact the CDC Division of Quarantine for information.

Regulations are found in 42 C.F.R. part 71.

LACEY ACT

The Lacey Act (16 U.S.C. 3371), significantly revised in 1981, makes it a violation of federal law to import, export, transport, sell, receive, acquire, or purchase any fish or wildlife taken or possessed in violation of any law, treaty, or regulation of the United States or any of the states, or any Indian tribe or any foreign country.

Any person who violates this law and with the exercise of due care should have known that the fish or wildlife was taken, possessed, transported, or sold in violation of any underlying law may be assessed a civil penalty of $10,000.

If the value of the fish or wildlife is less than $350 and the violation involves only the transportation, acquisition, or receipt of fish or wildlife taken or possessed in violation of any law, the penalty shall not exceed the maximum provided for violation of the underlying law or $10,000, whichever is less.

Criminal penalties of up to a $20,000 fine or 5 years imprisonment can be assessed for any person who knowingly imports or exports any fish or wildlife in violation of this act, or violates any provision of this act by knowingly engaging in the sale or purchase of fish or wildlife knowing that such were taken, possessed, transported, or sold in violation of any underlying law. Regulations are found in 50 C.F.R. parts 14 and 246.

INJURIOUS WILDLIFE

The injurious wildlife provision of the Lacey Act (18 U.S.C. 42) prohibits the importation, transportation, or acquisition of any wildlife (or their eggs) designated by the act as injurious into the United States without a permit. It is also illegal to ship injurious wildlife between the United States and any territory or between any two territories of the United States.

The mammals listed as injurious wildlife include:

1. Any species of flying fox or fruit bat of the genus *Pteropus*
2. Any species of mongoose or meerkat of the genera *Atilax, Cynictis, Helogale, Herpestes, Ichneumia, Mungos,* or *Suricata*
3. Any species of European rabbit of the genus *Oryctolagus*
4. Any species of Indian wild dog, red dog, or dhole of the genus *Cuon*

TABLE A3.1.   Orders of Mammals and U.S. Regulations that Apply to Them

Order	Regulations[a]
Artiodactyla	AWA; some CITES; some ESA; LAC; QUAR, except hippopotamuses
Carnivora	AWA; some CITES; some ESA; some INJ; LAC; some MMPA (polar bears and sea otters)
Cetacea	AWA; CITES; some ESA; LAC; MMPA
Chiroptera	AWA; some CITES; some ESA; some INJ; LAC; some PHSA
Dermoptera	AWA; LAC
Edentata	AWA; some ESA; some CITES; LAC
Hyracoidea	AWA; LAC
Insectivora	AWA; some CITES; some ESA; LAC
Lagomorpha	AWA; some CITES; some ESA; some INJ; LAC
Marsupialia	AWA; some CITES; some ESA; LAC
Monotremata	AWA; some CITES; LAC
Perissodactyla	AWA; some CITES; some ESA; LAC; QUAR (not Rhinocerotidae)
Pholidota	AWA; some ESA; some CITES; LAC
Pinnipedia	AWA; some CITES; some ESA; FSA (only *Callorhinus ursinus*); MMPA
Primates	AWA; CITES; most ESA; LAC; PHSA
Proboscidea	AWA; CITES; ESA; LAC
Rodentia	AWA (except rats and mice, guinea pigs, and hamsters); some CITES; some INJ; LAC; PHSA
Scandentia	AWA; LAC
Sirenia	AWA; CITES; ESA; LAC; MMPA
Tubulidentata	AWA; CITES; LAC

[a] Key to Abbreviations: AWA, Animal Welfare Act regulations; CITES, Convention on International Trade in Endangered Species of Wild Fauna and Flora; ESA, Endangered Species Act regulations; FSA, Fur Seal Act regulations; INJ, Lacey Act/Injurious Wildlife regulations; LAC, Lacey Act regulations; MMPA, Marine Mammal Protection Act regulations; PHSA, Public Health Service Act regulations; QUAR, USDA Quarantine/Importation regulations

5. Any species of multimammate rat or mouse of the genus *Mastomys*

6. Any raccoon dog, *Nyctereutes procyonoides*

Permits may be issued by the FWS to import otherwise prohibited injurious wildlife for zoological, educational, medical, or scientific purposes. Applications should be sent to the Special Agent in Charge of the FWS Regional Law Enforcement Office. Applicants must supply information about the premises where the wildlife will be kept and their qualifications and previous experience in caring for and handling captive wildlife. FWS will decide whether to issue a permit based on certain criteria, including: (1) whether the permit is for a bona fide activity; (2) whether the facilities are adequate to prevent escape and whether they have been inspected and approved; (3) whether the applicant can be expected to pro-vide adequate protection for public interests; and (4) if the wildlife is to be imported or acquired for exhibition purposes, whether the facility is open to the public.

Permits issued to import or ship injurious wildlife are subject to the following conditions: (1) all injurious wildlife possessed under a permit must be confined in the approved facilities on the authorized premises; (2) no injurious wildlife can be transferred in any way to another person who does not have a permit; and (3) the Director of FWS must be notified within 24 hours of any escape of any injurious wildlife, and a complete report must be filed within 10 days.

Regulations can be found in 50 C.F.R. part 16.

Table A3.1 lists the orders of mammals and the regulations that apply to them.

Appendix 4
Records, Studbooks, and ISIS Inventories

Alan Shoemaker and Nathan Flesness

Until the last few decades, maintenance and manipulation of vital statistics on wild animals held in captivity was not a widely practiced aspect of animal management. Rather, wild animals were commonly considered unlimited resources, and little attention was paid to incorporating record keeping into their husbandry or management. Relatively few older zoos can produce precise specimen data from the beginning of the twentieth century, even for important, nearly extinct species like the thylacine, *Thylacinus cynocephalus*, or quagga, *Equus quagga*, and many zoos have difficulty retrieving detailed data for specimens held during the 1950s and 1960s. This situation has improved greatly over the last fifteen years, and must continue to improve. Contemporary zoo-based species preservation and conservation programs now depend critically on quality specimen records.

Record Keeping

Record keeping should be an integral part of all zoological husbandry programs. Captive populations are increasingly becoming insurance policies against extinction in the wild, and the dwindling of wild populations also means that most future zoological exhibit specimens will descend from today's captive populations. Two-thirds of ISIS-registered zoological specimens are now captive-bred (ISIS 1990). Only permanent record systems on individually identified specimens will tell us what we have and who it is related to.

Prior to 1974 (the beginning of the International Species Information System—ISIS), standards within this area of animal management were quite varied, despite the fact that many national regulatory agencies required accurate retention of records and documents related to interstate and international commerce in and transportation of animals. In many instances, critical data on zoological specimens were known only by the director, curator, or keeper involved with the transaction or event, and were never recorded. Accordingly, the accuracy of these unwritten "data" faded over time, or they were lost following personnel changes. There were no uniform record-keeping procedures among zoos, and in the case of very large facilities, data maintained by divisions within a single institution often were contradictory.

As a matter of good standard practice, every specimen entering a collection should be formally accessioned, permanently identified, and documented, with special attention to information on its original provenance. This includes specimens acquired from other institutions and those accepted from the public as well as those born within the collection or otherwise incorporated into the permanent collection. Furthermore, this level of record keeping should include all captive-born young, regardless of whether they survive

to maturity, are stillborn or die shortly after birth, or are represented only by abortions or premature fetuses. Such data will be needed for analysis if problems generated by inbreeding or management surface later. For similar reasons, information on clutch size, fertility, and hatch rate should be recorded and retained.

Critical Data

1. Specimen Identification Each specimen should receive a unique accession number individually identifying it within the collection. Some zoos prefer to record all vertebrate taxa within a single record-keeping system, while others may maintain records within individual departments (mammals, birds, reptiles, etc.).

Accession (i.e., ISIS) numbers should be entirely numeric to facilitate computerization. When possible, record systems should be sequential; that is, begin with specimen 1 to indicate the first animal entering the collection or department and progress through 2, 3, 4, 5 . . . *n* to the present. Use of alphabetical or other nonnumeric characters is not recommended, as these have often caused confusion and sorting difficulties. Use of the accession number to encode other information is generally not desirable, although a simple year-of-accession-based scheme (i.e., 910001, 910002, for accessions during 1991) has proved successful for many institutions.

2. Gender The sex of all specimens should be noted, even if only to indicate that no determination has been made. When sex is confirmed surgically, this should be noted.

3. Parentage The accession numbers of the sires and dams of captive-born offspring should be recorded, regardless of whether they were born within the holding institution or at another location. In this way pedigrees can be constructed when genealogies need to be examined. When a studbook exists for the taxon, the assigned studbook numbers of the parents also should be recorded, for the same reason.

4. Age The specimen's age on arrival should be recorded, along with an indication of whether it is accurately known or an estimate (if an estimate, indicate the basis). When no responsible estimate even within several years is possible, indicate the life stage (i.e., "juvenile"). Age data are necessary for the increasingly important demographic analyses applied to captive populations.

5. Source and Provenance The date of arrival and origin of wildlife arriving from other locations should be recorded. Whenever possible, it is very important to record the accession numbers and other identifiers assigned by other institutions to this same specimen. It is also important to record information on any dealers or animal carriers used in transport or acquisition. Information on the purchase price also should be included. Whenever possible, data on the initial geographic origin of new specimens, whether

ld-caught or captive-bred, should be obtained and recorded. In-
tutions will know what they have only when specimens can be
aced through any captive pedigree back to the place of wild cap-
re of their ancestors.

6. Disposition The date and recipient of wildlife shipped to
her locations should be recorded. If possible, the accession num-
r and/or other identifiers assigned by them should be recorded,
these are valuable for later specimen tracing. If disposition is by
ath, the circumstances of death and any causal information or
topsy findings should be recorded, along with identification of
y museums or other institutions receiving specimen materials af-
r the specimen's death.

dditional Data

me important data are specific to particular taxa. Among the
ore common categories of information vital to management are
e types and locations of transponders, tattoos, tags, and bands;
use names; exhibit locations; and studbook numbers. Important
havioral considerations, especially rearing techniques (i.e., par-
t- or hand-reared) should be noted. The numbers of interna-
nal, national, state, or provincial permit(s) used to acquire or
move the wildlife should be listed for ease of reference.

udbooks

important exception to the generally poor record-keeping prac-
es of the past has been the compilation and maintenance of inter-
tional and regional zoological studbooks. In 1930 the last wild
pulations of the Caucasian subspecies of the European bison, *Bi-
n bonasus caucasicus,* were extirpated, just a few years after the
ss of the nominate race in Poland, *B. b. bonasus,* which was ex-
guished by poachers in 1922 (Slatis 1960). Fearing that the cap-
e population of Europe's only remaining wild bovine would suf-
r a similar fate unless carefully monitored, administrators of
ological parks in Europe established an international studbook
milar to those used for domestic livestock. Initiated in 1924 with
ta obtained after World War I by Heinz Heck Sr. (Mohr 1968),
is pedigree was first published in 1932 (von der Groeben 1932)
d became the first studbook designed specifically for the zoologi-
l park community. In 1959, a similar studbook for the Asian
ld horse, *Equus przewalskii* (also extinct in the wild), was pub-
hed by Mohr (1959). Since 1965, studbooks have become an
tegral part of the management of endangered species living in
ological parks.

Another reason studbooks are established is to keep records
ear when both pure and hybridized specimens of a species are
ld. Some hybrid young are intermediate in appearance between
eir two parents and may be easily distinguished from them. The
ung of other species may not be distinguished readily from ei-
er parent and, after multiple generations, become impossible to
stinguish from pure specimens. Hybridization, of course, is gen-
ally discouraged—especially between studbook-kept species or
bspecies.

It is fortunate and noteworthy that the zoological community
udbook standard is an expansion of the information typically
ntained in domestic-breed studbooks. Zoological studbooks also
ntain date of death—information not normally compiled in do-
estic-breed studbooks. Because of this important addition, zoo-
gical studbooks contain the minimum critical data necessary for
netic and demographic management of small populations.

efinition

udbook keeping involves the compilation of genealogical and
mographic data covering a species' history in captivity. This task
cludes numerically identifying individual specimens to record
rmanently data on their origins and dates of arrival from the
wild, parentage and date of birth (if captive-born), gender, important locally assigned identifiers, including accession numbers and
house names, dates of departure, identification of subsequent owners and holders, and dates and causes of death. Some studbooks
also include supplementary information such as rearing technique,
levels of inbreeding, and so forth. International studbooks must
be updated annually and republished in their entirety every three
years. Regional studbook standards are often even more stringent,
but may vary somewhat with the region.

Because captive population sizes and fecundity rates vary
greatly, the task of keeping a studbook ranges from the simple
and easy to the large and very challenging. All studbooks benefit
from computerization because of the automatic quality control
and greater efficiency that can be achieved, and because of the need
for sophisticated genetic and demographic analyses of the population data the studbook contains.

Computer programs that assist with studbook keeping and
printing have been developed by several individuals and groups.
They have varied greatly in ease of use, flexibility, analytic power,
and accuracy. Studbook keepers should select computer software
carefully to be sure it can meet both studbook production and
population analysis needs. Coordinated population management
requires extensive demographic and genetic analysis of the data set
the studbook represents. The SPARKS program, developed by ISIS
for the IBM PC and compatible microcomputers, is recommended
for zoological studbook and population analysis.

When studbooks were first developed, most were directed at
species that were highly endangered or extinct in the wild. Now
some studbooks are maintained on species that still may be common in the wild but are unavailable from nature. In a similar vein,
early studbooks were directed toward large, charismatic species,
but more recently smaller, less charismatic species have begun to
receive this level of treatment. Birds, reptiles, and amphibians are
now being managed through the use of studbooks. By 1990 well
over 150 species had studbooks either regionally or internationally.
The first studbooks were organized at the international level, but
today many of these are augmented by regional studbooks, or encompass only captive populations within a single region.

It should be noted that a studbook and a registry are not the
same. A studbook numerically identifies individual specimens and
tracks them throughout their entire lifetimes. A registry only summarizes the inventory of target species at various locations, and
does not distinguish between individual animals. As a result, the
quality and usefulness of the data in a registry are inferior to that
in a studbook; registry initiation is not encouraged.

Coordination and Initiation

Worldwide, international studbooks are overseen by a coordinator
(Peter Olney) sponsored by The Zoological Society of London
under the auspices of IUCN-The World Conservation Union and
IUDZG-The World Zoo Organization. IUCN policy on studbooks
is developed and expressed through the Conservation Breeding
Specialist Group of the Species Survival Commission (CBSG/SSC)
of IUCN. International studbooks must receive official endorse-
ment from these organizations. In North America, studbook keeping is further regulated by the American Zoo and Aquarium Association (AZA) through its Wildlife Conservation and Management
Committee (WCMC). In the case of international studbooks, the
AZA acts as a liaison between the international studbook office
and North American studbook keepers.

All potential studbooks initiated by AZA members must be approved by the AZA/WCMC prior to data collection. To assist interested parties in developing a studbook petition, the WCMC has
prepared a protocol document providing advice on the characteristics of candidate species, application procedures and petition requirements, and standards for preparing a studbook. In consider-

ing the merit of a studbook petition, the WCMC considers all aspects of the proposal, especially captive conservation priorities. Institutional and personnel resources are also investigated because of the workload and costs involved.

Applications and Standards

Studbooks now serve as the data bases for a growing number of coordinated captive management programs, such as the AZA's Species Survival Plan (SSP), the Joint Management of Species Group (JMSG) of zoos in the British Isles, the continental European zoos' Entwicklung Erhaltungzucht Programme (EEP), the Australasian zoos' Species Management Plan (SMP), the Japanese Association of Zoological Gardens and Aquaria's Species Survival Committee, and developing programs elsewhere. This makes studbook accuracy and timeliness even more important than before.

This increasing level of importance was the reason that North American institutions imposed an additional level of review by requiring that all studbooks based in AZA member institutions be approved by WCMC prior to data collection. AZA-member owners of captive wildlife who receive unsanctioned North American questionnaires are under no obligation to complete them. Through this requirement, all participating parties are assured that a studbook project has merit, involves an institution capable of providing adequate support, and will be maintained by an individual with the necessary skills, qualifications, and commitment to complete and maintain the project.

Standards for format and timeliness of studbook publication have been developed based on much experience. Persons desiring further information on studbook keeping or managed species should contact the AZA's Conservation Center.

ISIS

The International Species Information System (ISIS) grew out of widespread recognition that a central, timely source for pooled captive specimen data was needed and that zoological specimen records needed improvement. In 1973, U. S. Seal and D. G. Makey proposed to the AZA and AAZV (American Association of Zoo Veterinarians) that such a system be started. Both organizations endorsed the proposal and offered seed money. Development funds were raised from grant agencies and foundations, a computer system constructed under the auspices of the new Minnesota Zoological Garden, and invitations distributed to major zoos worldwide. ISIS began operations in 1974 with 51 North American and 4 European zoological institutions participating. The IUDZG endorsed ISIS shortly after operations commenced. The network of ISIS-participating institutions has expanded steadily, reaching 100 by 1979, 200 by 1984, and a total of 378 as of the end of 1990.

As of August 1993, 467 institutions (268 North American, 121 European, 42 Asian, 15 Australasian, 12 African, and 9 South American facilities) in a total of 52 countries participated in ISIS. They registered 187,747 live mammal, bird, reptile, and amphibian specimens of 4,200 species and subspecies with ISIS, along with almost 500,000 of those animals' ancestors.

ISIS supports its operations primarily through members' fees (operations grants from the AZA played a significant role in the past). Development efforts, such as improvement of software and services, have been supported by granting agencies and private foundations as well as by donations from participant institutions.

ISIS and Zoological Records

ISIS has thus far provided over 1,000,000 standardized, archive-quality multipart specimen inventory record forms to participating facilities. These forms have contributed substantially to improving the quality and standardization of zoological records. Since December of 1985, ISIS has offered an alternative to such paper forms.

Called ARKS, for "Animal Records Keeping System," this softwa package is designed for in-house use by zoological facilities on IB PC and compatible microcomputers. ARKS produces numero reports for use by the facility (specimens, taxa, collections, tra actions, local inbreeding, age pyramids, life tables, local pedigre reproductive history, siblings, enclosures, etc.), and also au mates participation in ISIS. Taxon reports produced by ARKS ha greatly simplified participation in studbooks for many facilities. of August 1993, 401 institutions in 44 countries had adopted ISI ARKS software.

ISIS has focused on assembling the specimen data necessary pooled inventories and for genetic and demographic populati management. These data include the same information collect for a much smaller number of species by zoological studboo Less emphasis has been placed so far on standardizing and pooli nutritional, behavioral, or general medical records, although I paper forms, ARKS, and the developing medical records compa ion system, MedARKS, do offer means for keeping such record Additionally, ISIS offers standardized record forms for clinical thology data, and operates an additional data base that provi pooled blood chemistry and hematology data on over 600 spec to the 45 institutions that participate in it.

ISIS collects and disseminates data based on individually ide tified specimens only. Individual specimen data are a far more po erful management tool than data on groups, and ISIS has stron encouraged identification and marking of individual specimens. dividual specimens are identified in ISIS records by specimen I assigned by the holding institution (up to 6 characters in lengt usually as some sort of accession number.

When a specimen is transferred to another institution, it is n mally assigned a new accession number (specimen ID) by the n institution. ISIS assembles a specimen's history using (primari this chain of sequential specimen IDs. It is therefore vital that ea successive acquiring institution report to ISIS the specimen ID us by the previous facility.

ISIS Services

ISIS's main reason for being is to provide information based on t pooling of records across participating institutions. At the time writing, ISIS is redesigning its central data base and designing hanced central services. Major services available at present inclu the following.

Pooled Inventory ISIS provides participants with semiann registries of all live specimens in the ISIS data base. Two levels detail are offered.

1. ISIS Species Distribution Report (SDR). This report is organiz taxonomically and contains numbers of all specimens held each participant facility, indicates births by facility for the l year, and provides summary sex distribution information at taxonomic levels. This report is useful for detailed surveys captive holdings, as well as for quick assessment of the capt status of a population.
2. SDR Abstracts. These are spiral-bound paper volumes total a few hundred pages that contain a condensation of the en mously longer data base. The Abstracts are organized by tax nomic class and contain the sex-specific holdings of all facilit (identified by abbreviations) and their births during the last months, as well as a one-line summary of proportion capti bred, total bred in the last 12 months, and the number born t died in the first 30 days. These reports are primarily a conveni format for who-has-what information.

Partial Studbooks Available on request from ISIS for any of t 4,200 registered taxa are "studbook-like" reports that show bir transfer, and death information for all individuals in the taxon corded with ISIS. These resemble a true studbook in format,

re of course limited to the information submitted by ISIS participants. They are typically current to within 1–2 months. For the
95% of captive species without formal studbooks, these reports are
the only existing source of such information, and are the only available international data set for tracing pedigree relationships or performing genetic or demographic analyses of the captive population.
When new formal studbooks are initiated, this ISIS information
offers a very good start, already compiled. These partial studbooks
are offered both as printed paper reports and as computer-readable
files, in SPARKS format (see below).

"In-House" Information Tools

ARKS: an increasingly powerful PC-based animal records software
package for use in collections management at one site.

MedARKS: a very thorough PC-based veterinary medical records
software package, offering many kinds of reports for improving
veterinary medical management of animal collections.

SPARKS: a powerful PC-based software package for maintaining
and producing studbooks and performing the demographic and
genetic analyses necessary for coordinated species management
programs. ISIS can supply a partial studbook for any taxon in
SPARKS format, and plans to be able to accept studbooks compiled in SPARKS for addition to ISIS's central data base and ar-
chive. SPARKS is therefore an important tool for developing more
efficient interchange of and future integration of data from ISIS and
studbook sources, as has been recommended by Glatston (1986)
and others.

ISIS paper data forms: a world standard animal records system for
those not yet able or willing to computerize their specimen records.

Institutional inventory: a traditional ISIS service offering inventory and acquisition/removal reports to participants. Before the
widespread adoption of ARKS, these reports were an important
resource for many facilities. Now, they serve primarily to double-
check submitted data. When needed for some purpose by an insti-

tution, these reports are available as of a specified month and can
be requested as an "institutional history," showing all recorded accessions and removals for some specified time interval.

Summary

Specimen records have always been important, but the rapid conversion of many zoological populations to dependence on captive
breeding for replacement stock makes them even more so. Assem-
bly and distribution of captive population-wide information from
these records is then the next important step. Both the studbook
and ISIS mechanisms help meet these needs.

Collecting near-comprehensive specimen data institution by institution, as ISIS does, complements the studbook approach of
collecting data taxon by taxon. As ISIS continues to expand its
capabilities, coverage, and services, improved interaction and data
interchange with the formal studbooks will result. This interchange should be mutually beneficial, and should contribute to
sound captive population management.

References

Glatston, A. R. 1986. Studbooks: the basis of breeding programmes. *Int. Zoo Yrbk.* 24/25:162–67.
ISIS. 1990. Species distribution report for 31 December 1990.
Apple Valley, Minn.: ISIS.
Mohr, E. 1959. Das Urwildferd. *Neue Brehm Buch.* no. 249.
———. 1968. Studbooks for wild animals in captivity. *Int. Zoo
Yrbk.* 8:159–66.
Slatis, H. M. 1960. An analysis of inbreeding in the European
bison. *Genetics* 45:275–87.
von der Groeben, G. 1932. Das Zuchtbuch. In *Ber. int. Ges. Er-
halt. Wisents* 5.

Appendix 5
Inter-Zoo Breeding Loans

Judith A. Block and Lorraine A. Perkins

Zoos have probably been giving, selling, trading, and loaning animals to one another since zoos began. How the two parties come to a decision about the type of transaction, what value to place on the animals, and what conditions they set depends on many factors. When an animal is sold, traded, or given away, the zoo has no further claim on that animal or its offspring. The loan—by which the animal, but not title to it, is transferred—has become increasingly popular among zoo managers who must look to a future when animals are no longer available from the wild and must increasingly be obtained from captive stock.

There are several types of special-purpose, usually temporary, loans of animals between zoos. In the exhibit loan, animals may be loaned for a specific period, such as the summer season. In the study or research loan, animals may be loaned for a special project. In the care and maintenance loan, an animal may be loaned for hand rearing, or while the lender is rebuilding an exhibit facility. Occasionally there are loans of animals for specialized medical care.

In the early 1970s, zoo managers began to consider the idea of retaining title to the genetic resources embodied in particular animals, thus setting the stage for captive breeding programs for conservation purposes and the development of formal, often long-term, animal loans.

The breeding loan is actually a special-purpose loan like those described above, but is focused primarily on the propagation of an animal over the long term. A major objective of breeding loan agreements is to ensure continued ownership of the animal and some or all of its offspring by one or both parties. Just as retention of ownership of the animal gives the lender recall rights and a claim on offspring, it also gives the lender some rights and responsibilities concerning the manner in which the animal is maintained and bred. Plans for maintenance and breeding strategies are thus major aspects of any loan arrangement, whether the loan involves one specimen and two neighboring zoos, or, directly or indirectly, the entire captive and wild populations of a species and zoos and governments all over the world.

Loans of all types should include formal, legally binding agreements between lender and borrower. These agreements often read the same for simple "next-door" loans as they do for complex international arrangements, but in the latter case the plans and strategies are contained in documents separate from the actual breeding loan agreement.

Formal breeding loan agreements are designed to address as many—or as few—of the points necessary to ensure that both borrower and lender have no doubts about their respective rights and responsibilities and that they are in accord. The creation, implementation, and testing of these agreements are new endeavors, and their legal and management implications are becoming understood through experience.

MAJOR ASPECTS OF THE LOAN AGREEMENT

A formal loan agreement should state the primary function(s) of the loan. The reason the animal is being loaned and borrowed is the standard by which all actions will be measured. Whatever the functions of a loan, concerns for the welfare and best care of the animal should be made explicit. The responsibilities and extent of control to be exercised by both lender and borrower should be addressed. Flexibility must be built into the loan agreement to allow for changes of plans or unforeseen developments through specific clauses that provide for amending or modifying the document.

The written loan agreement is a legal, binding document. Most of the words and phrases in the document have specific, narrow definitions developed (in other contexts) in courts of law, and these definitions take precedence over common everyday usage. For example, one cannot use the term "arbitration" and assign a zoo curator as a third party to settle a dispute when, in many states and other government units, arbitration is a formal procedure that can be carried out only in a strictly prescribed setting by authorized persons.

Loans may be between and among individuals, institutions, and governments (from the local to the national level). The legal structure and requirements of each party must be considered in the loan agreement that is negotiated. The person who signs such a document, committing an institution and its resources, must have the authority to do so.

The loan agreement in use at present in U.S. zoos, described below, generally follows a format developed in the late 1970s. Some zoos make modifications relating to specific considerations. The usual breeding loan agreement (hereafter BLA) is divided into four main sections: an introduction, obligations of the lender, obligations of the borrower, and obligations of both institutions. The general contents of each section are presented below, along with a brief discussion of common variations, and recommendations in some cases.

Introduction

At the outset, the participant institutions are identified as "loaning institution" and "receiving institution." The purpose of the loan should be specified in this first section. The introduction should include a clause specifying that all offspring resulting from the BLA that are the property of the lender also will be covered by the original

nal agreement. Such a clause eliminates potential confusion regarding loan termination (termination is discussed in a later section) and ensures that young are covered by all of the obligation clauses until such time as separate agreements may be drafted for them.

Obligations of the Lender

The loaning institution generally agrees to two primary conditions: it will not hold the receiving institution responsible for mishap (disease, injury, or death of the loaned specimen); and it will provide all pertinent information about the loaned specimen to the receiving institution. In some agreements, the lender agrees to grant right of first refusal to the receiving institution should the lender decide to dispose of (i.e., sell) title to the loaned specimen.

An infrequent but important stipulation used by some zoos states that the receiving institution is free from responsibility for mishap *provided* that such mishap is not due to negligence. How negligence is to be determined and the options for compensation are not stated, but procedures for dealing with such circumstances may not in fact need to be addressed by zoos unless or until cases are disputed in courts of law.

Obligations of the Borrower

The obligations to which the receiving institution agrees are more numerous, more complex, and more variable, but, in general, they address five or six basic issues.

First, the receiving institution agrees to care for the loaned specimen to the best of its ability by providing a situation conducive to the well-being and reproduction of the specimen. Second, a clause regarding the selection of a mate for the loaned specimen may be inserted. One of the following stipulations may be specified: American Zoo and Aquarium Association's Species Survival Plan (SSP) will determine choice of mate; the lender will name the specific individual to be mated with the loaned specimen; or the lender will have the right to approve the selection of a mate for the loaned specimen. An SSP determination can be difficult to obtain if animal-by-animal breeding plans have not yet been fully developed, and, regarding the second alternative, unforeseen circumstances may make the mate specified by the lender unavailable, necessitating, at least in theory, a new BLA. The authors recommend the last alternative.

The foregoing emphasizes the lender's awareness of the housing situation into which its loaned specimen is placed. Such knowledge can minimize the possibility of disputes, including conflicts about disease transmission and conspecific aggression as well as offspring apportionment.

The third, and most complex and important, issue addressed under the obligations of the borrower concerns the ownership of offspring that result from the BLA. There are many offspring-apportionment systems in use, but in keeping with the good-faith nature of the BLA, most are geared to equity for all concerned. How ownership of offspring is divided depends on the particular interests of the participating institutions and on the reproductive patterns of the species (e.g., single births, litters, or clutches). Each institution should carefully consider its future plans and determine what exactly it wants from the BLA and how this will affect the purpose of the loan (e.g., the loaning institution might not want to own any offspring unless the original animal cannot be brought back into its own breeding program).

The most common apportionment method states that the loaning institution will be the owner of the first viable offspring, with the receiving institution owning the second, and so on. If the participant institutions have an interest in offspring of a given gender, the division may be according to sex of offspring. If a receiving institution receives more than one loaned specimen from more than one institution, it may be specified that the owner of the dam will own the first offspring, the receiving institution the second, and the owner of the sire the third.

For most apportionment schemes, knowing the identity of the sire and dam is essential, and indeed is a requirement for all SSP animals. In group situations with multiple pairing possibilities, if parentage cannot be determined, ownership of offspring may be apportioned among the receiving institution and the other institutions that have contributed specimens to the group, according to their proportional contributions. Alternatively, the best method for the division of ownership of offspring may be to apportion "offspring-to-date" every few years. This method also may be used in larger breeding programs even when parentage is known.

When the litter or clutch size of a species is greater than one, it may be impossible to determine which is the "first" offspring. In this situation, the determination of birth order often is made arbitrarily, on a case-by-case basis. For BLAs involving species that frequently bear more than one offspring per litter, offspring apportionment may be litter-by-litter rather than one-by-one.

We do not recommend that institutions state in the BLA that "half of the offspring will be the property of the loaning institution, and half will be the property of the receiving institution," because how this clause should be interpreted is unclear.

As mentioned earlier, most BLA offspring apportionment plans specify "viable" offspring. Most, however, do not provide a definition of the term. The best method is to use a species-specific definition of viability, stating that offspring surviving "more than 30 days" or "to the age of 6 months" will be divided in the given manner. The ownership of offspring is assigned when the criteria of viability are met.

Another decision to be made is whether a new loan agreement should be produced for each offspring of loaned animals, or whether such offspring will be covered by the terms specified in the original agreement. Several institutions incorporate a clause into the introduction of their standard loan agreement stating that all offspring owned by the lender will be covered by the original agreement. Such a clause is quite useful as an interim measure until separate agreements are developed for progeny.

A fourth obligation of the receiving institution is to obtain permission from the loaning institution before subjecting the loaned specimen to any high-risk or stressful procedures, and to provide the lender with a written follow-up. It is also wise to specify that the loaned specimen is not to be transferred out of the receiving institution without the lender's prior knowledge and consent.

A fifth obligation of the receiving institution is to provide to the lender "timely notification" of births (or hatchings) or death, illness, or escape of the specimen(s) covered by the BLA. "Timely notification" generally ranges from 24 hours to 30 days, and varies from one agreement to another. In addition, some BLAs specify that the receiving institution must provide a yearly status report on the loaned specimen(s). If a loaned specimen dies, the receiving institution is required to perform a detailed necropsy and to provide its findings to the loaning institution. The carcass remains the property of the loaning institution. Finally, the receiving institution agrees to provide all information necessary to maintain appropriate studbooks and record-keeping systems, including ISIS data.

Obligations of Both Institutions

Most BLAs specify responsibility for the costs of transporting specimens to the receiving institution and of returning them to the loaning institution at the termination of the loan; usually the recipient of a given shipment must pay such costs. The proposed termination date also is indicated in this section of the agreement. Many simply state that the BLA "will remain in effect until terminated." A better method is to specify that the agreement will remain in effect "for the lifetime of the specimen," which includes the lifetimes of offspring owned by the lender if such a clause has been written into the introduction. All termination arrangements include the statement that either party may effect termination prior to any established time by providing advance written notice of such intent. Some BLAs also stipulate that if this option is exercised, the specific shipping information is to be provided by some period of time, usually 30 days, prior to the actual shipment. Some concern over this point has been raised: 30 days' notice of intent to ship a small specimen may be more than adequate, but 30 days may not be sufficient time for the recipient to prepare for receiving a very large animal. Thus the negotiated loan agreement should specify an acceptable period of time for notice of intent to ship the animal concerned.

In any BLA, there should be specified some method of dealing with differences of opinion among the parties. A commonly specified system of conflict resolution is that each participating institution will nominate five Professional Fellows of the AZA, who must agree to serve as arbitrators; then each participant must delete a name from the other's list until three names remain. These three Professional Fellows will then settle the dispute. This system is complicated. First, if Professional Fellows willing to serve cannot be found, the system will break down. Second, the participant institutions, in signing the BLA, agree to abide by the decisions of such arbitrators. It is unclear what might follow if both participants had misgivings about the decision reached. Third, the participants' legal structures may require arbitration through other channels. In that case, there are concrete definitions of and restrictions on the rights and obligations of arbitrators that would preempt the use of this procedure. We know of no actual experience to date in using this system.

Other BLAs specify that the signatories to the agreement themselves will resolve any conflicts between them. This arrangement, too, has inherent problems, such as the possibility that the signatories have vested interests in the outcome of a dispute. Further, if a zoo is required by its governing authority to obtain signatures from officials not directly involved with the zoo itself (e.g., mayor, city auditor, etc.), problems could arise because these signatories may be unfamiliar with the issues involved. This latter method of conflict resolution, however, is probably the better alternative. It is to be hoped that the professional ethics of the parties involved will enable them to arrive at a reasonable and equitable solution to any conflict.

BLAs generally specify that the welfare of the specimen will be the sole consideration in the settlement of any dispute among the parties. It is the authors' opinion that the welfare of the specimen might sometimes be secondary to larger goals (e.g., the SSP, or the health of other animals nearby). Furthermore, disputes of a strictly legal nature might involve jurisdiction rather than biology.

Finally, most agreements require the signature of an officer (usually the director) of the loaning institution and of the receiving institution. The agreement, like a contract, goes into effect on the date it is signed by the final signing party. Its terms become effective upon the date of shipment of the specimen.

As more breeding loans are undertaken in conjunction with regional or global strategies for captive population management, other sorts of formal agreements are coming into existence. A loan agreement between two (or more) parties must not contradict other obligations, such as cooperative management agreements.

Spirit and Intent

The basis of formal breeding loan agreements is the good faith and good will under which they are drafted and signed. They *are* legal documents, but it is noteworthy and laudatory that in more than a decade, no court cases have been required to test the letter of these documents.

Also, it is clear from our experience that the idea of a "standard" loan agreement, an idea we cherished at the start, has not been achieved. Common elements and a template have emerged (see "Sample Breeding Loan Agreement" below), but the applications have been varied and seem to be becoming more so. In the future, borrowers and lenders must improve their procedures for administering loans. A simple example of such an improvement would be the prompt notification of a lender when his or her animal dies; information about mating or injury would also be a useful refinement.

There are some factors, such as public relations or publication rights and public health and safety, that are not often incorporated into current loan agreements. If lenders are not credited in press releases or not acknowledged in popular and scientific articles, or if a public hazard suddenly is attributed to zoo animals, new clauses addressing these matters might need to be added routinely to loan agreements.

In the authors' view, the number of loans probably will decline in the future as the administration of captive breeding program continues to improve and curators become more confident of continued access to animals. Other sorts of transactions will be explored, such as restricted gifts, by which title is transferred but some rights are retained by the donor. It is to be hoped that there will be a constant reevaluation of the formal loan agreements that we create and by which we live.

BREEDING LOAN AGREEMENT

This Breeding Loan Agreement, entered into by

NATIONAL ZOOLOGICAL PARK (NZP) (Loaning Institution)

and

SAMPLE ZOOLOGICAL GARDENS (SZG) (Receiving Institution)

concerns the preservation and propagation of certain specimen(s) identified as follows:

Common name *(Scientific name)*

Sex	Loaning Institution Specimen I.D. Number	Receiving Institution Specimen I.D. Number	Studbook Number
female	NZP #703826		722

As appropriate and unless otherwise specified, the term specimen(s) used in this Agreement will include the progeny of said specimen(s). All permits and licenses for shipping, receiving, and holding of the specimen(s) shall be obtained by the loaning or receiving institutions as required by law.

A. Obligations of the Loaning Institution

1. It is agreed that in the event of disease, injury, or death of the specimen(s) and in the absence of negligence, the receiving institution, its agents and employees will be free of all responsibility to the loaning institution.

2. A copy of all appropriate information pertaining to the specimen(s), including, but not restricted to, ISIS data, behavioral traits, medical and reproductive history, diet, origin, and all other pertinent data will be provided by the loaning institution.

B. Obligations of the Receiving Institution

1. The receiving institution will provide the highest acceptable standards of housing, security for the specimen(s) and the public, diet, veterinary care, and other necessities conducive to the well-being and reproduction of the specimen(s). Under certain circumstances (bachelor herds, etc.) the specimen(s) may be placed in a non-reproductive situation, but will be maintained in compliance with the above, for subsequent reintroduction into a potential reproductive situation.

2. The receiving institution will undertake its best efforts to breed the specimen(s) with mates approved by the loaning institution.

3. Any live young born or hatched, either during the term of this Agreement or within a period after termination of this Agreement measured by the normal gestation or incubation period of the species will be divided between the participating institutions as follows:

NZP will own the first, third, fifth, and so forth of the viable young born;
SZG will own the second, fourth, sixth, and so forth of such viable young.

4. In the event of the specimen(s) being subjected to high-risk veterinary or husbandry procedures, permission must be obtained by telephone or telegraph from the loaning institution before the performance of such procedures. This provision is waived in the event of an emergency. Details of such procedures shall be provided in writing to the loaning institution within ten (10) days. For any research project in which the specimen(s) may be subjected to manipulation, stress, or high-risk procedures, prior permission must be obtained in writing from the appropriate official of the loaning institution.

5. The specimen(s) described in this document will not be transferred to another location outside the receiving institution's property without first obtaining permission from the loaning institution.

6. The loaning institution will be notified immediately by telephone or telegraph of mortality of the specimen(s), serious illness, or the escape of the specimen(s). The loaning institution will be notified of births or hatches as soon as reasonably possible.

7. In the event of the death of the specimen(s), a detailed necropsy will be performed by the receiving institution and the findings sent to the loaning institution.

8. The carcass and its parts remain the property of the loaning institution. The final disposition of the carcass and parts will be the decision and the responsibility of the loaning institution.

9. The receiving institution will provide all information necessary to maintain appropriate studbooks and record-keeping systems, including ISIS data.

10. A copy of all pertinent records will be sent to the loaning institution upon termination of this Agreement.

C. Obligations of Both Institutions

1. The receiving institution shall hold harmless the United States, the Smithsonian Institution (SI-NZP), and any of their respective officers, employees, and representatives from any damage, loss, injury or death occurring by reason of anything done or omitted to be done by the receiving institution in connection with the execution of this Agreement if such acts are not under the direct supervision and control of the loaning institution.

2. All transportation expenses incurred in shipping the specimen(s) to the receiving institution will be borne by the receiving institution; transportation expenses for returning the specimen(s) to the loaning institution will be borne by the loaning institution.

3. Unless one of the parties terminates this Agreement by giving the other party 30 days written notice, this Agreement will remain in effect for the lifetime of the specimen(s).

4. Prior to the shipping of the specimen(s), the receiving institution must be notified at least 14 days in advance; and the specific shipping information must be provided at least 24 hours in advance of actual shipment.

5. Neither this Agreement, nor any rights or privileges granted hereunder, shall be assigned without prior written consent by the undersigned parties hereto.

6. Consistent with applicable law, the undersigned or their designees shall be responsible for resolving any conflicts arising from the implementation of this Agreement.

7. This Agreement may be amended or modified by mutual consent of all parties hereto. Such amendments shall be incorporated into this Agreement as addenda.

Executed this the _____ day of _____, 199_____.

Signature _____
    Director
    National Zoological Park
    Washington, D.C. 20008 U.S.A.
    (Loaning Institution)

Signature _____
    Director
    Sample Zoological Gardens
    street address
    city, state, ZIP code, country
    (Receiving Institution)

CONTRIBUTORS

Mary E. Allen
Department of Nutritional Resources
National Zoological Park
Smithsonian Institution
Washington, D.C. 20008

Wilbur B. Amand
Zoological Society of Philadelphia
3400 West Girard Avenue
Philadelphia, Pennsylvania 19104

Cheryl S. Asa
Research Department
St. Louis Zoological Park
Forest Park
St. Louis, Missouri 63110

David J. Baer
USDA ARS
BHNRC EPNL
BARC—EAST
Bldg. 308, Room 226
Beltsville, Maryland 20705

Andrew J. Baker
Philadelphia Zoological Garden
3400 West Girard Avenue
Philadelphia, Pennsylvania 19104

Anne M. Baker
Burnet Park Zoo
500 Burnet Park Drive
Syracuse, New York 13204-2504

Jonathan D. Ballou
Department of Zoological Research
National Zoological Park
Smithsonian Institution
Washington, D.C. 20008

George F. Barrowclough
Department of Ornithology
American Museum of Natural History
Central Park West at 79th Street
New York, New York 10024

Kurt Benirschke
Department of Pathology
University of California, San Diego
Medical Center
200 West Arbor Drive
San Diego, California 92103

Joel Berger
Program in Ecology, Evolution and
    Conservation Biology
University of Nevada
1000 Valley Road
Reno, Nevada 89612

Judith Block
National Zoological Park
Smithsonian Institution
Washington, D.C. 20008

Daryl J. Boness
Department of Zoological Research
National Zoological Park
Smithsonian Institution
Washington, D.C. 20008

Mitchell Bush
Conservation and Research Center
National Zoological Park
1500 Remount Road
Front Royal, Virginia 22630

Kathy Carlstead
Department of Zoological Research
National Zoological Park
Smithsonian Institution
Washington, D.C. 20008

Jon Charles Coe
CLR Design
115 North Third Street
Philadelphia, Pennsylvania 19106

Larry Collins
Conservation and Research Center
National Zoological Park
1500 Remount Road
Front Royal, Virginia 22630

Carolyn M. Crockett
Regional Primate Research Center SJ-50
University of Washington
Seattle, Washington 98195

Scott Derrickson
Conservation and Research Center
National Zoological Park
1500 Remount Road
Front Royal, Virginia 22630

Donald A. Dewsbury
Department of Psychology
University of Florida
Gainesville, Florida 32611

James G. Doherty
Department of Mammalogy
The Wildlife Conservation Society
185th Street and Southern Boulevard
Bronx, New York 10460

John F. Eisenberg
The Florida Museum of Natural History
University of Florida
Gainesville, Florida 32611

Sue Ellis
IUCN/SSC/CBSG
138 Strasburg Reservoir Road
Strasburg, Virginia 22657

Daniel Q. Estep
Animal Behavior Associates, Inc.
4994 South Independence Way
Littleton, Colorado 80123-1906

Donna Fernandes
Commonwealth Zoological Corporation
1 Franklin Park Road
Boston, Massachusetts 02121

Joseph P. Flanagan
Houston Zoological Gardens
1513 North MacGregor
Houston, Texas 77030

Robert C. Fleischer
Department of Zoological Research
National Zoological Park
Smithsonian Institution
Washington, D.C. 20008

Nathan R. Flesness
International Species Inventory System
13000 Zoo Boulevard
Apple Valley, Minnesota 55124

Thomas J. Foose
International Rhino Foundation
The Wilds
14000 International Road
Cumberland, Ohio 43237

Steve Graham
P.O. Box 150
Bloxom, Virginia 23308

Theodore I. Grand
Departments of Pathology and Zoological
    Research
National Zoological Park
Smithsonian Institution
Washington, D.C. 20008

David Hancocks
Arizona-Sonora Desert Museum
2021 North Kinney Road
Tucson, Arizona 85743-8919

Donna FitzRoy Hardy
Department of Psychology
California State University, Northridge
18111 Nordhoff Street—PSYCH
Northridge, California 91330

Keith C. Hinshaw
Zoological Society of Philadelphia
3400 West Girard Avenue
Philadelphia, Pennsylvania 19104

J. Keith Hodges
Deutsches Primatenzentrum
6Mb H
Kellnerweg A
D-3400 Göttingen
Germany

Michael Hutchins
AZA Conservation Center
7970-D Old Georgetown Road
Bethesda, Maryland 20814

Donald W. Jackson
P.O. Box 4314
Elwyn, Pennsylvania 19063-7314

Penny Kalk
Collections Manager, Mammalogy
The Wildlife Conservation Society
185th Street and Southern Boulevard
Bronx, New York 10460

Kay A. Kenon
National Zoological Park Branch Library
Smithsonian Institution
Washington, D.C. 20008

James K. Kirkwood
Department of Veterinary Science
Institute of Zoology
The Zoological Society of London
Regent's Park
London NW1 4RY
United Kingdom

Devra G. Kleiman
Department of Zoological Research
National Zoological Park
Smithsonian Institution
Washington, D.C. 20008

Fred W. Koontz
Science Resource Center
The Wildlife Conservation Society
Bronx, New York 10460

Karl R. Kranz
Philadelphia Zoological Gardens
3400 West Girard Avenue
Philadelphia, Pennsylvania 19104

Michael D. Kreger
Animal Welfare Information Center
National Agricultural Library
Beltsville, Maryland

Barbara Lundrigan
Museum of Zoology
University of Michigan
Ann Arbor, Michigan 48109

Georgina M. Mace
Institute of Zoology
The Zoological Society of London
Regent's Park
London NW1 4RY
United Kingdom

Terry L. Maple
Zoo Atlanta
800 Cherokee Avenue S.E.
Atlanta, Georgia 30315

Edward J. Maruska
Cincinnati Zoo and Botanical Garden
3400 Vine Street
Cincinnati, Ohio 45220

Angela Meder
Eduard-Pfeiffer-Strasse, 54
D-7000 Stuttgart, Germany

Jane E. Meier
3048 Bonita Mesa Road
Bonita, California 91902

Jill D. Mellen
Metro Washington Park Zoo
4001 S.W. Canyon Road
Portland, Oregon 97221

Joy A. Mench
Department of Poultry Science
University of Maryland
College Park, Maryland 20742

Olav T. Oftedal
Department of Zoological Research
National Zoological Park
Smithsonian Institution
Washington, D.C. 20008

Lorraine A. Perkins
Zoo Atlanta
800 Cherokee Avenue S.E.
Atlanta, Georgia 30315

Sharon Pfeifer
Minnesota Department of Natural
    Resources
1200 Warner Road
St. Paul, Minnesota 55106

Edward D. Plotka
Marshfield Medical Research
    Foundation, Inc.
Marshfield, Wisconsin 54449

Ingrid Porton
St. Louis Zoological Park
Forest Park
St. Louis, Missouri 63110

Bruce W. Read
St. Louis Zoological Park
Forest Park
St. Louis, Missouri 63110

Clifford G. Rice
Ecologist
Threatened and Endangered Species Team
U.S. Army Construction Engineering
    Research Laboratories
P.O. Box 9005
Champaign, Illinois 61816-9005

Michael H. Robinson
National Zoological Park
Smithsonian Institution
Washington, D.C. 20008

Michaele M. Robinson
Medical Library
Mercy Hospital and Medical Center
4077 Fifth Avenue
San Diego, California 92103-2180

Mark A. Rosenthal
Lincoln Park Zoological Gardens
2200 North Cannon Drive
Chicago, Illinois 60614

Rebecca S. Roush
Department of Zoology
University of Wisconsin
1202 West Johnson Street
Madison, Wisconsin 53706

Oliver A. Ryder
Center for Reproduction of Endangered
      Species
Zoological Society of San Diego
P.O. Box 551
San Diego, California 92112-0551

John Seidensticker
Department of Mammalogy
National Zoological Park
Smithsonian Institution
Washington, D.C. 20008

Alan Shoemaker
Riverbanks Zoological Park
P.O. Box 1060
Columbia, South Carolina 29202

Elizabeth F. Stevens
Zoo Atlanta
800 Cherokee Avenue S.E.
Atlanta, Georgia 30315

Patrick Thomas
The Wildlife Conservation Society
185th Street and Southern Boulevard
Bronx, New York 10460

Warren D. Thomas
P.O. Box 1890
El Prado, New Mexico 87529

Katerina V. Thompson
College of Life Sciences
University of Maryland
College Park, Maryland 20742

Carl L. Tinkelman
Zoological Society of Philadelphia
3400 West Girard Avenue
Philadelphia, Pennsylvania 19104

Lou E. Tsipis
2700 Buckboard Drive
Hillsborough, North Carolina 27278

Kristin L. Vehrs
AZA Conservation Center
7970-D Old Georgetown Road
Bethesda, Maryland 20814

Eve Watts
San Francisco Zoological Society
1, Zoo Road
San Francisco, California 94132

Christen Wemmer
Conservation and Research Center
National Zoological Park
1500 Remount Road
Front Royal, Virginia 22630

David Wildt
Conservation and Research Center
National Zoological Park
1500 Remount Road
Front Royal, Virginia 22630

William A. Xanten
Department of Mammalogy
National Zoological Park
Smithsonian Institution
Washington, D.C. 20008

AUTHOR INDEX

Authors are listed as cited in the text. Works cited as "et al." are listed under the first author's name only. The letter *t* after a page number indicates a table; *n* indicates a note.

SUBJECT INDEX

The letter *t* after a page number indicates a table.

TAXONOMIC INDEX

The letter *t* after a page number indicates a table.